Thirteenth Edition

Legal Aspects

of Health Care Administration

George D. Pozgar, MBA, CHE, D.Litt.
Author, Speaker, Consultant
Gp Health Care
Annapolis, Maryland

Legal Review
Nina M. Santucci, MSCJ, JD

JONES & BARTLETT
LEARNING

World Headquarters
Jones & Bartlett Learning
5 Wall Street
Burlington, MA 01803
978-443-5000
info@jblearning.com
www.jblearning.com

Jones & Bartlett Learning books and products are available through most bookstores and online booksellers. To contact Jones & Bartlett Learning directly, call 800-832-0034, fax 978-443-8000, or visit our website, www.jblearning.com.

Substantial discounts on bulk quantities of Jones & Bartlett Learning publications are available to corporations, professional associations, and other qualified organizations. For details and specific discount information, contact the special sales department at Jones & Bartlett Learning via the above contact information or send an email to specialsales@jblearning.com.

23986-7

Production Credits

VP, Product Management: David D. Cella
Director of Product Management: Michael Brown
Product Specialist: Danielle Bessette
Production Manager: Carolyn Rogers Pershouse
Production Assistant: Brooke Haley
Senior Marketing Manager: Sophie Fleck Teague
Manufacturing and Inventory Control Supervisor: Amy Bacus
Composition: codeMantra U.S. LLC

Cover Design: Kristin E. Parker
Director of Rights & Media: Joanna Gallant
Rights & Media Specialist: Merideth Tumasz
Media Development Editor: Shannon Sheehan
Cover Image: © Marilyn Nieves/Getty Images
Printing and Binding: Edwards Brothers Malloy
Cover Printing: Edwards Brothers Malloy

Library of Congress Cataloging-in-Publication Data

Names: Pozgar, George D., author.
Title: Legal aspects of health care administration / George D. Pozgar, MBA, CHE, D.Litt.
Description: Thirteenth edition. | Burlington, MA: Jones & Bartlett Learning, [2019] |
  Includes bibliographical references and index.
Identifiers: LCCN 2018002863 | ISBN 9781284127171 (casebound)
Subjects: LCSH: Health services administration—Law and legislation—United States. |
  Medical laws and legislation—United States. | Medical personnel—Malpractice—United States. |
  BISAC: BUSINESS & ECONOMICS / Information Management.
Classification: LCC KF3821 .P69 2018 | DDC 344.7304/1—dc23
LC record available at https://lccn.loc.gov/2018002863

6048

Printed in the United States of America
22 21 20 19 18   10 9 8 7 6 5 4 3 2

I dedicate this book to Denise Mirafuentes.

Your life was an inspiration.

Your love for family, friends, caregivers, and the
many lives you have touched never failed.

Your unwavering faith in God and the challenges you faced
have forever changed the lives of so many.

Your life is a testimony to goodness, kindness, and compassion.

Though the thoughts I wish to impart continue to swirl in my mind,
words alone will never suffice.

So I leave you with this my dear friend,

Your signature phrase to "Live, Laugh, and Love" describes you well.

"The best and most beautiful things in the world cannot
be seen or even touched, they best be felt with the heart."

Helen Keller
ALOHA & MAHALO
Until We All Meet Again

Contents

Epigraph

 I consider ethics, as well as religion, as supplements to law in the government of man.

—**Thomas Jefferson,** President of the United States (1743–1826)

 In law a man is guilty when he violates the rights of others. In ethics he is guilty if he only thinks of doing so.

—**Immanuel Kant,** Philosopher (1724–1804)

 Books are the carriers of civilization. Without books, history is silent, literature dumb, science crippled, thought and speculation at a standstill. I think that there is nothing, not even crime, more opposed to poetry, to philosophy, ay, to life itself than this incessant business.

—**Henry David Thoreau,** Author, Poet, Philosopher (1817–1862)

 It is curious—curious that physical courage should be so common in the world, and moral courage so rare.

—**Mark Twain,** American Author, Humorist (1835–1910)

 In civilized life, law floats in a sea of ethics.

—**Earl Warren,** Chief Justice of the United States (1891–1974)

 How far you go in life depends on your being tender with the young, compassionate with the aged, sympathetic with the striving, and tolerant of the weak and the strong—because someday you will have been all of these.

—**George Washington Carver,** American Inventor (1864–1943)

Preface

He has achieved success who has lived well, laughed often and loved much; who has gained the respect of intelligent men and the love of little children; who has filled his niche and accomplished his task; who has left the world better than he found it, whether by an improved poppy, a perfect poem, or a rescued soul; who has never lacked appreciation of earth's beauty or failed to express it; who has always looked for the best in others and given them the best he had; whose life was an inspiration; whose memory a benediction.

—Bessie Stanley

Legal Aspects of Health Care Administration, Thirteenth Edition, as with the previous 12 editions, continues to be the most comprehensive and engaging book encompassing both the legal and ethical issues of healthcare administration. The Thirteenth Edition continues its tradition of providing a solid foundation in a wide range of current healthcare topics in an understandable format that carefully guides the reader through the complex maze of law and ethics, as well as an overview of practical ways to improve quality and safety in the delivery of patient care. As in previous editions, the Thirteenth Edition serves as a valuable tool for both undergraduate and graduate programs. Additionally, as has been well recognized by practicing healthcare professionals, Legal Aspects of Health Care Administration continues to be a valuable reference tool in their day-to-day work activities.

The author infuses life into the educational process through legal case studies that have been litigated in the courtroom or reported in the press, as well as real-world healthcare events through "reality checks" experienced by patients and healthcare professionals. The author's approach inspires dynamic discussion and excitement in the learning process, thus creating an atmosphere of interest and participation, which is conducive to learning.

Although the court cases relating examples of malpractice are often mirror images of the failures of medicine, this Thirteenth Edition provides a comprehensive resource from which the reader will learn how the law, ethics, and medicine intertwine. The contents of this book serve as a reminder to its readers of the need to learn from the mistakes and tragedies experienced by others to avoid repeating them. The legal cases and resulting headlines should stand as a reminder of the responsibility that caregivers bear to the profession they have chosen.

With revised estimates that as many as 400,000 patients die each year as a result of medical errors, according to a September 2013 study reported in the Journal of Patient Safety, it is mandatory that caregivers be ever mindful of the nature of the life-and-death settings within which they work. At the time of this writing the headlines continue to repeat themselves. For example, on December 4, 2014, an Oregon hospital's medication error led to the death of a 65-year-old patient. This error resulted in three employees being placed on administrative leave. The knowledge gained here will help prevent caregivers from becoming the next headline.

Although there will always be a "next time" for human error, the reader who grasps the contents in this book and understands its lessons will better understand how failures can turn to success and the pain of past mistakes can turn to hope. The application of the knowledge gained from this book and in the classroom learning process will serve to improve the competency of the reader and the quality of life for the patient through an educational process that will help prevent further injury in the healing process.

About the Book

Legal Aspects of Health Care Administration, Thirteenth Edition, lays a strong foundation in both health law and ethics. Chapter 1 begins with a review of hospitals through the ages, providing the reader with an overview of the historical development of hospitals as influenced by medical progress. This allows the reader to see the successes and failures of hospitals through the centuries and how history has a way of repeating itself, thus creating a need to learn from past mistakes in order to prevent repeating them. Chapter 2 continues with an introduction to government, law, and ethics.

Chapters 3 and 4 introduce the reader to negligence and intentional torts. Chapter 5 discusses tort reform and risk reduction, thus reducing the costs of health care. Chapter 6 reviews the criminal aspects of health care, and Chapter 7 reviews the basics of contract law as it pertains to healthcare professionals. The reader is then introduced to civil procedure and trial practice in Chapter 8. The reader's journey continues with a discussion of corporate structure and related legal issues in Chapter 9. A review of medical staff organization and physician liability is covered in Chapter 10, followed by nursing and the law and common nursing practice errors in Chapter 11. Chapter 12 reviews the legal risks of various other hospital departments and healthcare professions.

Information management and patient records are reviewed in Chapter 13. Issues related to patient consent, rights, and responsibilities are reviewed in Chapter 14, followed by a discussion of ethical theories, principles, virtues, and values. Chapter 15 concentrates on healthcare ethics, theories, principles, and values. This review is followed by procreation and ethical dilemmas in Chapter 16, and end-of-life issues in Chapter 17.

Legal reporting requirements are discussed in Chapter 18. Labor relations and employment-at-will, employee rights, and employee responsibilities are reviewed in Chapters 19 and 20, respectively. An overview of professional liability insurance, managed care, and national health insurance is provided in Chapters 21 and 22.

The practical application of the law and ethics in the healthcare setting is accomplished by interspersing the thoughts of great minds through *Quotes*, applicable *News Clippings*, provider and organizational experiences through *Reality Checks*, and patient experiences through legal rulings and summaries through *Case Law*. When reviewing the various cases, the reader should consider both the ethical and legal implications of a dilemma and how they intertwine with one another. It is important to recognize that the decisions in the cases described are generally governed both by applicable state and federal statutes and common law principles. When reviewing a case, the reader must keep in mind that the case law and statutes of one state are not binding in another state.

There is no one magical legal or ethics book that can possibly compress into its pages the plethora of issues that have bombarded the healthcare industry. This book is merely a beginning of the study of legal and ethical issues and is an adventure that all caregivers should take. Although there is always much more that could be discussed on any one topic, the reader will understand that this book provides a solid foundation for practical everyday use as well as further study in the law and ethics.

Each life is like a novel. Filled with moments of happiness, sadness, crisis, defeat, and triumph. When the last page has been written, will you be happy or saddened by what you read?

—Author Unknown

The *Thirteenth Edition* presents real-world life experiences that bring the reader through a journey of learning that provides an effective transitional stage from the classroom to the reality of the everyday work environment. When considering matters of law and ethics, healthcare professionals are usually considering matters of freedom in regard to personal choices, one's obligations to other sentient beings, or judgments about human character and the right to choose. The author's objective is to equip the reader with the background knowledge necessary to understand that legal and ethical behavior begins with recognizing that we have alternatives and choices in our behavior. To make good decisions, each individual must first understand that those decisions will only be as good as

🔍 *IT'S YOUR GAVEL . . .*

"It's Your Gavel" boxes offer the reader an opportunity to make their own decisions about actual court cases. Many chapters begin with a case that has been reviewed by the courts in state or federal jurisdictions. After reviewing each case and subsequent relevant material, readers can take on the role of the fact finder and render a decision. Then, at the end of the respective chapters, the actual court findings and reasoning for each case are given in "The Court's Decision" box.

the knowledge and understanding he or she possesses of right and wrong. This book is not an indictment of any profession or organization. There is a deluge of ethical issues in every aspect of human existence. Although cultural differences, politics, and religion influence who we are, it is all of life's experiences that affect who we become.

▶ Case Presentation Format

When reviewing the various cases in this book, the reader should consider what happened, why things went wrong, what the relevant legal issues are, and how the event could have been prevented. The reader should also consider how, if one fact in a particular case changed, the outcome might have been different. What would that fact be? The cases presented in the text have been chosen because of the frequency of their occurrence. The general format for each boxed case review is as follows:

Title: Each case has a title that signals the type of case to be reviewed.

Case Citation: The case citation describes where a court's opinion in a particular case can be located. It identifies the parties in the case, the text in which the case can be found, the court writing the opinion,

and the year in which the case was decided. For example, the case citation of *Bouvia v. Superior Court (Glenchur)*, 225 Cal. Rptr. 297 (Cal. Ct. App. 1986) is described as follows:

■ *Bouvia v. Superior Court (Glenchur)*: Identifies the basic parties involved in the lawsuit
■ 225 Cal. Rptr. 297: Identifies the case as being reported in volume 225 of the California Reporter on page 297
■ Cal. Ct. App. 1986: Identifies the case as being decided in the California Court of Appeals in 1986

Students who wish to research a specific case should visit a law school library, which provides access to various state and regional reporters.

Facts: A review of the material facts of the case is presented.

Issues: This is the disputed point or question the judge or jury must decide. The issues discussed in any given case are selected for review based on medical and legal pertinence to the healthcare professional. Although any one case in this text may have multiple issues, emphasis is placed on those issues considered to be more relevant for the reader in the context of the topic being discussed.

Holding: The court's ruling based on the facts, issues, and applicable laws pertaining to a case is summarized.

Reason: The rationale for the court's decision based on the facts, issues, and relevant laws surrounding a case is presented.

Author's Note: This book is not a definitive treatise, but rather a portrait of the ever-evolving story of health care through the study of law and ethics. It is educational in nature and should not be considered a substitute for legal advice on any particular issue. Moreover, each chapter presents an overview, rather than an exhaustive treatment, of the various topics discussed.

The author, legal reviewers, and/or the publisher cannot be responsible for any errors or omissions, including additions to, interpretations of, and/or changes in the regulations presented in this book.

Acknowledgments

The author especially acknowledges the staff at Jones & Bartlett Learning, whose guidance and assistance was so important in making this *Thirteenth Edition* a reality. Special thanks to Mike Brown, Director of Product Management at Jones & Bartlett Learning, who has once again been truly an amazing leader and mentor. I would like to thank Danielle Bessette, Product Specialist, who worked diligently and tirelessly with me on this *Thirteenth Edition*. I would also especially like to acknowledge Sophie Teague, Senior Marketing Manager, Brooke Haley, Production Assistant, and Merideth Tumasz, Rights & Media Specialist, who worked with me on the *Thirteenth Edition*. Thank you for allowing me to leave behind this legacy of writing.

I am grateful to the very special people in the more than 1,000 hospitals and ambulatory sites from Alaska to Puerto Rico with whom I have consulted, surveyed, and provided education over many years. Their shared experiences have served to remind me of the importance of making this book more valuable in the classroom and as a reference for practicing healthcare professionals.

To my students in healthcare law and ethics classes at the New School for Social Research, Molloy College, Long Island University–C.W. Post Campus, Saint Francis College, and Saint Joseph's College; my intern from Brown University; my resident in hospital administration from The George Washington University; and those I have instructed through the years at various seminars, I will always be indebted for your inspiration.

Many thanks are also extended to all of the special people at the National Library of Medicine and the Library of Congress for their guidance over the years in locating research materials.

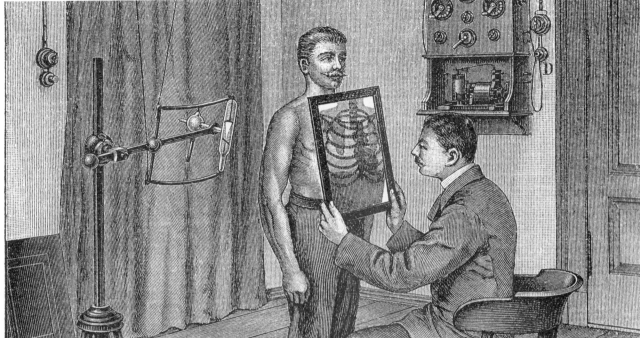

CHAPTER 1

Hospitals Through the Ages

I was created at the end of the Renaissance, watched pirates rule the oceans as Ivan the Terrible ruled Russia, and witnessed the arrest of Galileo for believing the Earth revolved around the Sun.

—I Am History

▶ LEARNING OBJECTIVES

The reader, upon completion of this chapter, will be able to:

■ Explain how societal conflicts due to politics, religion, and warfare have both impeded the growth of hospitals and contributed to their progress.
■ Describe how advances in medicine led to the rise of the modern-day hospital and improved the quality of patient care.
■ Describe how the knowledge gained from best practices (e.g., infection control) can lead to progress while at the same time result in patient harm if not consistently followed over time.

We can learn from history how past generations thought and acted, how they responded to the demands of their time and how they solved their problems. We can learn by analogy, not by example, for our circumstances will always be different than theirs were. The main thing history can teach us is that human actions have consequences and that certain choices, once made, cannot be undone. They foreclose the possibility of making other choices and thus they determine future events.

—Gerda Lerner [1]

This chapter provides the reader with notable historical events, from ancient civilizations to the present time, which continue to revolutionize the delivery of patient care. It provides a review of the advance of civilization as disclosed in the history of hospitals and medical achievements through the ages. A study of the past often reveals errors that then can be avoided, customs that persist only because of tradition, and practices that have been superseded by others that are more effective. The past may also bring to light long-abandoned practices, which may be revived to some advantage. The story of the birth and evolution of the hospital portrays the triumph of civilization over barbarism and the progress of civilization toward an ideal characterized by an interest in the welfare of the community.

This chapter reviews some of the most amazing medical discoveries and achievements in the history of medicine. It also describes some of the failures that continue to plague the healthcare industry. The importance of the study of history is undeniable. The Spanish philosopher George Santayana (1863–1952) recognized this all too well when he said, "Those who do not remember the past are condemned to repeat it." George Bernard Shaw (1856–1950), an Irish dramatist and socialist, recognized the tragedies of the history of civilization when he said, "If history repeats itself, and the unexpected always happens, how incapable must man be of learning from experience." Yes, Santayana and Shaw are right: If we do not learn from the mistakes of the past, we are doomed to repeat them. Progress in health care will only prevail so long as advances in medicine are practiced by each new generation. Although the struggle to progress is a road filled with many pitfalls, hope still looms.

Martin Makary wrote in the *Wall Street Journal* that "Medical errors kill enough people to fill four jumbo jets a week . . . To do no harm going forward, we must be able to learn from the harm we have already done."[2] If we do not learn from historical events to those of the present days, we are bound to

repeat them. This chapter takes the reader on a journey from the past to the present, from which to spring forward on a better road that returns the people's trust in the safety net of the nation's hospital systems. Here, we go "back into the future" to bring forth the fruits of healthier hospitals and healthier lives. Let the reader now travel that road.

▶ EARLY HINDU AND EGYPTIAN HOSPITALS

Two ancient civilizations, the Hindu (in what is now India) and the Egyptian, had crude hospitals. Hindu literature reveals that in the 6th century BC, Buddha appointed a physician for every 10 villages and built hospitals for the crippled and the poor. His son, Upatiso, built shelters for the diseased and for pregnant women. These examples probably moved Buddha's devotees to erect similar hospitals. Despite a lack of records, historians agree that hospitals existed in Ceylon as early as 437 BC.

During his reign from 273 to 232 BC, King Asoka built 18 hospitals that hold historical significance because of their similarities to the modern hospital. Attendants gave gentle care to the sick, provided patients with fresh fruits and vegetables, prepared their medicines, gave massages, and maintained their personal cleanliness. Hindu physicians, adept at surgery, were required to take daily baths, keep their hair and nails short, wear white clothes, and promise that they would respect the confidence of their patients. Although bedside care was outstanding for those times, medicine was only beginning to find its way.

Egyptian physicians were probably the first to use drugs such as alum, peppermint, castor oil, and opium. In surgery, anesthesia consisted of hitting the patient on the head with a wooden mallet to render the patient unconscious. Surgery was largely limited to fractures, and medical treatment was usually given in the home. Therapy away from home was often available in temples, which functioned as hospitals.

▶ GREEK AND ROMAN HOSPITALS

The term *hospital* derives from the Latin word *hospitalis*, which relates to guests and their treatment. The word reflects the early use of these institutions not merely as places of healing, but also as havens for the poor and weary travelers. Hospitals first appeared in Greece as *aesculapia*, named after the Greek god of medicine, Aesculapius. For many centuries, hospitals developed in association with religious institutions, such as the Hindu hospitals opened in Sri Lanka in the 5th century BC and the monastery-based European hospitals of the Middle Ages (5th century to 15th century AD). The Hotel-Dieu in Paris, a monastic hospital founded in 660 AD, is still in operation today.

In early Greek and Roman civilization, when medical practices were rife with mysticism and superstitions, temples also were used as hospitals. Every sanctuary had a sacred altar before which the patient, dressed in white, was required to present gifts and offer prayers. If a patient was healed, the cure was credited to miracles and divine visitations. If the patient remained ill or died, he or she was considered to be lacking in purity and unworthy to live.

Greek temples provided refuge for the sick. One of these sanctuaries, dedicated to Aesculapius, is said to have existed as early as 1134 BC at Titanus. Ruins attest to the existence of another, more famous Greek temple built several centuries later in the Hieron, or sacred grove, at Epidaurus. Here, physicians ministered to the sick holistically in body and soul. They prescribed medications such as salt, honey, and water from a sacred spring. They gave patients hot and cold baths to promote speedy cures and encouraged long hours of sunshine and sea air, combined with pleasant vistas, as an important part of treatment. The temple hospitals housed libraries and rooms for visitors, attendants, priests, and physicians. The temple at Epidaurus even boasted what might be described as the site of the first clinical records. The columns of the temple were inscribed with the names of patients, brief histories of their cases, and comments as to whether or not they were cured.

The aesculapia spread rapidly throughout the Roman Empire, as well as through the Greek world. Although some hospitals were simply spas, others followed the therapy outlined by the leading physicians of the day. Hippocrates, for example, a physician born about 460 BC, advocated medical theories that have startling similarity to those of the present day. He employed the principles of percussion and auscultation, wrote intelligently on fractures, performed numerous surgical operations, and described such conditions as epilepsy, tuberculosis, malaria, and ulcers. He also kept detailed clinical records of many of his patients. Physicians like Hippocrates not only cared for patients in the temples, but also gave instruction to young medical students.

▶ HOSPITALS OF THE EARLY CHRISTIAN ERA

Christianity and the doctrines preached by Jesus stressing the emotions of love and pity gave impetus to the establishment of hospitals, which, with the advance of Christianity, became integral parts of the church institution. These Christian hospitals, which replaced those of Greece and Rome, were devoted entirely to care of the sick, and accommodated patients in buildings outside the church proper.

A decree of Constantine in 335 AD closed the aesculapia and stimulated the building of Christian hospitals, which, during the 4th and 5th centuries, reached the peak of their development. Many were erected by the rulers of the period or by wealthy Romans who had converted to Christianity. By the year 500, most large towns in the Roman Empire had hospitals. Nursing, inspired by religion, was gentle and considerate, but soon began to discard the medical precepts of Hippocrates, Antyllus, and other early Greek physicians because of their pagan origins. Instead, health care turned toward mysticism and theurgy (the working of a divine agency in human affairs) as sources of healing.

Hospitals rarely succeeded during the centuries leading to the Middle Ages; only a few existed outside Italian cities. Occasional almshouses in Europe sheltered some of the sick, whereas inns along the Roman roads housed others. No provision appears to have been made for care of the thousands of helpless paupers who had been slaves and were later set free when Christianity was introduced into the Roman Empire.

▶ ISLAMIC HOSPITALS

The followers of Mohammed were almost as dedicated as the Christians in caring for the sick. In Baghdad, Cairo, Damascus, Cordova, and many other cities under their control, luxurious hospital accommodations were frequently provided. Harun al-Rashid, the glamorous caliph (a title for a religious or civil ruler claiming succession from Mohammad) of Baghdad (786–809 AD), built a system of hospitals and paid the physicians himself. Medical care in these hospitals was free. Approximately four centuries later, in 1160, a Jewish traveler reported that he had found as many as 60 dispensaries and infirmaries in Baghdad alone. The Persian physician Rhazes, who lived from approximately 850 to 923 AD, was skilled in surgery. He is believed to be the first to use the intestines of sheep for suturing and to cleanse patient wounds with alcohol. He also gave the first rational accounts of smallpox and measles.

Islamic physicians like Rhazes received much of their medical knowledge from the persecuted Christian sect known as the Nestorians. Nestorius (Archbishop of Constantinople from April 428 to August 431) was driven into the desert with his followers after having been appointed patriarch of Constantinople and took up the study of medicine. The school at Edessa, in Mesopotamia, with its two large hospitals, eventually came under the control of the Nestorians, where they established a remarkable teaching institution. Eventually driven out of Mesopotamia by the orthodox bishop Cyrus, they fled to Persia, where they established the famous school at Gundishapur, which is considered to be the true starting point of Islamic medicine. Gundishapur was home to the world's oldest known teaching hospital and also comprised a library and a university. It was located in the present-day province of Khuzestan, in southwestern Iran, not far from the Karun River.

Islamic medicine flourished up to about the 15th century. Physicians were acquainted with the possibilities of inhalation anesthesia. They instituted precautions against adulteration of drugs and developed a vast number of new drugs. Islamic countries also built asylums for the mentally ill 1,000 years before such institutions appeared in Europe. The people of Islam made a brilliant start in medicine, but never fulfilled the great promise that glowed in their early work in medical arts and hospitalization was never fulfilled. Wars, politics, superstitions, and a nonprogressive philosophy stunted the growth of a system that had influenced the development of hospitals.

▶ EARLY MILITARY HOSPITALS

Engraved on a limestone pillar dating back to the Sumerians (2920 BC) are pictures that depict, among other military procedures, the assemblage of the wounded. The Book of Deuteronomy records that Moses established outstanding rules for military hygiene. Out of the urgency of care for the wounded in battle came much of the impetus for medical progress. Hippocrates is quoted as saying that "war is the only proper school for a surgeon." Under the Romans, surgery advanced largely because of experience gained through gladiatorial and military surgery. Throughout the centuries, warfare has been a two-edged sword, producing tragic events while providing an environment for the advancement of surgery and medicine. From an ethical point of view, the question arises: What surgical and medical advancements might have been lost due to the failure of mankind to sit at the table of peace and compromise on differences based on logic and reason?

▶ MEDIEVAL HOSPITALS

Religion continued to be the most important factor in the establishment of hospitals during the Middle Ages. A number of religious orders created *hospitia*, or travelers' rests, and infirmaries adjacent to monasteries provided food and temporary shelter for weary travelers and pilgrims. One of these, the famous alpine hospice of St. Bernard, founded in 962, gave comfort to the weary and sent its renowned dogs to the rescue of lost mountain climbers.

The hospital movement grew rapidly during the Crusades, which began in 1096. Military hospital orders sprang up, and accommodations for sick and exhausted crusaders were provided along well-traveled roads. One body of crusaders organized the Hospitallers of the Order of St. John, which in 1099 established in the Holy Land a hospital capable of caring for 2,000 patients. Knights of this order took personal charge of service to patients and often denied themselves so that the sick might have food and medical care. For years, these institutions were the best examples of hospitals of that period.

Although physicians cared for physical ailments to afford relief, they rarely attempted to cure the sick. Dissection of a human body would have been sacrilege because the body was created in the image of God.

Finally, an active period of hospital growth came during the late 12th and early 13th centuries. In 1198, Pope Innocent III urged hospitals of the Holy Spirit to be subscribed for by the citizenry of many towns. He set an example by founding a model hospital in Rome, known as Santo Spirito, in Sassia. Built in 1204, it survived until 1922, when it was destroyed by fire. In Rome, nine other hospitals were founded shortly after completion of the one in Sassia; it is estimated that in Germany alone, 155 towns had hospitals of the Holy Spirit during early medieval times.

Although most hospitals constructed during the Middle Ages were associated with monasteries or founded by religious groups, a few cities, particularly in England, built municipal institutions. Like all hospitals of the period, the buildings were costly and often decorated with colorful tapestries and stained glass windows, but the interiors were frequently little more than large drafty halls with beds lining each side. Some hospitals were arranged on the ward plan, usually built in the shape of a cross. Floors were made of red brick or stone, and the only ventilation came from the cupola in the ceiling.

With the spread of leprosy during the 12th and 13th centuries, lazar houses sprang up, supplying additional hospital facilities. Made up of crude structures, lazar houses were usually built on the outskirts of towns and maintained for the segregation of lepers rather than for their treatment. Special groups of attendants, including members of the Order of St. Lazar, nursed the patients. The group represented an important social and hygienic movement because their actions served to check the spread of epidemics through isolation. The group is credited for virtually stamping out leprosy.

During the same period of hospital growth, three famous London institutions were established: St. Bartholomew's in 1137, St. Thomas's before 1207, and St. Mary of Bethlehem in 1247. St. Bartholomew's, founded by Rahere (reportedly the court jester of Henry I), cared for the sick poor but, unlike many hospitals of that day, was well organized. St. Thomas's Hospital was founded by a woman who was later canonized St. Mary Overie. It burned in 1207, was rebuilt 6 years later, and was constructed again on a new site in 1228. St. Mary of Bethlehem was the first English hospital to be used exclusively for the mentally ill.

The Hotel-Dieu of Paris was probably typical of the better hospitals of the Middle Ages. Built at the beginning of the 13th century, the hospital provided four principal rooms for patients in various stages of disease, as well as a room for convalescents and another for maternity patients. Illustrations by artists of the time show that two persons generally shared one bed.

Heavy curtains sometimes hung from canopies over the bed to afford privacy, but this advantage was more than offset by the fact that the draperies, which were never washed, spread infection and prevented free ventilation. The institution was self-contained, maintaining a bakery, herb garden, and farm. Often, patients who had fully recovered remained at the hospital to work on the farm or in the garden for several days in appreciation for the care they had received.

▶ THE "DARK AGE" OF HOSPITALS

Pictures and records of hospitals during the Middle Ages illustrate how many hospitals commonly crowded several patients into one bed regardless of the type or seriousness of the illness. A mildly ill patient might be placed in the same bed as an occupant suffering from a contagious disease. A notable exception to the general deterioration in medicine during this era was the effort of those monks who copied by hand and preserved the writings of Hippocrates and other ancient physicians.

The great Al-Mansur Hospital, built in Cairo in 1276, struck a contrast to the European institutions of the Middle Ages. It was equipped with separate wards for the more serious diseases and provided outpatient clinics. The handful of hospitals like Al-Mansur would lay the groundwork for hospital progress to come in later centuries.

▶ HOSPITALS OF THE RENAISSANCE

During the revival of learning around the close of the 14th century, hundreds of medical hospitals in Western Europe received the new, more inquiring surgeons that the Renaissance produced. New drugs were developed, and anatomy became a recognized study. Ancient Greek writings were printed, and dissection was performed by such masters as Leonardo da Vinci, known as the originator of cross-sectional anatomy, and Andreas Vesalius, author of *De Humani Corporis Fabrica* (On the Fabric of the Human Body), on human anatomy. Hospitals became more organized. Memoranda from 1569 describe the duties of the medical staff in the civil hospital of Padua, a city that was home to the most famous medical school of the 16th century. These read:

> There shall be a doctor of physic upon whom rests the duty of visiting all the poor patients in the building, females as well as males; a doctor of surgery whose duty it is to apply ointments to all the poor people in the hospital who have wounds of any kind; and a barber who is competent to do, for the women as well as the men, all the other things that a good surgeon usually does.[3]

The practice of surgery during the Renaissance became more scientific and progressive. Operations for lithotomy and hernioplasty were undertaken without the use of anesthetics, and surgery was practiced by the *long-robe surgeons*, a small group who were educated in the universities and permitted to perform all types of operations, and by the *short-robe surgeons*, the barbers who, in most communities, were allowed only to leech and shave the patient, unless permission was granted to extend the scope of treatment. Both groups were regarded as inferior to physicians.

In 1506, a band of long-robe surgeons organized the Royal College of Surgeons of Edinburgh. By 1540, both the long- and short-robe surgeons in England joined to form the Company of Barber-Surgeons of London. In 1528, Thomas Linacre, physician to Henry VIII, founded and became the first president of the Royal College of Physicians of England.

Although English physicians were organized during the 16th century, Henry VIII of England ordered that hospitals associated with the Catholic Church be given over to secular uses or destroyed. The sick were turned out into the streets. Conditions in hospitals became so intolerable that the king was petitioned to return one or two buildings for the care of patients. Henry consented and restored St. Bartholomew's in 1544. Practically the only hope for the sick poor from outlying towns was to journey many miles to London.

The dearth of hospitals in England continued throughout the 17th century, when the medical school was developed. The French and the English quickly accepted what had originated in Italy—the first attempt to make medical instruction practical. St. Bartholomew's took the lead in education by establishing a medical library in 1667 and permitted apprentices to walk the wards for clinical teaching under experienced surgeons.

In 1634, an outstanding contribution was made to nursing by the founding of the order of the Daughters of Charity of St. Vincent de Paul. Originating at the Hotel-Dieu of Paris as a small group of village girls who were taught nursing by the nuns, the order grew rapidly and was transplanted to the United States by Mother Seton in 1809.

▶ HOSPITALS OF THE 18TH CENTURY

During the 18th century, the building of hospitals began to revive. Because of poverty, the movement made slow progress in England, but a few hospitals were built and supported jointly by parishes. By 1732, there were 115 such institutions in England, some of them a combination of almshouse and hospital. As hospitals grew in number, new advances in health care began.

The Royal College of Physicians established a dispensary where medical advice was free and medicines were sold to the needy at cost. Controversies and lawsuits, however, brought an untimely end to this early clinic. Not discouraged by this experience, the Westminster Charitable Society created a similar dispensary in 1715. The same organization, in 1719, founded Westminster Hospital, an infirmary built by voluntary subscription, in which the staff gave its services gratuitously. Ten years later, the Royal College

of Physicians in Edinburgh opened the Royal Infirmary. London Hospital, another notable institution, was founded in 1740. Admission of charity patients to the London Hospital was apparently by an admission ticket. Among its historical relics is an admission card that had on the back of the card a representation of a biblical scene drawn by the artist William Hogarth.

In 1727, John Theophilus Desaguliers invented a machine for pumping fresh air into and foul air out of rooms. It was first used in prisons and public buildings and later installed in hospitals. Other mechanical improvements for the care of the sick were sadly wanting, but worse was the lack of cleanliness and the crude and careless treatment of patients.

In the Elizabethan period, with its materialistic and cold culture, the deterioration of hospital service that had set in under Henry VIII continued. The lowest point in the deterioration of hospitals came during the 18th and first half of the 19th centuries. Considering the increase in knowledge during the 18th century, development of educational opportunities, and steady growth in population and wealth, the few hospitals built at that time were inadequate. As far as hospital progress is concerned, the 18th century was not only decidedly uneventful; it was a period of regression. The full revival did not begin until well after the middle of the 19th century.

Antony van Leeuwenhoek (1632–1723) succeeded in making some of the most important discoveries in the history of biology. Although van Leeuwenhoek did not invent the first microscope, he was able to perfect it. His many discoveries included bacteria, free-living and parasitic microscopic protists, sperm cells, blood cells, and microscopic nematodes. His research opened up an entire world of microscopic life. Often referred to as the "father of microbiology," van Leeuwenhoek had a pronounced influence on the creation of the sciences of cytology, bacteriology, and pathology. His discoveries have forever improved patient care.

▶ EARLY HOSPITALS IN THE UNITED STATES

Manhattan Island claims the first account of a hospital in the New World, a hospital that was used in 1663 for sick soldiers. Fifty years later, in Philadelphia, William Penn founded the first almshouse established in the American colonies. The Quakers supported the almshouse, which was open only to members of that faith. However, Philadelphia was rapidly growing and in need of a public almshouse. Such an institution for the aged, the infirm, and persons with mental illness was established in 1732. The institution later became the historic Old Blockley, which, in turn, evolved into the Philadelphia General Hospital.

Philadelphia was the site of the first incorporated hospital in America, the Pennsylvania Hospital. Dr. Thomas Bond wanted to provide a place where Philadelphia physicians could treat their private patients. With the aid of Benjamin Franklin, Dr. Bond sought a charter for the Pennsylvania Hospital, which was granted by the Crown in 1751. Franklin assisted in designing the hospital. It included a central administration unit and two wings opened to the public. The first staff consisted of Dr. Phineas Bond, Dr. Lloyd Zachary, and the founder, Dr. Thomas Bond, all of whom gave their services without remuneration for 3 years.

Rich in the history of hospitals, Philadelphia is credited with the first quarantine station for immigrants (created in 1743) and the first lying-in hospital (established in 1762), a private institution owned by the noted obstetrician William Shippen. The quality of American health care seemed to be improving. However, by 1775 Dr. John Jones published a book calling attention to the frightful conditions that existed in hospitals. He charged that hospitals abroad were crowded far beyond capacity and that Hotel-Dieu of Paris frequently placed three to five patients in one bed—putting the convalescent with the dying and fracture cases with infectious cases. He estimated that one fifth of the 22,000 patients cared for at Hotel-Dieu died each year. Wounds were washed daily with a sponge that was carried from patient to patient. The infection rate was said to be 100%, and mortality after amputation was as high as 60%. Jones's call to action had a positive effect on American health care.

As late as 1769, New York City, with nearly 300,000 inhabitants, was without hospitals. In 1771, a small group of citizens, Dr. Jones among them, formed the Society of the New York Hospital and obtained a grant to build a hospital. The society purchased a five-acre site and made plans for a model structure that would allow a maximum of eight beds per ward and provide improved ventilation. The hospital fell into the hands of the British troops during the American Revolution and was used as a barracks and military hospital.

During postwar reconstruction, the New York Hospital broadened its services. Under the supervision of Dr. Valentine Seaman, the hospital began providing instruction in nursing, and in 1779, it introduced vaccination in the United States and established an ambulance service. Other early American hospitals of historic interest include the first psychiatric hospital in the New World, founded in Williamsburg, Virginia, in 1773, and a branch of federal hospitals created by the passage of the U.S. Marine Hospital Service Act in 1798. Under this act, two marine hospitals were established in 1802: one in Boston and another in Norfolk, Virginia.

The Massachusetts General Hospital (MGH), which pioneered many improvements in medicine, originated in Boston. Its first patient, admitted in 1821, was a 30-year-old sailor.

> More than a decade earlier, two Boston doctors had appealed to the city's "wealthiest and most influential citizens" to establish a general hospital. The War of 1812 delayed the dream, but on July 4, 1818, the cornerstone was finally laid. The original building, designed by Boston's leading architect, Charles Bulfinch, is still in use. One of the world's leading centers of medical research and treatment has grown up around it. The original domed operating amphitheater, where anesthesia was first publicly demonstrated in 1846, is now a Registered National Historic Landmark. MGH has achieved countless medical milestones, including the first successful reattachment of a human limb.[4]

In 1832, the Boston Lying-In Hospital opened its doors to women unable to afford in-home medical care. It was one of the nation's first maternity hospitals, made possible because of fundraising appeals to individuals and charitable organizations.

Despite the increased number of institutions providing care for the sick, the first half of the 19th century stands as a dark period in hospital history. Surgeons of the day had sufficient knowledge of anatomy to lead them to perform many ordinary operations, and as a result, more surgery was most likely undertaken than during any previous era. Although the medieval and ancient surgeons had sought to keep wounds clean, even using wine in an attempt to accomplish this purpose, 19th-century surgeons believed *suppuration* (the production and discharge of pus) to be desirable and encouraged it. Hospital wards were filled with discharging wounds, which made the atmosphere offensive enough to warrant the use of perfume. Some patient wards had multiple patients with multiple conditions allowing for the spread of infections, as depicted in **FIGURE 1-1**.

Nurses of that period are said to have used snuff to make conditions tolerable. Surgeons wore their operating coats for months without washing. The same bed linens served several patients. Pain, hemorrhage, infection, and gangrene infested the wards. Mortality from surgical operations rated as high as 90–100%. Nathan Smith, in the second decade of that century, advocated a bichloride of mercury solution for reducing infection, but his ideas were ignored.

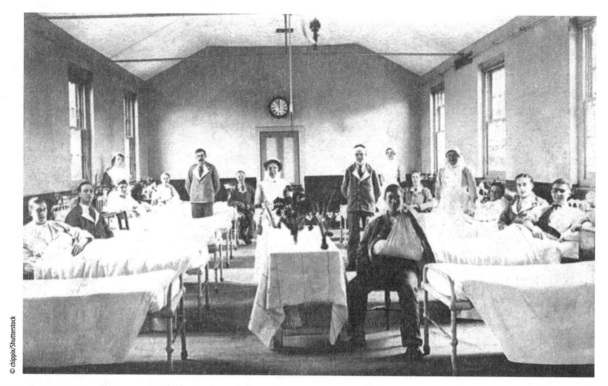

© chippix/Shutterstock

FIGURE 1-1 Patient ward.

▶ LATE 19TH CENTURY RENAISSANCE

Florence Nightingale, the famous English nurse, began her career by training at Kaiserswerth on the Rhine in a hospital and deaconess home established in 1836 by Theodor Fliedner and his wife. Florence Nightingale wrote disparagingly of her training there, particularly of the hygiene practiced. Returning to England, she put her own ideas of nursing into effect and rapidly acquired a reputation for efficient work.

By 1854, during the Crimean War, the English government, disturbed by reports of conditions among the sick and wounded soldiers, selected Florence Nightingale as the one person capable of improving patient care. Upon her arrival at the military hospital in Crimea with a small band of nurses whom she had assembled, she found that the sick were lying on canvas sheets in the midst of dirt and vermin. There was neither laundry nor hospital clothing and beds were made of straw. She proceeded to establish order and cleanliness. She organized diet kitchens, a laundry service, and departments of supplies, often using her own funds to finance her projects. Ten days after her arrival, the newly established kitchens were feeding 1,000 soldiers. Within 3 months, 10,000 soldiers were receiving clothing, food, and medicine. As a result of her work, the death rate substantially declined. She has been credited with observing:

A good nursing staff will perform their duties more or less satisfactorily under every disadvantage. But while doing so, their head will always try to improve their surroundings, in such a way as to liberate them from subsidiary work, and enable them to devote their time more exclusively to the care of the sick.[5]

Because of her organizational skills, many consider Florence Nightingale to be the first true healthcare administrator. Later she extended her administrative duties to include planning the details of sanitary engineering in a new military hospital.

As the field of nursing continued to progress, so did medicine. Dr. Crawford Williamson Long first used ether as an anesthetic in 1842 to remove a small tumor from the neck of a patient. He did not publish any accounts of his work until later. However, the discovery of an anesthetic is often attributed to Dr. W.T.G. Morgan, a dentist who developed sulfuric ether and arranged for the first hospital operation under anesthesia at MGH in 1846. Although not put to practical use immediately, ether soon took away some of the horror that hospitals had engendered in the public mind. Sir James Simpson first used chloroform as an anesthetic in 1847 for an obstetrical case in England.

The year 1847 was the year that the American Medical Association (AMA) was founded under the leadership of Dr. Nathan Smith Davis. The association, among its main objectives, strived to improve medical education, but most of the organization's tangible efforts in education began at the close of the century. The AMA was a strong advocate for establishing a code of ethics, promoting public health measures, and improving the status of medicine.

The culmination of Florence Nightingale's work came in 1860, after her return to England. There, she established the Nightingale School of Nursing at the St. Thomas's Hospital. From this school, a group of 15 nurses graduated in 1863. They later became the pioneer leaders of nurse training.

In 1886, the Royal British Nurses' Association (RBNA) was formed. The RBNA worked toward establishing a standard of technical excellence in nursing. A charter granted to the RBNA in 1893 denied nurses a register, although it did agree to maintain a list of persons who could apply to have their name entered thereon as nurses.[6]

The first formally organized American nursing schools were established in 1872 at the New England Hospital for Women and Children in Boston (Brigham and Women's Hospital), and then in 1873 at Bellevue, New Haven, and Massachusetts General Hospitals. In 1884, Alice Fisher was appointed as the first head of nurse training at Philadelphia Hospital's (renamed as the Philadelphia General Hospital in 1902) nurses' training program. She had the distinction of being the first Nightingale-trained nurse recruited to Philadelphia upon recommendation by Florence Nightingale.

Mrs. Bedford Fenwick, a nurse leader in the English nurse registration movement, traveled to Chicago in 1893 to arrange for nursing exhibits to be displayed in the women's building at the World's Fair.

This event showcased America's social, cultural, and scientific advances and its growing cultural parity with Western Europe. This was the first major exposition in which women played a prominent role. Integral to the fair was a series of Congresses that provided an international platform for discussion of social issues. The Congress on Hospitals, Dispensaries, and Nursing, a section of the International Congress of Charities, Correction, and Philanthropy, particularly focused on health care issues."[7]

As part of the Congress on Hospitals and Dispensaries, the nursing section included papers on establishing standards in hospital training schools, the establishment of a nurses association, and nurse registration. The group formulated plans to improve nursing curriculum and hospital administration in the first concerted attempt to improve hospitals through a national organization.

Progress in Infection Control

Dr. Ignaz Philipp Semmelweis of Vienna, Austria, unknowingly laid the foundation for Louis Pasteur's later work. In 1847, at the Vienna Lying-In Hospital, Europe's largest teaching obstetrical department, he boldly declared that the alarming number of deaths from puerperal fever was a result of infection transmitted by students who came directly from the dissecting room to take care of maternity patients. "Puerperal fever is due to an infection, most often of the placental site within the uterus. If the infection involves the bloodstream, it constitutes puerperal sepsis."[8] Semmelweis noted that Division 1 of the hospital was a medical student–teaching service and Division 2 was used for midwife trainees. Maternal deaths for Division 1 averaged 10%, whereas the rate for Division 2 averaged 3%. Medical students performed autopsies; midwives did not. As a result of these findings, an order was posted on May 15, 1847, requiring all students to scrub their hands in chlorinated lime until the cadaver smell was gone. The order was later revised to include hand washing between patients.

Despite having made bitter enemies, Semmelweis had the satisfaction of seeing the mortality rate in his obstetrical cases drop from 9.92% to 1.27% as a result of the aseptic technique he developed. A few years later, Louis Pasteur, a French chemist and microbiologist, demonstrated the scientific reason for Semmelweis's success when he proved that bacteria were produced by reproduction and not by spontaneous generation, as was then generally believed. From his work came the origin of modern bacteriology and clinical laboratories.

Despite the attention given to the control of infections in hospitals, adherence to hand-washing protocols continues to be a problem well into the 21st century, as noted by the following *reality check* and depicted in **FIGURE 1-2**.

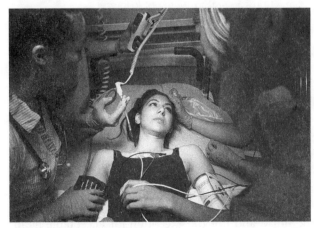

FIGURE 1-2 Patient Room.

☑ *FAILURE TO FOLLOW HAND HYGIENE GUIDELINES*

Sheri was a healthy 30-year-old female until she suddenly experienced neck pain with a numbness radiating down her left arm. She was diagnosed with cervical rib outlet syndrome and agreed to a surgical procedure by Dr. Botchit for removal of her first cervical rib. Sheri was admitted to a postsurgical care unit at a major teaching hospital. Upon entering her assigned four-bed room, she and her husband Bill observed a bloody suction bottle hanging from the wall at the head of her assigned bed. The bed rails were rusting with dried bloody body fluids from a previous patient. They were uneasy about having a surgical procedure performed but they decided the physician's skills were more important than an unclean room. Bill commented, "Well, at least the sheets appear clean."

Elda, the first patient on the left upon entering the room greeted Sheri and Bill. She said, "The room isn't very clean is it? Could you watch out for the nurses?" She then smiled as she removed Tylenol from her bedside table. She took a few and said, "I don't want my doctor to cancel my surgery, so I have to lower my temperature before the nurses retake my temperature. I think I have an infection. I have waited so long to get my surgery scheduled. I am just so worried my surgery will be canceled."

The morning following surgery, a third-year resident entered the room with three first-year residents and beginning with Elda, examined each of four postsurgical patients. Elda was a postsurgical amputee, who was later diagnosed with a staph infection. Sheri was the fourth patient to be examined in the room. Even though each of the patient's wounds had been examined and dressings changed, the physicians failed to change their surgical gloves between patients. Following examination of Sheri, they proceeded to remove their gloves and tossed them in Sheri's bedside wastebasket. They then washed their hands at the only sink in the room, which was by Sheri's bedside.

Sheri's temperature began to rise. Bill asked if a wound culture had been taken. Carol, the nurse manager after checking Sheri's chart said, said, "No culture was ordered." He asked, "Can you please have a culture ordered?" The nurse replied that she would call Dr. Green to see if he would order a blood culture." Bill asked, "Who is Dr. Green?" Carol replied, "Dr. Green is covering for Dr. Botchit while he is on vacation. Dr. Botchit left on a family skiing trip the day after surgery to Aspen, Colorado."

Bill learned the following day that the blood tests came back positive for a staph infection and learned that no antibiotics had been prescribed by Dr. Green. Bill became increasingly concerned about the lack of care and went back to the nursing station to describe his concern about the lack of treatment for Sheri. Carol suggested that he call Dr. Green.

Bill placed a call to Dr. Green and relayed his concern about his wife's deteriorating health. Dr. Green returning Bill's call said, "I hear you are unhappy with my care. I am merely providing coverage for Dr. Botchit. I have my own patients to be concerned with and treat." Bill replied, "Well if you are covering for another physician you need to address my wife's infection." Dr. Green replied, "I am doing a favor for Dr. Botchit by covering his patients as well as mine. I will get to the hospital when I can!"

Upon returning to his wife's bedside, Sheri looked up at him and said, "The priest was here and administered last rites to me." Looking at his mother-in-law, who was trying to be strong, holding back the tears, Bill devotedly said, "I will fix this." He called Dr. Field, who he knew was a physician educator at the medical center, and explained his concerns. Dr. Field said, "I can help. I will get a team of infectious disease specialists to Sheri's bedside. They are the best in the city, probably the world. But please do not use my name in any dispute that you may have with Dr. Botchit or Dr. Green." Sheri survived but the staph infection had taken its toll on her immune system.

Sheri and Bill never thought much about it at the time, but in hindsight, Elda's infection was most likely the contributing factor to the staph infections that eventually affected the other three patients in the room. History repeated itself. Despite being adopted by the hospital, the CDC hand-washing guidelines, which could have helped prevent the infection, were not followed,.

This *reality check* illustrates how the failure to follow established protocols in the prevention of infections can have disastrous consequences for patients. Progress in the delivery of patient care can move forward only as long as complacency does not stymie progress.

This case also provides an important lesson for patients who treat themselves, masking their physical symptoms, as in this case where the patient took Tylenol to hide her fever, an indicator that the patient may have an active infection. Staff should be alert to patients who self-treat and confiscate all home and store bought medications upon admission to the hospital. The lessons here also apply to family members, who must not honor patient requests for medications.

This *reality check* serves as a reminder that history continues to repeat itself. Strict adherence to CDC guidelines and hospital policy must become the norm and not the exception for acceptable hand hygiene in order to prevent the spread of infection by both caregivers and patients. *The Joint Commission's* (TJC) 2017 Hospital Accreditation Standards recognize the importance of complying with hand hygiene guidelines. The standards require hospitals and other accredited TJC organizations to follow current CDC or World Health Organization guidelines for hand hygiene.[9] When hand-washing guidelines have to be declared a TJC *national patient safety goal*, it would appear that caregivers have much to learn from Dr. Semmelweis, who determined in 1847 that poor hand-washing technique can be attributed to being a major cause of hospital-acquired infections. Dr. Ernst von Bergmann's introduction of steam sterilization in 1886 and Dr. William Stewart Halsted's introduction of rubber gloves in 1890 aided in reducing the incidence of hospital-acquired infections.

By the end of the century, Dr. Joseph Lister carried Pasteur's work a step further and showed that wound healing could be hastened by using antiseptics to destroy disease-bearing organisms and by preventing contaminated air from coming into contact with these wounds. Lister was not content with obtaining better results in his own surgical cases; he devoted his life to proving that suppuration is dangerous and that it could be prevented or reduced by the use of antiseptics to destroy disease-bearing organisms. Despite his successful work and eloquent pleas, his colleagues persisted in following their old methods. Years after his discovery, they continued to deride him and his technique, which consisted of spraying carbolic solution so profusely about the operating room that both surgeons and patients were drenched. The use of antiseptics and the techniques of using them continued to improve. Eventually even the skeptics were impressed by the clinical results in reducing infection rates. Surgeons, at last, realized that they could undertake major operations with less fear of morbidity and mortality.

Discovery of Anesthesia

As the 19th century neared its close, surgery was becoming more frequent. The discovery of anesthesia and the principle of antiseptics were two of the most significant influences in the development of surgical procedures in the modern hospital. Anesthesia improved pain control, and hygiene practices helped reduce the incidence of surgical site infections. Although patients did not immediately flock to hospitals as a result of these discoveries, these innovations set the stage for the remarkable growth of the 20th century.

Modern Hospital Laboratory

The study of cytology originated around the middle of the 19th century and influenced the development of the modern hospital clinical laboratory. The cell theory was first advanced in 1839 by the German anatomist Theodor Schwann and was further developed by Dr. Jacob Henle,

whose writings on microscopic anatomy appeared in 1850. Rudolf Virchow, known as the Father of Pathology, was the most eminent proponent of the cell theory. His studies in cellular pathology supported further research in the etiology of disease.

Changing Hospital Structure

With nursing, anesthesia, infection control, and cytology under way, a change in hospital structure began in the last quarter of the 19th century. Buildings of the Civil War days were still in use, with as many as 25 to 50 beds in a ward with little provision for segregating patients. In New York City in 1871, Roosevelt Hospital was constructed on the lines of a one-story pavilion with small wards, and this set the style for a new type of architecture that came to be known as the American plan. A noteworthy feature was ventilation by means of openings in the roof, which was an improvement in hospital construction. Hospitals had been characterized by a lack of provision for ventilation. Dr. W.G. Wylie, writing in 1877, said he favored this type of building, but he advocated that it be a temporary structure only, to be destroyed when it became infected.

As noted in the following *reality check*, hospital construction and building maintenance programs are essential in preventing the spread of infections.

All caregivers must be observant of the cleanliness of the environment within which they care for patients. **FIGURE 1-3** illustrates the not so uncommon finding of soiled vents and ducts by those who inspect hospitals. Such findings contribute to the spread of infections between staff and patients. Caregivers who observe such issues should notify designated staff members who are responsible for ensuring the correction of such environmental deficiencies.

FIGURE 1-3 Soiled vents and ducts.

☑ *STERILE SUPPLY STORAGE*

Mark was assigned a 3-day survey at Anytown Medical Center (AMC). During a tour of the hospital's facilities, Robin, AMC's survey coordinator, Bill, the building engineer, and Jack, the maintenance supervisor, accompanied Mark. While conducting the building tour, Mark had asked to see the neonatal intensive care unit (NICU). After being introduced to Helen, the NICU nurse manager, Mark and Robin gowned up to enter into the nursery with Helen. Bill and Jack waited in the hospital corridor. Mark noticed during his tour of the nursery a door marked "Sterile Supply Storage." Mark looked at Helen and asked, "Can we enter the storage room?" Helen replied, "Sure thing." Upon entry to the room Mark observed that cardboard boxes marked "sterile supply" were stored on the floor. He glanced up at the ceiling tiles and noticed that they were damp and had green and black mold. Mark asked for a flashlight to look at the air vents and ducts. He observed a significant amount of mold on the exhaust vents. He shined the flashlight up into the vent and observed that the air ducts had a buildup of mold. Robin, somewhat concerned, said, "We can get this all cleaned up before the end of the survey." Mark said, "I am also concerned that the sterile supplies stored on the floor, even though in cardboard boxes, have been compromised. The cardboard boxes are damp from mopping of the floor. Let's go out to the corridor and speak to Bill and Jack. After Mark described what he saw in the clean storage area, Bill replied, "Oh, there was a toilet that overflowed in a patient bathroom a few weeks ago in the floor above. Jack interrupting said, "Well, I do not recall seeing a maintenance slip from the NICU describing the problem."

The risks of infection in healthcare settings require healthcare organizations to provide continuing education and training for caregivers. Documentation of in-service training should be placed in employee personnel files. It is important for managers to be alert to and correct hazardous conditions observed in the working environment. Both hospital surveyors (e.g., TJC) and state inspectors, as part of their training, are required to observe the working environment and employees who may breach infection control protocols, such as following proper hand hygiene prior to caring for each patient. Breaches in protocol that are observed are included in both state and TJC formal reports pertaining to the hospital's compliance with infection control standards. Hospitals are required to develop, implement, monitor, and improve the environment to help prevent the spread of infections.

Changing Hospital Function

Promoted by the wealth of bacteriologic discoveries, hospitals began to care for patients with communicable diseases. During the decade from 1880 to 1890, the tubercle bacillus was discovered, and Louis Pasteur developed vaccines for anthrax and rabies. He also developed the process for pasteurization. Robert Koch isolated the cholera bacillus, diphtheria was first treated with antitoxin, the tetanus bacillus and the parasite of malarial fever were isolated, and inoculation for rabies was successful. "On March 24, 1882, Robert Koch announced to the Berlin Physiological Society that he had discovered the cause of tuberculosis."[10] Treatment of patients with some of these infections necessitated isolation, and hospitals were the logical place for observation of communicable diseases. Consequently, at the end of the century, in addition to their many surgical cases, hospitals were crowded with large numbers of patients suffering from scarlet fever, diphtheria, typhoid, and smallpox, all of which were contagious diseases.

Discovery of the X-Ray

Wilhelm Conrad Röntgen's discovery of the X-ray in 1895 was a major scientific achievement. The first use of the X-ray symbolizes the beginning of the period that necessitated equipment so costly that the average practitioner could not afford to install it. The natural result was the founding of community hospitals in which physicians could jointly use such equipment. Nineteenth-century inventions also included the clinical thermometer, the laryngoscope, the Hermann von Helmholtz ophthalmoscope, and innumerable other aids that have led to more accurate diagnoses.

Although the medical and nursing professions of the later half of the 19th century did not reap the full reward of their discoveries, they provided the 20th century with a firm foundation upon which to build.

▶ 20TH-CENTURY PROGRESS

The treatment of metabolic diseases and nutritional deficiencies, the importance of vitamins, and the therapy of glandular extracts played an important role in the advancement of medicine in the 20th century. As early as 1906, Frederick Gowland Hopkins began investigations into vitamins. Two years later, Carlos Finlay produced experimental rickets by means of a vitamin-deficient diet. This, in turn, was followed by Kurt Huldschinsky's discovery that rickets could be treated successfully with ultraviolet light. In quick succession came Casimir Funk's work with vitamins, Elmer McCollum's discovery of vitamins A and B, Joseph Goldberger's work in the prevention of pellagra, and Harry Steenbock's irradiation of foods and oils. Other outstanding contributions to the science of nutrition include Frederick

Banting's introduction of insulin in 1922, the studies in anemia carried out by Dr. George Hoyt Whipple and Dr. Frieda Robscheit-Robbins, a pathologist who worked with Dr. Whipple. This led to Dr. George R. Minot and Dr. William P. Murphy's successful treatment of pernicious anemia. This achievement was considered a major advancement in the treatment of noninfectious diseases. As a result of their research, Hoyt, Minot, and Murphy were awarded the Nobel Prize in Physiology or Medicine.

Dr. Willem Einthoven invented the electrocardiograph (ECG) in 1903. The machine measures the electrical changes that occur during contractions of the heart muscle. The ECG records these graphically, thus allowing the physician to diagnose abnormalities in a patient's heartbeat. He coined the term electrocardiogram for this process, marking the beginning of an era of diagnostic and therapeutic aids. Shortly after that invention came the first basal metabolism apparatus, then the Wassermann (August Von) test in 1906, and tests for pancreatic function. Invention of the fluoroscopic screen followed in 1908. Subsequently, the introduction of blood tests and examinations of numerous body secretions required well-equipped and varied laboratories. Concurrent with this progress in the field of internal medicine was the introduction of radium for the treatment of malignant growths, increasing the use of the clinical laboratory for microscopic examination of pathologic tissue and developments in antibiotics. The result of these many new aids was the conquest of diseases formerly regarded as incurable, which in turn, resulted in improved public confidence in hospitals. The discovery of the structure of DNA is by far one of the most famous scientific discoveries of the 20th century.

The discovery in 1953 of the double helix, the twisted-ladder structure of deoxyribonucleic acid (DNA), by James Watson and Francis Crick marked a milestone in the history of science and gave rise to modern molecular biology, which is largely concerned with understanding how genes control the chemical processes within cells. In short order, their discovery yielded ground-breaking insights into the genetic code and protein synthesis. During the 1970s and 1980s, it helped to produce new and powerful scientific techniques, specifically recombinant DNA research, genetic engineering, rapid gene sequencing, and monoclonal antibodies, techniques on which today's multi-billion dollar biotechnology industry is founded. Major current advances in science, namely genetic fingerprinting and modern forensics, the mapping of the human genome, and the promise, yet unfulfilled, of gene therapy, all have their origins in Watson and Crick's inspired work.[11]

The 20th century was also characterized by rapid growth in nursing education. The earlier schools were maintained almost entirely to secure nursing service at a low cost. The nurse's duties were often menial, hours long, and classroom and laboratory study almost entirely lacking. Nurses themselves had begun to organize for educational reforms. By 1910, training increasingly emphasized theoretical studies. This movement was largely a result of the work of organizations such as the American Nurses Association and the National League for Nursing, along with the organization of the Committee on the Grading of Nursing Schools. In 1943, the U.S. Cadet Nurse Corps was organized to spur enrollment of student nurses in nursing schools to help meet the shortages caused by enlistment of graduate nurses for military service. As a result, efforts increased to train practical nurses and nurses' aides in order to relieve the shortage of graduate nurses.

Reform in medical education began early in the century and was almost wholly a result of the efforts of the Council on Medical Education and Hospitals, which was established in 1905 by the AMA. Immediately after its organization, this council began inspection of medical schools. The council, by establishing standards and by grading the schools, brought about gradual elimination of most of the unethical, commercial, and unqualified institutions.

A great stimulus to the profession of hospital administration has been the work of the American Hospital Association. Organized in 1899 as the Association of Hospital Superintendents, it took its present name in 1907. Since its inception, the organization has concerned itself particularly with the problems of hospital management. As early as 1910, the association held educational programs for hospital chief executive officers and trustees. The American College of Surgeons was founded in 1913 under the leadership of Dr. Franklin H. Martin, the first director general of the organization. One of the most dramatic achievements of the American College of Surgeons was the hospital standardization movement that began in 1918. The founders drew up what was known as "The Minimum Standard," a veritable constitution for hospitals, setting forth requirements for the proper care of the sick. An annual survey of all hospitals having 25 or more beds made the standard effective. When the first survey was conducted, only 89 hospitals in the United States and Canada could meet the requirements.

The hospital standardization movement focused its efforts on the patient, with the goal of providing the patient with the best professional, scientific, and humanitarian care possible. The growth of this movement is remarkable, given that participation in hospital standardization programs is voluntary. Following several name changes over the years, The Joint Commission today conducts unannounced accreditation surveys, with emphasis on ongoing improvements in the quality of patient care.

The years following 1929 will long be remembered as one of the most trying periods in the history of hospitals. Due to critical economic conditions, many institutions found it difficult to keep their doors open. A declining bed occupancy and an ever-increasing charity load, coupled with steadily decreasing revenues from endowments and other sources of income, created hardships on private institutions. Fortunately, however, every economic crisis brings forth new ideas and means and methods of organization to benefit humanity.

In the latter half of the 20th century, competition among hospitals began to grow as for-profit hospital chains began to spring up and compete with nonprofit organizations. Advances in medical technology, such as computed tomography (CT), magnetic resonance imaging (MRI), positron emission tomography (PET) scanners, and robotic surgery, as well as an ever-growing list of new medications, have revolutionized the practice of medicine. During this period, less invasive surgical procedures and a trend toward care in outpatient settings has reduced the need for lengthy stays in hospitals and various long-term care facilities. Laparoscopic surgery, performed through one or more small incisions using small tubes and tiny cameras and surgical instruments, has proven to be one of the remarkable movements forward in the history of surgical procedures.

▶ HEALTH CARE AND HOSPITALS IN THE 21ST CENTURY

So how safe is your hospital? Two new rating systems help you check before you check in. Hospital safety score (hospitalsafetyscore.org), launched in June (2012), assigns grades of A, B, C, D or F to more than 2,600 U.S. hospitals based on 26 safety measures and standards—from hand-washing policies to foreign objects left in body cavities after surgery. Nearly half of the hospitals received a C or lower.

—Bill Hogan[12]

The struggle for hospitals to survive continues well into the 21st century but the news is not always kind. In the nation's capital, one would dream that it would represent the "model city of hope" for the healthcare system. But all to often we learn of its failures and not its progress. Howard University Hospital, for example, opened its doors in 1863 as Freedman's hospital, and it provided care to the freed African American slaves. It soon "became an incubator for some of the brightest African

American slaves." But over the past decade, the once-grand hospital that was the go-to place for the city's middle-class black patients has been beset by financial troubles, empty beds, and an exodus of respected physicians and administrators, many of whom said they are fed up with the way it is run."[13] This follows the closure of DC General Hospital, which many had hoped would be rebuilt. Other hospitals, including the VA system, have struggled and continue to struggle, some even to survive. The overflow of patients into the city's remaining hospitals affects the ability of those hospitals to handle the needs of patients. Many physicians now tell their patients, "My goal is to get you in and out of the hospital as fast as I can. I don't want you to get sicker." The challenges remain as history repeats itself.

The delivery of health care in the modern hospital continues to be the revolutionary product of a long and arduous struggle. The continuing stream of new medicines and treatments, as well as legal, financial, and human resource issues, continues to test the healthcare system. Many of today's healthcare *challenges* have carried over from the 20th century. The challenges include exorbitant malpractice awards, excessive insurance premiums, high expectations of society for miracle drugs and miracle cures, fairly balancing the mistakes of caregivers with the numerous successful events, negative press that increases public fear, and numerous ethical dilemmas involving abortion, human cloning, physician-assisted suicide, how to fairly distribute limited resources, and the dwindling number of rural hospitals, are but a few of the challenges of the 21st century.

According to a study written by Sy Mukherjee in *ThinkProgress*, there is an increased risk of dying in rural hospitals.

Critical access hospitals (CAHs) are medical providers located in America's most isolated regions, serving rural communities that do not otherwise have easily available access to care. Since the closest alternatives to these hospitals are usually over 35 miles away, they provide an essential resource for Americans living in secluded communities—and therefore receive enhanced funding from the federal government to carry out their work. But according to a Harvard School of Public Health study, death rates at these hospitals are significantly higher than national averages—and are on the rise.[14]

As advances in medicine rapidly move the nation's healthcare system in the direction of high-cost care and treatment, small rural hospitals are increasingly unable to meet the challenges of both procuring expensive capital equipment and attracting qualified specialists. This, in turn, is leading to the demise of rural hospitals' ability to provide the more complex care available in modern medical centers.

Translational Medicine

Translational medicine began to be recognized as a significant development at the end of the 20th century and well into the 21st century. Both the researcher and the practitioner began to better understand the importance of knowing each other's contribution in the healing process.

> The translation of biomedical discovery into clinical benefit is the essence of translational medicine, which continued to experience remarkable growth in 2012. The University of Dundee, Scot., for example, received almost £12 million ($19.2 million) for the completion of a Centre for Translational and Interdisciplinary Research, and a £24 million ($38.4 million) Institute for Translational Medicine was slated for development in Birmingham, Eng. Scientists continued to work to coordinate the application of new scientific knowledge in clinical practice with basic observations and questions in the laboratory.[15]

Minimally Invasive Surgery

The ever-evolving precision of *minimally invasive surgery* (MIS) will catapult medicine into a limitless future of exotic discoveries. MIS allows physicians to use a variety of techniques to operate with less damage to body tissues than with open surgery and is believed by some surgeons to be more noteworthy than the discovery of anesthesia. MIS is associated with less pain, a shorter hospital stay, fewer complications and medical errors, while improving the accuracy of complex

surgical procedures. Decision making during surgery often involves thousands of pieces of information that are considered during a surgical procedure. This can lead to increased physician fatigue and the possibility of human error. MIS reduces the fatigue factor by assisting the surgeon in the decision-making process by reducing the time required for a surgical procedure, and the surgeon concentrates on the surgical skills necessary for completing a successful surgery. The bells and whistles and blinking lights become less of a distraction, by allowing the surgeon to concentrate on the surgical field (e.g., patient's abdomen).

Robotic surgery provides a magnified 3-D view of the surgical site and helps the surgeon operate with precision, flexibility, and control. The popular da Vinci System robotic equipment is used for cardiac, colorectal, general, gynecologic, head and neck, thoracic, and urologic surgical procedures. It allows surgeons to operate through several small incisions with enhanced vision, precision, and control inside the human body.[16]

Surgical Simulation Training

Advances in *surgical simulation training* (SST) will enhance the training of residents, enabling them to transition more effectively to performing more precise surgical procedures with fewer errors and improved patient outcomes. Pilots are trained in a simulator before ever flying a plane. Surgeons have historically been in the dark stages of SST, even though "they are in charge of carrying out the procedures that may either save or kill the patient at hand."[17] The patient will one day no longer be the experimental subject in the hands of a surgeon-in-training. Surgical simulation, so long waited for, will produce a generation of surgeons who have practiced surgical procedures, just as pilots do before flying a plane.

Social Media Impacts on Caregivers

The advent of social media has raised concern among caregivers and hospitals. Patients post both positive and negatives reviews on the World Wide Web (e.g., Healthgrades, Facebook, GooglePlus, Twitter, YELP, ZocDoc). Reviews may include long waits and rude staff members, which can affect a physician's social media ratings. Patients who complete multiple forms prior to an office visit often discover the physician has not reviewed them. Instead, the physician conducts a hurried review of the documents at the time of a patient's scheduled appointment, reviewing with patients the ailments with which they are familiar and not addressing or leaving less time to discuss the patient's current concerns, reason for being there, and the treatment plan. Unfortunately, patients who experience long waits to see their physicians often tarnish their physician's reputation by posting negative remarks. It is not the wait time that should be judged. It is the skills of a physician in diagnosis and presentation of treatment options that makes the difference in the quality of life. Not only are physicians impacted by the challenges of social media, but hospitals are also concerned with their image in the community. All care organizations and caregivers must be sensitive to the fact that social media will not go away, and the concerns of patients need to be addressed in a positive way by addressing the concerns of the community.

National Health Insurance

The Patient Protection and Affordable Care Act (PPACA), passed by Congress and signed by President Barack Obama on March 23, 2010, was designed to ensure that more Americans receive healthcare benefits. The costs, however, associated with national health insurance continue to rise. Insurance premiums have risen by as much as 10% in 2017 for those who are not eligible for subsidies. "Aetna, Humana and United Health-Care Group said they would stop selling Obamacare policies in most states next year, citing financial losses due to a flood of older, sicker enrollees and not enough young, healthy people to offset the costs."[18]

As healthcare politics continue to rage on in Congress, the greatest health challenge of the 21st century requires that each member of society take a more responsible and proactive role in his or her health and well-being by maintaining a healthy lifestyle.

Boutique Medicine

The problem of accessibility to care is further exacerbated by an increasing number of physicians who turn to boutique medicine, a plan of care whereby a patient pays an annual retainer fee in exchange for expedited access to a physician for health care. As a result, physicians who elect to practice boutique medicine find it necessary to limit the number of patients they can treat due to the need to be readily available to patients in their practice. In other words, increased access leads to fewer patients, and arguably, better care for those who can afford the fees.

Medical Errors Plague Hospitals

The uncanny number of medical errors described in the following *news feature* quote illustrates the depth of the failure to understand what history has taught us.

Hospital-acquired infections (HAIs) continue to be a major concern in healthcare facilities. The results of a project known as the HAI Prevalence Survey were published in 2014.

The Survey described the burden of HAIs in U.S. hospitals, and reported that, in 2011, there were an estimated 722,000 HAIs in U.S. acute care hospitals. . . . Additionally, about 75,000 patients with HAIs died during their hospitalizations. More than half of all HAIs occurred outside of the intensive care unit.[20]

In a special issue of *Emerging Infectious Diseases*, Dr. William R. Jarvis, Associate Director for Program Development, Division of Health Care Quality Promotion (currently Hospital Infections Program), Centers for Disease Control and Prevention, writes:

Over the past two decades, acute-care facilities have become smaller and fewer, but the hospitalized patient population has become more severely ill and more immuno-compromised and thus at greater risk for hospital-acquired infections. At the same time, the proportion of the U.S. population 65 years of age has increased, as have the number of long-term care facilities and the number of beds in these facilities. This trend is expected to continue for the next 50 years. . . .

Infection control personnel will need to expand their efforts to match the expansion of the healthcare delivery system. Enhanced administrative support for programs to prevent infections and medical errors will be needed if we are to reduce the risk of infection and other adverse events and improve the quality of care in the entire spectrum of health-care delivery. Now, instead of the acute-care facility being the center of the infection control universe, the infection control department has become the center of the diverse health-care delivery system. Infection control departments will need to expand their surveillance of infections and adverse events and their prevention efforts to all settings in which health care is delivered.[21]

Infection control issues have been a reoccurring theme throughout the ages. Hospital-acquired infections are a leading cause of injury and unnecessary death. Such infections have been linked to unsanitary conditions in the environment and poor practices that can lead to cross-contamination between patients, visitors, and caregivers (e.g., hand-washing technique,[22] sterile gowning procedures, improper disposal of contaminated clothing, failure to follow recognized protocol for sterilizing hospital instruments, and equipment). The CDC has estimated that infections that are acquired by patients during their hospital stay, known as "nosocomial

DEATHS BY MEDICAL MISTAKES HIT RECORDS

It's a chilling reality—one often overlooked in annual mortality statistics: Preventable medical errors persist as the No. 3 killer in the U.S.—third only to heart disease and cancer—claiming the lives of some 400,000 each year. At a Senate hearing Thursday, patient safety officials put their best ideas forward on how to solve the crisis, with IT often at the center of discussions.

—McCann, Erin, *Healthcare IT News*, July 18, 2014[19]

bloodstream infections" are a leading cause of death in the United States. If we assume a nosocomial infection rate of 5%, of which 10% are bloodstream infections, and an attributable mortality rate of 15%, bloodstream infections would represent the eighth leading cause of death in the United States."[23] It has been estimated that the total number of infections have resulted in as many as 100,000 deaths and added billions of dollars in additional healthcare costs. These numbers do not reflect infections that have occurred in physicians' offices, nor do they account for the pain and disabilities suffered by patients who have been the recipient of a hospital-acquired infection.

HISTORY CHALLENGES US TO DO BETTER

The maintenance of hospitals today is a result of the human emotions of fear, pity, and sympathy, together with civic consciousness and religious zeal. If society has changed, human nature has remained much the same, for it was with these fundamental emotions which led ancient peoples to build hospitals for their sick and injured.

—Malcolm T. MacEachern, MD, CM, DSc, LLD

The pinnacle of the evolution of the hospital has not been reached, nor has the final page of its colorful history been written. As long as there remains a humanitarian impulse and as long as a society feels compassion, love, and sympathy for its neighbors, there will be hospitals. In the past, hospitals changed as conditions changed. In the future, they will continue to change to meet the needs of their communities. Healthcare leaders of the 21st century must understand their roots. They must understand the historical value of knowing the past and possess the vision to preserve the good, the courage to expunge the bad, and the passion to create an even better healthcare system, one that provides quality care for all. With each new discovery comes a new challenge.

CHAPTER REVIEW

1. The evolution of the hospital traveled a long, tortuous road, struggling along a hazardous path from India and Egypt to Greece and Rome, to the Islamic countries, to England, France, Germany, Spain, Italy, and on to America.

   - The existence of hospitals is evidence of a high degree of civilization, in which people are interested not only in the well-being of themselves and their families, but that of the greater community.

2. Religion played an important role in the development of hospitals.

   - Faith healing was practiced in India and Egypt thousands of years ago. Aesculapia (hospital temples) were numerous in ancient Greece and Rome and were dedicated to the god of medicine.
   - Hospitals in the early Christian era and in the Middle Ages were an integral part of the church.
   - Not until abuses crept into their administration under ecclesiastical authority in the 15th and 16th centuries were some of religious hospitals taken over and managed by civil bodies.

3. The development of the hospital has not been a smooth and easy advance.

   - Centuries of experiments, scientific discoveries, and public enlightenment were necessary to break down the barriers of ignorance and prejudice.
   - The evolution was accomplished in cycles, with alternating dark and golden ages.
   - Never has the hospital possessed the quality and quantity of scientific care for the sick that it has today, never before has its influence been so extensive and so widespread, and never before has it played such an important role in the life of the community.
   - During all of this growth and development, hospitals benefited by technical and scientific developments.

4. The primary function of the hospital is to care for the sick and injured.

   - The scope of services offered by hospitals continues to expand.
     a. Treating the sick and injured
     b. Preventing illness
     c. Prolonging purposeful life

5. National health insurance helps ensure more Americans will receive healthcare benefits, although the costs associated with it will require more collaboration among politicians, caregivers, and receivers of care well into the future.

▶ REVIEW QUESTIONS

1. Describe various historical events that have led to the growth of hospitals and at times impeded their progress over the centuries.
2. Describe advances in medicine that have contributed to improving the quality of patient care.
3. Who is often recognized as being the first hospital administrator and what major contributions did she make to nursing in the improvement of patient care?
4. What data did Semmelweis collect, and what was the significance of those data as related to performance improvement in the present-day hospital?
5. Describe how social media can have a negative or positive impact on caregivers and healthcare facilities.
6. Discuss the advancements in medicine and the challenges facing hospitals today.

▶ NOTES

1. Wisdom Quotes, "Gerda Lerner Quote," http://www.wisdomquotes.com/002320.html
2. "How to Stop Hospitals From Killing Us," *The Wall Street Journal*, September 21, 2012.
3. Malcolm T. MacEachern, *Hospital Organization and Management* (Berwyn, IL: Physician's Record Company, 1957), 10.
4. Mass Moments, "Massachusetts General Hospital Admits First Patient, September 3, 1821," http://www.massmoments.org/moment.cfm?mid=256
5. Mary Ann Byrnes, "Non-Nursing Functions: The Nurses State Their Case," *American Journal of Nursing* 82 (1982): 1089.
6. Carrie Howse, "Registration—A Minor Victory," *Nursing Times* 85 (1989): 32.
7. BioPortfolio, "Florence Nightingale in Absentia: Nursing and the 1893 Columbian Exposition," http://www.bioportfolio.com/resources/pmarticle/72474/Florence-Nightingale-In-Absentia-Nursing-And-The-1893-Columbian-Exposition.html
8. MedicineNet, "Medical Definition of Fever, puerperal," http://www.medicinenet.com/script/main/art.asp?articlekey=7921
9. The Joint Commission, 2017 Hospital Accreditation Standards, NPSG.07.01.01-07.06,01.
10. Centers for Disease Control and Prevention, "Historical Perspectives Centennial: Koch's Discovery of the Tubercle Bacillus," *Morbidity and Mortality Weekly Report* 31, no. 10 (1982): 121–123. http://www.cdc.gov/mmwr/preview/mmwrhtml/00000222.htm
11. U.S. National Library of Medicine, "Profiles in Science: The Francis Crick Papers," https://profiles.nlm.nih.gov/SC/Views/Exhibit/narrative/doublehelix.html
12. "Grading Hospital Safety," *AARP Bulletin*, November 2012.
13. Cheryl W. Thompson, "Howard: A Hospital in Turmoil," *The Washington Post*, March 26, 2017, at A1.
14. Sy Mukherjee, "*STUDY: An Increasing Number of Patients at Isolated Rural Hospitals Are Dying*, ThinkProgress, April 3, 2013. https://thinkprogress.org/study-an-increasing-number-of-patients-at-isolated-rural-hospitals-are-dying-175393ac39c5
15. Encyclopedia Britannica, "Translational Medicine: Year In Review 2012," https://www.britannica.com/topic/Translational-Medicine-1891925
16. da Vinci® Surgery, "Minimally Invasive Surgery," http://www.davincisurgery.com
17. Rifat Latifi. "Surgical Decision-making Process: More Questions Than Answers," http://sjs.sagepub.com/content/102/3/139.full
18. Insurers Exit ObamaCare, National Health Insurance, *AARP Bulletin*, October 2016.
19. Erin McCann, Deaths by Medical Mistakes Hit Records," *Healthcare IT News*, July 18, 2104. http://www.healthcareitnews.com/news/deaths-by-medical-mistakes-hit-records
20. Centers for Disease Control and Prevention, "Healthcare-Associated Infections: HAI Data and Statistics," https://www.cdc.gov/hai/surveillance/
21. William R. Jarvis, "Infection Control and Changing Health-Care Delivery Systems," Emerging Infectious Diseases, Centers for Disease Control and Prevention, http://www.cdc.gov/ncidod/eid/vol7no2/jarvis.htm
22. Centers for Disease Control and Prevention, "You're your Hands," CDC Features, Centers for Disease Control and Prevention, http://www.cdc.gov/Features/HandWashing/
23. Richard P. Wenzel and Michael B. Edmond, "The Impact of Hospital-Acquired Bloodstream Infections," http://www.cdc.gov/ncidod/eid/vol7no2/wenzel.htm

CHAPTER 2

Government, Law, and Ethics

As the patriots of seventy-six did to the support of the Declaration of Independence, so to the support of the Constitution and Laws, let every American pledge his life, his property, and his sacred honor—let every man remember that to violate the law, is to trample on the blood of his father, and to tear the character of his own, and his children's liberty. Let reverence for the laws, be breathed by every American mother, to the lisping babe, that prattles on her lap—let it be taught in schools, in seminaries, and in colleges; let it be written in Primers, spelling books, and in Almanacs—let it be preached from the pulpit, proclaimed in legislative halls, and enforced in courts of justice. And, in short, let it become the political religion of the nation; and let the old and the young, the rich and the poor, the grave and the gay, of all sexes and tongues, and colors and conditions, sacrifice unceasingly upon its altars.

—Abraham Lincoln

▶ LEARNING OBJECTIVES

The reader, upon completion of this chapter, will be able to:

- Explain the development and sources of law.
- Discuss how case law differs from statutory and administrative law.
- Describe what is meant by *conflict of laws*.
- Describe the three branches of government.
- Describe what is meant by *separation of powers*.
- Describe the organizational structure of the Department of Health and Human Services.
- Describe the functions of various government ethics committees.
- Explain the term *political malpractice*.

Laws are the very bulwarks of liberty; they define every man's rights, and defend the individual liberties of all men.

—J. G. Holland

This chapter introduces the reader to the development of law in the United States, the functioning of the legal system, and the roles of the three branches of government in creating, administering, and enforcing the law. It lays a foundation for the understanding of the legal system that is needed before one can appreciate or comprehend the specific laws and principles relating to health care. The reader is also introduced to the term *political malpractice*, as well as a variety of government ethics committees that address ethical conduct within the various branches of government.

▶ DEVELOPMENT OF LAW

Scholars often define the law as a system of principles and processes by which people in a society deal with disputes and problems, seeking to solve or settle them without resorting to force. Simply stated, laws are rules of conduct enforced by government, which imposes penalties when prescribed laws are violated.

U.S. Supreme Court Justice Oliver Wendell Holmes said that the law "is a magic mirror, wherein we see reflected not only our own lives but also the lives of those who went before us."[1] Chief Justice John Marshall, in delivering his opinion to the court in *Marbury v. Madison*, said,

The very essence of civil liberty certainly consists in the right of every individual to claim the protection of the laws, whenever he receives an injury. One of the first duties of government

is to afford that protection. [The] government of the United States has been emphatically termed a government of laws, and not of men. It will certainly cease to deserve this high appellation, if the laws furnish no remedy for the violation of a vested right.[2]

Laws govern the relationships between private individuals and organizations and between both of these parties and government. *Public law* is the term used to describe "The laws that cover administration, constitution, and criminal acts. It controls the actions between the citizens of the state and the state itself. It deals with the government's operation and structure."[3] The purpose of *public law* is to attain what society deems to be valid public goals. One important segment of public law, for example, is *criminal law*, which prohibits conduct deemed injurious to public order and provides for punishment of those proven to have engaged in such conduct.

In contrast, *private law* is concerned with the recognition and enforcement of the rights and duties of private individuals. Tort and contract actions are two basic types of private law. In a *tort action*, one party asserts that the wrongful conduct of another has caused harm, and the injured party seeks compensation for the harm suffered. A *contract action* involves a claim by one party that another party has breached an agreement by failing to fulfill an obligation. Either remuneration or specific performance of the obligation may be sought as a remedy. Without an organized, clear system of laws that regulate society, anarchy would clearly arise.

Public Policy as a Principle of Law

Public policy is the principle of law that holds that no one can lawfully do that which tends to be injurious to the public or against the public good. The sources of public policy "include legislation; administrative rules, regulations, or decisions; and judicial decisions. In certain instances, a professional code of ethics may contain an expression of public policy."[4]

▶ SOURCES OF LAW

The basic sources of law are *common law*, which is derived from judicial decisions; *statutory law*, which emanates from the federal and state legislatures; and *administrative law*, prescribed by administrative agencies. In those instances in which written laws are either silent, vague, or contradictory to other laws, the judicial system often is called on to resolve those disputes until such time as appropriate legislative action can be taken to clear up a particular legal issue. In the following sections, the sources of law that formed the foundation of our legal system are discussed.

Common Law

Common law refers to the body of principles that evolve from and expand upon judicial decisions that arise during the trial of court cases. Many of the legal principles and rules applied today by courts in the United States have their origins in English common law.

Because a law could never cover every potential human event that might occur in society, the judicial system is doubly necessary. It not only serves as a mechanism for reviewing legal disputes that arise in the written law, but it is also an effective review mechanism for those issues in which the written law is silent or in instances of a mixture of issues involving both written law and common law decisions. For example, in the *Cruzan v. Director, Missouri Department of Health* case, the U.S. Supreme Court based its decision on the consideration of existing statutory law and prior judicial decisions.[5]

Common Law in England

[handwritten: English Custom, Foreign Lit, Rule of strong kings]

[handwritten: English / Romans Saxons Normans Danes]

Law reflects to a large degree the civilization of those that live under it. Its progress and development are mirrors not merely of material prosperity but of the method of thought and of the outlook of the age.[6]

The common law of England is much like its language: as varied as the nations that peopled its land in different locations and different periods. Parts of the common law are derived from the Britons, Romans, Saxons, Danes, and Normans.

> To recount what innovations were made by the succession of these different nations, or estimate what proportion of the customs of each go to the composing of our body of common law, would be impossible at this distance of time. As to a great part of this period, we have no monuments of antiquity to guide us in our inquiry; and the lights which gleam upon the other part afford but dim prospect. Our conjectures can only be assisted by the history of the revolutions effected by these several nations.[7]

The Romans governed the island as a province from the time of Claudius (AD 43) until AD 448. It was a time of peace and cultivation of the arts. Roman laws were administered as laws of the country. When the Romans left Britain to attend to their own domestic safety, the Picts and the Scots clashed with inhabitants of southern England. Unable to oppose the attack, these southern inhabitants appealed to the Saxons for assistance. The Saxons, who came from German lands, drove the northern invaders back inside their own borders.[8] The Saxons also had to contend with Danish raiders from the 8th to the 11th centuries.

The law in England before the Norman Conquest in 1066 was dispensed primarily by tradition and local custom and mostly dealt with violent crimes. The kings during this period were concerned more with enforcing customary law than with amending it. The courts mainly consisted of open-air meetings where no records were maintained. "For the Anglo-Saxons justice was a local matter, administered chiefly in the shire courts, and was largely dependent upon local customs, preserved in the memory of those persons who declared the law in the court."[9] The Saxons operated with the goal of exterminating the Britons and destroying all their monuments and establishments. Subsequently, the native Briton customs and laws fell out of favor. The Britons were forced into the mountains of Wales, dividing the remainder of the dominion into seven independent kingdoms.[10]

These kingdoms were, for a time, independent of one another. A variety of laws grew among the Saxons themselves, as well as among the Danes, who, following a treaty in Northumberland, were considered in some measure to be part of the nation. Toward the later part of Saxon times, the kingdom was governed by a variety of laws (Mercian Law, West-Saxon Law, and Danish Law) and local customs. All British and Roman customs that survived the times were buried within one of the three laws, which governed all of England.[11]

Following their conquest in 1066, the Normans had little regard for Anglo-Saxon laws. They considered themselves apart from such laws.

> It is obviously impossible to attempt an adequate picture of Anglo-Saxon life. It was a wild time. Men lived in terror of the vast forests, where it was easy to be lost and succumb to starvation, of their fellow man who would plunder and slay, and above all of the Unknown, whose inscrutable ways seemed constantly to be bringing famine and disaster. The uncertainties of modern life pale into insignificance when regarded from the standpoint of these men. It is natural, therefore, that their law should reflect their reaction against the environment. It was

conservative and harsh. Violence, robbery and death formed its background.[12]

The principal change introduced by the Norman Conquest was that the king's court opened for disputes about land tenure. Land disputes involved the Saxons who held the land before the conquest and the Normans who dispossessed them. Evidence in such disputes was often the result of oral testimony from neighboring landowners. Although no professional judiciary yet existed, the king's representatives held trials before the county courts, and a cleric often presided.

Soon, a system of national law began to develop based on custom, foreign literature, and the rule of strong kings. The first royal court was established in 1178. This court, enlisting the aid of a jury, heard the complaints of the kingdom's subjects. Because there were few written laws, a body of principles evolved from these court decisions, which became known as *common law*. Judges used these court decisions to decide subsequent cases. As Parliament's power to legislate grew, the initiative for developing new laws passed from the king to Parliament.

Common Law in the United States

During the colonial period, English common law began to be applied in the colonies. In the vast new country with its abundance of natural resources, English common law could not be adopted exactly; the law was thus adapted to meet the needs of the new land. Compared to England, the New World glistened with land, timber, and minerals, so the law would have to aid the new society in mastering the land.

In an 1829 U.S. Supreme Court decision, Joseph Story wrote, "The common law of England is not to be taken in all respects to be that of America. Our ancestors brought with them its general principles, and claimed it as their birthright but they brought with them and adopted only that portion which was applicable to their situation."[13]

After the American Revolution, each state, with the exception of Louisiana, adopted all or part of the existing English common law and added to it as needed. Louisiana civil law, by contrast, is based to a great extent on French and Spanish laws and, especially, on the Code of Napoleon. As a result, there is no national system of common law in the United States, and common law on specific subjects may differ from state to state.

Case law, derived from judicial decisions, did not easily pass from colony to colony. There were no printed reports to make transfer easy, although in the 18th century, some manuscript materials did circulate among lawyers. These could hardly have been very influential. No doubt custom and case law slowly seeped from colony to colony. Travelers and word of mouth spread the knowledge of living law. It is hard to say how much this occurred, and thus, it is hard to tell to what degree there was a common legal structure.[14]

Judicial review became part of the law in the decade before the federal Constitution was adopted. Courts began to assert their power to rule on the constitutionality of legislative acts and to void unconstitutional statutes.

Today, cases are tried applying common law principles unless a statute governs. Although statutory law has affirmed many of the legal rules and principles initially established by the courts, new issues continue to arise, especially in private law disputes, which require decision making according to common law principles. Common law actions are initiated mainly to recover monetary damages or possession of real or personal property.

State Decisions Not Binding on Other States

When a higher state court has enunciated a common law principle, the lower courts within the state where the decision was rendered must follow that principle. A decision in a case that sets forth a new legal principle establishes a precedent. Trial courts or those on equal footing are not bound by the decisions of other trial courts. Also, a principle established in one state does not set precedent for another state. Rather, the rulings in one jurisdiction may be used by the courts of other jurisdictions as guides to the legal analysis of a particular legal problem. Decisions found to be reasonable are followed, and decisions found to be unreasonable are not followed.

For example, in *Lebron v. Gottlieb Memorial Hospital*,[15] the plaintiffs challenged the caps on noneconomic damages contained in an Illinois act. In this case, the Supreme Court of Illinois agreed with the plaintiffs that a $500,000 limit on noneconomic damages was arbitrary and violated the state's constitution.

The defendants referred the court's attention to statutes limiting noneconomic damages in medical malpractice cases that have been adopted in other states. The defendants contended that the limits on damages contained in the act are well within the range of reasonable limits adopted by these states. The court reviewed the statutes cited by the defendants and observed that the limitations on noneconomic damages adopted in other states vary widely.

For example, the California statute provides simply: "In no [medical malpractice] action shall the amount of damages for noneconomic losses exceed

Louisiana

two hundred fifty thousand dollars ($250,000)."[16] In contrast, the Florida statute sets up a more complex scheme, in which the damages cap may be as low as $150,000 and as high as $1.5 million, depending on whether the medical negligence is attributable to a practitioner or nonpractitioner, the negligence results in a permanent vegetative state or death, the negligence caused a catastrophic injury to the patient, or the negligence occurred during the provision of emergency care.[17]

On what basis defendants have determined that such disparate provisions are all reasonable is not known, and it is not for the Supreme Court of Illinois to judge the reasonableness of other states' legislation. The "everybody is doing it" mentality is hardly a valid test for the constitutionality of the statute. Although decisions from other jurisdictions can provide guidance, "This court's jurisprudence of state constitutional law cannot be predicated on the actions of our sister states."[18]

The position of a court or agency, relative to other courts and agencies, determines the place assigned to its decision in the hierarchy of decisional law. The decisions of the U.S. Supreme Court are highest in the hierarchy of decisional law with respect to federal legal questions. Because of the parties or the legal question(s) involved, most legal controversies do not fall within the scope of the Supreme Court's decision-making responsibilities. On questions of purely state concern—such as the interpretation of a state statute that raises no issues under the U.S. Constitution or federal law—the highest court in the state has the final word on interpretation of the law.

Common Law Principles

The following are explanations of some of the more important common law principles:

- *Precedent.* A precedent is a judicial decision that may be used as a standard in subsequent similar cases. A precedent is set when a court decision is rendered that serves as a rule for future guidance when deciding similar cases.

- *Res judicata.* In common law, the term *res judicata*—which means "the thing is decided"—refers to that which has been previously acted on or decided by the courts. According to *Black's Law Dictionary*, it is a rule where "a final judgment rendered by a court of competent jurisdiction on the merits is conclusive as to the rights of the parties and their privies, and, as to them, constitutes an absolute bar to subsequent action involving the same claim, demand, or cause of action."[19]

- *Stare decisis.* The common law principle *stare decisis* ("let the decision stand") provides that when a decision is rendered in a lawsuit involving a particular set of facts, another lawsuit involving an identical or substantially similar situation is to be resolved in the same manner as the first lawsuit. A lawsuit is decided by applying the rules and principles of prior cases. In this manner, courts arrive at comparable rulings. Sometimes, slight factual differences may provide a basis for recognizing distinctions between the precedent and the current case. In some cases, even when such differences are absent, a court may conclude that a particular common law rule is no longer in accord with the needs of society and may depart from precedent. Principles of law are subject to change, whether they originate in statutory or in common law. Common law principles may be modified, overturned, abrogated, or created by new court decisions in a continuing process of growth and development to reflect changes in social attitudes, public needs, judicial prejudices, or contemporary political thinking.

First Medical Malpractice Common Law Case

The first common law case in the United States in which a physician was held legally responsible for negligence occurred as early as 1794. In *Cross v. Guthery*,[20] the court heard that when Mrs. Cross complained that there was something wrong with her breast, her husband sent for Dr. Guthery. The doctor examined Mrs. Cross, diagnosed her ailment, and removed her breast. Shortly after the surgery, she bled to death. Guthery expressed his regrets to her husband and then sent him a bill for 15 pounds. Mr. Cross hired a lawyer, who persuaded a jury to dismiss Guthery's bill and award Mr. Cross 40 pounds as compensation for the loss of his wife's companionship. Since that time, physicians have experienced recurring periods of substantial increases in the number of malpractice cases. The first such increase occurred in the 15 years prior to the Civil War.[21] Another rise in the number of malpractice cases and ever-increasing concern about them occurred at the beginning of the 20th century. By 1941, *The Journal of the American Medical Association* published studies showing that 1,296 malpractices had occurred between 1900 and 1940, with more than 500 between 1930 and 1940. The increase in malpractice cases was attributed to substantial malpractice awards, high patient expectations, new diagnostic procedures, and erosion of the physician–patient relationship.[22]

The Harvard Medical Malpractice Study, commissioned by the state of New York to determine the rate of medical injury in New York hospitals, revealed that 3.7% of patients entering New York hospitals in 1984 were injured by the care provided. One tenth of those who were treated negligently filed malpractice suits.[23] The research group conducting the study suggested that "only one claim makes its way into the tort system for every eight cases of injury caused by medical negligence."[24] The study, which cost $3.1 million and ran 1,200 pages, was funded by the state and a grant from the Robert Wood Johnson Foundation. It involved 4 years of research and included the review of more than 30,000 medical records.[25]

The number of malpractice suits is staggering. Critics say that the system fails by making too little information known.[26] A report by the Physician Insurers Association of America, which represents 50 malpractice insurance companies covering 50% of private physicians in the United States, claims that breast cancer accounts for more medical malpractice claims than any other medical condition. Delayed diagnosis is common among both younger and older women. The report focuses on 487 lawsuits in which damages were awarded for delayed diagnosis. The most common reasons for delay were misdiagnosis, failure to follow up, and false-negative mammograms. The next most common medical diagnoses involving malpractice suits were infant brain damage, pregnancy, and heart attacks.[27] Not much has changed since this study was conducted. Misdiagnosis and failure to follow up remain high on the list of common malpractice claims. The long list of news articles on misdiagnoses continues to flow as physicians often rely on technology to make their diagnoses, as Ms. Sandra B. Goodman well describes in the *news feature* below.

Failure to diagnose a patient's disease is sometimes due to the difficulty associated with evaluating

vague symptoms that can often mimic more common and treatable ailments. The complexity associated with diagnosing rare autoimmune diseases, such as scleroderma and lupus, often results in a delayed diagnosis. In 2012, *misdiagnosis* accounted for 34% of malpractice claims. *Surgery* accounted for 24%, *treatment* 18%, obstetrics 11%, and medication related 4%, monitoring 3%, anesthesia 3%, and other 4% of claims made.[29] Actual numbers are increasingly difficult to determine due to unpublished out-of-court settlements.

Statutory Law *Hierarchical order / State Constitution*

Statutory law is written law emanating from a legislative body. Although a statute can abolish any rule of common law, it can do so only by express words. The principles and rules of statutory law are set in hierarchical order. The Constitution of the United States adopted at the Constitutional Convention in Philadelphia in 1787 is first in the hierarchy of enacted law. Article VI of the Constitution declares:

> This Constitution, and the Laws of the United States which shall be made in Pursuance thereof; and all Treaties made, or which shall be made, under the Authority of the United States, shall be the supreme Law of the Land; and the Judges in every State shall be bound thereby, any Thing in the Constitution or Laws of any State to the Contrary notwithstanding.[30]

The clear import of these words is that the U.S. Constitution, federal law, and federal treaties take precedence over the constitutions and laws of the states and local jurisdictions. Statutory law may be amended, repealed, or expanded by action of the legislature, as was the case with the *Bill of Rights*, which details the first 10 amendments to the U.S. Constitution, and other amendments to the Constitution, such as the 14th Amendment, which provides that a state cannot act to deny equal protection of the laws to any person. If a state or a political subdivision of a state, whether through its executive, judicial, or legislative branch, acts in such a way as to deny unfairly to any person the rights accorded to another, the amendment has been violated.

Fourteenth Amendment to the U.S. Constitution

Section 1. All persons born or naturalized in the United States, and subject to the jurisdiction thereof, are citizens of the United States

NEWS AS HANDS-ON DOCTORING FADES AWAY, PATIENTS LOSE

Doctors at a Northern California hospital, concerned that a 40-year-old woman with sky-high blood pressure and confusion might have a blood clot, ordered a CT scan of her lungs. To their surprise, the scan reveals not a clot but large cancers in both breasts that have spread throughout her body. Had they done a 'simple physical exam of the woman's chest, they would have been able to feel the tumors. So would the doctors who saw her during several hospitalizations over the previous two years, when the cancer might have been more easily treated.[28]

and of the state wherein they reside. No state shall make or enforce any law, which shall abridge the privileges or immunities of citizens of the United States; nor shall any state deprive any person of life, liberty, or property, without due process of law; nor deny to any person within its jurisdiction the equal protection of the laws.

Section 5. The Congress shall have power to enforce, by appropriate legislation, the provisions of this article.

States and local jurisdictions can only enact and enforce laws that do not conflict with federal law. Statutory laws may be declared void by a court; for example, a statute may be found unconstitutional because it does not comply with a state or federal constitution, because it is vague or ambiguous, or, in the case of a state law, because it is in conflict with a federal law.

In many cases involving statutory law, the court is called on to interpret how a statute applies to a given set of facts. For example, a statute may state merely that no person may discriminate against another person because of race, creed, color, or sex. A court may then be called on to decide whether certain actions by a person are discriminatory and therefore violate the law.

Administrative Law

Administrative law is the extensive body of public law issued by either state or federal agencies to direct the enacted laws of the federal and state governments. It is the branch of law that controls the administrative operations of government. Congress and state legislative bodies realistically cannot oversee their many laws; therefore, they delegate implementation and administration of the law to an appropriate administrative agency. Healthcare organizations, in particular, are inundated with a proliferation of administrative rules and regulations affecting every aspect of their operations.

The Administrative Procedures Act[31] describes the different procedures under which federal administrative agencies must operate.[32] The act prescribes the procedural responsibilities and authority of administrative agencies and provides for legal remedies for those wronged by agency actions. The regulatory power exercised by administrative agencies includes power to license, power of rate setting (e.g., Centers for Medicare and Medicaid Services [CMS]), and power over business practices (e.g., National Labor Relations Board [NLRB]).

Rules and Regulations

Administrative agencies have legislative, judicial, and executive functions. They have the authority to formulate rules and regulations considered necessary to carry out the intent of legislative enactments. Regulatory agencies have the ability to legislate, adjudicate, and enforce their own regulations in many cases.

Rules and regulations established by an administrative agency must be administered within the scope of authority delegated to it by Congress. Although an agency must comply with its own regulations, agency regulations must be consistent with the statute under which they are promulgated. An agency's interpretation of a statute cannot supersede the language chosen by Congress. An executive regulation that defines some general statutory term in a too restrictive or unrealistic manner is invalid. Agency regulations and administrative decisions are subject to judicial review when questions arise as to whether an agency has overstepped its bounds in its interpretation of the law.

§702: Right to Review

A person suffering legal wrong because of agency action, or adversely affected or aggrieved by agency action within the meaning of a relevant statute, is entitled to judicial review thereof. . . .[33]

§706: Scope of Review

To the extent necessary . . . the reviewing court shall decide all relevant questions of law, interpret constitutional and statutory provisions, and determine the meaning or applicability of the terms of an agency action. The reviewing court shall

(1) compel agency action unlawfully withheld or unreasonably delayed; and

(2) hold unlawful and set aside agency action, findings, and conclusions found to be

   (A) arbitrary, capricious, an abuse of discretion, or otherwise not in accordance with law;

   (B) contrary to constitutional right, power, privilege, or immunity;

   (C) in excess of statutory jurisdiction, authority, or limitations, or short of statutory right;

   (D) without observance of procedure required by law;

   (E) unsupported by substantial evidence in a case subject to sections 556 and 557 of this title or otherwise reviewed on the record of an agency hearing provided by statute; or

(F) unwarranted by the facts to the extent that the facts are subject to trial de novo by the reviewing court.

In making the foregoing determinations, the court shall review the whole record or those parts of it cited by a party, and due account shall be taken of the rule of prejudicial error.[34]

Recourse to an administrative agency for resolution of a dispute is generally required prior to seeking judicial review. The Pennsylvania Commonwealth Court held in *Fair Rest Home v. Commonwealth, Department of Health*[35] that the Department of Health was required to hold a hearing before it ordered revocation of a nursing home's operating license. The Department of Health failed in its responsibility when "in a revocation proceeding it [did] not give careful consideration to its statutorily mandated responsibility to hear testimony."[36]

Regulations and decisions of administrative agencies reviewed by the courts may be upheld, modified, overturned, or reversed and remanded for further proceedings. For example, the owner and operator of a licensed residential care facility brought an action challenging regulations, promulgated by the Arkansas Department of Human Services (DHS) through its Office of Long Term Care (OLTC), governing administration of medicines in residential care facilities.[37]

The owner challenged two OLTC regulations that required the following:

1. Under no circumstances shall an operator or employee or anyone solicited by an operator or employee be permitted to administer any oral medications, injectable medications, eye drops, eardrops, or topical ointments (both prescription and nonprescription drugs).

2. In addition, any owner and/or operator of a Residential Care Facility who is a licensed nurse who administers any medication to a resident will be in violation of operating an unlicensed nursing home.[38]

The circuit court in this case held that the regulations were invalid, and the DHS appealed. The Supreme Court reversed the circuit court's decision by holding the regulations reasonable in light of the distinctions between residential care facilities and nursing homes.

Conflict of Laws

When state and federal laws conflict, resolution can be sought in the appropriate federal court. The following case illustrates how federal and state laws may be in conflict. The plaintiff in *Dorsten v. Lapeer County General Hospital*[39] brought an action against a hospital and certain physicians on the medical board, alleging wrongful denial of her application for medical staff privileges. The plaintiff asserted claims under the U.S. Code for sex discrimination, violations of the Sherman Antitrust Act, and the like. The plaintiff filed a motion to compel discovery of peer review reports to support her case. The U.S. District Court held that the plaintiff was entitled to discovery of peer review reports despite a Michigan state law purporting to establish an absolute privilege for peer review reports conducted by hospital review boards.

▶ GOVERNMENT ORGANIZATION

The three branches of the federal government, as illustrated in **FIGURE 2-1**, are the legislative, executive, and judicial branches. A typical example of a state government organization is illustrated in **FIGURE 2-2**. A vital concept in the constitutional framework of government on both federal and state levels is the separation of powers. Essentially, this principle provides that no one branch of government is clearly dominant over the other two; however, in the exercise of its functions, each may affect and limit the activities, functions, and powers of the others.

Legislative Branch

On the federal level, legislative powers are vested in the *Congress* of the United States, which consists of the *Senate* and the *House of Representatives*. The function of the legislative branch is to enact laws, as well as amend or repeal existing legislation and to create new legislation. The legislature determines the nature and extent of the need for new laws and for changes in existing laws. Committees of both houses of Congress are responsible for preparing federal legislation. There are 16 standing committees in the Senate and 19 in the House of Representatives, all of whose membership are appointed by a vote of the entire body.

Legislative proposals are assigned or referred to an appropriate committee for study. The committees conduct investigations and hold hearings where interested persons may present their views regarding proposed legislation. These proceedings provide additional information to assist committee members in their consideration of proposed bills. A bill may be reported out of a committee in its original form, favorably or unfavorably; it may be reported out with recommended amendments; or the bill might be

THE GOVERNMENT OF THE UNITED STATES

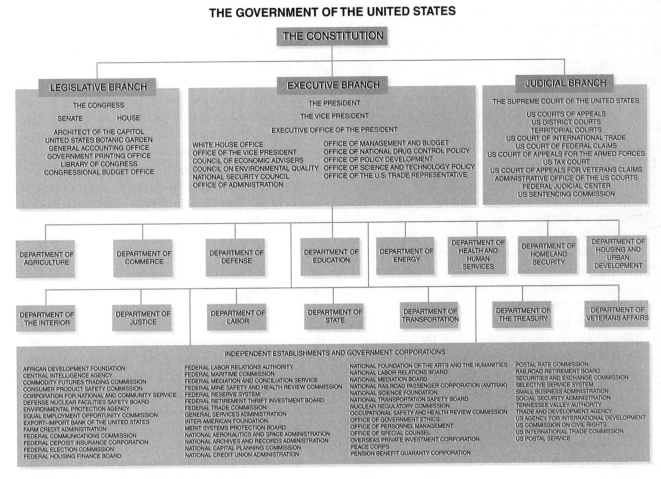

FIGURE 2-1 Government of the United States.

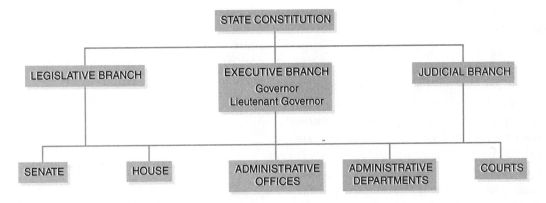

FIGURE 2-2 Example of a state government organization.

allowed to lie in the committee without action. Some bills eventually reach the full legislative body, where, after consideration and debate, they may be approved or rejected.

The U.S. Congress and all state legislatures are bicameral (consisting of two houses), except for the Nebraska legislature, which is unicameral. Both houses in a bicameral legislature must pass identical versions of a legislative proposal before the legislation can be brought to the chief executive (president or governor).

Executive Branch

The primary function of the *executive branch of government* on the federal and state level is to administer and enforce the law. The chief executive, either the president of the United States or the governor of a state, also has a role in the creation of law through the power to approve or veto legislative proposals.

The U.S. Constitution provides that the president of the United States holds the executive power.

The president serves as the administrative head of the executive branch of the federal government. The executive branch includes 15 executive departments (see Figure 2-1), as well as a variety of agencies, both temporary and permanent.

The cabinet is composed of 15 executive department heads.[40] Each department is responsible for a different area of public affairs, and each enforces the law within its area of responsibility. For example, the DHHS administers much of the federal health law enacted by Congress. Most state executive branches are also organized on a departmental basis. These departments administer and enforce state law concerning public affairs.

On a state level, the governor serves as the chief executive officer. The responsibilities of a state governor are provided for in the state's constitution. The Massachusetts State Constitution, for example, describes the responsibilities of the governor as presenting an annual budget to the state legislature, recommending new legislation, vetoing legislation, appointing and removing department heads, appointing judicial officers, and acting as Commander-in-Chief of the state's military forces (the Massachusetts National Guard).[41]

Judicial Branch

As I have said in the past, when government bureaus and agencies go awry, which are adjuncts of the legislative or executive branches, the people flee to the third branch, their courts, for solace and justice.[42]

—Justice J. Henderson, Supreme Court of South Dakota

The function of the judicial branch of government is *adjudication*—resolving disputes in accordance with law. As a practical matter, most disputes or controversies that are covered by legal principles or rules are resolved without resort to the courts.

Alexis de Tocqueville (1805–1859), a foreign observer commenting on the primordial place of the law and the legal profession, stated:

Scarcely any political question arises in the United States that is not resolved, sooner or later, into a judicial question.

—Alexis de Tocqueville (1805–1859)

The decision regarding which court has *jurisdiction*—the legal right to hear and rule on a particular case—is determined by such matters as the locality in which each party to a lawsuit resides and the issues of a lawsuit. Each state in the United States provides its own court system, which is created by the state's constitution and statutes. Most of the nation's judicial business is reviewed and acted on in state courts. Each state maintains a level of trial courts that have *original jurisdiction,* meaning the authority of a court to first conduct a trial on a specific case, as distinguished from a court with *appellate jurisdiction*, where appeals from trial judgments are held. This jurisdiction may exclude cases involving claims with damages less than a specified minimum, probate matters (i.e., wills and estates), and workers' compensation. Different states have designated different names for trial courts (e.g., superior, district, circuit, or supreme courts). Also on the trial court level are minor courts, such as city, small claims, and justice of the peace courts. States such as Massachusetts have consolidated their minor courts into a statewide court system.

Each state has at least one appellate court. Many states have an intermediate appellate court between the trial courts and the court of last resort, which is the state supreme court in most states. Where this intermediate court is present, there is a provision for appeal to it, with further review in all but select cases. A state's highest appellate tribunal is seen as the final arbiter for a state's system of jurisprudence. **FIGURE 2-3** depicts a typical state court system.

The trial court of the federal system is the U.S. District Court. There are 94 district courts in the 50 states (the larger states having more than one district court) and one in the District of Columbia. The Commonwealth of Puerto Rico also has a district court with jurisdiction corresponding to that of district courts in the different states. Generally, only one judge is required to sit and decide a case, although certain cases require up to three judges. The federal district courts hear civil, criminal, admiralty, and bankruptcy cases.

The *U.S. Circuit Court of Appeals* is the appellate court. There are 12 regional courts in various cities and the 13th judicial court is located in Washington, DC. Their main purpose is to review cases tried in federal district courts within their respective circuits, but they also possess jurisdiction to review orders of designated administrative agencies and to issue original writs in appropriate cases. These intermediate appellate courts were created to relieve the U.S. Supreme Court of deciding all cases appealed from the federal trial courts.

The *Supreme Court*, the nation's highest court, is the only federal court created directly by the Constitution. Eight associate justices and one chief justice sit on the Supreme Court.

The court has limited original jurisdiction over the lower federal courts and the highest state courts. In a

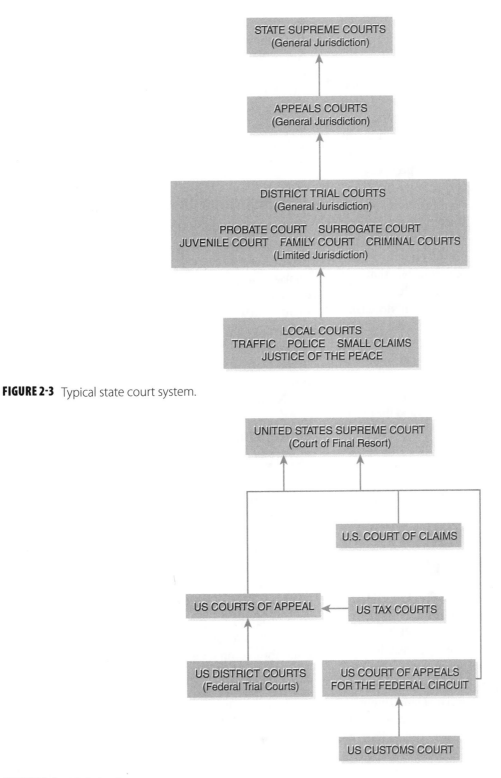

FIGURE 2-3 Typical state court system.

FIGURE 2-4 U.S. federal court system.

few situations, an appeal will go directly from a federal or state court to the Supreme Court, but in most cases, review must be sought through the discretionary *writ of certiorari*, an appeal petition. In addition to the aforementioned courts, special federal courts have jurisdiction over particular subject matters. The *U.S. Court of Claims*, for example, has jurisdiction over certain claims against the government. The *U.S. Court of Appeals* for the Federal Circuit has appellate jurisdiction over certain customs and patent matters. The *U.S. Customs Court* reviews certain administrative decisions by customs officials. Also, there is a *U.S. Tax Court* and a *U.S. Court of Military Appeals*. The federal court system is illustrated in **FIGURE 2-4**.

Separation of Powers

The concept of *separation of powers*, a system of checks and balances, is illustrated in the relationships among the three branches of government with regard to legislation. On the federal level, when a bill creating a statute is enacted by Congress and signed by the president, it becomes law. If the president vetoes a bill, it takes a two-thirds vote of each house of Congress to override the veto. The president also can prevent a bill from becoming law by avoiding any action while Congress is in session. This procedure, known as a *pocket veto*, can temporarily stop a bill from becoming law and may permanently prevent it from becoming law if later sessions of Congress do not act on it favorably.

The Supreme Court may declare a bill that has become law invalid if it violates the Constitution. "It is not entirely unworthy of observation, that in declaring what shall be the Supreme law of the land, the Constitution itself is first mentioned; and not the laws of the United States generally, but those only made in pursuance to the Constitution, have that rank."[43]

Even though a Supreme Court decision is final regarding a specific controversy, Congress and the president may generate new, constitutionally sound legislation to replace a law that has been declared unconstitutional. The procedures for amending the Constitution are complex and often time consuming, but they can serve as a way to offset or override a Supreme Court decision.

▶ DEPARTMENT OF HEALTH AND HUMAN SERVICES

The *Department of Health and Human Services* (DHHS) is a cabinet-level department within the executive branch of the federal government (**FIGURE 2-5**). The DHHS has been charged with the responsibility for developing and implementing appropriate administrative regulations for carrying out national health and human services policy objectives. The Department of Health and Human Services was created on April 11, 1953 to strengthen "the public health and welfare of the American people by making affordable and quality health care and childcare accessible, ensuring the safety of food products, preparing for public health emergencies, and advancing the diagnosis, treatment, and curing of life threatening illnesses."[44] It is also the main source of regulations governing the healthcare industry. The secretary of the DHHS, serving as the department's administrative head, advises the president with regard to health, welfare, and income security plans, policies, and programs. The DHHS is also responsible for many of the programs designed to meet the needs of senior citizens, including Social Security benefits (e.g., retirement, survivors, disability), Supplemental Security Income (which ensures a minimum monthly income to needy persons and is administered by local Social Security offices), Medicare, Medicaid, and programs under the Older Americans Act (e.g., in-home services, such as home health and home-delivered meals, and community services such as adult day care, transportation, and ombudsman services in long-term care facilities).

Administration on Aging

The Administration on Aging (AOA) is the principal agency designated to carry out the provisions of the Older Americans Act of 1965, which, as amended, focuses on improving the lives of senior citizens in areas of income, housing, health, employment, retirement, and community services. The AOA develops policies, plans, and programs designed to promote the welfare of the aging population. It promotes their needs by planning programs and developing policy, procedural direction, and technical assistance to states and Native American tribal governments.

Centers for Medicare and Medicaid Services

The *Centers for Medicare and Medicaid Services* (CMS), formerly the Health Care Financing Administration, was created to combine under one administration the oversight of the Medicare program, the federal portion of the Medicaid program, the State Children's Health Insurance Program, and related quality assurance activities.

Medicare is a federally sponsored health insurance program for persons 65 years of age, as well as certain diseases and disabilities of all disabled persons. It has four complementary parts A, B, C, and D:

Medicare Part A

Medicare Part A helps pay for the costs associated with hospital care. Part A can also help cover the cost of hospice, home health care and skilled nursing facilities. Part A pays about 80 percent of Medicare-approved, inpatient costs for the first 60 days of hospitalization. Patients who have longer hospital stays are required to pay a larger share of the costs, thus emphasizing the importance of having supplemental insurance.

Medicare Part B

Medicare Part B helps pay for medical costs associated with physician visits, some home health care, medical equipment, outpatient

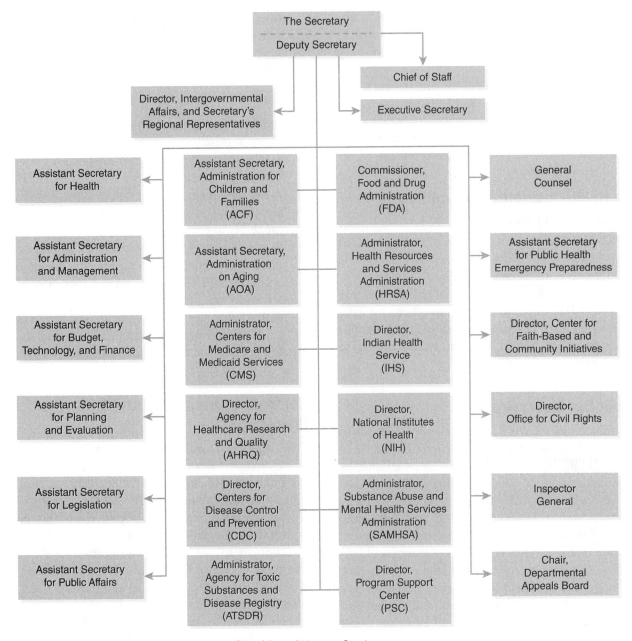

FIGURE 2-5 Organization of the Department of Health and Human Services.

procedures, rehabilitation therapy, laboratory tests, X-rays, mental health services, ambulance services, and blood. Preventive care, such as flu shots, are also covered.

Medicare Part C

Medicare Part C helps pay for hospital and medical costs not covered by Parts A and B. Part C private insurance plans are offered through private health insurance companies that are approved by Medicare. They are referred to as Medicare Advantage Plans. They generally cover more of the costs the patient would have to pay for out of pocket with Medicare Parts A and B. Part C plans also put a limit on what you pay out of pocket

in a given year. Some of these plans cover preventive dental, vision, and hearing costs.

Medicare Part D

Medicare Part D helps pay for prescription drugs and is available through private health insurance companies. Called prescription drug plans, they commonly cover brand-name and generic drugs. Coverage can differ from one insurance carrier to the next. Part D is optional and available to those who are enrolled in Medicare Parts A and B and most Medicare Advantage plans.

Medicaid, Title XIX of the Social Security Act Amendments of 1965, is a government program administered by the states that provides medical services (both institutional and outpatient) to the medically needy. Federal grants, in the form of matching funds, are issued to those states with qualifying Medicaid programs. Medicaid is jointly sponsored and financed by the federal government and several states. Medical care for needy persons of all ages is provided under the definition of need established by each state. Each state sets its own criteria for determining eligibility for services under its Medicaid program.

The Health Insurance Portability and Accountability Act of 1996

The CMS is responsible for implementing various provisions of the *Health Insurance Portability and Accountability Act of 1996* (HIPAA). The administrative simplification provisions of HIPAA require that the DHHS establish national standards for electronic healthcare transactions and national identifiers for providers, health plans, and employers. It also addresses the privacy of health data.

Public Health Service

The mission of the *Public Health Service* (PHS) is to promote the protection of the nation's physical and mental health. The PHS accomplishes its mission by coordinating with the states in setting and implementing national health policy and pursuing effective intergovernmental relations; generating and upholding cooperative international health related agreements, policies, and programs; conducting medical and biomedical research; sponsoring and administering programs for the development of health resources, the prevention and control of diseases, and alcohol and drug abuse; providing resources and expertise to the states and other public and private institutions in the planning, direction, and delivery of physical and mental healthcare services; and enforcing laws to ensure drug safety and protection from impure and unsafe foods, cosmetics, medical devices, and radiation-producing objects. Within the PHS are smaller agencies responsible for carrying out the purpose of the division and DHHS; these agencies are described next.

National Institutes of Health

The *National Institutes of Health* (NIH) is the principal federal biomedical research agency. NIH is considered to be the largest biomedical research agency in the world.

NIH's mission is to seek fundamental knowledge about the nature and behavior of living systems and the application of that knowledge

to enhance health, lengthen life, and reduce illness and disability. It is responsible for conducting, supporting, and promoting biomedical research.

The goals of the agency are:

- to foster fundamental creative discoveries, innovative research strategies, and their applications as a basis for ultimately protecting and improving health;
- to develop, maintain, and renew scientific human and physical resources that will ensure the nation's capability to prevent disease;
- to expand the knowledge base in medical and associated sciences in order to enhance the nation's economic well-being and ensure a continued high return on the public investment in research; and
- to exemplify and promote the highest level of scientific integrity, public accountability, and social responsibility in the conduct of science.[45]

Centers for Disease Control and Prevention

The *Centers for Disease Control and Prevention* (CDC) was established as an operating health agency within the Public Health Service by the Secretary of Health, Education, and Welfare on July 1, 1973. It is the lead federal agency charged with protecting the public health of the nation by providing leadership and direction in the prevention and control of diseases and other preventable conditions and responding to public health emergencies. It administers national programs for the prevention and control of communicable and vector-borne diseases and other preventable conditions. It develops and implements programs in chronic disease prevention and control, including consultation with state and local health departments. It develops and implements programs to deal with environmental health problems, including responding to environmental, chemical, and radiation emergencies. The CDC also serves to help other nations as they struggle with communicable diseases.

Food and Drug Administration

The *Food and Drug Administration* (FDA) is responsible "for protecting the public health by assuring the safety, effectiveness, quality, and security of human and veterinary drugs, vaccines and other biological products, and medical devices. The FDA is also responsible for the safety and security of most of our nation's food supply, all cosmetics, dietary supplements and products that give off radiation."[46]

Substance Abuse and Mental Health Services Administration

The *Substance Abuse and Mental Health Services Administration*'s mission is to reduce the impact of substance abuse and mental illness on America's communities.

Health Resources and Services Administration

The *Health Resources and Services Administration* (HRSA) is the primary federal agency for improving access to healthcare services for people who are uninsured, isolated, or medically vulnerable. Its mission is to improve health and achieve health equity through access to quality services, a skilled health workforce, and innovative programs. HRSA takes a comprehensive approach to addressing human immunodeficiency virus/acquired immune deficiency syndrome (HIV/AIDS) with activities taking place across multiple bureaus and offices designed to deliver care to people living with HIV or AIDS, expand and strengthen the HIV care workforce, and improve access to and the quality of HIV care and treatment.

Agency for Healthcare Research and Quality

The *Agency for Healthcare Research and Quality* (AHRQ) provides evidence-based information on healthcare outcomes, quality, cost, use, and access. Information from AHRQ's research helps people make more informed decisions and improve the quality of healthcare services.

Agency for Toxic Substances and Disease Registry

The mission of the *Agency for Toxic Substances and Disease Registry* (ATSDR) is to prevent or mitigate harmful exposures and related diseases by applying science, taking responsive action, and providing trustworthy health information.

Indian Health Service

The *Indian Health Service* (IHS) is an operating division within the DHHS that provides a comprehensive federal health program for American Indians and Alaska Natives who belong to federally recognized tribes. "The Indian Health Care Improvement Act (IHCIA), the cornerstone legal authority for the provision of health care to American Indians and Alaska Natives, was made permanent when President Obama signed the bill on March 23, 2010, as part of the Patient Protection and Affordable Care Act."[47]

▶ GOVERNMENT ETHICS

I weep for the liberty of my country when I see at this early day of its successful experiment that corruption has been imputed to many members of the House of Representatives, and the rights of the people have been bartered for promises of office.

—Andrew Jackson

Ethics and the law are not mutually exclusive—they are intertwined. Without the two, we would become a lawless land. The words of Abraham Lincoln and Andrew Jackson, so eloquently spoken, resonate true today. Political corruption, antisocial behavior, declining civility, and rampant unethical conduct have heightened discussions over the nation's moral decline and decaying value systems. The numerous instances of questionable political decisions, executives with shocking salaries, dishonesty at work and in school, the entertainment industry, and dishonest news reporting, have all contributed to this decline. Legislators, investigators, prosecutors, and the courts have been quick to speak moral truths but continue to be slow in action. The question remains: Can the decline in ethical behavior be reversed, as citizens struggle with a broken legal system inundated with new laws? The answer is more likely to be a return to practicing the virtues and values upon which this nation was founded. Ethics and the law are not mutually exclusive—they are intertwined throughout the text, providing an overview of government agencies designed to protect each individual's rights (e.g., the right to privacy and self-determination).

Executive Branch: Office of Government Ethics

The Office of Government Ethics (OGE) is an agency within the executive branch of government. The agency was established by the Ethics in Government Act of 1978. Originally within the Office of Personnel Management, OGE became a separate agency on October 1, 1989. The Office of Government Ethics exercises leadership in the executive branch to prevent conflicts of interest on the part of government employees, and to resolve those conflicts of interest that do occur. In partnership with executive branch agencies and departments, OGE fosters high ethical standards for employees and strengthens the public's confidence that the government's business is conducted with impartiality and integrity.[48]

The OGE website provides information about the agency and services it provides. The site helps people understand the executive branch ethics program and its effort to reach federal employees and the general public. Common ethical issues discussed on the website include gifts from outside sources, gifts between employees, conflicting financial interests, remedies for financial conflicts of interest, impartiality in performing official duties, seeking other employment, misuse of position, outside activities, postemployment, representation to government agencies and courts, supplementation of salary, financial disclosure, informal advisory letters and memorandum and formal opinions, DAEOgrams (memoranda to agency ethics officials providing guidance on how to interpret and comply with modifications or new issuances of ethics laws, policies, and procedures; copies of the memoranda released since 1992 are available in the DAEOgrams section of the OGE website), and contractors in the workplace.

> The public may lose confidence in the integrity of Government if it perceives that an employee's Government work is influenced by personal interests or by payments from an outside source. An executive branch employee's Government work may have the potential to benefit the employee personally, affect the financial interests of the employee's family, or involve individuals or organizations with which the employee has some past, present, or future connection away from the employee's Government job. Separately, an employee might be offered a payment from a non-Federal source, such as a former employer, either before or after entering Government. Accordingly:

> - An employee may be disqualified from working on a particular Government matter.
> - An employee may be prohibited from holding specified property.
> - An employee may be prohibited from accepting a payment from a non-Federal source.[49]

U.S. House of Representatives: Committee on Ethics

The Committee on Ethics is designated the "supervising ethics office" for the House of Representatives. The jurisdiction of the Committee on Ethics is derived from authority granted under House Rules and federal statutes.

> The Committee on Ethics is unique in the House of Representatives. Consistent with the duty to carry out its advisory and enforcement responsibilities in an impartial manner, the Committee is the only standing committee of the House of Representatives with its membership divided evenly by party. These rules are intended to provide a fair procedural framework for the conduct of the Committee's activities and to help ensure that the Committee serves the people of the United States, the House of Representatives, and the Members, officers, and employees of the House of Representatives.[50]

The scope of the Committee's jurisdiction under the various authorizing rules and statutes involves duties and responsibilities related to:

- Jurisdiction over all bills, resolutions, and other matters relating to the Code of Official Conduct.
- Recommend administrative actions to establish or enforce standards of official conduct.
- Investigate alleged violations of the Code of Official Conduct or of any applicable rules, laws, or regulations governing the performance of official duties or the discharge of official responsibilities.
- Report to appropriate federal or state authorities substantial evidence of a violation of any law applicable to the performance of official duties that may have been disclosed in a committee investigation.
- Consider requests for written waivers of the gift rule.
- Provide oversight over foreign gifts and gifts to superiors and other federal employees.
- Prohibit members, officers, and employees of the House of Representatives from soliciting or receiving gifts.[51]

The official Code of Conduct for the House of Representatives can be found on its Committee on Ethics website at ethics.house.gov.

Senate: Select Committee on Ethics

(a) The ideal concept of public office, expressed by the words, "a public office is a public trust," signifies that the officer has been entrusted with public power by the people; that the officer holds this power in trust to be used only for their benefit and never for the benefit of himself or of a few; and that the officer must never conduct his own affairs so as to infringe on the public interest. All official conduct of Members of the Senate should be guided by this paramount concept of public office.[52]

The U.S. Senate Select Committee on Ethics consists of six members of the Senate, three of whom shall be selected from members of the majority party and three shall be selected from members of the minority party.[53] The committee is responsible for investigating complaints involving a violation of the franking statute;[54] financial disclosure statements; outside employment with respect to members, officers, and employees of the Senate; foreign gifts and decorations; gifts to an official superior or receiving gifts from employees with a lower salary level; and prohibitions against members, officers, and employees of the Senate soliciting or receiving gifts.[55]

The Senate Select Committee on Ethics is authorized to receive and investigate allegations of improper conduct that may reflect upon the Senate, including violations of law, violations of the Senate Code of Official Conduct, and violations of rules and regulations of the Senate; recommend disciplinary action; recommend additional Senate rules or regulations to insure proper standards of conduct; and report violations of law to the proper federal and state authorities.[56]

U.S. Judicial Code of Conduct

As with other branches of government, federal judges are expected to abide by a code of conduct that includes ethical principles and guidelines. "The Code of Conduct provides guidance for judges on issues of judicial integrity and independence, judicial diligence and impartiality, permissible extrajudicial activities, and the avoidance of impropriety or even its appearance."[57] The Code of Conduct for United States Judges includes the following ethical canons:

> Canon 1: A Judge Should Uphold the Integrity and Independence of the Judiciary
>
> Canon 2: A Judge Should Avoid Impropriety and the Appearance of Impropriety in all Activities
>
> Canon 3: A Judge Should Perform the Duties of the Office Fairly, Impartially and Diligently
>
> Canon 4: A Judge May Engage in Extrajudicial Activities that are Consistent with the Obligations of Judicial Office
>
> Canon 5: A Judge Should Refrain from Political Activity[58]

Office of Congressional Ethics

The Office of Congressional Ethics (OCE) was created in March 2008 as an independent, nonpartisan office, governed by a board comprising private citizens, which provides more public review and insight into the ethical conduct of members of the House of Representatives. The OCE reviews allegations of misconduct against members, officers, and staff of the House and, when appropriate, refers matters to the House Committee on Ethics. The OCE is not authorized to determine if a violation occurred, nor is it authorized to sanction members, officers, or employees of the House or to recommend sanctions. The OCE is not able to provide advice or education on the rules and standards of conduct applicable to members, officers, and employees of the House.[59] The mission of the OCE and its board is to assist the House in upholding high standards of ethical conduct for its members, officers, and staff and, in so doing, to serve the American people. The board of directors consists of eight members, who are private citizens and cannot serve as members of Congress or work for the federal government.[60] Additional information regarding the work of the OCE is available at its website oce.house.gov.

As the reader will note, there are a variety of laws and agencies that provide oversight and regulations that are designed to protect the rights and safety of all citizens. Government is a reflection of the people it serves. Failure of the many to participate in the political process leads to government for the few who do.

State Ethics Committees

Many states have legislative ethics committees that hear complaints of ethics violations by legislators. They often investigate complaints and impose penalties for ethics-related violations. Duties vary among the state committees. A state-by-state review can be found at www.ncsl.org/research/ethics/table-of-legislative-ethics-committees.aspx. "State legislatures pass ethics laws that impose restrictions on themselves and lobbyists. To ensure these laws are kept, legislatures establish oversight entities that include ethics committees, ethics commissions or a combination of both. Internal ethics committees are an important way for legislatures to solidify their credibility with the public."[61]

▶ POLITICAL MALPRACTICE

 Nothing is politically right which is morally wrong.
—Daniel O'Connell (1755–1847)

Political malpractice is negligent conduct by an elected or appointed political official. Ronald Brownstein wrote in a news column in the *St. Petersburg Times*, "Practical steps are possible to help millions of low income families live healthier lives and receive more effective care when they need it. Ignoring that opportunity, while waiting for consensus on coverage, would be a form of political malpractice."[62] The likelihood of a successful negligence case against a member of Congress is doubtful. If such a case ever got through a courtroom door, the following four elements of negligence would have to be proven:

1. The first element necessary to prove political malpractice requires that the plaintiff(s) be able to establish there is a duty to care. Establishing this first element of negligence for a senator, for example, would be a difficult hurdle. The oath of office for a senator is so amorphous that it would be difficult to establish a duty to care, as illustrated in the following quotes.

Oath of Office
I do solemnly swear (or affirm) that I will support and defend the Constitution of the United States against all enemies, foreign and domestic; that I will bear true faith and allegiance to the same; that I take this obligation freely, without any mental reservation or purpose of evasion; and that I will well and faithfully discharge the duties of the office on which I am about to enter: So help me God.[63]

Looking beyond the oath of office:

For nearly three-quarters of a century, that oath served nicely, although to the modern ear it sounds woefully incomplete. Missing are the soaring references to bearing "true faith and allegiance;" to taking "this obligation freely, without any mental reservation or purpose of evasion"; and to "well and faithfully" discharging the duties of the office.[64]

Should a plaintiff be able to overcome this first element of negligence, thus proving a duty to care, the remaining elements could be just as difficult to establish.

2. The second element of political malpractice requires the plaintiff prove that the *duty to care was breached.* Arguably, politicians, for example, who agree to veto any program the President supports while he is in office, are contrary to the spirit of the law. The dilemma here requires the plaintiff(s) to prove what specific duty to care was breached.

3. The third element of political malpractice requires proof of harm.

4. The fourth element requires proof of a *causal connection* between the politician's breach of duty and the harm suffered. In other words, the plaintiff(s) must prove that the breach of duty was the proximate cause of the plaintiff's injury.

Senator Bob Dole, when speaking of Veterans Affairs Secretary Eric Shinseki regarding allegations of mismanagement, falsified records, and long waits for veterans in receiving health care, said, "If the facts reveal that he neglected his duties, then he should go."[65] By May 30, 2014, Secretary Shinseki, a retired general, resigned his office following the allegations with increasing pressure from Congress for him to resign. Like medical malpractice, political malpractice involves a failure to offer adequate healthcare services to help prevent the bureaucratic quagmire of regulations that hinders the provision of health care to those in need, as illustrated in the *reality check* **The Coal Miner**.

Flint, Michigan is not the only city concerned with questions that involve both political malpractice and criminal conduct facing government employees and officials regarding the health safety of drinking water. Residents of St. Joseph, Louisiana, for example, are concerned with drinking and bathing in murky brown water. The Louisiana health department claims tests show that there are no dangerous amounts of chemicals in St. Joseph's water supply. However, this does not ease the fears of those living there. It is an ethical dilemma involving trust. Government officials are not willing to drink the water, why should the public. While conducting a survey in Louisiana and 10 years before St. Joseph became the focus of public and media scrutiny, a hospital surveyor described his water pollution concerns, as described in the *reality check* **Hospital Water Questioned**.

The New Jersey Health Department's website references public concern over the safety of tap water in the Dover Township/Toms River area of Ocean County as far back as 1995 [www.nj.gov/health/eohs/dovertwp.shtml], where the occurrence of childhood cancer has been a concern for many years and linked to the drinking water. This website illustrates the difficulty in bringing closure to the people's concerns for the health and welfare of their children.

Community outrage continues because of the slow pace in addressing public concerns about

☑ THE COAL MINER

It was December 1989 when Larry, the hospital administrator, was making his morning visits to various departments, as he often did each day with both staff and patients. While visiting a medical unit he visited with Jimmy, one of the patients. Larry asked Jimmy, "Are we taking good care of you?" He said, "Yes." He then turned to a man who was on the opposite side of his bed and said, "This is my brother Bill." Bill, looking at Larry, choked up and asked, "Can you help my brother? He has given up the will to live. Please help my brother want to live." I looked at Jimmy lying there in his bed, fragile and struggling to breathe between each word, as he said, "I can no longer carry on this way. I am ready to move on. I'm a tired old man. I have fought so long. I've needed benefits for so many years for my family and myself. I have had many promises over of the years of people promising to help me. But up until this moment in time, no one was able to help me. I have black lung disease. I struggle to breathe." He then turned, looking over to Bill, and said, "My brother also has black lung disease. We worked together in the coalmines for many years. This is our reward." I looked at Jimmy and slowly back to Bill and said, "I will have my staff help facilitate you in getting the help you need." As we said our good-byes, I thought to myself, as I left the room, Jimmy has fought so long. He has asked for so little, a man forgotten by incompetent and corrupt bureaucratic leadership.

Michigan Governor Rick Snyder has admitted that the government failed the people. The following *news article* and *reality check* illustrate how the nation's government, on the highest levels, continues to fail the people throughout the nation, from as far north as Michigan to as far south as Louisiana.

📰 HOW WATER CRISIS IN FLINT, MI BECAME FEDERAL STATE OF EMERGENCY

Michigan Gov. Rick Snyder gave a State of the State address Tuesday night, following remarks he made a day earlier on how he's made mistakes in handling the Flint, Michigan water crisis.

"I'm sorry and I will fix it," Snyder said near the opening of his speech, directly addressing the residents of Flint. "Government failed you at the federal, state and local level."

—Jessica Durando, *USA Today*, January 20, 2016

contaminated water. Government officials elected as the guardians of the communities they serve continue down the slippery slope of distrust.

Ethicists in Public Service

Although not all cities may need to hire an ethicist in order to set priorities, it may be helpful in certain types of decisions. An independent, unbiased, professionally trained decision maker from who is an "outsider" may be more acceptable to councils, mayors, citizens, employees, or the press than one derived from inside the political arena. The city of Alexandria, Virginia, in 2008, "hired an ethics consultant for $9,000 per year. Cities must make decisions to set priorities when allocating scarce resources. City council members,

mayors, and city managers have available the advice of the city attorney and/or their professional organizations when faced with ethical dilemmas."[66] This is particularly helpful in the decision-making process when decisions involve a reduction or elimination of services to the public, especially services to the elderly, disabled, or less fortunate.[67]

▶ CHAPTER REVIEW

1. A law is a general rule of conduct that is enforced by the government. When a law is violated, the government imposes a penalty.

   ■ *Public laws* deal with the relationships between individuals and the government.

   ■ *Private laws* deal with relationships among individuals.

2. *Common law* is derived from judicial decisions. During the colonial period, the United States based its law on English common law, but states had the authority to modify their legal systems. As a result, there is no uniform system of common law among the states.

   ■ *Precedent*—a judicial decision that may be used as a standard in subsequent similar cases. A precedent is set when a court decision is rendered that serves as a rule for future guidance when deciding similar cases.

   ■ *Res judicata*—"the thing is decided"—refers to that which has been previously acted on

✔ *HOSPITAL WATER QUESTIONED*

Joe was in Shreveport, Louisiana. It was Sunday evening about 11:00 PM. Joe opened his computer to review his itinerary on his company's website when he noticed that the survey starting date for a small community hospital in south central Louisiana had been changed from Tuesday to Monday. The rush began. He packed his clothes, loaded his rental car, and checked out of the hotel, accidentally leaving his suits behind.

Joe arrived at the new hotel at about 2:00 AM. He checked in and unpacked. Joe turned on the water and found it was a mucky brown color. He called the front desk to question the water that flowed into the sink, tub, and toilet. After a bit of a chuckle, the desk associate said, "It's OK. It's always brown." Joe thought to himself, "Well, at least the hospital will have clear, clean water."

The following day, Carol, the survey coordinator, greeted Joe and his survey team in the hospital lobby. Carol escorted the survey team to a conference room, which was assigned to the team as a home base during the survey. The first thing Joe noticed was bottled water, apple juice, and orange juice packed in ice on the boardroom table. He thought, "Oh happy day." He then went to the small sink in the anteroom of the boardroom to wash his hands. Joe observed that the water was a brown in color, just a bit lighter than the water at the hotel. Before leaving the room, Carol said, "If you need anything, I'll be just across the hall." Joe quickly replied, "There is something I have some concern with—the quality of the water here in central Louisiana." Carol replied, "Oh no, it's OK. It's been tested by the health department." Joe replied, "Could you please show me any documentation you have on file that I can review." Carol replied, "OK, I'll see what we have on file." By the end of the survey, there was no health department paperwork available in the hospital for Joe to review. He suggested that an attempt be made to seek clarification from the health department, in writing, regarding the safe use of the hospital's water source.

or decided by the courts—a final judgment rendered by a court of competent jurisdiction on the merits is conclusive as to the rights of the parties and their privies, and, as to them, constitutes an absolute bar to subsequent action involving the same claim, demand, or cause of action.

- *Stare decisis*—common law principle ("let the decision stand") provides that when a decision is rendered in a lawsuit involving a particular set of facts, another lawsuit involving an identical or substantially similar situation is to be resolved in the same manner as the first lawsuit.

- *Original jurisdiction*—authority of a court to first conduct a trial.

- *Appellate jurisdiction*—authority of a court to hear appeals from trial court decisions.

3. *Statutory law* is written law that emanates from legislative bodies.

- A statute can abolish any rule of common law.
- The Constitution is the highest level of enacted law; it takes precedence over the constitutions and laws of specific states and local jurisdictions.
- Statutory law can be amended, repealed, or expanded by the legislature. States and local jurisdictions can only enact and enforce laws that do not conflict with federal laws.

4. *Administrative law* is public law issued by administrative agencies to administer the enacted laws of the federal and state governments.

- Administrative agencies implement and administer the administrative law.
- The rules and regulations established by an agency must be administered within the scope of the authority delegated to the agency by Congress.
- Agency regulations and decisions can be subject to judicial review.
- Each state has its own system of administrative law.

5. *Separation of powers* provides that no one branch of the government—legislative, executive, or judicial—will be clearly dominant over the other two.

- *Legislative branch* enacts, amends, and/or repeals existing laws.
- *Executive branch* administers and enforces the law.
- *Judicial branch* resolves disputes in accordance with the law.

6. The *Department of Health and Human Services* (DHHS) develops and implements administrative regulations for carrying out national health and human services policy objectives through various agencies within DHHS.

7. Ethics and the law are not mutually exclusive—they are intertwined. Government ethics committees include:

   ■ Executive branch: Office of Government Ethics
   ■ U.S. House of Representatives: Committee on Ethics
   ■ Senate: Select Committee on Ethics
   ■ Judicial branch: U.S. Judicial Code of Conduct
   ■ Office of Congressional Ethics

8. *Political malpractice* is negligent conduct by an elected or appointed political official.

▶ REVIEW QUESTIONS

1. Define the term *law* and describe the sources from which law is derived.
2. Define the legal terms precedent, res judicata, stare decisis, original jurisdiction, and appellate jurisdiction.
3. Describe the function of the three branches of government.
4. What is the meaning of separation of powers?
5. What is the function of an administrative agency?
6. Describe why the Department of Health and Human Services was created.

▶ NOTES

1. Bernard Schwartz, *The Law in America* (New York: McGraw-Hill, 1974), 1.
2. 5 U.S. (Cranch) 137, 163 (1803).
3. The Law Dictionary, "What is Public Law?" http://thelawdictionary.org/public-law/
4. *Pierce v. Ortho Pharmaceutical Corp.*, 417 A.2d 505, 512 (N.J. 1980).
5. *Cruzan v. Director, Missouri Department of Health,* 496 U.S. 261, 110 S.Ct. 2841 (1990).
6. A.K.R. Kiralfy, *Potter's Historical Introduction to English Law* (London, UK: Sweet & Maxwell, 1962), 9.
7. John Reeves, *History of the English Law* (London, UK: Reed and Hunter, 1814), 2.
8. *Id.*
9. George W. Keeton, *English Law* (Newton Abbot, UK: David & Charles, 1974), 70.
10. *Id.*
11. *Id.*
12. Kiralfy, *supra* note 6, at 9–10.
13. Schwartz, *supra* note 1, at 29.
14. Lawrence Friedman, *A History of American Law* (New York, NY: Touchstone Books, 1985), 92.
15. *Lebron v. Gottlieb Memorial Hospital*, Docket Nos. 105741, 105745 cons., (Ill. February 4, 2010).
16. Cal. Civ. Code §3333.2(b) (West 2009).
17. Fla. Stat. §766.118 (2009).
18. *People v. Caballes*, 221 Ill. 2d 282, 313 (2006).
19. *Black's Law Dictionary*, 6th ed. (Eagan, MN: 1990), 1305.
20. 2 Root 90, 92 (Conn. 1794).
21. U.S. Department of Health and Human Services, *Task Force on Medical Liability and Malpractice* (Washington, DC: Author, 1987), 3.
22. *Id.*
23. Zinman, "Study Finds Hospitals 'Harm' Some," *Newsday*, March 1, 1990, 17.
24. The Robert Wood Johnson Foundation, "The Tort System for Medical Malpractice: How Well Does It Work, What Are the Alternatives?" *Abridge*, Spring 1991, 2.
25. The Robert Wood Johnson Foundation, "Negligent Medical Care: What Is It, Where Is It, and How Widespread Is It?" *Abridge*, Spring 1991, 6.
26. D. Sharp, "Errors Renew the Call for Doctor Review," *USA Today*, March 27, 1995, 2.
27. K. Painter, "Breast Cancer Top Cause of Malpractice Complaints," *USA Today*, June 15, 1996, 1.
28. Sandra B. Goodman, "As Hands-on Doctoring Fades Away, Patients Lose," *The Washington Post*, May 20, 2014, E1.
29. Becker's Hospital Review, "Legal & Regulatory Issues: 29 Statistics on Medical Malpractice Payouts and Lawsuits," http://www.beckershospitalreview.com/legal-regulatory-issues/29-statistics-on-medical-malpractice-payouts-and-lawsuits.html
30. U.S. Constitution, art. 6, § 1, cl. 2.
31. 5 U.S.C.S. §§ 500–576 (Law. Co-op. 1989).
32. An "agency means each authority of the Government of the United States, … but does not include (A) the Congress; the Courts of the United States; …" 5 U.S.C.S. § 551(1) (Law. Co-op. 1989).
33. 5 U.S.C.S. § 702 (Law. Co-op. 1989).
34. 5 U.S.C.S. § 706 (Law. Co-op. 1989). https://www.gpo.gov/fdsys/pkg/USCODE-2010-title5/html/USCODE-2010-title5-partI-chap7-sec706.htm.
35. 401 A.2d 872 (Pa. Commw. Ct. 1979).
36. *Id.* at 873
37. *Department of Human Serv. v. Berry,* 764 S.W.2d 437 (Ark. 1989).
38. *Id.* at 439
39. 88 F.R.D. 583 (E.D. Mich. 1980).

40. Yahoo!, "U.S. Government Departments and Agencies," http://dir.yahoo.com/Government/U_S__Government/Executive_Branch/Departments_and_Agencies/

41. Donald Levitan and Elwyn E. Mariner, *Your Massachusetts Government*, 10th ed. (Newton Center, MA: Government Research Publications, 1984), 14.

42. *Heritage of Yankton, Inc. v. South Dakota Dep't. of Health*, 432 N.W.2d 68, 77 (S.D. 1988).

43. *Marbury v. Madison*, 5 U.S. (Cranch) 137, 180 (1803).

44. Government Publishing Office, "The United States Government Manual: Executive Branch: Departments," https://www.gpo.gov/fdsys/pkg/GOVMAN-2015-07-01/xml/GOVMAN-2015-07-01-117.xml

45. National Institutes of Health, "What We Do: Mission and Goals," https://www.nih.gov/about-nih/what-we-do/mission-goals

46. U.S. Food and Drug Administration, "FDA Fundamentals," http://www.fda.gov/AboutFDA/Transparency/Basics/ucm192695.htm

47. Indian Health Service, "Indian Health Care Improvement Act," http://www.ihs.gov/ihcia/

48. U.S. Office of Government Ethics, http://www.usoge.gov

49. U.S. Office of Government Ethics, "Financial Conflicts of Interest," https://www.oge.gov/web/oge.nsf/Financial+Conflicts+of+Interest

50. Committee on Ethics, "Committee Rules," http://ethics.house.gov/about/committee-rules

51. Committee on Ethics, "Jurisdiction," http://ethics.house.gov/jurisdiction

52. United States Senate Select Committee on Ethics, "Jurisdiction," http://www.ethics.senate.gov/public/index.cfm/jurisdiction

53. U.S. Senate Select Committee on Ethics, "Rules of Procedure," http://www.ethics.senate.gov/public/index.cfm/files/serve?File_id=551b39fc-30ed-4b14-b0d3-1706608a6fcb

54. Franking Commission, "What is the Frank?" https://cha.house.gov/franking-commission/what-frank.

55. U.S. Senate Select Committee on Ethics, "Jurisdiction," http://www.ethics.senate.gov/public/index.cfm/jurisdiction

56. Id.

57. U.S. Courts, "Code of Conduct," http://www.uscourts.gov/RulesAndPolicies/CodesOfConduct.aspx

58. USCourts.gov, "Code of Conduct for United States Judges," http://www.uscourts.gov/judges-judgeships/code-conduct-united-states-judges#f.

59. Office of Congressional Ethics, "Frequently Asked Questions," http://oce.house.gov/faq.html.

60. *Id.*

61. National Conference of State Legislatures, "State Ethics Committees," http://www.ncsl.org/research/ethics/table-of-legislative-ethics-committees.aspx

62. Ronald Brownstein, "Health Care Safety Net Stretched Thin," *St. Petersburg Times*, June 4, 2004, Section A, 13a.

63. U.S. Senate, "Oath of Office," http://www.senate.gov/artandhistory/history/common/briefing/Oath_Office.htm

64. *Id.*

65. Susan Page, "Veterans Affairs A 'Disaster'," *The Washington Post*, May, 23, 2014, 1A.

66. Ethics in Public Service, "Alexandria Hires Ethics Consultant," April 9, 2009, http://urpa5358group2.wordpress.com/2009/01/31/alexandria-hires-ethics-consultant/

67. Laura Olson, "URPA 5358 Group 2," January 2, 2009, http://urpa5358group2.blogspot.com

© photogl/Shutterstock

CHAPTER 3

Tort Law—Negligence

🔍 *IT'S YOUR GAVEL...*

THE COURT WAS APPALLED

The plaintiff, while in the custody of the defendant penal institution, alleged that because the defendant's employees failed to timely diagnose her breast cancer, her right breast had to be removed. The defendant contended that even if its employees were negligent, the plaintiff's cancer was so far developed when discovered that it would nevertheless have required removal of her breast.[1]

Pursuant to the defendant's policy of medically evaluating all new inmates, on May 26, Dr. Evans gave the plaintiff a medical examination. He testified that his physical evaluation included an examination of the plaintiff's breasts. However, he stated that his examination was very cursory.

The day following her examination, the plaintiff examined her own breasts. At that time, she discovered a lump in her right breast, which she characterized as being about the size of a pea. The plaintiff then sought an additional medical evaluation at the defendant's medical clinic. Testimony indicated that fewer than half of the inmates who sign the clinic list are actually seen by medical personnel the next day after signing their name. Also, those not examined on the day for which the list is signed are given no preference in being examined on the following day. Their names are simply deleted

(continues)

IT'S YOUR GAVEL...   (continued)

from the daily list, and their only recourse is to continually sign the list until they are examined. The evidence indicated that after May 27, the plaintiff constantly signed the clinic list and provided the reason she was requesting medical care.

A nurse finally examined the plaintiff on June 21. The nurse noted in her nursing notes that the plaintiff had a "moderate large mass in right breast." The nurse recognized that the proper procedure was to measure such a mass, but she testified that this was impossible because no measuring device was available. The missing measuring device to which she alluded was a simple ruler. The nurse concluded that Evans should again examine the plaintiff.

On June 28, Evans again examined the plaintiff. He recorded in the progress notes that the plaintiff had "a mass on her right wrist. Will send her to hospital and give her Benadryl for allergy she has."[2] Evans meant to write "breast" not "wrist."

He failed to measure the size of the mass on the plaintiff's breast. The plaintiff was eventually transferred to the Franklin Pre-Release Center (FPRC) on September 28. On September 30, when a nurse at FPRC examined the plaintiff; the nurse recorded that the plaintiff had a "golf ball"-sized lump in her right breast. The plaintiff was transported to the hospital on October 27, where Dr. Walker treated her. The plaintiff received a mammogram examination, which indicated that the tumor was probably malignant. This diagnosis was confirmed by a biopsy performed on November 9. The plaintiff was released from confinement on November 13.

On November 16, Dr. Lidsky, a surgeon, examined the plaintiff. Lidsky noted the existence of the lump in the plaintiff's breast and determined that the size of the mass was approximately 4 to 5 centimeters and somewhat fixed. He performed a modified radical mastectomy upon the plaintiff's right breast, by which nearly the plaintiff's entire right breast was removed. A suit was filed.

WHAT IS YOUR VERDICT?

Every instance of a man's suffering the penalty of the law is an instance of the failure of that penalty in effecting its purpose, which is to deter from transgression.

—Richard Whately

LEARNING OBJECTIVES

The reader, upon completion of this chapter, will be able to:

- Describe what a tort is and the objectives of tort law.
- Define negligence and explain the distinction between negligence and malpractice.
- Explain how the commission and omission of an act differ.
- Explain the elements necessary to prove a negligence case.
- Describe the importance of foreseeability in a negligence case.

This chapter introduces the reader to the study of tort law with an emphasis on negligence in healthcare settings. A tort is a civil wrong, other than a breach of contract, committed against a person (e.g., reputation, privacy), property (real or personal) for which a court provides a remedy in the form of compensation for damages suffered. Tort actions are a concern to caregivers both personally and professionally. Caregivers should be armed with the knowledge necessary to improve their understanding of their rights and responsibilities in the healthcare setting.

OBJECTIVES OF TORT LAW

The basic objectives of tort law are: (1) *preservation of peace* between individuals by providing a substitute for retaliation; (2) *culpability* (to find fault for wrongdoing); (3) *deterrence* (to discourage the wrongdoer [tortfeasor] from committing future wrongful acts, as well as, deter others from committing wrongdoing); and (4) *compensation* (to indemnify the injured party to a lawsuit).

Compensation for adverse medical outcomes typically takes the form of financial damages. When finding fault, the court must determine who should bear the cost of an unfavorable outcome—the patient-plaintiff or the provider-defendant. The plaintiff must prove negligence by the defendant. Conversely, the defendant argues a case to avoid fault determination. Underlying this adversarial proceeding is the assumption that when a defendant bears the cost of a negligent act, there will be a decline in similar acts. Although professional liability insurance helps to insulate a provider from financial loss, the fear is ever present that the monetary award may exceed the provider's coverage limits.

The three basic categories of tort law are (1) negligent torts; (2) intentional torts (e.g., assault, battery, false imprisonment, invasion of privacy, infliction of mental distress); and (3) strict liability, which is applied when the activity, regardless of fault, intentions, or negligence, is so dangerous to others that public policy demands absolute responsibility on the part of the wrongdoer (e.g., products liability). Negligence is reviewed in the next section.

NEGLIGENCE

Negligence is a tort, a civil or personal wrong. It is the unintentional commission or omission of an act that a reasonably prudent person would or would not do under given circumstances.

Commission of an act would include, for example:

- Administering the wrong medication
- Administering the wrong dosage of a medication
- Administering medication to the wrong patient
- Performing a surgical procedure without the patient's consent
- Performing a surgical procedure on the wrong patient or body part
- Performing the wrong surgical procedure

Omission of an act would include, for example:

- Failure to conduct a thorough history and physical examination
- Failure to assess and reassess a patient's nutritional needs
- Failure to administer medications as prescribed
- Failure to order diagnostic tests
- Failure to follow up on abnormal or critical test results
- Failure to conduct a "time out" to insure that the correct surgical procedure is being performed on the correct patient at the correct site

Negligence is a form of conduct caused by heedlessness or carelessness that constitutes a departure from the standard of care generally imposed on reasonable members of society. It can occur when, after considering the consequences of an act, a person does not exercise the best possible judgment; when one fails to guard against a risk that should be appreciated; or when one engages in behavior expected to involve unreasonable danger to others. Negligence or carelessness of a professional person (e.g., nurse practitioner, pharmacist, physician, physician assistant) is referred to as *malpractice*, whereas *criminal negligence* is the reckless disregard for the safety of another (e.g., willful indifference to an injury that could follow an act).

Thousands of deaths occur each year as a result of medical errors. Although medical errors often involve misdiagnosis, delayed diagnosis, failure to diagnose, surgical errors, and prescription errors, not all medical errors are necessarily malpractice. Most medical or surgical interventions involve some degree of risk. It is the responsibility of the treating professional to inform his or her patient as to the inherent risks, benefits, and alternatives of a proposed treatment or procedure.

FORMS OF NEGLIGENCE

The three basic forms of negligence in **FIGURE 3-1** are as follows:

1. *Malfeasance*: Performance of an unlawful or improper act (e.g., performing an abortion in the third trimester when prohibited by state law)
2. *Misfeasance*: Improper performance of an act, resulting in injury to another (e.g., administering the wrong dose of a medication, wrong site surgery (e.g., removal of a healthy kidney instead of the diseased kidney[3], removal of the healthy breast instead of the diseased breast[4], removal of the wrong leg during surgery[5])
3. *Nonfeasance*: Failure to act when there is a duty to act as a reasonably prudent person would in similar circumstances (e.g., failure to administer medications, failure to order diagnostic tests or prescribe necessary medications)

DEGREES OF NEGLIGENCE

The use of the terminology, "degrees of negligence," more aptly describes three generally accepted "degrees of care" that can affect the amount of damages in a negligence case.

FIGURE 3-1 Forms of negligence.

1. *Slight*: Minor deviation of what is expected under the circumstances.
2. *Ordinary*: Failure to do what a reasonably prudent person would or would not do under the circumstances.
3. *Gross*: The intentional or wanton omission of required care or performance of an improper act.

▶ ELEMENTS OF NEGLIGENCE

The following four *elements of negligence* (**FIGURE 3-2**) must be proven in order for a plaintiff to recover damages for negligence. When the four elements of negligence have been proven, the plaintiff is said to have presented a *prima facie case of negligence*, thus enabling the plaintiff to prevail in a lawsuit. The foundation of the columns in Figure 3-2 illustrates examples of negligent acts. The pillars represent each element of negligence that must be proven in order to establish that a negligent act has occurred. Any unproven element of negligence will defeat a lawsuit based on negligence.

1. Duty to care
   - Obligation to conform to a recognized standard of care.
2. Breach of duty
   - Deviation from the recognized standard of care.
   - Failure to adhere to an obligation.
3. Injury
   - Actual damages must be established.
   - If there are no injuries, monetary damages cannot be awarded the plaintiff(s).
4. Causation
   - Departure from the standard of care must be the cause of the plaintiff's injury.
   - The injury must be foreseeable.

Duty to Care

Duty to care is defined as a legal obligation of care, performance, or observance imposed on one to safeguard the rights of others. Duty can arise from a special relationship such as that between a physician, nurse, or pharmacist and a patient. The existence of this relationship implies that a caregiver–patient relationship was in effect at the time an alleged injury occurred. In the case of a physician, duty to care can arise from a simple telephone conversation or out of a caregiver's voluntary act of assuming the care of a patient. Duty also can be established by *statute* or *contract* between the plaintiff and the defendant.

Duty to care is depicted in **FIGURE 3-3**, where the pharmacy manager of General Hospital's pharmacy, prior to leaving work for the day, assigns responsibility to the pharmacist behind the counter, telling her, "You're in charge of the pharmacy, which includes the IV admixture room. Your duties and responsibilities are those as described in the pharmacy department policy and procedure manual. I will be leaving in an hour, so you should review them before I leave. If you have any questions after I leave, you can reach me on my cell phone." This assignment established a duty on the part of the pharmacist to adhere to the policies and procedures in the department manual.

Breach of duty, injury, and causation are further illustrated next under the relevant headings.

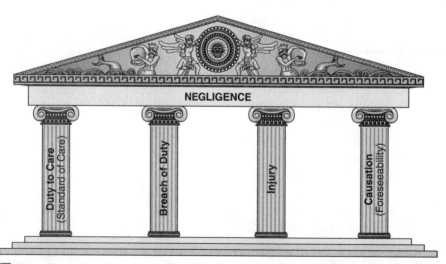

☑ Wrong Site Surgery (e.g., wrong side brain surgery: 3 occasions, same hospital, same year)
☑ Wrong Medication Dosage (e.g., Quaid twins given 20,000 units of heparin instead of 20)

FIGURE 3-2 The four elements of an act of negligence.

FIGURE 3-3 Duty to save.

Hastings Case: Duty to Stabilize the Patient

The surviving parents in *Hastings v. Baton Rouge Hospital*[6] brought a medical malpractice action for the wrongful death of their 19-year-old son. The action was brought against the hospital; Dr. Gerdes, the emergency department (ED) physician; and the thoracic surgeon on call, Dr. McCool. The patient was brought to the ED at 11:56 PM because of two stab wounds and weak vital signs. Gerdes decided that a thoracotomy (an incision into the pleural space of the chest) had to be performed. He was not qualified to perform the surgery and called Dr. McCool, who was on call that evening for thoracic surgery. Gerdes described the patient's condition, indicating that the patient had been stabbed in a major blood vessel. At trial, McCool claimed that he did not recall Gerdes saying that a major blood vessel could be involved. McCool asked Gerdes to transfer the patient to the Earl K. Long Hospital. Gerdes said, "I can't transfer this patient." McCool replied, "No. Transfer him." Kelly, an ED nurse on duty, was not comfortable with the decision to transfer the patient and offered to accompany him in the ambulance. Gerdes reexamined the patient, who exhibited marginal vital signs, was restless, and was draining blood from his chest. The ambulance service was called at 1:03 AM, and by 1:30 AM, the patient had been placed in the ambulance for transfer. The patient began to fight wildly, the chest tube came out, and the bleeding increased. An attempt to revive him from a cardiac arrest was futile, and the patient died after having been moved back into the ED. The patient virtually bled to death in the ED.

The duty to care in this case cannot be reasonably disputed. Louisiana, by statute, imposes a duty on hospitals licensed in Louisiana to make emergency services available to all persons residing in the state regardless of insurance coverage or economic status. The hospital's own bylaws provide that patient transfer should never occur without due consideration for the patient's condition. The 19th Judicial District Court directed a verdict for the defendants, and the plaintiffs appealed. The court of appeals affirmed the district court's decision. On further appeal, the Louisiana Supreme Court held that the evidence presented to the jury could indicate the defendants were negligent in their treatment of the victim. The findings of the lower courts were reversed, and the case was remanded for trial.

Hospitals are required to stabilize the patient prior to transfer. In this case, there was a surgeon on call who was available to treat this patient. McCool decided to practice telephone medicine and made the unfortunate decision to transfer the patient, which resulted in risking the life of an unstable patient, leading to his death.

Duty to Treat Emergency Patients

In *O'Neill v. Montefiore Hospital*,[7] the duty owed to the patient was clear. Mr. O'Neill had been experiencing pain in his chest and arms. He had walked with his wife to the hospital at 5:00 AM for care. After arriving at the hospital, O'Neill explained his pain. Upon learning that O'Neill was a member of the Hospital Insurance Plan (HIP), the ED nurse stated that the hospital had no connection with HIP. The nurse contacted Dr. Graig, an HIP physician, and explained O'Neill's symptoms. He allegedly suggested O'Neill be treated by an HIP physician later in the morning, at 8:00 AM. The nurse then handed the phone to O'Neill, who said to Dr. Graig, "Well, I could be dead by 8 o'clock." Following his phone conversation with Dr. Graig, O'Neill spoke to the nurse, indicating that he had been told to go home and come back when HIP was open. Mrs. O'Neill, concerned about her husband, asked that a physician see her husband immediately. The nurse again requested that they return at 8:00 AM. Mrs. O'Neill said he could be dead by 8:00 AM. No help was offered, and the O'Neills left the ED to return home. O'Neill paused occasionally on his way home to catch his breath. Shortly after arriving home, he fell to the floor and expired. The plaintiff sought recovery against the hospital for failure to render necessary emergency treatment and against the physician for his failure and refusal to treat O'Neill. Dr. Graig claimed that he had offered to come to the ED but that O'Neill said he would wait and see a HIP physician that morning.

The New York Supreme Court for Bronx County entered a judgment dismissing the plaintiff's complaint, and the plaintiff appealed the court's ruling. The New York Supreme Court, Appellate Division, reversed the lower court's decision and held that a physician who abandons a patient after undertaking examination or treatment can be held liable for malpractice. The proof of the record in this case indicated that the physician undertook to diagnose the ailments of the deceased by telephone, thus establishing at least the first element of negligence—duty to use due care. The finding of the trial court was reversed, and a new trial was ordered.

Duty to Hire Competent Employees

Texas courts recognize that an employer has a duty to hire competent employees, especially if they are engaged in an occupation that could be hazardous to life and limb and requires skilled or experienced persons. For example, the appellant in *Deerings West Nursing Center v. Scott*[8] was found to have negligently hired an employee that the appellant knew or should have known was incompetent, thereby causing unreasonable risk of harm to others. In this case, an 80-year-old visitor had gone to Deerings to visit her infirm older brother. During one visit, Nurse Hopper, a 6-foot-4-inch male employee of Deerings, confronted the visitor to prevent her from visiting. The visitor recalled that he was angry and just stared. She stated that upon his approach, she had thrown up her hands to protect her face, but he hit her on the chin, slapped her down on the concrete floor, and got on top of her, pinning her to the floor.

Hopper testified that he was hired sight unseen over the telephone by Deerings's director of nursing. Even though the following day, Hopper completed an application at the nursing facility, he still maintained that he was hired over the phone. In his application, he falsely stated that he was a Texas licensed vocational nurse (LVN). Additionally, he claimed that he had never been convicted of a crime. In reality, he had been previously employed by a bar, was not an LVN, had committed more than 56 criminal offenses of theft, and was on probation at the time of his testimony.

The trial court awarded the plaintiff a judgment of $35,000 for actual damages and $200,000 in punitive damages. The court of appeals held that there was sufficient evidence to support the findings that the employee's failure to obtain a nursing license was the proximate cause of the visitor's damages and that the hiring was negligent and also showed a heedless and reckless disregard of the rights of others.

It is common knowledge that the bleakness and rigors of old age, drugs, and the diseases of senility can cause people to become confused . . . and cantankerous. It is predictable that elderly patients will be visited by elderly friends and family. It is reasonable to anticipate that a man of proven moral baseness would be more likely to commit a morally base act on an 80-year-old woman. Fifty-six convictions for theft is some evidence of mental aberration. Hopper was employed not only to administer medicine but also to contend with the sometimes erratic behavior of the decrepit. The investigative process necessary to the procurement of a Texas nursing license would have precluded the licensing of Hopper. In the hiring of an unlicensed and potentially mentally and morally unfit nurse, it is reasonable to anticipate that an injury would result as a natural and probable consequence of that negligent hiring.[9]

Deerings West Nursing Center showed a clear duty of care. The appellant violated the very purpose of Texas licensing statutes by failing to verify whether Hopper held a current LVN license. The appellant then placed him in a position of authority, allowed him to dispense drugs, and made him a shift supervisor. This negligence eventually resulted in the inexcusable assault on an elderly woman.

Duty to Nursing Facility Patient

A concise statement of the duty a nursing facility owes to its residents is found in *Lagrone v. Helman*[10] where an action was brought against the operator of the nursing facility for injuries sustained by the resident in a fall. The trial court, which rendered judgment for the defendant, stated in its instructions to the jury, "It was the duty of the defendants to use reasonable care for the safety of the appellant, consistent with her age and physical condition." The plaintiff/appellant appealed the trial court's decision and the Supreme Court of Mississippi affirmed the trial court's decision. The resident was an ambulatory resident in the defendant nursing facility who suffered from cerebral arteriosclerosis, which subjected her to occasional dizzy spells. She had requested medication from a nurse employed by the facility and had followed her to the medicine cabinet. There were two conflicting statements as to what occurred next. The plaintiff claimed that, after obtaining the medicine, the nurse suddenly, carelessly, and negligently whirled around and struck her, knocking her down and causing her to suffer a fracture of her left hip. The facility claimed that the nurse handed the pill to the plaintiff, who dropped it, and in bending over to pick it up, became dizzy and fell to the floor. Although judgment was entered for the nursing facility, had the jury accepted the plaintiff's description of the facts, the result might have been liability for the nursing facility on the basis of respondeat superior.

Standard of Care

The standard of care describes what conduct is expected of an individual in a given situation. The general standard of acceptable care is based on what a *reasonably prudent person* would do or not do acting under the same or similar circumstances. The *reasonably prudent person* doctrine describes a hypothetical person who is put forward as the community ideal of what would be considered reasonable behavior. One's age, sex, physical condition, education, training, profession, knowledge, mental capacity, and requirements imposed by law determine the reasonableness of conduct. Deviation from the standard of care constitutes negligence if it can be shown that the resulting damages are caused by the breach of one's duty to care.

The courts often rely on the testimony of an expert witness when determining the standard of care required of a health professional in the same or similar communities. Expert testimony is necessary when the jury is not qualified to determine what a reasonably prudent professional's standard of care should be in a given situation. Most states hold those with special skills (e.g., physicians, nurse practitioners, physician assistants) to a higher standard of care, which is reasonable in light of their education and training. A *registered nurse*, for example, has the duty to exercise that degree of skill, care, and knowledge ordinarily possessed and exercised by other nurses. If a patient's injury is the result of a physician's negligent act, the standard of care required would be that degree of skill, care, and knowledge ordinarily possessed and exercised in the specialty the physician is practicing. In addition, an organization's policies and procedures, regulatory requirements, and accreditation standards (e.g., The Joint Commission) can be used to help establish the standard of care required.

Duty Set by Statute

Various state statutes can be used in establishing the duty to care. California Code of Regulations, Title 22, section 70217 reads in part:

> (a) . . . only registered nurses shall be assigned to Intensive Care Newborn Nursery Service Units, which specifically require one registered nurse to two or fewer infants. In the Emergency Department, only registered nurses shall be assigned to triage patients and only registered nurses shall be assigned to critical trauma patients.

· · ·

> (1) The licensed nurse-to-patient ratio in a critical care unit shall be 1:2 or fewer at all times. "Critical care unit" means a nursing unit of a general acute care hospital which provides one of the following services: an intensive care service, a burn center, a coronary care service, an acute respiratory service, or an intensive care newborn nursery service. In the intensive care newborn nursery service, the ratio shall be 1 registered nurse: 2 or fewer patients at all times.
>
> (2) The surgical service operating room shall have at least one registered nurse assigned to the duties of the circulating nurse and a minimum of one additional person serving as scrub assistant for each patient-occupied operating room. The scrub assistant may be a licensed nurse, an operating room technician, or other person who has demonstrated current competence to the hospital as a scrub assistant, but shall not be a physician or other licensed health professional who is assisting in the performance of surgery.
>
> (3) The licensed nurse-to-patient ratio in a labor and delivery suite of the perinatal service shall be 1:2 or fewer active labor patients at all times. When a licensed nurse is caring for antepartum patients who are not in active labor, the licensed nurse-to-patient ratio shall be 1:4 or fewer at all times.
>
> (4) The licensed nurse-to-patient ratio in a postpartum area of the perinatal service shall be 1:4 mother-baby couplets or fewer at all times. In the event of multiple births, the total number of mothers plus infants assigned to a single licensed nurse shall never exceed eight. For postpartum areas in which the licensed nurse's assignment consists of mothers only, the licensed nurse-to-patient ratio shall be 1:6 or fewer at all times.
>
> (5) The licensed nurse-to-patient ratio in a combined Labor/Delivery/Postpartum area of the perinatal service shall be 1:3 or fewer at all times the licensed nurse is caring for a patient combination of one woman in active labor and a postpartum mother and infant. The licensed nurse-to-patient ratio

for nurses caring for women in active labor only, antepartum patients who are not in active labor only, postpartum women only, or mother-baby couplets only, shall be the same ratios as stated in subsections (3) and (4) above for those categories of patients.

(6) The licensed nurse-to-patient ratio in a pediatric service unit shall be 1:4 or fewer at all times.

(7) The licensed nurse-to-patient ratio in a postanesthesia recovery unit of the anesthesia service shall be 1:2 or fewer at all times, regardless of the type of anesthesia the patient received.

(8) In a hospital providing basic emergency medical services or comprehensive emergency medical services, the licensed nurse-to-patient ratio in an ED shall be 1:4 or fewer at all times that patients are receiving treatment. There shall be no fewer than two licensed nurses physically present in the ED when a patient is present.

As in *Hastings v. Baton Rouge Hospital*, some duties are created by statute. As noted earlier, a Louisiana statute imposes a duty on licensed hospitals to make emergency services available to all persons residing in the state regardless of insurance coverage or economic status. Many such standards are created by administrative agencies under the provisions of a statute. To establish liability based on a defendant's failure to follow the standard of care required by statute, the following elements must be present:

1. The defendant must have been within the specified class of persons outlined in the statute.
2. The plaintiff must have been injured in a way that the statute was designed to prevent.
3. The plaintiff must show that the injury would not have occurred if the statute had not been violated.

Duty Set by Policies and Procedures

The standard of care that employees and agents of a healthcare entity must follow can be established through the healthcare organization's internal policies, procedures, rules, and regulations. The courts generally hold that such internal operational standards are indicative of, for example, a hospital's expectations of the proper procedures to be followed in rendering patient care and, hence, create a duty to adhere to those standards. Thus, if an employee fails to adhere to a hospital's written standards of care and a patient is injured, the employee who violates those standards can be considered negligent if the patient is injured as a result of that violation.

Ethics and the Standard of Care

The standard of care required by a caregiver can in part be influenced by the principles of ethics that apply to the caregiver's profession. For example, a decision concerning termination of resuscitation efforts is an area where the standard of care includes an ethical component. Under these circumstances, it occasionally may be appropriate for a medical expert to testify about the ethical aspects underlying the professional standard of care.

Community Versus National Standard of Care

The courts have been moving away from reliance on a community standard and applying an industry or national standard. This trend has developed as a result of the more reasonable belief that the standard of care should not vary with the locale where an individual receives care. It is unreasonable for any one healthcare facility and/or healthcare professional to set the standard simply because there is no local basis for comparison. Geographic proximity rules have increasingly given way to a national standard, with the standard in the professional's general locality becoming a factor in determining whether the professional has exercised that degree of care expected of the average practitioner in the class to which he or she belongs.

The ever-evolving advances in medicine and mass communications, the availability of medical specialists, the development of continuing education programs, and the broadening scope of government regulations continue to raise the standard of care required of healthcare professionals and organizations. As a result, many courts have adopted the view that the practice of medicine should be national in scope. In *Dickinson v. Mailliard*, the court stated:

> Hospitals must now be licensed and accredited. They are subject to statutory regulation. In order to obtain approval they must meet certain standard requirements. . . . It is no longer justifiable, if indeed it ever was, to limit a hospital's liability to that degree of care which is customarily practiced in its own community. . . . [M]any communities have only one

hospital. Adherence to such a rule, then, means the hospital whose conduct is assailed, is to be measured only by standards which it has set for itself.[11]

The Court of Appeals of Maryland, in *Shilkret v. Annapolis Emergency Hospital Association,* stated:

> [A] hospital is required to use that degree of care and skill which is expected of a reasonably competent hospital in the same or similar circumstances. As in cases brought against physicians, advances in the profession, availability of special facilities and specialists, together with all other relevant considerations, are to be taken into account.[12]

Evidence of the standard of care applicable to professional activities may be found in a variety of documents, such as regulations of government agencies (e.g., state licensure laws) and standards established by private organizations, such as The Joint Commission. Although the courts tend to prefer a broader standard of care, the community standard can be extremely important in any given situation.

> Assume for a moment that the question is whether a doctor in a remote area of Alaska has placed patients at an unnecessarily high risk by receiving telephone inquiries from nurses in Eskimo villages at even more remote areas and attempting to prescribe by phone. Clearly, such conduct would violate the standard of care in San Francisco and, in San Francisco, would place his patients in an "unnecessarily" high-risk situation. For the doctor in Alaska, on the other hand, this method of consultation may be the only possible one, and thus not at all unnecessary or a gross and flagrant violation.[13]

Hospital Must Meet Nationwide Standard

The parents in *Wickliffe v. Sunrise Hospital*[14] sued the hospital for the wrongful death of their teenage daughter, who suffered respiratory arrest while recovering from surgery. The Nevada Supreme Court held that the level of care to which the hospital must conform is a nationwide standard. The hospital's level of care is no longer subject to narrow geographic limitations under the so-called locality rule; rather, the hospital must meet a nationwide standard.

Furthermore, the Georgia Court of Appeals in *Hodges v. Effingham*[15] held that application of the locality rule was erroneous in an action against the hospital. The alleged failure of nurses to take an accurate medical history of the patient's serious condition and convey the information to the physician drew into question the professional judgment of the nurses. The jury should have been instructed as to the general standard of nursing required.

> There are no degrees of care in fixing responsibility for negligence, but the standard is always that care which a reasonably prudent person should use under like circumstances. The duty to exercise reasonable care is a standard designed to protect a society's members from unreasonable exposure to potentially injurious hazards; negligence is conduct that falls short of the reasonable care standard. Perfection of conduct is humanly impossible; however, and the law does not exact an unreasonable amount of care from anyone.[16]

Professionals Held to a Higher Standard

Most states hold those with special skills to a standard of care that is reasonable in light of their special abilities and knowledge. The plaintiff, for example in *Kowal v. Deer Park Fire District*[17] submitted affidavits from two doctors who stated that, to a reasonable degree of medical certainty, the death of the plaintiff's decedent "was caused by severe and extensive cerebral anoxia caused by . . . incorrect intubation," that the incorrect intubation of the decedent constituted medical malpractice. The failure to recognize that the patient's condition constituted a gross departure from good and accepted practice of what is a commonplace medical technique. Assuming that the deposition testimony of the defendants established prima facie evidence that they were not grossly negligent, the sworn opinion of the plaintiff's experts established that there were issues of fact that precluded the granting of summary judgment.

Specialists, in particular, are held to a higher standard of care than nonspecialists. Generally, the reliance of the public on the skills of a specialist and the wealth and sources of his or her knowledge is not limited to the geographic area in which he or she practices. Rather, his or her knowledge is a specialty; a person specializes to keep abreast. Any other standard for a specialist would negate the fundamental expectations and purpose of a specialty.

Expert Testimony to Establish Required Standard

Traditionally, in determining how a reasonably prudent person should perform in a given situation, the courts rely on the testimony of an expert witness as to the standard of care required in the same or similar communities.

Locality Cannot Be Limited to County Lines

The plaintiff's expert witness in *Stogsdill v. Manor Convalescent Home, Inc., and Hiatt, MD,*[18] who practiced about 12 miles from the convalescent home where the defendant physician treated the plaintiff, was found competent to testify. The defendant objected, stating the expert never practiced in the county where the malpractice occurred. The court overruled this objection on the grounds that locality cannot be construed so narrowly as to be determined by county lines. Expert testimony like that in *Stogsdil* is necessary when a jury is not trained or qualified to determine what the reasonably prudent professional's standard of care would be under similar circumstances.

Breach of Duty

Once a duty to care has been established, the plaintiff must demonstrate that the defendant breached that duty by failing to comply with the accepted standard of care. *Breach of duty* is the failure to conform to or the departure from a required duty of care owed to a person. The obligation to perform according to a standard of care can encompass either performing or failing to perform a particular act.

Breach of duty is illustrated in **FIGURE 3-4**, where the IV admixture room pharmacist checking the work of a pharmacy technician failed to follow up on his concern as to whether or not the medication in

FIGURE 3-4 Breach of duty.

the intravenous (IV) bag had been diluted in the correct dosage. Hospital policies and procedures often provide that when there are questions regarding an order, the pharmacy assistant must seek verification from the pharmacist when a medication order raises concern as to the medication ordered, dosage, and/or route to be administered (e.g., injection, IV). In this instance, failure to follow up established a breach of duty.

Hastings Case: Breach of Duty

The court in *Hastings v. Baton Rouge Hospital,*[19] which was discussed earlier, found there was a breach of duty when the patient did not receive adequate care. Hospital regulations provided that when a physician cannot be reached or refuses a call, the chief of service must be notified so that another physician can be obtained. This was not done. A plaintiff need not prove that the patient would have survived if proper treatment had been administered, only that the patient would have had a chance of survival. As a result of Dr. Gerdes's failure to make arrangements for another physician and Dr. McCool's failure to perform the necessary surgery, the patient had no chance of survival. The duty to provide for appropriate care under the circumstances was breached.

Failure to Provide a Safe Environment

In *Dunahoo v. Brooks,*[20] the nursing facility was found to have breached its duty when a patient tripped over an obviously ill-placed light cord. The court stated that because the defendant nursing facility operator had been aware of the 94-year-old plaintiff's infirmities and had agreed to provide her nursing care, the nursing facility assumed an obligation to exercise care commensurate with her physical condition. While the plaintiff was getting out of bed, she tripped and fell over a light cord that was loose on the floor in an area that the defendant knew the plaintiff frequently used. The cord was plugged into a socket on the floor 5 inches from the baseboard. The court was impressed with the ease with which the situation could have been corrected, noting that the cord could have been fastened down with a few nails and the outlet placed on the baseboard instead of nearly in the middle of the floor.

Responsibility to Protect Patient

The nursing facility was found negligent in *Booty v. Kentwood Manor Nursing Home, Inc.,*[21] when a 90-year-old resident wandered outside the facility, fell, and suffered a hip fracture. The resident's physical condition deteriorated, and he eventually died. The staff was aware of the resident's confusion and tendency to stray. The court found that the facility was responsible for taking reasonable steps to prevent injury to a mentally confused and physically fragile resident. The facility's alarm system might have alerted the staff of unauthorized resident departures, but it had been deactivated, and the doors were propped open for the convenience of the staff. The record demonstrated that inadequate supervision was the cause of resident's departure and that he most likely would not have suffered injury but for the nursing facility's breach of duty owed to the resident.

Injury

Injury includes physical harm, pain, suffering, and loss of income or reputation. A defendant may be negligent and still not incur liability if no injury or actual damages result to the plaintiff. Without harm or injury, there is no liability. The mere occurrence of an injury "does not establish negligence for which the law imposes liability, because the injury may be the result of an unavoidable accident, or an act of God, or some cause so remote to the person sought to be held liable for negligence that he cannot be charged with responsibility for the injury."[22]

FIGURE 3-5 portrays the administration of an incorrect dose of an IV medication that had been improperly diluted in the hospital's pharmacy, which led to the injury and ultimate death of an infant in General Hospital's nursery.

Hastings Case: Injury

Hastings went into cardiac arrest. An attempt to revive him was futile and the patient died after having been moved back to the ED. The patient virtually bled to death, thus establishing the third element required to establish proof that a negligent act had been committed.

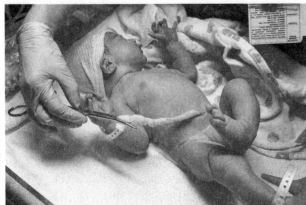

FIGURE 3-5 Injury.

Failure to Render Care

Injury was obvious in *Lucas v. HCMF Corp.*,[23] where the patient had been transferred to a nursing facility following hospitalization for several ailments, including early decubitus ulcers. The resident was returned to the hospital[24] days later. "At that time the ulcer on her hip had become three large ulcers that reached to the bone and tunneled through the skin to meet one another. The ulcer on her buttocks had grown from one inch in diameter to eight inches in diameter and extended to the bone. Additional ulcers had developed on each of her ribs, on her left arm and wrist, and on the left side of her face."[24] The standard of care in preventing and treating decubitus ulcers required that the resident be mobilized and turned every 2 hours to prevent deterioration of tissue. The treatment records reflected that the resident was not turned at all from September 22 through October 1, nor was she turned on October 4, 7, or 12. Failure to periodically turn the resident and move her to a chair had caused the deterioration in her condition.

Multiple Punctures in Starting Central Line

In the medical malpractice case of *Goodwin v. Kufoy*,[25] the internist failed to successfully start a central line in order for the patient to receive her prescribed medication intravenously. During the attempts to start the central line, the internist made an indeterminate number of puncture wounds at four different sites on the patient's body. The patient alleged that she experienced physical pain and suffering as a result of the multiple puncture wounds. Her pain, however, was managed successfully with medication, and no further treatment was sought.

The patient filed a lawsuit against the internist, and a medical review panel was formed. The medical review panel's opinion found that the patient failed to show that the treating internist had breached the standard of care.

The patient then brought her case to trial in district court. The trial court found that the patient failed to establish the applicable standard of care, failed to prove that the internist had breached any standard of care, and failed to prove that she suffered any damages as a result of the unsuccessful procedure.

The patient appealed, contending that the trial court erred in finding she failed to establish the standard of care. The plaintiff claimed the internist failed to obtain a consult from a specialist, after multiple puncture wounds to start a central line. The State of Louisiana Court of Appeal, 3rd Circuit, agreed that the patient had established the standard of care. However, the plaintiff did not prove that she suffered any damages as a result of the defendant's failed attempts to start a central line.

Causation

The element of causation requires that there be a reasonable, close, and causal connection or relationship between the defendant's negligent conduct and the resulting damages. In other words, the defendant's negligence must be a substantial factor causing the plaintiff's injury. *Proximate cause* is a term that refers to the relationship between a breach of duty and the resulting injury. The breach of duty must be the proximate/direct cause of the resulting injury. The mere departure from a proper and recognized procedure is not sufficient to enable a patient to recover damages unless the plaintiff can show that the departure was unreasonable and the proximate cause of the patient's injuries.

The courts generally apply the *but-for rule* to determine if the injury is directly the result of a defendant's act or omission of an act. A finding that an injury would not have occurred *but for* a defendant's act establishes that the particular act or omission is the proximate cause of the harm. If an injury would have occurred regardless of a defendant's negligent act, liability cannot be assigned to the defendant. "Thus, in a death case, if a defendant physician, by action or inaction, has destroyed any substantial possibility of the patient's survival, such conduct becomes a proximate cause of the patient's death. The law does not require the plaintiff to prove to a certainty that the patient would have lived had he received more prompt diagnosis and treatment for the condition causing the death."[26]

FIGURE 3-6 portrays a defense attorney successfully arguing that the cause of death of an infant in General Hospital's nursery was due to the failure of the pharmacist to properly verify that the IV medication had been properly diluted and labeled by the pharmacy technician in the hospital's pharmacy. The IV solution, containing the medication, was delivered to the nursery, where the nurse checked the label, unaware that the medication left the pharmacy mislabeled and improperly diluted, she administered it to the infant, who subsequently died. Those actions combined to establish the proximate cause of the injury, the fourth element of negligence—causation.

Hastings Case: Causation

Causation in the *Hastings v. Baton Rouge Hospital*,[27] discussed earlier, was well established. In the ordinary course of events, Hastings would not have bled to death in a hospital ED over a 2-hour period without some surgical intervention to save his life. "As a result of

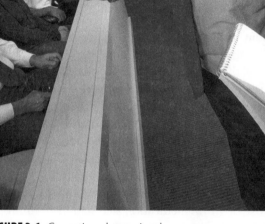

FIGURE 3-6 Causation determined.

© Junial Enterprises/Shutterstock

Dr. Gerdes's failure to obtain another surgeon and Dr. McCool's failure to operate, Cedric had no chance of living. Requiring his survivors to prove that surgery would have saved him would be an unreasonable burden."[28]

Failure to Alert Patient of Misread Computed Tomography Scan

On November 2, 1995, the plaintiff, in *St. Dic v. Brooklyn Hospital Center*,[29] was admitted to the hospital complaining of a severe headache, an inability to open her eyes, and the absence of feeling in her legs. A computed tomography (CT) scan was administered, which the defendant conceded was misread by the staff physician as normal. After discharging the plaintiff from its care, the defendant's radiologist reviewed the CT and concluded it was, in fact, not normal. The defendant did not contact the plaintiff to alert the defendant about the revised finding. The hospital conceded that its employee misread the CT. Failure to alert the plaintiff and the misreading were departures from accepted medical practice, the jury properly found that those conceded departures were the proximate causes of the plaintiff's injury. "The principal issue presented on this appeal is whether those conceded departures were the proximate causes of the plaintiff's injury. Contrary to the defendant's contention, the evidence adduced at trial was legally sufficient to support the jury's verdict on causation."[30]

Failure to Refer

In *Robinson v. Group Health Association, Inc.*,[31] the District of Columbia Court of Appeals held that there was a genuine issue of material fact as to whether the failure of a group health provider to treat a patient's diabetes aggressively resulted in the amputation of his leg below the knee. The testimony of the plaintiff's expert, as it related to the issue of proximate cause, was sufficient to allow the case to go to the jury. According to the expert witness, the failure of the provider to refer the patient for vascular evaluation resulted in his below-the-knee amputation. The expert testified to a reasonable degree of medical certainty, which he equated to a greater than 50% chance, that if there had been an early vascular consult, followed by an angioplasty and perhaps a partial foot amputation, a below-the-knee amputation could have been avoided. Although the provider presented contrary testimony, the plaintiff's expert testimony was found sufficient to permit a reasonable juror to find that there was a direct and substantial causal relationship between the provider's breach of the standard of care and the patient's injuries.

The primary wrong upon which a cause of action for negligence is based consists of the breach of a duty on the part of one person to protect another against injury, the proximate result of which is an injury to the person to whom the duty is owed. These elements of duty, breach, and injury are essentials of actionable negligence, and in fact, most judicial definitions of the term "negligence" or "actionable negligence" are couched in those terms. In the absence of any one of them, no cause of action for negligence will lie.[32]

Causation Not Established: Case Dismissed

Mrs. Stewart was admitted to the hospital with inflammation of the gallbladder, and the surgeon began antibiotics. Stewart, however, died early the next morning. The county medical examiner stated that the cause of death was a result of a blood-borne infection. The plaintiff's nurse provided expert testimony in a deposition that a registered nurse at the hospital failed to meet the nursing standard of care in treating the patient. A chart was produced identifying 11 instances in which the hospital nurse allegedly failed to meet the nursing standard of care, including failure to assess the need for oxygen therapy, failure to note abnormal breath sounds and severity or location of pain, failure to assess urinary retention, and failure to assess vital signs and nausea. The plaintiff, Stewart's husband, contended that the evidence established that the defendants violated the nursing standard of care and that their failures were the proximate cause of his wife's death. The defendants moved for dismissal and the superior court granted the motion. The Court of Appeals of Washington, Division Three, in *Stewart v. Newbold*,[33] found that the plaintiff—Stewart's husband—failed to establish any genuine issue on the question of proximate causation. The trial court properly dismissed the claims against the nurse and hospital.

Eliminating Causes

Another way to establish the causal relationship between the particular conduct of a defendant and a plaintiff's injury is through the process of eliminating causes other than the defendant's conduct. As an example, in *Shegog v. Zabrecky*,[34] Mr. Pereyra sought treatment for back pain from Dr. Zabrecky, a chiropractor at the Life Extension Center, in January 1987. Zabrecky ordered X-rays. The X-rays revealed that Pereyra was suffering from a fractured vertebra caused by a malignant tumor. Pereyra was referred to a surgeon, who performed two surgical procedures to remove the tumor. Pereyra underwent a series of radiation treatments, which were supervised by Dr. Usas. A CT scan revealed that the cancer had spread to his lungs. Dr. Usas and other consulting physicians recommended that chemotherapy be considered following the course of radiation treatments. Pereyra was advised that his chance of survival following chemotherapy was 50% or better. During the summer of 1987, Pereyra consulted with a number of physicians as to the best course of treatment. Pereyra continued to see Zabrecky throughout the summer and fall of 1987. Zabrecky recommended that Pereyra reject the chemotherapy treatments and undergo a course of treatment with neytumorin and neythymin (two compounds manufactured in Germany). The Food and Drug Administration had not approved either drug. Pereyra agreed to undergo the treatment. Zabrecky performed an initial enzyme study prior to treatment, but did not perform further tests after the course of treatment began. During the course of treatment, the cancer continued to spread. Additional radiation treatments were given. Pereyra's condition worsened, and he was admitted to the hospital. The physicians at the hospital had not been aware that Pereyra was injecting himself with drugs given to

🔍 *FAILURE TO ADMINISTER PROPER NOURISHMENT*

Citation: *Caruso v. Pine Manor Nursing Ctr.*, 538 N.E.2d 722 (Ill. App. Ct. 1989)

Facts

In Illinois, a nursing facility by statute has a duty to provide its residents with proper nutrition. Under the Nursing Home Care Reform Act, the owner and licensee of a nursing home are liable to a resident for any intentional or negligent act or omission of their agents or employees that injures a resident. The act defines neglect as a failure of a facility to provide adequate medical or personal care or maintenance, when failure results in physical or mental injury to a resident or in the deterioration of the resident's condition. Personal care and maintenance include providing food, water, and assistance with meals necessary to sustain a healthy life. The nursing facility in this case maintained no records of the resident's fluid intake or output. A nurse testified that such a record is a required nursing facility procedure that should have been followed for a person in the resident's condition, but was not.

The resident's condition deteriorated after staying 6.5 days at the facility. Upon leaving the facility and entering a hospital ED, the resident was diagnosed by the treating physician as suffering from severe dehydration caused by an inadequate intake of fluids. The nursing facility offered no alternative explanation for the resident's dehydrated condition.

The trial court found that the record supported a finding that the resident had suffered from dehydration as a result of the nursing facility's negligence. The defendant appealed the jury verdict.

Issue

Did the resident suffer harm as a result of Pine Manor Nursing Center's negligence?

Holding

The Illinois Appellate Court upheld the trial court's finding that the resident suffered dehydration due to the nursing facility's negligence.

Reason

The evidence demonstrated that the proximate cause of the resident's dehydration was the nursing facility's failure to administer proper nourishment; therefore, the jury reasonably concluded that the nursing facility's negligence caused the dehydration.

---

him by Zabrecky. Upon urging from his wife, Pereyra revealed this information to the physicians at the hospital. Pereyra died on December 17, 1987, approximately 6 weeks after he had begun treatment with neytumorin and neythymin. An autopsy revealed that Pereyra had died from necrosis of the liver caused by a toxic reaction to a foreign substance. Pereyra was taking only the drugs neytumorin and neythymin between July 1987 and his death. No cancer was found in the liver.

A lawsuit was filed against the defendants, seeking damages for negligent treatment. The alleged negligent acts included:

- Administering drugs statutorily prohibited for use
- Withholding information from treating physicians
- Failing to follow patient's blood work
- Advising the patient to use drugs that had expired
- Engaging in the unlicensed practice of medicine
- Inducing the patient to forgo appropriate therapy

The jury delivered a verdict for the plaintiff. The defendants appealed, claiming that the evidence introduced at trial did not support the jury's

finding as to causation. The appellate court held that Zabrecky's grossly negligent actions and the circumstantial evidence introduced supported the jury's finding of causation. Zabrecky violated a recognized standard of care by prescribing statutorily prohibited drugs. No evidence was presented that would have supported another cause of the patient's liver failure. Reports from treating physicians indicate that the plaintiff died of liver failure and not from cancer. The defendant's expert testified that necrosis of the liver can be caused by the injection of foreign substances. He also testified that the normal reaction time of the human liver to a foreign protein is, on average, 6 weeks.

One of the ways to establish the causal relationship between particular conduct of a defendant and a plaintiff's injury is the expert's deduction, by the process of eliminating causes other than the conduct, that the conduct was the cause of injury. . . . The submitted reports indicate that each physician deduced that the German drugs were the most probable cause of Pereyra's liver failure, even without analysis of the drugs.[35]

Foreseeability

Foreseeability is the reasonable anticipation that harm or injury is likely to result from a commission or omission of an act. The *test for foreseeability* is whether one of ordinary prudence and intelligence should have anticipated the danger to others caused by his or her negligent act. The test for foreseeability is not what the wrongdoer believed would occur; instead, it is whether the wrongdoer ought to have reasonably foreseen that the event in question, or some similar event, would occur.[36] The broad test of negligence is what a reasonably prudent person would or should normally foresee and would do in light of this foresight under the circumstances.[37]

Foreseeability involves guarding against that which is probable and likely to happen, not against that which is only remotely possible. There is no expectation that a person can guard against events that cannot reasonably be foreseen or that are so unlikely to occur that they would be disregarded.

When a defendant's action or actions breach the standard of care and injury is the result of the breach, the jury must make two determinations. First, was it foreseeable that harm would occur from the failure to meet the standard of care? Second, was the carelessness or negligence the proximate or immediate cause of the harm or injury to the plaintiff?

In *Hastings v. Baton Rouge Hospital*, it was highly probable that the patient would die if the bleeding was not stopped. The broad test of negligence is what a reasonably prudent person would foresee and would do in the light of this foresight under the circumstances.

In *Haynes v. Hoffman*,[38] the plaintiff brought a medical malpractice action against the defendant physician for his alleged negligence in prescribing a medication from which the plaintiff suffered an allergic reaction. The trial court returned a verdict in favor of the defendant, and the plaintiff appealed. The evidence at trial revealed that the plaintiff had not disclosed her history of allergies to the physician. The physician testified that, at the time of the physical examination, the plaintiff denied having any allergies. The plaintiff was found to have contributed to her injuries by failing to provide her physician information regarding her known allergies.

The question of foreseeability was an issue in *Ferguson v. Dr. McCarthy's Rest Home*.[39] In this case, the plaintiff, a resident in the defendant's nursing facility, suffered from paralysis of the left side of the body but was able to roll toward the left side in bed. The defendant had knowledge of this ability. A radiator, which was approximately the same height as the bed, was next to the plaintiff's bed. During the night, the plaintiff's left foot came in contact with the radiator, and she suffered third-degree burns. The court held that this kind of accident was foreseeable with respect to a person in the plaintiff's condition, particularly because the defendant had knowledge of the plaintiff's condition. The defendant should have shielded the radiator or not placed the plaintiff next to it.

Generally, the issue of foreseeability is for the trial court to decide. A duty to prevent a wrongful act by a third party will be imposed only where those wrongful acts can be reasonably anticipated.

▶ SUMMARY CASE

All the elements necessary to establish negligence were well established in *Niles v. City of San Rafael*.[40] On June 26, 1973, at approximately 3:30 PM, Kelly Niles, a young boy, got into an argument with another boy on a ball field, and he was hit on the right side of his head. He rode home on his bicycle and waited for his father, who was to pick him up for the weekend. At approximately 5:00 PM, his father arrived to pick him up. By the time they arrived in San Francisco, Kelly appeared to be in a great deal of pain. His father then decided to take him to Mount Zion Hospital, which was a short distance away. He arrived at the hospital ED at approximately 5:45 PM. On admission to the ED, Kelly was taken to a treatment room by a registered nurse. The nurse obtained a history of the injury and took Kelly's pulse and blood pressure. During his stay in the ED, he was irritable, vomited several times, and complained that his head hurt. An intern who had seen Kelly wrote, "pale, diaphoretic, and groggy," on the patient's chart. Skull X-rays were ordered and found to be negative except for soft tissue swelling that was not noted until later. The intern then decided to admit the patient. A second-year resident was called, and he agreed with the intern's decision. An admitting clerk called the intern and indicated that the patient had to be admitted by an attending physician. The resident went as far as to write "admit" on the chart and later crossed it out. A pediatrician who was in the ED at the time was asked to look at Kelly. The pediatrician was also the paid director of the Mount Zion Pediatric Outpatient Clinic.

Haskins talked to Kelly in the emergency room, but he did not examine Kelly or look at his chart. Then Haskins talked to Kelly's father, concluded he was a responsible person, and told him Kelly could go home. Haskins advised Niles to watch for dilation of the pupils in Kelly's eyes, and to be sure that Kelly could be aroused from sleep. The pediatrician asked Kelly a few questions and then decided to send him home.[41]

The physician could not recall what instructions he gave the patient's father, but he did give the father his business card. The pediatrician could not recall giving the father a copy of the ED's head injury instructions, an information sheet that had been prepared for distribution to patients with head injuries. The head injury pamphlet described under what circumstances the patient should be returned to the ED should any of the following signs appear:

1. A large, soft lump on the head
2. Unusual drowsiness (cannot be awakened)
3. Forceful or repeated vomiting
4. A fit or convulsion (jerking or spells)
5. Clumsy walking
6. Bad headache
7. One pupil larger than the other

Although Kelly exhibited several of these signs while he was in the ED, he was discharged. Kelly was taken back to his father's apartment at about 7:00 PM. A psychiatrist, a friend of Kelly's father, had stopped by later that evening. He examined Kelly and noted that one pupil was larger than the other. Because the pediatrician could not be reached, Kelly was taken back to the ED. A physician on duty noted an epidural hematoma during his examination and ordered that a neurosurgeon be called.

Today, Kelly can move only his eyes and neck. A lawsuit against Mount Zion and the pediatrician for $5 million was instituted. The city of San Rafael and the public school district also were included in the lawsuit as defendants. Expert testimony by two neurosurgeons during the trial indicated that the patient's chances of recovery would have been very good if he had been admitted promptly. This testimony placed the proximate cause of the injury with the hospital. The final judgment was $4 million against the defendants, $2.5 million for compensatory damages, and another $1.5 million for pain and suffering.

Case Lessons

Each case presented in this textbook illustrates actual experiences of plaintiffs and defendants, enabling the reader to apply the lessons learned to real-life situations. The many lessons in *Niles v. City of San Rafael* include the following:

- An organization can improve the quality of patient care rendered in the facility by establishing and adhering to policies, procedures, and protocols that facilitate the delivery of quality care across all disciplines.
- The provision of quality health care requires collaboration across disciplines.
- A physician must conduct a thorough and responsible examination and order the appropriate tests for each patient, evaluating the results of those tests and providing appropriate treatment prior to discharging the patient.
- A patient's vital signs must be monitored closely and documented in the medical record.
- Corrective measures must be taken when a patient's medical condition signals a medical problem.
- A complete review of a patient's medical record must be accomplished before discharging a patient. Review of the record must include review of test results, nurses' notes, residents' and interns' notes, and the notes of any other physician or consultant who may have attended the patient.
- An erroneous diagnosis leading to the premature dismissal of a case can result in liability for both the organization and physician.

Collaboration in Tort Reform

Physicians and, increasingly, advanced practice practitioners (e.g., physician assistants and nurse practitioners) are on the front lines of medicine but often have been excluded from the decision-making processes that threaten their autonomy and financial security. A concerted effort must be made to include them in the process of tort reform. The present system of punishment for all because of the inadequacies of the few has proven to be costly and far from effective.

The medical malpractice insurance crisis continues to be a major dilemma for the healthcare industry. Although there have been many approaches to resolving the crisis, there appears to be no one magic formula. The solution most likely will require a variety of efforts, including tort reforms, some of which have been reviewed earlier here.

⚲ *THE COURT'S DECISION*

The Ohio Court of Appeals held that the delay in providing the plaintiff treatment fell below the medically acceptable standard of care. The court was appalled that the physician had characterized his evaluation as a medical examination or had implied that what he described as a "cursory breast examination" should be considered a medically sufficient breast examination. It seemed incredible to the court that a physician would deliberately choose not to take the additional few minutes or seconds to thoroughly palpitate the sides of the breasts, which is a standard, minimally intrusive cancer detection technique. His admission that he merely "pressed" on the plaintiff's breasts, coupled with the additional admission that such acts would not necessarily disclose lumps in the breasts, constituted poor medical care.

It was probable that an earlier procedure would have safely and reliably conserved a large part of the plaintiff's right breast. Through inexcusable delays, the plaintiff lost this option and, instead, was medically required to have the entire breast removed. The court concluded that the defendant's negligence was the sole and proximate cause of the plaintiff's losses.[42]

▶ CHAPTER REVIEW

1. A *tort* is a civil wrong that is committed against a person or property for which a court provides a remedy in the form of an action for damages.
2. *Negligence* is a tort—a civil or personal wrong that is the unintentional commission or omission of an act that a reasonably prudent person would or would not do under the same or similar circumstances.
3. Forms of negligence
   - *Malfeasance*: the execution of an unlawful or improper act.
   - *Misfeasance*: the improper performance of an act that results in injury to another.
   - *Nonfeasance*: a failure to act when there is a duty to do so.
4. Degrees of negligence
   - *Ordinary negligence*: the failure to do what a reasonably prudent person would do or doing what a reasonably prudent person would not do under the circumstances of the act or omission in question.
   - *Gross negligence*: the intentional or wanton omission of care that should be provided or the performance of an improper act.
5. Elements of negligence
   - *Duty to care*: the legal obligation or obligatory conduct owed by one person to another. The standard of care is the conduct expected of an individual in a given situation.
   - *Breach of duty*: the failure to meet a prevailing standard of care.

   - *Injury*: without proof of harm or injury, a defendant cannot be found liable for negligence.
   - *Causation*: the defendant's negligence must be a substantial factor in having caused injury.
     - *Foreseeability*: the reasonable anticipation that harm or injury will result from an act or a failure to act.
     - *Test for foreseeability*: whether one should have reasonably anticipated that the event in question or a similar event would occur.

▶ REVIEW QUESTIONS

1. Describe the objectives of tort law.
2. Explain the difference between negligence and malpractice.
3. Describe the elements of a negligence that the plaintiff must establish in a negligence suit.
4. Describe the importance of causation in establishing liability in a negligence suit.

▶ NOTES

1. *Tomcik v. Ohio Dep't of Rehabilitation & Correction*, 62 Ohio Misc.2d 324, 598 N.E.2d 900 (Ohio Ct. App. 1991).
2. *Id*. at 904.
3. Clare Kitchen, "You're Taking Out Wrong Kidney, Surgeon Was Told," http://www .dailymail.co.uk/health/article-123005 /Youre-taking-wrong-kidney-surgeon-told .html#ixzz4sTYYdGM2

4. YourLawyer.com, "Wrong Breast and Wrong Kidney Removed as a Result of Two Inexcusable Surgical Errors," http://www.yourlawyer.com /articles/title/wrong-breast-and-wrong-kidney -removed-as-a-result-of-two-inexcusable -surgical-errors

5. NYTimes.com, "Doctor Who Cut Off Wrong Leg Is Defended by Colleagues," *The New York Times*, September 17, 1995. http://www .nytimes.com/1995/09/17/us/doctor-who -cut-off-wrong-leg-is-defended-by-colleagues .html

6. 498 So. 2d 713 (La. Ct. App. 1986).

7. 11 A.2d 132 (N.Y. App. Div. 1960).

8. 787 S.W.2d 494 (Tex. Ct. App. 1990).

9. *Id.* at 496.

10. 233 Miss. 654, 103 So. 2d 365 (1958).

11. 175 N.W.2d 588, 596 (Iowa 1970).

12. 349 A.2d 245 (Md. 1975).

13. *Greene v. Bowen*, 639 F. Supp. 544, 561 (E.D. Cal. 1986).

14. 706 P.2d 1383 (Nev. 1985).

15. 355 S.E.2d 104 (Ga. Ct. App. 1987).

16. 57A AM. JUR. 2D Torts § 26 (1989).

17. No. 2004-00863 (N.Y. App. Div. 2004).

18. 343 N.E.3d 589 (Ill. 1976).

19. 498 So. 2d 713 (La. Ct. App. 1986).

20. 128 So. 2d 485 (Ala. 1961).

21. 483 So. 2d 634 (La. Ct. App. 1985).

22. 57A AM. JUR. 2D Torts § 78 (1989).

23. 384 S.E.2d 92 (Va. 1989).

24. *Id.*

25. 974 So. 2d 815 (La. App. 2008).

26. *Brown v. Koulizakis*, 229 Va. 524, 331 SE.2d 440 at 446 (1985).

27. 498 So. 2d 713 (La. Ct. App. 1986).

28. *Id* at 71.

29. *St. Dic v. Brooklyn Hospital Center,* 12 A.D. 3rd 661 (2004).

30. *Id.* at 662.

31. 691 A.2d 1147 (D.C. App. 1997).

32. 57A AM. JUR. 2D Torts § 80 (1989).

33. 112 Wash. App. 1027 (2002).

34. 654 A.2d 771 (Conn. App. 1995).

35. *Id.* at 777.

36. *Clark v. Wagoner*, 452 S.W.2d 437, 440 (Tex. 1970).

37. 57A AM. JUR. 2D Torts § 134 (1989).

38. 296 S.E.2d 216 (Ga. Ct. App. 1982).

39. 142 N.E.2d 337 (Mass. 1957).

40. 116 Cal. Rptr. 733 (Cal. Ct. App. 1974).

41. *Id.*

42. *Supra, Tomcik v. Ohio Dep't of Rehabilitation & Correction.*

© tlegend/Shutterstock

CHAPTER 4

Intentional Torts

🔍 IT'S YOUR GAVEL...

FALSE ARREST

In *Desai v. SSM Healthcare*,[1] Dr. Desai was walking across a hospital parking lot, a shortcut to the St. Louis University Medical School's Institute of Molecular Virology, where he worked as part of his graduate studies. Two security guards, Mr. Mealey and Mr. Windam, stopped Desai and asked him for identification. Desai said that he was a doctor and that he did not have his identification with him. Following an argument, the two security guards grabbed Desai's arms and Windam slammed Desai's head against the trunk of a car. After handcuffing him, the security guards escorted Desai back to the security office where they were joined by the security guards' supervisor. The handcuffs were eventually removed after the security guards received verification that Desai was affiliated with the institute and confirmation from a nurse supervisor that he was a physician. Shortly thereafter, the university campus police arrived. One of the officers asked Desai to apologize to Mealey. Desai refused and said that he wanted the St. Louis city police called, because he wanted to file an official complaint of assault. At the request of the security guards, Desai was handcuffed again and arrested by the St. Louis police for trespassing. The security guards later admitted that they had Desai arrested to avoid trouble for themselves. Desai was not released from jail until noon the following day. While in jail, he suffered headaches and seizures. Desai brought suit against the hospital and security guards for false imprisonment, battery, and malicious prosecution.

(continues)

IT'S YOUR GAVEL... *(continued)*

The defendants moved to have the malicious prosecution count dismissed, and the motion was granted. The jury had returned a verdict totaling $75,000 in damages for the false imprisonment claim and found in favor of the defendants on the battery claim. The trial court sustained the defendants' motions for judgment notwithstanding the verdict, and the plaintiff appealed. Did the plaintiff meet his burden of establishing his case by substantial evidence?

WHAT IS YOUR VERDICT?

▶ LEARNING OBJECTIVES

The reader, upon completion of this chapter, will be able to:

■ Define intentional torts and describe the differences between intentional torts and negligence.

■ Identify various intentional torts and their application in the healthcare setting.

■ Explain the theories a plaintiff can use in pursuing a products liability case against a manufacturer.

■ Describe various theories a manufacturer may use when defending itself against a products liability case.

An *intentional tort* is one that is committed deliberately. Proof of intent is based on the premise that the defendant intended the harmful consequences of his or her behavior. An individual's reason to cause harm is irrelevant and does not protect him or her from responsibility for the damages suffered as the result of an intentional act.

There are two main differences between intentional torts and negligence. The first is *intent* is present in intentional but not in negligent wrongs. For a tort to be considered intentional, the act must be committed intentionally, and the wrongdoer must realize to a substantial certainty that harm would result. The second difference is less obvious. Although a negligent wrong may simply be the failure to act when there is a legal duty to act, an intentional wrong always involves a *willful* act that violates another's interests. Intentional wrongs include assault and battery, false imprisonment, defamation of character, fraud, invasion of privacy, and infliction of emotional distress (**FIGURE 4-1**).

▶ ASSAULT AND BATTERY

It has long been recognized by law that a person possesses a right to be free from aggression and the threat of actual aggression against one's person. The right to expect others to respect the integrity of one's body has roots in both common and statutory law. The distinguishing feature between assault and battery is that *assault* effectuates an infringement on the mental security or tranquility of another, whereas *battery* constitutes a violation of another's physical integrity.

Caregivers must be aware of the potential for assault and battery complaints that can arise when caring for patients. In addition, they have to be alert to potential problems that can occur between patients (e.g., problems caused by smoking; cultural, racial or religious bias; emotional conflicts). A healthcare facility has a particular duty to closely supervise those patients whose mental conditions make it probable that they will injure themselves or others.

The defendant in *United States v. Moore,*[2] an inmate at the Federal Medical Center in Rochester, had tested positive for the HIV antibody. He was convicted later by a jury for assault and battery for assaulting two federal correctional officers with his mouth and teeth. The defendant motioned the U.S. District Court for a judgment of acquittal and for a new trial. Evidence at trial showed that AIDS could be transmitted through body fluids such as blood and semen. The defendant had been informed that he had both the AIDS virus and the hepatitis antibody and that he potentially could transmit the diseases to other persons. He bit one officer on the leg twice, leaving a 4-inch saliva stain. He bit the second officer, leaving a mark that was visible 5 months later at trial. Expert testimony at trial indicated that any human bite can cause a serious infection and that blood is sometimes present in the mouth, particularly if an individual has ill-fitting teeth or gum problems. In the defendant's motion for a new trial, he claimed that the court erred in denying his requested Jury Instruction 12, which would have prohibited the officers' testimony as to medical instructions they were given to avoid infecting their families from being entered into evidence. The evidence was considered probative of the dangerousness of the bites inflicted by the defendant, and the probative value outweighed any prejudicial effect. The defendant's motions for a judgment of acquittal and a new trial were denied.

Assault

An *assault* is a deliberate threat coupled with the apparent present ability to do physical harm to another. No actual contact or damage is necessary. It is the deliberate

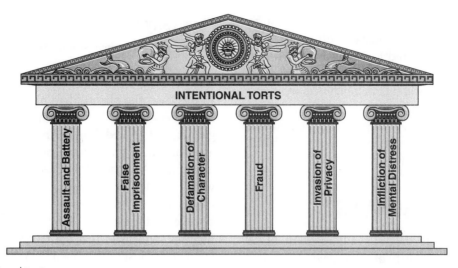

FIGURE 4-1 Intentional torts.

threat or attempt to injure another or the attempt by one to make bodily contact with another without his or her consent. To commit the tort of assault, two conditions must exist. First, the person attempting to touch another unlawfully must possess the apparent present ability to commit the battery. Second, the person threatened must be aware of or have actual knowledge of an immediate threat of a battery and must fear it.

Battery

A *battery* is the intentional touching of another's person in a socially impermissible manner, without that person's consent. It is intentional conduct that violates the physical security of another. An act that otherwise would be considered to be a battery may be permissible if proper consent has been given or if it is in defense of oneself or of a third party. The receiver of the battery does not have to be aware that a battery has been committed (e.g., a patient who is unconscious and has surgery performed on him or her without consent, either expressed or implied, is the object of a battery). The unwanted touching may give rise to a cause of action for any injuries brought about by the touching. No actual damages need be shown to impose liability.

The law provides a remedy if consent to a touching has not been obtained or if the act goes beyond the consent given. In the healthcare context, the principle of law concerning battery and the requirement of consent to medical and surgical procedures are critically important. Liability of organizations and healthcare professionals for acts of battery is most common in situations involving lack of patient consent to medical and surgical procedures.

It is of no legal importance that a procedure constituting a battery has improved a patient's health. If the patient did not consent to the touching, the patient may be entitled to such damages as can be proved to have resulted from commission of the battery.

Unauthorized Surgery

In *Perna v. Pirozzi*,[3] the New Jersey Supreme Court held that a patient who consents to surgery by one surgeon and is actually operated on by another has an action for medical malpractice or battery. Proof of unauthorized invasion of the plaintiff's person, even if harmless, entitles one to nominal damages. Patients, when signing informed consents, should be informed verbally and in the body of the written consent of the possibility of another physician participating in or conducting the surgical procedure.

Nurse Muffles Patient with Pillow

The registered nurse in *Wyatt v. Iowa Dep't of Human Services*[4] sought to muffle a patient's screams with a pillow in order to protect another patient, who suffered from a neurologic condition that rendered the patient highly susceptible to stimuli such as noise. The nurse was found not to have committed assault under Iowa's dependent adult abuse registry because the nurse did not have the intent necessary to commit abuse. She did not intend to harm the patient. She only intended to muffle the noise for protection of her other patient.

Physician Strikes Nurse

In *Peete v. Blackwell*,[5] punitive damages in the amount of $10,000 were awarded to a nurse in her action against a physician for assault and battery. Evidence showed that the physician struck the assisting nurse on the arm and cursed at her when he ordered her to turn on the suction. Dr. Peete appealed the trial court's decision asserting the evidence presented was insufficient to show the requisite "insult or other aggravating circumstances" required for an award of $10,000 in punitive damages. He contended that, even if sufficient evidence of aggravating circumstances were presented, the actual assessment of punitive damages was against the weight and preponderance of the evidence submitted. On appeal, the Supreme Court of Alabama upheld the judgment of the trial court.

▶ FALSE IMPRISONMENT

False imprisonment is the unlawful restraint of an individual's personal liberty or the unlawful restraint or confinement of an individual. The personal right to move freely and without hindrance is basic to the legal system. Any intentional infringement on this right may constitute false imprisonment. Actual physical force is not necessary to constitute false imprisonment; false imprisonment may occur when an individual who is physically confined to a given area reasonably fears detainment or intimidation without legal justification. Both intimidation and forced detainment may be implied by words, threats, or gestures. Excessive force used to restrain a patient may produce liability for both false imprisonment and battery.

To recover for damages for false imprisonment, a plaintiff must (1) be aware of the confinement and (2) have no reasonable means of escape. Availability of a reasonable means of escape may bar recovery. To lock a door when another is reasonably available to pass through is not imprisonment. However, if the only other door provides a way of escape that is dangerous, the law may consider it an unreasonable way of escape, and therefore, false imprisonment may be a cause of action. Whether false imprisonment has taken place will be a matter for the courts to decide. No actual damage needs to be shown for liability to be imposed.

Some occasions and circumstances allow for a person's confinement, such as when a person presents a danger to self or to others. Criminals are incarcerated, as are sometimes the mentally ill who may present a danger to themselves or others. Long-term care residents are sometimes restrained to prevent falls. Children are retained after school for disciplinary reasons. In these examples, the right to move about freely has been violated, but the infringement occurs for reasons that are justifiable under the law. Where legal justification is absent and an arrest or imprisonment is false, a person denied free movement is permitted to seek a remedy at law for any resulting injury.

Physically Violent Persons

In *Celestine v. United States,*[6] the right to move about freely had been violated; however, the infringement was permissible for reasons justifiable under the law. In this case, the plaintiff had brought an action alleging battery and false imprisonment because security guards had placed him in restraints. The plaintiff-appellant sought psychiatric care at a Veterans Administration (VA) hospital. He became physically violent while waiting to be seen by a physician. The VA security guards placed him in restraints until a psychiatrist could examine him. The U.S. Court of Appeals for the Eighth Circuit held that the record supported a finding that the hospital was justified in placing the patient under restraint. Under Missouri law, no false imprisonment or battery occurred in view of the common law principle that a person believed to be mentally ill could be restrained lawfully if such was considered necessary to prevent immediate injury to that person or others.

Contagious Diseases

Detaining patients without statutory protection can constitute false imprisonment. State health codes generally provide guidelines describing under what circumstances a patient may be detained. For example, patients with certain contagious diseases may be detained. Healthcare organizations should establish protocols for handling patients who have contracted a contagious disease. Also, statutes in most states allow persons with mental illness and intoxicated individuals to be detained if they are found to be dangerous to themselves or others. Those persons with mental illness, however, can be restrained only to the degree necessary to prevent them from harming themselves or others.

Intoxicated Persons

The patient in *Davis v. Charter by the Sea*[7] was found not entitled to a directed verdict on a false imprisonment claim. The claim arose from her overnight, involuntary detention at a hospital. Evidence that the patient was highly intoxicated, confused, incoherent, and experiencing a low diastolic blood pressure raised a jury question as to the existence of a medical emergency authorizing her detention.

Restraints

Restraints generally are used to control behavior when patients are disoriented or may cause harm to themselves (e.g., suicide, falling, contaminating wounds, pulling out intravenous lines) or to others. The use of restraints raises many questions of a patient's rights in the areas of autonomy, freedom of movement, and the accompanying health problems that can result from continued immobility. In general, a patient has a right to be free from any physical restraints imposed or psychoactive drugs administered for purposes of discipline or convenience and that are not required to treat a patient's medical symptoms.

Although the motivations for using restraints appear sound, there has been a tendency toward overuse. The fear of litigation over injuries sustained because of the failure to apply restraints further compounds the problem of overuse. As a result, regulations governing the use of restraints under the Omnibus Budget Reconciliation Act of 1987 make it clear that restraints are to be applied as a last resort rather than as a first option in the control of a patient's behavior. Because prescription drugs are sometimes used to restrain behavior, the regulations represent the first time that prescription drugs must, by law, "be justified by indications documented in the medical chart."[8]

To avoid legal problems, healthcare organizations should implement policies aimed at eliminating or reducing the use of restraints. Programs for the effective use of restraints should include the following:

- Policies that conform to federal and state guidelines, as well as those required by accrediting agencies
- Policies prescribing that the least restrictive device be used to maintain the safety of the patient, requiring the periodic review of patients under restraint, and requiring physician orders for restraints
- Procedures for implementing organizational policies (e.g., alternatives to be followed before resorting to restraints include family counseling to encourage increased visitations, environmental change, activity therapies, and patient counseling)
- Periodic review of policies and procedures, with revision as necessary
- Education and orientation programs for staff
- Educational programs for patients and their families
- Sound assessment of each patient's needs
- Informed consent from the patient or legal guardian
- Periodic patient monitoring to determine the need to continue the use of restraints
- Review of safe practices to prevent patient injury
- A mechanism for handling complaints of patients in restraint
- Documentation that includes the need for restraints, time-limited orders ("as needed" [PRN] orders are not acceptable), consents for the

application of restraints, patient monitoring, and reappraisal of the continuing need for restraints

In *Big Town Nursing Home, Inc. v. Newman*,[9] the court held that there was sufficient evidence to support a finding that a 67-year-old male resident had been falsely imprisoned in a facility against his will. He had attempted to leave the facility 3 days after he arrived, but was caught by the facility's employees and forcibly returned. He was placed in a patient care unit with persons who were addicted to drugs and alcohol and those who were mentally disturbed. He asked during the ensuing weeks that he be permitted to leave and attempted to leave five or six times. Eventually, he was confined to a restraint chair, his clothes were taken, and he was not permitted to use the telephone. The actions of the staff were described as being in utter disregard of the resident's legal rights. There was no court order for his commitment, and the agreement for his admission stated that he was not to be kept against his will. The court stated that the staff acted recklessly, willfully, and maliciously by unlawfully detaining him.

▶ DEFAMATION OF CHARACTER

Defamation of character is a communication to someone about another person that tends to hold that person's reputation up to scorn and ridicule. To be an actionable wrong, defamation must be communicated to a third person; defamatory statements communicated only to the injured party do not constitute grounds for an action. Slander is the verbal form of defamation and tends to form prejudices against a person in the eyes of third persons. Libel is the written form of defamation and can be presented in such forms as signs, photographs, letters, and cartoons.

Slander

Slanderous lawsuits are rare because of the difficulty in proving defamation, the small awards, and high legal fees. With slander, the person who brings suit generally must prove special damages; however, when any allegedly defamatory words refer to a person in a professional capacity, the professional need not show that the words caused damage, since it is presumed that any slanderous reference to someone's professional capacity is damaging.

Professionals who are called incompetent in front of others have a right to sue to defend their reputation. However, it is difficult to prove that an individual comment was injurious. If the person making an injurious comment cannot prove that the comment is true, then that person can be held liable for damages.

Libel

Libelous words must be communicated to a third person in order to be an actionable wrong. Defamatory statements communicated only to the injured party will not support an action. Truth of a statement is a complete defense.

In a libel or slander per se (on its face) action, a court will presume that certain words and accusations cause injury to a person's reputation without proof of damages. Words or accusations that require no proof of actual harm to one's reputation are (1) accusing someone of a crime, (2) accusing someone of having a loathsome disease, (3) using words that affect a person's profession or business, and (4) calling a woman unchaste. Healthcare professionals are, however, legally protected against libel when complying with a law that requires the reporting of patient information, such as malaria and smallpox. Damages typically consist of economic losses, such as loss of business or employment.

Performance Appraisals Not for General Publication

A statement in a hospital newsletter regarding the discharge of a nursing supervisor constituted libel per se in *Kraus v. Brandsletter*.[10] The newsletter indicated that the hospital's medical board had discharged the nursing supervisor after a unanimous vote of no confidence. Couching the board's determination in terms of a vote gave the impression that the board's determination had been based on facts that justified the board's opinion. The statement tended to injure the nurse's reputation as a professional because it did not refer to specifics of her performance, but rather to her abilities as a professional in general. The reasonable interpretation of the statement in the newsletter was that the supervisor was incompetent in her professional capacity, thus giving rise to a cause of action for libel per se.

On the flip side in the same case, an alleged statement that a physician said, "You nurses will receive your Christmas bonus early, your boss is going to get fired," was not slander per se in that it did not injure the nurse in her professional capacity.[11] In addition, the statement that she was going to be fired was true.

Performance Appraisal Statements Not Libelous

In *Schauer v. Memorial Care System*,[12] the plaintiff applied for and was given a supervisory position at

Memorial Hospital's new catheterization laboratory. In March 1989, she received an employment appraisal for the period of June 1988 through December 1988. At that time, Schauer's supervisor rated her performance as "commendable" in two categories and "fair" in eight categories, with an overall rating of "fair." Although Schauer did not lose her job as a result of the appraisal, she brought an action against the hospital and her former supervisor for libel and emotional distress as a result of the appraisal. The hospital moved for summary judgment on the grounds that the employment appraisal was not defamatory as a matter of law, the hospital had qualified privilege to write the performance appraisal, and the claim for emotional distress did not reach the level of severity required for a claim for intentional infliction of emotional distress. The trial court granted the hospital's motion for summary judgment, and Schauer appealed.

The Texas Court of Appeals held that the statements contained in the performance appraisal were not libelous and that the appraisal was subject to qualified privilege. Moreover, the hospital's conduct and the statements contained in the appraisal did not support the claim for intentional infliction of emotional distress.

To sustain her claim of defamation, Schauer had to show that the hospital published her appraisal in a defamatory manner that injured her reputation in some way. A statement can be unpleasant and objectionable to the plaintiff without being defamatory. The hospital argued that the statements contained in the appraisal were truthful, permissible expressions of opinion and not capable of a defamatory meaning. Schauer's supervisor prepared the appraisal as part of her supervisory duties. The appraisal was not published outside the hospital and was prepared in compliance with the hospital policy for all employees. Schauer disputed her overall rating of "fair" as being libelous. "Clearly, this is a statement of her supervisor's opinion and is not defamatory as a matter of law."[13]

In her performance appraisal, Schauer objected to the statement, "Ms. Schauer was not sensitive to employee relations."[14] Schauer conceded in her deposition that there were a number of interpersonal problems in the catheterization laboratory and that she did not get along with everyone. The court found that given these admissions, the statement was not defamatory.

As to the plaintiff's claim of emotional distress, the plaintiff failed to show that the hospital acted intentionally and recklessly. The Restatement of Torts, Second, § 46 (1977) provides:

> Liability has been found only where the conduct has been so outrageous in character, and

so extreme in degree, as to go beyond all possible bounds of decency, and to be regarded as atrocious, and utterly intolerable in a civilized community. . . . The liability clearly does not extend to mere insults, indignities, threats, annoyances, petty oppressions, or other trivialities. Complete emotional tranquility is seldom attainable in this world, and some degree of transient and trivial emotional distress is part of the price of living among people. The law intervenes only where the distress is so severe that no reasonable man could be expected to endure it.

Newspaper Articles

A libel suit was brought against the Miami Herald Publishing Company more than 2 years after its publication of an editorial cartoon depicting a nursing facility in a distasteful manner.[15] The cartoon was described in the following manner:

On October 29, 1980, *The Herald* published an editorial cartoon which depicted three men in a dilapidated room. On the back wall was written "Krest View Nursing Home," and on the side wall there was a board which read "Closed by Order of the State of Florida." The room itself was in a state of total disrepair. There were holes in the floor and ceiling, leaking water pipes, and exposed wiring. The men in the room were dressed in outfits resembling those commonly appearing in caricatures of gangsters. Each man carried a sack with a dollar sign on it. One of the men was larger than the other two and was more in the forefront of the picture. One of the others addressed him. The caption read: "Don't Worry, Boss, We Can Always Reopen It As a Haunted House for the Kiddies."[16]

The court held that the newspaper's editorial cartoon depicting persons resembling gangsters in a dilapidated building, identified as a particular nursing facility that had been closed by state order, was an expression of pure opinion and was protected by the First Amendment against the libel suit alleging that the cartoon defamed the owner of the facility.

In another newspaper libel case, the court in *Wisconsin Association of Nursing Homes v. Journal Co.*[17] would not compel the newspapers to accept and print an advertisement in the exact form submitted by the Wisconsin Association of Nursing Homes and various individual homes.

Plaintiffs allege in their complaint that the defendants published a series of "investigative reports" in the *Milwaukee Journal* which dealt with the quality of care and services in several nursing homes. Plaintiffs further characterized the conclusions of the article as being false and erroneous. As a result, the plaintiffs prepared a full-page advertisement which purported to respond to and refute the allegations set out in the above mentioned "reports." The defendant newspaper refused to publish the advertisement in the form presented, and referred the question of possibly libelous matter to the attention of plaintiffs' attorneys.[18]

The court held that it was within the newspaper's journalistic discretion to reject the advertisement on the ground that it contained possibly libelous material. "[T]he clear weight of authority has not sanctioned any enforceable right of access to the press. In sum, a court can no more dictate what a privately owned newspaper can print than what it cannot print."[19]

Unlike broadcasting, the publication of a newspaper is not a government-conferred privilege. As we have said, the press and the government have had a history of disassociation. We can find nothing in the United States Constitution, any federal statute, or any controlling precedent that allows us to compel a private newspaper to publish advertisements without editorial control merely because such advertisements are not legally obscene or unlawful.[20]

In a very different suit, the appellee in *Stevens v. Morris Communications Corp.*[21] alleged that a newspaper article, which identified her as a representative of a convalescent center at a city council meeting, had defamed her. She claimed that the article implied that she had responsibility for the convalescent center's problems of maintenance and disrepair. The court held that the newspaper article did not defame the appellee. Using the reasonable person test, the court found that it was highly unlikely that a reasonable person could have read the newspaper article as being defamatory.

The Georgia case of *Barry v. Baugh*,[22] however, presented a unique situation. The case involved a nurse who brought a defamation action, charging that a physician slandered her in the course of a consultation concerning the commitment of her husband to a mental institution. The nurse requested damages for mental pain, shock, fright, humiliation, and embarrassment. The nurse alleged that if the physician's statement were made known to the public, her job and reputation would be adversely affected. The court held that the physician's statement concerning the nurse did not constitute slander because the physician was not referring to the nurse in a professional capacity;[23] therefore, the plaintiff had to demonstrate damages in order to recover. The plaintiff was unable to show damages.

Defenses to a Defamation Action

Essentially, the two defenses to a defamation action are (1) truth and (2) privilege. When a person has said something that is damaging to another person's reputation, the person making the statement will not be liable for defamation if it can be shown that the statement is true. A privileged communication differs from a defamatory statement in that the person making the communication has a responsibility to do so. For example, many states have statutes providing immunity to physicians and healthcare institutions in connection with peer review proceedings. The person making the communication must do so in good faith, on the proper occasion, in the proper manner, and to persons who have a legitimate reason to receive the information.

An administrator's statements made to a physician's supervisor regarding the physician's alleged professional misconduct are not grounds for a defamation action as long as the statements are made in good faith. An administrator has a duty to report complaints about alleged professional misconduct of physicians working in the hospital. The administrator has qualified privilege to report such complaints to the physician's supervisor and other hospital officials as necessary.[24]

Two types of privilege may provide a defense to an action for defamation: absolute privilege and qualified privilege. Absolute privilege attaches to statements made during judicial and legislative proceedings as well as to confidential communications between spouses. Qualified privilege attaches to statements such as those made as a result of a legal or moral duty to speak in the interests of third persons and may provide a successful defense only when such statements are made in the absence of malice. If it can be shown that a speaker made a statement out of monetary gain, hatred, or ill will, the law will not permit the speaker to hide behind the shield of privilege to avoid liability for defamation.

Nurse Manager and Privileged Information

The defense of privilege is illustrated in the case of *Judge v. Rockford Memorial Hospital*,[25] whereby a nurse brought an action for libel. The action was based on a letter written to a nurses' professional registry by the director of nurses of the hospital to which the nurse had been assigned by the registry. In the letter, the director of nurses stated that the hospital did not wish to have the nurse's services available to them because of certain losses of narcotics during times when this particular nurse was on duty. The court refused the nurse recovery. Because the director of nurses had a legal duty to make the communication in the interests of society, the director's letter constituted a privileged communication. Therefore, the court held that the letter did not constitute libel because it was privileged.

Public Figures

It is important to note that public figures have more difficulty in pursuing defamation litigation than the average individual. A person who occupies a position of considerable public responsibility is considered a public figure for the purposes of the law of defamation and is generally more vulnerable to public scrutiny. Legal action against a public figure often will be denied in the absence of any showing of actual malice in connection with alleged defamatory references to a plaintiff. Actual malice applies only in cases involving public figures and encompasses knowledge of falsity or recklessness as to truth.

Television Station Sued by Board Chairman

The chairman of a publicly owned and operated county hospital in *Drew v. KATV Television*[26] brought a suit against a television station for defamation. The station reported during a news broadcast that the board chairman had been charged with a felony when he had been charged with two misdemeanor counts of solicitation to tamper with evidence (both of which were dismissed at trial). The second news report implied that the plaintiff was involved in a drug investigation being conducted at the hospital where he served as chairman of the board. The plaintiff occupied a position of considerable public responsibility, and he was considered a public figure for the purposes of the law of defamation. The circuit court dismissed the case on the defendant's motion for summary judgment, and the plaintiff appealed. The Arkansas Supreme Court held that the trial court properly ordered summary dismissal of the plaintiff's action against the television station in the absence of any showing of malice in connection with the allegedly defamatory references to the plaintiff during the news broadcasts.

ACCUSATORY STATEMENTS NOT DEFAMATORY

Citation: *Chowdhry v. North Las Vegas Hospital, Inc.,* 851 P.2d 459 (Nev. 1993)

Facts

On October 2, a young woman entered the emergency department of a hospital complaining of chest pain and shortness of breath. Dr. Lapica, the emergency physician on duty, saw her. Dr. Lapica diagnosed the patient as suffering from a possible pneumohemothorax, which required the placement of a chest tube to drain accumulated fluids. Lapica contacted Dr. Chowdhry, a physician who had recently performed surgery on the young woman and who was also the on-call thoracic surgeon at the hospital, and informed Chowdhry that his services were required at the hospital. The record revealed that Chowdhry refused to return to the hospital to treat the patient because he had recently left there and would treat her only if she were transferred to University Medical Center (UMC). Chowdhry testified that he could not return to the hospital because of a conflicting emergency at UMC.

Lapica then contacted the hospital's chief of staff, Dr. Wilchins, and told him that Chowdhry refused to come to the hospital and attend to the patient. Both physicians concluded that if the patient could be safely transported to UMC, the transfer should be affected so that Chowdhry could treat her.

The patient was ultimately transported to UMC where Lapica and Ms. Crow, the supervising nurse at the hospital, prepared incident reports detailing the events and submitted them to the administrator, Mr. Moore.

On October 3, Mr. Moore informed Dr. Silver, UMC's Chief of Surgery, that Chowdhry had refused to come to the hospital emergency department to treat the patient. The matter was directed to the hospital's surgery committee, which recommended summary suspension of Chowdhry's staff privileges.

On November 1, in response to Chowdhry's request, a hearing was held before the medical executive committee. As a result of the hearing, Chowdhry's staff privileges were reinstated, but a reprimand was placed in his file for jeopardizing himself, the patient, and the hospital. The hospital denied Chowdhry's subsequent request to have the reprimand expunged from his record, thus prompting Chowdhry to file an action against the hospital, Silver, Moore, Wilchins, and Lapica.

Chowdhry's complaint alleged theories of liability based upon negligence, breach of contract, conspiracy, defamation, and negligent and intentional infliction of emotional distress. The district court concluded that Chowdhry had no reasonable basis for bringing the action and awarded attorneys' fees and costs to the defendants, and Chowdhry appealed.

Issue

Did the district court err in dismissing the claims of defamation and infliction of emotional distress?

Holding

The Nevada Supreme Court held that the district court did not err in dismissing the claims of defamation and infliction of emotional distress.

Reason

Chowdhry's emotional distress claims are premised upon respondents' accusations of patient abandonment. Chowdhry testified that, as a result, "he was very upset" and could not sleep. Insomnia and general physical or emotional discomfort were found to be insufficient to satisfy the physical impact requirement for emotional distress. Thus, Chowdhry failed, as a matter of law, to present sufficient evidence to sustain verdicts for negligent or intentional infliction of emotional distress.

To establish a prima facie case of defamation, a plaintiff must prove (1) a false and defamatory statement by defendant concerning the plaintiff, (2) an unprivileged publication to a third person, (3) fault amounting to at least negligence, and (4) actual or presumed damages. The actual statements made by the various respondents were not that Chowdhry "abandoned" his patient, but that he "failed to respond" or "would not come" to the hospital to treat his patient. The record reflected that the respondents made the statements to hospital personnel and other interested parties (e.g., the patient's mother) in the context of reporting what was reasonably perceived to be Chowdhry's refusal to treat the patient at the hospital. The statements attributable to the respondents, taken in context, are not reasonably capable of a defamatory construction.

FRAUD

Fraud is a willful and intentional misrepresentation that could cause harm or loss to a person or property. It includes any cunning, deception, or artifice used in violation of legal or equitable duty to circumvent, cheat, or deceive another. The forms it may take and the means by which it may be practiced are as multifarious as human ingenuity can devise, and the courts consider it unwise or impossible to formulate an exact, definite, and all-inclusive definition of the action.

To prove fraud, the following facts must be shown:

1. An untrue statement known to be untrue by the party making it and made with the intent to deceive
2. Justifiable reliance by the victim on the truth of the statement
3. Damages as a result of that reliance

Concealment of Information

The plaintiff in *Robinson v. Shah*[27] was a patient of the defendant, Dr. Shah, from 1975 to 1986. During that period, Dr. Shah treated Robinson for various gynecologic disorders. On November 9, 1983, Dr. Shah performed a total abdominal hysterectomy and bilateral salpingo-oophorectomy on Robinson. Approximately 1 week following surgery, Robinson was discharged from the hospital and was assured that there were no complications or potential problems that might arise as a result of the surgery. She began to experience abdominal distress the day after she was discharged. She consulted Dr. Shah about her symptoms, and he ordered X-rays to be taken of Robinson's kidneys, ureter, and bladder in an effort to explain her discomfort.

The X-rays were taken at St. Joseph Memorial Hospital and were read and interpreted by Dr. Cavanaugh. After reading the X-rays, Dr. Cavanaugh called Dr. Shah, reporting the X-rays showed the presence of surgical sponges in Robinson's abdomen. Dr. Cavanaugh also sent Dr. Shah a copy of a written report reflecting his findings.

Dr. Shah decided to conceal from Robinson the findings of the X-rays. He intentionally lied, telling her that the X-rays were negative and that there were no apparent or unusual complications from the surgery. He at no time revealed that surgical sponges were left in Robinson's abdomen. Over the next several years, Robinson continued to see Dr. Shah for gynecologic checkups. Although Robinson continued to experience abdominal pain and discomfort, Dr. Shah failed to reveal the existence of the surgical sponges in her abdomen. Robinson eventually ceased seeing Dr. Shah as her physician in 1986.

Because of her ongoing concerns about the pain and discomfort in her abdomen, as well as intestinal, urologic, and gynecologic problems, she consulted other physicians. Although Robinson brought her complaints to the attention of other physicians, no one was able to diagnose the source of her problems. Finally, in 1993, one of the physicians attending to Robinson's problems diagnosed a pelvic mass, which he felt could be causing her discomfort. Robinson underwent pelvic sonograms and X-rays, which revealed the existence of surgical sponges in Robinson's abdomen.

Robinson filed a lawsuit contending that since November 18, 1983, Dr. Shah had knowledge of the presence of the surgical sponges in her abdomen and knew that future complications could arise from this condition. Despite this knowledge, the plaintiff contended, the defendant continued to conceal the existence of the surgical sponges in her abdomen.

The trial court found that the plaintiff was unable to discover the fact that the defendant negligently left surgical sponges in her abdomen and that this fact was fraudulently concealed from the plaintiff. The plaintiff appealed the trial court's decision.

The appeals court held that although the action in this case was filed more than 10 years after the fraud was perpetrated, the statute of limitations was not tolled because of the defendant's fraudulent concealment of information from the patient. The court decided that allowing such misrepresentation would only serve to encourage such behavior.

INVASION OF PRIVACY

Invasion of privacy is a wrong that invades the right of a person to personal privacy. Absolute privacy has to be tempered with reality in the care of any patient, and the courts recognize this fact. Disregard for a patient's right to privacy is legally actionable, particularly when patients are unable to protect themselves adequately because of unconsciousness or immobility.

The *right to privacy* is implied in the Constitution. It is recognized as a right to be left alone—the right to be free from unwarranted publicity and exposure to public view, as well as the right to live one's life without having one's name, picture, or private affairs made public against one's will. Healthcare organizations and professionals may become liable for invasion of privacy if, for example, they divulge information from a patient's medical record to improper sources or if they commit unwarranted intrusions into a patient's personal affairs.

The information in a patient's medical record is confidential and should not be disclosed without the patient's permission, with the exception of occasions when there is a legal obligation or duty to disclose the information (i.e., reporting of communicable diseases, gunshot wounds, and child abuse). Those who come into possession of the most intimate personal information about patients have both a legal and an ethical duty not to reveal confidential communications.

Employee/Patient Confidentiality Breached

Unfortunately, familiarity with an organization's healthcare environment tends to diminish the conscious concern employees should have for the protection of patient privacy. The plaintiff in *Vernuil v. Poirie*,[28] a former hospital employee, was awarded $15,000 in a legal action against her supervisor and hospital for invasion of privacy. The plaintiff claimed that while she was a patient and in the postoperative recovery room, her supervisor lifted her sheet in an attempt to view her abdominal incision. The court of appeals held that evidence sustained a finding of invasion of privacy. Because the supervisor's conduct occurred during the time and place of his employment, the hospital was jointly liable for damages. "Ensuring a patient's well-being from all others, including staff, while the patient is helpless under the effects of anesthesia is part of its normal business."[29]

▶ INFLICTION OF MENTAL DISTRESS

The intentional or reckless infliction of mental distress is characterized by conduct that is so outrageous that it goes beyond the bounds tolerated by a decent society. It is a civil wrong for which a tortfeasor can be held liable for damages. Mental distress includes mental suffering resulting from painful emotions such as grief, public humiliation, despair, shame, and wounded pride. Liability for the wrongful infliction of mental distress may be based on either intentional or negligent misconduct. A plaintiff may recover damages if he or she can show that the defendant intended to inflict mental distress and knew or should have known that his or her actions would give rise to it.

Recovery generally is permitted even in the absence of physical harm.

To prove the infliction of emotional distress, the plaintiff must establish the following:

1. The defendant's conduct was intentional or reckless.
2. The conduct was extreme and outrageous.
3. The conduct caused emotional distress to the plaintiff.
4. The emotional distress was severe.

All of these elements were present in *Lucchesi v. Stimmell*,[30] where the plaintiff brought a legal action against a physician for intentional infliction of emotional distress, claiming that the physician failed to be present during unsuccessful attempts to deliver her premature fetus and that he thereafter failed to disclose to her that the fetus was decapitated during attempts to achieve delivery by pulling on the hip area to free the head. The judge instructed the jury that it could conclude that the physician had been guilty of extreme and outrageous conduct for staying at home and leaving the delivery in the hands of a first-year intern and a third-year resident, neither of whom was experienced in breech deliveries.

Mother Shown Her Premature Infant

The mother of a premature infant who died shortly after birth went to her physician for a 6-week checkup. She noticed a report in her medical chart that stated that the child was past the fifth month in development and that hospital rules and state law prohibited disposal of the infant as a surgical specimen. The mother questioned her physician regarding the infant. The physician requested that his nurse take the mother to the hospital. An employee at the hospital took the mother to a freezer. The freezer was opened and the mother was handed a jar containing her premature infant. The circuit court found that the hospital, through its employees, committed intentional infliction of emotional distress. On appeal, the court of appeals in *Johnson v. Woman's Hospital*[31] held that the jury could find that the hospital's conduct in displaying the infant was outrageous conduct.

> As to the outrageous conduct theory we hold that there is evidence from which a jury could find that the conduct of the defendant hospital in displaying the infant in the manner and under circumstances described was outrageous conduct as defined by our Supreme Court in the Medlin case, supra, and that such conduct recklessly caused severe emotional

distress to plaintiff Mrs. Johnson. We are of the opinion that a recitation of the foregoing facts could be considered to cause the exclamation of "outrage!" from the general community.[32]

Verbal Abuse of a Patient

In another case, an action was brought in *Greer v. Medders*[33] by a patient and his wife against the physician for mental distress. In this case, the defendant physician had been providing on-call coverage for the attending physician, who was on vacation. When the patient, who had been admitted to the hospital, had not seen the covering physician for several days, he called the physician's office to complain. The physician later entered the patient's room in an agitated manner and became verbally abusive in the presence of the patient's wife and nurse. He said to the patient, "Let me tell you one damn thing, don't nobody call over to my office raising hell with my secretary. . . . I don't have to be here every damn day checking on you because I check with physical therapy. . . . I don't have to be your damn doctor."[34] When the physician left the room, the plaintiff's wife began to cry, and the plaintiff experienced episodes of uncontrollable shaking for which he received psychiatric treatment. The superior court entered summary judgment for the physician, and the plaintiff appealed. The Georgia Court of Appeals held that the physician's abusive language willfully caused emotional upset and precluded summary judgment for the defendant.

▶ PRODUCTS LIABILITY

Products liability is the accountability of a manufacturer, seller, or supplier of chattels to a buyer or other third party for injuries sustained because of a defect in a product. An injured party may proceed with a lawsuit against a seller, manufacturer, or supplier on three legal theories: (1) negligence, (2) breach of warranty (express or implied), and (3) strict liability. Many states have enacted comprehensive products liability statutes. These statutory provisions can be very diverse such that the U.S. Department of Commerce has promulgated a Model Uniform Products Liability Act (MUPLA) for voluntary use by the states. Three types of product defects that incur liability are design defects, manufacturing defects, and defects in marketing (e.g., providing improper instructions or making exaggerated claims about a product's use).

A $200 million settlement was reached over the deadly meningitis outbreak that was linked to a Massachusetts pharmacy. The funds were set aside for the victims of the outbreak and their families. The defendants in the New England Compounding Center (NECC) are facing criminal charges.

Negligence

Negligence, as applied to products liability, requires the plaintiff to establish duty, breach, injury, and causation. The manufacturer of a product is not liable for injuries suffered by a patient if they are the result of negligent use by the user. Product users must conform to the safety standards provided by the manufacturers of supplies and medical devices. Failure to follow proper safety instructions can prevent recovery in a negligence suit if injury results from improper use.

Because manufacturers are liable for injuries that result from unsafe product design, they generally provide detailed safety instructions to the users of their products. Failure to provide such instructions could be considered negligence on the part of the manufacturer.

Selling Equipment with a Known Hazardous Design

An action in *Airco v. Simmons National Bank, Guardian, et al.*[35] was brought against a physician partnership that provided anesthesia services to the hospital and Airco, Inc., the manufacturer of an artificial breathing machine used in the administration of anesthesia. It was alleged that the patient suffered irreversible brain damage because of the negligent use of the equipment and its unsafe design. The machine had been marketed despite prior reports of a foreseeable danger of human error brought about by the presence of several identical black hoses and the necessity of connecting them correctly to three ports of identical size placed closely

NEWS FRAMINGHAM: TRIAL DATE SET FOR NECC PHARMACY DEFENDANTS

BOSTON—A federal judge has set an April 10, 2017 trial date for the remaining 10 defendants in the criminal cases stemming from the deadly fungal meningitis outbreak in 2012.

In an order issued Tuesday, U.S. District Judge Richard G. Stearns set the spring date for the 10 who are facing charges ranging from mail and wire fraud to racketeering.

—Walter F. Roche, Jr., *MetroWest Daily News*, August 23, 2016 together. The machine lacked adequate labels and warnings, according to the reports. The jury awarded over $1 million in compensatory damages against the physician partnership and Airco, Inc. Punitive damages in the amount of $3 million were awarded against Airco, Inc. On appeal of the punitive damages award, the Arkansas Supreme Court held that the evidence for punitive damages was sufficient for the jury. The manufacturer acted in a persistent reckless disregard of the foreseeable dangers in use of the machine by continuing to sell it with the known hazardous design.

Tainted Tylenol Capsules

Negligence, as well as breach of warranty and strict liability, was not established in the well-publicized case of the 1980s involving a woman who died after ingesting Tylenol capsules tainted with potassium cyanide. The decedent's estate in *Elsroth v. Johnson & Johnson*[36] sued the manufacturer and the retail grocery store that sold the over-the-counter drug. The defendants moved for a summary judgment. The U.S. district court held that the retailer did not have a duty to protect the decedent from acts of tampering by an unknown third party. The manufacturer was not liable under an inadequate warning theory. Manufacturers are under a duty to warn of the dangers that may be associated with the normal and lawful use of their products, but they need not warn that their products may be susceptible to criminal misuse.

Negligent Use of a Bovie Plate

Negligent use of a product may lead to liability, as was the case in *Monk v. Doctors Hospital*.[37] In this case, the patient was admitted to the hospital for abdominal surgery. Prior to surgery, the patient asked the surgeon also to remove three moles from the right arm and one from the right leg. The surgeon instructed a hospital nurse to prepare a Bovie machine but was not present while the machine was set up. The nurse placed the contact plate of the Bovie machine under the patient's right calf in a negligent manner, and the patient suffered burns. Manufacturer instruction manuals, supplied to the hospital, supported the claim that the plate was placed improperly under the patient. The trial court directed a verdict in favor of the hospital and the physician. The appellate court found that there was sufficient evidence from which the jury could conclude that the Bovie plate was applied in a negligent manner. There also was sufficient evidence, including the manufacturer's manual and expert testimony, from which the jury could find that the physician was independently negligent.[38]

This case demonstrates the necessity for an organization to require conformity to the safety standards provided by the manufacturers of supplies and medical devices. As evidenced in the previous case, such failure can cause an organization and its staff to be held liable for negligence. This case should alert manufacturers of the necessity to provide appropriate safety instructions to the users of their products. It can be assumed that failure to provide such instructions could be considered negligence on the part of the supplier.

Defective Packaging

Cotita, a registered nurse, stuck himself with a syringe manufactured by the defendant-appellee, PharmaPlast. The syringe, although still in its sterile packaging, was missing the protective cap that normally covers the tip of the needle. Improper packaging allowed the needle to pierce its sterile plastic covering and penetrate the protective gloves Cotita was wearing. Because of the presence of the patient's blood on his gloves at the time of the needlestick, Cotita feared that he had been exposed to the human immunodeficiency virus (HIV). Subsequent tests revealed that Cotita was not HIV positive; nevertheless, he sued PharmaPlast, seeking damages for mental anguish stemming from his fear of contracting HIV.

PharmaPlast admitted defective packaging, and the district court granted summary judgment for the plaintiff on the issue of the defective state of the syringe. PharmaPlast asserted Cotita was negligent in his use of the syringe. Cotita objected to the introduction of evidence concerning his negligence.

The damage issue was tried before a jury that returned a verdict for $150,000 in Cotita's favor. This amount was reduced by 30%, a figure that the jury found reflected his negligence. Cotita maintained that the issue of his negligence should not have been considered by the jury or used to reduce the amount of his award.

On appeal, the U.S. Court of Appeals found no error in the district court's application of comparative fault. PharmaPlast presented evidence that the procedures used by the nurse were in violation of universal safety precautions and procedures that are standard in the healthcare industry. The district court here was entitled to determine that the application of comparative fault would ultimately encourage workers in the healthcare field to follow the established procedures for handling syringes.[39]

Failure to Warn

Merck pulled its painkiller, Vioxx, a drug it manufactured for the treatment of arthritis, off pharmacy shelves after participants in a study experienced adverse cardiovascular events compared to those taking a placebo. Merck officials had argued that Vioxx was not the cause of users' heart attacks and the company had properly warned doctors and consumers about its risks. Following a 3-year battle, Merck announced in November 2007 that it would pay $4.85 billion to settle plaintiff claims over injuries linked to Vioxx. The company paid the money into a fund, and people who claimed Vioxx injured them could petition for monetary relief.

Breach of Warranty

A *warranty* is a particular type of guarantee (a pledge or assurance of something) concerning goods or services provided by a seller to a buyer. Nearly everything purchased is covered by a warranty. To recover under a cause of action based on a breach of warranty theory, the plaintiff must establish whether there was an express or implied warranty.

Express Warranty

An *express warranty* includes specific promises or affirmations made by the seller to the buyer, such as "X" drug is not subject to addiction. If the product fails to perform as advertised, it is a breach of express warranty. For example, in *Crocker v. Winthrop Laboratories*,[40] the patient, Mr. Crocker, was admitted to the hospital for a hernia operation. His physician prescribed both Demerol and Talwin for pain. After discharge from the hospital, Crocker developed an addiction to Talwin and was able to obtain prescriptions from several physicians to support a habit he developed. He was eventually admitted to the hospital for detoxification. After 6 days, Crocker walked out of the hospital and went home. He became agitated and abusive, threatening his wife, and she eventually called a physician at his request. The physician arrived and gave Crocker an injection of Demerol. Crocker then retired to bed and subsequently died. Action was brought against the drug company for the suffering and subsequent wrongful death that occurred as the proximate result of the decedent's addiction to Talwin.

The district court rendered a judgment for the plaintiff and the court of appeals reversed. On further appeal, the Texas Supreme Court held that when a drug company positively and specifically represents its product to be free and safe from all dangers of addiction and when the treating physician relies on such representation, the drug company is liable when the representation proves to be false and injury results.

Implied Warranty

An *implied warranty* is a guarantee of a product's quality that is not expressed in a purchase contract. An implied warranty assumes that the item sold can perform the function for which it is designed. Implied warranties are in effect when the law implies that one exists by operation of law as a matter of public policy for the protection of the public. For example, *Jacob E. Decker & Sons v. Capps*[41] is a case involving the question of the liability of a manufacturer for selling tainted food products to the consumer for damages sustained by ingestion of contaminated sausage. One member of a family died and others became seriously ill as a result of eating contaminated food. The jury found that the sausage had been contaminated before being packaged by the defendant and that it was unfit for human consumption. The Texas Supreme Court decided that the defendant was liable for the injuries sustained by the consumers of the contaminated food under an implied warranty. Liability in such a case is based neither on negligence nor on a breach of the usual implied contractual warranty; instead, it is based on the broad principle of public policy to protect human health and life.

There was no implied warranty for contaminated blood where the patient in *Perlmutter v. Beth David Hospital*[42] contracted serum hepatitis from a blood transfusion. The plaintiff relied on an implied sales warranty as the basis of her suit. The court denied recovery, pointing out that even though a separate charge of $60 was made for the blood, the charge was incidental to the primary contract with the hospital for services. Because there was no claim of negligence, the court determined that blood provided by the hospital was a service, rather than a sale, and therefore, barred recovery by the patient. The rationale in this case did not extend to relieve commercial blood banks from liability on the basis of strict liability warranty theories. Action could have been instituted against the hospital if it had been shown that the hospital was negligent in handling the blood.

Strict Liability

Strict liability is a legal doctrine that causes some persons or entities to be responsible for the damages their actions or products cause, regardless of "fault" on their part. Strict liability often applies when people engage in inherently hazardous activities, such as blasting in a city. If the blasting injures a person, no matter how careful the blasting company is, it could be liable for the injuries suffered.

Strict liability also applies in cases involving the manufacturers of products such as drugs and medical equipment. Responsibility without fault makes possible an award of damages without proof of a manufacturer's negligence. The plaintiff only needs to show that he or she suffered injury while using the manufacturer's product in the prescribed way. The following elements must be established in order for a plaintiff to proceed with a case on the basis of strict liability:

1. The product must have been manufactured by the defendant.
2. The product must have been defective at the time it left the hands of the manufacturer or seller. The defect in the product normally consists of a manufacturing defect, a design defect in the product, or an absence or inadequacy of warnings for the use of the product.
3. The plaintiff must have been injured by the specific product.
4. The defective product must have been the proximate cause of injury to the plaintiff.

The number of drug-related lawsuits increased significantly between 2000 and 2006, as noted in the following news article.

📰 MORE DRUGS GET SLAPPED WITH LAWSUITS

Between 2000 and 2006, "more than 65,000 product liability lawsuits have been filed against prescription drug makers, the most of any industry," says researcher Thomson West.

The pace isn't likely to slow, given the number of drugs on the market, the millions of consumers taking them, and the skill of plaintiffs' lawyers . . ."
—Julie Schmit, *USA Today*, August 23, 2006

Products liability–related lawsuits are a worrisome concern for pharmaceutical manufacturers as lawyers continue to use TV advertisements to seek clients who believe they have been harmed by medications. At the same time, drug manufacturers, in an attempt to slow the surge of lawsuits, are including frightening disclaimers in their drug-related advertisements.

Manufacturer Responsible for Defective Latex Gloves

In *Green v. Smith & Nephew AHP, Inc.*,[43] Green began her employment at St. Joseph's Hospital in Milwaukee, where she worked as a radiology technologist. Hospital rules required Green to wear protective gloves while attending patients. To comply with these rules, Green wore powdered latex gloves manufactured by Smith & Nephew AHP (S&N). Initially, Green used one or two pairs of gloves per shift. However, upon her promotion to the computed tomography (CT) department, her use of gloves increased. Green's job required her to use approximately 40 pairs of gloves per shift. Green began suffering various health problems. Her hands became red, cracked, and sore, and began peeling. Green was eventually diagnosed with a latex allergy. Her symptoms grew increasingly severe, eventually culminating in an acute shortness of breath, coughing, tightening of the throat, and hospitalization on more than one occasion.

Green claimed that S&N should be held strictly liable for her injuries. She argued that although S&N could have significantly reduced the protein levels in and discontinued powdering its gloves by adjusting its production process, S&N nonetheless used a production process that maintained these defects in the gloves. These defects, Green alleged, created the unreasonable danger that S&N's gloves would cause consumers to develop an allergy to latex and suffer allergy-related conditions. The primary cause of an allergy to latex is latex gloves, and for this reason, an allergy to latex disproportionately affects members of the healthcare profession. According to Green's medical experts, the vast majority of people with an allergy to latex (up to 90%) are healthcare workers. In addition, although an allergy to latex is not common among the general population, Green's medical experts testified that it affects between 5 and 17% of all healthcare workers in the United States.

Although a manufacturer is not under a duty to manufacture a product that is absolutely free from all possible harm to every individual, it is the duty of the manufacturer not to place upon the market a defective product that is unreasonably dangerous to the ordinary consumer.

The jury returned a verdict in favor of Green, finding that S&N's gloves were defective and unreasonably dangerous, and that they caused Green's injuries. The jury awarded Green $1 million in damages. The court of appeals affirmed the circuit court judgment. S&N then petitioned the Wisconsin Supreme Court to review the court of appeals decision.

The Wisconsin Supreme Court affirmed the decision of the court of appeals. Strict products liability imposes liability without regard to negligence and its attendant factors of duty of care and foreseeability. Regardless of whether a manufacturer could foresee the potential risks of harm inherent in its defective and unreasonably dangerous product, strict products liability holds the manufacturer responsible for injuries caused by that product. When a manufacturer places a defective and unreasonably dangerous product into the stream of commerce, the manufacturer, not the injured consumer, should bear the costs of the risks posed by the product.

Negligent Handling of Blood

A blood bank was found strictly liable in *Weber v. Charity Hospital of Louisiana at New Orleans*[44] when a hospital patient developed hepatitis from a transfusion of defective blood during surgery. Evidence established that the blood bank collected, processed, and sold the blood to the hospital. Although the hospital administered the blood, absent any negligence in its handling or administration, it was not liable for the patient's injury. Many states have enacted statutes to exempt blood from the product category and thus remove blood products from the theory of strict liability.

Res Ipsa Loquitur

Liability also may be based on the concept of res ipsa loquitur (the thing speaks for itself) by establishing the following:

1. The product did not perform in the way intended.
2. The product was not tampered with by the buyer or third party.
3. The defect existed at the time it left the defendant manufacturer.

Mislabeled Pain Patches

A manufacturer mislabeled a box of Duragesic patches, a strong prescription medication for moderate to severe chronic pain, marking the box as containing 25-mg patches. In actuality, the box contained 100-mg patches. The patient placed a patch on her back to provide relief of severe back pain. Instead of receiving the 25-mg dosage recommended by her physician, she received 100 mg, four times the recommended dosage. The patient went into a coma and eventually died.

Products Liability Defenses

Defenses against recovery in a products liability case include:

1. Assumption of a risk (e.g., voluntary exposure to such risks as radiation treatments and chemotherapy treatments)
2. Intervening cause (e.g., an intravenous solution contaminated by the negligence

of the product user, rather than that of the manufacturer)
3. Contributory negligence (e.g., use of a product in a way for which it was not intended)
4. Comparative fault (e.g., injury as a result of the concurrent negligence of both the manufacturer and plaintiff)
5. Disclaimers (e.g., manufacturers' inserts and warnings regarding usage and contraindications of their products)

Courts often invalidate disclaimers and waivers of liability for products as being against public policy. Warranties are limited so that manufacturers and retailers are held responsible for personal injuries caused by the use of a product.

THE COURT'S DECISION

The Missouri Court of Appeals held that the evidence supported a finding that the security guards falsely imprisoned the physician and that the physician was entitled to punitive damages on the false imprisonment claim. The defendants' testimony provided the jury with sufficient evidence to establish that the plaintiff was held without justifiable cause. The testimony supported a finding that the arrest was self-serving and resulted in the false imprisonment.

▶ CHAPTER REVIEW

1. *Intentional wrongdoing* involves a willful act that violates another person's interests. Not only must the action be intentional, but the perpetrator must realize that the action will result in harm. Intentional torts include:

    ■ Assault and battery: *Assault* is the infringement on the mental security or tranquility of another person. *Battery* is the violation of another person's physical integrity. No actual physical harm needs to have occurred for an individual to be guilty of assault.
    ■ *False imprisonment* is the unlawful restraint of an individual's personal liberty or the unlawful restraint or confinement of an individual. For a false imprisonment charge to warrant recovery, the plaintiff must be aware of the confinement and have no reasonable means of escape.
    ■ *Defamation of character* is a false oral or written communication to someone other than the individual defamed that subjects

that individual's reputation to scorn and ridicule in the eyes of a substantial number of respectable people in the community. Two aspects of defamation of character are:

- *Libel*: written defamation.
- *Slander*: spoken (verbal) form of defamation.

- *Fraud* is a willful and intentional misrepresentation that could cause harm or loss to an individual or property. To prove fraud, the following elements must be established: (1) an untrue statement known to be untrue by the party making it and made with the intent to deceive; (2) a justifiable reliance by the victim on the truth of that statement; and, (3) damages as a result of that reliance.
- *Invasion of privacy* is a wrong that interferes with the right of an individual to personal privacy.
- *Infliction of mental distress* is conduct so outrageous that it goes beyond the bounds tolerated by a decent society. Mental distress can include mental suffering from painful emotions such as grief, public humiliation, despair, shame, and wounded pride.
- *Products liability* is the liability of a manufacturer, seller, or supplier of chattels to a buyer or other third party for injuries sustained because of a defect in a product.

2. Theories for a products liability lawsuit include:

- Negligence
- Failure to warn
- Breach of warranty
  - Express warranty
  - Implied warranty
- Strict liability: liability without fault that makes possible an award of damages without any proof of manufacturer negligence. The plaintiff needs only to show that he or she suffered injury while using the manufacturer's product in the prescribed way.

3. Products liability defenses include:

- Assumption of a risk
- Intervening cause
- Contributory negligence
- Comparative fault
- Disclaimers

▶ REVIEW QUESTIONS

1. Describe the various categories of intentional torts.

- Describe the difference between *assault* and *battery*.
- What is defamation of character? What two forms can it take?
- Under what circumstances can a patient be held in a hospital against his or her will?
- What is fraud? What three elements must be present to establish fraud?
- Describe how a patient's privacy can be invaded.
- What is the infliction of mental distress? Give an example.

2. What are the legal theories an injured party can pursue when filing a lawsuit against a seller, manufacturer, or supplier of goods?

3. Describe the defenses often used in a products liability case.

▶ NOTES

1. 865 S.W.2d 833 (Mo. Ct. App. 1993).
2. No. Crim. 4-87-44 (D. Minn. Sept. 3, 1987) (unpublished).
3. 457 A.2d 431 (N.J. 1983).
4. 744 N.W.2d 89 (Ia. 2008).
5. 504 So.2d 22 (Ala. 1986).
6. 841 F.2d 851 (8th Cir. 1988).
7. 358 S.E.2d 865 (Ga. Ct. App. 1987).
8. Judith Garrard et al., "Evaluation of Neuroleptic Drug Use by Nursing Home Elderly Under Proposed Medicare and Medicaid Regulations," *Journal of the American Medical Association* 265 (1991): 463.
9. 461 S.W.2d 195 (Tex. Ct. App. 1970).
10. 562 N.Y.2d 127 (N.Y. App. Div. 1990).
11. *Id.* at 129.
12. 856 S.W.2d 437 (Tex. Ct. App. 1993).
13. *Id.* at 447.
14. *Id.*
15. *Keller v. Miami Herald Publishing Company,* 778 F.2d 711 (11th Cir. 1985).
16. *Id.* at 713.
17. 285 N.W.2d 891 (Wis. Ct. App. 1979).
18. *Id.* at 893.
19. *Id.* at 894.
20. *Associates and Aldrich Co. v. Times Mirror Co.,* 440 F.2d 133, 136 (9th Cir. 1971).

21. 317 S.E.2d 652 (Ga. Ct. App. 1984).

22. 143 S.E. 489 (Ga. Ct. App. 1965).

23. *Id.*

24. *Miller-Douglas v. Keller*, 579 So. 2d 491 (La. Ct. App. 1991).

25. 150 N.E.2d 202 (Ill. App. Ct. 1958).

26. 739 S.W.2d 680 (Ark. 1987).

27. 936 P.2d 784 (Kans. App. 1997).

28. 589 So. 2d 1202 (La. Ct. App. 1991).

29. *Id.* at 1204.

30. 716 P.2d 1013 (Ariz. 1986).

31. 527 S.W.2d 133 (Tenn. Ct. App. 1975).

32. *Id.* at 140.

33. 336 S.E.2d 329 (Ga. App. 1985).

34. *Id.*

35. 638 S.W.2d 660 (Ark. 1982).

36. 700 F. Supp. 151 (S.D.N.Y. 1988).

37. 403 F.2d 580 (D.C. Cir. 1968).

38. *Id.*

39. 974 F.2d 598 (5th Cir. 1992).

40. 514 S.W.2d 429 (Tex. 1974).

41. 164 S.W.2d 828 (Tex. 1942).

42. 123 N.E.2d 793 (N.Y. 1955).

43. 629 N.W.2d 727 (2001).

44. 487 So. 2d 148 (La. Ct. App. 1986).

© alejandro dans neergaard/Shutterstock

CHAPTER 5

Tort Reform and Risk Reduction

▶ LEARNING OBJECTIVES

The reader, upon completion of this chapter, will be able to:

- Discuss the ways in which a provider can practice *defensive medicine*.
- Describe various tort reform programs designed to lower the cost of malpractice insurance.
- Describe various programs that can help reduce the number of malpractice claims.

The tort system has proven to be inadequate in the prevention of medical malpractice. Damage awards as deterrents to malpractice have failed to reduce the number of claims. Exorbitant jury awards and malpractice insurance premiums continue to cost the healthcare industry billions of dollars annually. Given the difficulties in the present tort system, we often become victims of the failures of medicine as opposed to beneficiaries of its many successes. Dr. Gregg Roslund writes in *Emergency Physician's Monthly*: "Do you think our medical liability system has been broken for a while? If so, you're not alone. And now, with the recent enactment of the Affordable Care Act, our resources are more limited, our decisions more scrutinized, and we're going to have to do more with less."[1] With changes in the political arena, it is unclear how changes in the Affordable Care Act will affect malpractice premiums and physician income.

Physicians have altered, limited, or closed their practices after having spent the most productive years of their lives training to practice medicine. Many obstetricians/gynecologists, for example, have dropped the high-risk obstetrics portion of their practices to reduce their malpractice premiums. As a result, it has become more difficult for patients to find a physician to get the care they need. Frivolous and unscrupulous malpractice actions have caused physicians to place limitations on their scope of practice.

Physicians who wish to practice their chosen specialty and remain financially independent often resort to the practice of defensive medicine. *Defensive medicine* involves overprescribing diagnostic tests and avoiding more risky, lawsuit-prone procedures, thus reducing the likelihood of litigation and the associated risks of higher insurance premiums. While defensive medicine provides the practitioner with a valuable legal defense in the event of a lawsuit, it is believed to be one of the most harmful effects produced by the threat of malpractice litigation. "The message the tort system is sending to doctors is not so much deterrence, in terms of practicing good medicine, but more just 'drive defensively,' because any patient you may see may be a litigant."[2]

The states have legislated a variety of tort reforms designed to help lower the economic impact of malpractice awards on the healthcare system. Out-of-court settlements make it difficult to evaluate the impact of these reforms on a state-by-state basis. A wide variety of legislative enactments designed to help lower malpractice insurance premiums by limiting malpractice awards are reviewed here. The Medical Malpractice Center provides helpful information on malpractice laws by state at its website (www.malpracticecenter.com/states/).

(NEWS) TRIALS, VERDICTS, AND MEDIATION IN MARYLAND'S U.S. DISTRICT COURT

Over the last decade or more, mediation has become an integral part of our civil justice system. While undoubtedly some cases are not (and should not be) resolved by mediation, but rather by trial, attorneys and litigants seem to have embraced mediation as a natural part of the litigation process and a highly satisfactory way to resolve disputes.

—Susan K. Gauvey and Heather R. Pruger, *Maryland Bar Journal*, July 2010

MEDIATION AND ARBITRATION

Among the many factors contributing to the malpractice crisis is the high cost of litigation. Trial by jury is lengthy and expensive. If case disputes can be handled out of court, the process and expense of a lawsuit can be significantly reduced. *Mediation* and arbitration are basically mechanisms for simplifying and expediting the settlement of claims. Mediation is the process whereby a third party, the mediator, attempts to bring about a settlement between the parties of a complaint. The mediator, however, cannot force a settlement. The U.S. District Court for the Southern District of New York describes mediation as follows:

- Mediation is a form of alternative dispute resolution.
- In mediation, parties and counsel meet, sometimes collectively and sometimes individually, with a neutral third party (the mediator) who has been trained to facilitate confidential settlement discussions.
- The parties articulate their respective positions and interests and generate options for a mutually agreeable resolution to the dispute.
- The mediator assists the parties in reaching their own negotiated settlement by defining the issues, probing and assessing the strengths and weaknesses of each party's legal positions, and identifying areas of agreement and disagreement.
- The main benefits of mediation are that it can result in an expeditious and less costly resolution of the litigation, and can produce creative solutions to complex disputes often unavailable in traditional litigation.[3]

Arbitration is the process by which parties to a dispute voluntarily agree to submit their differences to the judgment of an impartial mediation panel for resolution. It is used as a means to evaluate, screen, and resolve medical malpractice disputes before they reach the courts. Arbitration can be accomplished by mutual consent of the parties or statutory provisions. A decision made at arbitration may or may not be binding, depending on prior agreement between the parties or statutory requirements.

STATUTE OF LIMITATIONS

All states have precise deadlines for the filing of medical malpractice lawsuits. These deadlines are described as the *statute of limitations*, which sets a limit on the amount of time a plaintiff has to file a malpractice complaint. Time limits vary from state to state as noted at the following website:

www.alllaw.com/articles/nolo/medical-malpractice/state-laws-statutes-limitations.html.

Malpractice actions must be filed in a timely manner. The action filed in *Russell v. Williford*[4] was not filed in a timely manner under the statute of limitations. Reasonable diligence should have led the plaintiff to seek a second opinion or additional treatment much sooner when the abnormal condition in his left leg persisted. This simple action, if taken within 1 to 2 years after surgery instead of 27 years later, might have made the true problem with the plaintiff's leg known much sooner. Therefore, the plaintiff may not bring this action now, over a quarter of a century after the alleged act or omission. To allow the plaintiff to proceed under this set of facts on such an ancient claim would set a dangerous precedent.

▶ STRUCTURED AWARDS

Structured awards are set up for the periodic partial payment of judgments rather than paying the injured party a lump-sum payment. The purpose of a structured award is to provide compensation during a plaintiff's lifetime. It eliminates the potential for an unwarranted windfall to the plaintiff's beneficiaries in the event of early death. Some states have sought to deal with award limitations by mandating structured recoveries when awards exceed a certain dollar amount.

Structured awards provide that money awarded to the plaintiff be placed in a trust fund and invested appropriately so that the funds will be available to the plaintiff over an extended period of time. The rationale behind such legislation is that an immediate award of a large sum of money often is not necessary for a plaintiff to be well taken care of after suffering injuries. Instead, the prudent investment of a smaller amount of money can produce a recovery commensurate with the needs and the rights of the plaintiff. This, in turn, requires a smaller cash outlay by the defendant or the defendant's insurance company, thereby holding down the costs of malpractice insurance and the ultimate cost of medical care to the consumer.

▶ MEDICAL MALPRACTICE SCREENING PANELS

Medical malpractice screening panels are designed to evaluate the merits of medical injury claims and encourage the settlement of claims outside the courtroom. "Panels render an opinion on provider liability and, in some cases, on damages. In most states, the panel's decision on the merit of the claim is admissible in court."[5] Unlike binding arbitration, the decision of a screening panel is not binding and is imposed as a condition precedent to trial, whereas arbitration is conducted in lieu of a trial. Mandatory screenings of alleged negligence cases are useful in discouraging frivolous lawsuits from proceeding to trial.

The Alaska Supreme Court, in *Keyes v. Humana Hospital Alaska*,[6] held that a statute creating mandatory pretrial review of medical malpractice claims by an expert advisory panel did not impermissibly infringe on the plaintiff's constitutional right to a trial by jury. The statute was a reasonable legislative response to the medical malpractice insurance crisis.

The constitutionality of a Virginia statute, in *Speet v. Bacaj*,[7] provided that admission of a medical review panel's opinion into evidence did not infringe on the plaintiff's right to a trial by jury or impact on a jury's function in resolving the disputed facts in the case. The trial court jury instructions were correctly permitted in this case, where the lower court stated, "The opinion of the Medical Review Panel is not binding upon you. You should consider it along with the other evidence."[8]

▶ COLLATERAL SOURCE RULE

The *collateral source rule* is a common law principle that prohibits a court or jury from taking into account, when setting an award, that part of the plaintiff's damages covered by other sources of payment (e.g., health insurance for medical bills, disability). Several states have modified the collateral source rule so that evidence regarding other sources of payment to the plaintiff may be introduced for purposes of reducing the amount of the ultimate award to the plaintiff. The jury then would be permitted to assign the evidence such weight as it chooses. The award could be reduced to the extent that the plaintiff has received compensation from other sources.

Imposition of the collateral source rule can result in recoveries to plaintiffs far in excess of their economic loss. Such excessive payments contribute significantly to the high cost of malpractice insurance and the high cost of health care to the public. When evidence regarding collateral sources of payment is allowed to mitigate the damages payable to a plaintiff, excessive recoveries are discouraged.

▶ CONTINGENCY FEE LIMITATIONS

A *contingency fee* is payment for services rendered by an attorney predicated on the favorable outcome of a case. Payment is based on a preestablished percentage of the total award. Some states set this percentage by statute. California, in Section 6146 of the California Business and Professional Code, "caps contingency fees at a rate of forty percent of the first $50,000 recovered, thirty-three and one-third percent of the next $50,000 recovered, twenty-five percent of the next $500,000, and fifteen percent on anything over $600,000."[9] These are maximums, and the attorney and client are free to negotiate lower rates. Under a contingency agreement, if there is no award to the plaintiff, the attorney receives no payment for services rendered.

Physicians argue that the contingency fee arrangement serves to encourage an unreasonable number of lawsuits. Attorneys reason that if they or their clients must bear the initial cost of a lawsuit, only those lawsuits with obvious merit will be filed. The contingency fee structure allows those unable to bear the cost of litigation to initiate a suit for damages. Limiting contingency fees on a sliding scale basis, with the percentage decreasing as the award to the plaintiff increases, and/or providing for a lesser fee if a claim is settled prior to trial, appears to have merit.

▶ COUNTERSUITS: FRIVOLOUS CLAIMS

Healthcare providers, in some instances, have filed countersuits after being named in what they believe to be frivolous medical malpractice suits. The threat of countersuits, however, has not been helpful in reducing the number of malpractice claims. Remedies for such actions vary from one jurisdiction to the next. For a physician to prevail in a suit against a plaintiff or plaintiff's attorney, the physician must show the following:

1. The suit was frivolous.
2. The motivation of the plaintiff was not to recover for a legitimate injury.
3. The physician has suffered damages as a result of the suit.

It has been argued that defendants should be allowed to recover court costs and damage awards from both the plaintiff(s) and their attorneys for frivolous claims and counterclaims. Frivolous litigation is the practice of filing a lawsuit that lacks legal merit and has little chance of being successful. It consists of a claim made by the defendant(s) that there is insufficient evidence for the plaintiff(s) to proceed with a case.

A claim or defense may be frivolous because it has no underlying justification, either in fact or law. United States Rule 11 of the Federal Rules of Civil Procedure and similar state rules require an attorney to perform a due diligence investigation concerning the factual basis for a claim or defense. Congress enacted section 1912 of Title 28 of the U.S.C., which provides that in the U.S. Supreme Court and in the U.S. Courts of Appeals, where litigation by the losing party has caused damage to the prevailing party, the court may impose a requirement that the losing party must pay the prevailing party for those damages. The costs associated with filing a lawsuit include time spent in preparing and litigating a case, obtaining and analyzing medical records, obtaining expert witnesses, conducting depositions, and a variety of other costs associated with litigating a lawsuit.

In *Berlin v. Nathan*,[10] a radiologist, a surgeon, and a hospital were sued for alleged malpractice by a patient who sought $250,000 because the defendants did not diagnose a fracture of her little finger. The radiologist missed the break, but he claimed that it was not evident on the X-ray taken at the hospital and that there was no error on his part. Furthermore, the finger was placed in a splint just as if it had been broken, so the treatment was correct regardless of the diagnosis. The radiologist countersued, so the malpractice suit and countersuit were tried together. When the jury was selected, the patient withdrew the malpractice suit, but the radiologist persisted with his case. The jury awarded the radiologist $2,000 as compensation and $6,000 in punitive damages, presumably convinced that the patient and her attorneys acted improperly in bringing the lawsuit and that the attorneys were negligent in their investigation of the patient's case before filing suit.

When the case was taken to an appellate court, the decision of the lower court was reversed on the grounds that the physician failed to plead special damages and (because the countersuit had been filed prematurely) failed to plead a favorable result in the original suit. The appellate court went on to say that a showing of special damages is essential in a case of this type in order that the public's right to free access of the court system not be impeded by the threat of counter-litigation. The court reasoned that people who believe they have legitimate claims should not be dissuaded from using the court system solely because of the fear of liability in the event their claim is unsuccessful. However, a study conducted by researchers at the Harvard School of Public Health found that "most malpractice claims are meritorious, with 97% of claims involving medical injury. The press release from Harvard headlined: "Study casts doubt on claims that the medical malpractice system is plagued by frivolous lawsuits."[11]

The appellate court holding in the *Berlin* case represents the majority judicial view across the country regarding countersuits. Courts generally do not find in favor of the countersuing party because they fear that persons who otherwise would bring valid malpractice suits will be discouraged simply because of a concern over the possibility of a countersuit.

The courts, thus far, have not looked favorably on countersuits for frivolous negligence actions. Some state legislatures have taken limited action in this area. An Arkansas statute, for example, provides that in any civil action in which the court finds that there was a complete absence of a judicial issue of either law or fact raised by the losing party or his or her attorney, the court shall award, with certain stipulations, an attorney fee in an amount not to exceed $5,000 or 10% of the amount in controversy, whichever is less, to the prevailing party.[12]

▶ JOINT AND SEVERAL LIABILITY

The *doctrine of joint and several liability* provides that a person causing an injury concurrently with another person can be held equally liable for the entire judgment awarded by a court. This has been referred to as *pure joint and several liability*.

Some states have taken action to modify the doctrine by adopting a *modified joint and several liability* requirement, in which the defendant "is responsible for the entire verdict only if they are found to be at or above a specified percentage of fault. Twenty-eight (28) states practice Modified Joint and Several Liability (California, Colorado, Hawaii, Idaho, Illinois, Iowa, Louisiana, Maine, Minnesota, Mississippi, Missouri, Montana, Nebraska, Nevada, New Hampshire, New Jersey, New Mexico, New York, North Dakota, Ohio, Oklahoma, Oregon, South Carolina, South Dakota, Texas, Washington, West Virginia, and Wisconsin)."[13]

Some states require that each defendant in a multidefendant action should be limited to payment for the percentage of fault ascribed to him or her. This has been referred to as *pure several liability*. Presently, "Fourteen (14) states practice Pure Several Liability (Alaska, Arizona, Arkansas, Connecticut, Florida, Georgia, Indiana, Kansas, Kentucky, Michigan, Tennessee, Utah, Vermont, and Wyoming)."[14] A Wyoming statute, for example, provides that each defendant to a lawsuit is liable only for that proportion of the total dollar amount of damages according to the percentage of the amount of fault attributed to him or her.[15]

A Minnesota statute provides that a defendant whose fault is 15% or less may be jointly liable for a percentage of the whole award not greater than four times his or her percentage of fault.[16]

Fair Share Act

Governor Tom Corbett of Pennsylvania signed the Fair Share Act (42 Pa. Cons. Stat. § 7102) in 2011, which provides for a proportionate share of liability among joint tortfeasors and eliminates the common law doctrine of joint and several liability. Under the law, with few exceptions, each defendant is liable for "that proportion of the total dollar amount awarded as damages in the ratio of the amount of that defendant's liability to the amount of liability attributed to all defendants and other persons to whom liability is apportioned under subsection (a.2)" [42 Pa. Cons. Stat. § 7102(a.1)(1)].

▶ MALPRACTICE CAPS

Many states have attempted to stem the tide of rising malpractice awards by enacting laws that limit the total dollar damages allowable in malpractice actions. Some states have placed limitations on the amount of awards in order to discourage frivolous lawsuits. The impetus for malpractice caps is due, in part, because jury awards often vary substantially from jurisdiction to jurisdiction within and between states. As a result, negligence attorneys often attempt to try personal injury cases in those jurisdictions in which a jury is more likely to grant a higher award. Although there have been challenges to statutes limiting awards, it would appear that limitations on malpractice recoveries are mixed as to the constitutionally of such caps. Pennsylvania for example does not impose caps on damages in personal injury cases unless the case is brought against a Commonwealth agency. In fact, damages caps are otherwise unconstitutional under the Constitution of the Commonwealth of Pennsylvania.

The battle continues regarding the effectiveness of malpractice liability caps. States that have such statutes in place are finding that the caps do not resolve the issue of high malpractice insurance premiums for physicians. Although there have been challenges to statutes limiting awards, it would appear that limitations on malpractice recoveries are considered constitutional in some states and unconstitutional in others, as illustrated in the following cases.

Florida. Florida caps on medical malpractice damages were determined to be unconstitutional. The Florida Supreme Court ruled on June 8, 2017, that the Florida caps on medical malpractice damages were unconstitutional. Susan Kalitan had filed a lawsuit in 2008 against the North Broward Hospital District and other defendants after undergoing carpal-tunnel syndrome surgery and suffering a perforated esophagus during anesthesia. A jury awarded $4 million in noneconomic damages. The amount was reduced by about $2 million because of the caps in the 2003 law. On appeal, the 4th District Court of Appeal ruled that the damage caps were unconstitutional.[17] The Florida Supreme Court upheld the 4th District Court of Appeal's decision, which found that the state's malpractice caps on noneconomic damages violated the Equal Protection Clause of the Florida Constitution.

> We conclude that the caps on noneconomic damages in sections 766.118(2) and (3) arbitrarily reduce damage awards for plaintiffs who suffer the most drastic injuries. We further conclude that because there is no evidence of a continuing medical malpractice insurance crisis justifying the arbitrary and invidious discrimination between medical malpractice victims, there is no rational relationship between the personal injury noneconomic damage caps in section 766.118 and alleviating this purported crisis. Therefore, we hold that the caps on personal injury noneconomic damages provided in section 766.118 violate the Equal Protection Clause of the Florida Constitution.[18]

Section 766.118 sets noneconomic damages caps of $500,000 per claimant in personal injury or wrongful death actions arising from medical negligence. The noneconomic damages suffered by the injured patient in this case were severe. Such an award in this case could not be constitutionally limited by Section 766.188(2) and (3).

Idaho. The Idaho Supreme Court, in *Jones v. State Board of Medicine*,[19] held that the state's limitation on malpractice recoveries of $150,000 is not necessarily unconstitutional. The court also held that there was no inherent right to an unlimited amount of damages and that the state had a legitimate interest in controlling excessive medical costs caused by large malpractice recoveries and, thus, the statute could be held constitutional. Idaho has raised the limitation on noneconomic damages, such as pain and suffering, to $250,000 under Idaho Code § 6-1603. This limitation does not apply to economic damages such as medical expenses, and adjusts with inflation yearly based on adjustments made by the Idaho Industrial Commission.

California. The California Supreme Court, in *Fein v. Permanente Medical Group*,[20] found that provisions in the Medical Injury Compensation Reform Act of 1975, Section 3333.2 of the Civil Code, that limit noneconomic damages for pain and suffering in medical malpractice cases to $250,000 are not unconstitutional. The legislature did not place limits on a plaintiff's right to recover for economic damages, such as medical expenses and lost earnings resulting from an injury. Unlike other states, California's limitation does not adjust with inflation, and the limitation will remain at the 1975 rates until the law is amended. At the ballot box in 2014, California citizens voted to maintain the $250,000 cap on noneconomic damages.[21]

Virginia. A Virginia statute that places a cap of $750,000 on damages recoverable in a malpractice action was found not to violate the Seventh Amendment separation of powers principles or the Fourteenth Amendment due process or equal protection clauses.[22] Under Virginia Code § 8.01-581.15, Virginia's malpractice cap has been increasing incrementally over the years and is as of 2015 set at $2.15 million. The malpractice cap is scheduled to rise to $3 million by 2031. Further increases are scheduled after that date.

Illinois. In November 2006, the plaintiffs in *Lebron v. Gottlieb Memorial Hospital*, Abigaile Lebron (Abigaile), a minor, and her mother, Frances Lebron (Lebron), filed a medical malpractice and declaratory judgment action against the defendants—the hospital, physician, and nurse. According to the complaint, Lebron was under the care of the physician during her pregnancy. On October 31, 2005, Lebron was admitted to the hospital, where the physician delivered Abigaile by cesarean section. The nurse assisted in the delivery and provided the principal nursing care from the time of Lebron's admission. The plaintiffs alleged that as the direct and proximate result of certain acts and omissions by the defendants, Abigaile sustained numerous permanent injuries, including severe brain injury, cerebral palsy, cognitive mental impairment, inability to be fed normally such that she must be fed by a gastrostomy tube, and inability to develop normal neurologic function.

The plaintiffs sought a judicial determination of their rights with respect to Public Act 94-677 and a declaration that certain provisions of the act, applicable to the plaintiffs' cause of action, violate the Illinois Constitution. The plaintiffs challenged the caps on noneconomic damages contained in the act. The plaintiffs alleged that Abigaile sustained disability, disfigurement, and pain and suffering to the extent that damages for those injuries will greatly exceed the applicable limitations on noneconomic damages under the Act.

The Supreme Court of Illinois agreed with the plaintiffs that the $500,000 limit on noneconomic damages was arbitrary. Although agreeing with the defendants that noneconomic injuries are difficult to assess, imposing an arbitrary damages limitation in all cases, without regard to the facts, did not alleviate such difficulty.

The defendants referred the court's attention to statutes limiting noneconomic damages in medical malpractice cases that have been adopted in other states. The defendants contended that the limits on damages contained in the act are well within the range of reasonable limits adopted by these states. The court reviewed the statutes cited by the defendants and observed that the limitations on noneconomic damages adopted in other states vary widely, not only in the amount of the cap, but also regarding other specifics. "On what basis defendants have determined that such disparate provisions are all reasonable is not known, and it is not for the Supreme Court of Illinois to judge the reasonableness of other states' legislation. The 'everybody is doing it' mentality is hardly a litmus test for the constitutionality of the statute."[23]

A summary of medical malpractice damages caps, which vary from state to state, can be found at www.nolo.com/legal-encyclopedia/state-state-medical-malpractice-damages-caps.html. The state supreme courts of Florida,[24] Missouri,[25] Georgia,[26] Illinois,[27] Alabama, Oregon,[28] Washington,[29] and New Hampshire[30] have overturned limits on noneconomic damages.[31] The Florida Supreme Court, in a 5-2 decision, held that the way the caps reduced damages is "arbitrary and unrelated to a true state interest," and it "offends the fundamental notion of equal justice under the law." The court continued: "The statutory cap on wrongful death noneconomic damages fails because it imposes unfair and illogical burdens on injured parties when an act of medical negligence gives rise to multiple claimants."[32]

▶ NO-FAULT SYSTEM

A _no-fault system_ compensates injured parties for economic losses regardless of fault. It is intended to compensate more claimants with smaller awards. A no-fault system compensates victims of medical injury whether or not they can prove medical negligence. Proponents of the no-fault approach cite its advantages as providing a swifter and less expensive resolution of claims and a more equitable compensation for patients. "While several other countries have established a no-fault system for medical malpractice, no state has established an across-the-board no-fault medical malpractice system. But Florida and Virginia have established a voluntary no-fault system for children born severely impaired because of neurologic injuries suffered during the birthing process."[33]

A no-fault system of compensation does have drawbacks. Opponents of the no-fault system are concerned about the loss of whatever deterrent effect the present tort system exerts on healthcare providers. The system's lower administrative costs can be an incentive to file lawsuits and, therefore, may not produce the desired outcome of reducing the incidence of malpractice claims.

▶ REGULATION OF INSURANCE PRACTICES

Many believe that the _regulation of insurance practices_ is necessary to prevent windfall profits. Both the medical profession and the legal profession believe that insurance carriers have raised premiums disproportionately to their losses and that, despite their claims of substantial losses, they have reaped substantial profits. Additional information on insurance can be found at several websites including www.naic.org/documents/consumer_state_reg_brief.pdf.

▶ REDUCING THE RISKS OF MALPRACTICE

A variety of programs have been implemented to improve the quality of patient care, reduce the incidence of medical errors, and lower malpractice insurance premiums.

Risk Management

Risk management programs improve patient care and treatment practices, thus reducing the number of patient injuries and thereby minimizing the exposure of an organization to lawsuits. An effective risk management program includes a monitoring system that identifies potential risks to patients and staff. Liability insurers have been strong proponents of risk management and in many cases, insurers have reduced premiums for physicians and healthcare organizations that implement risk management programs that include: a grievance or complaint mechanism designed to process and resolve grievances by patients or their representatives; data collection with respect to negative healthcare outcomes; medical care evaluation mechanisms that include tissue review, blood utilization, and medical audit committees to periodically assess the quality of medical care being provided; and patient safety education programs to support staff.

Performance Improvement

There are a variety of labels ascribed to the quality improvement process, such as *continuous quality improvement* (CQI) and *performance improvement* (PI). CQI is the term given to the philosophy of management introduced into the U.S. business world in 1980 by an American statistician, Dr. W. E. Deming. Initially working in Japan, Deming was rediscovered by his own country when an NBC news documentary entitled *If Japan Can—Why Can't We?* was broadcast on June 24, 1980. A portion of the documentary highlighted Deming's efforts in helping to make Japanese management and products what some would call the best in the world. His concepts on improving quality, however, failed to catch the immediate attention of the business world in the United States. Through his years of research, Deming formulated step-by-step procedures for improving quality and decreasing costs. Since that time, there have been numerous variations on the CQI process of improving quality. CQI comes in a diversity of packages that contain sound business practices that have been developed over many years. CQI involves improving performance at every functional level of an organization's operation, using all available resources (human and capital). It combines fundamental management techniques, innovative improvement efforts, and specialized technical skills in a structure focused on continuously improving processes. CQI relies on people and involves everyone. CQI is concerned with providing a quality product, getting to market on time, providing the best service, reducing costs, broadening market share, and producing organizational growth.

Performance improvement is the terminology adopted by The Joint Commission, which describes "the systematic process of detecting and analyzing performance problems, designing and developing interventions to address the problems, implementing the interventions, evaluating the results, and sustaining improvement."[34] Successful PI programs require commitment by the organization's leadership to PI activities, regular inter- and intra-departmental meetings between caregivers, and continuing educational opportunities for self-improvement within and outside of the organization. PI should be part of an organization's culture and can be adopted by professional organizations and specialty societies when developing best-practice guidelines. "Many of the specialty societies either have drafted or are drafting practice guidelines for their medical area of expertise. For example,

the American Society of Anesthesiologists developed guidelines for intra-operative monitoring in 1986. During the following year, no lawsuits were brought for hypoxic injuries; in previous years hypoxic injury suits averaged six per year."[35]

Peer Review

Medical staff peer review is the evaluation of a physician's work competence and quality by his or her peers. It is a form of self-regulation and can be accomplished internally by qualified members of an organization's medical staff within their respective fields of expertise. In high-profile cases, an external group can conduct peer review activities in order to avoid giving the perception of bias and the appearance of wrongdoing and thus provide credibility to the process.

▶ COLLABORATION IN TORT REFORM

Physicians and, increasingly, advanced practice practitioners (e.g., physician assistant and nurse practitioners) are on the front lines of medicine but often have been excluded from the decision-making processes that threaten their autonomy and financial security. A concerted effort must be made to include them in the process of tort reform. The present system of punishment for all because of the inadequacies of the few has proven to be costly and ineffective.

The medical malpractice insurance crisis continues to be a major dilemma for the healthcare industry. Although many approaches have been taken to resolve the crisis, there appears to be no one magic formula. The solution most likely will require a variety of efforts, including tort reforms, some of which have been reviewed here.

▶ CHAPTER REVIEW

1. *Mediation* is the process wherein a third party attempts to bring about a settlement between parties. *Arbitration* is a process wherein parties agree to submit their differences to the judgment of an impartial mediation panel for resolution in lieu of trial.
2. *Structured awards* are those placed in a trust set up to provide compensation over a plaintiff's lifetime.
3. *Pretrial screening panels* are used to encourage out-of-court settlements. The panels give an opinion on provider liability and, in some cases, damages.

4. The *collateral source rule* is a common law principle that prohibits a court or jury, when setting an award, from taking into account that part of the plaintiff's damages that would be covered by other sources of payment.

5. A *contingency fee* is payment for an attorney's services predicated on the favorable outcome of a case. Many believe that a limitation on such fees would limit the windfall profits of attorneys, thus reducing the economic drain on the healthcare system.

6. Some healthcare providers have filed *countersuits* after being named in what they believe to be frivolous claims. The threat of such suits, however, has not proven to be helpful in reducing the number of malpractice claims.

7. The concept of *joint and several liability* holds that a person who caused an injury concurrently with another person can be held equally liable for the full judgment awarded by a court. Some states require that each defendant in a multidefendant action should be limited to payment for the percentage of fault ascribed to him or her.

8. Some states are attempting to limit the rising costs of malpractice awards by setting *malpractice caps*.

9. Proponents of a *no-fault approach* to reducing the costs associated with exorbitant malpractice awards cite as its advantages swifter and less expensive resolution of claims and more equitable compensation for patients.

10. *Statutes of limitations* specify the timeframe within which a lawsuit must be commenced.

11. Reducing the risks of malpractice can be accomplished by implementation of best practices, risk management, *performance improvement activities*, and peer review.

▶ REVIEW QUESTIONS

1. Describe various tort reform programs designed to lower the cost of malpractice insurance. Should there be limits placed on malpractice awards? Support your opinion.

2. Discuss what a structured award is and how it might reduce the costs associated with large-sum malpractice awards.

3. Discuss which of the schemes for tort reform discussed previously you consider most helpful in addressing the malpractice insurance crisis.

4. Describe how risk management, performance improvement, and peer review can be helpful in improving patient care and reducing the number of malpractice claims.

▶ NOTES

1. Gregg Roslund, MD, "The Medical Malpractice Rundown: A State-by-State Report," *Emergency Physicians Monthly*, July 21, 2014.

2. The Robert Wood Johnson Foundation, "The Tort System for Medical Malpractice: How Well Does It Work, What Are the Alternatives?" *Abridge*, Spring 1991, 2.

3. United States District Court Southern District of New York, "What Is Mediation," http://www.nysd.uscourts.gov/mediation.

4. No. 2003-CA-01573-COA (Miss. Ct. App. 2004).

5. The Robert Wood Johnson Foundation, "Legal Reform," *Abridge*, Spring 1991, 3.

6. 750 P.2d 343 (Alaska 1988).

7. 377 S.E.2d 397 (Va. 1989).

8. *Id.* at 401.

9. Eugen C. Andres and Jim Moore, "Requirements for Client Retainer Agreements," December 2013. http://www.ocbar.org/AllNews/NewsView/tabid/66/ArticleId/1207/December-2013-Requirements-for-Client-Retainer-Agreements.aspx.

10. 381 N.E.2d 1367 (1978).

11. Jack Cannon, "Frivolous Malpractice Lawsuits Uncommon: Harvard Study," http://www.healylawfirm.com/News-Articles/Irish-American-News/Frivolous-Malpractice-Lawsuits-Uncommon-Harvard-Study.shtml.

12. Ark. Code Ann. § 16-22-309 (Michie 1987).

13. Matthiesen, Wickert & Lehrer, S.C., "Joint and Several Liability and Contribution Laws in All 50 States," Updated September 15, 2017. https://www.mwl-law.com/wp-content/uploads/2013/03/contribution-actions-in-all-50-states.pdf.

14. *Id.*

15. Wyo. Stat. § 1-1-109 (1986).

16. Minn. Stat. § 604.02 (1988).

17. *North Broward Hospital District, etc., et al., Appellants, vs. Susan Kalitan*, 174 So. 3d 403 (2015).

18. *North Howard Hospital v. Kalitan*, No. SC15-1858 (June 8, 2017).

19. 555 P.2d 399 (Idaho 1976).

20. 695 P.2d 665 (Cal. 1985).

21.   Ballotpedia, "California Proposition 46, Medical Malpractice Lawsuits Cap and Drug Testing of Doctors (2014)," https://ballotpedia .org/California_Proposition_46,_Medical _Malpractice_Lawsuits_Cap_and_Drug _Testing_of_Doctors_(2014)

22.   *Boyd v. Bulala*, 877 F.2d 1191 (4th Cir. 1989).

23.   *Lebron v. Gottlieb Memorial Hospital*, Docket Nos. 105741, 105745 cons., (Ill. February 4, 2010).

24.   John Chapman, "Florida medical malpractice wrongful death damage caps overturned in state Supreme Court ruling," April 23, 2015. https://www.hop-law.com/florida-medical -malpractice-wrongful-death-damage-caps -overturned-state-supreme-court-ruling/.

25.   Stephen R. Clark and Kristin Weinberg, "Missouri Supreme Court Overrules 20 Years of Precedent in Holding Noneconomic Damages Cap Unconstitutional," January 4, 2013. http://www.fed-soc .org/publications/detail/missouri-supreme -court-overrules-20-years-of-precedent -in-holding-noneconomic-damages-cap -unconstitutional.

26.   The Cochran Firm, "Georgia Supreme Court Overturns Medical Malpractice Damage Cap," http://www.cochranfirm.com/georgia-supreme -court-overturns-medical-malpractice -damage-cap/.

27.   Kevin Sack, "Illinois Court Overturns Malpractice Statute," February 4, 2010. *The New York Times.* http://www.nytimes.com/2010/02/05/us /05malpractice.html.

28.   MedicalMalpracticeLawyers.com, "Oregon Supreme Court Overturns $12M Medical Malpractice Verdict, Applies $3M Cap," June 17, 2016. https://www.medicalmalpracticelawyers .com/hospital-medical-malpractice-2/oregon -supreme-court/.

29.   Zachary Matzo, "Washington Medical Malpractice Laws & Statutory Rules," http://www .alllaw.com/articles/nolo/medical-malpractice /laws-washington.html.

30.   Medical Malpractice Center, "New Hampshire Medical Malpractice Laws," http://www .malpracticecenter.com/new-hampshire/.

31.   Pamela Menaker, "Caps on Non-Economic Damages Held Unconstitutional," June 2, 2014. American Bar Association, *Litigation News.* https://apps.americanbar.org/litigation /litigationnews/top_stories/060214-non -economic-damage-caps.html.

32.   *Id.*

33.   George Coppolo and Saul Spigel, "Medical Malpractice-No-Fault Systems," December 8, 2003. *OLR Research Report.* https://www.cga .ct.gov/2003/olrdata/ins/rpt/2003-R-0885.htm.

34.   Glossary, The Joint Commission Hospital Accreditation Standards, 2017, GL–29.

35.   The Robert Wood Johnson Foundation, "Preventing Negligence," *Abridge*, Spring 1991, at 8.

© Orguz Dikbakan/Shutterstock

CHAPTER 6

Criminal Aspects of Health Care

WRONGFUL ADMINISTRATION OF CHEMOTHERAPY

The physician in the *United States v. Moon* was convicted by a trial court for healthcare fraud and making false statements regarding the administration of partial doses of chemotherapy medications to patients. These actions resulted in placing patients at risk of death or serious bodily harm. The physician was billing Medicaid and other insurance programs for full doses of the medications. The defendant-physician appealed the trial court's decision. At sentencing, the district court considered testimony from family members of deceased patients. The various families testified that their loved ones suffered emotional harm as a result of not knowing whether or not the medications administered were wrongfully administered. The defendant contended that the testimony of the patients' relatives was not "relevant" because they were not "victims" of the offenses for which the defendant was convicted.[1]

WHAT IS YOUR VERDICT?

Laws are made to restrain and punish the wicked; the wise and good do not need them as a guide, but only as a shield against rapine and oppression; they can live civilly and orderly, though there were no law in the world.

—John Milton (1608–1674)

▶ LEARNING OBJECTIVES

The reader, upon completion of this chapter, will be able to:

- Explain what criminal law is, its main objectives, and the classification of crimes.
- Describe the criminal procedure process from arrest through trial.
- Describe several of the more common crimes that occur in the healthcare setting.

Criminal law is society's expression of the limits of acceptable human and institutional behavior. A *crime* is any social harm defined and made punishable by law. The objectives of criminal law are as follows:

- Maintain public order and safety.
- Protect the individual.
- Use punishment as a deterrent to crime.
- Rehabilitate the criminal for return to society.

A crime is also defined as "any act which the sovereign has deemed contrary to the public good; a wrong which the government has determined is injurious to the public and, hence, prosecutable in a criminal proceeding."[2] Crimes are generally classified as misdemeanors or felonies. The difference between a misdemeanor and a felony is the severity of the crime. A *misdemeanor* is an offense punishable by less than 1 year in jail and/or a fine (e.g., petty larceny). A *felony* is a much more serious crime (e.g., rape, murder) and is generally punishable by imprisonment in a state or federal penitentiary for more than 1 year.

Criminal law has been seen as a system of regulating the behavior of individuals and groups in relation to societal norms, whereas civil law is aimed primarily at the relationships between private individuals and their rights and obligations under the law.[3]

Particular to healthcare organizations is the fact that patients are often helpless and at the mercy of others. Healthcare facilities are far too often places where the morally weak and mentally deficient prey on the physically and sometimes mentally helpless. The very institutions designed to make the public well and feel safe can sometimes provide the setting for criminal conduct. As a result, the U.S. Department of Justice and state prosecutors vigorously pursue and prosecute healthcare organizations and individuals for criminal conduct. There is a zero-tolerance policy for healthcare fraud, patient abuse, and other such crimes. Healthcare professionals must be observant of the actions of others and report suspicious conduct. In an effort to provide the reader with a review of criminal law as it applies to the healthcare industry, this chapter presents the procedural aspects of criminal law, as well as an overview of criminal cases that have occurred in healthcare facilities.

▶ CRIMINAL PROCEDURE

Criminal procedure regulates the process for addressing violations of criminal law. The following sections provide an overview of criminal procedure and the process for the prosecution of misdemeanors and felonies.

Arrest

Prosecution for a crime generally begins with the arrest of a person by a police officer or with the filing of a formal action in a court of law and the issuance of an arrest warrant or summons. On arrest, the suspect is taken to the appropriate law enforcement agency for processing and booking, which includes paperwork and fingerprinting. The police also prepare and file accusatory statements, such as a misdemeanor information and felony complaints, with the appropriate jurisdiction. When necessary, one or more detectives may be assigned to a case to gather evidence, interview both persons suspected of committing a crime and witnesses to a crime, and assist in preparing a case for possible trial. After processing has been completed, the person is either detained or released on bond. If the alleged offense is classified as a felony, the U.S. Constitution requires that the case be referred to a grand jury for an indictment. An *indictment* is the official charging instrument accusing the defendant of criminal conduct.

A prosecuting attorney represents the interests of the state, and a defense attorney represents the interests of the defendant. Although the specific process varies according to local law, in virtually every jurisdiction, unless a guilty plea has been accepted by the court, the process culminates with a trial. The defendant can appeal a lower court's decision by appealing to a higher court.

Criminal statutes spell out the specific elements that must be proven to constitute a criminal act. Unless the prosecuting authority proves all the elements of a particular crime, the defendant is not guilty of the offense charged. In a criminal case, the three general elements that must be established are as follows:

1. The act itself is a criminal act, known as *actus reus* or the guilty act.
2. The intent to commit the criminal act provides the requisite mental state, or the *mens rea*.
3. The attendant or surrounding circumstances of the crime demonstrate that the crime was committed by the defendant.

Arraignment

The *arraignment* is a formal reading of the *accusatory instrument* (a generic term that describes a variety of documents, each of which accuses the defendant of an offense) and includes the setting of bail. The accused should appear with counsel or have counsel appointed by the court if he or she cannot afford an attorney. After the charges are read, the defendant pleads guilty or not guilty as charged. A not guilty plea is normally offered on a felony complaint. On a plea of not guilty, the defense attorney and prosecutor formulate arguments to the judge when setting bail. After arraignment of the defendant, the judge sets a date for the defendant to return to court. Between the time of arraignment and the next court date, the defense attorney and the prosecutor confer about the charges and the evidence in the possession of the prosecutor. The defense will at that time offer mitigating circumstances in an attempt to negotiate with the prosecutor to reduce or drop the charges.

Indictment

A felony complaint or grand jury indictment commences a criminal proceeding. The accused can be tried for a felony after a *grand jury indictment* (**EXHIBIT 6-1**). The defendant can waive presentment to the grand jury and plead guilty by relinquishing his rights to a grand jury hearing and proceed to trial by jury. During a grand jury hearing, the prosecution presents evidence, which may lead to an indictment of the target if the grand jury finds reasonable cause to believe from the evidence presented that all the elements of a particular crime are present. The grand jury may request that witnesses be subpoenaed to testify. A defendant may choose to testify and offer information if he or she wishes. Actions of a grand jury are handed up to a judge, after which the defendant is notified to appear to be arraigned for any crimes charged in the indictment.

Conference

If the defendant does not plead guilty, both felony and misdemeanor cases are taken to conference, and plea-bargaining commences with the goal of an agreed upon disposition. If a disposition cannot be reached, the case is adjourned, motions are made, and further plea-bargaining takes place. After several adjournments, a case may be assigned to a trial court.

Criminal Trial

Most of the processes of a criminal trial are similar to those of a civil trial. They include jury selection, opening statements, presentation of witnesses and other evidence, summations, instructions to the jury by the judge, jury deliberations, verdict, and opportunity for appeal to a higher court. In a criminal trial, the jury verdict must be unanimous, and the standard of proof is that *guilt must be proven beyond a reasonable doubt*, whereas in a civil trial, the plaintiff need only prove a claim by a *preponderance* of the evidence.

Criminal History and False Statements

The record in *Hoxie v. Ohio State Med. Bd.* indicated that the physician had made false statements concerning his criminal history when he stated in a deposition that he had never been arrested. There was, however, sufficient evidence presented to support permanent revocation of his license to practice medicine. Certified records held by the state of California indicated that the physician had been arrested or detained by the Los Angeles Police Department multiple times in the 1970s and 1980s for possessing marijuana and phencyclidine piperidine (PCP), driving under the influence of alcohol and/or drugs, and driving with a suspended license. Although the physician asserted that documentation of his criminal past had been fabricated by police and was not credible, law enforcement investigation reports were generally admissible. The physician himself added to the reliability of the records by verifying all significant identifying information contained within the documents and records.[4]

Prosecutor

The role of the prosecutor in the criminal justice system is well defined in *Berger v. United States*:

> The United States Attorney is the representative not of an ordinary party to a controversy, but of a sovereignty whose obligation to govern impartially is as compelling as its obligation to govern at all; and whose interest, therefore, in a criminal prosecution is not that it shall win a case, but that justice will be done. As such, he is in a peculiar and very definite sense the servant of the law, the twofold aim of which is that guilt shall not escape or innocence suffer.[5]

IN THE COURT OF COMMON PLEAS
FIRST JUDICIAL DISTRICT OF PENNSYLVANIA
CRIMINAL TRIAL DIVISION

IN RE	**: MISC. NO 009901-2008**
COUNTY INVESTIGATING	**:**
GRAND JURY XXIII	**: C-17**

REPORT OF THE GRAND JURY

R. SETH WILLIAMS
District Attorney

This case is about a doctor who killed babies and endangered women. What we mean is that he regularly and illegally delivered live, viable, babies in the third trimester of pregnancy – and then murdered these newborns by severing their spinal cords with scissors. The medical practice by which he carried out this business was a filthy fraud in which he overdosed his patients with dangerous drugs, spread venereal disease among them with infected instruments, perforated their wombs and bowels – and on, at least two occasions, caused their deaths. Over the years, many people came to know that something was going on here. But no one put a stop to it.

There remained, however, a final difficulty. When you perform late-term "abortions" by inducing labor, you get babies. Live, breathing, squirming babies. By 24 weeks, most babies born prematurely will survive if they receive appropriate medical care. But that was not what the Women's Medical Society was about. Gosnell had a simple solution for the unwanted babies he delivered: he killed them. He didn't call it that. He called it "ensuring fetal demise." The way he ensured fetal demise was by sticking scissors into the back of the baby's neck and cutting the spinal cord. He called that "snipping."

☐ ☐ ☐

Gosnell's students parroted his grisly techniques. Massof himself admitted to us that, of the many spinal cords he cut, there were about 100 instances where he did so after seeing a breath or some sign of life. The shocking regularity of killing babies who were born alive, who moved and breathed, as testified to by Gosnell's employees, demonstrates that these murders were intentional and collaborative. In addition to the specific murder charges identified above, **we recommend that Kermit Gosnell, Lynda Williams, Sherry West, Adrienne Moton, and Steven Massof be charged with conspiracy to commit murder.**

☐ ☐ ☐

Section VII: Criminal Charges

Gosnell and his staff showed consistent disregard not only for the health and safety of their patients, but also for the laws of Pennsylvania. After reviewing extensive and compelling evidence of criminal wrongdoing at the clinic, the Grand Jury has issued a presentment recommending the prosecution of Gosnell and members of his staff for criminal offenses including:

- Murder of Karnamaya Mongar
- Murder of babies born alive
- Infanticide
- Violations of the Controlled Substances Act
- Hindering, Obstruction, and Tampering
- Perjury
- Illegal late term abortions
- Violations of the Abortion Control Act
- Violations of the Controlled Substances Act
- Abuse of Corpse
- Theft by Deception
- Conspiracy
- Corrupt Organization
- Corruption of Minors

☐ ☐ ☐

15. If authorities responsible for overseeing, monitoring, or licensing Gosnell or his operation should conduct serious self-assessments to determine why their departments failed to protect the women and babies whose lives were imperiled at Gosnell's clinic. Employees who failed to perform their jobs of protecting the public should be held accountable.

The employees of the state and local health departments and the prosecutors for the Board of Medicine are charged with protecting the public health. Very few that we ran across in this investigation came even close to fulfilling that duty. These people seemed oblivious to the connection between their dereliction and the deaths and injuries that Gosnell inflicted under their watch. Reproduced from Grand Jury Women's Medical, http://www.phila.gov/districtattorney/pdfs/grandjurywomensmedical.pdf.

EXHIBIT 6-1 Report of the grand jury.

The potential of the prosecutor's office is not always fully realized in many jurisdictions. In many cities, the combination of the prosecutor's staggering caseload and small staff of assistants prevents sufficient attention from being given to each case.[6]

Defense Attorney

The defense attorney generally sits in the proverbial hot seat, being perceived as the bad guy. Although everyone seems to understand the attorney's function in protecting the rights of those represented, the defense attorney often is not the most popular person in the courtroom.

> There is a substantial difference in the problem of representing the "run-of-the-mill" criminal defendant and one whose alleged crimes have aroused great public outcry. The difficulties in providing representation for the ordinary criminal defendant are simple compared with the difficulties of obtaining counsel for one who is charged with a crime, which by its nature or circumstances incites strong public condemnation.[7]

Criminal trials involving healthcare professionals and organizations often involve healthcare fraud, kickbacks, tampering with drugs, illegal use and sale of drugs, falsification of records, patient abuse, criminal negligence, manslaughter, murder, rape and sexual assault, and theft. Each of these criminal offenses is reviewed in the following paragraphs.

▶ HEALTHCARE FRAUD

Healthcare fraud involves an unlawful act, generally deception for personal gain. It encompasses an array of irregularities and illegal acts characterized by intentional deception. Healthcare fraud continues to be a major financial drain on the healthcare system. The primary agency for exposing and investigating healthcare fraud is the Federal Bureau of Investigation (FBI), with jurisdiction over both federal and private insurance programs.[9]

The Bureau seeks to identify and pursue investigations against the most egregious offenders involved in health care fraud through investigative partnerships with other federal agencies, such as Health and Human Services-Office of Inspector General (HHS-OIG), Food and Drug Administration (FDA), Drug Enforcement Administration (DEA), Defense Criminal Investigative Service (DCIS), Office of Personnel Management-Office of Inspector General (OPM-OIG), and Internal Revenue Service-Criminal Investigation (IRS-CI), along with various state Medicaid Fraud Control Units and other state and local agencies.[10]

Moreover, the Health Insurance Portability and Accountability Act of 1996 (HIPAA) provides for criminal and civil enforcement tools and funding dedicated to the fight against healthcare fraud. The Act requires the U.S. Attorney General and the U.S. Secretary of the Department of Health and Human Services (DHHS), acting through the Office of Inspector General (OIG), to establish a coordinated national healthcare fraud and abuse control program. The program provides a national framework for federal, state, and local law enforcement agencies; the private sector; and the public to fight healthcare fraud. Since its establishment in 1976, "OIG has been at the forefront of the Nation's efforts to fight waste, fraud and abuse in Medicare, Medicaid and

---

NEWS *LARGEST HEALTH CARE FRAUD . . .*

National Health Care Fraud Takedown Results in Charges Against over 412 Individuals Responsible for $1.3 Billion in Fraud Losses

Largest Health Care Fraud Enforcement Action in Department of Justice History

Attorney General Jeff Sessions and Department of Health and Human Services (HHS) Secretary Tom Price, MD, announced today the largest ever health care fraud enforcement action by the Medicare Fraud Strike Force, involving 412 charged defendants across 41 federal districts, including 115 doctors, nurses, and other licensed medical professionals, for their alleged participation in health care fraud schemes involving approximately $1.3 billion in false billings. Of those charged, over 120 defendants, including doctors, were charged for their roles in prescribing and distributing opioids and other dangerous narcotics. Thirty state Medicaid Fraud Control Units also participated in today's arrests. In addition, HHS has initiated suspension actions against 295 providers, including doctors, nurses, and pharmacists.

— Department of Justice, *Justice News*, July 13, 2017[8]

more than 100 other HHS programs. HHS-OIG is the largest inspector general's office in the Federal Government, with approximately 1,600 dedicated to combating fraud, waste and abuse and to improving the efficiency of HHS programs."[11]

The DHHS and the Department of Justice (DOJ) in 2009 created the Health Care Fraud Prevention and Enforcement Action Team (HEAT). With its creation, the fight against Medicare fraud became a Cabinet-level priority. The HHS Secretary and the Attorney General direct HEAT's work. By 2015, HEAT coordinated a national healthcare fraud takedown that uncovered $712 million in fraudulent billing.[12]

The *Department of Justice Health and Human Services Medicare Fraud Strike Force* is a multiagency team of federal, state, and local investigators that is designed to combat Medicare fraud. Medicare fraud is estimated to cost the nation $80 billion annually.[13] The success of cooperation of agencies on the federal and state levels was evident when the Medicare Fraud Strike Force in 2011 charged 111 defendants in 9 cities, including doctors, nurses, healthcare company owners and executives, and others, for their alleged participation in Medicare fraud schemes involving more than $225 million in false billing.[14]

The Obama administration in July 2012 announced the formation of a public-private partnership to aid in the prevention of healthcare fraud among the federal government, state officials, several leading private health insurance organizations, and other healthcare antifraud groups. The partnership is designed to share information and best practices in order to improve detection and prevent payment of fraudulent healthcare billings.

Attorney General Loretta E. Lynch and HHS Secretary Sylvia Mathews Burwell announced in 2016 that a "nationwide sweep led by the Medicare Fraud Strike Force in 36 federal districts, resulting in criminal and civil charges against 301 individuals, including 61 doctors, nurses and other licensed medical professionals, for their alleged participation in health care fraud schemes involving approximately $900 million in false billings."[15] The message is clear that those involved in healthcare fraud are being vigorously pursued. The public has been encouraged to report suspected Medicare fraud by calling 1-800-HHS-TIPS (1-800-447-8477) or TTY: 1-800-377-4950.

The federal government's initiative to investigate and prosecute healthcare organizations for criminal wrongdoing has resulted in the establishment of corporate compliance programs for preventing, detecting, and reporting criminal conduct. An effective corporate compliance program should include:

1. Developing appropriate policies and procedures
2. Appointing a compliance officer to oversee the compliance program
3. Communicating the organization's compliance program to employees
4. Providing for monitoring and auditing systems that are designed to detect criminal conduct by employees and other agents
5. Publicizing a reporting system whereby employees and other agents can report criminal conduct by others within the organization without fear of retribution
6. Taking appropriate steps to respond to criminal conduct and to prevent similar offenses
7. Periodically reviewing and updating the organization's corporate compliance program
8. Working with state and federal law enforcement and regulatory agencies and insurance companies to detect, prevent, and prosecute healthcare fraud

As noted in the following remarks by former Attorney General Eric Holder, healthcare fraud continues to present significant risks to patient health and is a financial drain on the healthcare system, leading to higher costs for legitimate care.

We are here to announce that Johnson & Johnson and three of its subsidiaries have agreed to pay more than $2.2 billion to resolve criminal and civil claims that they marketed prescription drugs for uses that were never approved as safe and effective—and that they paid kickbacks to both physicians and pharmacies for prescribing and promoting these drugs.

• • •

Put simply, this alleged conduct is shameful and it is unacceptable. It displayed a reckless indifference to the safety of the American people. And it constituted a clear abuse of the public trust, showing a blatant disregard for systems and laws designed to protect public health.

• • •

This settlement demonstrates that the Departments of Justice and Health and Human Services—working alongside a variety of federal, state, and local partners—will not tolerate such activities. No company is above the law. And my colleagues and I are determined to keep moving forward—guided by the facts and the law, and using every tool, resource, and authority at our disposal—to hold these corporations accountable, to safeguard the American people, and to prevent this conduct from happening in the future.[16]

Schemes to Defraud

A defendant is guilty of a scheme to defraud when he or she engages in a scheme constituting a systematic, ongoing course of conduct with intent to defraud more than one person or to obtain property from more than one person by false or fraudulent pretenses, representations, or promises, and so obtains property from one or more of such persons. To show intent in a scheme to defraud, one needs to establish the following three elements:

1. That on or about (date), in the county of (county), the defendant (defendant/s name) engaged in a scheme constituting a systematic ongoing course of conduct.
2. That the defendant did so with intent to defraud more than one person or to obtain property from more than one person by false or fraudulent pretenses, representations, or promises.
3. That the defendant so obtained property from one or more of such persons, at least one of whom has been identified.

Schemes to defraud come in many forms, such as when $12 million in Medicaid funds were fraudulently used in the names of the deceased, where "The Illinois Medicaid program paid an estimated 12 million for medical services for people listed as the deceased in other state records, according to the internal state government memo . . . Auditors identified overpayments for services to roughly 2,900 people after the date of their deaths."[17]

Healthcare fraud is committed when a dishonest provider or consumer intentionally submits or causes someone else to submit false or misleading information for use in determining the amount of healthcare benefits payable. Some examples of provider healthcare fraud include the following:

- Billing for services not rendered
- Falsifying a patient's diagnosis to justify tests, surgeries, or other procedures that are not medically necessary
- Misrepresenting procedures performed to obtain payment for noncovered services, such as cosmetic surgery

- Upcoding services (billing for a more costly service than the one actually performed)
- Upcoding medical supplies and equipment (billing for more expensive equipment than what was delivered to the patient)
- Unbundling (billing each stage of a procedure as if it were a separate procedure)
- Billing for unnecessary services (services that are not medically indicated)
- Accepting kickbacks for patient referrals
- Waiving patient co-pays or deductibles
- Overbilling the insurance carrier or benefit plan

There are many examples of healthcare fraud, and some of the most egregious are described next.

Fraud Results in 45-Year Prison Sentence

The U.S. Supreme Court refused to hear the appeal of Dr. Farid Fata, who was convicted of running a scheme that involved billing the government for medically unnecessary cancer and blood treatments. As a result of his scheme to defraud the government, and harm patients in the process, he will spend the next 45 years in prison.

> The defendant, Farid Fata, was a physician who intentionally misdiagnosed no fewer than 553 of his patients with cancer and other maladies they did not have, then administered debilitating treatments, noxious chemicals, and invasive tests—including chemotherapy, intravenous iron, and PET scans—they did not need. For this reprehensible conduct, Fata received no less than $17 million in ill-gotten payments from Medicare and other insurers. The district court accurately described Fata's conduct as "a huge, horrific series of criminal acts."[18]

Healthy Dose of Fraud

Patients were allegedly brought to California where they were paid to undergo surgeries that they did not need.

> In the scam, agents say, recruiters bring "patients" from across the nation to surgery centers in California where they give phony or exaggerated symptoms and doctors perform unnecessary operations on them. Then the surgery centers send inflated claims for the unnecessary procedures to the patients' insurance companies. When the insurers pay up, federal authorities say, the recruiters, the surgery centers and the patients split the proceeds.[19]

Individuals and corporate entities are continuously bombarding the public with fraudulent activities. Fraud has become so rampant that it has led to a decline of trust in corporate leadership.

Medicare and Medicaid Fraud

The jury in *United States v. Raithatha*[20] convicted the defendant for making false statements and scheming to defraud. The defendant, sentenced to 27 months of imprisonment, appealed his conviction and sentence.

The indictment filed against the defendant included charges for instructing billing staff to raise the *Current Procedural Terminology* (CPT) code on invoices when the physician actually provided a lower cost service; submitting invoices to insurance companies for services performed by other physicians, as if the defendant had performed them; submitting claims with a diagnosis listing an illness, when the patient did not have an illness; and causing patients to present themselves for medically unnecessary visits by refusing to authorize refills on prescriptions.

Charges also included making unannounced home visits to patients; approaching people on the street and ushering them into the clinic for unscheduled examinations; examining people who had come into the clinic for nonmedical reasons, such as to pay debts owed to the defendant; ordering medical tests not related to patients' conditions; falsely representing that other physician employees had specialties so that patients would be examined an additional time by a specialist; and refusing to provide test results until a follow-up appointment was scheduled and kept.

The defendant also was charged with defrauding Medicare/Medicaid by submitting a cost report for 1997 that included personal expenses unrelated to patient care (e.g., money that was actually spent to furnish and complete the defendant's home).

The defendant, on appeal, argued that there was insufficient evidence to sustain his conviction for defrauding or attempting to defraud. The defendant's staff members testified that the defendant instructed them to bill office visits covered by private insurance under CPT codes 99213 or 99203, regardless of the CPT code entered by the attending physician on the encounter form. Staff members were aware of the "up-coding" scheme, which resulted in higher reimbursement for the physician.

In addition, staff members testified that the defendant routinely ordered tests unrelated to his patients' conditions and supported the tests with false diagnoses. Zeren, a nurse practitioner working at the McKee Clinic, testified that after she performed sports physicals on children at local schools and found no indication of upper respiratory infections, the defendant, who had not been present at the examinations, falsely diagnosed them as having upper respiratory infections. A reasonable juror could have reasonably found the defendant physician guilty of defrauding or attempting to defraud Medicare/Medicaid. The conviction and sentence of the district court was affirmed.

False Medicaid Claims

In *United States v. Larm*,[21] a physician and his office manager were convicted on charges that they violated 42 U.S.C. § 139h(a)1 by submitting false Medicaid claims for medical services they never rendered to patients. Claims sometimes were submitted even when patients administered allergy injections themselves. In addition, more expensive serums were billed instead of the less expensive serums that were actually administered.

Home Care Fraud

Today, more Americans are living longer than ever before. As medicine has advanced, the average life expectancy has increased by 50%. There is an ever-increasing number of seniors receiving in-home care who are dependent on family and healthcare providers to attend to their physical, financial, emotional, and healthcare needs. Medicare home health benefits allow individuals with restricted mobility to remain at home, instead of in an institutional setting, by providing home care benefits. Home care services and supplies are generally provided by nurses, home nursing aides, speech therapists, and physical therapists under a physician-certified plan of care.

Home care is rapidly being recognized as a breeding ground for abuse. The numerous scams in home care fraud are caused by the difficulty in supervising services provided in the home, Medicare's failure to monitor the number of visits per patient, beneficiaries paying no co-payments except for medical equipment, and the lack of accountability to the patient by failing to explain services provided.

Home care fraud generally is not easy to detect. It involves charging insurers for more services than patients received, billing for more hours of care than were provided, falsifying records, and charging higher nurses' rates for care given by aides. The trend toward shorter hospital stays has created a multibillion-dollar market in home care services. This new market is providing opportunities for fraud.

Fraudulent Billing for Laboratory Tests

The *Court of Appeals of Georgia in Culver v. State*[22] found that a reasonable fact finder could conclude that the physician (Kell) maintained control over the laboratory and its Medicaid billings and received significant payments from the laboratory. The trier of fact (jury or judge as chosen by the defendant) also could find that although Medicaid paid the laboratory approximately $200 for each urine test conducted, the laboratory routinely charged self-pay patients $19.20 for what the laboratory employees described as the same test. Regulations prohibit providers from billing Medicaid for an amount greater than the lowest price routinely offered to the general public for the same service or item on the same date of service.

Physician Bills for Services Not Rendered

A physician in *State v. Cargille*[23] was found to have submitted false information for the purpose of obtaining greater compensation than was otherwise permitted under the Medicaid program. Sufficient evidence was presented to sustain a conviction of Medicaid fraud. The physician argued that he felt justified for multiple billings for single office visits because of the actual amount of time that he saw a patient. He believed that his method of reimbursement was more equitable than Medicaid. The court disagreed with the physician's reasoning.

Pharmacist Submits False Drug Claims

The pharmacist in *State v. Heath*[24] submitted claims for reimbursement on brand-name medications rather than on the less expensive generic drugs that were actually dispensed. A licensed pharmacist and former employee of the defendant contacted the Medicaid Fraud Unit of the Louisiana Attorney General's office and reported the defendant's conduct in substituting generic drugs for brand-name drugs. As a result of the complaint, the Medicaid Fraud Unit conducted a call out, in which the unit sent letters to Medicaid recipients in the pharmacy's surrounding area:

> In a recipient call out, the Medicaid Fraud Unit sends letters to Medicaid recipients in the general area of the pharmacy involved and asks them to bring all their prescription drugs to the welfare office on a specific date. The call out revealed that some of the prescription vials issued by the aforesaid pharmacies contained generic drugs while the labels indicated that they should contain brand-name drugs.[25]

The pharmacist eventually was convicted on three counts of Medicaid fraud.

Inaccurate Records and Controlled Drugs

The operator of a pharmacy, in a disciplinary proceeding before the California Board of Pharmacy, was found negligent because of inaccurate record keeping.[26] The pharmacist failed to keep accurate records of dangerous drugs, report thefts by employees, and report a burglary of pharmacy drugs. Such reporting is required by state statute.

Nursing Facility Stockholder Falsifies Records

The principal stockholder of a nursing home corporation in *Chapman v. United States, Department of Health and Human Services*[27] was convicted of making 19 false line-item cost entries in reports to the Kansas Medicaid agency. The record shows that Chapman acted deliberately to submit false data to the Kansas Medicaid agency so that nursing homes owned by him would be reimbursed for goods and services they did not provide. When an audit was scheduled that threatened to reveal the false claims, Chapman prepared false invoices and had checks issued, but not signed, in an effort to cover up the discrepancies that the state audit would reveal.[28]

The U.S. Court of Appeals found that the DHHS did not act unreasonably when it imposed a $2,000 penalty for each of the false Medicaid claims and proposed an additional settlement of $118,136 even though the state already had recovered the $21,115 in excessive reimbursement by setoff. The court concluded, "The penalty reflects a fair amount of leniency on the part of the Inspector General and the Administrative Law Judge (ALJ)."[29]

Inflating Insurance Claims

The North Carolina Court of Appeals held that a chiropractor's license was properly suspended for 6 months in *Farlow v. North Carolina State Board of Chiropractic Examiners*[30] for inflating the insurance claims of victims of an automobile accident. Dr. Farlow prescribed a course of treatment for several patients that was not justified by the injuries they received. Instead, the treatment was prescribed to inflate insurance claims.

Fraudulent Billing

The physician in *Richstone v. Novello*[31] was found to have willfully filed false reports, practiced with negligence on more than one occasion, practiced fraudulently, failed to maintain adequate records, and performed unnecessary medical tests and treatments. The physician was found to be morally unfit to practice medicine as well as unsuitable for retraining or probation. A hearing committee of the state decided to revoke the physician's license. The physician challenged the committee's actions.

Given evidence that the physician was found to have engaged in fraudulent billing, attempted to coerce a patient into dropping her complaint with the department of health, denied patients timely access to their records, performed substandard follow-up procedures, ordered excessive and medically unnecessary tests on patients, and falsified his application for reappointment to the hospital's medical staff, the Supreme Court, Appellate Division declined to disturb the hearing committee's decision to revoke the physician's license.

Abuse in Prescribing Controlled Substances

Evidence was sufficient in *United States v. Merrill*[32] to support a doctor's convictions for deaths resulting from healthcare fraud and the use of narcotics prescribed outside the course of professional practice in violation of the controlled substance act, where the record indicated that the doctor had written more than 33,000 prescriptions for controlled substances during the 3.5 years prior to his arrest. Furthermore, even if the patients who died had other substances in their systems, such as alcohol or illicit drugs, the medical examiner, who performed the autopsies on each of the patients, testified that the drugs of the same type as prescribed by the defendant were the cause of death.

Fraud and Ethics

Behind every act of healthcare fraud lies a lapse in ethics. One particular type of fraud occurs when physicians refer their patients to hospitals and ancillary healthcare providers when the physician has a financial interest in the provider to which the patient has been referred. The ethical risks inherent in physician self-referral were first noted in a 1986 Institute of Medicine study and again in a 1989 HHS Inspector General study. The 1989 study concluded that physicians who owned or invested in independent clinical laboratories referred Medicare patients for 45% more laboratory services than did physicians without financial interests. It was in 1989 that the Ethics and Patient Referrals Act was enacted, prohibiting unethical referrals, which were further defined in 1991 when

the American Medical Association (AMA) Council on Ethical and Judicial Affairs concluded that physicians should not refer patients to a healthcare facility in which they have a financial interest and do not directly provide services. In the following year, the AMA House of Delegates voted to declare self-referral unethical in most instances.

The Omnibus Budget Reconciliation Act of 1989 (effective January 1, 1992) backed the AMA's position on self-referral, barring the referral of Medicare patients to clinical laboratories by physicians who have, or whose family members have, a financial interest. The scope of the ban on self-referral was expanded with the enactment of the Omnibus Reconciliation Act of 1993 (effective January 1, 1995), which added 10 additional designated health services: physical therapy; occupational therapy; radiology services; radiation therapy services and supplies; durable medical equipment and supplies; parenteral and enteral nutrients, equipment, and supplies; orthotics, prosthetics, and prosthetic devices and supplies; home health services; outpatient prescription drugs; and inpatient and outpatient hospital services. The 1993 law also expanded and clarified exceptions and applied the referral limits to Medicaid.

Anti-kickback laws require proof of "knowing" and "willful" illegal remuneration (i.e., bribes or rebates) for patient referrals. Such conduct is illegal and can result in criminal sanctions. If an improper financial relationship exists, a loss of Medicare payment or a civil fine may serve as punishment. Because of the law's preventive nature, it has been highly effective in protecting the Medicare and Medicaid programs' integrity by motivating healthcare professionals to proactively comply with the law and to avoid financial arrangements that may unethically lead to substantial increases in use of service.

Unethical Pay to Referring Physicians

In *United States v. Greber*,[33] an osteopathic physician violated the Omnibus Budget Reconciliation Act when he unethically paid referring physicians after rendering services. The defendant, board certified in cardiology, was president of Cardio-Med, Inc., an organization that he founded. The company provided physicians with diagnostic services, one of which was Holter monitoring, a method of recording a patient's cardiac activity on tape, generally for a period of 24 hours. Cardio-Med billed Medicare for the monitoring service and, when payment was received, forwarded a portion to the referring physician. The government charged that the referral fee exceeded that permitted by Medicare and that there was evidence the physician received interpretation fees even though the defendant actually evaluated the monitoring data. After a trial by jury, the physician was convicted on 20 of 23 counts in an indictment charging mail fraud, Medicare fraud, and false statements. On appeal, the physician contended that the evidence was insufficient to support the guilty verdict. The court of appeals held that to the extent that payments made to the physician were made to induce referrals by that physician of Medicare patients to use payer laboratory services, Medicare fraud was established.

Physicians Victims of Fraud

Physicians are not immune from being the victims of fraud. The detection, investigation, and prosecution of financial crimes against physicians are not uncommon occurrences. They involve such areas as computer billing crime, bookkeeper/office manager theft, insurance fraud, cash larceny, checkbook scams, and patient record tampering.

Physicians should be aware of how to analyze larcenous transactions, identify embezzled funds, and recognize the criminal employee. Physicians should be wary of bookkeepers who make themselves appear indispensable because of their perceived ability to operate the office computer system. To avoid being victimized by employee fraud, physicians should do the following:

- Familiarize themselves with patient billing and recordkeeping practices.
- Avoid having one individual in charge of billing and collection procedures.
- Arrange for an annual audit of office procedures and records by an outside auditor.

▶ KICKBACKS

The Medicare and Medicaid Patient Protection Act of 1987, as amended (42 U.S.C. §1320a-7b; the "Anti-Kickback Statute"), provides for criminal penalties for certain acts impacting Medicare and state healthcare (e.g., Medicaid) reimbursable services. The Anti-Kickback Statute, as amended, prohibits certain solicitations or receipt of remuneration. The statute penalizes anyone who knowingly and willfully solicits, receives, offers, or pays anything of value as an inducement for referring an individual to a person for the furnishing or arranging for the furnishing of any item or service payable under the Medicare or Medicaid programs; and purchasing, leasing, or ordering or arranging for or recommending purchasing, leasing,

or ordering any good, facility, service, or item payable under the Medicare or Medicaid programs.

The OIG investigates violations of the Medicare and Medicaid Anti-Kickback Statute. Violators are subject to criminal penalties or exclusion from participation in the Medicare and Medicaid programs. The OIG specifically targets four billing practices: claims for services not provided, claims for beneficiaries not homebound, claims for visits not made, and claims for visits not authorized by a physician.

Laboratory Kickback

In the case of *United States v. Kats*,[34] the owner of Tech Diagnostic Medical Lab (Tech-Lab) agreed to kick back 50% of the Medicare payments received by Tech-Lab as a consequence of referrals from Total Health Care, a medical service company. Under the scheme, Total Health Care collected blood and urine samples from medical offices and clinics in southern California and sent them to Tech-Lab for testing. Tech-Lab billed Total Health Care, which in turn billed the private insurance carrier or the government-funded insurance programs Medi-Cal and Medicare for reimbursement. Tech-Lab then kicked back half of its receipts to Total Health Care. The owners of Tech-Lab and Total Health Care arranged an identical scheme with a community medical clinic; Kats, the appellant, subsequently purchased a 25% interest in the clinic and began collecting payments under the scheme. Kats was convicted of conspiracy to commit Medicare fraud and of receipt of kickbacks in exchange for referral of Medicare patients. He appealed the decision. The court of appeals, however, affirmed the charges against him.

Architectural Contract Kickback

In *United States v. Thompson*,[35] a jury convicted three members of a county council, which served as the governing body of a county hospital, for soliciting and receiving $6,000 in kickbacks from architects. The architects testified that the appellants and others sought a 1% kickback on a hospital project, financed by federal funds, in return for being awarded the architectural contract. Mr. Galloway, of the architectural firm of Galloway and Guthrey, delivered $6,000 to appellant Campbell at the Knoxville airport. The architects had informed the FBI, and an investigation was conducted. After the investigation, indictments, and trial by jury, the defendants were each sentenced to 1 year in prison. On appeal, the U.S. Court of Appeals for the Sixth Circuit held that the receipt of a kickback constituted an overt act in furtherance of a conspiracy to obstruct lawful government function and was a violation of the general conspiracy statute and a crime against the United States. It had been previously observed that "[t]o conspire to defraud the United States means primarily to cheat the government out of property or money, but it also means to interfere with or obstruct one of its lawful governmental functions by deceit, craft or trickery, or at least by means that are dishonest."[36] Proof that part of the architects' fee was reimbursed with federal funds was not necessary for a conviction. The criminal convictions were affirmed.

Ambulance Service Kickback

In *United States v. Bay State Ambulance and Hospital Rental Services*,[37] a city official was convicted in a federal district court for conspiring to commit Medicare fraud along with other defendants who were also convicted of making illegal payments. Bay State Ambulance and Hospital Rental Services, a privately owned ambulance company, gave cash and two automobiles to an official of a city-owned hospital. The gifts were given as an inducement to the city official for his recommendation that Bay State be awarded the Quincy City Hospital ambulance service contract, for which Bay State received some Medicare funds as reimbursement. The defendants appealed, and the U.S. Court of Appeals for the First Circuit held that the evidence was sufficient to sustain a conviction.

▶ TAMPERING WITH DRUGS

In *United States v. Milstein*,[39] the government established at trial that the defendant and others purchased Eldepryl, a medication used to treat Parkinson's

---

⬤NEWS *THE TOXIC PHARMACIST*

. . . Robert Courtney would, by law enforcement estimates, dilute 98,000 prescriptions for 4,200 patients. The sheer voraciousness of his dilutions suggests the compulsion of a pathological shoplifter. At times, Courtney diluted conservatively; at others, he reduced medications to trace amounts, seemingly taunting their recipients: Feel anything now? Though Courtney's highest profits came from diluting expensive chemotherapy medication—a plaintiff's lawyer says he pocketed as much as $50,000 in the treatments for a single cancer patient—Courtney adulterated a total of 72 different drugs, including fertility drugs, antibiotics, drugs to prevent nausea, and others to improve blood clotting.

—Robert Draper, "The Toxic Pharmacist," *The New York Times*, June 8, 2003[38]

---

disease, and the fertility drugs Pergonal and Metrodin, which were produced for distribution outside the United States; stripped them of their original factory packaging; and repackaged them with forged labels and packaging materials closely resembling those of drugs produced in accordance with Food and Drug Administration (FDA) requirements for the U.S. market. They then fraudulently sold the drugs in the United States to doctors, pharmacists, and pharmaceutical wholesalers. The conviction for distributing the misbranded drugs in interstate commerce with fraudulent intent was appropriate.

In another case, the chief medical officer of the Nebraska Department of Health and Human Services Regulation and Licensure entered an order revoking Poor's license to practice as a chiropractor in the state of Nebraska.[40] Poor engaged in a conspiracy to manufacture and distribute a misbranded substance, and he introduced into interstate commerce misbranded and adulterated drugs with the intent to defraud and mislead. He was arrested for driving under the influence and was convicted of that offense. In addition, Poor knowingly possessed cocaine. He conceded that these factual determinations were understood as beyond dispute.

Both the district and appellate courts found that Poor's conduct was clearly immoral. The appellate court stated that Poor's denial now, after taking advantage of a plea bargain, that he committed any of the acts he admitted to in the U.S. District Court is disturbing and is not consistent with the integrity expected by persons engaged in a professional occupation.

The Supreme Court of Nebraska, as a result of the seriousness of Poor's felony conviction and its underlying conduct, his subsequent lack of candor with respect to that conduct, and his lack of sound judgment demonstrated by his driving under the influence conviction, concluded that revocation of Poor's license was an appropriate sanction.

▶ INTERNET PHARMACY AND SALE OF DRUGS

The use of Internet pharmacies has been on the rise due to the high cost of drugs. Not only are patients purchasing bogus medications, but they also are obtaining questionable prescriptions from physicians through the Internet, as noted in *United States v. Nelson*,[41] where Fuchs operated an Internet pharmacy called NationPharmacy.com. Customers would obtain prescription and nonprescription drugs from the Internet pharmacy. In accord with federal law, all requests for prescription drugs must be reviewed by a physician. Dr. Nelson, the defendant in this case, agreed to review the prescriptions, approving 90 to 95% of prescription requests without examining his purported patients. Customers who used Fuchs's Internet pharmacy would have their orders routed through a brick-and-mortar pharmacy called Main Street Pharmacy. Dr. Nelson would physically visit Main Street Pharmacy to sign the prescription requests, and customers would receive prescriptions by mail and pay Fuchs directly.

Dr. Nelson was charged and convicted of both conspiracy to distribute controlled prescription drugs outside the usual course of professional practice, in violation of 21 U.S.C. § 846, and conspiracy to launder money, in violation of 18 U.S.C. § 1956(h). Dr. Nelson appealed his conviction, arguing that there was insufficient evidence to support a conviction because there was no evidence of a conspiracy. On appeal, the court determined that a reasonable jury could infer the existence of an agreement constituting a conspiracy to distribute prescription drugs outside the usual course of professional practice and to launder the proceeds of that distribution.

Federal law 21 U.S.C. § 841(a) makes it illegal for any person knowingly or intentionally:

1.   to manufacture, distribute, or dispense, or possess with intent to manufacture, distribute, or dispense, a controlled substance; or
2.   to create, distribute, or dispense, or possess with intent to distribute or dispense, a counterfeit substance.

(NEWS) MOST ONLINE PHARMACIES ARE FRAUDS, FDA WARNS

The FDA is warning consumers that almost all Internet pharmacies are fraudulent and probably are selling counterfeit drugs that could harm them.

• • •

Instead, they're getting fake drugs that are contaminated, are past their expiration date or contain no active ingredient, the wrong amount of active ingredient or even toxic substances. These drugs could sicken people, cause them to develop a resistance to their real medicine, cause no side effects or trigger harmful interactions with other medications.

—Associated Press, *The Washington Post*, October 2, 2012

(NEWS) RENEWED CRITICISM FOR GOOGLE OVER DRUG SITES

Several state attorneys general are pressing Google to make it harder for its users to find counterfeit prescription medicine and illegal drugs online, marking the second time in the past 3 years that the firm has drawn government scrutiny for its policies on rogue Internet pharmacies.

• • •

Google, which failed to persuade a California judge to dismiss the suits, entered settlement talks last month after attorneys for the shareholders obtained e-mails showing that top executives warned then-chief executive Eric Schmidt and co-founder Larry Page more than a decade ago about the risks of accepting such ads.

—Matea Golf and Tom Hamburger, *The Washington Post*, April 16, 2014

Dr. Richard Ruth, a 78-year-old physician, was sentenced to 15 to 30 years in prison, and his son Michael was sentenced 7 to 22 years in prison, for running what has been termed a "pill mill" involving the illegal distribution of tens of thousands of prescription drugs to, for example, drug addicts. The County Court Judge in this case "expressed bafflement at the Ruths' lack of remorse or acceptance of responsibility." "Your claims of victimization defy common sense," the judge said to Michael Ruth, 46.[42]

The illegal sale of drugs on the Internet continues to grow as unsuspecting patients search for cheaper drugs. Internet pharmacy is a risky business, as noted in the following *news report* and the case that follows.

Although Google reached a settlement to pay $500 million to avoid prosecution for aiding illegal online pharmaceutical ads, some state prosecutors want to see more from Google in preventing ads from unlicensed pharmacies. "Google acknowledged in the settlement that it had improperly and knowingly assisted online pharmacy advertisers allegedly based in Canada to run advertisements for illicit pharmacy sales targeting U.S. customers."[43]

Where greed is involved and money the reward, criminals believe the risks taken are worth the monetary reward gained, as is noted by how common Internet crimes have become. The various schemes to sell both tainted and illegal drugs on the Internet are becoming more creative.

Healthcare providers convicted of illegally selling prescription drugs face not only criminal penalties but the loss of their licenses to practice medicine, as was the case in *Brown v. Idaho State Board of Pharmacy*,[44] where the Idaho State Board of Health suspended the license of a pharmacist who admitted to using marijuana approximately twice a week. During a hearing by the Board, the hearing officer admitted into evidence a copy of a judgment of a conviction on Brown's plea of guilty to a criminal charge of possession of drug paraphernalia. The Idaho State Board of Pharmacy suspended Brown's license. On appeal, the Idaho Court of Appeals held that revocation of his license was supported by evidence that he engaged in the illegal use of marijuana and that he also had participated in the sale and delivery of a misbranded drug.

It is important to note that not only is the physician at risk for writing illegal prescriptions, but the pharmacist is at risk as well if he or she knowingly fills such prescriptions.

▶ FALSIFICATION OF RECORDS

As with healthcare fraud, falsification of medical and business records is grounds for criminal prosecution. Anyone who suffers damage as a result of falsification of records may claim civil liability, which could result in the provider's loss of Medicare and Medicaid funding.

False Entries in Operative Report

When a surgeon omitted a true entry in his operative report by not indicating that a nonphysician assisted in a patient's surgery, the surgeon was indicted for falsification of records. Two of the defendants, orthopedic surgeons Dr. Lipton and Dr. Massoff, in *People v.*

NEWS VA TREATMENT RECORDS FALSIFIED, PROBE FINDS

A VA investigation of one of its outpatient clinics in Colorado reveals how ingrained delays in medical care may be for an agency struggling to rapidly treat nearly 9 million veterans a year amid allegations that dozens have died because of delays.

Clerks at the Department of Veterans Affairs clinic in Fort Collins were instructed last year how to falsify appointment records so it appeared the small staff of doctors was seeing patients within the agency's goal of 14 days, according to the investigation.

—Gregg Zoroya, *USA Today*, May 4, 2014[45]

Smithtown General Hospital,[46] on the morning of July 3, 1975, performed an orthopedic procedure on a patient. The prosthesis used during surgery was supplied by a general sales manager, Mr. MacKay, who was present in the operating room during most of the operation, which began at 8:00 AM and ended at 11:30 AM. After completion of the operation, an X-ray of the patient revealed that the "head of the femur popped out of the acetabulum."[47] At the request of Lipton, the salesman was located at a golf course and asked to return to the hospital. On arriving back in the operating room, he found Massoff reopening the surgical site. Massoff attempted to remove the prosthesis. MacKay offered his assistance and successfully removed the prosthesis. Massoff then returned to his office. With the consent of Lipton, MacKay removed the cement from the bone shaft and reinserted the prosthesis. An indictment charged Lipton with the intent to defraud and to conceal the crimes of unauthorized practice of medicine and assault. A similar indictment was returned against a supervising nurse and the hospital for failure to make a true entry in the operating room register.

A motion to dismiss the indictments against the physicians and nurse charged with falsifying business records in the first degree was denied. A motion to dismiss the indictments for assault in the second degree was granted.

▶ PATIENT ABUSE

Patient abuse is the mistreatment or neglect of individuals who are under the care of a healthcare organization. Abuse is not limited to an institutional setting and may occur in an individual's home. Abuse can take many forms: physical, psychological, medical, and financial. To compound the issue, abuse is not always easy to identify because injuries often can be attributed to other causes, especially in elderly patients with their advanced age and failing health. In the hospital setting, patients are not generally as dependent on the facility operator in the same manner as a resident in a nursing facility. Patients are usually hospitalized only for brief time periods, whereas nursing facility residents may be dependent on the facility operator for years. Thus the potential for long-term abuse and neglect is far greater for nursing facility residents than hospital patients.

Unfortunately, the abuse of the elderly is not a localized or isolated problem; it permeates society. *Behind Closed Doors*, a landmark book on family violence, stated that the first national study of violence in American homes estimated that one in two homes is the scene of family violence at least once a year.[48]

We have always known that America is a violent society. . . . What is new and surprising is that the American family and the American home are perhaps as much or more violent than any other single institution or setting (with the exception of the military, and only then in the time of war). Americans run the greatest risk of assault, physical injury and even murder in their own homes by members of their own families.[49]

It is difficult to determine the extent of elder abuse because the abused elderly are reluctant to admit that their children or loved ones have assaulted them. According to a 2005 fact sheet by the National Center on Elder Abuse, "between 1 and 2 million Americans age 65 years or older have been injured, exploited, or otherwise mistreated by someone on whom they depended for care and protection."[50]

The plaintiffs in *In re Estate of Smith v. O'Halloran*[51] instituted a lawsuit in an effort to improve deplorable conditions at many nursing homes. The court concluded that:

The evidentiary record . . . supports a general finding that all is not well in the nation's nursing homes and that the enormous expenditures of public funds and the earnest efforts of public officials and public employees have not produced an equivalent return in benefits. That failure of expectations has produced frustration and anger among those who are aware of the realities of life in some nursing homes, which provide so little service that they could be characterized as orphanages for the aged.[52]

Abuse of nursing facility residents gave impetus to the strengthening of resident rights under the Omnibus Budget Reconciliation Act of 1989. The Act provides that a "resident has the right to be free from verbal, sexual, physical, or mental abuse, corporal punishment, and involuntary seclusion."[53] Although resident rights have been significantly strengthened, resident abuse is often in the headlines. For example, the headline, "Nurse's Aide Jailed for Punching Patient," topped a story about a nurse's aide who was jailed for punching a 91-year-old senile man in the nose.[54] The aide had been previously convicted of resident abuse.

Questions to ask in order to determine whether patients are being abused:

- Are physician time-limited orders for restraints documented in each patient's medical record?
- Are there an unusual number of patients who are physically restrained?
- Which restraints are commonly being used (e.g., physical, medication)?
- Are physical restraints applied correctly?
- What is the apparent physical and mental condition of restrained patients?
- Are physical restraints periodically released as required by law?
- Are patients able to move about and exercise, with assistance as necessary?
- Do staff members respond to requests for water and assist patients to the bathroom on a timely basis?
- How often are observations of restrained patients documented?
- Do patients show signs of overmedication?
- Are there signs of mental and physical abuse?
- Are there signs of harassment, humiliation, or threats from staff or patients?
- Are patients comfortable with staff?
- Do patients show skin breakdown due to bruises or other causes (e.g., failure to turn patients in bed)?
- Is there evidence of patient neglect (e.g., patients left in urine or feces without cleaning)?

Abusive Search

A nurse in *People v. Coe*[55] was charged with a willful violation of the public health law in connection with an allegedly abusive search of an 86-year-old resident at a geriatric center and with the falsification of business records in the first degree. The resident, Mr. Gersh, had heart disease and difficulty in expressing himself verbally. Another resident claimed that two $5 bills were missing. Nurse Coe assumed that Gersh had taken them because he had been known to take things in the past. The nurse proceeded to search Gersh, who resisted. A security guard was summoned, and another search was undertaken. When Gersh again resisted, the security guard slammed a chair down in front of him and pinned his arms while the defendant nurse searched his pockets, failing to retrieve the two $5 bills. Five minutes later, Gersh collapsed in a chair, gasping for air. Coe administered cardiopulmonary resuscitation but was unsuccessful, and Gersh died.

Coe was charged with violation of Section 175.10 of the New York Penal Law for falsifying records, because of the defendant's "omission" of the facts relating to the search of Gersh. These facts were considered relevant and should have been included in the nurse's notes regarding this incident. "The first sentence states, 'Observed resident was extremely confused and talks incoherently. Suddenly became unresponsive....' This statement is simply false. It could only be true if some reference to the search and the loud noise was included."[56] A motion was made to dismiss the indictment at the end of the trial.

The court held that the search became an act of physical abuse and mistreatment, the evidence was sufficient to warrant a finding of guilt on both charges, and the fact that searches took place frequently did not excuse an otherwise illegal procedure.

It may well be that this incident reached the attention of the criminal justice system only because, in the end, a man had died. In those instances that are equally volatile of residents' rights and equally contrary to standards of common decency but which do not result in visible harm to a patient, the acts are nevertheless illegal and subject to prosecution. A criminal act is not legitimized by the fact that others have, with impunity, engaged in that act.[57]

Repeated Instances of Physical Abuse

The revocation of a personal care home license was found to be proper in *Miller Home, Inc. v. Commonwealth, Department of Public Welfare*[58] because of repeated medication violations and resident abuse. Evidence was presented that the son of the personal care home's manager was hired as a staff member after having acted as a substitute, even though he had physical altercations with residents of the home. On one occasion, the manager's son punched a female resident, resulting in her hospitalization for broken bones around the eye, and on two prior occasions, he had been involved in less physical altercations that required police intervention.

A nursing facility orderly challenged a determination by the commissioner of the State Department of Health finding him guilty of resident abuse in *Reid v. Axelrod*.[59] The orderly maintained that the resident struck him with his cane and that he merely pushed the cane away to avoid being struck a second time. A co-employee testified that the orderly struck the resident in the chest after being hit with the cane. The court held that the determination was supported by substantial evidence and that the 3-year delay in conducting the hearing did not warrant dismissal of the petition charging the orderly with resident abuse. Public policy requires that residents must be protected from abusive healthcare workers.

The nursing facility resident in *Stiffelman v. Abrams*[60] died as a result of the following abuse:

". . . blows, kicks, kneeings, or bodily throwings intentionally, viciously, and murderously dealt him from among the facility's staff over a period of approximately two to three weeks prior to his death"; that the "beatings were repeated and were received by the decedent at ninety years of age and in a frail, defenseless, and dependent condition"; that the beatings so administered to the decedent were "physically and mentally tortuous"; that he was caused by them to live out his final days in agony and terror; and that his physical injuries included thirteen fractures to his ribs, subpleural hemorrhaging, and marked lesions to his chest, flanks, abdomen, legs, arms, and hands; that during and following the period of the beatings the decedent lay at the facility for days unattended and unaided as to the deterioration and grave suffering he was undergoing.[61]

The executors of the estate had brought suit against the operator and individual and corporate owners of the facility for damages for personal injuries resulting in the death of the resident. The executors were requesting, under Count I, $1.5 million in survival damages because of the physical and mental pain and suffering of the decedent, as well as $3 million for punitive damages, and under Count II, $1,504,084 in contractual breaches of the resident's admission contract with the facility. The executors claimed that certain standards of care and personal rights contained in the contract were violated. The trial court sustained the nursing facility's motion for dismissal of the case on the grounds that the plaintiffs failed to state a claim on which relief could be granted. On appeal, the judgment of the trial court was reversed with respect to Count I, and the dismissal of Count II was sustained. The case was remanded, requiring the executors to proceed under appropriate statutory authority and not under contract.

Forcible Administration of Medications

The medical employee in *In re Axelrod*[62] sought review of a determination by the commissioner of health that she was guilty of resident abuse. Evidence showed that the employee, after a resident refused medication, "held the patient's chin and poured the medication down her throat."[63] There was no indication or convincing evidence that an emergency existed that would have required the forced administration of the medication. The court held that substantial evidence supported the commissioner's finding that the employee had been guilty of resident abuse.

> Upon our review of the record, we conclude that the Commissioner's determination that the petitioner had been guilty of patient abuse was supported by substantial evidence. The record supports the respondent's findings that the petitioner forcibly administered medication to the patient; that there was no order directing the petitioner to administer the medication forcibly; and that there was no convincing evidence that the patient's refusal to take the medication constituted a medical emergency justifying the forcible administration of medication.[64]

Abuse and Revocation of License

The operator of a nursing facility appealed an order by the department of public welfare revoking his license because of resident abuse in *Nepa v. Commonwealth Department of Public Welfare*.[65] Substantial evidence supported the department's finding. Three former employees testified that the nursing facility operator had abused residents in the following incidents: he unbuckled the belt of one of the residents, causing his pants to drop, and then grabbed a second resident, forcing the two to kiss (petitioner's excuse for this behavior was to shame the resident because of his masturbating in public); on two occasions, he forced a resident to remove toilet paper from a commode after she had urinated and defecated in it (denying that there was fecal matter in the commode, petitioner's excuse was that this was his way of trying to stop the resident from filling the commode with toilet paper); and he verbally abused a resident who was experiencing difficulty in breathing and accused him of being a fake as he attempted to feed him liquids.[66]

The nursing facility operator claimed that the findings of fact were not based on substantial evidence and that, even if they were, the incidents did not amount to abuse under the code. The defendant attempted to discredit the witnesses with allegations

🔍 *ABUSE OF STROKE PATIENT*

Citation: *State v. Houle*, 642 A.2d 1178 (Vt. 1994)

Facts

The defendant, a licensed practical nurse (LPN), had criminal charges brought against her stemming from her treatment of a stroke patient. It was alleged that she had slapped the patient's legs repeatedly and shackled him to his bed at the wrists and ankles. By the time of trial, the patient had died of causes unrelated to the charged conduct. During the trial, the state presented testimony of eyewitnesses, including the patient's wife, hospital employees, and an investigator from the office of the attorney general. The defendant did not deny that she had restrained the patient, but claimed that her actions were necessary for the patient's protection, as well as her own, and that her actions were neither assaultive nor cruel. The defendant claimed that the trial court improperly admitted evidence that the patient submitted.

Issue

Was the evidence that the patient submitted admissible in prosecution of the defendant?

Holding

The Vermont Supreme Court held that the evidence that the patient gave was relevant and admissible.

Reason

The patient's awareness of what happened to him was relevant to the state's case because the trial court, in its instruction to the jury, defined cruelty as "intentional and malicious infliction of physical or emotional pain or suffering upon a person." By showing that the patient was aware of what had happened to him, the state allowed the jury to infer that he had suffered physical or emotional pain. The state presented a witness who was present when the incident occurred and who was able to describe the acts of abuse in detail. The credibility of this eyewitness testimony, and not what the patient's testimony would have been, was the focus of the trial.

from a resident and another employee that one of his former employees got into bed with a resident and that another had taken a picture of a male resident while in the shower and had placed a baby bottle and a humiliating sign around the neck of another resident. The court was not impressed. Although these incidents, if true, were reprehensible, they were collateral matters that had no bearing on the witnesses' reputation for truthfulness and therefore could not be used for impeachment purposes. The court held that there was substantial evidence supporting the department's decision and that the activities committed by the operator were sufficient to support revocation of his license.

> We believe Petitioner's treatment of these residents as found by the hearing examiner to be truly disturbing. These residents were elderly and/or mentally incapacitated and wholly dependent on Petitioner while residing in his home. As residents, they are entitled to maintain their dignity and be cared for with respect, concern, and compassion.
>
> Petitioner testified that he did not have adequate training to deal with the patients he received who suffered from mental problems. Petitioner's lack of training in this area is absolutely no excuse for the reprehensible manner in which he treated various residents. Accordingly, DPW's order revoking Petitioner's license to operate a personal care home is affirmed.[67]

▶ CRIMINAL NEGLIGENCE

Criminal negligence is the reckless disregard for the safety of others and the willful indifference to an injury that could follow an act. The neglect of elderly residents was noted in the *State v. Cunningham*,[68] where the defendant was the owner and administrator of a residential care facility that housed 30 to 37 mentally ill, mentally retarded, and elderly residents. The Iowa Department of Inspections and Appeals conducted routine inspections of the defendant's facility between October 1989 and May 1990. All of the surveys except for one resulted in a $50 daily fine assessed against the defendant for violations of the regulations. On August 16, 1990, a grand jury filed an indictment charging the defendant with several counts of wanton neglect of a resident in violation of Iowa Code section 726.7 (1989), which provides: "A person commits *wanton neglect* of a resident of a health care facility when the

person knowingly acts in a manner likely to be injurious to the physical, mental, or moral welfare of a resident of a health care facility. . . . Wanton neglect of a resident of a health care facility is a serious misdemeanor."

The district court held that the defendant had knowledge of the dangerous conditions that existed in the healthcare facility but willfully and consciously refused to provide or exercise adequate supervision to remedy or attempt to remedy the dangerous conditions. The residents were exposed to physical dangers and unhealthy and unsanitary physical conditions and were grossly deprived of much needed medical care and personal attention.

The district court sentenced the defendant to 1 year in jail for each of the five counts, to run concurrently. The district court suspended all but 2 days of the defendant's sentence and ordered him to pay $200 for each count, plus a surcharge and costs, and to perform community service. A motion for a new trial was denied, and the defendant appealed.

The Iowa Court of Appeals held that there was substantial evidence to support a finding that the defendant was responsible for not properly maintaining the nursing facility, which led to prosecution for wanton neglect of the facility's residents. *Substantial evidence* means evidence that would convince a rational fact finder that the defendant was guilty beyond a reasonable doubt. The defendant was found guilty of knowingly acting in a manner likely to be injurious to the physical or mental welfare of the facility's residents by creating, directing, or maintaining the following five hazardous conditions and unsafe practices:

1. There were fire hazards and circumstances that impeded safety from fire. For example, cigarette stubs were found in a cardboard box, and burn holes were found in patient clothing, on furniture, and in nonsmoking areas. Also, exposed electrical wiring was found, along with a bent and rusted fire door that could not close or latch.
2. The facility was not properly maintained and demonstrated many health and safety violations, including broken glass in patients' rooms; excessively hot water in faucets; dried feces on public bathroom walls and grab bars; no soap in the kitchen; insufficient towels and linens; dead and live cockroaches and worms in the food preparation area; and debris, bugs, and grease throughout the facility.

3. Dietary facilities were unsanitary and inadequate to meet the dietary needs of the residents. In one particular case, an ordered "no concentrated sweets" diet for a diabetic patient was not followed, subjecting the patient to life-threatening blood sugar levels.

4. There were inadequate staffing patterns and supervision in the facility. No funds were spent on employee training, and the defendant did not spend the minimum amount of time at the facility, as required by administrative standards.

5. Improper dosages of medications were administered to the residents. For example, physicians distributed an ongoing overdose of heart medication to one resident while failing to administer medication to another (which resulted in a seizure).[69]

The defendant argued that he did not create the unsafe conditions at the facility. The court of appeals disagreed. The statute does not require that the defendant create the conditions at the facility to sustain a conviction. The defendant was the administrator of the facility and responsible for the conditions that existed.

Cruelty to the Infirm

Cruelty to the infirm is the intentional neglect by any person, including a caregiver, causing unjustifiable pain or suffering to an infirm, aged patient. The defendants in *State v. Brenner*[70] were charged with cruelty to the infirm. The defendants brought a challenge stating that the criminal statutes under which they were charged were constitutionally vague. According to the court, Section 14.12 of Louisiana Revised Statutes defines *criminal negligence* as follows:

> *Criminal negligence* exists when, although neither specific nor general criminal intent is present, there is such disregard of the interest of others that the offender's conduct amounts to a gross deviation below the standard of care expected to be maintained by a reasonably careful man under like circumstances.[71]

Criminal negligence requires:

> . . . a gross deviation below the standard of care expected to be maintained by a reasonably careful man under like circumstances.

It calls for substantially more than the ordinary lack of care, which may be the basis of tort liability, and furnishes a more explicit statement of that lack of care, which has been variously characterized in criminal statutes as "gross negligence" and "recklessness."[72]

The state alleged that the administrator of the nursing facility neglected and mistreated residents by failing to ensure that the facility was maintained in a sanitary manner, necessary health services were performed, staff were properly trained, there were adequate medical supplies and sufficient staff, records were maintained properly, and the residents were adequately fed and cared for.

In addition to allegations of neglect and mistreatment of residents, other allegations charged the *director of nursing* with failing to properly train the staff at the facility in correct nursing procedures. The *controller* was alleged to have failed to purchase adequate medical supplies for proper treatment. The *admissions director* allegedly failed to exercise proper judgment regarding admission procedures, and the *physical therapist* allegedly failed to provide adequate physical therapy services. The defendants asserted that the term *neglect* was unconstitutionally vague. The Louisiana Supreme Court, on appeal by the defendants from two lower courts, held that the phrases "intentional or criminally negligent mistreatment or neglect" and "unjustifiable pain and suffering" were not vague and that they were sufficiently clear in meaning to afford a person of ordinary understanding fair notice of the conduct that was prohibited.[73]

This case clearly illustrates how various employees can be included in a legal action involving criminal negligence. It serves as a reminder about the responsibility of all employees to serve as advocates for all patients.

▶ HOMICIDE

Murder of Newborn Babies

In a highly publicized case, Dr. Kermit Gosnell was convicted of murdering newborn babies by snipping their spinal cords shortly after delivery. The jury, following a 2-month trial and 10 days of deliberation, convicted Gosnell of murder. Although it was expected that prosecutors would seek the death penalty, Gosnell made a deal with prosecutors promising not to appeal the jury's decision in exchange for life in prison without parole.

NEWS DOCTOR KILLED IN HOSPITAL ATTACK WAS COVERING SHIFT FOR CO-WORKER

In an instant, Dr. Henry Bello triggered a Code Silver at Bronx Lebanon Hospital, sending his one-time colleagues diving for cover on the hospital's top two floors while he repeatedly pulled his trigger, killing a doctor who had the misfortune of covering someone else's shift as a favor and injuring six others, including a patient.

—Coleen Long and Julie Watson, *The Washington Times*, July 3, 2017

All too often, places of healing become homicide scenes, as was the case at Bronx Lebanon Hospital in New York. Homicide includes all killings of humans and ranges from manslaughter to murder with varying degrees of each representing the severity of the crime. First-degree murder involves the deliberate and premeditated killing of another with malice aforethought. Second-degree murder is not deliberate and is not premeditated; however, it is the killing of another with malice aforethought. The tragedy of murder in institutions that are dedicated to the healing of the sick has been an all-too-frequent occurrence, as noted in the following examples.

NEWS 3 SHOT AT GEORGIA HOSPITAL; SUSPECT CAPTURED

Armed with a 3-year grudge and more guns than he could hold, a former substitute schoolteacher stormed a hospital looking to punish the nurse he blamed for his mother's death. The nurse, another employee and a bystander are dead . . .

—Daniel Yee, *The Capital*, March 29, 2008

NEWS DOCTOR AT BOSTON'S BRIGHAM AND WOMEN'S HOSPITAL DIES AFTER SHOOTING, SUSPECT DEAD

"Dr. Davidson was a wonderful and inspiring cardiac surgeon who devoted his career to saving lives and improving the quality of life of every patient he cared for," said a statement issued by the hospital, which is affiliated with Harvard Medical School. "It is truly devastating that his own life was taken in this horrible manner."

—HuffPost/AP, *The Huffington Post*, January 20, 2015[74]

Nurse Sentenced for Diabolical Acts

From 1993 to 1995, Majors worked as a licensed practical nurse (LPN) in the intensive care unit (ICU) of a county hospital. He may have been a competent nurse, but he had one problem: An incredibly high number of elderly patients died under his watch. By 1995, after rumors started to circulate that he was euthanizing patients, the hospital suspended him, and the state board of nursing suspended his license.

In 1994, 100 of the 351 people admitted to the hospital's four-bed ICU died. A large percentage of those who died were elderly. In comparison, during the previous 4 years, an average of only 27 patients per year died, out of an average of 354 admitted to the ICU each year.

Spurred on by her suspicions (and those of other nurses), Nurse Stirek conducted an analysis showing that Majors was present for more deaths than any other nurse, almost twice as many as the nearest contender. After Stirek showed her analysis to Ling, the hospital's president and chief executive officer, Ling suspended Majors from work, with pay. Later, Ling asked the police to investigate, and Majors was subsequently prosecuted.[75]

Majors was sentenced to spend life in prison for murdering six elderly patients, a crime the judge referred to as a paragon of evil at its most wicked. Majors had been entrusted with their care; in response, he committed diabolical acts that extinguished the frail lives of six people.

Fatal Injection of Pavulon

In a case involving Angelo, a registered nurse on the cardiac/intensive care unit at a Long Island hospital, the defendant was found guilty of second-degree murder for injecting two patients with the drug Pavulon. He was found guilty of the lesser charges of manslaughter and criminally negligent homicide in the deaths of two other patients. Angelo committed the murders in a bizarre scheme to revive the patients and be thought of as a hero.[76]

Fatal Injection of Lidocaine

In another case, *Hargrave v. Landon*,[77] the defendant, a nurse's aide, was convicted of murder in the first degree when he was found to have injected an elderly patient with a fatal dose of the drug lidocaine. He was sentenced to life imprisonment by the circuit court. The defendant appealed the judgment of the circuit court, alleging that his due process rights were violated during the trial when the trial court failed to grant his motion for change of venue. Because of what was termed the *carnival atmosphere* surrounding the trial, he argued the trial court should have sequestered the jury. In addition, the defendant claimed the trial court improperly admitted evidence of other crimes. Finally, he asserted the evidence was insufficient as a matter of law to sustain the conviction.[78]

The U.S. district court held that the nurse's aide failed to establish that he was denied an impartial jury because of adverse pretrial publicity, especially because the tenor of newspaper articles before his trial was primarily informative and factual and the articles treated the story objectively. The evidence was determined to have been sufficient to support the petitioner's conviction for murder.

Lethal Dose of Anesthesia

A licensed dentist and an oral surgeon in *People v. Protopappas*[79] were convicted in the superior court of second-degree murder for the deaths of three patients who died after receiving general anesthesia. The record revealed that the three patients received massive doses of drugs, which resulted in their deaths. The dosages had not been tailored to the patients' individual conditions. The dentist had also improperly instructed surrogate dentists, who were neither licensed nor qualified to administer general anesthesia, to administer preset dosages for an extended time with little or no personal supervision. In addition, the dentist had been habitually slow in reacting to resulting overdoses. In one case, the patient's general physician informed the defendant that the 24-year-old, 88-pound patient suffered from lupus, total kidney failure, high blood pressure, anemia, heart murmur, and chronic seizure

disorder, and should not be placed under anesthesia even for a short time. The defendant consciously elected to ignore that medical opinion. On appeal, the court of appeals found that there was sufficient evidence of implied malice to support the jury's findings that the dentist and the oral surgeon were guilty of second-degree murder.

> This is more than gross negligence. These are the acts of a person who knows that his conduct endangers the life of another and who acts with conscious disregard for life. . . . Many murders are committed to satisfy a feeling of a hatred or grudge, it is true, but this crime may be perpetrated without the slightest trace of personal ill-will.[80]

Not every charge of suspected murder ends in a conviction; however, there is a heavy price to be paid due to the mental anguish suffered by those charged with the crime.

Lethal Dose of Codeine

Evidence supported a finding that a nurse killed the plaintiff's decedent in *Havrum v. United States*.[81] After a bench trial in an action brought under the Federal Tort Claims Act, the trial court concluded that Williams, a nurse at a Veterans Affairs (VA) hospital, killed veteran Elzie Havrum. On appeal, the government challenged the sufficiency of the evidence.

Ms. Havrum was required to show that the VA hospital had a duty to protect Mr. Havrum from injury and that its failure to perform that duty caused his death. The government did not challenge the trial court's conclusion that the hospital breached its duty to protect Havrum from the nurse, who presented a danger to patients. The government contends, however, that Havrum failed to establish causation because the evidence did not support the court's finding that the nurse killed Havrum.

The trial court found that Williams gave Havrum a lethal dose of codeine, and that even disregarding the evidence of codeine poisoning, the circumstantial evidence indicated that Williams killed Havrum. The trial court relied, in part, on a study by the hospital's epidemiologist, Dr. Christensen, who investigated a suspected link between Williams and an increase in deaths on the ward where Williams customarily worked. The study concluded that patients who were under Williams's care were nearly 10 times more likely to die than patients not under his care. In addition, Williams was associated with many unexpected deaths that occurred in private rooms. Christensen also testified that he had never seen anything so unusual as the number of patients who died on the relevant ward from May through July 1992, between 1:00 AM and 3:00 AM (a period when fewer deaths generally occur). Williams was present for 11 of the 13 deaths in that interim, although he worked on only one third of the shifts.

Christensen concluded that there was only one chance in a million that the pattern of deaths on the ward was random and that there was a compelling correlation between the deaths and Williams for which Christensen could find no benign explanation. Although the court agreed with the government, the statistical evidence alone does not establish that Williams caused Havrum's death; that evidence is nevertheless probative. It was, moreover, only one aspect of the circumstantial evidence upon which the trial court relied in finding causation.

With regard to Havrum specifically, the court noted that his death was among those that Christensen found highly unusual. Havrum died on the ward in question at 1:15 AM in a private room with Williams present. Havrum was not expected to die, and the government offered no evidence that he faced death as part of some short-term natural progression. Although Havrum suffered from a serious illness, the admitting physician did not place him in intensive care and did not believe that his death was imminent. Havrum actually reported feeling better while he was in the hospital, but 16 hours after his admission, he was pronounced dead.

The trial court also referred to suspicious inconsistencies and alterations in the medical records. The court remarked that Williams first wrote a medical note indicating that he found Havrum in severe respiratory distress at about 1:15 AM, the same time that the physician pronounced him dead. The time in the note was then changed to 1:10 AM, a line was drawn through the note, and the note was marked "error R.W." Williams then wrote another medical note; this time he stated that he found Havrum in severe respiratory distress at about 1:10 AM and that the physician arrived at about 1:15 AM, just as Havrum stopped breathing. Although the government suggests possible innocent explanations for the changed entries and omissions, the trial court, which noted that Williams had been fired by another hospital for inserting a false entry into a patient's chart, was free to draw its own, less-innocent inferences from Havrum's hospital records. In addition, one permissible inference is that Williams's evident uncertainty about what to say and to note in the records indicates that there was, in fact, nothing particularly wrong with Havrum, and that Williams took his life. The appellate court concluded that, more likely than not, Williams did kill Havrum.

Removal of Life Support Equipment

There is generally a duty to provide life-sustaining equipment in the immediate aftermath of cardiopulmonary arrest; however, there is no duty to continue its use once it has become futile and ineffective to do so in the opinion of qualified medical personnel. Two physicians in *Barber v. Superior Court*[82] were facing murder charges for failing to continue treatment. The charges were based on their acceding to requests of the patient's family to discontinue life support equipment and intravenous tubes. The patient suffered a cardiopulmonary arrest in the recovery room after surgery. A team of physicians and nurses revived the patient and placed him on life support equipment. The patient suffered severe brain damage, which placed him in a comatose and vegetative state from which, according to tests and examinations by other specialists, he was unlikely to recover. On the written request of the family, the patient was taken off life support equipment. The family, his wife and eight children, made the decision together after consultation with the physicians. Evidence had been presented that the patient, before his incapacitation, had expressed to his wife that he would not want to be kept alive by a machine. There was no evidence indicating that the family was motivated in their decision by anything other than love and concern for the dignity of their loved one. The patient continued to breathe on his own. Showing no signs of improvement, the physicians again discussed the patient's poor prognosis with the family. The intravenous lines were removed, and the patient died sometime thereafter.

A complaint was filed against the two physicians. The magistrate who heard the evidence determined that the physicians did not kill the deceased, because their conduct was not the proximate cause of the patient's death. On motion of the prosecution, the superior court determined as a matter of law that the evidence required the magistrate to hold the physicians to answer and ordered the complaint reinstated. The court of appeals held that the physicians' omission to continue treatment, although intentional and with knowledge that the patient would die, was not an unlawful failure to perform a legal duty. The evidence amply supported the magistrate's decision.

🔍 NURSE INJECTS PATIENTS WITH LIDOCAINE

Citation: *People v. Diaz*, 834 P.2d 1171 (Cal. 1992)

Facts

The defendant, a registered nurse, was working on the night shift at a community hospital. During a 3½-week period, 13 patients on the night shift had seizures, cardiac arrest, and respiratory arrest; nine died. The unit closed, and the defendant went to work at another hospital. Within 3 days, a patient died after exhibiting the same symptoms as those of the patients in the previous hospital while the defendant was on duty. The defendant was arrested and tried for 12 counts of murder.

The testimony revealed that the defendant injected the patients with massive doses of lidocaine (a rhythm-controlling drug). Evidence showed that the defendant assisted the patients before they exhibited seizures, providing opportunity for the nurse to administer the drug. She was observed acting strangely on the nights of the deaths, and high concentrations of lidocaine were found in the patients' syringes. Moreover, syringes containing the drug and lidocaine vials were discovered in the defendant's home.

Pretrial investigation revealed that 26 other patients had died at the defendant's first hospital while under the nurse's care. All had the same symptoms. The defendant, who waived her right to trial by jury, was found guilty of the 12 counts of murder. The nurse appealed the judgment.

Issue

Did the expert testimony support the finding that an overdose of lidocaine caused the patients' deaths? Did the evidence prove that the defendant had the opportunity to give patients overdoses of lidocaine?

Holding

The California Supreme Court upheld the convictions.

Reason

The expert testimony about the levels of lidocaine in the patients' tissue, coupled with the nurse's testimony concerning the symptoms prior to the deaths, confirmed that the patients died from overdoses given to them by the defendant. Testimony showed that the defendant was the only nurse on duty the night each patient was poisoned, other nurses were there only on some of the nights, and only the defendant had the opportunity to administer the fatal doses.

▶ MANSLAUGHTER

Manslaughter is the commission of an unintentional act that results in the death of another person. It can be either voluntary or involuntary. *Voluntary manslaughter* is the intentional killing of another person without premeditation or malice aforethought, in what is commonly referred to as the "heat of passion," which is caused by the provocation of the victim (e.g., found having an affair with the defendant's spouse). *Involuntary manslaughter* is the result of a negligent act that occurs when the defendant did not intend to kill the victim but acted in a criminally negligent or reckless manner, such as performing a risky surgical procedure when the defendant was aware that he or she was not sufficiently competent to perform it. There are an endless number of cases where physicians have been charged with manslaughter, as follows.

- A physician was charged in patient's death from substandard tummy tuck. A medical board found, after reviewing the case, that the physician practiced internal medicine and was not a surgeon. He did not have adequate backup, including support staff, equipment to monitor vitals, or a crash cart, which would have had resuscitative drugs, oxygen, and a defibrillator to be used in the event the patient suffered distress during the procedure."[84]

- A cosmetic surgeon was "charged with involuntary manslaughter after allegedly giving a deadly cocktail of drugs during a liposuction procedure, authorities said."[85]

- A surgeon was convicted of manslaughter for delaying an operation and was "sentenced to 2½ years in prison, of which he must serve at least half, for delaying surgery for a man with a perforated intestine."[86]

- In Manhattan Beach, a plastic surgeon was charged with manslaughter after a liposuction patient died on the operating table. He was charged with recklessly performing liposuction on a patient he knew previously had had a heart transplant, causing her death during the operation.[87]

- A surgeon was charged with manslaughter over a kidney error in the death of a war veteran whose healthy kidney was accidentally removed instead of the diseased one.[88]

NEWS SURGEON CONVICTED OF PATIENT MANSLAUGHTER THROUGH NEGLIGENCE

The operation went smoothly but while recovering from surgery he developed abdominal pain and was transferred to Sellu's care. Sellu suspected there had been a rupture in the patient's bowel—a potentially life-threatening condition that requires surgery—but the surgeon ignored the urgency that the case demanded and the patient later died.

—Owen Bowcott, *The Guardian*, November 5, 2014[83]

NEWS FAMILY NEGLECTED WOMAN TO DEATH: AUTHORITIES SAY

The family of a 65-year-old woman has been charged with manslaughter after authorities say the woman's body was found covered in infected bedsores that left her ribs exposed, the *Tampa Bay Times* reports. The Hillsborough County Sheriff's Office says Mary Winston, a former nurse, had rheumatoid arthritis that was so severe she couldn't move. Her husband told authorities they should have sought professional medical care, but they were scared to let authorities see how badly her condition had deteriorated.

—Health News Florida Staff, *Health News Florida*, June 27, 2013[89]

Reviewing the various case studies and news clippings, there are a variety of manslaughter charges against both family members and healthcare workers. Dr. Conrad Murray, for example, was convicted of involuntary manslaughter in the death of Michael Jackson for providing him with the powerful operating room anesthetic *propofol* on a nightly basis to help him sleep. He had been sentenced to a 4-year prison term. After serving 2 years of his 4-year sentence, he was released from prison following a U.S. Supreme Court decision on state prison conditions that diverted him to the overcrowded Los Angeles County lockup. In another case, the *Boston Globe* reported a healthcare worker was ordered held on $20,000 bail on a manslaughter charge for allegedly ignoring a mentally ill client who was choking to death on a piece of steak. In another reported case, a physician was facing manslaughter charges for the alleged overdose of one of his patients who died of a *methadone* overdose.[90]

A study published in the *Journal of the Royal Society of Medicine* identified 85 reported cases of manslaughter from 1995 to December 2005 by searching newspaper databases, Medline, Embase, and the Wellcome library catalogue. The study concluded:

> The number of doctors prosecuted for manslaughter has risen steeply since 1990, but the proportion of doctors convicted remains low. Prosecution for deliberately violating rules is understandable, but accounts for only a minority of these cases. Unconscious errors—mistakes and slips (or lapses)—are an inescapable consequence of human actions and prosecution of individuals is unlikely to improve patient safety. That requires improvement to the complex systems of health care.[91]

Although charges are often reduced, the lessons are clear—healthcare professionals must be aware of the potential for criminal charges as they practice in healthcare settings.

▶ RAPE AND SEXUAL ASSAULT

Rape occurs when one person is forced, without giving consent, to have sexual intercourse with another. *Statutory* rape occurs when a person under the age of legal consent has sexual intercourse with another. An action was filed against a nursing home in *Dupree v. Plantation Pointe, L.P.*[92] after the plaintiff's mother was sexually assaulted at the nursing home by a dementia patient. A registered nurse testified that on the night of the incident, the nursing home was properly staffed and that no member of the nursing home staff did anything improper in the treatment of the assaulted resident. She stated measures were taken to protect residents from the dementia resident. Furthermore, she testified that only a doctor had the power to order restraints or transfer the patient and that the doctors did not do so. In addition, there was testimony that there was no penetration, that the resident suffered no physical injury, and that she was not even aware of the assault. The trial court did not err in finding that the nursing home had not breached its duty of care.

Dr. Earl Brian Bradley, a pediatrician, was indicted in 2010 for molesting, raping, and exploiting his pediatric patients. After trial he was sentenced on June 26, 2011 to 14 consecutive life terms in prison.[93] The hospital where he had worked had previously cleared Dr. Bradley after conducting an internal investigation following an accusation of inappropriate conduct with young patients. "Hence, administrators reportedly never informed the state's medical disciplinary board or law enforcement authorities of the allegations."[94] Whatever the circumstances of the investigation were, conducting a thorough investigation is mandatory for the safety of both staff and patients.

Although statistics are not reliable, rape cases in healthcare facilities are not infrequent occurrences. The hospital's responsibilities in an alleged rape involve the following:

- Notification of the parents if the patient is a minor
- Timely notification of law enforcement
- Following recognized procedures for examination of the patient
- Collecting and protecting physical evidence (e.g., body fluids)
- Thorough documentation (e.g., photographs and victim statements)
- Treatment of patient injuries
- Maintaining patient privacy and dignity
- Providing emotional support
- Referral for follow-up counseling
- Pregnancy counseling as appropriate

The American Congress of Obstetricians and Gynecologists recommends the following in evaluation and the treatment of victims of sexual assault:

Medical Issues

- Obtain informed consent.
- Assess and treat physical injuries.
- Obtain past gynecologic history.
- Perform physical examination, including pelvic examination, with appropriate chaperone.
- Obtain appropriate specimens and serologic tests for sexually transmitted infection testing.
- Provide appropriate infectious disease prophylaxis as indicated.
- If the assailant's HIV status is unknown, evaluate the risks and benefits of nonoccupational postexposure prophylaxis.
- Provide or arrange for provision of emergency contraception as indicated.
- Provide counseling regarding findings, recommendations, and prognosis.
- Arrange follow-up medical care and referrals for psychosocial needs.

Legal Issues

- Provide accurate recording of events.
- Document injuries.
- Collect samples as indicated by local protocol or regulation.
- Identify the presence or absence of sperm in the vaginal fluids and make appropriate slides.
- Report to authorities as required.
- Ensure security of chain of evidence.[95]

An article titled "Patient education: Care after sexual assault (beyond the basics)" contains more helpful information; it can be found at www.uptodate.com.

A hospital technologist in *Copithorne v. Framingham Union Hospital*[96] alleged that a staff physician raped her during the course of a house call. The technologist's claim against the hospital was summarily dismissed for lack of proximate causation. On appeal, the dismissal was found to be improper when the record indicated that the hospital had received notice of allegations that the physician assaulted patients on and off the hospital's premises. The hospital had instructed the physician to have another individual present when visiting female patients and had instructed nurses to keep an eye on him. The physician's sexual assault was foreseeable. There was evidentiary support for the proposition that failure to withdraw the physician's privileges caused the rape when the technologist asserted that it was the physician's good reputation in the hospital that led her to seek his services.

▶ THEFT

NEWS COUPLE IN 90S ALLEGE THEFT BY CAREGIVERS

Mann sees an empty spot where a treasured object once sat, and her eyes fill with tears. The mantelpiece in her living room, which used to display crystal vases and porcelain figurines. Her light-filled atrium, where small marble animals peeked out from among the orchids.
—Tara Bahrampour, *The Washington Post*, May 12, 2016

Theft is the illegal taking of another person's or organization's property. Patients at home and in healthcare facilities must be cautious of the potential for unscrupulous persons to take their personal belongings. Healthcare facilities, including home care agencies, must be alert to the potential threat of theft by dishonest persons, such as caregivers, visitors, and trespassers. The theft of patient valuables (e.g., cash, credit cards, jewelry, in-home valuables), supplies, drugs, and medical equipment is substantial, and it costs healthcare organizations millions of dollars each year.

The lengths to which thieves will go are listed here.

- A report published in the *Mayo Clinic Proceedings* says hospital workers have stolen drugs by siphoning medication from IV bags, taking leftover pills meant for the trash, and tampering with their patient's syringes, which has led to six infectious disease outbreaks in U.S. hospitals since 2004.[97]

- A Pennsylvania man is facing charges that he stole human skin worth about $350,000 from a Philadelphia hospital over a period of nearly 2 years, police said.[98]
- Police received a report that two wallets and an iPad had been stolen from a new mother's room in the maternity ward of Langley Memorial on March 30.[99]
- Foster said the thieves broke into at least one staff locker. They also stole cash, clothing, cellphones, office supplies, and staff identification badges, swipe cards, and personal alarms. After learning of the thefts, the hospital deactivated those security items.[100]

Medical Identity Theft

Medical identity theft is the unauthorized use or disclosure of patient information. "Medical identity theft occurs when someone uses another person's name or insurance information to get medical treatment, prescription drugs, or surgery. It also happens when dishonest people working in a medical setting use another person's information to submit false bills to insurance companies."[101] Thieves often use patient mail (e.g., credit card information, bank statements, patient bills, checking account information) to obtain information about the consumer, which they use to steal his or her identity for financial gain.

To improve the efficiency and effectiveness of the healthcare system, HIPAA included administrative simplification provisions that required DHHS to adopt national standards for electronic healthcare transactions and code sets, unique health identifiers, and security. At the same time, Congress recognized that advances in electronic technology could erode the privacy of health information. Consequently, Congress incorporated into HIPAA provisions that mandated the adoption of federal privacy protections for individually identifiable health information.[102]

More than 11 million records were reported breached in June 2016. "The bulk of these record breaches were

☑ *OR LOCKER ROOM THEFT*

It all started in the operating room's locker room. At first it was $2 from someone's wallet and $5 from another. It was sporadic at first, then the frequency of the thefts increased. Employees began to look at one another with suspicion. Finally, management was able to make a difficult decision. A *theft detection powder* that cannot be easily washed off was dusted on some of the money, and it was placed in a purse in an open locker. Greed finally took over as the person's thefts became more frequent and brazen. She eventually took the money that was marked with the powder. Unaware that the money had been dusted, the employee, an OR transporter responsible for wheeling patients into and out of the OR on a stretcher, eventually went to the hospital's coffee shop to spend some of the money. When the cashier noticed the greenish color on the thief's hands, he realized that this was the culprit who had been taking money from her coworkers, and he notified administration. The transporter admitted to taking the money, not only from the OR staff and her coworkers, but when she transported patients to and from their rooms, she would take money and other items from the patient's bedside cabinet. She admitted that patients were groggy when recently anesthetized, and this made it easy for her to steal from them. The employee was discharged without charges being pressed against her.

The legal and ethical issues swirling around this incident became a hot topic for discussion among the OR staff. The potential impact on public relations concerns mitigated the willpower of management to press charges.

attributable to a single hacking incident that included a large insurer database (10.3 million records)."[103]

The HIPAA Breach Notification Rule, 45 CFR §§ 164.400-414, requires HIPAA covered entities and their business associates to provide notification following a breach of unsecured protected health information. Similar breach notification provisions implemented and enforced by the Federal Trade Commission (FTC), apply to vendors of personal health records and their third party service providers, pursuant to section 13407 of the HITECH Act."[104]

As required by section 13402(e)(4) of the Health Information Technology for Economic and Clinical Health (HITECH) Act, the Secretary must post a list of breaches of unsecured protected health information affecting 500 or more individuals. These breaches

📰 *VA DRUG THEFTS PERSIST DESPITE NEW EFFORTS*

Federal authorities have launched dozens of new criminal investigations into possible opioid and drug theft by employees at Department of Veterans Affairs hospitals, a new sign the problem is not going away despite new prevention efforts.

—Hope Yen, *The Washington Times*, May 31, 2017

are now posted in a new, more accessible format that allows users to search and sort the posted breaches. Additionally, this new format includes brief summaries of the breach cases that Office of Civil Rights (OCR) has investigated and closed, as well as the names of private practice providers who have reported breaches of unsecured protected health information to the Secretary.[105]

Regarding notification, the DHHS requires: (1) *Individual Notice* to individuals whose data has been compromised in written form by first-class mail or email if the affected individual has agreed to receive such notices electronically; (2) *Media Notice* when a breach affects more than 500 residents of a state or jurisdiction; and, (3) *Notice to the Secretary* of DHHS in addition to notifying affected individuals and the media regarding breaches of unsecured protected health information.[106]

The Federal Trade Commission offers a brochure titled "Medical Identity Theft," at its website (www.consumer.ftc.gov) that can help the consumer detect identity theft, correct mistakes in medical records, protect medical information, and check for other identity theft concerns. Contact information for credit reporting companies is also available at the site.

Theft of Drugs

Perhaps one of the most tempting and accessible crimes for a healthcare professional involves the misuse or theft of drugs. Drugs can offer significant financial gain when they fall into the hands of the wrong people. As noted in *Chia v. Ohio Board of Nursing*,[107] where the appellant licensed nurse took a patient's Percodan tablets for her own use, the appellant pled no contest and was found guilty of theft of drugs and a felony of the fourth degree. The licensing board mailed to the appellant a notice of immediate suspension and opportunity for hearing. In that notice, the board informed the appellant that her license was immediately suspended as a result of her felony drug abuse conviction. The notice also informed the appellant that the board proposed further sanctions to her license and that she was entitled to a hearing regarding those sanctions if she requested one within 30 days. The appellant did not respond to the notice.

Without having heard from the appellant, the board mailed her a letter informing her that it would consider sanctions to her license at its regularly scheduled meeting in May. At that meeting, the board permanently revoked the appellant's nursing license. The appellant appealed the board's decision to the court of common pleas. That court affirmed the board's decision, finding that it was supported by reliable, probative, and substantial evidence and was in accordance with law. The board's notice clearly informed the appellant that her license was immediately suspended as a result of her felony drug conviction.

Theft of Resident's Money

The evidence presented in *People v. Lancaster*[108] was found to have provided a probable cause foundation for information charging felony theft of nursing home residents' money by the office manager. Evidence showed that on repeated occasions, the residents' income checks were cashed, or cash was otherwise received on behalf of residents; that the defendant, by virtue of her office, had sole responsibility for maintaining the residents' ledger accounts; and that frequently cash receipts were not posted to the residents' accounts.

In another case, there was sufficient evidence in *Miller v. Dunn*[109] to hold that a nurse assistant had misappropriated $15,000 from an 83-year-old nursing home resident. The record indicated that the funds were taken during those times the resident made visits to the hospital for respiratory problems. The patient had been diagnosed with dementia, and the resident's confusion was increasing. The nursing assistant actively procured the check in question, filling in the date, amount, and her name as payee. As a result, the nursing assistant was placed on the employee disqualification list for misappropriating funds.

Commingling Resident's Personal Funds

Criminal charges of theft were imposed because of misapplication of property in *State v. Pleasant Hill Health Facility*.[110] The facility commingled the residents' personal funds (Social Security checks and personal allowances) in a corporate account. There were times that the residents' funds remained in the corporate account for 3 to 6 months before being transferred to the residents' accounts, during which time the combined funds were used to pay corporate expenses. The facility described its relationship with the residents as debtor–creditor and not a trust relationship. The facility claimed that the funds were always available to residents, and they were never denied a request for their funds. The Maine Supreme Judicial Court held that the facility's handling of the residents' funds was not a debtor–creditor relationship but a trust relationship. Pleasant Hill's commingling of patients' personal need funds with corporate funds and use of the combined funds to pay corporate expenses constituted dealing with the money as its own and was a violation of the corporation's trust agreement. The facility argued

🔍 *THE COURT'S DECISION*

The U.S. Court of Appeals for the Sixth Circuit determined that the physician was found to have been properly convicted of healthcare fraud and making false statements, arising from administration of partial doses of chemotherapy medication while billing Medicaid and other insurance programs for full doses. The appeals court also disagreed with the defendant's contention that the district court considered an inappropriate factor when it heard testimony from family members.

that it ultimately transferred all of the residents' personal funds from a transfer account to the residents' accounts. The court concluded that a violation had occurred at the moment the residents' personal funds were deposited without segregating them from the corporation's own funds.

▶ CHAPTER REVIEW

1. The objectives of criminal law are to:

    - Maintain public order and safety
    - Protect individuals
    - Use punishment as a deterrent to crime
    - Rehabilitate criminals for return to society

2. A crime—a social harm defined and made punishable by law—is generally either a misdemeanor or a felony.

    - A *misdemeanor* is an offense generally punishable by less than 1 year in jail and/or a fine.
    - A *felony*, however, is punishable by imprisonment in a state or federal prison for a period of more than 1 year.

3. Criminal procedure involves

    - Arrest
    - Arraignment
    - Indictment
    - Conference
    - Criminal trial

4. Criminal trials involving healthcare professionals and organizations include: healthcare fraud, kickbacks, false claims, tampering with drugs, Internet pharmacy, falsification of records, patient abuse, criminal negligence, manslaughter, murder, rape, sexual abuse, and theft.

▶ REVIEW QUESTIONS

1. Discuss the objectives and classification of criminal offenses.
2. Discuss the criminal trial process.
3. Describe some of the more common criminal offenses that occur in healthcare settings.

▶ NOTES

1. 513 F.3d 527 (C.A. 6. Tenn. 2008).
2. Stephen H. Gifis, *Law Dictionary*, at 118–119 (1975).
3. "Model Penal Code: Selected Provisions," http://www1.law.umkc.edu/suni/CrimLaw/MPC_Provisions/model_penal_code_default_rules.htm.
4. No. 05AP-681 (Ohio App. 2006).
5. 295 U.S. 78, 88 (1935).
6. John Kaplan, *Criminal Justice Introductory Cases and Materials* (Eagan, MN: Foundation Press, 1973), 228.
7. *Id.* at 259.
8. U.S. Department of Justice, "National Health Care Fraud Takedown Results in Charges Against Over 412 Individuals Responsible for $1.3 Billion in Fraud Losses," https://www.justice.gov/opa/pr/national-health-care-fraud-takedown-results-charges-against-over-412-individuals-responsible.
9. Federal Bureau of Investigation, "What We Investigate: Health Care Fraud," https://www.fbi.gov/investigate/white-collar-crime/health-care-fraud.
10. *Id.*
11. Office of the Inspector General, "About Us," https://oig.hhs.gov/about-oig/about-us/index.asp.
12. U.S. Department of Health and Human Services, "Stop Medicare Fraud," https://www.stopmedicarefraud.gov/aboutfraud/heattaskforce/.
13. *Id.* note 8.
14. U.S. Department of Health and Human Services, News Release, February 17, 2011.
15. U.S. Department of Justice, "National Health Care Fraud Takedown Results in Charges against 301 Individuals for Approximately $900 Million in False Billing," June 22, 2016. https://www.justice.gov/opa/pr/national-health-care-fraud-takedown-results-charges-against-301-individuals-approximately-900.

16. Attorney General Eric Holder, "Attorney General Eric Holder Delivers Remarks at the Johnson and Johnson Press Conference," The United States Department of Justice, November 4, 2013. http://www.justice.gov/iso/opa/ag/speeches/2013/ag-speech-131104.html.

17. Carla K. Johnson and Sara Burnett, "$12 Million in Medicaid Funds Went to Deceased in Illinois," *The Washington Post*, April 20, 2014.

18. *USA v. Farid Fata*, No. 15-1935 (6th Cir. 2016).

19. ABC News, "A Healthy Dose of Fraud," http://www.peura.com/David/insurnce.htm.

20. 385 F.3d 1013 (C.A. 6, Ky. 2004).

21. 824 F.2d 780 (9th Cir. 1987).

22. 254 Ga. App. 297, 562 S.E.2d 201 (Ga. App. 2002).

23. 507 So. 2d 1254 (La. Ct. App. 1987).

24. 513 So. 2d 493 (La. Ct. App. 1987).

25. *Id*. at 495.

26. *Banks v. Board of Pharmacy*, 207 Cal. Rptr. 835 (Cal. Ct. App. 1984).

27. 821 F.2d 523 (10th Cir. 1987).

28. *Id*. at 529.

29. *Id*. at 530.

30. 322 S.E.2d 696 (N.C. Ct. App. 1985).

31. 726 N.Y.S.2d 188 (2001).

32. 513 F.3d 1293 (C.A. 11, Fla. 2008).

33. 760 F.2d 68 (3d Cir. 1985).

34. 871 F.2d 105 (9th Cir. 1989).

35. 366 F.2d 167 (6th Cir. 1966).

36. 265 U.S. 182, 188 (1924).

37. 874 F.2d 20 (1st Cir. 1989).

38. Robert Draper, "The Toxic Pharmacist," *The New York Times*, June 8, 2003. http://www.nytimes.com/2003/06/08/magazine/the-toxic-pharmacist.html?mcubz=0.

39. 401 F.3d 53 (C.A. 2, N.Y. 2005).

40. *Poor v. State*, No. S-02-472, 266 Neb. 183 (Neb. 2003).

41. No. 02-6183 (C.A. 10, Okla. 2004).

42. Carolyn Davis, "Souderton Doctor Jailed with Son in 'Pill Mill' Case," *The Philadelphia Inquirer*, June 7, 2014. http://articles.philly.com/2014-06-07/news/50390458_1_father-and-son-sentencing-motions.

43. Thomas Catan, "Con Artist Starred in Sting That Cost Google Millions," *The Wall Street Journal*, January 25, 2012. http://online.wsj.com/news/articles/SB10001424052970204624204577176964003660658.

44. 746 P.2d 1006 (Idaho Ct. App. 1987).

45. Gregg Zoroya, "VA Treatment Records Falsified, Probe Finds," *USA Today*, May 4, 2014. http://www.usatoday.com/story/news/nation/2014/05/04/va-healthcare-delays-treatment-phoenix-cheyenne-deaths/8602117/.

46. 402 N.Y.S.2d 318 (N.Y. Sup. Ct. 1978).

47. *Id*. at 320.

48. Richard J. Gelles, Murray A. Strauss, and Suzabbe K. Steinmetz, *Behind Closed Doors: Violence in the American Family* (New York, NY: Anchor Books, 1981).

49. *Id*.

50. National Center on Elder Abuse, "Fact Sheet: Elder Abuse Prevalence and Incidence," http://www.ncea.aoa.gov/resources/publication/docs/finalstatistics050331.pdf.

51. 557 F. Supp. 289 (D. Colo. 1983).

52. *Id*. at 293.

53. 42 C.F.R. § 483.13 (1989).

54. "Nurse's Aide Jailed for Punching Patient," *The Baltimore Sun*, June 29, 1990, §D, at 2.

55. 501 N.Y.S.2d 997 (N.Y. Sup. Ct. 1986).

56. *Id*. at 1001.

57. *Id*.

58. 556 A.2d 1 (Pa. Commw. Ct. 1989).

59. 559 N.Y.S.2d 417 (N.Y. App. Div. 1990).

60. 655 S.W.2d 522 (Mo. 1983).

61. *Id*.

62. 166 A.D. 913 (1990).

63. *Id*.

64. *Id*. at 573–574.

65. 121 Commonwealth Court 532 (1988).

66. *Id*. at 535.

67. *Id*. at 540.

68. *State v. Cunningham*, 493 N.W.2d 884 (Iowa Ct. App. 1992).

69. *Id*. at 887–888.

70. 486 So. 2d 101 (La. 1986).

71. *Id*. at 103.

72. *Id*.

73. *Id*. at 101, 104.

74. HuffPost/AP, Doctor at Boston's Brigham and Women's Hospital Dies after Shooting, Suspect Dead," January 20, 2015. http://www.huffingtonpost.com/2015/01/20/gunman-boston-hospital-shooting_n_6508430.html.

75. *Majors v. Engelbrecht*, 149 F.3d 709 (1998).

76. Carolyn Collwell, "The Verdict of Angelo: Murder Found in 2 Deaths," *Newsday*, December 15, 1989. http://www.newsday.com/long-island/serial-killer/the-verdict-on-angelo-murder-found-in-2-deaths-1.1875478.

77. 584 F. Supp. 302 (E.D. Va. 1984).

78. *Id*. at 305.

79. 246 Cal. Rptr. 915 (Cal. Ct. App. 1988).

80. *Id.* at 927.

81. 204 F.3d 815 (8th Cir. 2000).

82. 195 Cal. Rptr. 484 (Cal. Ct. App. 1983).

83. Owen Bowcott, "Surgeon convicted of patient manslaughter through negligence," *The Guardian,* November 5, 2013. https://www.theguardian.com/uk-news/2013/nov/05/surgeon-convicted-manslaughter-negligence-patient.

84. Alyssa Newcomb, "Oregon Doctor Charged in Patient's Death From Botched Tummy Tuck," *ABC News,* August 29, 2012. http://abcnews.go.com/Health/oregon-doctor-charged-death-botched-cosmetic-surgery/story?id=17104454.

85. Brandon Lowry, "Former Encino Cosmetic Surgeon Charged in Patient's Death," *ABC News,* August 20, 2013. http://www.nbclosangeles.com/news/local/Former-Encino-Cosmetic-Surgeon-Charged-in-Patients-Death-220456371.html.

86. Skeptical Scalpel, "Surgeon Convicted of Manslaughter for Delaying Operation," *Physicians Weekly,* November 18, 2013. http://www.physiciansweekly.com/surgeon-convicted-manslaughter-delaying-operation/.

87. Ned Berke, "Manhattan Beach Plastic Surgeon Charged With Manslaughter After Liposuction Patient Dies On Table," April 1, 2013. http://www.sheepsheadbites.com/2013/04/manhattan-beach-plastic-surgeon-charged-with-manslaughter-after-liposuction-patient-dies-on-table/.

88. Clare Dyer, "Surgeon charged with manslaughter over kidney error," *BMJ,* September 15, 2001. http://www.bmj.com/content/323/7313/590.2.

89. "Family Neglected Woman to Death: Authorities," *Health News Florida,* June 27, 2013. http://health.wusf.usf.edu/post/family-neglected-woman-death-authorities.

90. "Doctor Charged in Pain Med Death," *Health News Florida,* July 10, 2013. http://health.wusf.usf.edu/post/doctor-charged-pain-med-death.

91. R. E. Ferner and Sarah E. McDowell, "Doctors Charged with Manslaughter in the Course of Medical Practice, 1795–2005: A Literature Review," *Journal of the Royal Society of Medicine,* 99(6); (2006): 309–314.

92. No. 2002-CT-00556-SCT (Miss. 2004).

93. "Earl Bradley," https://en.wikipedia.org/wiki/Earl_Bradley.

94. Martha Neil, *ABA Law Journal,* April 19, 2010.

95. American Congress of Obstetricians and Gynecologists, "Committee Opinion: Sexual Assault," http://www.acog.org/Resources-And-Publications/Committee-Opinions/Committee-on-Health-Care-for-Underserved-Women/Sexual-Assault.

96. 520 N.E.2d 139 (Mass. 1988).

97. Cathy Puleo, "6 infectious disease outbreaks linked to hospital drug thefts: Patients at high risk," *Healthcare Business and Technology,* June 11, 2014. http://www.healthcarebusinesstech.com/infectious-disease-outbreaks/.

98. Jonathan Allen, "Pennsylvania Man Accused in Theft of Human Skin from Hospital," *Reuters,* May 30, 2014. http://news.yahoo.com/pennsylvania-man-accused-theft-human-skin-hospital-190051628.html.

99. "Thief Targets Mother in Langley Hospital Maternity Ward," *CBC News,* April, 17, 2013, http://www.cbc.ca/news/canada/british-columbia/thief-targets-mother-in-langley-hospital-maternity-ward-1.1323284.

100. Trevor Wilheim, "Police Make Arrest in Windsor Regional Hospital Thefts," *The Windsor Star,* January 29, 2014. http://blogs.windsorstar.com/2014/01/29/windsor-regional-hospital-targeted-again-by-thieves/.

101. Federal Trade Commission, "Medical Identity Theft: FAQs for Health Care Providers and Health Plans," https://www.ftc.gov/tips-advice/business-center/guidance/medical-identity-theft-faqs-health-care-providers-health-plans.

102. HHS.gov, "HIPAA for Professionals," Reviewed June 16, 2017. https://www.hhs.gov/hipaa/for-professionals/index.html.

103. Kira Caban, "Monthly Breach Barometer: Staggering 11 Million Patient Records Breached," July 5, 2016. http://www.protenus.com/blog/breach-barometer-june.

104. HHS.gov, "Breach Notification Rule," Reviewed July 26, 2013. https://www.hhs.gov/hipaa/for-professionals/breach-notification/index.html.

105. U.S. Department of Health and Human Services, Office for Civil Rights, "Breach Portal: Notice to the Secretary of HHS Breach of Unsecured Protected Health Information," https://ocrportal.hhs.gov/ocr/breach/breach_report.jsf.

106. *Id.* note 104.

107. No. 04AP-143 (Ohio App. 2004).

108. 683 P.2d 1202 (Colo. 1984).

109. 184 S.W.3d 122 (Mo. App. 2006).

110. 496 A.2d 306 (Me. 1985).

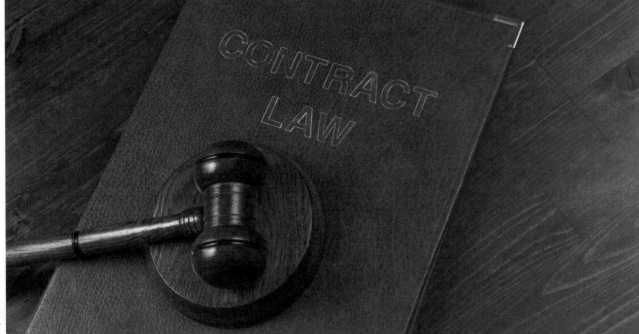

© Jerry Silwowski/Shutterstock

CHAPTER 7

Contracts and Antitrust

BREACH OF CONTRACT: BLOOD TRANSFUSION

Harvey was diagnosed with blockage in his carotid artery. Dr. Strickland recommended a surgical procedure. In anticipation of surgery, Harvey signed written forms entitled, "Refusal of Treatment, Release from Liability" and "Consent to Operation." The documents indicated that Harvey refused to have blood or blood products given to him and that he fully understood the attendant risks. The documents stated: "In all probability, my refusal for such treatment, medical intervention, and/or procedure (may)(will) seriously imperil my health or life." Hospital forms list Harvey's mother, Julia, as his emergency contact. The day before his surgery, Harvey signed another consent form indicating that he would not give permission to the doctor to use blood or blood products, even if it became necessary to administer blood.

Surgery was performed and appeared to have gone well. Harvey, however, later developed a blood clot and had a stroke while in the recovery room. Because Harvey was unconscious, hospital personnel located his mother in the waiting room and obtained her permission to perform a computed tomography (CT) scan and arteriogram. A second surgery was performed, and more blood clots were removed along the side of the carotid artery. Harvey was moved

(continues)

to the intensive care unit (ICU). He was intubated that evening by the on-call emergency room physician after the ICU nurse discovered Harvey was having trouble breathing. The next day, Harvey began bleeding from the surgical site and had lost approximately 30% of his blood volume. His heart rate was extremely high, and Dr. Strickland was concerned that if they could not get the heart rate down, Harvey would have a heart attack and die. When his hemoglobin level reached 8, Dr. Strickland recommended a blood transfusion to Harvey's mother, Julia, who initially declined because of her son's faith as a Jehovah's Witness. Ultimately, Julia consented to giving Harvey two units of blood. Harvey recovered fully from the procedures and later sued. Harvey filed a lawsuit against Dr. Strickland after receiving the unwanted blood. The lawsuit claimed breach of contract, lack of informed consent, medical malpractice, and medical battery. The trial court directed a verdict for Dr. Strickland. Harvey appealed the court's decision.[1]

WHAT IS YOUR VERDICT?

▶ LEARNING OBJECTIVES

The reader, upon completion of this chapter, will be able to:

- Explain what a contract is.
- Describe the elements of a contract.
- Describe how a hospital can be liable for the acts of a physician under contract.
- Explain the possible defenses and remedies for nonperformance of a contract.
- Describe under what circumstances an employee handbook could be considered a contract and how to avoid that assumption.

This chapter provides the reader with a general understanding of the purpose, types, elements, and importance of contracts as they pertain to healthcare organizations and caregivers. Attention also is given to the defenses and legal remedies for nonperformance of a contract.

▶ WHAT IS A CONTRACT?

A *contract* is a special kind of voluntary agreement, either written or oral, that involves legally binding obligations between two or more parties. A contract serves to provide one or more of the parties with a legal remedy if another of the parties does not perform his or her obligations pursuant to the terms of the contract. The major purpose of a contract is to specify, limit, and define the agreements that are legally enforceable. A contract forces the participants to be specific in their understandings and expectations of each other. Contracts, particularly those in writing, serve to minimize misunderstandings and offer a means for the parties to a contract to resolve any disputes that may arise.

▶ TYPES OF CONTRACTS

The following is a general description of the various types of contracts and a brief definition of each. Healthcare professionals should be knowledgeable about each type of contract because they are used commonly in the healthcare setting.

Express Contracts

An *express contract* is one in which the parties have an oral or written agreement. Both written and oral contracts are generally recognized and are equally legal and binding.

> *Oral Contract.* A court will not consider oral negotiations and agreements made before or at the same time a written contract is signed if the parties intended the document to be their complete and final agreement. Both written and oral contracts are generally recognized and are equally legal and binding.

> *Written Contract.* It is preferable to reduce important and complex contracts to writing. In certain instances, the courts will enforce only written contracts.

Implied Contract

An *implied contract* is one that is inferred by law. It is based on the conduct of the parties, such as a handshake or similar conduct. Much of the litigation concerning excesses of corporate authority involves questions of whether a corporation has the implied authority—incidental to its express authority—to perform a questioned act. In *Hungerford Hosp. v. Mulvey*, for example, even though its certificate of incorporation did not authorize the hospital to construct a medical office building, the hospital was permitted to construct the building on land that had been donated for maintaining and operating the hospital. The court, in recognizing a trend to encourage charitable hospitals to provide private offices for rental to staff members, held that such an act was within the implied powers of the hospital and that such offices aid in the work of a general hospital even though it went beyond the hospital corporation's *express powers*.[2]

Voidable Contract

A *voidable contract* is one in which one party, but not the other, has the right to escape from its legal obligations under the contract. It is considered to be a voidable contract at the option of that party. For example, a minor, not having the capacity to enter into a contract, can void the contract. However, the competent party to the contract may not void the contract. Contracts involving fraud or where one party to the contract is incapacitated, not legally of sound mind, or under undue influence or duress are voidable contracts.

Executed Contract

An *executed contract* is one in which all the terms and obligations of the parties to the contract have been fully performed.

Enforceable Contract

An *enforceable contract* is one that is a valid, legally binding agreement. If one party breaches it, the other will have an appropriate legal remedy.

Unenforceable Contract

An *unenforceable contract* is one in which, because of some defect, no legal remedy is available if breached by one of the parties to the contract.

Contracts for Realty, Goods, or Services

There are also contracts for *realty* (a contract for the purchase and sale, exchange, or other conveyance of real estate), *goods* (movable objects, with the exception of money and securities), and *services* (human energy).

⏺▶ ELEMENTS OF A CONTRACT

Whether contracts are executed in writing or agreed to orally, they must contain the following elements to be enforceable: (1) offer/communication, (2) consideration, and (3) acceptance.

The law will enforce contracts only when they are executed between persons who are competent—that is, those with the legal and mental capacity to contract. Certain classes of persons, such as minors, people with mental illness, and prisoners, traditionally have been considered unable to understand the consequences of their actions and have been deemed incompetent, or lacking in legal capacity, to make a binding contract.

Offer/Communication

An *offer* is a promise by one party to do (or not to do) something if the other party agrees to do (or not do) something. Preliminary negotiations are not offers. An offer must be communicated to the other party so that it can be accepted or rejected.

Consideration

Consideration requires that each party to a contract give up something of value in exchange for something of value. No side can have a free way out or the ability to obtain something of value without providing something in exchange. Only when legal consideration has been given will a court treat the agreement as a contract. The adequacy or inadequacy of consideration, or the price paid, normally will not affect the formation of a contract.

Acceptance

Upon proper acceptance of an offer, a contract is formed. A valid acceptance requires the following:

1. *Meeting of the Minds.* Acceptance requires a *meeting of the minds* (mutual assent); in other words, the parties must understand and agree on the terms of the contract. This means that each side must be clear as to the details, rights, and obligations of the contract.
2. *Definite and Complete.* Acceptance requires that mutual assent be found between the parties. The terms must be so complete that both parties understand and agree to what has been proposed.
3. *Duration.* Generally, the *offeror* (the one who makes the offer) may revoke an offer at any time prior to a valid acceptance. When the offeror does revoke the proposal, the revocation is not effective until the *offeree* (the person to whom the offer is made) receives it. Once the offeree has accepted the offer, any attempt to revoke the agreement is invalid.

4. *Complete and Conforming.* The acceptance must be a mirror image of the offer. In other words, the acceptance must comply with all the terms of the offer and not change or add any terms, unless agreed upon by both parties.

▶ BREACH OF CONTRACT

A *breach of contract* occurs when there is a violation of one or more of the terms of the contract. The basic elements that a plaintiff must establish in order to be successful in a breach of contract lawsuit are: (1) a valid contract was executed; (2) the plaintiff performed as specified in the contract; (3) the defendant failed to perform as specified in the contract; and, (4) the plaintiff suffered an economic loss as a result of the defendant's breach of contract.

▶ CORPORATE CONTRACTS

The ability of a corporation to enter into a contract is limited by its powers as contained in or inferred from its articles of incorporation (sometimes called a *charter*) or conferred upon it by general corporation law. Whenever a contract of any consequence is made with a corporation, appropriate corporate approval and authorization must be obtained. In the event that a contract is entered into with a corporation without the appropriate authority, the contract nevertheless may be ratified and made binding on the corporation by subsequent conduct or statements made on its behalf by its representatives.

When the chief executive officer (CEO) exceeds his limits of authority to execute a contract on behalf of the organization, the question arises as to who will be responsible for the costs of the contract. If the actions of the governing body give rise to a third party's reasonable belief that the CEO acts with the authority of the organization, and such belief causes the third party to enter into an agreement with the CEO, expecting that the organization will be obligated under the contract, the organization generally is responsible under the *concept of apparent authority*, which is the appearance of being the agent of another (employer or principal) with the power to act for the principal. However, if a third party deals with the CEO in the absence of indications of the CEO's authority created by the governing body and thereby unreasonably assumes that the CEO possesses the authority to bind the organization to a contract, then such third party deals with the CEO in an individual capacity and not as an agent of the organization.

Although there can be times when a CEO makes a decision that exceeds his or her authority, the governing body may subsequently approve such actions through ratification by accepting any resulting responsibility as though it had been authorized previously. Conversely, if the governing body, for example, has set a limitation on the amount of funds a CEO is authorized to expend on a capital budget item and the CEO exceeds that authorization, he could be held liable to the supplier for that purchase, if so made without prior approval of the governing body.

Physician Contracts

Hospitals have traditionally contracted with physician groups to provide specialty coverage in the emergency department, radiology, and anesthesia services, and hospital-operated out-patient clinics. It has been estimated that there are as many as 31,000 hospital-employed *physician hospitalists* caring for inpatients.[3] Statistics show that "One-in-four medical practices is now owned by a hospital or health system, and hospitals employed 38% of all U.S. physicians in 2015. 'That's a 50% increase between 2012 and 2015, growing from 95,000 employed physicians in 2012 to more than 140,000 employed physicians in 2015.'"[4] Physicians continue to lose medical independence and more costly hospital care. Physicians are increasingly seeking hospital employment to improve their lifestyle by having more control over working hours and to lessen their financial worries of maintaining a practice (e.g., malpractice insurance, government regulations, and the high costs associated with the day-to-day functioning of an office).

▶ PARTNERSHIP

A *partnership* comprises two or more persons who agree to carry on a business for profit and to share profits and losses in some proportion. According to *Black's Law Dictionary*, a partnership is "A voluntary contract between two or more competent persons to place their money, effects, labor, and skill, or some or all of them, in lawful commerce or business, with the understanding that there shall be a proportional sharing of the profits and losses between them."[5] A partnership, unlike a corporation, can be created by the parties' actions without a written or oral agreement.

The Uniform Partnership Act, which has been adopted by most states, describe a *partnership* and *partnership agreement* as follows:

(6) "Partnership" means an association of two or more persons to carry on as co-owners a business for profit formed under Section 202,

predecessor law, or comparable law of another jurisdiction.

(7) "Partnership agreement" means the agreement, whether written, oral, or implied, among the partners concerning the partnership, including amendments to the partnership agreement.[6]

There are a variety of partnerships in the healthcare industry, such as those between physicians when forming a physician general practice or specialty group. Hospital–physician partnerships can take the form of a joint venture, such as a freestanding *ambulatory surgery center*.

▶ AGENT

An *agent* is one who has the power to contract for and bind another person, the principal, to a contract. Corporations can act only through agents (e.g., their officers). An *apparent or ostensible agent* is one who a third person believes is acting on behalf of the principal. If a hospital undertakes to provide physician services to a community and the community reasonably believes that a physician is employed by the hospital to deliver services, then the hospital would generally be liable for the physician's negligent acts. For example, in *Jennison v. Providence St. Vincent Med. Ctr.*,[7] Jennison, having severe abdominal pain, was taken to the hospital emergency department. Unsure of the cause of Jennison's medical problems, Cook, Jennison's assigned physician, recommended surgery. Prior to surgery Cook asked Nunez, a member of an independent anesthesiology group at the hospital, to place a central venous catheter in Jennison.

An X-ray had been taken to confirm the correct placement of the central line. The X-ray showed that the tip of the central line had gone into the pericardial sac of Jennison's heart. A procedure had not been established to notify the treating physicians in a timely manner that the central line had been dangerously misplaced.

Upon the eventual discovery that the central line had been misplaced, it was pulled back to its proper position. Unfortunately, fluids had already infused through the central line and into the space between Jennison's heart and pericardial sac. The pressure of the fluid against her heart kept it from filling adequately. Jennison's blood pressure dropped, and she went into cardiac arrest. The doctors attempted to remove the excess fluid. During the procedure, Jennison suffered a second cardiac arrest. The doctors were again able to resuscitate her. However, due to the lack of oxygen to her brain, Jennison suffered a severe brain injury.

The jury returned a verdict in favor of the plaintiffs, finding the hospital 100% negligent, and the hospital appealed. The Court of Appeals of Oregon affirmed the findings of the trial court. The hospital presented itself as providing radiology services to the public. The public, looking to the hospital to provide such care, is unaware of and unconcerned with the technical complexities and nuances surrounding the contractual and employment arrangements between the hospital and the various medical personnel operating therein. Public policy dictates that the public has every right to assume and expect that the hospital is the medical provider it purports to be.

▶ INDEPENDENT CONTRACTOR

An *independent contractor* is an individual who agrees to undertake work without being under the direct control or direction of another. Independent contractors are personally liable for their own negligent acts. Whether a physician is an employee or an independent contractor is of primary importance in determining liability for damages. Generally, a healthcare organization is not liable for injuries resulting from negligent acts or omissions of independent physicians. There is no liability on the *theory of respondeat superior*, whereby a physician is an independent contractor as long as the physician is not an employee of the organization, is not compensated by the organization, maintains a private practice, and is chosen directly by his or her patients. The mere existence of an independent contractual relationship, however, is not sufficient to remove an organization from liability for the acts of certain of its professional personnel if the independent contractor status is not readily known to the injured party as noted in *Mduba v. Benedictine Hospital* next.

Hospital Liable for Physician's Negligence

A hospital can be liable for a physician's negligence, even if the physician is under contract to provide services to the hospital. The appellate division of the New York State Supreme Court in *Mduba v. Benedictine Hospital*[8] held that the hospital was liable for the emergency department physician's negligence whether the physician was an independent contractor or, even if under contract, the physician was considered to be an independent contractor. The court held that the patient had no way of knowing of the existence of a contract and relied on the relationship between the hospital and the physician in seeking treatment in the emergency department.

Agency Not Liable for Negligent Hiring

The employer, Patient Support Services, Inc. (PSS), in *Maristany v. Patient Support Services, Inc.,*[9] was found not liable for negligent hiring for injuries received by a patient under the care of one of its independent contractors. By contract dated January 29, 1994, the plaintiff retained the services of PSS to furnish an independent nurse, Terry, to care for her husband, Santiago, a postoperative brain surgery patient at defendant Presbyterian Hospital.

At approximately 10:00 PM, Terry assisted a hospital nurse in placing Santiago into a Posey-restraining vest. At approximately 3:30 AM, Terry returned from a break to find Santiago extremely agitated. Terry sought assistance and tried to restrain the patient physically, but the patient escaped from the vest, climbed over the rails, and fell to the floor, sustaining serious injury.

The plaintiffs did not contest that Terry's status was that of an independent contractor rather than an employee. Although an employer is generally not liable for the torts or negligent acts of an independent contractor under the doctrine of *respondeat superior*, the employer had a right to rely on the supposed qualifications and good character of the contractor and is not bound to anticipate misconduct on the contractor's part. The employer is not liable on the ground of its having employed an incompetent or otherwise unsuitable contractor unless it also appears that the employer either knew or, in the exercise of reasonable care, should have ascertained that the contractor was not properly qualified to undertake the work.

There was no competent proof that PSS had any reason to question Terry's qualifications. At the time of the incident, Terry had had her qualifying certificate for more than 10 years. She had received training in the use of Posey restraints and had previously cared for patients whose condition required these restraints. Because Terry had previously worked for PSS and had not given any indication of incompetence, there was no viability to the claim that PSS was negligent in assigning her to the care of Santiago.

▶ CONDITIONS

A *condition* to a contract is an act or event that must happen or be performed by one party before the other party has any responsibility to perform under the contract. An *express condition* is formally written into the contract in specific terms. An *implied condition* is one in which, although the parties may not have specifically mentioned the condition, it can reasonably be assumed that the parties intended the condition to be enforced.

▶ PERFORMANCE

Performance is the act of doing what is required by a contract. Each party to a contract is bound to perform the promises according to the stipulated terms contained in the contract. The effect of successful performance by each party to a contract is to discharge the parties bound to the contract from any future contractual liability.

③ NONPERFORMANCE DEFENSES

Under some circumstances, the law gives a person a *right not to perform* under a contract. Defenses permitting nonperformance of a contract include fraud, mistakes, duress, illegal contract, impossibility, and statute of limitations.

Fraud

A victim of fraud is not generally required to perform the agreed upon terms of a contract. *Contract fraud* occurs when at least one party in a contract knowingly misrepresents a material fact contained in the contract and intends that the other party rely on that misrepresentation. The second party must rely on the misrepresentation and suffer some damage before being excused from performing under the terms of the contract.

Mistakes of Fact and Law

A party to a contract is permitted to claim a mistake in fact or law in a contract as a defense under certain instances. There are two types of mistakes: mistake of fact and mistake of law. A *mistake of fact* is a mistaken belief that certain facts are true. Both parties must have made the mistake. If only one is in error (and it is not known to the other), mistake of fact is not generally a defense. *Mistake of law*, on the other hand, is an incorrect judgment of the legal consequences of the known facts. If the parties to a suit make a mistake as to the law involved, they must accept their plight without any remedy.

Duress

Duress is the use of unlawful threats or pressure to force an individual to act against his or her will. An act performed under duress is not legally binding.

Illegal Contract

An illegal contract is a contract whose formation, object, or performance is against the law or contrary to public policy that no court will uphold or enforce. No individual can recover damages when a contract is formed for illegal purposes. A contract must not violate the law. To be a valid contract, the purpose or object (purpose or design) of the contract must not violate state or federal policy and must not violate any statute, rule, or regulation. If the subject or purpose of a contract becomes illegal by some statute, rule, or regulation before actual formation of the contract, the contract is invalid. For example, the transference of property with the object of defrauding another is an unenforceable contract.

Impossibility to Perform

Contracts can become impossible to perform because (1) certain facts might have existed at the time the contract was executed or (2) they might have arisen subsequent to the formation of the contract. Contracts that are impossible to perform do not have to be carried out by the parties to a contract. A promise to perform a contract becomes impossible when, for example, the work to be performed is impossible to complete the terms of the contract because of a natural disaster or the law has changed, thus making performance of the work agreed upon illegal.

Statute of Limitations

A party who does not, within a timely period set by statute (*statute of limitations*), take action to enforce contract rights by suing for damages caused by a breach of contract can be barred from doing so.

▶ REMEDIES

What can a party do when another has breached the contract and refuses to or cannot perform? The general rule is that legal redress will attempt to make the injured party whole again.

Specified Performance

When an aggrieved party has subsequently complied with his or her obligations pursuant to the agreed upon terms of a contract, that party might seek specific performance as a remedy from the other party to the contract rather than monetary remuneration. The most satisfactory remedy available to an injured party may be to require specific performance by the other party to the contract.

Monetary Damages

Monetary damages, sometimes called *compensatory damages*, are awarded in an attempt to restore to the aggrieved party the money that it would have had if the other party had not breached the contract. This can include the cost of making a substitute contract with another party and the expense of delays caused by the breach.

General and Consequential Damages

General damages are those that can be expected to arise from a breach of a contract. The damages incurred must be foreseeable and common in the circumstances. *Consequential damages* are those that occur because of some unexpected, unusual, or strange development involved in the particular contract in dispute. The distinction between the two types is one of foreseeability. If it is found that the party who breached the contract could have foreseen the damages that followed, that person could be liable for consequential as well as general damages.

Duty to Mitigate Damages

When a party to a contract has breached the terms of a contract, the other party cannot stand idly by and let damages build indefinitely. Every injured party has a duty to mitigate (lessen) damages caused by the breach of another person or entity. Failure to do so will prevent the aggrieved party's recovery of damages that could have been mitigated.

Arbitration

Under the modern view of contract law, agreements in contracts to arbitrate subsequent disputes are valid.

▶ EMPLOYMENT CONTRACTS

An *employment contract* is a written document that sets forth the terms of the employment relationship. Such contracts are binding on both the employer and employee so long as the contract has been executed in a legal manner. The conditions of employment, including wages, hours, and type of work, are generally described in an employment contract. Depending on the level of employment and the responsibility of the new employee, the conditions of employment should include the terms of employment, the duties and responsibilities of the employee, compensation, confidentiality requirements (e.g., trade secrets and proprietary information), a noncompete clause, and provisions for termination of the agreement (e.g., an inability to perform one's duties and responsibilities).

A contract can be express or implied. Most employees work under employment contracts. For example, if an employee signs a document promising to abide by company policy and procedures, it likely constitutes an employment contract. Certain categories of employees (e.g., radiologists) often have the ability to negotiate their employment contracts. An employer's right to terminate an employee can be limited by express agreement with the employee or through a collective bargaining agreement to which the employee is a beneficiary.

The rights of employees have been expanding through judicial decisions in different states. Court decisions have been based on verbal promises, historical practices of the employer, and documents, such as employee handbooks, job descriptions, and administrative policy and procedure manuals that describe employee rights.

A job description is not intended to be an employment contract, nor does it dissolve the at-will employment relationship. It is a record of the basic purpose, typical level of authority, typical source of action, and representative function or duties of the job. It is designed to provide management and others with a clear understanding of the level of the job and its working relationships, skills, and requirements in relation to other jobs.

Employee Breaches Contract: Repayment of Tuition Required

The registered nurse in *Sweetwater Hosp. Ass'n v. Carpenter*[10] was found to have breached her contract with the hospital under which the hospital agreed to pay for her schooling as a nurse anesthetist in exchange for her agreeing to work for the hospital for 5 years following completion of her studies. The nurse agreed that if she failed to work at the hospital following completion of her studies, she would be responsible for cash advances by the hospital plus interest. Upon completion of her studies, the nurse sought employment elsewhere because it appeared to her that there were no nurse anesthetist positions available at the hospital.

As consideration for the loan, the contract provided that the defendant agreed to become or remain an employee of the hospital. The contract did not state in what capacity the defendant would become or remain an employee. There was nothing in the language of the contract stating that the hospital had an obligation to offer the defendant a nurse anesthetist position.

In this case, there was no proof by the defendant that the hospital breached the contract. The defendant breached her own contract by taking a job elsewhere without specifically getting proof that she was not going to be offered a job by the hospital. The defendant did not present herself for employment at the hospital after graduation. She accepted a position elsewhere. Because she did not accept employment at the hospital, she was not entitled to rely upon the forgiveness provisions contained in the contract. She was, therefore, obligated to repay the hospital.

Geographic Limitations on Practice Reasonable

The provisions of a covenant prohibiting the plaintiff in *Thompson v. Nason Hosp.*,[11] a pediatrician, from practicing pediatric medicine for a period of 2 years within a 10-mile radius of the defendant's office, and prohibiting her for a period of 1 year from soliciting patients of the defendant, were found to be reasonable as to both duration and geographic area. When the plaintiff entered into the employment contract, she agreed to be bound by the restrictive covenants in the event that her employment should end. The defendant had the right to terminate the plaintiff's employment for any reason whatsoever or for no reason upon 60 days' written notice to the plaintiff.

No Express Agreement: Right to Terminate

No express agreement was found to exist in *O'Connor v. Eastman Kodak Co.*,[12] in which the court held that an employer had a right to terminate an employee at will at any time and for any reason or no reason. The plaintiff did not rely on any specific representation made to him during the course of his employment interviews nor did he rely on any documentation in the employee handbook, which would have limited the defendant's common law right to discharge at will. The employee had relied on a popular perception of Kodak as a "womb-to-tomb" employer.

Restrictive Covenant Enforceable

The plaintiff-hospital, in *Sarah Bush Lincoln Health Ctr. v. Perket*,[13] sued its former director of physical medicine and rehabilitation to enforce a restrictive covenant in the employment contract precluding the director from accepting similar employment in the same county within 1 year of termination of employment.

The parties to the complaint entered into a contract whereby the defendant was employed as the plaintiff's director of physical medicine. The contract provided that during the director's employment and for a period of 1 year thereafter, the director would not, directly or indirectly, invest in, own, manage, operate, control, be employed by, participate in, or be connected in any manner with the ownership, management, operation, or control of any person, firm, or corporation engaged in competition with the hospital in providing health services or facilities within Coles County, including the provision of services in a private office, without prior written consent of the hospital. Following the termination, the defendant engaged in the business of providing physical medicine and rehabilitation services in Coles County. The plaintiff argued that unless the defendant was enjoined, the hospital would suffer irreparable injury. The circuit court granted the hospital's motion for preliminary injunction.

On appeal, the Illinois Appellate Court held that the grant of the preliminary injunction was proper and that the defendant was engaging in the business of providing physical medicine and rehabilitation services in Coles County. By hiring the defendant, the hospital was thereby bringing him in contact with a clientele that the hospital had established over a period of years. The hospital was naturally interested in protecting its clients from being taken over by the defendant as a result of these contacts.

Restrictive Covenant Not Enforceable

Not every restrictive covenant is enforceable; for example, a restrictive covenant in an employment contract between a hospital and neurosurgeon was found to be geographically too restrictive, whereby the neurosurgeon was not to practice within a 30-mile radius of the hospital. This restriction was determined to be excessive. Such a restriction was considered to be detrimental to public interest in that the restricted area was plagued with a shortage of neurosurgeons.[14]

> A restrictive covenant in an employment contract between a hospital and a physician is not per se unreasonable and unenforceable. Under the circumstances of this case, however, the geographic restrictive area is excessive and must be reduced to avoid being detrimental to the public interest. In addition, because the two-year period for the restrictive covenant in this case has expired, the request for injunctive relief is moot.[15]

The reader should understand that employment contracts that contain a restrictive covenant between a physician and a hospital, although not favored, are not per se unreasonable and unenforceable. The trial court must determine whether the restrictive covenant protects the legitimate interests of the employer, imposes no undue hardship on the employee, and is not adverse to the public interest.[16]

In another case, the restrictive covenant in *Comprehensive Psychology System P.C. v. Prince,*[17] limiting the ability of a psychologist from practicing his profession within 10 miles of his former employer's facility and from soliciting any of his patients, was determined not to be enforceable. The nature of the practice of psychology and the uniquely personal patient–psychologist relationship forbid restrictions that might interfere with an ongoing course of treatment. A psychologist who changes his office location, voluntarily or involuntarily, has a duty to inform patients of the change and the new location and phone number. To do otherwise may be akin to abandonment. Before unilaterally withdrawing from treating a patient, a doctor must provide reasonable notice of withdrawal to enable the patient to obtain substitute care. The limitations the plaintiff seeks to enforce against the defendant interfere with a critical patient–psychologist relationship and with the right of the patient to continued treatment from that psychologist.

Employee Handbook: A Contract (4)

In order for an employee handbook to constitute a contract, thereby giving enforceable rights to the employee, the following elements must be present:

1. A policy statement that clearly sets forth a promise that the employee can construe to be an offer.
2. The policy statement must be distributed to the employee, making him or her aware of the offer.
3. After learning about the offer and policy statement, the employee must "begin" or "continue" to work.

The plaintiff-employee in *Weiner v. McGraw-Hill*[18] brought suit against his employer for wrongful termination. The plaintiff allegedly was discharged without just and sufficient cause or the rehabilitative efforts specified in the defendant's handbook and allegedly promised at the time the plaintiff accepted employment. Furthermore, on several occasions when the plaintiff recommended that certain of his subordinates

🔍 *BREACH OF EMPLOYMENT CONTRACT*

Citation: *Dutta v. St. Francis Reg'l Med. Ctr.*, 850 P.2d 928 (Kan. Ct. App. 1993)

Facts

On July 1, 1987, Dr. Dutta, a radiologist, began working in the radiology department of the hospital as an employee of Dr. Krause, the medical director of the hospital's radiology department. On August 5, 1988, the hospital terminated Krause's employment as medical director. On August 8, 1988, Dutta and the hospital entered into a written employment contract with a primary term of 90 days. The contract provided that if a new medical director had not been hired by the hospital within the 90-day period, the agreement was to be automatically extended for a second 90-day period.

Following a period of recruitment and interviews, the hospital offered Dr. Tan the position. Tan and the hospital executed a contract making him the medical director of the radiology department. The contract granted Tan the right "to provide radiation oncology services on an exclusive basis subject to the exception of allowing Dutta to continue her practice of radiation oncology at the hospital." On April 24, 1989, the hospital notified Dutta that the 90-day contract had expired and that Tan was appointed as the new medical director. The letter provided in part:

> It is our intent at this time to establish an exclusive contract with Dr. Donald Tan for medical direction and radiation therapy at SFRMC. Your medical staff privileges to practice radiation therapy at SFRMC will not be affected by this action. You will be allowed to maintain your current office space for radiation oncology activities; however, you should make alternative arrangements for your billing and collection activities. [*Id.* at 931]

Dutta and Tan then practiced independently of each other in the same facility. On October 13, 1989, Tan became unhappy with this arrangement and requested exclusive privileges, stating he could not continue as medical director without exclusivity. On February 2, 1990, an exclusive contract was authorized by the hospital. Dutta was notified that she would no longer be permitted to provide radiation therapy services at the hospital after May 1, 1990. By letter, Dutta twice requested a hearing on the hospital's decision to revoke her right to use hospital facilities. Both requests were denied.

Dutta sued the hospital for breach of employment contract after the hospital entered into an exclusive agreement with Tan, thereby denying Dutta the use of the hospital's radiology department and equipment. Dutta presented evidence about the purpose of the requirement in her contract with the hospital that provided that the new medical director be mutually acceptable to both parties. A hospital administrator testified that the hospital and Dutta included the phrase "mutually acceptable" in the contract because "[w]e both agreed that we wanted the person being recruited to be compatible with Dutta" [*Id.* at 932].

Issue

Was the language, "mutually acceptable," ambiguous in the employment contract between the hospital and Dutta?

Holding

The Kansas Court of Appeals held that substantial evidence supported the jury's verdict that the hospital breached its written employment contract with Dutta by hiring a medical director who was not mutually acceptable to both the hospital and Dutta.

Reason

The language in the contract is ambiguous if the words in the contract are subject to two or more possible meanings. The determination of whether a contract is ambiguous is a question of law. Paragraphs 4 and 5 of the hospital's employment agreement with Dutta, dated August 8, 1988, read as follows:

> 4. During the term of this Agreement the Medical Center shall be actively recruiting for a full-time Medical Director for the Radiation Therapy department. . . . Dr. Dutta shall be involved in the interviewing process. The person selected for [the] above positions shall be mutually acceptable to the Medical Center and Dr. Dutta. Dr. Dutta may discuss potential business arrangements with each individual interviewed.

> 5. Once the full-time Medical Director or part-time radiation therapist is selected, Dr. Dutta will, in good faith, attempt to reach a satisfactory business arrangement with the selected individual. [*Id.* at 936]

The testimony of Dutta, the hospital administrator, and the attorney who represented Dutta in contract negotiations provides a factual basis for the jury to find that the phrase, "mutually acceptable," in the contract was intended by Dutta to ensure that the hospital would select a medical director who indicated a willingness to form a partnership or otherwise acceptable business relationship.

be dismissed, he allegedly was instructed to proceed in strict compliance with the handbook and policy manuals. The court held that although the defendant did not engage the plaintiff for a fixed term of employment, the plaintiff pleaded a good cause of action for breach of contract. Even the employment application that the plaintiff signed at the time of employment stated that he would be subject to the provisions of McGraw-Hill's *Handbook on Personnel Policies and Procedures.*

In *Watson v. Idaho Falls Consolidated Hospitals, Inc.,*[19] a nurse's aide was awarded $20,000 for damages when the hospital, as employer, violated the provisions of its employee handbook in the manner in which it terminated the plaintiff's employment. Although the nurse's aide had no formal written contract, the employee handbook and the hospital policies and procedures manual constituted a contract in view of evidence to the effect that these documents had been intended to be enforced and complied with by both employees and management. Employees read and relied on the handbook as creating terms of an employment contract. They were required to sign for the handbook to establish receipt of a revised handbook that explained hospital policy, discipline, counseling, and termination. A policy and procedure manual placed on each floor of the hospital also outlined termination procedures.

Employee Handbook: Not a Contract

An employee handbook is not always considered a contract, as noted in *Churchill v. Waters*[20] where it was not a contract because of a disclaimer in the handbook. A nurse brought a civil rights action against the hospital and hospital officials after her discharge. The federal district court held for the defendants, finding that the hospital employee handbook did not give the nurse a protected property interest in continued employment: "Absent proof that the handbook contained clear promises which indicated the intent to bind the parties, no contract was created."[21] The "handbook contained a disclaimer" expressly disavowing any attempt to be bound by it and stated that its contents were not to be considered conditions of employment. The handbook was presented as a matter of information only, and the language contained therein was not intended to constitute a contract between McDonough District Hospital and the employee. Although an employee handbook may delineate specific disciplinary procedures, that fact

does not, in and of itself, constitute an enforceable contract.[22]

In *Trieger v. Montefiore Med. Ctr.*[23] a memorandum was circulated by Trieger to department chairs at the hospital strongly criticizing management and urging his co-chairs "to set things right and reclaim their prerogatives and responsibilities." The memorandum read in part as follows:

> . . . the role of Chairman has eroded over the past decade, largely through autocratic, unilateral decision-making and administrative micro-management. Chairmen no longer recruit faculty to their staff. Senior administration writes a contract which details in legalistic terminology what the boundaries will be, often without any provision for academic pursuits or even a phrase of welcome and encouragement. The Administration insists that all revenues belong to Montefiore including honoraria paid for continuing medical education teaching. Monies received for Graduate Medical Education from federal and state sources, which are meant to pay for teaching support for house staff education are usually absent from teaching budgets. The crisis of failure to replace essential capital equipment has managed to impair our efficiency of operation and have us drift further down the spiral of deficit. We seem to have entered onto the stage of a non-reversible Greek tragedy. We have to deal with hiring freezes which further compromise our productivity. To my knowledge chairmen and attending staff have not received a cost of living increase in salary in nine years! How can you retain good faculty?[24]

The appellate court found that the trial court correctly determined that the memorandum was insubordinate and that it gave just cause for termination of the physician's employment contract. In addition, the physician's age discrimination claim was dismissed for lack of evidence sufficient to raise an issue of fact as to whether the hospital's reason for the doctor's dismissal, circulation of the insubordinate memorandum, was a pretext for discrimination. The doctor was terminated immediately after circulating the insubordinate memorandum, and there was no other evidence in the record to support the claim that the hospital's actions were false or contrived.

▶ MEDICAL STAFF BYLAWS: A CONTRACT

Medical staff bylaws can be considered a contract. The plaintiff, Dr. Bass, in *Bass v. Ambrosius*,[25] alleged that the hospital's termination of his staff privileges violated its own bylaws. The hospital contended that its bylaws did not constitute a contract between itself and Bass, and therefore, any violation of those bylaws would not support a breach of contract claim. The general rule that hospital bylaws can constitute a contract between the hospital and its staff is consistent with Wisconsin law that an employee handbook written and disseminated by the employer, and whose terms the employee has accepted, constitutes a contract between the employer and the employee. For instance, in *Ferraro v. Koelsch*,[26] an employee handbook was management's statement of what the company offered its employees and what it expected from its employees in return. It thus contained the essential elements of a binding contract: the promise of employment on stated terms and conditions by the employer and the promise by the employee to continue employment under those conditions. The court noted that a promise for a promise, or the exchange of promises, constitutes consideration to support any contract of this bilateral nature.

The bylaws at issue in *Bass v. Ambrosius*, required by Wis. Admin. Code § HSS 124.12(5) and approved by the hospital's board of directors, have the same contractual elements as did the handbook in *Ferraro*. First, the bylaws state that they provide the rules that govern the physicians and dentists practicing at the hospital. Second, members of the hospital's medical–dental staff must continuously meet the qualifications, standards, and requirements set forth in the bylaws. Third, an appointment to the medical–dental staff confers only those privileges provided by the letter of appointment and the bylaws. Fourth, all applicants for appointment to the medical–dental staff must submit a signed application acknowledging the requirement to familiarize themselves with the bylaws. Thus, Bass's application to the medical–dental staff acknowledged by his signature that he would conduct his professional activities according to the bylaws and rules and regulations of both the hospital and the medical–dental staff of the hospital. In a separate letter, as part of the application process, Bass agreed to conduct his activities according to the bylaws of the hospital, as well as the bylaws and rules and regulations of the hospital's medical–dental staff. For its part, the hospital promised that the medical–dental staff would be guided and governed by rules and regulations consistent with the bylaws, and it promised that any adverse action against a member of the medical–dental staff would comply with various procedural safeguards. The bylaws constituted a contract between Bass and the hospital. Accordingly, Bass was entitled to an order holding that the hospital had to comply with its bylaws before it could terminate his staff privileges.

In *Sadler v. Dimensions Health Corporation*,[27] Sadler, an obstetrician and gynecologist (OB/GYN), applied for medical staff privileges in the hospital's OB/GYN department. She was granted temporary privileges pending receipt of further information on her application. While practicing at the hospital, three incident reports concerning Sadler were filed. They involved her failure to respond to calls and initiate timely treatment, a broken humerus and permanent nerve injury following a birth, and a retained surgical sponge. The patient care committee (PCC) of the OB/GYN department reviewed the reports and concluded that continued observation of Sadler was warranted. The PCC met with Sadler to review five cases. Three involved nonindicated or precipitous cesarean sections, and two involved delayed responses to calls from the hospital staff. Following review, the PCC recommended that Sadler consult with more senior practitioners for second opinions before performing cesarean sections.

Two physician consultants were eventually retained by the OB/GYN department of the hospital to review charts of a variety of Sadler's cases. Random charts of other members of the OB/GYN department of the hospital were also reviewed. Following review, the consultants recommended in their report that Sadler be subjected to case-by-case pre-monitoring for surgical indications. The hospital's medical executive committee (MEC) reviewed the documentation regarding Sadler's performance. Based on that review, the MEC voted not to extend provisional privileges and to impose monitoring of Sadler until her provisional privileges expired. Sadler was notified by letter of the MEC decision not to extend her provisional privileges. She was advised that she had a right to request a hearing pursuant to the provisions of the bylaws. Sadler exercised that right, and an ad hoc committee (a hearing committee) was formed pursuant to the bylaws. The committee concluded that there was compelling evidence that the physician consistently disregarded hospital policies, was unprofessional in her dealings with staff, and deviated from acceptable standards in her hospital record keeping and clinical practice. In addition, she ignored efforts by the hospital to bring her into compliance.

The parties agreed that the bylaws of the medical staff of the hospital to which Sadler subscribed when she applied for privileges at the hospital constituted an enforceable contract between her and the hospital. Those bylaws provided a process by which Sadler could challenge her termination of clinical privileges. Sadler fully pursued the prescribed process.

Represented by counsel, she appeared before a panel of members of the medical staff who had no involvement with her case. She cross-examined witnesses under oath, called her own witnesses, offered evidence, and presented oral argument and posthearing written memoranda to the hearing committee. When the hearing committee agreed with the recommendation of the MEC that her privileges at the hospital should be terminated, she exercised her right under the bylaws to have that decision reviewed by the appellate review committee of the board of directors.

The court of appeals held that there was substantial evidence to support the conclusions of the hearing committee and the board of directors that the imposition of proctoring and monitoring upon Sadler and the termination of her hospital privileges were reasonable and proper.

Right to Hearing

A physician whose privileges are either suspended or terminated must exhaust all remedies provided in a facility's bylaws, rules, and regulations before commencing a court action. The U.S. Court of Appeals in *Northeast Georgia Radiological Associates v. Tidwell*[28] held that a contract with the hospital's radiologists, which incorporated the medical staff bylaws, sustained the plaintiffs' claim to a protected property interest entitling them to a hearing before the medical staff and the hospital authority.

▶ EXCLUSIVE CONTRACTS

An organization often enters into an exclusive contract with physicians or medical groups for the purpose of providing a specific service(s) to the organization. Such contracts generally grant the contracting party the exclusive right to perform the services contracted for by the organization. Exclusive contracts typically occur within the organization's ancillary service departments (e.g., anesthesiology, emergency services, pathology, radiology). Physicians who seek to practice at organizations in these ancillary areas but who are not part of the exclusive group have attempted to invoke the federal antitrust laws to challenge these exclusive contracts. These challenges generally have been unsuccessful.

In *Jefferson Parish Hospital v. Hyde*,[29] the defendant hospital had a contract with a firm of anesthesiologists that required all anesthesia services for the hospital's patients be performed by that firm. Because of this contract, the plaintiff anesthesiologist's application for admission to the hospital's medical staff was denied. Dr. Hyde commenced an action in the federal district court, claiming the exclusive contract violated Section 1 of the Sherman Antitrust Act. The district court rejected the plaintiff's complaint, but the U.S. Court of Appeals for the Fifth Circuit reversed the decision, finding the contract illegal per se. The Supreme Court reversed the Fifth Circuit, holding that the exclusive contract in question does not violate Section 1 of the Sherman Antitrust Act. The Supreme Court's holding was based on the fact that the defendant hospital did not possess "market power," and, therefore, patients were free to enter a competing hospital and to use another anesthesiologist instead of the firm. Thus, the court concluded that the evidence was insufficient to provide a basis for finding that the contract, as it actually operates in the market, had unreasonably restrained competition.

Similarly, the anesthesiologists in *Belmar v. Cipolla*[30] brought an action challenging a hospital's exclusive contract with a different group of anesthesiologists. The New Jersey Supreme Court held that under state law, the hospital's exclusive contract was reasonable and did not violate public policy.

> Although the experts at trial differed about the relative advantages and disadvantages of the exclusive contract between Community and defendant doctors, all agreed that an exclusive contract was a recognized method of providing anesthesiology services. At trial, plaintiffs relied on an amendment to the statement of policy of the American Society of Anesthesiologists that disapproves exclusive contracts between hospitals and anesthesiologists. The statement, apparently adopted in response to the use of nurse anesthetists by some hospitals, is advisory only and does not subject contracting anesthesiologists to ethical sanctions.[31]

Nurse Practitioner: Noncompetitive Clause

The respondent-hospital in *Washington County Memorial Hospital v. Sidebottom*[32] employed the appellant-nurse practitioner from October 1993 through April 1998. Prior to beginning her employment,

COMPETITION CLAUSE NOT OVERLY RESTRICTIVE

Citation: *Dominy v. National Emergency Servs.*, 451 S.E.2d 472 (Ga. App. 1994)

Facts

The appellee, National Emergency Services (NES), assigned appellant, Dr. Dominy, to the emergency department at Memorial Hospital and Manor (MHM) in Bainbridge, Georgia, where he was working in 1987 when that hospital terminated its contract with NES and contracted with another provider, Coastal Emergency Services, for emergency department physicians. Dominy continued to perform emergency medical services at MHM under contract with Coastal until 1989.

The contract provided: "The period of this Agreement shall be for one (1) year from the date hereof, automatically renewable for a like period upon each expiration thereof...." The only reasonable construction of this provision was that the parties intended to contract for Dominy's employment for automatically renewable 1-year terms upon the mutual assent of the parties. The fact that the agreement did not set out the mechanics by which mutual assent may be communicated did not invalidate the contract.

Dominy challenged the contract's noncompetition clause as overly restrictive. The covenant in this case provides, in pertinent part: "for a period of two (2) years after the termination of this agreement ... Physician shall not directly or indirectly solicit a contract to perform nor have any ownership or financial interest in any corporation, partnership, or other entity soliciting or contracting to perform emergency medical service for any medical institution at which Physician has performed the same or similar services under this Agreement or any prior Agreement between Physician and Corporation" [*Id.* at 474].

Issue

Was the contract's noncompetition clause overly restrictive?

Holding

The court of appeals held that the noncompetition clause was not overly restrictive.

Reason

The record reveals no attempt by either party to terminate the contract, and it is undisputed that Dominy received payment for his services at MHM and other benefits from NES consistent with the agreement until the hospital terminated its contract with NES. By their conduct, the parties assented to each of the contract's yearly renewals. Accordingly, the trial court properly granted summary judgment to NES.

As to the contract's noncompetition clause, this restriction prohibits Dominy from performing emergency medical services in only MHM in Bainbridge, Georgia, where he worked pursuant to a contract with NES, and from having an ownership or financial interest in an entity contracting to provide emergency medical services to that one hospital. He is not precluded from all practice of medicine, with staff privileges at MHM, nor is he prohibited from providing emergency medical services, directly or under contract to a provider of such services, to other hospitals in the immediate vicinity. The court found that such a restriction is reasonably limited in duration and territorial effect while it protects NES's interest in preventing Dominy from becoming its competitor immediately after termination of its contract with MHM.

the nurse entered into an employment agreement with the hospital. The agreement included a noncompetition clause providing, in part, that the nurse, during the term of the agreement and for a period of 1 year after the termination of her employment, would not within a 50-mile radius directly or indirectly engage in the practice of nursing without the express direction or consent of the hospital. In February 1994, the nurse requested the hospital's permission to work for the Washington County Health Department doing prenatal nursing care. Because the hospital was not then involved in providing prenatal care, the hospital gave her permission to accept

that employment but reserved the ability to withdraw the permission if the services the nurse was providing later came to be provided by the hospital. In January 1996, the nurse and the hospital entered into a second employment agreement that continued the parties' employment relationship through January 9, 1998. This agreement included a noncompetition clause identical to the 1993 employment agreement. It also provided for automatic renewal for an additional 2 years unless either party gave written termination notice no less than 90 days prior to the expiration of the agreement. On March 11, 1998, the nurse gave the hospital written notice of her resignation effective April 15. On April 16, the nurse began working as a nurse practitioner with Dr. Mullen, whose office is located within 50 miles of the hospital.

The Circuit Court prohibited the nurse from practicing nursing within a 50-mile radius of the hospital for a period of 1 year from April 15. The noncompetition clause in the nurse's employment agreement was found to be clear and unambiguous. The nurse had been notified by the hospital that the noncompetition clause in her contract would be enforced. On appeal, the judgment of the circuit court was affirmed.

▶ RESTRAINT OF TRADE

The increasing number of alternative delivery systems and resultant competition has created the potential for illegal activities to restrain trade. The emphasis on free enterprise and a competitive marketplace has resulted in careful scrutiny by the Federal Trade Commission (FTC), the federal agency responsible for monitoring the marketplace and enforcing federal antitrust laws.

The Antitrust Division of the U.S. Department of Justice has primary responsibility for enforcing federal antitrust laws, which includes investigation of possible violations of both the criminal and the civil provisions of the Sherman, Clayton, and Robinson–Patman Acts.

Federal Trade Commission

The FTC is authorized to enforce Section 5 of the FTC Act, which prohibits unfair methods of competition and unfair or deceptive acts or practices. Together with the Department of Justice, the FTC also enforces the Clayton Act sections that prohibit discrimination (e.g., in price), exclusive dealings and similar arrangements, certain corporate acquisitions of stock or assets, and interlocking directorates.

Sherman Antitrust Act

The Sherman Antitrust Act, named for its author Senator John Sherman of Ohio, proscribes that every contract, combination in the form of trust or otherwise, or conspiracy in restraint of trade or commerce among the several states is declared to be illegal. Those who attempt to monopolize or combine or conspire with any other person or persons to monopolize any part of the trade or commerce can be deemed guilty of a felony.[33] Areas of concern for healthcare organizations include reduced market competition, price fixing, actions that bar or limit new entrants to the field, preferred provider arrangements, and exclusive contracts.

A healthcare organization must be cognizant of the potential problems that may exist when limiting the number of physicians that it will admit to its medical staff. Because closed staff determinations can effectively limit competition from other physicians, the governing body must ensure that the decision-making process in granting privileges is based on legislative, objective criteria and is not dominated by those who have the most to gain competitively by denying privileges. Physicians have attempted to use state and federal antitrust laws to challenge determinations denying or limiting medical staff privileges. Generally, these actions claim that the organization conspired with other physicians to ensure that the complaining physician would not obtain privileges so that competition among physicians would be reduced.

Conspiracy to Terminate Physician's Privileges

In *Patrick v. Burget*,[34] the U.S. Supreme Court upheld a $2 million jury verdict in favor of a surgeon practicing in Oregon who claimed that other physicians conspired to terminate his staff privileges at the only hospital in town and thus drove him out of practice. The defendant physicians argued that their conduct should be immune from liability under the state action doctrine because Oregon, like many states, has state agencies that regulate the procedures that hospitals may use to grant or deny staff privileges. The Supreme Court rejected this state action defense in the light of the egregious facts of the case (the defendant physicians were also participants in the state processes) and the fact that Oregon's statutory scheme did not actively supervise medical staff determinations.[35]

Claim of Boycott Denied

On February 29, 1984, the defendant hospital in *Cogan v. Harford Memorial Hospital*,[36] owned by Upper Chesapeake Health Systems, Inc. (UCHS), contracted with Dr. Cogan to act as the chief of radiology for 5 years. In 1988, the hospital and Cogan renegotiated the contract. Cogan's compensation was increased, and the contract was extended until May 25, 1993, subject to termination by either party, providing a 120-day written notice. During the renegotiation, Cogan sought compensation on a fee-for-service basis, but the hospital was uncomfortable with such an arrangement.

In December 1990, Cogan began discussing with NMR of America, Inc. the possibility of opening a radiology clinic to provide testing with magnetic resonance imaging (MRI) separate from the hospital.

The hospital expressed opposition to such an arrangement. In response, Cogan tied discussions of a new MRI clinic to renegotiation of his contract on a fee-for-service arrangement. The hospital agreed to discuss a fee-for-service contract. Under the proposed contract, Cogan's radiology group would not maintain any financial or professional interest with any competing medical facility within 20 miles of a hospital owned by UCHS. The parties failed to reach an agreement.

On March 1, 1991, the hospital informed Cogan of its intention to terminate his employment contract as of June 28, 1991. In October 1991, Cogan formed Cogan & Smith, a partnership with Dr. Smith, his former associate at the hospital.

In November 1991, Cogan & Smith signed a contract in which it agreed to act as the managing director of a radiology clinic. The clinic had a lower volume of business than anticipated, and Cogan filed suit against UCHS. He contended that the hospital's policy against sending patients to facilities not accredited by The Joint Commission impeded the clinic's business. The hospital claimed that the policy affected no more than seven patients. Cogan contended it affected 15,000 patients. He characterized this policy as a group boycott against the clinic. Under the Sherman Antitrust Act, group boycotts may be considered anticompetitive.

Cogan contended that the defendants violated the Sherman Act, breached the contract between himself and UCHS, interfered with his contractual relations, wrongfully discharged him, and deprived him of his constitutional rights in violation of 42 U.S.C. § 1983, as amended, 15 U.S.C.A. §§ 1, 2.

The U.S. District Court held that the harm suffered by Cogan because he was unable to continue working at the hospital was not compensable under the Sherman Act. The court found no evidence showing that competition in any relevant market had been harmed, reduced, or impacted by the termination of Cogan's contract or the alleged group boycott of the MRI clinic by the implementation of the hospital's policy. The only harm asserted was Cogan's inability to continue working at the hospital. The injury he incurred as a competitor of the hospital was not the "type the antitrust laws were intended to prevent."[37]

Agreement for Professional Services Too Restrictive

In *Emergicare Systems Corporation v. Bourdon*,[38] Emergicare Systems Corporation (ESC) contracted to provide emergency department physicians to the Longview

Regional Hospital for several years; Dr. Bourdon was one of those physicians. On October 23, 1991, ESC sent a letter to Bourdon confirming that its contract with Longview Regional Hospital would terminate on November 8, 1991, and that pursuant to his agreement for professional services with ESC, his agreement with ESC would also terminate. Bourdon talked to the hospital administrator and to Metroplex Emergency Physicians, PA. Arrangements were made for him to continue his work at the emergency department as an employee of Metroplex.

ESC sued Bourdon and Metroplex. ESC alleged that Bourdon breached a covenant not to compete and that Metroplex interfered with its contractual agreement with Bourdon. Following a nonjury trial, judgment was rendered on February 15, 1996, that ESC take nothing from the defendants. ESC appealed. The covenant purports to restrict the physician from working within 5 miles of any clinic operated by ESC, whether the physician ever worked in that clinic or not. Also, the covenant purports to restrict the physician from working in any emergency department where ESC provides emergency department physicians for 1 year following termination of such contract. This could be at some indefinite future date, more than 1 year following the physician's termination of employment by ESC.

The trial court was correct in rendering the take-nothing judgment on the appellant's claims against Metroplex. The appeals court held that covenants not to compete that are unreasonable restraints of trade and that are unenforceable on grounds of public policy cannot form the basis of an action for tortious interference.

▶ HOSPITAL STAFF PRIVILEGES

Staff privileges are both professionally and economically important to healthcare professionals in the practice of their chosen professions. Healthcare organizations must be selective in the granting of staff privileges to maintain quality standards, but every effort must be made to prevent anticompetitive abuses. As competition increases between podiatrists and orthopedic surgeons, psychologists and psychiatrists, nurse midwives and obstetricians, nurse anesthetists and anesthesiologists, and so on, it must be understood that there is a clear difference in denying staff privileges to an individual on a quality basis and denying such privileges to an entire group of professionals; the latter will serve only to raise a red flag and increase the chances of scrutiny by the courts. Competition for patients increases the potential for denial

CONTRACT VIOLATES ANTITRUST LAWS

Citation: *Oltz v. St. Peter's Community Hosp.*, 19 F.3d 1312 (9th Cir. 1994)

Facts

Oltz, a nurse anesthetist, brought an antitrust action against physician anesthesiologists and St. Peter's Community Hospital after he was terminated. Oltz had a billing agreement with the hospital, which provided 84% of the surgical services in the rural community that it served. The anesthesiologists did not like competing with the nurse anesthetist's lower fees and, as a result, entered into an exclusive contract with the hospital on April 29, 1980, in order to squeeze the nurse anesthetist out of the market. This resulted in cancellation of the nurse anesthetist's contract with the hospital. Oltz filed a suit against the anesthesiologists and hospital for violation of the Sherman Antitrust Act, 15 U.S.C. § 1. The anesthesiologists settled for $462,500 before trial.

The case against the hospital proceeded to trial. The jury found that the hospital conspired with the anesthesiologists and awarded the plaintiff $212,182 in lost income and $209,649 in future damages. The trial judge considered the damage award to be excessive and ordered a new trial.

The hospital motioned the court to exclude all damages after June 26, 1982, which was the date that the hospital renegotiated its exclusive contract with the anesthesiology group. The court decided that Oltz failed to prove that the renegotiated contract also violated antitrust laws, thus ruling that Oltz was not entitled to damages after June 26, 1982. Because Oltz conceded that he could not prove damages greater than those offset by his settlement with the physicians, his claim for damages against the hospital was disposed of by summary judgment.

The judge who presided over Oltz's request for attorneys' fees restricted the amount that he could claim. Because Oltz had been denied damages from the hospital, the judge refused to award attorneys' fees or costs for work performed after the 1986 liability trial.

Issue

Was Oltz entitled to seek recovery for all damages resulting from destruction of his business after June 26, 1982?

Holding

The U.S. Court of Appeals for the Ninth Circuit held that Oltz was entitled to seek recovery for all damages.

Reason

Oltz introduced evidence that the initial exclusive contract violated antitrust laws and that such violation destroyed his practice. "Because the initial conspiracy destroyed his practice, Oltz is entitled to seek recovery for all damages resulting from the destruction of his business. . . . The legality of any subsequent agreements between the conspirators is irrelevant, because the April 29, 1980, contract severed the lifeline to Oltz's thriving practice . . ." [*Id.* at 1314].

of privileges to prevent competitors from effectively entering the marketplace and practicing their respective professions.

Restricting Medical Staff Privileges

Moratoriums and closed medical staffs, as used in the healthcare field, describe an organization's policy of prohibiting further appointments to its medical staff. Generally, a *moratorium* is for a specified period. It is lifted at such time as the purpose for which it was instituted no longer exists. A *closed staff* is of a more permanent nature and relates to the mission of the institution, such as a commitment to teaching and research. Such institutions are very selective in their medical staff appointments. Generally, physicians who are appointed have both prominent academic interests and abilities as well as national recognition for expertise in their specialties.

Organizations have adopted a moratorium policy in certain instances because of a high inpatient census and the difficulties that would be encountered in accommodating new physicians. If left unchecked, the closing of an organization's medical staff eventually could have the effect of discouraging a competitive environment in the physician marketplace and delivery of health care. The governing body should methodically and rationally review any request to close any department or specialty to new applicants for medical staff privileges. When considering *exclusive* contracts the organization also must consider its financial effect on both the physician as well as the organization. Closing the staff to competent community-based physicians does not necessarily equate to quality patient care.

Governing bodies that adopt a policy limiting the number of physicians by specialty or department must do so on a rational basis and take the following into consideration before closing or limiting medical staff privileges to new applicants:

- Effect on the organization's census
- Organization and community needs for additional physicians in medical and surgical specialties and subspecialties that have a few or dwindling number physicians on staff, which in turn, limits patient choice in selecting a physician
- Strain that additional staff will place on the organization's supporting departments (e.g., radiology and laboratory services)
- Effect of denying medical staff privileges to applicants who presently are located within the geographic area of the organization and serving community residents
- Effect on any contracts the organization may have with other healthcare delivery systems, such as health maintenance organizations
- Effect a moratorium will have on physician groups that may desire to add a partner
- The positive effect additional staff may have on the quality of care rendered in the organization
- Whether closing the staff will confine control of the organization's beds to the existing medical staff, allowing them to enhance their economic interests at the expense of their patients and other qualified physicians
- Effect of a limited moratorium by specialty as opposed to a comprehensive one involving all specialties (indiscriminately closing a staff in all departments and sections without a review could be considered an action in restraint of trade)
- Existence of a mechanism for periodic review of the need to continue a moratorium
- Effect that medical staff resignations during the moratorium may have on the organization's census
- Adopting a mechanism to encourage and recruit new physicians when a need is determined necessary to meet community needs
- Characteristics of the medical staff (is the staff aging and is there a need for highly trained physicians trained in new technology?)
- Potential for restraint of trade legal action under antitrust laws
- Effect on physicians without staff privileges whose patients are admitted to the hospital
- Formation of a committee composed of representatives from the governing body, medical staff, administration, and legal counsel to develop an appropriate moratorium policy
- Selection of a consultant to study the demographic marketplace, physician referral patterns, literature, and organization use; conduct a medical staff opinion poll; develop patient–physician population ratios; determine population shifts; develop a formula to determine optimal staffing levels by department and section; and provide this information to the governing body for use in determining the appropriateness of closing the staff in selected medical departments and/or sections
- Consideration of the support of the governing body, medical staff, and administration prior to taking any action that limits the acceptance of new physicians to the organization's professional staff
- Addressing of community concerns in order to assure diversity and the right and the ability of patients to choose a physician from the community with which they have a trust relationship, a right that must not be hindered by healthcare facilities that decide to limit applications from qualified medical staff applicants

The continuing pressures of new technology, third-party payers, a growing body of regulations, malpractice insurance rates, and a shortage of physicians in a variety of specialties emphasize the need for organizations to consider how they can effectively compete in the marketplace. The imposition of a moratorium could prove to be counterproductive to the long-term survival of an organization.

The governing body must ensure that any proposed action to close an organization's medical staff is based on objective criteria. Unless an organization can show closing its medical staff is based on legitimate patient care concerns and/or relates to the objectives of the organization, physicians could successfully challenge an organization's actions to impose a moratorium.

▶ TRANSFER AGREEMENTS

Healthcare organizations should have a written transfer agreement in effect with other organizations to help ensure the smooth transfer of patients from one facility to another when such is determined appropriate. A *transfer agreement* is a written document that sets forth the terms and conditions under which a patient may be transferred from one facility to another that is able to provide the kind of care required by the patient. Transfer agreements help to seamlessly facilitate moving patients between facilities when medically necessary.

Transfer agreements should be written in compliance with and reflect the provisions of the federal and state laws, regulations, and standards affecting healthcare organizations. Agreements that will aid in bringing about the maximum use of the services of each organization and in ensuring the best possible care for patients should be established. The basic elements of a transfer agreement include the following:

1.   *Identification of each party to the agreement*, including the name and location of each organization to the agreement.

2.   *Purpose of the agreement.*

3.   *Policies and procedures* for transfer of patients. (Language in this section of the agreement should make it clear that the patient's physician makes the determination as to the patient's need for the facilities and services of the receiving organization. The receiving organization should agree that, subject to its admission requirements and availability of space, it will admit the patient from the transferring organization as promptly as possible.)

4.   *Organizational responsibilities* for arranging and making the transfer. (Generally, the transferring organization is responsible for making transfer arrangements. The agreement should specify who would bear the costs involved in the transfer.)

5.   *Exchange of information.* (The agreement must provide a mechanism for the interchange of medical and other information relevant to the patient.)

6.   *Retention of autonomy.* (The agreement should make clear that each organization retains its autonomy and that the governing bodies of each facility will continue to exercise exclusive legal responsibility and control over the management, assets, and affairs of their respective facilities. It also should be stipulated that neither organization assumes any liability by virtue of the agreement for any debts or obligations of a financial or legal nature incurred by the other.)

7.   *Procedure for settling disputes.* (The agreement should include a method of settling disputes that might arise over some aspect of the patient transfer relationship.)

8.   *Procedure for modification or termination of the agreement.* (The agreement should provide that it could be modified or amended by mutual consent of the parties. It also

should provide for termination by either organization on notice within a specified period.)

9.   *Sharing of services.* (Depending on the situation, cooperative use of facilities and services on an outpatient basis [e.g., laboratory and X-ray testing] may be an important element of the relationship between organizations. The method of payment for services rendered should be carefully described in the agreement.)

10. *Publicity.* (The agreement should provide that neither organization will use the name of the other in any promotional or advertising material without prior approval of the other.)

11. *Exclusive versus nonexclusive agreement.* (It is advisable for organizations—when and where possible—to have transfer agreements with more than one organization. The agreement may include language to the effect that either party has the right to enter into transfer agreements with other organizations.)

▶ INSURANCE CONTRACT

Insurance is a form of risk management used primarily to hedge against the risk of potential loss. In an *insurance contract*, the insurer has an obligation to indemnify the insured for losses caused by specified events. In return, the insured must pay a fixed premium during the policy period. As noted, the interpretation of an insurance contract can give rise to a legal action when the insurer refuses to indemnify the insured.

Coverage Denied

The plaintiffs in *Truett v. Community Mut. Ins. Co.*[39] brought an action against the insurer to recover medical expenses. In June 1991, Truett was treated for migraine headaches. As of August 1, 1991, Truett was covered under an employee benefit plan through a group health insurance contract with Community Mutual Insurance Co. On August 29, 1991, Truett was hospitalized for dizziness, vomiting, and weakness on his left side. After extensive testing, Dr. Moorthy diagnosed Truett as suffering from a complicated migraine. Truett sought reimbursement for medical expenses he incurred during the course of his illness.

Community Mutual concluded on January 20, 1992, that Truett's medical expenses were not covered because the expenses were for the care of a

🔍 *THE COURT'S DECISION*

The Supreme Court of South Carolina found that the trial court erred in granting a directed verdict to Strickland on Harvey's breach of contract claim. Harvey relied on the documents he signed expressing his desire not to be administered blood.

> I, Charles Harvey, refuse to have blood or any blood products given to me.
> The risks attendant to my refusal have been fully explained to me and I fully understand that my chances for gaining normal health are seriously reduced, and that in all probability, my refusal for such treatment, medical intervention, and/or procedure (may) (will) seriously imperil my health or life.
> With the understanding, I hereby release the attending physician, the Lexington Medical Center and its employees and their respective agents, heirs, executors, administrators and assigns from any and all claims of whatsoever kind of any nature.[41]

"Dr. Strickland testified that although he knew Harvey was a Jehovah's Witness, Harvey had told him he would consider a blood transfusion."[42] The court determined that it was for the jury to determine whether an undocumented express contract was created after the written consent form was signed refusing blood and blood by-products. The trial court's grant of a directed verdict was reversed, and the matter was remanded for a new trial.

preexisting condition. Under the insurance policy, conditions that existed prior to the effective date of the policy were not covered if health problems related to the conditions were manifested after the effective date. Truett challenged this assessment to a Community Mutual appeals board. Dr. Morrow was recruited by Community Mutual to provide an expert assessment of Truett's case. The Community Mutual appeals board found that Truett's condition was preexisting because he had been treated in June 1991 for migraine headaches. Therefore, Community Mutual denied his coverage for his expenses. On September 1, 1992, Truett filed a complaint against Community Mutual to recover Truett's medical expenses. The court of common pleas entered summary judgment for Community Mutual, and Truett appealed.

The Ohio Court of Appeals held that the insurer's denial of coverage was not arbitrary or capricious. The appeals board had all of Truett's medical records from before and after the incident in question. It obtained Morrow's expert opinion that the complicated migraine was a continuation from Truett's previous bouts with normal migraines. The appeals board and Morrow relied on medical evidence in making their decisions and neither overlooked nor ignored relevant information. Thus, the decision was not arbitrary or capricious.

Today, national health insurance provides that "All Marketplace plans must cover treatment for pre-existing medical conditions. No insurance plan can reject you, charge you more, or refuse to pay for essential health benefits for any condition you had before your coverage started. Once you're enrolled, the plan can't deny you coverage or raise your rates based only on your health."[40]

▶ CHAPTER REVIEW

1. A *contract* is a written or oral agreement that involves legally binding obligations between two or more parties. The *purpose* of a contract is to provide legal recourse should one or more of the parties not perform its obligations as set forth under the contract.

2. Various types of contracts include:

   - *Express contracts*: Those in which the parties have an oral agreement or have reduced agreements to writing. Written contracts are always the most desirable form. Although oral contracts are generally recognized, the courts cannot always enforce them.
   - *Implied contracts*: Those that are inferred by law and are based on parties' conduct.
   - *Voidable contracts* allow one party, but not the other, to escape from legal obligations under the contract.
   - *Executed contracts* are those in which obligations have been performed fully.
   - An *enforceable contract* is one that is a valid, legally binding agreement. If one party breaches it, the other will have an appropriate legal remedy.
   - An *unenforceable contract* is one in which, because of some defect, no legal remedy is available if breached by one of the parties to the contract.
   - Contracts for *realty* (real estate or interests in real estate), *goods* (movable objects, with

the exception of money and securities), and *services* (human energy).

3. To be enforceable, contracts must contain:

   - An offer or communication
   - Consideration
   - Acceptance (If one or more of the parties who have entered into the contract are not considered competent, the contract will not be enforceable. Examples of those often found incompetent include minors, people with mental illness, and prisoners.)

4. In a contract lawsuit, the following elements must be established:

   - A valid executed contract
   - Plaintiff performed as specified in the contract
   - Defendant failed to perform as specified in the contract
   - Plaintiff suffered an economic loss as a result of the defendant's breach of contract

5. *Independent contractors* agree to perform work without being under the direct control or direction of another party.

   - An employer is liable for the torts or negligence of an independent contractor in certain circumstances; these include negligence of the employer in selecting, instructing, or supervising the contractor.

6. Defenses for not performing under a contract include:

   - Fraud
   - Mistake of fact or law
   - Duress
   - Impossibility to perform the contract
   - Expiration of the statute of limitations

7. Legal redress for breach of contract includes:

   - Specified performance of the duties set forth in the contract
   - Monetary (or compensatory) damages
   - General or consequential damages. General damages could be expected to result from the breach of the contract, whereas consequential damages are a result of unforeseen damages.

8. The right of an employer to terminate an employee can be limited through:

   - Employment contract
   - Collective bargaining agreement

9. *Employee handbooks and medical staff bylaws* can be binding contracts between employer and employee, unless such documents provide legally acceptable disclaimers.

10. *Exclusive contracts* allow organizations to contract with physicians and medical groups to provide specific services to the organization.

11. The *Federal Trade Commission* is a federal agency that monitors the marketplace and enforces federal antitrust laws with the goal of maintaining free enterprise in a competitive marketplace.

12. *Transfer agreement* is a written document that sets forth terms and conditions under which a patient may be transferred to an alternate facility for care.

13. *Insurance contract*

    - Insurer has an obligation to indemnify the insured for losses caused by specified events.
    - In return, the insured must pay a fixed premium during the policy period.
    - Interpretation of an insurance contract can give rise to a legal action when the insurer refuses to indemnify the insured.

▶ REVIEW QUESTIONS

1. Explain the importance of a "written" contract.
2. Explain the elements of a contract.
3. Describe the differences between an express and an implied contract.
4. Describe various defenses and remedies available for nonperformance of a contract.
5. Explain why and under what circumstances an employee handbook can be considered a contract.
6. Explain why employers should place disclaimers in employee handbooks.

▶ NOTES

1. *Harvey v. Strickland*, 350 S.C. 303, 566 S.E.2d 529 (2002).
2. 225 A.2d 495 (Conn. 1966).
3. http://www.nghs.com/what-is-a-hospitalist.
4. Number of Hospital Employed Physicians by 50% Since 2012, *HealthLeaders Media News*, September 8, 2016. http://www.healthleadersmedia.com/physician-leaders/number-hospital-employed-physicians-50-2012?page=0%2C2#.

5.   Henry Campbell Black, *Black's Law Dictionary*, 4th ed., (Eagan, MN: West Publishing, 1968), 1277.

6.   National Conference of Commissioners on Uniform State Laws, "Uniform Partnership Act (1997)," July 1996. http://www.uniformlaws.org /shared/docs/partnership/upa_final_97.pdf.

7.   25 P.3d 358 (2001).

8.   384 N.Y.S.2d 527 (N.Y. App. Div. 1976).

9.   693 N.Y.S.2d 143 (N.Y. App. Div. 1999).

10. No. E2004–00207-COA-R3-CV (Tenn. App. 2005).

11. P.C., 782 N.Y.S.2d 115 (N.Y. App. Div. 2004).

12. 492 N.Y.S.2d 9 (N.Y. 1985).

13. 605 N.E.2d 613 (Ill. App. Ct. 1992).

14. No. A75 September Term 2003 (N.J. 2005).

15. Community Hospital Group, Inc. v. Jay More, M.D., et al. (A-75/76-03).

16. 869 A.2d 901 (N.J. 2005).

17. 867 A.2d 1187 (N.J. App. 2005).

18. 457 N.Y.S.2d 193 (N.Y. 1982).

19. 720 P.2d 632 (Idaho 1986).

20. 731 F. Supp. 311 (D. Ill. 1990).

21. *Id.* at 321–322.

22. 570 N.E.2d 545 (Ill. App. Ct. 1991).

23. 789 N.Y.S.2d 42 (N.Y. App. Div. 2005).

24. Horty Springer, *Trieger v. Montefiore Med. Ctr.* March 9, 2004. https://www.hortyspringer.com /documents/trieger-v-montefiore-med-ctr/.

25. 520 N.W.2d 625 (Wis. App. 1994).

26. 368 N.W.2d 666, 668, 674 (1985).

27. 141 Md. App. 715 (2001).

28. 670 F.2d 507 (5th Cir. 1982).

29. 466 U.S. 2 (1984).

30. 475 A.2d 533 (N.J. 1984).

31. *Id.*

32. 7 S.W.3d 542 (Mo. App. 1999).

33. 15 U.S.C. § 1 (1982).

34. 108 S. CT. 1658 (1988).

35. 42 U.S.C.A. §§ 11101–11152 (1986).

36. 843 F. Supp. 1013 (D. Md. 1994).

37. *Id.* at 1018.

38. 942 S.W.2d 201 (Tex. App. 1997).

39. 633 N.E.2d 617 (Ohio Ct. App. 1993).

40. HealthCare.gov. "Coverage for pre-existing conditions," https://www.healthcare.gov/coverage /pre-existing-conditions/.

41. *Harvey v. Strickland*, 566 S.E.2d 529, 311 (2002).

42. *Id.* at 307.

© corgarashu/Shutterstock

CHAPTER 8
Civil Procedure and Trial Practice

CONFLICTING EVIDENCE

Gwendolyn was in Mississippi when she felt light-headed and as though her heart was racing. Gwendolyn's sister brought her to the BCH hospital. Dr. Dorrough diagnosed Gwendolyn as suffering from supraventricular tachycardia. As Gwendolyn was discharged, she was told to follow up with her physician and to return to the emergency room if she experienced any further problems. Gwendolyn returned to Georgia and was admitted to a medical center. She complained of dizziness, shortness of breath, and chest tightness and stayed at the medical center for over 5 hours. She was later transferred to St. Francis Hospital with a suspected diagnosis of acute pulmonary embolus. At St. Francis, Gwendolyn underwent emergency surgery. The surgery was unsuccessful, and Gwendolyn died of a pulmonary embolus.

The plaintiffs filed a complaint against Dorrough and BCH hospital. The complaint alleged that Dorrough and BCH breached their duty to provide proper care to Gwendolyn. The plaintiffs had two expert witnesses, Dr. Vance and Dr. Falk. Dorrough had one expert witness, Dr. Dupuis. The jury heard conflicting testimony from the expert witnesses concerning the events leading up to Gwendolyn's death.

(continues)

🔍 *IT'S YOUR GAVEL...*   *(continued)*

Vance testified that Dorrough did not meet the minimum standard of care based on the fact that there was a sustained rapid heart rate and abnormal laboratory findings. He stated that Gwendolyn suffered from sinus tachycardia and not supraventricular tachycardia. He defined sinus tachycardia as an increase in pulse rate in response to an underlying disease state. Falk stated that, in his opinion, if Gwendolyn had been properly diagnosed and given the drug heparin, she would not have embolized and would have survived.

Dupuis, the defendant's expert, testified that Dorrough did not fall below the standard of care. He testified that Gwendolyn had a rare condition in that the clot that ultimately killed her was in the heart and did not come from the legs. Dupuis stated that Gwendolyn's death was unavoidable despite the best of care.

The jury returned a verdict in favor of the plaintiffs and assessed damages in the amount of $1.5 million against Dorrough. He appealed, asserting that the verdict of the jury was not supported by credible or sufficient evidence.[1]

WHAT IS YOUR VERDICT?

Trials, especially jury trials, are vital to fostering the respect of the public in the civil justice system. Trials do not represent a failure of the system. They are the cornerstone of the civil justice system. Unfortunately, because of expense and delay, both civil bench trials and civil jury trials are disappearing.[2]

▶ LEARNING OBJECTIVES

The reader, upon completion of this chapter, will be able to:

- Discuss the pretrial discovery process.
- Describe the trial process.
- Describe the forms of evidence presented by the plaintiff.
- Describe defenses offered by the defendant.
- Explain the purpose of the judge's charge to the jury.
- Describe the types of damages and how they are awarded.

For many students and healthcare practitioners, this book will be their only formal introduction to the legal aspects of health care. This chapter, in particular, is valuable to readers in understanding the law and its application in the courtroom. Although many of the procedures that are followed leading up to and during a trial are discussed in this chapter, civil procedure and trial practice are governed by each state's statutory requirements. Cases on a federal level are governed by federal statutory requirements.

▶ PLEADINGS

The pleadings of a case are the written statements of fact and law filed with a court by the parties to a lawsuit. The pleadings generally include such papers as the complaint, demurrer, counterclaims, answer, and bill of particulars. The parties to a controversy are the plaintiff and the defendant. The *plaintiff* is the person who initiates an action by filing a complaint. The *defendant* is the person against whom a lawsuit is brought. Many cases have multiple plaintiffs and defendants.

Summons and Complaint

The *complaint* is the first pleading in a lawsuit. It sets forth the relevant allegations of fact that give rise to one or more legal causes of action, along with the damages requested. The complaint identifies the parties to a suit, states a cause of action, and includes a demand for damages. The essential elements of a complaint include the following:

1. A short, concise statement of the grounds on which the court's jurisdiction depends (the court's authority to hear the case)
2. A statement of the claim demonstrating that the pleader is entitled to relief
3. A demand for judgment for the relief to which the plaintiff deems him- or herself entitled

All of these elements apply to any counterclaim, cross claim, or third-party claims.

The *summons* is the legal document issued by a court and served on an individual announcing that a legal proceeding has been commenced. The summons provides the date and place where the defendant must appear to respond to and answer the complaint. In some jurisdictions, a complaint must accompany a summons (an announcement to the defendant that a legal action has been commenced).

A complaint can be served on a defendant either with the summons or within a prescribed time after the summons has been served. The formalities that must be followed when serving a summons so that appropriate jurisdiction over a defendant is obtained include the manner in which the summons is to be delivered, the time period within which the delivery must occur, and the geographic limitations within which service must be made. **EXHIBIT 8-1** is an example of a summons.

Improper Service of a Summons

Improper service of a complaint or summons is not effective if it is incorrectly served. Such failure does not prevent a complaint from being properly reserved as required by law in the state where the summons or complaint is served.

Improper service of a summons occurred on March 14, 1989, when a sheriff attempted to serve the writ on the defendant by leaving a copy with the receptionist at the hospital where he had worked. The defendant had terminated his relationship with the hospital on February 22, 1988. The plaintiff's attempted service of the writ of summons was therefore defective, because the defendant was not affiliated with the hospital where service of the summons was attempted. A copy of the complaint was left with a nurse at the intensive care unit of the hospital where the defendant was then a patient. The intensive care unit of a hospital, however, was not deemed the defendant-patient's place of residence. "Where service of process is defective, the proper remedy is to set aside the service. In that event, the action remains open, but it cannot proceed against a defendant unless the plaintiff can thereafter effect service on such defendant which is sufficient to vest jurisdiction in the court."[3]

Demurrer

A *demurrer* is a pleading in a lawsuit by the defendant challenging the legal adequacy of the plaintiff's complaint. The pleading represents preliminary objections that are constructed so as to preempt "answering" the plaintiff's complaint. A demurrer, for example, can be filed by one of the parties to a lawsuit claiming that the evidence presented by the other party is insufficient to sustain an issue or case.

Answer

After service of a complaint, a response is required from the defendant in a document termed the *answer*. The answer to a complaint requires the defendant to respond to each of the allegations contained in the complaint by stating his or her defenses and by admitting to or denying each of the plaintiff's allegations. If the defendant fails to answer the complaint within the prescribed time, the plaintiff can seek judgment by default against the defendant. However, in certain instances, a default judgment will be vacated if the defendant can demonstrate an acceptable excuse for failing to answer.

Personal appearance of the defendant to respond to a complaint is not necessary. To prevent default, the defendant's attorney responds to the complaint with an answer. The defense attorney attempts to show, through evidence, that the defendant is not responsible for the negligent act claimed by the plaintiff to have occurred. The answer generally consists of a denial of the charges made and specifies a defense or argument justifying the position taken. The defense can show that the claim is unfounded, for example, because: (1) the period within which a suit must be instituted has expired; (2) there is contributory negligence on the part of the plaintiff; (3) any financial obligation has been remunerated; (4) a general release was provided to the defendant; or (5) a contract was illegal and therefore null and void. The original answer to the complaint is filed with the court having jurisdiction over the case, and a copy of the answer is provided to the plaintiff's attorney.

Counterclaim

A *counterclaim* is generally filed with the answer denying the plaintiff's claims by alleging that it was the plaintiff and not the defendant who committed a wrongful act, and therefore, it is the defendant who is entitled to damages. For example, the plaintiff could sue a hospital for personal injuries and property damage caused by the negligent operation of the hospital's ambulance. The hospital could file a counterclaim on grounds that its driver was careful and that it was the plaintiff who was negligent and is liable to the hospital for damage to the ambulance.

Bill of Particulars

A *bill of particulars* is a written request by the defendant for more detailed information from the plaintiff regarding the allegation(s) and claim(s) made than is provided in the initial complaint. If a *counterclaim* has been filed, the plaintiff's attorney also can request a bill of particulars from the defendant. More specifically, a bill of particulars in a malpractice case may include a request that the plaintiff provide the defendant information that includes the following:

- Date and time the alleged malpractice occurred
- Specific injuries alleged

UNITED STATES DISTRICT COURT

For the
District of Columbia

______________________ *Plaintiff(s)*	)	
V.	)	Civil Action No.
The United States & ______________________ *Defendant(s)*	)	

SUMMONS IN A CIVIL ACTION

To: *(Defendant's name and address)*

A lawsuit has been filed against you.

Within 21 days after service of this summons on you (not counting the day you received it) – or 60 days if you are the United States or a United States agency, or an officer or employee of the United States described in Fed. R. Civ. P. 12 (a)(2) or (3) – you must serve on the plaintiff an answer to the attached complaint or a motion under Rule 12 of the Federal Rules of Civil Procedure. The answer or motion must be served on the plaintiff or plaintiff's attorney, whose name and address are:

If you fail to respond, judgment by default will be entered against you for the relief demanded in the complaint. You also must file your answer or motion with the court.

CLERK OF COURT

Date: ______________________ ______________________

EXHIBIT 8-1 Summons in a civil action.

Reproduced from Summons in a Civil Action http://www.uscourts.gov/uscourts/FormsAndFees/Forms/AO440.pdf. Accessed August 13, 2014.

Civil Action No. _____

PROOF OF SERVICE

(This section should not be filed with the court unless required by Fed. R. Civ. P. 4 (1))

This summons for *(name of individual and title, if any)* _____
was received by me on *(date)* _____

☐ I personally served the summons on the individual at *(place)* _____
on *(date)* _____; or

☐ I left the summons at the individual's residence or usual place of abode with *(name)* _____ a
person of suitable age and discretion who resides there, on *(date)* _____, and mailed a copy
to the individual's last known address; or

☐ I served the summons on *(name of individual)* _____, who is designated by law
to accept service of process on behalf of *(name organization)* _____ *on date*
_____; or

☐ I returned the summons unexecuted because _____; or

☐ Other (specify)

☐ I declare under penalty of perjury that this information is true.

My fees are $_____ for travel and $_____ for services, for a total of
$_____.

I declare under penalty of perjury that this information is true.

Date: _____

_____
Server's signature

_____
Printed name and title

_____
Server's address

Additional information regarding attempted service, etc.:

EXHIBIT 8-1 Summons in a civil action.

- Where the alleged malpractice occurred
- The commissions and/or omissions constituting the malpractice alleged to have occurred, for example:
  - Misdiagnosis or failure to diagnose
  - Failure to perform a test or diagnostic procedure
  - Failure to medicate, treat, or operate
  - A contraindicated test given or a contraindicated test or surgical procedure performed
  - Administration of a medicine or treatment or performance of a test or surgical procedure in a manner contrary to accepted standards of medical practice
  - Removal of the wrong body part
- How the alleged malpractice occurred
- A listing of injuries claimed to have been caused by the defendant's alleged malpractice
- A listing of any witnesses to the alleged malpractice
- A listing of damages claimed, for example:
  - Pain and suffering
  - Length of time the plaintiff was confined to bed
  - Required rehabilitation
  - Permanent disabilities
  - Economic damages (e.g., lost wages)
- The name and address of the plaintiff's employer

A death action rider may also be attached if the malpractice allegedly caused death. The rider may request such information as the length of time the decedent experienced pain; the date, time, and place of death; and a statement setting forth the cause of death.

▶ DISCOVERY

Discovery is the process of investigating the facts of a case before trial. The discovery process is available to promote more just trials by preventing unfair surprise. "Discovery rules were promulgated to prevent trial by ambush. To deny a party the right to know absolutely at some meaningful time before trial the names and addresses of all witnesses the opposing side proposes to call in its case-in-chief is an insult to this principle."[4] The objectives of discovery are as follows:

1. Obtain evidence that might not be obtainable at the time of trial.
2. Isolate and narrow the issues for trial.
3. Gather knowledge of the existence of additional evidence that may be admissible at trial.
4. Obtain leads to enable the discovering party to gather further evidence.

Discovery may be obtained on any matter that is not privileged and that is relevant to the subject matter involved in the pending action. The parties to a lawsuit have the right to discovery and to examine witnesses before trial.

Examination Before Trial

Examination before trial (EBT) is one of several discovery techniques used to enable the parties of a lawsuit to learn more regarding the nature and substance of each other's case. An EBT consists of oral testimony under oath and includes cross-examination. A deposition, taken at an EBT, is the testimony of a witness that has been recorded in a written format. Testimony given at a deposition becomes part of the permanent record of the case. Each question and answer is transcribed by a court stenographer and may be used at the subsequent trial. Truthfulness and consistency are important because answers from an EBT that differ from those given at trial can be used to attack the credibility of the witness.

Preparation of Witnesses

The manner in which a witness handles questioning at a deposition or trial is often as important as the facts of the case. Each witness should be well prepared before testifying. Preparation should include a review of all pertinent records. Helpful guidelines for witnesses undergoing an EBT, a court hearing, or examination during trial include the following:

- Review the records (e.g., medical records and other business records) on which you might be questioned.
- Do not be antagonistic in answering the questions. The jury may already be somewhat sympathetic toward a particular party to the lawsuit; antagonism may serve only to reinforce such an impression.
- Be organized in your thinking and recollection of the facts regarding the incident.
- Answer only the questions asked.
- Explain your testimony in simple, succinct terminology.
- Do not overdramatize the facts you are relating.
- Do not allow yourself to become overpowered by the cross-examiner.
- Be polite, sincere, and courteous at all times.
- Dress appropriately and be neatly groomed.
- Pay close attention to any objections your attorney may have as to the line of questioning being conducted by the opposing counsel. Do not answer any question objected to by your legal counsel unless the judge overrules the objection and says to you, "You may answer the question."
- Be sure to have reviewed any oral deposition in which you may have participated.
- Be straightforward with the examiner. Any answers designed to cover up or cloud an issue or fact will, if discovered, serve only to discredit any previous testimony that you may have given.
- Do not show any visible signs of displeasure regarding any testimony with which you are in disagreement.
- Be sure to have questions that you did not hear repeated and questions that you did not understand rephrased.
- If you are not sure of an answer, indicate that you are not sure or that you do not know the answer.

Attorney–Client Privilege

Attorney–client privilege protects from discovery the communications between the parties to a lawsuit and their attorneys. In order for such information be protected from discovery, the following three elements must be established:

1. Both parties must agree that the attorney–client relationship does or will exist.
2. The client must seek advice from the attorney in his or her capacity as a legal advisor.

3. Communication between the attorney and client must be identified to be confidential.

Attorney–client privilege is intended to ensure that a client remains free from the apprehension that consultations with a legal advisor will be disclosed. Such privilege encourages a client to talk freely with his or her attorney so that he or she may receive meaningful legal advice. Likewise, with regard to the work-product doctrine, not even the most liberal of discovery theories can justify unwarranted inquiries into the files and the mental impressions of an attorney. Courts are required to protect the integrity and fairness of the fact-finding process by requiring full disclosure of all relevant facts connected with the impending litigation while promoting full and frank consultation between a client and a legal advisor by removing the fear of compelled disclosure of information.

Incident and Investigative Reports

Hospital incident and investigation reports are generally not protected from discovery. The burden rests with the hospital to demonstrate incident and investigation reports are protected from discovery under attorney–client privilege and the work-product doctrine. If in connection with an accident or an event, a business entity, in the ordinary course of business, conducts an investigation for its own purposes, the resulting investigative report is producible in civil pretrial discovery. The determination as to whether a defendant's in-house report was prepared in the ordinary course of business or was a work product in anticipation of litigation is an important one. The fact that a defendant anticipates litigation resulting from an accident or event does not automatically qualify an in-house report as a work product. *A document that is not privileged does not become privileged by the mere act of sending it to an attorney or by marking the documents as "privileged information."*

Statistical Data Not Necessarily Privileged

The collection of statistical data is not necessarily protected from discovery during court proceedings. For example, the patient, Braverman, in *Braverman v. Columbia Hospital, Inc.*,[5] underwent surgery and was subsequently diagnosed with a nosocomial infection (hospital-acquired infection). She was hospitalized several times for treatment of the infection.

Braverman filed a lawsuit and sought a variety of documents from the hospital. The hospital objected on the grounds that some of the information sought by Braverman was a record of its review and evaluation procedures under Wis. Stat. § 146.38 and therefore was privileged. In its written decision, the trial court found that the infection control materials, including meeting minutes, infection rates, and the results of any investigations conducted by quality assurance/peer review committees, were privileged. Braverman appealed.

As mandated by Wis. Admin. Code § HFS 124.08, the hospital maintains an infection control committee (ICC). Its purpose is to influence and improve the quality of health care through the practice of infection control. The ICC recommends practices to reduce the risk of infection to patients, visitors, and healthcare workers. The hospital infection control practitioners compile infection statistics. The ICC conducts an investigation or study of any postoperative infection for purposes of quality assurance. The ICC coordinates its infection control processes in compliance with the bylaws and rules of the medical staff in order to reduce the risk of hospital-acquired infections.

Braverman argued that this kind of statistical data is not covered by Wis. Stat. § 146.38, which provides:

> (3) Information acquired in connection with the review and evaluation of health care services shall be disclosed and records of such review and evaluation shall be released, with the identity of any patient whose treatment is reviewed being withheld unless the patient has granted permission to disclose identity, in the following circumstances:
>
> . . . .
>
> (d) In a report in statistical form. The report may identify any provider or facility to which the statistics relate.[6]

The appeals court concluded that "We see this language as clear and unambiguous. And since Columbia's statistical data qualifies under the paragraph, we conclude that Braverman is entitled to discover this data."[7] Such information is exempt from the privilege. Braverman was entitled to discover the statistical reports of infection data.

▶ MOTIONS

The procedural steps that occur before trial are specifically classified as pretrial proceedings. After the pleadings have been completed, many states permit either party to move for a judgment on the pleadings. When this motion is made, the court will examine the entire case and decide whether to enter judgment according to the merits of the case as indicated in the pleadings.

In some states, the moving party is permitted to introduce sworn statements showing that a claim or defense is false or a sham. This procedure cannot be used when there is substantial dispute concerning the facts presented by the affidavits.

Motion to Dismiss

A defendant may make a motion to dismiss a case, alleging that the plaintiff's complaint, even if believed, does not set forth a claim or cause of action recognized by law. A motion to dismiss can be made before, during, or after a trial. Motions made before a trial may be made on the basis that the court lacks jurisdiction, that the case is barred by the statute of limitations, that another case is pending involving the same issues, and other similar matters. A motion by the defendant during trial may be made after the plaintiff has presented his or her case, on the grounds that the court has heard the plaintiff's case and the defendant is entitled to a favorable judgment as a matter of law. In the case of a motion made by the defendant at the close of the plaintiff's case, the defendant normally will claim that the plaintiff has failed to present a prima facie case (i.e., that the plaintiff has failed to establish the minimum elements necessary to justify a verdict even if no contrary evidence is presented by the defendant). After a trial has been completed, either party may move for a directed verdict on the grounds that he or she is entitled to such verdict as a matter of law.

Dismissal Denied

Procedural issues can result in a case being referred back to the trial court for further proceedings as noted in the following case, where Jean Pierrot, as personal representative of the deceased, filed a complaint alleging that Farrah, a 25-year-old pregnant woman, went to a hospital in the afternoon with complaints of abdominal pain. That evening, the hospital transferred Farrah involuntarily to Park Place, a behavioral health facility. The involuntary transfer of Farrah was allowed under the Florida Mental Health Act of 1971, commonly referred to as the Florida Baker Act, which allows for involuntary examination and commitment. Judges, law enforcement officials, physicians, or mental health professionals can initiate it. There must be evidence that the person possibly has a mental illness or may harm him- or herself or others. When Farrah arrived at Park Place she was in distress, complaining of severe abdominal pain and other symptoms. Over the next 2 days, Park Place employees committed various acts and omissions that resulted in her death.

The complaint alleged a wrongful death claim for violations of Farrah's rights as a patient under the Baker Act. Park Place, in response, disagreed and moved to dismiss Pierrot's wrongful death claim, arguing that the claim was one for medical malpractice and that Pierrot failed to comply with the pre-suit requirements of the Medical Malpractice Act.

The trial court dismissed Pierrot's claim, deciding that the main point of the claim was that Park Place failed to properly respond to Farrah's physical symptoms of severe abdominal pain, and therefore, the claim was one for medical negligence. Thus the court ruled Pierrot could not avoid the pre-suit requirements of the Medical Malpractice Act by pleading the claim under the Baker Act.

On appeal, Pierrot argued that a plaintiff claiming only violations of a mental health patient's rights under the Baker Act is not required to comply with the medical malpractice pre-suit requirements. Additionally, Pierrot contended the pre-suit requirements do not apply to his claim because Park Place was not a healthcare provider. The Court of Appeal of Florida agreed with both arguments.

According to the complaint, Park Place was a licensed mental health facility and not a healthcare provider. The court found that Park Place failed to establish that it was a healthcare provider for purposes of the pre-suit requirements. The case was reversed and remanded back to the trial court for further proceedings.[8]

This case illustrates the importance of preserving all causes of action and positions that the plaintiff's attorney may wish to argue at trial. Cases referred back to the trial court are difficult to follow up because further deliberations often prove to be more damaging than helpful. Defendants may decide that a settlement is less costly than a lawsuit that could drag on for years and gain the attention of the news media. The "Newspaper Clippings" dispersed throughout the text, often high-profile cases, are often settled out of the courtroom due to the negative impact they can have on the reputation of the healthcare provider(s).

Motion for Summary Judgment

A motion for summary judgment can be made when either party to a lawsuit believes that there are no triable issues of fact and that only issues of law need to be decided. This motion asks the court to rule that there are no facts in dispute and that the rights of the parties can be determined as a matter of law, on the basis of submitted documents, without the need for a trial. Summary judgment is generally granted when the evidence demonstrates that there are no genuine issues of material fact and the moving party is entitled to judgment as a matter of law. Although the courts are reluctant to look favorably on motions for summary judgment, they will grant them if the circumstances of a particular case warrant it. The plaintiff, for example, in *Thomas v. New York University Med. Ctr.*,[9] while under general anesthesia, slid off the operating table during a surgical procedure. The plaintiff's head was pulled out of a head-stabilizing device, causing his head to be lacerated by one of the pins. The plaintiff suffered trauma to his neck and required mechanical assistance to breathe for 6 days following the accident. The Supreme Court, Appellate Division, on motion by the plaintiff, determined that summary judgment on the issue of liability was warranted. It could easily be reasoned that anesthetized patients do not fall from operating tables in the absence of negligence. The defendants, who were in joint and exclusive control of the plaintiff, failed to explain their conduct in the operating room, and their failure to do so mandated summary judgment.

▶ PRETRIAL CONFERENCE

In many states, a pretrial conference can be ordered at the judge's initiative or on the request of one of the parties to the lawsuit. The *pretrial conference* is an informal discussion during which the judge and the attorneys eliminate matters not in dispute, agree on the issues, and settle procedural matters relating to the trial. Although it is not the purpose of the pretrial conference to compel the parties to settle the case, it often happens that cases are settled at this time.

▶ NOTICE OF TRIAL

The examination before trial may reveal sufficient facts that would discourage the plaintiff from continuing the case, or it may encourage one or both parties to settle out of court. Once a decision to go forward is reached, the case is placed on the court calendar.

Postponement of a trial may be secured with the consent of both parties and consent of the court. A case may not be postponed indefinitely without being dismissed by the court. If one party is ready to proceed and another party seeks a postponement, a valid excuse must be shown. Should a defendant fail to appear at trial, the judge can pass judgment against the defendant by default. A case also can be dismissed if the plaintiff fails to appear at trial.

▶ MEMORANDUM OF LAW

A *memorandum of law* (or *trial brief*) presents to the court the nature of the case, cites case decisions to substantiate arguments, and aids the court regarding points of law. Trial briefs are prepared by both the plaintiff's and the defendant's attorneys. A trial brief is not required, but it is a recommended strategy. It provides the court with a basic understanding of the position of the party submitting the trial brief before the commencement of the trial. It also focuses the court's attention on specific legal points that may influence the court in ruling on objections and on the admissibility of evidence in the course of the trial.

▶ THE COURTROOM AND THE JUDGE

A case is heard in the court that has jurisdiction over the subject in controversy. The judge presides over court proceedings, decides questions of law, and is responsible for ensuring that a trial is conducted properly, in an impartial manner, and that it is fair to both parties to a lawsuit. The judge determines what constitutes the general standard of conduct required of the defendant for the exercise of due care. The judge informs the jury of what the defendant's conduct should have been, thereby making a determination of the existence of a legal duty.

The judge decides whether evidence is admissible, charges the jury (defines the jury's responsibility in relation to existing law), and may take a case away from the jury (by directed verdict or make a judgment notwithstanding the verdict) when he or she believes that there are no issues for the jury to consider or that the jury has erred in its decision. This right of the judge with respect to the role of the jury narrows the jury's responsibility with regard to the facts of the case. The judge maintains order throughout the suit, determines issues of procedure and law, and is generally responsible for the conduct of the trial. On the appeals level, a panel of judges review the arguments of the defendant's and plaintiff's attorneys in order to make a determination as to whether the trial court's decision should be sustained, overruled, or sent back to the trial court with instructions for further proceedings.

▶ THE JURY

The *jury* reviews the facts of a case offered by opposing counsels and makes an impartial decision as to the guilt of the defendant(s). Members of the jury are selected from a jury list. They are summoned to court by a paper known as the *jury process*. The number of jurors who sit at trial is 12 in common law. If there are fewer than 12, the number must be established by statute.

Jury Selection Process

Counsel for both parties to a lawsuit question each prospective jury member for impartiality, bias, and prejudicial thinking. This process is referred to as the *voir dire*, the examination of jurors. Once members of the jury are selected, they are sworn in to try the case. The jury, when reviewing the facts of a case, determine what occurred, evaluate whether the plaintiff's damages were caused by the defendant's negligence, and decide whether the defendant exercised due care. The jury must pay close attention to the evidence presented by both sides of a suit in order to render a fair and impartial verdict. Jurors who fall asleep during the trial can be replaced with an alternate juror, as was the case in *Richbow v. District of Columbia*.[10] The juror in this case "had been sleeping through the evidence and appellant's counsel acknowledged that fact."[11]

Waiver of Trial by Jury

The right to a trial by jury is a constitutional right, but an individual may waive the right to a jury trial. If this right is waived, the judge acts as judge and jury, becoming the trier of facts and deciding issues of law.

A Jury Decision

A New York City jury awarded $26 million to a boy injured during surgery. What was it that so disturbed the jury that caused it to grant such a huge award? According to an article written by an alternate juror, who invited the jurors to his home 3 weeks after the trial:

> The defense lawyers were on their feet objecting they didn't want the jury to see Stephen. But that just raised a question for us: If his injuries were as slight as the defense had been insisting, why the resistance? The judge agreed that it was proper for Stephen to appear at his own trial, and the rear doors to the courtroom were opened.
>
> Most of the jurors had begun to cry. But we were also angry. The defense lawyers it seemed, had been trying to put one over on us, claiming that Stephen was a normal teenage boy with a few minor handicaps.
>
> For seven weeks, the jury had sat in that courtroom listening to the defense lawyers belittle Stephen's problems. We saw the doctors refuse to acknowledge Stephen's handicaps or to accept responsibility for them. To the jury at least, it seemed that the doctors had made mistakes, refused to admit them, and then tried to cover them up.[12]

▶ SUBPOENAS

A *subpoena* is a legal order requiring the appearance of a person and/or the presentation of documents to a court or administrative body. Attorneys, judges, and certain law enforcement and administrative officials, depending on the jurisdiction, may issue subpoenas. Subpoenas generally include: a reference number; names of the plaintiff(s) and defendant(s); the date, time, and place to appear; the name, address, and telephone number of the opposing attorney; and the documents requested if the subpoena is for records.

Some jurisdictions require the service of a subpoena at a specified time in advance of the requested appearance (e.g., 24 hours). In other jurisdictions, no such time limitation exists. A court clerk, sheriff, attorney, process server, or other person as provided by state statute can serve a subpoena.

A *subpoena ad testificandum* orders the appearance of a person at a trial or other investigative proceeding to give testimony. Witnesses have a duty to appear and may suffer a penalty for contempt of court should they fail to appear. They may not deny knowledge of a subpoena if they simply refused to accept it. The court may issue a bench warrant, ordering the appearance of a witness in court, if a witness fails to answer a subpoena. Failure to appear may be excused if extenuating circumstances exist.

A subpoena for records, known as a *subpoena duces tecum*, is a written command to bring records, documents, or other evidence described in the subpoena to a trial or other investigative proceeding. The subpoena is served on the individual or entity able to produce such records. Refusal to respond to a subpoena duces tecum is considered to be contempt of court and carries a penalty of a fine, imprisonment, or both.

▶ BURDEN OF PROOF

The *burden of proof* in a civil case is the obligation of the plaintiff to persuade the jury regarding the truth of his or her case. A preponderance of the credible evidence must be presented for a plaintiff to recover damages. Credible evidence is evidence that, in the light of reason and common sense, is worthy of belief. A preponderance of credible evidence requires that the prevailing side of the case carry more weight than the evidence on the opposing side. In a negligence case, the burden of proof requires that the plaintiff's attorney show that the defendant violated a legal duty by not following an acceptable standard of care and that the plaintiff suffered injury because of the defendant's breach. If the evidence presented does not support the allegations made, the case is dismissed. When a plaintiff, who has the burden of proof, fails to sustain such burden, the case can be dismissed despite the failure of the defendant to present any evidence to the contrary on his or her behalf. The burden of proof in some states shifts from the plaintiff to the defendant when it is obvious that the injury would not have occurred unless there was negligence.

The burden of proof in a criminal case requires that evidence presented against the defendant must be proven beyond a reasonable doubt by the prosecuting attorney. Note the terminology: reasonable doubt—not "all" doubt. In a criminal case, the burden of proof lies with the prosecution. The prosecution has the burden of proving each element of a crime beyond a reasonable doubt.[13] In a civil suit, the plaintiff has the burden of proving the case by a preponderance of the evidence. In other words, the evidence presented must demonstrate that, in a malpractice case for example, it is more likely than not that the defendant or defendants caused the patient's alleged injuries. The evidence presented by the plaintiff need only tip the scales of justice.

▶ RES IPSA LOQUITUR

Res ipsa loquitur ("the thing speaks for itself" or "circumstances speak for themselves") is the legal doctrine that shifts the burden of proof in a negligence case from the plaintiff to the defendant. It is an evidentiary device that allows the plaintiff to make a case legally adequate to go to the jury on the basis of well-defined *circumstantial evidence*, even though *direct evidence* is lacking. This does not mean that the plaintiff has fully proven the defendant's negligence—it merely shifts the burden of going forward in a lawsuit to the defendant, who must argue to dismiss the circumstantial evidence presented.

The general rule for negligence cases going forward on the basis of res ipsa loquitur does not require the plaintiff to eliminate all possible causes of a patient's injuries. The inference under the doctrine of res ipsa loquitur is that the circumstantial evidence offered is sufficient to shift the burden of proof from the plaintiff to the defendant because it is more probable than not that the defendant's actions were the cause of the patient's injuries. In other words, an inference of negligence is permitted from the mere occurrence of an injury when the defendant owed a duty and possessed the sole power of preventing the injury by the exercise of reasonable care.

The three elements necessary to shift the burden of proof from the plaintiff to the defendant under the doctrine of res ipsa loquitur are as follows:

1. The event would not normally have occurred in the absence of negligence.
2. The defendant had exclusive control over the instrumentality that caused the injury.
3. The plaintiff did not contribute to the injury.

Burns While Bathing Patient

An action was brought against the nursing facility in *Franklin v. Collins Chapel Correctional Hospital*[14] to recover damages for the wrongful death of an 82-year-old resident. Extensive thermal burns were discovered soon after an attendant bathed the resident. The complaint sought to invoke the doctrine of res ipsa loquitur because the injuries suffered by the resident do not occur in the absence of negligence, and the decedent was in the defendant's sole care, custody, and control.

The trial court entered a judgment for the nursing facility pursuant to a jury verdict, and the administrators of the estate appealed. The appeals court held that proof that the nursing facility had exclusive control over the bath wherein burns were allegedly suffered and that the burns normally would not occur absent negligence entitled the administrators to a jury instruction on the doctrine of res ipsa loquitur. The case was reversed and remanded for a new trial.

Burn by Electrocautery Unit

The patient in *Mack v. Lydia E. Hall Hospital*[15] was properly permitted to invoke the doctrine of res ipsa loquitur in her suit to recover damages for a third-degree burn on the side of her left thigh, which was caused by an electro-coagulator used during surgery.

The plaintiff, while under anesthesia, sustained third degree burns on the side of her left thigh during the course of a surgical procedure for the treatment of rectal cancer. The defendant Dr. Josef Jahr was the surgeon in charge of the operation. An electrical instrument called an electro-coagulator was used during the procedure to coagulate blood vessels and stop bleeding. A component part of the electro-coagulator known as a grounding pad was placed on the plaintiff's left thigh and remained there throughout the surgery. Electric current flowed through this grounding pad and the flow. Dr. Jahr controlled increase of that current. When the grounding pad was removed at the conclusion of the operation, a burn more than one-half-inch deep and over two inches in diameter was discovered on the skin directly underneath the area where the pad had been.[16]

The prerequisites for application of the doctrine were satisfied by the circumstantial evidence presented. The injury could not have occurred in the absence of negligence, the surgeon had exclusive control over the electro-coagulator, and the patient had not been a participant in the surgical procedure and therefore did not contribute to her injury.

RES IPSA LOQUITUR AND EXCLUSIVE CONTROL

Citation: *Seavers v. Methodist Medical Center of Oak Ridge*, 9 S.W.3d 86 (Tenn. 1999)

Facts

While in the intensive care unit (ICU), a nurse's note indicated that the grip in Seavers's right hand was weaker than that in her left hand. Both of her hands had been placed in wrist restraints and fastened to bed rails to prevent her from pulling out her endotracheal tube. When the endotracheal tube was removed and the appellant could speak, she complained that her right arm was numb; Seavers had suffered severe damage to her right ulnar nerve. The appellant and her husband filed suit against the medical center, alleging that the injury was the result of the nurses negligently restraining her arm. She later amended her complaint to include the theory of res ipsa loquitur.

The medical center filed a motion for summary judgment, supported by the affidavits of two experts. Both experts opined that the nerve damage in the appellant's right arm was "of unknown etiology" and that the injury could have developed during her stay in the ICU without any deviation from standards of professional care.

The appellant opposed the medical center's motion for summary judgment, arguing that there were genuine issues of material fact. The appellant's response was supported by the deposition of Natelson, a neurosurgeon, and the affidavits of both Natelson and Woodworth, a registered nurse who worked in the ICU. Both Natelson and Woodworth opined that the appellant was under the exclusive control and care of the medical center's nursing staff when the nerve injury occurred. Natelson and Woodworth stated that when treating ICU patients who are unconscious or under heavy sedation or restraint, the standard of professional care requires the protection of the patients' extremities so that injuries to the ulnar nerves do not occur. Based on their independent review of the appellant's medical records and electromyography (EMG) results, they opined that the injury was the type that would not have occurred if the nursing staff had upheld the standard of care.

Finding no genuine issues of material fact, the trial court granted the medical center's motion for summary judgment. A majority of the court of appeals affirmed the trial court's order granting summary judgment for the medical center. The court of appeals held that res ipsa loquitur did not apply because the appellant's injury was not within the common knowledge of laypersons.

Issue

Does the doctrine of res ipsa loquitur apply in this case?

Holding

The judgments of the lower courts were reversed, and the case was remanded to the trial court for further proceedings under the doctrine of res ipsa loquitur.

Reason

The parties agreed that the appellant was under the exclusive control and care of the medical center when the nerve injury occurred. The record further shows that the appellant's right arm and hand were fully functional when she entered the medical center's ICU and that no problem was detected until the ICU nurses noticed that the grip in her right hand was not as strong as the grip in her left hand. During that time, the appellant was heavily sedated, restrained, and under the complete care of the ICU nurses. Based on EMG results, the appellant has shown that the dysfunction in her right arm resulted from damage to her right ulnar nerve. According to Natelson, this injury was likely caused by prolonged pressure on the nerve from a hard object such as a bed rail. This theory was corroborated by evidence that the appellant's arms were strapped to the hospital bed during her stay in the ICU. The appellant satisfied the res ipsa loquitur requirements under Tennessee code and raised a genuine issue of material fact on the allegation of negligence. Summary judgment for the medical center was improper in this case.

Oxygen Mask Catches Fire

The oxygen mask in *Gold v. Ishak*[17] caught fire during surgery. In performing surgery, the physician used an electrocautery unit provided by the hospital. At some point during surgery, the oxygen mask caught on fire, and the patient was injured. A claim of negligent treatment was presented to a medical review panel, which concluded that the medical providers had complied with the requisite standard of care.

The plaintiff filed a complaint against the medical providers for medical malpractice. The trial court refused to apply the doctrine of res ipsa loquitur. On appeal, the trial court was found to have erred by refusing to apply the doctrine. The evidence presented at trial, as described here, clearly shows that the elements necessary for the inference of res ipsa loquitur had been established:

1. A fire under these circumstances is such that in the ordinary course of things would not have occurred if the medical providers had used proper care in relation to the electrocautery unit and oxygen mask.
2. The injuring instrumentality was under the management or exclusive control of the medical providers.
3. The patient could not have contributed to her injury, as she was not a participant in her surgery.

Expert testimony is not required because a fire occurring during surgery where an instrument that emits a spark is used near a source of oxygen is not beyond the realm of the layperson to understand. It is easily understandable to the common person that careless use of the two could cause a fire and result in bodily injury.

▶ OPENING STATEMENTS

During the opening statement, the plaintiff's attorney presents a summary of the allegations against the defendant and the credible evidence favorable to his or her client. The *opening statement* by the plaintiff's attorney provides, in capsule form (1) the facts of the case, (2) what he or she intends to prove by means of a summary of the evidence to be presented, and (3) a description of the damages to the plaintiff(s). The opening statement must be concise and relevant.

The defense attorney makes his or her opening statement indicating the position of the defendant and the points of the plaintiff's case he or she intends to refute. The defense attorney explains the facts as they apply to the case for the defendant.

▶ EXAMINATION OF WITNESSES

After conclusion of the opening statements, the judge calls for the plaintiff's witnesses. An officer of the court administers an oath to each witness, and direct examination begins. The attorney obtains information from each witness in the form of questions. On cross-examination by the defense, an attempt is made to challenge or discredit the plaintiff's witness. The defense may claim, for example, that the witness is biased toward the defendant, the plaintiff's witness lacks knowledge as to the facts of the case, or the witness's testimony is inconsistent with other facts presented in the case. Redirect examination by the plaintiff's attorney can follow the cross-examination, if so desired. The plaintiff's attorney may at this time wish to have his or her witness review an important point that the jury may have forgotten during cross-examination. The plaintiff's attorney may ask the same witness more questions in an effort to overcome the effect of the cross-examination. The defense attorney may then conduct a recross-examination of the witness, if necessary, in defense of the defendant.

A sampling of a seemingly endless number of questions that a defendant physician, for example, might expect to be asked during a personal injury case often includes the following:

1. Could you state for the court your name, residence, and any prior residences?
2. Where did you attend medical school?
3. Are you licensed in this state?
4. Are you licensed to practice medicine in any other state?
5. Where did you serve your internship?
6. Where did you serve your residency?
7. Is your practice general medicine?
8. Are you qualified to practice in any other specialty?
9. Are you board certified?
10. In what specialties are you board certified?
11. How does a physician obtain board certification?
12. Are you presently practicing medicine?
13. How long have you been in practice?
14. On or about _____ (date), did you have occasion to see the patient on a professional basis?
15. Where did you first see the patient?

16. Could you describe the patient's condition at the time?
17. What, if anything, did you do on that occasion?
18. Have you been practicing as a physician since that date?
19. What initial complaints did the patient present to you?
20. Describe the initial assessment you performed on the patient.
21. Did you see the patient daily, several times a day, at first?
22. Did you continue to see the patient?
23. How often did you see the patient?
24. Describe the treatment you rendered.
25. Did you find it necessary to refer the patient for consultation purposes?
26. Did there come a time when you found it necessary to refer, admit, or transfer the patient to a hospital, different hospital, rehab facility, or other healthcare entity?

The credibility of a witness may be impeached if prior statements are inconsistent with later statements or if there is bias in favor of a party or prejudice against a party to a lawsuit. As noted previously, either attorney to a lawsuit may ask the judge for permission to recall a witness for questioning.

▶ JUDICIAL NOTICE RULE

The *judicial notice rule* prescribes that well-known facts (e.g., fractures require prompt attention, two X-rays of the same patient may show different results) need not be proven. In other words, a court recognizes that a particular fact in a case is so commonly known by the average person that expert testimony is not necessary to establish the fact. The importance of this ruling is to prevent the parties to a lawsuit from endlessly arguing issues that are well known and accepted by the average person as fact. If a fact can be disputed, the rule does not apply. The need to order a computed tomography (CT) scan or magnetic resonance imaging (MRI), for example, as a diagnostic tool to diagnose a suspected skull fracture, can be considered a matter of common knowledge to which a court, in the absence of expert testimony, can take judicial notice. Should a patient have a serious fall and a fracture is indicated, under the foregoing rule, it is a matter of common knowledge that the ordinary physician in good standing, in the exercise of ordinary care and diligence, would have ordered the appropriate diagnostic tests.

The court applied the judicial notice rule in *Arthur v. St. Peter's Hospital*,[18] where the patient-plaintiff sought treatment in the emergency department of St. Peter's Hospital after an injury to his left wrist. After being examined, he was sent to the radiology department for X-rays of his wrist. He later was released after being advised that there were no fractures. As a result of continued swelling and pain, the plaintiff decided to seek care from another physician, who subsequently diagnosed a fracture of the navicular bone. The plaintiff sued, and the hospital motioned for summary judgment, stating that the physicians were independent contractors and not employees of the hospital. Copies of the emergency department record, X-ray report, and billing record contained the logo of the hospital. There was no notification on the records to identify the physicians as being independent contractors. The court took *judicial notice*, finding that people who seek medical help through hospital emergency departments are unaware of the status of the different professionals working there. Unless a patient had been put, in some manner, on notice that those physicians with whom he might come into contact during the course of his treatment were independent contractors, it would be natural to assume that they were employees of the hospital.

▶ EVIDENCE

Evidence consists of the facts proved or disproved during a lawsuit. The law of evidence is a body of rules under which facts are proven. The rules of evidence govern the admission of items of proof in a lawsuit. A fact can be proven by either direct or circumstantial evidence. Evidence must be competent, relevant, and material to be admitted at trial. In a negligence case, there must be reasonable evidence that the resulting injury does not occur in the ordinary course of patient care if proper care is rendered.

Evidence is generally offered in the form of oral testimony through witnesses, written or computer-generated documents, and physical evidence, such as digital imaging studies. The different forms of evidence are presented below.

Direct Evidence

Direct evidence is proof offered through direct testimony. It is the jury's function to receive testimony presented by witnesses and draw conclusions in the determination of facts. The law recognizes that a jury is composed of ordinary men and women and that some fact-finding will involve subjects beyond their knowledge. When a jury cannot otherwise obtain sufficient facts from which to draw conclusions, an expert witness who has special knowledge, skill, experience, or training can be called on to submit an opinion. The expert witness assists the jury when the issues to be resolved in the case are outside the experience of the average juror.

Laypeople are able to render opinions about a great variety of general subjects, but for technical questions, the opinion of an expert is necessary. During the examination of an expert witness, his or her training, experience, and special qualifications are explained to the jury. The experts will be asked to give an opinion concerning hypothetical questions based on the facts of the case. Should the testimony of two experts conflict, the jury will determine which expert opinion to accept. Expert witnesses may be used to assist a plaintiff in proving the wrongful act of a defendant or to assist a defendant in refuting such evidence. In addition, expert testimony may be used to show the extent of the plaintiff's damages or to show the lack of such damages. To qualify as an expert witness in a specified area, that person must have the appropriate training, experience, and qualifications necessary to explain and/or answer questions based on the facts of a particular case.

Not all negligence cases require testimony from an expert witness. Citing *Donovan v. State*: "If a doctor operates on the wrong limb or amputates the wrong limb, a plaintiff would not have to introduce expert testimony to establish that the doctor was negligent. On the other hand, highly technical questions of diagnoses and causation which lie beyond the understanding of a layperson require introduction of expert testimony."[19]

Admissibility of Expert Testimony

Expert testimony concerning what a reasonable patient wants to know and what doctors think patients want to know was found to be admissible in *Marsingill v. O'Malley*,[20] where the patient sued the physician for medical malpractice, alleging that information he had given her over the telephone, relating to her report of abdominal pain and nausea several months after stomach surgery, did not allow her to make an intelligent decision to seek emergency room treatment. Expert testimony by doctors who had extensive experience in interacting with patients was found to be relevant concerning the amount and kinds of information that patients generally want in late-night phone calls and was relevant to establish whether the physician had given the patient as much information as a reasonably prudent patient would want to know.

Pharmacist Not Always a Qualified Witness

The pharmacist in *Nail v. Laros*[21] was found not competent to render an expert opinion regarding the proper standard of care required of a physician practicing a medical specialty. The patient, Mrs. Nail, developed a staphylococcal infection following spinal surgery. The orthopedic surgeon, Dr. Laros, treated the patient with the antibiotic Ancef for 6 days. The patient was released from the hospital without any sign of an infection. The patient, while under the treatment of another orthopedic surgeon (Hanley), was discovered through blood tests to have contracted a staphylococcal infection at the operative site. The patient eventually developed osteomyelitis. She brought a lawsuit against Laros for negligence in diagnosing and treating her infection. Nail obtained an affidavit from a pharmacist (Neff), who stated an opinion that Laros should have treated the patient for a longer period on Ancef and that his failure to do so was the proximate cause of Nail's staphylococcal infection found by Hanley. The court reasoned that there was nothing in the record to support the pharmacist's claim of being an expert in this case. Neither his education nor his training qualified him to be an expert on equal footing with a board-certified orthopedic surgeon in diagnosing and treating infections associated with surgical implants. The court of appeals took judicial notice by ruling that the pharmacist cannot legally prescribe medication and is even prohibited from dispensing a dangerous drug, which by definition includes Ancef, without a valid prescription from a practitioner.

Gross Negligence

In medical malpractice cases where lack of care or want of skill is so gross as to be apparent or the alleged breach relates to noncomplex matters of diagnosis and treatment within the understanding of lay jurors by resort to common knowledge and experience, failure to present expert testimony on the accepted standard of care and degree of skill under such circumstances is not fatal to a plaintiff's prima facie case showing of negligence. The court in *McGraw v. St. Joseph's Hospital*[22] reviewed cases addressing hospital fall incidents and found that a majority of jurisdictions do not require expert testimony in cases such as the following:

1. A bed rail is left down contrary to the physician's order and the patient falls and is injured.
2. A patient known to be in weakened condition is left alone in a shower and falls.

3.   A nurse fails to respond to a sedated patient's call and the patient gets out of bed and falls.

A hospital owes the patient a duty to exercise reasonable care in rendering care, and in the performance of such duty, due regard must be given to the mental and physical condition of the patient of which the hospital, in the exercise of reasonable care, should have knowledge. If a patient requires professional care, then expert testimony as to the standard of care is necessary. The standard of nonmedical, administrative, ministerial, or routine care in a hospital need not be established by expert testimony. A jury is competent from its own experience to determine and apply a reasonable care standard.

Demonstrative Evidence

Demonstrative (real) evidence is proof furnished by things themselves. It is considered the most trustworthy and preferred type of evidence. It consists of tangible objects to which testimony refers (e.g., medical instruments and broken infusion needles) that can be requested by a jury. Demonstrative evidence is admissible in court if it is relevant, has probative value, and serves the interest of justice. It is not admissible if it will prejudice, mislead, confuse, offend, inflame, or arouse the sympathy or passion of the jury. Other forms of demonstrative evidence include photographs, motion pictures, X-ray films, drawings, human bodies as exhibits, pathology slides, fetal monitoring strips, safety committee minutes, infection committee reports, medical staff bylaws, rules and regulations, nursing policy and procedure manuals, census data, and staffing patterns. The plaintiff's attorney uses all pertinent evidence to reconstruct chronologically the care and treatment rendered.

Photographs

Photographs are a form of evidence. When presenting *photographs* as evidence, the photographer or a reliable witness who is familiar with the object photographed must testify that the picture is an accurate representation and a fair likeness of the object portrayed. The photograph must not exaggerate a client's physical condition, as such exaggeration could unfairly prejudice a jury. Photographs can be valuable legal evidence when they illustrate graphically the nature and extent of a medical injury.

Videos also are valuable evidence. The same principles that apply to photographs apply to videos. Videos must be accurately portrayed; the cutting and/or splicing of videos are suspect and may have no probative value. Videos are admissible in court, assuming

the matter being recorded, the time of the recording, and the manner in which such recording took place can be authenticated.

Under the Federal Rules of Evidence, Rule 1008—Functions of the Court and Jury provide:

> Ordinarily, the court determines whether the proponent has fulfilled the factual conditions for admitting other evidence of the content of a writing, recording, or photograph under Rule 1004 or Rule 1005. But in a jury trial, the jury determines — in accordance with Rule 104 (b) — any issue about whether:
>
> (a) an asserted writing, recording, or photograph ever existed;
> (b) another one produced at the trial or hearing is the original; or
> (c) other evidence of content accurately reflects the content.[23]

On the state level, the rules of evidence can differ from one state to another.[24]

Imaging Studies

Imaging studies are pictures of the interior of the object portrayed and are admissible under the same requirements as photographs and videos. Competent evidence must be offered to show that the scans and films are those of the patient, the object, or body part under consideration; that the images were taken in a recognized manner by a competent technician; and a competent physician trained to read the images interpreted them. The value of the images lies in the fact that they identify fractures, foreign objects, and other patient ailments.

Viewing Patient Injuries

Where an issue regarding personal injuries is involved, the plaintiff may be permitted to show to the jury the relevant wound or injury. The exhibition is allowable under the discretion of the court, which considers whether or not the jury will become biased and prejudiced as a result of the observation of the plaintiff's injuries.

The human body is considered the best evidence as to the nature and extent of the alleged injury/injuries. If there is no controversy about either the nature or the extent of an injury, presenting such evidence could be considered prejudicial, and an objection can be made as to its presentation to a jury.

Demonstrations are permitted in some instances to illustrate the extent of injuries. The resident in *Hendricks v. Sanford*[25] developed serious bedsores on her back. The defendant objected to the offer of the plaintiff to display her back to the jury. The court found that the plaintiff's injuries, which had healed, were completely relevant as evidence. Even though the injuries had healed and a skin graft had been performed, a declivity of approximately 3.5 inches in diameter and about the depth of a shallow ashtray was still discernible on the plaintiff's back.

Documentary Evidence

Documentary evidence is written information capable of making a truthful statement (e.g., drug manufacturer inserts, autopsy reports, birth certificates, and medical records). Documentary evidence must satisfy the jury as to authenticity, though proof of authenticity is not necessary if the opposing party accepts its genuineness. In some instances (e.g., wills), witnesses are necessary. In the case of documentation, the original of a document must be produced unless it can be demonstrated that the original has been lost or destroyed, in which case a properly authenticated copy may be substituted.

Medical Records

Preliminary questions that a witness might be asked on entering a medical record into evidence include the following:

1. Please state your name.
2. Where are you employed?
3. What is your position?
4. What is your official title?
5. Did you receive a subpoena for certain records?
6. Did you bring those records with you?
7. Can you identify these records?
8. Did you retrieve the records yourself?
9. Are these the complete records?
10. Were any records destroyed in the normal course of business? If your answer is yes, please describe for the jury which records were destroyed and why they were destroyed.
11. Are these the original records or copies of the originals?
12. How were these records prepared?
13. Are these records maintained under your care, custody, and control?
14. Were these records made in the regular course of business?
15. Was the record made at the time the act, condition, or event occurred or transpired?
16. Is this record regularly kept or maintained?

Manufacturer's Drug Inserts

A manufacturer's drug insert or manual describing the proper use of medical equipment is generally admissible in court as evidence. In *Mueller v. Mueller*,[26] a physician was sued by a patient who charged that she had suffered a deterioration of bone structure and ultimately a collapsed hip as a result of the administration of cortisone over an extended period. The jury decided that the physician's prolonged use of cortisone was negligent, and the physician appealed. "The busy doctor has no alternative but to prescribe these drugs according to the recommendations of the drug manufacturers. No one would expect him to stop his practice and conduct tests and experiments so that he could prescribe the drug solely from his own independent findings on its usefulness and possible side effects. Every doctor who testified in this trial admitted to the use of the drug manufacturer's recommendations as a guide in prescribing drugs."[27] The appeals court held that the manufacturer's recommendations are not only admissible but also essential in determining a physician's possible lack of proper care. "We see no reason for the courts to hesitate to use a standard so widely and favorably used in the medical profession."[28]

In another case, *Mulligan v. Lederle Laboratories*,[29] the plaintiff, a medical laboratory technician, brought an action against the drug manufacturer as the result of the side effects of the drug Varidase. The plaintiff developed several chronic health problems, including mouth sores, microscopic hematuria, and red cell cast, indicating kidney disease. The trial court awarded $50,000 in compensatory damages and $100,000 in punitive damages for the drug manufacturer's failure to warn of the side effects of Varidase. On appeal by the manufacturer, the appeals court held that the products liability action was not barred by a 3-year statute of limitations contained in an Arkansas products liability act and that the evidence was sufficient to award punitive damages. Evidence presented at trial indicated that several side effects were associated with the drug.

Statutes, Rules, and Regulations

Statutes, rules, and regulations can voice a duty that is owed to a particular class of persons who are protected by the statute or regulation. For example, assume a regulation specifies a nurse–patient ratio of no less than one registered nurse to care for no more than two patients in an ICU. This regulation is an expression of the duty imposed on the facility to provide adequate nursing care to patients. Patients are, therefore, a class of people identified within the regulation who are to have the benefits of the protection to be gained by having a predetermined minimum standard nurse–patient care ratio.

Policies and Procedures

The policies and procedures of a healthcare organization established for day-to-day operations are a form of documentary evidence. If a violation of a facility's policy and procedures causes injury to one whom the policy or procedure is designed to protect, such violation can give rise to evidence for negligent conduct.

Facebook Entries and Emails

A federal district court judge ruled in favor of the employer in *Lineberry v. Detroit Medical Center et al.*[30] The employer was found to have a reasonable belief that its employee was abusing her Family and Medical Leave Act (FMLA) leave when it concluded she was dishonest when she was confronted with questions about her Facebook postings of vacation pictures taken while on FMLA leave, and the employer was therefore entitled to terminate the employee. The Court granted summary judgment to the employer, dismissing the employee's suit accusing the hospital of interfering with her FMLA rights and retaliating against her for taking legally protected leave. The plaintiff had claimed that she had to use wheelchairs in all airports on her trip to Mexico. She was reminded that airports have cameras. Upon being shown her Facebook postings, she admitted that she had lied about the use of wheelchairs, as she had never used a wheelchair on her Mexico vacation. At her deposition, she testified:

Q. Is it not true that at the beginning of the [April 19, 2011] meeting, you told the group that you had used wheelchairs?

A. Yes.

Q. Then later on in the meeting, you admitted lying about that, correct?

A. Yes.

Q. Why did you initially lie to the group about using the wheelchair?

A. Because I had lied previously in an email [the March 7, 2011, email to Richards] and I wanted to remain consistent.

The plaintiff's acknowledgment of her behavior during family leave was sufficient evidence of the facts in this case upon which the defendants "could reasonably rely to support their decision to terminate Plaintiff. As such, Defendants are also entitled to summary judgment based on their honest belief that Plaintiff lied and misused her FMLA leave."[31]

Hearsay Evidence

Hearsay evidence is based on what another has said or done and is not the result of the personal knowledge of the witness. *Hearsay* consists of written and oral statements. When a witness testifies to the utterance of a statement made outside court and the statement is offered in court for the truth of the facts that are contained in the statement, this is hearsay and therefore objectionable.

The court in *Costal Health Services, Inc. v. Rozier*[32] held that a written report by an ombudsman (who did not testify at trial) concerning injuries and treatment of an 85-year-old patient was inadmissible as evidence. It contained hearsay accounts of conversations as well as impressions, opinions, and conclusions regarding the nursing facility's negligence when a patient wandered into another patient's room and was injured by that resident. However, the court found that the testimony about one patient's own account of his violent past, made to the nursing home personnel upon his admission, was admissible as original evidence, not as proof of the actual prior incidents, but to show the defendant's notice of the possibility of violent behavior on the part of that patient.

If a statement is offered not as proof of the facts asserted in the statement, but rather only to show that the statement was made, the statement can come into evidence. For example, if it is relevant that a conversation took place, the testimony relating to the conversation may be entered as evidence. The purpose of that testimony would be to establish that the conversation took place, not to prove what was said during the course of the conversation. If testimony is based on personal knowledge, it would be admissible as evidence.

Because of the ability to challenge hearsay evidence successfully, which rests on the credibility of the witness as well as on the competency and veracity of other persons not before the court, it is admitted as evidence in a trial under very strict rules.

There are many exceptions to the hearsay rule that allow testimony that ordinarily would not be admitted. Included in the list of exceptions are admissions made by one of the parties to the action, threats made by a victim, dying declarations, statements to refresh a witness's recollection if he or she is unable to remember the facts known earlier, business records, medical records, and other official records (e.g., certified copies of birth and death records). "Where hearsay

HEARSAY AND LOST CHANCE OF SURVIVAL

Citation: *Stroud v. Golson*, 741 So. 2d 182 (La. App. 2d Cir. June 16, 1999)

Facts

Dr. Mikey examined Stroud. After viewing X-rays, Mikey told Stroud that she might have lung cancer and referred her to Dr. Gullatt for follow-up care. A CT scan was performed at St. Francis Medical Center and Dr. Golson, a radiologist, interpreted Stroud's CT scan as negative for lung cancer. Approximately 1 year later, Stroud was hospitalized at St. Francis for a cerebral hemorrhage. X-rays and CT scans revealed inoperable cancer in Stroud's left lung.

Stroud was discharged from St. Francis and later died as a result of the cancer. The decedent's husband and sons filed a suit seeking damages arising from Golson's failure to properly interpret Stroud's CT scan. Before trial, the plaintiffs settled with Golson and his insurer.

On February 23, 1998, a trial by jury commenced against the Patients' Compensation Fund (PCF), which admitted medical negligence but claimed that Stroud would have died from the fast-acting cancer even if it had been diagnosed earlier. The jury returned a verdict finding that Stroud lost a less-than-even chance of survival because of Golson's negligence.

The defendant argued that the trial judge erred when he overruled the hearsay objection regarding Mr. Stroud's testimony concerning his wife's reasons for declining treatment after her cancer was diagnosed. The testimony at issue centered around the following exchange:

Mr. Thomas: Now, did your wife discuss—you—you and your wife discuss whether or not she should have treatment for her cancer?

Mr. Stroud: Yes, we did.

Mr. Thomas: And were you a part in making a decision with her with why she did not agree to have treatment?

Mr. Stroud: Yes.

Mr. Thomas: Share with the jury what she said about that.

Mr. Stroud: She, ah,—

Mr. Anzelmo: Your Honor, I object to hearsay.

The Court: I understand. But, I think it—it is hearsay but it's reliable. I'll allow it.

Mr. Thomas: Go ahead.

Mr. Stroud: Ah, I had a—my sister passed away in November '94 with lung cancer, and she found out in July of '94 that she had lung cancer. So she went and took the radium treatments, and she weighed 125 pounds and was eating and doing all right until she started taking the radium treatments, and by the end of the radium treatments she could hardly get about, and actually she just laid down and starved herself to death. She weighed 65 pounds when she passed away, and was bedridden all that time. And the wife felt that it was too far gone in her for any treatments to do any good, plus what few days she had left she didn't want to be like my sister.

Issue

Did the trial judge err when he overruled the hearsay objection regarding Stroud's testimony?

Holding

The appeals court found no abuse of discretion by the trial court.

Reason

Stroud suffered a great deal of mental anguish from the hopeless condition she faced, knowing that earlier detection was lost because her CT scan was not properly read. Her decision not to undergo the painful and debilitating chemotherapy, when the odds were so stacked against her recovery, was justified. It is a reasonable conclusion that Stroud would have, in all likelihood, opted for the treatment had the cancer been diagnosed sooner.

Stroud's testimony regarding statements his wife made provided statements of her then-existing state of mind. The testimony showed the motive behind Stroud's decision not to receive treatment, namely, her belief that the treatments would not be effective, as well as her desire to avoid the severe pain and discomfort that can accompany chemotherapy.

evidence is admitted without objection, its probative value is for the jury to determine."[33] This list of exceptions to hearsay evidence is by no means all-inclusive, and therefore, both federal and state statutes should be consulted.

A police officer's testimony that he overheard a drug dealer tell an informant, who was wearing a concealed transmitter, that he could obtain drugs for the informant from a pharmacist friend was properly admitted in a disciplinary proceeding in *Brown v. Idaho State Board of Pharmacy*.[34] The testimony was presented before the Idaho State Board of Pharmacy for proving a dealer's state of mind and explaining his subsequent visit to the pharmacy. The testimony was not subject to hearsay objection.

Medical Books as Hearsay Evidence

Medical books are considered hearsay because the authors are not generally available for cross-examination. Although medical books are not admissible as evidence, a physician may testify as to how he or she formed an opinion and what part textbooks played in forming that opinion. During cross-examination, medical experts may be asked to comment on statements from medical books that contradict their testimony.

▶ DEFENSES AGAINST PLAINTIFF'S ALLEGATIONS

When a plaintiff's case has been established, the defendant may put forward a defense against the claim for damages. The defendant's case is presented to discredit the plaintiff's cause of action and prevent recovery of damages. This section reviews various defenses available to defendants in a negligence suit (**FIGURE 8-1**) that may relieve a defendant from liability.

Ignorance of Fact and Unintentional Wrongs

Ignorance of the law excuses no man; not that all men know the law, but because it is an excuse every man will plead, and no man can tell how to confute him.

—John Selden (1584–1654)

Ignorance of the law is not a legal defense in a lawsuit; otherwise, the plaintiff would be rewarded by pleading ignorance. Arguing that a negligent act is

unintentional is not a defense. If such a defense were acceptable, all defendants would use it.

Assumption of the Risk

Assumption of the risk is knowing that a danger exists and voluntarily accepting the risk by exposing oneself to it, aware that harm might occur. Assumption of the risk may be implicitly assumed, as in alcohol consumption, or expressly assumed, as in relation to warnings found on cigarette packaging.

This defense provides that the plaintiff expressly has given consent in advance, relieving the defendant of an obligation of conduct toward the plaintiff and taking the chances of injury from a known risk arising from the defendant's conduct. For example, a provider who agrees to care for a patient with a communicable disease and then contracts the disease would not be entitled to recover from the patient for damages suffered. In taking the job, the individual agreed to assume the risk of infection, thereby releasing the patient from all legal obligations.

The following two requirements must be established in order for a defendant to be successful in an assumption of the risk defense:

1. The plaintiff must know and understand the risk that is being incurred.
2. The choice to incur the risk must be free and voluntary.

The patient in *Faile v. Bycura*[35] was awarded $75,000 in damages on her allegations that a podiatrist used inappropriate techniques during an unsuccessful attempt to treat her heel spurs. On appeal, it was held that the trial court erred in striking the podiatrist's defense of assumption of the risk. Evidence established that the patient signed consent forms that indicated the risks of treatment as well as alternative treatment modalities.

> Prior to both surgeries, Faile signed a consent form in which she acknowledged that the surgery would probably result in stiff toes. She further acknowledged that the surgery may not work and the heel spurs may have to be surgically removed at a later date. These consent forms were written out in Faile's own handwriting, and Faile testified one of Bycura's employees had discussed the risks with her. Faile also signed a form in which she acknowledged there were various methods for treating heel pain, but she was electing these treatments.[36]

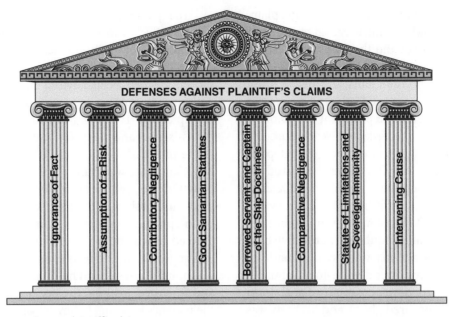

FIGURE 8-1 Defenses against a plaintiff's claims.

The appeals court reversed the judgment of the trial and the case was remanded for a new trial.

Contributory Negligence

Contributory negligence occurs when a person does not exercise reasonable care for his or her own safety. As a general proposition, if a person has knowledge of a dangerous situation and disregards the danger, then that person is contributorily negligent. Actual knowledge of the danger of injury is not necessary for a person to be contributorily negligent. It is sufficient if a reasonable person should have been aware of the possibility of the danger.

The rationale for contributory negligence is based on the principle that all persons must be both careful and responsible for their acts. A plaintiff is required to conform to the broad standard of conduct of the reasonable person. The plaintiff's negligence will be determined and governed by the same tests and rules as the negligence of the defendant. A person incurs the risk of injury if he or she knows of a danger, understands the risks involved, and voluntarily exposes him- or herself to such danger.

In some jurisdictions, contributory negligence, no matter how slight, is sufficient to defeat a plaintiff's claim. Generally, the defense of contributory negligence has been recognized in a medical malpractice action when the patient has failed to follow a physician's instructions; refuses or neglects prescribed treatment; or intentionally provides erroneous, incomplete, or misleading information that leads to the patient's injury.

Contributory negligence is established when: (1) the plaintiff's conduct falls below the required standard of personal care, and (2) there is a causal connection between the plaintiff's careless conduct and the plaintiff's injury. Therefore, the defendant contends that some, if not all, liability is attributable to the plaintiff's own actions. To establish a defense of contributory negligence, the defendant must show that the plaintiff's negligence was an active and efficient contributing cause of the injury.

This was not the case in *Bird v. Pritchard*,[37] in which the plaintiff, on July 3, 1970, slipped and fell, cutting her right hand on a mayonnaise jar and thus injuring the ulnar nerve. She was taken to Hocking Valley Memorial Hospital where she requested the services of Dr. Najm, a board-certified general surgeon. However, he was not available. The defendant, an osteopathic surgeon, was available, and he treated the patient's wound. The patient complained that the fourth and fifth fingers of her right hand were numb. The defendant cleaned the wound and advised the patient to see him on Monday, July 7. The patient did not return to the osteopathic surgeon, but went to see Najm that same Monday. A suit was filed, the court of common pleas rendered a judgment for the defendant, and the plaintiff appealed. The court of appeals held that the patient could not be found to have been contributorily negligent or to have assumed the risk. By the time of her scheduled visit, it was impossible to perform primary or secondary repair of the injured nerves that had not been treated on the initial visit when she had first complained of numbness. For contributory negligence to defeat the claim of the plaintiff, there must not only be negligent conduct by the plaintiff, but also a direct and proximate causal relationship between the negligent act and the injury the plaintiff received.

The Delaware Supreme Court affirmed a lower court's dismissal of a wrongful death action against a medical center's emergency department personnel in *Rochester v. Katalan*.[38] The decedent, Rochester, and a friend had been brought to the emergency department at approximately 6:30 PM under the custody of two police officers. Rochester and his friend, claiming to be heroin addicts suffering withdrawal symptoms, requested some form of medication. Rochester stated that he had a habit requiring four to five bags of heroin a day. His actions were symptomatic of withdrawal. He and his friend were loud, abusive, and uncooperative. Rochester complained of abdominal pains, his eyes appeared glassy, and his body was shaking, among other symptoms that he exhibited. The physician on duty in the emergency department asked whether Rochester had ever participated in a methadone clinic program. Rochester indicated that he had but that he had dropped out of it because he found a new supply source for heroin. The physician then ordered the administration of 40 mg of methadone. Rochester began beating his head against a wall, claiming that he was still sick and needed more methadone. The plea was granted, and the physician ordered a second dose of 40 mg of methadone. After eventually calming down, Rochester was taken to a cell by police officers. The following morning, it was impossible to awaken him, and he was later pronounced dead. It was discovered that he had never been an addict or in a methadone program; rather, the previous night he had been drinking beer and taking Librium. He had not told this to hospital authorities. Rochester's estate sued the physician, and the trial court dismissed the suit. The appellate court affirmed, saying that by Rochester's failure to provide the physician accurate information, he had contributed to his own death. On appeal, the plaintiff argued that the physician and staff could have done more to determine the truth of Rochester's assertions that he was a drug addict. The Delaware Supreme Court held that it already had assumed negligence in that respect. Rochester contributed to his own death by failing to provide a true account of the facts to the emergency department staff. He was guilty of negligent conduct, more accurately "willful" or "intentional" conduct, which was the proximate cause of his death, resulting from multiple drug intoxication. His estate was barred from recovering any monetary damages.

The patient, Cammatte, in *Jenkins v. Bogalusa Community Medical Center*,[39] was admitted to Bogalusa Community Medical Center on September 11 for the treatment of a severe gouty arthritic condition. He had been advised not to get out of bed without first ringing for assistance. On the morning of September 16, he got out of bed without ringing for assistance and went to a bathroom across the hall. As he returned to his room, he fell and fractured his hip. Cammatte was transferred to Touro Infirmary in New Orleans, where he underwent hip surgery and died on October 5, during recuperation, as a result of an apparent pulmonary embolism. The trial court entered judgment for the defendants, and the plaintiffs appealed. The appeals court found that the patient was in full possession of his faculties at the time he fell and fractured his hip. The accident was the result of the patient's knowing failure to follow instructions not to get out of bed without ringing for assistance. The injury in this case was not the result of any breach of the institution's duty to exercise due care.

In another case, the plaintiff in *Quinones v. Public Administrator*[40] sought to recover damages for the alleged negligence of the defendant's physicians for their failure to treat a fractured ankle. The plaintiff claimed that there was a nonunion of the fracture and that he was advised to put weight on his leg. As a result of this advice, the plaintiff claimed that there was an exacerbation of the original injury requiring two operative procedures, which resulted in the fusion of his left ankle. The defendant claimed that if there was any subsequent injury, it was because of the failure of the plaintiff to return for care. The New York Supreme Court entered a judgment in favor of the defendant hospital, and the plaintiff appealed. The New York Supreme Court, Appellate Division, held that a patient's failure to follow instructions does not defeat an action for malpractice where the alleged improper professional treatment occurred before the patient's own negligence.[41] Damages would be reduced to the degree that the plaintiff's negligence increased the extent of the injury.

Comparative Negligence

A defense of *comparative negligence* provides that the degree of negligence or carelessness of each party to a lawsuit must be established by the finder of fact and that each party then is responsible for his or her proportional share of any damages awarded. For example, when a plaintiff suffers injuries of $10,000 from an accident and the plaintiff is found 20% negligent and the defendant 80% negligent, the defendant would be required to pay $8,000 to the plaintiff. Thus, with comparative negligence, the plaintiff can collect for 80% of the injuries, whereas an application of contributory negligence would deprive the plaintiff of any monetary judgment. This doctrine relieves the plaintiff from the hardship of losing an entire claim when a defendant has been successful in establishing that the plaintiff contributed to his or her own injuries. A defense that provides that the plaintiff will forfeit an entire claim if he or she has been contributorily negligent is considered too harsh a result in jurisdictions that recognize comparative negligence.

Good Samaritan Statutes

Various states have enacted *Good Samaritan statutes*, which relieve physicians, nurses, dentists, and other healthcare professionals and, in some instances, laypersons from liability in certain emergency situations. Good Samaritan legislation encourages healthcare professionals to render assistance at the scene of emergencies. The language that grants immunity also supports the conclusion that the physician, nurse, or layperson covered by the act will be protected from liability for ordinary negligence in rendering assistance in an emergency.

Under most statutes, immunity is granted only during an emergency or when rendering emergency care. The concept of *emergency* usually refers to a combination of unforeseen circumstances that require spontaneous action to avoid impending danger. Some states have sought to be more precise regarding what constitutes an emergency or accident. According to the Alaska statute 09.65.090(a), the emergency circumstances must suggest that the giving of aid is the only alternative to death or serious bodily injury.

Apparently, this provision was inserted to emphasize that the actions of a Good Samaritan must be voluntary. To be legally immune under the Good Samaritan laws, a physician or nurse must render help voluntarily and without expectation of later pay.

Emergency Assistance

A physician *not on call* who responds to an emergency call by a *surgeon on call* to assist in the completion of a tubal ligation most likely will be immune from a negligence claim under the state's Good Samaritan law if he or she had a good faith belief that the patient was in a life-threatening situation. Such was the case in *Pemberton v. Dharmani*,[42] where the court of appeals held that the Michigan Good Samaritan statute merely requires a good faith belief by healthcare personnel that they are attending a life-threatening emergency

in order to be cloaked with the immunity provided by the statute, regardless of whether a life-threatening emergency actually exists. To construe the statute otherwise would controvert the purpose of the statute and render it meaningless. Healthcare personnel would be discouraged from giving treatment in emergency situations if an actual life-threatening situation were required to exist before they would be cloaked with immunity. Treatment may even be delayed in a given case, worsening the condition of the patient by waiting until the patient is in an obviously life-threatening situation before rendering treatment.[43]

Borrowed Servant Doctrine

The *borrowed servant doctrine* is a special application of the doctrine of respondeat superior and applies when an employer lends an employee to another for a particular employment. Although an employee remains the servant of the employer, under the borrowed servant doctrine, the employer is not liable for injury negligently caused by the servant while in the special service of another. For example, in certain situations, a nurse employed by a hospital may be considered the employee of the physician. In these situations, the physician is the special or temporary employer and is liable for the negligence of the nurse. To determine whether a physician is liable for the negligence of a nurse, it must be established that the physician had the right to control and direct the nurse at the time of the negligent act. If the physician is found to be in exclusive control of the nurse at the time of the alleged malpractice, the nurse is deemed to be the physician's temporary special employee and the *hospital is not generally considered liable* for the nurse's negligent acts.

Hospital Responsible for Resident's Negligence

The hospital in *Brickner v. Osteopathic Hospital*[44] was held vicariously liable for a surgical resident's failure to diagnose testicular cancer during exploratory surgery performed under the supervision of a staff physician. The hospital was not insulated from liability under the borrowed servant doctrine even though the supervising surgeon had authority over the resident during the operation. The hospital never relinquished control over the resident, who was required under the hospital's training program to assist in diagnosis and who could have taken a biopsy without express instructions of the operating surgeon. Liability was not precluded because of the hospital's lack of actual control over the resident's medical decision not to perform a biopsy.

🔍 *GOOD SAMARITAN STATUTE: PREEXISTING DUTY TO CARE*

Citation: *Deal v. Kearney*, 851 P.2d 1353 (Alaska 1993)

Facts

The plaintiff, Kearney, suffered a life-threatening injury and was taken by ambulance to the emergency department of Kodiak Island Hospital (KIH). The on-call emergency department physician, a family practitioner, examined Kearney. It was determined that a surgical consultation was necessary and Deal, a surgeon with staff privileges at the hospital, was called. After ordering certain tests, Deal was of the opinion that Kearney could not survive a transfer to Anchorage. Deal then performed emergency surgery that lasted for over 9 hours, ending the following morning.

The plaintiff was eventually transferred to Anchorage. His condition worsened, and he suffered loss of circulation and tissue death in both legs. The plaintiff alleged that KIH was negligent in failing to properly evacuate him to Anchorage. Kearney reached a settlement totaling $510,000. He also brought an action against Deal for negligent acts. Deal moved for summary judgment, claiming to be immune from suit under the Good Samaritan statute.

The trial court denied Deal's motion for summary judgment, ruling that the Good Samaritan statute was not applicable to Deal because he was acting under a preexisting duty to render emergency care to Kearney. Deal petitioned for review, and his petition was granted.

The superior court held that the immunity provided by the Good Samaritan statute is unavailable to physicians with a preexisting duty to respond to emergency situations. The court concluded that Deal was under a preexisting duty in the instant case by virtue of his contract with KIH, the duty being part of the consideration that Deal gave to KIH in exchange for staff privileges at the hospital. The court further found that the Good Samaritan statute did not apply to Deal in any event, because the actions allegedly constituting malpractice occurred during the follow-up care and treatment given to Kearney after surgery. By then, the court reasoned, Deal had become Kearney's treating physician and was no longer responding to an emergency situation. Deal appealed to the Alaska Supreme Court.

Issue

Does the Good Samaritan statute extend immunity to physicians who have a preexisting duty to render emergency care?

Holding

The Alaska Supreme Court held that the Good Samaritan statute does not extend immunity to physicians who have preexisting duty to render emergency care.

Reason

Alaska Statute 09.65.090(a) states:

> A person at a hospital or any other location who renders emergency care or emergency counseling to an injured, ill, or emotionally distraught person who reasonably appears to be "in immediate need of emergency aid in order to avoid serious harm or death is not liable for civil damages as a result of an act or omission in rendering emergency aid."

The legislature clearly intended this provision to encourage healthcare providers, including medical professionals, to administer emergency medical care, whether in a hospital or not, to persons who are not their patients, by immunizing them from civil liability. The clear inference of this recommendation is that the statute would not cover those with a preexisting duty to care.

The resident was performing a service for which he had been employed.

Physician Not Liable for Technician's Negligence

Oberzan brought a medical malpractice action against a hospital radiologist, Dr. Smith, for injuries allegedly incurred because of an X-ray technician's negligence in performing a barium enema.[45] The plaintiff alleged that either Dr. Smith or the X-ray technician, Davis, perforated his rectum during a barium enema procedure. Davis inserted the enema tip into the rectum of the plaintiff for the barium enema before Dr. Smith entered the X-ray room for the procedure. After Dr. Smith entered the room, the examination began. Immediately after Davis began injecting the barium, she noticed bleeding at the tip of the rectum.

Oberzan claimed the physician was vicariously liable for the employee's negligent conduct. The Kansas

Supreme Court held that the respondeat superior doctrine did not apply to the relationship between the technician employed by the hospital and the radiologist so as to impose vicarious liability on the radiologist.

Davis was not an employee of Dr. Smith. She was not under his direct supervision and control at the time the injury occurred. Dr. Smith did not select Davis to perform the insertion of the enema tip; she was assigned by the hospital. A master–servant relationship was not established because Dr. Smith was not exercising personal control or supervision over Davis.

Oberzan argued that Kansas law K.A.R. 28-34-86(a) provides that "the radiology department and all patient services rendered therein shall be under the supervision of a designated medical staff physician; wherever possible, this physician shall be attending or consulting radiologist." The plaintiff claimed this imposes a duty on radiologists to supervise patient services rendered in a hospital's radiology department. The plaintiff, however, failed to show that any of the statute's subsections require that the preparation of a patient for a barium enema be performed under the direct supervision of a physician. The purpose of K.A.R. 28-34-12(c) "is to establish an administrative head for the radiology department." Oberzan cited no authority in support of his position that the Kansas statute created a legal duty for a designated medical staff physician to personally control and supervise all activities that occur in a radiology department. Such an interpretation of the statute would create physician liability extending far beyond the intent of the regulation.

Captain of the Ship Doctrine

In the context of the operating room, the application of the borrowed servant doctrine generally is referred to as the *captain of the ship doctrine*. Historically, under this doctrine, the surgeon was viewed as being the one in command in the operating room. The rationale for this concept was provided in the Minnesota case of *St. Paul-Mercury Indemnity Co. v. St. Joseph Hospital*, when the court stated:

> [t]he desirability of the rule is obvious. The patient is completely at the mercy of the surgeon and relies upon him to see that all the acts relative to the operation are performed in a careful manner. It is the surgeon's duty to guard against any and all avoidable acts that may result in injury to his patient. In the operating room, the surgeon must be master. He cannot tolerate any other voice in the control of his assistants. In the case at bar, the evidence is clear that the doctor had exclusive control over the acts in question, and therefore the hospital cannot be said to have been a "joint master" or "comaster," even though the nurses were in its general employ and paid by it.[46]

In *Krane v. Saint Anthony Hospital Systems*,[47] the factual question that had to be determined was whether, at the time of the alleged negligent act, the operating surgeon had assumed control of a surgical nurse. If so, the responsibility of the surgeon supersedes that of the hospital. It was uncontradicted that the alleged negligent act of the surgical nurse took place over 2.5 hours into surgery, and there could be no factual dispute that the surgeon had assumed control over the nurse.

Several courts have developed a distinction between a nurse's clerical or administrative acts and those involving professional skill and judgment, which are considered medical acts. Some courts use this distinction in allocating liability for the acts of a nurse to either the surgeon or the hospital. If the act is characterized as administrative or clerical, it is the hospital's responsibility; if the act is considered to be medical, it is the surgeon's responsibility. This rule was followed in the Minnesota case of *Swigerd v. City of Ortonville*,[48] in which the court found that the hospital is liable as an employer for the negligence of its nurses in performing acts that are basically administrative. Administrative acts, although constituting a component of a patient's prescribed medical treatment, do not require the application of specialized procedures and techniques or the understanding of a skilled physician or surgeon.

Today's courts recognize that surgeons do not always have the right to control all persons within the operating room. An assignment of liability based on the theory of who had actual control over the patient more realistically reflects the actual relationship that exists in a modern operating room. For example, summary dismissal in *Thomas v. Raleigh*[49] was properly ordered for those portions of a patient's medical malpractice action that sought to hold a surgeon vicariously liable for throat injuries suffered by his patient because of the negligent manner in which an endotracheal tube was inserted during the administration of anesthesia. The patient's allegations that the surgeon exercised control over the administration of anesthesia were rebutted by evidence to the contrary. Liability of the surgeon could not be premised on the captain of the ship doctrine because that doctrine would not be recognized in West Virginia, where the surgery took place. Deposition testimony made it clear that Dr. Isaac had nothing to do with the anesthesia procedure. "In the present case Thomas presented no evidence to dispute the finding that Dr. Isaac had no control over the anesthesia procedure, and therefore the trial court's ruling on this matter was correct."[50]

Statute of Limitations

The *statute of limitations* refers to legislatively imposed time constraints that restrict the period after the occurrence of an injury during which a legal action must be commenced. Should a cause of action be initiated later than the period prescribed, the case cannot proceed. Many technical rules are associated with statutes of limitations. Statutes in each state specify that malpractice suits and other personal injury suits must be brought within fixed periods of time. An injured person who is a minor or is otherwise under a legal disability may, in many states, extend the period within which an action for injury may be filed. Computation of the period when the statute begins to run in a particular state may be based on any one or more of the following factors:

- The date that the physician terminated treatment
- The time of the wrongful act
- The time when the patient should have reasonably discovered the injury
- The date that the injury is discovered
- The date when the contract between the patient and the physician ended

The running of the statute will not begin if fraud (the deliberate concealment from a patient of facts that might present a cause of action for damages) is involved. The cause of action begins at the time fraud is discovered.

The statute of limitations does not generally begin to run in those cases where a patient is unaware that an act of malpractice has occurred. Such is the case when foreign objects are left in a patient during surgery. A New Hampshire patient in *Shillady v. Elliot Community Hospital*[51] sued the hospital for negligence in treatment that was administered 31 years earlier. A needle had been left in the patient's spine after a spinal tap in 1940. In 1970, an X-ray showed the needle. The patient had suffered severe pain immediately after the spinal tap, which had decreased over the intervening years to about three "spells" per year. The court held that the 6-year statute of limitations does not begin "until the patient learns or in the exercise of reasonable care and diligence should have learned of its

presence."[52] Therefore, the defendant's motion to dismiss the case on the grounds that the statute of limitations had run out was not granted.

Sovereign Immunity

Sovereign immunity is a legal doctrine by which federal and state governments historically have been immune from liability for harm suffered from the tortious conduct of government employees. For the most part, both federal and state governments have abolished sovereign immunity. Congress enacted the Federal Tort Claims Act (FTCA) of 1948 to provide redress for those who have been negligently injured by employees of the federal government acting within their scope of employment.

FTCA and Veterans Hospital

In an action under the FTCA,[53] the plaintiff was permitted to sue the Veterans Administration Hospital of Memphis, Tennessee, in a federal court for injuries sustained by an 83-year-old patient found lying in a hallway of the hospital. The patient suffered severe head injuries that required surgery. Damages in the amount of $80,000 were awarded to the plaintiff. The court held that the evidence was sufficient to raise a duty on the part of government employees attending the patient to use reasonable care to protect him from getting out of bed and injuring himself. This duty was breached, and the patient was injured. The proximate cause of the patient's injuries was related to the hospital's failure to put up the patient's bed rails and its failure to remind him to call a nurse if he needed help.

FTCA and Failure to Refer

Action was brought on behalf of a minor in *Steele v. United States*[54] who received treatment at a U.S. Army hospital and suffered injury because of the optometrist's failure to refer the child to an ophthalmologist for examination. The U.S. district court held that it was probable that an ophthalmologist would have diagnosed the child's problem and prevented the loss of his right eye. Recovery was permitted against the United States under the FTCA.

State Immunity Laws

The various states provide that government employees can be held liable for their tortious acts. The Texas Tort Claims Act, for example, allows an individual to file a private tort suit against a government entity.

🔍 STATUTE OF LIMITATIONS NOT APPLICABLE

Citation: *J.B. v. Sacred Heart Hosp. of Pensacola*, 635 So. 2d 945 (Fla. 1994)

Facts

The facts of this case reveal that the hospital on or about April 17, 1989, was requested by its medical staff to arrange transportation for the patient, diagnosed with acquired immunodeficiency syndrome (AIDS), to another treatment facility in Alabama. The social services department, unable to arrange ambulance transport, asked the patient's brother to provide the transportation. J.B., having visited his brother at the hospital when he was first admitted, was under the impression that his brother's diagnosis was Lyme disease. He had not been notified that there was a change in diagnosis. The patient was released to his brother from the hospital with excessive fever and a heparin lock in his arm. During the trip, J.B.'s brother began to thrash about and accidentally dislodged the dressing to his heparin lock, causing J.B. to reach over while driving in an attempt to prevent the lock from coming out of his brother's arm. In doing so, J.B. came in contact with fluid around the lock site. J.B.'s hand had multiple nicks and cuts as a result of a recent fishing trip. [*Id.* at 947]

The complaint, which was filed after the 2-year statute of limitation had tolled, alleged that the hospital was negligent in arranging for J.B. to transport his brother in that it knew of the patient's condition, the level of care that would be required in transporting him, and the risk involved. J.B. alleged that because he contracted the AIDS virus, his wife was exposed to it through him and his children have suffered a loss of relationship with him.

The Florida District Court ruled that J.B.'s complaint stated a claim for medical malpractice and was thus subject to the pre-suit notice and screening procedures set out in Florida statutes. Because J.B. did not follow those procedures, the court dismissed the complaint. On appeal, the Florida Circuit Court declined to rule on J.B.'s claim, concluding that the issues were appropriate for resolution by the Florida Supreme Court.

Issue

Was the claim of the patient's brother a claim for medical malpractice and therefore subject to a 2-year statute of limitations?

Holding

The Florida Supreme Court answered that the claim was not a claim for medical malpractice for purposes of the 2-year statute of limitations or pre-suit notice and screening requirements.

Reason

Florida statutes set a 2-year limitation period for medical malpractice actions. J.B.'s injury arose solely through the hospital's use of him as a transporter. Accordingly, this suit is not a medical malpractice action, and the 2-year statute of limitations is inapplicable. According to the allegations in J.B.'s complaint, the hospital was negligent in using J.B. as a transporter. The complaint does not allege that the hospital was negligent in any way in the rendering of, or the failure to render, medical care or services to J.B.

📰 WHAT SURGEONS LEAVE BEHIND

More than a dozen times a day, doctors sew up patients with sponges and other surgical objects mistakenly left inside. It's a deadly, yet easily avoidable phenomenon.

• • •

The consequences are enormous. Many patients carrying surgical sponges suffer for months or years before anyone determines the cause of the searing pain, digestive dysfunction and other typical ills.

—Peter Eisler, *USA Today*, March 8–10, 2013

The Texas Tort Claims Act ("The Act") is a set of statutes that determine when a governmental entity may be liable for tortious conduct under state law. Prior to the adoption of the Act, individuals could not recover damages from state or local governmental units for injuries resulting from the actions of a government employee or officer in the performance of a governmental function.[55]

The Mississippi Supreme Court, as demonstrated in the case below, determined there was no qualified immunity for public hospital employees making treatment decisions.

🔍 NURSE'S NEGLIGENCE: IMMUNITY DENIED

Citation: *Sullivan v. Sumrall by Ritchey*, 618 So. 2d 1274 (Miss. 1993)

Facts

In April 26, 1988, the patient was admitted to the hospital suffering from a severe headache. Her physician ordered a CT scan for the following morning and prescribed Demerol and Dramamine to alleviate pain. Referring to the patient's medical chart, the nurse stated in her deposition that the patient received injections of Demerol and Dramamine at 6:45 PM and 10:00 PM on April 26. The nurse checked on the patient at 11:00 PM. The patient's temperature and blood pressure were taken at midnight. Her blood pressure was recorded at 90/60, down from 160/80 at 8:00 PM. At 12:25 AM, 2 hours and 25 minutes after her last medication, the nurse administered another injection of Demerol and Dramamine because the patient was still complaining of pain. Although hospital rules require consultation with a patient's admitting physician when there is a question regarding the administration of medication, the nurse stated that she did not call the physician before administering another injection.

At 4:00 AM, when the nurse made an hourly check of the patient, she discovered that the patient was not breathing. She called a Code 99, which was an emergency signal that alerted designated staff to come to the assistance of the patient. In this case, an emergency department physician responded and revived the patient. The patient was diagnosed as having suffered "respiratory arrest, with what appears to be hypoxic brain injury." CT scans revealed no bleeding, but other tests revealed a grossly abnormal electroencephalogram (EEG). The patient was transferred to a nursing facility where she remained in a coma at the time of trial.

The patient's daughter and husband filed a complaint against the hospital, alleging that the hospital had been negligent in monitoring and medicating the patient, in failing to notify a physician when her vital signs became irregular, in failing to properly assess her condition and intervene, and in failing to exercise reasonable care. Later, the complaint was amended to include the nurse.

The defendant nurse filed a motion for summary judgment. She asserted that, as a matter of law, she was shielded from liability under the qualified immunity afforded public officials. The circuit court denied the motion, and the nurse appealed.

Issue

Is a nurse employed by a county hospital shielded by public official qualified immunity from a medical negligence action brought against her individually?

Holding

The Mississippi Supreme Court affirmed the decision of the circuit court denying the nurse's motion for summary judgment and remanded to the circuit court for further proceedings.

Reason

There is no qualified immunity for any public hospital employees making treatment decisions. Discretion exercised by medical personnel in making treatment decisions is not the sort of individual judgment sought to protect by the qualified immunity bestowed upon public officials.

Miss. Code Ann. § 41-13-11 expressly provides for the acquisition of liability insurance by boards and owners of community hospitals and waives immunity to the extent insurance is available to satisfy any judgment rendered. It is undisputed that Jones County Community Hospital carried such a policy. Thus, the hospital itself waived immunity to the extent of its liability coverage. The record is silent, however, as to whether Jones County Community Hospital also carried a liability policy for the benefit of its employees.

Intervening Cause

Intervening cause arises when the act of a third party, independent of the defendant's original negligent conduct, is the proximate cause of a patient's injury. If the negligent act of a third party is unforeseeable as a normal and probable consequence of the defendant's negligence, then the third party's negligence supersedes that of the defendant and relieves the defendant of liability. For example, in *DePesa v. Westchester Square Medical Center*,[56] a 49-year-old woman experiencing severe pain in her abdomen entered the emergency department at Westchester Square Medical Center (WSMC). There, she was prescribed Mylanta and sent home with the advice that she should contact her personal physician if her condition worsened. She took the Mylanta, but her condition continued to deteriorate, and after 20 more days, she went to the emergency department at a second hospital. She was admitted and was operated on for a perforated bowel and peritonitis. Although the evidence indicated that the operation itself was successful, she died at the hospital on May 25. The autopsy report indicated the presence of yellow fluid in the pleural cavity and peritoneal cavity and the cause of the death as status post-bowel resection, bronchopneumonia, and congestive heart failure.

The appellate court found that the trial court should have provided an instruction directing the jury to decide whether the postoperative care of the decedent by the second hospital, despite WSMC's negligence in misdiagnosing the patient's condition, was the proximate and superseding cause of death. WSMC's expert testified, based on the medical evidence, that while the decedent was recovering from surgery, employees at the second hospital administered almost double the amount of fluids that the decedent could output, resulting in congestive heart failure and her ultimate demise. WSMC's theory at trial was that the perforation of the bowel occurred at the second hospital, where staff allegedly administered substantially more fluid to the patient than she could excrete, that these causes of death were independent of WSMC's own negligence in failing to detect bowel conditions, and that such *intervening cause* would not have been foreseeable by a reasonably prudent person.

> Since plaintiff's expert's opinion presented an issue of fact as to whether fluid overload in decedent's system was a cause of her death, there is a triable issue as to whether the treatment rendered by nonparty Jacobi Hospital was an intervening cause, superseding, as a matter of law, any liability of defendant arising from defendant's emergency room treatment 20 days earlier.
>
> We have considered plaintiff's contentions for affirmative relief and find such relief to be unwarranted under the circumstances.[57]

Cause of Injury by Sterilized Needle Not Foreseeable

In *Cohran v. Harper*,[58] a patient sued a physician, charging him with malpractice for an alleged staphylococcal infection that she received from a hypodermic needle used by the physician's nurse. The nurse gave the patient an injection that resulted in osteomyelitis. The grounds of negligence included an allegation that the physician failed to properly sterilize the hypodermic needle that was used to administer penicillin. The evidence showed, without dispute, that a prepackaged sterilized needle and syringe were used in accordance with proper and accepted medical practice. The physician was not liable. There was inadequate proof that either the physician or his nurse was negligent. The court found that even if there was evidence that the needle was contaminated and that the patient's ailment was caused thereby, there was no evidence that the physician, his nurse, or anyone in his office knew, or by the exercise of ordinary care could have discovered, that the prepackaged needle and syringe were contaminated. The defense of intervening cause would have been an adequate defense against recovery of damages if it had been established that the needle was contaminated when packaged.

▶ CLOSING STATEMENTS

After completion of the plaintiff's case and the defendant's defense, the judge calls for closing statements. The defense proceeds first, followed by the plaintiff. Closing statements provide attorneys with an opportunity to summarize for the jury and the court what they have proven. They may point out faults in their opponent's case and emphasize points they want the jury to remember.

The court will grant a motion for a directed verdict if (1) there is no question of fact to be decided by the jury, or (2) the evidence presented failed to establish a legal basis for a verdict favoring the plaintiff. "In civil proceedings, either party may receive a directed verdict in its favor if the opposing party fails to present a prima facie case, or fails to present a necessary defense."[59]

▶ JUDGE'S CHARGE TO THE JURY

After the attorneys' summations, the court charges the jury before the jurors recess to deliberate. Because the jury determines issues of fact, it is necessary for the court to instruct the jury with regard to applicable law. This is done by means of a charge. The judge's charge describes the responsibility of the jury, the law applicable to the case heard by the jury, and advises the jury of the alternatives available to it. The following quote summarizes some important points in the judge's instruction to the jury.

> The judge will instruct the jury in each separate case as to the law of that case. For example, in each criminal case, the judge will tell the jury, among other things, that a defendant charged with a crime is presumed to be

innocent and the burden of proving his guilt beyond a reasonable doubt is upon the Government. Jurors must follow only the instructions of law given to them by the trial judge in each particular case.[60]

The trial judge's charge to the jurors in *Estes Health Care Centers v. Bannerman*,[61] in which a nursing facility resident died after transfer to a hospital after suffering burns in a bath, included:

The complaint alleges the defendant Jackson Hospital undertook to provide hospital and nursing care to the deceased, and that the defendant negligently failed to provide proper hospital and nursing care to the plaintiff's intestate. . . .

The defendants in response to these allegations . . . have each separately entered pleas of the general issue or general denial. Under the law, a plea of the general issue has the effect of placing the burden of proof on the plaintiffs to reasonably satisfy you from the evidence, the truth of those things claimed by them in the bill of the complaint. The defendants carry no burden of proof. . . .

As to the defendant Jackson Hospital, the duty arises in that in rendering services to a patient, a hospital must use that degree of care, skill, and diligence used by hospitals generally in the community under similar circumstances. . . .

Negligence is not actionable unless the negligence is the proximate cause of the injury. The law defines proximate cause as that cause which is the natural and probable sequence of events and without the intervention of any new or independent cause, produces the injury, and without which such injury would not have occurred. For an act to constitute actionable negligence, there must not only be some causal connection between the negligent act complained of and the injury suffered, but connection must be by natural and unbroken sequence, without intervening sufficient causes, so that but for the negligence of the defendant, the injury would not have occurred. . . .

If one is guilty of negligence, which concurs or combines with the negligence of another, and the two combine to produce injury, each negligent person is liable for the resulting injury. And the negligence of each will be deemed the proximate cause of the

injury. Concurrent causes may be defined as two or more causes which run together and act contemporaneously to produce a given result or to inflict an injury. This does not mean that the causes of the acts producing the injury must necessarily occur simultaneously, but they must be active simultaneously to efficiently and proximately produce a result. . . .

In an action against two or more defendants for injury allegedly caused by combined or concurring negligence of the defendants, it is not necessary to show negligence of all the defendants in order for recovery to be had against one or more to be negligent. If you are reasonably satisfied from the evidence in this case that all the defendants are negligent and that their negligence concurred and combined to proximately cause the injury complained by the plaintiffs, then each defendant is liable to the plaintiffs.[62]

When a charge given by the court is not clear enough on a particular point, it is the obligation of the attorneys for both sides to request clarification of the charge. When a jury retires to deliberate, the members are reminded not to discuss the case except among themselves.

Jury Instructions Must Not Be Prejudicial

The nursing assistant in *Myers v. Heritage Enterprises, Inc.*[63] was determined not to be in a professional position. The standard of care required by the nursing assistant was one of ordinary negligence. Therefore, the trial court should have instructed the jury that it had to decide how a reasonably prudent person would have acted under the circumstances. The trial court abused its discretion by instructing the jury on professional negligence rather than ordinary negligence. The instructions given misled the jury and resulted in prejudice to the plaintiff. The case was remanded for a new trial.

Court Erred in Jury Instructions

The medical malpractice action in *Houserman v. Garrett*[64] was filed after a gauze pad was discovered in the patient approximately 8 months after surgery. The trial court was found to have erred when it instructed the jury that the physician's conduct was negligent without any argument as to the surrounding circumstances (negligence per se). The physician alone was understood to be liable for failure to remove the pad from the patient's body. Without clarification elsewhere in the charge, it was hard to determine what, if anything, a physician could do to have defended himself.

It is undisputed that a nurse was responsible for counting the surgical sponges and surgical devices used in this procedure before and after the surgery and that she apparently did not include the pad in her presurgery count. In addition, she did not advise the physician, before the surgical site was closed, that a pad was unaccounted for.

The trial judge charged the jury that the nurse's count amounted only to an added precaution when, in fact, in light of the evidence, the jury was entitled to find that the nurse's count was valid evidence that the physician had satisfied one component of the standard of care. On appeal, the judgment was reversed, and the case was remanded to the trial court for further proceedings.

▶ JURY DELIBERATION AND DETERMINATION

After the judge's charge, the jury retires to the jury room to deliberate and determine the defendant's liability. The jury members return to the courtroom upon reaching a verdict, and their determinations are presented to the court.

If a verdict is against the weight of the evidence, a judge may dismiss the case, order a new trial, or set his or her own verdict. At the time judgment is rendered, the losing party has an opportunity to motion for a new trial.

▶ AWARDING DAMAGES

Monetary damages generally are awarded to individuals in cases of personal injury and wrongful death. Damages generally are fixed by the jury and are nominal, compensatory, hedonic, or punitive. General damages can be awarded as compensation "not only for physical pain but for fright, nervousness, grief, anxiety, worry, mortification, shock, humiliation, indignity, embarrassment, apprehension, terror or ordeal."[65]

1. *Nominal damages* are awarded as a mere token in recognition that a wrong has been committed when the actual amount of compensation is insignificant.
2. *Compensatory damages* are estimated reparation in money for detriment or injury sustained (including loss of earnings, medical costs, and loss of financial support).
3. *Hedonic damages* are those damages awarded to compensate an individual for the loss of enjoyment of life. Such damages are awarded because of the failure of compensatory damages to compensate an individual adequately for the pain and suffering that he or she has endured as a result of a negligent wrong.
4. *Punitive damages* are additional money awards authorized when an injury is caused by gross carelessness or disregard for the safety of others.

Plaintiffs seek recovery for a great variety of damages. Specific damages typically sought by plaintiffs include those for personal injuries, permanent physical disabilities, permanent mental disabilities, past and future physical and mental pain and suffering sustained and to be sustained, loss of enjoyment of life, loss of consortium where a spouse is injured in an accident, loss of child's services where a minor child is injured by an accident, medical and other health expenses reasonably paid or incurred or reasonably certain to be incurred in the future, past and future loss of earnings sustained and to be sustained, and permanent diminution in the plaintiff's earning capacity. The following cases illustrate a variety of damages sought by plaintiffs.

Punitive Damages/Mighty Engine of Deterrence

Punitive damages are awarded over and above that which is intended to compensate the plaintiff for economic losses resulting from the injury. Punitive damages cover such items as physical disability, mental anguish, loss of a spouse's services, physical suffering, injury to one's reputation, and loss of companionship. Punitive damages were referred to as that mighty engine of deterrence in *Johnson v. Terry*.[66]

The court in *Henry v. Deen*[67] held that allegations of gross and wanton negligence incidental to wrongful death in the plaintiff's complaint gave sufficient notice of a claim against the treating physician and physician's assistant for punitive damages. The original complaint, which alleged that the treating physician, the physician's assistant, and the consulting physician agreed to create and did create false and misleading entries in the patient's medical record, was sufficient to allege a civil conspiracy. The decision of the lower court was reversed, and the case was remanded for further proceedings.

In *Estes Health Care Centers v. Bannerman*, discussed earlier, the court stated:

> While human life is incapable of translation into a compensatory measurement,

the amount of an award of punitive damages may be measured by the gravity of the wrong done, the punishment called for by the act of the wrongdoer, and the need to deter similar wrongs in order to preserve human life.[68]

A punitive damage award in the amount of $1.7 million for the wrongful death of a patient from infected decubitus ulcers in *Payton Health Care Facilities, Inc. v. Estate of Campbell*[69] was found to be justified. The treating physician had agreed to a settlement prior to trial in the amount of $50,000. The decedent, a stroke victim, had been admitted to the Lakeland Health Care Center for nursing and medical care. While at the center, the patient developed several severe skin ulcers that eventually necessitated hospitalization in Lakeland General Hospital. The patient's condition deteriorated to such a state that further treatment was inadequate to prolong his life. Expert testimony had been presented that indicated that the standard of care received by the patient while at the nursing facility was an outrageous deviation from acceptable standards of care. There was sufficient evidence of the willful and wanton disregard for rights of others to permit an award of punitive damages against the companies who owned and managed the nursing facility. The cause of death was determined to be bacteremia with sepsis, caused by the extensive infected necrotic decubitus ulcers the patient developed at the nursing facility.

Punitive Damages Not Awarded

Punitive damages in *Brooking v. Polito*[70] were determined to be inappropriate in an action alleging failure to diagnose pancreatic cancer in a timely manner. It was undisputed that the defendants performed various tests on the decedent, which included blood tests, CT scans, MRI, and ultrasound. The tests had been analyzed, and the patient was treated accordingly.

Future Pain and Suffering

In *Luecke v. Bitterman*,[71] an award of $490,000 for future pain and suffering was found reasonable with respect to a 20-year-old patient who, as a result of a physician's negligent application of liquid nitrogen to remove a wart, suffered a 4 by 12–inch third-degree burn. The burn resulted in a scar on the right buttock extending to the back of the thigh. The plaintiff suffered excruciating pain and posttraumatic stress disorder.

Damages for Surviving Spouse and Children

Damages may be awarded given evidence of a patient's pain and the mental anguish of the surviving spouse and children. In *Jefferson Hospital Association v. Garrett*,[72] damages in the amount of $180,000 were found not to be excessive given evidence of the patient's pain and the mental suffering of the surviving spouse and children.

Damages/Emotional Distress

The court of appeals in *Haught v. Maceluch*[73] held that under Texas law, the mother was entitled to recover for her emotional distress, even though she was not conscious at the time her child was born. The mother had brought a medical malpractice action, alleging that the physician was negligent in the delivery of her child, causing her daughter to suffer permanent brain injury. The district court entered judgment of $1,160,000 for the child's medical expenses and $175,000 for her lost future earnings. The court deleted a jury award of $118,000 for the mother's mental suffering over her daughter's impaired condition. On appeal, the court of appeals permitted recovery, under Texas law, for mental suffering. The mother was conscious for more than 11 hours of labor and was aware of the physician's negligent acts, his absence in a near-emergency situation, and the overadministration of the labor-inducing drug Pitocin.

Damages/Not Excessive

The plaintiff in *Burge v. Parker*[74] suffered a laceration of his right foot on April 2 and was taken to St. Margaret's Hospital. A physician in the emergency department cleaned and stitched the laceration and released the patient with instructions to keep the foot elevated. Even though reports prepared by the fire medic who arrived on the scene of the accident and by ambulance personnel indicated the chief complaint as being a fracture of the foot, no X-rays were ordered in the emergency department. The admitting clerk had typed a statement on the admission form indicating possible fracture of the right foot. However, a handwritten note stated the chief complaint as being a laceration of the right foot. The patient returned to the hospital later in the day with his mother, complaining of pain in the right foot. His mother asked if X-rays had been taken. The physician said that it was not necessary. The wound was redressed, and the patient was sent home again with instructions to keep the foot elevated. The pain continued to worsen, and the patient was taken to see another physician on April 5. X-rays were ordered, and an orthopedic surgeon called for a consultation diagnosed three fractures and a compartment syndrome, a swelling of tissue in the muscle compartments. The swelling increased pressure on the blood vessels, thus decreasing circulation, which tends to cause muscles to die.

Approximately one-half pint of clotted blood was removed from the wound. By April 11, the big toe had to be surgically removed. It was alleged that the emergency department physician failed to obtain a full medical history, to order the necessary X-rays, and to diagnose and treat the fractures of the foot. As a result, the patient ultimately suffered loss of his big toe. The Macon County Circuit Court awarded damages totaling $450,000 for loss of a big toe, and the physician appealed. The Alabama Supreme Court found the damages not to have been excessive.

Award Was Fair and Just

In *Tesauro v. Perrige*,[75] Mrs. Tesauro, the appellee, went to Dr. Perrige, the appellant, to have a lower left molar removed. A blood clot failed to form, and the appellant administered an injection of alcohol near the affected area. The appellee began to experience pain, burning, and numbness on the left side of her face at the site of the injection. Several physicians diagnosed her as suffering from muscle spasms caused by a damaged trigeminal nerve. Over a 5-year period, the appellee was treated by a variety of specialists. In 1989, the plaintiff underwent radical experimental surgery. The surgery corrected the plaintiff's most oppressive symptoms. Although the most painful symptoms had been eliminated, the appellee continued to suffer numbness and burning on the left side of her face. A dental malpractice lawsuit was filed against Dr. Perrige alleging that he was negligent in administering the alcohol injection so close to the trigeminal nerve. The jury returned a verdict in favor of the plaintiffs in the amounts of $2,747,000 to Mrs. Tesauro and $593,000 to Mr. Tesauro for loss of consortium. Dr. Perrige appealed for a new trial to be based on the excessiveness of the jury verdict.

The superior court determined that the severity of the plaintiff's injury would support the compensatory award. The plaintiff spent 5 years trying to find a cure for her pain. Although much recovered, the plaintiff continued to suffer from numbness and burning. Her experience clearly fell into the category of severe injury. The severity of the injury had a huge impact on the marital relationship. The compensation awarded to Mr. Tesauro was, therefore, fair and just.

Damages Not Based on Prejudice and Passion

A medical malpractice action was brought against the employer of a physician, alleging that the physician's failure to properly treat an abscess some 3 weeks after an infant received a live polio vaccine resulted in suppression of the infant's immune system and the infant's contraction of paralytic polio. The jury in the circuit court returned a $16 million verdict in favor of the plaintiffs, and the defendant appealed. The case was transferred from the court of appeals to the state supreme court.[76] Was the $16 million verdict excessive, and did the trial court err in denying a new trial based on the alleged excessive verdict?

The Missouri Supreme Court held that there was no basis for a new trial on the grounds of excessiveness of the $16 million verdict. There is no formula for determining the excessiveness of a verdict. Each case must be decided on its own facts to determine what is fair and reasonable. A jury is in the best position to make such a determination. The trial judge could have set aside the verdict if a determination was made that passion and prejudice brought about an excessive verdict. The size of the verdict alone does not establish passion and prejudice. The appellant failed to establish that the verdict was: (1) glaringly unwarranted and (2) based on prejudice and passion. Compensation of a plaintiff is based on such factors as the age of the patient, the nature and extent of injury, diminished earnings capacity, economic condition, and awards in comparable cases. A jury is entitled to consider such intangibles that do not lend themselves to precise calculation, such as past and future pain, suffering, effect on lifestyle, embarrassment, humiliation, and economic loss.

Damages Excessive

A jury verdict totaling $12,393,130 was considered an excessive award in *Merrill v. Albany Medical Center*,[77] in which damages were sought with respect to the severe brain damage sustained by a 22-month-old infant as the result of oxygen deprivation. This occurred when the infant went into cardiac arrest during surgery for removal of a suspected malignant tumor from her right lung. Reduction of the amount to $6,143,130 was considered appropriate.

Damages Capped

The trial court in *Judd v. Drezga*[78] was found to have properly limited a brain-damaged infant's recovery of quality-of-life damages to $250,000. The Idaho cap on damages was designed to reduce healthcare costs, increase the availability of medical malpractice insurance, and secure the continued availability of healthcare resources—all legitimate legislative goals given the clear social and economic evil of rising healthcare costs and a shortage of qualified healthcare professionals. In attempting to meet its goals, the legislature had not unreasonably or arbitrarily limited recovery. Rather, it had chosen to place a limit on the recovery of noneconomic quality-of-life damages—one area where legislation had been shown to actually and substantially further these goals. Applying each individual test, the open courts, uniform operation of laws, and due process provisions of the constitution were not offended by the damage cap. Additionally, neither the right to a jury trial nor the constitutional guarantee of separation of powers was offended by the cap.

▸ JOINT AND SEVERAL LIABILITY

Joint liability is based on the concept that all joint or concurrent tortfeasors are actually independently at fault for their own wrongful acts. Both a hospital and its physicians can be held jointly liable for damages suffered by patients. In *Gonzales v. Nork & Mercy Hospital*,[79] the hospital was found negligent for failing to protect the patient, a 27-year-old man, from acts of malpractice by an independent, privately retained physician. The patient had been injured in an automobile accident and was operated on by Dr. Nork, an orthopedic surgeon. The plaintiff's life expectancy was reduced as a result of an unsuccessful and allegedly unnecessary laminectomy. It was found that the hospital knew or should have known of the surgeon's incompetence because the surgeon previously had performed many operations either unnecessarily or negligently. In such cases, the defendant produced false and inadequate findings as well as false-positive myelograms. He deceived his patients with this information and caused them to undergo surgery. Evidence was presented showing that the surgeon had performed more than three dozen similar operations unnecessarily or in a negligent manner. Even if the hospital was not aware of the surgeon's acts of negligence, an effective monitoring system should have been in place for monitoring his abilities. Consequently, the surgeon and hospital were jointly liable for damages suffered. An organization owes its patients a duty of care, and this duty includes the obligation to protect them from negligent and fraudulent acts of those physicians with a propensity to commit malpractice. The courts will not permit organizations to hide behind a cloak of ignorance in this responsibility.

Several liability should not be confused with *joint and several liability*. In several liability, each party to a lawsuit is liable only to the degree he or she has been determined to contribute to the injury. In other words, when there are multiple defendants in a lawsuit, each defendant's responsibility for damages will not exceed the degree or percentage that his or her carelessness contributed to the patient's injury. The *doctrine of joint and several liability*, however, provides that any one of the defendants to a lawsuit can be responsible to pay the full cost of damages awarded to the plaintiff(s).

▸ APPEALS

An appellate court reviews a case on the basis of the trial record, as well as written briefs and, if requested, concise oral arguments by the attorneys. A brief summarizes the facts of a case, testimony of the witnesses, laws affecting the case, and arguments of counsel. The party making the appeal is the *appellant*. The party answering the appeal is the *appellee*. After hearing oral arguments, the court takes the case under advisement until such time as the judges consider it and agree on a decision. An opinion is then prepared explaining the reasons for a decision.

Grounds for appeal can result from one or more of the following: the verdict was excessive or inadequate in the lower court; the evidence was rejected that should have been accepted; inadmissible evidence was permitted; testimony that should have been admissible was excluded; the verdict was contrary to the weight of the evidence; the court improperly charged the jury; the jury is confused by jury instructions; and/or the jury verdict is the result of bias, prejudice, and/or passion.

Notice of appeal must be filed with the trial court, the appellate court, and the adverse party. The party wishing to prevent execution of an adverse judgment until such time as the case has been heard and decided by an appellate court also should file a stay of execution.

The appellate court may modify, affirm, or reverse the judgment or reorder a new trial on an appeal. The majority ruling of the judges in the appellate court is binding on the parties of a lawsuit. If the appellate court's decision is not unanimous, the minority may render a dissenting opinion. Further appeal may be made, as set by statute, to the highest court of appeals. If an appeal involves a constitutional question, it eventually may be appealed to the U.S. Supreme Court.

When the highest appellate court in a state decides a case, a final judgment results, and the matter

THE COURT'S DECISION

The Supreme Court of Mississippi found that Dorrough's arguments were without merit, holding that the verdict by the jury was supported by the weight of the evidence. When evidence is in conflict, the jury is the sole judge of both the credibility of a witness and the weight of his or her testimony. The jury was presented with conflicting testimony concerning the alleged negligence of Dorrough. The jury, being the sole judge of the weight and credibility of the witnesses, determined that Dorrough was liable for the death of Gwendolyn and awarded damages.[80]

is ended. The instances when one may appeal the ruling of a state court to the U.S. Supreme Court are rare. A federal question must be involved, and even then, the Supreme Court must decide whether it will hear the case. A federal question is one involving the U.S. Constitution or a statute enacted by Congress, so it is unlikely that a negligence case arising in a state court would be reviewed and decided by the Supreme Court.

▶ EXECUTION OF JUDGMENTS

Once the amount of damages has been established and all the appeals have been heard, the defendant must comply with the judgment. If he or she fails to do so, a court order may be executed requiring the sheriff or other judicial officer to sell as much of the defendant's property as necessary, within statutory limitations, to satisfy the plaintiff's judgment.

▶ CHAPTER REVIEW

1. The pleadings of a case are the written statements of fact and law filed with a court by the parties to a lawsuit. Pleadings generally include such papers as a complaint, demurrer, answer, and bill of particulars.
   - If only questions of law are at issue, the judge will decide the case based on the pleadings.
   - If there are questions of fact, a trial will be held to determine those facts. In a negligence action, the first pleading filed with the court is a complaint, which identifies the parties to a suit, the cause of action, and the demand for damages.

2. Once a defendant receives a copy of the *complaint*, the defendant can file a preliminary objection before submitting an answer, or response, to the complaint. A formal objection to the lawsuit is called a *demurrer*, and it holds that the evidence presented by the plaintiff is insufficient to sustain an issue or case. The defendant can file a counterclaim if he or she has a claim against the plaintiff.

3. Before the trial, facts are investigated in a process called *discovery*. The discovery process helps to prevent surprises during trial.
   - *Examination before trial* is part of the discovery process that allows for witnesses to be examined prior to trial.
   - Generally, hospital incident and investigation reports are not protected from discovery.
   - Communications between client and attorney are protected under attorney–client privilege.

4. A *motion to dismiss* a case can be made before, during, or after the trial.
   - The motion alleges that the plaintiff's complaint does not set forth a claim or cause of action that is recognized by law.
   - If either party to a suit believes that there are no issues of fact in contention, only issues of law, they may make a motion for a *summary judgment*, in which the court is asked to rule without a trial.

5. The case is heard in the court that has jurisdiction over the subject in controversy.
   - The judge presides over court proceedings and decides questions of law.
   - The *jury* reviews the facts of a case offered by opposing counsels and makes an impartial decision as to the guilt of the defendant(s).

6. A *subpoena* is a legal order requiring a person to appear in court.

7. *Res ipsa loquitur* ("the thing speaks for itself" or "circumstances speak for themselves") is the legal doctrine that shifts the burden of proof in a negligence case from the plaintiff to the defendant.

8. The *judicial notice rule* prescribes that well-known facts need not be proven (e.g., fractures require prompt attention).

9. There are multiple types of evidence that can be presented at trial.
   - Direct evidence
   - Demonstrative evidence

- Documentary evidence
- Hearsay evidence

10. When the issues to be resolved in the case are outside the understanding or experience of the average juror, an expert witness is allowed to offer testimony to assist in explanation of technical matters. The testimony of two experts may conflict, in which case the jury will determine which opinion to accept. An expert witness must have experience and training sufficient to explain the facts or answer the questions of a particular case.

11. Types of defenses offered by the defendant(s):

- Ignorance of fact and unintentional wrongs
- Assumption of the risk
- Contributory negligence
- Comparative negligence
- Good Samaritan statutes
- Borrowed servant doctrine
- Captain of the ship doctrine
- Statute of limitations
- Sovereign immunity
- Intervening cause

12. Damages, which are usually determined by the jury, come in four forms:

- Nominal damages
- Compensatory damages
- Hedonic damages
- Punitive damages

▶ REVIEW QUESTIONS

1. Discuss the pretrial discovery process.
2. Describe the trial process.
3. Describe the role of the judge and jury in the trial process.
4. Explain the terms res ipsa loquitur and judicial notice rule.
5. Describe the forms of evidence presented by a plaintiff at trial.
6. Describe defenses to a lawsuit a defendant can offer at trial.
7. Explain the purpose of the judge's charge to the jury.
8. Describe the various types of damages that can be awarded to the plaintiff.

▶ NOTES

1. *Dorrough v. Wilkes*, 817 So. 2d 567 (2002).
2. The Honorable Susan K. Gauvey and Heather R. Pruger, "Trials, Verdicts and Mediation," *Maryland Bar Journal*, July 2010.
3. *Collins v. Park*, 423 Pa. Superior Ct. 601,606, 621 A.2d 996 (Pa. Super. Ct. 1993).
4. *Kern v. Gulf Coast Nursing Home of Moss Point, Inc.*, 502 So. 2d 1198, 1202 (Miss. 1987).
5. 244 Wis. 2d 112, 629 N.W.2d 66 (2001).
6. *Id.* at 111.
7. *Id.* at 112.
8. *Personal Representative, etc., Appellant, v. Osceola Mental Health, Inc., etc., et al. Appellee*, Court of Appeal of Florida, Fifth District, No. 5D11–2513 (Opinion filed January 11, 2013).
9. 725 N.Y.S.2d 35 (2001).
10. 600 A.2d 1063 (D.C. 1991).
11. *Id.* at 1070.
12. Steve Cohen, "Malpractice," *The New Yorker*, October 1 (1990): 43, 47.
13. NOLO, "What are the elements of a crime?" http://www.nolo.com/legal-encyclopedia/what-the-elements-crime.html.
14. 696 S.W.2d 16 (Tenn. Ct. App. 1985).
15. 503 N.Y.S.2d 131 (N.Y. App. Div. 1986).
16. *Id.* at 432.
17. 720 N.E.2d 1175 (Ind. App. 1999).
18. 405 A.2d 443 (N.J. Sup. Ct. 1979).
19. 445 N.W.2d 763 (Iowa 1989).
20. 128 P.3d 151 (Alas. 2006).
21. 854 S.W.2d 250 (Tex. Ct. App. 1993).
22. 488 S.E.2d 389 (W. Va. 1997).
23. The National Court Rules Committee, "Rule 1008 – Functions of the Court and Jury," https://www.rulesofevidence.org/article-x/rule-1008/.
24. Jeffrey Bellin, "The Virginia and Federal Rules of Evidence," April 9, 2015. https://papers.ssrn.com/sol3/papers.cfm?abstract_id=2591371.
25. 337 P.2d 974 (Or. 1959).
26. 221 N.W.2d 39 (S.D. 1974).
27. *Id.*
28. *Id.*
29. 786 F.2d 859 (8th Cir. 1986).
30. No. 11-13752 (E.D. Mich. Feb. 5, 2013).

31. *Id.*
32. 335 S.E.2d 712 (Ga. Ct. App. 1985).
33. *Spirito v. Temple Corp.*, 466 N.E.2d 491 (Ind. Ct. App. 1984).
34. 746 P.2d 1006 (Idaho Ct. App. 1987).
35. 346 S.E.2d 528 (S.C. 1986).
36. *Id.*
37. 291 N.E.2d 769 (Ohio Ct. App. 1973).
38. 320 A.2d 704 (Del. 1974).
39. 340 So. 2d 1065 (La. Ct. App. 1976).
40. 373 N.Y.S.2d 224 (N.Y. App. Div. 1975).
41. 320 A.2d 704 (Del. 1974).
42. 469 N.W.2d 74 (Mich. Ct. App. 1991).
43. *Id.* at 76.
44. 746 S.W.2d 108 (Mo. Ct. App. 1988).
45. *Oberzan v. Smith*, 869 P.2d 682 (Kan. 1994).
46. 4 N.W.2d 637–639 (Minn. 1942).
47. 738 P.2d 75 (Colo. Ct. App. 1987).
48. 75 N.W.2d 217 (Minn. 1956).
49. 358 S.E.2d 222 (W. Va. 1987).
50. *Id.* at 224.
51. 320 A.2d 637 (N.H. 1974).
52. *Id.*
53. *Wooten v. United States*, 574 F. Supp. 200 (W.D. Tenn. 1982).
54. 463 F. Supp. 321 (D. Alaska 1978).
55. Texas Municipal League, "Texas Tort Claims Act Q&A," February 2005, http://www.tml.org/legal-qna/2005February.pdf.
56. 657 N.Y.S.2d 419, 239 A.D.2d 287 (1997).
57. 248 A.D.2d 322 (1988).
58. 154 S.E.2d 461 (Ga. Ct. App. 1967).
59. Stephen H. Gifis, *Law Dictionary* (Hauppauge, NY: Barron's Educational Series, 1996), 145.
60. United States District Court Southern District of New York, "Handbook for Trial Jurors," http://www.nysd.uscourts.gov/jury_handbook.php.
61. 411 So. 2d 109 (Ala. 1982).
62. 657 N.Y.S.2d 419 (N.Y. App. Div. 1997).
63. 820 N.E.2d 604, 354 Ill. App.3d 241, 289 (Ill. App. Ct. 2004).
64. Nos. 1030587 & 1030789 (Ala. 2004).
65. *Capelouto v. Kaiser Foundation Hospitals* (1972) 7 Cal. 3d 889, 892-893 [103 Cal. Rptr. 856, 500 P.2d 880].
66. No. 537–907 (Wis. Cir. Ct. Mar. 18, 1983).
67. 310 S.E.2d 326 (N.C. 1984).
68. 411 So. 2d 109, 113 (Ala. 1982).
69. 497 So. 2d 1233 (Fla. Dist. Ct. App. 1986).
70. 16 A.D.3d 898, 791 N.Y.S.2d 686 (N.Y. App. Div. 2005).
71. 658 N.Y.S.2d 34 (N.Y. App. Div. 1997).
72. 804 S.W.2d 711 (Ark. 1991).
73. 681 F.2d 291 (5th Cir. 1982).
74. 510 So. 2d 538 (Ala. 1987).
75. 650 A.2d 1079 (Pa. Super. 1994).
76. *Callahan v. Cardinal Glennon Hosp.*, 863 S.W.2d 852 (Mo. 1993).
77. 512 N.Y.S.2d 519 (N.Y. App. Div. 1987).
78. 103 P.3d 135, 2004 UT 91 (Utah, 2004).
79. No. 228566 (Cal. Super. Ct. Sacramento Co. 1976).
80. *Roussel v. Robbins*, 688 So. 2d 714, 723–724 (Miss. 1996).

© Pavel L Photo and Video/Shutterstock

CHAPTER 9

Corporate Structure and Legal Issues

🔍 IT'S YOUR GAVEL...

NURSE ANESTHETIST: MEDICAL SUPERVISION REQUIRED

Mrs. LaCroix was admitted to the hospital's women's pavilion for the birth of her first child, Lawryn. She was admitted to the hospital under the care of Dr. Dulemba, her obstetrician. Prior to undergoing a cesarean section, LaCroix complained several times of breathing difficulty. When Dr. McGehee, the pediatrician, arrived, he noticed that LaCroix appeared to be in respiratory distress and heard her say, "I can't breathe." McGehee asked Nurse Blankenship, a certified registered nurse anesthetist (CRNA), if LaCroix was okay. She responded that LaCroix was just nervous. Mr. LaCroix claimed his wife whispered to him that she could not breathe. Mr. LaCroix then shouted, "She can't breathe. Somebody please help my wife." Blankenship asked that Mr. LaCroix be removed from the operating room because his wife was having what appeared to her to be a seizure.

Blankenship could not establish an airway. She told one of the nurses: "Get one of the anesthesiologists here now!" Dr. Green, who was in his car, was paged. Upon receiving the page, he immediately drove to the women's pavilion, where Dulemba had already started the cesarean section. When Lawryn was delivered, she was not breathing, and McGehee had to resuscitate her. Meanwhile, Blankenship worked to establish an airway for LaCroix. The intubation was, however, an esophageal intubation. Dulemba stated that he thought that the intubation was esophageal. LaCroix's blood pressure and pulse dropped, and she went into cardiac arrest. A physician and nurse from the hospital's emergency department responded to a code for assistance. McGehee testified that the emergency department physician said that he did not know how to resuscitate pregnant women and left without providing any medical care. Dulemba and a nurse began cardiopulmonary resuscitation on LaCroix. McGehee, having finished treating Lawryn, took control of the code. LaCroix suffered irreversible brain damage.

Blankenship and Dr. Hafiz, the Denton Anesthesiology Associates (DAA), PA, anesthesiologist on call for the women's pavilion on the day of LaCroix's incident, settled with the LaCroixes by paying $500,000 and $750,000, respectively. The trial court entered a judgment against the hospital, awarding the LaCroixes approximately $8.8 million in damages.[1]

Was the evidence sufficient to hold the hospital liable for medical negligence under a theory of corporate liability?

WHAT IS YOUR VERDICT?

It is of utmost importance that each organization recognizes that its successes lies with its ability to assure the staff, community, and patients that it holds itself accountable to ensuring the highest standards of quality professional care and the well-being of all that enter its hallowed halls.

—Gp

▶ LEARNING OBJECTIVES

The reader, upon completion of this chapter, will be able to:

- Explain from where a corporation derives its authority.
- Explain the difference between express, implied, and corporate authority.
- Discuss corporate organization and committee structure.
- Describe corporate ethics, the Sarbanes Oxley Act of 2002, and corporate compliance.
- Explain the terms corporate negligence, respondeat superior, and independent contractor.
- Describe the duties of healthcare organizations, the chief executive officer (CEO), and medical staff.
- Explain the purpose of corporate reorganization and the process of restructuring.
- Describe what is meant by parent holding company model.
- Describe what the Safe Harbor Act is designed to regulate.

This chapter introduces the healthcare professional to the responsibilities, as well as legal risks, of healthcare organizations and their governing bodies. Healthcare organizations are incorporated under state law as freestanding for-profit or not-for-profit corporations. Each corporation has a governing body (e.g.,

board of directors) that has ultimate responsibility for the operation of the organization. The existence of this authority creates certain duties and liabilities for governing boards and their individual members. The governing body is legally responsible for establishing and implementing policies regarding the management and operation of the organization. Responsibility for the day-to-day operations of an organization is generally accomplished by appointing a chief executive officer.

Not-for-profit healthcare organizations are exempt from federal taxation under Section 501(c)(3) of the Internal Revenue Code of 1986, as amended. Such federal exemption usually entitles the organization to an automatic exemption from state taxes as well. Such tax exemption not only relieves the organization from the payment of income taxes and sales taxes, but also permits the organization to receive contributions from donors, who then may obtain charitable deductions on their personal income tax returns.

The tax-exempt status of healthcare corporations is increasingly coming under scrutiny as they diversify their activities to generate higher revenues. The City of Pittsburgh initiated a challenge to the payroll tax exemption claimed by the University of Pittsburgh Medical Center (UPMC), which claims the exemption on the basis of its status as an "institution of purely public charity," or "IPPC," under Pennsylvania law. Questionable activities of UPMC's alleged offenses include: expanding business operations that include investment partnerships and more than 50 taxable corporations; not offering charitable services through many of its 400 doctors' offices and outpatient sites; closing facilities in locations with relatively high numbers of Medicare-eligible, Medicaid-eligible, or uninsured patients and opening or expanding facilities where there are proportionately more privately insured patients; paying more than 20 officers, directors, and key employees compensation in excess of $1 million, with the chief executive officer (CEO) receiving significantly more, as well as a lavish office space, private chef and dining room, private chauffeur, and private jet; turning over unpaid accounts to a collection agency or a law firm for further collections and legal action against its patients; and the list goes on. Failure of hospitals to show that their expanding joint ventures with physicians are not-for-profit activities, for example, could jeopardize their tax exempt status.

▶ AUTHORITY OF CORPORATIONS

Healthcare corporations—governmental, charitable, or proprietary—have certain powers expressly or implicitly granted to them by state statutes. Generally, the authority of a corporation is expressed in the law under which the corporation is chartered and in the corporation's articles of incorporation. The existence of this authority creates certain duties and liabilities for governing bodies and their individual members. Members of the governing body of an organization have both express and implied corporate authority.

Fiduciary Responsibility

Board members (trustees, directors) are not always fully aware of the fiduciary responsibilities and legal risks they undertake when serving on a corporate board. Although it is an honor to be a member of a hospital board, board members must be fully knowledgeable regarding their legal liability risks in their positions of trust and service to the organization.

> A person who has a relationship of trust or confidence with another is called a fiduciary. A fiduciary's relationship with an organization is one-sided, meaning that the relationship is designed to meet only the needs of the organization and the fiduciary must act without regard to his or her own needs. In hospitals and systems, board members are fiduciaries because they have been entrusted with overseeing the fulfillment of the organization's mission. They must be principally concerned about the performance of the nonprofit and that its interests are pursued faithfully.[2]

Corporate boards must act in the best interests of the healthcare entities they represent and the communities they serve. Their fiduciary responsibilities include: corporate finances; providing quality care and a safe work environment for staff, patients, and visitors; and periodically assessing the organization's progress, programs, and services. Trustees must be

fully informed by the CEO prior to making business decisions. They must abide by applicable laws, rules, regulations, and standards that regulate hospital operations. Trustees must be objective in their decision-making processes and free from the pressures and the all-to-often challenging demands and influences from within (e.g., professional staff requests designed to improve personal economic gain) and outside the organization. Board members must be free of conflicts of interest when discussing and making policy and financial decisions. Conflict of interest statements for trustees and staff should disclose on an annual basis known financial interest with any business entity that transacts business with the corporation or its subsidiary businesses, when applicable. Board members can be held liable for their actions or inactions when carrying out their fiduciary duties and responsibilities.

> The directors are entrusted with the management of the affairs of the railroad. If in the course of management they arrive at a decision for which there is a reasonable basis, and they acted in good faith, as the result of their independent judgment, and uninfluenced by any consideration other than what they honestly believe to be for the best interests of the railroad, it is not the function of the court to say that it would have acted differently and to charge the directors for any loss or expenditures incurred.[3]

The "Courts have properly decided to give directors a wide latitude in the management of the affairs of a corporation provided always that judgment, and that means an honest, unbiased judgment, is reasonable [sic] exercised by them."[4]

Express Corporate Authority

Express corporate authority is the power specifically delegated by statute. A healthcare corporation derives its authority to act from the laws of the state in which it is incorporated. The articles of incorporation set forth the purpose(s) of the corporation's existence and the powers the corporation is authorized to exercise in order to carry out its purposes.

Implied Corporate Authority

Implied corporate authority is the right to perform any and all acts necessary to exercise a corporation's expressly conferred authority and to accomplish the purpose(s) for which it was created. Generally, implied corporate authority arises from situations in which such authority is required or suggested as a result of a need for corporate powers not specifically granted in the articles of incorporation. A governing body, at its own discretion, may enact new bylaws, rules, and regulations; purchase or mortgage property; borrow money; purchase equipment; select employees; and adopt corporate resolutions that delineate decision-making responsibilities. These powers can be enumerated in the articles of incorporation and, in such cases, would be categorized as express rather than implied corporate authority.

Select Competent Physicians

The Florida Supreme Court held in *Insinga v. LaBella*[5] that the *corporate negligence doctrine* imposes on hospitals an implied duty to patients to select competent physicians who, although they are independent practitioners, would be providing in-hospital care to their patients through staff privileges. Hospitals are in the best position to protect their patients and consequently have an independent duty to provide staff privileges only to competent independent physicians.

In this case, an action was brought against Canton (who was masquerading as a physician, Dr. LaBella), a hospital, and others for the wrongful death of a 68-year-old woman whom Canton had admitted. The patient died while she was in the hospital. Canton was found to be a fugitive from justice in Canada where he was under indictment for the manufacture and sale of illegal drugs. He fraudulently obtained a medical license from the state of Florida and staff privileges at the hospital by using the name of LaBella, a deceased physician. Canton was extradited to Canada without being served process.

The surgeon in *Purcell & Tucson General Hospital v. Zimbelman*[6] performed inappropriate surgery because of his misdiagnosis of the patient's ailment. Prior malpractice suits against the surgeon revealed that the hospital had reason to know or should have known that the surgeon apparently lacked the skill to treat the patient's condition. The court held that the hospital had a clear duty to select competent physicians; to regulate the privileges granted to staff physicians; to ensure that privileges are conferred only for those procedures for which the physician is trained and qualified; and to restrict, suspend, or require supervision when a physician has demonstrated an inability to perform certain procedures. The hospital assumed the duty of supervising the competence of its physicians. The department of surgery

✔ QUESTIONABLE FUNDS TRANSFER

Jim, the administrator of East Campus Hospital, one of three hospitals in a multihospital system, was reviewing his mail and reports placed in his inbox by Carol, his secretary. He noticed what appeared to be a copy of correspondence that had been forwarded to him from the Bishop. The letter, describing a donation that had been made, read:

Dear Bishop John,

Enclosed is a contribution from David and his wife. He originally heard about our fundraising activities through the co-chairman of the fundraising appeal. The care he received at the East Campus Hospital was outstanding and he would like to make a contribution on our behalf.

Sincerely,

After reading his morning mail and reports, Jim placed the letter in his outbox for filing. Carol later picked up Jim's mail and other reports from his outbox. Later that afternoon, Carol walked back into Jim's office and inquired, "Did you read this letter forwarded to you from the corporate office?" Handing the letter to Jim, he replied, "Yes, I read it." Carol then asked, "Did you see anything that piqued your curiosity in this letter?" Jim replied that he had not. Carol, pointing at a strip of whiteout tape, urged Jim to look more closely. She then asked Jim to turn the letter over and read the words the tape was covering. He turned the letter over, noting what the letter had said. It appeared that only a copy of the original correspondence had been intended for Jim, not the original correspondence. With the missing words inserted, the correspondence read:

Dear Bishop John,

Enclosed is a contribution from David and his wife. He originally heard about our fundraising activities through the co-chairman of the fundraising appeal. The care he received at the East Campus Hospital was outstanding and he would like to make a contribution on our behalf, *earmarked for the East Campus Hospital*.

Sincerely,

The question arises as to why the whiteout tape was placed over the words, "earmarked for the East Campus Hospital." Jim was in a quandary as to what further action he should take to determine the amount of and the location of the funds earmarked for the hospital. Also, he could not absolutely determine who placed the whiteout tape on the correspondence. Was it the letter's author or addressee or corporate employee? To question the bishop directly would be tantamount to political suicide. Jim decided to ask the VP for financial affairs at the corporate offices about the amount of the donation and where it would appear on his hospital's financial statements. The VP, however, resisted discussing the matter with Jim. The hospital's controller, who had double reporting obligations to both Jim and the VP, stated that he was unaware of the specifics of the donation.

was acting for and on behalf of the hospital in fulfilling this duty. The court noted that it is reasonable to conclude that if the hospital had taken some action against the surgeon, the patient would not have been injured.

Ultra Vires Acts

Ultra vires is a Latin term meaning "beyond the powers." *Ultra vires acts* are those acts conducted by an organization that lie beyond the scope of authority of a corporation to perform. A governing body, which acts in and on behalf of the corporation, can be held liable for acting beyond its scope of authority, which is either expressed (e.g., in its articles of incorporation) or implied in law. If any action is in violation of a statute or regulation, it is illegal. An example of an illegal act would be the "known" employment of an unlicensed person in a position that by law requires a license. The state, through its attorney general, has the power to prevent the performance of an ultra vires act by means of an injunction.

▶ CORPORATE COMMITTEE STRUCTURE

Ultimate responsibility for the functioning of a healthcare corporation rests with the governing body. Ideally, the governing body includes representation from both the community and the organization's medical staff. The business of the governing body is generally conducted through a variety of committees. It should be noted that committee titles and responsibilities often vary from organization to organization based on size, complexity, and services rendered. Some of those committees are described here.

Executive Committee

The *executive committee* is a working group of the governing body that has delegated authority to act on behalf of the full board. It must act within the scope and authority assigned by the governing body. The duties and responsibilities of the committee should be delineated in the corporate bylaws. The functions of the executive committee generally include acting as a liaison between management and the full board, reviewing and making recommendations on management proposals, and performing special assignments as may be delegated by the full board from time to time. Business transactions and actions taken by the executive committee should be reported at regular sessions of the governing body and ratified. The executive committee generally has all the powers of the governing body, except such powers as the governing body may be prohibited from delegating in accordance with applicable laws.

Bylaws Committee

The *bylaws committee* reviews and recommends bylaw changes to the governing body. Bylaws generally are amended or rescinded by a majority vote of the governing body.

Finance Committee

The *finance committee* is responsible for overseeing the financial affairs of the organization and making recommendations to the governing body. This committee is responsible for directing and reviewing the preparation of financial statements, operating budgets, major capital requests, and so on. The governing body must approve actions of the finance committee.

Joint Conference Committee

The *joint conference committee* is a committee composed of an equal number of representatives from the executive committees of the governing body and medical staff, along with representation from administration and nursing. The committee acts as a forum for discussion of matters of policy and practice pertaining to patient care. The committee generally meets quarterly and reports on its activities to the governing body.

Nominating Committee

The *nominating committee* is generally responsible for developing and recommending to the governing body criteria for governing body membership. The requirements for membership to a governing body generally include a willingness to devote the time and energy necessary to fulfill the commitment as a board member, residence in the community or an identifiable association with the community served, demonstration of a knowledge of local healthcare issues, possession of the traits of good moral character and maturity, and professional and appropriate life experiences necessary to make managerial decisions in the healthcare setting.

Planning Committee

The *planning committee* is responsible for recommending to the governing body the use and development of organizational resources as they relate to the mission and vision of the organization. Specifically, the planning committee oversees the development of short-term and long-range goals, acquisition of major equipment, addition of new services based on identified community need, program development, and the preparation of progress reports for the full board. Major issues that the planning committee reviews include the organization's need to increase market share, expand services, downsize where appropriate, and integrate services across the entire continuum of care in a competitive marketplace.

The committee generally includes representation from the governing body, administration, medical staff, and nursing. When organizational planning affects the delivery of patient care services, a mechanism for obtaining employee and community input is incorporated into the planning process. Although there are times this does not occur, every effort should be made to include staff and community input when planning new services or major capital expenditures that are designed to serve the community. When planning a new emergency department for example, such input is of the utmost importance when addressing community concerns about the hospital's ability to provide adequate emergency services.

Patient Care Committee

The *patient care committee* reviews the quality of patient care rendered in the organization and makes recommendations for the improvement of such care. The committee is generally responsible for developing a process to identify patient and family needs and expectations and to establish a process to continuously improve customer relations. This process often includes development of a tool to identify patient and family needs and expectations; methodology for reviewing data; identification of patterns of concern; a mechanism for forwarding information to those responsible for implementing change in the organization; and continuing review, evaluation, and implementation of plans for improving organizational performance.

Audit and Regulatory Compliance Committee

The *audit and regulatory compliance committee* is responsible for the assessment of various functions and control systems of the organization and for providing management with analysis and recommendations regarding activities reviewed. Healthcare organizations must be vigilant in conducting their financial affairs. As the boards of several investment organizations have experienced in recent years, failure to do so can result in fines and imprisonment. An effective audit committee can be helpful in uncovering and thwarting poor or inept financial decision making. The committee should include members from the governing body and internal auditing staff. Responsibilities of the committee include developing corporate auditing policies and procedures; recommending independent auditors to the governing body; reviewing the credentials of the independent auditors and facilitating change in auditors as may be deemed appropriate; reviewing with independent auditors the proposed scope and general extent of their auditing duties and responsibilities; reviewing the scope and results of the annual audit with the independent auditors and the organization's management staff; setting, overseeing, reviewing, and acting on the recommendations of the internal audit staff; reviewing the internal accounting practices of the corporation, including policies and procedures; reviewing and evaluating financial statements (e.g., income statements, balance sheets, cash flow reports, investment accounts); promoting the prevention, detection, deterrence, and reporting of fraud; reviewing the means for safeguarding assets and, as appropriate, the existence of such assets; ensuring that financial reporting functions are in keeping with generally accepted accounting principles; and reviewing the reliability and integrity of financial and operating information.

Failure on the part of an audit committee to question management's representations may be the basis for committee malfeasance, because the committee and the governing body may be held liable for their failure to know what they were responsible for recognizing.

Safety Committee

The *safety committee* is generally charged with responsibility for overseeing the organization's safety management program. The committee reviews and acts on reports involving the organization's emergency preparedness, equipment management, fire safety, risk management, and utilities management programs.

▶ CORPORATE ETHICS

Corporate ethics describes the ethics of an organization and how it responds to internal or external circumstances affecting the organization's mission and values. Ethical behavior in an organization can be enhanced by providing staff members with a written code of ethics; providing training and education to improve each staff member's knowledge base, skills, and competencies; providing easy access to professional sources to assist in resolving ethical issues in the workplace; and providing systems for confidential reporting of breaches in ethical conduct within and outside of the organization. Although most healthcare organizations have published their mission, vision, and values statements, policy and practice continue to be distant relatives. Commitment to organizational ethics begins with the organization's leadership.

The purpose of organizational ethics in the healthcare setting is to promote responsible behavior in the decision-making process. Recent interest in organizational ethics is, in part, the result of concerns of government regulations (e.g., Sarbanes–Oxley Act, Emergency Medical Treatment and Active Labor Act) and accrediting agencies that certain unethical practices continue to plague the industry. These practices include billing scams, false advertising and marketing, and patient care issues (e.g., inappropriate patient transfers based on ability to pay, transferring patients before they have been clinically stabilized). Commitment to organizational ethics must begin with the organization's leadership.

Corporate Code of Ethics

The following list provides some value statements that should be considered when preparing an organization's code of ethics:

1. Employees and staff members will comply with the organization's code of ethics, which includes compassionate care; an understanding and acceptance of the organization's mission, vision, and values; and adherence to one's professional code of conduct.
2. The organization will be honest and fair in dealings with employees.
3. The organization will develop and maintain an environment that fosters the highest ethical and legal standards.
4. Employers and employees will be impartial when personal interests conflict with those of others.
5. Employees will be free to speak up without fear of retribution or retaliation.
6. The preservation of harmony will not become more important than the critical evaluation of ideas by "all" employees. The pitfalls of groupthink occur when a committee, for example, prefers harmony and conformity to rational resolutions to a stated problem in the decision-making process. This will not be acceptable conduct in the organization.
7. Employees will be provided with a safe environment within which to work.
8. The drive to increase revenues will not be tied to unethical activities, such as workforce cutbacks as a means to discharge employees when they are encouraged to speak up and then ostracized because of their honesty.
9. Employees will avoid conflict of interest situations by not favoring their own self-interests over those of others, including the organization.
10. Patients will be provided with care that is of the highest quality regardless of the setting.
11. All patients will be treated with honesty, dignity, respect, and courtesy.
12. Patients will be informed of the risks, benefits, and alternatives to care.
13. Patients will be treated in a manner that preserves their rights, dignity, autonomy, self-esteem, privacy, and involvement in their care.
14. Each patient's culture, religion, and heritage will be respected and addressed as appropriate.
15. The organization will provide assistance to patients and their families through a patient advocate.
16. The organization will provide appropriate support services for those with language barriers or physical disabilities (e.g., hearing and seeing impaired).
17. Patients will be provided with a "Patient's Bill of Rights and Responsibilities" on admission to the hospital.
18. Each patient's right to execute advance directives will be honored.

Sarbanes–Oxley Act

The Sarbanes–Oxley Act of 2002, commonly called SOX or SARBOX, was enacted as a response to the misconduct committed by executives at companies such as Enron, World Com, and Tyco, resulting in investor losses exceeding a half trillion dollars. To protect investors in public companies and improve the accuracy and reliability of corporate disclosures, SOX requires top executives of public corporations to vouch for the financial reports of their companies. The act encourages self-regulation and the need to promote due diligence; selecting a leader with morals and core values; examining incentives; constantly monitoring the organization's culture; building a strong, knowledgeable governing body; continuously searching for conflicts of interest in the organization; focusing attention on processes and controls that support accurate financial reporting through documented policies and procedures; and establishing strong standards of conduct and a code of ethics that encourages employees to report unethical or fraudulent behavior without fear of retribution.

The act covers issues such as establishing a public company accounting oversight board, auditor independence, corporate responsibility, and enhanced financial disclosure. Major provisions of SOX include certification of financial reports by CEOs and chief financial officers (CFOs); ban on personal loans to any executive officer or director; accelerated reporting of trades by insiders; prohibition on insider trades during pension fund blackout periods; public reporting of CEO and CFO compensation and profits; internal audit board independence; criminal and civil penalties for securities violations; obligation to have an internal audit function, which will need to be certified by external auditors; significantly longer jail sentences and larger fines for corporate executives who knowingly misstate financial statements; and codes of ethics and standards of conduct for executive officers and board members (most companies have expanded their code of ethics to include all employees and attach the document to their public reports).

Although not-for-profit organizations are not legally required to adopt SOX, the accountability and financial reporting requirements are being adopted by many not-for-profit hospitals. Two provisions of the Act that have universal application to both for-profit and not-for-profit corporations are:

- Section 802: prohibition from knowingly altering, destroying, mutilating, concealing, and impeding or covering up government investigations.
- Section 1107: Proscription of criminal penalties for retaliation against whistleblowers.

Corporate Compliance Program

The federal government's initiative to investigate and prosecute healthcare organizations for criminal wrongdoing, coupled with strong sanctions imposed after conviction, have resulted in healthcare organizations establishing *corporate compliance programs*. These programs establish internal mechanisms for preventing, detecting, and reporting criminal conduct. Sentencing incentives are in place for organizations that establish such programs. An effective compliance program should include the design, implementation, and enforcement of program policies, procedures, and processes to facilitate the prevention and detection of criminal conduct. An effective corporate compliance program should include the following elements:

1. Appointment of a corporate compliance officer to oversee the corporate compliance program.
2. Development of standards of conduct, policies, procedures, and processes to help reduce the risk of criminal conduct.
3. Assignment of duties, authority, and responsibility to employees with high integrity.
4. Communication and education of all employees and agents as to the organization's corporate compliance standards. This can be accomplished through required education programs, computer training modules, and disseminating publications that describe the organization's compliance program.
5. Utilization of monitoring and auditing systems designed to detect criminal conduct by employees and agents. This should include a program for publicizing a reporting system whereby employees and other agents are easily able to report criminal conduct by others within the organization without fear of retribution. A hotline number should be available to receive and review complaints. Procedures should be implemented to protect the anonymity of complainants from retaliation.
6. Policies must be consistently enforced through appropriate disciplinary mechanisms. Suspected illegal conduct should be handled through the corporate compliance officer.
7. The organization must take all reasonable steps to respond appropriately to any offense in order to prevent similar offenses.
8. An audit of the organization's corporate compliance program should be conducted annually. Policies, procedures, and processes should be redesigned as necessary. It is important that the corporate board participate in the review and evaluation process.
9. The integrity and effectiveness of a compliance program will hold up only as long as there is trust in management on all levels within the organization.

As noted in the following *reality check*, the duties and responsibilities of the compliance officer can be compromised when the corporation pays the salary of the compliance officer. As they say in the world of finance, "follow the money" and then you will know where loyalties lie.

▶ CORPORATE NEGLIGENCE

There are duties that a healthcare corporation itself owes to the general public and to its patients. These duties arise from statutes, regulations, principles of law developed by the courts, and the internal operating

✅ *COMPLIANCE OFFICER AND CONFIDENTIALITY*

The employee who decides to place confidence and trust in a corporate compliance officer must understand the following points, among others, prior to filing a complaint against any organizational practice, individual, and/or department within or entity owned by the organization:

- The compliance officer is hired by and is responsible to the corporation by which he or she is hired.
- Compliance officers often report directly to the organization's corporate counsel, CEO, and/or board of directors/trustees.
- The compliance officer is expected to abide by the laws of the land and follow the code(s) of ethics applicable to compliance officers in general and any ethical principles or codes of ethics that apply to his or her profession. For example, a compliance officer who is a lawyer is expected to adhere to those professional code(s) of ethics that apply to lawyers from both a professional and state licensing standpoint. Failure to do so can result in professional discipline and sanctions against the compliance officer.
- Compliance officers are expected to maintain confidentiality regarding the names of employees who file complaints.
- Organizations often have compliance hotlines to protect the identity of employees who file complaints.

The position of compliance officers is difficult; they must try to balance: (1) the confidentiality and privacy rights of employees; (2) satisfying the expectations of management and the governing body who pays the compliance officer's salary; and (3) adhering to applicable laws, rules, and regulations pertaining to the compliance officer's duties and responsibilities. Visualizing Lady Justice, these three demands weigh heavily on the compliance officer who sits alone on the opposite side of the scales.

When working for a salary paid by an organization, adhering to standards of ethical conduct is not necessarily consistent with a compliance officer's list of priorities, as Phil was about to learn.

Phil, having exhausted all other appeals in his complaint, called Beth, the compliance officer, to speak with her about a decision that the human resources department had made that he believed was out of compliance with the Federal Equal Pay Act. The office assistant, Mary, stated, "Beth will not be in the office until next week." Phil then scheduled a telephone conference with Beth for the following week. He asked Mary, "Will my telephone conference with Beth remain confidential?" Mary said, "Most certainly. Our office is here for you. Everything in our office is confidential."

The following week Phil called Beth to discuss his concern that certain professionals were getting paid more for performing the same work that he was. He described the specifics of his concern. Beth asked, "Is it OK for me to reveal your name to human resources so I can obtain the necessary records that I would need from them to see if you are being paid equally to others for the same work?" Phil agreed to Beth's request. During his discussion with Beth, Phil discussed several other corporate leadership concerns with her and asked that his conversations remain confidential. Beth replied, "If you wanted confidentiality, then you should have asked for it before speaking to me." Phil replied, "Confidentiality was promised prior to our discussion, and I am surprised at your response." Beth replied, "Well, you are wrong."

rules of the organization. A corporation is treated no differently than an individual. If a corporation has a duty and fails in the exercise of that duty, it has the same liability to the injured party that an individual would have.

> Corporate negligence is a doctrine under which the hospital is liable if it fails to uphold the proper standard of care owed the patient, which is to ensure the patient's safety and well-being while at the hospital. This theory of liability creates a non-delegable duty which the hospital owes directly to a patient. Therefore, an injured party does not have to rely on and establish the negligence of a third party.[7]

Corporate negligence occurs when a healthcare corporation fails to perform the duties it owes directly to a patient or to anyone else to whom a duty

may extend. If such a duty is breached and a patient is injured as a result of that breach, the organization can be held culpable under the theory of corporate negligence.

Hospitals once enjoyed complete tort immunity as charitable institutions. However, as hospitals evolved into more sophisticated corporate entities that expected fees for their services, their tort immunity receded. Courts first recognized that hospitals could be held liable for the negligence of their employees under the theory of respondeat superior. Liability was later extended for nonemployees who acted as a hospital's ostensible agents. In *Thompson v. Nason Hospital*,[8] the evolution continued. The Pennsylvania court recognized that hospitals are more than mere conduits through which healthcare professionals are brought into contact with patients. Hospitals owe some nondelegable duties directly to their patients, independent of the negligence of their employees or ostensible agents, such as a duty to do the following:

- Use reasonable care in the maintenance of safe facilities and equipment.
- Select and retain competent staff.
- Appoint competent physicians and other health-care professionals to the medical staff.
- Oversee all persons who practice medicine within the organization.
- Formulate, adopt, and enforce rules and policies to ensure quality care.

Darling—A Benchmark Case

A benchmark case in the healthcare field that has had a major impact on the liability of healthcare organizations was decided in 1965 in *Darling v. Charleston Community Memorial Hospital*.[9] The court enunciated a corporate negligence doctrine under which hospitals have a duty to provide an adequately trained medical and nursing staff. A hospital is responsible, in conjunction with its medical staff, for establishing policies and procedures for monitoring the quality of medicine practiced within the hospital.

The Darling case involved an 18-year-old college football player who was preparing for a career as a teacher and coach. The patient, a defensive halfback for his college football team, was injured during a play. He was rushed to the emergency department of a small, accredited community hospital where the only physician on emergency duty that day was Dr. Alexander, a general practitioner. Alexander had not treated a major leg fracture in 3 years.

The physician examined the patient and ordered an X-ray that revealed that the tibia and fibula of the right leg had been fractured. The physician reduced the fracture and applied a plaster cast from a point 3 or 4 inches below the groin to the toes. Shortly after the cast had been applied, the patient began to complain continually of pain. The physician split the cast and continued to visit the patient frequently while the patient remained in the hospital. Not thinking it was necessary, the emergency department physician did not call in any specialists for consultation.

After 2 weeks, the student was transferred to a larger hospital and placed under the care of an orthopedic surgeon. The specialist found a considerable amount of dead tissue in the fractured leg. During a period of 2 months, the specialist removed increasing amounts of tissue in a futile attempt to save the leg until it became necessary to amputate the leg 8 inches below the knee. The student's father did not agree

to a settlement and filed suit against the emergency department physician and the hospital. Although the physician later settled out of court for $40,000, the case continued against the hospital.

The documentary evidence relied on to establish the standard of care included the rules and regulations of the Illinois Department of Public Health under the Hospital Licensing Act; the standards for hospital accreditation, today known as The Joint Commission; and the bylaws, rules, and regulations of Charleston Hospital. These documents were admitted into evidence without objection. No specific evidence was offered that the hospital failed to conform to the usual and customary practices of hospitals in the community.

The trial court instructed the jury to consider those documents, along with all other evidence, in determining the hospital's liability. Under the circumstances in which the case reached the Illinois Supreme Court, it was held that the verdict against the hospital should be sustained if the evidence supported the verdict on any one or more of the 20 allegations of negligence. Allegations asserted that the hospital was negligent in its failure to: (1) provide a sufficient number of trained nurses for bedside care—in this case, nurses who were capable of recognizing the progressive gangrenous condition of the plaintiff's right leg; and (2) failure of its nurses to bring the patient's condition to the attention of the administration and staff so that adequate consultation could be secured.

Although these generalities provided the jury with no practical guidance for determining what constitutes reasonable care, they were considered relevant to aid the jury in deciding what was feasible and what the hospital knew or should have known concerning its responsibilities for patient care.

Evidence relating to the hospital's failure to review Alexander's work, to require consultation or examination by specialists, and to require proper nursing care was found to be sufficient to support a verdict for the patient. Judgment was eventually returned against the hospital in the amount of $100,000. The Illinois Supreme Court held that the hospital could not limit its liability as a charitable corporation to the amount of its liability insurance.

> [T]he doctrine of charitable immunity can no longer stand . . . a doctrine which limits the liability of charitable corporations to the amount of liability insurance that they see fit to carry permits them to determine whether or not they will be liable for their torts and the amount of that liability, if any.[10]

In effect, the hospital was liable as a corporate entity for the negligent acts of its employees and physicians. Among other things, the Darling case demonstrates the importance of the governing body's duty to establish a mechanism for the evaluation, counseling, and, when necessary, taking action against those physicians who pose an unreasonable risk of harm to patients. Physician review and monitoring is best accomplished through peer review. Most states provide statutory protection from liability for peer review activities conducted in a reasonable manner without malice.

Corporate Officer/Director

An officer or a director of a corporation is not personally liable for the torts of corporate employees. To incur liability, the officer or the director ordinarily must be shown to have in some way authorized, directed, or participated in a tortious act. The administrator of the estate of the deceased in *Hunt v. Rabon*[11] brought a malpractice action against hospital trustees and others for the wrongful death of the decedent during an operation at the hospital. A contractor had incorrectly crossed the oxygen and nitrous oxide lines of a newly installed medical gas system leading to the operating room. The trustees filed a *demurrer*—a pleading claiming that the facts of the case were not sufficient for an action against them individually as trustees. The lower court sustained the demurrer, and the plaintiff appealed. On appeal, the South Carolina Supreme Court held that the allegations presented were insufficient to hold the trustees liable for the wrongs alleged.

▶ DOCTRINE OF RESPONDEAT SUPERIOR

Respondeat superior ("let the master respond") is a legal doctrine holding employers liable, in certain cases, for the wrongful acts of their agents (employees). This doctrine also has been referred to as *vicarious liability*, whereby an employer is answerable for the torts committed by employees. In the healthcare setting, an organization, for example, is liable for the negligent acts of its employees, even though there has been no wrongful conduct on the part of the organization. "Hospitals are vicariously liable for the negligence of an independent contractor emergency-room physician where the patient enters the emergency room seeking treatment from the hospital rather than a specific physician of the patient's own choosing"[12]

For liability to be imputed to the employer, both of the following statements must be true:

1. A master–servant relationship must exist between the employer and the employee.
2. The wrongful act of the employee must have occurred within the scope of his or her employment.

The question of liability frequently rests on whether providers treating a patient are independent agents (responsible for their own acts) or employees of the organization. The answer to this depends on whether the organization can exercise control over the particular act that was the proximate cause of the injury. The basic rationale for imposing liability on an employer developed because of the employer's right to control the physical acts of its employees. It is not necessary that the employer actually exercise control, only that it possesses the right, power, or authority to do so.

When filing a lawsuit, the plaintiff's attorney generally names both the employer and employee. This occurs because the employer is generally in a better financial condition to cover the judgment. The employer is not without remedy if liability has been imposed against the organization as a result of an employee's negligent act. The employer, if sued, may seek *indemnification* (i.e., compensation for the financial loss caused by the employee's negligent act) from the employee.

Independent Contractor

An *independent contractor* relationship is established when the principal has no right of control over the manner in which the agent's work is to be performed. The independent contractor, therefore, is responsible for his or her own negligent acts. However, some cases indicate that an organization may be held liable for an independent contractor's negligence. For example, in *Mehlman v. Powell*,[13] the court held that a hospital could be found vicariously liable for the negligence of an emergency department physician who was not a hospital employee but who worked in the emergency department in the capacity of an independent contractor. The court reasoned that the hospital maintained control over billing procedures, maintained an emergency department in the main hospital, and represented to the patient that the members of the emergency department staff were its employees, which may have caused the patient to rely on the skill and competence of the staff.

In another case, a hospital was found vicariously liable for the negligent acts of independently contracted emergency department physicians. In *Schiavone v.*

Victory Mem. Hosp.,[14] the decedent was transported to the hospital emergency department by ambulance. "... the plaintiff's decedent was taken by ambulance to the Victory Memorial Hospital ... emergency room complaining of a burning sensation in the chest, belching, and pain in both arms. There, she was examined and treated by an emergency-room physician who rendered a diagnosis of gastritis and discharged her. The decedent died approximately 5 days later, allegedly of a myocardial infarction."[15] A suit was filed against the hospital. The New York Supreme Court, Appellate Division, ruled that the patient sought emergency treatment from the hospital, not from any specific physician of the patient's own choosing. Although the hospital could be vicariously liable for the alleged malpractice of the appellant even though he was an independent contractor with the hospital at the time of the occurrence, the cause of action was not filed on a timely basis against the hospital.

The doctrine of respondeat superior may impose liability on an organization for a nurse's acts or omissions that result in injury to a patient. Whether such liability attaches depends on whether the conduct of the nurse was wrongful and whether the nurse was subject to the control of the organization at the time the act in question was performed.

Determination of whether a nurse practitioner's conduct was wrongful in a given situation depends on the standard of conduct to which the nurse practitioner is expected to adhere. In liability deliberations, the nurse practitioner who is subject to the control of the organization at the time of the negligent conduct is considered an employee and not a borrowed servant of the organization.

▶ GOVERNING BODY RESPONSIBILITIES

Along with the corporate authority that is granted to the governing body, duties are attached to its individual members. These responsibilities are considered duties because they are imposed by law and can be enforced in legal proceedings. Governing body members are considered by law to have the highest measure of accountability. They have a fiduciary duty that requires acting primarily for the benefit of the corporation. The general duties of a governing body are both implied and express. Failure of a governing body to perform its duties may constitute mismanagement to such a degree that the appointment of a receiver to manage the affairs of the corporation may be warranted.

🔍 INDEPENDENT CONTRACTOR NEGLIGENT

Citation: *Hoffman v. Moore Reg'l Hosp., Inc.*, 441 S.E.2d 567 (N.C. Ct. App. 1994)

Facts
Hoffman was admitted to the hospital with an order for a renal arteriogram. After her admission, Hoffman was presented with a consent form for the procedure. The consent listed five radiologists on the form but did not specify which radiologist would perform the procedure. The list of radiologists was composed of members of the Pinehurst radiology group, which determined which radiologist would cover the hospital each day. Dr. Lina was assigned to perform Hoffman's procedure. Following the renal arteriogram, Lina determined that an angioplasty was necessary. Because of complications during the procedure, Hoffman had to be transferred to University Medical Center. Her condition deteriorated during the following year and she eventually died. Mr. Hoffman then sought to hold the hospital liable for the negligence of the radiologist under the theory of respondeat superior. The trial court dismissed the claim that the hospital was liable under the theory of respondeat superior.

Issue
Was the hospital liable for the malpractice of Lina under the theory of respondeat superior?

Holding
The North Carolina Court of Appeals held that the hospital was not liable for the negligence of Lina under the theory of respondeat superior.

Reason
The court of appeals held that Lina was not an employee of the hospital. He was not subject to supervision or control by the hospital. There was no evidence that Hoffman would have sought treatment elsewhere if she had known for a fact that Lina was not an employee.

The duty to supervise and manage is as applicable to the trustees as it is to the managers of any other business corporation. In both instances, there is a duty to act as a reasonably prudent person would act under similar circumstances. The governing body must act prudently in administering the affairs of the organization and must exercise its powers in good faith.

Appointment of a Chief Executive Officer

The governing body is responsible for appointing a CEO to act as its agent in the management of the organization. The CEO is responsible for the day-to-day operations of the organization. The CEO plans, directs, and coordinates the operational activities of the organization. The CEO must possess the competence and the character necessary to maintain satisfactory standards of patient care within the organization. The responsibilities and authority of the CEO should be expressed in an appropriate job description, as well as in any formal agreement or contract that the organization has with the CEO. Some state health codes describe the responsibilities of administrators in broad terms. They generally provide that the CEO/administrator shall be responsible for the overall management of the organization; enforcement of any applicable federal, state, and local regulations, as well as the organization's bylaws, policies, and procedures; appointment of, with the approval of the governing body, a qualified medical director; liaison between the governing body and medical staff; and appointment of an administrative supervisor to act during the CEO's absence from the organization.

The general duty of a governing body is to exercise due care and diligence in supervising and managing the organization. This duty does not cease with the selection of a CEO. A governing body can be liable if the level of patient care becomes inadequate because of the governing body's failure to properly supervise the management of the organization. With these responsibilities in mind, the governing body must closely monitor the effectiveness of the organization's leadership, beginning with the CEO. The Board should require a self-evaluation by the CEO on an annual basis, after which the board also reevaluates the CEO.

Hospital Administrator Licensure

There are no formal licensing requirements for hospital administrators, although there are common educational career paths to follow when seeking executive positions in hospitals. A master's degree in health services administration or a related field is often required. "Hospital administrators may also earn voluntary professional certification."[16] The American College of Healthcare Executives is the premiere professional organization offering a certification process.

> The American College of Healthcare Executives is an international professional society of 40,000 healthcare executives who lead hospitals, healthcare systems and other healthcare organizations. ACHE's mission is to advance its members and healthcare management excellence. ACHE offers its prestigious FACHE® credential, signifying board certification in healthcare management.[17]

Nursing Home Administrator Licensure

To comply with federal requirements, the various states have incorporated licensing requirements in their regulations. Administrators are licensed under the laws of their individual states. Statutes generally provide that the administrator of a nursing facility be licensed in accordance with state law. Alaska statutes, for example, require licensing of nursing home administrators.

> Sec. 08.70.080. License required. Only a licensed nursing home administrator may manage, supervise, or be generally in charge of a nursing home. The care provided by a nursing home or a licensed hospital providing nursing home care through the use of skilled nursing beds or intermediate care beds shall be supervised by a licensed nursing home administrator or by a person exempted from licensure requirements under this section.[18]

Licensure requirements include higher education, such as in New York State, which provides that "An applicant shall be deemed in fulfillment of Licensure Qualification 3 upon receipt of a baccalaureate or higher level degree from an accredited educational institution including, or supplemented by, 15 credit hours of required coursework in long-term care/health care, gerontology and personnel management."[19] In Massachusetts, 245 CMR 2.00 governs the licensure and practice of nursing home administrators and establishes the standards of conduct for the practice of nursing home administrators that include a written examination.[20]

The National Association of Long Term Care Administrator Boards (NAB) offers the nursing home administrator examination.[21] The NAB in July 2017 "will transition its examinations to a new structure: examinees will need to pass a 100-item 'core of knowledge' section and a 50-item line of service section."[22] The nursing home administrator exam "has been developed and administered by NAB for decades and is taken by over 2,000 candidates across the nation annually."[23]

States that require administrators to be licensed provide penalties ranging from fines to imprisonment for those administrators functioning without a license. The Alaska statutes cited earlier provide that "A person convicted of violating a provision of this chapter is guilty of a class B misdemeanor."[24]

A $5,000 fine was imposed on a nursing facility for operating without a licensed administrator for 54 days in *Magnolias Nursing and Convalescent Center v. Department of Health and Rehabilitation Services.*[25] The statute prohibiting operation of a nursing home without a licensed administrator was not considered vague, ambiguous, or unconstitutional.

Responsibility

The CEO is responsible for the supervision of the administrative staff and managers who assist in the daily operations of the organization. The CEO derives authority from the owner or governing body. The CEO of an organization owned and operated by a governmental agency may be an appointed public official. The CEO is responsible to lead and oversee the implementation of the company's long- and short-term plans in accordance with its strategy.

The CEO must implement the policies of the governing body, as well as interpret policies. Appropriate action must be taken where noncompliance with rules and regulations occurs. The CEO is responsible for making periodic reports to the governing body regarding policy implementation.

There may be occasions when the CEO believes that following a direction of the governing body may create a danger to the patients or others. If the CEO knows or should have known, as a reasonably prudent person, of a danger or unreasonable risk or harm that will be created by certain directed activity but nevertheless proceeds as directed, he or she could become personally liable for any resulting injury. The CEO, therefore, must take appropriate steps to notify the governing body of any policies that create dangers or unreasonable risks. Although the CEO cannot assume the functions of the professional staff, he or she must ensure that proper admission and discharge policies and procedures are formulated and carried out. The CEO must cooperate with the professional staff in maintaining satisfactory standards of medical care. The CEO is responsible to keep current as to regulatory

changes that affect organizational operations. Periodic meetings should be conducted to inform the staff of regulatory changes affecting their duties and responsibilities. The CEO should designate a representative for administrative coverage during those hours he or she is absent from the organization. This individual should be capable of dealing with administrative matters and be able to contact the CEO when major problems arise.

Tort Liability

The wrongful injury to another by the CEO in the performance of his or her duties can result in the CEO being liable to the one injured. Because the CEO is subject to the control of the organization, the organization also may be liable for the torts of the CEO that occur within the scope of his or her employment. When performing the duties that he or she was employed to perform, the CEO works for the benefit of the organization and not as an individual. Because the organization gains from the work performed by its employees, the law renders the organization legally responsible for the acts of employees while performing the work of the organization.

Liability for the Acts of Others

The CEO is not liable for the negligent acts of other employees as long as he or she personally took no part in the commission of the negligent act and was not negligent in selecting or directing the person committing the injury. However, under the doctrine of respondeat superior, a healthcare facility can be liable for an employee's negligent acts.

Case Reviews

Over the years, a fair number of cases have dealt with administrators and their management of healthcare organizations. In general, an administrator employed for the duration of satisfactory performance has no property right in the position, as was pointed out in *Bleeker v. Dukakis.*[26] The administrator of the Woodland Nursing Home had been hired through an oral agreement under which his continued employment was contingent upon satisfactory work performance. "The assistant commissioner determined that Woodland was being managed improperly and that the appellant should be replaced."[27] The administrator's appointment was considered to be at the will of the employer even though the nursing facility's policies provided a procedure for warning and an opportunity to correct work performance deficiencies.

✔ *ANESTHESIA ABUSE AND CEO DILEMMA*

Anytown Hospital has an outstanding reputation for surgical services. The operating room supervisor and a surgical nurse told Bob Wright, the CEO, that Dr. Flipton, an anesthesiologist, was abusing the use of anesthesia gases in the hospital's dental suite. He was reportedly seen by operating staff testing "laughing gas" by holding a mask against his face for short periods of time. This scene would be followed by a string of silly, seemingly meaningless jokes. Bob has repeatedly discussed this matter with the medical executive committee. The medical executive committee refuses to take any action without definitive action by the department chair. Bob suspects that if he pursues the matter further with the governing board, he could end up without a job. The governing body is generally unable to resolve disciplinary actions against a physician without support of the medical executive committee. Bob knows that if he pursues the matter further with the governing board, it will more likely result in a disgruntled board and medical staff. In this case, Bill knew enough to pick his battles, and this was one he could not win.

Dealing with the legal system can be a harrowing experience, even in those instances where the administrator is eventually exonerated from either negligence or criminal activity. Presented here are a few agonizing moments in the lives of some boards and their administrators.

- An administrator's license was revoked for concealment of the identities of the facility's owners in *Loren v. Board of Examiners of Nursing Home Administrators*.[28] The court found that the record contained substantial evidence to support the board's finding. The administrator had actively participated in a scheme to divert checks belonging to the nursing home to undisclosed partners of the home. The crime of knowingly filing false statements as to the facility's ownership with the intent of defrauding the U.S. government and the state of New York involved moral turpitude and subjected the administrator to disciplinary action.
- An administrator's plea to misdemeanor counts for mismanagement was considered a proper basis for suspending his nursing home license for 1 year.[29]
- A nursing facility's exclusion from a Medicaid rate incentive program was considered rationally

related to the encouragement of superior health care after the administrator was indicted for accepting excessive payments from the residents' relatives.[30]

- Although cases of alleged wrongdoing do not always end in a finding for the plaintiff, going through the ordeal is, at best, a most uncomfortable experience for the defendant. The court in *State v. Serebin*[31] held that the evidence of inadequate staffing and diet was found to be insufficient to support homicide charges against the administrator when the resident left the facility and died of exposure.

Leadership is responsible for leading, and that includes accepting responsibility for addressing those areas in the organization that need improvement, as noted in the following *reality check*.

Medical Staff Appointments and Privileging

The governing body is responsible for ensuring the medical staff bylaws, rules, and regulations include application requirements for clinical privileges and admission to the medical staff; a process for granting emergency staff privileges; requirements for medical staff consultations; a peer review process; a process for auditing medical records; a process for addressing disruptive physicians and substance abuse; and a process for instituting corrective action (disciplinary actions can take the form of a letter of reprimand, suspension, or termination of privileges).

✔ *CEO CHALLENGES BOARD-APPOINTED CONSULTANTS*

The hospital's board of directors had hired a consulting firm to review the quality of patient care being delivered at the hospital where Nathan was employed as the CEO. Following the 2-week review, the consultants presented Nathan and his leadership group with a verbal report. During the consultant's exit review, Nathan appeared somewhat agitated by the report as he sat restlessly in his seat. When the written preliminary report listing the hospital's deficiencies was presented to Nathan following the verbal report, he abruptly stood up and said, "This is not just about the hospital! This is about my job!" Nathan then angrily left the room, followed by his managers, with the exception of two. They never looked back—no goodbyes, just angry and disgruntled.

The governing body has a responsibility to appoint competent members to its professional staff. Failure of the governing body to properly screen a medical staff applicant's credentials can lead to liability for injuries suffered by patients as a result of that omission, as was the case in *Johnson v. Misericordia Community Hospital*,[32] where the patient brought a malpractice action against the hospital and its liability insurer for alleged negligence in granting orthopedic privileges to a physician who performed an operation to remove a pin fragment from the patient's hip. The Wisconsin Court of Appeals found the hospital negligent for failing to scrutinize the physician's credentials before approving his application for orthopedic privileges. The hospital failed to adhere to procedures established under both its own bylaws and state statute. The measure of quality and the degree of quality control exercised in a hospital are the direct responsibilities of the medical staff. Hospital supervision of the manner of appointment of physicians to its staff is mandatory, not optional. On appeal by the hospital, the Wisconsin Supreme Court affirmed the appellate court's decision, finding that if the hospital had exercised ordinary care, it would not have appointed the physician to the medical staff.

Ensure Medical Staff Competency

Healthcare organizations have a responsibility to ensure the competency of their medical staff and to evaluate the quality of medical treatment rendered on their premises. The California Court of Appeals in *Elam v. College Park Hospital*[33] reviewed a question as to "whether a hospital is liable to a patient under the doctrine of corporate negligence for negligent conduct of independent physicians and surgeons who, as members of the hospital staff, avail themselves of the hospital facilities, but who are neither employees nor agents of the hospital."[34] The Court of Appeals upheld that a hospital is liable to a patient under the doctrine of corporate negligence for the negligent conduct of independent physicians and surgeons who are neither employees nor agents of the hospital.

In *Dykema v. Carolina Emergency Physicians, P.C.*,[35] Dykema began having respiratory symptoms, cough, and shortness of breath for which Dr. King, his family physician, treated him. He sought a second opinion from the Center for Family Medicine ("Center"), part of the Greenville Hospital System. Dykema went to the Center with complaints of cough, shortness of breath, and tightness in the chest. A third-year medical student, Dr. Gemas, and Dr. Pearman, an attending faculty member, saw Dykema that day. Pearman prescribed antibiotics for persistent bronchitis and told Dykema to return in 1 week or sooner if his condition worsened.

Early Sunday morning, February 6, Mrs. Dykema called the Center concerning her husband's worsening condition and was advised to take him to the hospital the next day. She brought him to the hospital at approximately 1:00 PM on February 6, and Dr. Connell, a medical resident and employee of Greenville Hospital System, saw him. Connell diagnosed viral bronchitis and advised Dykema to continue his antibiotics and keep his follow-up appointment at the center on February 8. The next morning, February 7, Mrs. Dykema called the Center and spoke with a receptionist and requested that her husband be seen immediately because of his worsening condition. She was told there were no earlier appointments available and that she should keep the appointment on February 8. Dykema died on the morning of February 8, prior to his scheduled appointment. The cause of death was a progressive showering of pulmonary emboli, pieces of which moved to his lungs and caused a fatal blockage. The South Carolina Supreme Court held the defendant hospital was liable for the full $2 million in actual damages and reinstated the $500,000 award in punitive damages and finding that "the trial court's ruling that the statutory caps are inapplicable to this case is affirmed."[36]

Discipline Abusive Behavior

It is the responsibility of the CEO, medical board, and governing body to ensure that caregivers who engage in verbal or abusive behavior are appropriately disciplined. Accrediting bodies that claim a zero tolerance for such behavior must support surveyors who report inappropriate behavior. Furthermore, to punish an individual for reporting such behavior and abuse is tantamount to being complicit with allowing inappropriate behavior to continue. The healthcare industry has a long history of making excuses for allowing abusive behavior. Failure to effectively address such behavior cannot be tolerated in a civil society.

Disruptive physicians can have a negative impact on an organization's staff and ultimately affect the quality of patient care, as noted in the following *reality check*.

Implementing the appropriate policies and procedures to address conflict resolution are necessary to ensure a safe and functional environment for both

FAULTY CREDENTIALING PROCESS

Citation: *Candler Gen. Hosp., Inc. v. Persaud*, 442 S.E.2d 775 (Ga. Ct. App. 1994)

Facts

On or about February 15, 1990, the patient in this case was referred to Dr. Freeman for consultation and treatment of gallstones. Freeman recommended that the patient undergo a laparoscopic laser cholecystectomy procedure.

On February 16, 1990, Freeman requested and was granted temporary privileges to perform the procedure. The privileges were granted based on a certificate he had received after completing a laparoscopic laser cholecystectomy workshop, which he took on February 10, 1990. Freeman performed the cholecystectomy on February 20, 1990, with the assistance of Dr. Thomas.

A complaint by the administrator of the patient's estate, supported by an expert's affidavit, alleged that the cholecystectomy was negligently performed, and as a result, the patient bled to death. The complaint charged the hospital with negligence in permitting Freeman to perform the procedure on the decedent without having instituted any standards, training requirements, or "protocols," or otherwise instituted any method for judging the qualifications of a surgeon to perform the procedure. The complaint also alleged that the hospital knew or reasonably should have known that it did not have a credentialing process that could have assured the hospital of the physician's education, training, and ability to perform the procedure.

The trial court denied the hospital's motion for summary judgment, finding that the plaintiffs' evidence was sufficient to raise a question of fact regarding whether surgical privileges should have been issued by the hospital to Freeman. The hospital appealed.

Issue

Was there a material issue of fact as to whether the hospital was negligent in granting the specific privileges requested by Freeman?

Holding

The Georgia Court of Appeals held that there was a material issue of fact as to whether the hospital was negligent in granting the specific privileges requested, thus precluding summary judgment.

Reason

The court found that a hospital has a direct and independent responsibility to its patients to take reasonable steps to ensure that physicians using hospital facilities are qualified for the privileges granted. The hospital owed a duty to the plaintiffs' decedent to act in good faith and with reasonable care to ensure that the surgeon was qualified to practice the procedure that he was granted privileges to perform.

patients and employees. Criteria other than academic credentials (e.g., a physician's ability to work with others) must be considered before granting an applicant privileges on the hospital's professional staff. This *reality check* illustrates how disruptive physician behavior can be harmful to patients, staff, and hospital surveyors who are onsite to examine the hospital's quality of care.

Privileges Denied: Inability to Work with Others

The court, in *Ladenheim v. Union County Hospital District*,[37] held that the physician's inability to work with other members of the staff was sufficient grounds to deny him staff privileges. The physician's record was replete with evidence of his inability to work effectively with other members of the hospital staff. As stated in *Huffaker v. Bailey*,[38] most courts have found that the ability to work smoothly with others is reasonably related to the objective of ensuring patient welfare. The conclusion seems justified because healthcare professionals frequently are required to work together or in teams. A staff member who, because of personality characteristics or other problems, is incapable of getting along with others could severely hinder the effective treatment of patients.

In another case, the court, in *Pick v. Santa Ana-Tustin Community Hospital*,[39] held that the petitioner's demonstrated lack of ability to work with others in the hospital setting was sufficient to support the denial of his application for admission to the medical staff. There was evidence that the petitioner presented a real and substantial danger to patients treated by him and that the patients might receive less than a high quality of medical care.

✔ *THE ANGRY DOCTOR*

Dr. X came into my outer office standing in the doorway complaining that there were no beds available in the intensive care unit (ICU) for his patient whom he said was in critical condition.

I could hear his voice from my inner office. My secretary called me through the intercom and said "Dr. X is out here and says he wants to see you *now*. He wants you to discharge a patient from the ICU to a different nursing unit so he can move his patient in to an ICU bed."

I walked out of my office into the reception area. Before I could speak, Dr. X began an explosive tirade as to how his patient needed to be in the ICU more than the other patients already admitted. Dr. X said, "I want a patient moved from ICU to a different patient care unit. My patient is in critical condition." I suggested he calm down and stated that the priority for admission to the unit must to be reviewed with Alex, who is the director of the ICU. Dr. X became more angry and said, "Step outside and you and I will handle this." I then instructed my secretary to call security. She was so stunned that she sat there in a daze and failed to call security. Turning to Dr. X, I said, "Dr. X, it is time for you to leave and I will speak to Alex and he will make the appropriate accommodations for your patient. Alex will consult with you." He then stormed out of my office as Stu, the president of the medical staff walked in smiling and chuckling, "I see you met Dr. X. I heard him offer to go out to the parking lot with you. Lucky you didn't go with him. He just got back from Vietnam. I think he was used to being in charge and is having some difficulty readjusting to civilian life."

Dr. X was sent a letter of reprimand. There was no reply and thereafter he was seldom seen in the hospital.

—CEO

🌐 *ANGER MANAGEMENT COURSES ARE A NEW TOOL FOR DEALING WITH DOCTORS' RAGE IN THE O.R.*

For generations, bad behavior by doctors has been explained away as an inevitable product of stress or tacitly accepted by administrators. . . . but that time-honored tolerance is waning . . . as a result of regulations imposed in 2009 by The Joint Commission, the group that accredits hospitals. These rules require hospitals to institute procedures for dealing with disruptive behavior, which can take passive forms such as refusing to answer pages or attend meetings. The commission has called for a "zero tolerance" approach.

—Sandra G. Boodman, *The Washington Post*, March 4, 2013

Suspension Privileges

A physician who challenges a board's decision to suspend his medical staff privileges will find that a court will generally uphold the board's decision in a legal action. As was the case in *Bouquett v. St. Elizabeth's Corp.*,[40] where an ophthalmologist brought an action to challenge suspension of his medical staff privileges after a felony conviction in a federal court for conspiracy to distribute Dilaudid. He later was sentenced to 5 years of incarceration. On appeal, the Ohio Supreme Court held that the conviction of the ophthalmologist justified summary suspension of the physician's staff privileges pursuant to a hospital bylaw permitting summary suspension in the best interest of patient care in the hospital. A governing body has broad discretion in determining who shall be granted medical staff privileges. Unless an organization has been arbitrary and/or capricious or has abused its discretion, the courts generally will not interfere with a board's decision to suspend physicians convicted on drug-related felony charges.

Enforce Standards of Professional Ethics

Meyers applied for medical staff privileges. Shortly thereafter, the Credentials Committee, the Medical Executive Committee (MEC), and the board of the hospital approved Meyers for appointment to the medical staff. All initial appointments to the medical staff were provisional for 1 year.

Within a year of Meyers's initial appointment, the Credentials Committee began to evaluate Meyers for advancement to active staff. The Credentials Committee was concerned about Meyers's history: moving from hospital to hospital after disputes with hospital staff; his failure to fully, and in a timely manner, disclose disciplinary and corrective action taken against him in another state; and the quality of his patient care. The MEC voted to accept the Credentials Committee

☑ *DISRUPTIVE PHYSICIAN*

Stephen, a hospital administrative consultant, selected a complex case on the 10th floor orthopedic unit for review. Stephen reviewed the patient's record. Following several questions about the patient's care, a staff nurse asked, "Would you like Dr. Williams, the orthopedist, to discuss this case with you?" Stephen said, "Sure, that will be fine." Dr. Williams soon arrived and appeared a bit disturbed that he had been summoned. Stephen introduced himself and said that he just had a few questions he would like to ask.

Stephen asked Dr. Williams which diagnoses the patient related to the organization at the time of admission and which diagnoses were made during the course of the patient's hospitalization. Dr. Williams said, "I am treating the patient for her orthopedic problems, not all of these other diagnoses." Following a few questions with the physician, Stephen asked to interview the patient. Dr. Williams agreed, "OK." Stephen asked, "Could you please ask the patient if I could speak with her?" Dr. Williams said, "That's not necessary." Dr. Williams and Stephen walked to the entrance of the patient's room. Stephen waited outside the patient's room. Dr. Williams walked into the patient's room, returned to the hallway, and said, "The patient was sleeping, but I woke her up."

Upon entry to the patient's room, sensing that Dr. Williams had forgotten Stephen's name, Stephen introduced himself to the patient. Dr. Williams asked Stephen if he wanted him to leave the room. Stephen replied, "It's OK. I only have a few questions. You can stay if you would like."

The patient said, "Oh, I know what you do. My husband is a nurse." Stephen smiled and asked about her care. She said that it was excellent. She said the food could be better but she was pleased with her overall care. She talked about her hip fracture and back problems. Dr. Williams, interrupting the conversation, proceeded to tell the patient about her orthopedic issues. He described in explicit and frightening detail how the discs in her back were collapsing and how things could progress and how she could eventually be confined to a wheelchair.

Following his brief conversation with the patient, Stephen said, "You will be all OK." The patient smiled and said, "Thank you." Upon leaving the room, Dr. Williams asked, "What kind of doctor are you?" Stephen replied, "I am not a doctor; I am an administrative consultant." Not having listened to Stephen's answer, Dr. Williams said in a threatening manner, just outside the patient's room, "Don't you ever tell one of my patients they are going to be OK!" Stephen said calmly, "I was not speaking clinically; I was relating a compassionate goodbye to the patient." Stephen then extended his hand to Dr. Williams, saying, "Thank you for your time." Dr. Williams shook Stephen's hand and then quickly walked away down the corridor. Stephen later learned that this was not the first time that Dr. Williams had had behavioral issues with both patients and with the nursing staff. Questions arise as to: (1) what information should Stephen share with the corporate leaders regarding Dr. Williams' disruptive behavior on the patient care unit; and, (2) what action, if any, should the hospital take.

Dr. Williams eventually apologized to Stephen several months later for his conduct, stating that he thought Stephen was a physician and believed him to be out of place for saying that his patient would be OK.

decision to revoke Meyers's staff privileges. The MEC then recommended to the board the revocation of Meyers's privileges.

The board notified Meyers that a three-member board committee would conduct an independent review. This committee discussed concerns about Meyers's behavior and his inability to get along with others, in addition to questions about his surgical technique. The committee questioned Meyers about several incident reports concerning disruptive behavior, his history of problems at other hospitals, his failure to complete medical records, his hostility toward the operating room staff, and his failure to provide appropriate coverage for patients while he was unavailable. Meyers did acknowledge that he had a personality problem.

The three-member committee of the board voted to deny Meyers's appointment to active staff. The reasons cited for the committee's decision were Meyers's failure to satisfy requirements that he *abide by the ethics of the*

profession, work cooperatively with others, complete medical records in a timely manner, and abide by hospital standards. The committee outlined Meyers's pattern of rude, abusive, and disruptive behavior that included, but was not limited to, temper tantrums, attempted interference with the right of an attending physician to refer a patient to the surgeon of his choice or to transfer the patient, condescending remarks toward women, refusal to speak to a member of his surgical team during surgical procedures, and several instances of throwing a scalpel during surgery. The committee informed Meyers that this behavior could have an adverse effect on the quality of patient care. As for his failure to complete timely medical records, the committee stated that delinquent records can place patients at risk.

The committee issued its recommendation that Meyers not be reappointed to the hospital's staff because of his *failure to meet ethical standards* and his inability to work cooperatively with others. In May, the board adopted and affirmed the Fair Hearing Committee's recommendation. Ultimately, after further appeals, the board revoked Meyers's privileges.

Meyers brought suit, seeking a permanent injunction to require the hospital to reinstate him to staff. The court denied Meyers's motion. Quality patient care requires that physicians possess at least a reasonable ability to work with others. The board was concerned that Meyers's behavior would continue resulting in a patient injury.[41]

Duty to Be Financially Scrupulous

Healthcare organizations searching for alternate sources of income must do so scrupulously and not find themselves in what could be construed as questionable corporate activities. *Smith v. van Gorkum*[42] involved a board of directors that authorized the sale of its company through a cash-out merger for a tendered price per share nearly 50% over the market price. Although that might sound like a good deal, the governing body did not make any inquiry to determine whether it was the best deal available. In fact, it made no decision during a hastily arranged, brief meeting in which it relied solely on the CEO's report regarding the desirability of the move. The Delaware Supreme Court held that the board's decision to approve a proposed cash-out merger was not a product of informed business judgment and that it acted in a grossly negligent manner in approving amendments to the merger proposal.

A triable claim of illegal fee splitting was stated in *Hauptman v. Grand Manor Health Related Facility, Inc.*,[43] by the allegations of a psychiatrist that a nursing home barred him from continuing to treat its residents unless he joined a professional corporation, the members of which included owners of the nursing home. Under the proposed agreement, the nursing home would retain 20% of the fees collected on his behalf. Although Section 6509(a) of the New York Education Law does not prohibit members of a professional corporation from pooling fees, the statute did not apply to forced conscription into a corporation at the price of surrendering a portion of one's fees unwillingly. Likewise, Title 8, Section 29.1[b][4] of the New York Compilation of Codes and Rules expressly forbids a professional corporation from charging a fee for billing and office expenses based on a percentage of income from a practice. The psychiatrist's allegations also showed possible violation of New York Public Health Law § 2801(b), which prohibited exclusion of a practitioner on grounds not related to reasonable objectives of the organization.

A California bank, in *Lynch v. Redfield Foundation*,[44] refused to honor corporate drafts unless all trustees concurred. They could not agree, and funds in a noninterest-bearing account continued to grow in principal from $4,900 to $47,000 over a 5-year period. Although two trustees did try to carry on corporate functions despite a dissident trustee, their good faith did not protect them from liability in this case. The money could have been transferred to at least an interest-bearing account without the third trustee's signature. The trustees were held jointly liable to pay to the corporation the statutory rate of simple interest.

Duty to Require Competitive Bidding

Many states have developed regulations requiring competitive bidding for work or services commissioned by public organizations. The fundamental purpose of this requirement is to eliminate or at least reduce the possibility that abuses, such as fraud, favoritism, improvidence, or extravagance, will intrude into an organization's business practices. Contracts made in violation of a statute are considered illegal and could result in personal liability for board members, especially if the members become aware of a fraudulent activity and allow it to continue. The mere appearance of favoritism toward one contractor over another could give rise to an unlawful action. For example, a board member's pressing the administrator to favor one ambulance transporter over others because of his or her social acquaintance with the owner is suspect. An organization's governing body should avoid even the appearance of wrongdoing by requiring competitive bidding.

Duty to Avoid Conflicts of Interest

A *conflict of interest* involves those situations in which a person has opportunity to promote self-interests that could have a detrimental effect on an organization with which he or she has a special relationship (e.g., employee, board member). The potential for conflict of interest exists for individuals at all levels within an organization. Disclosure of potential conflicts of interest should be made so that appropriate action may be taken to ensure that such conflict does not inappropriately influence important organizational and/or healthcare decisions. Board members, physicians, and employees are required by most organizations to submit a form disclosing potential conflicts of interest that might negatively impact the organization's reputation or financial resources.

Governing body members must refrain from self-dealing and avoid conflict-of-interest situations. Each board member should submit in writing all

✔ *BOARD FAILS THE COMMUNITY*

At a time when many hospitals were on the brink of bankruptcy and struggling to survive, Brad, the administrator of Hospital A, one of three in a multihospital system, had a positive bottom line of approximately $6 million. The hospital was located in an upscale, affluent community. The corporate directors siphoned off funds from Hospital A for many years to support the operations and pet capital projects of two of the system's failing hospitals. Meanwhile, Hospital A was suffering from lack of supplies and funds for Hospital A's own capital projects, leading to a slow deterioration of Hospital A's facilities. The physicians and community members, aware of the positive bottom line, were disturbed that Hospital A's funds from operations and what few donations being made were allocated to fund the day-to-day operations of the system's two failing hospitals. As a result, it was difficult to get community members to donate to their own community hospital. The community had no trust their donations would remain in the community.

The needs of the hospital continued to suffer as corporate leadership was expanding nonrevenue-producing projects, relocating corporate offices to more costly sites, building lavish office suites, adding staff with vague job descriptions that only served to burden and penalize the revenue-producing entities, and jeopardizing patient care with their pet projects by deluging hospital staff with paperwork so they could produce even more paperwork to justify their own existence. Hospital staff felt that corporate staff had become an obstacle to the provision of quality patient care. No relief from battlefield fatigue seemed to be on the horizon.

Brad was able to work with a variety of local community leaders (e.g., a banker, lawyer, physician, newspaper editor, and real estate agent) to establish a fundraising board whose mission was to oversee the local fundraising process and help assure that donations were used for Hospital A's needs. Although many of the corporate leaders privately objected to the concept, the board reluctantly recognized the community fundraising board's existence, hoping to make inroads into the pockets of the wealthy. With halfhearted support by corporate leadership, the death of many of the board's founding fathers, and eventual resignation of *battle fatigued* Brad, who had developed community trust, the community board slowly faded out of existence under the leadership of the administrators that followed him.

Brad's dilemma regarding cash flow to other entities in the corporation was a decision made on the system's corporate level. When working in a multihospital system, the CEO of any one division of the system will face many agonizing nights about what he can and cannot control. This is but one of many ethics-driven dilemmas that occur in multihospital systems. The modern-day CEO understands that allocation of scarce resources is often politically driven. Thus, the CEO must have both the oral and written skills to justify to the corporate leadership the funding needed for the functioning of his division.

outstanding voting shares (where applicable) or any relationships or transactions in which the director might or could have a conflict of interest. Membership on the governing body or its committees should not be used for private gain. Board members are expected to disclose potential conflicts of interest and withdraw from the boardroom at the time of voting on such issues. Board members who suspect a conflict of interest by another board member have a right and a duty to raise pertinent questions regarding any potential conflict. Conflict of interest is presumed to exist when a board member or a firm with which he or she is associated may benefit or lose from the passage of a proposed action.

Membership on the governing body of a non-profit organization is deemed a public service. Neither the court nor the community expects or desires such public service to be turned to private gain. Thus, the standards imposed on board members regarding the investment of trust funds, self-dealing transactions, or personal compensation may be stricter than those for directors of business corporations.

The essential rules regarding self-dealing are clear. Generally, a contract between the organization and a trustee financially interested in the transaction is voidable by the organization in the event that the interested trustee spoke or voted in favor of the arrangement or did not disclose fully the material facts regarding his or her interest. This resolution of the self-dealing problem is based on the belief that if an interested board member does not participate in the governing body's action and does make full disclosure of his or her interest, the disinterested remaining members of the governing body are able to protect the organization's interests. Statutory provisions in some states specifically forbid self-dealing transactions altogether, irrespective of disclosure or the fairness of the deal.

Duty to Provide Adequate Insurance

One basic protection for tangible property is adequate insurance against negligence, fire, and other risks. This duty extends to keeping the physical plant of the corporation in good repair and appropriating funds for such purpose when necessary.

It is the duty of the governing body to purchase adequate insurance to cover the various risks associated with conducting organizational business, and thus protect the organization's assets. Organizations face as much risk of losing their tangible and intangible assets through judgments for negligence as they do through fires or other disasters. When this is true, the duty to insure against the risks of fire is as great as the duty to insure against the risks of negligent conduct.

Criminal Activity Insurance Settlement

Johns Hopkins Hospital agreed to a $190 million settlement as the result of Dr. Nikita Levy's secret taping of patients during pelvic examinations. An investigation was begun, and Dr. Levy was later found dead at home, which was attributed to suicide. The hospital stated that the settlement would be paid by insurance. But many legal and ethical questions remain unanswered—for example, how were Dr. Levy's activities able to go undetected for so many years? The "patient's rights to privacy," amongst many others, were severely violated. The pain and suffering will not be relieved by this settlement. It is difficult to place this case in any particular chapter; however, his chapter perhaps may be most appropriate, as ultimately, it is the hospital's responsibility to be ever vigilant for both negligent and criminal acts that impact the lives of the patients it serves to heal. Peer review should not merely be a process for meeting regulatory requirements. Hospital boards should continuously improve the process and consider the pros and cons of a profession's process of self-review.

Duty to Comply with Law

The governing body in general, and its agents (assigned representatives) in particular, are responsible for compliance with federal, state, and local laws regarding the operation of the organization. Depending on the scope of the wrong committed and the intent of the governing body, failure to comply could subject board members and/or their agents to civil liability and, in some instances, to criminal prosecution. The organization and its designated officers are responsible to address deficiencies identified during inspections by both governmental and nongovernmental agencies.

Failure to comply with applicable statutory regulations can be costly. This was the case in *People v. Casa Blanca Convalescent Homes*,[45] in which there was evidence of numerous and prolonged deficiencies in resident care. The nursing home's practice of providing inadequate staffing constituted not only illegal practice, but also unfair business practice in violation of Section 17200 of the California Business and Professions Code. The trial court was found to have properly assessed a fine of $2,500 for each of 67 violations, totaling $167,500, where the evidence showed that the operator of the nursing home had the financial ability to pay that amount.

Duty to Comply with Accreditation Standards

The governing body is responsible for compliance with applicable standards promulgated by accrediting bodies. Noncompliance could cause an organization to lose accreditation, which, in turn, could provide grounds for third-party reimbursement agencies such as Medicare, to deny payment for treatment rendered to patients.

The findings by The Joint Commission surveyors, for example, during accreditation surveys must be addressed and corrected. Consultative remarks are often offered during a survey to highlight an

---

(NEWS) *CARDIOLOGISTS FLAGGING WOEFUL PATIENT CARE SAY THEY PAID WITH THEIR JOBS*

San Jose, CA—When a California cardiologist and cardiac surgeon went to their superiors complaining of woeful patient care at their hospital, one had her job shifted to a satellite outpatient clinic, while the other's contract was terminated. Now, as their ensuing lawsuit—naming two additional cardiologists among the defendants—moves into its next phase, the plaintiffs have given an exclusive interview to *heartwire* detailing their experiences.

• • •

Some of their complaints have already been upheld. For example, the JC—a not-for-profit organization that accredits over 19,000 health care organizations in the U.S.—put the SCVMC on "conditional accreditation" for six months in 2010/2011.

—Lisa Nainggolan, *heartwire*, January 25, 2012

area of concern. Suggestions by surveyors should be addressed as determined to be appropriate by the organization. They should be regarded as being of considerable importance in identifying areas needing corrective action, as are the written reports provided by surveyors at the time of a survey.

Conflicts of Interests

The following *news report* describes how pervasive the conflicts of interest are between inspection agencies and accrediting bodies.

Hospital Accreditation and Conflicts of Interest

The mission of accrediting bodies is to improve the quality of care rendered in the nation's hospitals through its survey process. *The Joint Commission* (TJC), an accrediting body in the healthcare industry, for example, is dependent upon the hospitals it surveys/inspects to reimburse it for the costs of those surveys. Therefore, TJC, out of its own necessity for financial survival, must maintain satisfied clients, and in so doing, a conflict arises. How credible can a survey be when the accrediting body is dependent on the organizations it surveys for financial survival? Furthermore, hospitals evaluate the performance of the surveyors. The survival of the surveyor in his or her job is dependent upon satisfactory evaluations from the contracting hospitals. Conflicting interests here encourage surveyors/inspectors to be careful about what he or she scores because of fear of retaliation by both the organizations surveyed and the employer. Accrediting organizations are far from effective in protecting the consumer from the human errors that result in numerous deaths and injuries annually in the nation's hospitals.

The food inspection process is similar to that of the healthcare industry. Food makers often know when inspectors will audit their facilities, and they vigorously prepare for those inspections. This was also true for hospitals up until several years ago, when TJC decided to conduct unannounced surveys. This change occurred mostly due to criticism from its own surveyors, the Centers for Medicare and Medicaid Services, the public, and some of the surveyed organizations.

Food makers often score high in their inspections yet still have recalls and foodborne diseases from eating contaminated food or beverages. TJC, up until several years ago, scored hospitals. They discontinued the scoring process because of criticism, once again from its own surveyors and others. Because of the competition between hospitals, the surveyors were pressured to provide high scores by the organizations they surveyed. Large billboards could be seen on Florida highways advertising scores of 100, yet they may have not provided any better quality of care then a hospital that scored 80. One small town hospital advertised in a newspaper that it scored 100 on a TJC survey. This same hospital had no full-time emergency department physician. One young lady said, "I was home recently and saw plastered in a full page ad that my hometown hospital scored 100 in its most recent accreditation survey. I would not take my dog to that hospital. They killed my mom." As with hospitals, the food companies typically pay food industry inspectors, creating a conflict of interest for inspectors who might fear that they will lose business if they do not hand out high ratings.

Accreditation in both the healthcare and food industries is plagued by one major disturbing issue: There is a transparent conflict of interest between various inspecting agencies and the entities they inspect, placing the public's health at risk to benefit their bottom line. Someone has to regulate the regulators.

NEWS *FOOD INSPECTION IS OFTEN FLAWED*

The voluntary quality control system widely used in the nation's $1 trillion domestic food industry is rife with conflicts of interest, inexperienced auditors and cursory inspections that produce inflated ratings, according to food retail executives and other industry experts.

. . .

Suppliers "will hunt down the fastest, cheapest, easiest and least-intrusive third-party auditors that will provide the certificate" that will allow them to sell their product. . . . until that model flips, there will continue to be a false sense of security in terms of what these systems offer.

—Lena H. Sun, *The Washington Post*, October 22, 2010

The Joint Commission National Patient Safety Goals

TJC is striving to improve patient safety by identifying national patient safety goals, as well as adding and revising standards in the accreditation process. National patient safety goals have included improving the patient identification process (e.g., using two patient identifiers when administering medications); eliminating transfusion errors; improving the effectiveness of communication among caregivers; timely reporting of critical test results; improving the safety of medication use; reducing harm from anticoagulation therapy; reducing the risk of hospital-acquired infections; accurately reconciling medications; communicating each patient's medication list to the next provider; providing a reconciled medication list to each patient at discharge; reducing the risk of patient harm resulting from falls; preventing healthcare-associated pressure ulcers; identifying and addressing safety risks inherent in various patient populations served (e.g., adults, children); identifying individuals at risk for suicide; reducing the risks for falls and injury; and developing a *Universal Protocol for Preventing Wrong Site, Wrong Procedure, and Wrong Patient Invasive Procedures*. The protocol requires implementation of a process verifying the correct procedure, for the correct patient, at the correct site, including the marking of the procedure site with the patient's participation. *A preprocedure time-out* (immediately prior to surgery) requires that all participants involved in an invasive procedure unanimously agree that the correct patient is on the surgical table and is about to undergo the correct procedure at the correct site.

Periodically, TJC introduces new national patient safety goals into its survey process. Surveyors from TJC evaluate organizations at the time of an organization's accreditation survey, determining compliance with patient safety goals and the standards outlined in its accreditation manual. From time to time, goals are incorporated into the standards section of the accreditation manual. The goals encourage compliance with safe practices in the delivery of patient care and are designed to reduce the likelihood of medical errors. As a result of the frequency of questions asked regarding interpretation, implementation, and the periodic introduction of new goals into the survey process, TJC website (www.jointcommission.org) should be referenced for current information.

The Joint Commission Complaint Process

TJC has put into practice a patient complaint process that requires the healthcare organizations it accredits to educate employers and employees as to their right to report safety or quality concerns to TJC. TJC policy forbids accredited organizations from taking retaliatory actions against employees for having reported quality of care concerns to TJC. Patient complaints may be reported using the following means:

- Email (complaint@jointcommission.org)
- Fax (Office of Quality Monitoring at 630-792-5636)
- Mail (Office of Quality Monitoring, The Joint Commission, One Renaissance Boulevard, Oakbrook Terrace, IL 60181)
- Telephone (800-994-6610) for questions about how to file a complaint (8:30 AM to 5:00 PM, Central Time, weekdays). *Note*: Surveyors may query staff during the survey process as to what procedures an organization has in place for addressing quality of care concerns and how employees and patients are educated as to TJC's complaint process.

Duty to Provide Adequate and Competent Staff

Adequate staffing requires that managers not merely employ sufficient staff to provide patient care but also insure that each position is filled with an individual with the appropriate qualifications for the job for which he or she is hired. The importance of sound hiring practices is well borne out in the following *reality check*.

Under federal law, nursing homes must have sufficient nursing staff to provide nursing and related services adequate to attain and maintain the highest practicable physical, mental, and psychosocial well-being of each resident, as determined by resident assessments and individual plans of care. As nursing homes are increasingly filled with older, disabled residents with ever-increasing complex care requirements, demand for highly educated and trained nursing personnel continues to grow.[46] Organizations that fail to meet federal standards can lose certification as a provider of patient care. This, in turn, can lead to the denial of reimbursement under federal entitlement programs.

"Federal health officials have concluded that most nursing homes are understaffed to the point that patients may be endangered. For the first time, the government is recommending strict new rules that would require thousands of the homes to hire more nurses and health aides."[47] A report released by Representative Ciro Rodriguez and Representative Gene Green in 2002 found that the vast majority of Texas nursing homes are understaffed and fail to comply with federal standards.[48] The continuing problems of nursing home staffing prompted Representative

☑ *MATCHING RESPONSIBILITIES WITH QUALIFICATIONS*

An off-duty TJC surveyor entered a hospital in his hometown with his wife for urgent care. When he entered the emergency department (ED) reception waiting area, a sign was noted at the reception desk that read, "Please have a seat. There is a 3½ hour wait for nursing triage." The surveyor was unable to satisfy the receptionist that his wife needed urgent care. The receptionist insisted that his wife would have to wait her turn. The surveyor eventually spoke to the hospital's on-call night administrator. The surveyor explained current practice requires that triage be readily available for all patients. The administrator agreed and the surveyor's wife was attended to. The sign was later removed.

In another instance a surveyor noted that there was a two-step process before a triage nurse would examine a patient. The first step required the patient to sign in at the receptionist desk upon arriving in the ED, where the patient was required to write his or her name, date, and time on a sign-in sheet. The patient was then be requested to sit in the ED waiting area until summoned by a business office admissions intake clerk, who was responsible for gathering demographic and financial information. The clerk would then prioritize the order in which patients would be seen by a triage nurse, who would then determine who would be treated next in the ED treatment area. In speaking with two admissions clerks, the surveyor asked, "Do you feel comfortable making medical decisions as to in what order patients should be examined by a triage nurse?" The admissions clerk handing the surveyor a notice posted at her desk said, "We are provided this posting that lists 14 patient symptoms to look for to help us determine in what order they should be referred to a triage nurse." The surveyor asked, "Are you comfortable that this list provides you with sufficient information and training to make such a decision?" Simultaneously they both said, "No!" In this instance, the admitting clerk's responsibilities and qualifications to perform the assigned tasks were inadequate to perform the requirements of the job.

Waxman to introduce the Nursing Home Staffing Act of 2005 to establish minimum staff requirements for nursing homes receiving payments under the Medicare or Medicaid program.

> Many medical and regulatory investigators who work in nursing homes every day characterize the number of wrongful deaths in terms such as "massive" and "pervasive," based on their daily experience. Most of the deaths can be traced to an inadequate number of nurses and aides to provide life-sustaining care. The U.S. Department of Health and Human Services reported to Congress this year [2002] that nine out of 10 nursing homes have staffing levels too low to provide adequate care.[49]

The answer to staffing requires a continuing emphasis on recruitment and education, development of career ladders, respect for caregivers, salaries commensurate with the requirements of the job, and severe prosecution of those who seek financial gain by purposely understaffing their homes.

Deficient Nursing Care

The nursing facility in *Our Lady of the Woods v. Commonwealth of Kentucky Health Facilities*[50] was closed because of deficiencies found during an inspection of the facility, the most serious of which was the lack of continuous nursing care on all shifts. The court held that evidence that the nursing facility lacked continuous services required by regulation was sufficient to sustain an order to close the facility. Many witnesses testified concerning the deficiencies, and even the administrator admitted to the most serious violation—lack of continuous nursing services. The hearing officer, although noting that the quality of care provided to the facility's residents was satisfactory, concluded:

> The facts clearly reveal that the respondent has long violated one of the "essential functions of a nursing home" by not providing continuous graduate nursing supervision. To contend that such supervision can be provided from afar (by an "on-call" nurse) is to contend that a resident will never be confronted with a medical problem of such immediacy that his health or even his life would not be endangered while awaiting the arrival of the "on-call" professional. Such contention is unacceptable; the facility violated on a protracted basis one of its most substantive mandates. Absent proof that an adequate nursing staff could not be obtained (there is no such proof herein), it must be concluded that there is no justification for this violation.[51]

The court held that "deference is given to the trier of the fact, and agency determinations are to be upheld if the decision is supported by substantial, reliable, and probative evidence in the record as a whole."[52]

Timely Response to Patient Calls

Healthcare organizations must provide for adequate staffing. The court of appeals in *Leavitt v. St. Tammany Parish Hospital*[53] held that the hospital owed a duty to respond promptly to patient calls for help. The hospital breached its duty by having less than adequate staff on hand. In addition, the staff failed to at least verbally answer an assistance light to inquire what the patient needed.

Postoperative Care

The patient in *Czubinsky v. Doctors Hospital*,[54] recovering from anesthesia, went into cardiac arrest and sustained permanent damages. The court of appeals held that the injuries sustained by the patient were the direct result of the hospital's failure to properly monitor and render aid when needed in the immediate postoperative period. The registered nurse assigned to the patient had a duty to remain with her until the patient was transferred to the recovery room. The nurse's absence was the proximate cause of the patient's injuries. Failure of the hospital to provide adequate staff to assist the patient in the immediate postoperative period was an act in dereliction of duty—a failure that resulted in readily foreseeable permanent damages.

Nursing Facility Staffing

Residents in nursing facilities must be under the care and supervision of a physician. Provision should be made by the facility to obtain the services of at least one physician to oversee the quality of medical care.

States are more exacting than Medicare regulations in expressing nurse–resident ratios. In *Koelbl v. Whalen*,[55] regulations requiring the employment of sufficient personnel to provide for resident needs in nursing or convalescent homes were found to be sufficiently clear to avoid their being held unconstitutionally vague. State regulations vary in the methods used to establish staffing requirements. State regulations often are developed to ensure that the resident receives treatment, therapies, medications, and nourishment as prescribed in the resident care plans; the resident is kept clean, comfortable, and well groomed; and the resident is protected from accident, infection, and so forth.

In addition to nurses and physicians, a variety of other healthcare workers in nursing facilities support the care and services provided to residents. They include dietitians, physical therapists, social workers, activity directors, and others. The members of this group have specialized training and usually are licensed or certified by the state to practice their specialties. They differ from the medical or nursing staff in that they may not be involved with all residents, but rather limit their activities to residents needing their special skills.

Deficient Care Given

In *Montgomery Health Care Facility v. Ballard*,[56] three nurses testified that the nursing facility was understaffed. One nurse testified that she asked her supervisor for more help but did not get it. The estate of a nursing home resident that passed away as the result of multiple infected bedsores brought a malpractice action against the nursing home. First American Health Care, Inc., is the parent corporation of the Montgomery Health Care Facility. The trial court entered a judgment on a jury verdict against the home, and an appeal was taken. The Alabama Supreme Court held that reports compiled by the Alabama Department of Public Health concerning deficiencies found in the nursing home were admissible as evidence. Evidence showed that the care given to the deceased was deficient in the same ways as noted in the survey and complaint reports, which indicated deficiencies in the home, including:

> [I]nadequate documentation of treatment given for decubitus ulcers; 23 patients found with decubitus ulcers, 10 of whom developed those ulcers in the facility; dressings on the sores were not changed as ordered; nursing progress notes did not describe patients' ongoing conditions, particularly with respect to descriptions of decubitus ulcers; ineffective policies and procedures with respect to sterile dressing supplies; lack of nursing assessments; incomplete patient care plans; inadequate documentation of doctor's visits, orders or progress notes; AM care not consistently documented; inadequate documentation of turning of patients; incomplete "activities of daily living" sheets; "range of motion" exercises not documented; patients found wet and soiled with dried fecal matter; lack of bowel and bladder retaining programs; incomplete documentation of ordered force fluids.[57]

The defendants argued that the punitive damage award of $2 million against the home was greater than what was necessary to meet society's goal of punishing them. The Alabama Supreme Court, however, found the award not to be excessive. "The trial court also found that because of the large number of nursing home residents vulnerable to the type of neglect found in Mrs. Stovall's case, the verdict would further the goal of discouraging others from similar conduct in the future."[58]

Duty to Provide Timely Treatment

Healthcare organizations can be held liable for delays in treatment that result in injuries to their patients. For example, the patient in *Heddinger v. Ashford Memorial Community Hospital*[59] filed a malpractice action against the hospital and its insurer, alleging that a delay in treating her left hand resulted in the loss of her little finger. Medical testimony presented at trial indicated that if proper and timely treatment had been rendered, the finger would have been saved. The U.S. District Court entered judgment on a jury verdict for the plaintiff in the amount of $175,000. The hospital appealed, and the U.S. Court of Appeals held that even if the physicians who attended the patient were not employees of the hospital but were independent contractors, the risk of negligent treatment was clearly foreseeable by the hospital.

Provide Adequate Facilities, Equipment, and Supplies

Healthcare organizations are under a duty to exercise reasonable care to furnish adequate facilities, equipment, and supplies for use in the diagnosis or treatment of patients. Buildings and equipment should be maintained and operated to prevent fire and other hazards to personal safety. Patient rooms should be designed and equipped for adequate nursing care, comfort, and privacy. Mechanical, electric, and patient care equipment should be maintained in a safe operating condition.

Driftwood Convalescent Hospital, operated by Western Medical Enterprises, Inc., in *Beach v. Western Medical Enterprises, Inc.*,[60] was fined $2,500 in civil penalties because of nonfunctioning hallway

lights and the facility's failure to provide the type and amount of decubitus preventive equipment necessary for resident care as required by the California Health and Safety Code. The regulations required that equipment necessary for care of patients, as ordered or indicated, be provided.

Though no evidence was introduced to show that the decubitus equipment had been ordered by a physician, the phrase "as indicated" supports an inference that when a patient's condition requires certain equipment, the fact that no physician has ordered that equipment does not relieve the hospital (nursing facility) of the responsibility for providing equipment necessary for patient care.[61]

Provide a Safe Environment

Organizations are encouraged to create and maintain a *culture of safety* in order to reduce the risks of patient injuries and deaths as a result of common mistakes. Patients expect hospitals to provide a safe environment for medical care. Although healthcare organizations are aware of where systems break down, evidence suggests that they have been ineffective in preventing patient injuries that are often the result of human error or just plain carelessness.

Develop a Culture of Safety

Implementation of the following suggestions will help hospitals move toward a culture of safety:

- Ensure that accountability and responsibility have been assigned for monitoring an organization's safety initiatives.
- Involve the medical staff in the development and implementation of systems that are designed to create a culture of safety.
- Educate all staff as to their individual roles in establishing and maintaining a safe environment for patients.
- Encourage patients to question their care. Provide guidelines in patient handbooks as to the kinds

---

🔘 NEWS *DISARRAY AT VA HOSPITAL DETAILED IN NEW REPORT*

At the main health-care facility for veterans in the nation's capital, doctors have had to halt operating room procedures and dialysis treatments in the past year because of the lack of supplies, nurses have frantically run through the facility hunting for nasal oxygen tubes during an emergency, and sterile surgical items have been left in dirty or cluttered supply rooms, according to a new report.

—Aaron C. Davis, *The Washington Post*, April 14, 2017

of questions that patients should be asking caregivers (e.g., I don't recognize this medication, is it new? What is this medication for? Did you wash your hands before changing my surgical dressing? Is my nurse, Ms. X, off today?).

■ Appoint a safety officer to oversee the patient safety committee and day-to-day safety activities.

■ Establish a patient safety committee with responsibility for oversight of the organization's patient safety program. The patient safety committee is a multidisciplinary committee that includes representation from administration, nursing, and medical staff.

■ Set up a dedicated, 24-hour-a-day safety hotline.

■ Establish a voluntary event reporting system. Educate employees and patients as to reporting options (e.g., telephone, email). Assure employees that there will be no retaliation for reporting patient safety concerns.

■ Implement lifesaving initiatives that include: (1) establishing a rapid response team; (2) improving care for myocardial infarctions; (3) preventing adverse drug events; (4) preventing central line–associated bloodstream infections; (5) preventing surgical site infections; and (6) preventing ventilator-associated pneumonia.

■ Use the online tools released by Agency for Healthcare Research and Quality (AHRQ) to assist in evaluating and improving safe care.

Physical Environment

Each organization is responsible for providing a safe physical environment for patients, staff, and visitors. Responsibility for this function is often assigned to an organization's plant services/engineering department. Among other duties, the department is responsible for the provision of heat, water, electricity, and refrigeration and for maintenance of the organization's equipment and physical plant. The duties of the department may vary depending on the size of the organization and a particular organization's facilities.

An organization can be subject to corporate liability if it fails to ensure a patient's safety and well-being. Healthcare corporations are liable for injuries to both patients and employees arising from environmental hazards. For example, the license of a nursing facility operator was revoked in *Erie Care Center, Inc. v. Ackerman*[62] on findings of uncleanliness, disrepair, inadequate record keeping, and nursing shortages. The court held that although the violation of a single public health regulation may have been insufficient in and of itself to justify revocation of the nursing home's operating license, multiple violations, taken together, established the facility's practice and justified revocation.

In the following *reality check*, management failed in its responsibility to provide a safe working environment for its employees. The case in point here is that environmental issues need to be addressed in a timely manner.

✅ WINDOWS WIDE OPEN

With windows wide open, what happened to the pharmacy employees who were exposed to carbon monoxide from the tailpipes of ambulances backed up to the open windows of City Medical Center's ground floor pharmacy?

During a tour of City Medical Center, Bill, the surveyor-inspector asked to tour the pharmacy as part of the survey process. He was taken to the ground floor where the pharmacy was located. He was escorted into the pharmacy by several hospital staff members assigned to escort him during the 5-day survey process and respond to any questions he might have. As Bill entered the pharmacy, he noticed a strong odor of exhaust fumes.

He observed that windows were open along the length of the pharmacy's outside wall. He walked toward the open windows and counted and observed 8 to 10 ambulances that were parked and backed up to the open windows, some with engines running.

The odor from the fumes permeated the pharmacy. He noticed the admixture room where IV solutions were prepared for patients. He noticed the windows were open in this room as well. The room was quite warm, as was the rest of the pharmacy. There were no intake or ventilation systems in place other than the hoods under which the staff worked. There were no air conditioning or air exhaust systems in the room other than the open windows. Bill asked the staff, "Do these fumes bother you?" They replied, "Oh no, we don't notice it anymore." Bill asked, "How long have these windows been opened?" Their reply, "Not sure. Several years."

After touring and speaking to the staff working in the pharmacy, Bill turned to the pharmacy manager and asked, "Have you ever reported this to your manager." She replied, "Yes, I have. But it gets too hot in the pharmacy during the summer to keep them closed." Looking at his escorts, Bill said, "This is not a good situation. Employees have been exposed to exhaust fumes for way too long. And it is likely that the exhaust fumes contain carbon monoxide. Everyone working in

(continues)

✔ WINDOWS WIDE OPEN
(continued)

the pharmacy needs to be tested for carbon monoxide poisoning. The windows need to be closed and the ambulances removed to a safer location. And the intake and exhaust systems need to be addressed." One of the escorts replied, "Mayor X will not be happy with this." Bill replied, "This is not about the mayor, this is about the people working here."

The following morning Bill was asked by his escorts to go back to the pharmacy for another tour. He agreed to go back. He was presented with architectural drawings prepared during the night addressing the air intake and exhaust systems flaws. Not only were the drawings prepared but the necessary construction work was completed, with air-conditioning and exhaust ducts installed. The ambulances had been removed to a more appropriate location. Bill looked at the escorts and pharmacy manager and said, "Your work has only begun. Everyone here needs to be tested, and if necessary, treated for carbon monoxide poisoning." The question is: After each survey, do hospitals actually follow through with recommendations for improving the working environment and protect patients, staff, and visitors from harm?

City Medical Center could be liable for any harm suffered. The seriousness is easy to understand; knowingly failing to address such issues in a timely manner is gross negligence.

Unsafe Walking and Driving Conditions

The plaintiff in *Lutheran Hosp. of Ind. v. Blaser*[63] crossed the street one evening after visiting her husband in the hospital and was hit by a car as she was walking up the driveway to the hospital parking lot. She was struck from behind when the car was turning into the parking lot exit. The patient and her husband brought a negligence suit against the hospital as a result of the injuries she suffered.

Drivers, in general, could not determine that the driveway was not an exit until such time as they were alongside it or were in the process of turning into the driveway. Each night, three or four cars mistakenly mistook the exit for an entrance. Outside visual cues actually drew pedestrians to cross the highway mid-block in order to enter the lot. Neither security guards nor the parking lot attendants had attempted to dissuade pedestrians from crossing the street mid-block. The superior court found that the funneling of pedestrians and vehicular traffic into the exit driveway created a dangerous condition that the hospital should have reasonably foreseen, and the court entered judgment for the plaintiffs. The hospital appealed, claiming that although it maintained the driveway, it did not have control over the driveway.

The Indiana Court of Appeals held that the accident was sufficiently foreseeable to require the hospital to protect its invitees from such a mishap. The hospital had a legal duty to exercise reasonable care for the plaintiff's protection. The hospital's failure to post adequate safeguards or warnings to pedestrians and automobiles against the use of the exit driveway as an entrance to the parking lot was the proximate cause of the injuries suffered by the plaintiff.

Construction Hazards

The nursing facility's operating certificate in *Slocum v. Berman*[64] was revoked for violations of nursing home regulations relating to construction and safety standards. The most critical issues related to the facility's structure, which was neither protected wood frame nor fire resistive as required by regulation. This was a violation that adversely affected the health, safety, and welfare of the occupants. It was determined that the nursing home could not be made reasonably safe or functionally adequate for nursing home occupancy.

Fire Hazards

In *Stacy v. Truman Medical Center*,[65] the patients' families brought wrongful death actions against the medical center and one of its nurses. The wrongful death actions resulted from a fire in the decedents' room at the medical center. On the day of the fire, Ms. Stacy visited her brother, Stephen Stacy. When she arrived, Stephen, who suffered from head injuries and was not supposed to walk around, was sitting in a chair smoking a cigarette with the permission of one of the nurses. Ms. Stacy also lit a cigarette, and because she did not see an ashtray in the room, she used a juice cup and a plastic soup tray for her ashes.

At approximately 5:00 PM, a nurse came in and restrained Stephen in his chair with ties to prevent him from sliding out of the chair. Before Stacy left, she lit a cigarette, held it to Stephen's mouth, and extinguished it in the soup tray. When Ms. Stacy left, she believed there were one or two cigarette butts in the soup container. She did not recall dumping the soup tray into the wastebasket.

Shortly after 5:00 PM, a fire started in a wastebasket in the room. There was no smoke detector in the room. Another patient, Wheeler, was in the bed next to the windows. When Ms. Schreiner, the nurse in charge, discovered the fire, she did not think Wheeler was in immediate danger. She unsuccessfully tried to untie

Stephen from his restraints. Then she attempted to put out the fire by smothering it with a sheet. When her attempts to extinguish the fire failed, she ran to the door of the room and yelled for help, which alerted Nurses Cominos and Rodriguez. After calling for help, Ms. Schreiner resumed her attempts to smother the flames with bed linens. Subsequently, she and others grabbed Stephen by the legs and pulled him and his chair toward the hallway. In the process, Stephen's restraints burned through, and he slid from the chair to the floor. Schreiner and her assistants pulled him the remaining few feet out of the room and into the hallway. Schreiner tried to get back into the room but was prevented by the intense smoke, flames, and heat.

After initially entering the room, both Rodriguez and Cominos returned to the nurse's station to sound alarms and to call security; neither attempted to remove Wheeler from the room. Both ran directly past a fire extinguisher, but neither grabbed it before returning to the room. After Stephen was removed from the room, Cominos entered the room with a fire extinguisher and tried to rescue Wheeler but was unable to safely reach Wheeler. Wheeler died in the room from smoke inhalation. Stephen survived for several weeks and then died as a result of complications from infections secondary to the burns he sustained.

The medical center's policy in case of fire provided for the removal of patients from the room and out of immediate danger first. In its fire-training programs, the medical center used the acronym "RACE" to describe the chronology of steps to take in the event of a fire.

R—Rescue or remove the patient first.

A—An alarm should be sounded second.

C—Contain the fire third.

E—Extinguish the fire last.

The medical center's written smoking policy at the time of the fire stated: "No smoking shall be permitted in the Truman Medical Center Health Care Facility except in those areas specifically designated and posted as smoking areas. This shall be the responsibility of all employees and particularly supervisory and security employees." Nurse Cominos admitted that she was a supervisor and that she violated this portion of the smoking policy on the date of the fire by observing smoking and the use of a juice cup for an ashtray.

On appeal, the Missouri Supreme Court held that a causal connection between the medical center's negligence and the patients' deaths was sufficiently established.

Testimony was offered that training received by the medical center's nurses was below the standard of care and that attempting to put the fire out with linens would also be indicative of a lack of training. The medical center's expert, Fire Captain Gibson, testified that throwing dry sheets on the fire would have added to the problem by fueling the fire. The jury could have found that if the medical center's nurses had been properly trained, they would have followed their training and prevented Wheeler's death by removing him from the room, in accordance with their training acronym "RACE."

Storage Hazards for Medications and Medical Gases

Employees should be warned of any unusual hazards related to their jobs. For example, pregnant employees may abort because of exposure to anesthetic gases in the operating or delivery room, or the fetus of a pregnant employee may suffer cell damage because of exposure to chemotherapeutic agents and radioactive materials.

An employee's skin condition was found to be compensable in *Albertville Nursing Home v. Upton.*[66] The employee had developed a severe skin condition on his hands and feet as a result of daily exposure to various caustic cleaning solutions that he used while performing his duties in the nursing facility. The court held that the claimant was entitled to disability benefits for a period of 26 weeks.

A plan for the handling, safe storage, and disposal of hazardous materials to prevent user exposure should include policies and procedures (e.g., receipt, storage, and disposal of hazardous materials); engineering controls (e.g., vertical laminar flow hood for the preparation of chemotherapy medications); personal protective clothing and equipment (e.g., masks, gowns, foot and head coverings, gloves); work practices (who, where, when, and how hazardous materials are handled); medical surveillance of those who handle hazardous materials (e.g., hazardous material handling history and exposure follow-up by employee); inventory of the location, use, and security of all hazardous materials; orientation, education, training, and annual updates; and maintaining readily available, up-to-date material safety data sheets in appropriate locations for all staff.

Refuse generated by healthcare facilities can be divided into five separate categories: (1) infectious, (2) biohazardous, (3) hazardous, (4) radioactive, and (5) general (solid) waste. Each category poses its own particular problems for receiving, storing, handling, and disposal.

✔ MONITORING CHEMOTHERAPEUTIC AGENTS

So there I was, inspecting a newly opened infusion center for chemotherapy patients. I was impressed with the state-of-the-art medical equipment, facility cleanliness, and expertise of the physicians and nurses. I complimented the staff as to the design, comfort, working environment, and calming decor for both staff and patients.

After reviewing patient records, I asked to see the storage area for chemotherapy agents. I inquired as to the dollar value of the medications stored in the refrigeration systems. The figure was well over $250,000. I then asked, "How do you monitor the temperature to ensure the efficacy and safe usage of the chemo agents." An engineer replied. "There are alarms and continuous temperature recording devices that chart temperatures 24 hours a day 365 days a year." I inquired, who monitors the temperatures when the infusion center is closed, such as on weekends." The engineer replied, "An alarm will go off at the main switchboard." I asked, "Can we test the effectiveness of this system without causing panic at the switchboard?" The engineer replied, "Sure. We test the alarm system quarterly but can test now for you." The alarm was tested and there was no response from the central switchboard. After some discussion the staff decided that the system should be tested on a more regular basis. The words are often heard as to the need for *continuous quality improvement*. The staff was pleased that they learned of the problem now before there was a bigger issue with the storage of the chemotherapy agents.

Failure to Educate Staff

The plaintiff in *Parris v. Uni Med, Inc.*[67] was admitted to St. Francis Hospital with a decubitus ulcer. While there, he used a Mediscus bed, which was designed with air pockets to prevent decubitus ulcers. Upon discharge on May 31, 1987, the pressure ulcer was healing well. The plaintiff was readmitted on June 15. At the time of the June admission, his pressure ulcer was healing. Four days later, a nurse noted that the ulcer condition had worsened and a new pressure ulcer had formed. The nurse noticed that the dressing on the first site was touching the metal frame on the bed, thus putting pressure on his sacral area. The nurse called Uni Med, and a company employee made adjustments to the bed. Despite the observed improvement in the pressure ulcers at the time of discharge, the patient deteriorated, and surgery was required. Evidence showed that the beds were not monitored

regularly and that the nurses were not trained to turn the patients or adjust or regulate the beds.

The plaintiff brought a legal action against Uni Med, Inc., for pressure ulcers he sustained during his hospital stay. The jury found that the inadequate pressure setting on the bed was caused by its being improperly set up, thus causing worsening of the condition of the ulcers, necessitating surgery. An appellate court agreed that failure to set the bed up properly was the cause of the patient's pressure ulcers and subsequent surgery.

Failure to Properly Maintain Equipment

Hospitals must have appropriate procedures in place for the proper selection, training, handling, storage, and maintenance of medical equipment. The plaintiff, Thibodeaux, in *Thibodeaux v. Century Manufacturing Co.*,[68] a nurse's aide at the Rosewood nursing facility, sued Century Manufacturing Company after she was injured while operating a Saf-Kary chair lift, which was manufactured by Century. The plaintiff was injured when the chair fell and smashed her finger when the chair's lifting arm failed. The failure occurred when a patient was being lifted from a whirlpool bath. The plaintiff alleged that Century manufactured a defective chair lift that was the cause of her injuries.

Century argued that the chair lift was not defective in design and that the failure of the chair was caused by air in the Saf-Lift hydraulic system, resulting from the nursing facility's lack of maintenance. The plaintiff's expert witness testified that after inspecting the equipment, he found that the accident was caused by the safety lock failing to prevent the chair from disconnecting from the lift. Century theorized that this lack of maintenance caused the whole lift apparatus, including the chair still connected to the lifting arm of the lift column, to rapidly descend on Irene's finger. Approximately 4 months before the accident, a Century-licensed service technician performed an inspection of the equipment. He found leaks of hydraulic fluid, deteriorating seals and rings, a corroded lift base, and an air-contaminated lifting column.

He took the chair lift out of service and recommended that Rosewood not use it until repairs were made to restore it to safe operation. These findings were communicated to Rosewood in writing. Rosewood did not make the repairs.

The trial court, on a jury verdict, found that the sole cause of the accident was a result of poor maintenance on the part of the nursing facility. The plaintiff appealed.

The Louisiana Court of Appeal held that the evidence supported the conclusion that the accident was caused by the nursing facility's failure to properly maintain the equipment and that the injury was not the result of poor design. The nursing facility had been warned by the manufacturer of the need for repairs on the chair lift but failed to heed that warning.

Contracted Maintenance Services

In *Palka v. Servicemaster Management Services*,[69] Servicemaster Management Services contracted with Ellis Hospital to develop and implement a maintenance program for the hospital. Servicemaster's duties included the training, management, and direction of support service employees, including the maintenance department. There had been preexisting wall-mounted fans that had been inspected for safety prior to Servicemaster taking over. The plaintiff, a registered nurse employed by the hospital, was injured when one of the fans fell from the wall onto her. She sued Servicemaster for negligence. The jury rendered a verdict for the plaintiff, and Servicemaster appealed, alleging that they had no duty to her. The appellate division reversed and dismissed the complaint. The nurse appealed. The court of appeals reversed the decision of the appellate division and reinstated the jury verdict for the plaintiff. Servicemaster, by its contract with the hospital, assumed a duty to act. Servicemaster contracted with the hospital to perform certain services and performed those services negligently, which caused Palka's injury.

Prevent Falls

Falls are frequent occurrences in healthcare settings. They can occur anywhere from the time of arrival to the time of departure. Maintaining a safe environment, as well as providing ongoing staff and patient education, can reduce the frequency of falls. The following cases describe some of the more common falls.

PARKING LOT. The plaintiff, Harkins, in *Harkins v. Natchitoches Parish Hospital*,[70] tripped on a piece of black vinyl garden border material, hidden in the grass, and seriously injured herself. Although the plaintiff had surgery, she never regained full use of her right shoulder. The loss of use was permanent, and the shoulder continued to be painful. On appeal, the court held that a hospital owes a duty to its visitors to exercise reasonable care commensurate with the particular circumstances. Harkins established that she fell because she tripped on the black vinyl plastic gardening border, which was partially hidden by the grass. It was up to the hospital to exculpate itself from this presumption of liability. The appellate court agreed

with the trial judge. The failure to either remove the vinyl or place warning signs was a failure to exercise reasonable care.

HOSPITAL LOBBY. The plaintiff in *Blitz v. Jefferson Parish Hospital Service District*[71] brought a slip-and-fall suit against a hospital, alleging that her fall was caused by loose vinyl stripping in the front entrance of the hospital. The plaintiff testified that as she walked across the lobby, her foot got caught in vinyl stripping. She contended further that the vinyl stripping was defectively installed and maintained. An expert testified that there was an insufficient amount of vinyl adhesive on the underside of the vinyl trim stripping in contact with the top of the terrazzo floor. The plaintiff filed suit against the hospital and was awarded $80,000 after a bench trial. The hospital appealed, contending that the finding of liability was erroneous and that the trial judge erred in refusing to accept several defense witnesses as experts. The appellate court held that the evidence supported a liability determination.

STRETCHER SAFETY. On June 14, 1986, Hussey, in *Hussey v. Montgomery Memorial Hospital*,[72] became ill and was taken to the Montgomery Memorial Hospital by his wife. Upon arrival, he was seated on a stretcher in the emergency department. The stretcher had no side rails. Hussey fell from the stretcher and suffered a severe head injury. Hussey was eventually moved by ambulance to another hospital, where he was diagnosed with a dislocated clavicle, laceration of the skin, and two fractures of the lateral wall of the right orbit. The plaintiffs alleged that on several occasions, they questioned Dr. Andrews, the attending physician, as to whether there was any permanent brain damage. On each occasion, Andrews answered that there would not be any brain damage. Two months after the fall, the plaintiffs consulted with an attorney concerning a possible claim against the Montgomery Memorial Hospital but decided not to pursue a lawsuit at that time because they feared doing so might impair the plaintiff husband's ability to receive medical treatment. For the next 3.5 years, Hussey continued to see his medical providers. No physicians ever disclosed to the plaintiffs that Hussey may suffer permanent brain impairment. By April 1990, Hussey's behavior became severely erratic and unpredictable to the point that Mrs. Hussey took him to Sandhills Center for Mental Health. Hussey was examined and transferred to the Dartmouth Clinic. A physician at the clinic informed the plaintiffs that test results indicated permanent and residual brain impairment. On June 12, 1990, the plaintiffs filed a complaint alleging negligence against the hospital. The hospital filed a motion to dismiss on the grounds that the action was barred by the 3-year statute of limitations.

The trial judge granted the hospital's motion for summary judgment, and the plaintiffs appealed. The appellate court held that the action was time barred. The statute of limitations accrued on June 14, 1986, the date of Hussey's fall. The head injury was not latent. Hussey had a cause of action on the date he fell from the stretcher. Upon falling from the stretcher, he suffered a severe head injury and was rendered unconscious. A treating physician in the emergency department advised Hussey's wife that swelling in the brain caused her husband's condition. The probable cause of the accident was the hospital's negligence. On the date of the fall, it was apparent that there had been wrongdoing, most likely attributable to the hospital. The ultimate injuries sustained by Hussey were a direct result of the June 14, 1986, fall caused by the hospital's wrongdoing. Hussey's failure to pursue a cause of action on this date *resulted in the tolling of the statute of limitations.*

SAFE USE OF RESTRAINTS. Falls by patients often involve mixed allegations of a failure to restrain, supervise, assist, or attend the patient. Some plaintiffs have argued that, although restraints were applied, they were improperly applied. The plaintiff in *Smith v. Gravois Rest Haven, Inc.*[73] brought a lawsuit arising out of a fall and subsequent injuries suffered by his 78-year-old mother. The plaintiff's mother required use of a "posey" restraining device because of previous falls in the facility. There was sufficient evidence to establish that the restraints had been improperly applied.

WINDOW SAFETY. The plaintiffs in *Horton v. Niagara Falls Memorial Medical Center*[74] sought recovery against the hospital for injuries sustained by the plaintiff patient's fall from a second-story hospital window. The patient had been admitted to the hospital with a fever of unknown origin and was noted to be lacking in coordination and blurred vision. The patient had been placed in a private room with a single window that opened to a small balcony encircled by a 2- to 3-foot-high railing. Prior to the patient's fall, construction workers notified hospital personnel that the patient was standing on his balcony calling for a ladder. The patient was confused and disoriented. On learning of the incident, the attending physician advised a nurse to keep the patient under restraint and to keep an eye on him. The patient's wife was called, and she indicated that her mother would come to the hospital in 10 to 15 minutes to watch her husband. The patient fell shortly before the mother's arrival. The Niagara Supreme Court entered judgment for the plaintiffs,

and the hospital appealed. The New York Supreme Court, Appellate Division, held that the hospital had a duty to supervise the patient and prevent him from injuring himself.

SLIPPERY FLOORS. Slippery floors are a major source of lawsuits. To reduce liability caused by falls, floors should be maintained properly. The following actions should be taken to reduce patient falls: floors should not contain a dangerous amount of wax; caution signs (e.g., indicating slippery floors) should be used when and where appropriate; floors should be cared for and maintained properly on rainy and/or snowy days; broken floor tiles should be repaired promptly; foreign matter should be quickly and completely wiped from the floor; signs, ropes, and lights should be used where appropriate; and precautions should be taken for outdoor walkways to guard against dangers such as icy conditions and construction hazards.

The plaintiff in *Borota v. University Medical Center*,[75] a hospital visitor, brought an action against University Medical Center to recover for injuries she suffered as a result of slipping on a puddle of milk in the hospital corridor. The plaintiff claimed that the spill appeared fresh and that there were several spots of milk on the floor and on the walls. She also noted that the corridor was well lit. The trial court granted summary judgment for the hospital, and the plaintiff appealed. The Arizona Court of Appeals held that the plaintiff did not establish constructive notice that would indicate that the hospital was aware of the spilled milk. Although it is the responsibility and duty of a hospital to keep its premises reasonably safe for invitees, the hospital does not ensure their safety. The hospital is not liable for the injuries sustained by the plaintiff unless she can establish that either: (1) the hospital's employees caused the spill and failed to clean it on a timely basis; or (2) the milk was there for a long period and the hospital had constructive notice that the spill was there and yet failed to clean it. The plaintiff failed to show evidence that the milk was spilled by a hospital employee or that the hospital was aware of the spill.

LOADING DOCK SAFETY. In *Glowacki v. Underwood Memorial Hospital*,[76] a nurse, while employed as a pediatric transport nurse, was transporting a critically ill infant from the hospital. An isolette was needed for this purpose, and the nurse was responsible for wheeling it to the ambulance. The ambulance arrived at the hospital and drove to the emergency department area where it backed up to a loading platform. The bumper was separated from the concrete loading platform by intermittent rubber blocks, which left an open space of approximately 3.5 inches between the bumper and the dock. The nurse and driver began the process of lifting the isolette up into the ambulance. During this process, the nurse's foot became wedged into the space between the wooden bumper and the concrete platform.

A civil engineer testified at trial as an expert on behalf of the nurse that it was unsafe to have a hole or gap in the bumper system. The hospital produced a civil engineer who testified that there was no standard in the industry applicable to hospital bumpers. He admitted that any design should consider the nature of traffic going over it. The hospital's director of plant operations conceded that the hospital was aware of the spaces in the bumper system, but indicated there had never been a report of an incident since it was built.

The court charged the jury on principles of ordinary negligence and the liability of a property owner to business invitees for a dangerous condition on its property. The jury was also charged on contributory negligence. The jury returned a verdict finding that an unsafe condition existed on the hospital's platform, that the hospital was negligent, and that the negligence was a proximate cause of the nurse's accident. However, the court also found the nurse negligent and was found to be a proximate cause of the accident. The hospital was found 85% negligent and the nurse 15% negligent. The defendant argued that the court erred in denying its motion for a new trial on damages because the verdict of $908,000 constituted a miscarriage of justice; was against the weight of the evidence; and was the result of passion, prejudice, sympathy, or mistake. The appeals court disagreed. The nurse's symptoms from the day following the accident to the date of trial 8 years later never changed.

Duty to Safeguard Patient Valuables

Appropriate procedures should be developed for handling the personal property of patients. A healthcare facility can be held liable for the negligent handling of a patient's valuables. The following points should be remembered and followed when handling the personal belongings and valuables of patients: send the belongings home when feasible; deposit jewelry, wallets, and other appropriate items in the facility's safe; select one department to handle valuables; provide proper communication between the department handling lost-and-found articles and the department holding patient valuables for safekeeping; encourage patients to keep with them as little money, jewelry, and other valuables as possible; establish a valuables

procedure for deceased patients, patients entering the emergency department, and patients scheduled for a surgical procedure or other diagnostic tests; and provide prenumbered envelopes that list those items placed in each valuables envelope. Verification of the contents should be made between the employee delivering an envelope and the employee accepting the envelope for safekeeping. A receipt should be given to the patient making a deposit. Strikeouts or corrections should not be permitted on the envelope; this will help prevent claims of mishandling.

▶ CORPORATE REORGANIZATION AND MERGERS

Traditionally, hospitals have functioned as independent, freestanding corporate entities or as units or divisions of multihospital systems. Until recently, freestanding hospitals functioned as a single corporate entity, with most programs and activities carried out within such entity to meet increasing competition. As competition increases, both stand-alone hospitals and smaller hospital groups continue to merge with larger systems. In 2015 there were 102 separate merger agreements involving 265 hospitals. As the number of health system mergers increases, the Federal Trade Commission will closely scrutinize proposed mergers for antitrust violations.

Dependence on government funding and related programs (e.g., Medicare, Medicaid, and Blue Cross)

> (NEWS) ***PENN STATE, PINNACLEHEALTH DROP MERGER AFTER APPEALS COURT LOSS***
>
> Penn State Hershey (Pa.) Medical Center and PinnacleHealth System, Harrisburg, Pa., abandoned their proposed merger in the wake of renewed regulatory opposition from the Federal Trade Commission.
>
> In September, the 3rd U.S. Circuit Court of Appeals revived the FTC's antitrust challenge to the proposed hospital merger, paving the way for an administrative trial probing the alleged anti-competitive effects of the deal. Rather than endure a long, costly battle with regulators, the central Pennsylvania health systems terminated their agreement.
> —Erica Teichert, *Modern Healthcare*, October 22, 2016[77]

and the continuous shrinkage occurring in such revenues have forced hospitals to seek alternative sources of revenue. Greater competition from nonhospital sources also has contributed to this need to seek alternative revenue sources. It has become apparent that traditional corporate structures may no longer be appropriate to accommodate both normal hospital activities and those additional activities undertaken to provide alternative sources of revenue.

The typical hospital is incorporated under state law as a freestanding for-profit or not-for-profit corporation. The corporation has a governing body. The governing body has an overall responsibility for the operation and management of the hospital, with a necessary delegation of appropriate responsibility to the administrative employees and the medical staff.

Given the need to obtain income and to meet competition, hospitals often consider establishing business enterprises. They also may consider other nonbusiness operations, such as the establishment of additional nonexempt undertakings (e.g., hospices and long-term care facilities). Because hospitals have resources, including the physical plant, administrative talent, and technical expertise in areas that are potentially profitable, the first option usually considered is direct participation by the hospital in health-related business enterprises. There are, however, regulatory and legal pressures that present substantial impediments.

Taxation

Income earned by tax-exempt organizations from nonexempt activities is subject to unrelated business income taxes under the Internal Revenue Code. These taxes are similar to those paid by for-profit organizations. Tax-exempt status may be lost if substantial portions of the corporation's activities are related to nonexempt activities and/or if the benefits of the tax-exempt status accrue to individuals who control the entity either directly or indirectly. Care also must be taken to avoid the use of facilities exempt from real estate taxation for nonexempt enterprises because this may lead to a partial or complete loss of such exemption.

Third-Party Reimbursement

Medicare, Medicaid, Blue Cross, and other third parties that reimburse hospitals directly for patient care require that no reimbursement be available for activities unrelated to the provision of such care. Thus, costs associated with unrelated activities must be deducted from costs submitted to third-party payers

for reimbursement. The "carving out" of these costs can be detrimental to the hospital unless alternative revenues are found.

Certificate of Need

Generally, hospitals may not add additional programs or services and may not expend monies for the acquisition of capital in excess of specified threshold limits without first obtaining approval from appropriate state regulatory agencies. The process by which this approval is granted generally is referred to as the *certificate of need (CON) process*.

The National Health Planning and Resources Development Act of 1974, Public Law No. 93-641, sought to encourage state review of all plans calling for the construction, expansion, or renovation of health facilities or services by conditioning receipt of certain federal funds on the establishment of an approved state CON program. Most states responded to this law by instituting state CON programs that complied with federal standards.

> Certificate of Need (C.O.N.) programs are aimed at restraining health care facility costs and facilitating coordinated planning of new services and facility construction. Many "CON" laws initially were put into effect across the nation as part of the federal "Health Planning Resources Development Act" of 1974. Despite numerous changes in the past 30 years, most states retain some type of CON program, law or agency as of 2016.[78]

The CON process can be lengthy and expensive. Furthermore, it may not always result in approval of the request to offer the new program or service or to make the capital expenditure. Healthcare providers have criticized CON requirements because they require review of those expenditures by or on behalf of a healthcare facility but may allow, for example, groups of physicians or independent laboratories to make large expenditures for equipment or services without triggering the state review mechanism.

Disapprovals of CONs often occur because they do not comply with state health plans that are designed to limit programs and services and prevent over-bedding in predefined geographic areas. Some CON applicants have attempted to seek revisions in state health plans to obtain approval of their projects. *Nursing Home of Dothan v. Alabama State Health Planning & Development Agency*[79] was one such case. The nursing home filed a CON application with the State Health Planning and Development Agency (SHPDA) to construct a 110-bed nursing home. SHPDA informed Dothan that the state health plan failed to indicate a need for additional beds and advised Dothan to seek an amendment to the state health plan before proceeding with the CON process. The defendant filed the proposed amendment with the state health coordinating council, which approved the defendant's request for additional beds. The amendment, which required the governor's approval, was rejected. On appeal of the circuit court's finding for SHPDA, denying Dothan's proposed amendment to the state health plan and subsequent denial of the CON application, the appeals court held that the governor properly disapproved the requested amendment.

Disapproval of a CON application also can be based on the financial feasibility of the project. A CON proposal to construct a long-term care nursing facility with 65% Medicaid beds was found to have been properly denied in *National Health Corp. v. South Carolina Department of Health & Environmental Control*.[80] The Department of Health and Environmental Control's decision was considered proper, reasonable, and consistent with applicable laws and regulations. The unsuccessful applicant, National Health Corporation (NHC), failed to establish its project's financial feasibility because of the unavailability of Medicaid funding. Discrepancies also existed between its budgets and its cost reports.

The record contained clear evidence that Medicaid funds would not be available for the NHC beds. The board also found that inconsistencies in four budgets submitted by NHC and the discrepancies between those budgets and the cost reports submitted by NHC to the state health and human services finance commission raised serious questions regarding the financial feasibility of the NHC project.[81] The agency's competitor had shown the financial feasibility of its project and was, therefore, granted a CON.

There can be disagreement among justices within the same court as to whether an applicant has established the criteria for need within a specific geographic area. The record in *Heritage of Yankton, Inc. v. South Dakota Department of Health*[82] was found to have supported denial of a CON application for additional beds based on the argument that there was no need for additional beds in the service area. The Department of Health was found not to have acted arbitrarily and capriciously in denying the application: it provided valid reasons for rejecting new information submitted at a rehearing. The Department of Health rejected an argument that a bed shortage in the county demonstrated a need for more beds. The department argued that it had never considered county boundaries in determining bed need and that the population of the facility's service area is the proper area for consideration. In view of its policy to maintain high occupancy rates in all facilities, the department also rejected Heritage's claim that the department's formula forces the elderly to be separated from their families and home communities.

Justice Henderson stated in a dissenting opinion:

This health care facility submitted three items of new evidence, which had not been previously considered. This consisted of population projections for the area and an in-and-out migration data with information pertaining to the existence of alternative services. The Department, summarily, expressed that it refused to consider this new evidence. Instead of opening its mind and then opening the door of reconsideration with relevant evidence, the Department of Health chose to be unyielding with its grip on the single formula and methodology it employed. If this health facility's evidence had been reconsidered, an open mind would see that there was an extensive need for beds existing in the city of Yankton and Yankton county. . . .

I cannot in good conscience, join the majority opinion which prevents elderly citizens from having a bed, with medical care and treatment, administered compassionately, in a community where their children and grandchildren reside. I would elevate reality over a single methodology and accordingly dissent.

"[T]herefore never send to know for whom the bell tolls; it tolls for thee." John Donne (1573–1631), Devotions upon Emergent Occasions, Meditation XVII. My mind drifts to Ernest Hemingway. And a clod of dirt. Chipped away at the shores of Europe by the sea. "If a clod be washed away by the sea, Europe is the less . . ." *Supra*. All from whence Hemingway's great novel was born. And, yes, not a person is turned away from a bed of repose, in his older years, but South Dakota is lesser in spirit. A refrain also comes to my mind: "And crown thy good, with Brotherhood, from sea to shining sea."[83]

Financing

Even when a hospital has determined that it can and should add a program or service and when it is allowed to do so, it may lack the necessary capital financing.

The hospital could partner with private investors (who may, in fact, be members of the medical staff) to gain greater access to capital. Care must be taken, however, that no venture that includes physicians who refer to the hospital can be construed as providing an incentive or a reward for such referrals. Federal antifraud and abuse laws and regulations and similar state regulations impose severe penalties for such violations.

Recognizing the need to develop alternative sources of revenue, hospitals often establish an additional or restructured organization. Besides the need to develop alternative sources of capital, some restructurings come about simply because of the evolution of a multi-institutional system. Thus, when hospitals merge or consolidate, restructuring is virtually automatic. Also, when several hospitals fall under common ownership or when additional health enterprises are undertaken, restructuring usually evolves as more institutions are added to the system. In these instances, general legal principles applicable to corporations, as well as proper management considerations, will control the development of the appropriate corporate structure.

Corporate Restructuring

Assuming the existence of a single, not-for-profit, tax-exempt hospital, any restructuring undertaken normally involves the creation of at least one additional not-for-profit, tax-exempt entity. This entity may be referred to as a parent, or holding company, or a foundation. Its general function is to serve as the corporate vehicle to receive the ultimate benefits from the revenue-producing activities and to confer some or all of these benefits on the hospital. Under current rules regarding income taxation, income received directly (by providing goods or services) or indirectly (by means of dividends or other investment income) does not give rise to any tax obligation if the receiver of such benefit is exempt from taxation under any of several subsections of Section 501(c) of the Internal Revenue Code, provided that exempt activities are the organization's main source of income and expense.

Parent Holding Company Model

Under this model, a new not-for-profit corporation is formed in conformity with the laws of the state in which the hospital is located. This corporation then can seek to obtain a tax exemption under the Internal Revenue Code. The overall purposes of the corporation are general in nature but involve a promotion of the health and welfare of the public and also may directly involve benefit to a named

hospital or hospitals. In some states, when one organization exists to benefit a licensed hospital, such organization must itself be approved through a CON or similar process. The government of the parent holding company usually is derived from the governing body of the hospital. Qualifications for certain categories of exempt status under the Internal Revenue Code may require overlapping governing bodies between the hospital and the new entity. Section 509(a) of the Internal Revenue Code deals with the qualification of a tax-exempt entity as a "private and/or non private" foundation. Nonprofit is the preferred status, and the qualification for such status may depend in part on the relationship between the entity seeking tax exemption and the already exempt entity (i.e., the hospital).

Because there is no stock involved in a not-for-profit corporation (the ownership of which would confer control by one corporation over another), control of the not-for-profit hospital by the not-for-profit parent holding company generally arises when the parent holding company is the sole member of the hospital corporation. Membership carries with it the right to elect directors and thus creates the necessary linkage for the parent–subsidiary relationship.

As a tax-exempt entity, the parent holding company also may own one or more for-profit subsidiaries. Although such ownership cannot represent most activities of the parent holding company, the ownership of such entities would not in and of itself disqualify the parent holding company from achieving and maintaining a tax-exempt status. It is through the subsidiaries that for-profit activities are carried on. The for-profit ventures (which may be independent corporations, joint ventures with other investors, etc.) are tax-paying entities. The net revenues (after payment of taxes) are paid out as dividends to the entity owning the stock or other ownership interest (the parent holding company), which, being tax exempt, pays no taxes on the receipt of such dividends. The parent holding company may then, as a donation, confer benefits directly on the hospital or any other entity intended to benefit from the parent holding company. Again, it is important to monitor closely the activities of this corporation so that its participation in or ownership of for-profit entities does not destroy its tax-exempt status.

Controlled Foundation

An alternative structure to the parent holding company model is one in which the new, not-for-profit entity is controlled directly by the hospital. Instead of the parent holding company being a member of the hospital corporation, the reverse is true. The hospital is the member of the new entity. The structure described earlier to carry out for-profit activities would then fall under the controlled foundation. In many states, the regulators would view such a controlled foundation as nothing more than the alter ego of the hospital and therefore impose on this entity all regulatory restrictions, reimbursement restrictions, and the like.

Independent Foundation

The establishment of a separate not-for-profit corporation and the substructure for carrying out for-profit activities may be accomplished independent of the hospital. Even though members of the hospital's governing body are involved in the creation of the new not-for-profit entity, the two corporations themselves may not necessarily be linked. This "brother–sister" relationship frequently is found to be desirable when the governing body of a hospital does not favor the creation of a parent organization to control the hospital but nevertheless seeks to create a viable structure within which for-profit activities may be carried on outside the hospital. A concern frequently expressed in this brother–sister relationship is that the new entity, not being controlled directly by the hospital, or in the alternative, not controlling the hospital, may "run away" and not necessarily ultimately benefit the hospital as was originally intended. Whether such a concern materializes is naturally dependent on the degree to which the governing bodies of the two organizations overlap and the degree to which each organization remains responsive to the other. The use of this model also may have certain reimbursement advantages regarding earnings on donated monies. If reimbursement regulations ever change to offset charitable gifts from reimbursable activities, an independent organization also may prove useful.

General Considerations

The organizational structures just described are not intended to alter the way a hospital is managed or the way care is delivered. The driving force behind the creation of alternative structures is the desire to develop alternative sources of revenue and/or to streamline management of multi-institutional systems. In many states, substantial changes in the governance of a hospital require regulatory approval. The establishment of the alternative structures previously described normally does not require such regulatory approval as long as the hospital continues to be governed by a governing body and continues to carry out its functions in accordance with applicable laws, rules, and regulations.

After restructuring has taken place, many additional entities will require legal and accounting attention. These entities (normally corporations) must maintain minutes, books, and records; file tax returns; and make other such filings as are required by state laws and by federal and state income tax laws and regulations. It is important that the structures be viewed as running independent of one another. This includes establishing separate bank accounts, holding regular meetings among officers and directors, and maintaining appropriate minutes. Too often, the activities and records of one entity are difficult to discern from those of another, and then the benefits of the separate organizations may be lost. The concept of "piercing the corporate veil" may come into play when each corporate entity is not maintained separately and apart from every other entity. The corporate veil will be pierced when a court determines that the activities of the corporation are indistinguishable from the activities of either another corporation or the corporation's directors, officers, or members.

The parent corporation in *Boafo v. Hospital Corp. of America*[84] was held not liable for injuries sustained by a patient at a subsidiary hospital. Even though the parent corporation shared some officers with the subsidiary and furnished it with substantial administrative services, there was no basis for piercing the corporate veil of the parent, absent some showing that the subsidiary was a sham formed for the purpose of promoting fraud, defeating justice, concealing crime, or evading contractual or tort responsibility.

Although the hospital was a wholly owned subsidiary of a national management corporation, it was a fully capitalized corporate entity that was insured, owned the hospital property, autonomously managed and operated the hospital on a day-to-day basis, maintained its own payroll, and employed its own employees. Therefore, there was no basis for holding the parent corporation liable.

Medical Staff and Restructuring

Any discussion of corporate reorganization undertaken by a hospital must involve the medical staff. Although reorganization may have little or no direct impact on the medical staff, the perception of major change requires, at the very least, a full explanation and involvement in the process.

Many hospitals have come to realize that the medical staff presents a fertile area for developing relationships and projects leading to additional revenues. Projects such as imaging centers, laboratories, and durable medical equipment (DME) businesses may be organized in conjunction with one or more members of the medical staff. Other likely candidates to participate in joint ventures include existing laboratories, home care companies, DME companies, drug companies, surgical supply houses, and the like. As previously noted, ventures involving physicians are closely regulated. Laws and regulations have been designed to curb the practice of physicians and other professionals from referring patients to facilities or enterprises in which they have a financial interest.

Joint ventures with physician groups are not without risk, as was shown in *Arango v. Reyka*,[85] in which a hospital entered into a joint venture with an anesthesiology group and thus was vicariously liable for the malpractice of the members of that group. The hospital billed patients for anesthesiology services, retained 12% of all collections, owned and furnished anesthesiology equipment and medications used by the group, scheduled patients, and referred to the group as the hospital's department of anesthesiology. As a result, there existed a common purpose to provide anesthesiology services to hospital patients. Control was shared between the hospital and the group over the provision of anesthesia services, and there was a joint interest in the financial benefits and profits generated by the combination of their resources and services. The physicians had an obligation to maintain control over their medical judgment, but this did not prevent the creation of a joint venture contract.

Development of a business involving equity participation must be considered in the light of state and federal securities laws and other relevant laws, rules, and regulations to determine that there is full compliance. Shares of stock, shares in linked partnerships, and other similar equity participation interests may fall within the definition of a public offering of securities, requiring filings and/or registrations under state and federal securities laws.

Fundraising

A not-for-profit hospital generally raises funds. Any new not-for-profit corporation formed as part of restructuring also may be able to engage in fundraising if such entity obtains a tax exemption under the Internal Revenue Code.

Also, as part of a reorganization and despite the creation of a new entity as indicated, hospitals frequently determine that it is desirable to create an additional foundation, the sole purpose of which is fundraising for the hospital. This, therefore, may lead to as many as three organizations with both the capability and the intent to engage in fundraising to benefit the hospital. Obvious confusion may arise in the minds of the public being asked to give to these organizations. A coordinated approach to fundraising is critical to avoid such confusion.

Any organization engaged in fundraising may have local filing requirements at the state or other governmental level. Care must be taken so that the public is informed completely as to the ultimate beneficiary of such fundraising and the manner in which the monies raised will be spent. A donor to a charity may have a claim against that charity if the donor can show that he or she was misled regarding the ultimate beneficiary of the gift or the purposes for which the gift would be used. Members of the public may be reluctant to donate when capital is to be used to fund for-profit enterprises. The overall charitable purposes of the entity must be carried out, and the activities may not be so concentrated on the operation or participation in for-profit ventures that either the tax exemption is jeopardized or it is determined (usually by the state attorney general) that the funds have been raised improperly from the public.

Regulatory Authority Checklist

When considering restructuring, the following regulatory authority checklist may be helpful:

1. Not-for-profit corporations

    a. Not-for-profit corporation law
    b. Internal Revenue Code (exemption and taxpayer identification number)
    c. State and local tax laws on exemptions (including real property)
    d. Attorney general or similar charitable registration requirements
    e. Bylaws, organization minutes, and minutes of the first governing body meeting
    f. Bank account

2. For-profit corporations

    a. Business corporation law
    b. Taxpayer identification number
    c. Bylaws, organization minutes, minutes of the first governing body meeting, and issuance of stock
    d. Bank account

3. Hospitals

    a. Reimbursement regulations
    b. CON regulations
    c. Governing body bylaws and relationship to additional corporations
    d. Fraud and abuse laws, rules, and regulations

Competition and Restructuring

Because an organization exerts a certain amount of influence and dominance over its patient population, the participation in for-profit enterprises to which an organization's patients are referred may give rise to anticompetitive activities and antitrust claims. Patients must be permitted free choice of goods and services. For example, if an organization (through its reorganized structure) participates in a DME business and seeks to recommend such business to its patients on discharge, these patients must be allowed to choose an alternate supplier and must be advised that they are not required to use the vendor recommended by the organization. An organization should disclose its relationship to the DME company so that the patient knows the organization's involvement prior to making a choice.

Care must be taken that local vendors and merchants who have a traditional relationship with the organization or with the patients are not so affected by the proposed for-profit activity that ill will is generated within the community, leading to a potential legal claim regarding anticompetitive activity.

Restructuring requires a multidisciplinary approach. The issues to be considered include legal, financial, accounting, tax, regulatory, and reimbursement concerns. These disciplines must provide input on an ongoing basis, not merely at inception. Changing requirements and interpretations—especially in the areas of taxation and Medicare/Medicaid fraud and abuse regulations—mandate a continuous process of review and modification so that desired goals are not subverted by legal and financial problems.

> Nonetheless, a word of caution. Today's ventures require additional planning for the possibility that some, or part, of an enterprise might ultimately be found illegal. Therefore, potential buyers, and hopefully arrangements with them, as well as appropriate dissolution and unwinding provisions, now more than ever, need to be part of the fabric and documentation of any new joint venture. As well, the documentation of existing ventures must be reviewed in the light of current considerations and where necessary, needed revisions crafted.[86]

The Department of Justice and the Federal Trade Commission (FTC) periodically issue policy statements designed to educate and instruct members of the healthcare community on issues surrounding mergers and joint ventures. These statements outline the analysis the agencies will use to review conduct that falls outside antitrust safety zones. Restructuring is a complicated and lengthy process that requires involvement by legal council familiar with corporate restructuring.

Restructuring and acquisitions can lead to collusive practices that are harmful to consumers. Such was the case when the FTC determined that the

Hospital Corporation of America (HCA), a proprietary hospital chain, violated Section 7 of the Clayton Act, as amended, 15 U.S.C. § 18 (1982), by acquiring two hospital corporations in the Chattanooga area, Hospital Affiliates International, Inc., and Health Care Corporation, for $700 million. HCA already owned one hospital in the area. Hospital Affiliates International held management contracts with two other area hospitals.[87] This, in effect, gave HCA control of more than 5 of the 11 hospitals in the Chattanooga area. The management contract with one of the hospitals was canceled after the FTC began investigating HCA's acquisition of Hospital Affiliates. HCA sought judicial review by petitioning the court of appeals to set aside the decision of the FTC. The court of appeals held that there was substantial evidence to support the commission's determination that the acquisitions were likely to foster collusive practices harmful to consumers.

Restructuring is an undertaking that requires careful planning and legal and accounting advice, and should be undertaken not because it is "fashionable," but rather because it will provide the hospital with opportunities not available under its current structure.

THE COURT'S DECISION

The evidence was sufficient to hold the hospital liable for medical negligence under a theory of corporate liability. The evidence established that the hospital owed a duty to the plaintiff to have an anesthesiologist provide or supervise all anesthesia care, including having an anesthesiologist personally present or immediately available in the operating suite. The hospital's breach of this duty proximately caused the patient's brain damage.

The hospital's anesthesia department policies and procedures required that an anesthesiologist perform the preanesthesia evaluation, that an anesthesiologist discuss with the patient the anesthesia plan, and that an anesthesiologist supervise a CRNA by being "physically present or immediately available in the operating suite."

According to Dr. Via, chairman of the hospital's anesthesiology department in 1991, he complained to Mr. Ciulla, who was in charge of the DAA contract, about the lack of proper CRNA supervision in the women's pavilion. According to Ciulla, he renewed the contract in conjunction with the hospital's medical staff. According to Via, the hospital's medical executive committee recommended to Ciulla that he not renew DAA's contract and that he seek another anesthesia group for the women's pavilion. The hospital's board of directors renewed the contract anyway.[88]

▶ CHAPTER REVIEW

1. The governing body of a healthcare corporation:

    - Is incorporated under state law.
    - Has specific duties that include holding meetings, establishing policies, being financially scrupulous, providing adequate insurance, and paying taxes.
    - Oversees and controls corporate activities.
    - Is legally responsible for establishing and implementing policies for the management and operation of the organization.

2. Authority of corporations

    - Express corporate authority is delegated by statute.
    - *Implied corporate authority* is invoked in cases in which authority not specifically granted in the articles of incorporation is required to carry out its purpose.
    - *Ultra vires acts* are those in which a governing body acts beyond its expressed or implied scope of authority.

3. Corporate committee structure

    - *Executive committee* has the authority to act on behalf of the full board.
    - *Bylaws committee* reviews and recommends bylaws to the governing body.
    - *Finance committee* oversees financial affairs and makes recommendations to the governing body.
    - *Joint conference committee* acts as a forum for discussion of policy and practice matters.
    - *Nominating committee* develops and recommends criteria for governing body membership.
    - *Planning committee* makes recommendations for the use and development of an organization's resources.
    - *Patient care committee* reviews the quality of patient care and makes recommendations for its improvement.
    - *Audit and regulatory compliance committee* assesses various functions and control systems of the organization and provides management with analysis and recommendations for activities reviewed.
    - *Safety committee* oversees the organization's safety program.

4. *Organizational ethics* describes the ethics of an organization and how it responds to internal or external circumstances affecting the organization's mission.

    - The Sarbanes–Oxley Act of 2002 was enacted to protect investors by improving the accuracy and reliability of corporate disclosures.
    - The act requires top executives of public corporations to vouch for the financial reports of their companies and encourages self-regulation.
    - Corporate compliance programs establish internal mechanisms for preventing, detecting, and reporting criminal conduct.

5. Corporate negligence

    - A corporation itself owes duties to the general public and to its patients.
    - Duties arise from statutes, regulations, principles of law developed by the courts, and the internal operating rules of the organization.
    - A corporation is treated no differently than an individual. If a corporation has a duty and fails in the exercise of that duty, it has the same liability to the injured party as an individual would have.

6. Respondeat superior (vicarious liability)

    - An employer can be held responsible for the acts of its employees.
    - *Joint liability*: all joint or concurrent tort-feasors are independently at fault for their own wrongful acts.
    - *Independent contractor* relationship is one in which the principal has no right of control over the way in which the agent's work is to be performed.

7. Responsibilities of the governing body include selection of a CEO; medical staff appointments and privileging; being financially scrupulous; requiring competitive bidding; avoiding conflicts of interest; providing adequate insurance; complying with law and accreditation standards; providing adequate staff; providing timely treatment, adequate facilities, and properly maintained equipment; developing a culture of safety; providing a safe environment; and safeguarding patient valuables.

8. Corporate reorganization

    - The need to obtain income and meet competition has caused hospitals to consider establishing business enterprises.
    - Restructuring of a single not-for-profit, tax-exempt hospital normally involves the

formation of at least one additional not-for-profit, tax-exempt entity, which may be referred to as a parent, or holding company, or a foundation.

▶ REVIEW QUESTIONS

1. Explain from where a corporation derives its authority.
2. Explain the difference between express, implied, and corporate authority.
3. Discuss corporate organization and committee structure.
4. Describe corporate ethics, the Sarbanes–Oxley Act of 2002, and corporate compliance.
5. Explain the terms corporate negligence, respondeat superior, and independent contractor.
6. Describe the duties of healthcare organizations, the CEO, and medical staff.
7. Explain the purpose of corporate reorganization and the process of restructuring.
8. Describe what is meant by *parent holding company model*.

▶ NOTES

1. *Denton Reg'l Med. Ctr. v. LaCroix*, 947 S.W.2d 941 (Tex. Ct. App. 1997).
2. Paul S. Davidson and Tera Rica Murdock, "Legal Duties and Avoiding Liability: A Nonprofit Board Member Primer," *Trustee*, American Hospital Association, June 10, 2013. http://www.trusteemag.com/articles/662-legal-duties-and-avoiding-liability-a-nonprofit-board-member-primer.
3. *Casey v. Woodruff*, 49 N.Y.S.2d 642.
4. *FDIC v. Stahl*, 89 F.3d 1510 (Ct. App., 11th Circuit 1996).
5. 543 So. 2d 209 (Fla. 1989).
6. 500 P.2d 335 (Ariz. Ct. App. 1972).
7. *Thompson v. Nason Hosp.*, 591 A.2d 703, 707 (Pa. 1991).
8. *Id.*
9. 211 N.E.2d 253 (Ill. 1965).
10. *Id.* at 260.
11. 272 S.E.2d 643 (S.C. 1980).
12. *Abraham v. Dulit*, 679 N.Y.S.2d 707 255 A.D.2d 255, 345 (1998).
13. 46 U.S.I.W. 2227 (Md. 1977).
14. 738 N.Y.S.2d 87, 292 A.D.2d 365 (2002).
15. *Id.*
16. Learn.org, "Do Hospital Administrators Need Licenses?" http://learn.org/articles/What_is_a_Hospital_Administrator_License.html.
17. American College of Healthcare Executives, "About ACHE," http://www.ache.org/aboutache.cfm.
18. Alaska Department of Commerce, Community, and Economic Development, "Statutes and Regulations: Nursing Home Nursing Home Administrators," December 2012. https://www.commerce.alaska.gov/web/portals/5/pub/NHAStatute.pdf.
19. New York State Department of Health, "Nursing Home Administrator," https://www.health.ny.gov/professionals/nursing_home_administrator/.
20. Massachusetts Executive Office of Health and Human Services, http://www.mass.gov/eohhs/docs/dph/regs/245cmr002.pdf.
21. National Association of Long Term Care Administrator Boards, "Exam info," http://www.nabweb.org/examinations.
22. *Id.*
23. *Id.*
24. Sec. 08.70.170.
25. 438 So. 2d 412 (Fla. Dist. Ct. App. 1983).
26. 665 F.2d 401 (1st Cir. 1981).
27. *Id.* at 402.
28. 430 N.Y.S.2d 402 (N.Y. App. Div. 1980).
29. *Feuereisen v. Axelrod*, 473 N.Y.S.2d 870 (N.Y. App. Div. 1984).
30. *Cliff House Nursing Home, Inc. v. Department of Pub. Health*, 463 N.E.2d 578 (Mass. App. Ct. 1984).
31. 1986 Wis. L. Rev. 339, 338 N.W.2d 855 (Wis. Ct. App. 1983).
32. 301 N.W.2d 156 (Wis. 1981).
33. 183 Cal. Rptr. 156 (Cal. Ct. App. 1982).
34. JUSTIA, "*Elam v. College Park Hospital* (1982)," http://law.justia.com/cases/california/court-of-appeal/3d/132/332.html.
35. 348 S.C. 549, 560 S.E.2d 894 (2002).
36. *Id.*
37. 394 N.E.2d 770 (Ill. App. Ct. 1979).
38. 540 P.2d 1398, 1400 (Or. 1975).
39. 130 Cal. App. 3d 970 (1982).
40. 538 N.E.2d 113 (Ohio 1989).
41. *Meyers v. Logan Mem. Hosp.*, 82 F. Supp. 2d 707 (2000). 26
42. 488 A.2d 858 (Del. 1985).
43. 502 N.Y.S.2d 1012 (N.Y. App. Div. 1986).
44. 88 Cal. Rptr. 86 (Cal. Ct. App. 1970).
45. 206 Cal. Rptr. 164 (Cal. Ct. App. 1984).

46.   Charlene Harrington, "Educating and Licensing Nursing Home Administrators: Public Policy Issues," *The Gerontologist* 30 (1990): 582.

47.   Robert Pear, "U.S. Recommending Strict New Rules at Nursing Homes," *The New York Times*, July 23, 2000. http://www.nytimes.com/2000/07/23/us/us-recommending-strict-new-rules-at-nursing-homes.html.

48.   Minority Staff, Special Investigation Division, Committee on Government Reform, U.S. House of Representatives, "Many Nursing Homes Fail to Meet Federal Standards for Adequate Care," October 28, 2002. http://oversight-archive.waxman.house.gov/documents/20040830112134-57472.pdf.

49.   Andrew Schneider and Phillip O'Connor, "Nation's Nursing Homes Are Quietly Killing Thousands," *St. Louis Post-Dispatch*, October 12, 2002. http://www.highbeam.com/doc/1G1-120058452.html (accessed September 16, 2010).

50.   655 S.W.2d 14 (Ky. Ct. App. 1982).

51.   *Id.* at 26.

52.   *Id.* at 26.

53.   396 So. 2d 406 (La. Ct. App. 1981).

54.   188 Cal. Rptr. 685 (Cal. Ct. App. 1983).

55.   406 N.Y.S.2d 621 (N.Y. App. Div. 1978).

56.   565 So. 2d 221, 224 (Ala. 1990).

57.   *Id.* at 223–224.

58.   *Id.* at 226.

59.   734 F.2d 81 (1st Cir. 1984).

60.   171 Cal. Rptr. 846 (Cal. Ct. App. 1981).

61.   *Id.* at 852.

62.   449 N.E.2d 486 (Ohio Ct. App. 1982).

63.   634 N.E.2d 864 (Ind. Ct. App. 1994).

64.   439 N.Y.S.2d 967 (N.Y. App. Div. 1981).

65.   836 S.W.2d 911 (Mo. 1992).

66.   383 So. 2d 544 (Ala. Civ. App. 1980).

67.   861 S.W.2d 694 (Mo. Ct. App. 1993).

68.   625 So. 2d 351 (La. Ct. App. 1993).

69.   634 N.E.2d 189 (N.Y. 1994).

70.   696 So. 2d 19, 83–97 (La. App. 1997).

71.   636 So. 2d 1059 (La. Ct. App. 1994).

72.   441 S.E.2d 577 (N.C. Ct. App. 1994).

73.   662 S.W.2d 880 (Mo. Ct. App. 1983).

74.   380 N.Y.S.2d 116 (N.Y. App. Div. 1976).

75.   861 P.2d 679 (Ariz. Ct. App. 1993).

76.   636 A.2d 527 (N.J. Super. Ct. App. Div. 1994).

77.   Erica Teichert, "Penn State, PinnacleHealth drop merger after appeals court loss," *Modern Healthcare*, October 22, 2016. http://www.modernhealthcare.com/article/20161022/MAGAZINE/310229954.

78.   Richard Cauchi and Ashley Noble, "CON: Certificate of Need State Laws," National Conference of State Legislatures, August 25, 2016. http://www.ncsl.org/research/health/con-certificate-of-need-state-laws.aspx.

79.   542 So. 2d 935 (Ala. Civ. App. 1989).

80.   380 S.E.2d 841 (S.C. Ct. App. 1989).

81.   *Id.* at 845.

82.   432 N.W.2d 68 (S.D. 1988).

83.   *Id.* at 76–77.

84.   338 S.E.2d 477 (Ga. Ct. App. 1985).

85.   507 So. 2d 1211 (Fla. Dist. Ct. App. 1987).

86.   Carl Weissburg, "Joint Ventures: To Be or Not To Be," *Federation of American Health Systems Review* 22 (1989): 50.

87.   *Hospital Corp. of Am. v. Federal Trade Comm'n*, 807 F.2d 1381 (7th Cir. 1986).

88.   *Supra, Denton Reg'l Med. Ctr. v. LaCroix.*

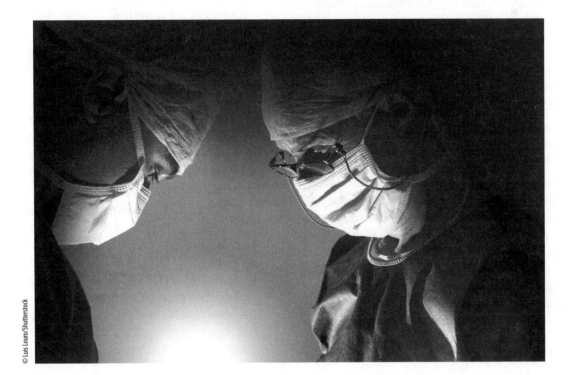

© Luis Louro/Shutterstock

CHAPTER 10

Medical Staff Organization and Malpractice

🔍 *RIGHT PATIENT, WRONG SURGERY*

The plaintiff was diagnosed with a herniated disk at L4-L5. His surgeon performed a laminectomy. During a review of the plaintiff's postoperative X-rays, the surgeon noted that he had mistakenly removed the disk at L3-L4. The plaintiff testified that after the surgery, his condition progressively worsened. The plaintiff's expert testified that removal of the healthy disk caused the space between L3-L4 to collapse and the vertebrae to shift and settle. Even the defendant's expert witness testified that the removal of the healthy disk would increase the likelihood that the plaintiff would be more susceptible to future injuries. The trial court directed a verdict against the defendant based on the defendant's admission and that of his expert that he was negligent and that his negligence caused at least some injury to the patient. The defendant appealed.[1]

WHAT IS YOUR VERDICT?

▶ LEARNING OBJECTIVES

The reader, upon completion of this chapter, will be able to:

- Describe medical staff organization and committee structure.
- Describe the credentialing and privileging process, and discuss the purpose of physician supervision and monitoring.
- Describe common medical errors involving patient assessment, diagnosis, treatment, discharge, and follow-up care.
- Explain how the physician–patient relationship can be improved.

This chapter provides an overview of medical staff organization, the credentialing process, a review of cases focused on the legal risks of physicians, and the principles of medical ethics. The medical malpractice cases presented highlight those areas in which physicians tend to be most vulnerable to lawsuits, with an emphasis on patient assessment, diagnosis, treatment, discharge, and follow-up care.

▶ MEDICAL STAFF ORGANIZATION

The medical staff is formally organized with officers, committees, and bylaws. At regular intervals, the various committees of the medical staff review and analyze their responsibilities, clinical experiences, and opportunities for improvement. The responsibilities of a variety of medical staff committees are described here.

Executive Committee. The executive committee oversees the activities of the medical staff. It is responsible for recommending to the governing body such things as medical staff structure, a process for reviewing credentials and appointing members to the medical staff, a process for delineating clinical privileges, a mechanism for the participation of the medical staff in performance improvement activities, a process for peer review, a mechanism by which medical staff membership may be terminated, and a mechanism for fair hearing procedures. The executive committee reviews and acts on the reports of medical staff departmental chairpersons and designated medical staff committees. Actions requiring approval of the governing body are forwarded to the governing body for

approval. Executive committee members generally include the chief of staff, medical staff officers, and department chairs. The chief executive and chief nursing officers are generally nonvoting members of the committee.

Bylaws Committee. The functioning of the medical staff is described in its bylaws, rules, and regulations, which must be reviewed and approved by the organization's governing body. Bylaws must be kept current, and the governing body must approve recommended changes. The bylaws describe the various membership categories of the medical staff (e.g., active, courtesy, consultative, and allied professional staff) as well as the process for obtaining privileges.

Blood and Transfusion Committee. The blood and transfusion committee develops blood usage policies and procedures. It is responsible for monitoring transfusion services and reviewing indications for transfusions, blood ordering practices, each transfusion episode, and transfusion reactions. The committee reports its findings and recommendations to the medical staff executive committee.

Credentials Committee. The credentials committee oversees the application process for medical staff applicants, requests for clinical privileges, and reappointments to the medical staff. The committee makes its recommendations to the medical executive committee.

Infection Control Committee. The infection control committee is generally responsible for the development of policies and procedures for investigating, controlling, and preventing infections.

Medical Records Committee. The medical records committee develops policies and procedures as they pertain to the management of medical records, including release, security, and storage. The committee determines the format of complete medical records and reviews medical records for accuracy, completeness, legibility, and timely completion. Medical records also are reviewed for clinical pertinence. The committee ensures that medical records reflect the condition and progress of the patient, including the results of all tests and therapy given, and makes recommendations for disciplinary action as necessary.

Pharmacy and Therapeutics Committee. The pharmacy and therapeutics committee is generally charged with developing policies and procedures relating to the selection, procurement, distribution, handling, use, and safe administration of drugs, biologicals, and diagnostic testing material. The committee oversees the development and maintenance of a drug formulary. The committee also evaluates and approves protocols for the use of investigational or experimental drugs. The committee oversees the tracking of medication errors and adverse drug reactions; the management, control, and effective and safe use of medications through monitoring and evaluation; and the monitoring of problem-prone, high-risk, and high-volume medications, utilizing parameters such as appropriateness, safety, effectiveness, medication errors, food–drug interactions, drug–drug interactions, drug–disease interactions, and adverse drug reactions. The committee also performs other activities that may be delegated to it by the medical executive committee.

Quality Improvement Council. The quality improvement council functions as a patient care assessment and improvement committee. The council generally consists of representatives from the organization's administration, governing body, medical staff, and nursing.

Tissue Committee. The tissue committee reviews all surgical procedures. Surgical case reviews address the justification and indications for surgical procedures. Representation on the tissue committee should include the departments of surgery, anesthesiology, pathology, nursing, risk management, and administration.

Utilization Review Committee. The utilization review committee monitors and evaluates utilization issues such as medical necessity and appropriateness of admission and continued stay, as well as delay in the provision of diagnostic, therapeutic, and supportive services. The utilization review committee ensures that each patient is treated at an appropriate level of care. Objectives of the committee include timely transfer of patients requiring alternate levels of care; promotion of the efficient and effective use of the organization's resources; adherence to quality utilization standards of third-party payers;

maintenance of high-quality, cost-effective care; and identification of opportunities for improvement.

▸ MEDICAL DIRECTOR

The medical director serves as a liaison between the medical staff and the organization's governing body and management. The medical director should have clearly written agreements with the organization, including duties, responsibilities, and compensation arrangements. State nursing home codes often provide for the designation of either a full-time or part-time physician to serve as medical director. The responsibilities of a medical director include enforcing the bylaws of the governing body and medical staff and monitoring the quality of medical care in the organization.

The medical director of an organization can be liable for failing to perform his or her duties and responsibilities. When a Texas nursing home was indicted by a grand jury in 1981 for the deaths of several residents, the medical director was also indicted.[2] His plea that he merely signed papers and attended meetings did not absolve him of the responsibility to ensure the adequacy and the appropriateness of medical services in the organization.

▸ MEDICAL STAFF PRIVILEGES

Medical staff privileges are restricted to those professionals who fulfill the requirements as described in an organization's medical staff bylaws. Although cognizant of the importance of medical staff membership, the governing body must meet its obligation to maintain standards of good medical practice in dealing with matters of staff appointment, credentialing, and the disciplining of physicians for such things as disruptive behavior, incompetence, psychological problems, criminal actions, and substance abuse.

Appointment to the medical staff and medical staff privileges should be granted only after there has been a thorough investigation of the applicant. The delineation of clinical privileges should be discipline-specific and based on appropriate predetermined criteria that adhere to national standards. The appointment, privileging, and credentialing process are discussed below.

Application

The application should include information regarding the applicant's medical school; internship; residency program; license to practice medicine; board certification; fellowship; medical society membership; malpractice coverage; unique skills and talents; privileges requested and specialty; availability to provide on-call emergency department coverage where applicable; availability to serve on medical staff and/or organization committees; medical staff appointments and privileges at other healthcare organizations; disciplinary actions against the applicant; unexplained breaks in work history; voluntary and/or involuntary limitations or relinquishment of staff privileges; and office location (geographic requirements should not be unreasonably restrictive; if the applicant does not meet the organization's geographic requirements for residence and office location, provision should be available in the bylaws for exceptions that might be necessary to attract high-quality consulting staff). Board certification alone is generally not acceptable criteria for determining eligibility for medical staff appointment.

> The primary function of physician board certification is to provide a platform for physician specialists to demonstrate a mastery of the core competencies required to provide the best possible care in a given medical specialty. The American Board of Physician Specialties (ABPS) governs 18 specialty boards that allow physicians to prove they possess the skill and experience necessary to practice their chosen specialties.[3]

Fellowship training and medical society membership are also not normally required for medical staff appointment.

Medical Staff Bylaws

The medical staff bylaws should be approved by the medical executive committee and governing body. All applicants for medical staff privileges should be required to sign a statement attesting to the fact that the medical staff bylaws have been read and understood and that the physician agrees to abide by the bylaws and other policies and procedures that may be adopted from time to time by the organization.

Physical and Mental Status

An applicant's physical and mental status should be addressed prior to the granting of medical appointments and staff privileges. Credentialed members of the medical staff should undergo a medical evaluation prior to reappointment to the medical staff.

Consent for Release of Information

Consent for release of information from third parties should be obtained from the applicant.

Certificate of Insurance

The applicant should provide evidence of professional liability insurance. The insurance policy should provide minimum levels of insurance coverage, with limits (e.g., $1 million to $3 million) determined by the organization.

State Licensure

A physician's right to practice medicine is subject to the licensing laws contained in the statutes of the state in which the physician resides. The right to practice medicine is not a vested right, but is a condition of a right subordinate to the police power of the state to protect and preserve public health. Although a state has the power to regulate the practice of medicine for the benefit of the public health and welfare, this power is restricted. Regulations must be reasonably related to public health and welfare and must not amount to arbitrary or unreasonable interference with the right to practice one's profession. Health professions commonly requiring licensure include chiropractors, dentists, nurses, nurse practitioners, pharmacists, physician assistants, optometrists, osteopaths, physicians, and podiatrists. A statute mandating that the Medical Board of California disclose to the public information regarding its licensees (Cal. Bus. & Prof. Code, § 803.1) and the statute mandating that the board post on the Internet information pertaining to its licensees (Section 2027) did not prohibit the board from posting on its website information regarding a licensee's completion of probation with a listing of the case number of the case from which the probation arose.[4] Grounds for the revocation of a license to practice medicine include: a clear demonstration of the lack of good moral character, deliberate falsification of a patient's medical record (to protect one's own interests at the expense of the patient), intentional fraudulent advertising, gross incompetence, sexual misconduct, substance abuse, performance of unnecessary medical procedures, billing for services not performed, and disruptive behavior.

National Practitioner Data Bank

Healthcare organizations must query the National Practitioner Data Bank (NPDB) for information on applicants seeking medical staff privileges and every

2 years on the renewal of appointments. The NPDB's principal purpose is to facilitate a more comprehensive review of professional credentials.

References

References should be checked thoroughly. Failure to do so can lead to corporate liability for a physician's negligent acts. Both written and oral references should be obtained from previous organizations with which the applicant has been affiliated. An action was brought against the hospital in *Rule v. Lutheran Hospitals & Homes Society of America*[5] for birth injuries sustained during an infant's breech delivery. The action was based on allegations that the hospital negligently failed to investigate the qualifications of the attending physician before granting him privileges. The jury's verdict of $650,000 was supported by evidence that the hospital failed to check with other hospitals where the physician had practiced. The physician's privileges at one hospital had been limited in that breech deliveries had to be performed under supervision.

Interview Process

Prior to interviewing the applicant, the following questions should be answered:

1. Have all documents been received prior to the interview?
2. Are there any unaccounted-for breaks or gaps in education or employment?
3. Has any disciplinary action or misconduct investigation been initiated or are any pending against the applicant by any licensing body?
4. Has the applicant's license to practice medicine in any state ever been denied, limited, suspended, or revoked?
5. Have the applicant's medical staff privileges ever been suspended, diminished, revoked, or refused at any healthcare organization?
6. Has the applicant ever withdrawn an application or resigned from any medical staff to avoid disciplinary action prior to a decision being rendered by an organization regarding application for membership?
7. Has the applicant ever been named as a defendant in a lawsuit?
8. Has the applicant ever been named as a defendant in a criminal proceeding?
9. Is the applicant available for emergency on-call coverage?
10. Does the applicant have back-up and cross-coverage?
11. Does the applicant have any special skills or talents?
12. Has the applicant reviewed medical staff bylaws, rules, and regulations, and, where applicable, departmental rules and regulations?
13. Does the applicant agree to abide by the medical staff bylaws, rules, regulations, and other policies and procedures set by the organization?
14. Is the applicant a team player? Can he or she work well with others?
15. Has the applicant ever been restricted from participating in any private or government (e.g., Medicare, Medicaid) health insurance program?
16. Has the applicant's malpractice insurance coverage ever been terminated by action of an insurance carrier?
17. Has the applicant ever been denied malpractice insurance coverage?
18. Have there been any settlements and/or judgments against the applicant?
19. Does the applicant have any physical or mental impairments that could affect his or her ability to practice the privileges requested?

Delineation of Clinical Privileges

The delineation of clinical privileges is the process by which the medical staff determines precisely what procedures a physician is authorized to perform. This decision is based on predetermined criteria as to what credentials are necessary to competently perform the privileges requested, including education and supervised practice to verify the skills necessary to perform the privileges being requested.

Limitations on Privileges Requested

Dr. Warnick, a pediatrician, obtained associate staff privileges at the Natchez Community Hospital in 1997. She later applied for full privileges through the hospital's credentials committee. Concern was raised about her alleged difficulty with the intubation of children. As a result, action on Warnick's request for full privileges was deferred. In May of 1998, the credentials committee recommended full privileges with the exception of neonatal resuscitation. After several in-hospital appeals, Warnick filed a lawsuit. The court determined that there was substantial evidence to support the hospital's suspension of Warnick's resuscitation privileges and her right to due process was not violated.

Hospitals licensed in Mississippi pursuant to statute are authorized to suspend, deny, revoke, or limit the hospital privileges of any physician practicing or applying to practice therein, if the governing board of such hospital, after consultation with the medical staff, considers such physician to be unqualified because of any of the acts set forth in Miss. Code Ann. § 73-25-93 (1998), provided that the procedures for such actions comply with the hospital and/or medical staff bylaw requirements for due process. In this case, the hospital and medical staff abided by the bylaws and requirements for due process, as evidenced by two hearings afforded to Warnick. She did not complain that she was unable to present all relevant evidence. Her claims were heard in a timely and meaningful manner.[6]

Practicing Outside Field of Competency

A physician should practice discretion when treating a patient outside his or her field of expertise or competence. The standard of care required in a malpractice case will be that of the specialty in which a physician is treating, whether or not he or she has been credentialed in that specialty.

In a California case, *Carrasco v. Bankoff*,[7] a small boy suffering third-degree burns over 18% of his body was admitted to the hospital. During his initial confinement, little was done except to occasionally dress and redress the burned area. At the end of a 53-day confinement, the patient was suffering hypergranulation of the burned area and muscular-skeletal dysfunction. The surgeon treating him was not a board-certified plastic surgeon and apparently was not properly trained in the management of burn cases. At trial, the patient's medical expert, a plastic surgeon who assumed responsibility for care after the first hospitalization, outlined the accepted medical practice in cases of this nature. The first surgeon acknowledged this accepted practice. The court held that there was substantial evidence to permit a finding of professional negligence because of the defendant surgeon's failure to perform to the accepted standard of care and that such failure resulted in the patient's injury.

Governing Body Responsibility

The governing body has the ultimate duty, responsibility, and authority to select the organization's professional staff and ensure that applicants to the organization's medical staff are qualified to perform the clinical privileges requested. The duty to select members of the medical staff is legally vested in the governing body as the body charged with managing the organization. In light of the importance of staff appointments, the courts have prohibited an organization from acting unreasonably or capriciously in rejecting physicians for staff appointments or in limiting their privileges.

Misrepresentation of Credentials

There was reliable, probative, and substantial evidence in *Graor v. State Medical Board*[8] to support the Ohio State Medical Board's decision to permanently revoke a physician's license for misrepresenting his credentials by claiming that he was board certified in internal medicine. The evidence submitted supported that, in many instances, the physician falsely indicated that he had American Board of Internal Medicine certification. The board contended that the hearing examiner addressed the physician's credibility and found many statements to support her conclusion that the physician intended to misrepresent his board status.

Appeal Process

An appeal process should be described in the medical staff bylaws to cover issues such as the denial of professional staff privileges, grievances, and disciplinary actions. The governing body should reserve the right to hear any appeals and be the final decision maker within the organization. A physician whose privileges are either suspended or terminated must exhaust all remedies provided in a hospital's bylaws, rules, and regulations before considering legal action. The physician in *Eidelson v. Archer*[9] failed to pursue the hospital's internal appeal procedure before bringing a suit. As a result, the Alaska Supreme Court reversed a superior court's judgment for the physician in his action for damages.

Reappointments

Each physician's credentials and departmental evaluations should be reviewed at a minimum of every 2 years. The medical staff must provide effective mechanisms for monitoring and evaluating the quality of patient care and the clinical performance of physicians. For problematic physicians, consideration should be given to privileges with supervision, a reduction in privileges, suspension of privileges with purpose (e.g., suspension pending further training), or termination of privileges.

▶ COMMON MEDICAL ERRORS

The NPDB 2012 Annual Report shows that between 2003 and 2012, the number of adverse actions reported to the NPDB related to physicians and dentists increased from 6,149 to 7,765, representing a 26% increase. The trend indicates that a small percentage of physicians are responsible for a large proportion of malpractice dollars paid to injured parties.[10]

This section provides an overview of some of the more common medical errors as they relate to patient assessment, diagnosis, treatment, and follow-up care. Infections, obstetrics, and psychiatry are discussed later in this chapter to introduce the reader to other common physician risks in the practice of medicine. As with many cases reviewed in the text, there are often multiple headings under which a case could be placed. For example, a poor assessment could lead to ordering the wrong lab tests, resulting in inappropriate treatment and follow-up care, which could result in patient injury or even death. It is important that the reader begin to critically analyze each case and see its application in the overall provision of quality patient care.

It is not enough to perform an assessment and order and get the correct lab test that supports a physician's order for a potassium infusion, which is started by a nurse. Quality care requires that each caregiver be aware of all the hazards that could lead to patient harm the moment he or she walks into that patient's room (e.g., is the infusion infiltrating the patient's tissue?).

The reader should keep in mind when reading this section that "Ethical values and legal principles are usually closely related, but ethical obligations typically exceed legal duties . . . The fact that a physician charged with allegedly illegal conduct is acquitted or exonerated in civil or criminal proceedings does not necessarily mean that the physician acted ethically."[11]

▶ PATIENT ASSESSMENTS

Patient assessments involve the systematic collection and analysis of patient-specific data that are necessary to determine a patient's care and treatment plan. A patient's plan of care is dependent on the quality of those assessments conducted by the practitioners of the various disciplines (e.g., physicians, nurse practitioners, dietitians, physical therapists).

The physician's assessment must be conducted for elective admissions within 24 hours of a patient's admission to the hospital. Emergency patients are, out of necessity, evaluated and treated promptly on arrival to the hospital's emergency department. The findings of the clinical examination are of vital importance in determining the patient's plan of care. The assessment is the process by which a doctor investigates the patient's state of health, looking for signs of trauma and disease. It sets the stage for accurately diagnosing the patient's medical problems. A cursory and negligent assessment can lead to a misdiagnosis of the patient's health problems and/or care needs and, consequently, to poor care.

Failure to conduct a thorough patient assessment and reassessment can result in disciplinary action against a physician, as noted in the following case.

🔍 *PHYSICIAN FAILS TO CONDUCT A COMPLETE ASSESSMENT*

Citation: *Moheet v. State Bd. of Regis. for Healing Arts*, 154 S.W.3d 393 (Mo. Ct. App. 2005).

Facts

J.D., a 40-year-old male suffering from high blood pressure, felt a sudden and severe headache while driving. Soon after he returned home, he asked his son Jason to call an ambulance. When the paramedics arrived, they took J.D.'s history, which included hypertension (high blood pressure), and a list of J.D.'s medications, one of which was to treat the hypertension.

The nurse manager of the emergency department, Bouldin, RN, was waiting to perform triage on J.D. when he arrived. Bouldin filled in an Emergency Room Record form (the "E.R. form") with J.D.'s vital signs. J.D.'s blood pressure was 170/130 at 4:50 PM. J.D.'s wife gave Nurse Brooks J.D.'s medical history, which in addition to high blood pressure, included depression, alcoholism, and left arm numbness.

Dr. Moheet was on duty in the emergency room that day. At 5:05 PM, Dr. Moheet began examining and taking a history from J.D. He observed that J.D. was lying on a backboard in a cervical collar, holding onto the side rails of the gurney, clenching his teeth, and going into spasms. When asked why he was in the emergency room, J.D. responded that he was having neck pain that radiated into the back part of his head. Dr. Moheet asked J.D. if he had hurt himself, and he said that he fell while sledding in the snow (referring to an incident the previous day when sledding with his children). He complained of numbness in the left arm. Dr. Moheet was hampered in taking J.D.'s medical history because J.D. was unhappy with the questions and repeatedly requested pain medication.

(continues)

🔍 PHYSICIAN FAILS TO CONDUCT A COMPLETE ASSESSMENT *(continued)*

Dr. Moheet checked J.D.'s breathing, pulse, lung sounds, and abdomen. He then did a neurologic check, which included checking his ability to feel sensations. J.D. had decreased sensation in the thumb, outer forearm, middle finger, and on the inner side of the left hand. To Dr. Moheet, these sensory changes suggested radiculopathy (nerve impingement due to a cervical disk problem). J.D. was given an injection for pain. Dr. Moheet sent J.D. for X-rays. Although J.D. had informed the nurse of a sudden onset of head pain, Dr. Moheet did not order a computed tomography (CT) scan of the head. J.D.'s reflexes were normal. When it was determined that J.D. did not have a neck fracture, the collar, cushion, and backboard were removed, and he was returned to the emergency room.

At 6:40 PM, Dr. Moheet again examined J.D. and checked his neurologic responses. At this time, J.D. was sitting upright on the gurney, and he told Dr. Moheet that he was feeling 50% better. Dr. Moheet told J.D. of his diagnosis of a C-6 radiculopathy (pinched sixth nerve) on the left side. He told J.D. that the X-ray was negative and that he was being discharged with a muscle relaxant and an anti-inflammatory painkiller. J.D.'s wife asked whether those medications would cause a problem with J.D.'s blood pressure. Dr. Moheet said they would not. Dr. Moheet did not consider this mention of blood pressure to be a reason to further examine the patient. J.D. was given a soft collar for his neck and was released to go home.

Dr. Moheet later charted his findings for J.D. based on his notes. Dr. Moheet did not know J.D.'s blood pressure when he treated him and did not review the ambulance records or the E.R. form. Dr. Moheet expected his nurses to inform him of any abnormalities in the patient's vital signs. J.D. did not inform Dr. Moheet that he had high blood pressure nor did he mention that he had stopped taking his medication.

At approximately 6:30 the next morning, J.D.'s wife found J.D. unconscious on the bedroom floor and could not revive him. An ambulance crew responded and took J.D.'s blood pressure four times between 7:16 and 7:50 AM. The readings were extremely high: 220/120; 200/128; 210/118; and 228/108. The ambulance crew gave J.D. a drug for hypertension and took him to the hospital.

At the hospital, a CT scan was taken, and emergency room personnel informed Dr. Boland, a neurosurgeon, that J.D. had an abnormal CT scan, was comatose, and needed emergency neurosurgical treatment. Dr. Boland diagnosed a spontaneous intraventricular hemorrhage in the fourth ventricle of his brain (a hemorrhagic stroke). The blood from the hemorrhage had clotted and blocked the flow of spinal fluid. The excess fluid in his brain built up tremendous pressure, causing J.D. to lapse into a coma. Dr. Boland believed that J.D. had already suffered the hemorrhage and had stopped bleeding by the time he arrived at the emergency room the first time and was seen by Nurse Bouldin and Dr. Moheet.

Dr. Boland told J.D.'s wife that J.D. needed an emergency procedure to avoid imminent death. His wife authorized the procedure. The procedure was performed in the emergency department due to the urgency. J.D. spent a week in neuro-intensive care, a week in a step-down area, and a week on a rehabilitation floor. At the time of the hearing, J.D. was deceased; but neither party has discussed whether the cause of death was related to the stroke.

The State Board of Registration for the Healing Arts Administrative Hearing Commission found cause to discipline Dr. Moheet's medical license by subjecting it to a public reprimand.

The pertinent parts of the Board's complaint alleged the following:

1. While J.D. was in the emergency room the day before the admission, licensee knew or should have known that J.D.'s blood pressure was very high.
2. Failure to ascertain a patient's vital signs, including blood pressure, in the practice of emergency medicine is below the standard of care.
3. Licensee's failure to assess J.D.'s blood pressure in the emergency room constitutes gross negligence.
4. Because of licensee's failure to assess J.D.'s blood pressure in the emergency room, J.D. was deprived of timely diagnosis and treatment of the bleed, reducing the likelihood of a favorable clinical outcome.
5. While J.D. was in the emergency room the day before the admission, licensee failed to do a complete physical examination of the patient.
6. While J.D. was in the emergency room the day before the admission, licensee failed to obtain appropriate laboratory tests.
7. Licensee's failure to adequately assess, diagnose and treat J.D. when he presented in the emergency room was below the standard of care for an emergency department physician.
8. Licensee's conduct, as set forth herein, constitutes incompetency and gross negligence in the practice of medicine.

Dr. Moheet appealed the decision of the Administrative Hearing Commission.

Issue

Did the Administrative Hearing Commission have cause to discipline Dr. Moheet's medical license by subjecting it to a public reprimand.

Holding

The Missouri Court of Appeals affirmed the Administrative Hearing Commission's decision.

Reason

Dr. Moheet had adequate notice of the charges against him in that he was fully aware of the link between his failure to obtain an adequate medical history and the possibility of harm to the patient. He had sufficient notice of the allegation of his failure to obtain an adequate patient history, and his own pleading showed that he knew the charges he would be defending against.

The testimony of the expert witnesses, combined with the other evidence in the record, constituted competent and substantial evidence to support the commission's finding of conduct that might be harmful to a patient. There is ample evidence in the record to support a finding of gross negligence.

To ensure a comprehensive process for assessing patient care needs, the organization should conduct a self-check that includes written policies and procedures that describe the requirements for screenings and assessments by profession. For example, criteria for nutritional screens and assessments should be developed and approved by the medical staff. Patients on special diets should be monitored to ensure that they receive the appropriate food tray. Functional screens should be developed and implemented that include a patient's neurologic and functional status (e.g., range of motion, strength).

Unsatisfactory History and Physical

Failure to obtain an adequate family history and perform an adequate physical examination violates a standard of care owed to the patient. In *Foley v. Bishop Clarkson Memorial Hospital*,[12] the spouse sued the hospital for the death of his wife. During her pregnancy, the patient was under the care of a private physician. She gave birth in the hospital on August 20, 1964, and died the following day. During July and August, her physician treated her for a sore throat. There was no evidence in the hospital record that the patient had complained about a sore throat while in the hospital. The hospital rules required a history and physical examination to be written promptly (within 24 hours of admission). No history had been taken, although the patient had been examined several times in regard to the progress of her labor. The trial judge directed a verdict in favor of the hospital.

On appeal, the appellate court held that the case should have been submitted to the jury for determination. A jury might reasonably have inferred that if the patient's condition had been treated properly, the strep throat infection could have been combated successfully and her life saved. It also reasonably might have been inferred that if a history had been taken promptly when she was admitted to the hospital, the sore throat would have been discovered and

hospital personnel would have been alerted to watch for possible complications of the nature that later developed. Quite possibly, this attention also would have helped in diagnosing the patient's condition, especially if it had been apparent that she had been exposed to a strep throat infection. The court held that a hospital must guard not only against known physical and mental conditions of patients, but also against conditions that reasonable care should have uncovered.

In another case, the physician in *Moheet v. State Board of Registration for the Healing Arts*[13] had adequate notice of the charges against him, in that he was fully aware of the link between his failure to obtain an adequate medical history and the possibility of harm to the patient. He had sufficient notice of the allegation of his failure to obtain an adequate patient history, and his own pleading showed that he knew the charges he would be defending against. The testimony of the expert witnesses, combined with the other evidence in the record, constituted competent and substantial evidence to support the commission's finding of conduct that might be harmful to a patient. There is ample evidence in the record to support a finding of gross negligence.

There was substantial evidence in *Solomon v. Connecticut Medical Examining Board*[14] to support disciplinary action against a physician where the record indicated that the physician failed to adequately document patient histories, perform thorough physical examinations, adequately assess the patient's condition order appropriate laboratory tests, or secure appropriate consultations. The Connecticut Medical Examining Board found that the physician had administered contraindicated medications to patients and did not practice medicine with reasonable skill and safety and that his practice of medicine posed a threat to the health and safety of any person. The board concluded that there was a basis on which to subject the physician's license to disciplinary action.

🔍 *CARELESSNESS RESULTS IN PATIENT'S DEATH*

Citation: *Gibson v. Moskowitz*, M.D., 523 F.3d 657 (2008)

Facts

Vaughn, an inmate of a correctional facility in Michigan, began acting strangely. Prison officials moved him from his prison cell to an observation room. There, he was placed under the care of Dr. Moskowitz, a psychiatrist. Moskowitz assessed Vaughn on a Friday and prescribed medication to treat schizophrenia. He then ordered continued observation over the weekend. There was no evidence in the record that Vaughn's abnormal temperature was addressed.

When Moskowitz returned to work on Monday, he learned that Vaughn's condition had worsened. Although Moskowitz left open the possibility that Vaughn might have a "heat problem," his plan on Monday morning was to "keep observing Mr. Vaughn" and to give the medication more time to work.

Vaughn's condition continued to deteriorate on Monday. At 12:30 PM, Foster, a prison guard, reported to the treatment team that Vaughn vomited in the bathroom after trying to drink a large amount of water from the bathroom sink. By Monday afternoon, Vaughn's room had reached 96 degrees. At the end of his Monday shift, Moskowitz concluded that "with cool temperature and more fluids Vaughn could be taken care of and . . . the dehydration could be prevented." Moskowitz's plan was to give the medication still more time to work, to transfer Vaughn to a cooler room, and eventually, to move Vaughn to a psychiatric hospital. Moskowitz "didn't feel that Vaughn's status was life threatening."

By the time Vaughn made it to a cooler room on Monday evening his condition had taken yet another turn for the worse. Vaughn began vomiting and dry heaving, both of which continued into the night until he died from dehydration early Tuesday morning.

Gibson, the representative of Vaughn's estate, filed this an action against Moskowitz and other defendants. The estate settled its claims against 14 defendants, with the exception of Moskowitz, for $600,000. The estate took its claims against Moskowitz to trial, and the jury returned a verdict against Moskowitz awarding Gibson $2 million in compensatory damages, later reduced by $500,000 to account for settlements with the other defendants, and $3 million in punitive damages.

Moskowitz conceded that Vaughn's medical needs had become serious by Monday, January 28, and he argued that they were not serious on Friday, January 25—when officials moved Vaughn to the observation room, when Moskowitz began treating Vaughn, and when the jury ascribed initial liability to Moskowitz.

Dr. Shiener, the estate's psychiatric expert, explained to the jury that the drugs Moskowitz prescribed to treat Vaughn's schizophrenia "also affect the part of the brain that regulates temperature." When patients on this type of medication are put into a hot environment, they develop a "positive feed-back," which means they can't convect the heat or get rid of the heat, and their body heats up out of control, which leads to a dangerous situation. Dr. Burns, another expert, corroborated Shiener's testimony by describing how some people cannot deal with heat as well as other people due to the impact on the heat dissipation center in their brains.

Vaughn had a weight loss of 42 pounds over several days, which lead to his death. A reasonable jury could find that Vaughn's medical needs were serious on Friday the 25th.

Issue

Did Moskowitz subjectively ignore Vaughn's medical needs? Does the evidence support the compensatory and punitive damages award?

Holding

The United States Court of Appeals, Sixth Circuit found that Moskowitz subjectively ignored Vaughn's medical needs and that the evidence supported the compensatory damages award.

Reason

A reasonable jury could fairly conclude that Moskowitz knew of and disregarded the risk to Vaughn's health. This was enough for Nurse Blankstrom to reach the conclusion—which she initially shared with Moskowitz at noon on Monday—that Vaughn was suffering from severe dehydration. She informed him that she had taken Vaughn's vitals, which were all abnormal. And she relayed her opinion that "the vomiting ultimately points to a possibility that he was becoming dehydrated."

Blankstrom also asked Moskowitz to examine Vaughn—which he did, concluding that the problem "was not the medication or symptoms or side effects from the medication" and she arranged for Vaughn's medical team to meet to discuss Vaughn's treatment. Blankstrom described for the team that Vaughn was exhibiting signs of dehydration and needed immediate medical help. And she asked Moskowitz to evaluate Vaughn one more time because Vaughn was deteriorating and might be dehydrated. Despite this request, Moskowitz never reexamined Vaughn.

Even if sufficient evidence supported the jury's liability determination, Moskowitz argued that the evidence does not support the amount of compensatory damages.

The district court was found not to have abused its discretion in letting this $1.5 million award stand. Vaughn's condition deteriorated over the course of several days, beginning late Thursday/early Friday and ending with his death early Tuesday morning. He suffered cramping, vomiting, confusion, delirium, and disorientation during this time. He did not sleep, he sweated profusely and he looked physically ill. His vital signs were all abnormal, and he lost over 40 pounds from the onset of his dehydration until his death. Along with this physical pain, his experts testified, Vaughn would have suffered extreme mental anguish. Moskowitz's failure to respond to Vaughn's deteriorating condition when others testified that Vaughn's condition would have been apparent and supports the award.

In the final analysis, failure to fully assess and timely reassess a patient's condition can lead to an improper diagnosis and treatment plan. The wrong assessment in this case resulted in the wrong diagnosis and treatment plan, ultimately resulting in the patient's death.

Assessment of Unconscious Patient

In *Ramberg v. Morgan*,[15] a police department physician, at the scene of an accident, examined an unconscious man who had been struck by an automobile. The physician concluded that the patient's insensibility was a result of alcohol intoxication, not the accident, and ordered the police to remove him to jail instead of the hospital. The man, to the physician's knowledge, remained semiconscious for several days and finally was taken from the cell to the hospital at the insistence of his family. The patient subsequently died, and the autopsy revealed massive skull fractures. The court found that any physician should reasonably anticipate the presence of head injuries when a car strikes a person. Failure to refer an accident victim to another physician or a hospital is actionable neglect of the physician's duty. Although a physician does not ensure the correctness of the diagnosis or treatment, a patient is entitled to such thorough and careful examination as his or her condition and attending circumstances permit, with such diligence and methods of diagnosis as usually are approved and practiced by healthcare professionals of ordinary or average learning, judgment, and skill in the community or similar localities.

Failure to Obtain a Second Opinion

Dr. Goodwich, an obstetrician and gynecologist (OB/GYN), in *Goodwich v. Sinai Hospital*,[16] had clinical practice patterns that were subject to question by his peers on a wide variety of medical matters. Dr. Goldstein (Chairman of the Department of Obstetrics and Gynecology) met with him on several occasions in 1988 regarding those concerns. It was suggested to Goodwich that he obtain second opinions from board-certified OB/GYNs; he orally agreed to do so. This agreement was presented to Goodwich in writing on two occasions in 1988. Goodwich failed to comply with the agreement, and Goldstein held a second meeting with him and his attorney in February 1990. As a result of continued noncompliance, Goldstein asked the Director of Quality, Risk, and Utilization Management to determine how often Goodwich failed to obtain a second opinion. The investigation uncovered several instances of noncompliance. Goldstein then met with Goodwich for a third time. Goodwich agreed that he would obtain a second opinion in high-risk obstetrical cases. Goldstein confirmed the agreement in writing on April 23, 1992.

Goldstein left the hospital in June 1992, and Dr. Taylor was appointed acting Chief of Obstetrics and Gynecology. He asked for a recheck of Goodwich's compliance with the second-opinion agreement. By January, the hospital appointed Dr. Currie as the Chief of Obstetrics and Gynecology. Because of Goodwich's continuing failure to obtain second opinions, Currie informed Goodwich in writing that pursuant to Article IV, Sec. 7C of the bylaws, rules, and regulations of the hospital's medical staff, his privileges were temporarily abridged. The letter also advised Goodwich that the medical ethics committee (MEC) would consider a permanent abridgment of his privileges. The MEC met and abridged Goodwich's privileges for 3 months. The abridgement of Goodwich's privileges was reported to the Maryland State Board of Physician Quality Assurance and the NPDB.

Goodwich appealed the MEC decision to two different physician panels and the hospital's governing board. Both physician panels and the governing board affirmed the MEC's decision to abridge Goodwich's privileges. Goodwich then sued the hospital for breach of contract, intentional interference with contractual relations, and tortious interference with prospective economic benefit after restrictions were placed on his practice privileges at the hospital. The circuit court entered summary judgment for the hospital on the grounds of statutory immunity. Goodwich appealed, and the court of special appeals held that the hospital acted reasonably, as required for immunity under the federal Health Care Quality Improvement Act of 1986. The record was replete with documentation of questionable patient management and continual failure to comply with second-opinion agreements.

Assessments Sometimes Require Referral to a Specialist

A physician has a duty to refer his or her patient whom he or she knows or should know needs referral to a physician familiar with and clinically capable of treating the patient's ailments. To recover damages, the plaintiff must show that the physician deviated from the standard of care and that the failure to refer resulted in injury.

The California Court of Appeals found that expert testimony is not necessary where good medical practice would require a general physician to suggest a specialist's consultation.[17] The court ruled that because specialists were called in after the patient's condition grew worse, it is reasonable to assume that they could have been called in sooner. The jury was instructed by the court that a general practitioner has a duty to suggest calling in a specialist if a reasonably prudent general practitioner would do so under similar circumstances.

A physician is in a position of trust, and it is his or her duty to act in good faith. If a preferred treatment in a given situation is outside a physician's field of expertise, it is his or her duty to advise the patient. Failure to do so could constitute a breach of duty. Today, with the rapid methods of transportation and easy means of communication, the duty of a physician is not fulfilled merely by using the means at hand in a particular area of practice.

A directed verdict for the defendants in *Vito v. North Medical Family Physicians, P.C.*,[18] following the plaintiff's proof, was found to be in error in an action alleging that the defendants were negligent in various aspects of their treatment of the plaintiff's lower back injury. The plaintiff established through expert testimony that the defendant physician failed to refer him to a specialist from 1996 to 2000 and that such failure was a departure from good medical practice and that the longer a herniation existed, the worse the prognosis. There is a rational process by which the jury could have found that Dr. Bonavita was negligent in failing to refer the plaintiff to a specialist to determine

the cause of his pain. The physician allegedly failed to keep proper business records and continued to prescribe OxyContin to the plaintiff, and this negligence caused the plaintiff's damages. The court denied the defendants' motion for a directed verdict, reinstated the complaint, and granted a new trial before a different justice.

Aggravation of Patient's Condition

Aggravation of a preexisting condition through negligence may cause a physician to be liable for malpractice. If the original injury is aggravated, liability will be imposed only for the aggravation, rather than for both the original injury and its aggravation. In *Nguyen v. County of Los Angeles*,[19] an 8-month-old girl was taken to the hospital for tests on her hip. She had been injected with air for a hip study and suffered respiratory arrest. She later went into cardiac arrest and was resuscitated, but she suffered brain damage that was aggravated by further poor treatment. The Los Angeles Superior Court jury found evidence of medical malpractice, ordering payments for past and future pain and suffering, as well as medical and total care costs that projected to the child's normal life expectancy.

The plaintiff in *Favalora v. Aetna Casualty & Surety Co.*[20] sued the hospital and the radiologist for injuries the patient sustained when she fell while undergoing an X-ray examination. The morning after her admission to the hospital, the patient was taken from her room in a wheelchair to the radiology department. When preparations for the GI series were complete, two technicians brought the patient to the X-ray room. She then waited for the arrival of the radiologist. When he arrived, the patient was instructed to walk to the X-ray table and stand on the footboard. The technician instructed her to drink a glass of barium. A second cup of barium was handed to her by the technician who then took the exposed film to a nearby pass box leading to the adjacent darkroom, obtained a new film, and repeated the X-ray process. While the technician was depositing the second set of exposed film in the pass box, the patient suddenly fainted and fell to the floor. The technician heard a noise, immediately turned on the lights, and found the patient lying on the floor. The patient was placed on the X-ray table, and X-rays were taken that revealed a fracture of the neck and of the right femur. As a result, a preexisting vascular condition was aggravated, causing a pulmonary embolism, which, in turn, necessitated additional surgery.

The failure of the radiologist to secure the patient's medical history before the X-ray examination was considered negligence, constituting the proximate cause of the patient's injuries. Although a defendant is generally required to compensate a patient for the amount of aggravation caused, it is often difficult to determine what monetary damages should be awarded.

▶ DIAGNOSIS

Medical diagnosis is not always an easy task. Making an accurate diagnosis involves the process of identifying a patient's illness. Patient assessments, reassessments, and test results (e.g., imaging and laboratory studies) are some of the tools of medicine that assist providers in diagnosing the possible causes of a patient's symptoms and medical problems. An accurate diagnosis provides the practitioner with alternative treatment options. The cases presented here describe a variety of lawsuits that have occurred due to misdiagnoses.

Failure to Order Diagnostic Tests

A plaintiff who claims that a physician failed to order proper diagnostic tests must show the following:

1. It is standard practice to use a certain diagnostic test under the circumstances of the case.
2. The physician failed to use the test and therefore failed to diagnose the patient's illness.
3. The patient suffered injury as a result.

Ophthalmologist Fails to Order Tests

In *Gates v. Jensen*,[21] a lawsuit was brought against Dr. Hargiss, an ophthalmologist, and others for failure to disclose to Mrs. Gates that her test results for

⦿ *HOW NOT TO BECOME A MEDICAL MYSTERY*

No one wants to be a medical mystery. But it's easy to become one.

While diagnosis may seem straightforward, the process can be surprisingly complex, strewn with cognitive land mines, logistical roadblocks, and red herrings. These complexities—and wrong turns—help create the medical mysteries.

—Tresa Baladas

glaucoma were borderline and that her risk of glaucoma was increased considerably by her high blood pressure and myopia. Hargiss failed to perform a field vision test and to dilate and examine the eye. He wrote off the patient's problem of difficulty in focusing and gaps in vision as being related to difficulties with her contact lenses. Gates visited the clinic 12 times during the following 2 years with complaints of blurriness, gaps in her vision, and loss of visual acuity. Gates eventually was diagnosed with glaucoma. By the time Gates was properly treated, her vision had deteriorated from almost 20/20 to 20/200. The court held that a duty of disclosure to a patient arises whenever a physician becomes aware of an abnormality that may indicate risk or danger. The facts that must be disclosed are those facts the physician knows, or should know, of which a patient needs to be aware to make an informed decision on the course of future medical care.

Once a physician concludes that a particular test is indicated, it should be performed and evaluated as soon as practicable. Delay may constitute negligence. The law imposes on a physician the same degree of responsibility in making a diagnosis as it does in prescribing and administering treatment.

Misdiagnosis of Appendicitis

Failure to order diagnostic tests resulted in the misdiagnosis of appendicitis in *Steeves v. United States*.[22]

In this case, physicians failed to order the appropriate diagnostic tests for a child who was referred to a Navy hospital with a diagnosis of possible appendicitis. Judgment in this case was entered against the United States, on behalf of the U.S. Navy, for medical expenses and for pain and suffering. The patient was given a test that indicated a high white blood cell count. A consultation sheet was given to the mother, indicating the possible diagnosis. The physician who examined the patient at the Navy hospital performed no tests, failed to diagnose the patient's condition, and sent him home at 5:02 PM, some 32 minutes after his arrival on July 21. The patient was returned to the emergency department on July 22, at about 2:30 AM, and was once again sent home by an intern who diagnosed the patient's condition as gastroenteritis. No diagnostic tests were ordered. The patient was returned to the Navy hospital on July 23, at which time diagnostic tests were performed. The patient was subsequently operated on and found to have a ruptured appendix.

Holding the Navy hospital liable for the negligence of the physicians who acted as its agents, the court pointed out that a wrong diagnosis will not in and of itself support a verdict of liability in a lawsuit. However, a physician must use ordinary care in making a diagnosis. Only where a patient is examined adequately is there no liability for an erroneous diagnosis. In this instance, the physicians' failure to perform further laboratory tests the first two times the child was brought to the emergency department was found to be a breach of good medical practice.

Efficacy of Test Questioned

A medical malpractice action was brought against Mambu in *Sacks v. Mambu*[23] for failure to make a timely diagnosis of Sacks's colon cancer. It was alleged that Mambu was negligent in that he failed to properly screen Sacks for fecal occult blood to determine whether there was blood in the colon.

Because of complaints of fatigue by the patient, Mambu ordered blood tests that revealed a normal hemoglobin, the results of which suggested that Sacks had not been losing blood. However, by late July 1984, Sacks experienced symptoms of jaundice. Mambu ordered an ultrasound test, and Sacks was subsequently diagnosed with a tumor of the liver. He was admitted to the hospital and diagnosed with having colon cancer. By the time the cancer was detected, it had invaded the wall of the bowel and had metastasized to the liver. Sacks died in March 1985.

The trial court entered judgment on a jury verdict for Mambu, and the plaintiff appealed. The Pennsylvania Superior Court upheld the decision of the trial court. The jury determined that the physician's failure to administer the test had not increased the risk of harm by allowing the cancer to metastasize to the liver before discovery and, therefore, was not a substantial factor in causing the patient's death. Although the presence of blood in the stool may be suggestive of polyps, cancer, and a variety of other diseases, not all polyps and cancers bleed. Physicians are therefore in disagreement as to the efficacy of the test.

In another case, at the age of five the plaintiff began to complain about chest pains and trouble breathing. The symptoms reported and the initial testing suggested that the plaintiff either had asthma or cystic fibrosis. Without further testing, the plaintiff's physician reached a diagnosis of cystic fibrosis and ordered treatment based on that diagnosis. Treatment included daily prescription medication and over 3,000 hours of painful percussion and vibration chest therapy. During percussion and vibration therapy a machine was used to palpitate the chest of the plaintiff in order to break up any secretions in the lungs and clear his airways for improved breathing.

In addition to the treatment, the diagnosis took a psychological toll on the patient. The patient was told that he would never be able to have children, his life expectancy was approximately 30 years, and he would eventually have to undergo lung transplant surgery. When the plaintiff entered his preteen years his parents began to question the diagnosis and educated themselves on the disease.

After reaching out to the physician multiple times with no response, the parents decided to get a second opinion from a consulting physician. The consulting physician ordered a new test specifically to diagnose cystic fibrosis. The new test came back negative. In the opinion of the consulting physician the plaintiff was never appropriately tested and did not have cystic fibrosis. In this case the jury found in favor of the plaintiff, and awarded him $2 million, which was the cap on medical malpractice damages at the time in Virginia.[24]

Failure to Promptly Review Test Results

Can a physician's failure to promptly review test results be the proximate cause of a patient's injuries? The answer is yes. In *Smith v. U.S. Department of Veterans Affairs*,[25] the plaintiff, Smith, was first diagnosed as having schizophrenia in 1972.

He had been admitted to the Veterans Affairs (VA) hospital psychiatric ward 15 times since 1972. His admissions grew longer and more frequent as time passed. On the occasion of his March 17, 1990, admission, he had been drinking in a bar, got into a fight, and was eventually taken to the VA hospital. Dr. Rizk was assigned as Smith's attending physician. Smith developed an acute problem with his respiration and level of consciousness. It was determined that his psychiatric medications were responsible for his condition. Some medications were discontinued, and others were reduced. An improvement in his condition was noted.

By March 23, Smith began to complain of pain in his shoulders and neck. He attributed the pain to more than 20 years of service as a letter carrier and to osteoarthritis. His medical record indicated that he had similar complaints in the past. A rheumatology consultation was requested and carried out on March 29. The rheumatology resident conducted an examination and noted that Smith reported bilateral shoulder pain increasing with activity as an ongoing problem since 1979. Various tests were ordered, including an erythrocyte sedimentation rate (ESR).

Smith was incontinent and complained of shoulder pain. By the afternoon, he was out of restraints, walked to the shower, and bathed himself. On returning to his room, he claimed that he could not get into bed. He was given a pillow and slept on the floor. By the morning of April 4, Smith was lying on the floor in urine and complaining of numbness. His failure to move was attributed to his psychosis. By evening, it was noted that Smith could not lift himself and would not use his hands.

On April 5, a medical student noted that Smith was having difficulty breathing and called for a pulmonary consultation. By evening, Smith was either unwilling or unable to grasp a nurse's hand and continued to complain that his legs would not hold him up.

On the morning of April 6, Smith was complaining that his neck and back hurt and that he had no feeling in his legs and feet. Later that day, a medical student noted that the results of Smith's ESR was 110 (more than twice the normal rate for a man his age). His white blood cell count was 18.1, also well above the normal rate. A staff member noted on the medical record that Smith had been unable to move his extremities for approximately 5 days. A psychiatric resident noted that Smith had been incontinent for 3 days and had a fever of 101.1°F.

On the morning of April 7, Smith was taken to University Hospital for magnetic resonance imaging of his neck. Imaging revealed a mass subsequently identified as a spinal epidural abscess. By the time it was excised, it had been pressing on his spinal cord too long for any spinal function to remain below vertebrae 4 and 5.

The plaintiff brought suit alleging that the physicians' failure to promptly review his test results was the proximate cause of his paralysis. Following a bench trial, the U.S. District Court agreed, holding that the negligent failure of physicians to promptly review laboratory test results was the proximate cause of the plaintiff's quadriplegia.

Of primary importance was the plaintiff's ESR of 110; the test results were available on the patient care unit by April 2 but were not seen, or at least not noted in the record, until April 6. An elevated ESR generally accounts for one of three problems: infection, cancer, or a connective tissue disorder. Most experts agreed that, at the very least, a repeat ESR should have been ordered. The VA's care of the plaintiff fell below the reasonable standard of care in that no one read the laboratory results until April 6. The fact that the tests were ordered mandates the immediate review of the results. Although it cannot be known with certainty what would have occurred had the ESR been read and acted upon on April 2, it is certain that the plaintiff had a chance to fully recover from his infection. By April 6, that chance was gone.

Due to the absence of notes from Rizk in the plaintiff's chart, it is impossible to know whether Rizk was aware of the plaintiff's symptoms. However, it appears that the absence of notes by Rizk indicated that Rizk's care of the plaintiff was negligent, and the failure to review the lab results constituted negligence under the relevant standard of care. That led to the failure to make an early diagnosis of the plaintiff's epidural abscess, which was the proximate cause of the patient's eventual paralysis. It was foreseeable that ignoring a high ESR could lead to serious injury.

A mechanism should be in place to expeditiously notify the patient's physician of abnormal test results. Computer systems help ensure physicians are notified of critical lab data so that appropriate care decisions can be implemented.

Timely Diagnosis

A physician can be liable for reducing a patient's chances for survival. The timely diagnosis of a patient's condition is as important as the need to accurately diagnose a patient's injury or disease. Failure to do so can constitute malpractice if a patient suffers injury as a result of such failure.

Failure to Read X-Ray Report

On February 5, 1988, Mr. Griffett was taken to the emergency department with a complaint of abdominal pain.[26] Two emergency department physicians evaluated him and ordered X-rays, including a chest X-ray. Dr. Bridges, a radiologist, reviewed the chest X-ray and noted in his written report that there was an abnormal density present in the upper lobe of Griffett's right lung.

Griffett was referred to Dr. Ryan, a gastroenterologist, for follow-up care. Ryan admitted Griffett to the hospital for a 24-hour period and then discharged him without having reviewed the radiology report of the February 5 chest X-ray. On March 1, 1988, Griffett continued to experience intermittent pain. A nurse in Ryan's office suggested that Griffett go to the hospital emergency department if his pain became persistent.

In November 1989, Dr. Baker examined Griffett, who was complaining of pain in his right shoulder. Baker diagnosed Griffett's condition as being cancer of the upper lobe of his right lung. The abnormal density on the February 5, 1988, chest X-ray was a cancerous tumor that had doubled in size from the time it had been first observed. The tumor was surgically removed in February 1990; however, Griffett died in September 1990.

Dr. Muller, an internist and expert witness for the plaintiff, testified that Griffett would have had a greater likelihood of survival if Ryan had made an earlier diagnosis. The defendants objected to Muller's testimony, arguing that the plaintiff failed to establish that Muller was an expert witness capable of testifying as to the proximate cause of Griffett's alleged shorter life span.

The trial court initially overruled the defendants' objection to Muller's testimony. The jury returned a verdict for the plaintiff in the amount of $500,000. On a motion from the defendants, the trial court set aside the verdict, ruling that it erred by allowing Muller to testify as to causation.

The plaintiff appealed, and the Virginia Supreme Court held that the plaintiff had sufficiently identified

🔍 WRONGFUL DEATH

Citation: *Powell v. Margileth*, 524 S.E.2d 434 (Va. 2000)

Facts

On January 9, 1992, Dr. Massey, a specialist in otolaryngology, measured a node in Mr. Powell's neck as 4 cm by 3 cm and ordered a CT scan. The CT scan conducted on January 11, 1992, indicated that the size of the left cervical mass was a result of an enlarged internal jugular node, which most likely was an abscess. On January 14, 1992, Massey aspirated fluid from the enlarged node. Although he discussed the CT scan with Powell and ordered cultures, he did not suggest a need for an examination to rule out cancer. Because Powell told Massey that he had experienced some exposure to cats, Massey referred Powell to Dr. Margileth, an infectious disease specialist experienced in the diagnosis and treatment of cat scratch disease. On January 27, 1992, Margileth performed tests for tuberculosis and cat scratch disease and measured the swelling in the left anterior-superior neck. He advised Powell that he had cat scratch disease and prescribed antibiotics. The results of the CT scan had been furnished to Margileth.

On February 18, 1992, Massey palpitated the nodule in Powell's neck, which measured 4 cm × 3 cm × 2.8 cm. Massey performed another examination on April 7, 1992, during the course of which he suggested the possibility of cancer.

In June 1992, Powell discovered a second lump in his neck and, in July, went for help to the VA Medical Center Hospital. A needle aspiration of the two lumps resulted in the diagnosis of cancer, representing a progression from stage III in January 1992 when the CT scan was conducted, to stage IV in July 1992. Powell underwent radiation therapy, surgery, and other treatment but died of cancer 3 years later at the age of 40.

The trial court held that there was not sufficient evidence that would allow a jury of reasonable persons to conclude that the defendant's breach of the standard of care (1) proximately caused Powell's injuries; (2) adversely altered the required method of treatment; or (3) adversely affected Powell's lifespan.

Issue

Did the trial court err in granting the defendant's motion to strike the plaintiff's evidence?

Holding

The appeals court ruled that there was adequate evidence that would allow a jury of reasonable persons to conclude that the defendant's breach of the standard of care proximately caused the decedent's injuries. The case was remanded for a new trial.

Reason

Dr. Holder, one of the plaintiff's expert witnesses, testified that the defendant's misdiagnosis of cat scratch disease caused his patient delay in diagnosis and treatment of his cancer from January until July and that if Powell had been informed of the possibility of cancer in January and options were offered in terms of biopsy for fine-needle aspirations, then Powell would have had a diagnosis of cancer probably in the first week of February. When asked whether the delay in diagnosis and treatment was a direct and proximate cause of the injuries to Powell, Holder answered, "Yes, it was."

Dr. Ali, who had treated Powell, said he would have had approximately a 75% chance of surviving 5 years compared with the 15% to 20% chance he had in July 1992. Dr. Tercilla, a professor at the Medical College of Virginia, testified that, in his opinion, if Powell had been treated in January as opposed to July, he would have had a higher likelihood of being in control of this disease than he had when he presented at the VA hospital. Dr. Kipreos, a pathologist at the VA center, stated that in her opinion, if Margileth had requested a fine-needle aspiration in January 1992, rather than misdiagnosing Powell with cat scratch disease, Powell's cancer would have been diagnosed at that time.

Muller as an expert witness capable of testifying as to the question of causation. Evidence was sufficient to establish that the failure to diagnose lung cancer, in connection with the emergency department visit, was the proximate cause of the patient's death. The duty to review an X-ray contained in a patient's medical record should not vary between an internist and a gastroenterologist. Evidence showed that Ryan's negligence destroyed any substantial possibility of Griffett's survival.

Radiologists Fail to Make a Timely Diagnosis

A medical malpractice action was brought against a university hospital through its interventional radiologists and other medical employees who failed to timely diagnose and treat the patient's internal bleeding, which is alleged to have occurred during the performance of an angioplasty that resulted in a hematoma around the patient's spinal cord, causing paralysis and subsequent loss of use of his limbs. The trial court was found to have erred in directing a verdict against the plaintiff where excluded expert testimony was sufficient to establish evidence of a national standard of care and breach of that standard. The expert had 40 years of experience as a board-certified general surgeon.[27]

Failure to Monitor Patient

A medical malpractice action was brought against two obstetricians, a pediatrician, and the hospital in *Ledogar v. Giordano*[28] because of a newborn infant's prenatal and postnatal hypoxia, which allegedly caused brain damage resulting in autism. The record contained sufficient proof of causation to support a verdict in favor of the plaintiff when an expert obstetrician testified that both obstetricians were negligent in failing to perform a cesarean section at an earlier time, that the hospital staff departed from proper medical standards of care by not monitoring the fetal heartbeat at least every 15 minutes, and that, with a reasonable degree of medical certainty, it was probable that the fetus suffered hypoxia during labor.

Imaging Studies

Misdiagnosis in general, and especially misdiagnosis related to medical imaging, represents a significant segment of malpractice litigation. Malpractice lawsuits generally involve allegations of misdiagnosis and can often be the result of the failure to order appropriate imaging tests, misinterpretation of an imaging study, failure to consult with a radiologist, failure to review imaging studies, delay in relaying test results,

and failure to relay imaging results. Although the following cases describe many of these issues, they are not exhaustive of the problems that can arise in imaging-related lawsuits.

Failure to Order Appropriate Imaging Studies

The failure to order a proper set of X-rays is as legally risky as the failure to order X-rays. In *Betenbaugh v. Princeton Hospital*,[29] the plaintiff was taken to the hospital because she injured the lower part of her back. One of the defendant physicians directed that an X-ray be taken of her sacrum. No evidence of a fracture was found. When the patient's pain did not subside, the family physician was consulted. He found that the films taken at the hospital did not include the entire lower portion of the spine and sent her to a radiologist for further study. On the basis of additional X-rays, a diagnosis of a fracture was made, and the patient was advised to wear a lumbosacral support. Two months later, the fracture was healed. The radiologist who had taken X-ray films on the second occasion testified that it was customary to take both an anterior-posterior and a lateral view when making an X-ray examination of the sacrum. In his opinion, the failure at the hospital to include the lower area of the sacrum was a failure to meet the standard required. The family physician testified that if the patient's fracture had been diagnosed at the hospital, then appropriate treatment could have been instituted earlier and thus the patient would have suffered less pain and recovery time would have been reduced. The evidence was sufficient to support findings that the physicians and the hospital were negligent by not having taken adequate X-rays and that such negligence was the proximate cause of the patient's additional pain and delay in recovery.

Image Misinterpretation Leads to Death

The deceased, Jane Fahr, in *Setterington v. Pontiac General Hospital*,[30] was concerned about a lump in her thigh. She had a CT scan taken at Pontiac General Hospital in August 1987. The radiologist, Dr. Mittner, did not mention that the lump could be cancerous. In reliance on the radiologist's report, Dr. Sanford, the plaintiff's treating physician, regarded the condition as a hematoma and believed that a biopsy was not warranted. In late January 1988, Fahr returned to Pontiac General Hospital for another CT scan because the lump seemed to be enlarging. The radiologist, Dr. Khalid, did not include the possibility of a malignant tumor in his report. As a result, Sanford continued to believe that Fahr had a hematoma.

In early September 1988, Fahr returned to Sanford, who had another CT scan performed. Dr. Kayne, the radiologist, found an enlarged hematoma. In a follow-up discussion with Sanford, Kayne assured Sanford that the lump did not appear to be dangerous or invasive. As a result, Sanford concluded that Fahr had a hematoma with a leaking blood vessel. In October 1988, the tumor was biopsied and the cancer diagnosed. By December 1988, chest scans revealed metastasis. Fahr died on July 6, 1990, at the age of 32. Setterington, Fahr's personal representative, brought a malpractice action against Sanford and Pontiac General Hospital, alleging that they failed to timely diagnose and treat Fahr.

The jury found that the radiologists were agents of defendant Pontiac General Hospital and breached the standard of care. The jury also concluded that the breach was a proximate cause of Fahr's death. The jury returned a verdict for the plaintiff in the amount of just over $251,000. The trial court denied the plaintiff's motion for a new trial as to damages, as well as the defendant's motion for a new trial.

The court found that the evidence as to the malpractice of Khalid and Kayne supported the jury's finding that they were professionally negligent. Kayne failed to diagnose the cancer in September 1988. With a proper diagnosis, there could have been a full month or more of treatment before metastasis was visible in December. As to Khalid, whose malpractice was 7 months earlier, the conclusion is even stronger.

The hospital provided the plaintiff with the radiologists. The evidence supports the jury's finding that an agency relationship existed between the radiologists and the hospital. Fahr did not have a patient–physician relationship with the radiologists independent of the hospital setting. Rather, the radiologists just happened to be on duty when Fahr arrived at the hospital. Moreover, the evidence showed that the radiology department is held out as part of the hospital, leading patients to understand that the services are being rendered by the hospital.

Failure to Consult with Radiologist

The internist in *Lanzet v. Greenberg*[31] failed to consult with the radiologist after his conclusion that the patient suffered from congestive heart failure and an enlarged heart. This factor may have contributed to the death of the patient while on the operating table. Although the case against the internist "was not as strong as that against the operating-room physicians, the proofs allowed the jury to infer that Dr. Oen's failure to consult with the radiologist and to realize that 'this is not a normal conducting system of the heart'

was in reasonable probability a factor that further contributed to the patient's failure to withstand the heart episode when it occurred on the operating table."[32]

Failure to Read Images

The patient in *Tams v. Lotz*[33] had to undergo a second surgical procedure to remove a laparotomy pad that had been left in the patient during a previous surgical procedure. The trial court was found to have properly directed a verdict with respect to the patient's assertion that the surgeon who performed the first operation failed to read a postoperative X-ray report, which allegedly would have put him on notice both that the pad was present and that there was a need for emergency surgery to remove the pad, therefore averting the need to remove a portion of the patient's intestine.

Delay in Conveying Imaging Results

On April 20, Mr. Carrasco[34] was taken to the Tri City Community Hospital (Tri City) emergency department by ambulance, complaining of back pain. He was admitted for observation and then released on April 21. On April 22, Carrasco returned to Tri City complaining of continued back pain and the inability to stand. A chest X-ray taken on April 22 revealed a significantly widened mediastinum and an increase in the size of the cardiac silhouette. On April 24, the radiologist reported that the X-ray revealed that in the setting of back pain, an aortic dissection should be considered.

Carrasco's condition deteriorated on April 24 and he was air lifted to Methodist Hospital in San Antonio for care. A CT scan was taken that revealed an aneurysm of the thoracic aorta, and Carrasco underwent emergency surgery. The following day, Carrasco suffered a pericardial effusion, had emergency surgery, coded, and died.

Tri City and the emergency department physician were sued. Tri City filed a motion for summary judgment, asserting that the plaintiffs failed to show it breached the standard of care owed to the patient. The trial court granted summary judgment on this ground.

Because Carrasco's condition did not deteriorate until April 24, an inference could be made that the rupture occurred sometime on April 24. The Texas Court of Appeals found that the evidence presented was sufficient to reverse the trial court's judgment and remand the case for trial.

Failure to Communicate Imaging Results

The court of appeals in *Washington Healthcare Corp. v. Barrow*[35] held that evidence was sufficient to sustain a finding that the hospital was negligent in failing to provide a radiology report demonstrating pathology on patient Barrow's lung in a timely manner. An X-ray of the patient taken on April 4, 1982, disclosed a small nodular density in her right lung. Within a year, the cancerous nodule had grown to the size of a softball.

The most significant testimony at trial was that of Theresa James, a medical student who worked for Dr. Oweiss, the defendant, until April 23, 1982. James testified that her job entailed combing through Oweiss's mail and locating abnormal X-ray reports, which she then would bring to his attention. James claimed that she received no such report while working for the physician, thus accounting for 19 days after the X-ray was taken. James stated that the X-ray reports were usually received within 4 or 5 days after being taken. Dr. Odenwald, who dictated the patient's report on April 4, 1982, gave testimony to corroborate her testimony. Odenwald, of Groover, Christie and Merritt, PC (GCM), who operated the radiology department at the Washington Hospital Center (WHC), stated that the X-ray reports usually were typed and mailed the same day that they were dictated. The jury could have determined that if the report did not reach Oweiss by April 23, 1982, then it did not reach him by May 3, 1982. The patient's record eventually was found; however, it was not in the patient's regular folder. Therefore, one could infer that the record was negligently filed.

Questions also arise as to why Oweiss did nothing to follow up on the matter in ensuing months. Oweiss testified that he did receive the report by May 3, 1982, and that he informed Mrs. Barrow of its contents. Barrow stated that although her folder was on the physician's desk at the time of her visit, he did not relay to her any information regarding an abnormal X-ray. Oweiss, however, was severely impeached at trial, and the jury chose not to believe him. Considering the entire record, there was reasonable probability that WHC was negligent and that Oweiss had not received the report. The plaintiff settled with Oweiss, the patient's personal physician, in the amount of $200,000 during pendency in the district court, and the action against him was dismissed with prejudice. The record did not support WHC's request of indemnification from Oweiss. The trial court directed a verdict in favor of GCM, leaving WHC as the sole defendant. The court of appeals remanded WHC's cross claim for indemnification from GCM for further findings of fact and conclusions by the trial court.

Misdiagnosis

Misdiagnosis is the most frequently cited injury event in malpractice suits against physicians.

Medicine is not an exact science and linking a patient's symptoms to a specific ailment is complicated at best. Sometimes things go wrong despite all the advances of modern medicine. Although diagnosis is a medical art and not an exact science, early detection can be critical to a patient's recovery. Misdiagnosis may involve the diagnosis and treatment of a disease different from that which the patient actually suffers or the diagnosis and treatment of a disease that the patient does not have. Misdiagnosis in and of itself will not necessarily impose liability on a physician, unless deviation from the accepted standard of care and injury can be established. The reader is presented here with a variety of cases that illustrate how things can go wrong due to poor judgment and negligent acts that result in patient injuries.

Mitral Valve Malfunction

In *Lauderdale v. United States*,[36] the federal government was held liable under the Federal Tort Claims Act for the death of a patient whose mitral valve malfunction was misdiagnosed at a military medical clinic. Under applicable Alabama law, the physician failed to conduct the necessary tests to determine the cause of a suspected heart problem. The physician never indicated to the patient that the problem was severe, that the treatment with digoxin was tentative, and that his well-being mandated that he return in a week. The patient subsequently died. He was found not to have been contributorily negligent by failing to return to the clinic. The patient had not been sufficiently advised of the urgency of a return visit. This failure was considered the proximate cause of the patient's death because his illness might have been treated successfully.

🔍 *FAILURE TO FORM A DIFFERENTIAL DIAGNOSIS*

Citation: *Corley v. State Department of Health & Hospitals*, 749 So. 2d 926 (La. App. 1999)

Facts

Corley began experiencing low back pain on February 11, 1988. He sought medical treatment from Dr. Gremillion. Corley complained that he had been experiencing low back pain and abdominal discomfort for approximately 4 months. At Corley's request, Gremillion ordered X-rays of the lower spine, chest, kidneys, and gallbladder, as well as an upper gastrointestinal series. Gremillion, feeling that a specialist should see Corley, gave him a written referral to a medical center for an orthopedic evaluation.

On March 2, 1988, Corley went to the medical center's emergency department with his wife. The Corleys presented admitting personnel with Corley's records from Gremillion, including X-rays and other test reports. Dr. Fuller, an emergency department physician, took a history from Corley and reviewed Gremillion's notes and the X-ray reports. He also conducted a routine physical examination and had X-rays made of Corley's lower back. Fuller's impression was that Corley was suffering from low back pain. Fuller continued Corley on the medication prescribed by Gremillion and made an appointment for him with the orthopedic clinic on March 16, 1988. On that date, a fourth-year resident, Dr. Bridges, saw Corley in the orthopedic clinic. Bridges conducted a physical exam, which was normal, and started Corley on a conservative course of treatment for low back pain.

Dr. Mehta next saw Corley on April 20, 1988. Mehta's notes reflect that his physical exam of Corley was normal but that he felt that Corley had a posture problem and referred him to physical therapy for correction of his posture. The notes do not reflect whether Mehta reviewed any of Corley's previous medical records, X-rays, or reports.

On September 14, 1988, Corley was seen by a surgical resident, Dr. White, who, during the course of the examination, ordered a CT scan of Corley's lower back. Dr. Ellis, a radiologist at the medical center, interpreted the CT scan as showing arthritis consistent with fibrosis or spinal stenosis and possible edema of the right L5 nerve root, which, according to White, may or may not have been the cause of Corley's back pain. White did not review any of the previous medical records, X-rays, or reports. Corley's last visit to the medical center was September 21, 1988. On that date, White reviewed the results of the CT scan with Corley, continued him on an anti-inflammatory drug, and encouraged him to continue his back exercises.

On October 26, 1988, Corley, plagued by constant back pain and beginning to experience difficulty breathing, consulted Dr. Maxwell, a chiropractor, who did a full spinal X-ray that revealed a markedly diminished right lung area. Maxwell sent Corley to his father, also a chiropractor, who confirmed that there was a potential problem with Corley's right lung and recommended that he see a pulmonary specialist.

On October 31, 1988, Corley presented to Gremillion complaining of chest congestion and shortness of breath. Gremillion diagnosed him with bronchitis and implemented treatment. Corley returned to Gremillion on November 14, 1988, with complaints of shortness of breath and marked weight loss. Subsequent diagnostic testing confirmed the presence of a very large mass (cancer) in Corley's right chest. Prior to his death on January 23, 1990, Corley received radiation and chemotherapy treatment.

Corley's surviving spouse and son instituted a malpractice action seeking wrongful death and survival damages. The trial court rendered judgment in favor of the plaintiffs and against the medical center in the amount of $400,000. The defendants, the state, and the medical center appealed.

Issue

The primary issue on appeal is whether the trial court committed error in finding that the physicians at the medical center deviated from the applicable standard of care by failing to properly diagnose Corley's condition, a large cancerous mass in his mediastinum, during the course of their treatment of his low back pain.

Finding

The physicians at the medical center fell below the standard of care when they failed to properly diagnose Corley's condition.

Reason

The evidence was in Gremillion's X-rays and medical report when Corley first arrived at the medical center. When Corley did not respond to conservative treatment, there had to be another explanation for his low back pain. The physicians did not expand their inquiry, which they should have done under a differential diagnosis assessment. A physician is required to take a "thorough" history based on a patient's presenting signs and symptoms. If the findings from the medical history and physical exam support a diagnosis, one should be made and treatment instituted. When, in treating a patient, a diagnosis cannot be made, at that time, a differential diagnosis should be made, which includes all reasonable, plausible, and foreseeable causes, signs, and symptoms noted. After forming a differential diagnosis, it is the physician's duty to rule out all imminent, serious, and life-threatening causes related to the signs and symptoms. Failure to eliminate these causes can subject a patient to a foreseeable risk of harm and would further constitute a breach of the applicable standards of care.

Appendicitis

Misdiagnosis does not always end in a verdict for the plaintiff. Summary judgment was properly entered in dismissing an action alleging that a physician had been negligent in failing to diagnose a pregnant patient's appendicitis in *Fiedler v. Steger*.[37] The testimony of expert witnesses for both parties established that diagnosis of appendicitis during pregnancy is difficult, that it probably would not have been diagnosed on the dates in question, and that the appendix had probably ruptured postpartum.

Diabetic Acidosis

A case before the Mississippi Supreme Court, *Hill v. Stewart*,[38] involved a patient who became ill and was admitted to the hospital. The physician was advised of the patient's recent weight loss, frequent urination, thirst, loss of vision, nausea, and vomiting. Routine laboratory tests were ordered including a urinalysis, but not a blood glucose test. On the following day, a consultant diagnosed the patient's condition as severe diabetic acidosis. Treatment was given, but the patient failed to respond to the therapy and died. The attending physician was sued for failing to test for diabetes and for failing to diagnose and treat the patient on the first day in the hospital.

The attending physician said in court that he suspected diabetes and admitted that when diabetes is suspected, a urinalysis and a blood sugar test should be performed. An expert medical witness testified that failure to do so would be a departure from the skill and care required of a general practitioner. The expert also stated that the patient in this case probably would have had a good chance of survival if treated properly. The state supreme court reversed the directed verdict for the physician by a lower court and remanded the case for retrial. There was sufficient evidence presented to permit the case to go to the jury for decision.

Once a physician concludes that a particular test is indicated, it should be performed and evaluated as soon as practicable. Delay may constitute negligence. The law imposes on a physician the same degree of responsibility in making a diagnosis as it does in prescribing and administering treatment.

Pathologist Fails to Diagnose Cancer

Condon, in *Anne Arundel Med. Ctr., Inc. v. Condon*, underwent a routine mammogram, which was ordered by her gynecologist on July 1, 1988. The mammogram revealed suspicious lesions in her right breast. Advised by her physician that her breast needed further examination, the patient selected Dr. Moore, a surgeon, to perform a biopsy at AA Medical Center (AAMC). The biopsy was ultimately performed on July 19, 1988. Dr. Williams, who was a pathologist working for Weisburger, MD, a pathology corporation providing contract pathology services to the hospital, performed an evaluation of the tissue. Williams reported noncancerous lesions in the right breast. Based on the pathology report, the surgeon advised the patient that she did not have cancer but that she should undergo frequent mammograms.

On February 7, 1990, the patient returned to her surgeon complaining of an inflammation of her right breast in the same area of her previous biopsy. The surgeon again recommended and performed a biopsy on February 15. Condon was advised that the biopsy results indicated invasive carcinoma of the breast. On February 23, 1990, Condon underwent a bilateral modified radical mastectomy.

Condon brought a malpractice action against Williams and AAMC, alleging the pathologist incorrectly interpreted the first biopsy specimen and that the pathologist's failure to interpret invasive carcinoma was a departure from the standard of care required and was the proximate cause of her injuries. On the eve of trial, December 9, 1992, counsel for the pathologist settled the claim against his client for $1 million. The circuit court entered judgment on a jury verdict in favor of the plaintiff. AAMC appealed, claiming that the release of the agent Williams served to act as a release for AAMC. The appellant claimed that the common law rule, which states that the release of an agent discharges the principal from liability, should, therefore, apply. The Court of Special Appeals of Maryland agreed.[39]

Radiologist Misreads Patient's X-Rays

In *Boudoin v. Nicholson, Baehr, Calhoun, & Lanasa*,[40] expert testimony supported a finding of loss of chance to survive. A diagnostic radiologist's improper reading of a patient's X-ray resulted in a loss of chance to survive a chest wall cancer. Boudoin had suffered a minor shoulder injury while lifting an object at his job as a pipefitter. Because the pain did not subside after a few days, on May 19, he went to see Dr. Nicholson, the family practitioner who had treated him since he was 18. Based on Boudoin's complaint of pain in the outer chest and a physical examination, Dr. Nicholson took a chest X-ray that, in his opinion, showed nothing remarkable and diagnosed Boudoin's injury as a muscle strain and prescribed accordingly. Nevertheless, he sent the X-ray to be evaluated by a diagnostic radiologist, Hendler. The radiology report returned to Nicholson read in part:

CHEST: Cardiac, hilar, and mediastinal shadows do not appear unusual. Both lung fields and angles appear clear. A 3.5-cm. broad-based benign osteomatous projection is noted at the level of the vertebral border of the inferior aspect of the left scapula.

IMPRESSION: 1—No evidence of active pulmonary or cardiac pathology.

Boudoin did not contact Nicholson again until January 1989, when he complained of discomfort in his neck and pain in his right shoulder blade and arm. Nicholson again ruled out serious injury through a cervical X-ray, resulting in a diagnosis of cervical spasm, degenerative disks, and bilateral spondylosis.

On April 18, 1989, Boudoin returned to Nicholson complaining of night sweats, weight loss, and pain in his left chest. A chest X-ray showed a large abnormal mass. Boudoin was given both the 1988 X-ray and the one just taken and was immediately sent to see a pulmonologist, Dr. Rosenberg. While Boudoin was undergoing a breathing test, Rosenberg called Mrs. Boudoin into his office and showed her the tumor as it appeared on the X-rays taken 11 months apart and also had her read Hendler's May 1988 report. Rosenberg told Mrs. Boudoin that the tumor could have been removed easily when it was as small as it first appeared. Although the tumor initially appeared to be on Boudoin's left lung, innumerable tests and examinations established that the cancer was malignant and was in the pleura, the tissue lining the chest wall. No sign of metastasis was found in the lymph nodes of the chest or other tissues.

Dr. Rigby surgically removed the tumor, now measuring 20 by 17.5 by 7 cm on May 10, 1989, along with a large portion of the chest wall and four ribs. Because a 4- or 5-mm metastatic deposit was found in Boudoin's right diaphragm, a section of that tissue also was removed. There was no sign of cancer on the lungs. A metal plate was implanted to replace the structural support lost with the removal of the ribs. After recovering from his surgery, Boudoin underwent concurrent radiation and chemotherapy. X-rays and examinations done every other month through March 1990 showed no signs of recurrence. Four months later, however, abnormalities were detected, and a second surgery, performed on July 20, 1990, revealed that the tumor had spread. As a result of the significant spread of cancer, the only tissue removed during surgery was a biopsy sample, which confirmed a malignant recurrence. Boudoin and his family were informed that even with chemotherapy, the prognosis was very poor. Further treatment was restricted to alleviating pain until Boudoin's death on December 18, 1990.

Hendler appealed an award of $560,000 based on a jury's finding that the physician's improper reading of Boudoin's X-ray resulted in a loss of chance to survive a chest wall cancer. The appeals court affirmed the finding of liability and causation but reduced the amount of the award.

Failure to Make a Timely Diagnosis

The plaintiff, Jane Doe, in *Doe v. McNulty*[41] was exposed to HIV as the result of sexual contact. The plaintiff consulted her defendant-physicians, but they failed to diagnose her condition as being positive for either HIV or AIDS. The disease weakened her immune system, and she developed pneumonia and was admitted to a hospital. The patient was eventually diagnosed with AIDS. The patient's infectious disease expert, Dr. Hill, claimed that proper diagnosis prior to her acute episode would have provided greater opportunity for improved long-term treatment. The defendants admitted that they negligently failed to timely diagnose the patient's condition.

The defendants' expert witness, Dr. Lutz, testified from his review of the patient's medical record that the patient's diagnosis could not have been determined based on the symptoms as described in the record. Lutz never examined the patient and based his determination on the documentation contained in the medical record. Lutz did, however, agree that if the patient's immune system had not been totally destroyed, preventive treatment could have resulted in a longer life span.

The civil district court entered judgment on a jury verdict of $700,000 in general damages, which included pain and suffering, mental anguish, disability, and the loss of the enjoyment of life, and $314,000 for medical and special damages. The defendants appealed.

The Louisiana Court of Appeal held that the evidence supported the jury's finding that the defendants failed to timely diagnose the plaintiff's condition. The medical defendants agreed that they negligently failed to timely diagnose the patient's condition. The plaintiff's expert witness testified that within the "reasonable medical probability" standard and the "more-likely-than-not" standard, if the plaintiff had been properly diagnosed and treated no later than August 18, 1990, which was the date the medical defendants should have diagnosed and treated the patient, then she would not have contracted pneumonia. She would have worked, as well as lived, for another year.

Wrongful Diagnosis of AIDS

A service member brought an action under the Federal Tort Claims Act in *Johnson v. United States*,[42] alleging that on or about October 8, 1986, Army physicians and medical personnel negligently and wrongly advised her that she had AIDS after she had donated blood to a public blood drive sponsored by the Walter Reed Hospital, which resulted in her having an unnecessary and unwanted abortion. In November 1986, prior to being notified of this error, the plaintiff discovered that she was pregnant. On November 21, 1986, physicians at Walter Reed Hospital advised the plaintiff that her child would most certainly be born with AIDS and would not live beyond 5 years. The physicians indicated that under these circumstances, it would be better for the plaintiff to have an abortion than to carry the child to term. As a result of this counseling, and for no other reason, the plaintiff had an abortion on December 4, 1986. It was not until February 3, 1987, nearly 4 months later, that a physician at Walter Reed Hospital told the plaintiff that there had been an error in the paperwork, and she did not have AIDS.

The United States moved to have the case dismissed on the grounds that the action was barred by the Feres Doctrine. Under this doctrine, the United States is not liable under the Federal Tort Claims Act for injuries that arise out of or are in the course of activity incident to service. The district court held that the donation of blood was not incident to service and, therefore, the Feres Doctrine did not bar the action.

▶ TREATMENT

This section focuses on negligence cases that relate to medical treatment and various legal and ethical issues that healthcare professionals encounter when treating patients. *Medical treatment* is the attempt to restore the patient to health following a diagnosis. It is the application of various remedies and medical techniques, including the use of medications for the purpose of treating an illness or trauma. Treatment can be *active treatment*, directed immediately to the cure of the disease or injury; *causal treatment*, directed against the cause of a disease; *conservative treatment*, designed to avoid radical medical therapeutic measures or operative procedures; expectant treatment, directed toward relief of untoward symptoms but leaving cure of the disease to natural forces; palliative treatment, designed to relieve pain and distress with no attempt to cure; *preventive/prophylactic treatment*, aimed at the prevention of disease and illness; specific treatment, targeted specifically at the disease being treated;

supportive treatment, directed mainly to sustaining the strength of the patient; or *symptomatic treatment*, meant to relieve symptoms without effecting a cure (i.e., intended to address the symptoms of an illness but not its underlying cause, as in scleroderma, lupus, or multiple sclerosis, for example).

Medical practice guidelines are evidence-based best practices that are developed to assist physicians in the diagnosis and treatment of their patients. It should be remembered that best practices are not ironclad rules. Skillful medical judgment demands that the physician determine how to use best practices and interpret the information.

Choice of Treatment

There can be *two schools of thought* regarding which treatment would be in the best interest of the patient. The potential for liability affects the choice of treatment a physician will follow with his or her patient. Use of unprecedented procedures that create an untoward result may cause a physician to be found negligent even though due care was followed. A physician will not be held liable for exercising his or her judgment in applying a course of treatment supported by a reputable and respected body of medical experts even if another body of expert medical opinion would favor a different course of treatment. The *two schools of thought doctrine* is only applicable in medical malpractice cases in which there is more than one method of accepted treatment for a patient's disease or injury. Under this doctrine, a physician will not be liable for medical malpractice if he or she follows a course of treatment supported by reputable, respected, and reasonable medical experts.

A physician's efforts do not constitute negligence simply because they were unsuccessful in a particular case. A physician cannot be required to guarantee the results of his or her treatment. The mere fact that an adverse result may occur following treatment is not in and of itself evidence of professional negligence.

Selecting the Wrong Treatment

Although there can be two schools of thought on how to treat a patient, the failure of an attending physician to carefully recognize recommendations of consulting physicians, who determine a different diagnosis and recommend a different course of treatment in a particular case, can result in liability for damages suffered by the patient. That was the case in *Martin v. East Jefferson General Hospital*[43] in which the attending physician continued to treat the patient for a viral infection despite three other physicians' diagnoses of lupus and their recommendations that the attending physician treat the patient for collagen vascular disease.

The trial court found that lupus had been more probable than not the cause of the patient's death, and that her chances of recovery had been destroyed by the physician's failure to rule out that diagnosis. Damages totaling $150,000 were awarded to the plaintiff.

If a consulting physician has suggested a diagnosis with which the treating physician does not agree, it would be prudent to consider obtaining the opinion of a second consultant who could either confirm or disprove the first consultant's theory. Failure to diagnose and properly treat a suspected illness is an open door to liability.

Delay in Treatment

A physician may be liable for failing to respond promptly if it can be established that such inaction caused a patient's death.[44] A patient afflicted with lung cancer was awarded damages in *Blackmon v. Langley*[45] because of the failure of the examining physician to inform the patient in a timely manner that a chest X-ray showed a lesion in his lung. The lesion eventually was diagnosed as cancerous. The physician contended that because the evidence showed the patient had less than a 50% chance of survival at the time of the alleged negligence, he could not be the proximate cause of injury. The Arkansas Supreme Court found that the jury was properly entitled to determine that the patient suffered and lost more than would have been the case had he been notified promptly of the lesion.

Untimely Cesarean Section

The attending physician in *Jackson v. Huang*[46] was negligent in failing to perform a timely cesarean section. The attending physician applied too much traction when he was faced with shoulder dystocia, a situation in which a baby's shoulder hangs under the pubic bone,

(NEWS) *LAB RESULTS BURIED IN FILES*

When a woman has a pelvic exam, she expects her doctor to let her know if there's a problem. But that didn't happen for Charlene Hutchens in 2002 or in 2003. It wasn't until 2004 that she learned she had advanced cervical cancer.

—Carol Gentry, *Health News Florida*, June 5, 2010.

arresting the progress of the infant through the birth canal. As a result, the infant suffered permanent injury to the brachial plexus nerves of his right shoulder and arm. On appeal of this case, no error was found in the trial court's finding of fact when such finding was supported by testimony of the plaintiff's expert witness. The trial judge accepted the testimony of Dr. Forte, the expert witness, who testified that the defendant possessed the necessary skill and knowledge relevant to the practice of obstetrics and gynecology. The defendant, because of prolonged labor and weight of the baby, should have anticipated the possibility of shoulder dystocia and performed a timely cesarean section.

Failure to Treat Known Condition

A medical malpractice action was filed against the physician in *Modaber v. Kelley*[47] for personal injuries and mental anguish caused by the stillbirth of a child. The circuit court entered judgment on a jury verdict against the obstetrician, and an appeal was taken. The Virginia Supreme Court held that the evidence was sufficient to support a finding that the obstetrician's conduct during the patient's pregnancy caused direct injury to the patient. Evidence at trial showed that the physician failed to treat the mother's known condition of toxemia, including the development of high blood pressure and the premature separation of the placenta from the uterine wall, and that the physician thereafter failed to respond in a timely fashion when the mother went into premature labor. The court also held that injury to the unborn child constituted injury to the mother and that she could recover for the physical injury and mental anguish associated with the stillbirth. The court found that the award of $750,000 in compensatory damages was not excessive.

Failure to Treat Evolving Emergency

The Bureau of Professional Medical Conduct (BPMC), in *Bell v. New York State Department of Health*,[48] upon investigation of a complaint charged that the physician failed to properly treat and respond to his patient's evolving emergency cardiac condition despite symptoms and circumstances indicating the need for immediate hospitalization. The physician denied the allegations, and the State Board for Professional Medical Conduct (committee) conducted a hearing.

When the patient visited the physician in September 1994, he was suffering from high blood pressure and taking medication for that condition. From 1994 to 1996, the patient was treated for various medical conditions, including high cholesterol and hypertension. On May 29, 1997, the patient visited the physician complaining of chest pains, anxiety panic attacks, and shortness of breath. During that visit, the physician performed an electrocardiogram (ECG), ordered chest X-rays, and referred the patient to a cardiac specialist for consultation. The physician also ordered a test for cardiac enzymes; however, the results were not available for several days. The physician prescribed asthma medication and sent the patient home. The next day, the physician attempted to call the patient to inquire about his condition but was unable to reach him.

Less than a week later, on June 2, 1997, the patient returned to the physician's office complaining of continued chest pain. At that time, the physician arranged a visit with the cardiologist for the same day. The cardiologist reviewed the patient's medical history; performed an ECG; reviewed the May 29, 1997, ECG; and concluded that the patient had a myocardial infarction followed by postinfarction angina. The patient was immediately sent to the hospital.

The physician was not present at the hearing and did not call any witnesses to rebut BPMC's expert witness. Expert opinion revealed that the physician's response to the patient's symptoms on May 29, 1997, and June 2, 1997, failed to meet medically acceptable standards of care. On February 21, 2001, the committee sustained the charge of negligence.

The physician's license was suspended for 2 years; however, the suspension was stayed, and the physician was placed on probation. On appeal, the Supreme Court of New York found that given the serious nature of the patient's complaints and symptoms and the potential consequences, the committee's conclusions were found by the court to be supported by substantial evidence. According to Greenburg (one of the defendants in the case), the physician's course of conduct in performing an ECG, ordering a cardiac enzyme test, and referring the patient to a cardiologist demonstrated that the physician suspected that the patient was experiencing cardiac problems. However, given the patient's symptoms and history, it was Greenburg's opinion that the physician failed to adhere to medically acceptable standards of treatment by failing to obtain the results of the cardiac enzyme test expeditiously and not referring the patient to an emergency department immediately.

Failure to Respond to Emergency Calls

Physicians on call in an emergency department are expected to respond to requests for emergency assistance when such is considered necessary. Failure to respond is grounds for negligence should a patient suffer injury as a result of a physician's failure to respond.

Issues of fact in *Dillon v. Silver*[49] precluded summary dismissal of an action charging that a woman's death from complications of an ectopic pregnancy occurred because of a gynecologist's refusal to treat her despite a request for aid by a hospital emergency department physician. Although the gynecologist contended that no physician–patient relationship had ever arisen, the hospital bylaws not only mandated that the physician accept all patients referred to him, but also stated that the emergency department physician had authority to decide which service physician should be called and required the service physician to respond to such a call.

Medication Errors

Thousands of brand name and generic drugs in use have led to an increase in medication errors. Such errors are a leading cause of patient injuries. Physicians should encourage the limited and judicious use of all medications and periodically document the reason for their continuation. They should be alert to any contraindications and incompatibilities among prescription, over-the-counter drugs, and herbal supplements. The negligent administration of medications is often a result of errors, such as the wrong medication, the wrong patient, the wrong dosage, and the wrong route.

Wrong Dosage

Expert testimony in *Leal v. Simon*,[50] a medical malpractice action, supported the jury's determination that the physician had been negligent when he reduced the dosage of a resident's psychotropic medication, Haldol. The resident, a 36-year-old man who had been institutionalized his entire life, was a resident in an intermediate-care facility. The drug was used for controlling the resident's self-abusive behavior. Expert medical testimony showed that the physician failed to familiarize himself with the resident's history, failed to secure the resident's complete medical records, and failed to wean the resident slowly off the medication.

Abuse in Prescribing Medications

The board of regents in *Moyo v. Ambach*[51] determined that a physician prescribed methaqualone fraudulently and with gross negligence to 20 patients. The board of regents found that the physician did not prescribe methaqualone in good faith or for sound medical reasons. His abuse in prescribing controlled substances constituted the fraudulent practice of medicine. Expert testimony established that it was common knowledge in the medical community that methaqualone was a widely abused and addictive drug. Methaqualone should not have been used for insomnia without first trying other means of treatment. On appeal, the court found that there was sufficient evidence to support the board's finding.

Wrongful Supply of Medications

Damages were awarded in *Argus v. Scheppegrell*[52] for the wrongful death of a teenage patient with a preexisting drug addiction. It was determined that the physician wrongfully supplied the patient with prescriptions for controlled substances in excessive amounts, with the result that the patient's preexisting drug addiction worsened, causing her death from a drug overdose. The Louisiana Court of Appeal held that the suffering of the patient caused by drug addiction and deterioration of her mental and physical condition warranted an award of $175,000. Damages of $120,000 were to be awarded for the wrongful death claims of the parents, who not only suffered during their daughter's drug addiction caused by the physician in wrongfully supplying the prescription, but who also were forced to endure the torment of their daughter's slow death in the hospital.

Surgery

Operating rooms, hidden behind closed doors, are often the scenes of negligent acts. A Wyoming man was awarded $1.175 million after doctors removed the wrong cervical disk during spinal surgery.[53] The potential for negligence in the surgical setting seems to be the never-ending story, as illustrated in the cases described in this section. Wrong surgery, wrong site, wrong patient, foreign objects left in patients, and hidden mistakes all continue to be common occurrences.

As noted in the following news clipping, surgical instruments inadvertently left in patients are reported by hospitals accredited by The Joint Commission. The various states also require the reporting of surgical errors, such as wrong patient, wrong surgery, and wrong site.

Wrong-site surgical mistakes have multiple causes, including draping the wrong surgical site, marking the wrong surgical site, and failure to mark the surgical site as required by hospital policy. A process for reducing the possibility of wrong-site surgery includes the following:

- Clearly mark the correct surgical site. If the actual site cannot be marked, a mark should be placed in close proximity to the surgical site.

NEWS JOINT COMMISSION ALERT: PREVENTING RETAINED SURGICAL ITEMS

The Joint Commission today issued a Sentinel Event Alert urging hospitals and ambulatory surgery centers to take a new look at how to avoid mistakenly leaving items such as sponges, towels, and instruments in a patient's body after surgery.

Known in medical terminology as the unintended retention of foreign objects (URFOs) or retained surgical items (RSIs), this is a serious patient safety issue that can cause death or harm patients physically and emotionally. The Joint Commission has received more than 770 voluntary reports of URFOs in the past seven years.

—Elizabeth Eaken Zhani, *The Joint Commission,*
October 17, 2013[54]

- Both the operating surgeon and patient must participate in and confirm the marking of the preoperative marking process. This may not always be possible when emergency surgery is required (e.g., the patient may be in a comatose state from an accident).
- The patient's medical record must be available to help determine the correct site prior to the start of surgery.
- The patient's imaging studies relating to the surgical procedure to be performed must be available for review prior to surgery. This will help to determine that the correct surgical site has been identified.
- Anesthesia is not administered until the operating surgeon is in the operating suite.
- The surgical team (all disciplines) conducts a "time-out" prior to the start of surgery to verify that the correct patient is on the surgical table, the correct surgical site has been marked, and the correct procedure has been identified.

Phantom Surgeon

Here, the list of surgical mistakes begins with the phantom surgeon. Watkins was referred to Dr. Eliachar, attending surgeon, who diagnosed a deviated septum and advised that a surgical procedure be performed. When asked by the patient whether he would be performing the procedure, Eliachar testified that he would operate with the assistance of residents. On the morning of Watkins's surgery, Eliachar was scheduled to perform four elective surgeries in two adjoining operating rooms. The anesthesiologist was Dr. Popovich, who also was involved in more than one surgery at the time and, like Eliachar, moved between operating rooms during the patients' procedures. The nurse anesthetist, Woods, assisted Popovich in Popovich's absence. Dr. Popovich did not inform the patient that a nurse anesthetist would perform the intubation/extubation and that he would not be present throughout the operation. The chief resident of the ear, nose, and throat department, Dr. Guay, performed the surgery on Watkins. Eliachar, who was listed in the operative records and discharge summary as the performing surgeon, allegedly supervised Guay's work as he moved between the adjoining operating rooms.

Guay testified that he first met the patient on the day of the surgery in the preoperative holding area minutes before the patient was transported to the operating room. He also testified that Eliachar assigned the surgery to him and that Eliachar did not scrub up that morning. Guay, upon meeting the patient, told the patient that he would be operating on her with Eliachar. During the operation, which began at 7:30 AM and ended at 11:10 AM, the patient was under a general anesthesia and was intubated by the nurse anesthetist. According to Eliachar, it was the surgeon's ultimate responsibility to ensure that the patient maintained an adequate airway during and after the operation, yet Eliachar could not recall whether he was present when the patient was extubated. He believed that the nurse anesthetist extubated the patient. Popovich was not present for the extubation and did not evaluate the patient between the operating room and the postanesthesia care unit (PACU). The nurse anesthetist stated that the patient was extubated at approximately 10:30 AM in the operating room and that he and Guay then transported the patient to PACU. On the way to the PACU at 10:35 AM, the patient's heart rate was 85 beats per minute according to the records of nurse Woods, yet the nurse's notes from PACU indicate that at 10:35 AM, when the patient was admitted to the PACU, her heart rate was 50 beats per minute. The nurse anesthetist's records also indicate that the patient was awake and responsive when he transported her to the PACU, yet the PACU records indicate that the patient was unresponsive, emitting a large amount of clear urine, and not moving. At 10:40 AM, the nurse anesthetist's records indicate that the patient's heart rate was 78 to 80 beats per minute, while the PACU nurse's record states 30 beats per minute, a rate that is admittedly life-threatening according to the nurse anesthetist. When the heart rate hit 30 beats per minute, the nurse anesthetist recalls, resuscitative measures were begun

on the patient. The patient was given cardiopulmonary resuscitation and was reintubated at 10:50 AM. The patient was left in a persistent vegetative state.

The jury found for the plaintiffs on the fraud and battery. The evidence presented demonstrated Eliachar represented to Watkins that he would be operating on her. Watkins specifically asked Eliachar whether he would be performing the surgery. When making the representation to the patient, Eliachar knew that he was scheduled to perform simultaneous surgeries on that date; as the performing surgeon of record, he had the responsibility to monitor the patient throughout the entire operation, including the postoperative procedures on his patient. He admittedly knew the extubation parameters and would have prevented Watkins's premature extubation had he been the surgeon in the operating room at the time. Based on this evidence, the elements of fraud were demonstrated. The appeals court held that the trial court did not err in denying the motion for directed verdict on that issue.[55]

Wrong Patient Surgery

In *Southwestern Kentucky Baptist Hospital v. Bruce*,[56] a patient admitted for conization of the cervix was taken mistakenly to the operating room for a thyroidectomy. The physician was notified early during surgery that he had the wrong patient on the operating room table. The operation was terminated immediately. The thyroidectomy was not completed, and the incision was sutured. The patient filed an action for malpractice and recovered $10,000 from the physician and $90,000 from the hospital. That the patient mistakenly answered to the name of another patient who had been scheduled for a thyroidectomy did not excuse the failure of the surgeon, the anesthesiologist, and the surgical technician to determine the identity of the patient by examining her identification bracelet. The Kentucky Supreme Court held that the verdict was not excessive in view of the injuries, which consisted of a 4-inch incision along the patient's neck, which became infected and required cosmetic surgery.

Wrong Site Surgery

The patient in *Holdsworth v. Galler*[57] had a 2-cm cancerous tumor on the left side of his colon. Unfortunately, the surgeon erroneously performed right-sided colon surgery to remove the tumor. After the surgeon recognized the error, he performed the required left-sided abdominal surgery 3 days later. At the first surgery on the patient's right side, the surgeon removed the end of the patient's small intestine, his entire right colon, and the majority of his transverse colon;

consequently, 40 to 45% of the colon was removed. Three days following the wrong-site surgery, the patient had to undergo left-sided surgery, after which he was left with approximately 20% of his colon. The patient developed complications and died 6 weeks thereafter.

In another wrong site case, *Jones v. Malinowski*,[58] it was determined that the costs of raising a normal healthy child were recoverable. The plaintiff had had three previous pregnancies. The first pregnancy resulted in a breech birth, the second child suffered brain damage, and the third child suffered from heart disease. For economic reasons, the plaintiff had undergone a bipolar tubal laparoscopy, which is a procedure that blocks both fallopian tubes by cauterization. The operating physician misidentified the left tube and cauterized the wrong structure, leaving the left tube intact. As a result of the negligent sterilization, Malinowski became pregnant. The court of appeals held that the costs of raising a healthy child are recoverable and that the jury could offset these costs by the benefits derived by the parents from the child's aid, comfort, and society during the parents' life expectancy.[59]

Wrong Surgery Site: Fraud

The physician-petitioner in *In re Muncan*[60] did not review either the patient's CT scan or magnetic resonance imaging films prior to surgery. In addition, he did not have the films with him in the operating room on the day of surgery. Had he done so, he would have discovered that the CT scan report erroneously indicated that there was a mass in the patient's left kidney when, in fact, such mass was located in the patient's right kidney. During surgery, the physician did not observe any gross abnormalities or deformities in the left kidney and was unable to palpate any masses. Nonetheless, he removed the left kidney. The physician was later advised that he had removed a healthy kidney and that he may have removed the wrong kidney. The physician discharged the patient with a postoperative diagnosis of left renal mass, failing to note that he had in fact removed a tumor-free kidney. In September 1999, when another CT scan revealed the presence of a 6- by 7-cm mass in the patient's right kidney, the physician deemed this to be a new tumor that was not present on the CT scan conducted 4 months earlier. The diagnosis, however, appeared highly suspect given the medical testimony that this new tumor was in the same location and had the same consistency and appearance as the tumor appearing in the prior CT study. The record also makes clear that it was highly unlikely that a tumor of this dimension could have achieved such size during the relatively brief period between the two CT studies.

A hearing committee of the State Board for Professional Medical Conduct sustained allegations that the physician practiced with gross negligence on more than one occasion. The committee suspended the physician's license to practice medicine for 48 months, stayed said suspension for 42 months, and placed the physician on probation. Upon appeal to the Administrative Review Board for Professional Medical Conduct (ARB), the ARB affirmed the committee's findings as to guilt and penalty and, further, sustained the specification alleging fraudulent practice. The physician commenced an action to annul that portion of the ARB's determination pertaining to the charge of fraudulent practice. The Supreme Court of New York, Appellate Division, Third Department held that the evidence was sufficient to support an inference of fraud. The physician knew he removed the wrong kidney and instead of taking steps to rectify the situation, intentionally concealed his mistake.

Foreign Objects Left in Patients

Physicians who change an organization's procedures governing surgical operations can be liable for those acts should they result in patient injury, even if they are performed by an organization's employees. In *Martin v. Perth Amboy General Hospital*,[61] a patient sued the hospital, cardiovascular surgeon, and nurses for leaving a laparotomy pad in his stomach. The surgeon, Dr. Lev, who performed the operation, was assisted by two other physicians, a scrub nurse, and a circulating nurse. Before the laparotomy pads were brought into the operating room, a strip of radiopaque material was embedded between the folds of the laparotomy pads that would show on an X-ray if a pad was left in the abdomen. Rings were attached to the laparotomy pads to prevent errors in counts made by the nurses; however, before the pads were used, the nurses, at the direction of the operating surgeon, removed the rings. The sponge count at the end of the operation indicated that no sponges were missing. Lev contended that the charge against him adopted the captain of the ship doctrine, which is not recognized by the state of New Jersey. If Lev had not ordered the rings to be removed by the nurses, the court would have agreed that the charge was contrary to state judicial decisions. By exercising control over the nurses to the extent of directing them to remove the rings and thus eliminating the safeguards provided by the hospital to ensure a proper count by its employees, the surgeon became the nurses' temporary or special employer with regard to their duties involving the laparotomy pads used during the operation. Thus, the surgeon was equally liable with the hospital for the nurses' subsequent negligence in counting the pads.

The most common methods of preventing operating room objects from being left in a surgical wound are:

1. Sponge and instrument counts
2. Use of surgical sponges with radiopaque threads
3. Use of X-rays for detecting foreign objects left in an operative wound

Procedure Improper

In *Ozment v. Wilkerson*,[62] Mrs. Wilkerson was suffering from Crohn's disease, a chronic ailment that affects the colon and small intestine. Part of the treatment for the disease is to allow the patient's gastrointestinal (GI) system to rest, and this means that the patient cannot eat. The patient is given a concentrated caloric solution intravenously. To deliver the needed nutritional solution, Dr. Ozment needed to place a central venous catheter into Wilkerson's body. Wilkerson's pericardial sac was punctured during the procedure.

As a result, a condition known as cardiac tamponade (accumulation of fluids in the pericardial sac) occurred. Wilkerson required emergency surgery to correct this condition and to repair the puncture. The defendants, following a jury verdict favorable to the plaintiffs, filed an appeal.

The Alabama Supreme Court held that expert testimony supported the jury's finding that the catheter was inserted incorrectly. The plaintiff's expert, Dr. Moore, testified that the tip of the catheter should have been placed in the superior vena cava and should not have extended into the heart. Moore also stated that placing the tip of the catheter in the atrium, or against the wall of the atrium, was a deviation from the standard of care ordinarily exercised by a physician in the same line of practice under similar circumstances. Moore stated that the intravenous central line perforated the right atrium and caused the cardiac tamponade. Moore's testimony provided sufficient evidence from which the jury could determine that Ozment inserted the catheter incorrectly and had thereby breached his duty of care to Wilkerson.

🔍 NEEDLE FRAGMENT LEFT IN PATIENT

Citation: *Williams v. Kilgore*, 618 So. 2d 51 (Miss. 1992)

Facts

On March 31, 1964, the patient-plaintiff was admitted to the medical center for treatment of metastatic malignant melanoma on her left groin. On April 6, 1964, an unknown resident performed a bone marrow biopsy. The needle broke during the procedure and a fragment lodged in the patient. The patient was told that the needle would be removed the following day, when surgery was to be performed to remove a melanoma from her groin. The operating surgeons, Dr. Peede and Dr. Kilgore, were informed of the presence of the needle fragment prior to surgery. A notation by Peede stated that the needle fragment had been removed.

The needle fragment, however, had not been removed. The patient remained asymptomatic until she was hospitalized for back pain in September 1985. During her hospitalization, the patient learned that the needle fragment was still in her lower back. The needle fragment was finally removed in October 1985. The physician's discharge report suggested that there was a probable linkage between the needle fragment and recurrent strep infections that the patient had been experiencing. Although the patient's treating physicians had known as early as 1972 that the needle fragment had not been removed, there was no evidence that the patient was aware of this fact.

The defendant physicians argued that the statute of limitations had tolled under Mississippi Code, thus barring the case from proceeding to trial. The circuit court entered a judgment for the physicians, and the plaintiff appealed.

Issue

Was the plaintiff's malpractice action time barred?

Holding

The Mississippi Supreme Court held that the plaintiff's action was not time barred and was, therefore, remanded for trial.

Reason

A patient's cause for action begins to accrue, and the statute of limitations begins to run when the patient can reasonably be held to have knowledge of the disease or injury. In this instance, the patient began to experience infections and back pain in 1985. Moreover, this is the date she discovered that the needle was causing her problems, never having been informed previously that the needle from the 1964 biopsy procedure remained lodged within her.

Inadequate Airway

In *Ward v. Epting*,[63] the anesthesiologist failed to establish and maintain an adequate airway and properly resuscitate a 22-year-old postsurgical patient, which resulted in the patient's death from lack of oxygen. Expert testimony based on autopsy and blood gas tests showed that the endotracheal tube had been removed too soon after surgery and that the anesthesiologist, in an attempt to revive the patient, reinserted the tube into the esophagus. The record on appeal was found to have contained ample evidence that the anesthesiologist failed to conform to the standard of care and that such deviation was the proximate cause of the patient's death.

Improper Positioning of Arm

The plaintiff in *Wick v. Henderson*[64] experienced pain in her left arm upon awakening from surgery; an anesthesiologist told her that her arm was stressed during surgery. According to the plaintiff, she sustained an injury to the ulnar nerve in her left upper arm. A malpractice action was filed against the hospital and the anesthesiologist. The plaintiff sought recovery on theory of res ipsa loquitur. There was testimony that the main cause of the injury was the mechanical compression of the nerve by improper positioning of the arm during surgery. The trial court granted the defendants a directed verdict, resulting in dismissal of the case.

On appeal, the Iowa Supreme Court held that the res ipsa loquitur doctrine applied. The plaintiff must prove two foundational facts in order to invoke the doctrine of res ipsa loquitur. She must prove, first, that the defendants had exclusive control and management of the instrument that caused her injury, and, second, that it was the type of injury that ordinarily would not occur if reasonable care had been used. As to control, the plaintiff can show an injury resulting from an external force applied while she lay unconscious in the hospital. It is within common knowledge and experience of a layperson that an individual does not enter the hospital for gallbladder surgery and leave with ulnar nerve injury.

Sciatic Nerve Injury

The plaintiff in *Lacombe v. Dr. Walter Olin Moss Regional Hospital*[65] was admitted to the hospital for a bladder suspension operation. Upon regaining consciousness in the recovery room, the plaintiff began complaining of severe pain in her right buttock, shooting down the back of her right leg. The plaintiff was eventually diagnosed with sciatic nerve injury. It is undisputed that the injury is permanent. A medical malpractice claim was filed against the hospital and the physicians involved in the surgery. A medical review panel rendered a decision finding no breach of the standard of care.

The plaintiff then filed a malpractice suit against the hospital and physicians. By the time of trial, all of the defendants, except the hospital, had been dismissed from the litigation. After trial, the trial judge rendered judgment in favor of the plaintiff. The trial judge found that, applying the doctrine of res ipsa loquitur to the evidence, the plaintiff had proven her case. Accordingly, he found the hospital responsible under the theory of respondeat superior for the negligent conduct of its agents (the personnel who prepared the plaintiff for surgery and the physicians who conducted the operation).

The hospital contended that the trial court incorrectly applied the doctrine of res ipsa loquitur. The facts established by the plaintiff also must reasonably permit the jury to discount other possible causes and to conclude it was more likely than not that the defendant's negligence caused the injury.

The Louisiana Court of Appeal agreed with the trial court that the evidence warranted an inference that negligence on the part of the defendant caused the injury and that an inference of res ipsa loquitur could be applied. Expert testimony established that the plaintiff was suffering from a sciatic nerve injury and that the injury was permanent. Experts on both sides agreed that sciatic nerve injury was not a known risk of this surgery. The testimony indicated that the plaintiff went into the hospital without the injury and came out with it.

Preventing Surgical Mishaps

The number of surgical errors can be reduced by adhering to the following practices:

- Requiring that second opinions are obtained as necessary and relevant; literature is searched; and other resources are used to provide current, timely, and accurate diagnoses and treatment options for each patient
- Ensuring each operating surgeon present during a specific procedure is qualified and has been credentialed to perform his or her role in the surgical procedure in which he or she is about to participate
- Informing patients regarding the risks, benefits, and alternatives to anesthesia, surgical procedures, and the administration of blood or blood products

- Executing consent forms and placing them in the patient's record
- Assigning responsibility for ensuring that appropriate surgical equipment, supplies, and staffing are available prior to the administration of anesthesia
- Completing pertinent and thorough history and physical exams and reviewing them prior to surgery
- Conducting a preanesthesia assessment
- Ensuring a process exists by which there is correlation of pathology and diagnostic findings
- Continuously monitoring vital signs, airway, and surgical site assessments during the procedure

▶ DISCHARGE AND FOLLOW-UP CARE

The premature discharge of a patient is risky business. The intent of discharging patients more expeditiously is often a result of a need to reduce costs. As pointed out by Dr. Nelson, an obstetrician and board member of the American Medical Association, such decisions "should be based on medical factors and ought not be relegated to bean counters."[66]

As noted in *Doan v. Griffith*,[67] discharge instructions must be clear and complete. In this case, an accident victim was admitted to the hospital with serious injuries, including multiple fractures of his facial bones. The patient contended that the physician was negligent in not advising him at the time of discharge that his facial bones needed to be realigned by a specialist before the bones became fused. As a result, his face became disfigured. Expert testimony demonstrated that the customary medical treatment for the patient's injuries would have been to realign his fractured bones surgically as soon as the swelling subsided and that such treatment would have restored the normal contour of his face. The appellate court held that the jury reasonably could have found that the physician failed to provide timely advice to the patient regarding his need for further medical treatment and that such failure was the proximate cause of the patient's condition.

Untimely Discharge

Barbara Jupiter, executrix of the estate of Warren Jupiter, brought an action against the Department of Veterans Affairs (VA) in *Jupiter v. U.S.*[68] The suit alleged that Mr. Jupiter sustained personal injury, pain, and suffering prior to his death, which was allegedly caused by the negligence of the defendant's agents and

employees while he was a patient at the VA hospital. A bench trial was conducted over a period of 7 days.

Mr. Jupiter had elected to undergo bariatric surgery for weight loss at the VA hospital. One step in the operation was claimed to be a departure from the accepted practice of performing bariatric surgery, and it was this step that lead to an infection, and ultimately, resulted in the Jupiter's death. The record showed that the distal stomach was removed at that time. The removal of the distal stomach was determined to be a departure from the standard of care.

Evidence in this case included testimony from 14 witnesses, medical records, reports of approximately 6,000 pages, and multiple anatomic diagrams and images. One witness, Dr. Randall, who had performed over 6,000 bariatric surgeries, testified that in his opinion there was no surgical reason for removing the distal stomach. He explained that the basis for that opinion was the positive postoperative management opportunities of which Jupiter was deprived by the removal of the distal stomach. Jupiter was discharged with an elevated white blood cell (WBC) count without timely treatment. Dr. Randall was of the opinion that the elevated WBC count indicated that there was an ongoing infection at the time Jupiter was discharged.

Jupiter was readmitted to the VA hospital on June 13, 2003, and an evaluation of his condition revealed a urinary tract infection (UTI), which was successfully treated. By June 23, 2003, even though his WBC count remained high, he was discharged from the VA hospital and sent to St. Alban's Hospital. Dr. Telzak testified that that decision departed from accepted medical practice. Additionally, he testified that the early departure from the VA hospital on May 14, 2003, also was unacceptable medical practice because no determination was made as to why his WBC count remained elevated. His testimony was further supported by the fact that several months later, in November of 2003, an abdominal CT scan evidenced a gastric leak and fluid in the ultra-abdominal cavity. This, he testified, was the cause of the elevated WBC count on June 23.

The surgeon had failed to address Jupiter's condition 2 months earlier when there were signs of infection. Furthermore, he was indifferent as to whether or not his recommendation to address the possibility of an internal gastric leak attributable to his surgery was addressed. He claimed it was the medical service's responsibility and not his. His testimony is startling given the testimony of Dr. Weinshel, the Deputy Chief of Staff of the VA hospital who, when asked whether the department of surgery was responsible for the patient's follow-up care, answered "sure."[69]

The failure to make or attempt to make a differential diagnosis which the undiagnosed elevated white blood count, the fever (the inexplicable failure to take his temperature for weeks), his progressive debilitation, failure to thrive, anorexia, virtually cried out for is, that if that were done and the relationship between an intra-abdominal leak and the infection was revealed and corrective surgery performed at or about June 2003, the likelihood of a successful outcome was better than it was when that surgery was finally performed approximately 5 months later, in November. Tr.76, 195-96.

The court concluded that the defendant's negligence was the proximate cause of the patient's pain and suffering. The plaintiff's estate was awarded $5.9 million.

Failure to Provide Follow-up Care

Failure to provide follow-up care can result in a lawsuit if such failure results in injury to a patient. In *Truan v. Smith*,[70] the Tennessee Supreme Court entered judgment in favor of the plaintiffs, who had brought action against a treating physician for damages alleged to have been the result of malpractice by the physician in the examination, diagnosis, and treatment of breast cancer. In January or February of 1974, the patient noticed a change in the size and firmness of her left breast, which she attributed to an implant. She later noticed discoloration and pain on pressure. While being examined by the defendant on March 25, 1974, for another ailment, the patient brought her symptoms to the physician's attention but received no significant response, and the physician made no examination of the breast at that time. The patient brought her symptoms to the attention of her physician for the second time on May 6, 1974. She had been advised by the defendant to observe her left breast for 30 days for a change in symptoms, which at the time of the examination included discomfort, discoloration, numbness, and sharp pain. She was given an appointment for 1 month later. The patient, on the morning of her appointment, June 3, 1974, called the physician's office and informed the nurse that her symptoms had not changed and that she would like to know whether she should keep her appointment. The nurse indicated that she would pass on her message to the physician. The patient assumed she would be called back if it was necessary to see the physician.

By late June, the symptoms became more acute, and the patient made an appointment to see the defendant physician on July 8, 1974. The patient also was scheduled to see a specialist on July 10, 1974, at which time she was admitted to the hospital and was diagnosed as having a malignant mass. A radical mastectomy was performed. Expert witnesses expressed the opinion that the mass had been palpable 7 months before the removal. When the defendant undertook to give the plaintiff a complete physical examination and embarked on a wait-and-see program as an aid in diagnosis, the physician should have followed up with his patient, who died before the conclusion of the trial.

The state supreme court held that the evidence was sufficient to support a finding that the defendant was guilty of malpractice in failing to inform his patient that cancer was a possible cause of her complaints and in failing to make any effort to see his patient at the expiration of the observation period instituted by him.

Failure to Follow Up on Test Results

The patient in *Downey v. University Internists of St. Louis, Inc.*[71] entered the hospital in December of 1996 for heart bypass surgery. Two chest X-rays were taken during this hospitalization. The X-rays were interpreted as showing a lesion in the patient's left lung and that a neoplasm could not be completely ruled out. If clinically warranted, CT scanning could be performed. No further tests or evaluations were ordered in response to these reports. A jury found that the now-deceased patient had a material chance of surviving his cancer and that his chance of survival was lost as a result of the physician's negligence. The jury, however, did not award damages to compensate for the harm suffered. The Missouri Court of Appeals found that the verdict of no-damage award was inconsistent with the evidence and remanded the case for a new trial.

Abandonment

Lack of patient care follow-up can sometimes be the result of the physician abandoning his patient for a variety of reasons. It can be the result of a personality conflict or it could be pure negligence in following up on the patient's care needs. The relationship between a physician and a patient, once established, continues until it is ended by the mutual consent of the parties, the patient's dismissal of the physician, the physician's withdrawal from the case, or agreement that the physician's services are no longer required. A physician who decides to withdraw his or her services must provide the patient with reasonable notice so that the services of another physician can be obtained. Premature termination of treatment is often the subject of a legal action for *abandonment*—the unilateral termination of a physician–patient relationship by the physician without notice to the patient. The following elements should be established in order for a patient to recover damages for abandonment:

- Medical care was unreasonably discontinued.
- The discontinuance of medical care was against the patient's will. Termination of the physician–patient relationship must have been brought about by a unilateral act of the physician. There can be no issue of abandonment if the relationship is terminated by mutual consent or by dismissal of the physician by the patient.
- The physician failed to arrange for care by another physician.
- Foresight indicated that discontinuance might result in physical harm to the patient.
- Actual harm was suffered by the patient.

▶ INFECTIONS

The Centers for Disease Control and Prevention estimates that nearly 2 million patients are stricken annually with hospital-acquired infections. There are estimates that as many as 90,000 of these patients die annually as a result of these infections.[72]

The mere fact that a patient contracted an infection after an operation will not, in and of itself, cause a surgeon to be liable for negligence. The reason for this, according to the Nebraska Supreme Court in *McCall v. St. Joseph Hospital*,[73] is as follows:

> Neither authority nor reason will sustain any proposition that negligence can reasonably be inferred from the fact that an infection originated at the site of a surgical wound. To permit a jury to infer negligence would be to expose every doctor and dentist to the charge of negligence every time an infection originated at the site of a wound. We note the complete absence of any expert testimony or any offer of proof in this record to the effect that a staphylococcus infection would automatically lead to an inference of negligence by the people in control of the operation or the treatment of the patient.[74]

Several cases that have lead to infection-related lawsuits are reviewed below.

Failure to Effectively Manage Infections

Making a case for using clinical guidelines is demonstrated in *McKowan v. Bentley*,[75] in which the patient, Mrs. Bentley, sought advice about gastric bypass surgery from Dr. McKowan in January 1993. On March 8, 1993, McKowan, assisted by Dr. Day, performed gastric bypass surgery on Bentley to alleviate her morbid obesity. Bentley was discharged from the hospital 2 days later with no indication of complications. On March 14, Bentley returned to see McKowan with redness and swelling around her incision. McKowan removed the sutures and found that Bentley had a wound infection. There was no indication that she had an intra-abdominal infection at that time. On March 15, the drainage from her wound changed in character, and she was admitted to the hospital. McKowan operated on Bentley and drained the abscesses. Bentley had exploratory surgery on March 17 so that the doctors could see the extent to which the surgery had successfully reduced her infection. McKowan operated again and found no disruption of the wound site.

On March 18, another follow-up surgery was performed. Following that surgery, Bentley was placed on a ventilator and began receiving total parenteral nutrition intravenously.

On March 22, surgery was again performed on Bentley. This time, McKowan cut the front part of the stomach and placed a gastrostomy tube in the lower stomach. On March 26, purulent drainage was discovered around the gastrostomy tube. The gastrostomy site was repaired. Bentley showed some improvement on March 27.

At that point, McKowan went on vacation and Dr. Day took over Bentley's care. On March 28, Day performed surgery to remove purulent material in the abdomen. On May 30, Bentley's sister transferred her to University of Alabama Hospital in Birmingham, where she died.

Mr. Bentley filed a malpractice case. At trial, the plaintiff presented expert testimony from Dr. Kirchner, who testified that Bentley died because McKowan and Day did not properly manage her postoperative infection. Kirchner testified that the conduct of both physicians in managing the massive intra-abdominal infection fell below the legally imposed standard of care in Alabama. Testimony of the plaintiff's expert was emphatic, stating that the defendants disregarded obvious signs of grave complications; omitted obvious, simple, effective measures for stopping the infection that eventually killed the patient; and repeatedly applied inappropriate measures virtually certain to exacerbate the infection. The jury awarded Mr. Bentley $2 million in punitive damages. The defendants contended that the award was excessive. The defendants' motion for a new trial was denied.

Poor Infection Control Technique

A jury verdict in the amount of $300,000 was awarded in *Langley v. Michael*[76] for damages arising from the amputation of the plaintiff's thumb. Evidence that the orthopedic surgeon failed to deeply cleanse, irrigate, and debride the injured area of the patient's thumb constituted proof of a departure from that degree of skill and learning ordinarily used by members of the medical profession and that this failure directly contributed to the patient's loss of the distal portion of his thumb.

Preventing the Spread of Infection

A district court of appeals held in *Gill v. Hartford Accident & Indemnity Co.*[77] that the physician who performed surgery on a patient in the same room as the plaintiff should have known that the patient's infection was highly contagious. The failure of the physician to undertake steps to prevent the spread of the infection to the plaintiff and his failure to warn the plaintiff led the court to find that hospital authorities and the plaintiff's physician caused an unreasonable increase in the risk of injury. As a result, the plaintiff suffered injuries causally related to the negligence of the defendant.

▶ PSYCHIATRY

The major risk areas of behavioral health professionals include commitment, electroshock, duty to warn, and suicide. Matters relating to admission, consent, and discharge are governed by statute in most states. Several areas where behavioral healthcare lawsuits occur more frequently are described next.

Commitment

The recent emphasis on patient rights has had a major impact on the necessity to perform an appropriate assessment prior to commitment. State statutes often provide requirements granting an individual's rights to legal counsel and other procedural safeguards (e.g., patient hotline) governing the admission, retention, and discharge of patients.

Most states have enacted administrative procedures that must be followed. The various statutes often require that two physicians certify the need for commitment. Physicians who participate in the commitment of a patient should do so only after first examining the patient and reaching their own conclusions. Reliance on another's examination and recommendation for commitment could give rise to a claim of malpractice. Commitment is generally necessary in those situations in which a person may be in substantial danger of injuring himself or herself or third persons.

Involuntary Commitment

In *In re Detention of Meistrell*,[78] proof of dangerousness was found adequate to support an order for involuntary commitment. There was testimony that on two occasions, the patient jumped off a teeter-totter, causing his two small children to fall to the ground. A substantial risk of physical harm to others also was demonstrated by testimony that the patient threatened his wife's ex-husband.

Involuntary Commitment Ordered

There was clear and convincing evidence in *Luis A. v. Pilgrim Psychiatric Center*[79] that the patient remained extremely psychotic and delusional. This was manifested by his own testimony denying that the victim of the crime in which he participated in 1990 was dead. Furthermore, he denied his attempted suicide on two prior occasions, his substance abuse problems, and his mental illness. The evidence showed that the patient believed that the reason he was reincarcerated upon violating his probation in 2000 was a conspiracy by certain individuals against him rather than the fact that he tested positive for marijuana and violated his curfew. The evidence demonstrated that the patient would likely relapse to his substance abuse. He posed a substantial threat of physical harm to himself and others if release from the care and control of the facility was permitted. Proof was demonstrated that if released, he intended to reside with his elderly mother, who had a significant history of mental illness herself and was incapable of properly caring for him out of an institutional setting or of preventing deterioration in his mental health status. Expert medical opinion indicated that such would inevitably occur. The application to retain the respondent on an involuntary basis was granted.

Continuation of Commitment

In *In re Todd*,[80] a psychiatrist filed a petition for additional detention of a patient previously ordered admitted to a state hospital for pretrial psychiatric examination. The circuit court, after hearing testimony from the appellant's son, a social worker at the hospital, and the psychiatrist, ordered detention, and the detainee appealed. The episode that gave rise to the involuntary commitment occurred when the appellant threw eggs at a house and various businesses and also broke some windows at a house with a tire iron. She lightly bumped a police car and was charged with second-degree property damage. During her involuntary detention, she refused to take her medications, which were necessary because of her illness. The psychiatrist indicated his concern that, on release, she might harm her invalid husband. Detention was considered necessary until such time as drugs could control the detainee's illness. The court of appeals held that the testimony of the psychiatrist established clear and convincing evidence to meet a required standard that the detainee's actions presented risk of serious harm to herself or others.

Involuntary Commitment of Invalid

In *In re Carl*,[81] a New York Supreme Court found a patient to be mentally ill and authorized his involuntary retention. On appeal, however, the New York Supreme Court, Appellate Division, held that the state had not shown by clear and convincing evidence that the patient's instability caused him to pose a substantial threat of physical injury to himself or others. The examining physician's testimony indicated that the patient did not pose a direct threat of physical harm to himself or others but that it was questionable whether he would be able to provide for the essentials of life. The patient testified that he was aware of food needs, of where to get food, and how he would pay for it. He indicated that he would not sleep outside and that he had a bed in a rooming house where he had been paying rent for 2 years.

Commitment by a Spouse

The plaintiff's husband in *Bencomo v. Morgan*[82] filed a petition to have his wife declared incompetent. In a letter supporting the petition, the defendant physician, who had treated the wife 10 years previously, stated that she was badly in need of a psychiatric examination. The plaintiff wife attempted to sue the physician for libel and slander. The court held that the plaintiff had no cause for action because it was her husband who initiated the commitment procedures.

Commitment by a Parent

The U.S. Supreme Court in *Parham v. J.R.*[83] held that the risk of error inherent in a parental decision to have a child institutionalized for mental health care is sufficiently great that an inquiry should be made by a neutral fact finder to determine whether statutory requirements for admission are satisfied. Although a formal or quasiformal hearing is not required and

an inquiry does not need to be conducted by a legally trained judicial or administrative officer, such inquiry must probe a child's background using all available sources. It is necessary that a decision maker have the authority to refuse to admit a child who does not satisfy medical standards for admission. A child's continuing need for commitment also must be reviewed periodically by a similarly independent procedure.

Patient Due-Process Rights

The principles of due process were violated in *Birl v. Wallis*[84] when an involuntarily committed patient was conditionally released and once again confined without notice and opportunity for a hearing. Remand was required to permit the drafting of reconfinement procedures that would protect the patient's due-process rights.

Release Denied

In *State v. Wenk*,[85] Wenk was charged with one count of attempt to entice a child for immoral purposes in October 1977. He entered a plea of not guilty. While awaiting trial and out on bail, Wenk was charged with three additional felonies involving an 11-year-old boy—one count of abduction and two counts of first-degree sexual assault. Ultimately, Wenk withdrew his pleas of not guilty but maintained a plea of not guilty by reason of a mental disorder. The trial court agreed with Wenk and found him not guilty as a result of his mental disorder. The trial court also found him dangerous and that he needed to be committed. Wenk successfully petitioned for conditional release in 1979. Five years later, Wenk waived his right to contest the motion seeking revocation of his conditional release after his probation agent instituted proceedings against him when it was discovered that Wenk failed to remain drug free and to abstain from contacting his ex-wife.

Wenk, at the age of 76, again petitioned the trial court seeking conditional release. As a result of his request, the trial court appointed two experts to examine Wenk: Palermo, a psychiatrist, and Smail, a psychologist. At the hearing, the state called Smail, who testified that Wenk could be released if certain conditions were placed on him. Also admitted into evidence were Palermo's report and the report of Chapman, a clinical psychologist employed by the state institution. Both of these reports recommended that Wenk be released, but only if certain conditions were placed upon him. Following the close of testimony, the assistant district attorney stated that he was unsure whether he had met his burden of proof, but he urged the court to place conditions on Wenk if the trial court decided to release him.

The trial court, disagreeing with the doctors' ultimate recommendations, found that Wenk was still dangerous. He had a long-standing substance abuse problem, and although Wenk had not abused drugs while he was confined, the trial court believed his drug relapse that occurred during his earlier conditional release indicated he still posed a danger to the community if released. As a result, the trial court, in denying the petition, found that the state had met its burden of proof to a reasonable certainty by evidence that is clear and convincing that Wenk still remained dangerous.

Wenk argued that all of the expert witnesses who examined him opined that he could be released under certain conditions. The court remained unpersuaded by his arguments. None of the doctors believed Wenk should be unconditionally released. Each recommended his release only under certain conditions. In Chapman's report, the doctor noted that Wenk had been previously diagnosed as suffering from bipolar disorder, as well as inhalant dependence. Chapman reasoned that Wenk could be conditionally released because Wenk's mental illness appeared to be in remission. With regard to Wenk's addiction to toluene, a paint thinner, Chapman acknowledged that Wenk used this drug when he engaged in his sexual criminal conduct, but Chapman's report contained the mistaken entry that during the 4 years Wenk was on conditional release, Wenk reported that he had no temptation to inhale. Wenk's records clearly show that Wenk was recommitted, in part, as a result of his probation agent's discovery of his drug addiction. Consequently, the doctor's opinion that Wenk could be conditionally released was premised on his mistaken belief that Wenk had no difficulty with drugs during his previous release. Either Wenk minimized his toluene abuse when discussing his history with Chapman or Chapman failed to investigate the record.

Smail testified that Wenk's inhalant dependence was in remission. He did, however, admit that all of Wenk's criminal acts took place while he was under the influence of toluene. Smail's recommendation in favor of conditional release was also based on Wenk's statement to him that he had no personal concerns about resuming his abuse of inhalants. This self-serving opinion was not only overly optimistic but also, given Wenk's past conduct, not borne out by his history.

Palermo's report acknowledged that Wenk was abusing drugs when recommitted, but notwithstanding this history, Palermo recommended that Wenk be conditionally released, although he failed to set forth in his report any conditions that needed to be imposed on Wenk when he was released. This gaping hole in Palermo's report could easily have caused the trial court to lack confidence in the doctor's opinion.

The Wisconsin Court of Appeals determined that the record supported the trial court's decision. The differences of opinion between the doctors and the trial court lay with their prediction of Wenk's likely behavior when released. While the trial court acknowledged that predicting a person's future behavior is a difficult task, it pointed out that the past predictions of the psychiatric experts were wrong. Further, the trial court stated that its prediction for Wenk's future behavior was based on his past conduct, conduct that strongly suggested it was quite likely that Wenk would again abuse drugs, posing too great a danger to the community to release him.

Untimely Discharge

A trial court decided that an insanity acquittee suffering from schizophrenia, paranoid type, in remission, failed to meet his burden of proving that he should be discharged, even though a psychiatric review board had recommended discharge. Two psychiatrists testified that as long as the patient was taking his medication, he was in no danger to himself or to others. The appeals court decision, based on the entire record, found that the acquittee had not proven by a preponderance of the evidence that there was a mechanism in place to provide for continuation of the required medication if he was released from supervision. The court considered the violent nature of the underlying crimes (e.g., attempt to commit sexual assault in the first degree and kidnapping in the first degree), which was precipitated by the acquittee's mental illness. It was unclear whether the patient would continue to show the same progress after being discharged from the board's supervision.[86]

Electroshock Therapy

Most states have laws and regulations governing the use of electroshock therapy and other treatments for psychiatric patients. Failure to abide by these statutory and regulatory guidelines may result in liability to the organization and treating physician.

Duty to Warn

In *Tarasoff v. Regents of the University of California*,[87] a former patient allegedly killed a third party after revealing his homicidal plans to his therapist. His therapist made no effort to inform the victim of the patient's intentions. The California Supreme Court held that when a therapist determines or reasonably should determine that a patient poses a serious danger of violence to others, there is a duty to exercise reasonable care to protect the foreseeable victims and to warn them of any impending danger. Discharge of this duty also may include notifying the police or taking whatever steps are reasonably necessary under the circumstances.

Under Nebraska law, the relationship between a psychotherapist and a patient gives rise to an affirmative duty to initiate whatever precautions are reasonably necessary to protect the potential victims of a patient. This duty develops when a therapist knows or should know that a patient's dangerous propensities present an unreasonable risk of harm to others.[88]

Exceptions to Duty to Warn

The Maryland Court of Special Appeals in *Shaw v. Glickman*[89] held that a plaintiff could not recover against a psychiatric team on the theory that they were negligent in failing to warn the plaintiff of the patient's unstable and violent condition. The court held that making such a disclosure would violate statutes pertaining to privilege against disclosure of communications relating to treatment of mental or emotional disorders. The court found that a psychiatrist may have a duty to warn the potential victim of a dangerous mental patient's intent to harm. However, the duty could be imposed only if the psychiatrist knew the identity of the prospective victim.

The psychiatrist in *Currie v. United States*[90] was found not to have had a duty to seek the involuntary commitment of a patient who evidenced homicidal tendencies. Absent control over the patient, the federal government could not be held liable for a murder that the patient committed at his former place of employment. The psychiatrist had warned the patient's former employer and law enforcement officials that he could be dangerous.

There was no duty on the part of the hospital or treating psychiatrists in *Sharpe v. South Carolina Department of Mental Health*[91] to warn the general public of the potential danger that might result from a psychiatric patient's release from a state hospital. There was no identifiable threat to a decedent who was shot by the patient approximately 2 months after the patient's release from voluntary commitment under a plan of outpatient care. In addition, there was nothing in the record indicating that the former patient and the decedent had known each other prior to the patient's release.

Suicidal Patients

Organizations have a duty to exercise reasonable care to protect suicidal patients from foreseeable harm. This duty exists whether the patient is voluntarily admitted or involuntarily committed. The District Court in *Abille v. United States*[92] held that evidence supported a finding that the attending physician had not authorized a change in status of a suicidal patient to permit him to leave the ward without an escort. The nursing staff allowed him to leave the ward, and he found a window from which he jumped. This constituted a breach of the standard of due care under the law in Alaska, where the act or omission occurred.

The attendant in *Fernandez v. State*[93] left a patient alone in her room for 5 minutes when the patient appeared to be asleep. During the attendant's absence, the patient injured herself in a repeated suicide attempt. The court found that even if the hospital assumed a duty to observe the patient continually, such a 5-minute absence would not constitute negligence. Therefore, the hospital could not be held liable for the patient's injuries.

However, in a case in which a patient with a 14-year history of mental problems escaped from a hospital and committed suicide by jumping off a roof,[94] the record showed that the patient was to be checked every 15 minutes. There was no evidence that such checks had been made. The appellate court ruled that the facts showed a prima facie case of negligence.

The New York Supreme Court, Appellate Division, in *Eady v. Alter*,[95] held that an intern's notation on the hospital record that the patient tried to jump out the window was sufficient to establish a prima facie case against the hospital. The patient succeeded in committing suicide by jumping out the window approximately 10 minutes after having been seen by the intern. Testimony had been given that the patient was restrained inadequately after the reported attempted suicide.

Flawed Evaluation

John Doe was at his father's home seeking help in overcoming a heroin addiction. Doe was acting noticeably withdrawn and began vomiting. The plaintiff-father took his son to a local hospital to be evaluated for drug withdrawal. Doe tested negative for the presence of drugs in his blood and was discharged with instructions to attend a drug rehab program. The following day, the father became aware that his son had attempted suicide. He called the office of a drug rehab program for help and was advised to take Doe to the hospital's crisis center.

The crisis center referred the father and his son to the hospital's emergency department. The father explained to the emergency department nurse that his son had attempted suicide by cutting his wrist. Doe's wrist was bandaged. The father and his son proceeded to the crisis center. Following an interview by a nurse and physician, the physician and nurse advised the father that his son was not suicidal but was "acting out" and looking for attention. Hospitalization was not offered, and the plaintiff was advised to follow up with a drug rehab program. Doe's medical records contain no information regarding voluntary hospitalization being recommended or offered, nor do the records reflect that the son refused any offer of voluntary hospitalization.

They returned home, and Doe went to bed. When the father checked Doe at about 6:00 AM, he was gone. He telephoned the home of his ex-wife and was relieved to learn that his son was there. The father agreed to pick him up before the mother left for work. A few minutes later, the mother called and told the father that their son had left the house. The father immediately went to look for his son. While searching for his son, he noticed flashing lights on a nearby highway. When he went to see what was happening, he saw paramedics administering cardiopulmonary resuscitation to his son. The father was told that his son jumped in front of a dump truck and was killed.

A lawsuit was filed against the defendants alleging negligence, malpractice, and infliction of emotional distress. At trial, the physician testified that the deceased declined voluntary admission to the hospital. However, in a deposition prior to trial, he testified that he could not recall whether Doe had declined voluntary admission or not. On cross-examination, the physician conceded that he had never specifically recommended hospitalization to Doe. The nurse testified that voluntary hospitalization was offered as an option to the plaintiff and his son but was not recommended. That option, if in fact offered, was not recorded in the hospital record.

The plaintiff's medical experts testified that (1) because of Doe's two suicide attempts, he needed hospitalization; (2) additional steps should have been taken prior to ruling out major depression; (3) in all probability, Doe would not have killed himself had he been hospitalized earlier and put on medications; and (4) Doe's prior suicide attempts should have been taken more seriously. They opined that the failure to hospitalize Doe and keep him under close supervision was a deviation from accepted standards of medical practice. The defendants' expert testified to the contrary but conceded on cross-examination that Doe had at least three high-risk factors for suicide.

The trial largely turned to a contest between the experts. The jury, by its verdict, accepted the opinions of the plaintiff's experts. The court found, after a review of the record, no reason to disturb the jury's verdict. The plaintiff, as administrator of the estate of his late son, recovered a verdict of $425,000 against the defendants for their failure to provide appropriate evaluation and hospitalization of Doe.[96]

Inadequate Care

The hospital system in *Pinnacle Health System v. Dep't of Public Welfare*[97] was found to have been properly denied Medicaid reimbursement for providing inpatient psychiatric services that fell below the requisite standard. In this case, patients were not examined daily as required by a psychiatrist. Professionals who work in the healthcare setting recognize that this is not an uncommon occurrence. This case is typical of what has driven up healthcare costs in the United States.

▶ PRINCIPLES OF MEDICAL ETHICS

The medical profession has long subscribed to a body of ethical guidelines developed primarily for the benefit of the patient. As a member of this profession, a physician must recognize responsibility to patients first and foremost, as well as to society, to other health professionals, and to self.

The following principles adopted by the American Medical Association are not laws, but rather standards of conduct that define the essentials of honorable behavior for the physician.

Code of Medical Ethics

I. A physician shall be dedicated to providing competent medical care, with compassion and respect for human dignity and rights.

II. A physician shall uphold the standards of professionalism, be honest in all professional interactions, and strive to report physicians deficient in character or competence, or engaging in fraud or deception, to appropriate entities.

III. A physician shall respect the law and also recognize a responsibility to seek changes in those requirements that are contrary to the best interests of the patient.

IV. A physician shall respect the rights of patients, colleagues, and other health professionals, and shall safeguard patient confidences and privacy within the constraints of the law.

V. A physician shall continue to study, apply, and advance scientific knowledge; maintain a commitment to medical education; make relevant information available to patients, colleagues, and the public; obtain consultation; and use the talents of other health professionals when indicated.

VI. A physician shall, in the provision of appropriate patient care, except in emergencies, be free to choose whom to serve, with whom to associate, and the environment in which to provide medical care.

VII. A physician shall recognize a responsibility to participate in activities contributing to the improvement of the community and the betterment of public health.

VIII. A physician shall, while caring for a patient, regard responsibility to the patient as paramount.

IX. A physician shall support access to medical care for all people.[98]

The following correspondence in the form of a *reality check* describes one episode of a frustrated patient's journey of being passed from physician to physician, eventually finding one she thought would help her find the answers to her mysterious disease.

What happened to the first principle in the code of medical ethics for physicians?

I. A physician shall be dedicated to providing competent medical care, with compassion and respect for human dignity and rights.

The physician failed to respond. The patient considered contacting the hospital governing body as well as regulatory and accreditation agencies but never pursued the option because her painful disease consumed her life.

The patient's hope for answers and possible treatment in this *reality check* were dashed. The patient began to lose trust in the medical profession. I listened as she explained to me, "I was troubled as I stood looking at the *code of medical ethics* that hung so prominently in the physician's waiting room. All the right words were there, only one thing was missing." I asked

✓ MY HOPES FOR HELP CRUMBLE

"When I went to your office, it was with great hopes that someone was finally going to piece together all of the bizarre symptoms I have been experiencing over the last several months and get to the cause of my pain.

I was quite frankly shocked by how I was treated as a patient—especially one experiencing a health crisis. A medical student examined me. He wrote my history and current health problems on a small "yellow sticky pad." You were not in the room when he examined me, and then I saw you for approximately 10 minutes. You took the business card of my New York doctor and said you were going to call him, and then call me regarding what you thought the next steps should be.

I called you on Friday because my local doctor said that you had not called, and I was told you were on vacation until yesterday. I had asked that you call me. You never did. I called you yesterday again, but you did not answer nor did you return my call. On Monday, I received a letter from a medical student, I assume. Although I empathize with the demands on your time, I have never seen a handwritten letter, which I received, informing me of test results I provided to you prior to my appointment with you. You never mentioned the liver enzyme elevations or my February test from New York. Moreover, no mention was made regarding any plan to help me alleviate immediate problems.

Doctor, I am not a complainer or a person with a low pain tolerance. Since moving here, I've had fainting episodes, severe chest pain and pressure, leg and arm pain and stiffness, congestion on the left side when the pain kicks in, and by 3 o'clock I have to go home and lie down because I'm so weak and tired. I cannot continue to exist like this. It is not normal. If you're too busy and don't want to take me as a patient, you will not offend me. Frankly, I need attention now to get these things resolved. Testing my cholesterol in a month will not address the problem. I've been treated for that for three years.

Please call or write to me so I can get another doctor if I have to."

—Anonymous

her what was missing. She looked at me and emphatically said, "practice."

▶ PHYSICIAN–PATIENT RELATIONSHIP

The following suggestions can help improve the physician–patient relationship and decrease the probability of malpractice suits:

- Personalized treatment. A patient is more inclined to sue an impersonal physician than one with whom he or she has developed a good relationship.
- Conduct a thorough assessment/history and physical examination that includes a review of all body systems.
- Develop a problems list and comprehensive treatment plan that addresses the patient's problems.
- Provide sufficient time and care to each patient.
- Take the time to explain treatment plans and follow-up care to the patient, his or her family, and other professionals who are caring for your patient. Provide a copy of each update to the patient.
- Request consultations when indicated and refer if necessary.
- Closely monitor the patient's progress and, as necessary, make adjustments to the treatment plan as the patient's condition warrants.

THE COURT'S DECISION

The Illinois Appellate Court held that the evidence was sufficient to support a determination that the defendant's negligence caused the plaintiff's pain and suffering.

> Finally, defendant requests that we reduce the amount of the jury's award. A jury's award should not be disturbed on review as excessive unless it is shocking to the judicial conscience. (*Altszyler v. Horizon House Condominium Association* (1988), 175 Ill. App. 3d 93, 124 Ill. Dec. 723, 529 N.E.2d 704.) Plaintiff, a 29 year-old man with a family has suffered pain and restricted bodily movement for the past eight years. Moreover, based upon his life expectancy, he will probably continue to endure pain and suffering for the remainder of his life. Under these circumstances, we cannot say that the jury usurped its authority in determining this award.[99]

- Maintain timely, legible, complete, and accurate records. Do not make erasures.
- Do not guarantee treatment outcome.
- Provide for cross-coverage during days off.
- Do not overextend your practice.
- Avoid prescribing over the telephone.
- Do not become careless because you know the patient.
- Seek the advice of counsel should you suspect the possibility of a malpractice claim.
- Maintain the patient's privacy rights.

▶ CHAPTER REVIEW

1. A healthcare organization's bylaws set forth, among other things, the responsibilities of the medical staff. The committees of the staff review and analyze their responsibilities, clinical experiences, and opportunities for improvement.
2. In cases where a medical staff member's credentials are not screened properly, the healthcare organization can be held liable for injuries to patients as a result of the lack of investigation.
3. The application process includes an evaluation of the applicant's physical and mental status, the applicant's release of information from third parties, the applicant's provision of a certificate of insurance, provision of evidence of an applicant's state licensure, a query of the National Practitioner Data Bank for information on the applicant, evaluation of the applicant's references, a thorough interview of the applicant, and approval by the governing body.
4. The medical staff must determine what procedures a physician is authorized to perform. This determination, known as delineation of privileges, is based on set criteria for credentials required to perform with competence the privileges requested.
5. To commence a court action for issues such as initial denial of medical staff privileges, grievances, and disciplinary actions, a physician must first exhaust all remedies set forth in the hospital's bylaws, rules, and regulations.
6. Physician monitoring is most effectively practiced through peer review. The governing body of a hospital has a duty to create a means through which the medical staff can evaluate, counsel, and, when appropriate, take action against a physician whose actions pose an unreasonable risk of harm to a patient.
7. A physician is not liable for exercising his best judgment in following a course of treatment

that is supported by a reputable and respected body of medical experts. However, a physician is at risk for liability if he or she uses an unprecedented procedure that results in harm.

8. Common medical errors include: patient assessment, diagnosis, treatment, discharge, and follow-up care.

9. Infection control concerns include the failure to effectively manage infections and substandard infection control techniques.

10. Behavioral health risks include:

- Commitment issues
- Untimely discharge
- Electroshock therapy
- Duty to warn
  - If a therapist determines or should reasonably determine that a patient poses a serious threat of violence or danger to a third party, the therapist must exercise reasonable care to protect the third party and warn him or her of the impending danger.
- Flawed evaluation
- Inadequate care

▶ REVIEW QUESTIONS

1. Describe various principles identified in the medical code of ethics.
2. Explain medical staff organization and committee structure.
3. Describe the privileging and credentialing process.
4. Understand and describe common medical errors and how they lead to litigation.
5. Explain how the physician–patient relationship can be improved.
6. Describe common legal issues for behavioral health professionals.
7. Discuss the more common legal risks facing behavioral health professionals.

▶ NOTES

1. *Bombagetti v. Amine*, 627 N.E.2d 230 (Ill. App. Ct. 1993).
2. 42 C.F.R. § 482.12(a)(7).
3. American Board of Physician Specialties, "How Specialty Certification Helps Physicians Differentiate Their Credentials," http://www.abpsus.org/specialty-certification.

4. *Szold v. Medical Board of California*, 127 Cal. App. 4th 591, 25 Cal. Rptr. 3d 665 (Cal. App. 2005).
5. 835 F.2d 1250 (8th Cir. 1987).
6. *Warnick v. Natchez Community Hospital, Inc.*, No. 2003-CA-01513-SCT (Miss. 2004).
7. 33 Cal. Rptr. 673 (Cal. Ct. App. 1963).
8. No. 04AP-72 (Ohio Ct. App. 2004).
9. 645 P.2d 171 (Alaska 1982).
10. U.S. Department of Health and Human Services, "National Practitioner Data Bank 2012 Annual Report," http://www.npdb.hrsa.gov/resources/annualRpt.jsp.
11. American Medical Association, "Opinion 1.02 - The Relation of Law and Ethics," http://www.ama-assn.org/ama/pub/physician-resources/medical-ethics/code-medical-ethics/opinion102.page?
12. 173 N.W.2d 881 (Neb. 1970).
13. No. WD63543 (Mo. Ct. App. 2004).
14. 85 Conn. App. 854 (Conn. App. 2004).
15. 218 N.W.2d 492 (Iowa 1928).
16. 653 A.2d 541 (Md. App. 1995).
17. *Valentine v. Kaiser Found. Hosps.*, 15 Cal. Rptr. 26 (Cal. Ct. App. 1961) (*dictum*).
18. No. CA 04-02238 (N.Y. App. Div. 2005).
19. No. C538628 (L.A. Co. Cal. Super. Ct.).
20. 144 So. 2d 544 (La. Ct. App. 1962).
21. 595 P.2d 919 (Wash. 1979).
22. 294 F. Supp. 466 (D.S.C. 1968).
23. 632 A.2d 1333 (Pa. Super. Ct. 1993).
24. *Johnson v. MCV Associated*, CL10004982-00, Richmond City Circuit Court, March 22, 2012.
25. 865 F. Supp. 433 (N.D. Ohio 1994).
26. *Griffett v. Ryan*, 443 S.E.2d 149 (Va. 1994).
27. *Snyder v. George Washington Univ.*, 890 A.2d 237 (D.C. App. 2006).
28. 505 N.Y.S.2d 899 (N.Y. App. Div. 1986).
29. 235 A.2d 889 (N.J. 1967).
30. 568 N.W.2d 93 (Mich. App. 1997).
31. 126 N.J. 168, 594 A.2d 1309 (N.J. 1991).
32. *Id.*
33. 530 A.2d 1217 (D.C. 1987).
34. *Gomez v. Tri City Community Hosp.*, 4 S.W.3d 281 (Tex. App. 1999).
35. 531 A.2d 226 (D.C. 1987).
36. 666 F. Supp. 1511 (Ala. 1987).
37. 713 P.2d 773 (Wyo. 1986).
38. 209 So. 2d 809 (Miss. 1968).
39. *AA Medical Center v. Condon*, 649 A.2d 1189 (Md. App. 1994).
40. 698 So. 2d 469 (La. App. 4 Cir. 1997).
41. 630 S.2d 825 (La. Ct. App. 1983).

42. 735 F. Supp. 1 (D.D.C. 1990).
43. 582 So. 2d 1272 (La. 1991).
44. *John v. Jarrard*, 927 F.2d 551 (11th Cir. 1991).
45. 737 S.W.2d 455 (Ark. 1987).
46. 514 So. 2d 727 (La. Ct. App. 1987).
47. 348 S.E.2d 233 (Va. 1986).
48. 291 A.D.2d 744, 738 N.Y.S.2d 137 (N.Y. App. Div. 2002).
49. 520 N.Y.S.2d 751 (N.Y. App. Div. 1987).
50. 542 N.Y.S.2d 328 (N.Y. App. Div. 1989).
51. 523 N.Y.S.2d 645 (N.Y. App. Div. 1988).
52. 489 So. 2d 392 (La. Ct. App. 1986).
53. Chad Baldwin, "Medical News Summary: $1.175 Million Awarded in a Medical Malpractice Case," *Casper Star Tribune*, May 13, 2005, http://www.wrongdiagnosis.com/news/_1_175_million_awarded_in_a_medical_malpractice_case.htm.
54. Elizabeth Eaken Zhani, "Joint Commission Alert: Preventing Retained Surgical Items," The Joint Commission, October 17, 2013, http://www.jointcommission.org/joint_commission_alert_preventing_retained_surgical_items/.
55. *Watkins v. Cleveland Clinic Foundation*, 719 N.E.2d 1052 (Ohio App. 1998) (April 1995).
56. 539 S.W.2d 286 (Ky. 1976).
57. 785 A.2d 25 (2001).
58. 473 A.2d 429 (Md. 1984).
59. *Id.* at 431.
60. 745 N.Y.S.2d 304 (N.Y. App. Div. 2002).
61. 250 A.2d 40 (N.J. Super. Ct. App. Div. 1969).
62. 646 So. 2d 4 (Ala. 1994).
63. 351 S.E.2d 867 (S.C. Ct. App. 1987).
64. 485 N.W.2d 645 (Iowa 1992).
65. 617 So. 2d 612 (La. Ct. App. 1993).
66. Anita Manning, "AMA Calls Drive-Thru Birth Risky," *USA Today*, June 21, 1995: 1.
67. 402 S.W.2d 855 (Ky. Ct. App. 1966).
68. No. 05 CV 4449 (United States District Court, E.D. New York, December 20, 2012).
69. *Id.* (Tr. at 273).
70. 578 S.W.2d 73 (Tenn. 1979).
71. No. ED83231 (Mo. App. 2004).
72. John P. Burke, "Infection Control: A Problem for Patient Safety," *New England Journal of Medicine* 348 (2003): 651–656.
73. 165 N.W.2d 85 (Neb. 1969).
74. *Id.* at 89.
75. 773 So. 2d 990 (1999).
76. 710 S.W.2d 373 (Mo. Ct. App. 1986).
77. 337 So. 2d 420 (Fla. Dist. Ct. App. 1976).
78. 733 P.2d 1004 (Wash. Ct. App. 1987).
79. Nos. 2004-04404 & 2004-03036 (N.Y. App. Div. 2004).
80. 767 S.W.2d 589 (Mo. Ct. App. 1988).
81. 511 N.Y.S.2d 144 (N.Y. App. Div. 1987).
82. 210 So. 2d 236 (Fla. Dist. Ct. App. 1968).
83. 442 U.S. 584 (1979).
84. 619 F. Supp. 481 (D. Ala. 1985).
85. 637 N.W.2d 417 (2001).
86. *State v. Corr*, 867 A.2d 124, 87 (Conn. App. Ct. 2005).
87. 551 P.2d 334 (Cal. 1976).
88. See *Lipari v. Sears, Roebuck & Co.*, 497 F. Supp. 185 (D. Neb. 1980).
89. 415 A.2d 625 (Md. Ct. Spec. App. 1980).
90. 836 F.2d 209 (4th Cir. 1987).
91. 354 S.E.2d 778 (S.C. Ct. App. 1987).
92. 482 F. Supp. 703 (N.D. Cal. 1980).
93. 356 N.Y.S.2d 708 (N.Y. App. Div. 1974).
94. *Fatuck v. Hillside Hosp.*, 356 N.Y.S.2d 105 (N.Y. App. Div. 1974).
95. 380 N.Y.S.2d 737 (N.Y. App. Div. 1976).
96. *Vasilik v. Federbush*, 742 A.2d 591 (N.J. Super. Ct. App. Div. 1999).
97. 942 A.2d 189 (Pa. Cmwlth. 208).
98. American Medical Association, "AMA Code of Medical Ethics," Revised June 2001. https://www.ama-assn.org/sites/default/files/media-browser/principles-of-medical-ethics.pdf.
99. *Bombagetti v. Amineat* at 233.

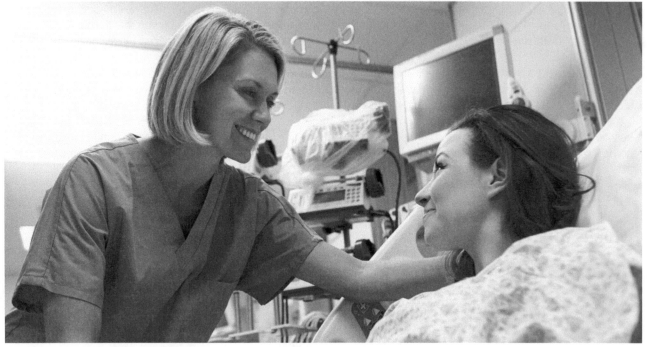

© Monkey Business Images/Shutterstock

CHAPTER 11

Nursing and the Law

🔍 IT'S YOUR GAVEL...

CHANCE OF SURVIVAL DIMINISHED

On the afternoon of May 20, the patient, Mr. Ard, began feeling nauseated. He was in pain and had shortness of breath. Although his wife rang the call bell several times, it was not until sometime later that evening that someone responded and gave Ard medication for the nausea. The nausea continued to worsen. Mrs. Ard then noticed that her husband was having difficulty breathing. He was reeling from side to side in bed. Believing that her husband was dying, she continued to call for help. She estimated that she rang the call bell for 1.25 hours before anyone responded. A code was eventually called. Unfortunately, Mr. Ard did not survive the code. There was no documentation in the medical records for May 20, between 5:30 PM and 6:45 PM, that would indicate that any nurse or physician checked on Ard's condition. This finding collaborated Mrs. Ard's testimony regarding this time period.

A wrongful death action was brought against the hospital, and the district court granted judgment for Mrs. Ard. The hospital appealed.

Ms. Krebs, an expert in general nursing, stated that it should have been obvious to the nurses from the physicians' progress notes that the patient was a high risk for aspiration. This problem was never addressed in the nurses' care plan or in the nurses' notes.

(continues)

IT'S YOUR GAVEL...   *(continued)*

On May 20, Ard's assigned nurse was Ms. Florscheim. Krebs stated that Florscheim did not perform a full assessment of the patient's respiratory and lung status. There was nothing in the record indicating that she completed such an evaluation after he vomited. Krebs also testified that a nurse did not conduct a swallowing assessment at any time. Although Florscheim testified that she checked on the patient around 6:00 PM on May 20, there was no documentation in the medical record. Ms. Farris, an expert witness for the defense, testified on cross-examination that if a patient was in the type of distress described by Mrs. Ard and no nurse checked on him for 1.25 hours, that would fall below the expected standard of care.[1]

Dr. Bruce Iteld, a member of the medical review panel and an expert in the fields of medicine and cardiology, testified that with Devon Ard's history and with reports of nausea, vomiting, rolling around in bed, paleness, and blueness he would have wanted to be notified by the attending nurse had he been the treating physician.

He would have transferred him back to intensive care immediately. He would have done this because it looked like he was going to have a respiratory and cardiac arrest. Possibly, had he been transferred to the cardiac unit his chances of going into a code would have been averted. When asked whether this would be more probable than not he replied:

> This is a very sick gentleman and already had two respiratory problems . . . I think he would have had a much better chance of survival in the intensive care unit.[2]

WHAT IS YOUR VERDICT?

To Be a Nurse: Swedish Hospital, Seattle, Washington

- *Excellence is about who we are, what we believe in, what we do with every day of our lives. And in some ways we are a sum total of those who have loved us and those who we have given ourselves to.*
- *Nursing is the honor and privilege of caring for the needs of individuals in their time of need. The responsibility is one of growth to develop the mind, soul, and physical well-being of oneself as well as the one cared for.*
- *In memory of all those patients that have enriched my life and blessed me with their spirit of living—while they are dying.*
- *There are many things I love about being an RN, but as a Recovery Room nurse, my favorite, by far, is being able to tell a groggy but anxious patient, "It was benign."*
- *I have been with a number of people/patients when they die and have stood in awe. Nursing encompasses the sublime and the dreaded. We are regularly expected to do the impossible. I feel honored to be in this profession.*
- *To get well, I knew I had to accept the care and love that were given to me—when I did healing washed over me like water.*
- *Thank you!*
- *In the caring for one another, both are forever changed.*
- *A friend takes your hand and touches your heart.*
- *To all of you whose names were blurred by the pain and the drugs.*
- *Don't ever underestimate your role in getting patients back on their feet.*
- *Through all of this I was never alone.*

—Swedish Hospital, Seattle, Washington,
Unknown Authors

▶ LEARNING OBJECTIVES

The reader, upon completion of this chapter, will be able to:

- Describe how the scope of nursing practice continues to evolve.
- Describe common categories of nursing staff.
- Explain the process of obtaining nurse licensure.
- Describe a variety of the legal risks nurses encounter.
- Describe the ways in which a nurse is a patient advocate.

This chapter provides an overview of nursing practice, nurse licensure, and various nursing specialties, as well as a review of cases focused on the legal risks of nurses. The cases presented highlight cases where nurses have been vulnerable to lawsuits.

▶ SCOPE OF PRACTICE

The role of the nurse continues to evolve and expand due to a shortage of primary care physicians in rural and inner-city areas, ever-increasing specialization, improved technology, public demand, and expectations within the profession itself.

The following timeline describes many of the key historical events that have led to the continuing expansion of the roles and duties of nurses in patient care settings.

NEWS *THE ROLE OF NURSES EXTENDS BEYOND THE HOSPITAL WARD*

A nurse is a doctor's best friend, according to Marvin M. Lipman, Consumers Union's chief medical adviser. This advice was given to him by a hospital ward's head nurse when he was a third-year medical student making contact with patients for the first time, along with the suggestion that he'd do well not to forget it.

Over the years, those words continued to echo in Lipman's mind . . . he has seen nurses go that extra step to make a patient comfortable or more at ease.

—Consumers Union of United States Inc., *The Washington Post*, May 30, 2011

NOTEWORTHY EVENTS IN THE EXPANDING SCOPE OF NURSING PRACTICE

1901—New York began to organize for passage of nurse practice legislation.

1903—North Carolina enacted the first nurse registration act.

1905—The development of the hospital economics course at Teachers College, Columbia University, ushered in a new era in preparation of nurse leaders in America. This 1-year certificate course was extended to a 2-year post–basic training program in 1905. The commitment of key nursing leaders to advancing educational preparation for nurse faculty fostered the subsequent development of baccalaureate education in nursing during the first quarter of the 20th century.

1937—The American Nurses Association (ANA) began recommending that nurses use their professional organization to improve every phase of their working lives.

1938—New York enacted the first exclusive practice act. This act required mandatory licensure of everyone who performed nursing functions as a matter of employment.

1946—The ANA convention adopted an economic security program and called for collective action on such items as a 40-hour workweek and higher minimum wages.

1952—All states, including the District of Columbia and U.S. territories, had enacted nurse practice acts.

1955—The ANA approved a model definition for nursing practice.

1957—The California Nurses Association met with representatives of medical and hospital associations to draw up a statement supporting nurses in performing venous punctures.

1966—The Michigan Heart Association favored the use of defibrillators by coronary care nurses.

1968—The Hawaii nursing, medical, and hospital associations approved nurses performing cardiopulmonary resuscitation.

1970—The ANA amended its model definition for nursing practice to include nursing diagnosis.

1971—Idaho revised its nurse practice act by allowing diagnosis and treatment as part of the scope of practice for nurse practitioners (NPs).

1972—New York expanded its nurse practice act and adopted a broad definition of nursing.

1973—The first ANA guidelines for NPs were written for geriatric NPs. These were later modified and adapted to apply to other practitioners.

1975—Missouri revised statutes (1975) authorized a nurse to make an assessment of persons who are ill and to render a nursing diagnosis. The 1975 act not only described a much broader spectrum of nursing functions, but it also qualified this description with the phrase, "including, but not limited to."

1980—The ANA published a model nurse practice act for state legislators to provide for consistency in individual state nurse practice acts.

1985—New York revised its definition of nursing by providing that a registered professional nurse who has the appropriate training and experience may provide primary healthcare services as defined under the statutory authority of the public health law and as approved by the hospital's governing authority. The term primary healthcare services means taking histories and performing physical examinations, selecting clinical laboratory tests and diagnostic radiology procedures, and choosing regimens of treatment. These provisions do not alter a physician's responsibility for patient care.

1989—New York allowed NPs to diagnose, treat, and write prescriptions within their area of specialty with minimum physician supervision.

(continues)

NOTEWORTHY EVENTS IN THE EXPANDING SCOPE OF NURSING PRACTICE *(continued)*

1990—The ANA again amended its model definition for nursing practice to include the advanced NP as well as the registered nurse (RN).

2014—Doctor of Nursing programs continue to expand.

2015—RNs treat patients, advise patients, and provide emotional support to patients and their family members during difficult times. RNs document patients' medical histories and symptoms, help doctors perform diagnostic tests, administer treatment and medications, and follow up with patients during rehabilitation.[3]

2015—Nurses take on expanded roles at Massachusetts General Hospital from admission to after discharge.

2017—The Veteran's Administration allows nurse practitioners to have an expanded role in treatment decisions.

Nurses who exceed their scope of practice as defined by applicable statutes (e.g., nurse practice acts) can be found to have violated licensure provisions and thus be subject to disciplinary action. Nurses, however, generally have not encountered lawsuits for exceeding their scope of practice unless negligent conduct is an issue. The expanding scope of nursing practice is accompanied by increased ethical and legal risks.

Nurses are at risk for inappropriate professional relationships due to the broadening scope of nursing practice amidst rapid societal changes and pressures. The complexities of professional nursing relationships have outpaced awareness of ethical considerations of boundary issues. In addition, because professional nursing is founded on a caring ethic and nurses become intimately involved in life experiences of clients and families, nurses may be at risk for confusion over boundaries and inappropriate relationships. Boundaries, which historically were unclear, are increasingly recognized as an issue for the profession.[4]

A nurse who exceeds his or her scope of practice as defined by state nurse practice acts can be found to have violated licensure provisions or to have performed tasks that are reserved by statute for another healthcare professional. Because of increasingly complex nursing and medical procedures, it is sometimes difficult to distinguish the tasks that are clearly reserved for the physician from those that may be performed by the professional nurse. Nevertheless, many physicians want nurses to have a greater role in the treatment of patients.

Nursing Diagnosis

Various states recognize that nurses can render a nursing diagnosis. This was the case in *Cignetti v. Camel*,[6] where the defendant physicians ignored a nurse's assessment of a patient's diagnosis, which contributed to a delay in treatment and injury to the patient. The nurse testified that she told the physician that the patient's signs and symptoms were not those associated with indigestion. The defendant physician objected to this testimony, indicating that such a statement constituted a medical diagnosis by a nurse. The trial court permitted the testimony to be entered into evidence. Section 335.01(8) of the Missouri Revised Statutes (1975) authorizes an RN to make an assessment of persons who are ill and to render a nursing diagnosis. On appeal, the Missouri Court of Appeals affirmed the lower court's ruling, holding that evidence of negligence presented by the hospital nurse, for which an obstetrician was not responsible,

NURSES TAKE ON NEW AND EXPANDED ROLES IN HEALTH CARE

Massachusetts General Hospital is known for medical innovations such as the first public demonstration of surgical anesthesia and the first replantation of a severed arm.

Today, the venerable Boston hospital is testing out another innovation, but this time it's in the field of nursing. When a patient arrives at Massachusetts General Hospital (MGH) now, he or she is assigned an attending registered nurse (ARN) for the duration of the hospital stay and after discharge. The ARN builds a relationship with the patient and his or her caregivers, and ensures that all members of the patient's health care team follow a shared care plan. Unlike other RNs, ARNs are designed to promote continuity of care, ideally with a five-day, eight-hour work schedule.

—Lisa Rein, Robert Wood Johnson Research Foundation, January 29, 2015[5]

was admissible to show the events that occurred during the patient's hospital stay.

▶ NURSE LICENSURE

Each state has its own nurse practice act that defines the practice of nursing. Although most states have similar definitions of nursing, differences generally revolve around the scope of practice permitted. The scope of practice of a licensed practical nurse (LPN) is generally limited to routine patient care under the direction of an RN or a physician.

An RN is one who has passed a state registration examination and is licensed to practice nursing. The scope of practice of a registered professional nurse includes, for example, patient assessment, patient teaching, health counseling, executing medical regimens, and operating medical equipment as prescribed by a physician, dentist, or other licensed healthcare provider.

The common organizational pattern of nurse licensing authority in each state is to establish a separate board, organized and operated within the guidelines of specific legislation, to license all professional and practical nurses. Each board is, in turn, responsible for the determination of eligibility for initial licensing and relicensing; for the enforcement of licensing statutes, including suspension, revocation, and restoration of licenses; and for the approval and supervision of training institutions. A licensing board has the authority to suspend a license; however, it must do so within existing rules and regulations.

Requirements for Licensure

Formal professional training is necessary for nurse licensure in all states. The course requirements vary, but all courses must be completed at board-approved schools or institutions. Each state requires that an applicant pass a written examination, which is generally administered twice annually. A licensing board may draft examinations, or a professional examination service or national examining board may prepare them. Some states waive their written examination for applicants who present a certificate from a national nursing examination board. Graduate nurses are generally able to practice nursing under supervision while waiting for the results of their examination. The four basic methods by which boards license out-of-state nurses are (1) reciprocity, (2) endorsement, (3) waiver, and (4) examination.

Reciprocity

This is a formal or informal agreement between states whereby a nurse licensing board in one state recognizes licensees of another state if the board of that state extends reciprocal recognition to licensees from the first state. To have reciprocity, the initial licensing requirements of the two states must be essentially equivalent.

Endorsement

Although some nurse licensing boards use the term endorsement interchangeably with reciprocity, the two words have different meanings. In licensing by *endorsement*, boards determine whether out-of-state nurses' qualifications are equivalent to their own state requirements at the time of initial licensure. Many states make it a condition for endorsement that the qualifying examination taken in another state be comparable to their own. As with *reciprocity*, endorsement becomes much easier when uniform qualification standards are applied by the different states.

Waiver

Some states license nurses by waiver and examination. When applicants do not meet all the requirements for licensure but have equivalent qualifications, the specific prerequisites of education, experience, or examination may be waived.

Examination

Some states will not recognize out-of-state licensed nurses and make it mandatory that all applicants pass a licensing examination. Most states grant temporary licenses for nurses, which may be issued pending a decision by a licensing board on permanent licensure or may be issued to out-of-state nurses who intend to be in a jurisdiction for a limited, specified time.

Graduates of schools in other countries are required to meet the same qualifications as nurses trained in the United States. Many state boards have established special training, citizenship, and experience requirements for students educated abroad; others insist on additional training in the United States. Nurses who complete their studies in a foreign country are required to pass an English proficiency examination and/or a licensing examination administered in English. A few states have reciprocity or endorsement agreements with some foreign countries.

Suspension and Revocation of License

Nurse licensing boards have the authority to suspend or revoke the license of a nurse who is found to have violated specified norms of conduct. Such violations may include procurement of a license by fraud; unprofessional, dishonorable, immoral, or illegal conduct; performance of specific actions prohibited by statute; and malpractice.

Suspension and revocation procedures are most commonly contained in the licensing act; in some jurisdictions, however, the procedure is left to the discretion of the board or is contained in the general administrative procedure acts. For the most part, suspension and revocation proceedings are administrative, rather than judicial, and do not carry criminal sanctions.

Practicing Without a License

Healthcare organizations are required to verify that each nurse's license is current. The mere fact that an unlicensed practitioner is hired would not generally in and of itself impose additional liability unless a patient suffered harm as a result of the unlicensed nurse's negligence. However, a person posing as a nurse could face criminal charges.

▶ NURSING CAREERS

The next several pages describe a variety of nursing careers and case law examples of the risks some have encountered. Specific attention is given to registered nurses, traveling nurses, nurse managers, licensed practical nurses, certified nursing assistants, float nurses, agency nurses, special duty nurses, student nurses, and advanced practice nurses.

Registered Nurse

An RN is a nurse who has graduated from an accredited nursing program and has passed a national licensing exam, known as the NCLEX (*National Council Licensure Examination*)-RN. NCLEX examinations are developed and owned by the *National Council of State Boards of Nursing, Inc.* (NCSBN), which administers these examinations on behalf of its member boards. NCSBN is a not-for-profit organization whose membership comprises the boards of nursing in the 50 states, including the District of Columbia, and four U.S. territories. There are also nine associate members.

Nurses wishing to practice in a particular state should contact the state's nurse licensure body for information for specific registration and nurse licensing requirements.

Traveling Nurse

A traveling nurse is one who travels to work in temporary nursing positions in different cities and states. There are a variety of traveling professionals, such as physical therapists and physicians. The traveling

professional often has opportunities that include higher wages, professional growth and development opportunities, and the adventure of traveling. Their skills are often enhanced due to their exposure to intriguing assignments in prominent medical centers. Travelers may work as independent contractors or elect to work with one or more recruitment agencies, which act as intermediaries between the nurse and healthcare provider.

Licensed Practical Nurse

An LPN, as well as a licensed vocational nurse (LVN), provides routine nursing care (e.g., vital signs, injections, assisting patients with personal hygiene needs, and wound dressings) under the direction of an RN or physician. To be licensed, they must graduate from a state-approved program and pass a licensing exam. Nurses wishing to practice in a particular state should contact the state's nurse licensure body for information regarding specific registration and nurse licensing requirements.

Nurse Manager

The *chief nursing officer* (CNO) is a qualified RN who has administrative authority, responsibility, and accountability for the function, activities, and training of the nursing staff. CNOs are generally responsible for maintaining standards of practice, maintaining current policy and procedure manuals, making recommendations for staffing levels based on need, coordinating and integrating nursing services with other patient care services, selecting nursing staff, and developing orientation and training programs.

A nurse manager who knowingly fails to supervise an employee's performance or assigns a task to an individual whom he or she knows, or should know, is not competent to perform the task can be held personally liable if injury occurs. The employer will be liable under the doctrine of respondeat superior as the employer of both the manager and the individual who performed the task in a negligent manner. The manager is not relieved of personal liability even though the employer is liable under the doctrine of respondeat superior.

In determining whether a nurse with supervisory responsibilities has been negligent, the nurse is measured against the standard of care of a competent and prudent nurse in the performance of supervisory duties. Those duties include the setting of policies and procedures for the prevention of accidents in the care of patients.

Failure to Supervise

Nursing managers must properly supervise the care rendered to patients by their subordinates. Failure to do so can lead to disciplinary action by a state regulatory agency. This was the case in *Hicks v. New York State Department of Health*,[7] in which the court held that evidence was sufficient to support a finding that a practical nurse was guilty of resident neglect for failing to ensure that the resident was properly cared for during her assigned shift. The record demonstrated that the petitioner was responsible for ensuring that the nursing aides' tasks were properly accomplished by conducting a visual check of each resident while making rounds at the end of her shift. The nurse's record indicated that a security guard found a resident lying in the dark, half in his bed and half still restrained in an overturned wheelchair. The nurse's record indicated that the resident was covered in urine and stool. The commissioner of health denied the petitioner's request to expunge the patient neglect report and assessed a penalty of $200, of which the petitioner was required to pay $50.

Certified Nursing Assistant

A certified nursing assistant (CNA) provides patient care, generally involving activities of daily living. CNAs work under the supervision of an RN or LPN. The CNA aids with positioning, turning, and lifting, and performs a variety of tests and treatments. The CNA establishes and maintains interpersonal relationships with patients and other hospital personnel while ensuring confidentiality of patient information. Those who wish to become a CNA in a particular state should be sure to contact the state's nurse licensure body or a local healthcare facility for guidance and information for educational programs and certification requirements. The failure of CNAs and nursing aides to follow applicable nursing procedures and protocols can result in patient injuries, as noted in the following cases.

Failure to Follow Policy

Failure to follow hospital policy can result in a successful lawsuit for the plaintiff, as was the case where Ovitz, a 73-year-old resident of a convalescent center, died after immersion in a tub of hot water that had been prepared by a nursing assistant.[8] Ovitz had paralysis of his left side and could articulate only the words "yes" and "no." The nursing assistant checked the water with his hand and bathed the resident. Later in the day, a nurse noticed that the resident's leg was bleeding and his skin was sloughing off. The paramedics were contacted, and they transferred the resident to a hospital after determining that the patient had suffered third-degree burns. Dr. Drueck, the surgeon at the hospital, observed that Ovitz had suffered third-degree burns over 40% of his body, primarily on his back, buttocks, both sides, genitals, and lower legs.

Ovitz developed pneumonia during his hospitalization and died. There was testimony from Drueck that the cause of death was a result of complications following the burns. The center's bathing policy to prevent accidents was to avoid making the water too hot. The center's daily temperature logs indicated that it knew that the water temperature in the system at times fluctuated above its bathing policy, sometimes exceeding 110°F, yet the center failed to take adequate measures to protect residents from exposure to excessive water temperatures. The center's own written policy was violated when the nursing assistant left the resident unattended in his bath. The appellate court held that revocation of the center's license was warranted in this case.

Patient Fall

In *Bowe v. Charleston Area Medical Center*,[9] a nurse's aide brought an action against a medical center for retaliatory discharge and breach of contract. The nurse's aide assisted a patient to the bathroom and placed him on the commode. She left him unattended for about 10 minutes. When she returned, the patient was found lying on the floor in a pool of blood. The patient apparently hit his head on the sink when he fell. Following an investigation of the incident, the hospital found that the aide had been grossly negligent and thus terminated her employment. The human resources director had authorized the employee's termination because of a provision in the employee handbook that makes gross negligence a dischargeable offense. The aide claimed that she had been terminated because of her complaints about the lack of patient care on the oncology unit to which she had been assigned. There was no specific evidence that could substantiate that she filed a grievance regarding patient care.

The West Virginia Supreme Court of Appeals held that (1) the evidence established that patient neglect by the plaintiff prompted an investigation that led to her subsequent discharge, and (2) the disclaimer in the employee handbook adequately shielded the employer from any contractual liability based on the employee handbook. The evidence showed that the aide, contrary to the medical center's policy, had assisted a patient in getting on a commode and then left him unattended, resulting in a fall and his subsequent death. Leaving the patient unattended for 10 minutes on the commode was clearly against hospital policy.

The nurse's aide failed to establish that her discharge was a retaliatory act or that it contravened some public policy.

The hospital's disclaimer specifically stated that the employee handbook was not intended to create any contractual rights. Employment was subject to termination at any time by either the employee or employer. The disclaimer in the employee handbook read:

> Because of court decisions in some states, it has become necessary for us to make it clear that this handbook is not part of a contract, and no employee of the Medical Center has any contractual right to the matters set forth in this handbook. In addition, your employment is subject to termination at any time by either you or by the Medical Center.[10]

Patient Transfer

The nursing assistant in *Kern v. Gulf Coast Nursing Home of Moss Point, Inc.*[11] was attempting to give a resident a whirlpool bath. The resident had been placed in a special rolling seat and was being lifted by a hydraulic lifting device that was used to place residents in the whirlpool. In the process of lifting the resident, the seat, which had been connected to the lift, disconnected. The resident fell to the floor, hitting her head and breaking her hip. The trial court entered a verdict in the amount of $20,000 for the plaintiff and the plaintiff appealed, stating that the award was inadequate. The Mississippi Supreme Court held that, based on the facts of this case, the verdict was not so low as to shock the conscience of the court.

Leaving Patient Unattended

The record in *Jones v. Axelrod*[12] indicated that a nurse's aide, while transferring a nursing home patient to her bed from a wheelchair, left the patient sitting on the edge of the bed. The patient subsequently fell to the floor. The aide acknowledged that the patient required restraints. The supervisor testified that the act of leaving the patient unrestrained and unattended on the edge of the bed was improper and inconsistent with safe procedure. Sufficient evidence supported a determination by the commissioner of health that the conduct of the nurse's aide constituted patient neglect.

Float Nurse

A *float nurse* is healthcare professional who rotates from unit to unit based on staffing needs. "Floaters" can benefit an understaffed unit, but they also may present a liability if they are assigned to work in an area outside their expertise. If a patient is injured because of a floater's negligence, the standard of care required of the floater will be that required of a nurse on the assigned patient care unit. The nurse manager must assess the float nurse's ability to perform the tasks for those patient care units to which he or she is assigned.

> Spend a few minutes finding out what the float nurse can do and negotiate an assignment that renders safe patient care. If you fail to accurately assess the float nurse and therefore make an inappropriate assignment, you could be found negligent in the event that patient injury occurred as a result of the assignment.[13]

State codes, such as the California Code of Regulations, Title 22: *Nurse Staffing Development*, describe the concerns and safety of patients regarding all nurses, including floating nurse assignments.

> (A) Assignments shall include only those duties and responsibilities for which competency has been validated.
>
> (B) A registered nurse who has demonstrated competency for the patient care unit shall be responsible for nursing care as described in subsections 70215(a) and 70217(h)(3), and shall be assigned as a resource nurse for those registered nurses and licensed vocational nurses who have not completed competency validation for that unit.
>
> (C) Registered nurses shall not be assigned total responsibility for patient care, including the duties and responsibilities described in subsections 70215(a) and 70217(h)(3), until all the standards of competency for that unit have been validated.
>
> (3) The duties and responsibilities of patient care personnel who may be temporarily re-directed from their assigned units are subject to the restrictions in (A), (B), and (C) of subsection (a)(2) above.
>
> (4) Orientation and competency validation shall be documented in the employee's file and shall be retained for the duration of the individual's employment.[14]

Agency Nurse

Healthcare organizations are at risk for the negligent conduct of agency staff. Because of the need for patient safety, it is important to be sure that agency workers have the necessary skills and competencies to carry out the duties and responsibilities assigned by the organization.

Agency nurses must have both competency and performance evaluations to verify the nurse's ability to perform the tasks assigned by the hospital. The agency nurse must be periodically assessed by the agency on a regular, predetermined time basis with written verification of licensure and competencies made available to the hospital. Competency and performance evaluations must be performed regularly based on federal, state, and accreditation standards, such as those required by The Joint Commission.

It was reported that an agency nurse was found guilty of gross negligence and manslaughter as the result of placing a do-not-resuscitate order in the wrong patient record at the Leicester Royal Infirmary. As a result of this error the medical staff was "stopped from giving life-saving treatment to the boy by Dr. Hadiza Bawa-Garba before the error was noticed by a junior doctor. The court heard earlier in the trial that Bawa-Garba had confused Jack for another patient she had treated that day, in what the prosecutor, Andrew Thomas QC, described as a "remarkable error."[15]

Special Duty Nurse

A *special duty nurse* is a healthcare professional employed by a patient or patient's family to perform nursing care for the patient. An organization is generally not liable for the negligence of a special duty nurse unless a master–servant relationship can be determined to exist between the organization and the special duty nurse. If a master–servant relationship exists between the organization and the special duty nurse, the doctrine of respondeat superior may be applied to impose liability on the organization for the nurse's negligent acts.

A special duty nurse may be required to observe certain rules and regulations as a precondition to working in the organization. The observance of organization rules is insufficient, however, to establish a master–servant relationship between the organization and the nurse. Under ordinary circumstances, the patient employs the special duty nurse, and the organization has no authority to hire or fire the nurse. The organization does, however, have the responsibility to protect the patient from incompetent or unqualified special duty nurses.

Student Nurse

Student nurses are entrusted with the responsibility of providing nursing care to patients. They are personally liable for their own negligent acts, and the facility is liable for their acts on the basis of respondeat superior. A student nurse is held to the standard of a competent professional nurse when performing nursing duties. The courts, in several decisions, have taken the position that anyone who performs duties customarily performed by professional nurses is held to the standards of professional nurses. Every patient has the right to expect competent nursing services, even if students provide the care as part of their clinical training. It would be unfair to deprive a patient of compensation for an injury simply because the nurse was a student.

▶ ADVANCED PRACTICE NURSES

The practice of nursing continues to expand with an ever-increasing number of specialties, along with professional organizations and certifying boards. Discussed here are a variety of legal risks of advanced practice nurses, including nurse practitioners, clinical nurse specialists, certified nurse anesthetists, and certified nurse midwifes, who possess an advanced degree that allows them to treat patients in areas beyond those provided to RNs.

Nurse Practitioner

Nurse practitioners (NPs) are RNs who have completed the necessary education to engage in primary healthcare decision making.

> According to the American Association of Nurse Practitioners (AANP 2016), nurse practitioners (NPs) are licensed, autonomous clinicians focused on managing people's health conditions and preventing disease. As advanced practice registered nurses (APRNs), NPs often specialize by patient population, including pediatric, adult-gerontological, and women's health. NPs may also subspecialize in areas such as dermatology, cardiovascular health, and oncology.[16]

The NP is trained in the delivery of primary health care and the assessment of psychosocial and physical health problems, such as the performance of routine examinations and the ordering of routine diagnostic tests. A physician may not delegate a task to an NP when regulations specify that the physician must perform it personally or when the delegation is prohibited under state law or by an organization's own policies.

The potential risks of liability for the NP are as real as the risks for any other nurse. The standard of care required most likely will be set by statute. If not, the courts will determine the standard based on the reasonable person doctrine (i.e., What would a reasonably prudent NP do under the similar circumstances?). The standard would be established through the use of expert testimony of other NPs in the field. Because of

THE ROLE OF NURSES EXTENDS BEYOND THE HOSPITAL WARD

Studies have found that [nurse practitioners'] ability to diagnose illnesses, order and interpret tests, and treat patients is equivalent to that of primary-care physicians. They also tend to spend more time with patients during routine office visits than physicians, and they are more likely to discuss preventive health measures. As of 2010, 140,000 NPs were working in the United States.

Nurse practitioners are poised to become even more visible with the passage last year of the Patient Protection and Affordable Care Act, which could add nearly 35 million people to the ranks of the insured.

—Consumers Union of United States Inc.,
The Washington Post, May 30, 2011

potential liability problems and pressure from physicians, historically, hospitals have been reluctant to use NPs to the full extent of their training. Such reluctance has been diminishing as the competency of NPs has been well demonstrated in practice.

As described in the following case, the negligence of an NP can be imputed to a physician if the physician is the employer of the nurse.

Clinical Nurse Specialist

A clinical nurse specialist (CNS) is a professional RN with an advanced academic degree, experience, and expertise in a clinical specialty (e.g., obstetrics, pediatrics, psychiatry). Furthermore, the CNS acts as a resource for the management of patients with complex needs and conditions. The CNS participates in staff development activities related to his or her clinical specialty and makes recommendations to establish standards of care for those patients. The CNS functions as a change agent by influencing attitudes, modifying behavior, and introducing new approaches to nursing practice. The CNS collaborates with other members of the healthcare team in developing and implementing the therapeutic plan of care for patients.

Certified Registered Nurse Anesthetist

Administration of anesthesia by a nurse anesthetist requires special training and certification. Nurse-administered anesthesia was the first expanded role for nurses requiring certification. Certified registered nurse anesthetists (CRNAs)

are advanced practice registered nurses (APRNs) licensed as independent practitioners. CRNAs practice both autonomously and in collaboration with a variety of health providers on the interprofessional team to deliver high-quality, holistic, evidence-based anesthesia and pain care services. Nurse anesthetists care for patients at all acuity levels across the lifespan in a variety of settings for procedures including, but not limited to, surgical, obstetrical, diagnostic, therapeutic, and pain management. CRNAs serve as clinicians, researchers, educators, mentors, advocates, and administrators.[17]

Oversight and availability of an anesthesiologist are required by most organizations. The major risks for nurse anesthetists include improper placement of an airway, failure to recognize significant changes in a patient's condition, and the improper use of anesthetics (e.g., wrong anesthetic, wrong dose, wrong route). Medical supervision of nurse anesthetists is generally required in hospital settings. Failure to properly supervise a nurse anesthetist can lead to a lawsuit if a patient is injured because of a negligent act.

Certified Nurse Midwife

A certified nurse midwife (CNM) provides comprehensive prenatal care, including delivery, for patients who are at low risk for complications. A CNM is nationally certified through the North American Registry of Midwives. A CNM is trained to manage normal prenatal, intrapartum, and postpartum care. Provided that there are no complications, normal newborns also are cared for by a CNM. In addition, CNMs often provide primary care for women's issues from puberty to postmenopause. Controversy continues to surround the use of midwives. This is attributed to the lack of a safer environment that hospitals can provide during high-risk pregnancies. Although unforeseen events can occur during any delivery, physicians are more apt to accept home deliveries for low-risk pregnancies provided pertinent state licensing laws, rules, and regulations address the concerns associated with midwife deliveries.

The American College of Nurse-Midwives "reviews research, administers and promotes continuing education programs, and works with organizations, state and federal agencies, and members of Congress to advance the well-being of women and infants through the practice of midwifery."[18] Dr. Thomas Gellhaus, MD, FACOG, president of the American Congress of Obstetricians and Gynecologists stated, "Every year, more than 1 million babies are born to mothers who were unable to access adequate prenatal care. These

⚖ *NEGLIGENCE IMPUTED TO PHYSICIAN*

Citation: *Adams v. Krueger*, 856 P.2d 864 (Idaho 1993)

Facts

The plaintiff went to her physician's office for diagnosis and treatment. A nurse practitioner (NP) who was employed by the physician performed her assessment and diagnosed the plaintiff as having genital herpes. The physician prescribed an ointment to help relieve the patient's symptoms. The plaintiff eventually consulted with another physician who advised her that she had a yeast infection, not genital herpes.

The plaintiff and her husband filed an action against the initial treating physician and his NP for their failure to correctly diagnose and treat her condition. The action against the physician was based on his failure to review the NP's diagnosis and treatment plan. The trial court found in favor of the plaintiff and the defendants appealed. The court of appeals affirmed, and further appeal was made.

Issue

Did the trial court err by imputing the nurse's negligence to the physician?

Holding

The Idaho Supreme Court held that the negligence of the nurse was properly imputed to the physician.

Reason

The Idaho Supreme Court held that the physician and NP stood in a master–servant relationship and that the nurse acted within the scope of her employment. Consequently, her negligence was properly attributed to her employer/physician.

In the present case, it was undisputed that the physician and the NP stood in relation as master and servant and that the NP, at all relevant times, acted within the scope of her employment. Consequently, her negligence was properly charged, or attributed, to the physician in applying the comparative negligence statute. Accordingly, we find no error. *Id.* at 867.

women and babies face unnecessary risks simply because care is inaccessible."[19] Pending approval by Congress is H.R.1209 *Improving Access to Maternity Care Act*. The bill provides in part:

> This bill amends the Public Health Service Act to require the Health Resources and Services Administration to designate maternity care health professional shortage areas and review these designations at least annually.
>
> The Department of Health and Human Services must collect and publish data on health professional shortage areas so availability of maternal health professionals can be compared by professional category and geographic region.
>
> A maternity care health professional shortage area is: (1) an area determined to have a shortage of providers of full scope maternity care health services or of hospital or birth center labor and delivery units, or (2) a population group determined to have a shortage of such providers or facilities.
>
> Full scope maternity care health services include care during labor, birthing, prenatal care, and postpartum care.[20]

Several legal cases involving midwives are reviewed next.

Practicing Without a License

The plaintiff in *Morris v. Dep't of Prof'l Regulation*[21] held herself out as a lay midwife in Illinois from 1983 through August 2001. The plaintiff performed prenatal exams on her patients, helped them deliver their babies at home, and provided postpartum and newborn care.

> Defendant issued plaintiff a license to practice as a registered nurse on February 24, 1999. Plaintiff began working at Provena St. Joseph Hospital as a registered nurse in the labor and delivery unit, but continued her practice as a direct-entry midwife on the side. Provena St. Joseph Hospital terminated plaintiff on July 5, 2000, after learning that she had been practicing midwifery on a patient who, following a home birth with plaintiff, was admitted to the hospital for postpartum bleeding.[22]

The plaintiff was never licensed to perform midwifery care and, therefore, failed to comply with the state nursing act's licensing requirements. The purpose of the nursing act is to promote public health, safety, and welfare by ensuring that those individuals who engage in the conduct described in the act are properly trained and licensed. The Department of Professional Regulation ordered the plaintiff to cease and desist the practice of midwifery. The plaintiff's nursing license was suspended, followed by probation and a fine of $2,500. In addition the nurse was required to complete a 12-hour ethics course.

On appeal, the appellate court affirmed the orders requiring the nurse to cease and desist the practice of midwifery and suspending her nursing license and fining her. The defendant, however, failed to provide an argument or citation to any authority explaining the relevance of the 12-hour ethics course as to the purposes of the Nursing Act and thus vacated the defendant's requirement that plaintiff complete an ethics course.[23]

Standard of Care Required

The plaintiff-appellant in *Ali v. Community Health Care Plan, Inc.*[24] claimed that the trial court improperly charged the jury on the standard of care to be applied in this case. Specifically, the plaintiff contended that the effect of the trial court's charge was to establish a lower standard of care by which the jury would determine whether negligence existed in the case. The plaintiff asserted that the standard of care to be applied should have been that of a reasonably prudent professional engaged in the practice of obstetrics and gynecology, and not that of a reasonably prudent nurse midwife engaged in the practice of obstetrics and gynecology. The defendant responded that the trial court's charge did not establish a lower standard of care and that the jury instruction was correct because it was in accordance with the actual evidence presented in the case. The Supreme Court of Connecticut, agreeing with the defendant, concluded that the trial court charged the jury with the correct standard of care. The question properly presented to the jury was whether the defendant's conduct met the standard of care applicable to her as a nurse midwife.

▶ LEGAL RISKS OF NURSES

This section describes some of the more common legal risks of nursing. Nurses are with their patients 24 hours per day. From admission to discharge, the nurse is continuously at risk for negligent acts.

If the patient has a sudden emergency, a nurse may be liable if he or she doesn't take appropriate immediate steps. This may involve actions like administering a medication or calling for help. Similarly, a nurse is under a duty to monitor a patient's condition. If the nurse notices something of concern, or should notice it, then the nurse may be liable for malpractice for not notifying the attending doctor.[25]

The number of adverse actions reported for nurses to the *National Practitioner Data Bank* (NPDB) was 12,298 in 2003, which nearly doubled to 22,742 in 2012. The number of adverse actions by nurses reported to the NPDB between 2009 and 2011 increased 25%, from 16,951 to 22,597, reflecting the implementation of Section 1921 of the Social Security Act, which expands the information gathered by the NPDB to include adverse licensure actions taken against all licensed healthcare practitioners. The information gathered includes any negative actions by state licensing agencies, peer review organizations, and private accreditation organizations.[26] The NPDB initially had difficulty in obtaining statistics from the various sates that did not meet reporting requirements. Secretary of Health and Human Services Kathleen Sebelius

> was the first HHS Secretary to publish a list of State agencies that fail to meet the Data Bank reporting requirements. She also took the unprecedented step of calling on Governors to do their part to assure that State reports to the Data Bank are complete and accurate. Through these extensive efforts, we have received more than 16,000 State licensure reports on health professions that had never been reported before.[27]

Dilemma of Two Standards of Care

Given two standards of care, should a hospital adopt the least restrictive standard? This generally would not be a good idea. For example, in *Edwards v. Brandywine Hosp.*,[28] Mr. Edwards went to the emergency department complaining of pain in his hip. He was admitted, and a heparin lock (a device that allows multiple IV fluids to be introduced at a common point) was placed in his left hand. The heparin lock was left in place for 3 or 4 days. This was in violation of regulations promulgated by the Pennsylvania Department of Health requiring hospitals to develop written standards regarding such antiseptic practices as changing IV catheter sites. The regulations state that these standards should comply with standards described in the American Hospital Association's publication, *Infection*

Control in the Hospital (1979), which recommends that IV catheter sites be changed every 48 hours in order to reduce the risk of infection. The hospital was subject to corporate liability for adopting a 72-hour rule.

Following discharge, Edwards noticed a red spot at the site of the heparin lock. He returned that day to the hospital for physical therapy. His therapist referred him to the emergency department for evaluation. The emergency department physician examined Edward's hand and took a specimen of pus from the site of the heparin lock and sent it to the laboratory for evaluation. Edwards was provided with oral antibiotics and sent home. The laboratory results showed that Edwards had a *Staphylococcus* (staph) infection. The emergency department physician entered this information on the patient's record.

Edwards returned to the hospital a few days later and was admitted with leg pains. A second laboratory test was ordered, which again showed the presence of a staph infection. The patient was treated over a period with IV antibiotics and eventually discharged with a good bill of health, only to return a week later with pain and a fever. Following treatment and various hospitalizations over the next several years, Edwards's physicians decided to remove his artificial hip and treat him with massive doses of antibiotics. In order to be ambulatory, Edwards now needs the aid of assistive devices (e.g., crutches).

A suit was brought against the physicians and hospital. The trial court took notice of the health department's regulation regarding catheter site changing and ruled that the hospital's admitted failure to move the heparin lock for at least 3 days constituted negligence per se. The physicians settled with the plaintiff, leaving the hospital as the only defendant. At the close of the plaintiff's case, the trial court granted the defendant's motion for a directed verdict. The trial court held that although the negligence per se ruling established the hospital's breach of a duty to care, the plaintiff could not prove causation.

The superior court reversed the trial court's directed verdict for the defendant, finding that the evidence presented at trial by the plaintiff was sufficient to allow the claim of causation to go to the jury. The kind of causation evidence the trial court expects cannot be produced. No witness could possibly testify that she saw a *S. aureus* bacterium crawl into Mr. Edwards's hand through the heparin lock site on his third day in the hospital and then multiply into the infection that spread to his artificial hip—yet the trial court's ruling implied that such showing was necessary to get to the jury.

Once a plaintiff has introduced evidence that a defendant's negligent act or omission increased the risk of harm to a person in the plaintiff's position and that, in fact, harm was sustained, it becomes a question for the jury as to whether or not that increased risk was a substantial factor in producing the harm.

Is there an issue of corporate negligence? Yes. The plaintiff claimed that the hospital was subject to corporate liability for adopting a 72-hour rule for changing placement of IV catheters. The plaintiff introduced evidence showing that a 48-hour rule was appropriate, but that the hospital adopted a rule allowing IVs to remain in place at the same site for 72 hours. If Edwards could prove that the 72-hour rule was inadequate, that the hospital should have known that it was inadequate, and that following this rule caused him harm, then he has made a proper claim for corporate negligence.

Should the nurse have been faulted for following hospital policy? No. A nurse following hospital rules cannot be faulted. If hospital policy required changing the site of the catheter every 48 hours and the nurse failed to do so, then the nurse could be held negligent and the hospital liable under the theory of respondeat superior.

When faced with the dilemma of two standards for rendering patient care, an organization may find it more attractive to adopt the one that is least restrictive or labor intensive. This could prove to be a costly decision for both the patient and the organization by increasing (1) the risk of patient injury and (2) the organization's exposure to corporate liability for any injury suffered from following the less restrictive standard.

Patient Misidentification

National patient safety goals provide that proper identification of a patient be conducted prior to performing any procedure. Such was not the case in *Meena v. Wilburn*,[29] where the patient injured her leg and developed an ulcer because of poor blood circulation. As a result of the plaintiff's diabetic condition, the ulcer did not heal. Dr. Maples, a vascular surgeon, performed surgery. Two days following surgery, Dr. Meena was at the hospital covering for one of his partners, Dr. Petro, who had asked him to remove the staples from one of his patients, 65-year-old Slaughter. Slaughter shared a semiprivate room with the plaintiff. Meena testified that he went and picked up Slaughter's chart at the nurse's desk and asked one of the nurses which bed Slaughter was in. Meena claimed that he was led to believe that she was in the bed next to the window. He picked up the chart and asked Greer, a nurse, to accompany him to the plaintiff's room.

Shortly thereafter, Meena received an emergency call at the nursing station. He said that he asked Greer to take out the staples because he had to respond to an emergency call at another hospital. Greer conceded during her testimony that, before removing staples from a patient, a nurse should read the chart, be familiar with the chart, look at the patient's wrist band, and compare the arm band to the chart—all of which she failed to do. Greer rationalized her failure: "When the doctor I work for is standing at the foot of a patient's bed, I would have no doubt—no reason to doubt what he tells me to do."

Greer began to remove the plaintiff's staples. She soon realized that there was a problem. The plaintiff's skin split open, revealing the layer of fat under the skin. Greer stopped the procedure and left the room to check the medical records maintained at the nursing station. She realized that she had removed staples from the wrong patient. At that point, she encountered Maples and explained to him what had happened. Maples immediately restapled the skin.

Following discharge, the plaintiff's health began to falter, and she developed a fever of 101°F. The tissue where the staples had been removed became infected. The plaintiff was ultimately readmitted to the hospital; she remained there for approximately 22 days. Her condition gradually improved, and presumably, she recovered completely with the exception of some scarring and skin indention.

A complaint was filed against Meena and Greer. After 4 days of trial, the jury returned a verdict against Meena and assessed damages in the amount of $125,000. The jury declined to hold the nurse liable for the plaintiff's injuries. Meena appealed, claiming that the jury's exoneration of the nurse, who removed the surgical staples, was grounds for a new trial on the issue of the physician's liability. Further, Meena argued the jury was bound to return a verdict against both defendants, inasmuch as the defendants were sued as joint tort-feasors. The Mississippi Supreme Court held that the jury's exoneration of Greer was not grounds for a new trial on the issue of the physician's liability.

Misidentifying Infants

The patient identification process failed in *De Leon Lopez v. Corporacion Insular de Seguros*.[30] In this case, Dulce had been discharged from the hospital a day before her twins. When she returned to pick up her twins the following day, she noticed that they did not appear to be identical as they did the prior day. "She asked the nurse why the babies did not 'look alike.' The nurse explained that infants change from one day to the next, and assured the anxious mother that the babies were indeed her twin daughters. The nurse also remarked disparagingly that Dulce must be a 'primeriza,' that is, a first-time mother. Their concerns assuaged, the parents took the babies home."[31]

Approximately a year and a half later Gloria, Dulce's sister, had taken one of her other nieces to her physician's office with her. Her niece commented to her saying she saw one of her cousins across the room. Gloria approached Mrs. Hernandez, the mother of the young child, and they discussed when and where Mrs. Hernandez had the child who was with her. It turned out that Mrs. Hernandez's twins were delivered at the same hospital and time as Dulce. Following some blood tests, Dulce and Mrs. Hernandez learned that each had the other's child. The two babies had been inadvertently or negligently switched after birth.

Following a lawsuit, damages were awarded by the United States District Court for Puerto Rico for the inadvertent switching of two babies. On appeal, the United States Court of Appeals, First Circuit, held: "The record shows, beyond any legitimate question, that the Hospital was negligent and that its negligence set into motion a particularly unfortunate chain of events; thus, the court below did not err in directing a verdict on liability."[32]

Patient Monitoring and Observation

Nurses have the responsibility to observe the condition of patients under their care and report any pertinent findings to the attending physician. Failure to note changes in a patient's condition can lead to liability on the part of the nurse and the organization. The recovery room nurse in *Eyoma v. Falco*,[33] who had been assigned to monitor a postsurgical patient, left the patient and failed to recognize that the patient stopped breathing. Nurse Falco had been assigned to monitor the patient in the recovery room. She delegated that duty to another nurse and failed to verify that the other nurse accepted that responsibility.

> Nurse Falco admitted she never got a verbal response from the other nurse, and when she returned there was no one near the decedent. She acknowledged that Dr. Brotherton told her to watch the decedent's breathing, but claimed she was not told that the decedent had been given narcotics. She maintained that upon her return she checked the decedent and observed his respirations to be eight per minute.
>
> Thereafter, Dr. Brotherton returned and inquired about the decedent's condition.

Falco informed the doctor that the patient was fine. However, upon his personal observation, Dr. Brotherton realized that the decedent had stopped breathing. . . .

Decedent, because of oxygen deprivation, entered a comatose state and remained unconscious for over a year until his death.[34]

The jury held the nurse to be 100% liable for the patient's injuries. The Superior Court of New Jersey, Appellate Division affirmed the judgment as to liability, holding that there was sufficient evidence to support the verdict. The appellate court also held that the trial court's judgment to limit damages for *loss of enjoyment of life* be reversed and remanded for a new trial.

Failure to Monitor Vital Signs

In *McCann v. ABC Insurance Co.*,[35] an attempt to deliver a baby by forceps was unsuccessful. The obstetrician, Dr. Merrill, testified that he listened to the baby's heart tone immediately after the failed forceps delivery and that the baby's heart rate was normal. The baby was then delivered by cesarean section. At birth, the baby was not breathing and had no detectable heartbeat. The baby was resuscitated and transferred to another hospital where he was in a clinically brain-dead state within 24 hours. Evidence at trial established that during delivery, the baby suffered a severe hypoxic event that caused the death. The plaintiffs instituted a lawsuit against the obstetrician; the hospital and the trial court granted a motion for a directed verdict at the end of the trial and dismissed Merrill, and an appeal was taken.

The plaintiffs' cause of action was dependent on whether the plaintiffs could show that Merrill or the hospital was negligent in failing to timely diagnose the existence of the hypoxic event. The sole claim against Merrill was the allegation that he failed to properly monitor the baby's heartbeat or make sure that the nurse properly monitored the baby's heartbeat after the fetal monitor had been removed. Evidence presented indicated that the standard of care would require that fetal heartbeats be monitored every 10 minutes following removal of the fetal monitor. The evidence presented indicated that this did not occur. Both the defendants' and plaintiffs' medical experts agreed that Merrill did not breach the standard of care required in treating McCann. The plaintiffs' expert testified by deposition that the duty to monitor was a nursing responsibility.

Testimony was needed to show that Merrill breached the standard of care required in treating McCann. Because the plaintiffs failed to provide such testimony, the trial court was found to have correctly granted the directed verdict.

Plaintiffs' cause of action against . . . Hospital was predicated primarily upon its failure to have policies and procedures regarding the continuous monitoring of fetal heart tones and its failure to adequately and continuously monitor the unborn infant. The basic thrust of the case was that none of the parties auscultated the baby every 10 minutes after the fetal monitoring device was removed, as required by the standards of the American College of Obstetrics and Gynecology (ACOG). Thus the issue in this case is not whether the baby would have died from other causes even if the Caesarean section had been performed faster, but rather the issue is whether the baby had lost a chance of survival. . . . [Because] the nurses' negligent inaction has terminated any chance of survival, conjecture as to other possible causes of death is inadmissible.[36]

In *Brandon HMA, Inc. v. Bradshaw*,[37] the patient, Bradshaw, had been admitted to Rankin Medical Center (RMC) under the care of Dr. Bobo for treatment of bacterial pneumonia. A general surgeon inserted a chest tube in Bradshaw's left side to drain some fluid that had accumulated. Because of the pain and discomfort associated with a chest tube, Extra Strength Tylenol and Lorcet Plus were prescribed for pain. Bobo also prescribed Ativan to relieve anxiety. During the afternoon and evening following insertion of the chest tube, two nurses periodically checked Bradshaw, took her vital signs, and noted that she exhibited "no distress." Around 11:00 PM, Lewis, an LPN, was assigned by Nail, the floor's charge nurse, to provide care to Bradshaw. Before checking on Bradshaw, Lewis reviewed the notes and a tape left by the previous nurse that detailed Bradshaw's condition. Around midnight, Lewis made his first visit to Bradshaw's room, took her vital signs, and noted she was experiencing some pain on her left side. Sometime before 1:00 AM, a respiratory therapist checked on Bradshaw and did not notice any problems, but did note that Bradshaw was restless. Shortly after, at 1:00 AM, Lewis made his second visit to Bradshaw's room. She continued to complain of pain in her chest. Lewis, however, did not take her vital signs. He gave her an Extra Strength Tylenol and made a note indicating that the patient was complaining of pain on the left side and appeared to be in distress. At 2:00 AM during Lewis's next visit, Bradshaw again complained that she could not sleep and that the pain had increased. Despite her complaints, Lewis again failed to take her vital signs. Instead, he consulted Nail and administered an injection of Ativan to relieve Bradshaw's anxiety and restlessness. Forty minutes later, Bradshaw again complained of increased pain. Lewis noticed that she was sitting up in bed and her respiration had become short and rapid. Feeling that the earlier Lorcet Plus was wearing off, Lewis administered another dose. Lewis again failed to check Bradshaw's vital signs.

Nail, while in Bradshaw's room at 3:00 AM, did not note any problems. When Lewis returned to Bradshaw's room at 3:30 AM, her condition had significantly worsened. She was nauseated, disoriented, covered in sweat, and did not follow verbal commands. Lewis checked her vital signs and found that her temperature had fallen to 95.8°F. Realizing the seriousness of Bradshaw's condition, Lewis left the room to find Nail. At this point, testimony among RMC's employees varies. Lewis and Washington, a nurses' aide, testified that Lewis found Nail and Washington conversing in the hallway. According to the two testimonies, Nail and Lewis discussed Bradshaw's condition and returned to the room at 3:40 AM.

When Lewis and Nail returned to the room, they found that Bradshaw was cyanotic, had stopped breathing, and had no pulse. Nail called a "code" and started cardiopulmonary resuscitation (CPR). The code team arrived and revived Bradshaw by administering epinephrine. Bradshaw was transferred to the intensive care unit where she remained comatose for 2 weeks. She was eventually transferred to a rehabilitation center for treatment. While in treatment, magnetic resonance imaging scans of Bradshaw's brain were ordered and showed evidence of brain damage as a result of lack of oxygen. Bradshaw's present condition as a result of the cardiopulmonary arrest and hypoxic brain damage is permanent and severe.

Bradshaw filed suit against Brandon HMA, Inc., for negligent nursing care. Bradshaw alleged that nursing personnel failed to properly monitor her and report vital information to her physician and allowed her condition to deteriorate to a critical stage before providing urgently needed care and implementing life support. The jury found in favor of Bradshaw and awarded $9 million in damages. The judge entered a final judgment on the jury verdict, and Brandon filed an appeal.

On appeal, the Supreme Court of Mississippi upheld the judgment of the circuit court. The court found that $9 million did not seem excessive. Bradshaw will live out her years with both emotional and physical pain, and her present existence will not remotely resemble her former life.

Although a nurse's failure to closely monitor a patient's vital signs can lead to a patient's injury or death, not every patient injury can be attributed this failure, as noted in the following case.

🔍 *FAILURE TO REPEAT VITAL SIGNS*

Citation: *Porter v. Lima Mem'l Hosp.*, 995 F.2d 629 (6th Cir. 1993)

Facts

During an automobile accident, Liesl, an infant, was thrown to the floor of her mother's car. Rescue squad personnel examined the infant and found nothing seriously wrong. Liesl was transported with her mother, Mrs. Porter, to Hospital A's emergency department. Ogelsbee, an RN, took Liesl's vital signs and recorded them on the medical chart. She reported the vital signs to Dr. Singh, the emergency room physician on duty. The only observable sign of injury was a small bruise on the right side of Liesl's head. Ogelsbee reported this to Singh, who found all of Liesl's extremities functioning normally and ordered several laboratory tests and X-rays. He did not, however, order any spinal X-rays and failed to diagnose spinal instability. Ogelsbee did not repeat the vital signs during or after Singh's examination, claiming that she received no physician's instruction in this regard. After reviewing the X-rays and laboratory tests, Singh discharged Liesl and provided her mother with written instructions concerning her head injuries. While awaiting a ride home, Liesl's mother reported a short period of irregular breathing by Liesl to one of the nurses. The nurse examined Liesl and determined that nothing was wrong. Porter testified that the nurse told her that "babies just breathe funny." When she reached home, Porter noted that Liesl's condition was worsening.

Mrs. Porter decided to take Liesl to Hospital B, where physicians determined that Liesl's legs were not moving. They ordered X-rays and laboratory tests, and eventually, another hospital staff physician diagnosed a subluxation at her first and second lumbar vertebrae, which resulted in Liesl's paralysis from the waist down. Experts who testified in trial agreed that Liesl suffered paralysis sometime after Singh's examination and before her arrival at Hospital B.

Singh was the primary person who could have prevented the spinal injury by diagnosing Liesl's unstable spine before it became critically injured. Singh settled for $2.5 million. The district court denied the hospital's motion for judgment, notwithstanding the verdict in favor of the mother, but ordered a new trial, at which the jury found the hospital not liable for the infant's injuries. Both the hospital and the mother appealed.

Issue

Did the conduct of Hospital A's nurses proximately cause the infant's paralysis?

Holding

The U.S. Court of Appeals for the Sixth Circuit held that the nurses' failure to repeat vital signs was legally insufficient to establish a connection between the failure to repeat vital signs and the eventual paralysis.

Reason

The experts on both sides generally agreed that the nurses had no independent duty, apart from a physician's instructions, to immobilize the infant. The plaintiff's experts made it clear that the physician is ultimately responsible for determining the patient's medical diagnosis and then to order the necessary and appropriate medical treatment. Singh did not diagnose any spinal cord injury and discharged the baby after examining and X-raying the infant. It was Singh who was responsible for treating Liesl's spinal cord injury, or at least he was responsible for ordering Liesl to be immobilized and hospitalized for further care and workup. The vital signs had no causal relationship to the paralysis.

This case illustrates the importance of conducting thorough assessments and reassessments of a patient's symptoms and injuries between all caregivers. The circumstances under which a patient is transported to a hospital will assist the staff at the receiving hospital to better determine each patient's care needs. Communication between a patient's caregivers (e.g., paramedics, nurses, physicians) is an essential element in improving the quality of patient care.

Delay in Monitoring Fetus

The plaintiffs' experts in *Northern Trust Co. v. University of Chicago Hospitals and Clinics*[38] supported their contention that an obstetrical nurse's delay in placing a fetal monitor and an additional delay caused by the unavailability of a second operating room for a cesarean section caused an infant's mental retardation. Although there was contrary expert opinion, there was no error in the trial court's denial of the hospital's motion for judgment notwithstanding the verdict.

> With respect to the first theory of negligence challenged by UCH, the time at which the fetal monitor was attached,[7] we disagree with UCH's contention that plaintiffs presented merely conclusory, and therefore "worthless," medical testimony that the delay in the monitor's placement by the obstetrical nurse was a proximate cause of Marshawn's injury. To the contrary, there was appropriate and sufficient expert testimony in this regard to support the jury's verdict.[39]

Monitor Alarm Disconnected

In *Odom v. State Department of Health and Hospitals*,[40] the appeals court held that the decedent's cause of death was directly related to the absence of being placed under the watch of a heart monitor. Jojo was born 12 weeks prematurely at the HPL Medical Center. Jojo remained in a premature infant's nursery and

was eventually placed into two different foster homes prior to his admission to Pinecrest foster home. While Jojo was a Pinecrest resident, Mr. and Mrs. Odom adopted Jojo. He was unable to feed himself and was nourished via a gastrostomy tube. Because he suffered from obstructive apnea, he became dependent on a tracheostomy (trach) tube.

At Pinecrest, Jojo was assigned to Home 501. Means, while making patient rounds, "found Jojo with his trach out of the stoma but still tightly attached to his neck. Immediately, she hollered at Johnson for help. Ogle and Johnson responded rapidly. Johnson immediately sent Means to call Fowler for help and asked if anyone knew CPR. Ogle answered that she thought she did and started CPR through Jojo's mouth, unaware that Jojo had a trach."[41] Wiley, a nurse, responding from another home, immediately began CPR on Jojo. She noticed that Jojo was breathless and immediately reinserted the trach tube. She then noticed that Jojo was still hooked to a monitor.

No one had heard the heart monitor's alarm sound. Means asserted that the monitor was on, because she saw that the monitor's red lights were blinking, indicating the heart rate and breathing rate. She stated that she took the monitor's leads off of Jojo to put the monitor out of the way, but the alarm did not sound. CPR efforts continued while Jojo was placed on a stretcher and sent by ambulance to HPL. Jojo was pronounced dead at HPL's emergency department at 7:02 PM.

The Odoms filed a petition against Pinecrest, alleging that Jojo's death was caused by the negligence and fault of Pinecrest, its servants, and employees. Judgment was for the plaintiffs. The trial court's reasons for judgment were enlightening because it stated that the monitor should have been on but was, however, disconnected by the staff and that this was the cause, in fact, of Jojo's injury. The appeals court found that the record supported the trial court's findings. There was overwhelming evidence upon which the trial court relied to find that the monitor was turned off, in breach of the various physicians' orders with which the nurses should have complied. The monitor was supposed to be on Jojo to warn the nurses of any respiratory distress episodes that he might experience. A forensic pathologist's report showed the cause of Jojo's death to be hypoxia, secondary to respiratory insufficiency, secondary to apnea episodes. Thus, Jojo's cause of death was directly related to the absence of being placed under the watch of a heart monitor.

Defective Monitoring Equipment

Failure to report defective equipment can cause a nurse to be held liable for negligence if the failure to report is the proximate cause of a patient's injuries. The defect must be known and not hidden from sight. Healthcare facilities must have in place a policy for reporting defective medical equipment by the user of the equipment, as well a policy for the repair, replacement or, when necessary, disposal of defective medical equipment.

Delay in Reporting Patient's Condition

An organization's policies and procedures should prescribe the guidelines for staff members to follow when confronted with a physician or other healthcare professional whose action or inaction jeopardizes the well-being of a patient. Guidelines in place, but not followed, are of no value, as the following cases illustrate. Such was the case in *Goff v. Doctors General Hospital*,[42] in which the court held that nurses who knew that a woman they were attending was bleeding excessively were negligent in failing to report the circumstances so that prompt and adequate measures could be taken to safeguard her life.

The plaintiff in *Utter v. United Hospital Center, Inc.*[43] suffered an amputation that the jury determined resulted from the failure of the nursing staff to properly report the patient's deteriorating condition. The nursing staff, according to written procedures in the nursing manual, was responsible for reporting such changes. It was determined that deviation from hospital policy constituted negligence.

In *Cuervo v. Mercy Hospital, Inc.*,[44] Cuervo was admitted to Mercy Hospital by Dr. Iglesias to undergo routine diagnostic cardiac tests. After performing the catheterization on Cuervo, Iglesias decided to perform a balloon angioplasty procedure; Iglesias was not authorized to perform this procedure. Unfortunately, in carrying out this procedure, Iglesias inserted the catheter into the wrong artery in Cuervo's right leg. This compromised the blood flow to the leg, causing loss of pulse and sensation. This error was compounded when Mercy Hospital's nurses on Cuervo's floor were unable to reach Iglesias for 6 hours and never attempted to reach Dr. Milian, the backup physician, to alert them of Cuervo's deteriorating condition.

The following day, Dr. Pena attempted an arteriogram to treat the right leg. Regrettably, Pena accessed the wrong artery in the left leg, compromising the blood flow to that leg as well. Shortly thereafter, Cuervo began to lose pulse and sensation in his left leg. The hospital's nurses never reported this condition to the physicians. Sometime later, Milian performed surgery to attempt to restore circulation to the right leg; the surgery was unsuccessful. Two hours later, surgery was performed on the left leg; the surgery failed to restore circulation to that leg. Thereafter, both legs required amputation.

Cuervo sued the physicians and hospital, asserting that the hospital was negligent based on the nurses' failure to promptly notify a physician of his condition and asserting corporate negligence against the hospital based on the unauthorized procedure. Cuervo's experts testified at deposition that if the nursing staff had contacted a physician when the symptoms were first detected, the amputations would not have been necessary. Relying on the same experts' testimony, the hospital filed a motion for summary judgment, asserting that any acts or omissions of its nurses were not the proximate cause of Cuervo's injuries. The hospital's motion for summary judgment did not raise any issue as to whether the hospital breached its duty to Cuervo by allowing a medical doctor to perform unauthorized procedures or by failing to provide adequate nursing care. The hospital's motion solely disputed causation. The trial court granted the motion and entered final summary judgment in the hospital's favor. The summary judgment was therefore reversed and the cause remanded for a jury trial.

On appeal, District Court of Appeal of Florida, Third District determined that when both parties to a lawsuit rely on testimony from the same experts and then draw diametrically opposed conclusions, the jury should be given opportunity to weigh the evidence and determine whether the hospital's conduct was the proximate cause of the patient's injuries. It is for the jury to decide if Mercy Hospital's conduct was a proximate cause of Mr. Cuervo's injuries. The case was therefore remanded for trial by jury.

In *Hiatt v. Grace*,[45] on appeal by the hospital and the nurse, the Kansas Supreme Court held that there was sufficient evidence to authorize the jury to find that the nurse was negligent in failing to timely notify the physician that delivery of the plaintiff's child was imminent. This delay resulted in an unattended childbirth with consequent injuries. The trial court had awarded the plaintiff $15,000 in damages.

In *Citizens Hospital Association v. Schoulin*,[46] an accident victim sued the hospital and the attending physician for their negligence in failing to discover and properly treat his injuries. The court held that there was sufficient evidence to sustain a jury verdict that the hospital's nurse was negligent in failing to inform the physician of all the patient's symptoms, to conduct a proper examination of the plaintiff, and to follow the directions of the physician. Thus, because the nurse was the employee of the hospital, the hospital was liable under the doctrine of respondeat superior.

In another case, arising from the death of a hospital patient following hernia surgery, evidence supported findings that both the patient's treating physician and the hospital deviated from their applicable standards of care and that the deviations were the cause of the patient's death. The applicable standard of care required the nurse to notify the physician if the patient complained of restlessness and had a heart rate fluctuating between 120 and 136. If the cardiologist had been called, it was probable that the patient could have been successfully treated. Hospital personnel had deviated from the standard of care when they observed bleeding from the patient and did not inform the physician, and the physician deviated from the standard of care when he failed to call a cardiac consult for the patient. In addition, a nursing expert testified that the nurse had deviated from the standard of care when he failed to call the physician when the patient pulled off his oxygen mask and complained of difficulty breathing.[47]

The failure of nurses to follow adequate nursing procedures in treating decubitus ulcers was found to be a factor leading to the death of a nursing facility resident in *Montgomery Health Care v. Ballard*.[48] Two nurses testified that they did not know that decubitus ulcers could be life threatening. One nurse testified that she did not know that the patient's physician should be called if there were symptoms of infection. Such allegations would indicate that there was a lack of training and supervision of the nurses treating the patient. The seriousness of such failure was driven

home when the court allowed $2 million in punitive damages.

Delay in Treatment

Howerton was the only patient in the labor and delivery room on March 27 at Mary Immaculate Hospital. Dr. O'Connell, Howerton's obstetrician, directed hospital nurses to administer Pitocin (a drug to induce labor) to Howerton.[49] When Dr. O'Connell examined her at 2:25 PM, she thought that Howerton was in the early stages of labor and directed that Pitocin be continued. At 3:00 PM, Howerton testified that she experienced intense abdominal pains. Mr. Howerton went to the nurses' station and described to the nurses that his wife was in severe pain. The nurses said that it would take a few minutes because they were in the middle of a shift change. Later, Howerton's mother went to the nurses' station and stated that her daughter needed help now. She received the same response from the nurses. Two of the nurses eventually came to the room at 3:15 PM after Howerton's father demanded their help. There was a further delay in contacting the doctor because one nurse suggested they not call the doctor yet. Then, at 3:23 PM, another nurse, who disagreed, paged Dr. O'Connell. When Dr. O'Connell answered the emergency page at 3:25 PM, she was advised that the undelivered baby's heart rate was in the 60s to 70s (a normal heart rate being from 120 to 160) and that the mother was having abdominal pain. Dr. O'Connell, while driving to the hospital, called the labor room at 3:30 PM and learned that the baby's heart rate remained in the 60s to 70s. Dr. O'Connell was able to deliver Howerton's daughter Kacie by cesarean section at 3:55 PM. After Kacie's delivery, it was discovered that the mother's uterus had ruptured in three places during labor, resulting in extensive neurologic damage to Kacie.

A lawsuit was filed and at trial, Holder, a nurse expert witness, opined that the labor and delivery room nurses should have immediately gone to Howerton when they were notified of the worsening pain, evaluated her condition, and notified her physician. Dr. Juskevitch, who testified as an expert witness, stated that the intensity of labor pains prior to delivery of the baby could indicate a ruptured uterus or a separation of the placenta. Dr. Juskevitch explained that a tearing of the uterus presented challenges to the unborn baby, which began when the first tear occurred at 3:00 PM, and were evident at 3:17 PM when the nurses went into the room and realized that the baby's heart rate was erratic. Dr. Juskevitch opined that if Dr. O'Connell had been informed at 3:09 PM, the baby would have been delivered by 3:39 PM. Because O'Connell was not advised by the nurses of the change in the mother's condition until 3:25 PM, the baby was not delivered until 3:55 PM, 30 minutes after O'Connell responded to the delayed page. This delayed delivery took place 46 minutes after the doctor should have been called at 3:09 PM. According to Dr. White, a child neurologist called as an expert witness by the plaintiff, testified that if the baby had been delivered by 3:40 PM, she would have sustained no neurologic damage.

When the jury was unable to agree on a verdict following deliberation for over 2 days, the court discharged the jury, declared a mistrial, and, after additional argument, finally struck the plaintiffs' evidence and entered summary judgment for the defendant, and the plaintiffs appealed.

The Supreme Court of Virginia concluded that the evidence was sufficient to raise a jury issue regarding the nurses' negligence, holding that the trial court erred in striking the plaintiffs' evidence and in entering summary judgment for the defendant. The case was remanded for a new trial.

Failure to Follow Orders

Nurses have periodically found themselves in a lawsuit because of their failure to follow orders. Several cases below involve the failure to follow written orders, verbal orders, and a supervisor's orders.

Written Orders

In July 1998, Kitchen became a resident of Wickliffe nursing home.[50] She had been a patient of the appellant, Dr. Muenster, since 1963. While Kitchen resided in the nursing home, Muenster continued to act as her treating physician. When Kitchen entered Wickliffe, she had been receiving Coumadin, a blood thinner that requires monitoring by specific blood tests on a periodic basis. These blood tests were needed in order to adjust the dosage of Coumadin if necessary. Muenster had written the orders for the nurses to conduct blood tests every Wednesday. On July 29, 1998, the nurses administered these tests and faxed the results to Muenster. Kitchen continued to receive Coumadin at the dosage prescribed by Muenster even though the nurses apparently failed to conduct subsequent weekly blood tests. Likewise, Muenster did not receive any reports concerning the blood test results. During this time, Muenster made no further effort to check up on the resident. On August 19, 1998, Kitchen was found in distress and was transported to a hospital, where she went into renal failure and later lapsed into a coma and died as a result of toxic levels of Coumadin.

The appellees filed suit against Muenster and Wickliffe, alleging negligence and wrongful death. After appellees settled with Wickliffe, the case proceeded against Muenster. Following trial, the jury returned a verdict in favor of the physician, and the plaintiffs/appellees moved for a new trial. The appellees maintained that Muenster had a responsibility to follow up and make sure that the nurses fulfilled his orders. The appellees argued that if the jury found the nurses negligent in failing to follow the physician's orders, then the jury also should have found the physician negligent on the basis that he controlled the performance of the nurses.

Muenster claimed that there was absolutely no evidence to establish that he had a right to control or direct the performance of the nurses beyond the issuance of the orders in question. Thus, the negligence of the nurses could not be imputed to him. The trial court granted the appellees' motion for a new trial. The Ohio Court of Appeals found that other than the issuance of treatment orders, there was no evidence presented at trial that established Muenster had the right to control and direct the performance of the nurses at the nursing home.

Verbal Orders

The evidence in *Redel v. Capital Reg. Med. Ctr.*[51] noted that nurses failed to follow the treating doctor's orders and established a submissible case of medical negligence against the hospital. It was established that, following bilateral knee replacement surgery, the action of nurses caused permanent drop foot in the patient. They failed to follow the doctor's *verbal orders* to watch the patient closely and to place him in one continuous passive motion machine at a time during physical therapy.

> Plaintiffs' claim of negligence was based on Nurse Mote's failure to follow Dr. Galbraith's orders to administer CPM therapy to only one of Patient's legs at a time and to monitor Patient closely to the extent Patient was disoriented. Thus, it was unnecessary for Plaintiffs to offer expert testimony that it was a violation of the standard of care to use two CPM machines at once or to apply CPM therapy when Patient was disoriented.[52]

Verify Orders

Failure to take correct telephone orders can be just as serious as failure to follow, understand, and/or interpret a physician's order(s). Nurses must be alert in transcribing orders because there are periodic contradictions between what physicians claim they ordered and what nurses allege was ordered. Orders should be read back, once transcribed, for verification purposes. Verification of an order by another nurse on a second telephone is helpful, especially if an order is questionable. Any questionable orders must be verified with the physician initiating the order. Physicians must authenticate their verbal order(s) by signing the written order in the medical record. Nurses who disagree with a physician's order should not carry out an obviously erroneous order. In addition, they should confirm the order with the prescribing physician and report to the supervisor any concerns they may have with a particular order.

Supervisor's Orders

Failure of a nurse to follow the instructions of a supervising nurse to wait for her assistance before performing a procedure can result in the revocation of the nurse's license. The nurse in *Cafiero v. North Carolina Board of Nursing*[53] failed to heed instructions to wait for assistance before connecting a heart monitor to an infant. The heart monitor was connected incorrectly and resulted in an electrical shock to the infant. The board of nursing, under the nursing practice act of the state, revoked the nurse's license. The board had the authority to revoke the nurse's license even though her work before and after the incident had been exemplary. The dangers of electric cords are within the realm of common knowledge. The record showed that the nurse failed to exercise ordinary care in connecting the infant to the monitor.

Leaving Patient Unattended

The Navy veteran in *Vanhoy v. United States*[54] successfully underwent coronary bypass surgery at the Veterans Affairs Medical Center. However, he was injured as a result of being left unattended for several hours by nursing personnel in the intensive care unit. "During that time, the endotracheal tube that was supplying Mr. Vanhoy with oxygen became dislodged, causing him to go into respiratory and cardiac arrest. Medical records indicate that he was likely extubated for more than twenty-one minutes before his condition was discovered and attempts were made to reintubate him."[55] The veteran suffered anoxic brain injury following a complication with his endotracheal tube and was left permanently disabled. An action was brought under the *Federal Tort Claims Act*.

The Federal Tort Claims Act (June 25, 1946, ch. 646, Title IV, 60 Stat. 812, "28 U.S.C. Pt. VI Ch. 171" and 28 U.S.C. § 1346(b) ("FTCA") is a 1946 federal statute that permits private parties to sue the United States in a federal court for most torts committed by persons acting on behalf of the United States. Historically, citizens have not been able to sue their state—a doctrine referred to as sovereign immunity. The FTCA constitutes a limited waiver of sovereign immunity, permitting citizens to pursue some tort claims against the government.[56]

The trial court awarded a lump-sum payment of $3.5 million to the veteran for future medical care and services. On appeal, the trial court was found to have properly required the federal government to make an immediate lump-sum payment of future medical damages to the veteran.

Failure to Record Patient's Care

The plaintiff in *Pellerin v. Humedicenters, Inc.*[57] went to the emergency department at Lakeland Medical Center complaining of chest pain. An emergency department physician, Dr. Gruner, examined her and ordered a nurse to give her an injection consisting of 50 mg of Demerol and 25 mg of Vistaril. Although the nurse testified that she did not recall giving the injection, she did not deny giving it, and her initials were present in the emergency department record as having administered the medication. The nurse admitted that she failed to record the site and mode of injection. She said she might have written this information in the nurse's notes, but no such notes were admitted into evidence.

The plaintiff testified she felt pain and a burning sensation in her hip during an injection. The burning persisted and progressively worsened over the next several weeks. The pain spread to an area approximately 10 inches in diameter around the injection site. She could not sleep on her right side, work, perform household chores, or participate in sports without experiencing pain.

The appeals court found that there was sufficient evidence to support a jury finding that the nurse had breached the applicable standard of care in administering an injection of Vistaril into Pellerin's hip. The jury awarded the plaintiff $90,304.68 in total damages. The nurse admitted that she failed to record the site and mode of injection in the emergency department records. According to the testimony of two experts in nursing practice, failing to record this information is below the standard of care for nursing.

Medication Errors

Nurses are required to handle and administer a vast variety of drugs that are prescribed by physicians and dispensed by an organization's pharmacy. Medications may range from aspirin to highly dangerous drugs (e.g., potassium chloride) administered through IV solutions. Medications must be administered in the prescribed manner and dose to prevent serious harm to patients. The risks of medication errors for nurses include: (1) selecting the right patient; (2) administering the right medication; (3) in the right dose; (4) by the right route; (5) at the right time; (6) documenting the patient's response to the medication administered; (7) determining the patient's reaction to the medication to be sure there is no adverse reaction to the medication; and (8) taking the appropriate action if the patient has an adverse reaction to the medication administered.

The practice of pharmacy includes the ordering, preparation, dispensing, and administration of medications. These activities may be carried out only by a licensed pharmacist or by a person exempted from the provisions of a state's pharmacy statutes. Nurses are exempted from the various pharmacy statutes when administering a medication on the oral or written order of a physician.

Failure to Administer Drugs

The trial court in *Lloyd Noland Hospital v. Durham*[58] did not err in denying a hospital's motion for a new trial based on the hospital's argument that it did not breach an applicable standard of care in failing to administer a preoperative antibiotic to a patient. The record contained ample evidence of the existence of a standing order that required the nursing staff to administer preoperative antibiotics to patients prior to being treated.

In *Kallenberg v. Beth Israel Hospital*,[59] a patient died after her third cerebral hemorrhage because of the failure of the physicians and staff to administer necessary medications. When the patient was admitted to the hospital, her physician determined that she should be given a specific drug to reduce her blood pressure and make her condition operable. For an unexplained reason, the drug was not administered. The patient's blood pressure rose, and after the final hemorrhage, she died. The jury found the hospital and physicians negligent by failing to administer the drug and ruled that the negligence caused the patient's death. On appeal, the appellate court found that the jury had sufficient evidence to decide that the negligent treatment had been the cause of the patient's death.

Failure to Document Drug Wastage

The nurse in *Matthias v. Iowa Board of Nursing*[60] failed to conform to minimum standards of practice by neglecting to document the loss or wastage of controlled substances. The minimum standard of acceptable practice requires nurses to count controlled substances each shift, to document all loss or wastage of controlled substances, and to obtain the signature of a witness to the disposal of controlled substances. Iowa Code allows a professional license to be suspended or revoked when the licensee engages in professional incompetency. Iowa Administrative Code section 655 4.19(2)(c), which regulates the actions of the board, defines professional incompetency as including "[w]illful or repeated departure from or failure to conform to the minimum standards of acceptable and prevailing practice of nursing in the state of Iowa."

Matthias argued that the board erred as a matter of law because it failed to find that she knowingly or willfully failed to conform to the minimum standards of practice regarding documentation of loss or wastage of controlled substances. The Iowa Court of Appeals found that there was substantial evidence supporting the board's finding that Matthias engaged in repeated departures from the minimum standards of nursing. The board, therefore, did not need to find that the departure was also willful.

Administering Drugs Without a Prescription

In *People v. Nygren*,[61] evidence was considered sufficient to establish probable cause for charging the director of nursing and a charge nurse with second-degree assault in the administration of unprescribed doses of Thorazine to a resident at a time when the patient was incapable of providing consent. There was probable cause to believe that the defendants committed the offense charged and that it would have been established if the prosecution had been permitted to present its witnesses, two of whom would have testified that the nurses administered the unprescribed doses of the drug. The treating physician told the special investigator from the attorney general's office that Thorazine never had been prescribed for the resident while he was in the nursing facility. The resident was mentally retarded and incapable of consenting to administration of the drug. Medical evidence of the amount of Thorazine in the resident's blood was consistent with stupor and impairment of physical and mental functions.

Administering Wrong Medication

In *Abercrombie v. Roof*,[62] a solution was prepared by a nurse employee and injected into the patient by a physician. The physician made no examination of the fluid, and the patient suffered permanent injuries as a result of the injection. An action was brought against the physician for malpractice. The patient claimed that the fluid injected was alcohol and that the physician should have recognized its distinctive odor. In finding for the physician, the court stated that he was not responsible for the misuse of drugs prepared by an employee unless the ordinarily prudent use of his faculties would have prevented injury to the patient.

Failure to Clarify Orders

A nurse is responsible for making an inquiry if there is uncertainty about the accuracy of a physician's medication order in a patient's record. In the Louisiana case of *Norton v. Argonaut Insurance Co.*,[63] the court focused attention on the responsibility of a nurse to obtain clarification of an apparently erroneous order from the patient's physician. The medication order, as entered in the medical record, was incomplete and subject to misinterpretation. Believing the order to be incorrect because of the dosage, the nurse asked two physicians present on the patient care unit whether the medication should be given as ordered. The two physicians did not interpret the order as the nurse did and, therefore, did not share the same concern. They advised the nurse that the attending physician's instructions did not appear out of line. The nurse did not contact the attending physician but instead administered the misinterpreted dosage of medication. As a result, the patient died from a fatal overdose of the medication.

The court upheld the jury's finding that the nurse had been negligent in failing to verify the order with the attending physician prior to administering the drug. The nurse was held liable, as was the physician who wrote the ambiguous order that led to the fatal dose. The court noted that it is the duty of a nurse to make absolutely certain what the physician intended, regarding both dosage and route. This clarification was not sought from the physician who wrote the order.

Administration of the Wrong Dosage

The nurse in *Harrison v. Axelrod*[64] was charged with patient neglect because she administered the wrong dosage of the drug Haldol to a patient on seven occasions while she was employed at a nursing facility. The patient's physician had prescribed a 0.5-mg dosage of Haldol. The patient's medication record indicated that the nurse had been administering dosages of 5.0 mg, the dosage sent to the patient care unit by the pharmacy. A Department of Health investigator testified that the nurse admitted that she administered the wrong dosage and that she was aware of the facility's medication administration policy, which she breached by failing to check the dosage supplied by the pharmacy against the dosage ordered by the patient's doctor. The nurse denied that she made these admissions to the investigator. The commissioner of the Department of Health made a determination that the administration of the wrong dosage of Haldol on seven occasions constituted patient neglect.

On appeal, the New York Supreme Court, Appellate Division, held that the evidence established that the nurse administered the wrong dosage of the prescribed drug Haldol to the patient. This was a breach of the facility's medication administration policy and was sufficient to support the determination of patient neglect.

NEGLIGENT DRUG OVERDOSE

Citation: *Harder v. Clinton, Inc.*, 948 P.2d 298 (Okla. 1997)

Facts

Kayser was admitted to a nursing home on July 14, 1992. On the evening of September 30, she was transferred to a hospital after ingesting an overdose of tolbutamide, a diabetic medication. She was diagnosed as being in a hypoglycemic coma caused by the lowering of her blood sugar from ingestion of the medication. An IV device was inserted in the dorsum area of her right foot to treat the coma. Gangrene later developed in the same foot, which eventually required an above-the-knee amputation.

As Kayser's guardian, Harder, Kayser's sister, brought a suit against the nursing home for harm caused to Kayser by an overdose of the wrong prescription administered to her while she was in the nursing home's care and custody. At the close of Harder's case, which followed a res ipsa loquitur pattern of proof, the trial court directed a verdict for the nursing home. The trial court ruled that Harder's evidence fell short of establishing a negligence claim because her proof failed to show all the requisite foundational elements for res ipsa loquitur.

(continues)

NEGLIGENT DRUG OVERDOSE   *(continued)*

Issue

Did the trial court err when it directed a verdict for the nursing home based on its ruling that Harder had not satisfied the requirements for a res ipsa loquitur submission?

Holding

By the evidence adduced at trial, Harder met the standards for submission of her claim based on the doctrine of res ipsa loquitur pattern of proof.

Reason

In light of the circumstances that surround the injurious event, it seems reasonably clear that Kayser's ingestion of a tolbutamide overdose would not have taken place in the absence of negligence by the nursing home's staff. The record shows that Kayser had not been prescribed any diabetes medication while a resident at the nursing home and that she had never been prescribed that type of hypoglycemic drug. Testimony indicates Kayser was at the nursing home when she ingested the prescribed medication. There is no direct evidence that anyone else supplied to her the harm-dealing dosage or that the substance in question was kept in her room (or elsewhere within her control). Neither is there indication that any other cause contributed to the coma. According to Dixon, a licensed practical nurse and a medication clerk at the nursing home are responsible for the administration of medication to its residents. The administration of the wrong medication in an amount so excessive as to harm a resident is below the applicable standard of care.

Harder's evidence laid the requisite res ipsa loquitur foundation facts from which it could be inferred that the injury—from an overdose of the wrong prescription—was one that would not ordinarily occur in the course of controlled supervision and administration of prescribed medicine in the absence of negligence. The responsibility for producing proof that would rebut the inferences favorable to Harder's legal position was thus shifted to the defendant.

Administering by the Wrong Route

The nurse in *Fleming v. Baptist General Convention*[65] negligently injected the patient with a solution of Talwin and Atarax subcutaneously, rather than intramuscularly. The patient suffered tissue necrosis as a result of the improper injection.

> On October 19, 1971, Mrs. Fleming was taken to defendant's emergency room before dawn for an injection for migraine. A member of the hospital staff prepared the injection and administered it into the left thigh. Plaintiff experienced immediate pain and by the time she had returned home the injection site began discoloring. She consulted Dr. Cosby about the condition that afternoon. The following day she was admitted to the hospital for treatment of the problem. The deterioration of the flesh at the injection site continued to grow progressively worse. The skin and subcutaneous tissue down to the fascia deteriorated and gangrene set in. The skin and subcutaneous tissue eroded and, after the tissue death had run its course, the plaintiff required two skin grafts to close the wound.[66]

The suit against the hospital was successful. On appeal by the defendant, the court held that the jury's verdict for the plaintiff found adequate support in the testimony of the plaintiff's expert witness on the issues of negligence and causation.

Failure to Discontinue Medication

A healthcare organization will be held liable if a nurse continues to inject a solution into a patient after noticing its ill effects. In the Florida case of *Parrish v. Clark*,[67] the court held that a nurse's continued injection of saline solution into an unconscious patient's breast after the nurse noticed ill effects constituted negligence. After something was observed to be wrong with the administration of the solution, the nurse had a duty to discontinue its use.

Failure to Identify Correct Patient

A patient's identification bracelet must be checked prior to administering medications. To ensure that the patient's identity corresponds to the name on the patient's bracelet, the nurse is responsible for addressing the patient by name when approaching the patient's bedside to administer any medication. Should a patient unwittingly be administered another patient's medication, the attending physician should be notified, and appropriate documentation placed on the patient's chart.

Failure to Note Order Change

In *Larrimore v. Homeopathic Hospital Association*,[68] the physician wrote an instruction on the patient's order sheet changing the method of administration from intramuscular to oral. When a nurse on the patient unit who had been off duty for several days was preparing to medicate the patient by injection, the patient objected and referred the nurse to the physician's new order. The nurse, however, told the patient she was mistaken and administered the medication intramuscularly.

> The entry on the order sheet of October 1, 1959, which constitutes direct orders from the physician to the nursing staff, states:
>
> "Discontinue parenteral Ansolysen at eight p.m. Give oral Ansolysen, 20 milligrams, at eight p.m., 10-1-59, then 20 milligrams at eight p.m. and two p.m., on 10-2-59."
>
> The entry on the order sheet for October 2, 1959, states:
>
> "Continue Ansolysen by mouth today and 10-3-59."
>
> The entry on the order sheet for October 4, 1959, states:
>
> "Increase Ansolysen, 30 milligrams at eight p.m., 30 milligrams at two p.m., and 30 milligrams at 8 p.m., on 10-5-59."[69]

The doctor had "stated that after his order for oral administration of the drug, it was clear that it was now only a matter of time before the patient's ultimate demise would occur."[70] The court went on to say that the jury could find the nurse negligent by applying ordinary common sense to establish the applicable standard of care.

Failure to Follow Infection-Control Procedures

Failure to follow proper infection-control procedures (e.g., proper hand-washing techniques) can result in cross-contamination among patients, staff, and visitors. Staff members who administer to patients, moving from one patient to another, must wash their hands after changing dressings and carrying out routine procedures.

Cross-Contamination

The patient in *Helmann v. Sacred Heart Hospital*[71] was returned to his room following hip surgery. The patient's roommate complained of a boil under his right arm. A culture was taken of drainage from the wound and was identified as *Staphylococcus aureus*. The infected roommate was transferred immediately to an isolation room. Until this time, hospital employees administered to both patients regularly, moving from one patient to another without washing their hands as they changed dressings and carried out routine procedures. On the day the roommate was placed in isolation, the plaintiff's wound erupted, discharging a large amount of purulent drainage. A culture of the drainage showed it to have been caused by the presence of *S. aureus*. The infection penetrated into the patient's hip socket, destroying tissue and requiring a second operation. The court ruled that there was sufficient circumstantial evidence from which the jury could have found that the patients were infected with the same *S. aureus* strain and that the infection was caused by the hospital's employees' failure to follow sterile techniques in ministering to its two patients.

Improper Sterilization

The patient in *Howard v. Alexandria Hosp.*[72] brought a medical malpractice action against the hospital, seeking damages arising out of an operation performed with unsterile instruments. During her stay in the recovery room, the operating surgeon reported to the patient that she had been operated on with unsterile instruments. Allegedly, the nurse in charge of the autoclave used to sterilize the instruments did not properly monitor the sterilization process. Because of the patient's fear of a variety of diseases, she was administered several human immunodeficiency virus tests. The patient was evaluated by an infectious disease specialist and was administered antibiotics intravenously. Following her discharge, the patient was placed on several medications and, as a result, developed symptoms of pseudomembranous enterocolitis. Testimony described the patient's symptoms as resulting from the administration of the antibiotics. One expert testified that the patient had reason to be concerned for at least 6 months following the surgical procedure because of her risk of being infected with a variety of diseases. The hospital argued that the patient suffered no physical injury from the surgical procedure and the instruments used during the procedure. The circuit court entered summary judgment for the hospital on the grounds that no physical injury had been shown.

The Virginia Supreme Court held that the patient suffered injury resulting from measures taken to avoid infection following discovery of the use of unsterile instrumentation, even though the patient did not sustain any infection from use of the instruments. The case was reversed and remanded for a new trial on all issues.

Injury can be either physical or mental. It is clear that because of the hospital's use of inadequately sterilized instruments, the plaintiff sustained positive physical and mental injury. As the direct result of the nurse's negligence, IV tubes and needles invaded the plaintiff's body. She experienced physical pain and the discomforts of headache, nausea, vomiting, fever, chills, and unusual sweating.

Negligent Procedures

The following cases review several of the many procedures that can result in negligent acts that involve nurses. Case law helps to facilitate the learning process. As with any medical–legal case review, it is reemphasized here that the lessons to be learned from the mistakes of others help in the prevention of similar mistakes, regardless of the profession.

Burns from Bovie Machine

The negligent use of a Bovie plate led to liability in *Monk v. Doctors Hospital*,[73] in which a nurse had been instructed by the physician to set up a Bovie machine. The nurse placed the contact plate of the Bovie machine under the patient's right calf in a negligent manner, and the patient suffered burns. The patient introduced instruction manuals issued by the manufacturer supporting a claim that the plate was placed improperly. These manuals had been available to the hospital. The trial court directed a verdict in favor of the hospital and the physician. The appellate court found that there was sufficient evidence from which the jury could conclude that the Bovie plate was applied in a negligent manner. There was also sufficient evidence, including the manufacturer's manual and expert testimony, from which the jury could find that the physician was independently negligent.

Arm Laceration

The plaintiffs in *Morris v. Children's Hospital Medical Center*[74] alleged in their complaint that, while hospitalized at Children's Hospital Medical Center, the patient suffered a laceration to her arm as a result of treatment administered by the defendants and their agents that fell below the accepted standard of care. Morris alleged from personal observation that the laceration to her daughter's arm was caused by the jagged edges of a plastic cup that had been split and placed on her arm to guard an IV site. A nurse, in her affidavit, who stated her qualifications as an expert, expressed her opinion that the practice of placing a split plastic cup over an IV site as a guard constituted a breach of the standard of nursing care.

Negligent Injection

In *Bernardi v. Community Hospital Association*,[75] a 7-year-old patient was in the hospital after surgery for the drainage of an abscessed appendix. The attending physician left a written postoperative order requiring an injection of tetracycline every 12 hours. During the evening of the first day after surgery, the nurse, employed by the hospital and acting under this order, injected the prescribed dosage of tetracycline in the patient's right gluteal region. It was claimed that the nurse negligently injected the tetracycline into or adjacent to the sciatic nerve, causing the patient to permanently lose the normal use of the right foot. The court did not hold the physician responsible. It concluded that if the plaintiff could prove the nurse's negligence, the hospital would be responsible for the nurse's act under the doctrine of respondeat superior. The physician did not know which nurse administered the injection because he was not present when the injection was given, and he had no opportunity to control its administration. The hospital was found liable under respondeat superior. The hospital was the employer of the nurse: Only it had the right to hire and fire her, and only it could assign the nurse to certain hours, designated areas, and specific patients.

Cutting IV Tube Results in Amputation

A nurse employed by the defendant in *Ahmed v. Children's Hospital of Buffalo*[76] amputated nearly one-third of a 1-month-old infant's index finger while cutting an IV tube with a pair of scissors. Surgery to reattach the amputated portion of the finger was unsuccessful. The plaintiffs were awarded $87,000 for past pain and suffering and $50,000 for future damages. The defendant moved to set aside the verdict and sought a new trial, claiming that damages were excessive. The trial court rejected much of the testimony presented by the plaintiffs.

An appeals court determined that it was the jury's function to assess the credibility of witnesses and to evaluate the testimony regarding the child's pain, suffering, and disability. The trial court was found to have improperly invaded the jury's province to evaluate the nature and extent of the injury. The appellate court found that the jury's award of damages did not deviate materially from what would be reasonable compensation. The jury's verdict was reinstated.

Foreign Objects Left in Patients

There are many cases involving foreign objects left in patients during surgery. The hospital in *Ross v. Chatham County Hospital Authority*[77] was properly denied summary dismissal of an action in which a patient sought to recover damages for injuries suffered when a surgical instrument was left in the patient's abdomen during surgery. This incident occurred as a result of the failure of the operating room personnel to conduct an instrument and sponge count after surgery. The borrowed servant doctrine did not insulate the hospital from the negligence of its nurses because the doctrine applies only to acts involving professional skill and judgment. Foreign objects negligently left in a patient's body constitute an administrative act. A standard nursing check-off procedure should be used to account for all sponges and/or instruments used in the operating room. Preventive measures of this nature will reduce a hospital's risk of liability.

The decedent's estate in *Holger v. Irish*[78] sued the surgeon and the hospital that employed the nurses who assisted the surgeon during the operation performed on the deceased. During the course of performing colon surgery, the surgeon placed laparotomy sponges in the decedent's abdomen. After he had removed the sponges at the end of surgery, the two nurses assisting him counted them and verified that they had all been removed. Two years later, a sponge was discovered in the patient's abdomen. It was removed, and the 92-year-old patient died. The jury decided in favor of the defendants, and the decedent's estate appealed. The court of appeals reversed the decision, and the Oregon Supreme Court reviewed the case.

The Oregon Supreme Court held that the surgeon was not vicariously liable, as a matter of law, for the negligence of the operating room nurses. There was no evidence presented that the nurses were the defendant's employees or that they were under the supervision or control of the defendant regarding their counting of the sponges. It was their sole responsibility to count the sponges. The nurses had been hired and trained by the hospital, which paid for their services.

Shared Responsibility for Sponge Counts

Romero v. Bellina[79] describes how both nurses and surgeons are responsible for sponge counts. Bellina performed laser surgery on Romero at the hospital. During surgery, Bellina was assisted by Markey and Toups, surgical nurses employed by the hospital. Before the final suturing of the incision, the nurses erroneously informed Bellina that all the lap pads had been accounted for.

The day after the procedure, Romero complained of severe abdominal pain. A few months later, she discovered a mass in her abdomen near the area where the surgery was performed. She visited her treating physician, Dr. Blue, who determined through an X-ray that the mass in her abdomen was a lap sponge from the surgery with Bellina. Romero underwent corrective surgery with a different physician to remove the sponge.

The plaintiffs settled their claims with the hospital, and the case proceeded to trial against Bellina. After a bench trial, the trial court rendered judgment in favor of the plaintiffs for $170,966.41, and Bellina filed an appeal.

In ruling against Bellina, the trial court held that a surgeon's duty to remove foreign objects placed in a patient's body is an independent, nondelegable duty. The trial court found that Bellina was 70% at fault and the nurses employed by the hospital were 30% at fault. On appeal, Bellina argued that the trial judge erred in concluding that, in Louisiana, a surgeon cannot rely on surgical nurses to count sponges to make sure none are left inside a patient. Prevailing case law in Louisiana, however, holds that a surgeon has a nondelegable duty to remove all sponges placed in a patient's body.

The Louisiana Court of Appeal held that although nurses have an independent duty, apart from the surgeon's duty, to account for the sponges, and that they can be concurrently at fault with the surgeon for leaving a sponge in the patient's body, the nurses' count is a remedial measure that cannot relieve the surgeon of his or her nondelegable duty to remove the sponge in the first instance. Bellina had an independent, nondelegable duty to remove from the patient's body the foreign substance that he had placed into her.

Current jurisprudence more accurately reflects the modern team approach to surgery, whereby the nurses' count is a remedial measure that does not discharge the surgeon's independent duty to ensure that all sponges are removed before an incision is closed.

The lesson in this case illustrates the importance of building redundancy in the delivery of health care to protect patients from harm. The responsibility of accounting for sponges, instruments, and other foreign objects lies with both the surgeon and nurse and, in some instances, the operating room technician. Even though some jurisdictions may free the surgeon of such responsibility, organizations should adopt a higher standard, assigning responsibility to both the nurse and surgeon and, where applicable, the operating room technician.

Patient Falls

Patients are highly susceptible to falling, and the consequences of falling are generally more serious with older age groups. Among senior citizens, falls represent the fifth-leading cause of death, and the mortality rate from falls increases significantly with age. For those age 75 years and older, the mortality rate from falls is five times higher than for those age 65 to 74 years, and the rate increases such that persons older than age 80 years have an even greater chance of experiencing a fatal fall.

Standards for the application of both physical and chemical restraints have been evolving over the past decade, and they are becoming more stringent. Because of patient rights issues, injuries, and the improper and indiscreet use of restraints, organizations are attempting to develop restraint-free environments.

Failure to Follow Policy

The plaintiffs, in *Estate of Hendrickson v. Genesis Health Venture, Inc.*,[80] filed an action for negligence, breach of contract, and negligent infliction of emotional distress against Genesis ElderCare Network Services, Inc. (GENS), among others.

Hendrickson suffered a massive stroke while she was a patient at a hospital in the summer of 1996. The stroke left her totally dependent on others for her daily care. During one of her admissions to Salisbury Center, a nursing home, operated by the defendant GENS, Ferguson went into Hendrickson's room while making rounds and found Hendrickson dead, her head wedged between the mattress and the adjacent bed rail.

A jury found that Hendrickson's death was caused by negligence. On appeal, GENS argued that the plaintiff failed to show that GENS knew or should have known of the risk of injury to Hendrickson from the side rails. The North Carolina Court of Appeals disagreed, finding that there was evidence tending to show that nursing assistants employed by GENS were aware that Hendrickson, on several occasions before her death on October 30, had slid to the edge of the bed and become caught between the edge of the mattress and the bed rail. Plaintiffs offered evidence showing that GENS had a restraint policy in effect that required a restraint assessment form for any resident for whom the use of restraints was required. The nursing staff was required to document the effectiveness of less restrictive measures. The assessment was required to be reviewed by a restraint alternative team/committee. Evidence was offered showing that no restraint assessment form had been completed for Hendrickson. In addition, her medical records contained no nursing notes documenting the use of less restrictive measures than the bed rails. The defendant argued that the bed rails were required for positioning and safety and were not restraints, so that no restraint assessment was required. Although the evidence was conflicting as to whether the bed rails were used as a restraint or as a safety measure, evidence indicated that the rails should have been considered a restraint in connection with Hendrickson's care, as per organization policy.

The court of appeals concluded that the plaintiffs offered sufficient evidence to sustain a finding by the jury that defendant GENS was negligent in failing to conform to its own policies with respect to the use of physical restraints and that such negligence was the proximate cause of Hendrickson's death.

Failure to Raise Bed Rails

The plaintiff in *Polonsky v. Union Hospital*[81] suffered a fall and fractured her hip after the administration of a sleeping medication commonly known by the trade name Dalmane. The superior court awarded damages in the amount of the statutory limit of $20,000, and the hospital appealed. The appeals court held that from the Dalmane warning provided by the drug manufacturer and the hospital's own regulation regarding bedside rails, without additional medical testimony, the jury could draw an inference that the hospital's nurse failed to exercise due care when she failed to raise the bed rails after administering Dalmane.

Nurse Followed Safe Procedures

The fall of a patient is not always attributable to negligence. The New York Court of Appeals held that the evidence in *Stoker v. Tarentino*[82] did not support discipline of a nurse on a charge that a wheelchair resident was improperly left alone in the bathroom. The negligence charge against the petitioner was predicated on a wheelchair resident having been left alone in the bathroom after the petitioner assisted another nurse in moving the resident from the bed to the wheelchair to the bathroom. All the nurses who testified agreed that there was no order, written or verbal, requiring the nurse to remain with the resident while she was in the bathroom. Policies and procedures of the nursing facility and the health department contained no instructions concerning toilet procedures with respect to wheelchair residents. The court held that disciplinary action against the nurse should be annulled and expunged from the petitioner's personnel file.

Fall from Examination Table

A judgment for the plaintiff was affirmed in *Petry v. Nassau Hospital*,[83] which was an action to recover damages for personal injuries suffered by the plaintiff's wife. The patient had been placed on a narrow examination table in the emergency department of the defendant hospital and fell from the table. The table had no side rails in place to protect the patient from falling, and the patient had been left unattended by the nurse in charge.

▶ DUTY TO QUESTION DISCHARGE

A nurse is not only a caregiver, but often takes on the role of a patient advocate. For example, a nurse has a duty to question the discharge of a patient if he or she has reason to believe that such discharge could be injurious to the health of the patient. Jury issues were raised in *Koeniguer v. Eckrich*[84] by expert testimony that the nurses had a duty to attempt to delay the patient's discharge if her condition warranted continued hospitalization. By permissible inferences from the evidence, the delay in treatment that resulted from the premature discharge contributed to the patient's death. Summary dismissal of this case against the hospital by a trial court was found to have been improper.

▶ DUTY TO REPORT PHYSICIAN NEGLIGENCE

An organization can be liable for failure of nursing personnel to take appropriate action when a patient's personal physician is clearly unwilling or unable to cope with a situation that threatens the life or health of the patient. In a California case, *Goff v. Doctors General Hospital*,[85] a patient was bleeding seriously after childbirth because the physician failed to suture her properly. The nurses testified that they were aware of the patient's dangerous condition and that the physician was not present in the hospital. Both nurses knew the patient would die if nothing was done, but neither contacted anyone except the physician. The hospital was liable for the nurses' negligence in failing to notify their supervisors of the serious condition that caused the patient's death. Evidence was sufficient to sustain the finding that the nurses who attended the patient and who were aware of the excessive bleeding were negligent and that their negligence was a contributing cause of the patient's death. The measure of duty of the hospital toward its patients is the exercise of that degree of care used by hospitals generally. The court held that nurses who knew that a woman they were attending was bleeding excessively were negligent in failing to report the circumstances so that prompt and adequate measures could be taken to safeguard her life.

🔍 *SWOLLEN BEYOND RECOGNITION*

Citation: *NKC Hosps., Inc. v. Anthony*, 849 S.W.2d 564 (Ky. Ct. App. 1993)

Facts

The decedent, Mrs. Anthony, was in her first pregnancy under the primary care of Dr. Hawkins, her personal physician. Anthony was in good health, 26 years of age, employed, and about 30 weeks along in her pregnancy. On September 5, 1989, Anthony's husband took her to the emergency department of Norton Hospital. She was experiencing nausea, vomiting, and abdominal pain. Because of her pregnancy, she was referred to the hospital's obstetrical unit. In the obstetrical unit, Anthony came under the immediate care of Moore, a nurse, who performed an assessment.

Hawkins was called, and she issued several orders, including an IV start, blood work, urinalysis, and an antinausea prescription. Later that night, a second call was made to Hawkins, giving her the test results and informing her that the patient was in extreme pain. Believing that Anthony had a urinary tract infection, antibiotics were ordered along with an order for her discharge from the hospital.

That same night, a third call was made to Hawkins because of the pain that Anthony was experiencing, as observed by Moore. Anthony's husband also talked with Hawkins about his wife's pain. Moore became concerned about Hawkins's discharge order. Although aware of Moore's evaluation, Hawkins prescribed morphine sulfate but was unrelenting in her order of discharge. Love, the resident physician on duty, did not see or examine the patient, although a prescription for morphine was ordered and administered pursuant to the telephoned directions of Hawkins. At approximately 2:00 AM, the morphine was administered to Anthony. She rested comfortably for several hours but awakened in pain again. At 6:00 AM, the patient was discharged in pain.

During trial testimony, Hale, a nursing supervisor, admitted that it was a deviation from the standard of nursing care to discharge a patient in significant pain. Moore, who was always concerned about the patient's pain, had grave reservations about her discharge. She suggested that Love examine Anthony. She even consulted her supervisor, Nurse Hale.

At approximately 10:00 AM, Anthony was readmitted to the hospital. Upon readmission, Hawkins began personal supervision of her patient. It was determined that Anthony had a serious respiratory problem. The next day, the patient was transferred to the hospital's intensive care unit.

(continues)

SWOLLEN BEYOND RECOGNITION   *(continued)*

The following day, the baby was delivered by cesarean section. It was belatedly determined at that time that Anthony's condition was caused by a perforation of the appendix at the large bowel, a condition not detected by anyone at the hospital during her first admission. Almost 3 weeks later, while still in Norton Hospital, Anthony died of acute adult respiratory distress syndrome, a complication resulting from the delay in the diagnosis and treatment of her appendicitis.

Judgment was brought against the hospital. At trial, Dr. Fields, an expert witness for the estate of Anthony, testified that the hospital deviated from the standard of care. Pertinent testimony of Fields follows from the trial transcript:

Question: Had Margaret [Anthony] received care at Norton's Hospital which was within, which would have been within the standard of care, what would have been the outcome?

Answer: She would have had a prompt appendectomy performed following ruling out of various other conditions, such as kidney infection, and the appendix would have been removed, the antibiotic therapy instituted promptly in the intravenous fashion, her dehydrated state would have been corrected, she would never have suffered the pulmonary complication known as acute adult respiratory distress syndrome.

Question: Within a degree of medical probability, sir, would she be alive today?

Answer: Yes.

Question: Was the discharge of Margaret Anthony from the hospital on the early morning hours of September 6, 1989, a deviation from the standard of care for the hospital?

Answer: Yes, sir. [*Id.* at 566]

Fields's testimony tagged Norton Hospital with negligence as its actions were ". . . below the standard of care for any institution . . ." and he explained:

Every patient who presents herself to the labor and delivery area, the emergency room, or any area of the hospital, would be seen by a physician before anything is undertaken, and certainly before she is allowed to leave the institution. Furthermore, to provide the patient with medication in the form of a prescription without the physician ever seeing the patient is below any standard I'm acquainted with. [*Id.* at 567]

An award of more than $2 million was returned, with the apportionment of causation attributable to Hawkins as 65% and to the hospital as 35%. The hospital argued that the trial court erred in failing to grant its motions for directed verdict and for judgment notwithstanding the verdict because of the lack of substantial causation in linking the negligence of the hospital to Anthony's death.

Issue

Was the negligence of the hospital superseded by the negligence of the patient's primary care physician, and was the award excessive?

Holding

The Kentucky Court of Appeals held that negligence of the hospital was not superseded by the negligence of the patient's primary care physician and that the award for pain and suffering was not excessive.

Reason

The hospital's negligence is based on acts of omission, by failing to have Mrs. Anthony examined by a physician and by discharging her in pain. The hospital should have foreseen the injury to Anthony because its own staff was questioning the judgments of Hawkins while, at the same time, failing to follow through with the standard of care required of it. The defense that the hospital's nurses were only following a "chain of command" by doing what Hawkins ordered is not persuasive. The nurses were not the agents of Hawkins. All involved had their independent duty to Anthony.

The evidence presented a woman conscious of her last days on Earth, swollen beyond recognition, tubes exiting almost every orifice of her body, in severe pain, and who deteriorated to the point where she could not verbally communicate with loved ones. Among the last things she did was write out instructions about the care for her newborn child. The trial court, when confronted with a motion for a new trial on excessive damages, must evaluate the award mirrored against the facts. It is said, if the trial judge does not blush, the award is not excessive. No question, the award was monumental, but so was the injury.

Telephone assessments and reassessments are risky business, and they can come at a high price, as illustrated in this case. Nurses, although skilled caregivers, are often in a position where they also play a role as patient advocate. Therefore they, as with all caregivers, should be trained and their competencies assessed to determine their understanding as to what policies and procedures should be followed when there is a need to question another caregiver's patient care.

🔍 *THE COURT'S DECISION*

The trial court judge determined that the nursing staff had breached the standard of care required in the case of Mr. Ard. On appeal, the Court of Appeal of Louisiana, Fifth Circuit, concluded there was ample evidence to support the trial judge's decision. The nursing staff did indeed breach the standard of care required. The "negligence of the nurses lessened Devon Ard's chance of survival by his not being transferred to the intensive care unit prior to his being coded."[86] Testimony indicated that Ard would have had a much better chance of survival if he had been transferred to the intensive care unit.

The plaintiffs' appealed the amount of the award. The Appeals court determined that the trial court did abuse its discretion by awarding inadequate amounts for general damages. The Court of Appeal of Louisiana, Fifth Circuit, determined that the general damages award by the trial court should be raised from $50,000 to $150,000.[87]

▶ CHAPTER REVIEW

1. The *scope of nursing practice* is defined in state nurse practice acts, which describe the actions, duties, and limits of nurses in their particular roles.
2. Nurse practice acts
   - Although states have similar definitions of nursing, each state has its own individual *nurse practice act*.
   - These acts define the practice of nursing and outline a nurse's authority to act in that state.
3. *Nurse licensure* varies slightly from state to state, but each requires that an applicant receive formal professional training and pass a written examination. The basic methods by which boards license out-of-state nurses are: *reciprocity, endorsement, waiver, and examination.*
4. A variety of nursing careers exist, including registered nurse, traveling nurse, licensed practical nurse, nurse manager, certified nursing assistant, float nurse, agency nurse, special duty nurse, and nursing student.
5. Advanced practice nurses, who have undergone the requisite training and certification, can enjoy expanded roles, including the following:
   - *Nurse practitioner*—an RN who has completed the necessary education to engage in primary healthcare decision making
   - *Clinical nurse specialist*—an RN with an advanced academic degree, experience, and expertise in a clinical specialty (e.g., obstetrics, pediatrics, psychiatry)
   - *Certified nurse anesthetist*—an RN who administers anesthesia
   - *Certified nurse midwife*—an RN who provides comprehensive prenatal care, including delivery for patients who are at low risk for complications

6. Common legal risks for nurses include: the dilemma of two standards of care; patient misidentification; patient monitoring and observation; delay in reporting a patient's condition; delay in treatment; failure to follow orders; leaving a patient unattended; failure to record patient's care; medication errors; failure to follow infection control procedures; negligent procedures; and patient falls.
7. Duty to question discharge
8. Duty to report physician negligence

▶ REVIEW QUESTIONS

1. Describe why the scope of nursing has been changing.
2. Describe the various roles of advanced practice nurses.
3. Describe the various legal risks for nurses.
4. Describe the various errors that can occur in the administration of medications.
5. Discuss why it is important to report significant changes in a patient's condition to the treating physician.
6. If a nurse disagrees with a physician's written orders, discuss what action the nurse should take to protect the patient's safety.
7. Discuss under what circumstances a nurse has a duty to question a patient's care.

▶ NOTES

1. *Ard v. East Jefferson Gen. Hosp.*, 636 So. 2d 1042 (La. Ct. App. 1994).
2. *Id.*, 1046–1047.
3. CareerProfiles, "Registered Nurse (RN)," http://www.careerprofiles.info/nurse-career.html.

4. Minnesota Nurses Association, "MNA Position Statement: Professional Relationships and Boundaries in Nursing Practice," MNA Ethics Committee, June 3, 1996. http://www.mnnurses.org/sites/default/files/documents/mna-position-statements-294.pdf.

5. Robert Wood Johnson Foundation, "Nurses Take on New and Expanded Roles in Health Care," January 20, 2015. http://www.rwjf.org/en/library/articles-and-news/2015/01/nurses-take-on-new-and-expanded-roles-in-health-care.html.

6. 692 S.W.2d 329 (Mo. Ct. App. 1985).

7. 570 N.Y.S.2d 395 (N.Y. App. Div. 1991).

8. *Moon Lake Convalescent Center v. Margolis*, 535 N.E.2d 956 (Ill. App. Ct. 1989).

9. 428 S.E.2d 773 (W. Va. 1993).

10. *Id.* at 779.

11. 502 So. 2d 1198 (Miss. 1987).

12. 519 N.Y.S.2d 738 (N.Y. App. Div. 1987).

13. RN.com, "Critical Thinking: Mastering the Art of Floating," August 2, 2011, Updated August 5, 2014. https://lms.rn.com/courses/2039/page147.html.

14. Thompson Reuters, "California Code of Regulations, § 70214. Nursing Staff Development," https://govt.westlaw.com/calregs/Document/IE9E78290D4BB11DE8879F88E8B0DAAAE?viewType=FullText&originationContext=documenttoc&transitionType=CategoryPageItem&contextData=(sc.Default)&bhcp=1

15. The Guardian, "Nurse found guilty of gross negligence manslaughter," November 2, 2015. https://www.theguardian.com/uk-news/2015/nov/02/nurse-found-guilty-of-gross-negligence-manslaughter.

16. Nurse Practitioner Schools, "What is a Nurse Practitioner?" https://www.nursepractitionerschools.com/faq/what-is-np.

17. American Association of Nurse Anesthetists, "Scope of Nurse Anesthesia Practice," http://www.aana.com/resources2/professionalpractice/Pages/Scope-of-Nurse-Anesthesia-Practice.aspx.

18. American College of Nurse-Midwives, "About American College of Nurse-Midwives (ACNM)," http://www.midwife.org/About-ACNM—American-College-of-Nurse-Midwives.

19. American College of Obstetricians and Gynecologists, "Certified Nurse-Midwives/Certified Midwives, Ob-Gyns Applaud House Committee Action on Maternity Care Provider Shortage Bill," September 14, 2016. http://www.acog.org/About-ACOG/News-Room/News-Releases/2016/Certified-Nurse-Midwives-Applaud-House.

20. Congress.gov, "H.R.1209 - Improving Access to Maternity Care Act," November 14, 2016. https://www.congress.gov/bill/114th-congress/house-bill/1209.

21. *Morris v. The Department of Professional Regulation*, 824 N.E.2d 1151 (Ill. App. 1 Dist. 2005).

22. *Id.* at 1155.

23. *Id.* at 1161.

24. 801 A.2d 775 (Ct. 2002).

25. Coulter Boeschen, "Nursing Malpractice," http://www.nolo.com/legal-encyclopedia/nursing-malpractice-30076.html.

26. U.S. Department of Health and Human Services, Health Resources and Services Administration, "National Practitioner Data Bank 2012 Annual Report," October 2014, http://www.npdb.hrsa.gov/resources/reports/2012NPDBAnnualReport.pdf.

27. https://www.npdb.hrsa.gov/resources/npdbstats/npdbStatistics.jsp#contentTop.

28. 652 A.2d 1382 (Pa. Super. 1995).

29. 603 So. 2d 866 (Miss. 1992).

30. 931 F.2d 116 (1st Cir. 1991).

31. *Id.*

32. *Id.*

33. 247 N.J. Super. 435, 589 A.2d 653 (N.J. Super. App. Div. 1991).

34. *Id.* at 655.

35. 640 So. 2d 865 (La. App. 4 Cir. 1994).

36. *Id.* at 872.

37. 809 So. 2d 611 (2001).

38. 290 Ill.Dec. 445 355 Ill. App.3d 230, 355 Ill. App.3d 230, 821 N.E.2d 757 (2004).

39. *Id.* at 769.

40. 733 So. 2d 91 (La. App. 3 Cir. 1999).

41. *Id.* at 94–95.

42. 333 P.2d 29 (Cal. Ct. App. 1958).

43. 236 S.E.2d 213 (W. Va. 1977).

44. 694 So. 2d 98 (Fla. App. 1997).

45. 523 P.2d 320 (Kan. 1974).

46. 262 So. 2d 303 (Ala. 1972).

47. *Leblanc v. Walsh*, 922 So. 2d 1248 (La. App. 2006).

48. 565 So. 2d 221 (Ala. 1990).

49. *Howerton v. Mary Immaculate Hospital, Inc.* 264 Va. 272, 563 S.E.2d 671 (2002).

50. *Kitchen v. Wickliffe Country Place*, No. 2000-L-051 (Ohio App. 11th 2001).

51. No. ED 84559, 165 S.W.3d 168 (Mo. App. 2005).

52. *Id.* at 769.

53. 403 S.E.2d 582 (N.C. Ct. App. 1991).

54. No. 06-31318, 514 F.3d 447 (C.A. 5, La. 2008).

55. *Id.*

56. Wikipedia.org, "Federal Tort Claims Act," https://en.wikipedia.org/wiki/Federal_Tort_Claims_Act.

57. 696 So. 2d 590 (La. App. 1997).
58. No. 1030422 (Supreme Court of Alabama 2005).
59. 357 N.Y.S.2d 508 (N.Y. App. Div. 1974).
60. No. 2-153/01-1019 (Iowa Ct. of App. 2002).
61. 696 P.2d 270 (Colo. 1985).
62. 28 N.E.2d 772 (Ohio 1940).
63. 144 So. 2d 249 (La. Ct. App. 1962).
64. 599 N.Y.S.2d 96 (N.Y. App. Div. 1993).
65. 742 P.2d 1087 (Okla. 1987).
66. *Id.* at 1090
67. 107 Fla. 598, 145 So. 2d 848 (Fla. 1933).
68. 181 A.2d 573 (Del. 1962).
69. *Id.* at 364.
70. *Id.* at 364.
71. 381 P.2d 605 (Wash. 1963).
72. 429 S.E.2d 22 (Va. 1993).
73. 403 F.2d 580 (D.C. Cir. 1968).
74. 597 N.E.2d 1110 (Ohio Ct. App. 1991).
75. 443 P.2d 708 (Colo. 1968).
76. 661 N.Y.S.2d 164 (N.Y. App. Div. 1997).
77. 367 S.E.2d 793 (Ga. 1988).
78. 851 P.2d 1122 (Or. 1993).
79. 798 So. 2d 279 (2001).
80. 151 N.C. App. 139, 565 S.E.2d 254 (2002).
81. 418 N.E.2d 620 (Mass. App. Ct. 1981).
82. 478 N.E.2d 184 (N.Y. 1985).
83. 48 N.Y.S.2d 227 (N.Y. App. Div. 1944).
84. 422 N.W.2d 600 (S.D. 1988).
85. 333 P.2d 29 (Cal. Ct. App. 1958).
86. *Ard v. East Jefferson Gen. Hosp., supra.*
87. *Id.*

© Monkey Business Images/Shutterstock

CHAPTER 12

Hospital Departments and Allied Professionals

DYING AT THE HOSPITAL'S DOOR ... TROUBLING QUESTIONS*

While communications were breaking down among a child's parent, a 9-1-1 dispatcher, and hospital personnel, the child's condition was quickly deteriorating. Twelve hours later, the 3-year-old girl was brain dead, and she expired 3 days later. Although there are several central issues involved in this story, the frustrating dialogue that took place is particularly important.

The 9-1-1 dispatcher answers the phone:

Dispatcher: 9-1-1; is this an emergency?

Parent: Yes, it's an emergency. I need an ambulance. I have a 3-year-old daughter that's passed out on me.

Dispatcher: OK. Where do you need the ambulance?

Parent: I'm right in front of the emergency exit at Coral Springs Hospital.

Dispatcher: You're right in front of the emergency exit?

Parent: Yes, that's exactly where I am. And they won't do a … thing in this place.

The dispatcher phones the hospital emergency department:

Dispatcher: There's a guy that says he's right outside your emergency exit. And he needs an ambulance. He says his 3-year-old daughter is passed out.

Hospital: This is a guy who wants to be seen quicker. We're busy—so he figured if he called 9-1-1 he'd be seen quicker.

Dispatcher: Well, he's saying he needs an ambulance right away. Is somebody going to go out there, or not?

Hospital: There's nothing we can do.[1]

The parents-plaintiffs filed a lawsuit.

WHAT IS YOUR VERDICT?

---

* *Miami Herald*, April 16, 1995, by Ronnie Green. Copyright 1995 by *Miami Herald*.

▶ LEARNING OBJECTIVES

The reader, upon completion of this chapter, will be able to:

- Describe a variety of legal issues that occur in patient care settings.
- Discuss the purpose of the Emergency Medical Treatment and Active Labor Act.
- Describe the purpose of certification and licensure, and the reasons for revocation of licenses.
- Explain the importance of a multidisciplinary approach to patient care.

This chapter presents an overview of selected departments and healthcare professions. Although it describes a variety of legal issues, there is no intensive review of any specific department or profession. Many of the cases presented here could have been discussed in more than one subject area; they are discussed here to illustrate that no healthcare profession is exempt from the long arm of the legal system. Healthcare professionals are held to the prevailing standard of care required in their profession, which includes proper assessments, reassessments, diagnosis, treatment, and follow-up care.

▶ PARAMEDICS AND FIRST RESPONDERS

Emergency Medical Services (EMS) personnel (**FIGURE 12-1**) are reported to have treated "nearly 20 million patients a year…Many of these patients have complicated medical or traumatic conditions that require considerable knowledge, skill, and judgment to be treated effectively in the out-of-hospital setting." The regulations that describe the scope of practice for emergency services personnel vary from state to state. The National EMS Model describes the various activities EMS personnel can legally perform, as regulated by law through certification and licensure. The regulations that affect the EMS vary from state to state.[2] According to Dr. Severo Rodriquez, Executive Director of the National Registry of Emergency Medical Technicians, "For a third consecutive year, growth continued as more EMS professionals than ever before recognized the value of maintaining their National EMS Certification. More than 98,000 providers renewed their EMS Certification during the 2016 recertification cycle, making it the strongest year in the organization's history."[3]

The National EMS Scope of Practice Model identifies the psychomotor skills and knowledge necessary for the minimum competence of each nationally identified level of EMS provider. This model will be used to develop the National EMS Education Standards, national EMS certification exams, and national EMS educational program accreditation. Under this model, to be eligible for State licensure, EMS personnel must be verifiably competent in the minimum knowledge and skills needed to ensure safe and effective practice at that level. This competence is assured

FIGURE 12-1 Fire fighters and paramedics assisting an injured man.

by completion of a nationally accredited educational program and national certification.[4]

The scope of practice does not define every activity of a licensed individual, such as lifting and moving patients, taking blood pressure readings, and bleeding control. The scope of practice focuses on activities regulated by law (for example, starting an intravenous line, administering a medication).[5]

The scope of practice for first responders is a continuing concern as the risks associated with their profession continue to change. The need for continuing education is therefore a high priority concern in maintaining and improving their skills. First responders are always at risk when responding to those in need of emergency services. Illicit drugs and chemical hazards are often an issue from industry fires to routine emergency roadside accidents. Carfentanil, for example, is another chemical substance on a long list of hazardous materials that was recently reported as presenting a hazard to all first responders as well as members of the general public. Carfentanil is a synthetic opioid approximately 10,000 times more potent than morphine and 100 times more potent than fentanyl. In those situations where there is a chemical hazard present, such as carfentanil, EMS and law enforcement personnel are required to follow safety protocols to avoid accidental exposure to themselves and the public.[6]

The four levels of EMS personnel reviewed here are emergency medical responder, emergency medical technician, advanced emergency medical technician, and paramedic.

Emergency Medical Responder

The primary focus of the emergency medical responder (EMR) is to initiate immediate lifesaving care to critical patients who access the emergency medical system. This individual possesses the basic knowledge and skills necessary to provide lifesaving interventions while awaiting additional EMS response and to assist higher-level personnel at the scene and during transport. The minimum skill sets of an EMR include airway and breathing, insertion of airway adjuncts intended to go into the oropharynx, use of positive pressure ventilation devices such as the bag-valve-mask, suction of the upper airway, supplemental oxygen therapy, pharmacologic interventions, such as use of unit-dose autoinjectors for the administration of lifesaving medications intended for self or peer rescue in hazardous materials situations, medical/cardiac care, use of an automated external defibrillator, trauma care, manual stabilization of suspected cervical spine injuries, and manual stabilization of extremity fractures, bleeding control, and emergency moves.[7]

Emergency Medical Technician

The primary focus of the emergency medical technician (EMT) is to provide basic emergency medical care and transportation for critical and emergent patients who access the emergency medical system. This individual possesses the basic knowledge and skills necessary to provide patient care and transportation.

The minimum skill sets of an EMT include: airway and breathing (e.g., insertion of airway adjuncts intended to go into the oropharynx or nasopharynx); use of positive-pressure ventilation devices, such as manually triggered ventilators and automatic transport ventilators; pharmacologic interventions, including assisting patients in taking their own prescribed medications and administration of the over-the-counter medications with appropriate medical oversight (e.g., oral glucose for suspected hypoglycemia, aspirin for chest pain of suspected ischemic origin); and trauma care, including application and inflation of the pneumatic anti-shock garment (PASG) for fracture stabilization.[8]

Advanced Emergency Medical Technician

The primary focus of the advanced emergency medical technician (AEMT) is to provide basic and limited advanced emergency medical care and transportation for critical and emergent patients who access the emergency medical system.

The minimum skill sets of an AEMT include: airway and breathing, such as insertion of airways that are not intended to be placed into the trachea and tracheobronchial suctioning of an already intubated patient; patient assessment; and pharmacologic interventions, such as establishing and maintaining peripheral intravenous access, establish and maintaining intraosseous access in a pediatric patient, administration of (nonmedicated) intravenous fluid therapy, administration of sublingual nitroglycerin to a patient experiencing chest pain of suspected ischemic origin, administration of subcutaneous or intramuscular epinephrine to a patient in anaphylaxis, administration of glucagon to a hypoglycemic patient, administration of intravenous D_{50} to a hypoglycemic patient, administration of inhaled beta agonists to a patient experiencing difficulty breathing and wheezing, administration of a narcotic antagonist to a patient suspected of narcotic overdose, and administration of nitrous oxide for pain relief.[9]

Paramedic

A paramedic is a healthcare professional, predominantly in the prehospital and out-of-hospital environment, and working mainly as part of *emergency medical services* (EMS), such as on an ambulance. A paramedic is an allied health professional whose primary focus is to provide advanced emergency medical care for critical and emergent patients who access the emergency medical system. This individual possesses the complex knowledge and skills necessary to provide patient care and transportation. The minimum skill sets of a paramedic include: airway and

breathing, such as performance of endotracheal intubation, performance of percutaneous cricothyrotomy, decompression of the pleural space, and performance of gastric decompression; pharmacologic interventions, such as insertion of an intraosseous cannula, enteral and parenteral administration of approved prescription medications, accessing indwelling catheters and implanted central IV ports for fluid and medication administration, administration of medications by IV infusion, maintaining an infusion of blood or blood products, and percutaneous means to access via needle-puncture; and medical/cardiac care, such as performance of cardioversion, manual defibrillation, and transcutaneous pacing.[10]

Many states have enacted legislation that provides civil immunity to paramedics who render emergency lifesaving services. Immunity does not, however, extend to negligent acts. A variety of paramedic-related lawsuits are presented here.

Wrong Drug Dosage Administered

The plaintiff in *Malone v. City of Seattle*[11] alleged that the defendant was negligent in providing care to the plaintiff after an automobile accident. The plaintiff, on appeal, contended that the trial court wrongfully instructed the jury regarding a 1971 civil immunity statute. The following is an excerpt from the relevant Washington statute:

> No act or omission of any physician's trained mobile intensive care paramedic . . . done or omitted in good faith while rendering emergency lifesaving service . . . to a person who is in immediate danger of loss of life shall impose any liability upon the trained mobile intensive care paramedic . . . or upon a . . . city or other local governmental unit.[12]

📰 CHICAGO CITY COUNCIL APPROVES $1.75M SETTLEMENT IN AMBULANCE CASE

The Chicago City Council today approved a $1.75 million settlement with the family of a 13-year-old girl who died a decade ago after city paramedics allegedly botched her care amid an asthma attack.

Paramedics in July 2002 incorrectly inserted a tube meant to help Arielle Starks breathe, said Jeffrey Levine, deputy corporation counsel.

—Hal Dardick, *Chicago Tribune*, February 15, 2012

One of the issues raised was whether the legislature intended the statute to apply only to the rendition of cardiopulmonary resuscitation (CPR) emergency treatment by a paramedic. The court of appeals indicated that although the definition contained in the statute places special emphasis on the paramedic's training in all aspects of CPR, the act does not limit the paramedic to CPR. The act implicitly recognizes that paramedics may encounter different emergencies.

Protected by Good Samaritan Statute

The daughter of a deceased patient in *Dunlap v. Young*[13] had brought a wrongful death action against EMS personnel for the death of her mother. The critically ill patient died after receiving care for respiratory distress in the ambulance while en route to the hospital.

Under the Good Samaritan statute, an Illinois court found that EMS personnel were not negligent in their treatment of the decedent. They had acted promptly to get the patient to the hospital. Although EMS personnel had failed to intubate the patient, she had been provided with oxygen and assisted respiration.

Inability to Diagnose Extent of Injury

In *Morena v. South Hills Health Systems*,[14] the Pennsylvania Supreme Court held that paramedics were not negligent in transporting a victim of a shooting to the nearest available hospital rather than to a hospital located 5 or 6 miles away where a thoracic surgeon was present. The paramedics were not capable of diagnosing the extent of the decedent's injury. Except for a children's center and a burn center, there were no emergency trauma centers specifically designated for the treatment of particular injuries.

Lidocaine Administered 44 Times Normal Dosage

In *Riffe v. Vereb Ambulance Service, Inc.*,[15] a wrongful death action was filed by appellants against Vereb Ambulance Service, St. Francis Hospital, and Custozzo. The complaint alleged that, while responding to an emergency call, defendant Custozzo, an EMT employed by Vereb, began administering lidocaine to Anderson, as ordered over the telephone by the medical command physician at the defendant hospital. While en route to the hospital, Anderson was administered lidocaine at 44 times the normal dosage. Consequently, normal heart function was not restored, and Anderson was pronounced dead at the hospital shortly thereafter.

The superior court held that the liability of medical technicians could not be imputed to the hospital. The court noted the practical impossibility of the hospital carrying ultimate responsibility for the quality of care and treatment given patients by EMS. The focus of training and monitoring of such services must lie with EMS regional and local councils pursuant to and subject to regulations promulgated by the department of health.

Although hospitals, as facilities, participate in the overall operation of EMS services, the hospital command facility derives its function from the law and regulations relating to the operation of EMS. The networking of EMS and command facilities is such that they have a common interrelated function that is apart from the administration of the hospitals to which they are attached. Because EMS may be involved with several hospitals depending on specialization, and even allowing for patients' directions, a hospital's legal responsibility for the operation of any given EMS becomes too tenuous.

Failure to Transport Patient

The deceased's parents in *Lemann v. Essen Lane Daiquiris*[16] filed a wrongful death action after paramedics failed to transport their son to the hospital for evaluation after they had treated him following a fight in the parking lot of a bar. It was determined that the parents failed to establish that the paramedics breached their duty to care when they did not transport their son to the hospital. Although police officers at the scene testified that the deceased was intoxicated and had slurred speech and erratic behavior, paramedics testified that they found him to be alert and oriented. In addition, he twice refused to be transported to the hospital and signed a waiver form that acknowledged his refusal to the paramedics to transport him to the hospital.

Paramedic License Denied

The South Dakota Board of Medical and Osteopathic Examiners was found not to have acted arbitrarily in denying the petitioner's application for a paramedic license. The record indicated that the board had considered the petitioner's multiple felony convictions along with extensive evidence of her current conduct. Considering her six felony convictions, the board was not arbitrary and capricious in concluding that Benton did not meet her burden of proving good moral character and an absence of unprofessional or dishonorable conduct.

The appeals court was advised that the petitioner recently received a pardon for her convictions and that she had completed paramedic training in Nebraska. The board did not have the benefit of that information at the time it heard the matter, and those facts were not in the record. The appeals court could only deal with matters presented in the record and, therefore, remanded the matter to the circuit court with directions to remand to the board for further proceedings.[17]

▶ EMERGENCY DEPARTMENT

Emergency departments (see **FIGURE 12-2**) are high-risk areas that tend to be a main source of lawsuits for hospitals. Results of the Harvard Medical Practice Study revealed that the hospital emergency department is "a real hot spot" for negligence.[18] In this study, 70% of adverse events occurring in the emergency department were because of negligence. Hospital emergency departments, which are heavily used by patients as primary care clinics, are a major source of adverse events because of poor follow-up care. Suits that end up in a courtroom are few in number compared with the number of out-of-court settlements.

Federal and state regulations, as well as standards set by accrediting agencies, may be considered by the courts to establish the duty and standard of care required in emergency department settings. Emergency departments are required to provide emergency care to those patients who present themselves with the need for such care. Hospitals, for example, under the *Emergency Medical Treatment and Active Labor Act* (EMTALA) are required to first provide stabilizing treatment and transfer to an appropriate healthcare facility when necessary.

The courts recognize a general duty to care for all patients presenting themselves to hospital emergency departments. Not only must hospitals accept, treat, and transfer emergency department patients if such

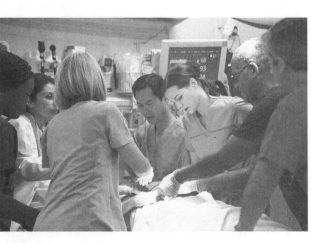

FIGURE 12-2 Hospital emergency room.

© Monkey Business Images/Shutterstock

NEWS $216.7 MILLION MEDICAL MALPRACTICE VERDICT IN FLORIDA

A Florida jury yesterday awarded a whopping $100.1 million in punitive damages to a Tampa man who was left brain-damaged and disabled after hospital emergency room doctors misdiagnosed stroke symptoms for a headache. Including compensatory damages of $116.7 million, the jury awarded Allan Navarro $216.7 million. The verdict is the third largest U.S. medical malpractice award ever, according to data compiled by Bloomberg.

—Peter Lattman, *The Wall Street Journal*, October 4, 2006

is necessary for the patients' well-being, but they also must adhere to the standards of care they have set for themselves, as well as to national standards.

Emergency Medical Treatment and Active Labor Act

In 1986, Congress passed EMTALA, which prohibits Medicare-participating hospitals from "dumping" patients out of emergency departments. The act provides that:

> [i]n the case of a hospital that has a hospital emergency department, if any individual (whether or not eligible for benefits under this subchapter) comes to the emergency department and a request is made on the individual's behalf for examination or treatment for a medical condition, the hospital must provide for an appropriate medical screening examination within the capability of the hospital emergency department, including ancillary services routinely available to the emergency department, to determine whether or not an emergency medical condition . . . exists.[19]

The term *emergency medical condition* under EMTALA has been defined as:

> (A) a medical condition manifesting itself by acute symptoms of sufficient severity (including severe pain) such that the absence of immediate medical attention could reasonably be expected to result in (i) placing the health of the individual (or, with respect to a pregnant woman, the health of the woman

or her unborn child) in serious jeopardy, (ii) serious impairment to bodily functions, or (iii) serious dysfunction of any bodily organ or part; or

(B) with respect to a pregnant woman who is having contractions, (i) that there is inadequate time to effect a safe transfer to another facility before delivery, or (ii) that transfer may pose a threat to the health or safety of the woman or the unborn child.[20]

Under EMTALA, hospital emergency rooms are subject to two principal obligations, commonly referred to as (1) the appropriate medical screening requirement and (2) the stabilization requirement. The appropriate medical screening requirement obligates hospital emergency rooms to provide an appropriate medical screening to any individual seeking treatment to determine whether the individual has an emergency medical condition. If an emergency medical condition exists, the hospital is required to provide stabilization treatment before transferring the individual.

Screening Determined Appropriate

On May 4, 2000, Nolen, pregnant with triplets, arrived at the hospital for a labor check at the direction of her physician, Dr. Zann. She complained of cramping and a mucous discharge that she feared signaled the onset of labor. After an initial assessment was performed, Dr. Zann arrived and performed an examination. He concluded that Nolen's lower uterine segment was consistent with what he expected from a normal pregnancy in this circumstance. Dr. Zann discharged Nolen from the hospital. He instructed Nolen to keep her scheduled appointment with her perinatologist, Dr. Scott, the next morning.

After leaving the hospital, Nolen testified at deposition that she began cramping. She made no effort to contact Dr. Zann or the hospital after this change in condition. When she reached Dr. Scott's office the next morning, Nolen fully described the events of the previous day and her change in condition after leaving the hospital. Dr. Scott examined Nolen and sent her back to the hospital to suppress her preterm labor. Nolen was transferred on May 7 to Broward General Hospital where she went into preterm labor. Her first baby was stillborn, and her other two babies subsequently failed to survive. Nolen contended that the hospital did not have a standard written screening procedure or, alternatively, that the hospital did not follow its screening procedure, either of which, she contended, violated EMTALA.

The record shows that Nolen received superior care from the hospital, primarily from her private physician, who provided care beyond the screening mandated by EMTALA. Nolen's argument that the hospital was required to have a written screening procedure failed because a written procedure is not required by the terms of EMTALA.[21]

Stabilizing the Patient

Patients can be transferred after being medically screened by a physician, stabilized, and cleared for transfer by the receiving institution. *Stabilized* means "with respect to an emergency medical condition . . . to provide such medical treatment of the condition as may be necessary to assure, within reasonable medical probability, that no material deterioration of the condition is likely to result from or to occur during the transfer of the individual from a facility."[22]

Failure to Stabilize the Patient

The plaintiff in *Huckaby v. East Ala. Med. Ctr.*[23] brought an action against the hospital alleging that the patient was transferred from the hospital's emergency department before her condition was stabilized. The patient went to the hospital, suffering from a stroke. The complaint alleged that the patient's condition was critical and materially deteriorating. The attending emergency department physician, Dr. Wheat, informed the patient's family that she needed the services of a neurosurgeon but that the hospital had problems in getting neurosurgeons to accept patients. Upon the recommendation of Wheat, the patient was transferred to another hospital where she expired soon after arrival. The plaintiff alleged that Wheat did not inform the family regarding the risks of transfer, and that the transfer of the patient in an unstable condition was the proximate cause of her death. Did the plaintiff have a cause of action under EMTALA?

The U.S. District Court held that the plaintiff stated a cause of action under EMTALA for which monetary relief could be granted. For the plaintiff to overcome the defendant's motion to dismiss the case, the plaintiff had to demonstrate that, under EMTALA, the patient: (1) went to the defendant's emergency department; (2) was diagnosed with an emergency medical condition; (3) was not provided with adequate screening; and (4) was discharged and transferred to another hospital before her emergency condition was stabilized. The plaintiff met this standard.

Failure to follow EMTALA can result in civil penalties. In addition, any individual who suffers personal harm as a direct result of a participating hospital's violation of a requirement may, in a civil action against the participating hospital, obtain those damages available for personal injury under the law of the state in which the hospital is located.

Inappropriate Transfer

In *Burditt v. U.S. Department of Health and Human Services*,[24] EMTALA was violated by a physician when he ordered a woman with dangerously high blood pressure (210/130) and in active labor with ruptured membranes to be transferred from the emergency department of one hospital to another hospital 170 miles away. The physician was assessed a penalty of $20,000. Dr. Louis Sullivan, secretary of the Department of Health and Human Services at that time, issued this statement:

> This decision sends a message to physicians everywhere that they need to provide quality care to everyone in need of emergency treatment who comes to a hospital. This is a significant opinion and we are pleased with the result.[25]

The American Public Health Association, in filing an amicus curiae, advised the appeals court that if Burditt wants to ensure that he will never be asked to treat a patient not of his choosing, then he ought to vote with his feet by affiliating only with hospitals that do not accept Medicare funds or do not have an emergency department.

Screening and Discharge Appropriate

Fifteen-year-old Nydia, in *Marshall v. East Carroll-Parish Hospital Service District*,[26] was brought by ambulance to the hospital emergency department because she "wouldn't move" while at school after the bell rang. Upon her arrival, hospital personnel took her history and vital signs. She was unable to communicate verbally but cooperated with hospital staff. She was examined by Dr. Horowitz, who diagnosed Nydia as having a respiratory infection and discharged her. He informed Nydia's mother, Ms. Marshall, that her daughter's failure to communicate was of unknown etiology and advised her to continue administering the medications that had been prescribed by the family physician on the previous day and to return to the emergency department if her condition deteriorated. The complaint alleged that, later that same day, Nydia's symptoms continued to worsen, and she was taken to the emergency department at a different hospital, where she was diagnosed as having suffered a cerebrovascular accident.

The action claimed that the hospital violated EMTALA by failing to provide Nydia with an appropriate medical screening examination and failing to stabilize her condition prior to discharge. The hospital moved for summary judgment and submitted supporting affidavits from Dr. Horowitz and a registered nurse who participated in Nydia's treatment in the hospital's emergency department. The district court granted summary judgment for the hospital on grounds that no material fact issues were in dispute.

Marshall, on appeal, claimed that hospital personnel knew that Nydia had an emergency medical condition and were concerned about the cursory examination provided by Dr. Horowitz and that Nydia should have been admitted to the hospital for observation of her unexplained altered mental status. Marshall argued that Dr. Horowitz committed malpractice by failing to accurately diagnose an emergency medical condition.

EMTALA was not intended to be used as a federal malpractice statute but, instead, was enacted to prevent *patient dumping* (the practice of refusing to treat patients unable to pay for care). An EMTALA-appropriate medical screening examination is not judged by its proficiency in accurately diagnosing a patient's illness, but rather by whether it was performed equitably in comparison to other patients with similar symptoms. If a hospital provides an appropriate medical screening examination, it is not liable under EMTALA even if the physician who performed the examination made a misdiagnosis that could subject him or her and the employer to liability in a medical malpractice action. The affidavits submitted by the hospital stated that Nydia was given an appropriate medical screening examination that would have been performed on any other patient and that she was not diagnosed as having an emergency medical condition.

The court determined that the hospital was entitled to summary judgment as a matter of law because there was no material fact issue as to whether Dr. Horowitz conducted an appropriate medical screening examination. The stabilization and transfer provisions of EMTALA are triggered only after a hospital determines that an individual has an emergency medical condition. The hospital has no duty under EMTALA to stabilize a condition that was not diagnosed during an appropriate screening examination. The physician here did not diagnose an emergency situation; therefore, this case is not an EMTALA issue. However, an issue in malpractice under the state's tort law can be raised.

Discharge Found Appropriate

In *Holcomb v. Humana Med. Corp.*,[27] the administrator of the estate of a deceased patient, Smith, sued the hospital, alleging a violation of EMTALA. Smith entered the emergency department on May 4, 1990, a week after giving birth, with a complaint of a fever, aching, sore throat, and coughing. Both a physician assistant (PA) and a physician examined Smith. The examination revealed that Smith had a temperature of 104.3°F, a pulse of 146, respirations of 32, and a blood pressure of 112/64. Diagnostic tests ordered included a white blood cell count, urine analysis, and chest X-ray. After reviewing Smith's complaints and medical history, results of the physical examination, and test results, the physician diagnosed the patient as having a viral infection. The physician ordered Tylenol and intravenous (IV) fluids as treatment. Smith was maintained in the emergency department overnight. The physician conducted a second physical examination during the night. By morning, Smith's vital signs had returned to normal. She was discharged with instructions for bed rest, fluids, and a request to return to the hospital if her condition worsened.

After returning home, Smith reported that she was feeling better but then took a turn for the worse and was admitted to Jackson Hospital on May 6, 1990. She was diagnosed with endometritis and subsequently died on May 9, 1990.

Was the patient inappropriately discharged from the emergency department under provisions of EMTALA? The U.S. District Court for the Middle District of Alabama held that there was no EMTALA violation. The patient was appropriately examined and screened. The care rendered was standard for any patient based on the complaints given. In addition, the plaintiff failed to demonstrate that an emergency condition existed at the time the patient was discharged on May 4.

EMTALA Claim Against Hospital Valid

The decedent in *Ballachino v. Anders*[28] went to the hospital on May 15, 1990, with complaints of chest pain and repeated episodes of loss of consciousness. The physicians allegedly failed to provide an appropriate medical screening examination and failed to determine whether an emergency medical condition existed. The patient's survivor and representative brought an action against the hospital and physicians, alleging violations of EMTALA and medical malpractice. EMTALA requires that a Medicare-provider hospital offer an appropriate medical screening examination to determine whether an emergency medical condition exists for any individual who presents to the emergency department seeking treatment. If the hospital determines that an emergency medical condition exists, then it must either stabilize the patient or provide for transfer of the patient to a facility capable of meeting the patient's medical needs.

The United States District Court, W.D. New York held that there is no private right of action against the individual physicians under EMTALA. However, the representative's complaint did state a claim against the hospital under EMTALA. The enforcement provision of EMTALA is explicitly limited to actions against a Medicare-participating hospital. Although the physicians were alleged to have acted in concert in rendering professional medical and surgical care and treatment to the decedent while at the hospital, the physicians importantly are nowhere alleged to have provided any emergency screening examination. The plaintiff clearly alleged that the defendants negligently failed to provide an appropriate medical screening examination and failed to determine whether an emergency medical condition existed for the decedent. The court was faced with the question of whether any emergency screening examination occurred at all. The plaintiff also alleged that the hospital failed in its stabilization and transfer procedures. The District Court determined that all of the allegations taken together stated an EMTALA claim against the hospital.

Wrong Record—Grave and Fatal Mistake

Dr. McManus had not realized that he had made a grave and fatal mistake. Dr. McManus had looked at the wrong chart. . . .

Terry Trahan, in *Trahan v. McManus*,[29] was taken to the hospital after being injured in an automobile accident. Terry's parents were informed about the accident and asked to come to the hospital. Mrs. Trahan drove to the hospital and consulted with Dr. McManus, the emergency department physician who treated Terry. McManus assured Trahan that it would be all right to take her son home because there was nothing more that could be done for him at the hospital.

Upon ordering discharge, however, McManus had not realized that he had made a *grave and fatal mistake*. McManus had looked at the wrong chart in determining Terry's status. McManus had looked at a chart that indicated that the patient's vital signs were normal. In fact, the correct chart showed that Terry had three broken ribs as a result of the accident. His blood pressure was 90/60 when he was admitted to the emergency department. Forty-five minutes after being admitted, Terry's blood pressure had dropped to 80/50, and his respiration rate had doubled. Terry's vital signs clearly indicated that he was suffering from internal hemorrhaging.

In the 7 hours following his discharge, Terry's condition continued to worsen. Terry complained to his parents about severe pain. He could not turn from his back to his side without the aid of his father. Several hours after being brought home from the hospital, Mr. Trahan noticed that Terry's abdomen was swelling. Mrs. Trahan immediately called the hospital. Mr. Trahan asked Terry if he wanted to sit up. Terry replied, "Well, we can try." Those were Terry's final words. Terry slumped in his father's arms and his head fell forward. When Mr. Trahan attempted to lift Terry's head, Terry's face was white. Mr. Trahan immediately laid his son down on the bed, realizing for the first time that his son was not breathing and had no pulse. He attempted CPR as Mrs. Trahan called for an ambulance. Mr. Trahan continued CPR until the ambulance arrived a few minutes later. Terry was pronounced dead on arrival at the hospital.

Subsequently, during a medical review panel proceeding in which the Trahans participated, McManus admitted liability by tendering his $100,000 limit of liability, pursuant to the Medical Malpractice Act.

A jury returned a verdict absolving McManus of any liability, finding that Terry's injuries would have occurred despite the physician's failure to use reasonable care in his treatment of Terry. The Trahans appealed. On appeal, the jury's determination was found to be clearly erroneous when it concluded that the physician's actions were not the cause-in-fact of Terry's death. The record is replete with testimony, including McManus's own admissions, that he acted negligently when he discharged Terry, that his actions led to Terry's death, and that there was treatment available that could have made a difference.

Duty to Contact On-Call Physician

Hospitals are expected to notify specialty on-call physicians when their particular skills are required in the emergency department. A physician who is on call and fails to respond to a request to attend a patient can be liable for injuries suffered by the patient because of his or her failure to respond.

Failure to Contact On-Call Physician

In *Thomas v. Corso*,[30] a patient had been brought to the hospital emergency department after he was struck by a car. A physician did not attend to him even though he had dangerously low blood pressure and was in shock. There was some telephone contact between the nurse in the emergency department and the physician who was providing on-call coverage. The physician did not act upon the hospital's call for assistance until the patient was close to death. Expert testimony was not necessary to establish what common sense made

evident—the patient struck by a car may have suffered internal injuries and should have been evaluated and treated by a physician. Lack of attention in such cases is not reasonable care by any standard. The concurrent negligence of the nurse, who failed to contact the on-call physician after the patient's condition worsened, did not relieve the physician of liability for his failure to respond to his on-call duty. Because of the nurse's negligence, the hospital is liable under the doctrine of respondeat superior.

Physician's Failure to Respond to ED Call

Treatment rendered by hospitals is expected to be commensurate with that available in the same or similar communities or in hospitals generally. In *Fjerstad v. Knutson*,[31] the South Dakota Supreme Court found that a hospital could be held liable for the failure of an on-call physician to respond to a call from the emergency department. An intern, who attempted to contact the on-call physician and was unable to do so for 3.5 hours, treated and discharged the patient. The hospital was responsible for assigning on-call physicians and ensuring that they would be available when called. The patient died during the night in a motel room as a result of asphyxia resulting from a swelling of the larynx, tonsils, and epiglottis that blocked the trachea. Testimony indicated that the emergency department's on-call physician was to be available for consultation and was assigned that duty by the hospital. Expert testimony also was offered that someone with the decedent's symptoms should have been hospitalized and that such care could have saved the decedent's life. The jury believed that an experienced physician would have taken the necessary steps to save the decedent's life.

Timely Response Required

Not only are hospitals required to care for emergency patients, but they also are required to do so in a timely fashion. In *Marks v. Mandel*,[32] a Florida trial court was found to have erred in directing a verdict against Marks, the plaintiff. It was decided that the relevant inquiry in this case was whether the hospital and the supervisor should bear ultimate responsibility for failure of the specialty on-call system to function properly. Jury issues had been raised by evidence that the standard for on-call systems was to have a specialist attending the patient within a reasonable period of being called.

> Extensive trial testimony proved that the local and national standard for on call systems is

to have a specialist actually attending to the patient within thirty minutes of the call to the physician. Palmetto General had a published policy which adopted this standard. In the case at bar, however, the fact that a thoracic surgeon eventually attended to Marks was a matter of coincidence and not a result of the on call system. The system failed. A jury should decide whether the failure was a breach of the standard of care owed to Michael Marks.[33]

Notice of Inability to Respond to Call

In *Millard v. Corrado*,[34] the Missouri Appellate Court found that on-call physicians owe a duty to provide reasonable notice when they will be unavailable to respond to calls. Physicians who cannot fulfill their on-call responsibilities must provide notice as soon as practicable once they learn of the circumstances that will render them unavailable. Imposing a duty on on-call physicians to notify hospital staff of their unavailability "does not place an unreasonable burden on the medical profession."[35] In this case, a mere telephone call would have significantly reduced the 4-hour period between an accident and life-saving surgery. The record shows in this case "that at the time of the accident, AMC expected "on call" physicians to respond to calls within thirty minutes. It was also reasonably foreseeable that AMC would be presented with a patient requiring the care of a general surgeon during Dr. Corrado's absence."[36]

Whatever slight inconvenience may be associated with notifying the hospital of the on-call physician's availability is trivial when compared with the substantial risk to patients. The Missouri Court of Appeals determined that:

> Applying these principles to the present case, we hold that the public policy of Missouri and the foreseeability of harm to patients in the position of Mrs. Millard support the recognition of a duty flowing from Dr. Corrado to Mrs. Millard. Accordingly, we hold that "on call" physicians owe a duty to reasonably foreseeable emergency patients to provide reasonable notice to appropriate hospital personnel when they will be unavailable to respond to calls. This duty exists independently of any duties flowing from a physician–patient relationship. Physicians who cannot fulfill their "on call" responsibilities must provide notice as soon as practicable once they learn of circumstances that will render them unavailable.[37]

Objectives of Emergency Care

The objectives of emergency care are the same regardless of severity. No matter how seemingly trivial the complaint, each patient must be examined. Treatment must begin as rapidly as possible, function is to be maintained or restored, scarring and deformity minimized. Every patient must be treated regardless of ability to pay.

> As the Sixth Circuit points out, there are many reasons other than indigence that might lead a hospital to give less than standard attention to a person who arrives at the emergency room doors. These might include: prejudice against the race, sex, or ethnic group of the patient; distaste for the patient's condition (e.g., acquired immune deficiency syndrome [AIDS] patients); personal dislike or antagonism between medical personnel and the patient; disapproval of the patient's occupation; or political or cultural opposition. If a hospital refuses treatment to persons for any of these reasons, or gives cursory treatment, the evil inflicted would be quite akin to that discussed by Congress in the legislative history, and the patient would fall squarely in the statutory language.[38]

Patient Leaves Emergency Department Without Notice

The patient and her sister became upset with the care offered, left the hospital, and went home without proper discharge. The patient died 2 days later at home. The county coroner's office initiated a postmortem examination and determined the patient died from meningoencephalitis. The patient made a conscious decision to leave the hospital on her own accord without the knowledge or permission of the hospital. She did not tell the doctors, nurses, or anyone else that she was leaving the emergency room; she just left without informing anyone.

In a wrongful death medical malpractice action alleging negligence, the trial court properly granted the hospital summary judgment because under Ohio law, an emergency room nurse has no duty to interfere with a patient who refuses treatment and decides to leave the emergency department without notifying hospital staff.[39]

Failure to Admit

Roy went to the emergency department complaining of chest pains. The attending physician, Dr. Gupta, upon examination, determined that Roy exhibited normal vital signs. Gupta performed an electrocardiogram that showed ischemic changes indicating a lack of oxygen to the heart tissue. He applied a transdermal nitroglycerin patch and gave her a prescription for nitroglycerin. After monitoring her progress, he sent her home. Several hours later, she returned to the emergency department, experiencing more chest pains. She was admitted to the hospital, and it was determined that she was having a heart attack. Three days later, Roy died of a massive myocardial infarction.

Gupta was found negligent in failing to hospitalize Roy or failing to inform her of the serious nature of her illness. The trial court found that had Roy been hospitalized on her first visit, her chances of survival would have been increased. On appeal, the Louisiana Court of Appeal held that Gupta was negligent by failing to advise Roy that she should be hospitalized for chest pains. All of the medical expert witnesses, except Dr. Kilpatrick, a defense witness, testified that Roy should have been admitted. Kilpatrick testified that such a decision varied greatly among physicians. The trial court disregarded his testimony because of his hostile responses to questioning.

The trial judge was not convinced by Gupta's explanation of why Roy was not hospitalized. He focused on Gupta's failure to have X-rays taken during the first visit, which might have allowed him to determine whether the ischemic changes were a result of her hypertension medication or indicated the beginning of a heart attack. The relative simplicity of the technique and its obvious availability lent credence to the trial judge's belief that the requisite attention was not paid to Roy's complaints. The law does not require proof that proper treatment would have been the difference between Roy's living or dying: It requires only proof that proper treatment would have increased her chances of survival.[40]

Documentation Sparse and Contradictory

An ambulance team found 26-year-old Feeney intoxicated and sitting on a street corner in South Boston. Feeney admitted to alcohol abuse but denied that he used drugs. He was physically and verbally combative, and he had trouble walking and speaking intelligibly. His condition interfered with conducting an examination, and he was transported by ambulance to the hospital.

Documentation at the hospital between 10:45 PM and 11:30 PM was sparse and contradictory. The minimum standard for nursing care required monitoring the patient's respiratory rate every 15 minutes. It was doubtful that this occurred. This monitoring would

have more than likely permitted the nursing staff to observe changes in the patient's breathing patterns and/or the onset of respiratory arrest. The emergency department physician failed to evaluate the patient and to initiate care within the first few minutes of Feeney's entry into the emergency facility. The emergency physician had an obligation to determine who was waiting for physician care and how critical the need was for that care. Had the standards been maintained, respiratory arrest might have been averted. According to the autopsy report, respiratory arrest was the sole cause of death.

The failure to provide adequate care rationally could be attributed to the staff nurse assigned to the area in which the patient lay, as well as to the physicians in charge. The hospital was implicated on the basis of the acts or omissions of its staff.[41]

Telephone Medicine Can Be Costly

The diagnosis and treatment of patients by telephone can be costly. As noted in *Futch v. Attwood*,[42] the record shows that on the morning of February 28, 1990, Lauren, a 4-year-old diabetic child, awoke her mother, Wanda. She had vomited two or three times, and her glucose reading was high. Wanda administered Lauren's morning insulin and intended to feed her a light breakfast before bringing her to see Dr. Attwood, a pediatrician, at about 9:45 AM. According to the plaintiff, Attwood did not check Lauren's blood sugar level or her urine to determine whether ketones were present. If Atwood had done so, Lauren's condition could have been quickly corrected by the simple administration of insulin. Instead of administering insulin, however, Attwood prescribed the use of Phenergan suppositories to address Lauren's symptoms. Lauren's symptoms of nausea continued, and she was taken to the hospital emergency department. Hospital personnel contacted Attwood. Attwood returned the call and again prescribed a Phenergan injection. Attwood did not go to the hospital and had not been given Lauren's vital signs when he suggested such an injection; furthermore, he failed to order any blood or urine tests.

Wanda returned home with Lauren at approximately 8:00 PM and put her to bed, waking her around midnight to administer the prescribed medication. Lauren woke but went back to sleep. Early the next morning, Wanda awoke and found Lauren with labored breathing. While attempting to wake up the 4-year-old, the only responses, according to the plaintiff's brief, were "huh" followed by moaning. Wanda telephoned Attwood and informed him of her daughter's far worsened condition. Attwood admitted Lauren to the hospital at 6:30 AM that morning.

Hospital records revealed that Lauren's glucose level was 507 at the time of admission, with her blood acid revealing diabetic ketoacidosis. At approximately 9:13 AM, Lauren went into respiratory arrest as a result of her brain swelling and rupturing into the opening at the base of her neck. Lauren was immediately transported by helicopter to Children's Hospital in New Orleans and diagnosed with ketoacidotic coma, cerebral edema, and bilateral pulmonary edema. She was pronounced dead at 5:07 PM on March 2, 1990.

Lauren and her mother were virtually inseparable, except when Wanda was at school. All of this changed in Lauren's last few days when she was rushed to New Orleans. During Lauren's 2.5 days of illness, every moment seemed worse than the previous. The mother witnessed her daughter's decline in health, and her protracted wait was punctuated only by various traumatic episodes: Lauren's respiratory intubation; her respiratory failure and consequent code blue; numerous medical staff scurrying in and out to see Lauren behind doors closed to Wanda; and, finally, Wanda's being asked to consider whether she would prefer to "pull the plug" on her daughter or to watch her linger indefinitely. Confronted with this dilemma, the young mother opted not to punish her daughter with more torment. She decided to let her go and did. For Wanda, the period following Lauren's death has been marked by the inevitable sense of loss of a daughter and by the guilt of a mother whose unrelenting loss compels her to ask what she might have done differently to save her child's life.

The trial court allocated $98,000 for the conscious pain and suffering. The defendant complained that the award of $98,000 was excessive. On appeal, the appellate court could not find that the trial court had erred in concluding what sum was fair.

Improving Emergency Department Patient Care

Emergency department care can be improved and lawsuits minimized by doing the following:

- Treating each patient courteously and promptly, regardless of ability to pay
- Providing adequate staff to care for patients
- Requiring timely response by on-call physicians
- Not taking lightly any patient's complaint
- Triaging, assessing, and treating seriously ill patients first
- Communicating with the patient and family to ensure a complete and accurate picture of the patient's symptoms and complaints are obtained
- Providing an appropriate examination of the patient based on the presenting complaint(s) and symptoms (failure to do this may be the single most common and sometimes fatal mistake in emergency departments)
- Obtaining patient consent for procedures when possible
- Providing a mechanism for obtaining consultations when necessary
- Requiring that hospitals determine what types of patients and levels of care they can safely address
- Knowing when to admit or stabilize and transfer a patient
- Maintaining thorough and complete medical records for each patient treated
- Ensuring that each patient's records treated in other settings within the organization (e.g., ambulatory care settings) are readily available
- Establishing criteria for admission and discharge
- Ensuring all patients are assessed and treated by a physician prior to discharge
- Ensuring that patient education is provided in the emergency department prior to discharging each patient
- Ensuring all documentation is completed prior to each patient's discharge
- Providing a procedure for reading X-rays and other imaging studies when there is no radiologist readily available
- Instituting a preventive maintenance program for emergency department equipment
- Determining which diagnoses can be safely addressed within the organization
- Assuring open lines of communications between hospitals and emergency medical services personnel when addressing transport and care issues
- Making appropriate arrangements, when required, for transfer
- Providing continuing education programs for all staff members
- Requiring mandatory administrative rounds to the emergency department by the risk manager, medical director, chief nursing officer, and chief executive officer

Emergency Rooms Vital to Public Safety

McBride, in *Simmons v. Tuomey Regional Medical Center*,[43] was involved in an accident while driving his moped. Upon learning of the accident, Simmons, McBride's daughter, rushed to the scene, where she found emergency services personnel attending to an injury to the back of her father's head. McBride was taken to Tuomey where Simmons signed an admission form for her father. The admission form contained the following provision:

The Physicians Practicing in this Emergency Room are not Employees of the Tuomey Regional Medical Center. They are Independent Physicians, as are All Physicians Practicing in this Hospital.

While in Tuomey's emergency department, Drs. Cooper and Anderson examined McBride. Despite McBride's confused state, the physicians decided to treat his contusions and release him from the hospital. The physicians, apparently attributing McBride's confusion to intoxication, did not treat his head injury.

The next day, McBride returned to Tuomey where his head injury was diagnosed as a subdural hematoma. Ultimately, McBride was transported to Richland Memorial Hospital. Approximately 6 weeks later, McBride died of complications from the hematoma.

When Simmons brought suit, Tuomey moved for summary judgment by alleging that it was not liable because the physicians were independent contractors. Tuomey relied on its June 1987 contract with Coastal Physicians Services, which set forth the procedures by which Coastal would provide emergency department physicians to Tuomey. The carefully worded contract referred numerous times to physicians as independent contractors and stated that Tuomey agreed not to exercise any control over the means, manner, or methods by which any physician supplied by Coastal carries out his duties. The trial court accorded great weight to the Coastal–Tuomey contract when it granted Tuomey's motion for summary judgment. Simmons appealed, arguing that the trial court erred in granting summary judgment on the issues of actual agency, apparent agency, and nondelegable duty.

The operation of emergency departments is such an important activity to the community that hospitals should be liable for the negligence of emergency department caregivers. Few things are more comforting in today's society than knowing that immediate medical care is available around the clock at any hospital. As the Texas Court of Appeals astutely observed:

> Emergency rooms are aptly named and vital to public safety. There exists no other place to find immediate medical care. The dynamics that drive paying patients to a hospital's emergency rooms are known well. Either a sudden injury occurs, a child breaks his arm or an individual suffers a heart attack, or an existing medical condition worsens, a diabetic lapses into a coma, demanding immediate medical attention at the nearest emergency room. The catch phrase in legal nomenclature, "time is of the essence," takes on real meaning.

Generally, one cannot choose to pass by the nearest emergency room, and after arrival, it would be improvident to depart in hope of finding one that provides services through employees rather than independent contractors. The patient is there and must rely on the services available and agree to pay the premium charged for those services.[44]

The public not only relies on the medical care rendered by emergency departments, but also considers the hospital as a single entity providing all of its medical services. A set of commentators observed:

> [T]he hospital itself has come to be perceived as the provider of medical services. According to this view, patients come to the hospital to be cured, and the doctors who practice there are the hospital's instrumentalities, regardless of the nature of the private arrangements between the hospital and the physician. Whether or not this perception is accurate seemingly matters little when weighed against the momentum of changing public perception and attendant public policy.[45]

Public reliance and public perceptions, as well as the regulations imposed on hospitals, have created an absolute duty for hospitals to provide competent medical care in their emergency departments. Hospitals contributed to the shift in public perception through commercial advertisements. By actively soliciting business, hospitals effectively removed themselves from the sterile world of altruistic agencies.

Given the cumulative public policies surrounding the operation of emergency departments and the legal requirement that hospitals provide emergency services, hospitals must be accountable in tort for the actions of caregivers working in their emergency departments. The court in this case agreed with a New York court, which wrote:

> In this Court's opinion it is public policy, and not traditional rules of the law of agency or the law of torts, which should underlie the decision to hold hospitals liable for malpractice which occurs in their emergency rooms. In this regard the observation of former U.S. Supreme Court Justice Oliver Wendell Holmes is apt: "The true grounds of decision are consideration of policy and of social advantage, and it is vain to suppose that solutions can be attained merely by logic and the general propositions of law which nobody disputes. Propositions as to public policy rarely are

unanimously accepted, and still more rarely, if ever, are capable of unanswerable proof."[46]

The appeals court in Tuomey held that hospitals have a nondelegable duty to render competent service to the patients of their emergency departments. The trial court's grant of summary judgment was reversed, and the case was remanded for further proceedings.

State Regulations

Legislation in many states imposes a duty on hospitals to provide emergency care. The statutes implicitly, and sometimes explicitly, require hospitals to provide some degree of emergency service.

If the public is aware that a hospital furnishes emergency services and relies on that knowledge, the hospital has a duty to provide those services to the public. Two Mexican children, burned in a fire at home, were refused admission or first aid by a local hospital. A lawsuit was filed claiming that additional injury occurred as a result of the failure to render care.[47] The trial court dismissed the suit. On appeal, the Arizona Court of Appeals found the defendants liable, claiming that it was the custom of the hospital to render aid in such a case. The Arizona Supreme Court, in finding the defendants liable, reasoned that

state statutes and licensing regulations mandate that a hospital may not deny a patient emergency care.

State statutes, such as the New York State Emergency Medical Services Act, provide that every hospital shall admit persons in need of immediate hospitalization. Any licensed medical practitioner who refuses to treat a person arriving at a general hospital for emergency medical treatment will be guilty of a misdemeanor and subject to up to 1 year in prison and a fine. EMTs, paramedics, and ambulance drivers are expected to report any refusals by hospitals to treat emergency patients. Patients may be transferred only after they have been stabilized if it is deemed by the attending physician to be in the best interest of the patient.

▶ LABORATORY

An organization must provide for clinical laboratory services in order to meet the needs of its patients (**FIGURE 12-3**). Each healthcare organization is responsible for the quality and timeliness of the services provided. Because it is often necessary to contract out a variety of tests according to an organization's needs, the healthcare organization must be committed to ensuring that contracted laboratory services are with a reputable licensed laboratory.

FIGURE 12-3 Laboratory staff at work.

© Tyler Olson/Shutterstock

An organization's laboratory provides data that are vital to each patient's diagnosis and treatment. Among its many functions, a laboratory monitors therapeutic ranges; measures blood levels for toxicity; places and monitors instrumentation on patient units; provides education for the nursing staff (e.g., glucose monitoring); provides valuable data used in research studies; provides data in selecting, for example, the most effective and economical antibiotic for treating patients; serves in a consultative role; and provides valuable data regarding the nutritional needs of patients. The importance of laboratory data in the care and treatment of patients is illustrated in the following *reality check*.

In order to improve timely reporting of lab results, performance improvement processes should be implemented that include pertinent data collection that can be used to measure and evaluate the quality and timeliness of test results. The end user, the provider/caregiver, depends on the efficacy and timeliness of laboratory data, which is crucial in the decision-making process for rendering quality care.

Confusion of Laboratory Specimens

Scientists at the Centers for Disease Control and Prevention in a laboratory accident had the potential to expose its workers to the deadly Ebola virus.

A worker at CDC's biosafety level 4 lab in Atlanta—where scientists wear spacesuit-like, full-body protective gear that filters the air they breathe—accidentally confused some specimens and sent an un-killed sample from an Ebola experiment to a lower-level lab with minimal protections. The agency's investigation of the incident has now found that the sample sent to the biosafety level 2 lab at CDC

✔ *IMPORTANCE OF LABORATORY RESULTS*

I was reviewing a patient record during the patient care conference and asked why the patient was admitted. The patient's nurse replied, "The patient was diagnosed with an impending stroke." Looking at the patient's lab results I said, "The patient's glucose is high." The nurse again replied, "Yes, but we are more concerned about the impending stroke." I said, "I see the patient was admitted at 11:00 PM. Do you know when the patient ate last before her admission to the hospital?" The nurse, asking for and looking at the record replied, "She ate last at 4:00 PM prior to her 11:00 PM lab results." Looking at the laboratory manager, who was also a working laboratory technologist, I asked, "Is it normal for a patient who ate last at 4:00 PM to have an abnormally high blood glucose at 11:00 PM?" The laboratory manager replied, "It is not normal for it to be that high." I followed up, "So the patient has been here 3 days, has there been any follow-up blood tests to determine if the blood glucose is back to normal?" The survey coordinator interrupting, "At the moment we are more concerned about the impending stroke." I then asked, "Do you know if the patient has diabetes?" The nurse said confidently that the patient did not have diabetes.

I continued, "Looking at the history and physical I see the physician wrote that the family medical history has been marked as unremarkable. Did your nursing assessment, care, and conversations with the patient reveal anything different as to the patient's family history and the patient's present condition?" In other words, do you know if the patient might have a predisposition to a stroke based on the family history?" The nurse replied, "The parents died of natural causes." I then asked to interview the patient if she agreed.

The nurse left the conference room to speak to the patient and shortly thereafter returned to the conference room and said, "Mrs. … said she was willing to talk to you."

After introducing myself to the patient and my purpose for being at the hospital, I asked the patient about her care at the hospital. The patient said, "I am very happy with the care I am receiving at the hospital." During our conversation I had the opportunity to ask about her parents. She explained how her father passed away as the result of a heart attack and her mother passed away as the result of a stroke. We talked a bit more on a happier note and I thanked her for the opportunity to speak with her.

Returning to the conference room, I sat down with the staff and said, "My concern here is that the high blood glucose laboratory results were not sufficiently addressed. The patient had other blood tests but there was no follow-up on the one abnormal glucose reading. All the other tests were found to be normal. If the patient's blood glucose is under control, the patient's deficits will be less severe should her impending stroke occur. I am also concerned that the patient's family history was written on the patient's record as "unremarkable."

I asked for the laboratory to have representation at this conference today. Technologists are rarely represented in these sessions yet some have estimated that as many as 70% of medical decisions are based on laboratory results. Thank you for attendance here today.

—Anonymous

likely never contained any live Ebola virus because it is now believed that animals used in the experiment no longer had detectable live virus in their bodies at the time of the mistake.[48]

Test Results and Misdiagnosis

Laboratory tests results are not always reported correctly. *False positives* can lead to unnecessary treatments, and *false negatives* can lead to delays in treatment. Some of the more common laboratory errors include a mix-up of samples, failure to properly identify patient information on sample containers, errors in reading and interpreting test results, and contamination of samples during collection and testing. Unnecessary testing is also a concern for both laboratories and patients. The Department of Justice, Office of Public Affairs, for example, reported that two cardiovascular disease testing laboratories agreed to pay $48.5 million "to resolve allegations that they violated the False Claims Act by paying remuneration to physicians in exchange for patient referrals and billing federal health care programs for medically unnecessary testing."[49]

The accuracy of laboratory testing of a variety of specimens (e.g., blood, tissue) continues to be a challenge for laboratories in various settings. Georgetown University Hospital, for example, in 2010 had to shut down its lab that performs genetic analysis for breast cancer patients. Tissue samples for 249 women were independently retested while federal officials investigated laboratory procedures. The laboratory employees involved in the testing were found not to have followed proper procedures in processing samples.[50]

NEWS LAB DILUTED SOLUTION USED TO DETECT ZIKA

For a public health lab to commit such an error once would be an embarrassment in the high-stakes testing of Zika, which has potentially devastating consequences for pregnant women, scientists and federal health officials say. That the District lab—which is also a first line of defense in screening bioterrorism threats—repeated the mistake daily, and without anyone catching it for more than six months, amounts to a more systemic and worrisome failure, experts said.
—Aaron C. Davis, *The Washington Post*
February 26, 2017

Blood Transfusions

Historically, the possibility of diagnosing AIDS from a blood transfusion was considered an unlikely risk in 1983. The case against Georgetown University and the American Red Cross in *Kozup v. Georgetown University*[51] was dismissed, where it was alleged that the death of a premature infant was a result of causes related to AIDS contracted through a blood transfusion given in January 1983, without the parents' informed consent. The court reasoned that there was no basis where a reasonable jury would have found that the possibility of contracting AIDS from a blood transfusion in 1983 was a material risk. Dismissal also was justified on the basis that the transfusion was the only method of treating the child for a life-threatening condition.

A hemophiliac patient in *McKee v. Miles Laboratories*[52] contracted AIDS from a coagulation protein, which was provided by the defendants, and subsequently died. The defendants moved for summary judgment, contending that at the time the plaintiff's decedent contracted AIDS, there were no tests that would have revealed the presence of the AIDS virus. The plaintiff argued that there was a genuine issue of material fact as to whether an alternative testing method was available when the decedent contracted AIDS in 1983. The district court held that the provision of blood and blood by-products was a service and not a sale and that the lack of any test to purify or screen blood or blood by-products for human immunodeficiency virus (HIV) demonstrated that the supplier did not violate industry standards.

The methods available for testing for HIV during the early 1980s were analyzed carefully in *Kozup*, in which the court determined it was not until 1984 that the medical community reached a consensus as to the proposition that HIV was transmitted by blood. The district court in *McKee* held there was no need to rehash the same chronologic medical history of AIDS that *Kozup* so methodically composed. The plaintiff in *McKee* appealed the district court's decision to the U.S. Court of Appeals for the Sixth Circuit in *McKee v. Cutter Laboratories*.[53] The court of appeals upheld the district court's decision that the manufacturer was not negligent.

Testing for HIV is mandatory today, as noted in *J.K. & Susie L. Wadley Research Inst. v. Beeson*.[54] In January 1983, a blood center knew that blood from homosexual or bisexual males should not be accepted under any circumstances. The blood center's written policy provided that donors who volunteer that they are gay should not be permitted to donate blood. On April 22, 1983, Kraus, a cardiologist, discovered that Mr. B, the patient, had severe blockage of two major arteries in his heart and recommended cardiac bypass surgery.

During surgery, B received seven units of blood by transfusion. In May 1987, B had chest pain and trouble breathing. On June 5, 1987, B was hospitalized. Kraus consulted with two specialists in pulmonary medicine about the unusual pneumonia evident in X-rays of B's lungs. Because there was a possibility that the lung infection was secondary to AIDS, B was tested for HIV. Although B had not yet been formally diagnosed, physicians started him on therapy for AIDS.

B was formally diagnosed as HIV positive. His wife was then tested for HIV, and she learned that she was also HIV positive. On July 2, 1987, B expired. On April 21, 1989, the plaintiffs, Mrs. B and her son, filed suit against the blood center, alleging that her husband contracted HIV from the transfusion of a unit of blood donated at the blood center on April 19, 1983, by a donor identified at trial as Doe. The parties stipulated at trial that Doe was a sexually active homosexual male with multiple sex partners.

The plaintiffs contend that the blood center's negligence in testing and screening blood donors was the proximate cause Mrs. B's contraction of HIV. At trial, the jury awarded the plaintiffs $800,000 in damages. The blood center filed an appeal arguing the evidence of causation was legally insufficient to support the jury verdict.

The Texas Court of Appeals held that the evidence supported a finding that the blood center's negligence in the collection of blood was the proximate cause of B's HIV infection. The court held that the blood center, despite its knowledge about the dangers of HIV-contaminated blood, failed to reject gay men, that the blood center's donor screening was inadequate, and that these omissions were substantial factors in causing Mr. and Mrs. B's HIV infections. The blood center's own technical director admitted that there was "strong evidence" that the blood accepted from Doe was contaminated with HIV. Another recipient of components of Doe's blood was diagnosed as HIV positive less than 6 months after Mr. B was diagnosed as HIV positive.

Suits often arise as a result of a person with AIDS claiming that he or she contracted the disease as a result of a transfusion of contaminated blood or blood products. In blood transfusion cases, the standards most commonly identified as having been violated concern blood testing and donor screening. An injured party generally must prove that a standard of care existed, that the defendant's conduct fell below the standard, and that this conduct was the proximate cause of the plaintiff's injury.

The most common occurrences that lead to lawsuits in the administration of blood involve transfusion of mismatched blood, improper screening and transfusion of contaminated blood, unnecessary administration of blood, and improper handling procedures (i.e., inadequate refrigeration and storage procedures).

The patient-plaintiff had a blood specimen drawn and sent to SmithKline laboratories for testing for the HIV. The laboratory informed the physician that his patient tested positive for HIV. On June 13, 1988, the patient was informed that he had AIDS. Not believing that his symptoms mimicked those of an individual with AIDS, the patient was retested for HIV. On three separate occasions (July 1, 1988; July 15, 1988; and July 22, 1988), involving two separate laboratories, he tested negative for the virus. In September 1990, the plaintiff later filed a lawsuit against his physician and SmithKline for the negligent interpretation and reporting of his blood samples as being HIV positive.

The circuit court ruled that the plaintiff stated a claim upon which relief could be granted in alleging that the defendants caused him to suffer major depression. The defendants appealed. On appeal, the West Virginia Supreme Court of Appeals ruled that the plaintiff stated a claim for the negligent infliction of emotional distress. The Supreme Court found that, "Given the well-known fact that AIDS had replaced cancer as the most feared disease in America and, as defendant-SmithKline acknowledged, a diagnosis of AIDS is a death sentence, conventional wisdom mandates that fear of AIDS triggers genuine—not spurious—claims of emotional distress."[55]

Failure to Follow Transfusion Protocol

Fowler, in *Fowler v. Bossano*,[56] gave birth to twins on March 26, 1996. As a result of premature birth, the twins were transferred to Lake Charles Memorial Hospital (LCMH) and were cared for by Bossano, a neonatologist. The infants experienced complications and problems associated with premature birth, including respiratory and feeding difficulties. The twins' treatment included blood transfusions. Bossano stated that the twins proceeded through these difficulties and began to make progress, but then Ryan (one of the twins) took a turn for the worse. According to Bossano, Ryan's condition generally continued to deteriorate until he died on May 25. Bossano stated that the most likely cause of death was a viral infection. At his urging, an autopsy was performed, and the pathologist found the presence of cytomegalovirus (CMV). Bossano stated that he learned that the lab at the hospital did not, at that time, screen for the presence of the virus in the blood used for transfusions.

Ryan's parents instituted proceedings under the Medical Malpractice Act, convening a medical review panel against Bossano and LCMH. The panel determined that the evidence presented did not support a finding that Bossano breached the standard of care. As for the hospital, the panel found that the evidence showed that it failed to comply with the appropriate standard of care with regard to the testing of blood. The child most likely expired from an overwhelming CMV viral infection resulting from blood product usage.

The formal policy of the hospital's blood bank for selecting components for neonatal transfusion provided that blood products, such as irradiated or CMV-negative products are available upon request but are not routinely used. The 16th edition of *Standards for Blood Banks and Transfusion Services* by the American Association of Blood Banks (AABB) provides, in Section 18.500, that "Where transfusion-associated CMV disease is a problem, cellular components should be selected or processed to reduce that risk to infant recipients weighing less than 1200 grams at birth, when either the infant or the mother is CMV antibody-negative or that information is unknown."

The hospital's policy did not provide for compliance with the applicable AABB policy at that time, so LCMH had the obligation to properly inform the medical staff and ensure that all such infants who might be affected could be readily identified. Bossano should have been able to make a correct medical assumption that all high-risk infants receiving blood products in the neonatal intensive care unit would receive CMV-negative blood products.

The Fowlers decided to file suit naming both Bossano and the hospital as defendants. They sought damages associated with a survival action and those for wrongful death. The jury found for the plaintiffs. LCMH breached the applicable standard of care by failing to test the blood used for this transfusion for CMV. The evidence presented was sufficient to support the jury's determination that the hospital's breach of the standard of care was the cause of Ryan's death.

Mismatched Blood

A laboratory technician in *Barnes Hospital v. Missouri Commission on Human Rights*[57] had been discharged because of inferior work performance. On three occasions, the employee allegedly mismatched blood. The employee filed a complaint with the Commission on Human Rights, alleging racial discrimination as a reason for his discharge by the hospital. The hospital appealed, and the circuit court reversed the commission's order. The technician appealed to the Missouri Supreme Court, which held that the evidence did not support the ruling of racial discrimination by the Missouri Commission on Human Rights.

In *Dodson v. Community Ctr.*, 633 So. 2d 252 (La. Ct. App. 1993), the patient was scheduled to undergo surgery at a medical center. In anticipation of the surgery and out of fear of contracting AIDS through blood transfusions from unknown donors, the patient arranged to have three known donors donate blood earmarked for his use should transfusion be required. After surgery, the patient was transfused with 2 pints of blood. However, the blood used was not the blood obtained from the patient's voluntary donors. The blood had been taken from the hospital's general inventory, which had been obtained from the community blood center. The patient subsequently learned that as a result of the transfusions, he had been infected with hepatitis C. A lawsuit was brought and the plaintiff was awarded $325,000 in general damages. The defendant appealed the amount of the award. The Louisiana Court of Appeal held that the award of damages was not excessive. In reasons for judgment, the trial court found that the patient was a credible witness. The plaintiff did not exaggerate his symptoms, fears, or worries about his condition. The court believed the patient when he said he felt like a leper and feared infecting his wife, child, and friends with the disease. The trial court arrived at what it determined to be an appropriate award for general damages. After careful review of the record and in light of the vast discretion of the trial court to assess general damages, the court found that there was no abuse of discretion.

Blood Transfusion Constitutes a Provision of Service

In *Roberts v. Suburban Hospital Association*,[58] the Maryland Court of Special Appeals held that a blood transfusion constituted provision of a service (i.e., the rendering of health care rather than the sale of a product) and was subject to the exhaustion of Maryland's Health Claims Arbitration Act. The *Roberts* case involved the contraction of AIDS by a hemophiliac through the transfusion of contaminated blood. The court stated: "A transfusion is not just a sale of blood which the patient takes home in a package. The transfusion of the blood—the injecting of it into the patient's bloodstream—is what he really needs and pays for, and that involves the application of medical skill."[59]

The risk of an HIV infection through a blood transfusion has been reduced significantly through health history screening and blood donation testing. All blood donated in the United States has been tested for HIV antibodies since May of 1985. Blood units that test positive for HIV are removed from the blood transfusion pool.

Blood Transfusions and the Feres Doctrine

The plaintiff, D.B.S., in *C.R.S. v. United States*,[60] claimed that he had been infected with the AIDS virus while undergoing abdominal surgery at a army hospital while he was on active duty. He had received a minimum of nine units of blood during surgery. He recovered and completed his tour of duty.

D.B.S. later married plaintiff N.A.S. and had three children. The youngest, plaintiff C.R.S., was determined not to be developing normally. A blood test was conducted and C.R.S. tested positive for HIV. D.B.S. and N.A.S. later tested positive for HIV. The plaintiffs alleged that the blood transfusion given to D.B.S. was the source of the AIDS virus. D.B.S. claimed the virus spread to his wife and most likely to his daughter in utero or through breastfeeding.

The plaintiffs brought this action against the United States, alleging medical malpractice, lack of informed consent, breach of express and implied warranties, assault and battery, and violation of various constitutional and civil rights."[61] The government made motions for summary judgment claiming the plaintiffs are barred by the *Feres* doctrine (barring members of the military from successfully suing the federal government under the Federal Tort Claims Act where the injuries arise out of or are in the course of activity incident to military service). The Feres doctrine was found not to be appropriate in this case to bar the claim from moving forward.

> Even if the Feres doctrine would apply to bar the claims of D.B.S. arising during his period of military service, it would not apply to any claims that may have arisen under state law after his discharge. The Supreme Court made clear in Brown that the Feres doctrine does not bar tort suits for injuries after discharge from the military even if there is an arguable relationship between the injury and the plaintiff's prior military service.[62]

Refusal to Work with Certain Blood Specimens

AIDS is spread by direct contact with infected blood or body fluids, such as vaginal secretions, semen, and breast milk. Currently, there is no evidence that the virus can be transmitted through food, water, or casual body contact. HIV does not survive well outside the body. High-risk groups include those who have had unprotected sexual encounters, intravenous drug users, and those who require frequent transfusions of blood and blood products, such as hemophiliacs.

Situations may arise from time to time in which employees may refuse to treat AIDS patients. There are two basic approaches that can be taken in dealing with such problems. The most beneficial course of action for the employee and the institution would be to embark on a program of educating the staff. The alternative and less desirable response to the problem may require that disciplinary steps be initiated against the employee. Such action could be justified on the basis that a healthcare organization has a right to manage its workforce by assigning staff in a responsible manner to carry out its mission of caring for the sick.

The supervisor, in *Stepp v. Review Board of the Indiana Employment Security Division*,[63] had discussions with Stepp for refusing to test specimens with AIDS warning labels attached to them. The supervisor instructed the employee as to the appropriate safety protocols she needed to follow when working with such warnings on specimens. Stepp continued to refuse to perform the tests. She was eventually terminated from her job for failing to perform her assigned tasks. Stepp decided to appeal the supervisor's decision to terminate her to the Review Board of the Indiana Employment Security Division. The review Board determined Stepp was dismissed for just cause. Stepp then appealed the Board's decision to the Court of Appeals of Indiana. The Court upheld the Board's decision finding that Stepp was dismissed for just cause and that the laboratory did not waive its right to compel employees to perform assigned tasks. "Furthermore, Stepp was warned, suspended, then discharged for insubordination. She was clearly required to perform a task which she refused to do."[64]

Employees who have contracted HIV and whose symptoms constitute a risk to others should not be placed in positions that threaten the health and safety of patients and employees. The court in *School Board of Nassau County v. Airline* noted that "a person who poses a significant risk of communicating an infectious disease will not be otherwise qualified for his or her job if reasonable accommodations will not eliminate the risk."[65]

In the final analysis, many competing issues (e.g., humanitarian, legal, moral, ethical, and religious) pertain to the rights of patients and caregivers who have contracted AIDS, as well as those who have not, and employers. As the search for answers continues, the debates and controversies persist, regardless of the type of infectious disease (more recently, the Zika virus). It is hoped that solutions that meet the needs of those who have been infected with an infectious disease and those who are involved with providing health care to them will be forthcoming.

Failure to Diagnose Cervical Cancer

Cervical cancer is often curable when diagnosed in its early stages. A *Pap smear screening* makes early stage diagnosis of cervical cancer possible when properly performed and accurately read. Because of any one or more of the following, the opportunity for early diagnosis and treatment is lost: (1) the failure of a physician to order and/or review the results of Pap smears; (2) the carelessness on the part of laboratory staff in performing the test; (3) the failure of a pathologist to either review the test or make an accurate diagnosis; and/or (4) the failure to communicate test results to physicians and patients. In addition to these failures,

the failure of a patient's physician to thoroughly follow up on a patient's test results can lead to late-stage treatment and sometimes early death, as noted in the following case.

Surgical Specimens

Procedures to reduce the risk of surgical specimen discrepancies and mix-ups of patient specimens can help prevent a wrong diagnosis for the patients involved. For example, two patients in different operating rooms at the same hospital at the same time could have breast biopsies performed in the laboratory on a stat basis. If the tissue slides are incorrectly labeled, the pathology

---

🔍 *LOST CHANCE OF SURVIVAL*

Citation: *Sander v. Geib, Elston, Frost Prof'l Ass'n*, 506 N.W.2d 107 (S.D. 1993)

Facts

The patient had several gynecologic examinations, including Pap smears, in 1977, 1978, 1980, 1984, 1986, and 1987. The patient's physician performed the examinations. Specimens for the Pap test were submitted to a laboratory for evaluation. The laboratory procedure included a clerk assigning each specimen a number when it was received. A cytotechnologist would then screen the specimen. If the specimen was determined to be abnormal, it would be marked for review by a pathologist. Out of the Pap tests that were determined to be normal, only 1 in 10 was actually viewed by a pathologist. The pathologist made recommendations based on the classification of the Pap tests. A biopsy would be recommended if the Pap test was determined to be Class IV.

Except for the Pap test in 1987, which showed premalignant cellular changes, all of the patient's other Pap tests were determined to be negative. In 1986, the laboratory made a notation to the patient's physician that "moderate inflammation" was present. The patient's physician, who was treating her with antibiotics for a foot inflammation, thought that the medication would also treat the other inflammation. In September 1987, the patient returned to her physician complaining of pain, erratic periods, and tiredness. After completing a physical, her physician took a Pap test, which he sent to the laboratory. He also referred her to a gynecologist. The pathologist recommended a biopsy. Biopsies and further physical examinations revealed squamous cell carcinoma that had spread to her pelvic bones. Her Pap tests were reexamined by the laboratory, which reported that the 1986 smear showed that malignancy was highly likely. The patient was referred to the University of Minnesota to determine whether she was a viable candidate for radiation treatment. The cancer, however, had spread, and the patient was not considered a candidate for radiation treatment because she had no chance of survival. When the university reviewed all of the available slides, they found cellular changes back to 1984.

The patient sued in 1988, alleging that the laboratory failed to detect and report cellular changes in her Pap tests in time to prevent the spread of the cancer. Before trial, the patient died. Her husband and sister were substituted as plaintiffs, and the complaint was amended to include a wrongful death action. After trial, a jury awarded $3.7 million in damages, which were reduced to $1 million by the circuit court. The jury found against the laboratory, and the laboratory appealed.

Issue

Was it erroneous for the trial court to submit to the jury the 1988 negligence claim based on the 1984 slide?

Holding

The South Dakota Supreme Court upheld the jury verdict and restored the $3.7 million damage award.

Reason

The court determined that evidence relating to negligence claims pertaining to Pap tests taken more than 2 years before filing the action was admissible because the patient had a continuing relationship with the clinical laboratory as a result of her physician submitting her Pap tests to the laboratory over a period of time.

readings sent back to the operating room could result in each patient getting the other patient's results. Assuming one patient is cancer free and the other is not, the wrong patient gets a mastectomy and the other wakes up believing she does not have cancer.

Procedures must be in place to ensure that the correct specimens are placed in the correct containers and are labeled properly at the surgical table. Specimens, including blood, must not leave one's possession until labeled. A strict chain of custody for each specimen must be maintained.

A pathology report discrepancy can occur when one pathologist renders a diagnosis and a second pathologist, looking at the same tissue, renders a different diagnosis. The pathology interpretation of the tissue reviewed can alter a clinician's treatment plan and the patient's prognosis. A review of discrepancies between pathologists and/or a physician's diagnosis should be reviewed on an inter- and intradepartmental basis in order to improve the quality of patient care.

Transfusion of Wrong Blood

The patient-plaintiff, Mrs. Bordelon, in *Bordelon v. St. Francis Cabrini Hospital*,[66] was admitted to the hospital to undergo a hysterectomy. Prior to surgery, she provided the hospital with her own blood in case it was needed during surgery. During surgery, Bordelon did indeed need blood, but was administered donor blood other than her own. Bordelon filed a lawsuit claiming that the hospital's failure to provide her with her own blood resulted in her suffering mental distress. The hospital filed a peremptory exception claiming that there was no cause of action. The Ninth Judicial District Court dismissed the suit because the plaintiff did not allege that she suffered any physical injury.

On appeal by the plaintiff, the court of appeal held that the plaintiff did in fact state a cause of action for mental distress. It is well-established in law that a claim for negligent infliction of emotional distress unaccompanied by physical injury is a viable claim of action. It is indisputable that HIV can be transmitted through blood transfusions even when the standard procedure for screening for the virus is in place. Bordelon's fear was easily associated with receiving someone else's blood and, therefore, a conceivable consequence of the defendant's negligent act.[67] The hospital had a duty to ensure that Bordelon received her own blood when it accepted that as a condition of her hospitalization. It is undisputed that the hospital breached that duty by administering the wrong blood.

MEDICAL ASSISTANT

A *medical assistant* is an unlicensed person who provides administrative, clerical, and/or technical support to a licensed practitioner. A medical assistant can obtain a certificate in medical assisting, which can take a year to complete. A medical assistant also can pursue an associate degree from an accredited program, which requires 2 years of coursework.[68] The *American Association of Medical Assistants* describes the education, certification, and continuing education process at its website [www.aama-ntl.org]. As with any profession, the laws affecting medical assistants can vary from state to state. Florida, for example, provides in its 2016 Florida Statutes 458.3485 a definition for a medical assistant and describes the following duties of a medical assistant:

> (1) DEFINITION.—As used in this section, "medical assistant" means a professional multiskilled person dedicated to assisting in all aspects of medical practice under the direct supervision and responsibility of a physician. This practitioner assists with patient care management, executes administrative and clinical procedures, and often performs managerial and supervisory functions. Competence in the field also requires that a medical assistant adhere to ethical and legal standards of professional practice, recognize and respond to emergencies, and demonstrate professional characteristics.
>
> (2) DUTIES.—Under the direct supervision and responsibility of a licensed physician, a medical assistant may undertake the following duties:
>
> A. Performing clinical procedures, to include:
>   1. Performing aseptic procedures.
>   2. Taking vital signs.
>   3. Preparing patients for the physician's care.
>   4. Performing venipunctures and nonintravenous injections.
>   5. Observing and reporting patients' signs or symptoms.
> B. Administering basic first aid.
> C. Assisting with patient examinations or treatments.
> D. Operating office medical equipment.
> E. Collecting routine laboratory specimens as directed by the physician.
> F. Administering medication as directed by the physician.

G. Performing basic laboratory procedures.
H. Performing office procedures including all general administrative duties required by the physician.
I. Performing dialysis procedures, including home dialysis.

A licensed practitioner is generally required to be physically present in the treatment facility, medical office, or ambulatory facility when a medical assistant is performing procedures. Employment of medical assistants is expected to grow much faster than the average for all occupations as the health services industry expands. This growth is a result, in part, of technologic advances in medicine and a growing and aging population. Increasing use of medical assistants in the rapidly growing healthcare industry will most likely result in continuing employment growth for the occupation.

Medical assistants work in physicians' offices, clinics, nursing homes, and ambulatory care settings. The duties of medical assistants vary from office to office, depending on the location and size of the practice and the practitioner's specialty. In small practices, medical assistants are usually generalists, handling both administrative and clinical duties. Those in large practices tend to specialize in a particular area, under supervision. Administrative duties often include answering telephones, greeting patients, updating and filing patients' medical records, filling out insurance forms, handling correspondence, scheduling appointments, arranging for hospital admission and laboratory services, and handling billing and bookkeeping. Clinical duties vary according to state law and include assisting in taking medical histories, recording vital signs, explaining treatment procedures to patients, preparing patients for examination, and assisting the practitioner during examinations. Medical assistants collect and prepare laboratory specimens or perform basic laboratory tests on the premises, dispose of contaminated supplies, and sterilize medical instruments. They instruct patients about medications and special diets, prepare and administer medications as directed by a physician, authorize drug refills as directed, telephone prescriptions to a pharmacy, prepare patients for X-rays, perform electrocardiograms, remove sutures, and change dressings.

Medical assistants who specialize have additional duties. Podiatric medical assistants make castings of feet, expose and develop X-rays, and assist podiatrists in surgery. Ophthalmic medical assistants help ophthalmologists provide eye care. They conduct diagnostic tests, measure and record vision, and test eye muscle function. They also show patients how to insert, remove, and care for contact lenses, and they apply eye dressings. Under the direction of the physician, ophthalmic medical assistants may administer eye medications. They also maintain optical and surgical instruments and may assist the ophthalmologist in surgery.[69]

Poor Communications

In 1987, the patient-plaintiff in *Follett v. Davis*[70] had her first office visit with Dr. Davis. In the spring of 1988, Follett discovered a lump in her right breast and made an appointment to see Davis; however, the clinic had no record of her appointment. The clinic's employees directed her to radiology for a mammogram. Davis or any other physician at the clinic did not offer Follett an examination nor was she scheduled for an examination as a follow-up to the mammogram. A technician examined Follett's breast and confirmed the presence of a lump in her right breast. After the mammogram, clinic employees told her that she would hear from Davis if there were any problems with her mammogram.

The radiologist explained in his deposition that the mammogram was not normal. Davis reviewed the mammogram report and considered it to be negative for malignancy. He was unaware of the lump in the patient's breast, and there was no evidence that clinic employees informed him about it. The clinic, including Davis, never contacted Follett about her lump or the mammogram. On April 6, 1990, Follett called the clinic and was told that there was nothing to worry about unless she heard from Davis. On September 24, 1990, Follett returned to the clinic after she had developed pain associated with the lump. A mammogram performed on that day gave results consistent with cancer. Three days later, Davis made an appointment for Follett with a clinic surgeon for a biopsy and treatment. Davis subsequently transferred her care to other physicians. Follett's biopsy had confirmed the diagnosis of cancer in October 1990.

Follett filed a lawsuit and the trial court granted summary judgment to Davis on the grounds that Follett failed to file her complaint within the applicable statute of limitations and she appealed.

The Indiana Court of Appeals determined that the evidence demonstrated that, had clinic procedures been properly followed, Davis or another physician at the clinic would have made an accurate diagnosis. Follett timely filed her proposed complaint within 2 years of her last visits to Davis and the clinic. The trial court therefore improperly granted summary judgment.

▶ NUTRITIONAL SERVICES

Healthcare organizations are expected to provide patients with diets that meet their individual needs (**FIGURE 12-4**). Some university hospitals stress the importance of good nutrition. University Hospitals in Cleveland describe the importance of nutritional services by promoting "the idea that proper nutrition can improve health and well-being. Our registered dietitians offer nutrition education and counseling for patients with conditions such as diabetes, seizure disorders, or immune disorders, and work to incorporate dietary plans into the patients' course of treatment."[71] Massachusetts General Hospital nutritional "experts from the Department of Nutrition and Food Services aid the general public with management of specific dietary needs in many different areas, including cardiac care, diabetes, and childhood and adult obesity. They also provide nutritional care and advice about lifestyle maintenance and good nutrition, often through classes available on the hospital's main campus and at community health centers."[72] Healthcare organizations have traditionally failed to recognize or promote the importance of good nutritional care. New York-Presbyterian Hospital, in their nutrition program, states:

> Our vision is to go beyond the expectations of our patients and customers with the clinical expertise, service, compassion, education, and caring that one expects from a premier clinical nutrition and food service department.

MALNUTRITION: A SERIOUS CONCERN FOR HOSPITALIZED PATIENTS

The problem of malnutrition in hospitalized patients was revealed in a 1974 article, "The Skeleton in the Hospital Closet," by Charles Butterworth, Jr., MD, and published in *Nutrition Today*. Citing several cases of neglect in nutrition care, Butterworth pointed out that changes in practice were urgently needed to properly diagnose and treat undernourished patients and prevent iatrogenic malnutrition.

—Theresa A. Fessler, MS, RD, CNSD,
Today's Dietitian, July, 2008

Networking, our team focuses on best practices in the spirit of unity where each team member autographs their work with pride and quality.[73]

The Joint Commission standards require that "food and nutrition products are consistent with each patient's care, treatment, and services."[74] Failure to address the nutritional needs of patients can lead to negligence suits, as noted in the cases presented here.

Malnutrition

The daughter of the deceased in *Lambert v. Beverly Enterprises, Inc.*[75] filed an action claiming that her

FIGURE 12-4 Preparation of patient's diet plan.

© create jobs 51/Shutterstock

father had been mistreated. The deceased allegedly suffered malnutrition as a direct result of the acts or omissions of personnel. In addition, the plaintiff's father suffered actual damages that included substantial medical expenses and mental anguish as a result of the injuries he sustained. A motion to dismiss the case was denied.

▶ PHARMACY

The practice of pharmacy essentially includes preparing, compounding, dispensing, and retailing medications. These activities may be carried out only by a pharmacist with a state license or by a person exempted from the provisions of a state's pharmacy statutes. The entire stock of drugs in a pharmacy is subject to strict government regulation and control. The pharmacist is responsible for developing, coordinating, and supervising all pharmacy activities and reviewing the drug regimens of each patient.

Medication Errors

Medication errors are considered to be a leading cause of medical injury in the United States. Antibiotics, chemotherapeutic drugs, and anticoagulants are three categories of drugs responsible for many drug-related adverse events. Because of the immense variety and complexity of medications now available, it is practically impossible for nurses or doctors to keep up with the information required for safe medication use. The pharmacist has become an essential resource in modern hospital practice.[76] It is therefore mandatory that

(NEWS) *FDA FINDS WIDESPREAD SAFETY ISSUES AT SPECIALIZED PHARMACIES*

Federal inspectors have found dozens of potentially dangerous safety problems at 30 specialized pharmacies, months after tainted steroid shots made by a Massachusetts pharmacy triggered the worst drug disaster in decades.

• • •

FDA officials say the inspections show that compounders, in many cases, are failing to ensure the safety of their products, despite months of stepped-up scrutiny from state and federal regulators as well as consumer groups.
—Lena H. Sun, *The Washington Post*, April 12, 2013

hospital pharmacies "have an adequate number of personnel to ensure quality pharmaceutical services, including emergencies."[77]

The prevention of medication errors requires recognition of common causes and the development of practices to help reduce the incidence of errors. With thousands of drugs, many of which look and sound alike, it is understandable why medication errors are so common. The following list describes some of the more common types of medication errors.

- Prescription errors include wrong patient, wrong drug, wrong dose, wrong frequency, wrong route, transcription errors (often as a result of illegible handwriting and improper use of abbreviations), inadequate review of drug ordered (e.g., known drug allergies, drug–drug and food–drug interaction[s]), and inadequate review of medication for appropriateness.
- Dispensing errors include improper preparation of medication, failure to properly formulate medications, dispensing expired medications, mislabeling containers, wrong patient, wrong dose, wrong route, and misinterpretation of physician's order.
- Administration errors include wrong patient, wrong route, double-dosing (drug administered more than once), failure to administer medications, wrong frequency, administering discontinued drugs, administering drugs without an authorized order, and wrong dose (e.g., IV rate).
- Documentation errors include transcription errors (often as a result of illegible handwriting and improper use of abbreviations), inaccurate transcription to medication administration record (MAR), charted but not administered, administered but not documented on the MAR, discontinued order not noted on the MAR, and medication wasted and not recorded.

The *Institute for Safe Medication Practices* (ISMP) is a nonprofit organization based in Philadelphia devoted entirely to medication error prevention and safe medication use. The organization's website (www.ismp.org) should be visited on a regular basis to assist in the prevention of medication errors. The website provides information in its newsletters, describes consulting services, educational programs, professional development, self-assessments, and ISMP guidelines.

Government Control of Drugs

The power and authority to regulate drugs, packaging, and distribution rest primarily with federal and state governments. Consequently, there are often two sets of regulations and standards governing the same activity. In general, states have attempted to enact laws that comply with federal laws. For example, most states have adopted the Uniform Controlled Substances Act (UCSA). This law is based on and is in conformity with the federal Controlled Substances Act. Several states have modified the UCSA in various ways, frequently setting more stringent standards than are required under the federal law.

Controlled Substances Act

The Comprehensive Drug Abuse Prevention and Control Act of 1970, commonly known as the Controlled Substances Act (CSA), was signed into law on October 27, 1970, as Public Law No. 91-513. This law replaced virtually all preexisting federal laws dealing with narcotics, depressants, and stimulants.

> The CSA places all substances that are regulated under existing federal law into one of five schedules. This placement is based upon the substance's medicinal value, harmfulness, and potential for abuse or addiction. Schedule I is reserved for the most dangerous drugs that have no recognized medical use, while Schedule V is the classification used for the least dangerous drugs. The act also provides a mechanism for substances to be controlled, added to a schedule, decontrolled, removed from control, rescheduled, or transferred from one schedule to another.[78]

Federal Food, Drug, and Cosmetic Act

The Federal Food, Drug, and Cosmetic Act (FDCA) applies to drugs and devices carried in interstate commerce and to goods produced and distributed in federal territory. The Act's requirements apply to almost every drug that would be dispensed from a pharmacy, because nearly all drugs and devices, or their components, are eventually carried in interstate commerce.

Section 502 of the Act sets forth the information that must appear on the labels or the labeling of drugs and devices. The label must contain, among other special information: (1) the name and place of business of the manufacturer, packer, or distributor; (2) the quantity of contents; (3) the name and quantity of any ingredient found to be habit forming, along with the statement, "Warning—may be habit-forming"; (4) the established name of the drug or its ingredients; (5) adequate directions for use; (6) adequate warnings and cautions concerning conditions of use; and (7) special precautions for packaging.

The regulation implementing the labeling requirements of Section 502 exempts prescription drugs from the requirement that the label bear "adequate directions for use for laymen" if the drug is in the possession of a pharmacy or under the custody of a practitioner licensed by law to administer or prescribe *legend drugs*, those that can only be obtained by prescription.[79] This particular exemption only applies to prescription drugs meeting the other requirements. Ordinary household remedies in the custody or possession of a practitioner or pharmacist would not fall under the labeling exemption.

If the drug container is too small to bear a label with all of the required information, the label may contain only the quantity or proportion of each active ingredient and the lot or control number. The prescription label may appear on the outer container of such drug units. The lot or control number may appear on the crimp of a dispensing tube, and the remainder of the required label information may appear on other labeling within the package.

Besides the label itself, each drug must be accompanied by labeling, on or within the sealed package from which it is to be dispensed, bearing full prescribing information including indications; dosage; routes, methods, and frequency of administration; contraindications; side effects; precautions; and any other information concerning the intended use of the drug necessary for the prescriber to use the drug safely. This information usually is contained in what is known in the trade as the *package insert*.

State Regulations

In addition to federal laws affecting the manufacture, use, and handling of drugs, the different states have controlling legislation. All states regulate the practice of pharmacy, as well as the operation of pharmacies. State regulations generally provide that: (1) each healthcare organization must ensure the availability of pharmaceutical services to meet the needs of patients; (2) pharmaceutical services must be provided in accordance with all applicable federal and state laws and regulations; (3) pharmaceutical services must be provided under the supervision of a pharmacist; (4) space and equipment must be provided within the organization for the proper storage, safeguarding, preparation, dispensing, and administration of drugs; (5) each organization must develop and implement written policies and procedures regarding accountability, distribution, and assurance of quality of all drugs; and (6) each organization must develop and follow current written procedures for the safe prescription and administration of drugs.

State laws require that pharmacies be licensed and that they be under the supervision of a person licensed to practice pharmacy. The pharmacist usually can be either an employee of the organization or a consultant. The authority of an organization to operate a pharmacy is conditioned on compliance with licensing requirements affecting the pharmacy premises and its personnel. The statutes applying to pharmacies usually empower regulatory agencies, such as the state pharmacy board, to issue rules and regulations as necessary.

Each organization is subject to liability for the negligent acts of its professional and nonprofessional employees in the handling of drugs and medications within the organization. Both the pharmacist and the organization are subject to criminal liability, as well as civil liability, for the violation of statutory directives. Most states have regulations that dictate in detail the dispensing, distribution, administration, storage, control, and disposal of drugs within healthcare organizations.

Storage of Drugs

Drugs must be stored in their original containers and must be labeled properly. The label should indicate the patient's full name, physician, prescription number, strength of the drug, expiration date of all time-dated drugs, and the address and telephone number of the pharmacy dispensing the drug. Medication containers must be safely and securely stored in an area that can be closely monitored by the nursing staff. Medications containing narcotics or other dangerous drugs must be stored under double lock (e.g., a locked box within the medicine cabinet). The keys to the medicine cabinet and narcotics box must be in the possession of authorized personnel. Medications for external use only must be marked clearly and kept separate from medications for internal use. Medications that are to be taken out of use must be disposed of according to federal and state laws and regulations.

Hospital Formulary

Healthcare organizations use a formulary system, whereby physicians and pharmacists create a formulary listing of drugs used in the institution. The formulary contains the brand names and generic names of drugs. Under the formulary system, a physician agrees that his or her prescription, which calls for a

✔ OUTPATIENT CHEMOTHERAPY UNIT

Jill was inspecting a newly opened chemotherapy infusion center (CIC) for cancer patients. She toured the center and was amazed at the up-to-date equipment, cleanliness, and expertise of the physicians and nurses on the unit. Jill complimented the staff about the design, efficiency, and comforting environment for both staff and patients.

Following Jill's tour and review of the CIC's operations manuals and patient records, she asked to see the storage area for chemotherapy agents. Jill inquired about the monetary value of the chemo agents stored in the refrigerator. The figure was well over $100,000 at that moment. Jill then asked Mike, the nurse manager, "How do you monitor the refrigerator temperature to protect the efficacy of the chemo agents?" Mike replied, "We have an alarm system that continuously monitors the temperature through a recording device that charts the temperature 24 hours a day 365 days a year."

Jill then asked how many days a week is the clinic open. Mike replied, "We are open Monday to Friday." Jill then asked, "What happens if the chemo storage refrigerator temperature goes above normal." Mike replied, "An alarm will go off." Jill, making further inquiry, asked, "Who will hear the alarm on weekends?" Mike replied, "Well, we really wouldn't know until Monday morning when we come to work."

Jill then asked, "If the temperature goes above the normal range, how will that affect the efficacy of the chemo agent." Mike replied, "It could be problematic as to the efficacy of the agents stored in the refrigerator and costly to the hospital. The chemo agents, depending on how high the temperature went and for how long, may have to be discarded according to protocol and new chemo agents ordered. It also would affect the scheduling of patients. The high cost of the chemo agent and obtaining a replacement supply of chemo agents could pose a problem. Rescheduling patients would be difficult because we are running a tight schedule already."

Jill suggested that if the alarm sounded, it should be forwarded to a central station, preferably the hospital switchboard operator, who would then contact the on-duty engineer and cancer center on-call staff member. The engineer on duty in the hospital should respond to the alarm. A determination would then be made regarding how a power outage might affect the chemo agents by a designated staff member knowledgeable about the chemo agents stored in the refrigerator. Jill went on to remind Mike about the importance of documenting evidence of continuing education of staff regarding the safe handling, storage, and administration of chemotherapy; use of spill kits; proper disposal; and procedures to follow in the event of accidental exposure.

brand-name drug, may be filled with the generic equivalent of that drug (i.e., a drug that contains the same active ingredients in the same proportions). If there is a medical contraindication to prescribing a generic drug for a particular patient, the physician may prescribe the brand-name drug. Hospitals that dispense and administer a generic drug for financial reasons when a brand-name drug is requested for medical reasons most likely will be liable for any harm suffered by the patient as a result of being administered the generic equivalent of the brand-name drug. However, there would be difficulty in proving that the use of a generic drug was the cause of an injury a patient might incur as the result of the use of a generic equivalent of a brand-name drug.

Dispensing and Administration of Drugs

The *dispensing of medications* is the processing of a drug for delivery or for administration to a patient pursuant to the order of an appropriately licensed healthcare practitioner. It consists of checking the directions on the label with the directions on the prescription or order to determine accuracy; selecting the drug from stock to fill the order; counting, measuring, compounding, or preparing the drug; placing the drug in the proper container; and adding any required notations to a written prescription.

The *administration of medications* is an act in which an authorized person, in accordance with federal and state laws and regulations, gives a single dose of a prescribed drug to a patient. The complete act of administration includes removing an individual dose from a previously dispensed, properly labeled container (including a unit-dose container); verifying it with

INSIDE A PHARMACY WHERE A FATAL ERROR OCCURRED

Lewis typed up a prescription label with erroneous dosage instructions. About 36 hours later, Smith died of what an autopsy found was an accidental methadone overdose.

It may be impossible to fix blame precisely for Smith's death, in part because Walgreens in December settled the lawsuit with his family in a confidential agreement that bars any discussion of the case. However, the depositions and interviews gathered before the settlement suggest that both a technician with limited experience and a pharmacist coping with a heavy workload figured in the tragedy.

—Kevin McKoy, *USA Today*, February 12, 2008

the physician's order; giving the individual dose to the proper patient; and recording the time and dose given.

Each dose of a drug administered must be recorded on the patient's clinical records. A separate record of narcotic drugs must be maintained. The narcotic record must contain the following information: date and time administered, physician's name, signature of person administering the dose, and the balance of the narcotic drug on hand.

In the event that an emergency arises requiring the immediate administration of a particular drug, the patient's record should be documented properly, showing the necessity for administration of the drug on an emergency basis. Procedures should be in place for handling emergency situations.

Drug Substitution

Drug substitution may be defined as the dispensing of a different drug or brand in place of the drug or brand ordered. Several states prohibit this, and penal sanctions, including loss of license, are imposed for violation of the law.

Expanding Role of Pharmacist

Historically, the role of the pharmacist was centered on the management of the pharmacy and the accurate dispensing of drugs. The duties and responsibilities of pharmacists have moved well beyond the concept of filling prescriptions and dispensing drugs. Schools of pharmacy have recognized the ever-expanding role of the pharmacist into the clinical aspects of patient care—so much so that educational requirements are becoming more stringent, with emphasis on clinical education and application. Pharmacists now, among other duties, maintain patient medication profiles and monitor patient profiles, looking for incompatibilities between drug–drug and food–drug interactions.

Pharmacists have an ever-expanding clinical role in the delivery of patient care. For example, pharmacists often maintain a separate telephone line in hospitals for caregivers and practitioners to use to discuss medication usage. Pharmacists play an important role when they respond and participate in reviving patients in cardiac arrest. Their knowledge of drugs, potential drug interactions, and proper dosing can be the difference between life and death. Some hospitals have reported improved code outcomes when pharmacists attend and participate in patient codes. A variety of legal cases, as they apply to pharmacy, are presented in the following sections. Additional recent legal cases of interest to pharmacists can be found at the American Society for Pharmacy Law's website (www.aspl.org).

Duty to Monitor Patient's Medications

In *Baker v. Arbor Drugs Inc.*,[80] a Michigan court imposed a duty on a pharmacist to monitor a patient's medications. The patient filled three different prescriptions by the same physician at the same pharmacy. The pharmacy maintained a computer system that detected drug–drug interactions. The pharmacy advertised to consumers that it could, through the use of a computer-monitoring system, provide a medication profile for its customers that would alert its pharmacists to potential drug–drug interactions. Because the pharmacy advertised and used the computer system to monitor the medications of its customers, the pharmacist voluntarily assumed a duty of care to detect the harmful drug–drug interaction that occurred in this case, where it was determined without question that decedent suffered injury when he suffered a stroke due to the adverse drug interaction between two drugs, Parnate and Tavist-D.

Warning Patients About Medication Usage

A Pennsylvania court held that a pharmacist failed to warn the patient about the maximum dosage of a drug the patient could take.[81] This failure resulted in an overdose, causing permanent injuries. Expert testimony focused on the fact that a pharmacist who receives inadequate instructions as to the maximum recommended dosage has a duty to ascertain whether the patient is aware of the limitations concerning the use of the drug. The pharmacist in this case should have contacted the prescribing physician to clarify the prescription. The Supreme Court of Pennsylvania held:

> It is not for this Court to delineate the precise bounds of a medical professional's responsibilities. It is for the medical community to determine what degree of vigilance is required in this respect. They are in the best position to balance the interests and prescribe a standard of conduct which is consistent with the best interests of the patient.
>
> In the instant case the testimony of the medical experts, both physicians and pharmacists, established that the conduct of Morgan Pharmacy's pharmacists fell below the level of reasonable conduct in the practice of pharmacy. The jury heard the evidence and found that Morgan Pharmacy was not only negligent but more negligent [than] Dr. Stack.[82]

Refuse to Honor Questionable Prescription

In *Hooks v. McLaughlin*,[83] the Indiana Supreme Court held that a pharmacist had a duty to refuse to refill prescriptions at an unreasonably faster rate than prescribed pending directions from the prescribing physician. The Indiana code provides that a pharmacist is immune from civil prosecution or civil liability if he or she, in good faith, refuses to honor a prescription because, in his or her professional judgment, the honoring of the prescription would aid or abet an addiction or habit.[84]

Limited Duty to Warn

The rules and regulations promulgated by a state board of pharmacy generally do not require a duty on the part of pharmacists to warn of every potentially adverse drug reaction. For example, the Georgia State Board of Pharmacy rules do not require that a pharmacist warn about all of the potential side effects of a medication.

> Upon receipt of a Prescription Drug Order and following a review of the patient's record, the dispensing Pharmacist shall personally offer to discuss matters which will enhance or optimize drug therapy with each patient. . . . Such discussion . . . shall include appropriate elements of patient counseling, based on the professional judgment of the pharmacist. Such elements may include but are not limited to the following: . . . (v) common severe side or adverse effects or interactions and therapeutic contraindications that may be encountered . . . [Ga. Comp. R. & Regs. r. 480-31-.01(c)(1)].

The Georgia Court of Appeals in Chamblin v. K-Mart Corp. found that the pharmacy was properly granted summary judgment with respect to claims arising from a patient's extreme allergic reaction, namely, Stevens–Johnson syndrome, to a prescription drug—Daypro, a nonsteroidal anti-inflammatory drug—even though it was alleged that the pharmacist failed to warn the patient of the potential side effects of the drug.[85]

> . . . Chamblins have not cited any evidence in the record establishing that the employees of the K-Mart pharmacy did not make an offer of counseling.
>
> Brock deposed [612 S.E.2d 29] that he was aware of the regulations regarding patient counseling and that he made a point of talking to customers about their prescriptions, but he did not specifically recall Jan Chamblin. Further, it is unlikely that Brock would have discussed the risk of Stevens-Johnson syndrome if he had counseled Chamblin, as the Chamblins'

own expert witness, Dr. Guerra, testified that it was an extremely rare allergic reaction that could be caused by almost any drug.

Accordingly, because the trial court properly found that K-Mart did not have a duty to warn Chamblin of every potential side effect of Daypro, we affirm the grant of summary judgment to K-Mart.

2. Based on our holding in Division 1 that the rules and regulations promulgated by the Board did not establish a generalized duty on the part of pharmacists to warn of every potentially adverse reaction to a drug, we find that the trial court properly denied the Chamblins' motion for summary judgment on the issue of negligence per se.[86]

Refusal to Fill Prescription

The plaintiff, in *Sellars v. Walgreen Co.*,[87] filed a complaint on behalf of himself and the wrongful death beneficiaries of his mother against Walgreen Co., alleging that a Walgreens pharmacist negligently caused the death of his mother for refusing to fill her prescription without first receiving promise of payment. Walgreen filed for summary judgment with the Lee County Circuit Court, which the court granted. The plaintiff appealed, alleging that the court erred in granting summary judgment because there were genuine issues of material fact.

The Court of Appeals of the State of Mississippi found no error in the County Court's decision to grant summary judgment for the defendants, finding no issue of material fact that established a legal duty or standard of care owed by Walgreens to the deceased.

Failure to Consult with the Patient's Physician

The pharmacist in *Warren v. Walgreen*[88] was found negligent for failing to warn a deceased patient about possible drug interactions when filling two prescriptions over 2 days. In this case, the pharmacist increased the dosage of the second drug without consulting a physician.

The family and estate of Eric Warren sued Walgreen's and Mr. Warren treating physician on a wrongful death claim for negligently giving him Tramadol and Methadone and failing to warn the high school Wrestling coach that taking the medications together might kill him, which doing so did when he took the medications.[89]

Intravenous Admixture Service

Intravenous fluids, with or without added medications, are generally prepared in an IV admixture room by pharmacists and technicians. Pharmacists are expected to oversee the work of pharmacy technicians. Medications prepared in admixture rooms include antibiotics, chemotherapy, and electrolytes, as well as intravenous nutrition solutions that are tailored for each patient's needs. Elements crucial to the process of preparing sterile products include stability of the mixtures, sterility, solubility of added ingredients, considerations of incompatibilities, storage, and proper labeling. Proper disposal is a key consideration for the protection of personnel and the environment. Labeling of IV admixtures should include: patient's name and identification number, date of birth, room number, drug and strength, infusion period, flow rate (e.g., this may vary from patient to patient based on such concerns as congestive heart failure), information that is required by the healthcare entity (e.g., hospital, outpatient infusion center), and any other specific requirements that might be required by state and federal law and regulations.

A sterile compounding environment is maintained with the use of laminar flow hoods and aseptic techniques. Vertical and horizontal laminar flow hood cabinets are utilized in the preparation of intravenous fluids. The cabinets are designed for creation of a bacterial dust–free air space. They are utilized for work with low-risk substances and materials, when protection of working material from the environment is required, or when working with an item requires a sterile working space. The hoods are maintained daily and are certified periodically for proper functioning.

Aseptic technique is the key to producing a sterile product. The American Society of Health-System Pharmacists and the Occupational Safety and Health

ERROR THAT LED TO BABY'S DEATH SLIPPED THROUGH MANY HANDS

The mistakes that led up to Alyssa Shinn's death on Nov. 9 started the night before when pharmacist Pamela Goff mishandled the entry of Alyssa's prescription into the pharmacy's computer. It ended with neonatal intensive care unit nurses hanging an IV bag containing zinc at 1,000 times the amount prescribed the preemie.

—Annette Wells, *Las Vegas Review Journal*, August 5, 2007

Administration, amongst others, provide guidelines and regulations in order to provide for a safe working environment.

An observational study of the accuracy in compounding IV admixtures at five hospitals showed that "Of every 100 errors, 2 were judged to be potentially clinically important. In five U.S. hospital pharmacies, the observed error rate for compounding i.v. admixtures was 9%."[90]

Medications and Helpful Tips

The following medication checklist is helpful in reducing the number of adverse events:

- There is a process for documenting a complete listing of a patient's current medications upon admission to the hospital or other healthcare setting.
- The attending physician decides which medications should be continued during a patient's stay.
- Handwriting is legible and printed if necessary for readability.
- Felt-tip pens are avoided.
- Orders are clear.
- A zero is added prior to a decimal.
- Abbreviations are avoided except were permitted by hospital policy.
- A process is in place for validating interpretation of illegible medication orders.
- Hold orders (e.g., the temporary discontinuance of a medication) are accompanied by a time frame. In one case, a physician placed a hold order on the patient's Coumadin without any monitoring parameters prior to the patient undergoing an endoscopy procedure. Coumadin was never reordered following the procedure. The patient subsequently suffered a stroke.[91]
- Medications are properly diluted before administering.
- Drugs are safely stored, ordered, and distributed.
- Potentially dangerous look-alike drugs are separated in the pharmacy.
- High-risk drugs are easily identified and standardized when feasible.
- Look-alike medications are repackaged or relabeled, as necessary, in the pharmacy.
- Medications are labeled as to dosage and expiration date.
- Medications are administered at the proper time in the prescribed dosage by the correct route (e.g., IV, intramuscular, oral).
- A complete list of medications is available to the next provider when the patient is transferred from one setting to another (e.g., patient care unit, service,

practitioner, or level of care within or outside the organization, such as an ambulatory care setting).

- Upon discharge, the attending physician instructs the patient as to which drugs should be continued or discontinued.
- Risk reduction activities are in place to reduce the likelihood of adverse drug reactions and medication errors.
- There is a mechanism for monitoring the effect of medications on patients.
- Responsibility for ensuring the integrity of crash carts has been assigned.
- There are appropriate medications and equipment on crash carts for treating both children and adults.
- Staff members are appropriately trained in the testing and use of equipment contained in or on the crash cart.
- Staff members who participate in codes are periodically tested for competency.
- A mechanism is in place for approving and overseeing the use of investigational drugs.
- Causes and trends of medication errors are tracked and changes made in the process as necessary to improve outcomes.
- Educational processes have been implemented to reduce the likelihood of medication errors and adverse drug events.

▸ PHYSICAL THERAPY

Physical therapy is the art and science of preventing and treating neuromuscular or musculoskeletal disabilities through the evaluation of an individual's disability and rehabilitation potential; the application of physical agents (heat, cold, ultrasound, electricity, water, and light); and the use neuromuscular procedures that, through their physiologic effect, improve or maintain the patient's optimum functional level (**FIGURE 12-5**). Because of different physical disabilities brought on by various injuries and medical problems, physical therapy is an extremely important component of a patient's total health care. Physical therapists, therefore, have a legal duty as any other health professional to adhere to an accepted standard of care when providing care and treatment. Negligence occurs when the physical therapist fails to provide rehabilitation or treatment at the accepted standard of care that other physical therapists in similar circumstances would have provided.

Areas of liability concern for physical therapists include: failure to obtain a completed prescription from the prescribing physician, failure to follow physician's orders or to clarify such orders, aggressive

FIGURE 12-5 Physical therapist treating a patient.

treatment (e.g., use of heavy weights), and treatment burns from hot packs. Adherence to the physician's treatment plan as prescribed and seeking clarification when necessary, review of patient's history and risk assessments, preparation of equipment to be used, and observation and feedback from the patient will go a long ways in reducing the number of injuries suffered by physical therapy patients. Various physical therapy–related lawsuits are reviewed here.

Incorrectly Interpreting Physician's Orders

Pontiff, in *Pontiff v. Pecot & Assoc.*,[92] filed a petition for damages against Pecot and Associates and Morris. Pontiff alleged Pecot and Associates had been negligent in failing to properly train, supervise, and monitor its employees, including Morris, and that Pecot and Associates was otherwise negligent. Pontiff alleged that employee Morris failed to exercise the degree of care and skill ordinarily exercised by physical therapists, failed to heed his protests that he could not perform the physical therapy treatments she was supervising, and failed to stop performing physical therapy treatments after he began to complain he was in pain. Pontiff claimed he felt a muscle tear while he was exercising on the butterfly machine, a resistive exercise machine.

Pontiff's expert, Boulet, a licensed practicing physical therapist, testified that Morris deviated from the standard of care of physical therapists by introducing a type of exercise that, according to her, was not prescribed by Dr. deAraujo, the treating physician. She stated that Pecot added resistive or strengthening exercises to Pontiff's therapy and these were not a part of the physician's prescription. Pecot argued that resistive exercises were implicitly part of the prescription, even if her interpretation of the prescription was not reasonable.

Legally, under Louisiana law, a physical therapist may not treat a patient without a written physical therapy prescription. Ethically, the Physical Therapists' Code of Ethics, Principle 3.4, states that any alteration of a program or extension of services beyond the program should be undertaken in consultation with the referring practitioner. Because resistive exercises were not set forth in the original prescription, Boulet stated that consultation with the physician was necessary before Pontiff could be advanced to that level. Only in the case where a physician has indicated on the prescription that the therapist is to evaluate and treat would the therapist have such discretion. There was no such indication on the prescription written by deAraujo.

Davis, a physical therapist in private practice and Pecot's expert witness, testified that the program that Pecot designed for Pontiff was consistent with how she interpreted the prescription for therapy that the physician wrote. Davis, however, did not at any time state that Pecot's interpretation was a reasonable one. In fact, Davis herself would not have interpreted the prescription in the manner that Pecot did. Davis testified only that Pecot's introduction of resistive exercises was reasonable based on her interpretation of the prescription.

It is clear that Pecot, as a licensed physical therapist, owed a duty to Pontiff, her client. Pecot's duty is defined by the standard of care of similar physical therapists and the American Physical Therapy Association. If Pecot found the prescription to be ambiguous, she had a duty to contact the prescribing physician for clarification. The appeals court found that the trial court was correct in its determination that Pontiff presented sufficient evidence to show that this duty was breached and that Pecot's care fell below the standard of other physical therapists.

Termination of Contracted Services

The physical therapist in *Armintor v. Community Hospital of Brazosport*[93] was properly enjoined from entering the hospital's premises after termination of an oral contract to furnish services to hospital patients in need of physical therapy. Substantial evidence supported the court's finding that the hospital's attempt to establish a hospital-based physical therapy program would have been disrupted if the independent therapist had been permitted to continue treating patients. The court considered the exclusion of a therapist an administrative matter within the board's discretion. The therapist's entering the hospital without the permission of a staff physician would constitute trespass and would be in violation of hospital policy.

Neglect

In *Zucker v. Axelrod*,[94] a physical therapist had been charged with resident neglect for refusing to allow an 82-year-old nursing facility resident to go to the bathroom before starting his therapy treatment session. Undisputed evidence at a hearing showed that the petitioner refused to allow the resident to be excused to go to the bathroom. The petitioner claimed that her refusal was because she assumed that the resident had gone to the bathroom before going to therapy and that the resident was undergoing a bladder-training program. The petitioner had not mentioned when she was interviewed after the incident or during her hearing testimony that she considered bladder training a basis for refusing to allow the resident to go to the bathroom. It is uncontroverted that the nursing facility had a policy of allowing residents to go to the bathroom whenever they wished to do so. The court determined that the evidence supported a finding of resident neglect.

Physical Therapist License Revoked

The license of a physical therapist was found to have been properly revoked by the Bureau of Professional and Occupational Affairs, State Board of Physical Therapy after the therapist had been disciplined in other states. In New Jersey, the board of physical therapy denied Girgis a license to practice physical therapy. The Michigan Board of Physical Therapy imposed a $1,000 fine on Girgis. The South Carolina Board of Physical Therapy suspended Girgis's license indefinitely. The New Hampshire Governing Board of Physical Therapy suspended Girgis's license for 5 months. The Montana Board of Physical Therapy Examiners revoked Girgis's license. The Medical Licensing Board of Indiana put Girgis's license on indefinite probation for no less than 2 years and later indefinitely suspended it for no less than 6 months and imposed a $500 fine because Girgis failed to comply with the terms of his probation. The Hawaii Board of Physical Therapy suspended Girgis's license for 5 months. The Florida Department of Health accepted Girgis's voluntary relinquishment of his Florida license.

Whether Girgis was incompetent, negligent, abusive, or a risk to patients in Pennsylvania was found to be wholly irrelevant. The sole inquiry is whether his license to practice physical therapy was suspended, revoked, or otherwise disciplined in another jurisdiction. Because he does not dispute that he was disciplined in eight states, the board did not err in disciplining him in Pennsylvania.[95]

▶ PHYSICIAN ASSISTANT

A *physician assistant* (PA) is a medical professional who is a graduate of an accredited PA educational training program and is nationally certified and state licensed to practice medicine, and, when required, by a state's regulations, under the supervision of a physician.

- According to California law, all care provided to a patient by a PA is the ultimate responsibility of the supervising physician.
- Current law allows a physician to supervise no more than four PAs at any moment in time.
- According to regulations, the physician must be in the same facility with the PA or be immediately available by electronic communications.
- Before authorizing a PA to perform any medical procedure, the physician is responsible for evaluating the PA's education, experience, knowledge, and ability to perform the procedure safely and competently. In addition, the physician should verify that a PA has a current California license issued by the Physician Assistant Board (Board website: www.pac.ca.gov).
- PAs may not own a medical practice. (Please see Section 13400 and following of the Corporations Code.)

- PAs may not hire their supervisors. PAs are dependent practitioners who act as agents on behalf of a supervising physician.[96]

The scope of a PA's practice must be in accordance with state law. For example, Californian law provides:

The scope of a given PA's practice is limited by his/her supervising physician. Whatever medical specialty a physician practices (e.g., general practice, cardio-thoracic surgery, dermatology, etc.) limits the PA's scope of practice. The Delegation of Services Agreement between the PA and the supervising physician then further defines exactly what tasks and procedures a physician is delegating to the PA. These tasks and procedures must be consistent with the supervising physician's specialty or usual and customary practice and with the patient's health and condition.[97]

One of the solutions to the shortage of physicians has been to train PAs, as well as nurse practitioners, to perform the more routine and repetitive medical procedures. PAs are generally licensed to administer injections, perform routine history and physical examinations, order and interpret tests, diagnose and treat patient ailments (e.g., assist in surgery, suture minor lacerations), prescribe medications, and provide patient education and counseling. A physician may not delegate a task to a PA in those instances where regulations specify that the physician must perform the task or when delegation of a task is prohibited under state law or by an organization's policies by which the PA is employed. The legal risks for PAs are as real as for any other physician.

PAs are responsible for their own negligent acts. The employer of a PA can be held liable for the PA's negligent acts on the basis of respondeat superior. Guidelines and procedures should be established, as with any professional, to provide a standard mechanism for reviewing a PA's skills and performance. The reader is encouraged to review applicable laws that regulate a PA's scope of practice, which may vary from state to state (e.g., Title 16 California Code of Regulations Section 1399.541). Due to the ever-increasing shortage of physicians, the educational requirements and scope of practice for PAs will most likely continue to expand.

Allan Navarro, in *Navarro v. Carrollwood Emergency Physicians,* was examined by a PA in the emergency room. The PA determined that the patient's head pain was due a sinus infection. The emergency physician on duty did not examine Navarro and sent him home based on the PA's evaluation. In fact, Navarro had suffered a stroke and subsequently went into a coma for 4 months. He survived but was paralyzed in three limbs. A jury awarded Navarro 216.7 million.[98] The lessons are clear for all caregivers, quality assessments are frontline to the decision-making process, which includes the recommended treatment for the patient.

▶ RADIOLOGY AND RELATED LAWSUITS

Medical imaging–related lawsuits include ordering unnecessary tests, physician kickbacks, patient falls, the negligent handling of equipment, improper lead shielding, and misdiagnosis. Lawsuits against radiologic technologists are rare. It has been reported "fewer than nine malpractice payments involving an X-ray technician are awarded each year. In more than half of these cases, payments do not exceed $50,000. These findings come from analysis of X-ray technician malpractice payments reported to the National Practitioner Data Bank over 18 years."[99]

JURY AWARDS $3 MILLION IN MALPRACTICE SUIT

When Lynn Flaherty visited her family doctor's office in Mt. Lebanon on Dec. 4, 2001, she had been having headaches and a nasal discharge – symptoms consistent with a sinus infection.

But the physician's assistant who saw her failed to make that diagnosis or to prescribe antibiotics. Instead, according to Mrs. Flaherty's attorney, his client received a prescription for steroids, was told to undergo additional testing and return in a week.

But just five days later, she developed stroke-like symptoms, including facial drooping and disorientation, said one of her attorneys, Stephen Del Sole.

• • •

But Mr. Del Sole said that the doctors in the office failed to follow the protocol they laid out in employing a physician's assistant.

On paperwork submitted with the state, Dr. DeGiovanni and Dr. Montini said they would see every patient treated by Ms. Egidi [Physician's Assistant].

"The testimony was undisputed that that did not happen," Mr. Del Sole said. "Clearly, the doctor would have treated her differently."

—Paula Reed Ward, *Pittsburgh Post-Gazette,* November 24, 2007

Unnecessary Tests and Physician Kickbacks

The Department of Justice, Office of Public Affairs reported that Diagnostic Imaging Services, which is headquartered in Hicksville, New York, agreed to pay $13.65 million to the federal government and an additional total of $1.85 million to New York and New Jersey "to resolve allegations that its diagnostic testing facility falsely billed federal and state health care programs for tests that were not performed or not medically necessary and by paying kickbacks to physicians."[100]

> The settlement announced today resolves allegations that DIG submitted claims to Medicare, as well as the New Jersey and New York Medicaid Programs, for 3D reconstructions of CT scans that were never performed or interpreted. Additionally, DIG allegedly bundled certain tests on its order forms so that physicians could not order other tests without ordering the additional bundled tests, which were not medically necessary.[101]

Patient Falls

For example, the plaintiff in *Cockerton v. Mercy Hospital Medical Center*[102] was admitted to the hospital for the purpose of surgery to correct a problem with her open bite. Her physician ordered postsurgical X-rays for her head and face to be taken the next day. A hospital employee took the plaintiff from her room to the X-ray department by wheelchair. A nurse assessed her condition as slightly drowsy. An X-ray technician took charge of the plaintiff in the X-ray room. After the plaintiff was taken inside the X-ray room, she was transferred from a wheelchair to a portable chair for the procedure. Upon being moved, the plaintiff complained of nausea, and the technician observed that the plaintiff's pupils were dilated. The technician did not use the restraint straps to secure the plaintiff to the chair. At some point during the procedure, the plaintiff had a fainting seizure, and the technician called for help. When another hospital employee entered the room, the technician was holding the plaintiff in an upright position; she appeared nonresponsive. The plaintiff only remembered being stood up and having a lead jacket placed across her back and shoulders. The technician maintains that the plaintiff did not fall. At the time the plaintiff left the X-ray room, her level of consciousness was poor. The plaintiff's physician noticed a deflection of the plaintiff's nose. Because the plaintiff had fainted in X-ray, an incident report was completed by request of the plaintiff's physician. The following day, the deflection of the plaintiff's nose was much more evident. A specialist was contacted, and an attempt was made to correct the deformity. The specialist made an observation that it would require a substantial injury to the nose to deflect it to that severity.

The plaintiff instituted proceedings against the hospital, alleging that the negligence of the nurses or technicians allowed her to fall during the procedure and subsequently caused injury. The trial court did not require expert testimony concerning the standard of care given by the technician. The jury concluded that the hospital was negligent in leaving the plaintiff unattended or failing to restrain her, which proximately caused her fall and injury. The jury returned a verdict of $48,370, and the hospital appealed.

The Iowa Court of Appeals held that the patient was not required to present expert testimony on the issue of the hospital's negligence. The conduct in question was simply the way the technician handled the plaintiff during the X-ray examination. The X-ray technician testified that during the X-ray, the plaintiff appeared to have a seizure episode. She also testified that she left the plaintiff unattended for a brief period and that she did not use the restraint straps that were attached to the portable X-ray chair. Using the restraint straps would have secured the plaintiff to the portable chair during the X-ray examination. The court found that substantial evidence existed to establish a causal connection between the hospital's conduct and the plaintiff's injury.

Improper Lead Shielding

Improper lead shielding when constructing imaging rooms can lead to lawsuits. Five lawsuits were filed in January 2014 against a hospital alleging that X-ray staff was exposed to excess radiation. The plaintiffs claimed "some walls in and around a radiology imaging center in the new emergency department were built without the required lead shielding, elevating the workers' risk of health problems, including cancer."[103] The plaintiffs did not prevail in their lawsuit where the Court of Appeals in June 2015 ruled in favor of the defendants.[104]

Misdiagnosis

A study to determine the most common causes of malpractice suits against radiologists was reported in the journal of the Radiological Society of North America (RSNA). The most common errors were related to misdiagnosis. Breast cancer was found to be the most frequently missed diagnosis, followed by non-spinal fractures, spinal fractures, lung cancer, and vascular disease. The category next in frequency was procedural complications, followed by inadequate communication with either patient or referrer. Failure

X-RAY CASSETTE FALLS ON PATIENT'S HEAD

Citation: Schopp v. Our Lady of the Lake Hospital, Inc., 739 So. 2d 338, 98 1382 (La. App. 1 Cir. 6/25/99)

Facts

On August 2, 1993, Sophie Schopp stumbled coming from her bathroom and fell, striking her head. She was unable to get up, so she lay on the floor until approximately 8:00 AM, when a home health aide came to her home for her daily visit. Her doors were locked, but Schopp told Montgomery to go across the street and get a key, which she did. Emergency medical services arrived shortly thereafter and took Schopp to the hospital. Her friend and neighbor, Guwang, followed in her car. Schopp's friend, Haper, also came to the hospital that morning.

Schopp was taken for skull X-rays, and when she returned, the X-ray technologist, Coates, told Haper and Guwang that there had been "a little accident." Haper testified that Coates said that the X-ray plate fell on her head. He pointed to Schopp's head and showed Haper where it had fallen on her. Haper stated she saw no mark or bruise and thought nothing more of it. Guwang testified, however, that she pushed back Schopp's hair and saw a blue mark on the left side of her forehead.

A computed tomography scan showed that Schopp had a large acute subdural hematoma. Dr. Perone, a board-certified neurosurgeon, performed surgery to evacuate the hematoma. Although Schopp seemed to improve initially following the surgery, her health declined thereafter, and she died on August 16, 1993.

Schopp's sons filed suit against the hospital (defendant) and two of the defendant's X-ray technologists, Coates and Smith. The plaintiffs later dismissed Coates and Smith but proceeded to jury trial against the hospital. The jury rendered a verdict in favor of the plaintiffs, and an appeal was taken for wrongful death.

Issue

Was Schopp's death caused by the negligence of hospital staff dropping an X-ray cassette on her head while she underwent a skull X-ray?

Holding

Schopp's death was caused by the negligence of hospital staff dropping an X-ray cassette on her head while she underwent a skull X-ray.

Reason

Although there was conflicting testimony as to the cause of death, Morris apparently gave the most convincing testimony regarding Schopp's injury. Morris stated that although he did not operate, he made the diagnoses that led to surgery. He pointed out he was the one who diagnosed the subdural hematoma. He stated that there was no doubt in his mind that the incident in the X-ray room caused the hematoma. He believed that the cartridge was dropped on Schopp's head based on her statements to him and the alarmed tone in the nurse's voice when she called him to report the X-ray incident. He saw the soft tissue swelling on Schopp's head and noted that the hematoma was in the exact place she had shown him where the cartridge struck her.

In this case, there were two versions of the X-ray room incident—either the cartridge tilted less than an inch and barely brushed Schopp's head, leaving no mark, or it was dropped from some distance and struck her with enough force to leave a soft tissue injury. The jury chose to believe the second version.

to recommend additional testing was found to be a rare cause of malpractice lawsuits in this study.[105]

▶ RESPIRATORY THERAPIST

Respiratory therapy is the allied health profession responsible for the treatment, management, diagnostic testing, and control of patients with cardiopulmonary deficits. A respiratory therapist is a person employed in the practice of respiratory care who has the knowledge and skill necessary to administer such care (**FIGURE 12-6**). Respiratory therapists are responsible for their negligent acts, and a respiratory therapist's employer is responsible for the

negligent acts of the therapist under the legal doctrine of respondeat superior.

Failure to Remove Endotracheal Tube

The court, in *Poor Sisters of St. Francis v. Catron*,[106] held that the failure of nurses and an inhalation therapist to report to the supervisor that an endotracheal tube had been left in the plaintiff longer than the customary period of 3 or 4 days was sufficient to allow the jury to reach a finding of negligence.

It is clear that, while in most cases the nursing staff is not negligent in following the orders

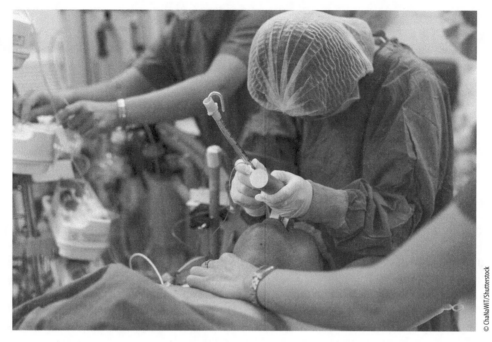

FIGURE 12-6 Insertion of Endotracheal Tube

given by the attending physician, an exception to this rule exists when the nurse or other hospital employee knows the doctor's orders are not in accordance with normal medical practice. *Toth v. Community Hospital at Glen Cove*, (1968) 22 N.Y.2d 255, 292 N.Y.S.2d 440, 239 N.E.2d 368.[107]

The patient experienced difficulty speaking and underwent several operations to remove scar tissue and open her voice box. At the time of trial, she could not speak above a whisper and breathed partially through a hole in her throat created by a tracheotomy. The hospital was found liable for the negligent acts of its employees and the resulting injuries to the plaintiff.

Neither the nurses in ICU nor the inhalation therapists reported Weller's treatment of Catron to their supervisors although they were aware the endotracheal tube was being left in the patient longer than the customary three to four day period. Similarly, the nurses did not bring to Weller's attention the fact that the tube was being left in longer than usual.[108]

Multiple Use of Same Syringe

The respiratory therapist in *State University v. Young*[109] was suspended for using the same syringe for drawing blood from several critically ill patients. The therapist had been warned several times of the dangers of that practice and that it violated the state's policy of providing quality patient care. The arbitrator's penalty was a 2-month suspension without pay.

The State University of New York thereupon commenced this proceeding to vacate so much of the arbitrator's award as imposed that penalty, as violative of the State's strong public policy to protect and care for its patients, particularly those who are unable to care for themselves. The Supreme Court concluded that the lesser penalty imposed by the arbitrator did, in fact, violate that public policy, and vacated that portion of the arbitrator's award.[110]

Restocking the Code Cart

Dixon had been admitted to the hospital and was diagnosed with pneumonia in her right lung. Dixon's condition began to deteriorate, and she was moved to the intensive care unit (ICU). A code blue was eventually called, signifying that her cardiac and respiratory functions were believed to have ceased. During the code, a decision was made to intubate, which is to insert an endotracheal tube into Dixon so that she could be given respiratory support by a mechanical ventilator. As Dixon's condition stabilized, Dr. Taylor, Dixon's physician at that time, ordered that she gradually be weaned from the respirator. Blackham, a respiratory therapist employed by the hospital, extubated Dixon at 10:15 PM. Taylor left Dixon's room to advise her family that she had been extubated. Blackham decided an oxygen mask would provide better oxygen to Dixon but could not locate a mask in the ICU, so he left the ICU and went across the hall to the critical care unit (CCU). When Blackham returned to Dixon's room with the oxygen mask and placed it on Dixon, he realized that she was not breathing properly. Blackham realized that she would have to be reintubated as quickly as possible.

A second code was called. Shackleford, a nurse in the cardiac CCU, responded to the code. Shackleford recorded on the code sheet that she arrived in Dixon's room at 10:30 PM. She testified that Blackham said he had too short of a blade and he needed a medium, a Number 4 MacIntosh laryngoscope blade, which was not on the code cart. The code cart is a cart equipped with all the medicines, supplies, and instruments needed for a code emergency. The code cart in the ICU had not been restocked after the first code that morning, so Shackleford was sent to obtain the needed blade from the CCU across the hall. When Shackleford returned to the ICU, the blade was passed to Taylor, who had responded to the code and was attempting to reintubate Dixon. Upon receiving the blade, Taylor was able to quickly intubate Dixon. Dixon was placed on a ventilator, but she never regained consciousness. After the family was informed that there was no hope that Dixon would recover the use of her brain, the family requested that no extraordinary measure be taken to prolong her life.

A medical negligence claim was filed against Taylor and the hospital. The jury found that Taylor was not negligent. Evidence presented at trial established that the hospital's breach of duty in not having the code cart properly restocked resulted in a 3-minute delay in the intubation of Dixon. Reasonable minds could accept from the testimony at trial that the hospital's breach of duty was a cause of Dixon's brain death, without which the injury would not have occurred. Foreseeability on the part of the hospital could be established from the evidence introduced by the plaintiff that the written standards for the hospital require every code cart be stocked with a Number 4 MacIntosh blade. This evidence permits a reasonable inference that the hospital should have foreseen that the failure to have the code cart stocked with the blade could lead to critical delays in intubating a patient. Accordingly, there was substantial evidence that failure to have the code cart stocked with the proper blade was a proximate cause of Dixon's injuries.[111]

▶ CHIROPRACTOR

A chiropractor is required to exercise the same degree of care, judgment, and skill exercised by other reasonable chiropractors under like or similar circumstances. He or she has a duty to determine whether a patient is treatable through chiropractic means and to refrain from chiropractic treatment when a reasonable chiropractor would or should be aware that a patient's condition will not respond to chiropractic treatment. Although the American Chiropractic Association says that neck manipulation is a safe procedure, there are associated risks with chiropractics as with any medical procedure. Failure to conform to the standard of care can result in liability for any injuries suffered.

Lawsuits against chiropractors often involve a failure to properly diagnose a patient's medical condition and harm as a result of treatments, such as manipulation of the spine and neck. For example, a patient stated that she knew she was in trouble shortly after a chiropractor began to manipulate her neck. She said she knew what was happening and told the chiropractor, "Stop. I'm having a stroke."[112] The patient stated that if she had been told that there would be a risk of a stroke she would not have continued with the treatment.[113] As with any medical procedure, the chiropractor should inform each patient as to the risks, benefits, and alternatives associated with a suggested procedure. All patients should sign a consent form acknowledging that they have been informed of the risks, benefits, and alternatives to the recommended procedure.

▶ DENTISTRY

Dental malpractice includes the failure to diagnose (e.g., temporomandibular joint disorder, oral cancer); misdiagnosis; improper treatment; failure to

NEWS VA HOSPITAL MAY HAVE INFECTED 1,800 VETERANS WITH HIV

A Missouri VA hospital is under fire because it may have exposed more than 1,800 veterans to life-threatening diseases such as hepatitis and HIV . . .

Dr. Gina Michael, the association chief of staff at the hospital, told the affiliate that some dental technicians broke protocol by hand washing tools before putting them in cleaning machines. . . .

In June, Palomar Hospital in San Diego, California, has sent certified letters to 3,400 patients who underwent colonoscopy and other similar procedures, informing the patients that there may be a potential of infection from items used and reused in the procedures.

—CNN Wire Staff, *CNN U.S.*, June 30, 2010

follow acceptable standards of dental care (e.g., sterile techniques that are common to the practice of dentistry, such as equipment sterilization); infections; complications from the administration of anesthesia; extraction of the wrong tooth (teeth); failure to refer to a specialist; and complications that arise out of various dental procedures, such as dental implants, failed root canal, nerve damage involving the jaw, face, chin, lips, and tongue. Injuries can involve high-speed drills damaging the tongue, which can result in permanent loss of sensation or taste, and failure to supervise staff.

Professional competence or conduct that adversely affects a dentist's membership on the hospital's medical-dental staff must be reported to the National Practitioner Data Bank (NPDB). Adverse actions involve the reduction, restriction, suspension, revocation, or denial of clinical privileges or membership in a healthcare entity.[114] Adverse actions must be submitted to the NPDB and appropriate state licensing board within 30 days of such actions taken by a hospital.[115] There were 13,729 adverse actions against dentists between 2005 and 2015.[116] A variety of dental malpractice cases are reviewed here.

Drill Bit Left in Tooth

The patient in *Mazor v. Isaacman*[117] visited the defendant dentist in August 1997 for routine root canal surgery. After the surgery, the patient began experiencing constant pain in the tooth in which the root canal was performed. The dentist explained to the patient that such pain was ordinarily felt after root canal surgery. In February 1999, the patient visited another dentist, who discovered that a piece of a drill bit had been left inside the patient's tooth during the previous root canal. The patient filed a lawsuit against the defendant-dentist for dental malpractice. The defendant-dentist filed a motion to dismiss, arguing that the patient did not bring the claim within the 1-year statute of limitations. This motion was granted, and the patient appealed. The Tennessee Court of Appeals reversed the finding, holding that the patient had 1 year from the time she discovered or should have discovered the foreign object in which to file her lawsuit.

Tennessee Code Annotated § 29-26-116(a)(4) (2000) states that "where a foreign object has been negligently left in a patient's body . . . the action shall be commenced within one (1) year after the alleged injury or wrongful act is discovered or should have been discovered." This statute has been interpreted to require only that the plaintiff bring the action within one year after the foreign object was discovered or should have been discovered.

Failure to Refer

Dr. Smith told O'Neal that tooth number 14, an upper left molar, should be extracted. O'Neal advised Smith that another dentist warned her that tooth number 14 should not be pulled because it was embedded in the sinus. Smith responded that all of her top teeth were in the sinus and that extraction was no problem. O'Neal relented to Smith's judgment, and tooth number 14 was extracted. Complications developed in the extraction process, resulting in an oral antral perforation of the sinus cavity wall. Four days after the extraction, Smith began root canal work, even though the antral opening wound was not healed. Three weeks after the extraction, a tissue mass developed in the tooth socket and the patient was referred to Dr. Herbert, an oral surgeon.

Herbert testified that the degree of infection inhibited proper healing and closure of the extraction site. After several more months, O'Neal was referred to Dr. Berman, an ear, nose, and throat specialist. Because of the continual deterioration, Berman performed a surgical procedure that sealed the extraction site. The surgery required hospitalization.

O'Neal brought a malpractice action against Smith.[118] The trial court entered judgment in favor of O'Neal. Smith appealed, arguing that the evidence was factually insufficient to support the judgment. An expert witness had testified that Smith was negligent for not referring the patient to an oral surgeon for the necessary extraction because of the known risks of roots embedded in the sinus floor. Smith was also negligent for not referring the patient to a specialist when the antral perforation first occurred and later by not referring her to a specialist when the fistula and the infection manifested. On appeal, expert testimony was found sufficient to support a jury finding that the defendant was negligent in the treatment of his patient.

Lack of Consent

The plaintiff in *Gaskin v. Goldwasser*[119] brought a suit against an oral surgeon alleging dental malpractice. The oral surgeon had removed 19 of the teeth remaining in the plaintiff's mouth. The defendant admitted that 5 of the 19 teeth were removed without the consent of the patient. The circuit court entered a judgment for the plaintiff on a jury verdict for damages resulting from the extraction of the five lower teeth. On appeal, the appellate court held:

> In conclusion, we find the cumulative errors committed during trial warrant reversal. The jury should have been instructed regarding the proper use of evidence of the plaintiff's

past conduct, that being to assess the amount of damage sustained. The counts alleging willful and wanton misconduct and battery for the unauthorized removal of the five lower teeth were supported by the evidence and, thus, were improperly dismissed. The trial court properly directed a verdict on liability for removal of the five teeth.[120]

The patient was entitled to have the allegation of willful and wanton misconduct and battery for unauthorized removal of the lower teeth submitted to the jury. The case was remanded for a new trial.

Failure to Prescribe Antibiotics

In *Pasquale v. Miller*,[121] the plaintiff brought a suit against the defendant, Dr. Miller, for dental malpractice. Miller treated the plaintiff for swollen gums. He removed tissue from the patient's gums and used sutures to control the bleeding. Although it was common practice to prescribe antibiotics prior to or following gum surgery, Miller failed to prescribe antibiotics in either case. The following May, after the plaintiff experienced a persistent fever, she was diagnosed as having contracted subacute bacterial endocarditis. The plaintiff was treated in the hospital for nearly a month. Miller claimed that the bacterial infection could have resulted from a number of causes. The trial court, upon a jury verdict, found for the plaintiff. An appeals court held that the evidence supported a finding of causation.

The plaintiff's expert witnesses testified that her endocarditis was related to the dental surgery and that one of the risks of not prescribing an antibiotic is that bacteria can flow through the bloodstream to the heart. The jury rejected testimony from Miller that endocarditis could have been caused by something other than failure to administer antibiotics prior to or following gum surgery.

Failure to Follow Sterile Technique

In *Kirschner v. Mills*,[122] there was sufficient evidence to support a charge that the dentist failed to wear protective gloves while performing a medical examination. That charge was supported by testimony of the patient, whom a hearing panel found to be credible, that the dentist did not wear gloves during the examination. The violation of accepted practice also was supported by the testimony of the dentist's own expert, a fellow dentist, who opined that it was necessary to wear gloves any time you put your hands on a patient.

Practicing Outside Scope of Competency

Brown, in *Brown v. Belinfante*,[123] sued Dr. Belinfante and the Atlanta Orthofacial Surgicenter, LLC, after Belinfante performed several elective cosmetic procedures including a face-lift, eyelid revision, and facial laser resurfacing. Belinfante is not a physician. He is licensed to practice dentistry in Georgia and was employed by the Surgicenter. Brown claims that after the cosmetic procedures, she could not close her eyes completely, developed chronic bilateral eye infections, and required remedial corrective surgery. Among other things, Brown alleged that Belinfante's performance of the cosmetic procedures constituted negligence per se because he exceeded the scope of the practice of dentistry.

The Georgia Court of Appeals held that cosmetic procedures of this nature do not fall within Georgia statutes. The primary purposes of the Georgia Dental Act are to define and regulate the practice of dentistry. The statute limits the scope of the practice of dentistry. Such limitation protects the health and welfare of patients who submit themselves to the care of dentists by guarding against injuries caused by inadequate care or by unauthorized individuals. Brown falls within that class of persons that the statute was intended to protect, and the harm complained of was of the type the statute was intended to guard against. In performing the elective cosmetic procedures, Belinfante violated the Dental Practice Act by exceeding the statutory limits of the scope of dentistry and, therefore, committed negligence per se.

Failure to Supervise Dental Assistant

The plaintiff in *Hickman v. Sexton Dental Clinic*[124] brought a malpractice action against a dental clinic for a serious cut under her tongue. The dental assistant, without being supervised by a dentist, placed a sharp object into the patient's mouth, cutting her tongue while taking impressions for dentures. The court of common pleas entered a judgment on a jury verdict in favor of the plaintiff, and the clinic appealed. The court of appeals held that evidence presented was sufficient to infer without the aid of expert testimony that there was a breach of duty to the patient. Tepper presented the following testimony regarding denture impressions:[125]

> Q. You also stated that you have taken, I believe, thousands?
>
> A. Probably more than that.
>
> Q. Of impressions?

A. Yes, sir.

Q. This never happened before?

A. No, sir, not a laceration.

Q. Would it be safe and accurate to say that if someone's mouth were to be cut during the impression process, someone did something wrong?

A. Yes, sir.

The testimony of Dr. Tepper, the clinic dentist, was found pertinent to the issue of the common knowledge exception in which the evidence permits the jury to recognize breach of duty without the aid of expert testimony.

Dental Hygienist Administers Nitrous Oxide

A dental hygienist alleged that her employer-defendant allowed dental hygienists to administer nitrous oxide to patients. Under New York state law, dental hygienists may not administer nitrous oxide. The Department of Education's Office of Professional Discipline investigated the complaint by using an undercover investigator. The investigator made an appointment for teeth cleaning. At the time of her appointment, she requested that nitrous oxide be administered. Agreeing to the investigator's request, the dental hygienist administered the nitrous oxide. There were no notations in the patient's chart indicating that she had been administered nitrous oxide.

A hearing panel found the dental hygienist guilty of administering nitrous oxide without being properly licensed. In addition, the hearing panel found that the dental hygienist had failed to accurately record in the patient's chart that she administered nitrous oxide.

The New York Supreme Court, Appellate Division, held that the investigator's report provided sufficient evidence to support the hearing panel's determination. There is adequate evidence in the record to support a finding that the dentist's conduct was such that it could reasonably be said that he permitted the dental hygienist to perform acts that she was not licensed to perform.[126]

▶ PODIATRIST

Podiatry is that branch of medicine involving the study of, diagnosis, and medical treatment of disorders of the feet, ankles, and lower extremities.

Although the scope of practice is based on a state's licensing laws, podiatrists generally provide the following services: perform complete medical histories and physical examinations, order and interpret imaging studies, prescribe medications, perform minor surgery and set fractures, prescribe and fit orthotics, and prescribe physical therapy as required. The legal concerns of podiatrists, similar to those of surgeons, include misdiagnosis and negligent surgery. The podiatrist, for example, in *Strauss v. Biggs*[127] was found to have failed to meet the standard of care required of a podiatrist, and that failure resulted in injury to the patient. The podiatrist, by his own admission, stated that his initial incision in the patient's foot had been misplaced. The trial court was found not to have erred in permitting the jury to consider additional claims that the podiatrist acted improperly by failing to refer the patient, stop the procedure after the first incision, inform the patient of possible nerve injury, and provide proper postoperative treatment. Testimony of the patient's experts was adequate to show that such alleged omissions violated the standard of care required of podiatrists.

▶ SECURITY

Hospitals have a duty to implement reasonable security measures to protect patients, visitors, and staff from the criminal acts of third parties. However, if an attack and injury to a patient is not foreseeable, the hospital's actions cannot be the proximate cause of the patient's injuries. For example, the patient in *Lane v. St. Joseph's Regional Medical Center*[128] was sitting in the emergency department waiting room when a teenage boy, D.G., arrived with his mother. After they had all sat in the waiting room for a short period, D.G. walked up to Lane and began to hit her on her right arm and shoulder. Lane's son-in-law, who had accompanied her to the emergency room, jumped to her aid and struck D.G., knocking him to the floor. The attack stopped, and nothing further happened. Lane suffered some injuries as a result of the attack. The evidence in this case depicts a situation in which the attack upon Lane by D.G. was unexpected and that no other evidence was designated to the trial court from which it could have concluded that the specific actions of D.G. on the day in question were foreseeable. The court was bound to conclude that the attack and injury were not foreseeable, that the center's actions were not the proximate cause of Lane's injuries, and that the center is entitled to judgment as a matter of law.

🔍 *FAILURE TO PROVIDE ADEQUATE SECURITY*

Citation: *Hanewinckel v. St. Paul's Property & Liab.*, 611 So. 2d 174 (La. App. 1992)

Facts

The plaintiff, a nurse anesthetist, arrived at the hospital at approximately 5:25 AM. After parking her car and before she shut off the engine, a man jumped into the driver's seat and began to drive off. The nurse jumped from the car but her attacker caught her and started to beat her. An employee pulling into the parking lot saw what was happening and alerted security. The plaintiff suffered a broken left wrist, 12 teeth either knocked out or broken, severe bruises on her face, and cuts on her legs and knees. She also suffered mental distress from which she had not recovered.

The nurse sued the owner of the parking lot and the security force for breach to protect her from a criminal attack committed on the premises. The trial court found that the defendant had a duty to provide reasonable and adequate security in the parking area and that it had breached this duty.

Issue

Did the hospital breach a duty by failing to adequately patrol its parking lot?

Holding

The court of appeals affirmed the decision for the plaintiff, finding that the hospital breached its duty to the employee by failing to patrol the parking lot.

Reason

The hospital took on the responsibility of maintaining a security force to cover the parking lot. As such, the hospital assumed liability, giving a warranty that, through employment of a security service, their work would be carried out in a non-negligent manner. The evidence indicated that other witnesses had seen the attacker in or near the parking lot 5 hours earlier in the day, yet no security personnel spotted him. The court found that the security force breached its duty by negligently failing to provide adequate security, which should have included random patrolling of all of the areas. After the attacker was reported to security earlier in the day, nothing other than a brief walk-through of the lot was done.

Hospitals clearly have a duty to care and that duty was breached in this case. The duty here was to provide adequate security in parking areas. This duty extends beyond parking and includes both inside and outside hospital property. Where there is a nearby security concern off hospital grounds, hospital security must have a cooperative relationship with law enforcement agencies.

▶ LICENSURE AND CERTIFICATION OF HEALTHCARE PROFESSIONALS

An overview of the education, certification, licensure, and credentialing process that apply to healthcare professionals, such as physicians, nurses, and EMS personnel are reviewed in this section.

Licensure

Licensure can be defined as the process by which a competent authority grants permission to a qualified individual or entity to perform certain restricted activities that would be illegal without a license. As it applies to healthcare personnel, *licensure* refers to the process by which state licensing boards, agencies, or departments grant to individuals who meet certain predetermined standards the legal right to practice in a healthcare profession and to use a specified healthcare practitioner's title. The commonly stated objectives of licensing laws are to limit and control admission to the different healthcare occupations and to protect the public from unqualified practitioners by promulgating and enforcing standards of practice within the professions. The scope of practice of a particular profession represents the patient care activities that a licensed individual can legally perform.

The authority of states to license healthcare practitioners is found in its regulating power. Implicit in the power to license is the authority to collect license fees, establish standards of practice, require certain minimum qualifications and competency levels of applicants, and impose on applicants other requirements necessary to protect the general public welfare. This authority, which is vested in the legislature, may be delegated to political subdivisions or to state boards, agencies, and departments. In some instances, the scope of the delegated power is made specific in the legislation; in others, the licensing authority may have wide discretion in performing its functions. In either case, however, the authority granted by the legislature may not be exceeded.

Suspension and Revocation of License

Licensing boards have the authority to suspend or revoke the license of a healthcare professional found to have violated specified norms of conduct. Such violations may include procurement of a license by fraud; unprofessional, dishonorable, immoral, or illegal conduct; performance of specific actions prohibited by statute; and malpractice. Suspension and revocation procedures are most commonly contained in a state's licensing act; in some jurisdictions however, the procedure is left to the discretion of the board or is contained in the general administrative procedure acts.

Certification of Healthcare Professionals

The *certification* of healthcare professionals is the recognition by a governmental or professional association that an individual's competencies meet the standards of that group in delivering quality patient care. Some professional groups establish their own minimum standards for certification in those professions that are not licensed by a particular state. Certification by an association or group is a self-regulation credentialing process. Certification exams are designed to verify that an individual has achieved minimum competency standards to assure safe and quality patient care.

▶ HELPFUL ADVICE FOR CAREGIVERS

If we do not hang together, we will all hang separately.
—Benjamin Franklin (1706–1790)

Teamwork is the process of working cooperatively with others. In the healthcare setting, caregivers must work together to improve patient outcomes. The healthcare worker today works in an environment where change is the norm. Technologic change is occurring at a pace faster then the human mind can absorb, thus requiring teamwork among individuals with a wide variety of skill sets. The following list provides some helpful advice that will promote teamwork and improve patient care.

- Abide by the ethical code of one's profession.
- Do not criticize the professional skills of others.
- Maintain complete and adequate medical records.
- Inform the patient of the risks, benefits, and alternatives to proposed procedures.
- Provide each patient with medical care comparable with national standards.
- Be a good listener, and allow each patient sufficient time to express fears and anxieties.
- Foster a sense of trust and feeling of significance.
- Communicate with the patient and other caregivers.
- Seek the aid of professional medical consultants when indicated.
- Obtain informed consent for diagnostic and therapeutic procedures.
- Do not indiscriminately prescribe medications or diagnostic tests.
- Practice the specialty in which you have been trained.
- Keep patient information confidential.
- Check patient equipment regularly, and monitor it for safe use.
- When terminating a professional relationship with a patient, give adequate written notice to the patient.
- Authenticate all telephone orders.
- Obtain a qualified substitute when you will be absent from your practice.
- Investigate patient incidents promptly.
- Develop and implement an interdisciplinary plan of care for each patient.
- Safely administer patient medications.
- Closely monitor each patient's response to treatment.
- Provide cost-effective care without sacrificing quality.
- Provide education and teaching to patients.
- Participate in continuing education programs.

🔍 THE COURT'S DECISION

The parents were offered an out-of-court settlement totaling $200,000. This tragedy might have been prevented if the patient had been screened and triaged by a person competent to determine the patient's need for immediate care. Failure to assign triage responsibility to a competent individual can lead to lawsuits that involve not only the hospital, but also the supervisor who assigns responsibilities to unqualified staff members. First-level managers who have knowledge of such practices and allow them to occur also can be held liable for negligence.

▶ CHAPTER REVIEW

1. Healthcare professionals are required to adhere to the prevalent standards of care required within their professions. This includes proper assessment, reassessment, diagnosis, treatment, and follow-up care.

2. Lawsuits arise in a wide variety of patient care settings (e.g., emergency transport services, emergency department, physical therapy, radiology) and office practices (e.g., chiropractic, dentistry). Other patient care–related services include laboratory, pharmacy, podiatry, nutritional, and respiratory care.

3. Emergency medical services lawsuits involving paramedics include, for example, the wrong dosage of drugs administered, inability to diagnose a patient's extent of injury, and failure to transport a patient.

4. Some of the more common issues involving emergency department lawsuits include failure to conduct an adequate physical examination, failure to admit a patient, insufficient or contradictory medical documentation, failure to render care, and inappropriate discharge or transfer.

5. When the skills of a specialist are required in an emergency department, hospitals are required to notify an on-call specialty physician for assistance.

6. Healthcare organizations are responsible for the quality and timeliness of the services provided by their clinical laboratories. When laboratory services are contracted, such as often occurs in nursing facilities, the contracted lab should be properly vetted to ensure that it is a reputable licensed laboratory.

7. The nutritional needs of each patient must be met during his or her stay in an organization's facility. Organizations are responsible for the provision of nourishing, palatable, well-balanced diets. Each diet should meet the daily nutritional and special dietary needs of the respective patient.

8. Medication errors are common as a result of many factors, including the vast number of drugs available and their similar names and appearances. These errors constitute a leading cause of injury. In addition to federal laws regarding the manufacture, use, and handling of drugs, states also have legislation designed to regulate pharmacies.

9. In addition to their regular duties to manage the pharmacy and accurately dispense medications, pharmacists are required to maintain patient medication profiles and monitor these profiles for incompatibilities between drug–drug and food–drug interactions.

10. Physical therapists evaluate patients' disabilities and potential for rehabilitation for the purpose of preventing and treating neuromuscular or musculoskeletal disabilities.

11. Physician assistants are responsible for their own negligent actions; in addition, their employers also can be held responsible for their negligent acts based on respondeat superior.

12. Lawsuits in the practice of dentistry involve, for example, failure to: refer; obtain patient consent; prescribe antibiotics; sterilize equipment; practice within one's scope of competency; and supervise office staff.

13. Hospitals have a duty to implement reasonable security measures to protect patients, visitors and staff from the criminal acts of third parties.

14. *Licensure* of healthcare professionals is the process through which licensing boards, agencies, or departments grant to individuals who meet certain criteria the legal right to practice in a healthcare profession and use the title of a healthcare practitioner.

15. Certification is an external verification of the competencies that an individual has achieved and typically involves an examination process.

16. Credentialing is a process by which an individual is permitted to perform a specific procedure in a designated setting (e.g., hospital).

▶ REVIEW QUESTIONS

1. Describe the four common levels of EMS personnel (emergency medical responder, emergency medical technician, advanced emergency medical technician, and paramedic).

2. Describe the wide variety of legal issues that occur in the emergency department setting.

3. Discuss the purpose of the Emergency Medical Treatment and Active Labor Act.

4. Should medical advice be dispensed on the telephone? Explain your opinion.

5. Describe negligence-related risks when providing laboratory, nutritional, pharmacy, physical therapy, podiatry, radiology, respiratory, chiropractic, dentistry, and podiatric services.

6. Discuss why a hospital has a duty to provide adequate security on its premises.

7. Describe the purpose of licensure, certification, and credentialing.

8. Describe the importance of teamwork in the provision of patient care.

▶ NOTES

1. Ronnie Green, "Dying at the Hospital's Door: A Child Lost, Troubling Questions," *The Miami Herald*, April 16, 1995, p. 14A.

2. National Scope of Practice EMS Model, National Safety Highway Safety Administration. https://www.ems.gov/education/EMSScope.pdf.

3. Dr. Severo Rodriquez, A Letter from the Executive Director, *2016 Report, National Registry of Emergency Medical Technicians*, 2016 at 04.

4. National Scope of Practice EMS Model, National Safety Highway Safety Administration at 9.

5. National Scope of Practice EMS Model, National Safety Highway Safety Administration at 10.

6. Drug Enforcement Administration, Officer Safety Alert: Carfentanil: A Dangerous New Factor in the U.S. Opioid Crisis," https://www.dea.gov/divisions/hq/2016/hq092216_attach.pdf.

7. *Id.* at 23.

8. *Id.* at 24.

9. *Id.* at 26.

10. *Id.* at 27–18.

11. 600 P.2d 647 (Wash. Ct. App. 1979).

12. 1971 Wash. Laws § 1783.

13. 187 SW.3d 828 (2006).

14. 462 A.2d 680 (Pa. 1983).

15. 650 A.2d 1076 (Pa. Super. 1994).

16. 933 S.2d 627 (La. 2006).

17. *In re Application of Benton*, No. 23232 (S.D. 2005).

18. The Robert Wood Johnson Foundation, "Negligent Medical Care: What Is It, Where Is It, and How Widespread Is It?" *Abridge* (Spring 1991):7.

19. 42 U.S.C.A. § 1395dd(a) (1992).

20. 42 U.S.C.A. § 1395dd(e)(1) (1992).

21. *Nolen v. Boca Raton Community Hospital, Inc.*, 373 F.3d 1151 (2004).

22. 42 U.S.C.A. § 1395dd(3)(A) (1992).

23. 830 F. Supp. 1399 (M.D. Ala. 1993).

24. 934 F.2d 1362 (5th Cir. Tex. 1991).

25. "Courts Uphold Law, Regulations Against Patient Dumping," *Nation's Health* (August 1991):1.

26. 134 F.3d 319 (5th Cir. 1998).

27. 831 F. Supp. 829 (M.D. Ala. 1993).

28. 811 F. Supp. 121 (W.D. N.Y. 1993).

29. 689 So. 2d 696 (La. App. 1997).

30. 288 A.2d 379 (Md. 1972).

31. 271 N.W.2d 8 (S.D. 1978).

32. 477 So. 2d 1036 (Fla. Dist. Ct. App. 1985).

33. *Id.* at 1039.

34. 14 S.W.3d 42 (Mo. App. 1999).

35. *Id.* at 48.

36. *Id.*

37. *Id.* at 49.

38. *Cleland v. Bronson Health Care Group*, 917 F.2d 266, 272 (6th Cir. 1990).

39. *Griffith v. University Hospitals of Cleveland*, No. 84314 (Ohio Ct. App. 2004).

40. *Roy v. Gupta*, 606 So.2d 940 (La. Ct. App. 1992).

41. *Feeney v. New England Medical Center, Inc.*, 615 N.E.2d 585 (Mass. App. Ct. 1993).

42. 698 So. 2d 958 (La. App. 1997).

43. 498 S.E.2d 408 (1998).

44. *Baptist Mem'l Hosp. Sys. v. Sampson*, 969 S.W.2d 945, 947 (Tex. 1998).

45. Martin C. McWilliams, Jr. and Hamilton E. Russell III, Hospital Liability for Torts of Independent Contractor Physicians, 47 S.C. L. REV. 431, 473 (1996).

46. *Martell v. St Charles Hosp.*, 523 N.Y.S.2d 342, 352 (N.Y. Sup. Ct. 1987).

47. *Guerrero v. Copper Queen Hosp.*, 537 P.2d 1329 (Ariz. 1975).

48. https://www.usatoday.com/story/news/2015/02/04/cdc-releases-ebola-lab-incident-report/22754861/.

49. U.S. Department of Justice, "Two Cardiovascular Disease Testing Laboratories to Pay $48.5 Million to Settle Claims of Paying Kickbacks and Conducting Unnecessary Testing," *Justice News*, April 9, 2015. https://www.justice.gov/opa/pr/two-cardiovascular-disease-testing-laboratories-pay-485-million-settle-claims-paying.

50. Lena H. Sun, *The Washington Post*, August 6, 2010.

51. 663 F. Supp. 1048 (D.D.C. 1987).

52. 675 F. Supp. 1060 (D.C. Ky. 1987).

53. 866 F.2d 219 (6th Cir. 1989).

54. 835 S.W.2d 689 (Tex. Ct. App. 1992).

55. *Bramer v. Dotson*, 437 S.E.2d 775 (W. Va. 1993).

56. 797 So. 2d 160 (2001).

57. 661 S.W.2d 534 (Mo. 1983).

58. 532 A.2d 1081 (Md. Ct. Spec. App. 1987).

59. *Id.* at 1088.
60. 761 F. Supp. 665 (D.C. Minn. 1991).
61. *Id.* at 667.
62. *Id.* at 670.
63. 521 N.E.2d 350 (Ind. Ct. App. 1988).
64. *Id.* 354.
65. 107 S. Ct. 1131 (1987).
66. 640 So. 2d 476 (La. App. 3d Cir. 1994).
67. *Id.* at 479.
68. Angie Best-Boss, "What Kind of Degree Should a Medical Assistant Have?" https://www.medical assistantschools.com/articles/what-kind-of -degree/.
69. U.S. Department of Labor, Bureau of Labor Statistics, "Medical Assistants," http://www.bls .gov/oco/ocos164.htm.
70. 636 N.E.2d 1282 (Ind. Ct. App. 1994).
71. University Hospitals, "Nutrition Services," http:// www.uhhospitals.org/services/nutrition-services.
72. Massachusetts General Hospital, "Nutrition," http://www.massgeneral.org/nutrition/.
73. NewYork-Presbyterian, "Food and Nutrition: Welcome," http://www.nyp.org/nutrition/.
74. 2017 Hospital Accreditation Standards, The Joint Commission, PC.02.02.03 (element 7).
75. 753 F. Supp. 267 (W.D. Ark. 1990). Institute of Medicine, To Err Is Human: Building a Safer Health System, http://www.nationalacademies .org/hmd/~/media/Files/Report%20Files /1999/To-Err-is-Human/To%20Err%20is%20 Human%201999%20%20report%20brief .pdf and http://scholarlycommons.law.case.edu /cgi/viewcontent.cgi?article=1354&context =healthmatrix.
76. C.F.R., Title 42, Subpart C § 482.25, 2011.
77. Drug Enforcement Agency, "Controlled Substances Act," http://www.justice.gov/dea/pubs /csa.html.
78. 21 C.F.R. § 1.106.
79. 544 N.W.2d 727 (Mich. Ct. App. 1996).
80. *Riff v. Morgan Pharmacy*, 508 A.2d 1247 (Pa. Super. Ct. 1986).
81. *Riff v. Morgan Pharmacy*, 353 Pa. Superior Ct. 34 (1986)
82. 642 N.E.2d 514 (Ind. 1994).
83. Ind. Code § 25-26-13-16(b)(3) (1993).
84. *Chamblin v. K-Mart Corp.*, 272 Ga. App. 240, 612 S.E.2d 29 (2005).
85. *Id.* at 28–29.
86. 971 So. 2d 1278 (Miss. App. 2008).
87. 2007 WL 4293465 (Ariz. Super. Ct., Oct. 11, 2007).
88. More Law Lexapedia, "*Estate of Eric Warren v. Walgreen's et al.*," http://www.morelaw.com /verdicts/case.asp?s=AZ&d=34159.
89. E.A. Flynn, R.E. Pearson, and K. Barker, "Observational study of accuracy in compounding i.v. admixtures at five hospitals," *American Journal of Health-System Pharmacy* 54 (1997): 904–912.
90. Matthew Grissinger, "Hold That Order," *PSNet*, https://psnet.ahrq.gov/webmm/case/171 /hold-that-order#references.
91. 780 So. 2d 478 (2001).
92. 659 S.W.2d 86 (Tex. Ct. App. 1983).
93. 527 N.Y.S.2d 937 (N.Y. App. Div. 1988).
94. *Girgis v. Board of Physical Therapy*, No. 361 C.D 2004 (Pa. Cmwlth. 2004).
95. http://www.medpointmanagement.com/wp -content/uploads/2015/02/Article-Highlights -Supervision-of-PA.pdf.
96. CA.gov, "Frequently Asked Questions about Supervising Physician Assistants," http://www .pac.ca.gov/supervising_physicians/faqs.shtml#1.
97. *Navarro v. Carrollwood Emergency Physicians*; Oct. 3, 2006; Circuit Court, Hillsborough County, Fla.
98. Lisa Tortorello, "X-Ray Technicians: Missing in Malpractice Cases," June 7, 2011. http://www .xrayschools.com/articles/xray-technicians -missing-in-malpractice-cases.html.
99. U.S. Department of Justice, Office of Public Affairs, "Diagnostic Imaging Group to Pay $15.5 Million for Allegedly Submitting False Claims to Federal and State Health Care Programs," June 25, 2014. https://www.justice.gov/opa/pr/diagnostic -imaging-group-pay-155-million-allegedly -submitting-false-claims-federal-and-state.
100. *Id.*
101. 490 N.W.2d 856 (Iowa Ct. App. 1992).
102. John Huotari, "Inadequate Shielding Exposed Workers to Excess Radiation at MMC Imaging Center, Lawsuits Allege," *Oakridge Today*, January 15, 2014. http://oakridgetoday.com/2014/01/15 /inadequate-shielding-exposed-workers-to -excess-radiation-at-mmc-imaging-center -lawsuits-allege/.
103. John Huotari, "Appeals Court Rules in Favor of Covenant Health, Other Defendants in Excessive Radiation Lawsuit," *Oak Ridge Today*, June 25, 2015. http://oakridgetoday.com/2015/06/25 /appeals-court-rules-in-favor-of-covenant-health -other-defendants-in-excessive-radiation-lawsuit/.

104. Jeremy S. Whang, Stephen R. Baker, Ronak Patel, Lyndon Luk, and Alejandro Castro III, "The Causes of Medical Malpractice Suits against Radiologists in the United States," *RSNA Radiology* 266(2), 2013. http://pubs.rsna.org/doi/abs/10.1148/radiol.12111119?etoc=&#.

105. 435 N.E.2d 305 (Ind. Ct. App. 1982).

106. *Id.* at 309.

107. *Id.* at 309.

108. 566 N.Y.S.2d 79 (N.Y. App. Div. 1991).

109. *Id.* at 512.

110. *Dixon v. Taylor*, No. 9224SC760 (Filed 20 July 1993).

111. Susan Berger, "How Safe of the Vigorous Neck Manipulations Done by Chiropractors?" *The Washington Post*. http://www.washingtonpost.com/national/health-science/how-safe-are-the-vigorous-neck-manipulations-done-by-chiropractors/2014/01/06/26870726-5cf7-11e3-bc56-c6ca94801fac_story.html.

112. *Id.*

113. National Practitioner Data Bank, "NPDB Research Statistics: Definitions and Terms," https://www.npdb.hrsa.gov/resources/definitions.jsp.

114. National Practitioner Data Bank, "What You Must Report to the NPDB," https://www.npdb.hrsa.gov/hcorg/whatYouMustReportToTheDataBank.jsp.

115. National Practitioner Data Bank, "NPDB Research Statistics," https://www.npdb.hrsa.gov/resources/npdbstats/npdbStatistics.jsp#contentTop.

116. No. W2000-01485-COA-R3-CV (Tenn. App. 2002).

117. *Smith v. O'Neal*, 850 S.W.2d 797 (Tex. Ct. App. 1993).

118. 520 N.E.2d 1085 (Ill. App. Ct. 1988).

119. *Id.* at 1015.

120. 599 N.Y.S.2d 58 (N.Y. App. Div. 1993).

121. 711 N.Y.S.2d 65 (N.Y. Sup. Ct., App. Div., 3d Dep't. 2000).

122. 557 S.E.2d 339 (2001).

123. 295 S.C. 164, 367 S.E.2d 453 (S.C. 1988).

124. *Id.* at 455–456.

125. *Lowenberg v. Sobol*, 594 N.Y.S.2d 874 (N.Y. App. Div. 1993).

126. 525 A.2d 992 (Del. 1987).

127. No. 71A05-0310-CV-525 (Ind. App. 2004).

128. 817 N.E. 266 (2004).

© Condor 36/Shutterstock

CHAPTER 13

Information Management and Patient Records

RELEASE OF CONFIDENTIAL INFORMATION

Sanfiel, a psychiatric nurse, had his professional license suspended for 5 years after he intentionally disclosed confidential patient information to the news media. Sanfiel testified that he knew the information he possessed was confidential and that he understood the danger in disclosing psychiatric records to unauthorized persons. He also knew that a nurse could be disciplined for disclosing such information, yet he intentionally released information to the news media. The state board of nursing suspended Sanfiel's nursing license and placed him on probation for 5 years for disclosing confidential patient information. The question arises: Was the state board of nursing authorized to suspend Sanfiel's license because of his disclosure of information to the news media?

WHAT IS YOUR VERDICT?

▶ LEARNING OBJECTIVES

The reader, upon completion of this chapter, will be able to:

- Describe the contents of medical records.
- Explain the importance of maintaining complete and accurate records.
- Explain the ownership of and who can access a patient's medical record.
- Describe the advantages and disadvantages of electronic medical records.
- Describe why the medical record is important in legal proceedings.
- Describe a variety of ways in which medical records have been falsified.
- Explain what is meant by the medical record battleground.
- Describe the purpose of the *Privacy Act of 1974* and the *Health Insurance Portability and Accountability Act of 1996* and how they affect hospital and physician practices.

Healthcare organizations are required to maintain a medical record for each patient in accordance with accepted professional standards and practices. The effective and efficient delivery of patient care requires that an organization determine its information needs. Organizations that do not centralize their information needs will often suffer scattered databases, inconsistent reports, and inefficiencies in the use of economic resources.

The medical record is the principal means of communication among healthcare professionals in matters relating to patient care. Medical records provide pertinent information regarding the daily care and treatment of each patient; document each patient's illness, symptoms, diagnosis, and treatment; serve as a planning tool for patient care; protect the legal interests of patients, caregivers, and healthcare organizations; provide a database for use in statistical reporting, continuing education, and research; and provide information necessary for third-party billing. Records must be complete, accurate, current, readily accessible, and systematically organized.

Licensure rules and regulations contained in federal and state statutes often describe the requirements and standards for the maintenance, handling, signing, filing, and retention of medical records. Failure to maintain a complete and accurate medical record reflecting the treatment rendered may affect the ability of an organization and/or physician to obtain third-party reimbursement (e.g., from Medicare, Medicaid, or private insurance carriers). Under federal and state laws, the medical record must reflect accurately

the treatment for which the organization or physician seeks payment. Thus, the medical record is important to the organization for medical, legal, and financial reasons. This chapter reviews several topics relating to the medical record.

▶ INFORMATION MANAGEMENT

All organizations, regardless of mission or size, develop and maintain information management systems, which often include financial, medical, and human resource data. *Information management* is a process intended to facilitate the flow of information within and between departments and caregivers. An information management plan must address the information necessary in the care of each patient; process information in a logical manner to allow for quality patient care; address third-party payer needs; set goals and establish priorities; improve accuracy of data collection and medical record entries; provide uniformity of data collection and definitions; limit duplication of entries; deliver timely and accurate information; provide easy access to information; improve the security and confidentiality of information; improve collaboration across disciplines in the organization through information sharing; establish disaster plans for the recovery of information; orient and train staff on the information management system; and conduct an annual review of the plan that addresses the scope, organization, objectives, and effectiveness of the information management plan.

▶ MEDICAL RECORD CONTENTS

The medical record is an essential tool in the delivery of quality patient care. Therefore, caregivers and healthcare organizations must strive to maintain the integrity and accuracy of records. The inpatient medical record includes, for example, the admission record, which describes pertinent demographic information; consent and authorization for treatment forms; advance directives; history and physical examination, including a preliminary/working diagnosis and findings that support the diagnosis; patient screenings and assessments (e.g., nursing, functional, nutritional, social, and discharge planning); treatment plans; physicians' orders; progress notes; nursing notes; diagnostic reports; consultation reports; vital signs charts; anesthesia assessments; operative reports; medication administration records; discharge planning documentation; patient education; and discharge summaries. The patient's care record is the key communications tool between caregivers who attend to the patient's needs throughout the day and night during a patient's hospitalization.

▶ DOCUMENTATION OF CARE

The importance of maintaining records of treatment rendered to a patient must not be underestimated. It may be many years after a patient has been treated before litigation is initiated; therefore, it is imperative that patient records of treatment in the physician's office, as well as in the healthcare facility, be maintained. A jury could consider lack of documentation as sufficient evidence for determining guilt in a negligence case.

Record Entries Accuracy

Medical record entries must be accurate. Such was not the case in *Tulier-Pastewski v. State Board for Professional Medical Conduct*,[1] where two hospital administrators testified and showed undisputed proof that the physician had recorded a patient was alert during the purported examination when the patient was actually sedated and asleep. Evidence also indicated that the physician failed to properly document medical histories and current physical status. Although the physician asserted that evidence of failure to document did not support the findings of negligence because there was no expert testimony that her omissions actually caused or created a risk of harm to a patient, an expert witness testified that the missing information as to certain patients was needed for proper assessment of the patient's condition and choice of treatment. This testimony, together with the importance of cardiac information when treating patients with chest pain, provided a rational basis for the conclusion by the administrative review board for professional medical conduct that the physician's deficient medical recordkeeping could have affected patient care. The physician was found to be practicing medicine negligently on more than one occasion.

Nurse's Charting

Nurses tend to access medical records more often than any other healthcare professional, simply because of the amount of time they spend delivering care to the patient. The nurse monitors the patient's illness, response to medication, display of pain and discomfort, and general condition. The patient's care, as well as the nurse's observations, should be recorded on a regular basis. A nurse who has doubt as to the appropriateness of a particular order should verify with the prescribing physician the intent of the prescribed order.

Documentation and Reimbursement

When charting, professionals should be familiar with diagnosis-related groups (DRGs). DRGs refer to a methodology developed by professors at Yale University for classifying patients in categories according to age, diagnosis, and treatment resource requirements. It is the basis for the prospective payment system, contained in the 1983 Social Security Amendments for reimbursing inpatient hospital costs for Medicare beneficiaries. The key source of information for determining the course of treatment of each patient and the proper DRG assignment is the medical record. Reimbursement is based on preestablished average prices for each DRG. As a result of this reimbursement methodology, poor recordkeeping can precipitate financial disaster for a hospital. The potential financial savings for Medicare are substantial. Under this system of payment, if hospitals can provide quality patient care at a cost lower than the price established for a DRG, they keep the excess dollars paid. This is an incentive for hospitals to keep costs under control.

> The DRGs, as they are now defined, form a manageable, clinically coherent set of patient classes that relate a hospital's case mix to the resource demands and associated costs experienced by the hospital. DRGs are defined based on the principal diagnosis, secondary diagnoses, surgical procedures, age, sex and discharge status of the patients treated. Through DRGs, hospitals can gain an understanding of the patients being treated, the costs incurred and within reasonable limits, the services expected to be required. The classification of patients into DRGs is a constantly evolving process. As coding schemes change, as more comprehensive data are collected or as medical technology or practice changes, the DRG definitions will be reviewed and revised.[2]

Methodical, precise, and logical documentation of a patient's care is important in coding the correct DRG for reimbursement purposes and helping to prevent costly malpractice lawsuits.

Charting by Exception

Some hospitals institute a practice of charting by exception, whereby hospital policy instructs its nurses to engage in *charting by exception*, a system whereby nurses notes record concise and significant changes in a patient's condition. It should be noted that "Nurses' notes with few explanations, little description of key findings, or no mention of periodic patient checks could be construed as negligence by a plaintiff's attorney guided by the premise, not charted, not done."[3] In *Lama v. Borras*,[4] Dr. Borras, while operating on Mr. Lama, discovered that the patient had an extruded disc and attempted to remove the extruded material. Either because Borras failed to remove the offending material or because he operated at the wrong level, the patient's original symptoms returned several days after the operation. On May 15, Borras operated again but did not order preoperative or postoperative antibiotics. On May 17, a nurse's note indicated that the bandage covering the patient's surgical wound was extremely bloody, which, according to expert testimony, indicates the possibility of infection. On May 18, the patient was experiencing local pain at the site of the incision, another symptom consistent with an infection. On May 19, the bandage was soiled again. A more complete account of the patient's evolving condition was not available because the hospital instructed nurses to engage in charting by exception, a system whereby nurses did not record qualitative observations for each of the day's three shifts, but instead made such notes only when necessary to chronicle significant changes in a patient's condition.

On May 21, Dr. Piazza, an attending physician, diagnosed the patient's problem as discitis—an infection of the space between discs—and responded by prescribing antibiotic treatment. Lama was hospitalized for several additional months while undergoing treatment for the infection.

After moving from Puerto Rico to Florida, Lama filed a tort action in the U.S. District Court for the district of Puerto Rico. Although the plaintiff did not claim that the hospital was vicariously liable for any negligence on the part of Borras, he alleged that the hospital failed to prepare, use, and monitor proper medical records.

The jury returned a verdict awarding the plaintiff $600,000 in compensatory damages. The district court ruled that the evidence was legally sufficient to support the jury's findings, and an appeal was taken.

The U.S. Court of Appeals for the First Circuit upheld the decision of negligence based on the charting-by-exception policy, but the jury had to decide whether the violation of the regulation was a proximate cause of harm to Lama. Before deciding the case, the jury considered several important factors. For example, the jury may have inferred from the evidence presented that, as part of the practice of charting by exception, the nurses did not regularly record certain information important to the diagnosis of an infection, such as the changing characteristics of the surgical wound and the patient's complaints of postoperative pain. Furthermore, because there was evidence that the patient's hospital records described possible signs of infection that deserved further investigation (e.g., an excessively bloody bandage and local pain at the site of the wound), the jury could have reasonably inferred that the intermittent charting failed to provide the sort of continuous danger signals that would most likely spur early intervention by the physician.

Failure to Maintain Records

Failure to maintain patient records may occur when healthcare professionals are particularly busy, overwhelmed, preoccupied, or careless in recording significant events related to patient care. In *Braick v. New York State Department of Health*,[5] a physician was under review by a hearing committee of the New York State Review Board for Professional Medical Conduct. The committee reviewed 122 specifications of misconduct, which included gross negligence, failure to adequately maintain patient records, and failure to obtain informed consent. The committee revoked the physician-petitioner's license. In reaching its decision, the committee found the bureau of professional medical conduct's expert credible, including his opinion that the physician was ultimately responsible for what happened to his patients during the relevant surgeries, and the committee rejected the efforts of the physician and his expert to shift responsibility to nurses.

The petitioner appealed to the administrative review board for professional medical conduct, which affirmed the committee's determination and penalty. An appeals court found the physician's license had been properly revoked.

Medical Record Battleground

The contents of a medical record must not be tampered with after an entry has been made; therefore, the record should be used wisely. The record should be complete and accurate, as its purpose is to record the patient's course of care, not to be used as an instrument for registering complaints about another individual or the organization. Those individuals who choose to make derogatory remarks about others in a patient's record might find themselves in a courtroom trying to defend such notations in the record. Inappropriate comments written during a time of anger may have been based on inaccurate information, which could,

🔊 NEWS HOSPITAL WORKERS PUNISHED FOR PEEKING AT CLOONEY FILE

George Clooney and his companion got top billing when they were treated at a New Jersey hospital after a motorcycle accident last month. But while some nurses clamored to see the celebrity patients, other staff members were busy prying into the couple's medical records, hospital officials said yesterday.

That curiosity proved to be costly. After an internal investigation, the hospital, Palisades Medical Center in North Bergen, has suspended 27 employees for a month without pay for violating a federal law on patient confidentiality.

—Bruce Lambert and Nate Schweber, *The New York Times*, October 10, 2007

in turn, be damaging to one's credibility and future statements.

▶ PRIVACY ACT OF 1974

The *Privacy Act of 1974*, codified at 5 U.S.C. 552, was enacted to safeguard individual privacy from the misuse of federal records, to give individuals access to records concerning themselves that are maintained by federal agencies, and to establish a Privacy Protection Safety Commission. Section 2 of the Privacy Act reads as follows:

> [a] The Congress finds that (1) the privacy of an individual is directly affected by the collection, maintenance, use, and dissemination of personal information by Federal agencies; (2) the increasing use of computers and sophisticated information technology, while essential to the efficient operations of the Government, has greatly magnified the harm to individual privacy that can occur from any collection, maintenance, use, or dissemination of personal information; (3) the opportunities for an individual to secure employment, insurance, and credit, and his right to due process, and other legal protections are endangered by the misuse of certain information systems; (4) the right to privacy is a personal and fundamental right protected by the Constitution of the United States; and (5) in order to protect the privacy

of individuals identified in information systems maintained by Federal agencies, it is necessary and proper for the Congress to regulate the collection, maintenance, use, and dissemination of information by such agencies. [b] The purpose of this Act is to provide certain safeguards for an individual against an invasion of personal privacy by requiring Federal agencies, except as otherwise provided by law, to (1) permit an individual to determine what records pertaining to him are collected, maintained, used, or disseminated by such agencies; (2) permit an individual to prevent records pertaining to him obtained by such agencies for a particular purpose from being used or made available for another purpose without his consent; (3) permit an individual to gain access to information pertaining to him in Federal agency records, to have a copy made of all or any portion thereof, and to correct or amend such records; (4) collect, maintain, use, or disseminate any record of identifiable personal information in a manner that assures that such action is for a necessary and lawful purpose, that the information is current and accurate for its intended use, and that adequate safeguards are provided to prevent misuse of such information.

▶ HEALTH INSURANCE PORTABILITY AND ACCOUNTABILITY ACT

The *Health Insurance Portability and Accountability Act of 1996* (HIPAA) (Public Law 104-191) was enacted by Congress to protect the privacy, confidentiality, and security of patient information. According to the Centers for Medicare and Medicaid Services, Title I of HIPAA protects health insurance coverage for workers and their families when they change or lose their jobs. Title II of HIPAA, the *administrative simplification* (AS) provisions, requires the establishment of national standards for electronic healthcare transactions and national identifiers for providers, health insurance plans, and employers. The AS provisions also address the security and privacy of health information. The standards are meant to improve the efficiency and effectiveness of the nation's healthcare system by encouraging the widespread use of electronic data interchange in health care.

As a result of the continuing advances in portable technology, an ever-increasing number of healthcare entities are making good use of mobile devices. Texting, the use of e-mails, and various computer applications are revolutionizing the ways in which healthcare providers interact with one another and their patients. The use of these devices comes with hidden costs of compliance, especially if they lead to a reportable breach under HIPAA or state laws. HIPAA privacy and security officers have been struggling to keep up with the use of the devices to protect patient privacy and avoid HIPAA compliance issues. Managers of health information privacy and security should to be aware of the concerns encompassing the use of mobile devices, as it relates to HIPAA compliance requirements, audits and enforcement, privacy, and security breaches and how to prevent them.

HIPAA standards are applicable to all health information in all of its formats (e.g., electronic, paper, verbal). It applies to both electronically maintained and electronically transmitted information. HIPAA privacy standards include restrictions on access to individually identifiable health information and the use and disclosure of that information, as well as requirements for administrative activities such as training, compliance, and enforcement of HIPAA mandates.

Privacy Provisions

The HIPAA privacy provisions took effect on April 14, 2003. Key privacy provisions include the following:

- Patients must be able to access their record and request correction of errors.
- Patients must be informed of how their personal information will be used.
- Patient information cannot be used for marketing purposes without the explicit consent of the involved patients.
- Patients can ask their health insurers and providers to take reasonable steps to ensure that their communications with the patient are confidential. For instance, a patient can ask to be called at his or her work number, instead of a home or cell phone number.
- Patients can file formal privacy-related complaints to the U.S. Department of Health and Human Services (DHHS), Office for Civil Rights.
- Health insurers or providers must document their privacy procedures, but they have discretion on what to include in their privacy procedure.
- Health insurers or providers must designate a privacy officer and train their employees.

- Providers may use patient information without patient consent for the purposes of providing treatment, obtaining payment for services, and performing the nontreatment operational tasks of the provider's business.

Security Provisions

The HIPAA security provisions took effect April 20, 2005. The security provision complements the privacy provision. HIPAA defines three segments of security safeguards for compliance: administrative, physical, and technical. Key provisions are as follows.

Administrative Safeguards

- Policies and procedures must be designed to clearly show how the entity will comply with the act.
- Entities that must comply with HIPAA requirements must adopt a written set of privacy procedures and designate a privacy officer to be responsible for developing and implementing all required policies and procedures.
- Policies and procedures must reference management oversight and organizational buy-in to comply with the documented security controls.
- Procedures should clearly identify employees or classes of employees who will have access to protected health information (PHI).
- Access to PHI in all forms must be restricted to only those employees who have a need for it to complete their job function.
- Procedures must address access authorization, establishment, modification, and termination.
- Entities must show that an appropriate ongoing training program regarding the handling of PHI is provided to employees performing health plan administrative functions.
- Covered entities that outsource some of their business processes to a third party must ensure that their vendors have a framework in place to comply with HIPAA requirements.
- Care must be taken to determine whether the vendor further outsources any data-handling functions to other vendors, while monitoring whether appropriate contracts and controls are in place.
- A contingency plan should be in place for responding to emergencies.
- Covered entities are responsible for backing up their data and having disaster recovery procedures in place.
- The recovery plan should document data priority and failure analysis, testing activities, and change control procedures.

- Internal audits play a key role in HIPAA compliance by reviewing operations, with the goal of identifying potential security violations.
- Policies and procedures should specifically document the scope, frequency, and procedures of audits.
- Audits should be both routine and event-based.
- Procedures should document instructions for addressing and responding to security breaches that are identified either during the audit or the normal course of operations.

Physical Safeguards

- Responsibility for security must be assigned to a specific person or department.
- Controls must govern the introduction and removal of hardware and software from the network.
- When equipment is retired, it must be disposed of properly to ensure that PHI is not compromised.
- Access to equipment containing health information should be carefully controlled and monitored.
- Access to hardware and software must be limited to properly authorized individuals.
- Required access controls consist of facility security plans, maintenance records, and visitor sign-in and escorts.
- Policies are required to address proper workstation use.
- Workstations should be removed from high-traffic areas, and monitor screens should not be in direct view of the public.
- If the covered entities use contractors or agents, they too must be fully trained on their physical access responsibilities.

Technical Safeguards

- Information systems housing PHI must be protected from intrusion.
- When information flows over open networks, some form of encryption must be used.
- If closed systems/networks are used, existing access controls are considered sufficient, and encryption is optional.
- Each covered entity is responsible for ensuring that the data within its systems have not been changed or erased in an unauthorized manner.
- Data corroboration, including the use of check sum, double-keying, message authentication, and digital signature, may be used to ensure data integrity.

- Covered entities must also authenticate the entities with which it communicates.
- Authentication consists of corroborating that an entity is who it claims to be.
- Covered entities must make documentation of their HIPAA practices available to the government to determine compliance.
- Information technology documentation should also include a written record of all configuration settings on the components of the network because these components are complex, configurable, and always changing.
- Documented risk analysis and risk management programs are required.

Patient Health Information Data Breaches

Section 13402(e)(4) of the Health Information Technology for Economic and Clinical Health Act (*HITECH Act*) provides that the Secretary of Health and Human Services must post a listing of breaches of unsecured PHI that affect 500 or more individuals. The format for postings includes brief summaries of each case breached that the Office of Civil Rights (OCR) has investigated and closed, as well as the names of private practice providers who have reported breaches of unsecured PHI to the Secretary. Breaches reported to the Secretary are posted on the DHHS website (https://ocrportal.hhs.gov/ocr/breach/breach_report.jsf). The complaint portal for registering data breaches can be found at https://ocrportal.hhs.gov. Answers to questions regarding privacy complaints are also available by calling the DHHS, Office for Civil Rights (1-800-368-1019, TDD: 1-800-537-7697).

Failure to safeguard PHI led to a $650,000 fine with the Catholic Health Services of the Archdiocese of Philadelphia.

Catholic Health Care Services of the Archdiocese of Philadelphia (CHCS) has agreed to settle potential violations of the Health Insurance Portability and Accountability Act of 1996 (HIPAA) Security Rule after the theft of a CHCS mobile device compromised the PHI of hundreds of nursing home residents. CHCS provided management and information technology services as a business associate to six skilled nursing facilities. The total number of individuals affected by the combined breaches was 412. The settlement includes a monetary payment of $650,000 and a corrective action plan.[6]

The corrective action plan requires implementation of the following policies and procedures:

D. Minimum Content of the Policies and Procedures

The Policies and Procedures shall include, but shall not be limited to the following:

1. Policies regarding encryption of ePHI.
2. Policies regarding password management.
3. Policies regarding security incident response.
4. Policies regarding mobile device controls.
5. Policies regarding information system review.
6. Policies regarding security reminders.
7. Policies regarding log-in monitoring.
8. Policies regarding a data backup plan.
9. Policies regarding a disaster recovery plan.
10. Policies regarding an emergency mode operation plan.
11. Policies regarding testing and revising of contingency plans.
12. Policies regarding applications and data criticality analysis.
13. Policies regarding automatic log off.
14. Policies regarding audit controls.
15. Policies regarding integrity controls.[7]

▶ PATIENT OBJECTS TO RECORD ENTRIES

Patients periodically object to notations made by their physicians in their medical records, as noted in the following case. In *Dodds v. Johnstone*,[8] during a physical exam conducted on October 30, 2000, the appellee indicated in her progress notes that she believed the appellant had been using cocaine prior to her last office visit. Appellee's notes read: "I believe by physical exam the patient was using cocaine on Friday before her office visit." The appellant filed a complaint in which she alleged that the appellee was negligent in her diagnosis of the appellant and that, as a result, she incurred a loss of compensation for her automobile accident claim and suffered severe emotional distress. The patient "testified that she has not sought counseling of any sort as a result of the mental stress and has not experienced any limitation in her activities as a result of the notation."[9] The court reviewed the record of proceedings before the trial court and found that there was no genuine issue of material fact as to negligent infliction of severe emotional distress, loss of employment opportunities, or a decreased insurance

settlement as a result of the notation in the patient's medical records."[10]

▶ OWNERSHIP AND RELEASE OF MEDICAL RECORDS

Healthcare providers who handle medical records must fully understand ownership and privacy concerns. Medical records are the property of the provider of care and are maintained for the benefit of the patient. Ownership resides with the organization or professional rendering treatment. Although medical records typically have been protected from public scrutiny by a general practice of nondisclosure, this practice has been waived under a limited number of specifically controlled situations. Both applicable law and the courts recognize that individuals have a right to privacy and to be protected from the mass dissemination of information pertaining to their personal or private affairs. The right of privacy generally includes the right to be kept out of the public spotlight. The *Privacy Act of 1974* was enacted to safeguard patient privacy from the misuse of federal records and to give individuals access to records concerning themselves that are maintained by federal agencies.

Requests by Patients

Patients have a legally enforceable interest in the information contained in their medical records and, therefore, have a right to access their records. Patients may have access to review and obtain copies of their records, X-rays, and laboratory and diagnostic test results. Access to information includes that maintained or possessed by a healthcare organization or a healthcare practitioner who has treated or is treating a patient. Organizations and physicians can withhold records if the information could reasonably be expected to cause substantial and identifiable harm to the patient (e.g., patients in psychiatric hospitals, institutions for the mentally disabled, or alcohol and drug treatment programs).

Changes to HIPAA released by the DHHS 45 CFR Parts 160 and 164 adopt rules on individuals' right of access to PHI that include, in part, the following:

■ Expand individuals' rights to receive electronic copies of their health information and to restrict disclosures to a health plan concerning treatment for which the individual has paid out of pocket in full.
■ Require modifications to, and redistribution of, a covered entity's notice of privacy practices.[11]

Failure to Release Patient Records

Failure to release a patient's record can lead to legal action. The patient, for example, in *Pierce v. Penman*[12] brought a lawsuit seeking damages for severe emotional distress when physicians repeatedly refused to turn over her medical records. The defendants had rendered professional services to the plaintiff for approximately 11 years. The patient moved and found a new physician, Dr. Hochman. She signed a release authorizing Hochman to obtain her records from the defendant physicians. Hochman wrote a letter requesting her records but never received a response. The defendants claimed that they never received the request. The patient changed physicians again and continued in her efforts to obtain a copy of the records. Eventually, the defendants' offices were burglarized, and the plaintiff's records were allegedly taken. The detective in charge of investigating the burglary stated that he was never notified that any records were taken. The court of common pleas awarded the patient $2,500 in compensatory damages and $10,000 in punitive damages. On appeal, the superior court upheld the award.

Requests by Third Parties

The medical record is a peculiar type of property because of the wide variety of third-party interests in the information contained in medical records. Healthcare organizations may not generally disclose information without patient consent. Policies regarding the release of information should be formulated to address the rights of third parties, such as insurance carriers processing claims, physicians, medical researchers, educators, and governmental agencies. Several cases are listed here where the right to privacy is nullified due to, for example, criminal investigations, Medicaid fraud, and substance abuse.

Criminal Investigation

The psychotherapist–patient privilege that exists under the federal rules of evidence can be overcome if the need for a psychiatric history outweighs a privacy interest. In *In re Brink*,[13] the hospital sought to quash a grand jury request for the medical records pertaining to blood tests administered to a person under investigation. The court of common pleas held that physician–patient privilege did not extend to medical records subpoenaed pursuant to a grand jury investigation. A proceeding before a grand jury is considered secret in nature, inherently preserving the confidentiality of patient records.

Medicaid Fraud

Patient records may be obtained during investigations into such alleged criminal actions as Medicaid fraud. The defendant physician, Dr. Edwin Ekong, in the *People v. Ekong*,[14] was held in contempt of court for failing to comply with a subpoena duces tecum that was issued by a grand jury for Medicaid patient records in his possession. The physician contended that he could not release the files because of physician–patient privilege. The Appellate Court of Illinois, Third District disagreed, holding that the grand jury was permitted to obtain the patient files and records that were in his possession because he was under investigation for Medicaid fraud.

Substance Abuse Records

The federal Drug Abuse and Treatment Act of 1972[15] and federal regulations provide that patient records relating to drug and alcohol abuse treatment must be held confidential and not disclosed except in specific circumstances. Unlike other medical records, drug and alcohol abuse records cannot be released until the court has determined whether a claimed need for the records outweighs the potential injury to the patient, patient–physician relationship, and treatment services being rendered. Because of these strict requirements, the courts have been reluctant to order the release of such records unless absolutely necessary.

▶ USE OF PATIENT DATA COLLECTED

Caregivers are responsible for assuring that the information critical to a patient's care is readily available to all caregivers in the opening pages of the record. Provider mistakes often occur because of the unwieldy, unorganized, and voluminous amount of information gathered on patients. Caregivers who fail to use the information collected when assessing patient needs may find themselves in a lawsuit. For example, consider the patient who advised her physician that she was allergic to latex. Hospital staff, failing to take note of the allergy, inserted a latex catheter into the patient. As a result, the patient developed interstitial cystitis. Expert testimony was sufficient to establish to a reasonable degree of medical certainty that the catheter "caused" the patient's chronic bladder disorder.[16]

Failure to Read Nursing Notes

A physician can breach his or her duty of care by failing to read nursing notes. In *Todd v. Sauls*,[17] Mr. Todd was admitted to Rapides General Hospital on October 3, 1988, and the following day, Dr. Sauls performed bypass surgery. Postoperatively, Todd sustained a heart attack. During the following days, Todd did not ambulate well and suffered a weight loss of 19.5 pounds.

On October 17, the medical record indicated that Todd's sternotomy wound and the mid-lower left leg incision were reddened and his temperature was 99.6°F. Sauls did not commonly read the nurses' notes, instead preferring to rely on his own observations of the patient. In his October 18 notes, he indicated that there was no drainage. The nurses' notes, however, show that there was drainage at the chest tube site. Contrary to the medical records showing that Todd had a temperature of 101.2°F, Sauls noted that the patient was afebrile.

On October 19, Sauls noted that Todd's wounds were improving and he did not have a fever. The nurses' notes indicated otherwise, with redness at the surgical wounds and a temperature of 100°F. No white blood cell count had been ordered. Again on October 20, the nurses' notes indicated wound redness and a temperature of 100.8°F. No wound culture had yet been ordered. Dr. Kamil, one of Todd's treating physicians, noted that Todd's nutritional status needed to be seriously confronted and suggested that Sauls consider supplemental feeding. Despite this, no follow-up to his recommendation appears, and the record is void of any action by Dr. Sauls to obtain a nutritional consult.

Todd was transferred to the intensive care unit on October 21 because he was gravely ill with profoundly depressed ventricular function. The nurses' notes for the following day describe the chest tube site as draining foul-smelling, bloody purulence. The patient's temperature was recorded to have reached 100.6°F. This is the first time that Sauls had the test tube site cultured. On October 23, the culture report from the laboratory indicated a staph infection, and Todd was started on antibiotics for treatment of the infection.

On October 25, at the request of family, Todd was transferred to St. Luke's Hospital. At St. Luke's, Dr. Leatherman, an internist and invasive cardiologist, treated Todd. Dr. Zeluff, an infectious disease specialist, examined Todd's surgical wounds and prescribed antibiotic treatment. Upon admission to St. Luke's, every one of Todd's surgical wounds was infected. Despite the care given at St. Luke's, Todd died on November 2, 1988. The family brought a malpractice suit against the surgeon. The district court entered judgment on a jury verdict for the defendant, and the plaintiff appealed claiming the surgeon breached his duty of care owed to the patient by failing to (1) aggressively treat the surgical wound infections; (2) read the nurses' observations of infections;

and (3) provide adequate nourishment, allowing the patient's body weight to rapidly waste away.

The Louisiana Court of Appeal held that Sauls committed medical malpractice when he breached the standard of care he owed to Todd. He was effectively ineligible for a heart transplantation, which was his only chance of survival because of the infections and malnourishment caused by Sauls's malpractice. Sauls's testimony convinced the court that he failed to aggressively treat the surgical wound infections, that he chose not to take advantage of the nurses' observations of infection, and that he allowed Todd's body weight to waste away, knowing that extreme vigilance was required because of Todd's already severely impaired heart. Sauls's medical malpractice exacerbated an already critical condition and deprived Mr. Todd of a chance of survival. An impaired nutritional status depresses the body's immune system and adversely affects the body's ability to heal wounds. Sauls had a responsibility to make certain that Todd received adequate calories and proteins.

▶ RETENTION OF RECORDS

The retention of patient records is necessary in providing continuing patient care by caregivers regardless of care setting (e.g., inpatient, outpatient, emergency). Retention of patient records is vital to a patient's ongoing care and treatment as noted in the following *reality check*.

Retaining a patient's medical records for long periods of time may seem unwieldy, but computers make the task practical, and they also increase efficiency for many other information management processes.

The length of time medical records must be retained varies from state to state. A California court, for example, revoked the license of a nursing facility for failure to keep adequate records. In *Yankee v. State Department of Health*,[18] the facility claimed that the word *adequate* was unclear and therefore the requirement was invalid. The court stated that the word adequate is not so uncertain as to render a penal statute invalid. Healthcare organizations, with the advice of an attorney, should determine how long records should be maintained, taking into account patient needs, statutory requirements, future need for such records, and the legal considerations of having the records available in the event of a lawsuit.

Failure to Preserve X-rays

The plaintiff in *Rodgers v. St. Mary's Hosp. of Decatur*[19] filed a complaint for damages against a hospital,

☑ *DESTRUCTION OF ONCOLOGY RECORDS*

During a review of a patient record on an outpatient oncology unit, Bill reviewed the nurse's detailed handwritten notes on an outpatient nursing care sheet that were maintained separate from the patient's medical record. The patient had multiple entries on the record regarding a variety of medical issues that had occurred during the patient's chemotherapy infusion. Bill noted that these notes were separate from the patient's permanent medical record. He asked Lilly, the patient's nurse, "Are these notes incorporated into the patient's permanent medical record after the patient is discharged from the outpatient chemotherapy unit?" Lilly responded that they were discarded after the physician reviews them.

Bill asked why they were not incorporated into the patient's permanent record. Lilly replied, "The physician wants them discarded." Bill inquired further, "Is this in keeping with the hospital records retention policy?" Lilly replied, "I don't think so. But the physician said he did not want them in the patient's permanent record."

Looking at Carol, a nursing manager and one of Bill's escorts that had accompanied him during the outpatient oncology unit review, he asked, "Is this your policy?" Carol replied, "No, it is not hospital policy." Lilly interrupted, "But the physician said he is the unit director and wants the handwritten notes destroyed at the end of each day."

Bill then asked, "Is this patient scheduled for additional treatments?" Lilly replied that the patient would be back for additional chemotherapy treatments. Bill then asked, "Would these notes be helpful to you or other nurses when administering the patient treatment in the future?" The nurse replied, "Most definitely in this particular case." Carol interrupted, "I did not know this was happening. I will be sure that these records are saved."

Bill replied, "Yes, I understand. But my bigger concern is to be sure this is not happening in other patient care settings." Carol said she would follow up with administration to correct the problem.

alleging that the hospital breached its statutory duty to preserve for 5 years all of the X-rays taken of his wife. He alleged that the hospital's failure to preserve the X-ray was a breach of its duty arising from the state's X-ray retention act and from the hospital's internal regulations. The plaintiff asserted that because the hospital failed to preserve the X-ray, he was unable to prove his case in a lawsuit. The circuit court entered judgment in favor of the hospital, and the plaintiff appealed.

The Illinois Supreme Court held that a private cause of action existed under the X-ray retention act and that the plaintiff stated a claim under the act. The act provides that hospitals must retain X-rays and other such photographs or films for a period of 5 years. The hospital also argued that the loss of one X-ray out of a series of six should not be considered a violation of the statute. The court disagreed, finding the statute requires all X-rays be preserved, not just some of them.

▶ ELECTRONIC MEDICAL RECORDS

To significantly reduce the tens of thousands of deaths and injuries caused by medical errors every year, health care organizations must adopt information technology systems that are capable of collecting and sharing essential health information on patients and their care, says a new report by the Institute of Medicine of the National Academies. These systems should operate seamlessly as part of a national network of health information that is accessible by all health care organizations and that includes electronic records of patients' care, secure platforms for the exchange of information among providers and patients, and data standards that will make health information uniform and understandable to all, said the committee that wrote the report.[20]

The HITECH Act is designed to promote the widespread adoption and interoperability of health information technology. HITECH was enacted under Title XIII of the American Recovery and Investment Act of 2009 (Public Law 111-5). Under the Act, the DHHS is promoting the expansion and adoption of health information technology through program funding. For more detailed information see the DHHS website at www.healthit.gov.

Healthcare organizations undergoing computerization must determine user needs, design an effective system, select appropriate hardware and software, develop user training programs, develop a disaster recovery plan (e.g., provide for emergency power systems and back-up files), and provide for data security. A reliable electronic information system requires knowledge-based planning and design. Solid planning and design can lead to improved patient care.

Advantages

Computers have become an economic necessity, and they play an important role in the delivery of health care by assisting healthcare providers in improving the quality of care. Electronic medical records provide timely access to patient information that includes demographics, problems lists, history and physical exams, vital signs, diagnostic test results (e.g., laboratory and radiology), and consultant reports. Other of the many advantages of electronic records include order entries for medications and diagnostic tests, generation of critical alerts (e.g., out-of-range test values and drug–drug and food–drug interactions), computer-assisted diagnosis and treatment, generation of reminders for follow-up testing, assistance in standardizing treatment protocols, improving the ability to timely share information with treating providers, improved productivity and quality, reduced charting costs, support for clinical education and research, generation and transmission of electronic prescriptions, and indefinite storage of medical records.

Large medical centers are generating more than 100,000 orders a week. At the Brigham and Women's Hospital in Boston, laboratory and pharmacy results, pulmonary function, electroencephalography, and many other results-generating areas are based around the system. A strong aspect of the order-entry capability is its use of medical logic and medical expertise technology. The system flags cases where there have been duplicate physician orders and signals an allergy alert resulting in an order cancellation.[21]

Clearly, computers offer many advantages to today's health care.

Disadvantages

Computers may be an economic necessity, but they are not perfect and have thus far proven to be costly investments. Computerization increases the risk of lost confidentiality and unauthorized disclosure of information. The rapid growth of the Internet has led to an explosion of technology crime and related illegal activities (**FIGURE 13-1**). Increases in cybercrime have led to a need for high-end technology products and services to combat these problems. Billions of dollars are spent annually to protect networks and critical infrastructures from cyber-based threats.

Although the number of healthcare organizations installing electronic medical records systems is growing rapidly, the ability to have a completely paperless electronic system remains a challenge. Organizations often find themselves with a hybrid system with various elements of a patient's care recorded in both paper and electronic format. Although computerization is costly, the road to progress is reaping rewards by improving patient care and treatment.

Patient History and Physical

When the caregiver can ask one question and one checkmark is placed in the electronic medical record, that one checkmark can populate many fields and multiple pages. This may give the impression that

FIGURE 13-1 Cyber Security.

© Mohd Khairil/Shutterstock

numerous questions were asked of the patient and thus indicate that a complete and thorough history of the patient was completed, when in fact, one question was asked of a patient sitting in a hospital emergency department corridor. The computer automatically populated many fields of inquiry where such questions were never directly asked.

▶ LEGAL PROCEEDINGS AND THE MEDICAL RECORD

The ever-increasing frequency of personal injury lawsuits mandates that healthcare organizations maintain complete, accurate, and timely medical records. The integrity and completeness of the medical record are important in reconstructing the events surrounding alleged negligence in the care of a patient. Medical records aid police investigations, provide information for determining the cause of death, and indicate the extent of injury in workers' compensation or personal injury proceedings.

When healthcare professionals are called as witnesses in a proceeding, they are permitted to refresh their recollections of the facts and circumstances of a particular case by referring to the medical record. Courts recognize that it is impossible for a medical witness to remember the details of every patient's treatment. The record, therefore, may be used as an aid in relating the facts of a patient's course of treatment.

If a medical record is admitted into evidence in legal proceedings, the court must be assured the information is accurate, it was recorded at the time the event took place, and it was not recorded in anticipation of a specific legal proceeding. When a medical record is introduced into evidence, its custodian, usually the medical records administrator, must testify as to the manner in which the record was produced and the way in which it is protected from unauthorized handling and change. If a record can be shown to be inaccurate or incomplete or that it was made long after the event it purports to record, its credibility as evidence is diminished.

Records Authorship Questioned

The records purportedly relating to Belber's treatment for a fractured wrist in *Belber v. Lipson*[22] were found not admissible as business records. Dr. Conway, a witness at trial who had possession of certain records, had no personal knowledge of the circumstances under which the records were prepared. Dr. Conway did not create

the records and he did not testify as to the circumstances of their composition. Whether such records and other documents are admitted or excluded is governed by the facts and circumstances of the particular case, as well as by the applicable rules of evidence. Admission of a business record requires "the testimony of the custodian or other qualified witness."[23]

A jury determined that Dr. Felix, the physician who treated Belber, had been negligent in repairing his wrist fracture. He argued that Dr. Conway's documents should have been admitted into evidence. There was, however, no evidence in the trial record that these documents were in fact the medical records of Dr. Spinzia, who had provided follow-up care and treatment of Belber's wrist. "Both parties tried to obtain Spinzia's records during pretrial discovery but were told that the records had been destroyed in an accident."[24] In summary, there was no evidence of how the records came into Dr. Conway's hands. The United States Court of Appeals, First Circuit, affirmed the finding of the circuit court, which found that the records were not admissible at trial.

Without a witness to testify as to the authenticity of records produced for trial, such records are not admissible as evidence.

> Obviously a writing is not admissible . . . merely because it may appear upon its face to be a writing made by a physician in the regular course of his practice. It must first be shown that the writing was actually made by or under the direction of the physician at or near the time of his examination of the individual in question and also that it was his custom in the regular course of his professional practice to make such a record.[25]

▶ FALSIFICATION OF RECORDS

When handling medical records, professionals must recognize that tampering with records sends the wrong signal to jurors and can shatter one's credibility, and that altered records can create a presumption of guilt.

Falsifying Medical Records

The evidence in *Dimora v. Cleveland Clinic Foundation*[26] showed that the patient had fallen and broken five or six ribs; yet, upon examination, the physician noted in the progress notes that the patient was smiling and laughing pleasantly, exhibiting no pain upon deep palpation of the area. Other testimony indicated that she was in pain and crying. The discrepancy between the written progress notes and the testimony of the witnesses who observed the patient was sufficient to raise a question of fact. The court then considered the possible falsification of documents by the physician in an effort to hide the possible negligence of hospital personnel. The testimony of the witnesses, if believed, would have been sufficient to show that the physician falsified the record or intentionally reported the incident inaccurately in order to avoid liability for the negligent care of the patient. The intentional alteration or destruction of medical records to avoid liability for medical negligence is sufficient to show actual malice, and punitive damages may be awarded regardless of whether the act of altering, falsifying, or destroying records directly causes compensable harm.[27]

In another case, the court in the *Matter of Jasca-levich*[28] held:

> We are persuaded that a physician's duty to a patient cannot but encompass his affirmative obligation to maintain the integrity, accuracy, truth and reliability of the patient's medical record. His obligation in this regard is no less compelling than his duties respecting diagnosis and treatment of the patient since the medical community must, of necessity, be able to rely on those records in the continuing and future care of that patient.
>
> Obviously, the rendering of that care is prejudiced by anything in those records, which is false, misleading or inaccurate. We hold, therefore, that a deliberate falsification by a physician of his patient's medical record, particularly when the reason therefore is to protect his own interests at the expense of his patient's, must be regarded as gross malpractice endangering the health or life of his patient.[29]

Tampering with Medical Records

Dr. McCroskey faced a lawsuit for the alleged tampering with documents. The state board of medical examiners, in a disciplinary hearing in *State Board of Medical Examiners v. McCroskey*,[30] issued a letter of admonition to Dr. McCroskey based on a series of incidents arising out of the care of a patient's stab wound. Although the patient's condition was initially thought to be stable, he bled to death several hours after his admission to the hospital. Dr. McCroskey was the attending surgeon on the date of the incident and, therefore, responsible for the accurate completion of the patient's medical record. Dr. McCroskey declined to accept the letter of admonition, and a formal disciplinary hearing was held.

Dr. McCroskey erased and wrote over a preoperative note made by another physician concerning the patient's estimated blood loss. Specifically, the original record entry was completed by a surgical resident on the date of the patient's death and stated that the patient's blood loss just prior to surgery was "now greater than 3000 cc." Sometime after the autopsy, Dr. McCroskey changed the record to read that the patient's blood loss was "now greater than 2000 cc."[31] After listening to conflicting expert testimony, the administrative law judge (ALJ) concluded that the physician had not violated generally accepted standards of medical practice by adding the note to the patient's medical record days or weeks after the patient's death and then backdating the note to the date of the death.

On review of the ALJ's decision, the board accepted the ALJ's evidentiary finding that many physicians date a medical record entry to reflect the date of the medical event, rather than the date on which the entry was made. The board disagreed, however, with the ALJ's conclusion that this fact brought McCroskey's conduct within generally accepted standards of medical practice. Instead, the board determined that backdating a medical record entry falls below accepted standards of documentation. Having thus found two acts that fell below generally accepted standards of medical practice, the board concluded that Dr. McCroskey committed unprofessional conduct and issued a letter of admonition. On appeal, the court of appeals held that the board erroneously rejected the ALJ's findings.

On further appeal by the board, the Colorado Supreme Court held that the findings of the board were supported by substantial evidence. Because of the expertise of the board, it was in a position to determine the seriousness of the physician's conduct by placing the events in their proper factual context.

> All three of the inquiry panel's witnesses testified that the generally accepted standard of practice requires that a medical record entry be dated with the date it is made. Even one of McCroskey's witnesses acknowledged that misdating the medical record was "certainly something that should not have been done." McCroskey did not simply backdate a trivial note in a patient's medical record. Instead McCroskey's actions took place in the context of a patient's death, which resulted in a coroner's autopsy, peer review activities, publicity, and several legal actions. McCroskey was the

ALTERATION AND DESTRUCTION OF MEDICAL RECORDS

Citation: *Moskovitz v. Mount Sinai Med. Ctr.*, 635 N.E.2d 331 (Ohio 1994)

Facts

On November 10, 1987, Figgie removed a left Achilles tendon mass from Moskovitz. The tumor was found to be a rare form of cancer. A bone scan revealed that the cancer had metastasized. Moskovitz's care was transferred to Figgie's partner, Makley, an orthopedic surgeon specializing in oncology at University Hospitals. Makley received Figgie's original office chart, which contained seven pages of notes documenting Moskovitz's course of treatment from 1985 through November 1987. Makley thereafter referred Moskovitz to radiation therapy at University Hospitals and sent along a copy of page 7 of Figgie's office notes to the radiation department at University Hospitals.

One month later, Makley's office forwarded the chart to Figgie's office; a copy was then sent to Moskovitz's psychologist. In January 1988, Makley's secretary requested that Figgie's office return the chart to Makley. At this time, it was discovered that the original chart had mysteriously vanished. The problem arose on October 21, 1988, when Moskovitz filed a complaint for discovery seeking to ascertain information relative to a potential claim for medical malpractice. Moskovitz claimed that she had never refused to have the tumor biopsied, but discrepancies were noted in her medical record.

In his January 30, 1989, deposition, Makley produced a copy of page 7 of Figgie's office chart. That copy was identical to the copy ultimately recovered by the plaintiff's counsel from the radiation department records at University Hospitals. The copy produced by Makley contained a typewritten entry dated September 21, 1987, which stated: "Mrs. Moskovitz comes in today for her evaluation on the radiographs reviewed with Dr. York. He was not impressed that [the mass on Moskovitz's left leg] was anything other than a benign problem, perhaps a fibroma. We [Figgie and York] will therefore elect to continue to observe."

However, Figgie's photostatic copy revealed that a line had been drawn through the sentence "We will therefore elect to continue to observe." The copy further revealed that beneath the entry, Figgie had interlineated a handwritten notation: "As she does not want excisional Bx [biopsy] we will observe." The September 21, 1987, entry was followed by a typewritten entry dated September 24, 1987, which states: "I [Figgie] reviewed the X-rays with Dr. York. I discussed the clinical findings with him. We [Figgie and York] felt this to be benign, most likely a fibroma. He [York] said that we could observe and I concur." At some point, Figgie also had added to the September 24, 1987, entry a handwritten notation, "see above," referring to the September 21, 1987, handwritten notation that Moskovitz did not want an excisional biopsy. Figgie, at his deposition on March 2, 1989, produced records, including a copy of page 7 of his office chart. Because his original chart had been lost between December 1987 and January 1988, Figgie had made this copy from the copy of the chart that had been sent to Moskovitz's psychologist. The September 21, 1987, entry in the records produced by Figgie did not contain the statement "We will therefore elect to continue to observe." That sentence had been deleted (whited out) on the original office chart from which the psychiatrist's copy (and, in turn, Figgie's copy) had been made, in a way that left no indication on the copy that the sentence had been removed from the original records.

Figgie maintained that he did not discover the mass on the left Achilles tendon until February 23, 1987, and that Moskovitz continually refused a workup or biopsy.

During discovery, another copy of page 7 of Figgie's office chart, identical to the copy produced by Makley during his deposition, showed that the final sentence in the September 21, 1987, entry had been deleted from Figgie's original office chart sometime between November and mid-December 1987, the alteration presumably occurring while Figgie possessed the original chart.

Eventually, Figgie's entire office chart was reconstructed from copies obtained through discovery. The reconstructed chart contains no indication that a workup or biopsy was recommended by Figgie and refused by Moskovitz at any time prior to August 10, 1987. In a videotaped deposition before her death, Moskovitz claimed that she never refused to have the tumor biopsied. The panel found in favor of the defendants participating in that proceeding with the exception of Figgie, and the trial court agreed. A panel of arbitrators unanimously found that:

1. The evidence supported a finding that plaintiffs' . . . decedent had a very good chance of long-term survival if the tumor was found to be malignant at a time when it was less than one centimeter in size. The evidence supported the fact that the tumor had not grown in size as of May 7, 1987. If Dr. Figgie had performed a biopsy prior to this date, the cancer would not have metastasized and the decedent would have recovered.
2. Dr. Figgie's office chart, which is the primary reference material in analyzing a physician's conduct, is filled with contradictions and inconsistencies.

(continues)

🔍 *ALTERATION AND DESTRUCTION OF MEDICAL RECORDS* *(continued)*

3. Even if Dr. Figgie was first informed of the growth on February 23, 1987, he still fell below acceptable standards of care because he did not conduct further investigation until . . . X-rays performed in September 1987. All handwritten entries which appear on or prior to September 24, 1987, indicating that a biopsy was recommended or that the decedent refused further workup were subsequent changes of the records done to justify Figgie's conduct. The sentence "We will therefore elect to continue to observe" on the September 21, 1987 entry was whited out and the handwritten entry "as she does not want excisional biopsy we will observe" was a subsequent alteration of the records. [*Id.* at 338]

The court of appeals upheld the finding of liability against Figgie on the wrongful death and survival claims. The court of appeals found that the appellant was not entitled to punitive damages as a matter of law. The court of appeals reversed the judgment of the trial court as to the award of damages and remanded the case for a new trial only on the issue of compensatory damages.

Issue

Is an intentional alteration or destruction of medical records to avoid liability sufficient to show actual malice? Can punitive damages be awarded regardless of whether the act of altering or destroying records directly causes compensable harm?

Holding

The Ohio Supreme Court held that the evidence regarding the physician's alteration of the patient's records supported an award of punitive damages, regardless of whether the alteration caused actual harm.

Reason

The intentional alteration or destruction of medical records to avoid liability for medical negligence is sufficient to show actual malice, and punitive damages may be awarded regardless of whether the act of altering, falsifying, or destroying records directly causes compensable harm. The jury's award of punitive damages was based on Figgie's alteration or destruction of medical records. The purpose of punitive damages is not to compensate a plaintiff, but to punish and deter certain conduct. The court warned others to refrain from similar conduct through an award of punitive damages.

Figgie's alteration of records exhibited a total disregard for the law and the rights of Moskovitz and her family. Had the copy of page 7 of Figgie's office chart not been recovered from the radiation department records at University Hospitals, the appellant would have been substantially less likely to succeed in this case. The copy of the chart and other records produced by Figgie would have tended to exculpate Figgie for his medical negligence while placing the blame for his failures on Moskovitz.

attending physician responsible for the accuracy of the patient's medical record, and yet he engaged in conduct that cast doubt upon the medical record's integrity. Under these circumstances, the Board was justified in considering McCroskey's conduct to violate the standard of care.[32]

Falsifying Business Records

Falsification of medical or business records is grounds for criminal indictment, as well as for civil liability. In *People v. Smithtown General Hospital*,[33] a motion to dismiss indictments against a physician and a nurse charged with falsifying business records in the first degree was denied. The surgeon was charged because he omitted to make a true entry in his operative report, and the nurse was charged because she failed to make a true entry in the operating room log.

Another such incident occurred in a rest home, where employees attempted to cover up the death of an elderly woman who had wandered away from the home and was found frozen in a drainage ditch.[34] The deceased patient had been brought back into the home, was dressed in a nightgown, and was placed in her bed. On the basis of the account given by employees, a physician signed the death certificate stating that the 77-year-old patient died in her sleep. An anonymous tip to the county examiner's office prompted an autopsy, and the patient was found to have frozen to death.

Nurse Changes Record Entries

In a well-publicized case that involved the death of a child, the nurse replaced her original notes with a second set of notes that were much more detailed and indicated that she had seen the patient more frequently than was reported in her original notes.[35] Rewriting one's notes in a patient's medical record casts doubt as to the accuracy of other entries in the record. It is easier to explain why one did not chart all activities than it is to explain why a new entry was recorded and an original note replaced.

Alteration of Records

Alteration of patient records with the intent to deceive another for personal gain is considered fraud. Fraud can also be considered an intentional tort. For example, writing a postprocedure note before actually beginning the procedure is, in reality, falsifying a patient's record even though it might be considered normal practice for the physician. A physician who claims that notes are revised following the procedure if necessary is placing the patient in jeopardy if he fails to do so and that failure leads to injury during post–follow-up care. Thus all entries in a patient's care record should be timed, dated, and signed.

NEWS *FALSIFIED PATIENT RECORDS ARE UNTOLD STORY OF CALIFORNIA NURSING HOME CARE*

A supervisor at a Carmichael nursing home admitted under oath that she was ordered to alter the medical records of a 92-year-old patient, who died after developing massive, rotting bedsores at the facility.

In Santa Monica, a nursing home was fined $2,500 by the state for falsifying a resident's medical chart, which claimed that the patient was given physical therapy 5 days a week. The catch? At least 28 of those sessions were documented by nurse assistants who were not at work on those days.

—Marjie Lundstrom, *The Sacramento Bee*, September 18, 2011

Failure to Record Patient's Condition

The plaintiff in *Gerner v. Long Island Jewish Hillside Med. Ctr.*[36] gave birth to her infant son at the defendant medical center. Dr. Geller, the attending pediatrician, arrived at the hospital 6 hours later. Geller, having noted and confirmed a slightly jaundiced condition, ordered phototherapy for the baby. After 3 days of treatment, the child's bilirubin count fell to a normal level, and Geller ordered the patient discharged. The child today is brain damaged, with permanent neurologic dysfunction.

The plaintiff alleged medical malpractice on the part of both the medical center and Geller for failing to diagnose and treat the jaundice in a timely manner. Following examination before trial, the medical center motioned and was granted summary judgment. The plaintiff and Geller appealed.

The New York Supreme Court, Appellate Division, held that questions of fact precluded summary judgment for the hospital. A number of allegations were raised as to negligence attributed solely to hospital staff. For example, notes of attending nurses at the nursery failed to record any jaundiced condition or any reference to color until the third day after birth, despite the parents' complaints to hospital personnel about the baby's yellowish complexion. Additionally, Geller ordered a complete blood count and bilirubin test as soon as he learned of the first recorded observation by a nurse of a jaundiced appearance. Test results, which showed a moderately elevated bilirubin count, were not reported by the laboratory until 10 hours after the blood sample was drawn, and another 3 hours passed before Geller's order for phototherapy was carried out. An issue was thus raised as to whether the 13-hour delay in commencement of the treatment was the proximate cause of the infant's injuries.

▶ ILLEGIBLE HANDWRITING

Illegible handwriting is as ancient as the first stylus. Perhaps the simplest, but one of the most potentially dangerous, problems with medical records is illegible entries. Unfortunately, poor penmanship can cause injury to patients. Medical errors because of poor handwriting can lead to extended length of hospital stays and, in some cases, the death of patients. A Harvard study found that "penmanship was among the causes of 220 prescription errors out of 30,000 cases."[37] As physician offices and hospitals have increasingly switched to computerized medical records, illegible handwriting concerns are diminishing.

The seriousness of handwriting mix-ups was well-noted when a Texas jury ordered a physician, drugstore, and pharmacist to pay $225,000 to the family. In this case, the 42-year-old patient died as a result of a handwriting mix-up on the medication prescribed for his heart. The patient had been given a prescription for 20 mg of Isordil to be taken four times per day; the pharmacist misread the physician's handwriting and filled the prescription with Plendil, a drug for high blood pressure, which is usually taken at no more than 10 mg per day. As a result, Vasquez was given the wrong medication at eight times the recommended dosage. He died 2 weeks later from an apparent heart attack.[38]

▶ TIMELY COMPLETION OF MEDICAL RECORDS

Not only must the chart be accurate, but healthcare professionals must promptly complete records after patients are discharged. Persistent failure to conform to a medical staff rule requiring physicians to complete records promptly can be the basis for suspension of medical staff privileges, as was the case in *Board of Trustees Memorial Hospital v. Pratt*.[39]

▶ CONFIDENTIAL AND PRIVILEGED COMMUNICATIONS

Beyond the medical record lies an even more complex issue within healthcare organizations: communication. The duty of an organization's employees and staff to maintain confidentiality encompasses both verbal and written communications and applies to consultants, contracted individuals, students, and volunteers. Information about a patient, regardless of the method in which it is acquired, is confidential and should not be disclosed without the patient's permission. All healthcare professionals who have access to medical records have a legal, ethical, and moral obligation to protect the confidentiality of the information in the records, as well as verbal communications between physicians and patients. Communication between physicians and communication that occurs in peer review activities also falls under strict confidentiality procedures.

The *Health Care Quality Improvement Act of 1986*[40] insulates certain medical peer review activities affecting medical staff privileges from antitrust liability. Peer review is protected as long as there is reasonable belief that it is conducted in the furtherance of quality care. In enacting this legislation, Congress recognized that without such antitrust immunity, effective peer review might not be possible. Privileged communications statutes do not protect from discovery the records maintained in the ordinary course of doing business and rendering inpatient care. Such documents often can be subpoenaed after showing cause.

The *Health Care Quality Improvement Act of 1986*, Title IV, SEC. 401 [42 U.S.C. 11101] findings by Congress are as follows:

(1) The increasing occurrence of medical malpractice and the need to improve the quality of medical care have become nationwide problems that warrant greater efforts than those that can be undertaken by any individual State.

(2) There is a national need to restrict the ability of incompetent physicians to move from State to State without disclosure or discovery of the physician's previous damaging or incompetent performance.

(3) This nationwide problem can be remedied through effective professional peer review.

(4) The threat of private money damage liability under Federal laws, including treble damage liability under Federal antitrust law, unreasonably discourages physicians from participating in effective professional peer review.

(5) There is an overriding national need to provide incentive and protection for physicians engaging in effective professional peer review.[41]

The burden to establish privilege is on the party seeking to shield information from discovery. The party asserting the privilege has the obligation to prove, by competent evidence, that the privilege applies to the information sought.

Attorney–Client Privilege

Attorney–client privilege generally will preclude discovery of memoranda written to an organization's general counsel by the organization's risk management director. In *Mlynarski v. Rush Presbyterian–St. Luke's Medical Center*,[42] a memorandum written by the risk management coordinator to the hospital's general counsel was barred from discovery. There was undisputed evidence that the risk management coordinator had consulted with and assisted counsel in determining the legal action to pursue and the advisability of settling a claim that she had been assigned to investigate. Information contained in the memorandum was available from witnesses whose names and addresses were made available to the plaintiff. If the hospital later at trial decided to attempt to impeach those witnesses based on the coordinator's testimony, privilege would be waived and the hospital would be required to produce the relevant reports.

Physician–Patient Confidentiality

Patients enter the physician–patient relationship assuming that information acquired by physicians will not be disclosed, unless the patient consents or the law requires disclosure. Mutual trust and confidence are essential to the physician–patient relationship. An action alleging a breach of physician–patient confidentiality is analogous to invasion of privacy, and plaintiffs are entitled to recover damages, including emotional damages, for the harm caused by the physician's unauthorized disclosure.

In such a case, *Berger v. Sonneland*,[43] Berger revealed information during her initial appointment with Dr. Sonneland regarding her medical and personal history. When questioned about her personal history, Berger said that she had previously been married to Dr. Hoheim, a physician in Montana. She described her relationship with her ex-husband as extremely strained.

After meeting with Berger, Sonneland contacted Hoheim and discussed Berger's use of pain medications. Based on information provided by Sonneland, Hoheim filed a motion in a Montana court seeking to modify the custody orders relating to the couple's two children.

Berger sought damages for Sonneland's breach of physician–patient confidentiality. The court granted Sonneland's motion for summary judgment because Berger failed to establish any objective symptoms of emotional distress. Berger moved for reconsideration, urging the court to apply invasion of privacy principles rather than principles related to the tort of negligent infliction of emotional distress.

During the course of events in this case, an appellate court held that a tort action exists for damages resulting from the unauthorized disclosure of confidential information obtained within the physician–patient relationship. The Supreme Court of Washington remanded the case for further proceedings.

> When accepting Berger's factual allegations as true, and drawing all reasonable inferences in her favor, there is sufficient evidence to raise a question of fact as to whether Berger suffered emotional distress as a result of Sonneland's disclosure of confidential information about her. The Court of Appeals should be affirmed, summary dismissal of Berger's medical malpractice claim should be reversed, and the case should be remanded for trial.[44]

HIV Confidentiality

The unauthorized disclosure of confidential HIV-related information could subject an individual to civil and/or criminal penalties. Information regarding a patient's diagnosis as being HIV positive must be kept confidential and should be shared with other healthcare professionals only on a need-to-know basis. Each person has a right to privacy as to his or her personal affairs.

The patient's right to privacy is well described in *Estate of Behringer v. Medical Center at Princeton*,[45] where the plaintiff-surgeon was entitled to recover damages from the hospital and its laboratory director for the unauthorized disclosure of his condition during his stay at the hospital. The hospital and the director had breached their duty to maintain confidentiality of the surgeon's medical records by allowing placement of the patient's test results in his medical chart without limiting access to the chart, which they knew was available to the entire hospital community. "The medical center breached its duty of confidentiality to the plaintiff, as a patient, when it failed to take reasonable precautions regarding the plaintiff's medical records to prevent the patient's AIDS diagnosis from becoming a matter of public knowledge."[46]

The hospital in *Tarrant County Hospital District v. Hughes*[47] was found to have properly disclosed the names and addresses of blood donors in a wrongful death action alleging that a patient contracted AIDS from a blood transfusion administered in the hospital. The physician–patient privilege expressed in the Texas Rules of Evidence did not apply to preclude such disclosure because the record did not reflect that any such relationship had been established. The disclosure was not an impermissible violation of the donors' right of privacy. The societal interest in maintaining an effective blood donor program did not override the plaintiff's right to receive such information. The order prohibited disclosure of the donors' names to third parties.

In *Doe v. University of Cincinnati*,[48] a patient who was infected with HIV-contaminated blood during surgery brought an action against a hospital and a blood bank. The trial court granted the patient's request to discover the identity of the blood donor, and the defendants appealed. The court of appeals held that the potential injury to a donor in revealing his identity outweighed the plaintiff's modest interest in learning of the donor's identity. A blood donor has a constitutional right to privacy not to be identified as a donor of blood that contains HIV. At the time of the plaintiff's blood transfusion in July 1984, no test had been developed to determine the existence of AIDS antibodies. By May 27, 1986, all donors donating blood through the defendant blood bank were tested for the presence of HIV antibodies. Patients who received blood from donors who tested positive were to be notified through their physicians. In this case, the plaintiff's family was notified because of the plaintiff's age and other disability.

Any new HIV-related regulations must continue to address the rights and responsibilities of both patients and healthcare workers. Although this will require a delicate balancing act, it must not be handled as a low-priority issue by legislators.

Disclosure of Physician's HIV Status

The physician, John Doe, in *Application of Milton S. Hershey Med. Ctr.*,[49] was a resident in obstetrics and gynecology (OB/GYN) at the medical center. In 1991, he cut his hand with a scalpel while he was assisting another physician. Because of the uncertainty that blood had been transferred from Doe's hand wound to the patient through an open surgical incision, he agreed to have a blood test for HIV. His blood tested positive for HIV, and he withdrew himself from participation in further surgical procedures. The medical center and Harrisburg Hospital, where Doe also participated in surgery, identified those patients who could be at risk. The medical center identified 279 patients, and Harrisburg identified 168 patients who fell into this category. Because hospital records did not identify those surgeries in which physicians may have accidentally cut themselves, the hospitals filed petitions in the Court of Common Pleas, alleging that there was, under the Confidentiality of HIV-Related Information Act [35 P.S. § 7608(a)(2)], a "compelling need" to disclose information regarding Doe's condition to those patients who conceivably could have been exposed to HIV. Doe argued that there was no compelling need to disclose the information and that he was entitled to confidentiality under the act.

The court issued an order for the selective release of information by: (1) providing the name of Doe to physicians and residents with whom he had participated in a surgical procedure or obstetrical care; (2) providing a letter to the patients at risk describing Doe as a resident in OB/GYN; and (3) setting forth the relevant period of such service. The physicians were prohibited under the HIV Act from disclosing Doe's name. The superior court affirmed the decision of the trial court, and Doe appealed.

The Pennsylvania Supreme Court held that a compelling need existed for at least a partial disclosure of the physician's HIV status. There was no question that Doe's HIV-positive status fell within the HIV Act's definition of confidential information. There were, however, exceptions within the HIV Act that allowed for disclosure of the information. In this case, there was a compelling reason to allow disclosure of the information. All the medical experts who testified agreed that there was some risk of exposure and that some form of

notice should be given to those patients at risk. Even the expert witness presented by Doe agreed that there was at least some conceivable risk of exposure and that giving a limited form of notice would not be unreasonable. Failure to notify patients at risk could result in the spread of the disease to other noninfected individuals through sexual contact and through exposure to other body fluids. Doe's name was not revealed to the patients, only the fact that a resident physician who participated in their care had tested HIV positive. "No principle is more deeply embedded in the law than that expressed in the maxim Salus populi suprema lex, . . . (the welfare of the people is the supreme law), and a more compelling and consistent application of that principle than the one presented would be quite difficult to conceive" (*Id.* at 163).

Right to Know and Confidentiality

Healthcare professionals and others working with AIDS patients have a right to know when they are caring for patients with highly contagious diseases. There are times when the duty to disclose outweighs the rights of confidentiality. The U.S. Court of Appeals for the Tenth Circuit in *Dunn v. White*[50] declared there is no Fourth Amendment impediment to a state prison's policy of testing the blood of all inmates for HIV. Under the U.S. Supreme Court's drug-testing decisions, the proper analysis is to balance the prisoner's interest in being free from bodily intrusion inherent in a blood test against the prison's institutional rights in combating the disease. The U.S. Court of Appeals held that in or out of prison, a person has only a limited privacy interest in not having his or her blood tested. The court cited *Schmerber v. California*,[51] which rejected a Fourth Amendment challenge to the blood testing of a suspected drunken driver. Against the prisoner's minimal interest, prison authorities have a strong interest in controlling the spread of HIV.

HIV Status "Improperly" Disclosed to Employer

A legal action was filed alleging that a physician had disclosed, in a worker's compensation report, the patient's HIV status to his employer without his consent. Learning of the employee's HIV disease, his supervisor and restaurant owner had agreed that the employee's HIV disease could pose a public relations nightmare and that the employee would have to be discharged. The employee was notified by mail that he had been replaced as general manager and would, thereafter, be considered an employee on unpaid leave without benefits. The employee's termination from his employment caused him to suffer physical, mental, and emotional distress. Evidence supported a finding of medical malpractice where the testimony of expert witnesses for both sides established that the standard of care was breached by the physician's disclosure of the patient's HIV status without his consent. The plaintiff-employee had a constitutionally protected interest in the privacy of his medical records and his right to privacy.[52]

HIV Status "Properly" Disclosed to Employer

The trial court properly dismissed a claim for breach of medical confidentiality and unreasonable violation of privacy by an HIV-positive patient seeking damages from a consulting physician for disclosing his HIV status in a medical record that was forwarded to the employer. The patient, a veterinary assistant who had developed an infection after being bitten by a cat, sought treatment for a work-related injury. Thus, notwithstanding his assertion that Kentucky Revised Statute (KRS) 214.181 conferred an absolute right to privacy with respect to his HIV status, the matter was governed by provisions of the Kentucky Workers' Compensation Act, KRS 342.020(8) and 803 Kentucky Administrative Regulation (KAR) 25-010, under which the patient was required to execute a release for medical information concerning his treatment for the work-related injury. Because the employer was required by law to pay the work-related medical bills, the very same law gave the employer the right to know the pertinent medical information.[53]

News Media

The Pennsylvania Superior Court, in *Stenger v. Lehigh Valley Hospital Center*,[54] upheld the order of the court of common pleas denying the petition of The Morning Call, Inc., which challenged a court order closing judicial proceedings to the press and public in a civil action against a hospital and physicians. A patient and her family had contracted AIDS after the patient received a blood transfusion. The access of the media to pretrial discovery proceedings in a civil action is subject to reasonable control by the court in which the action is pending. The protective order limiting public access to pretrial discovery material did not violate the newspaper's first amendment rights. The discovery documents were not judicial records to which the newspaper had a common law right of access. Good cause existed for nondisclosure of information about the intimate personal details of the plaintiffs' lives, the disclosure of which would cause undue humiliation.

Privileged Information: Statements Protected

The court, in *Wylie v. Mills*,[55] adopted the privilege used in several federal jurisdictions that prevents disclosure of confidential, critical, evaluative, and deliberative material whenever the public interest in confidentiality outweighs an individual's need for full discovery. In applying the privilege to information contained in a corporate report on an accident in which an employee was involved, the court held that self-evaluation privilege protected the report from discovery. Without such protection, candid expressions of opinion or suggestions as to future policy would not be forthcoming as a result of a fear that these statements may be used against the employer in a subsequent litigation. The standard used for disclosure of confidential investigative records sets forth the following factors that should be taken into consideration: (1) the extent to which the information may be available from other sources, (2) the degree of harm that the litigant will suffer from its unavailability, and (3) the possible prejudice in the agency's investigation. The court adopted the holding that the plaintiffs had not made a strong showing of a particular need that outweighs the public interest in the confidentiality of the quality assessment committee. The court decided that the information sought by the plaintiff was readily discoverable.

Credentialing Files Privileged

An action was filed against a healthcare provider in *Abels v. Ruf*[56] for the negligent credentialing of a physician who allegedly committed medical malpractice. The credentialing file relative to the physician in question was privileged. There was no dispute that the provider's credentialing documents fell within the scope of records of the provider's peer review committee, and it was clear that the legislature had dictated that such documents were not obtainable from the provider. The Ohio Court of Appeals found that the trial court abused its discretion in ordering the appellant to provide certain credentialing documents to plaintiffs-appellees in discovery that may have been generated by the appellant's peer review committee.

The trial court in *Hammonds v. Ruf*[57] erred when it ordered that certain portions of a physician's credentialing file be disclosed to medical malpractice plaintiffs because the documents were obtainable from original sources. The trial court abused its discretion in ordering the documents in question to be disclosed by the physician in violation of a clear statutory mandate prohibiting such disclosures.

🔍 *JOINT COMMISSION REPORTS PRIVILEGED FROM DISCOVERY*

Citation: *Humana Hosp. Corp. v. Spears Petersen*, 867 S.W.2d 858 (Tex. Ct. App. 1993)

Facts

The plaintiff, Garcia, sued Dr. Garg for negligently performing an injection, battery, fraud, and lack of informed consent. Garcia also sued Humana Corporation for negligence in credentialing, supervising, and monitoring Garg's clinical privileges. The plaintiff's attorney requested documents from Humana, including reports prepared by The Joint Commission. The Joint Commission is a voluntary organization that surveys healthcare organizations for the purpose of accreditation.

Humana objected to releasing the reports of The Joint Commission and filed for a protective order preventing disclosure. The Joint Commission reports contained recommendations describing the hospital's noncompliance with certain of its published standards. Humana argued that The Joint Commission reports are privileged information under Texas statute. Under Texas law, the records and proceedings of a medical committee are considered confidential and are not subject to a court subpoena. The plaintiff argued that The Joint Commission is not a medical committee as defined in the Texas statute. The hospital's chief operating officer testified that the accreditation process with The Joint Commission is voluntary and the hospital chooses to have the accreditation survey. During the survey, The Joint Commission looks at certain quality care standards it has developed for hospitals. Humana argued that release of The Joint Commission's recommendations would do more than "chill" the effectiveness of such accreditation. The plaintiff argued that even if the information was privileged, it had already been disclosed to a third party, the hospital, thus waiving its rights to nondisclosure. The trial court denied Humana's motion for a protective order that, if granted, would have permitted it to withhold from discovery any information pertaining to credentialing, monitoring, or supervision practices of the hospital regarding its physicians. Humana appealed.

Issue

Are accreditation reports prepared by The Joint Commission privileged from discovery?

Holding

The Texas Court of Appeals held that the accreditation reports were privileged.

Reason

The purpose of privileged communications is to encourage an open and thorough review of a hospital's medical staff and operations of a hospital with the objective of improving the delivery of patient care. The plaintiff argued that The Joint Commission is not a medical committee as defined in the Texas statute. The court of appeals found that the determinative factor is not whether the entity is known as a "committee" or a "commission" or by any other particular term, but whether it is organized for the purposes contemplated by the statute and case law. The Joint Commission is organized for the purposes of improving patient care. Both Texas statute and case law recognize that the open, thorough, and uninhibited review that is required for such committees to achieve their purpose can only be realized if the deliberations of the committee remain confidential.

Ordinary Business Documents

Privileged communications statutes do not protect from discovery the records maintained in the ordinary course of doing business and rendering inpatient care. Such documents often can be subpoenaed after showing cause.

Committee Minutes Discoverable

When a plaintiff seeks case information that does not regard a committee's action or its exchange of honest self-critical study but, instead, regards merely factual accountings of otherwise discoverable facts, such information is not protected by any privilege because it does not come within the scope of information entitled to that privilege. This does not mean that the plaintiff is entitled to the entire study because it may contain evidence of policy making, remedial action, proposed courses of conduct, and self-critical analysis that the privilege seeks to protect in order to foster the ability of hospitals to regulate themselves unhindered by outside scrutiny and unconcerned about the possible liability ramifications that their discussions might bring about. As such, the trial court must make an in-camera inspection of such records and determine to what extent they may be discoverable.

In one such case, the plaintiff, a patient, brought an action against a hospital seeking to recover for injuries he sustained as a result of a nosocomial infection he allegedly contracted at the hospital.[58] The plaintiff claimed that his infection was a result of an act or omission on the part of the hospital in failing to protect him from such infections. During the discovery phase of the proceedings, the plaintiff filed a motion for production of documents seeking studies done by the hospital regarding the nosocomial infection rates per patients admitted. The hospital objected to this request, and the plaintiff obtained an order to compel the hospital to produce the documents. The court of appeal, on review, reversed the trial court's ruling, determining that statutes rendering hospital records confidential barred the information from disclosure.

The Louisiana Supreme Court, however, held that the records sought by the plaintiff were not entirely privileged from disclosure. The reliance of the court of appeal on La. R.S. 13:3715.3(A) and 44:7(D) was partially misplaced. These provisions were intended to provide confidentiality to the records and proceedings of hospital committees, not to insulate from discovery certain facts merely because they have come under the review of any particular committee. Such an interpretation could cause any fact that a hospital chooses to unilaterally characterize as privileged to be barred from discovery. The plaintiff sought facts relating to nosocomial infection rates in the defendant's hospital. A nosocomial infection is the same malady that gave rise to the plaintiff's injuries. Such facts would be highly relevant to the plaintiff's case or highly likely to lead to such evidence.

Peer Review Documents "Privileged"

In *Estate of Hussain v. Gardner*,[59] discovery was sought regarding the statements given by a physician to the hospital's internal peer review committee regarding the management and treatment of a patient. In this medical malpractice action, the plaintiff alleged that the defendant-physician deviated from accepted medical standards in the care and treatment of the decedent during surgical procedures. The New Jersey Superior Court held that the statements given by the defendant were protected.

In *In re Investigation of Liberman*,[60] long-term patient Liberman fell and injured her head while unattended. She later died, apparently as a result of complications from the fall. The attorney general (AG) commenced a criminal investigation into Liberman's death, with more than 15 employees being questioned by the AG. The AG obtained and executed an investigatory search warrant for hospital documents. Before the documents left the hospital's premises, however, some of the documents were sealed because the hospital deemed them privileged peer review documents.

A hearing was held in district court regarding the AG's motion for permission to unseal the documents.

The district court was persuaded that the privilege statute asserted by the hospital did not apply because the documents were seized pursuant to a search warrant. The district court allowed the AG to unseal the documents, but the district judge stayed the decision to give the hospital an opportunity to appeal to the circuit court.

On appeal, the circuit court ruled that the peer review documents were protected by peer review privilege and that the privilege could be enforced even against documents seized pursuant to a search warrant. The court determined that the legislature intended the privilege to apply regardless of whether the documents were seized pursuant to a subpoena or a search warrant.

The Michigan statute MCL 333 § 21515 provides:

(1) peer review information is confidential; (2) peer review information is to be used "only for the purposes provided in this article"; (3) peer review information is not to be a public record; and (4) peer review information is not subject to subpoena.

The legislation commands that a hospital maintain a peer review process for the purpose of improving patient care. Allowing a prosecutor to obtain a hospital's peer review materials pursuant to a search warrant would be to allow the prosecutor's general investigative powers to override the specific privilege of confidentiality that covers such materials. Accordingly, the Michigan Court of Appeals concluded that documents created by a peer review body exclusively for peer review purposes are not subject to disclosure pursuant to a search warrant in a criminal investigation.

Peer Review Documents "Not Privileged"

The identity of peer review committee members and individuals who may have given information to such committees is not always considered privileged. A state, for example, may access peer review reports relating to a physician suspected of criminal negligence.[61] In a civil action, a hospital may be required to identify all persons who have knowledge of an underlying event that is the basis of a malpractice action, whether or not they were members of a peer review committee.[62]

The surgeon in *Robinson v. Magovern*[63] brought an action under the Sherman Antitrust Act, as well as under state law, seeking recovery because he had been denied hospital privileges. The plaintiff moved in the U.S. District Court for an order compelling the defendants and certain third-party witnesses to respond to discovery requests and deposition questions. The defendants objected, claiming that the information sought was privileged and that the Pennsylvania Peer Review Protection Act seeks to foster candor and discussion at medical review committee meetings through grants of immunity and confidentiality. The court held that although there was a powerful interest in confidentiality embodied in the Pennsylvania Peer Review Protection Act, the Act would not be applied to shield from discovery events surrounding the denial of staff privileges, including what occurred at meetings of the hospital's credentials committee and executive committee. The need for evidence was greater than the need for confidentiality in this case. The defendants' objections were overruled, and the motion to compel was granted.

In a similar case, the physician in *Ott v. St. Luke Hospital of Campbell County, Inc.*[64] brought a civil rights suit because his application for medical staff privileges was denied. The physician contended that he was not invited to several peer review committee meetings or given an opportunity to be heard. The hospital filed for a protective order that would bar discovery of the proceedings of the peer review committee. The hospital argued that such committees would become ineffective if their deliberations were discoverable and that the privilege claimed by the hospital is recognized in Section 311.377 of the Kentucky Revised Statutes Annotates (1990).

The U.S. district court held that where there was no real showing that the peer review committee's functions would be impaired substantially, and where the benefit gained for correct disposal of the litigation by denying privilege was overwhelming, the hospital would not be permitted to assert privilege. The hospital's motion was therefore denied. The court indicated that it cannot permit the discharge of its responsibility to conduct a search for the truth to be thwarted by rules of privilege in the absence of strong countervailing public policies.

Staff Privileging Documents "Discoverable"

In *May v. Wood River Township Hospital*,[65] the patient's guardian sued the hospital and physicians, alleging that the hospital was negligent in providing care to the patient and in granting staff privileges to Dr. Marrese. The circuit court granted the guardian's motion and ordered the hospital to answer certain interrogatories. The hospital appealed.

The hospital submitted a memorandum of law and an affidavit stating that all documents concerning the granting of associate staff privileges to Marrese were kept for the purpose of improving the quality of patient care and were protected by the Illinois Code of Civil Procedure.

The trial court denied the hospital's motion for a protective order and granted the plaintiff's motion to compel, ordering the hospital to answer all of the plaintiff's interrogatories. The court determined that nothing related to work done, communications between executive committee members during their meetings, or discussions related to Marrese is protected; in addition, the minutes of the committee were not protected as long as this information existed or was created before the actual decision to grant privileges to Marrese. The hospital urged on appeal, however, that no Illinois case has interpreted the code as being inapplicable to the credentialing process.

The Illinois Appellate Court held that the code of civil procedure did not protect information generated prior to the physician's application for staff privileges or his application for the privileges. The same is true of a host of materials that might be considered by the committee, for example:

- Whether staff privileges were granted, denied, or revoked at other hospitals.
- Whether licenses to practice medicine were awarded, denied, suspended, or revoked in a given state.
- Whether an applicant has ever been sued for malpractice.

These facts would exist independent of a peer review process. That which is nonprivileged cannot be converted to being privileged simply by handing the facts to a committee. On the other hand, if the committee sought to generate new opinions or information for consideration by the committee, a privilege could attach. For example, if the committee interviewed a colleague of Marrese's to elicit an opinion on Marrese's ability as a physician, that opinion could be privileged. If, however, the same opinion had been stated earlier in a deposition in a malpractice case and the committee reviewed the deposition, no privilege could attach to conceal the deposition from the discovery process.

Staff Credentialing Documents "Not Discoverable"

The underlying action in *McGee v. Bruce Hospital System*[66] involved a wrongful death claim. A circuit court order granted the plaintiffs a motion instructing the defendant, Bruce Hospital System, to produce the credentialing files and clinical privileges for each of the defendant-physicians. The defendant-physicians contended that such documentation is protected by South Carolina confidentiality statute [S.C. CODE ANN. § 40-71-20 (Supp. 1992)]. The trial judge found that the materials sought were discoverable.

On appeal, the South Carolina Supreme Court held that: (1) applications for staff privileges and supporting documents of appropriate training were protected by the confidentiality statute; (2) the confidentiality statute did not preclude discovery of general policies and procedures for staff monitoring; and (3) the patient could discover a listing of clinical privileges either granted or denied by the hospital. The overriding public policy of the confidentiality statute is to encourage healthcare professionals to monitor the competency and professional conduct of their peers in order to safeguard and improve the quality of patient care. The underlying purpose behind the confidentiality statute is not to facilitate the prosecution of civil actions but to promote complete candor and open discussion among participants in the peer review process.

Section 40-71-20 of the South Carolina statute does not preclude the discovery of the general policies and procedures for staff monitoring. The information contained in the written rules, regulations, policies, and procedures for the medical staff would not compromise the statutory goal of candid evaluation of peers in the medical profession.

The outcome of the decision-making process is not protected. The confidentiality statute was intended to protect the review process, not to restrict the disclosure of the result of the process. Accordingly, the plaintiffs were entitled to a listing of clinical privileges either granted or denied by the hospital.

▶ CHARTING: SOME HELPFUL ADVICE

The medical record is the most important document in a malpractice action. Both the plaintiff and defendant use it as a basis for their actions and defense in a lawsuit. The following suggestions on documentation should prove helpful when charting in a patient's record.

- A medical record has many authors. Entries made by others must not be ignored. Good patient care is a collaborative, interdisciplinary team effort. Entries made by healthcare professionals provide valuable information in treating the patient.
- The medical record describes the care rendered to a patient. It should provide a clear timeline of patient care needs and how they were addressed from the time of admission to the time of discharge. It should include a complete and accurate medical history and physical, medications at the time of admission, allergies, over-the-counter drugs, vitamins, differential diagnoses, treatment plan, care rendered, and follow-up instructions.

- Medical record entries should be timely, legible, clear, and meaningful to a patient's course of treatment. Illegible medical records not only damage one's ability to defend oneself in a court action, but also can have an adverse effect on the credibility of other healthcare professionals who read the record and act on what they read.
- Progress notes should describe the symptom(s) or condition(s) being addressed, the treatment rendered, the patient's response, and status at the time inpatient care is discontinued. All notes must be dated and signed in order to provide an accurate history of the patient's care and treatment during the hospital stay. Follow-up on other caregiver notes should be described in the progress notes (e.g., observations of consultants, dietitians, nurses, pharmacists, physical therapists, and respiratory therapists).
- Long, defensive, or derogatory notes should not be written. Only the facts should be related. Criticism, complaints, emotional comments, and extraneous remarks have no place in the medical record. Such remarks can precipitate a malpractice suit.
- Erasures and correction fluid should not be used to cover up entries. Do not tamper with the chart in any form. A single line should be drawn through a mistaken entry, the correct information entered, and the correction signed and dated.
- Charts related to pending legal action should be placed in a separate file under lock and key. Legal counsel should be notified immediately of any potential lawsuit.
- Reasoning for not following the advice of a consultant should be noted in the medical record, not to discredit the consultant, but to show that due consideration was given to the consultant's medical opinion.

🔍 THE COURT'S DECISION

Sanfiel violated Florida Administrative Code by violating the confidentiality of information or knowledge concerning a patient. Florida Code Rule 59S-8.005 states in part that unprofessional conduct includes violating the confidentiality of information or knowledge concerning a patient. The board reasonably interpreted this provision to apply to the circumstances present in this case. Sanfiel knew that a nurse could be disciplined for disclosing such information, yet he intentionally released the information to the news media. It is reasonable to characterize Sanfiel's actions as unprofessional conduct.[67]

▶ CHAPTER REVIEW

1. *Information management* is the process of facilitating the flow of information within and among departments and caregivers.

2. The medical record is the principal means of communication among healthcare professionals in matters relating to patient care.

3. The contents of inpatient medical records provide evidence of a patient's care from admission to discharge (e.g., admission record, authorization for treatment forms, advance directives, history and physical examination, treatment plans, physicians' orders, progress notes, nursing notes, diagnostic reports, consultation reports, vital signs charts, anesthesia assessments, operative reports, medication administration records, discharge planning documentation, patient education, and discharge summary).

4. Patient care documentation must be complete and accurate. Federal funding can be denied for inaccurate record keeping.

5. The Privacy Act of 1974 was enacted in part to safeguard individual privacy from the misuse of federal records and to give individuals access to records concerning themselves that are maintained by federal agencies.

6. HIPAA requires the establishment of national standards for electronic healthcare transactions and national identifiers for providers, health insurance plans, and employers. HIPAA provisions also address the privacy and security of health information.

7. Medical records are maintained for the benefit of patients and are considered the property of the healthcare provider. Patients, providers of care, and third parties such as insurance carriers generally have access to patient records for billing purposes. They are also available for criminal investigations.

8. The requirements for the length of time medical records must be retained are based on statutory requirements, advice from legal counsel, patient needs, future need for the records, and legal considerations.

9. Although electronic medical records improve the ease and efficiency with which data are compiled and shared, they also pose confidentiality risks.

10. Records can be used as important evidentiary tools. The integrity and completeness of a medical record can be crucial in reconstructing the events surrounding alleged negligence.

11. Falsification of medical or business records is grounds for both criminal indictment and civil liability.

▶ REVIEW QUESTIONS

1. Describe the importance of information management planning.

2. Describe the importance and contents of medical records.

3. Explain the importance of maintaining complete and accurate records.

4. Discuss how the Privacy Act of 1974 and the Health Insurance Portability and Accountability Act of 1996 safeguard a patient's privacy.

5. Explain the ownership of and who can access a patient's medical record.

6. Describe the advantages and disadvantages of electronic medical records.

7. Describe why the medical record is important in legal proceedings.

8. Describe a variety of ways in which medical records have been falsified.

9. Explain what is meant by the medical record battleground.

▶ NOTES

1. No. 94969 (Supreme Court of N.Y. App. Div. 2004).

2. Centers for Medicare and Medicaid Services, "Design and development of the Diagnosis Related Group (DRG)," October 1, 2016. https://www.cms.gov/ICD10Manual/version 34-fullcode-cms/fullcode_cms/Design_and _development_of_the_Diagnosis_Related _Group_(DRGs)_PBL-038.pdf.

3. NSO, "Charting By Exception: The Legal Risks." http://www.nso.com/risk-education /individuals/articles/Charting-By-Exception -The-Legal-Risks.

4. 16 F.3d 473 (1st Cir. 1994).

5. No. 94189 (N.Y. App. Div. 2004).

6. U.S. Department of Health and Human Services, Office for Civil Rights, "Business Associate's Failure to Safeguard Nursing Home Residents' PHI Leads to $650,000 HIPAA Settlement," June 29, 2016. http://www.hhs.gov/hipaa/for -professionals/compliance-enforcement /agreements/catholic-health-care-services/.

7. U.S. Department of Health and Human Services, "Resolution Agreement," https://www.hhs.gov/sites/default/files/chcs-racap-final.pdf.

8. 2004 Ohio 3163 (Ohio Ct. App. 2004).

9. *Id.*

10. *Id.*

11. "Rules and Regulations," Federal Register 78, no. 17 (Friday, January 25, 2013), http://www.gpo.gov/fdsys/pkg/FR-2013-01-25/pdf/2013-01073.pdf.

12. 515 A.2d 948 (Pa. Super. Ct. 1986).

13. 536 N.E.2d 1202 (Ohio Com. Pl. 1988).

14. 582 N.E.2d 233 (Ill. App. Ct. 1991).

15. 21 U.S.C. § 1175 (1972).

16. *EHCA Dunwoody, L.L.C. v. Daniel*, 627 S.E.2d 830 (Ga. App. 2006).

17. 647 So. 2d 1366 (La. App. 3d Cir. 1994).

18. 328 P.2d 556 (Cal. Ct. App. 1958).

19. 597 N.E.2d 616 (Ill. 1992).

20. Institute of Medicine, "Reducing Medical Errors Requires National Computerized Information Systems; Data Standards Are Crucial to Improving Patient Safety," November 20, 2003, http://www8.nationalacademies.org/onpinews/newsitem.aspx?RecordID=10863.

21. John P. Glaser, "Brigham and Women's Wager on Huge PC Network Pays Solid Returns," *Health Management Technology*, October 1994: 7.

22. 905 F.2d 549 (1st Cir. 1990).

23. Federal Rules of Evidence, 28 § 803(6) (1988).

24. *Id.* at 551.

25. *Masterson v. Pennsylvania R. Co.*, 182 F.2d 793, 797 (3d Cir. 1950) (decided under the Federal Business Records Act).

26. 683 N.E.2d 1175 (Ohio App. 1996).

27. *Moskovitz v. Mount Sinai Med. Ctr.*, 635 N.E.2d 331 (Ohio 1994).

28. 442 A.2d 635 (N.J. Super. Ct. 1982).

29. *In re Jascalevich*, 182 N.J. Super. 445, 442 A.2d 635, 644–645 (1982).

30. 880 P.2d 1188 (Colo. 1994).

31. *Id.* at 1192.

32. *Id.* at 1196.

33. 402 N.Y.S.2d 318 (N.Y. Sup. Ct. 1978).

34. "Deceit Found in Fatality at Rest Home," *New York Times*, February 5, 1995: 35.

35. Ronnie Greene, "Examiner: Treatment 'Appropriate,'" *The Miami Herald*, April 16, 1995: 14A.

36. 609 N.Y.S.2d 898 (N.Y. App. Div. 1994).

37. Esme M. Infante, "Doctors' Rx: Write Right," *USA Today*, June 14, 1994: 1.

38. *Estate of Vasquez v. Albertsons, Inc., et al.*, Morelaw Lexapedia, http://www.morelaw.com/verdicts/case.asp?s=TX&d=7970; Mimi Hall, "Doctor Held Liable for Fatal Handwriting Mix-Up," *USA Today*, October 21, 1999.

39. 262 P.2d 682 (Wyo. 1953).

40. 42 U.S.C.A. § 11101–11152 (1989).

41. Social Security, "Title IV—Health Care Quality Improvement Act of 1986," https://www.ssa.gov/OP_Home/comp2/F099-660.html.

42. 572 N.E.2d 1025 (Ill. App. Ct. 1991).

43. *Berger v. Sonneland*, 1 P.3d 1187 (2000).

44. *Suzan Berger, Respondent, v. John Sonneland, M.D., Petitioner*, 144 Wash.2d 91, 26 3d 258, 271 (July 05, 2001).

45. 592 A.2d 1251 (N.J. Super. Ct. Law Div. 1991).

46. *Id.* at 1255.

47. 734 S.W.2d 675 (Tex. Ct. App. 1987).

48. 538 N.E.2d 419 (Ohio Ct. App. 1988).

49. 639 A.2d 159 (Pa.1993).

50. No. 88-2194 (10th Cir. Aug. 1, 1989) (unpublished).

51. 384 U.S. 757 (1966).

52. *Francies v. Kapla*, 127 Cal. App. 4th 1381, 26 Cal. Rptr. 3d 501 (Cal. Ct. App. 2005).

53. *Meld v. Barnett*, 157 S.W.3d 596 (Ky. 2005).

54. 554 A.2d 954 (Pa. Super. Ct. 1989).

55. 195 N.J. Super. 332 , 478 A.2d 1273 (N.J. Super. Ct. App. Div. 1984).

56. C. A. No. 22265 (Ohio App. 2005).

57. C. A. No. 22109 (Ohio Ct. App. 2004).

58. *Smith v. Lincoln Gen. Hosp.*, 605 So. 2d 1347 (La. 1992).

59. 624 A.2d 99 (N.J. Super. Ct. App. Div. 1993).

60. 646 N.W.2d 199 (Mich. App. 2002).

61. *People v. Superior Court*, 286 Cal. Rptr., 478 (Cal. Ct. App. 1991).

62. *Moretti v. Lowe*, 592 A.2d 855 (R.I. 1991).

63. 521 F. Supp. 842 (W.D. Pa. 1981).

64. 522 F. Supp. 706 (E.D. Ky. 1981).

65. 629 N.E.2d 170 (Ill. App. Ct. 1994).

66. 439 S.E.2d 257 (S.C. 1993).

67. *Proenza Sanfiel v. Department of Health*, 749 So. 2d 525 (Fla. App. 1999).

CHAPTER 14

Patient Consent, Rights, and Responsibilities

🔍 IT'S YOUR GAVEL...

BLOOD REFUSED WAS ADMINISTERED

Mrs. Hughes, a 39-year-old Jehovah's Witness, was admitted to the hospital to undergo a hysterectomy. At the time of her admission to the hospital, Mrs. Hughes signed forms expressing her desire not to receive any blood or blood products. She also verbally expressed this intention to her treating physician, Dr. Ances. Unanticipated problems arose during surgery that, in Dr. Ances' opinion, required blood transfusions to save Mrs. Hughes' life. Dr. Ances contacted Mr. Hughes, Mrs. Hughes' husband, to discuss the emergency situation and his wife's need for blood. While on the phone, Mr. Hughes, also a Jehovah's Witness, authorized transfusions.

On May 14, 1991, the hospital initiated an emergency hearing before a judge for the purpose of having a temporary guardian appointed for Mrs. Hughes to allow additional transfusions after the surgery. She was unconscious and incapable of expressing her desires at the time.

Dr. Ances testified that Mrs. Hughes, who had been his patient for 6 weeks, told him she did not want blood products. He informed her that a time could arise when blood might be needed to save her life. He also told her that, given the procedure and the size of the uterus, it was unlikely that she would need blood during the surgery. Dr. Ances was aware that Mrs. Hughes had signed hospital forms refusing blood. Dr. Ances told the judge that he assumed Mrs. Hughes was aware of the ramifications of refusing the blood and therefore did not specifically discuss them with her. After hearing testimony from Dr. Ances and Mrs. Hughes' family, the judge found that the evidence was unclear as to whether she would want blood or blood products if it meant saving her life. As a result, the judge appointed the hospital's risk manager as temporary guardian for the limited purpose of giving consent to the administration of blood and blood products. The order explicitly extended only until Mrs. Hughes regained consciousness and became competent to make her own decisions.

Mrs. Hughes received blood transfusions during the time she was unconscious. She later filed a lawsuit claiming she was administered blood transfusions contrary to her written instructions. Did the court err in making a temporary emergency decision to appoint a medical guardian?[1]

WHAT IS YOUR VERDICT?

▶ LEARNING OBJECTIVES

The reader, upon completion of this chapter, will be able to:

- Discuss the difference between verbal, written, and implied consent.
- Describe the role of the patient, physician, nurse, and hospital in informed consent.
- Describe the theories under which the validity of consent might be proven.
- Explain how consent differs among competent patients, minors, guardians, and incompetent patients.
- Discuss the importance of understanding patient rights.
- Discuss the importance of understanding patient responsibilities.

This chapter provides an overview of patient consent, rights, and responsibilities. Every person possesses certain rights guaranteed by the Constitution of the United States and its amendments, including the freedoms of speech, religion, and association, and the right not to be discriminated against on the grounds of race, creed, color, or national origin. The Supreme Court has interpreted the Constitution as also guaranteeing certain other rights, such as the right to privacy and self-determination, and the right to accept or reject medical treatment.

With rights come responsibilities. The patient, for example, has a right to receive emergency care, while at the same time, he or she has a responsibility to let the caregiver know the limits of that care, as noted in the opening case in which the patient had objections to the administration of blood.

▶ PATIENT CONSENT

[N]o right is held more sacred, or is more carefully guarded, by the common law, than the right of every individual to the possession and control of his own person.

—Union Pacific Ry. Co. v. Botsford[2]

Consent, in the healthcare setting, is the voluntary agreement by a person who possesses sufficient mental capacity to make an intelligent choice to allow a medical procedure and/or treatment proposed by another to be performed on himself or herself. Consent changes a touching that otherwise would be nonconsensual to one that is consensual. Consent can be either express or implied.

- *Express consent* can take the form of a verbal agreement, or it can be accomplished through the execution of a written document authorizing medical care.
- *Implied consent* is determined by some act or silence, which raises a presumption that consent has been authorized.

Consent must be obtained from the patient, or from a person authorized to consent on the patient's behalf, before any medical procedure can be performed. Every individual has a right to refuse to authorize a touching. Touching of another without authorization to do so could be considered a battery. Not every touching results in a battery. When a person voluntarily enters a situation in which a reasonably prudent person would anticipate a touching (e.g., riding in an elevator, rushing through a crowded subway, or in an emergency department), consent is implied. Consent is not required for the normal, routine, everyday touching and bumping that occurs in life. In the process of caring for patients, it is inevitable that they will be touched. Most touching in the healthcare setting is considered routine. Typical routine touching includes bathing, administering medications, dressing changes, and so forth. This section reviews the many issues relating to consent.

INFORMED CONSENT

NEWS SURGERY TO EASE PAIN SOUNDED REALLY SIMPLE

To Beth Israel, It sounded like a no-brainer . . .
  "If I knew what could have happened, I'd never have had the surgery. To go from shots to surgery was probably stupid."
  Other people's experiences, she observed, are no substitute for a careful consideration of the possible risks and benefits of surgery.
    —Sandra G. Goodman, *The Washington Post*, July 4, 2017

Informed consent is a legal doctrine that provides that a patient has the right to know the potential risks, benefits, and alternatives of a proposed procedure. *Canterbury v. Spence*,[3] in 1972, set the "reasonable man" standard, which required informed consent for treatment. Patients must be informed of the risks, benefits, and alternatives associated with recommended treatments. Where there are two or more medically acceptable treatment options, the competent patient has the absolute right to know about and select from the available treatment options after being informed of the risks, benefits, and alternatives of each.

The informed consent doctrine provides that a physician has a legal, ethical, and moral duty to respect patient autonomy and to provide only such medical care as authorized by the patient. An authorization from a patient who does not understand the treatment to which he or she is consenting is not effective consent.

The right to be free from unwanted medical treatment has long been recognized by the courts. The right to control the integrity of one's own body spawned the doctrine of informed consent.[4] The U.S. Supreme Court, in *Cruzan v. Director, Missouri Dep't of Health*,[5] held that a competent adult patient has the right to decline any and all forms of medical intervention, including lifesaving or life-prolonging treatment.

Verbal Consent

Verbal consent, if proved, is as binding as written consent because there is, in general, no legal requirement that a patient's consent be in writing. However, oral consent is more difficult to corroborate.

Verbal Consent for Surgery Adequate

The plaintiff in *Siliezar v. East Jefferson General Hospital*[6] argued that the defendants breached the standard of care by failing to obtain written consent for a surgical procedure. The trial judge found that the plaintiff failed to sustain her burden of proof and that the defendants were liable to her for damages. On appeal, the appellees admitted that they breached hospital policy by failing to obtain written consent prior to surgery. The physician testified that he explained the surgical procedure, as well as the risks of the procedure. He testified that after he explained the procedure and its risks, he left a written consent form for the patient to sign. He explained that although it is the policy of the clinic to obtain a written consent prior to performing surgery, the patient did not sign the consent form. The surgeon testified that he did not know why the form was not signed but that the patient did not refuse to sign the form.

At trial, a nurse testified that she placed the patient in an operating room and prepared her for surgery. Although she was not in the room when the surgeon discussed the surgical procedure with the plaintiff, she testified that she was in the next room and was able to hear the physician explain the procedure to the plaintiff. The nurse also had no explanation as to why the consent was not signed. She did state that the patient never said she did not want surgery and did not ask the physician to stop the procedure. The nurse testified that while the physician performed the surgery, he explained to the patient what he was doing.

Louisiana statutes do not require that a patient's consent be written. Verbal consent was sufficient. The verbal consent included the information required by statute, and the patient was given an opportunity to ask questions and those questions were answered. The plaintiff claimed that she was told that surgery would not be performed. The trial judge did not find her testimony to be credible. The appellate court found that the defendants did not commit malpractice by failing to obtain written consent prior to surgery.

Written Consent

A written consent form should be executed when a proposed treatment may involve some unusual risk(s) to the patient. A written consent provides visible proof of a patient's wishes. Because the function of a written consent form is to preserve evidence of informed consent, the nature of the treatment, the risks, the benefits, and the consequences involved should be incorporated into the consent form. States have taken the view that consent, to be effective, must be informed consent and should include the following elements:

- Nature of the patient's illness or injury
- Procedure or treatment consented to
- Purpose of the proposed treatment
- Risks and probable consequences of the proposed treatment
- Probability that the proposed treatment will be successful
- Alternative methods of treatment and their associated risks and benefits
- Risks and prognosis if no treatment is rendered
- An indication that the patient understands the nature of any proposed treatment, the alternatives, the risks involved, and the probable consequences of the proposed treatment
- Signatures of the patient, physician, and witnesses
- Date the consent is signed

Healthcare professionals have an important role in the realm of informed consent. They can be instrumental in averting major lawsuits by being observant as to the doubts, changes of mind, confusion, or misunderstandings expressed by a patient regarding any proposed procedures he or she is about to undergo.

Implied Consent

Although the law requires consent for the intentional touching that stems from medical or surgical procedures, exceptions do exist with respect to emergency situations. Implied consent will generally be presumed when immediate action is required to prevent death or permanent impairment of a patient's health. If it is impossible in an emergency to obtain the consent of the patient or someone legally authorized to give consent, the required procedure may be undertaken without liability for failure to procure consent.

Unconscious patients are presumed under law to approve treatment that appears to be necessary. It is assumed that such patients would have consented if they were conscious and competent. However, if a conscious patient expressly refuses to consent to certain treatment, such treatment may not be instituted after the patient becomes unconscious. Similarly, conscious patients suffering from emergency conditions retain the right to refuse consent.

If a procedure is necessary to protect one's life or health, every effort must be made to document the medical necessity for proceeding with medical treatment without consent. It must be shown that the emergency situation constituted an immediate threat to life or health.

In *Luka v. Lowrie*,[7] a case involving a 15-year-old boy whose left foot had been run over and crushed by a train, consultation by the treating physician with other physicians was an important factor in determining the outcome of the case. On the boy's arrival at the hospital, the defending physician and four house surgeons decided it was necessary to amputate the foot. The court said it was inconceivable that, had the parents been present, they would have refused consent in the face of a determination by five physicians that amputation would save the boy's life. Thus, despite testimony at the trial that the amputation may not have been necessary, professional consultation before the operation supported the assertion that a genuine emergency existed and consent could be implied.

Consent also can be implied in nonemergency situations. For example, a patient may voluntarily submit to a procedure, implying consent, without any explicitly spoken or written expression of consent. In the Massachusetts case of *O'Brien v. Cunard Steam Ship Co.*,[8] a ship's passenger who joined a line of people receiving injections was held to have implied his consent to a vaccination. The rationale for this decision is that individuals who observe a line of people and who notice that injections are being administered to those at the head of the line should expect that if they join and remain in the line, they would receive an injection. The plaintiff entered the line voluntarily. The plaintiff had opportunity to see what was taking place at the head of the line and could have exited the line, but chose not to do so. The jury appropriately determined this to be consent to the injection. The O'Brien case contains all of the elements necessary to imply consent to a voluntary act: the procedure was a simple vaccination, the proceedings were visible at all times, and the plaintiff was free to withdraw up to the instant of the injection.

Whether a patient's consent can be implied is frequently asked when the condition of a patient requires some deviation from an agreed-on procedure. If a patient expressly prohibits a specific medical or surgical procedure, consent to the procedure cannot be implied. The same consent rule applies if a patient expressly prohibits a particular extension of a procedure, even though the patient voluntarily submitted to the original procedure.

Statutory Consent

Many states have adopted legislation concerning emergency care. An emergency in most states eliminates the need for consent. When a patient is clinically unable to give consent to a lifesaving emergency treatment, the law implies consent on the presumption that a reasonable person would consent to lifesaving medical intervention.

When an emergency situation does arise, there may be little opportunity to contact the attending physician, much less a consultant. The patient's records, therefore, must be complete with respect to the description of his or her illness and condition, the attempts made to contact the physician as well as relatives, and the emergency measures taken and procedures performed. If time does not permit a court order to be obtained, a second medical opinion, when practicable, is advisable.

Judicial Consent

Judicial consent may be necessary in those instances where there is concern as to the absence or legality of consent. Judicial intervention is periodically necessary to grant consent on an emergency basis when a court is not in session. A judge should be contacted only after alternative methods have been exhausted and the matter cannot wait for a determination during the normal working hours of the court. Some courts (e.g., Massachusetts trial courts) require an attorney to initiate the call to the justice and to certify that there are no alternatives, other than a judicial response, available in the matter.

Physicians and Informed Consent

Informed consent is predicated on the duty of the physician to disclose to the patient sufficient information to enable the patient to evaluate a proposed medical or surgical procedure before submitting to it. Informed consent requires that a patient have a full understanding of that to which he or she has consented. A physician's explanation of treatment options should take into consideration the patient's ability to understand the description of the risks of treatment and the probable consequences of each treatment.

A patient who undergoes surgery in a teaching hospital may have a resident participating in the surgical procedures. Patients who prefer the attending physician to perform the surgery, often because of his or her reputation, should make an inquiry as to who will be performing the surgery. Consent forms in such

YOUR DOCTOR IS HERE AND THERE

Hospitals debate the wisdom and ethics of allowing surgeons to operate on two patients in different rooms at the same time.

The controversial practice has been standard in many teaching hospitals for decades, its safety and ethics largely unquestioned and its existence unknown to those most affected: people undergoing surgery.

—Sandra G. Boodman, *The Washington Post*, July 7, 2017

settings should include the name(s) and role of the participating surgeon(s). Dr. James Rickert, an Indiana orthopaedic surgeon, recommends in surgical cases that the patient ask the surgeon, "Are you going to be in the room the entire time during my surgery? . . . If the doctor's not willing to say yes, vote with your feet."[9]

Informed consent should include what a reasonable person would consider material to his or her decision of whether or not to undergo treatment. The needs of each patient can vary depending on age, maturity, and mental status. Florida statute § 766.103 (3) (a) (2) notes that reasonable care on the part of a physician in obtaining informed consent for treatment consists of providing the patient with information sufficient to give a reasonable person a general understanding of the proposed procedure, the medically acceptable alternative procedures, and the substantial risks and hazards inherent in the proposed procedure that are recognized by other physicians in the same or similar community who perform similar procedures. A physician is not under a duty to elucidate upon all of the possible risks, only those of a serious nature. Expert testimony is required to establish whether a reasonable physician in the community would make the pertinent disclosures under the same or similar circumstances.

The ethical rationale underlying the doctrine of informed consent is firmly rooted in the notions of liberty and individual autonomy. Informed consent protects the basic right of the patient to make the ultimate informed decision regarding the course of treatment to which he or she knowledgeably consents. The focus of informed consent must involve the patient receiving informed consent as a result of active personal interaction with the physician. Consent forms should be used as a supplement to the oral disclosure of risks, benefits, and alternatives to the proposed procedure that a physician normally gives. Ideally, the consent should be the result of an active process of dialogue between the patient and physician.

Informed consent is not merely a tool to avoid lawsuits; rather, it is designed to allow patients to make an informed decision. The emphasis on "informed" must not be to avoid a lawsuit by meeting some legal requirement, with little regard to the patient's level of understanding. The use of consent forms in this manner has contributed to the view that what was intended as a process of dialogue and discussion has developed into an event in which papers are signed and minimal legal requirements are satisfied. The consent form often is used as a legal protection for the physician for unforeseen mishaps that might occur during surgery.

Physicians Must Disclose Alternatives

The patient-plaintiff in *Stover v. Surgeons*[11] suffered damage to her heart valves as a result of childhood rheumatic fever. Dr. Ford, one of a group of physicians that the patient consulted after her condition worsened, informed the patient she needed a heart valve replacement. Dr. Ford stated that he briefly reviewed the details of the surgery with the patient. The plaintiff claims she was never informed about the risks associated with installing mechanical valves, including the Beall valve that was implanted in her heart. Thromboemboli, strokes, and the lifelong use of anticoagulants, which are common adverse effects of valve replacements, were never discussed with her. Dr. Zikria, who performed the surgery, could not recall discussing any risks, other than clotting. Following surgery, the patient suffered severe, permanent brain damage from multiple episodes of thromboemboli directly caused by valve

NEWS UNREPORTED ROBOTIC SURGERY INJURIES OPEN NEW QUESTIONS FOR FDA

When Sheena Wilson, 45, underwent robotic surgery for a hysterectomy in May, she didn't know the Intuitive Surgical Inc. system used by her doctor was previously tied to a variety of injuries for the same procedure.

• • •

"If I had known there were other people who had injuries, I would never have done this surgery," said Wilson, who has filed suit against Intuitive and her doctor. "Whatever they have in place is not working."
—Robert Langreth, *Bloomberg*, December 30, 2013[10]

implantation. She then sued for lack of informed consent. The jury returned a verdict for her and the physicians appealed. The Pennsylvania Superior Court held that the physicians had to discuss alternative prostheses with the patient where they represented medically recognized alternatives. Evidence that the heart valve actually implanted was no longer in general use at the time of operation was relevant and material to the issue of informed consent. The court reasoned that alternative valves were available and never discussed with the patient. Although the physicians argued that the choice of prosthesis should belong to them, the court held that if there are other recognized, medically sound alternatives, the patient must be informed about the risks and benefits of them in order to make a sound judgment regarding treatment, including the desire to execute a waiver of consent. The agreement between the physician and the patient is contractual. Consent is not valid if the patient does not understand the operation to be performed and its seriousness. Here the physicians failed to inform the patient about the recognized risks of the valve that was implanted.

Paternalism Fails

The patient-plaintiff in *Matthies v. Mastromonaco*,[12] an elderly woman living alone in a senior citizens' residence, fell and fractured her hip and was taken to the hospital. An orthopaedic surgeon, the defendant, reviewed the patient's history, condition, and X-rays and decided that, rather than using a pinning procedure for her hip involving the insertion of four steel screws, it would be better to adopt a conservative course of treatment, bed rest.

Prior to her injury, the plaintiff maintained an independent style of living. She did her own grocery shopping and other household duties and had been able to climb steps unassisted.

Expert testimony at trial indicated that bed rest was an inappropriate treatment. The defendant was of the opinion that given the frail condition of the patient and her age, she would be best treated in a nursing home and, therefore, opted for a more conservative treatment. At the heart of the informed consent issue was the plaintiff's assertion that she would not have consented to bed rest if she had been informed of the probable effect on the quality of her life.

The New Jersey Supreme Court held that it is necessary to advise a patient when considering alternative courses of treatment. The physician should have explained medically reasonable invasive and noninvasive alternatives, including the risks and likely outcomes of those alternatives, even when the chosen course is noninvasive.

In an informed consent analysis, the decisive factor is not whether a treatment alternative is invasive or noninvasive, but whether the physician adequately presents the material facts so that the patient can make an informed decision. That conclusion does not imply that a physician must explain in detail all treatment options in every case. The standard obligates the physician to disclose only that information material to a reasonable patient's informed decision.[13] If the patient's choice is not consistent with the physician's recommendation, the physician has the option of withdrawing from the case. The patient, then, has the option to seek another physician who is comfortable with the alternative treatment preferred by the patient.

🔍 *PHYSICIAN'S DUTY TO ADVISE: DELICATE MEDICAL JUDGMENT*

Citation: Mathias v. St. Catherine's Hosp., Inc., 569 N.W.2d 330 (Wis. App. 1997)

Facts

Mathias, a patient of Dr. Witt's at St. Catherine's Hospital, delivered a full-term son by cesarean section on February 2, 1993, while she was under general anesthesia. In the operating room, Dr. Witt indicated that he needed a particular instrument that would be used in a tubal ligation. The nurses, Ms. Snyder and Ms. Perri, employees of St. Catherine's, looked at Mathias's chart. Ms. Snyder informed Dr. Witt that she could not find a signed consent form for the procedure. In deposition testimony, Ms. Snyder stated that Witt replied, "Oh, okay."

Dr. Witt performed a tubal ligation. Three days after the procedure a nurse brought Mathias a consent form that had to be signed, telling Mathias the form was "just to close up our records." The nurse testified in her deposition that she signed Ms. Perri's name on that same consent form and backdated it to February 2, the day the surgery was performed. The trial court noted that these actions after the surgery were immaterial to the issue of the hospital's duty to Mathias. The trial court granted summary judgment dismissing St. Catherine's from the malpractice action. Mr. and Ms. Mathias appealed the summary judgment, contending that the hospital owed a duty to Mathias to prevent her physician from performing a tubal ligation for which there was no signed consent.

Issue

Did the hospital owe a duty to Mathias to prevent her physician from performing a tubal ligation for which there was no consent? Did the trial court err in granting summary judgment to St. Catherine's?

Holding

The trial court's grant of summary judgment was affirmed.

Reason

The duty to advise a patient of the risks of treatment lies with the physician and not the hospital. This duty is codified in Wisconsin Statute § 448.30, which requires the following:

> Any physician who treats a patient shall inform the patient about the availability of all alternate, viable medical modes of treatment and about the benefits and risks of these treatments. The physician's duty to inform the patient under this section does not require disclosure of:
>
> 1. information beyond what a reasonably well qualified physician in a similar medical classification would know,
> 2. detailed technical information that in all probability a patient would not understand,
> 3. risks apparent or known to the patient,
> 4. extremely remote possibilities that might falsely or detrimentally alarm the patient,
> 5. information in emergencies where failure to provide treatment would be more harmful to the patient than treatment, or
> 6. information in cases where the patient is incapable of consenting.

This statute is the cornerstone of the hospital's duty in this case. The court noted that the legislature limited the application of the duty to obtain informed consent to the treating physician. The Mathiases sought to extend the duty of ensuring informed consent to the hospital.

The duty to inform rests with the physician and requires the exercise of delicate medical judgment. It is the physician—not the hospital—who has the duty to obtain informed consent. The surgeon, not the hospital, has the education, training, and experience necessary to advise each patient of the risks associated with a proposed procedure. The physician is in the best position to know the patient's medical history and to evaluate and explain the risks of treatment options.

Adequacy of Consent

When questions arise as to whether the risks, benefits, and alternatives to treatment are adequate, the courts require that physicians reveal to their patients the information that skilled physicians of good standing would provide under the same or similar circumstance. The plaintiff in *Ramos v. Pyati*[14] had injured his thumb while at work. The plaintiff was diagnosed as having a ruptured thumb tendon. The plaintiff consented to a surgical repair of the thumb.

During surgery, the defendant discovered that scar tissue had formed, causing the ends of the tendons in the thumb to retract. As a result, the surgeon decided to use a donor tendon to make the necessary repairs to the thumb. He chose a tendon from the ring finger. On discovering additional disability from the surgery, the plaintiff filed a suit alleging that his hand was rendered unusable for his employment as a mechanic and that the defendant had breached his duty by not advising him of the serious nature of the operation, by not exercising the proper degree of care in performing the operation, and by failing to discontinue surgery when he knew or should have known that the required surgery would most likely cause a greater disability than the already injured condition of the thumb.

The plaintiff testified that although he signed a written consent form authorizing surgery on his thumb, he did not consent to a graft of his ring finger tendon or any other tendon. The plaintiff's expert witness testified that the ring finger is the last choice of four other tendons that could have been selected for the surgery. The circuit court entered a judgment for the plaintiff, and the defendant appealed. The appellate court upheld the judgment for the plaintiff, finding that the plaintiff had not consented to use of the ring finger tendon for repair of the thumb tendon.

Lack of Consent

Four children, in *Riser v. American Medical Intern, Inc.*,[15] brought a medical malpractice action against Lang, a physician who performed a femoral arteriogram on their 69-year-old mother, Riser, who subsequently died of a stroke 11 days following the procedure. Riser had been admitted to De La Ronde Hospital experiencing impaired circulation in her lower arms and hands. The patient had multiple medical diagnoses, including diabetes mellitus, end-stage renal failure, and arteriosclerosis. Her physician, Dr. Sottiurai, ordered bilateral arteriograms to determine the cause of the patient's impaired circulation. Because De La Ronde Hospital could not accommodate Sottiurai's request, Riser was transferred to Dr. Lang, a radiologist at St. Jude Hospital. Dr. Lang performed a femoral arteriogram, *not* the bilateral brachial arteriogram ordered by Sottiurai. The procedure seemed to go well, and the patient was prepared for transfer back to De La Ronde Hospital. However, shortly after the ambulance departed the hospital, the patient suffered a seizure in the ambulance and was returned to St. Jude. Riser's condition deteriorated, and she died 11 days later. The plaintiffs claimed in their lawsuit that Riser was a poor risk for the procedure.

The district court ruled for the plaintiffs and Dr. Lang appealed. On appeal, the Louisiana Court of Appeal found no error in the trial court's decision. Testimony revealed that Dr. Lang breached the standard of care by performing a procedure that he knew or should have known would have had no practical benefit to the patient or her referring physician.

As to informed consent, a reasonably prudent person in the position of Riser would have refused to undergo the procedure if he or she had known of the strong possibility of a stroke. Informed consent requires that the physician reveal to the patient all material risks. The consent form itself did not contain express authorization for Dr. Lang to perform the femoral arteriogram. Sottiurai ordered a brachial arteriogram, not a femoral arteriogram. Two consent forms were signed; neither form authorized the performance of a femoral arteriogram. O'Neil, one of Riser's daughters, claimed that, following the arteriogram, her mother said, "Why did you let them do that to me?"[16]

Although Dr. Lang claims that he explained the procedure to Riser and O'Neil, the trial court, faced with this conflicting testimony, chose to believe the plaintiffs. The defendants argued that the plaintiffs had not established a causal connection between the arteriogram and the stroke. There was conflicting testimony between the pathologists who testified at trial as to the cause of the patient's death. The judge chose to believe the pathologist's testimony that it was more probable than not that the stroke resulted from the arteriogram performed by Dr. Lang.

Hospitals and Informed Consent

Hospitals generally do not have an independent duty to obtain informed consent or to warn patients of the risks of a procedure to be performed by a physician who is not an agent of the hospital. It is the treating physician who has the education, expertise, skill, and training necessary to treat a patient and determine what information a patient should have in order to give informed consent. Hospital employees do not normally possess the knowledge of a particular patient's medical history, diagnosis, or other circumstances that would enable the employee to fully disclose all pertinent information to the patient. Ohio Revised Code, for example, provides:

> 2317.54 Informed consent to surgical or medical procedure or course of procedures.
>
> No hospital, home health agency, ambulatory surgical facility, or provider of a hospice care program or pediatric respite care program shall be held liable for a physician's failure to obtain an informed consent from the physician's patient prior to a surgical or medical procedure or course of procedures, unless the physician is an employee of the hospital, home health agency, ambulatory surgical facility, or provider of a hospice care program or pediatric respite care program.[17]

Although hospitals do not generally have responsibility of providing patients with informed consent, there are cases where hospitals have been found to owe a duty to provide patients with informed consent. For example, the patient-plaintiff, Keel, in *Keel v. St. Elizabeth Medical Center, Ky.*,[18] filed a medical malpractice action alleging that the hospital failed to provide him with informed consent when he went there for a computed tomography (CT) scan. The scan involved the injection of a contrast dye material. Prior to the test, Keel was given no information concerning any risks attendant to the procedure. The dye was injected, and the scan was conducted. However, the plaintiff developed a thrombophlebitis at the site of the injection.

The plaintiff argued that expert medical testimony was not required in order to prove the absence of informed consent. The hospital argued that the question of informed consent, like the question of negligence, must be determined against the standard of practice among members of the medical profession.

The circuit court granted summary judgment to the hospital on the grounds that the plaintiff failed to present expert testimony on the issue. The plaintiff appealed.

The Kentucky Supreme Court held that expert testimony was not required to establish lack of informed consent and that the hospital had a duty to inform the patient of the risks associated with the procedure. In view of the special circumstances of this case, the court found it significant that the hospital offered Keel no information whatsoever concerning any possible hazards of this particular procedure, while at the same time the hospital admits that it routinely questions every patient about to undergo a dye injection as to whether he or she has had any previous reactions to contrast materials. The questions to patients regarding reactions to CT scans demonstrated that the hospital recognized the substantial possibility of complications. The inconsistencies here were found to be apparent without the need for expert testimony.

Right to Refuse Treatment

Vega, a Jehovah's Witness, in *Stamford Hospital v. Nelly E. Vega*,[19] executed a release requesting that no blood or its derivatives be administered to her during her hospitalization. Vega's husband also signed the release. She delivered a healthy baby. Following the delivery, Vega bled heavily. Her obstetrician, Dr. Sood, recommended a dilation and curettage (D&C) to stop the bleeding. Although Vega agreed to permit Dr. Sood to perform the D&C, she refused to allow a blood transfusion.

Vega's condition continued to worsen. Eventually, when she was having difficulty breathing, her physicians placed her on a respirator in the intensive care unit. Because Dr. Sood and other physicians involved in Vega's care believed that it was essential that she receive blood in order to survive, the hospital filed a complaint requesting that the court issue an injunction that would permit the hospital to administer blood transfusions. The trial court convened an emergency hearing at the hospital. Vega's physicians testified that, with reasonable medical certainty, she would die without blood transfusions. Her husband testified that, on the basis of his religious beliefs as a Jehovah's Witness, he continued to support his wife's decision to refuse transfusions. The court, relying on the state's interests in preserving life and protecting innocent third parties and noting that Vega's life could be saved by a blood transfusion, granted the hospital's request for an injunction permitting it to administer blood transfusions. Vega recovered and was discharged from the hospital.

The Connecticut Supreme Court determined that the hospital had no common law right or obligation to thrust unwanted medical care on a patient who, having been sufficiently informed of the consequences, competently and clearly declined that care. The hospital's interests were sufficiently protected by Vega's informed choice, and it was not for the court to override that choice. Vega's common-law right of bodily self-determination was entitled to respect and protection. The trial court improperly issued an injunction that permitted the hospital to administer blood transfusions to Vega. The question as to state interests in saving the life of a healthy mother and child was left for another day. Justice J. Palmer, in a concurring opinion, stated, "By declining the opportunity to address the issue of the state's interest in such a case, we leave unanswered—without good cause, in my judgment—a question that is central to the fundamental issue presented by this appeal and one that was raised both in the trial court and on appeal."[20]

Nurses and Informed Consent

In general, a nurse has no duty to advise a patient as to a particular procedure to be employed; advise the patient as to the risks, benefits, and alternatives to a recommended procedure; or obtain a patient's informed consent prior to surgery merely because the physician directed a nurse to have the patient sign a consent form.

The plaintiff, Davis, in *Davis v. Hoffman*,[21] experienced pain in her lower abdomen and consulted Dr. Hoffman. He diagnosed her to be suffering from a fibroid uterus and prescribed a D&C procedure designed to remove the fibroids. Hoffman further suggested a laparoscopy and hysteroscopy to search for cancer. The plaintiff claimed that she specifically informed Hoffman and Puchini (the doctor's nurse) that she did not consent to a hysterectomy. They responded that they would awaken her during the operation to obtain her consent before proceeding to a hysterectomy. The plaintiff underwent a procedure that resulted in a hysterectomy, during which no one awakened Davis to discuss and explore possible alternatives. The plaintiff brought an action for lack of informed consent against Hoffman, Puchini, and the hospital.

In response to the plaintiff's allegation that the hospital committed battery by lack of informed consent to the hysterectomy, the hospital asserted that Pennsylvania law places no duty on a hospital to obtain a patient's consent to an operation. The hospital argued that Pennsylvania courts have applied the doctrine of informed consent only to physicians, not to hospitals. The plaintiff responded that the hospital gratuitously undertook to obtain her consent prior to the operation. Although the consent form authored and printed by the hospital was used, there was no suggestion that the deficiency in consent was in any way causally inadequate in the form. Rather, any failure was attributed to the omissions in the way the form was filled in or in the way the patient was not informed as to the next phase of the operation. Thus, the form was causally irrelevant and could not be a basis for finding liability.

Because nurses do not have a duty to obtain informed consent in Pennsylvania, the plaintiff had not stated a claim for battery by lack of informed consent against Puchini. Pennsylvania law generally imposes no duty on persons other than surgeons to obtain informed consent prior to surgery.

Validity of Consent

Some courts have recognized that the condition of a patient may be taken into account to determine whether the patient has received sufficient information to give consent. The individual responsible for obtaining consent must weigh the importance of giving full disclosure to the patient against the likelihood that such disclosure will seriously and adversely affect the condition of the patient.

The courts generally use a "subjective" or "objective" test to determine whether a patient would have refused treatment if the physician had provided adequate information as to the risks, benefits, and alternatives of the procedure. Under the subjective test theory, the court examines whether the "individual patient" would have chosen the procedure if he or she had been fully informed. In the *objective test*, the plaintiff must prove that a "reasonable person" would not have undergone the procedure if he or she had been properly informed. As described in the following cases, the courts favor the objective test.

Subjective Standard

The *subjective standard* relies solely on the patient's testimony. Patients must show that they would not have consented to the procedure(s) had they been advised of the particular risk in question. Proponents of the subjective standard argue that a patient should have the right to make medical decisions regarding his or her care regardless of whether the determination is rational or reasonable. The subjective standard, however, potentially places the physician in jeopardy of the patient's hindsight and bitterness. The subjective standard is premised on the credibility of a patient's testimony.

Objective Standard

When applying the *objective standard*, the finder of fact may take into account the characteristics of the plaintiff, including the plaintiff's idiosyncrasies, fears, age, medical condition, and religious beliefs. Accordingly, the objective standard affords the ease of applying a uniform standard and yet maintains the flexibility of allowing the finder of fact to make appropriate adjustments to accommodate the individual characteristics and idiosyncrasies of an individual patient. The standard to be applied in informed consent cases is whether a reasonable person in the patient's position would have consented to a procedure or treatment in question if adequately informed of all significant perils. Under the objective analysis, the plaintiff's testimony is only one factor when determining the issue of informed consent. The issue is not whether a particular patient would have chosen a different course of treatment; the issue is whether a *reasonable patient* would have chosen a different course of treatment.

Warren, in *Warren v. Schecter*,[22] was diagnosed as having a stomach ulcer. Dr. Schecter recommended surgery to remove the portions of the stomach containing the ulcer. One of the significant risks of gastric surgery is decreased calcium absorption, leading to early and severe metabolic bone disease. It was Dr. Schecter's role as the surgeon to advise Warren of the risks of surgery in order to obtain informed consent. Although he did not discuss these risks with her, he did advise Warren that she might experience bowel obstructions, dumping syndrome involving nausea, and the slight risk of death from anesthesia. Based on the risks disclosed to Warren, she consented to the surgery, which Dr. Schecter performed.

Following surgery, Warren developed dumping syndrome, a side effect that occurs in approximately 1% of the patients who undergo this procedure. Warren returned to Dr. Schecter, who recommended a second surgery to relieve the pain and discomfort from the first surgery. The second surgery would enhance the risk of bone disease. However, Dr. Schecter again failed to advise Warren of the risk of metabolic bone disease. Warren was eventually taken to a hospital emergency department where she was advised that she had suffered a fracture of one of her lumbar vertebrae

and that previous surgeries led to osteoporosis that resulted in a fracture.

Warren filed an action for medical negligence, alleging that Dr. Schecter was liable under an informed consent theory for performing surgery without advising her of the risk of metabolic bone disease. Warren claimed that had Dr. Schecter warned her of the risk of metabolic bone disease, she would not have consented to surgery. The jury decided that: (1) Dr. Schecter did not disclose to Warren all relevant information that would enable her to make an informed decision regarding surgery; (2) a reasonably prudent person in Warren's position would not have consented to surgery if adequately informed of all the significant perils; and (3) Dr. Schecter's negligence was a cause of injury to Warren.

On appeal, the plaintiff was found entitled to compensation for all damages proximately resulting from the physician's failure to give full disclosure of the risks of surgery. The patient was entitled to recover because she would not have consented to any surgery had the true risk been disclosed. A plaintiff meets the burden of establishing a causal relationship between the physician's failure to inform and the injury to the plaintiff by demonstrating that a prudent person in the plaintiff's position would have declined the procedure if adequately informed of the risks. Under the objective standard, Warren had only to prove that a prudent person in her position would not have consented if adequately informed of the risks. Dr. Schecter failed to provide Warren with the risks and benefits of the surgical procedures prior to obtaining her consent for the operations.

🔍 *OBJECTIVE TEST PREFERRED*

Citation: *Ashe v. Radiation Oncology Assocs.*, 9 S.W.3d 119 (Tenn. 1999)

Facts

Ashe underwent a double mastectomy and chemotherapy in 1988. By 1993, she began experiencing problems with a cough and a fever. She returned to her oncologist, Dr. Kuzu, where she presented a variety of symptoms, including fever, cough, weight loss, and decreased appetite. A chest X-ray and a CT scan revealed the presence of a mass in her left lung.

Ashe underwent surgery, and the upper portion of her left lung was removed. She underwent chemotherapy and was referred to the defendant, Dr. Stroup, who prescribed radiation treatment. Ashe agreed to radiation treatment and was later diagnosed with radiation myelitis caused by a permanent radiation injury to her spinal cord. She is now a paraplegic. Dr. Stroup did not inform Ashe that the radiation treatment might result in a permanent injury to her spinal cord.

Ashe filed an action alleging claims for medical malpractice and lack of informed consent. Dr. Perez, Ashe's expert, testified that the risk of spinal cord injury was 1 to 2%. Perez testified that the applicable standard of care required physicians to warn patients about the risk of radiation injury to the spinal cord. Ashe testified that she would not have consented to radiation therapy had she been informed of the risk of paralysis. On cross-examination, defense counsel pointed out that the plaintiff did equivocate in her deposition on the issue of consent. Her deposition testimony indicated that she did not know what she would have done had she been warned about the risk of spinal cord injury. She then testified on redirect examination that if Dr. Stroup had said to her, "'Patty, if you do this, there is a risk that you will be in a wheelchair 6 months from now,' I would have told him, 'I will take my chances.' I would not have it done."

The trial court found that the plaintiff's trial testimony conflicted with her deposition testimony regarding whether she would have consented to the procedure had she been warned of the risk of spinal cord injury. The trial court, therefore, struck the trial testimony and granted the defendant a directed verdict on the informed consent claim. The plaintiff's malpractice claim went to the jury. The jury was unable to reach a verdict, and a mistrial was declared.

The plaintiff appealed to the court of appeals. The court of appeals held that, as part of the plaintiff's informed consent claim, she was required to prove that a reasonable person knowing of the risk for spinal cord injury would have decided not to have the procedure performed. The court held that the discrepancy between the trial and deposition testimony went to the issue of credibility and that the trial testimony should not have been stricken. The Court of Appeals reversed the trial court's grant of a directed verdict on the informed consent claim and remanded the case for a new trial.

Issue

What was the appropriate standard to be employed in this case where the patient alleges the physician did not provide informed consent?

Finding

The Tennessee Supreme Court held that informed consent cases are better resolved on an objective basis. The standard to be applied in informed consent cases is whether a reasonable person in the patient's position would have consented to the procedure or treatment in question if adequately informed of all significant perils. The decision of the Court of Appeals was affirmed, and the case was remanded to the trial court for a new trial.

Reason

In Tennessee, the plaintiff in an informed consent medical malpractice case has the burden of proving: (1) what a reasonable medical practitioner in the same or similar community would have disclosed to the patient about the risk posed by the proposed procedure or treatment; and (2) that the defendant departed from the norm.

The issue with which the court was confronted was whether an objective, a subjective, or a hybrid subjective/objective test should be employed when assessing causation in informed consent cases. The majority of jurisdictions in Tennessee having addressed this issue follow an objective standard.

Under the objective analysis, the plaintiff's testimony is only one factor when determining the issue of informed consent. The issue is not whether Ashe would herself have chosen a different course of treatment—the issue is whether a reasonable patient in Ashe's position would have chosen a different course of treatment. The jury, therefore, should have been allowed to decide whether a reasonable person in Ashe's position would have consented to the radiation therapy had the risk of paralysis been disclosed.

Assessing Decision-Making Capacity

A patient is considered competent to make medical decisions regarding his or her care unless a court determines otherwise. The clinical assessment of decision-making capacity involves the patient's ability to:

- Understand the risks, benefits, and alternatives of a proposed test or procedure
- Evaluate the information provided by the physician
- Express his or her treatment preferences
- Voluntarily make decisions regarding his or her treatment plan without undue influence by family, friends, or medical personnel

Admission Consent Forms

Admission consent forms signed at the time of admission are designed to record the patient's consent to routine services, general diagnostic procedures, and the everyday routine touchings of the patient. Concerns for their use arise from the potential of unwarranted reliance on them for specific and potentially high-risk procedures or treatments.

Consent for Specific Procedures

There are a variety of consent forms designed to more specifically describe the risks, benefits, and alternatives of particular invasive and noninvasive procedures. Such forms include consent for anesthesia, cardiac catheterization, surgery, radiation therapy, blood and blood by-products, chemotherapy, CT and magnetic resonance imaging (MRI) scans, endoscopy, and colonoscopy.

Limited Power of Attorney

A *limited power of attorney* authorizes, for example, school officials, teachers, and camp counselors to act on a parents' or legal guardian's behalf when seeking emergency care for an injured student or camper. Such consent for treatment provides limited protection in the care of a particular child. Temporary consent indicates a parent or guardian's intent to have a school official, teacher, or counselor to seek emergency treatment when necessary for the child for whom consent is provided.

Who May Consent

Consent of the patient ordinarily is required prior to treatment. However, when the patient is either physically unable or legally incompetent to consent and no emergency exists, consent must be obtained from a person who is empowered to consent on the patient's behalf. The person who authorizes treatment of another must have sufficient information to make an intelligent judgment on behalf of the patient.

Competent Patients

A competent adult patient's wishes concerning his or her person may not be disregarded. The court in *In re Melideo*[23] held that every human being of adult years has a right to determine what shall be done with his or her own body and cannot be subjected to medical treatment without his or her consent. When there is no compelling state interest that justifies overriding an adult patient's decision, that decision should be respected.

The Pennsylvania Supreme court affirmed a trial judge's decision to appoint a temporary guardian to consent to blood transfusions when a patient is unconscious. The court reasoned that medical intervention necessary to preserve life requires nothing less than a "fully conscious contemporaneous decision by the patient. . . ."[24]

In *Fosmire v. Nicoleau*,[25] the New York Supreme Court, Suffolk County, issued an order authorizing blood transfusions for a patient who had refused them. The plaintiff applied for an order vacating the court's order. The appeals court held that the patient's constitutional rights of due process were violated when the trial court issued an order authorizing blood

transfusions in the absence of notice or opportunity for the patient or her representatives to be heard. The right of a competent patient to refuse medical treatment, even if premised on fervently held religious beliefs, is not unqualified and may be overridden by compelling state interests. However, a state's interest in preserving a patient's life in and of itself may not, under certain circumstances, be sufficient to overcome the patient's express desire to exercise her religious belief and forego a blood transfusion. The appellate division held, in part, that the state's interest would be satisfied if the other parent survived.

The New York Court of Appeals, New York's highest court, went further by stating that the citizens of the state have long had the right to make their own medical care choices without regard to their medical condition or status as parents. The court of appeals held that a competent adult has both a common law and statutory right under public health law to refuse lifesaving treatment. Citing the state's authority to compel vaccination to protect the public from the spread of disease, to order treatment for persons who are incapable of making medical decisions, and to prohibit medical procedures that pose a substantial risk to the patient alone, the court of appeals did note that the right to choose is not absolute. However, if there is no compelling state interest to justify overriding a patient's refusal to consent to a medical procedure because of religious beliefs, states are reluctant to override such a decision.

Guardianship

A *guardian* is an individual who, by law, is vested with the power and charged with the duty of taking care of a patient by protecting the patient's rights and managing the patient's estate. Guardianship is often necessary in those instances in which a patient is incapable of managing or administering his or her private affairs because of physical and/or mental disabilities or because he or she is under the age of majority.

Temporary guardianship can be granted by the courts if it is determined that such is necessary for the well-being of the patient. The court in *In re Estate of Dorone*[26] granted temporary guardianship. In this case, the physician and administrator petitioned the court on two occasions for authority to administer blood. A 22-year-old male patient brought to the hospital center by helicopter after an automobile accident was diagnosed as suffering from an acute subdural hematoma with a brain contusion. It was determined that the patient would die unless he underwent a cranial operation. The operation required the administration of blood; however, the parents would not consent to the administration because of their religious beliefs. After a hearing by telephone, the court of common pleas appointed the hospital's administrator as temporary guardian, authorizing him to consent to the performance of blood transfusions during emergency surgery. A more formal hearing did not take place because of the emergency situation that existed. Surgery was required a second time to remove a blood clot, and the court once again granted the administrator authority to authorize administration of blood. The superior court affirmed the orders, and the parents appealed.

The Pennsylvania Supreme Court held that the judge's failure to obtain direct testimony from the patient's parents and others concerning the patient's religious beliefs were not in error when death was likely to result from withholding blood. The judge's decisions granting guardianship and the authority to consent to the administration of blood were considered absolutely necessary in the light of the facts of this case. Nothing less than a fully conscious decision by the patient himself would have been sufficient to override the evidence of medical necessity in this case.

Parental Consent

Parents generally have the right to authorize medical care for minor children, generally under the age of 18 years. Consent laws for minors often vary from state to state and should be referenced as necessary. Children who are emancipated have a right to make their own medical care decisions. While parents may have a right to refuse medical care in certain instances, such refusal is reportable by the caregiver to the state if such refusal can result in harm to the child.

When a medical or surgical procedure is to be performed on a minor, the question arises as to whether the minor's consent alone is sufficient and, if not, from whom consent should be obtained. The courts have held, as a general proposition, that the consent of a minor to medical or surgical treatment is ineffective and that the physician must secure the consent of the minor's parent or someone standing in loco parentis; otherwise, he or she will risk liability. Although parental consent should be obtained before treating a minor, treatment should not be delayed to the detriment of the child. Several courts have held the consent of a minor to be sufficient authorization for treatment in certain situations. In any specific case, a court's determination that the consent of a minor is effective and that parental consent is unnecessary will depend on such factors as the minor's age, maturity, mental status, and emancipation and the procedure involved, as well as public policy considerations.

Emancipated Minors

Parental consent is not necessary when the minor is married or otherwise emancipated. Most states have enacted statutes making it valid for married and emancipated minors to provide effective consent. In *Carter v. Cangello*,[27] the California Court of Appeals held that a 17-year-old girl who was living away from home, in the home of a woman who gave her free room and board in exchange for household chores, and who made her own financial decisions legally could consent to medical procedures performed on her. The court made this decision knowing that the girl's parents provided part of her income by paying for her private schooling and certain medical care. The physician was privileged under statute to act on the minor's consent to surgery, and such privilege insulated him from liability to the parents for treating their daughter without their consent.

Many states have recognized by legislation that treatment for conditions such as pregnancy, venereal disease, and drug dependency does not require parental consent. State legislatures have reasoned that a minor is not likely to seek medical assistance when parental consent is demanded, and that insisting on parental consent for the treatment of these conditions would increase the likelihood that a minor would delay or go without treatment to avoid explanation to the parents.

The Right to Choose

Abraham Cherrix was 16 years old when he was diagnosed in August of 2005 with Hodgkin's disease. He was treated with chemotherapy. In February of 2006, he learned that chemotherapy had not cured his disease. Doctors recommended a higher dosage of chemotherapy combined with radiation and culminating in stem cell therapy. The treatment program offered Abraham less than a 50% chance of survival. Abraham and his family chose to pursue alternative treatment in Mexico. Cherrix's oncologist reported the family's decision to the Accomack County Department of Social Services (ACDSS). Cherrix's parents were accused of medical neglect by ACDSS. A judge granted the ACDSS temporary joint custody with the Cherrixes. The parents faced charges in the Juvenile and Domestic Court for parental neglect. The family obtained a stay from the Circuit Court.[28]

The Accomack Virginia Circuit Court Judge cleared Abraham's parents of all charges of medical neglect and allowed Abraham to pursue alternative treatment under a doctor of the family's choice. A board-certified oncologist who is experienced in alternative cancer treatment will monitor Abraham.

The family will provide the court updates on Abraham's care every 3 months until he is cured or turns 18. The questions to be asked in this case include: Whose body is it anyway? Did the state go too far? The judge must have thought so.

> The judge agreed to allow me to see an oncologist of my choice! My alternative treatments WILL continue. He also ruled that my parents were not guilty of medical neglect, and social services no longer has any jurisdiction over my case! Free, happy, and ready to live, that's me![29]

Incompetent Patients

When there is doubt as to a patient's capacity to consent, the consent of the legal guardian or next of kin should be obtained. If there are no relatives to consult, application should be made for a court order that would authorize a proposed procedure. It may be the duty of the court to assume responsibility of guardianship for a patient who is non compos mentis. The most frequently cited conditions indicative of incompetence are mental illness, mental retardation, senility, physical incapacity, and chronic alcohol or drug abuse.

A person who is mentally incompetent cannot legally consent to medical or surgical treatment. Therefore, consent of the patient's legal guardian must be obtained. When no legal guardian is available, a court that handles such matters must be petitioned to permit treatment. Subject to applicable statutory provisions, when a physician doubts a patient's capacity to consent, even though the patient has not been judged legally incompetent, the consent of the nearest relative should be obtained. If a patient is conscious and mentally capable of giving consent for treatment, the consent of a relative without the consent of the competent patient would not protect the physician from liability.

Right to Refuse Treatment: Religious Beliefs

As part of their religious beliefs, Jehovah's Witnesses generally have refused the administration of blood, even in emergency situations. Case law over the past several decades has developed to a point where any person, regardless of religious beliefs, has the right to refuse medical treatment.

The plaintiff, Bonita Perkins, in *Perkins v. Lavin*,[30] was a Jehovah's Witness. She gave birth at the defendant-hospital on September 26, 1991, and was discharged 2 or 3 days later. After going home, she began hemorrhaging and returned to the hospital. She specifically informed the defendant's employees that she was not to be provided any blood or blood derivatives and completed and signed a form to that effect:

> I request that no blood or blood derivatives be administered to (plaintiff) during this hospitalization, notwithstanding that such treatment may be deemed necessary in the opinion of the attending physician or his assistants to preserve life or promote recovery. I release the attending physician, his assistants, the hospital and its personnel from any responsibility whatever for any untoward results due to my refusal to permit the use of blood or its derivatives.[31]

As a result of the plaintiff's condition, it became necessary to perform an emergency D&C on her. She continued to bleed, and her condition deteriorated dramatically. Her blood count dropped, necessitating administration of blood products as a lifesaving measure. Her husband, who was not a Jehovah's Witness, consented to a blood transfusion, which was administered. The plaintiff recovered and filed an action against the defendant for assault and battery and intentional infliction of emotional distress. The plaintiff's claim as to assault and battery was sustained. The claim as to the intentional infliction of emotional distress was overruled.

The plaintiff specifically informed the defendant that she would consider a blood transfusion an offensive contact. The plaintiff submitted sufficient evidence to the trial court to establish that there was, at least, a genuine issue as to whether the defendant intentionally invaded her right to be free from offensive contact. Because of the plaintiff's recognition that the defendant acted to save her life, a jury may find that she is entitled to only nominal damages.

Exculpatory Agreements

An exculpatory agreement is an agreement that relieves one from liability when he or she has acted in good faith. Exculpatory agreements in the medical setting are generally considered invalid.

In *Cudnik v. William Beaumont Hospital*,[32] Mr. Cudnik underwent radiation therapy in March and April of 1985 after undergoing surgery for prostate cancer. Before receiving therapy, he signed a consent document that provided in part:

> Further, my physician has fully explained to me the possibilities of reactions and the possible side effects of the treatment.

I understand that there is no guarantee given to me as to the results of radiation therapy. Understanding all of the foregoing, I hereby release the physicians and staff of the Department of Radiation Oncology and William Beaumont Hospital from all suits, claims, liability, or demands of every kind and character which I or my heirs, executors, administrators [sic] or assigns hereafter can, shall, or may have arising out of my participation in the radiation therapy treatment regimen.[33]

SPOUSAL CONSENT

Citation: *Greynolds v. Kurman*, 632 N.E.2d 946 (Ohio Ct. App. 1993)

Facts

On July 29, 1987, Mr. Greynolds suffered a transient ischemic attack (TIA), a sudden loss of neurologic function caused by vascular impairment to the brain. As a result of the TIA, Greynolds had garbled speech and expressive and perceptive aphasia (a medical term used to describe the loss of the power of expression by speech, writing, or signs, or of comprehending spoken or written language). Greynolds was taken to an emergency department, where Dr. Litman met him. At Dr. Litman's request, Dr. Rafecas, a cardiologist, examined Greynolds. Dr. Rafecas determined that because of Greynold's past medical history, which included previous TIAs, he was at a high risk for a stroke and sought to pinpoint the exact source of vascular insufficiency to the brain.

On August 3, 1987, after receiving the results of noninvasive tests, Dr. Rafecas ordered a cerebral angiogram. Dr. Kurman performed the angiogram. During the procedure, Greynolds suffered a stroke that left him severely disabled.

Greynolds and his wife filed a medical malpractice action against Dr. Rafecas and Dr. Kurman, asserting that Dr. Rafecas negligently recommended the procedure and that Dr. Kurman performed the procedure without obtaining the informed consent of the patient. Dr. Kurman argued that the trial court erred by refusing to enter judgment for him consistent with the answer to jury question number 3 (*Id.* at 949):

Question No. 1: Do you find there was a failure to obtain informed consent?

Answer: Yes.

Question No. 2: If you answered Interrogatory No. 1 yes, then state specifically in what manner Dr. Kurman's care fell below the recognized standards of the medical community.

Answer: Mr. Greynolds was not in our estimation capable of comprehending the consent form. Therefore, Dr. Kurman should have obtained consent from the next-of-kin, specifically, Mrs. Greynolds.

Question No. 3: If you answered yes to interrogatory No. 1 and you found that Mr. Greynolds did not consent to the procedure, do you find that a reasonable person would have consented to the procedure?

Answer: Yes.

Kurman moved the trial court to grant him a judgment notwithstanding the verdict because the jury's answer to interrogatory question number 3 was not consistent with the jury's verdict. The trial court overruled Kurman's motion and entered judgment for the plaintiffs, and Kurman appealed.

Issue

Was there sufficient evidence to support a judgment for the plaintiffs?

Holding

The court of appeals held that the evidence was sufficient to support a judgment in favor of the patient and his wife.

Reason

The jury needed to determine that the risks involved in the cerebral angiogram were not disclosed to Greynolds, that the risks involved in the procedure materialized and caused his stroke, and that a reasonable person in the position of Greynolds would have decided against having the angiogram had the risks associated with the procedure been disclosed to him. The jury concluded that Greynolds did not consent to the angiogram because he "was not . . . capable of comprehending the consent form," and further noted that Kurman should have sought consent from the next of kin, specifically, the spouse. Given the evidence of Greynolds's condition when he signed the consent forms, his past medical history, and the fact that he was at an increased risk to suffer complications during an angiogram, the court found that there was sufficient evidence to support a finding of lack of informed consent.

In early 1989, Cudnik returned to the hospital complaining of back discomfort, whereupon he was diagnosed as suffering from a postradiation ulcer burn at the site where he previously received radiation treatment. An action was brought against the hospital claiming that the negligent administration of radiation therapy caused or contributed to Cudnik's death. The defendant moved for summary judgment, and the Oakland Circuit Court granted the hospital's motion after concluding that the exculpatory agreement between the parties precluded the plaintiff's claims.

The plaintiff appealed, claiming that the hospital should be held vicariously liable for the medical malpractice of its employees or agents. As a general proposition, the parties to a contract may enter into an exculpatory agreement provided that it does not violate the law or contravene public policy. The question in this case is whether the plaintiff's claim of medical malpractice is precluded by the exculpatory agreement between the two parties.

The court of appeals held that the exculpatory agreement executed by the patient prior to receiving radiation therapy was invalid and unenforceable to absolve a medical care provider from liability for medical malpractice. The agreement in this case is clearly against public policy. Furthermore, the majority of jurisdictions have held that exculpatory agreements involving patient care are unenforceable.

Some exculpatory agreements in the medical setting are considered valid. For example, experimental procedures may require a different standard because, by their very nature, they require a deviation from generally accepted medical practices. In a case involving the patient's last hope of survival, the New York Supreme Court held that "the parties may covenant to exempt the physician from liability for those injuries which are found to be the consequences of the nonnegligent, proper performance of the procedure."[34] The Cudnik case does not appear to involve an experimental procedure.

Proving Lack of Consent

The burden of establishing proof on a complaint of lack of informed consent is on the plaintiff. The plaintiff must establish both of the following:

1. A reasonably prudent person in the patient's position would not have undergone the treatment if fully informed.
2. The lack of informed consent is the proximate cause of the injury or condition for which recovery is sought.

In a lawsuit, testimony would be necessary to establish the extent of the patient's actual knowledge and understanding of the treatment rendered. It is possible for a patient, after treatment, to claim a lack of advance knowledge about the nature of a physician's treatment, and it is possible that a jury will believe the patient and impose liability on the physician and/or the organization.

Informed Consent Claims and Defenses

Defenses available to defendants who have been sued based on failure to provide their patients with sufficient information to make an informed decision include the following:

1. *Risks not disclosed are commonly known* and do not warrant disclosure.
2. *Patient assured the medical practitioner that he or she would undergo the treatment* or procedure regardless of the risk involved, or the patient assured the medical practitioner that he or she did not want to be informed of the matters to which he or she would be entitled to be informed.
3. *Consent was not reasonably possible* by or on behalf of the patient.
4. The practitioner, after considering all of the attendant facts and circumstances, used reasonable discretion as to the manner and extent as to which *alternatives or risks should be disclosed* to the patient because the practitioner reasonably believed that the manner and extent of such disclosure could reasonably be expected to adversely and substantially affect the patient's condition.

A patient's condition during surgery may be recognized as different from that which had been expected and explained, requiring a different procedure from the one to which the patient initially consented. The surgeon may proceed to treat the new condition; however, the patient must have been aware of the possibility of extending the procedure.

The patient in *Winfrey v. Citizens & Southern National Bank*[35] brought a suit against the deceased surgeon's estate, alleging that during exploratory surgery, the surgeon performed a complete hysterectomy without the patient's consent. The superior court granted summary judgment for the surgeon's estate, and the patient appealed. The court of appeals held that even though the patient may not have read the consent document, when no legally sufficient excuse appeared, she was bound by the terms of the consent document that she voluntarily executed. The plain wording of the binding consent authorized the surgeon to perform additional or different operations or procedures that he might consider necessary or advisable in the course of the operation. Relevant sections of the consent signed by the patient included the following:[36]

1. I authorize the performance on (patient's name) of the following operation/laparoscopy, possible laparotomy . . .
2. I consent to the performance of operations and procedures in addition to or different from those now contemplated, which the above named doctor or his associates or assistants may consider necessary or advisable in the course of the operation. . . .
3. I acknowledge that the nature and purpose of the operation, possible alternative methods of treatment, the risks involved, and the possibility of complications have been fully explained to me.

▶ PATIENT RIGHTS

Patient rights may be classified as either legal—those emanating from law—or human statements of desirable ethical principles, such as the right to be treated with dignity and respect. "Among the most important human needs is the desire for respect and dignity. That need doesn't change when a person becomes ill or disabled. Indeed, it may grow even stronger."[37]

The rights of patients discussed here do not exist in a vacuum without limitations—they are tethered to moral obligations and responsibilities that have their roots in the law, ethics, moral principles, and religious values. To kill another human being, for example, is wrong, and punishment will follow if the life of another is taken.

Patients have a right to receive a clear explanation of tests, diagnoses, prescribed medications, prognosis, and treatment options.[38] Most federal, state, and local programs (e.g., Medicare, Medicaid) specifically require, as a condition for receiving funds under such

© Isak55/Shutterstock

programs, an affirmative statement on the part of the organization that it will not discriminate.

Know One's Rights

The continuing trend of consumer awareness, coupled with increased governmental regulations, makes it advisable for caregivers to understand the scope of patient rights. Patients have a right to make their own healthcare decisions. Healthcare organizations may no longer passively permit patients to exercise their rights, but must educate patients about their rights. Each individual has a right to make decisions concerning his or her medical care, including the right to accept or refuse medical or surgical treatment and the right to formulate advance directives.

Patients have a right at the time of admission to be provided in writing a copy of their rights and responsibilities. The patient's rights and responsibilities are documented in a statement most often referred to as The Patient's Bill of Rights. Access to a copy of a patient's rights and responsibilities should be available to the general public when so requested. A limited random sample of three hospitals conducted by the author in two states revealed that staff members were often reluctant to provide and suspicious as to why a copy of the patient's bill of rights was being requested. All three hospitals would not provide a copy onsite; one hospital, after a second visit, reluctantly provided a copy via email.

Patient's Bill of Rights

A patient's bill of rights often includes the following:

1. Receive an explanation of their rights.
2. Receive assistance in understanding their rights, including an interpreter.
3. Receive treatment without discrimination as to race, color, religion, sex, national

origin, disability, sexual orientation, or source of payment.

4. Receive considerate and respectful care in a clean and safe environment, free of unnecessary restraints.

5. Receive emergency care, if needed.

6. Know the names, positions, and functions of any hospital staff involved in their care and refuse treatment, examination, or observation by them.

7. Receive complete information about their diagnosis, treatment, and prognosis.

8. Receive all the information they need to give informed consent for any proposed procedure or treatment, including the risks, benefits, and alternatives to care or treatment.

9. Designate an individual to give informed consent if they are too ill to do so.

10. Discontinue care or refuse treatment.

11. Receive an explanation as to what can be expected if care is refused.

12. Refuse to consent or decline to participate in research.

13. Expect privacy while in the hospital and confidentiality of all information and records regarding their care.

14. Participate in all decisions about their treatment and discharge from the hospital.

15. Review and obtain a copy of their medical records.

16. Receive an itemized bill and explanation of all charges.

17. Complain, without fear of reprisal, about the care and services they are receiving.

18. Know the hospital's relationships with outside parties that may influence a patient's treatment and care. These relationships may be with educational institutions, insurers, and other healthcare providers.

19. Know about hospital resources, such as patient representatives or ethics committee, that can assist in resolving problems and questions about their hospital stay and care.

20. Be informed of any unanticipated outcomes or mistakes that may affect the patient's health status (e.g., administration of the wrong medication).

21. Understand, participate in, and receive a copy of discharge instructions that address: the need for home or alternate level of care placement, as appropriate; diet and medication instructions; equipment needs (e.g., wheelchair); and follow-up care with the primary care physician(s) and specialist(s), as required.

22. Be provided a copy of medical records information that may be necessary for follow-up care with the primary care physician(s).

Explanation of Rights

Patients have a right to receive an explanation of their rights and responsibilities. An organization's description of patient rights and responsibilities should be viewed as a document with legal significance, whether or not the state in question has adopted a similar code. The rights of patients must be respected at all times. Each patient is an individual with unique healthcare needs. Any restrictions on a patient's visitors, mail, telephone, or other communications must be evaluated for their therapeutic effectiveness and fully explained to and agreed upon by the patient or patient representative.

Know Caregivers

The Joint Commission Standards require that "The hospital respects the patient's rights to receive information about the individual(s) responsible for, as well as those providing, his or her care, treatment, and services."[39]

Ask Questions

Patients have the right to ask questions regarding their care from entry to the hospital through the time of departure. Questions regarding care could include, for example, "I saw blood in my IV tubing. Is this okay? Is it infiltrating?" or "My wound dressing seems wet. Is this okay? Should the dressing be changed?" Patients should not hesitate to ask for verification that advance directives are available in the medical record, confirmation that contact information for the designated surrogate decision maker is available in the medical record in the event the patient becomes incapacitated and cannot make healthcare decisions, clarification of caregiver's instructions, interpretation of caregiver's illegible handwriting, instructions for medication usage (e.g., frequency, dosing, drug–drug or drug–food interactions, contraindications, side effects), clarification of physician's orders (e.g., diet), explanation of treatment plans, a copy of the organization's handwashing policy, a description of the hospital's procedures to prevent wrong-site surgery, consultations and second opinions, and accurate and complete discharge instructions. This listing is but a sampling of the many questions that patients have a right to ask during the course of their care in any healthcare setting.

✔ *A PATIENT'S RIGHT TO ASK QUESTIONS*

Hillary was the lead consultant assigned to speak at a state-sponsored conference. The purpose of the conference was to review new and revised standards designed to encourage patients to ask questions about their care. They were scheduled to be effective on January 1. Hillary scheduled four junior consultants to speak with her on a variety of topics.

Rebecca, one of the more junior of the consultants, addressed the right of patients to ask questions. She spoke about the newly designed program that would require healthcare providers to encourage patients to speak-up and ask questions about any concerns they may have regarding their care. Following her presentation, Rebecca asked for questions from the audience. One participant commented, "I really don't understand the need for this regulation. Patients don't seem to have a problem complaining." Rebecca attempted to continue answering the questions of what appeared to be a generally disgruntled person. Hillary listened intently but appeared to be at a loss for words.

Jerome attempted to rescue Rebecca from the constant interruptions of that day's apparently self-appointed antagonist in the audience. Jerome raised his hand, and after being recognized by Rebecca, he responded, "Many patients are not afraid to ask questions and complain when they believe things are not going right. These often are ambulatory patients who can leave a particular provider if they become dissatisfied. Other, more seriously ill in-patients may fear some sort of retaliation if they complain. This is often the case in long-term care facilities." A caregiver in the audience strongly disagreed. Jerome responding, "I realize this is not the case with all patients. This fear can often arise, however, with an elderly person or extremely ill individual who is weak and feels vulnerable to upsetting someone, believing that his or her care could be compromised if he or she asks too many questions or complains. Seniors have sometimes been abused at home or other care settings and are often not willing to risk further confrontation."

Figuring a picture is worth a thousand words, Jerome had asked for an overhead projector and proceeded to show the following newspaper clippings illustrating why some patients have developed a fear to ask questions.

- "NHS patients 'frightened to complain about poor treatment' because they fear they'll be branded troublemakers, watchdog finds"
- "Patients 'Afraid to Complain' for Fear of Repercussions"
- "Hospital Patients too Afraid to Complain"
- "Patients Still Afraid to Make Complaints"
- "Older People Are Afraid to Complain, Says Ombudsman"

After the session was over, the audience member who had raised the issue approached Jerome and said, "All caregivers are not like the ones you displayed." Jerome said, "I agree. However, these news clippings illustrate for you why some patients are fearful." The participant not assuaged to reason stomped away and continued to disparage the conference speakers to others in the conference room.

Admission

It is well established by both federal and state law, as well common law, that patients have a right to receive emergency care and inpatient admission if such is required for the health and safety of the patient. Healthcare providers receiving funds from programs such as Medicare and Medicaid are expected to have an affirmative statement that provides it will not discriminate against patients on the basis of age, race, creed, color, or national origin. Patients also have a right to have their care needs responded to within a reasonable time frame; delays in responding to a patient's needs can put a patient's life at risk and put the organization at legal risk for injuries the patient suffers as a result of the delay.

Emergency Care

Emergency care is well recognized as a patient right. Even though regulations and court decisions recognize the right to emergency care, some caregivers who resent treating patients whom they consider routine have made disparaging remarks regarding their care needs, as noted in the *reality check*.

Most caregivers are sympathetic toward patients. There is, however, a need for healthcare organizations to strive to do better when screening new employees and applicants to the organization's medical staff. Appropriate educational programs should address the ongoing care needs of patients and how caregivers can work more efficiently in the high-stress environment associated with caring for the sick and disabled.

Government Hospitals

Veterans and military hospital centers are owned and operated by the federal government. They receive government funding through public taxation. There are 212 reported such hospitals in the United States.[40]

☑ *YOUR DAD RAISES THE COSTS OF HEALTH CARE*

My dad lived in a small rural country town in southwest Pennsylvania near coalmines and brickyards. At 14 he had to leave school after his dad had passed away and work to support his mom, brothers, and sisters. He had been a heavy smoker most of his life. In addition, he was exposed to secondary smoke from a country bar that he lived above from the age of 18 until he passed away at the age of 76. The smoke would seep through our floorboards from two stories below.

While visiting with him I noticed that he was having difficulty breathing. I was able to convince him to go to the hospital emergency department. It was a Sunday, and it was his only option. After undergoing a physical examination, a variety of blood tests, and chest X-rays, the emergency department physician came out to greet me and took the liberty to say, "Well, your dad is okay. There is nothing wrong with him. It is people like your dad that raise the costs of health care. They run to the emergency department with every little problem." Needless to say, I was shocked and speechless but relieved that Dad was okay. I said nothing to the physician out of respect for my dad, but I hope the physician is reading these words today.

Unfortunately, relief was short lived. Dad received a call the following day. He was asked to follow up with his family physician because the radiologist noted a shadow on his chest X-ray. I had returned home to New York, and dad called me and asked what I thought. I attempted to reassure him, but knowing his history of smoking, I keep silent as the sadness invaded my body.

Dad was diagnosed with lung cancer. Although he refused chemotherapy, he did agree to radiation treatments. Mom relayed to me how his big event of the week was when he returned home from his radiation treatments with a smile on his face, would say, "Those cookies they gave me were actually pretty good." Yes, there are a lot of compassionate people who work in the hospital, but there are a few that give it a bad name.

—Administrator

Whether a person is entitled to admission to a particular governmental facility depends on the statute establishing that organization. Governmental hospitals, for example, are, by definition, creatures of some unit of government; their primary concern is providing service to the population within the jurisdiction of that unit. Military hospitals, for example, have been established to care for those persons who are active members of the military and their immediate family members.

Although persons who are not within the statutory classes have no right of admission, hospitals and their employees owe a duty to extend reasonable care to those who present themselves for assistance and are in need of immediate attention. With respect to such persons, governmental hospitals are subject to the same rules that apply to private hospitals. For example, the patient in *Stoick v. Caro Community Hospital*[41] brought a medical malpractice action against a government physician in which she alleged that the physician determined that she was having a stroke and required hospitalization but that he refused to hospitalize her. The plaintiff's daughter-in-law called the defendant, Caro Family Physicians, P.C., where the patient had a 1:30 PM appointment. She was told to take the patient to the hospital. On arriving at the hospital, there was no physician available to see the patient, and a nurse directed her to Dr. Loo's clinic in the hospital. On examination, Loo found right-sided

facial paralysis, weakness, dizziness, and an inability to talk. He told the patient that she was having a stroke and that immediate hospitalization was necessary. Loo refused to admit her because of a hospital policy that only the patient's family physician or treating physician could admit her. The plaintiff went to see her physician, Dr. Quines, who instructed her to go to the hospital immediately. He did not accompany her to the hospital. At the hospital, she waited approximately 1 hour before another physician from the Caro Family Physicians arrived and admitted her. Loo claimed that he did not diagnose the patient as having a stroke and that there was no bad faith on his part.

The circuit court granted the physician's motion for summary judgment on the grounds of governmental immunity. The court of appeals reversed, holding that the plaintiff did plead sufficient facts constituting bad faith on the part of Loo. His failure to admit or otherwise treat the patient is a ministerial act for which governmental immunity does not apply and may be found by a jury to be negligence.

Assessments and Reassessments

Patients have a right to expect their physician will conduct an appropriate history and physical examination based on the patient's presenting complaints. Nurses and physicians perform the assessment and reassessment process to determine a patient's ongoing health status from admission to discharge. The initial assessment is important for diagnosing a patient's medical condition. A cursory assessment can lead to a misdiagnosis and inappropriate treatment plan. Some patients find that it can take years to obtain a diagnosis. One patient found: "It took almost my whole life to get the right diagnosis because no one person had asked me enough questions."[42]

Participate in Care Decisions

Patients have the right to choose the medical care they wish to receive. They have a right to know their treatment options and to accept or refuse care. As medical technology becomes more advanced, care decisions become more complicated to make. Although patients have a right to make their own care and treatment decisions, they often face conflicting religious and moral values in their decision-making process. Often, it is difficult to make a choice when two roads may seem equally right.

Informed Consent

Patients have a right to receive all of the information necessary to make an informed decision prior to consenting to a proposed procedure or treatment. As discussed earlier in this chapter, this information should include the possible risks and benefits of the procedure or treatment. The right to receive information from the physician includes information about the illness, the suggested course of treatment, the prospects of recovery in terms that can be understood, the risks of treatment, the benefits of treatment, alternative care options, and proof of consent.

Right to Treatment

Patients have a right to treatment. Patients have a right not to be discriminated against in the provision of treatment. The ethics committee of the American Academy of Dermatology, for example, states that "it is unethical for a physician to discriminate against a class or category of patients and to refuse the management of a patient because of medical risk, real or imagined."[43] All patients should receive the same compassionate and competent care provided to other patients.

Surgeon Refuses to Treat HIV Patient

The hospital's on-call surgeon in *Fiske v. US Health Corp. of Southern Ohio*[44] had a duty to treat patients who came to the emergency room and required his services. The surgeon's alleged refusal to treat

a patient because of his HIV-positive status constituted an act of omission that could provide the basis for an action in negligence. In view of the hospital's absolute duties to emergency room patients to provide competent medical care, it could be held vicariously liable for the negligence (both acts of commission and acts of omission) of the surgeon. Thus, notwithstanding the hospital's assertion that the surgeon's refusal to treat the patient was a willful or intentional act that was outside the scope of his employment, the trial court was found to have improperly dismissed the patient's vicarious liability claim against the hospital.

Refuse Treatment

. . . the individual's right to make decisions vitally affecting his private life according to his own conscience . . . is difficult to overstate . . . because it is, without exaggeration, the very bedrock on which this country was founded.

—Wons v. Public Health Trust[45]

Adult patients who are conscious and mentally competent have the right to refuse medical care to the extent permitted by law, even when the best medical opinion deems it essential to life. If a patient rejects treatment, the hospital should take all reasonable steps to inform the patient of the risks of refusing treatment. Every person has the legal right to refuse to permit a touching of his or her body. Failure to respect this right can result in a legal action for assault and battery. Coercion through threat, duress, or intimidation must be avoided.

A patient's right to make decisions regarding his own health care is addressed in the Patient Self-Determination Act of 1990.[46] The Act provides that each person has a right under state law (whether statutory or as recognized by the courts of the state) to make decisions concerning his or her medical care, including the right to accept or refuse medical or surgical treatment.

A competent patient's refusal to consent to a medical or surgical procedure must be adhered to, whether the refusal is grounded on lack of confidence in the physician, fear of the procedure, doubt as to the value of a particular procedure, or mere whim. The U.S. Supreme Court stated that the "notion of bodily integrity has been embodied in the requirement that informed consent is generally required for medical treatment" and the "logical corollary of the doctrine of informed consent is that the patient generally possesses the right not to consent, that is, to refuse treatment."[47] The common law doctrine of informed consent is viewed as generally encompassing the right of a competent individual to refuse medical treatment.

The question of liability for performing a medical or surgical procedure without consent is separate and distinct from any question of negligence or malpractice in performing a procedure. Liability may be imposed for a nonconsensual touching of a patient, even if the procedure improved the patient's health.

The courts perform a balancing test to determine whether to override a competent adult's decision to refuse medical treatment. The courts balance state interests, such as preservation of life, protection of third parties, prevention of suicide, and the integrity of the medical profession, against a patient's rights of bodily integrity and religious freedom. The most frequently used state right to intervene in a patient's decision-making process is for the protection of third parties. The state of Illinois, in *In re Fetus Brown*,[48] asserted that its interest in the well-being of a viable fetus outweighed the patient's rights to refuse medical treatment. The state argued that a balancing test should be used to weigh state interests against patient rights. The appellate court held that it could not impose a legal obligation upon a pregnant woman to consent to an invasive medical procedure for the benefit of her viable fetus.

A patient's refusal to consent to care and treatment for any reason, religious or otherwise, should be noted in the medical record, and a release form should be executed (**EXHIBIT 14-1**). The completed release provides

🔍 *IT'S YOUR GAVEL...*

A MOTHER'S RIGHT: A CHILD'S DEATH

Citation: *Harrell v. St. Mary's Hosp., Inc.*, 678 So. 2d 455 (Fla. Dist. Ct. App. 1996).

Facts

Harrell, a Jehovah's Witness, was 6 months pregnant when physicians discovered a life-threatening blood condition that could deteriorate and place both her life and the life of the fetus in jeopardy. Because of religious beliefs, Harrell objected to a blood transfusion. After an emergency hearing, the court ruled that a blood transfusion could be given to Harrell if it was necessary to save the life of the fetus and that after the child was born, a blood transfusion could be given to the child if necessary to save the child's life. The Harrells appealed.

Issue

The child was delivered by cesarean section and died 2 days later. No blood transfusion was given to Harrell or to the child. As a result, the hospital and the state claimed that the appeal of the trial court's order is moot. Because of the hospital's misunderstanding about its standing to bring such proceedings, the Florida District Court of Appeals addressed the issue as capable of repetition yet evading review.

Holding

The Florida District Court of Appeals concluded that a healthcare provider must not be forced into the position of having to argue against the wishes of its own patient.

Reason

The Florida Constitution guarantees that a competent person has the constitutional right to choose or refuse medical treatment. In cases where these rights are litigated, a party generally seeks to invoke the power of the state, through the exercise of the court's judicial power, either to enforce the patient's rights or to prevent the patient from exercising those rights. The state has a duty to ensure that a person's wishes regarding medical treatment are respected.

Harrell argued that the hospital should not have intervened in her private decision to refuse a blood transfusion. She claimed that the state never had been a party in this action and had not asserted any interest and that the hospital had no authority to assume the state's responsibilities.

Patients do not lose their right to make decisions affecting their lives when they enter a healthcare facility. A healthcare provider's function is to provide medical treatment in accordance with the patient's wishes and best interests, not supervening the wishes of a competent adult. A healthcare provider cannot act on behalf of the state to assert state interests. The Florida court found that when a healthcare provider, acting in good faith, follows the wishes of a competent and informed patient to refuse medical treatment, the healthcare provider is acting appropriately and cannot be subjected to civil or criminal liability.

documented evidence of a patient's refusal to consent to a recommended treatment. A release will help protect the organization and physicians from liability should a suit arise as a result of a failure to treat. The best possible care must be rendered to the patient at all times within the limits imposed by the patient's refusal.

Should a patient refuse to sign the release, documentation of the refusal should be placed on the form, and the form should be included as part of the patient's permanent medical record. Advice of legal counsel should be sought in those cases where refusal of treatment poses a serious threat to a patient's health. With the advice of legal counsel, the organization should formulate a policy regarding treatment when consent has been refused. An administrative procedure should be developed to facilitate application for a court order when one is necessary and there is sufficient time to obtain one.

Each patient has a right to refuse treatment and be told what effect such a decision might have on his or her health. The responsibility of caregivers requires balancing risks and benefits. This balancing can lead to situations in which healthcare professionals view their obligations to a patient differently from the patient's own assessment. Forcing a patient to undergo an unwanted procedure can result in a failure to respect the patient's right to self-determination. For example, the patient in *Matter of Dubreuil*,[49] at the time of her admission, signed a standard consent form that included her agreement to have a blood transfusion if necessary. The following day, she was scheduled for a cesarean section, but she

---

REFUSAL OF CARE AND TREATMENT

(Leave Against Medical Advice)

Hospital _____

Address _____

Phone _____

The patient meets all of the following criteria:

1. The patient is over the age of 18 years of age.
2. The patient exhibits no evidence of:
   - Altered levels of consciousness
   - Alcohol or drug ingestion that would impair judgment
3. The patient understands the nature of his or her medical condition, including the risks, benefits, and of alternative treatments, as well as the consequences of refusing care or treatment alternatives.

Acknowledgement of Information (Initial each of the following lines)

_____ I have been advised that medical care on my behalf is necessary, and that refusal of care and assistance could be hazardous to my health, including disability or death.

_____ I acknowledge that I may have a medical problem which may require additional medical attention, and that an ambulance is available to transport me to the hospital. Instead, I elect to seek alternative medical care and/or refuse evaluation, treatment, and/or transport.

Release of Liability (Initial on line)

_____ By signing this form, I am releasing _____ (name of hospital or healthcare facility) of any liability or medical claims resulting from my decision to refuse care against medical advice.

_____ I have read and understand the Acknowledgement of Information and Release of Liability.

_____ If I change my mind, or my condition changes, I will call 911 in an emergency and request that I be taken to the _____ Hospital emergency room or call my private doctor for follow-up care as appropriate.

Signature: _____ Date: _____

Witness Information

Signature: _____ Name (printed): _____ Date: _____

Signature: _____ Name (printed): _____ Date: _____

EXHIBIT 14-1 Refusal of care and treatment.

would not consent to a blood transfusion because of her religious beliefs. During the course of the delivery, after she had lost a significant amount of blood, it was determined that she needed a transfusion to save her life, but she would not give her consent. Her estranged husband was contacted, and upon his arrival at the hospital, he gave his consent for the transfusion. After the first transfusion, physicians determined that she would need more blood, so they petitioned the circuit court for an emergency hearing to determine whether they could give the transfusion despite the patient's lack of consent. The trial court decided to allow the hospital to administer blood as they deemed necessary. The patient moved for a rehearing, and the circuit court denied a rehearing. The patient then sought review by the Florida Supreme Court, arguing that her federal and state constitutional rights of privacy, self-determination, and religious freedom had been denied. The Florida Supreme Court ruled that a competent person has a right to refuse medical treatment, including all decisions relevant to his or her health. A healthcare provider must comply with the patient's wishes unless supported by a court order to do otherwise. Here, the state interest was the protection of the children as innocent third parties. However, in this case, there would have been no abandonment because under Florida law, when there are two living parents, they share equally in the responsibilities of parenting. Had the patient died, her husband would have assumed the care of the children.

Pain Management

Pain is an unpleasant sensation ranging from mild, localized discomfort to acute systemic pain with both physical and emotional components. Some describe the physical part of pain as throbbing, hurting, tenderness, a burning sensation, dull, stabbing, numbing, sharp, and shooting. For others, it has been indescribable, making day-to-day living unbearable. The feeling of pain results from specific nerve fibers carrying pain impulses to the brain. The sensation of acute physical hurt or discomfort caused by injury or illness often includes varying degrees of emotional suffering.

Pain is the body's way of alerting the patient that something is not quite right. A pain rating scale (**FIGURE 14-1**) is a visual tool often used to help a patient describe his or her pain level. It helps the caregiver know how effective treatment is and whether a change in a patient's treatment plan is necessary. The pain assessment scale is often used because of its ease of use in performing a task. Just as important as the severity of pain are its locations and type. A diagram of the body should be used so that the patient can more easily identify the various locations of his or her pain. The severity of pain can be described to the physician to assist in diagnosing and treating the patient.

Pain management is the process whereby caregivers work with the patient to develop a pain control plan. The process involves educating the patient about the importance of pain management in the course of healing. With current treatments, pain often can be prevented, or at least controlled. A pain control treatment program should be developed in collaboration between the caregiver and the patient; include alternative and/or complementary strategies for pain management; include family and caregivers as appropriate in the decision-making process; and include

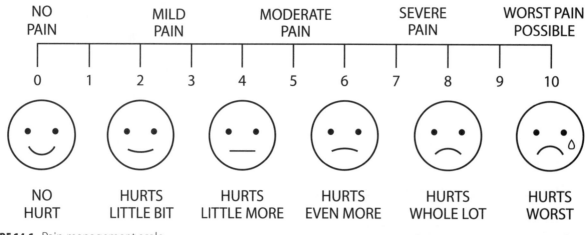

FIGURE 14-1 Pain management scale.
© Oxy_gen/Shutterstock

an explanation of the medications, anesthesia, other treatments, risks, benefits, and alternatives (e.g., acupuncture). In addition, the plan should ensure that the patient can request changes in treatment if pain persists, is able to refuse the recommended pain treatment(s), and receives pain medication in a timely manner.

Quality Care

Healthcare professionals are expected to monitor the quality of each patient's care, beginning with the history and physical, through the development of the treatment plan, and, ultimately, to the delivery of care to the patient. The patient has a right to expect that the quality of care rendered will be based on best practices recognized in the healthcare industry. The *reality check* "A Patient's Journey" describes how a breakdown in the quality of care can come in many forms, beginning in the physician's office and ending in an uncomfortable hospital stay.

Appoint a Surrogate Decision Maker

Patients have a right to appoint a surrogate decision maker should they become incapacitated or unable to make decisions.

Have Special Needs Addressed

Hospital policy should address how patients with special needs can be addressed. Patients who have physical and psychological disabilities should have these needs addressed at the time of their admission to the hospital. Whenever possible, arrangements should be available for a language interpreter, sign language interpreter for the hearing impaired, and pertinent documents written in braille for the blind. These are helpful tools in addressing patients with special needs. Information should be provided at the time of the patient's admission (e.g., employee handbook written in commonly used languages of the community the hospital serves, bulletin boards). A listing of

---

✅ A PATIENT'S JOURNEY

During the past 5 years, I have filled out numerous standardized forms requiring answers to questions that have been repeatedly asked by a wide variety of physician specialists and other caregivers. I had been told that my most recent specialist had great credentials. He came highly recommended. I grew more hopeful as I drove to his office during the early morning rush hour in Washington, DC. I would finally meet someone who cared and understood my disease processes.

As I walked into his office, I noted that my medical chart was lying on the desk in front of him. The sight of it on his desk comforted me, thinking that he had actually read the answers. His staff had said he wanted them several weeks prior to my appointment because he needed time to familiarize himself with my case. Several minutes into the conversation, I realized that he had not reviewed my medical chart. The forms that I had so painstakingly completed, hoping for an answer to my illness, had not been read. He inquired as to what medications I was taking. My husband accompanied me that day and noticed that the list of medications was laid in front of him; he didn't hesitate to point that out to the physician. The doctor asked questions within a predetermined range, one was, "What is your pain on a scale of 1 to 10?" How do I answer that? I am off your scale. I cannot remember not being in pain for the past 5 years. I sometimes wonder what it must be like to be pain-free. I don't know that feeling anymore. Hello, is anyone out there?

Eventually, I was admitted to the hospital for the first time. My nerve endings felt frayed, my stomach churned, worries were multiplying, and my thoughts turned to, "Is it time to get more bad news?" I was extremely ill. The sitting area in the admissions office was uncomfortable and uninviting. Privacy was minimal and soft music was nonexistent. I wondered what was going to happen to me next.

Things got worse when I was finally admitted to a room. Now, I had to stay in an unfamiliar room staring at drab, nondescript walls, and was dependent upon people who hardly had the time to dispense medications. Most physicians and other staff members were rushing about engaged in their everyday tasks. No one seemed to have time for me.

Confusion set in, and the fear of being in a strange place served only to increase my anxiety and fears. Unfamiliar people looked at me, touched me, and repeatedly asked me the same questions over and over again. The questioning seemed never ending. And then I wondered, "Do these people ever talk to each other?" The surroundings were sterile and unfriendly, adding to my uneasy feelings.

Why can't healthcare facilities be more patient friendly to those they serve? Why must I worry about complaining and fear of retribution? Provisions should be made for a serene environment with calming colors and carefully chosen people to gently ease answers from a frightened patient. More attention is needed in making a patient's room a calm and inviting place, which would help to soothe and carry the patient through troubling times.

—Anonymous

employees and community members who would be willing to help patients with special needs for improving the communication process should be maintained by the hospital and other healthcare settings as appropriate. The Joint Commission standards also address the patients' rights to effective communications in their accreditation manual (2017 Hospital Accreditation Standards RI.01.01.03).

Without alternative ways to address patients with special needs, it would be difficult to understand what the patient's wishes are and what he or she is consenting to in the hospital or other care setting.

Execute Advance Directives

Patients must be informed of their right to execute advance directives. The advance directives must be honored within the limits of the law and the organization's mission, philosophy, and capabilities.

Compassionate Care

Patients have a right to receive considerate and compassionate care from caregivers. There appears to be less time for compassion in the practice of medicine than at the turn of the 20th century. Providers of care seem to have taken the assembly line approach to patient care with little thought to the need to help alleviate their patients' fears. Dr. Robert E. Rakel, of the Department of Family Medicine at Baylor College of Medicine in Houston, wrote in the *Journal of the American Board of Family Practice*, "It has been said that more mistakes in medicine are made by those who do not care than by those who do not know."[50]

The caring function of family medicine emphasizes our personalized approach to health care and our commitment to understanding the patient as a person, respecting the person as an individual, and showing compassion for his or her discomfort. Compassion, from the word *patior*, literally means "to suffer with," to share in another's distress and to be moved to give relief. Compassion reflects the physician's willingness to share the patient's anguish and to attempt to understand what the sickness means to that person.[51]

It seems with the progress of medicine there has, at the same time, been a decline in compassion for the patient. Patients fill out numerous forms prior to their visit to the physician's office and yet the caregiver often fails to read the information the patient has provided.

Confidentiality

The Code of Federal Regulations provide that "The patient has right to the confidentiality of his or her

> ## (NEWS) *HOSPITAL TO PUNISH SNOOPING ON SPEARS*
>
> UCLA Medical Center is taking steps to fire at least 13 employees and has suspended at least six others for snooping in the confidential medical records of pop star Britney Spears during her recent hospitalization in its psychiatric unit, a person familiar with the matter said Friday.
>
> In addition, six physicians face discipline for peeking at her computerized records, the person said.
>
> —Charles Ornstein, *Los Angeles Times*, March 15, 2008

clinical records."[52] Patients have a right to expect that information regarding their care and treatment will be kept confidential. Information received by a caregiver in a confidential capacity relating to a patient's health should not be disclosed without the patient's consent.

Confidentiality requires that the caregiver safeguard a patient's confidences within the constraints of law. An exception to the rule of confidentiality of patient communications is the implied right to make available to others involved in the patient's care the information necessary to that care. Caregivers must be cautious not to discuss any aspect of a patient's care with others not involved in the case. Written permission must be obtained before a patient's medical record can be made available to anyone not associated with the patient's care.

The phlebotomist in *Bagent v. Blessing Care Corp.*[53] revealed the results of a patient's pregnancy test to the patient's sister at a public tavern. Although there was an attempt by the hospital to have the case dismissed for the phlebotomist's breach of confidentiality, invasion of privacy, and the negligent infliction of emotional distress, the appeals court determined that there were triable issues of fact precluding dismissal of the case. It was asserted that the phlebotomist had been trained to maintain the confidentiality of patient information and that she knew that she had violated the patient's rights.

Privacy and HIPAA

Patients have a right to receive a "Notice of Privacy Standards," a requirement under the Health Insurance Portability and Accountability Act (HIPAA) (45 CFR 164.520).

> The HIPAA Privacy Rule gives individuals a fundamental new right to be informed of the privacy practices of their health plans and of most of their health care providers, as well as to be informed of their privacy rights with

respect to their personal health information. Health plans and covered health care providers are required to develop and distribute a notice that provides a clear explanation of these rights and practices. The notice is intended to focus individuals on privacy issues and concerns, and to prompt them to have discussions with their health plans and health care providers and exercise their rights.[54]

The issues of confidentiality and privacy have both ethical and legal implications. Caregivers must safeguard each patient's right to privacy and the right to have information pertaining to his or her care kept confidential.

HIPAA permits disclosures of certain patient information. However, such disclosures are only permitted when reasonable steps have been taken to minimize the release of confidential information. For example, sign-in sheets may not display medical information that is not necessary for sign-in purposes.

Disclosure may be made under compelling circumstances (e.g., suspected child abuse) to a person with a legitimate interest in the patient's health. The issues of confidentiality and privacy are both ethical and legal. Caregivers must safeguard each patient's right to privacy and the right to have information pertaining to his or her care to be kept confidential.

Disclosures Permitted Without Patient Authorization

A healthcare provider may disclose patient information (e.g., diagnoses, anesthesia history, surgical and other invasive procedures, drug allergies, medication usage, laboratory test results, imaging studies) in the following situations:

- Disclosure of patient information to other providers who may be caring for the patient in order to provide safe healthcare treatment
- Disclosure of patient information to third-party payers so that providers can obtain payment for services rendered
- Disclosure of patient information for healthcare operations
- Disclosure of patient information as may be required by a law enforcement agency
- Disclosure of patient information as may be required to avert a serious threat to public health or safety
- Disclosure of patient information as required by military command authorities for their medical records
- Disclosure of patient information to workers' compensation or similar programs for processing of claims

- Disclosure of patient information in response to a subpoena for a legal proceeding
- Disclosure of patient information to a coroner or medical examiner for purposes of identification

Limitations on Disclosures

Some of the individual rights a patient has regarding disclosure of access to his or her medical information are as follows:

- Right to request restrictions or limitations regarding information used or disclosed about treatment or care.
- Right to an accounting of nonstandard disclosures: The patient has a right to request a list of the disclosures made of information released regarding his or her care.
- Right to amend: If a patient believes that medical information regarding his or her care is incorrect or incomplete, he or she has a right to request that the information be corrected.
- Right to inspect and copy medical information that may be used to make care decisions.
- Right to file a complaint with the provider, or the Secretary of the Department of Health and Human Services (DHHS) in Washington, DC, if the patient believes his or her privacy rights have been violated.
- Right to a paper copy of a notice pertaining to the patient.
- Right to know of restrictions on rights.

The limitations of space and financial restraints make it difficult to continuously preserve a patient's right to privacy in many hospital settings (e.g., emergency departments). Nevertheless, healthcare organizations have a responsibility to provide for a reasonable amount of privacy for patients.

Patient Advocate

Patients have a right to have a patient advocate from admission to discharge, regardless of the setting in which a patient is being treated (e.g., hospital, nursing facility, outpatient center, physician's office). Admission to a hospital is a fearful event for many patients. Patients often have one thought in mind upon admission to a hospital and that is to be discharged healthier than when they were admitted. The constant bombardment of negative news articles involving such concerns as medication errors, hospital-acquired infections, and wrong-sided surgery adds to those fears. This can lead to a patient's failure to fully hear, understand, and/or remember the information provided during his or her stay and follow-up discharge instructions. A patient advocate, such as a family member, friend, or professional advocate, can be helpful in advocating for the patient during the stressful events associated with a hospital stay.

Many states have established, by legislation, ombudsperson programs. Ombudspersons are responsible for the investigation of reports of resident abuse in nursing facilities. The primary impetus for the program came from the Nixon Administration, and gradually the program spread throughout the country. It was not until 1978 that the Older Americans Act Amendments (PUB. L. No. 95-478) mandated that every state have an ombudsperson program and that a certain amount of the Older Americans Act funds from Title III-B (the Social Services section) had to be allocated to the ombudsperson program.

All caregivers should consider themselves patient advocates, and they should be attuned to each patient's attentiveness and understanding of patient care instructions. Reinforcement of instructions may be necessary based on a patient's cognitive, language, and physical limitations, such as speech, sight, and hearing. The Joint Commission standards also require that "When a patient is unable to make decisions about his or her care, treatment, and services, the hospital involves a surrogate decision-maker in making these decisions."[55]

Nightingale Connects Patient Advocates

The mission of Nightingale Connects Patient Advocates (NCPA) "is to enable patients and family members or guardians to be more informed so that they can become better self advocates."[56] NCPA "operates in a non-medical capacity, offering excellent navigational support for working with medically licensed providers, insurance companies, and others and with whom your care must be coordinated. Although we are staffed with nurses, our services are non-medical."[57]

Ethics Consultation

Patients' rights in many hospitals allow for patients and/or their families to access an ethics committee for consultation when faced with challenging treatment decisions that involve ethical dilemmas. Dilemmas often arise when two or more choices often have some degree of a negative outcome. Conflict can arise when there is a difference of opinion between families and care providers, or when the family is unsure about what course of treatment is best for the patient. Ethics committee consultation can provide an objective perspective, and their recommendations should not be considered as binding.

Ethics consultations are helpful when, for example, making end-of-life decisions.

Chaplaincy Services

Today I will take the time to be happy and will leave my footprints and my presence in the hearts of others.

—Author Unknown

Patients have a right to chaplaincy services and have their spiritual needs addressed. The purpose of a pastoral care program is to affirm the valuable role of spiritual care as an integral part of a patient's healing process. Accordingly, a chaplaincy program will make available to patients and their families spiritual support while they are in the hospital, in accordance with their wishes. The clergy and pastoral care volunteers are important members of the healing team.

A multifaith chapel is available in many hospitals, as are televised services. Some hospitals provide spiritual devotions and reflections that are broadcast daily. Music and meditation are often provided as an adjunct for pain management and stress reduction at the bedside.

Chaplains are often available as a first-call option for ethics consultations. The hospital chaplain acts as a liaison between the patient and area clergy. Consults with the patient care team contribute to the holistic care of patients, family, and staff through assessment, pastoral conversation, and other interventions. Caregivers often refer patients to a chaplain if they are experiencing life-changing events; lack effective social, psychological, or spiritual support; have complicated personal relationships; express spiritual or religious concerns; are in a remorseful state of mind; express hopelessness, worthlessness, anger, or depression; or receive news of life-threatening conditions. Chaplains also are available to meet with families at times of death of the patient.

Organizational policies and procedures should address the psychosocial, spiritual, and cultural variables that influence one's understanding and perception of illness. Hospital pastoral care departments should provide a patient information brochure at the time of admission that describes the services offered and how to access them. For example, an introductory statement to such a brochure could be worded to include the following:

- When a loved one is hospitalized—or when you require hospitalization yourself—it is perfectly normal to feel anxious, worried, and sometimes overwhelmed.

- We know how you feel. At times like this, it's good to have a helping hand. The hospital's pastoral care department is here to help you cope with the emotional struggle associated with hospitalization.
- No matter what your religious affiliation, a representative of the pastoral care department is always available, ready to offer spiritual and emotional support.
- Someone will lend an ear and offer comforting words. He or she will help you draw on your spiritual strength in these times of need.

Services offered by a chaplaincy program should offer pastoral support to patients and their families at time of crisis, which may include prayer, scripture reading, and counseling; provide for enhanced communications among patients, their families, and hospital personnel; be available to clinical staff for counseling and support during or after emotional emergency situations; and provide appropriate referrals to the social service department, the local clergy, and community agencies as needed. Documentation should be included in the patient's medical record to indicate that the patient's spiritual needs have been addressed.

Discharge Orders

Patient discharge orders and instructions for follow-up care must be provided to the patient prior to discharge from the hospital. Accreditation standards, such as those promulgated by The Joint Commission provide that "The hospital has a process that addresses the patient's need for continuing care, treatment, and services after discharge or transfer."[58] The Code of Federal Regulations provides that "The patient has the right to participate in the development and implementation of his or her plan of care."[59] The complete Code of Federal Regulations, including those for hospitals that address patients' rights can be found online at www.ecfr.gov.

Discharge or Detainment

Patients have a right to be discharged and not detained in a healthcare setting. An unauthorized detention of a patient could subject the offending organization to charges of false imprisonment. Although patients have a right not to be held against their will, there are circumstances where reasonable detainment can be justified (e.g., a minor's release only to a parent or authorized guardian). When discharging a patient, a physician should issue and sign all discharge orders. If there is no need for immediate care, the patient should be advised to seek follow-up care with his or her family physician.

Release from Hospital Contraindicated

The plaintiff in *Somoza v. St. Vincent's Hospital*[60] was admitted to the hospital during the 29th week of her pregnancy. She was admitted under the care of her private attending physician, defendant Dr. Svesko. She presented herself to the hospital with complaints of severe abdominal pain. Upon the plaintiff's admission to the hospital, Dr. Gutwein (a resident physician at the hospital) examined her. According to the notations she made on the plaintiff's chart, Gutwein independently formed the impression that the plaintiff might be suffering from either left pyelonephritis, premature labor, or polyhydramnios. Gutwein recorded a written plan and orders requiring that the plaintiff be hooked up to a fetal monitor. The plaintiff also was to undergo a number of diagnostic tests, including a renal pelvic sonogram. The results of the sonogram were abnormal, and the radiologist recommended a follow-up sonogram. However, the attending physician did not order a follow-up. Despite the abnormal sonogram and various findings on the physical examinations, Svesko decided to release the plaintiff from the hospital because her pain had subsided. He orally conveyed this order to Gutwein. According to Gutwein, she did not formulate an opinion as to the correctness of the decision to discharge because she was of the opinion that it was not her place to make such a decision. Instead, pursuant to Svesko's instruction, on her early morning rounds, Gutwein simply signed an order discharging the plaintiff from the hospital. Four days later, the

NEWS DON'T LEAVE THE HOSPITAL UNTIL YOU KNOW WHAT COMES NEXT

Being discharged from a hospital can be overwhelming. Make sure you have someone with you to ask questions, take notes and stand up for your interests—especially if you feel unprepared to leave in your current state said Julie Gray, a care manager with Aging and Wisdom in Seattle.

—Judith Grahm, *The Washington Post*, September 6, 2016

plaintiff returned to the hospital with severe pain and soon thereafter delivered twin girls. The twins were diagnosed with cerebral palsy resulting from their premature birth. The plaintiff brought a medical malpractice action against the hospital and Svesko arising out of the premature birth of the twins. The defendants filed a motion for summary judgment, and it was denied. The defendants appealed.

The New York State Supreme Court, Appellate Division, held that there were material issues of fact as to whether the mother's symptoms exhibited during her physical assessment contraindicated her release from the hospital and that ordinary prudence required further inquiry by the resident physician, Gutwein.

The plaintiffs presented an affidavit by expert witness Dr. Sherman, which stated "the failure of the hospital staff to discharge without another physical examination, in my opinion, with a reasonable degree of medical certainty, is a departure from good and accepted medical practice. The resident clearly had an obligation to examine even a private patient in the face of a changing cervix and not just to discharge her pursuant to some attending physician's order."[61] A hospital whose staff carry out a physician's order may be held responsible where the hospital staff knows, or should know, that the orders are so clearly contraindicated by normal practice that ordinary prudence requires inquiry into the correctness of the orders. In this case, the plaintiff's release from the hospital was so clearly contraindicated by normal practice that ordinary prudence required further inquiry by Gutwein into the correctness of the discharge order.

Failure to Override Physician's Discharge Order

Greer, in *Greer v. Bryant*,[62] while at the Philadelphia College of Osteopathic Medicine (PCOM) and under the care of her physician, Dr. Bryant, was diagnosed with preeclampsia, a condition characterized by high blood pressure in the mother that poses a risk to the unborn child. On September 20, the patient suffered symptoms of fetal distress and was examined by the hospital's interns and residents. Tests ordered at the time of her visit revealed that the fetus was suffering from "decelerations," a periodic lowering of the heartbeat. Following her examination, Greer was instructed to return to the hospital on September 23. During that visit, it was noted that the fetus was experiencing "poor beat-to-beat variability." Greer was once again sent home with instructions to return to the hospital on September 27. However, on September 26, Greer, experiencing severe pains,

called the hospital emergency department. She was told to wait until her scheduled appointment the following day. Her appointment was subsequently canceled because of weather. Upon the insistence of her sister, Greer went to the hospital on September 27, where she delivered her child. The infant, suffering from "severe meconium aspiration" (inhalation by the fetus of its own fecal matter while in utero), died several days later.

The plaintiff alleged that the hospital, through its negligence, contributed to her child's death. Greer sued Bryant and PCOM separately. She alleged that based on the prenatal test results during her September 23 visit to PCOM, she should have been delivered on that date by Bryant. The plaintiff argued that even if the test results had been communicated to Bryant and he decided to send her home, the residents should have recognized the serious condition of the fetus and, if necessary, sought approval from their superiors to keep her at the hospital.

Bryant made an offer to settle, and the plaintiff accepted. The Court of Common Pleas, upon jury verdict, entered judgment for the mother, finding PCOM 41% liable to the plaintiff. PCOM appealed. The plaintiff's expert witness, Dr. Gabrielson, opined in her medical report that Greer should have been admitted and the child delivered despite the private physician's instructions to send her home.

The Pennsylvania Superior Court determined that the jury could find that the hospital's staff was negligent by not reporting the fetal distress of the unborn child to Bryant and that the plaintiff's expert witness did not exceed her scope of opinion in her medical report. Although a resident and intern claimed that they had called Bryant, neither could testify as to the content of their conversation with him. Bryant testified that he did not recall receiving any telephone calls. He stated that if he had been aware of the decelerated heart rate, he would have ordered delivery of the child. "Since many of the critical events occurred on September 23, the jury could have determined that PCOM's employees' crucial nonfeasance occurred on that date . . . we must assume that the jury drew this inference" (*Id.* at 1002).

Transfer

Patients have a right to be transferred to an appropriate facility when the admitting facility is unable to meet a patient's particular needs. This will at times necessitate the transfer of the patient to another healthcare organization that has the special services the patient requires. For this reason, it is important for each organization to execute transfer agreements with other healthcare organizations.

Healthcare organizations should have a written transfer agreement in effect with other organizations to help ensure the smooth transfer of patients from one facility to another when such is determined appropriate by the attending physician(s). Generally speaking, a transfer agreement is a written document that sets forth the terms and conditions under which a patient may be transferred to a facility that more appropriately provides the kind of care required by the patient. It also establishes procedures to admit patients of one facility to another when their condition warrants a transfer. Transfer agreements should be written in compliance with and reflect the provisions of the many federal and state laws, regulations, and standards affecting healthcare organizations. The parties to a transfer agreement should be particularly aware of applicable federal and state regulations.

Patients have a right to choose a receiving facility, whenever possible. The Medicaid patient in *Macleod v. Miller*[63] was entitled to an injunction preventing his involuntary transfer from the nursing home. The patient had not been accorded a pretransfer hearing, as was required by applicable regulations. In addition, it was determined that the trauma of transfer might result in irreparable harm to the patient. The appeals court remanded the case to the trial court with directions to enter an order prohibiting the defendants from transferring the plaintiff pending exhaustion of his administrative remedies.

In another case, a 97-year-old resident petitioned for review of a decision by the Department of Consumer and Regulatory Affairs to involuntarily discharge her from a community residence facility.[64] The resident had lived in the facility for 8 years. The basis for the agency's decision was that the resident's discharge was essential to be in accordance with her prescribed level of care, pursuant to D.C. Code Annotated Section 32-1421(a). The facility presented, as evidence, three medical certification forms completed by Dr. Choisser, the treating physician. Two forms indicated in an ambiguous check-off system that the resident required an intermediate level of care. This was contradicted by a letter written by Choisser that stated, "I see no reason why she should not continue to reside in Chevy Chase House with complete safety. . . . It is my opinion that a change in her residence, at this stage in her life, would prove harmful to her emotionally, and I strongly suggest that she be left as she is."[65] The court held that the need for the discharge was not proven by clear and convincing evidence.

Access Medical Records

The courts have taken the view that patients have a legally enforceable interest in the information contained in their medical records and, therefore, have a right to access their records. Some states have enacted legislation permitting patients access to their records. Patients may generally have access to review and/or obtain copies of their records, X-rays, and laboratory and diagnostic tests. Access to information includes that maintained or possessed by a healthcare organization and/or a healthcare practitioner who has treated or is treating a patient. Organizations and physicians can withhold records if it is determined that the information could reasonably be expected to cause substantial and identifiable harm to the patient (e.g., patients in psychiatric hospitals, institutions for the mentally disabled, or alcohol and drug treatment programs).

Know Hospital's Adverse Events

The Florida Supreme Court, in the cases *Florida Hospital Waterman, Inc., etc. v. Teresa M. Buster, et al.* and *Notami Hospital of Florida, Inc., etc. v. Evelyn Bowen, et al.*, ruled that hospitals under Amendment 7 (approved by the voters on November 2, 2004, and codified as article X, section 25 of the Florida Constitution) must reveal their records about past acts of malpractice that have been performed at the hospital. In Florida, patients now have a right to know, ask about, and/or receive records about adverse medical incidents that have happened at the hospital. Amendment 7 to the Florida Constitution reads in part:

> Section 25. Patients' rights to know about adverse medical incidents.
>
> (a) . . . patients have a right to have access to any records made or received in the course of business by a health care facility or provider relating to any adverse medical incident.
>
> (b) In providing such access the identity of patients involved shall not be disclosed, and any privacy restrictions imposed by federal law shall be maintained.

Know Third-Party Relationships

Patients have a right to know the hospital's relationships with outside parties that may influence their care and treatment. These relationships may be with educational institutions, insurers, and other healthcare providers.

Patient Education

Patients have a right to be provided education as it relates to their care and treatment. Patient education should begin with a caregiver's first contact with the patient and should include a family member as necessary or if requested by the patient. Education should be conducted in all settings (e.g., inpatient, ambulatory, emergency department, home care) with those caregivers involved in the patient's care on a collaborative basis. Patient education involves the establishment of trust, which emanates from patient recognition that the caregivers are knowledgeable and competent. Greetings, gestures, manner of taking information, and attitude are important ingredients in establishing a good relationship with the patient. Evidence of patient education should be placed in the patient's medical record and should include an assessment of the patient's readiness/willingness, ability, and need to learn about his or her care and treatment. Patient education should include the provision of information on medication safety, nutrition, medical equipment use, access to community resources, how to obtain further care if necessary, and responsibilities of the patient and family. The caregiver must ascertain whether the patient understands the care instructions provided.

Transparency and Hospital Charges

Patients have a right to transparency when requesting information about hospital emergency room, outpatient, and inpatient treatment charges. In August of 2013, the North Carolina legislature signed into law the Health Care Cost Reduction and Transparency Act (House Bill 834) requiring hospitals to submit pricing information on services to allow patients to compare treatment costs. Under the Act, hospitals and ambulatory surgical facilities are required to provide financial information annually for their 50 most common episodes of care to the North Carolina Health Information Exchange (Exchange), which allows free public access to its most current information. The Act is intended to allow patients to compare treatment costs among different providers.

Failure to Disclose Insurance Applicants' HIV Status

Unbeknownst to Wyoming residents Gary and Renna Pehle, husband and wife, they were infected with HIV at the time they applied for life insurance from the Farm Bureau Life Insurance Company in 1999. At the time of the application, Farm Bureau collected the initial premium and arranged for blood tests from the Pehles in furtherance of the application. Blood samples were forwarded for analysis to an independent laboratory, LabOne, which, in turn, reported the HIV status to the insurance company. On receipt of the information, Farm Bureau sent a notice of rejection to the Pehles and advised them that it would disclose the reason for their rejection to their physician if they so wished. The Pehles took no action. Two years later, Renna Pehle was diagnosed with AIDS, and, on inquiry, she and her husband learned that Farm Bureau records showed the HIV infection at the time of the life insurance rejection. The Pehles sued, alleging that the defendants were negligent in failing to tell them they were HIV positive. A federal court, balancing all the interests involved as Wyoming law requires, concluded that if an insurance company, through independent investigation by it or a third party for purposes of determining policy eligibility, discovers that an applicant is infected with HIV, the company has a duty to disclose to the applicant information sufficient to cause a reasonable applicant to inquire further.[66]

▶ PATIENT RESPONSIBILITIES

Patients have responsibilities as well as rights. The following description of patient responsibilities provides

---

✔ TRANSPARENCY NOT SO TRANSPARENT

I traveled to Florida for a continuing education program on patient care in my specialty. I unfortunately forgot my asthma inhaler. When I got off the plane after landing and not knowing where to go, as I was new to the area and it was late evening, I decided to go to a local hospital emergency department for a prescription. I was in no distress but was concerned that I had forgotten my inhaler. I unfortunately made the mistake of believing that an emergency room was an appropriate place to go for help and advice when traveling. I sat in a hallway, had my temperature and blood pressure taken, and inhaled some albuterol. My visit from beginning to end was about 20 minutes.

Upon returning home, I received an emergency room bill in excess of $3,000, so now I was distressed. Although I have an insurance policy, there is a $2,000 deductible that I was responsible to pay. I decided to request more detail on my bill. After a less than pleasant experience with the billing department I decided also to request a copy of my medical record. For a hospital that claimed transparency on its website, it took me 6 weeks and several annoying phone conversations with hospital staff to obtain the billing information and a copy of what turned out to be an 18-page barely readable computerized medical record that listed yes and no answers to questions I was never specifically asked. I couldn't believe it and said to my husband, "Wow, the bill says $27 for the medication and I have to pay $2,973 to inhale it."

In summary, I discovered there was no transparency, despite what the hospital publicized on its website. Transparency is an overused platitude that has little meaning. For me, I totally understand the U.S. citizen's frustration with the healthcare system.

—Anonymous

the reader with a sense of the ever-changing emphasis on patients' responsibilities from both a historical and contemporary perspective.

Historical Perspective

The following is an excerpt from Cornwall General Hospital's "Rules for Patients," which were posted in that hospital in 1897:[67]

1. Patients on admission to the Hospital must have a bath, unless orders to the contrary are given by the Attending Medical Attendant.

• • • •

6. Patients must be quiet and exemplary in their behaviour and conform strictly to the rules and regulations of the Hospital, and carry out all orders and prescriptions of the various officers of the establishment.

• • • •

8. No male patient shall, under any pretense whatever, enter the apartments or wards for the females, nor shall a female patient enter the apartments or wards for males, without express orders from the Medical Attendant or Lady Superintendent.

• • • •

10. Every patient shall retire to bed at 9 P.M. from First May to First November, and at

8 P.M. from November to May; and those who are able shall rise at 6 A.M. in the Summer and 7 A.M. in the Winter.

11. Such patients as are able, in the opinion of the physicians and surgeons, shall assist in nursing others, or in such services as the Lady Superintendent may require.

• • • •

13. Patients must not take away bottles, labels or appliances when leaving the Hospital.

14. No patients shall enter into the basement story, operating theater, or any of the officers' or attendants' rooms, except by permission of an officer of the Hospital.

• • • •

17. Any patient bringing spirituous liquors into the Hospital or the grounds, or found intoxicated, will be discharged.

18. Whenever patients misbehave or violate any of the standing rules of the Hospital, the Attending Physician may remove or discharge them, as provided by clauses 91 and 93 of Rules for Medical Staff.

Contemporary Perspective

Today, patient responsibilities are stated somewhat differently than those described previously. A 1997 report to the President by the Advisory Commission on Consumer Protection and Quality in the Health Care Industry states, "In a health care system that protects consumers' rights, it is reasonable to expect and encourage consumers to assume reasonable responsibilities. Greater individual involvement by consumers in their care increases the likelihood of achieving the best outcomes and helps support a quality improvement, cost-conscious environment."[68] The following paragraphs describe a variety of patient responsibilities.

Practice a Healthy Lifestyle

Living a healthy lifestyle involves both a right and a responsibility. Each person must take responsibility for living well through exercise, diet, stress control, and maintaining positive social relationships, which will help prepare people for whatever health obstacles the future may hold. Recognizing what is right and what is wrong for one's health is not enough—it must be practiced.

Maintain Current Medical Records

Patients should maintain a record of physical ailments (e.g., cardiovascular disease) and treatments (e.g., surgical procedures) and a current listing of medications, including dosages and frequency. Drug allergies should be included on the list. Medication records should be reviewed periodically to be sure the listing is current. A copy should be provided to treating physicians and treating facility.

Keep Appointments

Patients should be sure to keep their appointments. When necessary to cancel an appointment, be sure to notify the caregiver of the cancellation. Failure to notify the caregiver results in longer delays for other patients who may already be finding it difficult to schedule appointments.

Provide Full Disclosure of Medical History

Patients must provide all information relevant to one's medical condition, medical complaints, symptoms, location and severity of pain, previous pain control concerns, past illnesses, treatments, surgical or other invasive procedures, hospitalizations, medications, and allergies. Information provided must be accurate, timely, and complete. (The court of appeal in *Fall v. White*[69] affirmed the superior court's ruling that the patient had a duty to provide the physician with accurate and complete information and to follow the physician's instructions for further care or tests.)

Accurately Describe Symptoms

Patients must accurately describe the location and severity of their symptoms, as well as any previous treatments, allergies, and surgery. Failure to do so can lead to the wrong diagnosis and treatment plan.

RESPONSIBILITY TO DISCLOSE INFORMATION

Citation: *Oxford v. Upson County Hosp., Inc.*, 438 S.E.2d 171 (Ga. Ct. App. 1993)

Facts

Oxford brought a lawsuit against the Upson County Hospital and nurses, claiming that their medical malpractice caused her injury from a fall in the hospital's bathroom. Oxford had been admitted to the hospital after having been diagnosed with gastroenteritis and dehydration. Nothing on her chart indicated that she had experienced dizziness. Testimony at the trial indicated that Oxford told her nurse that she had to go to the bathroom. Oxford did not inform the nurse that she felt dizzy. After the nurse escorted her to the bathroom, Oxford fainted while sitting on the toilet. As she fainted, she hit her head on the bathroom wall.

Two nurse experts testified that it is a patient's responsibility to communicate to the staff any symptoms the patient is experiencing. Oxford had told her physician prior to her hospitalization about feeling dizzy, but he had not related this information to the hospital's staff.

After a jury verdict for the hospital, Oxford appealed, arguing that the trial court's jury charges on causation, failure to exercise ordinary care, and comparative negligence were wrong.

Issue

Was there sufficient evidence to warrant the judge's charges to the jury?

Holding

The Georgia Court of Appeals affirmed the jury verdict and found that the judge's charges on the issues had been sufficient. The court followed its determination in *Carreker v. Harper*, 196 Ga. App. 658, 659, 396 S.E.2d 587 (1990), that when a patient fails to disclose all information related to her condition and fails to exercise ordinary care for her safety by seeking medical attention for her worsening condition, a charge of comparative negligence is applicable. In this case, the court did not require that Oxford diagnose herself, but she should have told the staff about her symptoms so that they could have treated her using their professional judgment.

Communicate Care Preferences

Patients are responsible for communicating to staff their care preferences, including who has been selected as a decision maker in the event the patient becomes incapacitated and unable to make decisions for himself/herself.

Stay Informed

A patient has the responsibility to understand caregiver instructions and ask questions when information is unclear. Consider the following case where a patient had been sedated during the performance of a colonoscopy at an endoscopy center. He decided to drive himself home against medical advice. Claims against the clinic and a nurse were dismissed with respect to fatal injuries that the patient received during a one-car collision. The trial court correctly ruled that the nurse had no duty to prevent the patient from leaving its premises once she repeatedly warned the patient not to drive. The nurse was justified in relying upon the patient's false representations that he had a friend available to drive him home. She was not required to keep the patient in a gown in the recovery room once she learned the truth, and she was not required to use other options to prevent him from driving, such as putting him in a taxi cab, putting him in a hotel, calling the police, admitting him to the hospital, personally driving him home, taking his keys away from him, or physically restraining him. The center and the nurse owed no legal duty to the patient to do more than warn him that he should not drive. The center is not an insurer of the patients' safety. The patient acted recklessly in ignoring the advice he was given and suffered the consequences. The circuit court correctly found no duty to ensure that no patient drives after the procedure.[70]

Report Unexpected Changes in Health Status

If a patient experiences changes in health status, it is his or her responsibility to report these changes to healthcare providers.

Adhere to the Agreed-Upon Treatment Plan

Patients must state whether they clearly understand their plan of care. If they decide to refuse treatment, patients must accept responsibility for the potential consequences. Patients should work collaboratively with their healthcare providers in developing and carrying out agreed-upon treatment plans. Following the recommended treatment plan is the patient's responsibility, as are the consequences of failing to adhere to the caregiver's instructions.

Avoid Self-Administration of Medications

Patients are not to self-administer medications not prescribed by the physician, including those they may have brought to the hospital.

Actively Participate in Care

When in doubt, patients should ask questions and/or seek a second opinion. Patients should, for example, participate in marking the site of a surgical or other invasive procedure to help prevent treatment errors.

Comply with Hospital Policy

Patients are required to adhere to the rules and regulations in patient handbooks and posted instructive materials. The number of visitors, for example, should be limited as requested by hospital policy and to protect the privacy of other patients.

Respect

Patients should show the same respect for other patients and health workers that they expect for themselves. This includes being considerate of the rights of others (e.g., noise control, no-smoking rules, respect for the rights and property of others).

Understand That Medical Science Has Limits

While there have been great strides in medicine, patients must recognize that medicine has its boundaries. In addition, medicine is performed by humans, who are fallible, which means that there are limits to their capabilities.

Ask Questions

The necessity and responsibility to ask questions cannot be overstated. A knowledgeable patient is a good patient. If a caregiver's instructions are unclear or confusing, patients should seek clarification and a written copy of the proposed treatment plan. Patients have a responsibility to ask questions and understand explanations. Such questions include: "What is this medication for?", "What diet am I on?", or "Since you are going to change my dressing, did you wash your hands?"

✅ *20 TIPS TO HELP PREVENT MEDICAL ERRORS*[71]

What You Can Do to Stay Safe

The best way you can help to prevent errors is to be an active member of your healthcare team. That means taking part in every decision about your health care. Research shows that patients who are more involved with their care tend to get better results.

Medicines

1. Make sure that all of your doctors know about every medicine you are taking.
2. Bring all of your medicines and supplements to your doctor visits.
3. Make sure your doctor knows about any allergies and adverse reactions you have had to medicines.
4. When your doctor writes a prescription for you, make sure you can read it.
5. Ask for information about your medicines in terms you can understand—both when your medicines are prescribed and when you get them.
6. When you pick up your medicine from the pharmacy, ask: Is this the medicine that my doctor prescribed?
7. If you have any questions about the directions on your medicine labels, ask.
8. Ask your pharmacist for the best device to measure your liquid medicine.
9. Ask for written information about the side effects your medicine could cause.

Hospital Stays

10. If you are in a hospital, consider asking all healthcare workers who will touch you whether they have washed their hands.
11. When you are being discharged from the hospital, ask your doctor to explain the treatment plan you will follow at home.

Surgery

12. If you are having surgery, make sure that you, your doctor, and your surgeon all agree on exactly what will be done.
13. If you have a choice, choose a hospital where many patients have had the procedure or surgery you need.

Other Steps

14. Speak up if you have questions or concerns.
15. Make sure that someone, such as your primary care doctor, coordinates your care.
16. Make sure that all of your doctors have your important health information.
17. Ask a family member or friend to go to appointments with you.
18. Know that "more" is not always better.
19. If you have a test, do not assume that no news is good news.
20. Learn about your condition and treatments by asking your doctor and nurse and by using other reliable sources.

⚖ *THE COURT'S DECISION*

The Superior Court of New Jersey held that the trial judge's decision to appoint a temporary medical guardian for Mrs. Hughes was legally supportable. The doctrine of informed consent was developed to protect the right of self-determination in matters of medical treatment. Self-determination encompasses the right to refuse medical treatment and is a right protected by common law as well as by the federal and state constitutional right to privacy. The New Jersey Supreme Court has addressed the right to decline medical treatment in situations where the patient is opposed to prolonging an otherwise irreversible condition. The distinguishing factor in this case, however, is that the transfusion can preserve a healthy young woman's life, not prolong a painful and imminent death. In New Jersey, the decision maker must determine and effectuate, insofar as possible, the decision that the patient would have made if competent.

Even though the facts in this case indicate that Mrs. Hughes advised Dr. Ances and family members of her desire not to receive blood or blood products, and even though Mrs. Hughes directed the hospital and her physician, in writing, to refrain from giving her a transfusion, a doubt existed as to whether she had made a fully informed decision to refuse blood if this meant her death. Any glimmer of uncertainty as to Mrs. Hughes' desires in an emergency situation should be resolved "in favor of preserving life.

Mrs. Hughes and a witness signed the consent form, but there was no indication in the space provided that the consequences of her refusal had been explained to her in the context of this particular operation. These proposed forms must contain an unequivocal statement that under any and all circumstances, blood is not to be used and an acknowledgment that the consequences of the refusal were fully supplied to the patient. The court emphasized that this case arose in the context of elective surgery. This was not an emergency situation where the physician and patient did not have time to fully discuss the potential risks of the surgery and the depth of the patient's religious beliefs. A Jehovah's Witness patient has an obligation to make medical preferences unequivocally known to the treating physician, including the course to follow if life-threatening complications should arise. This protects the patient's right to freedom of religion and self-determination, as well as the hospital's obligation to preserve life whenever possible.[72]

▶ CHAPTER REVIEW

1. *Patient consent* is an agreement by the patient to allow something proposed by another to be performed on his or her body.

2. Consent can be expressed verbally or in writing. It can be implied by statute or granted by the courts in cases where emergency care is needed to save the life of the patient.

3. Oral consent, although binding, is often difficult to corroborate, whereas written consent provides visible proof of a patient's wishes.

4. *Implied consent* is generally presumed when immediate action is required to prevent death or permanent impairment of a patient's health. In such cases, documentation justifying the need to treat before obtaining consent should be maintained.

5. *Statutory consent* provides that when a patient is clinically unable to give consent to a lifesaving emergency treatment, the law implies consent on the presumption that a reasonable person would consent to lifesaving medical intervention.

6. *Judicial consent* may be necessary in those instances where there is concern as to the absence or legality of consent.

7. *Informed consent* is a legal concept that provides that a patient has a right to know the potential risks, benefits, and alternatives of a proposed procedure.

8. Validity of consent:

   - *Subjective standard*: informed consent is determined by patient testimony.
   - *Objective standard*: resolves the issue of informed consent in terms of what a reasonably prudent person in the patient's position would have decided if suitably informed of the risks, benefits, and alternatives of the procedure.

9. Liability for performing a medical or surgical procedure without consent is distinct from a question of negligence or malpractice in performing the procedure.

   - A physician can be found liable for imposing nonconsensual treatment, even if that treatment improved the patient's health.

10. Consent of a minor:

    - Not generally valid to proceed with medical or surgical treatment.
    - Not generally required if the minor is married or otherwise emancipated.

11. Consent for *incompetent patients*, assuming there is no designated family member or surrogate decision maker, can be obtained through application to a court for an order designating a decision maker to make the patient's healthcare decisions.

12. Regardless of religious beliefs, patients have the right to refuse medical treatment. If a patient refuses treatment:

    - The refusal should be noted in the patient's medical record.
    - A release form should be executed that protects the provider from liability should the patient's refusal to accept care result in injury.

13. An *exculpatory agreement* is an agreement that relieves one from liability when he or she has acted in good faith. However, these are generally considered invalid in the medical setting.

14. Defenses to claims that informed consent was lacking include:

   - Risk not disclosed is commonly known and does not warrant disclosure.
   - Patient stated he would undergo the procedure regardless of the risk involved.
   - Consent was not reasonably possible by or on behalf of the patient.
   - The practitioner, after considering all of the attendant facts and circumstances, used reasonable discretion as to the manner and extent as to which *alternatives or risks should be disclosed.*

15. Each patient should be informed of his or her rights and responsibilities at the time of admission. If a patient does not understand his or her rights and responsibilities, they should be explained to the patient.

16. Patient rights include the right to: admission, assessments, and reassessments, participate in care decisions, informed consent, treatment, refuse treatment, pain management, quality care, know one's rights, know caregivers, an explanation of rights, ask questions, have special needs addressed, execute advance directives, compassionate care, confidentiality, privacy, a patient advocate, an ethics consultation, chaplaincy services, discharge, transfer, access medical records, know hospital's adverse events, know third-party relationships, and patient education.

17. Patient responsibilities include maximizing healthy habits, such as exercising, not smoking, and eating healthy; being involved in healthcare decisions; working collaboratively with healthcare providers in developing treatment plans; disclosing relevant information and clearly communicating wants and needs; recognizing the risks and limits of medicine and the human fallibility of healthcare professionals; showing respect for other patients, caregivers, and visitors; making a good faith effort to meet financial obligations; providing caregivers with relevant medical complaints, symptoms, past illnesses, treatments, and hospitalizations; making it known whether one clearly understands the plan of care and course of treatment; following the agreed-upon treatment plan; and speaking up and asking questions.

18. Caregivers should consider themselves as patient advocates because of their position to help patients who are often helpless and unable to speak for themselves.

▶ REVIEW QUESTIONS

1. Discuss the rights and responsibilities of patients as reviewed in this chapter.
2. Discuss the distinction between verbal, written, and implied consent.
3. Describe the role of the patient, physician, nurse, and hospital in obtaining informed consent.
4. Explain how consent differs among competent patients, minors, guardians, and incompetent patients.
5. Explain the available defenses for defendants as it relates to informed consent.
6. Can a patient consent to a procedure and then withdraw it? Discuss your answer.
7. Discuss under what circumstances parental consent for a minor might not be necessary.
8. Describe the rights and responsibilities of patients as reviewed in this chapter.
9. Why should caregivers consider themselves as patient advocates?
10. Describe what patients can do to help prevent medical errors.

▶ NOTES

1. *Matter of Hughes*, 611 A.2d 1148 (N.J. Super. Ct. 1992).
2. 141 U.S. 250, 251 (1891).
3. 464 F.2d 772 (D.C. Cir. 1972).
4. *In re Duran*, 769 A.2d 497 (Pa. 2001).
5. 497 U.S. 261 (1990).
6. No. 04-CA-939 (La. Ct. App. 5 Cir. 1/11/05).
7. 136 N.W. 1106 (Mich. 1912).
8. 28 N.E. 266 (Mass. 1891).
9. Sandra G. Boodman, *The Washington Post*, July 11, 2017: E-4.
10. Robert Langreth, "Unreported Robot Surgery Injuries Open Questions for FDA," *Bloomberg*, December 30, 2013. http://mobile.bloomberg .com/news/2013-12-30/unreported-robot -surgery-injuries-open-questions-for-fda.html.
11. 635 A.2d 1047 (Pa. Super. Ct. 1993).
12. 733 A.2d 456 (1999).
13. *Id.* at 461.
14. 534 N.E.2d 472 (Ill. App. Ct. 1989).
15. 620 So. 2d 372 (La. Ct. App. 1993).
16. *Id.* at 380.
17. Title 23, XXIII, Courts - Common Pleas.
18. 842 S.W.2d 860 (Ky. 1992).
19. *Stamford Hosp. v. Vega*, 236 Conn. A.2d 646 (1996).

20. *Id.* at 668.
21. 972 F. Supp. 308 (D.C. Pa. 1997).
22. 67 Cal. Rptr. 2d 573 (Cal. App. 1997).
23. 390 N.Y.S.2d 523 (N.Y. Sup. Ct. 1976).
24. *In re Estate of Darone*, 349 Pa. Super. Ct. 59, 502 A.2d 1271 (1985), aff'd, 517 Pa. 3, 534. A.2d 452, 455 (1987).
25. 536 N.Y.S.2d 492 (N.Y. App. Div. 1989).
26. 534 A.2d 452 (Pa. 1987).
27. 164 Cal. Rptr. 361 (Cal. Ct. App. 1980).
28. Abraham Cherrix, "My Journey," Home Page, http://scienceblogs.com/insolence/2013/02/19/the-long-strange-case-of-abraham-cherrix-continues/.
29. Cherrix, *supra* note 1.
30. 648 N.E.2d 839 (Ohio App. 9 Dist. 1994).
31. *Id.* at 840.
32. 525 N.W.2d 891 (Mich. App. 1994).
33. *Id.* at 893.
34. *Colton v. New York Hosp.*, 414 N.Y.S.2d 866 (1979).
35. 254 S.E.2d 725 (Ga. Ct. App. 1979).
36. *Id.* at 727.
37. National Caregivers Library, "Respect and Dignity," http://www.caregiverslibrary.org/caregivers-resources/grp-emotional-issues/respect-and-dignity-article.aspx.
38. New York State Department of Health, "Your Rights as a Hospital Patient in New York State," Revised February 2017. https://www.health.ny.gov/publications/1449/.
39. 2107 Hospital Accreditation Standards, The Joint Commission, RI.01.04.01.
40. American Hospital Association, "Fast Facts on US Hospitals," http://www.aha.org/research/rc/stat-studies/fast-facts.shtml.
41. 421 N.W.2d 611 (Mich. Ct. App. 1988).
42. Karen Asp, "Is Your Doctor Missing the Mark?" *Shape Magazine*, March 2013.
43. Ethics Committee of the American Academy of Dermatology, *Ethics in Medical Practice* (Washington, DC: American Academy of Dermatology, 1992), 6.
44. Case No. 04CA2942 (Ohio Ct. App. 2005).
45. 500 So. 2d 679, 687 (Fla. Dist. Ct. App. 1987), aff'd 541 So. 2d 96 (Fla. 1989).
46. Public Law 101–508, November 5, 1990, sections 4206 and 4751 of the Omnibus Budget Reconciliation Act.
47. *Cruzan v. Director, Missouri Dep't of Health*, 497 U.S. 261, 269 (1990).
48. 689 N.E.2d 397 (Ill. App. Ct. 1997).
49. 629 So. 2d 819 (Fla. 1993).
50. Robert E. Rakel, "Compassion and the Art of Family Medicine: From Osler to Oprah" *Journal of the American Board of Family Medicine* 13(6): 440-8 (2000).
51. *Id.*
52. Condition of participation: Patient's rights, 42 e-CFR § 482.13(d)(1), October 9, 2016.
53. 844 N.E.2d 649 (Ill. App. 2006).
54. U.S. Department of Health and Human Services "Notice of Privacy Practices for Protected Health Information," December 3, 2002, Revised April 3, 2003. http://www.hhs.gov/ocr/privacy/hipaa/understanding/coveredentities/notice.html.
55. 2017 Hospital Accreditation Standards, The Joint Commission, PC.01.02.01 (Element 6).
56. Nightingale Connects Patient Advocates, "What We Are All About." http://www.nightingaleconnects.com.
57. *Id.*
58. 2017 Hospital Accreditation Standards, The Joint Commission, PC.04.01.01, 2016.
59. Condition of participation: Patient's rights, 42 e-CFR § 482.13(b)(1), October 9, 2016.
60. 596 N.Y.S.2d 789 (N.Y. App. Div. 1993).
61. *Id.* at 791.
62. 621 A.2d 999 (Pa. Super. Ct. 1993).
63. 612 P.2d 1158 (Colo. Ct. App. 1980).
64. *Henson v. Department of Consumer and Regulatory Affairs*, 560 A.2d 543 (D.C. 1989).
65. *Id.* at 545.
66. The plaintiffs in *Pehle v. Farm Bureau Life Insurance Company, Inc.*
67. "Rules for Patients, Cornwall General Hospital, 1897," http://www.archives.gov.on.ca/english/on-line-exhibits/health-records/big/big_06_patient_rules.aspx.
68. President's Advisory Commission on Consumer Protection and Quality in the Health Care Industry, "Consumer Bill of Rights and Responsibilities," Chapter Eight, Consumer Responsibilities, July 17, 1998, http://www.hcqualitycommission.gov/cborr/chap8.html.
69. 449 N.E.2d 628 (Ind. Ct. App. 1983).
70. *Young v. Gastro-Intestinal Center, Inc.*, No. 04-595 (Ark. 2005).
71. Agency for Healthcare Research and Quality, "20 Tips to Help Prevent Medical Errors: Patient Fact Sheet," May 2017. http://www.ahrq.gov/patients-consumers/care-planning/errors/20tips/index.html.
72. *Matter of Hughes, supra.*

© marekuliasz/Shutterstock

CHAPTER 15

Healthcare Ethics

To laugh often and love much; to win the respect of two intelligent persons and the affection of children; to earn the approbation of honest citizens and endure the betrayal of false friends; to appreciate beauty; to find the best in others; to give of one's self; to leave the world a bit better, whether by a healthy child, a garden patch or a redeemed social condition; to have played and laughed with enthusiasm and sung with exultation; to know even one life has breathed easier because you have lived—this is to have succeeded.

—Bessie Anderson Stanley

▶ LEARNING OBJECTIVES

The reader, upon completion of this chapter, will be able to:

- Describe the concepts of ethics and morality.
- Describe how an understanding of ethical theories, principles, and virtues is helpful in resolving ethical dilemmas.
- Explain the relationship between spirituality and religion.
- Discuss situational ethics and how one's moral character can change as circumstances change.
- Explain how one's reasoning skills influence the decision-making process.

■ Discuss the purpose of an ethics committee and its consultative role in the delivery of patient care.

 Ethics is nothing else than the reverence for life.
—Albert Schweitzer

Why introduce the study of ethics here? The law is the outcome, the result of mistakes, as reviewed in this book, and the cases presented demonstrate how the law is invoked as a result of unfortunate mistakes in the delivery of health care. They also describe the resulting pain for caregivers, patients, and their families. The practice of ethics helps to lead you in the right direction—toward making better choices. This chapter provides the reader with an overview of healthcare ethics and moral principles. The terms *ethics* and *morals* are derived from the Greek and Latin terms (roots) for *custom*. The intent of this chapter is not to burden the reader with the philosophical arguments surrounding ethical theories, moral principles, and virtues; however, as with the study of any new subject, "words are the tools of thought." Therefore, the necessary vocabulary is presented to the reader in order to lay a foundation for applying the abstract theories and principles of ethics and making practical use of them.

An ethical dilemma arises in situations where a choice must be made among unpleasant alternatives. It can occur whenever a choice involves giving up something good and suffering something bad, no matter what course of action is taken. Ethical dilemmas often require caregivers to make decisions that may break some law, religious standard, or custom. For example, should I choose life knowing that an unborn child will be born with severe disabilities, or should I choose abortion and thus prevent pain for both parent and child? Should I adhere to my spouse's wishes not to be placed on a respirator, or should I choose life over death, disregarding her wishes and right to self-determination? How should I allocate scarce financial resources when there is such a wide range of demands for building projects, expanded patient care programs, equipment, staff, and numerous other budget items competing for limited dollars?

▶ ETHICS

 How we perceive right and wrong is influenced by what we feed on.
—Author Unknown

Ethics is the branch of philosophy that seeks to understand the nature, purpose, justification, and the founding principles of moral rules and the systems they comprise. Ethics focuses on the rightness or wrongness of actions, as well as the goodness and badness of motives and ends. Ethics seeks to understand and to determine how human actions can be judged as right or wrong. Ethical judgments can be made based on our own experiences or based on the nature of our principles of reason.

Ethics encompasses the decision-making process of determining the ultimate actions: What should I do, and is it the right thing to do? It involves how individuals decide to live, how they exist in harmony with the environment, and how they live with each other when so few have so much and so many have so little.

Ethics is also referred to as a moral philosophy, the discipline concerned with what is morally good or bad, right or wrong. The term is also applied to any theoretical system of moral values or principles. Ethics is less concerned with factual knowledge than with virtues and values—namely, human conduct, as it ought to be, as opposed to what it actually is.

> *Microethics* involves an individual's view of what is right and wrong based on personal life experiences.
> *Macroethics* involves a more global view of right and wrong.

Because no person lives in a vacuum, solving ethical dilemmas involves consideration of ethical issues from both a micro- and macroethical perspective.

The term *ethics* is used in three different, but related, ways, signifying (1) philosophical ethics, which involves inquiry about ways of life and rules of conduct; (2) a general pattern or "way of life," such as religious ethics (e.g., Judeo-Christian ethics); and (3) a set of rules of conduct or "moral code," which involves professional ethics and unethical behavior.

The scope of healthcare ethics encompasses numerous issues, including the right to choose or refuse treatment and the right to limit the suffering one will endure. Incredible advances in technology and the resulting capability to extend life beyond the point of what some may consider a reasonable quality of life have complicated the process of healthcare decision making. The scope of healthcare ethics is not limited to philosophical issues but embraces economic, medical, political, and legal dilemmas.

Bioethics addresses such difficult issues as the nature of life, the nature of death, what sort of life is worth living, what constitutes murder, how we should treat people who are especially vulnerable, and the responsibilities that we have to other human beings. It is about making the right judgments in difficult situations.

We study ethics to assist us in making sound judgments, good decisions, and right choices—or if not right choices, at least better choices. To those in the healthcare industry, ethics is about anticipating and recognizing healthcare dilemmas and making good judgments and decisions based on the patient's needs and wishes and the universal values that work in unison with the laws of the land, our Constitution; where the Constitution remains silent, we rely on the ability of caregivers to make the right choices using the wisdom of Solomon to "do good."

▶ MORALITY

Aim above morality. Be not simply good; be good for something.

—Henry David Thoreau

Morality is a code of conduct. It is a guide to behavior that all rational persons put forward for governing their behavior. Morality describes a class of rules held by society to govern the conduct of its individual members. A moral dilemma occurs when moral ideas of right and wrong conflict.

Morals are ideas about what is right and what is wrong; for example, killing is wrong, whereas healing is right, and causing pain is wrong, whereas easing pain is right. Morals are deeply ingrained in culture and religion and are often part of their identities. Morals should not be confused with cultural habits or customs, such as wearing a certain style of clothing.

Moral judgments are those judgments concerned with what an individual or group believes to be the right or proper behavior in a given situation. They involve assessing another person's moral character based on how he or she conforms to the moral convictions established by the individual and/or group. What is considered right varies from nation to nation, culture to culture, religion to religion, and one person to the next. In other words, there is no universal morality that is recognized by all people in all cultures at all times.

A *code of conduct* generally prescribes standards of conduct, states principles expressing responsibilities, and defines the rules expressing duties of professionals to whom they apply. Most members of a profession subscribe to certain moral standards written into a formal document called a *code of ethics*. Codes of conduct often require interpretation by caregivers as

they apply to the specific circumstances surrounding each dilemma.

Michael D. Bayles, a famous author and teacher, describes the distinction among standards, principles, and rules:

- *Standards* (e.g., honesty, respect for others, conscientiousness) are used to guide human conduct by stating desirable traits to be exhibited and undesirable ones (dishonesty, deceitfulness, self-interest) to be avoided.
- *Principles* describe responsibilities that do not specify what the required conduct should be. Professionals need to make a judgment about what is desirable in a particular situation based on accepted principles.
- *Rules* specify specific conduct; they do not allow for individual professional judgment.

Morality Legislated

When it is important that disagreements be settled, morality is often legislated. Law is distinguished from morality by having explicit rules and penalties and officials who interpret the laws and apply penalties when laws are broken. There is often considerable overlap in the conduct governed by morality and that governed by law. Laws are created to set boundaries for societal behavior. They are enforced to ensure that the expected behavior happens.[1]

Moral Dilemmas

Moral dilemmas arise when rights, duties, and loyalties conflict and, consequently, not everyone is satisfied with a particular decision, as noted in the following *reality check*, where politics and ethics collide.

An understanding of the concepts presented here will help the caregiver in conflict resolution when addressing ethical dilemmas. Caregivers often find that there seems to be no right or wrong answer. The best answer when attempting to resolve an ethical dilemma is based on the wishes known and the information available at the time a decision must be made.

▶ ETHICAL THEORIES

Ethics, too, are nothing but reverence for life. This is what gives me the fundamental principle of morality, namely, that good consists in maintaining, promoting, and enhancing life, and that destroying, injuring, and limiting life are evil.

—Albert Schweitzer

✔ *THE SURVEYOR–HOSPITAL DILEMMA*

And so there we were in Politics Hospital, sent to survey the quality of care provided to patients. During the survey, there seemed to be a lack of interest in constructive suggestions about how the hospital could improve its services. However, there was one caveat to this—so long as the surveyors' observations would not be cited in a formal report, management was content to receive a surveyor's comments.

Survey team members who scored and included their observations in a formal report knew they were being watched closely, as though they were the ones being surveyed. Scribes were assigned by hospital management to record each surveyor's mannerisms, style, and comments while evaluating the hospital's compliance with the standards they are required to meet for accreditation purposes. The real concern of management seemed to be more how the surveyors would score the hospital's delivery of care to patients than how they could improve services based on surveyor findings and suggestions for improvement. They were pleasant when things were going well, argumentative when they were not.

Not only do the surveyors evaluate the hospital, the hospital also evaluates the surveyors. These evaluations are then forwarded to the surveyors' home office. A lower hospital score often results in a low surveyor score. Thus the dilemma and how the quality of a survey can be compromised.

The challenge in this situation involves the integrity of both the surveyor and the hospital. If the surveyor is reluctant to score a particular observation because of a hospital's relentless argumentative stature for an A+ (100%), then the quality of the survey will be compromised. However, if a hospital views a survey as an opportunity to learn and improve patient care services, it is likely that it can be a win-win situation for both the surveyors and the hospital, ultimately benefiting the patients. The pressure is on for both hospital management and surveyors. The answer to the quality of the survey and the resolution of the ethical dilemmas that arise during the process can only be resolved when both the hospital and surveying organization's leadership recognize the importance of ethics in the survey process.

—Anonymous

Theories and principles of ethics introduce order into the way people think about life. They are the foundations of ethical analysis and provide guidance in the decision-making process. The various theories present differing viewpoints that assist caregivers in making difficult decisions that impact the lives of others. Ethical theories help caregivers to predict the outcome of alternative choices, when following their duties to others, in order to reach an ethically correct decision.

Normative Ethics

Normative ethics is the attempt to determine what moral standards should be followed so that human behavior and conduct may be morally right. Normative ethics is primarily concerned with establishing standards or norms for conduct and is commonly associated with general theories about how one ought to live. One of the central questions of modern normative ethics is whether human actions are to be judged right or wrong solely according to their consequences.

The determination of a universal moral principle for all humanity is a formidable task and most likely not feasible due to the diversity of people and cultures. However, there is a need to have a commonly held consensus as to right and wrong to avoid chaos. Thus, there are generally accepted moral standards around which laws are drafted.

General normative ethics is the critical study of major moral precepts concerning such matters as what things are right, what things are good, and what things are genuine. It is the determination of correct moral principles for all autonomous rational beings.

Applied ethics is the application of normative theories to practical moral problems. It attempts to explain and justify specific moral problems such as abortion, euthanasia, and assisted suicide.

Descriptive ethics, also known as comparative ethics, deals with what people believe to be right and wrong, whereas normative ethics prescribes how people ought to act.

Meta-ethics is the branch of ethics that seeks to understand the nature of ethical properties, statements, attitudes, and judgments ethical terms and theories and their application—"A classification within western philosophy that attempts to discover the origin or cause of right and wrong." An example question within meta-ethics is: "How can we know what is right and wrong?" There are almost as many different answers as there are different people answering the question. Some individuals may say that right and wrong are dictated by holy books, or philosophy books, or political books, or by popular speakers, but there is not yet a good explanation within philosophy that can illustrate the origins and nature of right and wrong that is verifiable and acceptable to everyone.[2]

Consequential Ethics

The *consequential theory of ethics* emphasizes that the morally right action is whatever action leads to the maximum balance of good over evil. From a contemporary standpoint, theories that judge actions by their consequences have been referred to as consequential ethics. Consequential ethical theories revolve around the premise that the rightness or wrongness of an action depends on the consequences or effects of an action. The theory of consequential ethics is based on the view that the value of an action derives solely from the value of its consequences. The goal of a consequentialist is to achieve the greatest good for the greatest number. It involves asking the following questions:

- What will be the effects of each course of action?
- Will the effects be positive or negative?
- Who will benefit?
- What action will cause the least harm?

Utilitarian Ethics

Happiness often sneaks in a door you did not think was open.

—John Barrymore

The *utilitarian ethics* approach involves the concept that the moral worth of an action is solely determined by its contribution to overall usefulness. It describes doing the greatest good for the greatest number of people. It is thus a *form of consequential ethics*, meaning that the moral worth of an action is determined by its outcome, and thus, the ends justify the means. The utilitarian commonly holds that the proper course of an action is one that maximizes utility, commonly defined as maximizing happiness and reducing suffering.

Nonconsequential Ethics

The *nonconsequential theory of ethics* denies that the consequences of an action or rule are the only criteria for determining the morality of an action or rule. In this theory, the rightness or wrongness of an action is based on properties intrinsic to the action, not on its consequences. In other words, the nonconsequentialist

believes right or wrong depends on the intention, not the outcome.

Situational Ethics

Situational ethics is concerned with the outcome or consequences of an action in which the ends can justify the means. Why do good people behave differently in similar situations? Why do good people sometimes do bad things? The answer is fairly simple: One's moral character can sometimes change as circumstances change—thus the term *situational ethics*.

Why good people do bad things became a reality for Eddie Adams. He was the photojournalist who had photographed the event described in the news clipping below during the Vietnam War for which he received the Pulitzer Prize. Mr. Adams regrets taking the photo because he believes it sent the wrong message about what the picture more accurately depicts.

A person, therefore, may contradict what he believes is the right thing to do and do what is wrong. The values held ever so strongly in one situation may conflict with the same values given a different set of facts. For example, if your plane crashed high in the Andes mountains and the only source of food for survival would be the flesh of those who did not survive, you may, if you wish to survive, have to give up your belief that it is morally wrong to eat the flesh of another human being. Given a different set of circumstances, with an abundance of food, you would most likely find it reprehensible to eat human flesh. Thus, there are no effective hard and fast rules or guidelines to govern ethical behavior.

🅝🅔🅦🅢 VIET CONG EXECUTION

"And out of nowhere came this guy who we didn't know." Gen. Nguyen Ngoc Loan, chief of South Vietnam's national police, walked up and shot the prisoner in the head. His reason: The prisoner, a Viet Cong lieutenant, had just murdered a South Vietnamese colonel, his wife, and their six children.

The peace movement adopted the photo as a symbol of the war's brutality. But Adams, who stayed in touch with Loan, said the photo wrongly stereotyped the man. "If you're this general and you caught this guy after he killed some of your people ... how do you know you wouldn't have pulled that trigger yourself? You have to put yourself in that situation. . . . It's a war."

—*1969 Spot News, Newseum*, Washington, DC

As applied to healthcare decision making, each situation may have a different fact pattern, resulting in moral decisions being made on a case-by-case basis. For example, a decision not to use extraordinary means to sustain the life of an unknown 84-year-old may result in a different decision if the 84-year-old is one's mother. To better understand this concept, consider the desire to live and the extreme measures one will take in order to do so. Remember that ethical decision making is the process of determining the right thing to do in the event of a moral dilemma.

Deontological Ethics

Act in such a way that you always treat humanity, whether in your own person or in the person of any other, never simply as a means, but always at the same time as an end.

—Immanuel Kant

Deontological ethics is commonly attributed to the German philosopher Immanuel Kant (1724–1804). Kant believed that although doing the right thing is good, it might not always lead to or increase the good and right thing sought after. It focuses on one's duties to others and others' rights. It includes telling the truth and keeping your promises. Deontological ethics is often referred to as duty-based ethics. It involves ethical analysis according to a moral code or rules, either religious or secular. Deontology is derived from the Greek word meaning "duty." Kant's theory differs from consequentialism in that consequences are not the determinant of what is right; therefore, doing the right thing may not always lead to an increase in what is good.

> Duty-based approaches are heavy on obligation, in the sense that a person who follows this ethical paradigm believes that the highest virtue comes from doing what you are supposed to do—either because you have to, e.g., following the law, or because you agreed to, e.g., following an employer's policies. It matters little whether the act leads to good consequences; what matters is "doing your duty."[3]

Ethical Relativism

"*Ethical relativism* is the theory that holds that morality is relative to the norms of one's culture. That is, whether an action is right or wrong depends on the moral norms of the society in which it is practiced. The same action may be morally right in one society but be morally wrong in another."[4] What is acceptable in one society may not be considered as acceptable in another society. Slavery may be considered an acceptable practice in one society and unacceptable and unconscionable in another. The administration of blood may be acceptable to one's religious beliefs and not acceptable to another within the same society. The legal rights of patients vary from state to state, as is well borne out, for example, by Oregon's Death with Dignity Act.

Caregivers must be aware of cultural, religious, and legal issues that can affect the boundaries of what is acceptable and what is unacceptable practice, especially when delivering health care to persons with beliefs different from their own. As the various cultures merge together in common communities, the education and training of caregivers becomes more complex.

Virtue-Based Ethics

The most important human endeavor is the striving for morality in our actions. Our inner balance, and even our very existence depends on it. Only morality in our actions can give beauty and dignity to our lives.

—Albert Einstein

Virtue-based ethics focuses on the inherent character of a person rather than on the specific actions that he or she performs. A *virtue* is normally defined as some sort of moral excellence or beneficial quality. In traditional ethics, virtues are those characteristics that differentiate good people from bad people. Virtues, such as honesty and justice, are abstract moral principles. A morally virtuous person is one who does the good and right thing by habit, not by a set of rules of conduct. In other words, the character of a virtuous person is naturally good, as exhibited by his or her unswerving good behavior and actions.

Virtue-based ethical theories place much less emphasis on which rules people should follow and instead focus on helping people develop good character traits, such as kindness and generosity. Virtue theorists also emphasize the need for people to learn how to break bad habits of character, such as greed or anger.[5]

▶ PRINCIPLES OF HEALTHCARE ETHICS

You cannot by tying an opinion to a man's tongue, make him the representative of that opinion; and at the close of any battle for principles, his name will be found neither among the dead, nor the wounded, but the missing.

—E.P. Whipple[6] (1819–1886)

Ethical principles are universal rules of conduct, derived from ethical theories that provide a practical basis for identifying what kinds of actions, intentions, and motives are valued. Ethical principles assist caregivers in making choices based on moral principles that have been identified as standards considered important when addressing ethical dilemmas. Ethical principles provide a framework within which particular ethical dilemmas can be analyzed and decisions made. As noted by the principles discussed in the following sections, caregivers, in the study of ethics, will find that difficult decisions often involve choices between conflicting ethical principles.

Autonomy

No right is held more sacred, or is more carefully guarded, by the common law, than the right of every individual to the possession and control of his own person, free from all restraint or interference of others, unless by clear and unquestioned authority of law.

—*Union Pac. Ry. Co. v. Botsford*, 141 U.S. 250, 251 (1891)

The *principle of autonomy* involves recognizing the right of a person to make one's own decisions. *Auto* comes from a Greek word meaning "self" or the "individual." In this context, *autonomy* means recognizing an individual's right to make his or her own decisions about what is best for him or herself. Autonomy is not an absolute principle, meaning that the autonomous actions of one person must not infringe upon the rights of another.

Respect for autonomy has been recognized in the Fourteenth Amendment to the Constitution of the United States. The law upholds an individual's right to make his or her own healthcare decisions. A patient has the right to refuse to receive health care even if it is beneficial to saving one's own life. Patients can refuse treatment, refuse to take medications, refuse blood or blood by-products, and refuse invasive procedures regardless of the benefits that may be derived from them. They have a right to have their decisions followed by family members who may disagree simply because they are unable to "let go" of a loved one.

Autonomous decision making can be affected by one's disabilities, mental status, maturity, or incapacity to make decisions. Although the principle of autonomy may be inapplicable in certain cases, one's autonomous wishes may be carried out through an advance directive and/or an appointed healthcare agent in the event of one's inability to make decisions.

Beneficence

Beneficence describes the principle of doing good, demonstrating kindness, showing compassion, and helping others. In the healthcare setting, caregivers often demonstrate beneficence by balancing benefits against risks. Doing good requires knowledge of the beliefs, culture, values, and preferences of the patient—what one person may believe to be good for a patient may be harmful. For example, a caregiver may decide that a patient should be told frankly, "There is nothing else that I can do for you." This could be injurious to the patient if the patient really wants encouragement and information about care options from the caregiver. Compassion here requires the caregiver, for example, to explain to the patient, "I am not aware of new treatments for your illness; however, I have some ideas about how I can help treat your symptoms and make you more comfortable. In addition, I will keep you informed about any significant research that may be helpful in treating you."

Paternalism

Paternalism is a form of beneficence. People, believing that they know what is best for another, often make decisions that they believe are in that person's best interest. It may involve, for example, withholding information from someone, believing that the person would be better off not knowing. Paternalism can occur as a result of one's age, cognitive ability, and level of dependency. A patient or employee's rights to self-determination is compromised when a third party imposes their wishes against those of another person, as noted in the following *reality check*.

Paul Ramsey, in *The Patient as Person* (1970), discusses the question of paternalism. As physicians are faced with many options for saving lives, transplanting organs, and furthering research, they also must wrestle with new and troubling choices—for example, who should receive scarce resources (e.g., organ transplants), determining when life ends, and what limits should be placed on care for the dying.

Medical Paternalism

Medical paternalism often involves physicians unwittingly making decisions for patients who are capable of making decisions on their own. Physicians, by the nature of their work, are in a situation where they can influence a patient's healthcare decisions by selectively telling the patient what they choose, based on their personal beliefs. This directly violates a patient's autonomy. The problem with paternalism is that it involves

✅ *PATERNALISM AND BREACH OF CONFIDENTIALITY*

Vicky traveled with her husband, Dan, to a work assignment in Michigan. While visiting with her brother in Michigan, Vicky believed that her potassium was low, which had been a frequent occurrence for her for many years. Vicky's brother suggested she could have her blood tested at a local blood drawing station. Dan later learned Vicky's potassium was low.

Later that morning, while at work, Joan, Dan's colleague, called Bill, Dan's supervisor, to discuss Vicky's blood tests. Bill, however, had overslept and had not yet arrived at work. Joan decided to speak to the supervisor on call. After that conversation, Joan, being led by three staff members from the organization, tracked Dan down on several occasions that morning. On the first occasion, at approximately 10:15 AM, Dan was surveying the organization's family practice center when Joan arrived. She rudely called Dan aside, excusing the organization's staff from the immediate area. Joan said, with surprise, "Dan, you are working?" Dan, even more surprised at the question, "Yes, I have been working." Joan replied, "Well, anyway, the corporate office wants to speak to you." Dan said he would call during lunch hour. Joan, somewhat agitated, walked away.

Joan again tracked Dan down with an entourage of the organization's staff at 11:30 AM. She located Dan while he was in the organization's transfusion center. Again she rudely entered the conference room where Dan was discussing the care being rendered to a cancer patient. She once again asked in a stern tone of voice, "Could everyone please leave the room. I need to talk to Dan." The organization's staff left the room and the nurse said, "I finally reached Bill and he wants you to call him." Dan inquired, "Is he pulling me off this assignment?" The nurse replied, "Yes, he is. I spoke to Bill, and he has decided that out of concern for Vicky you should be removed from this particular assignment. He wants you to call him." Dan replied, "I don't understand why you did this, calling Bill and continuously interrupting my work and sharing with others confidential information about my wife. I will wrap up my review of this patient with the staff and then call Bill." As Joan left the conference room, Dan said, "I trusted you and you shared confidential information about my wife?" Joan, realizing that she had no right to share the information quickly walked away.

Dan called Bill during his lunch break. During that call Bill said, "I am going to remove you from your assignment because I think your wife's health needs should be addressed, and this could be disruptive to the survey." Dan replied, "The only disruption has been the nurse tracking me down with staff from the organization and not conducting her work activities. My wife has been ill for 9 years. Joan never even heard about her disease. We have been traveling together for many years and you should not be questioning our decisions regarding her healthcare needs. It has nothing to do with my job." Bill replied, "My decision stands. You can opt to take vacation time for the remainder of the week."

At the annual training conference in Chicago for surveyors, Jim approached Dan smiling, "That hospital I completed for you in Michigan was very interesting. They said you were very thorough. Then they told me I was as tough as you. I think they were hoping someone would fill in for you that would be easier on them."

Paternalism does replace one's right to decide his or her destiny. The issues of autonomy trust, confidentiality, fairness, and the right to privacy have been clearly violated in this case.

a conflict between the patient's right to choose and the physician's desire to save a patient's life.

Nonmaleficence

Nonmaleficence is an ethical principle that requires caregivers to avoid causing patients harm. It derives from the ancient maxim *primum non nocere*, translated from the Latin, "first, do no harm." Physicians today still swear by the oath of Hippocrates, pledging to do no harm. Medical ethics requires healthcare providers to "first, do no harm." A New Jersey court, in *In re Conroy*,[7] found that "the physician's primary obligation is . . . First do no harm." If there is no cure for a patient's disease, the caregiver is often faced with a reoccurring dilemma. Do I tell the patient he or she is terminal and possibly cause serious psychological harm, or do I do my best to give the patient hope?

The principle of nonmaleficence is shattered when a physician is placed in the position of ending life by removing respirators, giving lethal injections, or by writing prescriptions for lethal doses of medication. Helping patients die violates the physician's duty to save lives. Allowing death to follow its natural course can help solve the dilemma. In this instance, the patient's caregivers can help ease the transition from life to death by providing comfort care and addressing the patient's spiritual needs. For those who believe in an afterlife of peace and happiness, the transition will more likely be easier when one accepts that the patient is leaving one life and moving on to a better place.

🅝ABUSING ASSISTED SUICIDE LAWS

The debate surrounding legalizing assisted suicide is largely cast as one focusing on an individual who genuinely wants to end his or her life because of the pain and suffering they're experiencing due to a terminal medical condition. But this issue is wholly different—the possible cold-blooded and brutal abuse of those laws by bureaucrats in insurance companies against patients whom they determine are too expensive to keep alive.

• • •

And then there are the doctors. Healers who pledge to do no harm are now facing a system which will eventually expect them to do just that.

—Tammy Bruce, *The Washington Times*, June 7, 2017

Tuskegee Syphilis Experiment

The Tuskegee Syphilis Study, conducted by the U.S. Public Health Service between 1932 and 1972, was designed to analyze the natural progression of untreated syphilis in African American men. The participants were not warned during the study that penicillin was available as a cure for syphilis. They believed that they were receiving adequate care and unknowingly, they suffered unnecessarily. The Tuskegee Syphilis Study used disadvantaged, rural black men to investigate the untreated course of the disease, one that is by no means confined to that population. The study should have recognized from the beginning that selection of research subjects, regardless of race, must be closely monitored to ensure that specific classes of individuals (e.g., terminally ill patients, welfare patients, racial and ethnic minorities, or persons confined to institutions) are not selected for research studies based on their availability, compromised position, or manipulability. Rather, they must be selected for reasons directly related to the research being conducted. The ethical principle of *nonmaleficence* requires all people to avoid causing harm. In this case the failure to alert those involved in the research study that a cure was available was both ethically and legally wrong.

National Research Act of 1974

Because of publicity from the Tuskegee Syphilis Study, the National Research Act (NRA) of 1974 was passed. The NRA created the National Commission for the Protection of Human Subjects of Biomedical

and Behavioral Research.[8] One of the commission's charges was to identify the basic ethical principles that should underlie the conduct of biomedical and behavioral research involving human subjects and to develop guidelines to ensure that such research is conducted in accordance with those principles.[9] The commission was directed to consider:[10]

1. the boundaries between biomedical and behavioral research and the accepted and routine practice of medicine,
2. the role of assessment of risk–benefit criteria in the determination of the appropriateness of research involving human subjects,
3. appropriate guidelines for the selection of human subjects for participation in such research, and
4. the nature and definition of informed consent in various research settings.

Justice

Justice is the obligation to be fair in the distribution of benefits and risks. Justice demands that persons in similar circumstances be treated similarly. A person is treated justly when he or she receives what is due, is deserved, or can legitimately be claimed. Justice involves how people are treated when their interests compete with one another.

Distributive justice is a principle requiring that all persons be treated equally and fairly. No one person, for example, should get a disproportional share of society's resources or benefits. There are many ethical issues involved in the rationing of health care. This is often a result of limited or scarce resources, limited access as a result of geographic remoteness, or a patient's inability to pay for services combined with many physicians who are unwilling to accept patients who are perceived as "no pays" with high risks for legal suits.

Senator Edward M. Kennedy, speaking on health care at the John F. Kennedy Presidential Library in Boston, Massachusetts, on April 28, 2002, stated:

> It will be no surprise to this audience that I believe securing quality, affordable health insurance for every American is a matter of simple justice. Health care is not just another commodity. Good health is not a gift to be rationed based on ability to pay. The time is long overdue for America to join the rest of the industrialized world in recognizing this fundamental need.

Speaking at the Democratic National Convention on August 25, 2008, Senator Kennedy said:

And this is the cause of my life—new hope that we will break the old gridlock and guarantee that every American—North, South, East, West, young, old—will have decent quality health care as a fundamental right and not a privilege.

Although Senator Edward Kennedy did not live to see the day his dream would come true, President Barack Obama signed into law the final piece of his administration's historic and highly controversial healthcare bill on March 23, 2010, a bill that continues to be challenged in the courts and plays a troublesome role between political parties and their constituencies.

▶ VALUES

A *value* is a standard of conduct. Values are used for judging the goodness or badness of actions. *Ethical values* imply standards of worth. They are the standards by which we measure the goodness in our lives. *Intrinsic value* is something that has value in and of itself (e.g., happiness). *Instrumental value* is something that helps to give value to something else (e.g., money is valuable for what it can buy).

All people make value judgments when they make choices among alternatives. Values are the motivating power of a person's actions, and they are necessary to survival, both psychologically and physically. Values may change as needs change. If one's basic needs for food, water, clothing, and housing have not been met, one's values may change such that a friendship, for example, might be sacrificed if one's basic needs can be better met as a result of the sacrifice. If mom's estate is being squandered at the end of her life, a financially well-off family member may want to take more aggressive measures to keep mom alive despite the financial drain on her estate. Another family member, who is struggling financially, may more readily see the futility of expensive medical care and find it easier to let go. Values give purpose to each life. They make up one's moral character.

▶ PILLARS OF MORAL STRENGTH

I am part of all I have met.

—Alfred Tennyson

There is a deluge of ethical issues in every aspect of human existence. Although cultural differences, politics, and religion influence who we are, it is the sum of our life's experiences that affect who we become. If we have courage to do right, those who have influenced our lives were most likely courageous. If we are compassionate, it is most likely because we have been influenced by the compassionate.

The *Pillars of Moral Strength,* illustrated in **FIGURE 15-1**, describes a virtuous person. What is it that sets each person apart? In the final analysis, it is one's virtues that build moral character. We begin our discussion here with an overview of those virtues that have value when addressing difficult healthcare dilemmas.

Courage

Courage is the greatest of all virtues, because if you haven't courage, you may not have an opportunity to use any of the others.

—Samuel Johnson

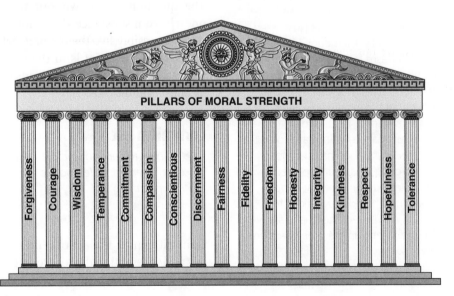

FIGURE 15-1 Pillars of moral strength.

Courage is the mental or moral strength to persevere and withstand danger. "Courage is the ladder on which all the other virtues mount."[11] It is the strength of character necessary to continue in the face of fears and challenges in life. It involves balancing fear, self-confidence, and values. Without courage, we are unable to take the risks necessary to achieve the things most valued. A courageous person has good judgment and a clear sense of his or her strengths, evaluates danger, and perseveres until a decision is made and the right goal that is being sought has been achieved. The *reality check* presented next describes the courage of a young lady facing a difficult journey in her battle with cancer.

Wisdom

You can't inherit wisdom. You can't be taught wisdom. You cannot learn wisdom. Wisdom is a God given gift that often comes with age.

—Gp

Wisdom is the judicious application of knowledge. Wisdom begins first by learning from the failures and successes of those who have preceded us. Marcus Tullius Cicero (106–43 BC), a Roman philosopher and politician, is reported to have said, "The function of wisdom is to discriminate between good and evil." In the healthcare setting, when the patient's wishes and end-of-life preferences are unknown, wisdom with good judgment and without bias or prejudice springs forth more easily. As Gerda Lerner, an American author, historian, and teacher, so profoundly said:

> We can learn from history how past generations thought and acted, how they responded to the demands of their time and how they solved their problems. We can learn by analogy, not by example, for our circumstances will always be different than theirs were. The main thing history can teach us is that human actions have consequences and that certain choices, once made, cannot be undone. They foreclose the possibility of making other choices and thus they determine future events.[12]

Wisdom often comes with age, therefore, "Count your age by friends, count your life by smiles."[13]

Temperance

Being forced to work, and forced to do your best, will breed in your temperance and self-control, diligence and strength of will, cheerfulness and content, and a hundred virtues which the idle will never know.

—Charles Kingsley[14]

Temperance involves self-control and restraint. It embraces moderation in thoughts and actions. Temperance is evidenced by orderliness and moderation in everything one says and does. It involves the ability to control one's actions so as not to go to extremes. The question arises, without the ability to control oneself from substance abuse, for example, how can a person possibly live the life of a virtuous person? The old adage, "the proof is in the pudding," lies in one's actions. A virtuous person stands out from the crowd by actions and deeds.

Commitment

I know the price of success: dedication, hard work, and an unremitting devotion to the things you want to see happen.

—Frank Lloyd Wright

Commitment is the act of binding oneself intellectually and/or emotionally to a course of action (e.g., pursue a career, adherence to a religious belief) or person

---

✓ MY JOURNEY: HOW LUCKY AM I?

No words can be scripted to say what I have been through, so I will just speak from my heart and off the cuff. From the day the doctor said to me, "Denise, you have a rare cancer and we are sorry, there is nothing we can do," I did not waver in my faith in God. He was in me, he was through me and he was around me. I just asked the doctor, "What do I do?" And yet, although he said a whole bunch of words, I wasn't focused so much on what was being said. It's like a calmness was over me, not much worry, just a feeling of I will never be ALONE on this new journey I'm about to experience. I felt calm. Not until I looked at my loved ones' FACES did I realize, oh my, this can be bad. But again, a feeling came over me that I will not face this ALONE. God has plans for me and I will surrender in his grace, and as time passed, I realized how lucky and blessed I am, for most people who may feel that death may be close by, I didn't feel that way. What I felt was WOW!! Everyone gets to show me their love in the NOW and not in the later when I am no longer HERE. How lucky am I?

—Denise

(e.g., marriage, family, patient care). It is an agreement or pledge to do something. It can be ongoing or a pledge to do something in the future.

Compassion

 Compassion is the basis of morality.

—Arnold Schopenhauer

Compassion is the profound awareness of and sympathy for another's suffering. The ability to show compassion is a true mark of moral character. Compassion is expected of all caregivers. Those who lack compassion have a weakness in their moral character. Dr. Linda Peeno showed her compassion as she testified before the Committee on Commerce on May 30, 1996. She stated that she had been hired as a claims reviewer for several health maintenance organizations (HMOs). Here is her story in part:

> I wish to begin by making a public confession. In the spring of 1987, I caused the death of a man. Although this was known to many people, I have not been taken before any court of law or called to account for this in any professional or public forum. In fact, just the opposite occurred. I was rewarded for this. It brought me an improved reputation in my job and contributed to my advancement afterwards. Not only did I demonstrate that I could do what was asked, expected of me, I exemplified the good company employee. I saved a half a million dollars.
>
> Since that day, I have lived with this act and many others eating into my heart and soul. The primary ethical norm is do no harm. I did worse, I caused death. Instead of using a clumsy bloody weapon, I used the simplest, cleanest of tools: my words. This man died because I denied him a necessary operation to save his heart. I felt little pain or remorse at the time. The man's faceless distance soothed my conscience. Like a skilled soldier, I was trained for the moment. When any moral qualms arose, I was to remember, "I am not denying care; I am only denying payment."[15]

Duty-based ethics required Dr. Peeno to follow the rules of her job. In so doing, a life was lost. Although Dr. Peeno came forward with her story, the lack of compassion for others plagues the healthcare industry in a variety of settings. Caregivers need to show the same compassion for others as they would expect for themselves.

 Never apologize for showing feeling. When you do so, you apologize for the truth.

—Benjamin Disraeli

Detachment

Detachment, or lack of concern for a patient's needs, is what often translates into mistakes that can result in patient injuries. Those who have excessive emotional involvement in a patient's care may be best suited to work in those settings where patients are most likely to recover and have positive outcomes (e.g., maternity wards). As with all things in life, there needs to be a comfortable balance between compassion and detachment. Caregivers need to show the same compassion for others as they would expect for themselves or their loved ones.

Conscientiousness

 The most infectiously joyous men and women are those who forget themselves in thinking about and serving others.

—Robert J. McCracken

A *conscientious* person is one who has moral integrity and a strict regard for doing what is considered the right thing to do. *Conscience* is a form of self-reflection on and judgment about whether one's actions are right or wrong, good or bad. It is an internal sanction that comes into play through critical reflection. This sanction often appears as a bad conscience in the form of painful feelings of remorse, guilt, shame, disunity, or disharmony as the individual recognizes that his or her acts were wrong. Although a person may conscientiously object and/or refuse to participate in some action (e.g., abortion), that person should not obstruct others from performing the same act if the others have no moral objection to it.

Discernment

 Get to know two things about a man. How he earns his money and how he spends it. You will then have the clue to his character. You will have a searchlight that shows up the innermost recesses of his soul. You know all you need to know about his standards, his motives, his driving desires, and his real religion.

—Robert J. McCracken

Discernment is the ability to make a good decision without personal biases, fears, and undue influences from others. A person who has discernment has the

✅ COMPASSION: MY FEARS V. YOUR RIGHTS

Annie was 27 when she began experiencing severe pain in her abdomen while visiting family in May of 1970. After complaining of pain to Mark, her husband, in June of 1970, he scheduled Annie for an appointment with Dr. Roberts, a gastroenterologist, who ordered a series of tests. While conducting a barium scan, a radiologist at Community Hospital noted a small bowel obstruction. Dr. Roberts recommended surgery, and Annie agreed to it.

After the surgery, on July 7, Dr. Brown, the operating surgeon, paged Mark over the hospital intercom as he walked down a corridor on the ground floor. Mark, hearing the page, picked up a house phone and dialed zero for an operator. The operator inquired, "May I help you?" "Yes," Mark replied. "I was just paged." The operator replied, "Oh, yes. Dr. Brown would like to talk to you. I will connect you with him. Hang on. Don't hang up." (Mark's heart began to pound.) Dr. Brown asked, "Is this you, Mark?" Mark replied, "Yes, it is." Dr. Brown replied, "Well, surgery is over. Your wife is recovering nicely in the recovery room." Mark was relieved but for a moment. "That's good." Mark sensed Dr. Brown had more to say. Dr. Brown continued, "I am sorry to say that she has carcinoma of the colon." Mark replied, "Did you get it all?" Dr. Brown reluctantly replied, "I am sorry, but the cancer has spread to her lymph nodes and surrounding organs." Mark, in tears, asked, "Can I see her?" Dr. Brown replied, "She is in the recovery room." Before hanging up, Mark told Dr. Brown, "Please do not tell Annie that she has cancer. I want her to always have hope." Dr. Brown agreed, "Don't worry, I won't tell her. You can tell her that she had a narrowing of the colon."

Mark hung up the phone and proceeded to the recovery room. After entering the recovery room, he spotted his wife. His heart sank. Tubes seemed to be running out of every part of her body. He walked to her bedside. His immediate concern was to see her wake up and have the tubes pulled out so that he could take her home.

Later, in a hospital room, Annie asked Mark, "What did the doctor find?" Mark replied, holding back the tears, "He found a narrowing of the colon." "Am I going to be okay?" "Yes, but it will take a while to recover." "Oh, that's good. I was so worried," said Annie. "You go home and get some rest." Mark said, "I'll be back later," as Annie fell back to sleep.

Mark left the hospital and went to see his friends, Jerry and Helen, who had invited him for dinner. As Mark pulled up to Jerry and Helen's home, he got out of his car and just stood there looking up a long stairway leading to Jerry and Helen's home. They were standing there looking down at Mark. It was early evening. The sun was setting. A warm breeze was blowing, and Helen's eyes were watering. Those few moments seemed like a lifetime. Mark discovered a new emotion, as he stood there, speechless. He knew then that he was losing a part of himself. Things would never be the same.

Annie had additional surgery a few months later in a futile attempt to extend her life. By November, Annie was admitted to the hospital for the last time. Annie was so ill that even during her last moments she was unaware that she was dying. Dr. Brown entered the room and asked Mark, "Can I see you for a few moments?" "Yes," Mark replied. He followed Dr. Brown into the hallway. "Mark, I can keep Annie alive for a few more days, or we can let her go." Mark, not responding, went back into the room. He was now alone with Annie. Shortly thereafter, a nurse walked into the room and gave Annie an injection. Mark asked, "What did you give her?" The nurse replied, "Something to make her more comfortable." Annie had been asleep; she awoke, looked at Mark, and said, "Could you please cancel my appointment to be sworn in as a citizen? I will have to reschedule. I don't think I will be well enough to go." Mark replied, "Okay, try to get some rest." Annie closed her eyes, never to open them again.

Mark had so many questions that went through his mind. Should he have told Annie about the seriousness of her illness? There were so many questions unanswered to this day. So many ethical dilemmas leading to poor judgments in an effort to give hope when hope was gone. Yes, Annie's rights were violated. Mark will never know how his remaining few months would have been, if only Annie knew how she wanted to spend her remaining days of her life.

As for Mark, he lives with regret. But his fears, his hope, and his compassion ruled that day. In his mind at that time, he wanted to spare his wife the grief of passing away at such a young age.

—Anonymous

📰 WHAT WENT WRONG?

The son of a prominent Boston doctor . . . was on his way to becoming a leading surgeon in his own right when a bizarre blunder interrupted his climb: he left his patient on the operating table so he could cash his paycheck. A series of arrests followed exposing a life of arrogance, betrayal, and wasted promise.

—Neil Swidey, "What Went Wrong," *The Boston Globe*, March 21, 2004

NEWS *TEACHING DOCTORS TO CARE*

At Harvard and other medical schools across the country, educators are beginning to realize that empathy is as valuable to a doctor as any clinical skill. . . . [D]octors who try to understand their patients may be the best antidote for the wide-spread dissatisfaction with today's health care system.

—Nathan Thornburgh, "Teaching Doctors to Care," *Time Magazine*, March 29, 2006

wisdom to decide the best course of action when there are many possible actions from which to choose.

Fairness

 Do all the good you can, By all the means you can, In all the ways you can, In all the places you can, At all the times you can, To all the people you can, As long as you ever can.

—John Wesley[16]

In ethics, fairness requires each person to be objective, unbiased, dispassionate, impartial, and consistent with the principles of ethics. Fairness is the ability to make judgments free from discrimination, dishonesty, or one's own bias. It is the ability to be objective without prejudice or bias. We often tolerate mediocrity. We sometimes forget to thank those who just do their jobs, and we often praise the extraordinary, sometimes despite questionable faults. To be fair, it is important to see the good in all and to reward that good.

Fidelity

 Nothing is more noble, nothing more venerable, than fidelity. Faithfulness and truth are the most sacred excellences and endowments of the human mind.

—Cicero

Fidelity is the virtue of faithfulness, being true to our commitments and obligations to others. A component of fidelity, veracity, implies that we will be truthful and honest in all our endeavors. It involves being faithful and loyal to obligations, duties, or observances. The opposite of fidelity is infidelity, meaning unfaithfulness.

Freedom

 You can only protect your liberties in this world by protecting the other man's freedom. You can only be free if I am free.

—Dorothy Thompson

Freedom is the quality of being free to make choices for oneself within the boundaries of law. Freedoms enjoyed by citizens of the United States include the freedom of speech, freedom of religion, freedom from want, and freedom from physical aggression.

Honesty/Trustworthiness/Truth Telling

 Lies or the appearance of lies are not what the writers of our Constitution intended for our country, it's not the America we salute every Fourth of July, it's not the America we learned about in school, and it is not the America represented in the flag that rises above our land.

—Message from the Internet

Honesty and trust involve confidence that a person will act with the right motives. It is the assured reliance on the character, ability, strength, or truth of someone or something. To tell the truth, to have integrity, and to be honest are most honorable virtues. Veracity is devotion to and conformity with what is truthful. It involves an obligation to be truthful.

Truth telling involves providing enough information so that a patient can make an informed decision about his or her health care. Intentionally misleading a patient to believe something that the caregiver knows to be untrue may give the patient false hopes. There is always apprehension when one must share bad news; the temptation is to gloss over the truth for fear of being the bearer of bad news. To lessen the pain and the hurt is only human, but in the end, truth must win over fear.

Integrity

 Nearly all men can stand adversity, but if you want to test a man's character, give him power.

—Abraham Lincoln

Integrity involves a steadfast adherence to a strict moral or ethical code and a commitment not to compromise that code. A person with integrity has a staunch belief in and faithfulness to, for example, his or her religious beliefs. Patients and professionals alike often make healthcare decisions based on their integrity and their strict moral beliefs. For example, a Jehovah's Witness generally refuses a blood transfusion because it is against his or her religious beliefs, even if such refusal may result in death. A provider of health care may refuse to participate in an abortion because it is against his or her moral beliefs. A person without personal integrity lacks sincerity and moral conviction and may fail to act on professed moral beliefs. The integrity of the numbers of an employee satisfaction survey that were presented to employees during an annual education conference is highlighted in the next *reality check.*

Kindness

 When you carry out acts of kindness, you get a wonderful feeling inside. It is as though something inside your body responds and says, yes, this is how I ought to feel.

—Harold Kushner

Kindness involves the quality of being considerate and sympathetic to another's needs. The failure of a patient to follow a physician's plan of care can lead to frustration on the part of the caregiver. Patients who, for example, fail to follow a physician's medication orders for blood pressure medication can experience erratic spikes in their blood pressure. If this information should come to the doctor's attention, the physician may become less empathetic with patients who complain their blood pressure is out of control. The responsibility for good care rests with both the caregiver, in relating to the patient the importance of complying with the treatment plan, and the patient, in complying with the physician's instructions. Ultimately, patient care outcomes can improve if patients adhere to their prescribed treatment plans. Caregivers need to understand the potential for noncompliance and address those concerns when developing treatment plans. This is especially important with seniors and patients with cognitive disorders.

✅ *36,000 FEET OVER TEXAS*

A few weeks before Frank was to travel to Dodge City, Texas, for a work assignment, he received a call from Dr. Layblame: "Hi Frank. This is Dr. Layblame. Can you be ready for an early afternoon departure from Dodge City on Friday?" Frank replied, "Well you know we have been instructed not to leave early, and the last flight leaves at 4:30 PM. Anyway, I don't mind flying out Saturday morning." Dr. Layblame replied, "Well, it's only an hour early. If you do most of your work the night before and during lunch on Friday, we should be able to finish up work by 2:30 PM. The airport is small and close to the hospital. Besides, my team has to drive to Louisiana and we would like to get there so we can go out to dinner and enjoy the evening. I am the tour leader, so it should not be a problem." Frank said OK and scheduled a 4:30 PM return flight.

While Frank was on a flight to Washington, DC following his work assignment, Ronald, Frank's supervisor, was dictating a voicemail message to him. When Frank returned home at about 10:30 that evening, he retrieved his voicemail messages. Ronald had left Frank a message at 4:30 PM earlier that day asking Frank, "Call me as soon as you get this message. I will be in my office until about 5:30 PM. If you miss me, you can reach me over the weekend. My cell phone number is xxx/xxx-xxxx."

Frank called Ronald that evening and the next morning; however, Ronald never answered, nor did he return his call. Frank called Ronald on Monday morning. As luck would have it, Ronald was out of the office for the day. Frank called Ronald again on Tuesday morning and Ronald answered. Frank asked, "Ronald, you called?" He replied, "Yes, I did. How were you able to get to the airport on Friday and catch a 4:30 PM flight without leaving your job early? I had your flight schedule and you left the survey early. You could not possibly have traveled to the airport in time to catch your flight without leaving early."

Frank replied, "I did not schedule the exit time from the survey. The physician team leader determined the time of the exit. He said that he was conducting a system tour and would like to get the exit briefing started as soon as possible. He asked for everybody to be ready to exit by having draft reports ready the night before." Ronald replied, "Dr. Layblame told me the team had to exit early because you scheduled an early flight."

Frank asked, "Just one question Ronald, why would you leave a message for me at 4:30 PM to call you at 5:30 PM when you knew I was 36,000 feet high in the sky? And why didn't you call the team leader at the beginning of the assignment and not after it was completed? Since you know flight schedules, why would you wait until the assignment was completed to raise this issue? Sounds a bit peculiar, don't you think? Sort of like observing a protocol not being followed in the OR, knowingly doing nothing about it, and then chastising the OR team after the surgery is completed for not following protocol. This is a serious business we are in. You need to ask yourself why you would allow an event to occur if you believed it to be wrong." *Honesty, trust,* and *integrity* require that all persons act with the right motives.

☑ EMPLOYEE SATISFACTION SURVEY

The human resources department manager was reporting on an employee satisfaction survey at a leadership roundtable session with the organization's employees. To maintain employee confidentiality, a third-party consulting firm had conducted the survey. Approximately 49% of employees had responded to the survey, compared with 47% three years earlier. The HR manager commented that it is was the first satisfaction survey conducted in 3 years and that the results were excellent, with a 4.2% rise in overall employee satisfaction.

Management was all smiles as they sat listening to the report. The HR manager had actually briefed the organization's leadership prior to the roundtable session. Following the report, she asked if there were any questions. The silence was deadly—no one responded. Finally, one employee, Richard, placed his hands on the table to stand up, but he felt a nudge on his right shoulder from Phil, a physician friend. Phil whispered, "Richard, are you sure you want to ask any questions? There is nothing to gain here." Richard, looking down with a smile, said, "I agree, but I can't help myself."

Richard then stood up and asked the HR manager, "Do you know what the employee turnover rate has been during the past 3 years?" She responded, "Well, ugh, yes, it was about 30%." Richard replied, "So, then, does this report reflect that we have had a 30% turnover?" The manager replied, "Good point, I will have to get back to you on that." When he returned to his seat, Phil said, "Do you really think you will ever hear back an answer to your question?" Richard smiled and replied, "Not really." Richard was right; she never did get back to him.

Employees are often reluctant to ask questions when their questions are solicited by leadership. The HR manager never followed up with Richard regarding the validity of the survey data. He remembered Phil's advice to him several months later, "Let sleeping dogs lie." And so he did.

—Anonymous

Respect

 Respect for ourselves guides our morals; respect for others guides our manners.

—Laurence Sterne

Respect is an attitude of admiration or esteem. Kant was the first major Western philosopher to put respect for persons, including oneself as a person, at the center of moral theory. He believed that persons are ends in themselves with an absolute dignity, which must always be respected. In contemporary thinking, respect has become a core ideal, extending moral respect to things other than persons, including all things in nature.

Caregivers who demonstrate respect for one another and their patients will be more effective in helping them cope with the anxiety of their illness. Respect helps to develop trust between the patient and caregiver and improve healing processes. If caregivers respect the family of a patient, cooperation and understanding will be the positive result, encouraging a team effort to improve patient care.

Hopefulness

Hope is the last thing that dies in man; and though it be exceedingly deceitful, yet it is of this good use to us, that while we are traveling through life, it conducts us in an easier and more pleasant way to our journey's end.

—Francois de La Rochefoucauld

📰 MICROSOFT AND JOHNS HOPKINS TEAM UP TO BUILD A SMARTER, SAFER ICU

Developed by the Johns Hopkins Armstrong Institute for Patient Safety, Project Emerge looks to eliminate all harms from the hospital environment, from medical complications like pneumonia to emotional harms such as a lack of respect and dignity.

—John Hopkins Medicine, *Under the Dome*, Issue 9, March 2016[17]

Hopefulness in the patient care setting involves looking forward to something with the confidence of success. Caregivers have a responsibility to balance truthfulness while promoting hope. The caregiver must be sensitive to each patient's needs and provide hope.

Tolerance

There is a criterion by which you can judge whether the thoughts you are thinking and the things you are doing are right for you. The criterion is: Have they brought you inner peace? If they have not, there is something wrong with them—so keep seeking! If what you do has brought you inner peace, stay with what you believe is right.

—Peace Pilgrim

Tolerance can be viewed in two ways, positive or negative. (1) *Positive tolerance* implies that a person accepts differences in others, and that one does not expect others to believe, think, speak, or act as him- or herself. Tolerant people are generally free of prejudice and discrimination. Recognizing this fact, Thomas Jefferson incorporated theories of tolerance into the U.S. Constitution. (2) *Negative tolerance* implies that one will reluctantly put up with another's beliefs. In other words, they simply tolerate the views of others.

Although tolerance can be viewed as a virtue, not all tolerance is virtuous nor is all intolerance necessarily wrong. An exaggerated tolerance may amount to a vice, whereas intolerance may sometimes be a virtue. For example, tolerating everything regardless of its repugnance (e.g., persecution for religious beliefs) is no virtue, and having intolerance for that which should not be tolerated is not a vice (e.g., continuously and knowingly failing to follow required handwashing policies prior to surgical procedures).

Forgiveness

Forgiveness is a virtue of the brave.

—Indira Gandhi

Forgiveness is a virtue. It is the willingness to pardon someone who has wronged you in some way. It is also a form of mercy. Forgiveness is to forgive and let loose the bonds of blame. It is a form of cleansing souls for both those who forgive and those who accept the forgiveness offered.

Forbearing one another, and forgiving one another, if any man have a quarrel against any: even as Christ forgave you, so also do ye.

—Colossians 3:13 (King James Version [KJV])

▶ RELIGIOUS ETHICS AND SPIRITUALITY

The Great Physician: Dear Lord, You are the Great Physician, I turn to you in my sickness asking for your help. I place myself under your loving care, praying that I may know your healing grace and wholeness. Help me to find love in this strange world and to feel your presence by my bed both day and night. Give my doctors and nurses wisdom that they may understand my illness. Steady and guide them with your strong hand. Reach out your hand to me and touch my life with your peace. Amen.

—University of Pennsylvania Health System

Religion serves a moral purpose by providing codes of conduct for appropriate behavior through revelations from a divine source. These codes of conduct are enforced through fear of pain and suffering and/or hope for reward in the next life for adhering to religious codes and beliefs. Evidence of belief in an afterlife, dating between 58,000 and 68,000 BC, was found in Neanderthal burial sites, where various implements and supplies were buried with the deceased. The prospect of divine justice helps us to tolerate the injustices in this life where goodness is no guarantee of peace, happiness, wellness, or prosperity.

Religion often is used as a reason to justify what otherwise could be considered unjustifiable behavior. Political leaders often use religion to legitimize and consolidate their power. Leaders in democratic societies speak of the necessity to respect the right to "freedom of religion." Militarily, political leaders often use religion to further their political aspirations, using "God is on our side" propaganda. Jihad often is referred to as a holy war against infidels (nonbelievers), the purpose of which is to expand the territories of Muslim nations. This, however, is not unique to Muslim nations. Many political leaders have used religion to justify their actions. Religious persecution has plagued humanity throughout the centuries.

Spirituality, in the religious sense, implies that there is purpose and meaning to life; spirituality generally refers to faith in a higher being. For a patient, injury and sickness are frightening experiences. This fear is often heightened when the patient is admitted to a hospital or nursing home. Healthcare organizations can help reduce patient fears by providing emotional and spiritual support. It is a well-proven fact that patients who are able to draw on their spirituality and religious beliefs tend to have a more comfortable and often improved healing experience. To assist both patients and caregivers in addressing spiritual needs, patients should be provided with information as to how their spiritual needs can be addressed.

Difficult questions regarding a patient's spiritual needs and how to meet those needs are best addressed on admission by first collecting information about the patient's religious or spiritual preferences. Caregivers often find it difficult to discuss spiritual issues for fear of offending a patient who may have beliefs different from their own. However, if caregivers know from admission records a patient's religious beliefs, the caregiver can share with the patient those religious and spiritual resources available in the hospital and community.

⬤NEWS *MANY THINK GOD'S INTERVENTION CAN REVIVE THE DYING*

When it comes to saving lives, God trumps doctors for many Americans. An eye-opening survey reveals widespread belief that divine intervention can revive dying patients. And, researchers said, doctors "need to be prepared to deal with families who are waiting for a miracle."

—Lindsey Tanner, "Many Believe God Can Revive the Dying," *The Capital*, August 19, 2008

A variety of religious beliefs are presented here to note the importance of better understanding why patients differ in decision-making processes, how religion affects one's beliefs, and to encourage further study of the ways in which each religion affects the decision-making process. Hospitals often maintain a directory of contacts for various religious groups for referral and consultation purposes.

Judaism

Jewish Law is the unchangeable 613 mitzvot (commandments) that God gave to the Jews. Halakhah (Jewish Law) comes from three sources: (1) the Torah (the first five books of the Bible); (2) laws instituted by the rabbis; and (3) long-standing customs. The *Jewish People* is another name for the Children of Israel, referring to the Jews as a nation in the classical sense, meaning a group of people with a shared history and a sense of a group identity rather than a specific place or political persuasion.[18]

Judaism is a monotheistic religion based on principles and ethics embodied in the Hebrew Bible (Old Testament). The notion of right and wrong is not so much an object of philosophical inquiry as an acceptance of divine revelation. Moses, for example, received a list of 10 laws directly from God. These laws were known as the Ten Commandments. Some of the Ten Commandments are related to the basic principles of justice that have been adhered to by society since they were first proclaimed and published. For some societies, the Ten Commandments were a turning point, where essential commands such as "thou shalt not kill" or "thou shalt not commit adultery" were accepted as law. When caring for the dying, family members will normally want to be present and prayers said. If a rabbi is requested, the patient's own rabbi should be contacted first.[19]

Hinduism

Hinduism is a polytheistic religion with many gods and goddesses. Hindus believe that God is everything and is infinite. The earliest known Hindu Scriptures were recorded around 1200 BC. Hindus believe in reincarnation and that one's present condition is a reflection of one's virtuous behavior, or lack thereof, in a previous lifetime.

When caring for the dying, relatives may wish to perform rituals at this time. In death, jewelry, sacred threads, or other religious objects should not be removed from the body. Washing the body is part of the funeral rites and should be carried out by the relatives.[20]

Buddhism

Buddhism is a religion and philosophy encompassing a variety of traditions, beliefs, and practices, largely based on teachings attributed to the Indian prince named Siddhartha Gautama (563–483 BC). He went on a spiritual quest and eventually became enlightened at the age of 35, and from then on, he took the name Buddha. Simply defined, Buddhism is a religion to some and a philosophy to others that encourages one "to do good, avoid evil, and purify the mind."

When caring for the dying, Buddhists like to be informed about their health status in order to prepare themselves spiritually. A side room with privacy is preferred.[21]

Falun Gong

Falun Gong, also referred to as *Falun Dafa*, is a traditional Chinese spiritual discipline belonging to the Buddhist school of thought. It consists of moral teachings, meditation, and four exercises that resemble tai chi and are known in Chinese culture as qigong. Falun Gong does not involve physical places of worship, formal hierarchies, rituals, or membership, and it is taught without charge. The three principles practiced by the followers are *truthfulness*, *compassion*, and *forbearance/tolerance* toward others. Falun Gong claims followers in 100 countries.

Zen

Zen evolved from Buddhism in Tibet. It emphasizes dharma practice (from the master to the disciple) and experiential wisdom based on learning through the reflection on doing, going beyond scriptural readings.

In Zen, Buddhism learning comes through a form of seated meditation known as zazen, where practitioners perform meditation to calm the body and the mind, experience insight into the nature of existence, and thereby gain enlightenment.

Taoism

Taoists believe that ultimate reality is unknowable and unperceivable. The founder of Taoism is believed to be Lao Tzu (6 BC). Taoist doctrine includes the belief that the proper way of living involves being in tune with nature. Everything is ultimately interblended and interacts. Taoist ethics include compassion, frugality, and humility. They emphasize the importance of meditation in daily life, which can be a challenge in the hospital setting.

Christianity

Christians accept both the Old and New Testament as being the word of God. The New Testament describes Jesus as being God, taking the form of man. He was born of the Virgin Mary and sacrificed his life by suffering crucifixion. After being raised from the dead on the third day, he ascended into Heaven, from which he will return to raise the dead, at which time the spiritual body will be united with the physical body. His death, burial, and resurrection provide a way of salvation through belief in Him for the forgiveness of sin. God is believed to be manifest in three persons: the Father, Son, and Holy Spirit.

The primary and final authority for Christian ethics is found in the life, teachings, ministry, death, and resurrection of Jesus Christ. He clarified the ethical demands of a God-centered life by applying the obedient love that was required of Peter. The Ten Commandments are accepted and practiced by both Christians and Jews.

Christians, when determining what the right thing to do is, often refer to the Golden Rule, which teaches, "do unto others as you would have them do unto you," a common principle in many moral codes and religions.

There have been and continue to be numerous interpretations of the meaning of the scriptures and its different passages. This has resulted in a plethora of churches with varying beliefs. As noted later, such beliefs can affect a patient's wishes for health care. However, the heart of Christian beliefs is found in the book of John:

 For God so loved the world, that he gave his only begotten and Son, that whosoever believeth in him should not perish, but have everlasting life.

—John 3:16 (KJV)

The Apostle Paul proclaimed that salvation cannot be gained through good works, but through faith in Jesus Christ as savior. He recognized the importance of faith in Christ over good works in the pursuit of salvation.

That if thou shalt confess with thy mouth the Lord Jesus, and shalt believe in thine heart that God hath raised him from the dead, thou shalt be saved.

—Romans 10:9 (KJV)

The Apostle Paul, however, did not dismiss the importance of good works. Good works are described as the fruit of one's faith. In other words, good works follow faith.

When caring for the dying, services of the in-house chaplain and/or one's religious minister should be offered to the patient. A Catholic priest should be offered when last rites need to be administered to those of the Catholic faith.

Islam

The Islamic religion believes there is one God: Allah. Muhammad (570–632 AD) is considered to be a prophet/messenger of God. He is believed to have received revelations from God. These revelations were recorded in the Qur'an, the Muslim Holy Book. Muslims accept Moses and Jesus as prophets of God. The Qur'an is believed by Muslims to supersede that of the Torah and the Bible. Muslims believe that there is no need for God's grace and that their own actions can merit God's mercy and goodness. Humans are believed to have a moral responsibility to submit to God's will and to follow Islam as demonstrated in the Qur'an.

When caring for the dying, patients may want to die facing Mecca and be with relatives. Many Muslims follow strict rules in respect of the body after death.[22]

Religious Beliefs and Duty Conflict

Religious beliefs and codes of conduct sometimes conflict with the ethical duty of caregivers to save lives. Jehovah's Witnesses, for example, believe that it is a sin to accept a blood transfusion since the Bible states that we must "abstain from blood" (Acts 15:29).

A principal tenet of the Jehovah's Witness faith is the belief that receiving blood or blood products into one's body precludes resurrection and everlasting life after death. Current Jehovah's Witness doctrine, in part, states that blood must not be transfused. In order to respect this belief, bloodless surgery is available in a number of hospitals to patients who find it against their religious beliefs to receive a blood transfusion.

The right to refuse a blood transfusion or any other treatment must be honored even in emergent situations where the patient is unconscious. Whether for a parent or child, it may become necessary to seek a court's guidance to make exceptions for such transfusions. Because time is of the essence in many cases, it is important that the legal system (e.g., legislative bodies and the courts) work with hospitals and religious bodies to provide guidance in advance in order to protect caregivers while also respecting the rights of patients.

▶ SECULAR ETHICS

Unlike religious ethics, secular ethics are based on codes developed by societies that have relied on customs to formulate their codes. The Code of Hammurabi, for example, carved on a black Babylonian column 8 feet high, now located in the Louvre in Paris, depicts a mythical sun god presenting a code of laws to Hammurabi, a great military leader and ruler of Babylon (1795–1750 BC). Hammurabi's code of laws is an early example of a ruler proclaiming to his people an entire body of laws. The following excerpts are from the Code of Hammurabi.

Code of Hammurabi

215
If a physician make a large incision with an operating knife and cure it, or if he open a tumor (over the eye) with an operating knife, and saves the eye, he shall receive ten shekels in money.
218
If a physician make a large incision with the operating knife, and kill him, or open a tumor with the operating knife, and cut out the eye, his hands shall be cut off.
219
If a physician make a large incision in the slave of a freed man, and kill him, he shall replace the slave with another slave.
221
If a physician heal the broken bone or diseased soft part of a man, the patient shall pay the physician five shekels in money.

▶ PROFESSIONAL ETHICS

My life is my message.

—Mahatma Gandhi

Professional ethics are standards or codes of conduct established by the membership of a specific profession. Most professions have a code of ethics designed to describe what is right and wrong conduct, including acceptable behaviors and expectations of a profession's membership. Professionals are expected to follow ethical guidelines in the practice of their profession.

Healthcare professionals are governed by ethical codes that demand a high level of integrity, honesty, and responsibility. It is the direct caregiver who is often confronted with complex ethical dilemmas in the delivery of patient care. Because of the ethical dilemmas facing healthcare providers, professional codes of ethics have been developed to provide guidance.

> Codes of ethics are created in response to actual or anticipated ethical conflicts. Considered in a vacuum, many codes of ethics would be difficult to comprehend or interpret. It is only in the context of real life and real ethical ambiguity that the codes take on any meaning.
> Codes of ethics and case studies need each other. Without guiding principles, case studies are difficult to evaluate and analyze; without context, codes of ethics are incomprehensible. The best way to use these codes is to apply them to a variety of situations and see what results. It is from the back and forth evaluation of the codes and the cases that thoughtful moral judgments can best arise.[23]

The Center for the Study of Ethics in the Professions at the Illinois Institute of Technology received a grant from the National Science Foundation to put a collection of over 850 codes of ethics on the Internet. This center's website includes links to the ethical codes of professional societies, corporations, government agencies, and academic institutions. Additional information can be found at their website (ethics.iit.edu/ecodes/about).

The contents of codes of ethics vary depending on the risks associated with a particular profession. For example, ethical codes for psychologists define relationships with clients in greater depth because of the personal one-to-one relationship they have with their clients.

Laboratory technicians and technologists, on the other hand, generally have little or no personal contact with patients but can have a significant impact on their care. In their ethical code, laboratory technologists pledge accuracy and reliability in the performance of tests. The importance of this pledge was borne out in a March 11, 2004, report by the *Baltimore Sun*, whereby state health officials discovered that a hospital's laboratory personnel overrode controls in testing equipment showing results that might be in error and then mailed them to patients anyway.

Several cases involving ethical misconduct by health professionals are reviewed next.

Documentation Falsified

The nurse in *Williams v. Bd. of Exam'rs for Prof. Nurses*[24] improperly, incompletely, or illegibly documented the delivery of nursing care and failed to adhere to established standards in the practice setting to safeguard patient care, which included, falsely documenting that she was in the patient's home during lunch hours when in fact she was not. The Board of Examiners for Professional Nurses determined that the nurse was guilty of conduct derogatory to the morals or standing of the profession of registered nursing. The West Virginia Board of Examiners for Registered Professional Nurses has the power to deny, revoke, or suspend any license to practice upon proof that the nurse is guilty of conduct derogatory to the morals or standing of the profession of registered nursing. Conduct that qualifies as derogatory to the morals or standing of the nursing profession includes improperly, incompletely, or illegibly documenting the delivery of nursing care.

The board proved that the nurse improperly documented the delivery of nursing care. Williams specifically charted that she was in the client's home during lunch hours. The agency, however, in reviewing its time sheets found that a homemaker was in the patient's home during lunch hours. Upon its review of the board's action, the circuit court upheld the board's action. The appellate court affirmed the order of the circuit court.

Psychologist's Sexual Misconduct

The defendant-psychologist in *Gilmore v. Board of Psychologist Examiners*[25] claimed that sexual improprieties with clients did not take place during treatment sessions. The board of psychologist examiners however disagreed and revoked the psychologist's license for sexual improprieties. The psychologist

petitioned for judicial review. She argued that therapy had terminated before the sexual relationships began. The court of appeals held that evidence supported the board's conclusion that the psychologist violated an ethical standard in caring for her patients. When a psychologist's personal interests intrude into the practitioner–client relationship, the practitioner is obliged to recreate objectivity through a third party. The board's findings and conclusions indicated that the petitioner failed to maintain that objectivity.

Attorney–Minister Misconduct

A minister was paid by an attorney to attend a hospital chaplain's course in furtherance of a plan whereby the minister could gain access to the emergency areas of a hospital in order to solicit patients and their families for the purpose of aiding the attorney in gaining legal cases based on negligence and malpractice. The improper solicitations were a part of organized schemes that lasted for years with multiple offenses, including two different schemes that led to at least 22 improper solicitations. Disbarment was decided to be appropriate with respect to an attorney who hired the ordained minister as a paralegal.[26]

▸ ETHICS COMMITTEE

I expect to pass through the world but once. Any good therefore that I can do, or any kindness I can show to any creature, let me do it now. Let me not defer it, for I shall not pass this way again.

—Stephen Grellet[27]

Healthcare ethics committees address legal–ethical issues that arise during the course of a patient's care and treatment. They serve as a resource for patients, families, and staff and offer objective counsel when dealing with difficult healthcare issues. Ethics committees provide both educational and consultative services to patients, families, and caregivers. They enhance, but do not replace, important patient/family–physician relationships; nevertheless, they afford support for decisions made within those relationships. The numerous ethical questions facing health professionals involve the entire life span, from the right to be born to the right to die. Ethics committees concern themselves with issues of morality, patient autonomy, legislation, and states' interests.

Although ethics committees first emerged in the 1960s in the United States, attention was focused on ethics committees as a result of the 1976 landmark

Quinlan case,[28] where the parents of Karen Ann Quinlan were granted permission by the New Jersey Supreme Court to remove Karen from a ventilator after she had been in a coma for a year. She died 10 years later at the age of 31, having been in a persistent vegetative state the entire time. The Quinlan court looked to a prognosis committee to verify Karen's medical condition. It then factored in the committee's opinion with all other evidence to reach the decision to allow withdrawing her life-support equipment. To date, ethics committees do not have sole surrogate decision-making authority; however, they play an ever-expanding role in the development of policy and procedural guidelines to assist in resolving ethical dilemmas. Most organizations describe the functioning of the ethics committee and how to access the committee at the time of admission in patient handbooks and informational brochures.

Committee Structure

To be successful, an ethics committee should be structured to include a wide range of community leaders in positions of political stature, respect, and diversity. The ethics committee should comprise a multidisciplinary group of people, whose membership should include an ethicist when available, educators, clinicians, legal counsel, and political leaders as well as members of the clergy, a quality improvement manager, and corporate leaders from the business community. Ethics committees, all too often, are comprised mostly of hospital employees and members of the medical staff with a token representation from the community.

Objectives of Ethics Committees

The objectives of an ethics committee include: providing support and guidance to patients, families, and decision makers; reviewing ethical dilemmas, as requested; providing assistance in clarifying situations that are ethical, legal, or religious in nature and extend beyond the scope of daily practice; assisting in clarifying issues to discuss alternatives and compromises; promoting the rights of patients; assisting the patient and family in coming to consensus in care decisions that best meet the patient's needs; promoting policies and procedures that maximize patient-centered outcomes; and enhancing the ethical tenor of both the healthcare organization and professional staff.

Committee Functions

The functions of ethics committees are multifaceted and include development of policy and procedure guidelines to assist in resolving ethical dilemmas; staff and community education; conflict resolution; case reviews, support, and consultation; and political advocacy. The degree to which an ethics committee serves each of these functions varies in different healthcare organizations.

Policy and Procedure Development

The ethics committee is a valuable resource for developing hospital policies and procedures to provide guidance to healthcare professionals when addressing ethical dilemmas.

Educational Role

The ethics committee helps to develop resources for educational purposes to help both in-hospital and ambulatory staff develop the appropriate competencies for addressing legal, ethical, and spiritual issues. Educational programs on ethical issues should be provided to committee members, staff, patients, and the community (e.g., informed consent, do-not-resuscitate (DNR) orders, preparation of advance directives, surrogate decision making).

Understanding the spiritual needs of patients of varying beliefs should be a component of the education, policy development, and consultative functions of ethics committees. Most hospitals provide staff with resources that describe various religious beliefs and how to access those resources for patients of various religions.

Consultation and Conflict Resolution

Ethics consultations are helpful in resolving uncertainty and disagreements over healthcare dilemmas. Ethics committees often provide consultation services for patients, families, and caregivers struggling with difficult treatment decisions and end-of-life dilemmas. Always mindful of its basic orientation toward the patient's best interests, the committee provides options and suggestions for resolution of conflict in actual cases. Consultation with an ethics committee is not mandatory, but is conducted at the request of a physician, patient, family member, or other caregiver.

The ethics committee strives to provide viable alternatives that will lead to the optimal resolution of dilemmas confronting the continuing care of the patient. It is important to remember that an ethics committee functions in an advisory capacity and should not be considered a substitute proxy for the patient.

Requests for Consultations

Requests for ethics consultations often involve clarification of issues regarding decision-making capacity, informed consent, advance directives, and withdrawal of treatment. Consultations should be conducted in a timely manner considering, for example, who requested the consultation, what the issues are, whether there is a problem that needs referral to another service, and what specifically is being requested of the ethics committee.

When conducting a consultation, all patient records must be reviewed and discussed with the attending physician, family members, and other caregivers involved in the patient's treatment. If an issue can be resolved easily, a designated member of the ethics committee should be able to consult on the case without the need for a full committee meeting. If the problem is unusual, problematic, or delicate, or has important legal ramifications, a full committee meeting should be considered. Others who can be invited to an ethics committee case review, as appropriate, include the patient, if competent; relatives, agents, or surrogate decision makers; and caregivers.

Preevaluation case consultations should take the following into consideration: the patient's current medical status, diagnosis, and prognosis; the patient's mental status and ability to make decisions, understand the information that is necessary to make a decision, and clearly understand the consequences of his or her choice; benefits and burdens of recommended treatment or alternative treatments; life expectancy, treated and untreated; views of caregivers and consultants; pain and suffering; quality-of-life issues; and the financial burden on family (e.g., if the patient is in a comatose state with no hope of recovery, should the spouse deplete his or her finances to maintain the spouse on a respirator?).

Decisions concerning patient care must take into consideration the patient's personal assessment of the quality of life; current expressed choices; advance directives; competency to make decisions; ability to process information rationally to compare risks, benefits, and alternatives to treatment; ability to articulate major factors in decisions and reasons for them; and ability to communicate.

The patient must have all of the information necessary to allow a reasonable person to make a prudent decision on his or her own behalf. The patient's choice must be voluntary and free from coercion by family, physicians, or others.

Family members must be identified, and the following questions must be considered when making decisions: Do family members understand the patient's wishes; is the family in agreement with the patient's wishes; does the patient have an advance directive; has the patient appointed a surrogate decision maker; are there any religious proscriptions; are there any financial concerns; and are there any legal factors (applicable state statutes and case law)?

When an ethics committee is engaged in the consulting process, its recommendations should be offered as suggestions, imposing no obligation for acceptance on the part of the patient, organization, its governing body, medical staff, attending physicians, or other persons. An example of an ethics committee consultation form is presented in **EXHIBIT 15-1**.

When conducting a formal consultation, ethics committees should identify the ethical dilemma (i.e., reasons why the consult was requested); be sure that the appropriate "Consultation Request" form has been completed; identify relevant facts (e.g., diagnosis and prognosis, patient goals and wishes, regulatory and legal issues, professional standards and codes of ethics); identify stakeholders; identify moral issues (e.g., human dignity, common good, justice, beneficence, respect for autonomy, informed consent, medical futility); identify legal issues; consider alternative options; conduct consultation (review, discuss, and provide reasoning for recommendations); review and follow up; include family members in committee discussion; ask family members what their hopes and expectations are; and document consultations.

Expanding Role of the Ethics Committee

The role of an organization's ethics committee is evolving into more than a group of individuals who periodically gather together to meet regulatory requirements and review and address advance directives and end-of-life issues. The function of an organizational ethics committee has an ever-expanding role as noted here.

The wide variety of ethical issues that an ethics committee can be involved in is somewhat formidable. Although an ethics committee cannot address every issue that one could conceivably imagine, the ethics committee should periodically reevaluate its scope of activities and effectiveness in addressing ethical issues.

- Dilemma of blind trials: Who gets the placebo when the investigational drug looks very promising?
- Informed consent: Are patients adequately informed regarding the risks, benefits, and alternative procedures that may be equally effective, knowing that one procedure may be more risky or

damaging than another (e.g., lumpectomy versus a radical mastectomy)?

- What is the physician's responsibility for informing the patient of his or her education, training, qualifications, and skill in treating a medical condition or performing an invasive procedure?
- What is the role of the ethics committee when the medical staff is reluctant or fails to take timely action, knowing that one of its members practices questionable medicine?
- Should a hospital's medical staff practice evidence-based medicine or follow its own best judgment?
- To what extent should the organization participate in and/or support genetic research?
- How should the ethics committee address confidentiality issues?
- To what extent should medical information be shared with the patient's family?
- To what extent should the organization's leadership control the scope of issues that the ethics committee addresses?
- Who provides information to the patient when mistakes are made relative to his or her care?

Although organizational politics may prevent an ethics committee from becoming involved in many of the issues just described, ethics committees need to review their functions periodically and redefine themselves. The ethics committee's involvement in the organizational setting has been for the most part strictly advisory. However, its full potential and value to an organization has yet to be fully understood and accepted. The ethics committee membership should provide a full assessment of its activities on an annual basis to the organization's leadership, along with suggested goals for expanding its role within the organization.

Ethics Committee Serves as Guardian

The Kentucky Supreme Court ruled in *Woods v. Commonwealth*[29] that Kentucky's Living Will Directive, allowing a court-appointed guardian or other designated surrogate to remove a patient's life support systems, is constitutional. The patient in this case, Woods, had been placed on a ventilator after having a heart attack. It was generally agreed that he would never regain consciousness and would die in 2 to 10 years. After a recommendation of the hospital ethics committee, Woods's guardian at the time asked for approval to remove Woods's life support. The Kentucky Supreme Court affirmed an appeals court decision, holding that:

- *If there is no guardian* and the family, physicians, and ethics committee all agree with the surrogate, there is no need to appoint a guardian.
- *If there is a guardian* and all parties agree, there is no need for judicial approval.
- *If there is disagreement*, the parties may petition the courts.[30]

Removal of life support will be prohibited, absent clear and convincing evidence that the patient is permanently unconscious or is in a persistent vegetative state.

Convening the Ethics Committee

The ethics committee is not a decision maker, but is instead a resource that provides advice to help guide others in making wiser decisions when there is no clear best choice. A unanimous opinion is not always possible when an ethics committee convenes to consider the issues of an ethical dilemma; however, consultative advice as to a course of action to resolve the dilemma is often the role of the ethics committee. Any recommendations for issue resolution reached by the ethics committee must be communicated to those most closely involved with the patient's care. Sensitivity to each family member's values and assisting them in coping with whatever consensus decision is reached is crucial when end-of-life decisions are being made. Unresolved issues often need to be addressed and a course of action followed. Each new consultation presents new opportunities for learning and teaching others how to cope with similar issues. Guidelines for resolving ethical issues will always be in a state of flux. Each new case presents new challenges and learning opportunities.

Making a decision and suggesting a course of action requires accepting the fact that there will be elements of right and wrong in the final decision. The idea is to cause the least pain and provide the greatest benefit.

Failure to Convene Bioethics Committee

In a medical malpractice suit, the Stolles (appellants) sought damages from physicians and hospitals (appellees) for disregard of their instructions not to use "heroic efforts" or artificial means to prolong the life of their child, Mariel, who was born with brain damage. The Stolles argued that such negligence resulted in further brain damage to Mariel, prolonged her life, and caused them extraordinary costs that will continue as long as the child lives.

Date: _____ Time: _____

Caller: _____ Reason for call: _____

Action taken: _____

Patient: _____ Age: _____

Record #: _____ Consultation requested by: _____

Relationship (e.g., caregiver, spouse): _____

Attending physician: _____

Other physicians: _____

Will the patient participate in the consultation?   Yes   No

Does the patient have decision-making capacity? Yes   No   Explain: _____

Surrogate decision maker?   Yes   No   If yes, name: _____

Phone #: _____ Advance directives (e.g., living will)? _____

Availability of advance directive: _____

Consultation participants:

❑ Family/relationship: _____

❑ Physicians: _____

❑ Nurses: _____

❑ Ethics committee members (e.g., chaplain, social worker, community representative): _____
_____
_____
_____

Medical Treatment/Care Information:

Diagnoses: _____ Prognosis: _____ Course of illness: _____

Treatment options appropriate: _____

Treatment options medically beneficial: _____

Treatment options available: _____

Would the patient have wanted the treatment? _____

Ethical issues: _____

Other persons to contact for input, if any: _____

Consultative guidance: _____

Guidance communicated?   Yes   No   If yes, to whom? _____

Consultation noted on the medical record?   Yes   No

Disposition: _____
_____
_____

Form completed by: _____ Date/Time: _____

EXHIBIT 15-1 Ethics Committee Consultation

The Stolles had executed a written "Directive to Physicians" on behalf of Mariel in which they made known their desire that Mariel's life not be artificially prolonged under the circumstances provided in that directive.

Mariel suffered a medical episode after regurgitating her food. An unnamed, unidentified nurse–clinician administered chest compressions for 30 to 60 seconds, and Mariel survived. The Stolles sued, alleging the following, among other things:

- Appropriate medical entries were not made in the medical record to reflect the Stolles' wishes that caregivers refrain from "heroic" life-sustaining measures.
- Lifesaving measures were initiated in violation of the physician's orders. The hospital did not follow the physician's orders, which were in Mariel's medical chart, when chest compressions and mechanically administered breathing to artificially prolong Mariel's life were applied, and a bioethics committee meeting was not convened to consider the Stolles' wishes and the necessity of a do-not-resuscitate (DNR) order.

The central issue in this case is whether appellees are immune from liability under the Texas Natural Death Act. Section 672.016(b) of the Texas Natural Death Act provides the following: "A physician, or a health professional acting under the direction of a physician, is not civilly or criminally liable for failing to effectuate a qualified patient's directive" [Tex. Health & Safety Code Ann. A4 672.016(b) (Vernon 1992)]. A "qualified patient" is a "patient with a terminal condition that has been diagnosed and certified in writing by the attending physician and one other physician who have personally examined the patient." A "terminal condition" is an "incurable condition caused by injury, disease, or illness that would produce death regardless of the application of life-sustaining procedures, according to reasonable medical judgment, and in which the application of life-sustaining procedures serves only to postpone the moment of the patient's death."

Mariel was not in a terminal condition, as appellees alleged. The Stolles failed to cite any authority that would have allowed the withdrawal of life-sustaining procedures in a lawful manner. The Texas Natural Death Act, therefore, provided immunity to the caregivers for their actions in the treatment and care of Mariel.[31]

Patient Not in a Persistent Vegetative State

A guardian may only direct the withdrawal of life-sustaining medical treatment, including nutrition and hydration, if the incompetent ward is in a persistent vegetative state and the decision to withdraw is in the best interests of the ward.

In *Spahn v. Eisenberg*,[32] Edna's sister and court-appointed guardian, Spahn, sought permission to direct the withholding of Edna's nutrition, claiming that her sister would not want to live in this condition; however, the only testimony presented at trial regarding Edna's views on the use of life-sustaining medical treatment involves a statement made 30 years

earlier. At that time, Spahn and Edna were having a conversation about their mother, who was recovering from depression, and Spahn's mother-in-law, who was dying of cancer. Spahn testified that during this conversation, Edna said to her that she would rather die of cancer than lose her mind. Spahn further testified that this was the only time that she and Edna discussed the subject and that Edna never said anything specifically about withholding or withdrawing life-sustaining medical treatment. The "ethics committee" at the nursing facility where Edna lived met to discuss the issue of withholding artificial nutrition from Edna. "The committee approved the withholding of the nutrition if no family member objected. However, one of Edna's nieces refused to sign a statement approving the withdrawal of nutrition."[33]

The record speaks very little about what Edna's desires would be, and there was no clear statement of what her desires would be today under the current conditions. Her friends and family never had any conversations with her discussing her feelings or opinions about withdrawing nutrition or hydration, and she did not execute any advance directives expressing her wishes while she was competent.

The court therefore held that a guardian may only direct the withdrawal of life-sustaining medical treatment, including nutrition and hydration, if the incompetent ward is in a persistent vegetative state and the decision to withdraw is in the best interests of the ward. In this case, where the only indication of Edna's desires was made at least 30 years earlier and under different circumstances, there is no a clear statement of intent such that Edna's guardian may authorize the withholding of her nutrition.

▶ REASONING AND DECISION MAKING

Reason guides our attempt to understand the world about us. Both reason and compassion guide our efforts to apply that knowledge ethically, to understand other people, and have ethical relationships with other people.

—Molleen Matsumura

Reasoning is the process of forming conclusions, judgments, or inferences based on one's interpretation of facts or premises that help support a conclusion. Reasoning includes the capacity for logical inference and the ability to conduct inquiry, solve problems, evaluate, criticize, and deliberate about how we should act, and to reach an understanding of other people, the world, and ourselves.[34] *Partial reasoning* involves bias for or against a person based on one's relationship with that person. *Circular reasoning* describes a person who has already made up his mind on a particular issue and sees no need for deliberation (i.e., "Don't confuse me with the facts"). For example, consider the following: "Mr. Smith has lived a good life. It's time to pull the plug. He is over 65 and, therefore, should not have any rights to donated organs. Donated organs should be given to younger people." The rightness or wrongness of this statement is a moral issue and should be open for discussion, fact-finding, evaluation, reasoning, and consensus decision making.

Ethical dilemmas often arise when ethical theories, principles, and values are in conflict. Healthcare dilemmas often occur when there are alternative choices, limited resources, and differing values among patients, family members, and caregivers. An ethical dilemma arises when, for example, the principles of autonomy and beneficence conflict with one another. Coming to an agreement may mean sacrificing one's personal wishes and following the road where there is consensus. Consensus building can happen only when the parties involved can sit and reason together. The process of identifying the various alternatives to an ethical dilemma, determining the pros and cons of each choice, and making informed decisions requires a clear, unbiased willingness to listen, learn, and, in the end, make an informed decision.

There are often competing medical dilemmas in the healthcare setting, as noted in *Estate of Behringer v. Medical Center at Princeton*[35] where the physician posed a risk to the patient.

> The patient and doctor occupy unequal positions in the relationship. The doctor is trained to recognize, diagnose, and avoid contracting the patient's disease. The doctor stands in a position of trust, a fiduciary position in relation to the patient. A small but palpable risk of transmitting a lethal disease to the patient gives the doctor an ethical responsibility to perform only procedures that pose no risk of transmission. The patient, on the other hand, has no corresponding ethical duty to the doctor. The patient is neither trained nor expected to ascertain the provider's health status. While secretive patients may transmit their diseases to unwary doctors, doctors are responsible for both their own health and the health of their patients.[36]

In this case, An HIV-infected surgeon in New Jersey was unable to recover on a discrimination claim when the hospital restricted his surgical privileges. The New Jersey Superior Court determined that the hospital acted properly when suspending the surgeon's surgical privileges and ultimately barring the surgeon from performing surgery. The court held that the risk of a surgical accident involving an HIV-positive surgeon and implications thereof would be a legitimate concern to a surgical patient that would warrant disclosure of the risk. The risk of transmission of HIV from the surgeon to the patient can be exacerbated during surgery if the surgeon, for example, cuts himself with a scalpel and his blood contaminates the patient.[37]

▶ MORAL COMPASS GONE ASTRAY

The world is a dangerous place. Not because of the people who are evil; but because of the people who don't do anything about it.

—Albert Einstein

Political corruption, antisocial behavior, declining civility, and rampant unethical conduct have heightened discussions over the nation's moral decline and decaying value systems. The numerous instances of questionable political decisions; numbers-cooking executives with exorbitant salaries, including healthcare executives working for both for-profit and nonprofit organizations; cheating at work and in school; and the proliferation of X-rated websites have contributed to this decline. Legislators, investigators, prosecutors, and the courts have been in a position to make change. The question, however, remains: Can this boat be turned around, or are we just plugging the holes with new laws and creating more leaks in a misdirected, sinking boat? The answer is more likely to be a return to practicing the values upon which this nation was founded.

The continuing trend of consumer awareness of declining value systems, coupled with increased governmental regulations, mandates that caregivers understand ethics and the law and their interrelationships.

It has been said that if you do not learn from history, you are doomed to repeat it. If you have not learned and do not apply the generally accepted moral principles (e.g., do good and do no harm) described in this chapter, you will not have a moral compass to guide you.

Be careful of your thoughts, for your thoughts inspire your words. Be careful of your words, for your words precede your actions. Be careful of your actions, for your actions become your habits. Be careful of your habits, for your habits build your character. Be careful of your character, for your character decides your destiny.

—Chinese Proverb

WE NO LONGER HAVE MORAL COMPASS

Hartford Police Chief Daryl Roberts questioned the city's "moral compass" a week after bystanders and drivers maneuvered around the motionless body of 78-year-old victim of a hit-and-run crash . . . .

"At the end of the day we've got to look at ourselves and understand that our moral values have now changed," Roberts said. "We have no regard for each other."

—WFSB.com, "Chief: 'We No Longer Have Moral Compass,'" Hartford, CT, June 6, 2008

Although you cannot control the amount of time you have in this lifetime, you can control your behavior by adopting those virtues that will define who you are, what you will become, and how you will be remembered or forgotten.

Become who you want to be and how you want to be remembered. The formula is easy and well described in the previous quote, attributed to a Chinese proverb. Read it. Reread it. Write it. Memorize it. Display it in your home, at work, and in your car, and most of all, practice it, always remembering it all begins with thoughts.

My words fly up, my thoughts remain below: Words without thoughts never to heaven go.

—William Shakespeare

Control your thoughts, and do not let them control you. As to words, they are the tools of thought. They can be sharper than any double-edged sword and hurt, or they can do good and heal. It is never too late to change your thoughts, as long as you have air to breathe. Your legacy may be short, but it can be powerful.

Helpful Hints

The reason for studying ethical and legal issues is to understand and help guide others through the decision-making process as it relates to ethical dilemmas. The following are some helpful guidelines when faced with ethical dilemmas:

- Be aware of how everyday life is full of ethical decisions and that numerous ethical issues can arise when caring for patients.
- Help guide others to make better choices.
- Ask your patient how you might help him or her.
- Be aware of why you think the way you do. Do not impose your beliefs on others.

- Ask yourself whether you agree with the things you do. If the answer is no, ask yourself how you should change.
- When you are not sure what to do, the wise thing to do is to talk it over with another person, preferably someone whose opinion you trust.
- Value the truth in all healthcare settings.

▶ CHAPTER REVIEW

1. *Ethics* is the branch of philosophy that seeks to understand the nature, purposes, justification, and founding principles of moral rules and the systems they comprise.

    - Ethics involves making sound judgments, good decisions, and right choices.
    - *Microethics* involves an individual's view of what is right and wrong based on his or her life experiences.
    - *Macroethics* involves a more generalized view of right and wrong.
    - *Bioethics* addresses such difficult issues as the nature of life, the nature of death, what sort of life is worth living, what constitutes murder, how we should treat people who are especially vulnerable, and the responsibilities we have to other human beings.

2. Morality is a code of conduct and a guide to good behavior.

    - *Moral judgments* are those judgments concerned with what an individual or group believes to be the right or proper behavior in a given situation.
    - There is no universal morality.
    - Morality is often legislated when differences cannot be resolved because of conflicting moral codes with varying opinions as to what is right and what is wrong.
    - Laws are created to set boundaries for societal behavior.

3. Theories of ethics

    - *Normative ethics* is the attempt to determine what moral standards should be followed so that human behavior and conduct may be morally right.

        - *General normative ethics* is the critical study of major moral precepts of such matters as what things are right, what things are good, and what things are genuine.

- *Applied ethics* is the application of normative theories to practical moral problems.
- *Descriptive ethics*, also known as comparative ethics, deals with what people believe to be right and wrong.
- *Meta-ethics* seeks to understand ethical terms and theories and their application.

- *Consequential ethical theory* emphasizes that the morally right action is whatever action leads to the maximum balance of good over evil.

  - *Utilitarian ethics* involves the concept that the moral worth of an action is solely determined by its contribution to overall utility.

- *Nonconsequential ethics* denies that the consequences of an action or rule are the only criteria for determining the morality of an action or rule.
- *Situational ethics* refers to a particular view of ethics in which absolute standards are considered less important than the requirements of a particular situation.
- *Deontological ethics* focuses on one's duties to others. Deontology is an ethical analysis according to a moral code or rules.
- *Ethical relativism* is the theory that holds that morality is relative to the norms of one's culture.
- *Virtue-based ethics* focuses on the inherent character of a person rather than on the specific actions he or she performs.

  - *Virtue*: that which has moral excellence or beneficial quality.
  - Characteristics that differentiate good people from bad people.

4. *Principles of ethics* are universal rules of conduct.

- *Autonomy*: the right of a person to make one's own decisions.
- *Beneficence*: the principle of doing good, demonstrating kindness, showing compassion, and helping others.

  - Paternalism is a form of beneficence that can involve withholding information from a person because of the belief that doing so is in the best interest of that person.
  - Medical paternalism involves making choices for patients who are capable of making their own choices; it directly violates patient autonomy.

- *Nonmaleficence*: ethical principle that requires caregivers to avoid causing patients harm.
- *Justice*: the obligation to be fair in the distribution of benefits and risks.

  - *Distributive justice*: a principle that requires treatment of all persons equally.

5. *Values* are standards of conduct. Values are used for judging the goodness or badness of some action.

- *Intrinsic value* is something that has value in and of itself (e.g., compassion, honesty, respect).
- *Instrumental value* helps to give value to something else (e.g., money).

6. The pillars of moral strength that build moral character include: courage, wisdom, temperance, commitment, discernment, fairness, fidelity, freedom, honesty, integrity, kindness, respect, hopefulness, tolerance, and forgiveness.

7. *Religious ethics* serves a moral purpose by providing codes of conduct for appropriate behavior through revelations from a divine source.

8. *Secular ethics* is based on codes developed by societies that have relied on customs to formulate their codes of ethics.

9. *Professional ethics* is a set of standards or codes of conduct established by the membership of a specific profession.

10. Healthcare ethics committees

- Address legal-ethical issues that arise during the course of a patient's care and treatment.
- Serve as a hospital resource to patients, families, and staff, offering an objective counsel when dealing with difficult healthcare issues and decisions.
- Committees should be structured to include a wide range of community leaders.
- Goals of the ethics committee include:

  - Promote patient rights.
  - Assist patient and family in resolving ethical dilemmas.
  - Educate and advise healthcare providers, patients, and families on how to analyze ethical dilemmas.
  - Serve as a hospital resource designed to offer objective counsel.

- The committee performs functions by:

  - Developing policy and procedure guidelines to assist in resolving ethical dilemmas
  - Educating staff and community

- Resolving conflicts
- Reviewing cases
- Offering support and consultation
- Offering political advocacy
- Providing consultation services when conflict arises

11. Reasoning is the process of forming conclusions, judgments, or inferences based on one's interpretation of facts or premises.

   - *Partial reasoning* involves bias for or against a person based on one's relationship with that person.
   - *Circular reasoning* describes a person who has already decided the correctness of something.

▶ REVIEW QUESTIONS

1. Describe how ethical theories differ and how ethical principles are helpful to caregivers and the ethics committee in resolving ethical dilemmas.
2. Describe how spirituality and religion help to shape one's healthcare choices.
3. Describe the term *situational ethics* and how decisions can change as circumstances change.
4. Describe the consultative role of the ethics committee when addressing ethical dilemmas.

▶ NOTES

1. "The Definition of Morality," *Stanford Encyclopedia of Philosophy*, 2005, http://plato.stanford.edu/entries/morality-definition/.
2. Larry N. Gowdy, "Meta-Ethics," October 15, 2013. http://www.ethicsmorals.com/metaethics.html.
3. Jason Gillikin, "Workplace Example of Duty Based Ethics," *Houston Chronicle*, http://smallbusiness.chron.com/workplace-example-duty-based-ethics-11972.html.
4. Manuel Velasquez, Claire Andre, Thomas Shanks, Michael Meyer, "Ethical Relativism," Santa Clara University, http://www.scu.edu/ethics/practicing/decision/ethicalrelativism.html.
5. Clare Booth Luce (1903–1987), *Readers Digest*, 1979.
6. American essayist.
7. 464 A.2d 303, 314 (N.J. Super. Ct. App. Div. 1983).
8. The National Commission for the Protection of Human Subjects of Biomedical and Behavioral Research, "The Belmont Report: Ethical Principles and Guidelines for the Protection of Human Subjects of Research," http://www.hhs.gov/ohrp/humansubjects/guidance/belmont.html (accessed October 14, 2010).
9. *Id.*
10. *Id.*
11. Albert Schweitzer, *Cultural Philosophy II: Civilization and Ethics* (London, UK: A. & C. Black, 1929).
12. Wisdom Quotes, "Gerda Lerner Quote," http://www.wisdomquotes.com/002320.html.
13. Author Unknown, from *Achieve Your Dreams*.
14. British Anglican clergyman, teacher, and writer (1819–1875).
15. "Important Issue Facing House-Senate Conference on Health Care Reform," http://www.fenichel.com/Ganske.shtml.
16. Evangelist and founder of Methodism (1703–1791).
17. Johns Hopkins University, "Microsoft and Johns Hopkins Team Up to Build a Smarter, Safer ICU," *Under the Dome*, March 2016. http://www.johnshopkinssolutions.com/microsoft-and-johns-hopkins-team-up-to-build-a-smarter-safer-icu/.
18. Tracey R. Rich, "Halakhah: Jewish Law," http://www.jewfaq.org/halakhah.htm.
19. St. George's Healthcare, "A Guide to Faith and Culture," http://www.stgeorges.nhs.uk/docs/Diversity/MultiFaithGuidance2006.pdf.
20. *Id.*
21. *Id.*
22. *Id.*
23. Illinois Institute of Technology, "Center for the Study of Ethics in the Professions," http://ethics.iit.edu/research/codes-ethics-collection.
24. No. 31328 (W.Va. 2004).
25. 725 P.2d 400 (Or. Ct. App. 1986).
26. *Florida Bar v. Barrett*, No. SC03-375 (Fla. 2005).
27. French/American religious leader (1773–1855).
28. *In re Quinlan*, 70 N.J. 10, 355 A.2d 647 (1976).
29. 1999-SSC0773 (August 24, 2004).
30. *Id.*
31. *Stolle v. Baylor College of Medicine*, 981 S.W.2d 709 (1998).
32. 563 N.W.2d 485 (1997).
33. *Id.*
34. George Lakoff and Mark Johnson, *Philosophy in the Flesh* (New York: Basic Books, 1999), 3–4.
35. 249 N.J. Super. 597, 592 A.2d 1251 (N.J. Super. Ct. L, 1991).
36. *Id.* at 605; footnotes omitted.
37. *Id.* at 1255.

© artlomp/Shutterstock

CHAPTER 16

Procreation and Ethical Dilemmas

TEXAS RESTRICTIONS ON WOMEN'S RIGHTS

The U.S. Supreme Court reviewed both the admitting privileges and Ambulatory Surgery Center requirements in Texas Health Bill HB 2. The first provision of HB 2 required:

> [A] physician performing or inducing an abortion . . . must, on the date the abortion is performed or induced, have active admitting privileges at a hospital that . . . is located not further than 30 miles from the location at which the abortion is performed or induced. Tex. Health & Safety Code Ann. §171.0031(a) (West Cum. Supp. 2015)

> Previously, Texas law required abortion facilities to maintain a written protocol "for managing medical emergencies and the transfer of patients requiring further emergency care to a hospital." 38 Tex. Reg. 6546 (2013).

The second provision of HB 2, referred to as the "surgical center requirement," required:

[T]he minimum standards for an abortion facility must be equivalent to the minimum standards adopted under [the Texas Health and Safety Code section] for ambulatory surgical centers. Tex. Health & Safety Code Ann. §245.010(a)

Preexisting Texas law already contained numerous detailed regulations covering abortion facilities, including a requirement that facilities be inspected at least annually. The record contains nothing to suggest that HB 2 would be more effective than preexisting Texas law at deterring wrongdoers. Should the U.S. Supreme Court overturn Texas Law HB 2?

WHAT IS YOUR VERDICT?

▸ LEARNING OBJECTIVES

The reader, upon completion of this chapter, will be able to:

- Discuss the 1973 Supreme Court ruling in *Roe v. Wade* and the continuing controversy over abortion.
- Describe the flow of abortion cases beginning with *Roe v. Wade*, concentrating on counseling, spousal consent, parental consent, and funding.
- Define and explain the legal issues of sterilization, artificial insemination, and surrogacy.
- Describe the legal and moral issues of wrongful birth, wrongful life, and wrongful conception.

There are numerous ethical questions involving the entire life span, from the right to be born to the right to die. This chapter reviews a variety of issues surrounding procreation, with the primary emphasis on abortion. Discussed to a lesser extent are issues relating to sterilization; artificial insemination; wrongful birth, wrongful life, and wrongful conception; and surrogacy.

This chapter focuses on some of the common questions facing healthcare providers where ethics and the law intersect. When reviewing this chapter, the reader should apply the ethical theories, principles, and values previously reviewed.

▸ ABORTION

We shall have to fight the politician, who remembers only that the unborn have no votes and that since posterity has done nothing for us we need do nothing for posterity.

—William Ralph Inge (1860–1954)[1]

Abortion is the premature termination of pregnancy. It can be classified as spontaneous or induced. It may occur as an incidental result of a medical procedure, or it may be an elective decision on the part of the patient. In addition to having substantial ethical, moral, and religious implications, abortion has proven to be a major political issue and will continue as such in the future. More laws will be proposed, more laws will be passed, and more lawsuits will wind their way up to the U.S. Supreme Court.

A consensus regarding when life begins has not been reached. There has been no final determination as to the proper interplay among a mother's liberty, the interests of the fetus, and the state's interests in protecting life. In abortion cases, the law presupposes a theory of ethics and morality, which, in turn, presupposes deeply personal ideas about being and existence. Answers to such questions as when life begins define ethical and religious beliefs, and these beliefs often determine how we govern ourselves. Abortion in this context is less a question about constitutional law and more about who we are as a people. This is a decision the Supreme Court cannot make. Taking these issues out of the public discourse threatens to foment hostility, stifle the search for answers, distance people from their Constitution, and undermine the credibility of that document.[2]

With more than 1 million abortions performed annually in the United States, it is certain that the conflict between "pro-choice" and "pro-life" advocates will continue to pervade America's landscape. The issues are numerous, and emotions run high. Common ethical concerns include: when does life begin; who decides; who protects the fetus; what are the rights of the child or woman who has been raped; what are the rights of the spouse; what are the rights of the father of an unwed child or woman; what are the rights of society and the state to interfere with another's rights; should the principles of autonomy and right to self-determination prevail; should an abortion be considered murder; can the use of contraception be considered a form of killing by preventing a birth that might have otherwise occurred; what are the religious implications for a woman who chooses to undergo an abortion; is it morally acceptable to save the life of the mother by aborting the fetus; is an abortion for mere convenience morally wrong; should a child or woman who has been raped have a right to abortion; what role should education play in the woman's decision to undergo an abortion; what alternatives should the woman be taught before undergoing an abortion; at what age should the decision to abort be that of the mother; how should the feelings of guilt that may accompany an abortion and how those feelings may haunt the mother through the years be discussed; should the feelings that might occur after giving birth be explained to the victim of a rape (e.g., anger, resentment); and when does control over one's body begin and when does it end?

These are but a few of the many questions yet to be fully resolved. As the following pages point out, for each new issue decided in the courts, numerous new issues arise, all of which seem to involve both legal and moral questions about what is acceptable behavior in American society.

Right to Abortion

In *Roe v. Wade* in 1973, the Supreme Court gave strength to a woman's right to privacy in the context of matters relating to her own body, including how a pregnancy would end.[3] However, the Supreme Court also has recognized the interest of the states in protecting potential life and has attempted to spell out the extent to which the states may regulate and even prohibit abortions.

In *Roe v. Wade*, the U.S. Supreme Court held the Texas penal abortion law unconstitutional, stating: "State criminal abortion statutes . . . that except from criminality only a lifesaving procedure on behalf of the mother, without regard to the stage of her pregnancy and other interests involved, is violating the Due Process Clause of the Fourteenth Amendment."[4]

First Trimester

During the first trimester of pregnancy, the decision to undergo an abortion procedure is between the woman and her physician. A state may require that abortions be performed by a licensed physician pursuant to law; however, a woman's right to an abortion is not unqualified because the decision to perform the procedure must be left to the medical judgment of her attending physician. "For the stage prior to approximately the end of the first trimester, the abortion decision and its effectuation must be left to the medical judgment of the pregnant woman's attending physician."[5]

Second Trimester

In *Roe v. Wade*, the Supreme Court stated, "[f]or the stage subsequent to approximately the end of the first trimester, the State, in promoting its interest in the health of the mother, may, if it chooses, regulate the abortion procedure in ways that are reasonably related to maternal health."[6] Thus, during approximately the fourth to sixth months of pregnancy, the state may regulate the medical conditions under which the procedure is performed. The constitutional test of any legislation concerning abortion during this period would be its relevance to the objective of protecting maternal health.

Third Trimester

The Supreme Court reasoned that by the time the final stage of pregnancy has been reached, the state has acquired a compelling interest in the product of conception, which would override the woman's right to privacy and justify stringent regulation even to the extent of prohibiting abortions. In the *Roe* case, the Supreme Court formulated its ruling as to the last trimester in the following words: "For the stage subsequent to viability, the State in promoting its interest in the potentiality of human life, may, if it chooses, regulate, and even proscribe, abortion except where it is necessary, in appropriate medical judgment for the preservation of the life or health of the mother."[7]

Thus, during the final stage of pregnancy, a state may prohibit all abortions except those deemed necessary to protect maternal life or health. The state's legislative powers over the performance of abortions increase as the pregnancy progresses toward term.

Abortion Review Committee Too Restrictive

1973: The Supreme Court went on to delineate what regulatory measures a state lawfully may enact during the three stages of pregnancy. In the companion decision, *Doe v. Bolton*,[8] where the Court considered a constitutional attack on the Georgia abortion statute, further restrictions were placed on state regulation of the procedure. The provisions of the Georgia statute establishing residency requirements for women seeking abortions and requiring that the procedure be performed in a hospital accredited by The Joint Commission were declared constitutionally invalid. In considering legislative provisions establishing medical staff approval as a prerequisite to the abortion procedure, the Court decided that "interposition of the hospital abortion committee is unduly restrictive of the patient's rights and needs that . . . have already been medically delineated and substantiated by her personal physician. To ask more serves neither the hospital nor the State."[9]

The Court was unable to find any constitutionally justifiable rationale for a statutory requirement of advance approval by the abortion committee of the hospital's medical staff. Insofar as statutory consultation requirements are concerned, the Court reasoned that the acquiescence of two copractitioners has no rational connection with a patient's needs and, further, unduly infringes on the physician's right to practice.

Thus, by using a test related to patient needs, the Court, in *Doe v. Bolton*, struck down four preabortion procedural requirements commonly imposed by state statutes: (1) residency, (2) performance of the abortion in a hospital accredited by The Joint Commission, (3) approval by an appropriate committee of the medical staff, and (4) consultations.

Funding

Some states have placed an indirect restriction on abortion through the elimination of funding. Under the Hyde Amendment, the U.S. Congress, through appropriations legislation, has limited the types of medically necessary abortions for which federal funds may be spent under the Medicaid program. Although the Hyde Amendment does not prohibit states from funding nontherapeutic abortions, this action by the federal government opened the door to state statutory provisions limiting the funding of abortions.

Not Required for Elective Abortions

1977: In *Beal v. Doe*,[10] the Pennsylvania Medicaid plan was challenged based on denial of financial assistance for nontherapeutic abortions. The Supreme Court held that Title XIX of the Social Security Act (the Medicaid program) does not require the funding of nontherapeutic abortions as a condition of state participation in the program.[11] The state has a strong interest in encouraging normal childbirth, and nothing in Title XIX suggests that it is unreasonable for the state to further that interest. The Court ruled that it is not inconsistent with the Medicaid portion of the Social Security Act to refuse to fund unnecessary (although perhaps desirable) medical services.

1977: In *Maher v. Roe*,[12] the Supreme Court considered the Connecticut statute that denied Medicaid benefits for first-trimester abortions that were not medically necessary. The Court rejected the argument that the state's subsidy of medical expenses incident to pregnancy and childbirth created an obligation on the part of the state to subsidize the expenses incident to

nontherapeutic abortions. The Supreme Court voted six to three that the states may refuse to spend public funds to provide nontherapeutic abortions for women.

Not Required for Therapeutic Abortions

1980: The Supreme Court, in *Harris v. McRae*,[13] upheld five to four the Hyde Amendment, which restricts the use of federal funds for Medicaid abortions. Under this case, the different states are not compelled to fund Medicaid recipients' medically necessary abortions for which federal reimbursement is unavailable, but may choose to do so. Justice Marshall, dissenting, stated that the Court's decision marked a retreat from *Roe v. Wade* and represented a cruel blow to the most powerless members of our society.

Funding Bans Unconstitutional in California

The California Supreme Court held that funding bans were unconstitutional; the court asked rhetorically:

> If the state cannot directly prohibit a woman's right to obtain an abortion, may the state by discriminatory financing indirectly nullify that constitutional right? Can the state tell an indigent person that the state will provide him with welfare benefits only upon the condition that he join a designated political party or subscribe to a particular newspaper that is favored by the government? Can the state tell a poor woman that it will pay for her needed medical care but only if she gives up her constitutional right to choose whether or not to have a child?[14]

Funding Discrimination Prohibited in Arizona

2002: The Arizona Supreme Court, in *Simat Corp. v. Arizona Health Care Cost Containment Sys.*,[15] found that the state's constitution does not permit the state and the Arizona Health Care Cost Containment System (AHCCCS) to refuse to fund medically necessary abortion procedures for pregnant women suffering from serious illness while funding such procedures for victims of rape or incest or when the abortion was necessary to save the woman's life (A.R.S. § 35-196.02. AHCCCS). After the state has chosen to fund abortions for one group of indigent, pregnant women for whom abortions are medically necessary to save their lives, the state may not deny the same option to another group of women for whom the procedure is also medically necessary to save their health. An example is cancer, for which chemotherapy or radiation therapy ordinarily cannot be provided if the patient is pregnant, making an abortion necessary before proceeding with the recognized medical treatment. Other therapy regimens that must at times be suspended during pregnancy include those for heart disease, diabetes, kidney disease, liver disease, chronic renal failure, inflammatory bowel disease, and lupus. In many of the women suffering from these diseases, suspension of recognized therapy during pregnancy will have serious and permanent adverse effects on their health and decrease their life span. In such a situation, the state is not simply influencing a woman's choice but is actually conferring the privilege of treatment on one class and withholding it from another.

A woman's right to choose preservation and protection of her health and, therefore, in many cases, her life is at least as compelling as the state's interest in promoting childbirth. The court's protection of the fetus and promotion of childbirth cannot be considered so compelling as to outweigh a woman's fundamental right to choose and the state's obligation to be evenhanded in the design and application of its healthcare policies. The majority of states that have examined similar Medicaid funding restrictions have determined that their state statutes or constitutions offer broader protection of individual rights than does the U.S. Constitution, and they have found that medically necessary abortions should be funded if the state also funds medically necessary expenses related to childbirth. The case was remanded to the trial court for further proceedings consistent with this opinion.

States May Protect Viable Fetus

1979: The Supreme Court, in *Colautti v. Franklin*,[16] voted six to three that the states may seek to protect a fetus that a physician has determined could survive outside the womb. Determination of whether a particular fetus is viable is, and must be, a matter for judgment of the responsible attending physician. State abortion regulations that impinge on this determination, if they are to be constitutional, must allow the attending physician the room that he or she needs to make the best medical judgment.

Abortions After 20 Weeks Prohibited

Governor Nikki Haley signed bill A183, R196, H3114 into law, prohibiting abortions 20 or more weeks post fertilization, thus amending the code of laws of South Carolina by adding Article 5 to Chapter 41, Title 44,

enacting the "South Carolina Pain-Capable Unborn Child Protection Act." The South Carolina bill has no provisions for rape or incest. South Carolina is the 13th state to enforce such a ban, along with Alabama, Arkansas, Indiana, Kansas, Louisiana, Mississippi, Nebraska, North Dakota, Oklahoma, Texas, West Virginia, and Wisconsin. The Act provides in part:

> Section 44-41-440. Except in the case of a medical emergency or fetal anomaly, no abortion must be performed or induced or be attempted to be performed or induced unless the physician performing or inducing it has first made a determination of the probable post-fertilization age of the unborn child or relied upon such a determination made by another physician. In making such a determination, the physician shall make such inquiries of the woman and perform or cause to be performed such medical examinations and tests as a reasonably prudent physician, knowledgeable about the case and the medical conditions involved, would consider necessary to perform in making an accurate diagnosis with respect to post-fertilization age.
>
> Section 44-41-450. (A) No person shall perform or induce or attempt to perform or induce an abortion upon a woman when it has been determined, by the physician performing or inducing or attempting to perform or induce the abortion or by another physician upon whose determination that physician relies, that the probable post-fertilization age of the woman's unborn child is twenty or more weeks, except in the case of fetal anomaly, or in reasonable medical judgment, she has a condition which so complicates her medical condition as to necessitate the abortion of her pregnancy to avert her death or to avert serious risk of substantial and irreversible physical impairment of a major bodily function, not including psychological or emotional conditions. No such greater risk must be considered to exist if it is based on a claim or diagnosis that the woman will engage in conduct which she intends to result in her death or in substantial and irreversible physical impairment of a major bodily function.[17]

Abortions in South Carolina may be performed after 20 weeks only if the mother's life is in jeopardy. There are no exceptions for rape or incest. Physicians who perform illegal abortions can face a $10,000 fine and up to 3 years in prison.

Parental Consent

A majority of states require parental consent for minors seeking an abortion. Notification of one parent is generally required 24 to 48 hours prior to the abortion. In 1976, the Supreme Court ruled in *Danforth v. Planned Parenthood*[18] that a Missouri statute requiring all women under age 18 to obtain written consent of a parent or person in loco parentis prior to an abortion is unconstitutional. The Court, however, failed to provide any definitive guidelines as to when and how parental consent may be required if the minor is too immature to fully comprehend the nature of the procedure. Later, in a 1979 case, the Supreme Court, in *Bellotti v. Baird*,[19] ruled eight to one that a Massachusetts statute requiring parental consent before an abortion could be performed on an unmarried woman under age 18 was unconstitutional. Justice Stevens, joined by Justices Brennan, Marshall, and Blackmun, concluded that the Massachusetts statute was unconstitutional because under that statute, as written and construed by the Massachusetts Supreme Judicial Court, no minor, no matter how mature and capable of informed decision making, could receive an abortion without the consent of either both parents or a superior court judge, thus making the minor's abortion subject in every instance to an absolute third-party veto. Supreme Court rulings that followed these two cases are presented here.

Notifying Parent for Immature Minor Constitutional

The Supreme Court, in *H. L. v. Matheson*,[20] by a six to three vote, upheld a Utah statute that required a physician to "notify, if possible" the parents or guardian of a minor on whom an abortion was to be performed. In this case, the physician advised the patient that an abortion would be in her best medical interest but, because of the statute, refused to perform the abortion without first notifying her parents. The Supreme Court ruled that although a state may not constitutionally legislate a blanket, unreviewable power of parents to veto their daughter's abortion, a statute setting out a mere requirement of parental notice, when possible, does not violate the constitutional rights of an immature, dependent minor.

Consent Not Required for Emancipated Minor

An Alabama trial court in *In re Anonymous*[21] was found to have abused its discretion when it refused a minor's request for waiver of parental consent to obtain an abortion. The record indicated that the minor was within 1 month of her 18th birthday, lived by herself most of the time, and was employed full time.

Parental Notification Not Required

The issue in *Planned Parenthood v. Owens*[22] was whether the Colorado Parental Notification Act (Colorado Revised Statute §§ 12-37.5-101, et seq. [1998]), which requires a physician to notify the parents of a minor prior to performing an abortion upon her, violates the minor's rights protected by the U.S. Constitution. The act, a citizen-initiated measure, was approved at Colorado's general election. The act generally prohibits physicians from performing an abortion on an unemancipated minor until at least 48 hours after written notice has been delivered to the minor's parent, guardian, or foster parent.

The U.S. District Court decided that the act violated the rights of minor women protected by the Fourteenth Amendment. The Supreme Court, for more than a quarter of a century, has required that any abortion regulation except from its reach an abortion medically necessary for the preservation of the mother's health. The act fails to provide such a health exception.

Minor's Decision to Abort Found Sufficient

In a Florida case, the minor in *In re Doe*[23] was determined to be sufficiently mature to decide whether to terminate her pregnancy, thus precluding notification of her pregnancy to a parent or guardian, which placed her less than 1 year from being outside the scope of notification law. The minor was a good student, was employed part time, and had formulated a plan for her future. Although she admitted that her pregnancy was the result of an immature decision, her acknowledgment supported her belief that she had sufficient maturity concerning whether or not to terminate pregnancy.

Justices Send Abortion Case Back to Lower Court

The U.S. Supreme Court, in a unanimous ruling, determined that the U.S. Court of Appeals for the First Circuit erred when it declared unconstitutional a New Hampshire state law requiring that a minor notify her parents before obtaining an abortion. The Court sent the case, *Ayotte v. Planned Parenthood of Northern New England*,[24] back to the appeals court and told it to find a way to include an exception to the law for a medical emergency. Justice Sandra Day O'Connor wrote the majority opinion, her last as an associate justice.

Minor's Decision to Abort Not Sufficient

Proceedings were brought in *In re petition of Doe*,[25] in which the juvenile sought judicial waiver of a statutory requirement that the physician notify her parent or guardian prior to terminating her pregnancy. The juvenile failed to prove by clear and convincing evidence that she was sufficiently mature to warrant waiving the requirement for parental notification of the abortion. A U.S. District Judge in Tallahassee upheld a Florida law requiring abortion providers to notify a minor's parent or legal guardian prior to performing an abortion. The law requires doctors to notify in person or by phone the parents or legal guardians of minors seeking an abortion at least 48 hours in advance of performing the procedure or 72 hours in advance by certified mail if the parents or guardians cannot be reached. The law allows for exceptions in cases of medical emergency, if the minor is married or has children, if a judge determines the minor is mature enough to make her own decision, if the juvenile is a victim of abuse, or if notification is not in the juvenile's best interests. The juvenile in this case failed to demonstrate any knowledge regarding specific immediate or long-term physical, emotional, or psychological risks of having an abortion. Furthermore, there was no evidence that the juvenile had sought advice or emotional support from any adults or that she had considered what she would do if any physical or emotional complications were to arise from the abortion. The juvenile's concerns that her parents would not understand and would be upset about her pregnancy amounted to nothing more than generalized fear of telling her parents and did not establish that notification would not be in her best interests.

Spousal Consent

A provision of the Florida Therapeutic Abortion Act that required a married woman to obtain the husband's consent before abortion was found to be unconstitutional. The state's interest was found not to be sufficiently compelling to limit a woman's right to abortion. The husband's interest in the baby was held to be insufficient to force his wife to face the mental and physical risks of pregnancy and childbirth.[26]

Spousal Consent Requirement Unconstitutional

In *Doe v. Zimmerman*,[27] the court declared unconstitutional the provisions of the Pennsylvania Abortion Control Act, which required that the written consent of the husband of a married woman be secured before performing an abortion. The court found that these provisions impermissibly permitted the husband to withhold his consent either because of his interest in the potential life of the fetus or for capricious reasons.

Father of Fetus Could Not Stop Abortion

The natural father of the fetus in *Doe v. Smith*[28] was found not entitled to an injunction to prevent the mother from submitting to an abortion. Although the father's interest in the fetus was legitimate, it did not outweigh the mother's constitutionally protected right to an abortion, particularly in the light of the evidence that the mother and father had never married. The father had demonstrated substantial instability in his marital and romantic life. The father was able to beget other children and, in fact, did produce other children.

Spousal Consent Undue Burden

The Supreme Court ruled in *Planned Parenthood v. Casey*,[29] that spousal consent would be an undue burden on the woman. The Supreme Court ruling, as enunciated in *Roe v. Wade*, reaffirmed the following:

- The constitutional right of women to have an abortion before viability of the fetus, as first enunciated in *Roe v. Wade*.
- The state's power to restrict abortions after fetal viability, as long as the law contains exceptions for pregnancies that endanger a woman's life or health.
- The principle that the state has legitimate interests from the outset of the pregnancy in protecting the health of the woman and the life of the fetus.

The Supreme Court rejected the trimester approach in *Roe v. Wade*, which limited the regulations states could issue on abortion depending on the development stage of the fetus. In place of the trimester approach, the Court will evaluate the permissibility of state abortion rules based on whether they unduly burden a woman's ability to obtain an abortion. A rule is an undue burden if its purpose or effect is to place a substantial obstacle in the path of a woman seeking an abortion before the fetus attains viability. The Supreme Court ruled that it is not an undue burden to require the following:

- A woman be informed of the nature of the abortion procedure and the risks involved.
- A woman be offered information on the fetus and on the alternatives to abortion.
- A woman give her informed consent before the abortion procedure.

- Parental consent be given for a minor seeking an abortion, providing for a judicial bypass option if the minor does not wish to or cannot obtain parental consent.
- A 24-hour waiting period before any abortion can be performed.

Abortion Counseling

Abortion counseling continues to be an emotionally charged debate that involves a woman's right to choose and the right to life. The arguments are both compelling and the division between opposing viewpoints appear to have no end. Here, case law, right or wrong, continues to develop and expand as new legislation is enacted by the various states and the courts issue new rulings.

Physician Counseling of Patient Upheld

The Supreme Court, in *City of Akron v. Akron Center for Reproductive Health*,[30] voted six to three that the different states cannot (1) mandate what information physicians give abortion patients or (2) require that abortions for women more than 3 months' pregnant be performed in a hospital.

With respect to a requirement that the attending physician must inform the woman of specified information concerning her proposed abortion, it is unreasonable for a state to insist that only a physician is competent to provide the information and counseling relative to informed consent. A state may not adopt regulations to influence a woman's informed choice between abortion and childbirth. With regard to a second-trimester hospital requirement, this could significantly limit a woman's ability to obtain an abortion. This is especially true in view of the evidence that a second-trimester abortion may cost more than twice as much in a hospital as in a clinic.

Prohibition of Abortion Counseling Not Unconstitutional

Federal regulations that prohibit abortion counseling and referral by family planning clinics that receive funds under Title X of the Public Health Service Act were found not to violate the constitutional rights of pregnant women or Title X grantees in a five to four decision by the Supreme Court in *Rust v. Sullivan*.[31] Proponents of abortion counseling argued (1) that the regulations impermissibly burden a woman's privacy right to abortion, and (2) that by prohibiting the delivery of abortion information, even as to where such information could be obtained, the regulations

deny a woman her constitutionally protected right to choose under the First Amendment. The question arises: How can a woman make an informed choice between two options when she cannot obtain information about one of them? In *Sullivan*, however, the Supreme Court found that there was no violation of a woman's or provider's First Amendment rights to freedom of speech. The plaintiff had argued that the government may not condition receipt of a benefit on the relinquishment of constitutional rights. The Court extended the doctrine that government need not subsidize the exercise of the fundamental rights to free speech.

Abortion Waiting Period Not Burdensome

The Supreme Court, in *Planned Parenthood of Southeastern Pennsylvania v. Casey*,[32] determined that in asserting an interest in protecting fetal life, a state may place some restrictions on previability abortions, as long as those restrictions do not impose an "undue burden" on the woman's right to an abortion. The Court determined that the 24-hour waiting period, the informed consent requirement, and the medical emergency definitions did not unduly burden the right to an abortion and were therefore constitutional.

The Utah Abortion Act Revision, Senate Bill 60, provides for informed consent by requiring that certain information be given to the pregnant woman at least 24 hours prior to the performance of an abortion. The law allows for exceptions to this requirement in the event of a medical emergency.

A 106-page complaint was filed challenging the constitutionality of the new Utah law.[33] It was determined that the 24-hour waiting period did not impose an undue burden on the right to an abortion. On appeal, a U.S. District Court held that the Utah abortion statute's 24-hour waiting period and informed consent requirements do not render the statute unconstitutionally vague. Because Senate Bill 60 is less restrictive than the Pennsylvania abortion statute, the plaintiffs may not prevail unless they can show material differences between the circumstances of Utah and Pennsylvania.

It would be extremely difficult in light of the Casey decision to bring a good faith facial challenge to the constitutionality of Utah's 24-hour waiting period and informed consent requirements. In an emergency situation, there is no requirement of informed consent or a 24-hour waiting period. The plaintiffs' contention that Senate Bill 60, when read together with provisions from Utah's 1991 abortion law, does not clearly provide that a woman can obtain an abortion in a medical emergency, is without merit.

> The abortion issue is obviously one that invokes strong feelings on both sides. Individuals are free to urge support for their cause through debate, advocacy, and participation in the political process. The subject also might be addressed in the courts so long as there are valid legal issues in dispute. Where, however, a case presents no legitimate legal arguments, the courthouse is not the proper forum. Litigation, or the threat of litigation, should not be used as economic blackmail to strengthen one's hand in the political battle. Unfortunately, the court sees little evidence that this case was filed for any other purpose.[34]

> Senate Bill 60, the duly enacted law of the people of Utah, has not been enforced for nearly nine months. That will change today. The court hereby adopts the report and recommmendation of the magistrate judge, lifts the injunction, and dismisses plaintiffs' case in its entirety with prejudice.[35]

Incompetent Persons

An abortion was found to have been proper by a family court in *In re Doe*[36] for a profoundly retarded woman. She became pregnant during her residence in a group home as a result of a sexual attack by an unknown person. The record supported a finding that if the woman had been able to do so, she would have requested the abortion. The court properly chose welfare agencies and the woman's guardian ad litem (a guardian appointed to prosecute or defend a suit on behalf of a party incapacitated by infancy, mental incompetence, etc.) as the surrogate decision makers, rather than the woman's mother. The mother apparently had little contact with her daughter over the years.

Narrowing of Abortion Rights

Webster v. Reproductive Health Services[37] began the U.S. Supreme Court's narrowing of abortion rights by upholding a Missouri statute providing that no public facilities or employees should be used to perform abortions. The court stated the statute did not prevent women from obtaining abortion services from private healthcare providers.

The court also upheld Missouri Revised Statutes section 188.029 requiring physicians to conduct viability tests before performing abortions, when there was reason to believe the fetus had reached at least 20 weeks of gestational age.

Partial-Birth Abortion

1998: The Supreme Court, in *Women's Medical Professional Corp. v. Voinovich*,[38] denied certiorari for the first partial-birth case to reach the federal appellate courts. This case involved an Ohio statute that banned the use of the intact dilation and extraction (D&E) procedure in the performance of any previability or postviability abortion. The Sixth Circuit Court of Appeals held that the statute banning any use of the D&E procedure was unconstitutionally vague. It is likely that a properly drafted statute will eventually be judged constitutionally sound.

Partial-Birth Abortion Ban Unconstitutional

1999: The defendants in *Little Rock Family Planning Services v. Jegley*[39] appealed a district court decision holding Arkansas's Partial-Birth Abortion Ban Act of 1997 unconstitutional. The act prohibited knowingly performing a partial-birth abortion. Arkansas code defines partial-birth abortion as an abortion in which the person performing the abortion partially vaginally delivers a living fetus before taking the life of the fetus and completing the delivery. Under this definition, any physician who knowingly partially vaginally delivers a living fetus and then takes the life of the fetus and completes delivery would violate the act. Because both the D&E procedure and the suction curettage procedure used in second-trimester abortions often include what the Act prohibits, physicians performing those procedures would have violated the Act. The Act provided that, in addition to committing a felony, a physician who knowingly performed a partial-birth abortion would be subject to disciplinary action by the state medical board. The federal district court held the Act unconstitutional because it was unconstitutionally vague, imposed an undue burden on women seeking abortions, and did not adequately protect the health and lives of pregnant women. The circuit court agreed, holding the Act unconstitutional.

2002: The U.S. Supreme Court, in *Stenberg v. Carhart*,[40] struck down a Nebraska ban on partial-birth abortion, finding it an unconstitutional violation of *Roe v. Wade*. The court found these types of bans to be extreme descriptive attempts to outlaw abortion—even early in pregnancy—that jeopardize women's health.

Following *Stenberg v. Carhart*, a Virginia statute that attempted to criminalize partial-birth abortion also was held to be unconstitutional under the Fourteenth Amendment because it lacked an exception to protect a woman's health.[41]

Partial-Birth Abortion Statute Vague

2000: New Jersey's partial-birth abortion statute was void for vagueness, in that it did not define the proscribed conduct with certainty and could be easily construed to ban the safest, most common, and most readily available conventional abortion procedures. The statute also was unconstitutional because it created an undue burden on a woman's right to obtain an abortion, in that its broad language covered many conventional, constitutionally permissible methods of abortion and it failed to contain a health exception.[42]

Partial-Birth Abortion Act: First Federal Restrictions

2003: President George W. Bush, on November 6, signed the first federal restrictions banning late-term partial-birth abortions. The partial-birth abortion, also referred to as the D&E procedure, is a late-term abortion involving partial delivery of the fetus before it is aborted. The ban, referred to as the Partial-Birth Abortion Act of 2003, was passed by both houses of Congress. The ban permits no exceptions when a woman's health is at risk or the fetus has life-threatening disabilities. A U.S. District Court in Nebraska issued a restraining order on the ban.

Partial-Birth Abortion Act: Supreme Court Asked to Review

On September 26, 2005, the Bush administration asked the Supreme Court to review an appellate court's decision holding the Partial-Birth Abortion Act of 2003 unconstitutional.

Partial-Birth Abortion Ban Unconstitutional

The Partial-Birth Abortion Act, 18 U.S.C. Section 1531, in *National Abortion Fed'n v. Gonzages*,[43] was found to be unconstitutional because it lacked any exception to preserve the health of the mother, where such exception was constitutionally required. Also, the act was unconstitutional because it imposed an undue burden on a woman's right to choose previability abortion and was constitutionally vague.

Texas Standards for Physicians and Abortion Facilities

The United States Supreme Court, in *Whole Woman's Health v. Hellerstedt*, 136 S.Ct. 2292 (2016), in a five-to-three decision struck down Texas abortion restrictions that the high Court determined would have overly restricted in the delivery of abortion services and placed an undue burden for women seeking an abortion. The 2013 Texas law that the court struck down would have required all abortions to take place in ambulatory surgical centers, or mini-hospitals, instead of regular clinics. The two provisions of the Texas law HB 2 required:

> [a] physician performing or inducing an abortion . . . must, on the date the abortion is performed or induced, have active admitting privileges at a hospital that . . . is located not farther than 30 miles from the location at which the abortion is performed or induced.[44]
>
> . . . the minimum standards for an abortion facility must be equivalent to the minimum standards adopted under [the Texas Health and Safety Code section] for ambulatory surgical centers.[45]

The ruling is believed by some to be the most restrictive since *Roe v. Wade* and *Planned Parenthood of Southeastern Pa. v. Casey* in 1992.

The Texas House of Representatives later passed Senate Bill HB No. 644, prohibiting partial-birth abortions and regulates the disposition of the bodies of abortion victims. Section 171.102 of the Act reads: "A Person may not intentionally perform a dismemberment abortion unless the dismemberment abortion is necessary in a medical emergency." Texas Governor Greg Abbott later signed the bill into law, parts of which took effect in August of 2017. The Center for Reproductive Rights has pledged to fight the new law.

Physicians and Clinics Under Pressure

Physicians and abortion clinics often have been the targets of antiabortion demonstrations, as noted in *Beverly v. Choices Women's Medical Center*,[46] where a physician's picture was published in an abortion calendar without her consent. The physician brought a civil rights action against the for-profit medical center for publication of her picture. The calendar was disseminated to the public by the center. The center derived approximately 50% of its income from abortions. The plaintiff was awarded $50,000 in compensatory damages and $25,000 in punitive damages. The physician testified that the publication of her picture caused her to suffer physical and mental injury. She also testified as to the effect of the publication on her lifestyle and career decisions.

Antiabortion Demonstrations

The San Diego police became aware that Operation Rescue planned to stage several antiabortion demonstrations in the city.[47] The purpose of the demonstrations was to disrupt operations at the target clinics and ultimately to cause the clinic to cease operations. In each of the three demonstrations at issue, protesters converged on a medical building, blocking entrances, filling stairwells and corridors, and preventing employees and patients from entering.

For each arrest, the officers warned the demonstrators that they would be subjected to pain-compliance measures if they did not move, that such measures would hurt, and that they could reduce the pain by standing up, eliminating the tension on their wrists and arms. The officers then forcibly moved the arrestees by tightening Orcutt police nunchakus (two sticks of wood connected at one end by a cord used to grip a demonstrator's wrist) around their wrists until they stood up and walked. All arrestees complained of varying degrees of injury to their hands and arms. Several subsequently filed suit, claiming that the police violated the Fourth Amendment by using excessive force in executing the arrests. The judge allowed the case to proceed to the jury to determine whether any particular use of force was unconstitutional. After viewing a videotape of the arrests, the jury concluded that none involved excessive force and returned a verdict for the city. An appeal was taken.

The U.S. Court of Appeals for the Ninth Circuit held that the police did not use excessive force. The videotape created an extensive evidentiary record: "Thanks to videotaped records of the actual events, plus the testimony of witnesses on both sides, the jury had more than a sufficient amount of evidence presented to them from which they could formulate their verdicts. The extensive use of video scenes of exactly what took place removed much argument and interpretation of the facts themselves."[48] The city clearly had a legitimate interest in quickly dispersing and removing the lawbreakers with the least risk of injury to police and others. The arrestees were part of a group of more than 100 protesters operating in an organized and concerted effort to invade private property, obstruct business, and hinder law enforcement.

Obstructing Access to Abortion Clinics

Abortion clinics and others sought enforcement of an injunction precluding antiabortion groups from blockading or obstructing access to abortion clinics. The order required the defendants to appear before the court to show cause as to why they should not be cited for contempt for violating and inducing others to violate an injunction order. The defendants, Tucci, Terry, and Mahoney, spoke at a rally. Tucci was introduced as a leader of Operation Rescue National and spoke about how the group had closed down clinics successfully. He also solicited funds for his organization. Terry said that they needed contributions to keep their work going. The defendants appeared before the court at two hearings to show cause regarding why they should not be cited in contempt for violating the court's injunction.[49] The questions posed are: (1) Can antiabortion leaders and groups be fined for violating an injunction barring them from blockading or obstructing access to abortion clinics? and (2) Can antiabortion groups be ordered to pay damages to compensate an abortion clinic for property damage resulting from an abortion clinic blockage that violated an injunction?

The U.S. District Court for the District of Columbia held that leaders and groups would be fined for violating the injunction. In addition, antiabortion groups are liable to abortion clinics for property damages resulting from blockades. The defendants violated provisions of the injunction "barring all defendants and those acting in concert with them 'from inducing, encouraging, directing, aiding, or abetting others' to trespass on, blockade, or obstruct access to or egress from facilities at which abortions are performed and other medical services are rendered."[50] In blockading the clinics, the defendants violated District of Columbia trespass law, which states, "Any person who, without lawful authority, shall enter, or attempt to enter, any public or private dwelling . . . against the will of the lawful occupant or of the person lawfully in charge thereof . . . shall be guilty of a misdemeanor" (D.C. Code § 22-3102).

The participants in the blockades were under court order not to trespass on the clinics and were ordered by clinic personnel and the police at the time of the blockades to leave the property. Their presence on the property clearly constituted trespass.

Physicians Brought Separate Actions Against Demonstrators

Two physicians in *Murray v. Lawson*[51] brought separate actions to obtain injunctions against antiabortion protesters who had been picketing their residences. In the first action, the defendant discovered the personal address of Dr. Murray and visited the house, where the physician's 14-year-old son answered the door. The defendant told the son to tell his father to stop performing abortions. A month later picketers walked on the sidewalk in front of Murray's home, carrying posters stating, among other things, that he scars and kills women and their fetuses. Murray filed suit seeking damages and injunctive relief. After the hearing, the medical center where Murray performed abortions was burned to the ground. After a bomb threat, the defendant and another picketer protested in front of the Murray house.

The chancery division ordered a permanent injunction prohibiting the defendant and all others from picketing within 300 feet of the Murray home. The defendants appealed, claiming that the injunction impinged upon their freedom of speech. The appellate division affirmed, finding that the injunction did not violate freedom of speech. On appeal, the New Jersey Supreme Court heard the case.

The New Jersey Supreme Court held residential privacy represents a sufficient public policy interest to justify injunctive restrictions. The court further held that because a state has a significant interest in protecting the residential privacy of its citizens, it is justified in imposing injunctive relief.

Law Barring Protests Near Clinics Struck Down

2014: The Supreme Court in *McCullen v. Coakley*[52] unanimously struck down a Massachusetts law barring protests near abortion clinics. The law, enacted in 2007, created 35-foot buffer zones around entrances to abortion clinics. State officials said the law was a response to a history of harassment and violence at abortion clinics. The court ruled that buffer zones around abortion clinics in Massachusetts violated the First Amendment. The court left open the possibility that states may use other methods to address harassment and violence at clinics.[53]

Continuing Controversy

Right-to-life advocates argue that life comes from God and that no one has a right to deny the right to life. Pro-choice advocates argue that a woman has a right to choose preservation and protection of her health and, therefore, in many cases, her life is at least as compelling as the state's interest in promoting childbirth. The protection of a fetus and promotion of childbirth cannot be considered so compelling as to outweigh a woman's fundamental right to choose and the state's obligation to be evenhanded in the design and application of its healthcare policies.

Hundreds of thousands of men and women from more than 60 countries marched in Washington, DC, on April 25, 2004, supporting women's reproductive rights. The rally included slogans such as "Pro Choice–Pro Child," "It's Your Choice . . . Not Theirs," "My Family My Choice," "My Body My Choice," "Justice for All," "Who Decides?," and "Keep Abortion Legal."

Pro-choice advocates argue that women have the right to choose. They also point out the fact that abortions are safer to perform when they are legal. In 1972, for example, the year before *Roe v. Wade* was upheld, the number of deaths from abortions in the United States is estimated to have reached the thousands; by 1985, the figure was six.[54] In addition, pro-choice advocates argue that women who have a right to an abortion when pregnancy threatens the life of the mother also have the right to an abortion when pregnancy is the result of incest or rape. There will most likely be a continuing stream of court decisions, as well as political and legislative battles, well into the 21st century. Given the emotional, religious, and ethical concerns, as well as those of women's rights groups, it is certain that the controversies and ethical dilemmas surrounding abortion will continue for many years to come.

⦿ PA. ABORTION PROVIDER CONVICTED OF MURDER

The case, which has unfolded since early March inside Courtroom 304 here, has garnered national attention and inflamed passions on all sides of the abortion divide.

"Some abortionists may have cleaner sheets than Gosnell, and better sterilized equipment and better trained accomplices, but what they do—What Gosnell did—kill babies and hurt women is the same," Rep. Christopher H. Smith (R-NJ) said in a statement.

Meanwhile, abortion-rights groups insisted that Gosnell's crimes are an anomaly and that the abysmal conditions inside his clinic persisted only because numerous regulators ignored red flags for years.

—Brady Dennis, *The Washington Post*, May 14, 2013

State Abortion Statutes

As noted in the previously mentioned cases, the effect of the Supreme Court's 1973 decisions in *Roe* and *Doe* was to invalidate all or part of almost every state abortion statute then in force. The responses of state legislatures to these decisions have been varied, but it is clear that many state laws had been enacted to restrict the performance of abortions as much as possible. Although *Planned Parenthood v. Casey* was expected to clear up some issues, it is evident that the states have been given more power to regulate the performance of abortions. In Oregon for example, Governor Kate Brown, in August 2017, joining California and New York, signed into law the *Reproductive Health Equity Act HB3391*. The health bill, approved by the state legislature in July 2017, requires Oregon insurance companies to cover reproductive procedures. The Oregon bill requires insurers to cover abortions at no cost to the patient. The statute also includes contraception, vasectomies, STD screenings, and postnatal care. All patients are covered, regardless of gender, gender identity, or immigration status. This includes abortions for immigrants who are otherwise ineligible under the state's Medicaid program.

> SECTION 7. (1) An individual may not, on the basis of actual or perceived race, color, national origin, sex, sexual orientation, gender identity, age or disability, be excluded from participation in, be denied the benefits of or otherwise be subjected to discrimination by any health benefit plan issued or delivered in this state, in the receipt of medical assistance as defined in ORS 414.025 or in the coverage of or payment for the services, drugs, devices, products and procedures described in section 2 of this 2017 Act.[55]

Abortion and Conflicting Beliefs

The difficulty in the abortion dilemma arises because beliefs, religion, culture, education, and life experiences differ from person to person. Good people cannot be considered bad people merely because their beliefs differ from those of another.

The *morality of abortion* is not a legal or constitutional issue; it is a matter of philosophy, ethics, and theology. It is a subject where reasonable people can, and do, adhere to vastly divergent convictions and ethical principles. Our obligation is to define the the rights and liberty of all, not to mandate our own moral code.[56]

The landscape of women's rights, differing religious beliefs, ethics, and values of the human race will forever be a dark side in human history, causing the natural phenomena of creation to be forever debated and, as to the *sanctity of life*, it will forever be written as a black mark in the annals of human history. As described in Wikipedia, "In religion and ethics, inviolability or sanctity of life is a principle of implied protection regarding aspects of sentient life which are said to be holy, sacred, or otherwise of such value that they are not to be violated." In the final analysis, the prevention of conception and the abortion of a fetus/unborn child, depending on your beliefs, will continue to be a contentious topic.

▶ STERILIZATION

Sterilization is a surgical technique that is used to prevent a male or female from being able to produce offspring. Sterilization most often is accomplished by either a vasectomy for men or a tubal ligation for women. A vasectomy is a surgical procedure in which the vas deferens is severed and tied to prevent the flow of seminal fluid into the urinary canal. A tubal ligation is a surgical procedure in which the fallopian tubes are cut and tied, preventing passage of the ovum from the ovary to the uterus. Sterilizations are often chosen for such reasons as birth control, economic necessity to avoid the additional expense of raising a child, therapeutic purposes to prevent harm to a woman's health (e.g., to remove a diseased reproductive organ), and genetic reasons to prevent the birth of a defective child.

Elective Sterilization

Voluntary, or elective sterilizations of competent individuals present few legal problems, as long as proper consent has been obtained from the patient and the procedure is performed properly. Civil liability for performing a sterilization of convenience may be imposed if the procedure is performed in a negligent manner, as was the case in *McLaughlin v. Cooke*,[57] where the physician was found negligent for mistakenly cutting a blood vessel in the patient's scrotum while he was performing a vasectomy. Excessive bleeding at the site of the incision was found to have occurred because of the physician's negligent postsurgical care. On appeal, the jury's finding of negligence was supported by testimony that the physician's failure to intervene sooner and to remove a hematoma had been the proximate cause of tissue necrosis.

Negligent Sterilization

The parents in *Goforth v. Porter Medical Associates, Inc.*[58] brought a medical malpractice action for expenses resulting from the negligence of the physician in performing a sterilization. The physician assured the plaintiff that she was sterile. The patient subsequently became pregnant and delivered a child. The plaintiff argued that as a result of the physician's negligence, she incurred $2,000 in medical bills and will incur $200,000 for the future care of the child. The district court dismissed the case. On appeal, the Oklahoma Supreme Court held that the parents could not recover the expenses of raising a healthy child; however, they could maintain an action for expenses resulting from the negligent performance of sterilization and the unplanned pregnancy.

In a 2003 case, Chaffee performed a partial salpingectomy on Seslar. The purpose of the procedure was to sterilize Seslar, who had already borne four children, so that she could not become pregnant again. After undergoing the surgery, however, Seslar conceived and delivered a healthy baby. Seslar sued Chaffee. The trial court permitted Seslar to seek damages including the expenses of raising and educating her child born following the unsuccessful sterilization procedure, and Chaffee appealed. The court of appeals held that damages for the alleged negligent sterilization procedure could not include the costs of raising a normal healthy child. Although raising an unplanned child is costly, all human life is presumptively invaluable. A child, regardless of the circumstances of birth, does not constitute harm to the parents so as to permit recovery for the costs associated with raising and educating the child. As with a majority of jurisdictions, the court held that the value of a child's life to the parents outweighs the associated pecuniary burdens as a matter of law. Recoverable damages may include pregnancy and childbearing expenses but not the ordinary costs of raising and educating a normal, healthy child conceived after an allegedly negligent sterilization procedure.[59]

Therapeutic Sterilization

If the life or health of a woman may be jeopardized by pregnancy, terminating her ability to conceive or terminating her husband's ability to impregnate may avoid the danger. Such a procedure is referred to as a therapeutic sterilization—one performed to preserve life or health. The medical necessity for sterilization renders the procedure therapeutic. Sometimes, a diseased reproductive organ has to be removed to preserve the life or health of the individual. The operation results in sterility, although this is not the primary reason for the procedure. Such an operation technically should not be classified as a sterilization because it is incidental to the medical purpose.

Involuntary: Eugenic Sterilization

The term *eugenic sterilization* refers to the involuntary sterilization of certain categories of persons described in statutes without the need for consent by, or on behalf of, those subject to the procedure. Persons classified as mentally deficient, feeble minded, and, in some instances, epileptic are included within the scope of the statutes. Several states also have included certain sexual deviates and persons classified as habitual criminals. Such statutes ordinarily are said to be designed to prevent the transmission of hereditary defects to succeeding generations, but several statutes also have recognized the purpose of preventing procreation by individuals who would not be able to care for their offspring.

Although there have been many judicial decisions to the contrary, the U.S. Supreme Court, in *Buck v. Bell*,[60] specifically upheld the validity of such eugenic sterilization statutes provided that certain procedural safeguards are observed. The U.S. Supreme Court determined:

> It is better for all the world, if instead of waiting to execute degenerate offspring for crime, or to let them starve for their imbecility, society can prevent those who are manifestly unfit from continuing their kind. The principle that sustains compulsory vaccination is broad enough to cover cutting the Fallopian tubes. *Jacobson v. Massachusetts*, 197 U.S. 11. Three generations of imbeciles are enough.[61]

Several states have laws authorizing eugenic sterilization. The decision in *Wade v. Bethesda Hospital*[62] strongly suggests that in the absence of statutory authority, a state cannot order sterilization for eugenic purposes. At the minimum, eugenic sterilization statutes provide: a grant of authority to public officials supervising state institutions for the mentally ill or prisons and to certain public health officials to conduct sterilizations; a requirement of personal notice to the person subject to sterilization and, if that person is unable to comprehend what is involved, notice to the person's legal representative, guardian, or nearest relative; a hearing by the board designated in the particular statute to determine the propriety of the prospective sterilization (at the hearing, evidence may be presented, and the patient must be present or represented by counsel or the nearest relative or guardian); and an opportunity to appeal the board's ruling to a court.

The procedural safeguards of notice, hearing, and the right to appeal must be present in sterilization statutes to fulfill the minimum constitutional requirements of due process. An Arkansas statute was found to be unconstitutional because it did not provide for notice to the incompetent patient and opportunity to be heard or for the patient's entitlement to legal counsel.[63]

Current statutes do not authorize castration and often specifically prohibit it. Most eugenic sterilization statutes provide for vasectomy or salpingectomy. This prohibition against castration, along with provisions granting immunity only to persons performing or assisting in a sterilization that conforms to the law, is an added safeguard for persons subject to sterilization. Civil or criminal liability for assault and battery may be imposed on one who castrates or sterilizes another without following the procedure required by law.

Sterilization for Convenience

Like abortion, voluntary sterilization is the subject of many debates concerning its moral and ethical propriety. Some healthcare institutions have adopted policies restricting the performance of such operations at their facilities. The U.S. Court of Appeals for the First Circuit ruled, in *Hathaway v. Worcester City Hospital*,[64] that a governmental hospital may not impose greater restrictions on sterilization procedures than on other procedures that are medically indistinguishable from sterilization with regard to the risk to the patient or the demand on staff and facilities. The court relied on the Supreme Court decisions in *Roe v. Wade*[65] and *Doe v. Bolton*,[66] which accorded considerable recognition to the patient's right to privacy in the context of obtaining medical services. The extent to which hospitals may prohibit or substantially limit sterilization procedures is not clear, but it appears likely that hospitals will be allowed considerable discretion in this matter.

Kansas enacted legislation declaring that hospitals are not required to permit the performance of sterilization procedures and physicians and hospital personnel may not be required to participate in such procedures or be discriminated against for refusal to participate. Such legislation, which more frequently is enacted in relation to abortion procedures, often is referred to by the term *conscience clause* and was not found objectionable in Supreme Court decisions striking down most state abortion laws.

Wrongful Birth, Life, and Conception

There is substantial legal debate regarding the impact of an improperly performed sterilization. Suits have been brought on such theories as wrongful birth, wrongful life, and wrongful conception. Wrongful life suits are generally unsuccessful, primarily because of the court's unwillingness, for public policy reasons, to permit financial recovery for the "injury" of being born into the world.

However, some success has been achieved in litigation by the patient (and his or her spouse) who allegedly was sterilized and subsequently proved fertile. Damages have been awarded for the cost of the unsuccessful procedure; pain and suffering as a result of the pregnancy; the medical expense of the pregnancy; and the loss of comfort, companionship services, and consortium of the spouse. Again, as a matter of public policy, the courts have indicated that the joys and benefits of having the child outweigh the costs incurred in raising a child.

There have been many cases in recent years involving actions for wrongful birth, wrongful life, and wrongful conception. Such litigation originated with the California case in which a court found that a genetic testing laboratory can be held liable for damages from incorrectly reporting genetic tests, leading to the birth of a child with defects.[67] Injury caused by birth had not been previously actionable by law. The court of appeals held that medical laboratories engaged in genetic testing owe a duty to the parents and their fetus to use ordinary care in administering available tests for the purpose of providing information concerning potential genetic defects of the fetus. Damages in this case were awarded based on the child's shortened life span.

Wrongful Birth

In a wrongful birth action, the plaintiffs claim that but for a breach of duty by the defendant(s) (e.g., improper sterilization), the child would not have been born. A wrongful birth claim can be brought by the parent(s) of a child born with genetic defects against a physician who or a laboratory that negligently fails to inform them, in a timely fashion, of an increased possibility that the mother will give birth to such a child, therefore precluding an informed decision whether to have the child.

Recovery for damages was permitted for wrongful birth but not wrongful life in *Smith v. Cote*.[68] The physician in this case was negligent because he failed to test in a timely fashion for the mother's exposure to rubella and to advise her of the potential for birth defects. Therefore, she was entitled to maintain a cause of action for wrongful birth. However, for compelling reasons of public policy, the mother would not be permitted to assert on the child's behalf a claim for damages based on wrongful life.

In *Proffitt v. Bartolo*,[69] the parents of a handicapped child stated a cause of action for wrongful birth against a physician who allegedly failed to properly interpret a rubella test performed during the mother's first trimester of pregnancy, thereby precluding the option of abortion. The physician had a duty to advise the parents so that they would have an opportunity to exercise the option of an abortion. If it could be established that the physician breached such a duty and that the parents would have terminated the pregnancy, the necessary causal connection would be demonstrated, and the parents would be entitled to recover for their extraordinary costs of raising the handicapped child and for any emotional harm that they might have suffered as a result of their child's handicap.

Recovery for damages was permitted for wrongful birth in *Keel v. Banach*,[70] where the Alabama Supreme Court held that a cause of action for wrongful birth is recognized in Alabama and compensable losses are any medical and hospital expenses incurred as a result of the physician's negligence, physical pain suffered by the mother, loss of consortium, and mental and emotional anguish suffered by the parents. The basic rule of tort compensation is that the plaintiffs should be placed in the position where they would have been without the defendant's negligence. A jury could conclude that the defendants, in failing to inform the mother of the possibility of giving birth to a child with multiple congenital deformities, directly deprived her and her husband of the option to accept or reject a parental relationship with the child and thus caused them to experience mental distress.

The Alabama Supreme Court said that it agreed with the Illinois Supreme Court, finding the following:

> Many courts have accepted wrongful birth as a cause of action on the theory that it is a logical and necessary extension of existing principles of tort law.... Some courts have recognized the cause of action because of the expanding ability of medical technology to accurately detect and predict genetic or other congenital abnormalities before conception or birth. Imposing liability on individual physicians or other health care providers, these courts say, vindicates the societal interest in reducing and preventing the incidence of such defects.... Other courts have expressed concern that refusing to recognize

this cause of action would frustrate the fundamental policies of tort law: to compensate the victim, to deter negligence, and to encourage due care.... The Alabama legislature passed a new Medical Liability Act in 1987, regarding medical negligence causes of action. Nowhere in that Act are wrongful birth cases excluded as they are in the laws passed in Missouri and Minnesota.[71]

The state of Georgia did not recognize a cause of action for wrongful birth filed by the parent of a child born with Down's syndrome in *Etkind v. Suarez*.[72] Throughout her pregnancy, Dr. Etkind was a patient of Dr. Suarez. After giving birth to a child with Down's syndrome, she and her husband filed suit against Suarez and his partnership, asserting a wrongful birth claim. The claim, brought by the parents of an impaired child, alleged that but for the treatment or advice provided by the defendant, the parents would have aborted the fetus. The trial court granted the defendants' motion for judgment on the pleadings. A cause of action for wrongful birth is not recognized in Georgia.

In a New Jersey case, *Canesi ex rel. v. Wilson*,[73] the New Jersey Supreme Court reviewed the dismissal of an action for wrongful birth on the claim of the parents that, had the mother been informed of the risk that a drug, Provera, which she had been taking before she learned that she was pregnant, might cause the fetus to be born with congenital anomalies, such as limb reduction, she would have decided to abort the fetus. It was alleged that the physicians failed to disclose the risks associated with the drug. The physicians argued that the informed consent doctrine requires that the plaintiffs establish that the drug in fact caused the birth anomalies. The court rejected the argument and distinguished the wrongful birth action from one based on informed consent:

> In sum, the informed consent and wrongful birth causes of action are similar in that both require the physician to disclose those medically accepted risks that a reasonably prudent patient in the plaintiff's position would deem material to her decision. What is or is not a medically acceptable risk is informed by what the physician knows or ought to know of the patient's history and condition. These causes of action, however, have important differences. They encompass different compensable harms and measures of damages. In both causes of action, the plaintiff must prove

that a reasonably prudent patient in her position, if apprised of all material risks, would have elected a different course of treatment or care. In an informed consent case, the plaintiff must additionally meet a two-pronged test for proximate causation: she must prove that the undisclosed risk actually materialized and that it was medically caused by the treatment. In a wrongful birth case, on the other hand, a plaintiff need not prove that the doctor's negligence was the medical cause of her child's birth defect. Rather, the test of proximate causation is satisfied by showing that an undisclosed fetal risk was material to a woman in her position; the risk materialized, was reasonably foreseeable and not remote in relation to the doctor's negligence; and, had plaintiff known of that risk, she would have terminated her pregnancy. The emotional distress and economic loss resulting from this lost opportunity to decide for herself whether or not to terminate the pregnancy constitute plaintiff's damages.[74]

In addressing the issue of proximate cause, the court noted:

[T]he nature of the wrongful birth does not depend on whether a defendant caused the injury or harm to the child. Rather, the appropriate inquiry was viewed as to whether the defendant's negligence was the proximate cause of the parent's loss of the option to make an informed and meaningful decision either to terminate the pregnancy or to give birth to a potentially defective child. . . .

The appropriate proximate cause question, therefore, is not whether the doctor's negligence caused the fetal defect; the congenital harm suffered by the child is not compensable. Rather the determination to be made is whether the doctor's inadequate disclosure deprived the parents of their deeply personal right to decide for themselves whether to give birth to a child who could possibly be afflicted with a physical abnormality. There is sufficient evidence in the record of this case to enable the jury to make that determination.[75]

With the increasing consolidation of hospital services and physician practices, a case could be made for finding a hospital liable for the physician's failure to obtain informed consent where the hospital actually owns or controls the physician's practice or where both the hospital and the physician's practice are owned or controlled by another corporation that sets policy for both the hospital and the physician's practice.

Wrongful Life

Wrongful life claims are initiated by the parent(s) or child based on harm suffered as a result of being born. The plaintiffs generally contend that the physician or laboratory negligently failed to inform the child's parents of the risk of bearing a genetically defective infant and hence prevented the parents' right to choose to avoid the birth.[76] Because there is no recognized legal right not to be born, wrongful life cases are generally not successful.

[L]egal recognition that a disabled life is an injury would harm the interests of those most directly concerned, the handicapped. Disabled persons face obvious physical difficulties in conducting their lives. They also face subtle yet equally devastating handicaps in the attitudes and behavior of society, the law, and their own families and friends. Furthermore, society often views disabled persons as burdensome misfits. Recent legislation concerning employment, education, and building access reflects a slow change in these attitudes. This change evidences a growing public awareness that the handicapped can be valuable and productive members of society. To characterize the life of a disabled person as an injury would denigrate both this new awareness and the handicapped themselves.[77]

A cause of action for wrongful life was not cognizable under Kansas law in *Bruggeman v. Schimke*.[78] A child born with congenital birth defects was not entitled to recover damages on the theory that physicians had been negligent when, after a prior sibling was born with congenital anomalies, they mistakenly advised the parents that the first child's condition was not because of a known chromosomal or measurable biochemical disorder. A fundamental principle of law is that human life is valuable, precious, and worthy of protection. A legal right not to be born rather than to be alive with deformities cannot be recognized. The Kansas Supreme Court held that there was no recognized cause for wrongful life.

A wrongful life action was brought against the physicians in *Speck v. Finegold* on behalf of an infant born with defects.[79] The court held that regardless of whether the claim was based on wrongful life or otherwise, no legally cognizable cause of action was stated on behalf of the infant even though the defendants' actions of negligence were the proximate cause of her defective birth. The parents could recover pecuniary expenses that they had borne and would bear for care and treatment of their child and that resulted in the natural course of things from the commission of the tort. The tort in this case was the failure of the urologist to perform a vasectomy properly and the failure of the obstetrician/gynecologist to perform an abortion properly. Recovery for negligence was allowed because the plaintiff parents did set forth a duty owed to them by the physicians and breached by the physicians with resulting injuries to the plaintiffs. Claims for emotional disturbance and mental distress were denied.

In *Pitre v. Opelousas General Hospital*,[80] the parents of a child born with a congenital defect filed a malpractice suit seeking damages for themselves and their child, alleging that the surgeon had been negligent in performing a tubal ligation. The suit also claimed that the hospital and the physician failed to inform Pitre that the operation was unsuccessful. A pathology report revealed that the physician had severed fibromuscular tissue, rather than the fallopian tissue, during the surgical procedure. The parents were not informed of this finding. The mother became pregnant and gave birth to an albino child. The court of appeals dismissed the child's claim for wrongful life and struck all the parents' individual claims with the exception of expenses associated with the pregnancy and the husband's loss of consortium.

The Louisiana Supreme Court held that the physician owed a duty to warn the parents regarding the failure of the tubal ligation, the physician did not have a duty to protect the child from the risk of albinism, and the parents were entitled to damages relating to the pregnancy and the husband's consortium. Special damages relating to the child's deformity were denied.

In *Kassama v. Magat*,[81] Kassama alleged that Dr. Magat failed to advise her of the results of an alpha-fetoprotein blood test that indicated a heightened possibility that her child might be afflicted with Down's syndrome. Had she received that information, Kassama contends, she would have undergone an amniocentesis, which would have confirmed that prospect. Kassama claims, if that occurred, she would have chosen to terminate the pregnancy through an abortion.

The Supreme Court of Maryland decided that for purposes of tort law, an impaired life was not worse than nonlife, and, for that reason, life itself was not,

and could not, be considered an injury. There was no evidence that the child was not deeply loved and cared for by her parents or that she did not return that love.

Wrongful birth is based on the premise that being born, and having to live, with the affliction is a disadvantage and thus a cognizable injury. The injury sued upon is the fact that the child was born; she bears the disability and will bear the expenses only because, but for the alleged negligence of Magat, her mother was unable to terminate the pregnancy and avert her birth. The issue here is whether Maryland law is prepared to recognize that kind of injury—the injury of life itself.

The child has not suffered any damage cognizable at law by being brought into existence. One of the most deeply held beliefs of society is that life, whether experienced with or without a major physical handicap, is more precious than nonlife. No one is perfect, and each person suffers from some ailments or defects, whether major or minor, which make impossible participation in all the activities life has to offer. Our lives are not thereby rendered less precious than those of others whose defects are less pervasive or less severe. Despite their handicaps, the Down's syndrome child is able to love and be loved and to experience happiness and pleasure—emotions that are truly the essence of life and that are far more valuable than the suffering that may be endured.

The right to life and the principle that all are equal under the law are basic to our constitutional order. To presume to decide that a child's life is not worth living would be to forsake these ideals. To characterize the life of a disabled person as an injury would denigrate the handicapped themselves. Measuring the value of an impaired life as compared to nonexistence is a task that is beyond mortals.

Unless a judgment can be made based on reason, rather than the emotion of any given case, that nonlife is preferable to impaired life—that the child-plaintiff would, in fact, have been better off had he or she never been born—there can be no injury, and if there can be no injury, whether damages can or cannot be calculated becomes irrelevant.

The crucial question, a value judgment about life itself, is too deeply immersed in each person's own individual philosophy or theology to be subject to a reasoned and consistent community response in the form of a jury verdict.

In another case, the mother, in her capacity as guardian for her minor son, brought a wrongful life action on behalf of the child against a physician. It was alleged that because the physician failed to adequately and timely diagnose the child's condition, the mother was denied the opportunity to decide whether to terminate the pregnancy while she was legally allowed to do so. The court, in deciding whether to render a verdict in the child's favor or what damages, if any, should be awarded, a jury would be faced with an imponderable question: Is a severely impaired life so much worse than no life at all that the child is entitled to damages? The civil justice system places inestimable faith in the ability of jurors to reach a fair and just result under the law, but even a jury collectively imbued with the wisdom of Solomon would be unable to weigh the fact of being born with a defective condition against the fact of not being born at all—in other words, nonexistence. It is simply beyond the human experience to analyze this position. The court declined to recognize a cause of action for wrongful life brought by or on behalf of a child born with a congenital defect. It was untenable to argue that a child who already had been born should have the chance to prove that it would have been better if he had never have been born at all.[82]

Wrongful Conception

Wrongful conception refers to a claim for damages sustained by the parents of an unexpected child based on an allegation that conception of the child resulted from negligent sterilization procedures or a defective contraceptive device.[83] Damages sought for a negligently performed sterilization could include pain and suffering associated with pregnancy and birth, the expenses of delivery, lost wages, father's loss of consortium, damages for emotional or psychological pain, suffering resulting from the presence of an additional family member in the household, the cost and pain and suffering of a subsequent sterilization, and damages suffered by a child born with genetic defects.

The most controversial item of damages claimed is that of raising a normal healthy child to adulthood. The mother in *Hartke v. McKelway*[84] had undergone sterilization for therapeutic reasons to avoid endangering her health from pregnancy. The woman became pregnant as a result of a failed sterilization. She delivered a healthy child without injury to herself. It was determined that "the jury could not rationally have found that the birth of this child was an injury to this plaintiff. Awarding child rearing expense would only give Hartke a windfall."[85]

The cost of raising a healthy newborn child to adulthood was recoverable by the parents of the child conceived as a result of an unsuccessful sterilization by a physician employee at Lovelace Medical Center. The physician in *Lovelace Medical Center v. Mendez*[86] found and ligated only one of the patient's two fallopian tubes and then failed to inform the patient of the unsuccessful operation. The court held that:

[T]he Mendezes' interest in the financial security of their family was a legally protected interest which was invaded by Lovelace's negligent failure properly to perform Maria's sterilization operation (if proved at trial), and that this invasion was an injury entitling them to recover damages in the form of the reasonable expenses to raise Joseph to majority.[87]

Some states bar damage claims for emotional distress and the costs associated with the raising of healthy children but will permit recovery for damages related to negligent sterilizations. In *Butler v. Rolling Hills Hospital*,[88] the Pennsylvania Superior Court held that the patient stated a cause of action for the negligent performance of a laparoscopic tubal ligation. The patient was not, however, entitled to compensation for the costs of raising a normal healthy child. "In light of this Commonwealth's public policy, which recognizes the paramount importance of the family to society, we conclude that the benefits of joy, companionship, and affection which a normal, healthy child can provide must be deemed as a matter of law to outweigh the costs of raising that child."[89]

As the Court of Common Pleas of Lycoming County, Pennsylvania, in *Shaheen v. Knight*, stated:

Many people would be willing to support this child were they given the right of custody and adoption, but according to plaintiff's statement, plaintiff does not want such. He wants to have the child and wants the doctor to support it. In our opinion, to allow such damages would be against public policy.[90]

Prevention of Wrongful Birth, Life, and Conception Lawsuits

The occurrence of an unplanned pregnancy is not necessarily the result of negligence on the part of a physician. Although slight, there is known to be a given failure rate of sterilizations. Physicians can prevent lawsuits by informing each patient, both orally and through written consent, as to the likelihood of an unsuccessful sterilization, as well as the inherent risks in the procedure.

▶ ARTIFICIAL INSEMINATION

Artificial insemination is the process by which sperm are placed into the reproductive tract of a female, for the purpose of impregnating the female by means other than sexual intercourse. There are two sources of sperm for impregnation of a female: (1) homologous artificial insemination, which uses the husband's semen to impregnate the female; and (2) heterologous artificial insemination (HAI), which uses semen from a donor other than a woman's husband.

The absence of answers to many questions concerning HAI may discourage couples from seeking to use the procedure and physicians from performing it. Some of the questions concern the procedure itself, while others concern the status of the offspring, the effect of the procedure on the marital relationship, and the risk of multiple births that could pose financial challenges. A further complication includes the potential for legal actions for multiple births. This may even lead to the loss of a physician's license to practice medicine, such as occurred when the Medical Board of California revoked Dr. Michael Kamrava's medical license.

Dr. Kamrava had transplanted multiple embryos that resulted in the birth of octuplets. The Medical Board determined that Dr. Kamrava had acted beyond the reasonable judgment of a physician by implanting a number of embryos that exceeded existing guidelines. "The Board subsequently found Kamrava guilty of gross negligence, repeated negligent acts, and inadequate medical records in the first case. In the additional two cases, Kamrava was found guilty of gross negligence and repeated negligent acts in one case and guilty of repeated negligent acts in the other case."[91]

Consent

The Oklahoma heterologous artificial insemination statute specifies that husband and wife must consent to the procedure.[92] It is obvious that the wife's consent must be obtained; without it, the touching involved in the artificial insemination would constitute a battery. Besides the wife's consent, it is important to obtain the husband's consent to ensure against liability accruing if a court adopted the view that without the consent of the husband, heterologous artificial insemination was a wrong to the husband's interest, for which he could sustain a suit for damages.

The Oklahoma statute also deals with establishing proof of consent. It requires that the consent be in writing and executed and acknowledged by the physician performing the procedure and by the local judge who has jurisdiction over the adoption of children, as well as by the husband and wife.

In states without specific statutory requirements, medical personnel should attempt to avoid the potential for liability by obtaining the written consent of the couple requesting the heterologous artificial insemination procedure. The hospital's legal counsel should be consulted with in order to ensure that hospital policy is in compliance with statutory requirements.

Confidentiality

Another problem that directly concerns medical personnel involved in heterologous artificial insemination birth is preserving confidentiality. This problem is met in the Oklahoma heterologous artificial insemination statute, which requires that the original copy of the consent be filed pursuant to the rules for the filing of adoption papers and is not to be made a matter of public record.[93]

▶ SURROGACY

Surrogacy is a method of reproduction whereby a woman agrees to give birth to a child she will not raise but hand over to a contracted party, who is often unable to conceive a natural child of her own. A surrogate "may be the child's genetic mother (the more traditional form of surrogacy), or she may, as a gestational carrier, carry the pregnancy to delivery after having been implanted with an embryo. In some cases surrogacy is the only available option for parents who wish to have a child that is biologically related to them."[94]

Surrogacy raises many ethical and legal issues to consider before searching for a surrogate mother. For example, is it right to enter a contract with a woman, taking advantage of her circumstances by offering her money in exchange for bearing a child and then transferring all parental rights and physical custody of the child to the "commissioning couple"? Although the long-term effects of surrogacy contracts are not known, the adverse psychological impact could be detrimental to the child who learns that he or she is the offspring of someone who gave birth for financial gain. Would the child want to search for his or her gestational mother? Should records be kept, and should the child have access to those records? After the child is taken, the surrogate mother may be negatively impacted by feelings of isolation or loss and with the reality of the sale of her body. One might ask: How does this differ from circumstances in which a donor would legally (which is not the case at present) be allowed to sell an organ strictly for financial purposes, thus allowing a donee to live as a result of the purchase?

Finally, some believe that the surrogacy contract is based on principles that are contrary to the objectives of our laws. The surrogate contract is perceived to be illegal when a fee is involved because it is compared with baby selling, which is illegal in all states. Court decisions and legislation in the United States have historically been split on how they address surrogacy contracts. In the District of Columbia, as of April 7, 2017, surrogacy contracts are legal and enforceable.

Chapter 16 Procreation and Ethical Dilemmas

THE COURT'S DECISION

The United States Supreme Court struck down on June 27, 2016, Texas restrictions on a woman's right to choose to have an abortion. The Court determined that the two provisions of Texas' House Bill 2 violated the federal Constitution. The provisions of HB 2 did not offer medical benefits sufficient to justify the burdens placed upon women seeking a previability abortion.[97]

"The bill sets guidelines for parents and surrogates entering into surrogacy arrangements and establishes how the intended parents should establish their parentage rights."[95]

A BILL 21-16
ENGROSSED ORIGINAL
IN THE COUNCIL OF THE DISTRICT OF COLUMBIA

To amend Chapter 4 of Title 16 of the District of Columbia Official Code to permit collaborative reproduction and surrogacy agreements, establish requirements for surrogates, intended parents, and the contents of surrogacy agreements, establish parentage of a child, provide for court orders of parentage, and establish the effect of a subsequent marriage or domestic partnership, dissolution of a marriage or domestic partnership, death of an intended parent, and withdrawal of consent.[96]

For a state-by-state analysis of surrogacy laws, visit the following websites: TheSurrogacyExperience.com or AllAboutSurrogacy.com.

▶ CHAPTER REVIEW

1. *Abortion* is the premature termination of a pregnancy, either spontaneous or induced. *Roe v. Wade* is the Supreme Court's ruling that, within certain guidelines, women are allowed to make decisions regarding how their pregnancies will end. According to *Roe v. Wade*:

   ■ First trimester, an abortion decision is between a woman and her physician.

   ■ Second trimester, a state may regulate the medical conditions under which an abortion is performed.

   ■ Third trimester, a state can prohibit all abortions except those deemed necessary to protect maternal life or health.

2. States' and women's rights regarding reproductive decision have been further shaped and defined by a number of landmark rulings.

   ■ In 1992, in *Planned Parenthood v. Casey*, the Supreme Court nearly overturned *Roe v. Wade*. It did reject the trimester approach in favor of the Court evaluating the permissibility of state abortion rules based on whether they unduly burden a woman's ability to obtain an abortion. A rule is considered an undue burden if its purpose or effect is to place a substantial obstacle in the path of a woman seeking an abortion before the fetus is viable.

3. A *partial-birth abortion* is a late-term abortion that involves partial delivery of the fetus prior to its being aborted. An Arkansas statute failed to prohibit this manner of abortion largely as a result of its broad coverage. The Act was determined to be unconstitutional because it was unconstitutionally vague, imposed an undue burden on women seeking abortions, and did not adequately protect the health and lives of pregnant women.

4. In *Utah Women's Clinic, Inc. v. Leavitt*, the court determined that imposition of a 24-hour waiting period—except in the event of a medical emergency—does not impose an undue burden on the right to an abortion.

5. In *Doe v. Zimmerman*, the court declared unconstitutional the provisions of the Pennsylvania Abortion Control Act, which required that the written consent of the husband of a married woman be secured before the performance of an abortion.

6. Individuals have a right to refuse to participate in abortions for reason of conscience or religious or moral conviction.

7. Several states have placed restrictions on abortions by reducing funding.

8. *Sterilization* is defined as the termination of the ability to produce offspring.

   ■ *Vasectomy* is a surgical procedure performed on men in which the vas deferens is severed and tied to prevent the flow of seminal fluid into the urinary canal.

   ■ *Tubal ligation* is a surgical procedure performed on women in which the fallopian tubes are cut and tied. This prevents the passage of the ovum from the ovary to the uterus.

   ■ *Therapeutic sterilization* is performed to preserve life or health.

■ *Eugenic sterilization* is the involuntary sterilization of certain categories of persons. It is often performed to prevent the transmission of hereditary defects and, in some states, is performed to prevent procreation by persons who would not be able to care for their offspring.

9. Wrongful birth, wrongful life, and wrongful conception have led to a variety of lawsuits.

■ *Wrongful birth actions* claim that, but for breach of duty by the defendant, a child would not have been born.

■ *Wrongful life suits* are those in which a parent or child claims to have suffered harm as a result of being born—are generally unsuccessful.

■ *Wrongful conception* actions claim that damages were sustained by parents of an unexpected child based on the allegation that the child's conception was the result of negligent sterilization procedures or a defective contraceptive device.

10. Physicians can avoid liability in wrongful conception/pregnancy actions by obtaining oral and written consent that indicates that the physician has disclosed the inherent risks of the sterilization procedure.

11. *Artificial insemination* most often takes the form of the injection of seminal fluid into a woman to induce pregnancy.

■ *Homologous artificial insemination* is when the husband's semen is used in the procedure.

■ *Heterologous artificial insemination* is when the semen is from a donor other than the husband.

12. *Surrogacy* is a method of reproduction whereby a woman agrees to give birth to a child she will not raise but will instead hand over to a contracted party.

▶ REVIEW QUESTIONS

1. Discuss the legal and ethical issues involved in *Roe v. Wade*.

2. Do you agree that individual states should be able to place reasonable restrictions or waiting periods?

3. Should a married woman be allowed to abort without her husband's consent?

4. Describe the various forms of sterilization.

5. Do you think *Roe v. Wade* is an example of legislating morality? Why or why not?

6. Do you agree that eugenic sterilization should be allowed? Why or why not?

7. Describe surrogacy and the legal and ethical issues that can arise.

8. Describe how wrongful birth, wrongful life, and wrongful conception differ.

▶ NOTES

1. English Clergy, Dean of Westminster.
2. *Causeway Medical Suite v. Ieyoub*, 109 F.3d 1096 (1997).
3. 410 U.S. 113 (1973).
4. *Id.* at 164.
5. *Id.*
6. *Id.*
7. *Id.*
8. 410 U.S. 179 (1973).
9. *Id.* at 198.
10. 432 U.S. 438 (1977).
11. *Id.*
12. 432 U.S. 464 (1977).
13. 448 U.S. 297 (1980).
14. *Committee to Defend Reproductive Rights v. Myers*, 625 P.2d 779, 798 (Cal. 1981).
15. 56 P.3d 28 (Ariz. 2002).
16. 99 S. Ct. 675 (1979).
17. South Carolina General Assembly, "A183, R196, H3114 Status Information," updated June 28, 2016. http://www.scstatehouse.gov/sess121_2015-2016/bills/3114.htm.
18. 428 U.S. 52 (1976).
19. 443 U.S. 622 (1979).
20. 101 S. Ct. 1164 (1981).
21. 515 So. 2d 1254 (Ala. Civ. App. 1987).
22. 107 F. Supp. 2d 1271 (2000).
23. 921 So. 2d 753 (Fla. App. 2006).
24. 546 U.S. 320 (2006).
25. 973 So. 2d 548 (Fla. App. 2008).
26. *Poe v. Gerstein*, 517 F.2d 787 (5th Cir. 1975).
27. 405 F. Supp. 534 (M.D. Pa. 1975).
28. 486 U.S. 1308 (1988).
29. *Planned Parenthood v. Casey*, 112 S. Ct. 2792 (1992).
30. 103 S. Ct. 2481 (1983).
31. 111 S. Ct. 1759 (1991).
32. 112 S. Ct. 2791 (1992).
33. *Utah Women's Clinic, Inc. v. Leavitt*, 844 F. Supp. 1482 (D. Utah 1994).

34. 844 F. Supp. 1482 (D. Utah 1994) at 1494.

35. *Id.* at 1495.

36. 533 A.2d 523 (R.I. 1987).

37. 492 U.S. 490 (1989).

38. 118 S. Ct. 1347 (1998).

39. 192 F.3d 794 (8th Cir. 1999).

40. 192 F.3d 1142 (8th Cir. 1999), 120 S. Ct. 2597 (2000).

41. *Richmond Med. Ctr. for Women v. Hicks*, 409 F.3d 619 (C.A. 4, Va. 2005).

42. *Planned Parenthood of Cent. N.J. v. Farmer*, 220 F.3d 127 (3rd Cir. 2000).

43. 437 F.3d. 278 (C.A. 2, N.Y. 2006).

44. Tex. Health & Safety Code Ann. § 171.0031(a) (West Cum. Supp. 2015).

45. Tex. Health & Safety Code Ann. § 245.010(a).

46. 565 N.Y.S.2d 833 (N.Y. App. Div. 1991).

47. *Forrester v. City of San Diego*, 25 F.3d 804 (9th Cir. 1994).

48. *Id.* at 807.

49. *NOW v. Operation Rescue*, 816 F. Supp. 729 (D. D.C. 1993).

50. *Id.* at 734.

51. 642 A.2d 338 (N.J. 1994).

52. 134 S. Ct. 2518, 573 US __, 189 L. Ed. 2d 502 - Supreme Court 2014

53. Adam Liptak and John Schwartz, "Court Rejects Zone to Buffer Abortion Clinic," *The New York Times*, June 26, 2014. http://www.nytimes.com /2014/06/27/us/supreme-court-abortion-clinic -protests.html.

54. Lawrence Terenzi, "Abortion: A World View," *Self*, November 1992: 54.

55. Oregon Legislative Assembly, "House Bill 3391," https://olis.leg.state.or.us/liz/2017R1/Downloads /MeasureDocument/HB3391.

56. *American Acad. of Pediatrics v. Lungren*, 940 P.2d 797 (1997).

57. 774 P.2d 1171 (Wash. 1989).

58. 755 P.2d 678 (Okla. 1988).

59. *Chaffee v. Seslar*, 786 N.E.2d 705 (2003).

60. 224 U.S. 200 (1927).

61. *Id.* at 24.

62. 337 F. Supp. 671 (E.D. Ohio 1971).

63. *McKinney v. McKinney*, 805 S.W.2d 66 (Ark. 1991).

64. 475 F.2d 701 (1st Cir. 1973).

65. 410 U.S. 113 (1973).

66. *Id.*

67. 165 Cal. Rptr. 477 (Cal. Ct. App. 1980).

68. 513 A.2d 341 (N.H. 1986).

69. 412 N.W.2d 232 (Mich. Ct. App. 1987).

70. 624 So. 2d 1022 (Ala. 1993).

71. *Id.* at 1031.

72. 519 S.E.2d 210 (Ga. 1999).

73. 730 A.2d 806 (N.J. 1999).

74. *Id.* at 18.

75. *Id.*

76. *Smith v. Cote*, 513 A.2d 344 (N.H. 1986).

77. *Id.* at 353.

78. 718 P.2d 635 (Kan. 1986).

79. 408 A.2d 496 (Pa. Super. Ct. 1979).

80. 530 So. 2d 1151 (La. 1988).

81. 136 Md. App. 38 (2002).

82. *Willis v. Wu*, No. 25915 (S.C. 2004).

83. *Cowe v. Forum Group, Inc.*, 575 N.E.2d 630, 631 (Ind. 1991).

84. 707 F.2d 1544 (D.C. Cir. 1983).

85. *Id.* at 1557.

86. 805 P.2d 603 (N.M. 1991).

87. *Id.* at 612.

88. 582 A.2d 1384 (Pa. Super. Ct. 1990).

89. *Id.* at 1385.

90. 11 Pa. D. & C.2d 41, 46 (Lycoming Co. Ct. Com. Pl. 1957).

91. Medical Board of California, News Releases 2011, http://www.mbc.ca.gov/About_Us/Media _Room/2011/news_releases_2011.pdf.

92. Okla. Stat. Ann. 10, §§ 551–553.

93. *Id.*

94. "Surrogacy and Child Rights," https://scholar .google.com/scholar?q=surrogacy+and +child+rights&hl=en&as_sdt=0&as_vis=1&oi =scholart&sa=X&ved=0ahUKEwjWrLOzv -nXAhUkhOAKHZYzCKgQgQMINTAA.

95. Washington D.C. Council Bill 210016, "Collaborative Reproduction Amendment Act of 2015," Engrossed December 20, 2016. https://beta .code.dccouncil.us/dc/council/code/titles/16 /chapters/4/.

96. *Id.*

97. *Whole Woman's Health v. Hellerstedt*, 136 S.Ct. 2292 (June 27, 2016).

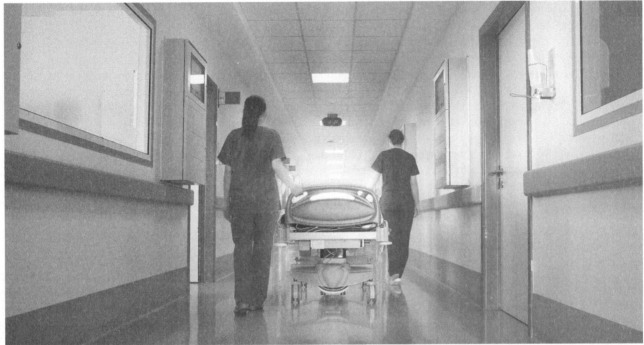

© sfam_photo/Shutterstock

CHAPTER 17

End-of-Life Issues

> *When we finally know we are dying, and all other sentient beings are dying with us, we start to have a burning, almost heart breaking sense of the fragility and preciousness of each moment and each being, and from this can grow a deep, clear, limitless compassion for all beings.*
>
> —Sogyal Rinpoche

▶ LEARNING OBJECTIVES

The reader, upon completion of this chapter, will be able to:

- Discuss the human struggle to survive and the right to autonomous decision making.
- Describe how patient autonomy has been impacted by case law and legislative enactments.
- Discuss the following concepts: preservation of life with limits, euthanasia, advance directives, futility of treatment, withholding and withdrawal of treatment, and do-not-resuscitate orders.
- Explain end-of-life issues as they relate to autopsy, organ donations, research, experimentation, and clinical trials.
- Describe how human genetics and stem cell research can have an impact on end-of-life issues.

The human struggle to survive and dreams of immortality have long been instrumental in inspiring medicine to develop the means to prevent and cure illness. Advances in medical technology have resulted in

✔ *END OF LIFE OR BEGINNING OF LIFE?*

My mother is 92 years old, and she is more active and is enjoying life more than when she was much younger. Her advanced age has actually proven to be something of an advantage, as it has given her the time and freedom to do some of the things she couldn't do while she was raising a family. It has been a joy to me, as her son, and to the rest of the family to witness her joy and vigor. Even strangers have found her stamina to be an inspiration as to the value of the end years of life.

Three years ago, however, it wasn't so. Mother was critically ill, comatose on a respirator in an intensive care unit. Survival was not considered likely. I am embarrassed to say that I was making arrangements for a funeral. I am even more embarrassed because I am a physician and did not see how she could survive for long except as a vegetable.

Then the unlikely occurred. She recovered! Her condition rapidly and surprisingly improved dramatically, including both her physical and mental status, and she promptly resumed a life even more active than before. It would have been a tragedy to deprive her of these joyous years of her life after she worked and sacrificed so much for others most of her life. I had thought it would be an act of mercy to disconnect the respirator when her condition had looked so hopeless. I was so wrong. I learned that we must not make life and death decisions casually. Life is a beautiful mystery with many wonderful surprises if we will let them happen.

Advances in medical technology have made it possible to survive to an older age. Although our bodies may physically decline over time, our treasure trove of life experiences accrues over time. Our knowledge and judgment may often be better than when we were younger. Furthermore, the aged may be a source of comfort and joy to their children, grandchildren, and even great-grandchildren. As long as we are alive, we have value.

—Anonymous

the power to *prolong a productive life*, as well as to *delay inevitable death*. Those victims of long-term pain and suffering, as well as patients in vegetative states and irreversible comas, are the most directly affected. Although rising survival rates can be a substantial financial burden to the family, the following *reality check* provides some perspective about the value of life regardless of age.

End-of-life issues continue to cause the most controversy and debate facing healthcare providers. Although it is well settled that competent terminally ill patients may refuse life-sustaining treatment, physician-assisted suicide remains a major point of contention. The competing concerns of privacy, morality, patient autonomy, legislation, and states' interests swirl around those involved in the decision-making process. The scope of healthcare ethics is not limited to philosophical issues but embraces economic, political, and medical dilemmas.

The primary emphasis in this chapter is placed on a patient's autonomy and one's right to choose when to proceed with treatment or discontinue it. Discussed to a lesser extent are issues relating to autopsy, organ donations, research and experimentation, surrogacy, and human genetics.

▶ PATIENT AUTONOMY

No right is held more sacred, or is more carefully guarded, by the common law, than the right of every individual to the possession and control of his own person, free from all restraint or interference of others, unless by clear and unquestioned authority of law.[1]

Medical ethics does not require that a patient's life be preserved at all costs and in all circumstances. The ethical integrity of the profession is not threatened by allowing competent patients to decide for themselves whether a particular medical treatment is in their best interests. If the doctrine of informed consent and right of privacy has as its foundations the right to bodily integrity and control of one's own fate, then those rights are superior to the institutional considerations of hospitals and their medical staffs. A state's interest in maintaining the ethical integrity of a profession does not outweigh, for example, a patient's right to refuse care, such as the refusal to be administered a blood transfusion. Desmond Tutu, Archbishop Emeritus of Capetown, South Africa, a Nobel Peace Prize laureate, believing that people should have the right to make their own choices, said, "Now, as I turn 85 Friday, with my life closer to its end than to its beginning, I wish to help give people dignity in dying. Just as I have argued firmly for compassion and fairness in life, I believe that terminally ill people should be treated with the same compassion and fairness when it comes to their deaths."[2]

This section reviews a variety of ethical and legal issues that inevitably arise when one approaches the end of life. To analyze end-of-life questions, it is necessary to consider first what rights a competent patient possesses. Both case law and statutory law have presented a diversity of policies and points of view. Courts often point to common law and the early case of *Schloendorff v. Society of New York Hospital*[3] to support their belief in a patient's right to self-determination. The *Schloendorff* court stated:

Every human being of adult years and sound mind has a right to determine what shall be done with his own body and a surgeon who performs an operation without his patient's consent commits an assault, for which he is liable in damages, except in cases of emergency where the patient is unconscious and where it is necessary to operate before consent can be obtained.[4]

This *right of self-determination* was emphasized in *In re Storar*[5] when the court announced that every human being of adult years and sound mind has the right to determine what shall be done with his or her own body. The *Storar* case was a departure from the New Jersey Supreme Court's rationale in the case of *In re Quinlan*.

The *Quinlan* case was the first to significantly address the issue of whether euthanasia should be permitted when a patient is terminally ill. The *Quinlan* court, relying on *Roe v. Wade*,[6] announced that the constitutional right to privacy protects a patient's right to self-determination. The court noted that the right to privacy "is broad enough to encompass a patient's decision to decline medical treatment under certain circumstances, in much the same way as it is broad enough to encompass a woman's decision to terminate pregnancy under certain conditions."[7] Karen's father was granted full power to make decisions regarding Karen's treatment. After the concurrence of the guardian and family, if Karen's physicians concluded that there was no reasonable possibility of her emerging from her comatose condition to a cognitive, sapient state and that her life support apparatus should be withdrawn, they were to consult with the ethics committee of the institution where Karen was then hospitalized. If that consultative body concurred in the prognosis, the life support system could be withdrawn without any civil or criminal liability on the part of any participant, whether it is the guardian, physician, hospital, or others. In addressing itself to the question of possible homicide, the court concluded that there is a valid distinction between withdrawing life support systems in cases such as Karen's and the infliction of deadly harm either on one's self or another.

The *Quinlan* court, in reaching its decision, applied a test balancing the state's interest in preserving and maintaining the sanctity of human life against Karen's privacy interest. It decided that, especially in light of the prognosis (physicians determined that Karen Quinlan was in an irreversible coma), the state's interest did not justify interference with her right to refuse treatment. Thus, Karen Quinlan's father, appointed as her legal guardian, requested that

the respirator be turned off. Opponents of euthanasia argued that before the Quinlan decision, any form of euthanasia was defined as murder by the U.S. legal system. Although acts of euthanasia did take place, the law was applied selectively, and the possibility of criminal sanctions against active participants in euthanasia was enough to deter most physicians from assisting a patient in committing euthanasia.

Despite intense criticism by legal and religious scholars, the *Quinlan* decision paved the way for courts to consider extending the right to decline treatment to incompetents as well. State courts recognize the right but differ on how this right is to be exercised.

In the same year as the *Quinlan* decision, the case of *Superintendent of Belchertown State School v. Saikewicz*[8] was decided. In this case, the court, using the balancing test enunciated in *Quinlan*, approved the recommendation of a court-appointed guardian that it would be in Saikewicz's best interests to end chemotherapy treatment. Saikewicz was a mentally retarded, 67-year-old patient suffering from leukemia. The court found from the evidence that the prognosis was grim, and even though a "normal person" would probably have chosen chemotherapy, it allowed Saikewicz to die without treatment to spare him the suffering. Although the court also followed the reasoning of the *Quinlan* opinion in giving the right to an incompetent to refuse treatment, based on either the "objective best interests" test or the "subjective substituted judgment" test (the latter of which it favored because Mr. Saikewicz had always been incompetent), the court departed from *Quinlan* in a major way. It rejected the *Quinlan* approach of entrusting a decision concerning the continuance of artificial life support to the patient's guardian, family, attending physicians, and a hospital ethics committee.

The *Saikewicz* court asserted that even though a judge might find the opinions of physicians, medical experts, or hospital ethics committees helpful in reaching a decision, there should be no requirement to seek out their advice. The court decided that questions of life and death with regard to an incompetent should be the responsibility of the courts, which would conduct detached but passionate investigations. The court took a "dim view of any attempt to shift the ultimate decision-making responsibility away from duly established courts of proper jurisdiction to any committee, panel, or group, ad hoc or permanent."[9]

This main point of difference between the *Saikewicz* and *Quinlan* cases marked the emergence of two different policies on the incompetent's right to refuse treatment. One line of cases has followed

Saikewicz and supports court approval before physicians are allowed to withhold or withdraw life support. Advocates of this view argue that it makes more sense to leave the decision to an objective tribunal than to extend the right of a patient's privacy to a number of interested parties, as was done in *Quinlan*. They also attack the *Quinlan* method as being a privacy decision effectuated by popular vote.[10]

Six months after *Saikewicz*, the Massachusetts Appeals Court narrowed the need for court intervention in *In re Dinnerstein*[11] by finding that no-code orders are valid to prevent the use of artificial resuscitative measures on incompetent, terminally ill patients. The court was faced with the case of a 67-year-old woman who was suffering from Alzheimer's disease. It was determined that she was permanently comatose at the time of trial. Furthermore, the court decided that *Saikewicz*-type judicial proceedings should take place only when medical treatment could offer a reasonable expectation of effecting a permanent or temporary cure of or relief from the illness.

The Massachusetts Supreme Judicial Court attempted to clarify its *Saikewicz* opinion with regard to court orders in *In re Spring*.[12] It held that such different factors as the patient's mental impairment and his or her medical prognosis with or without treatment must be considered before judicial approval is necessary to withdraw or withhold treatment from an incompetent patient. The problem in all three cases is that there is still no clear guidance regarding exactly when the court's approval of the removal of life support systems would be necessary. *Saikewicz* seemed to demand judicial approval in every case. *Spring*, however, in partially retreating from that view, stated that it did not have to articulate what combination of the factors it discussed, thus making prior court approval necessary.

The inconsistencies presented by the Massachusetts cases led most courts since 1977 to follow the parameters set by *Quinlan*, requiring judicial intervention. In cases where physicians have certified the irreversible nature of a patient's loss of consciousness, a neurologic team could certify the patient's hopeless neurologic condition, at which point a guardian would be free to take the legal steps necessary to remove life support systems. The main reason for the appointment of a guardian is to ensure that incompetents, like all other patients, maintain their right to refuse treatment.

Most holdings indicate that because a patient has the constitutional right of self-determination, those acting on the patient's behalf can exercise that right when rendering their best judgment concerning how the patient would assert the right. This substituted judgment doctrine could be argued on standing grounds, whereby a second party has the right to assert the constitutional rights of another when that second party's intervention is necessary to protect the other's constitutional rights. The guardian's decision is sound if based on the known desires of a patient who was competent immediately before becoming comatose.

Courts adhering to the *Quinlan* rationale have recognized that fact, and in 1984, the highest state court of Florida took the lead and accepted the living will as persuasive evidence of an incompetent's wishes. In *John F. Kennedy Memorial Hospital v. Bludworth*,[13] the Florida Supreme Court allowed an incompetent patient's wife to act as his guardian, and in accordance with the terms of a living will he executed in 1975, she could substitute her judgment for that of her husband. She asked to have a respirator removed. The court declined the necessity of prior court approval, finding that the constitutional right to refuse treatment had been decided in *Satz v. Perlmutter*.[14] The court required the attending physician to certify that the patient was in a permanent vegetative state, with no reasonable chance for recovery, before a family member or guardian could request termination of extraordinary means of medical treatment.

In keeping with *Saikewicz*, the decision maker would attempt to ascertain the incompetent patient's actual interests and preferences. Court involvement would be mandated only to appoint a guardian in one of the following cases:

- Family members disagree as to the incompetent's wishes
- Physicians disagree on the prognosis
- The patient's wishes cannot be known because he or she always has been incompetent

The decision in *John F. Kennedy Memorial Hospital v. Bludworth* increased the desire of the public, courts, and religious groups to know when a patient is considered to be legally dead and what type of treatment can be withheld or withdrawn. Most cases dealing with euthanasia speak of the necessity that a physician diagnose a patient as being either in a persistent vegetative state[15] or terminally ill.[16]

▶ CONSTITUTIONAL RIGHT TO REFUSE CARE

The Missouri Supreme Court applied the *Westchester* ruling and held that the family of 32-year-old Nancy Cruzan, who was in a persistent vegetative state since 1983, could not order physicians to remove artificial nutrition.[17] In 1983, she had sustained injuries in a car accident, in which her car overturned, and after which she was found face down in a ditch without respiratory or cardiac function. Although unconscious, her breathing and heartbeat were restored at the site of the accident. On examination at the hospital to which she was taken, a neurosurgeon diagnosed her as having suffered cerebral contusions and anoxia. It was estimated that she had been deprived of oxygen for 12 to 14 minutes. After remaining in a coma for 3 weeks, Cruzan went into an unconscious state. At first, she was able to ingest some food orally. Thereafter, surgeons implanted a gastrostomy feeding and hydration tube, with the consent of her husband, to facilitate feeding her. She did not improve, and until December 1990, she lay in a Missouri state hospital in a persistent vegetative state that was determined to be irreversible, permanent, progressive, and ongoing. She was not dead, according to the accepted definition of death in Missouri, and physicians estimated that she could live in the vegetative state for an additional 30 years. Because of the prognosis, Cruzan's parents asked the hospital staff to cease all artificial nutrition and hydration procedures. The staff refused to comply with their wishes without court approval. The state trial court granted authorization for termination, finding that Cruzan had a fundamental right—grounded in both the state and federal constitutions—to refuse or direct the withdrawal of death-prolonging procedures. Testimony at trial from a former roommate of Cruzan indicated to the court that she had stated that if she were ever sick or injured, she would not want to live unless she could live halfway normally. The court interpreted that conversation, which had taken place when Cruzan was 25 years old, as meaning that she would not want to be forced to take nutrition and hydration while in a persistent vegetative state.

The case was appealed to the Missouri Supreme Court, which reversed the lower court decision. The court not only doubted that the doctrine of informed consent applied to the circumstances of the case, it moreover would not recognize a broad privacy right from the state constitution that would support the right of a person to refuse medical treatment in every circumstance. Because Missouri recognizes living wills, the court held that Cruzan's parents were not entitled to order the termination of her treatment because "no person can assume that choice for an incompetent in the absence of the formalities required under Missouri's Living Will statutes or the clear and convincing, inherently reliable evidence absent here."[18] The court found that Cruzan's statements to her roommate did not rise to the level of clear and convincing evidence of her desire to end nutrition and hydration.

In June 1990, the U.S. Supreme Court heard oral arguments and held that:

- The U.S. Constitution does not forbid Missouri from requiring that there be clear and convincing evidence of an incompetent's wishes as to the withdrawal of life-sustaining treatment.
- The Missouri Supreme Court did not commit constitutional error in concluding that evidence adduced at trial did not amount to clear and convincing evidence of Cruzan's desire to cease hydration and nutrition.
- Due process did not require the state to accept the substituted judgment of close family members, absent substantial proof that their views reflected those of the patient.[19]

In delivering the opinion of the Supreme Court, Justice William Rehnquist noted that although most state courts have applied the common law right to informed consent or a combination of that right and a privacy right when allowing a right to refuse treatment, the Supreme Court analyzed the issues presented in the *Cruzan* case in terms of a Fourteenth Amendment liberty interest, finding that a competent person has a constitutionally protected right grounded in the due process clause to refuse lifesaving hydration and nutrition. Missouri provided for the incompetent by allowing a surrogate to act for the patient in choosing to withdraw hydration and treatment. Moreover, it put procedures into place to ensure that the surrogate's action conforms to the wishes expressed by the patient when he or she was competent. Although recognizing that Missouri had enacted a restrictive law, the Supreme Court held that right-to-die issues should be decided pursuant to state law, subject to a due process liberty interest, and in keeping with state constitutional law. After the Supreme Court rendered its decision, the Cruzans returned to Missouri probate court, where on November 14, 1990, Judge Charles Teel authorized physicians to remove the feeding tubes from Cruzan. The judge determined that testimony presented to him early in November demonstrated clear and convincing evidence that Nancy would not have wanted to live in a persistent vegetative state. Several of her coworkers testified that she told them before her accident that she would not want to live like a vegetable. On December 26, 1990, two weeks after her feeding tubes were removed, Nancy Cruzan died.

▶ LEGISLATIVE RESPONSE

After the *Cruzan* decision, states began to rethink existing legislation and draft new legislation in the areas of living wills, durable powers of attorney, healthcare proxies, and surrogate decision making. Pennsylvania and Florida were two of the first states to react to the *Cruzan* decision. The new Pennsylvania law is applied to terminally ill or permanently unconscious patients. The statute, the Advance Directive for Health Care Act,[20] deals mainly with individuals who have prepared living wills. It includes in its definition of life-sustaining treatment the administration of hydration and nutrition by any means if it is stated in the individual's living will. The statute mandates that a copy of the living will be given to the physician to be effective. Furthermore, the patient must be incompetent or permanently unconscious. If there is no evidence of the presence of a living will, the Pennsylvania probate codes allow an attorney-in-fact who was designated in a properly executed durable power of attorney document to give permission for "medical and surgical procedures to be utilized on an incompetent patient."[21]

The Supreme Court stated in *Cruzan* that only 15% of the population has signed a living will or other type of medical directive. In light of that fact, more states will have to address the problem of surrogate decision making for an incompetent. Legislation would not only have to include direction to consider evidence of an incompetent's wishes that had been expressed when he or she was competent, but also should include provisions for consideration and protection of an incompetent who never stated what he or she would want done if in a terminally ill or persistent vegetative state.

Unless there is some national uniformity in the legislation, patients and their families will shop for states that will allow them to have medical treatment terminated or withdrawn with as few legal hassles as possible. For example, on January 18, 1991, a Missouri probate court judge authorized a father to take his 20-year-old brain-damaged daughter, Christine Busalacchi, from the Missouri Rehabilitation Center to Minnesota for testing by a pro-euthanasia physician, Dr. Cranford. Cranford, who practiced at the Hennepin County Medical Center, was the center of controversy in Minnesota. In January 1991, Pro-Life Action Ministries demanded Cranford's resignation, claiming that he "desires to make Minnesota the killing fields for the disabled."[22] He, however, viewed himself as an advocate of patients' rights. Although the situation involving Cranford is resolved, it is clear that the main reason Busalacchi sought authorization to take his daughter to Minnesota is that he believed that he would have to deal with fewer legal impediments there to allow his daughter to die.

Because of the continuing litigation concerning the right-to-die issue, it is clear that the public must be educated about the necessity of expressing their wishes concerning medical treatment while they are competent. Uniformity with regard to the legal instruments available for demonstrating what a patient wants should be a common goal of legislators, courts, and the medical profession. If living wills, surrogates, and durable powers of attorney were to be enacted pursuant to national, rather than individual state guidelines, the result should be a greater ease in resolving the myriad conflicting issues in this area. Some states have addressed the problem by statutorily providing for these instruments, thereby enabling individuals to have a say in the medical care they should receive if they become unable to speak for themselves.

Chief Justice Dore of the Washington Supreme Court voiced his opinion that a legislative response to right-to-die issues could be better addressed by the legislature.

> The United States Supreme Court, in *Cruzan*, questioned whether a federally protected right to forgo nutrition and hydration existed. The Cruzan Court confronted the same philosophical issues that we face today and wisely recognized and deferred to the Legislature's superior policymaking abilities. As was the case in *Cruzan*, our legislature is far better equipped to evaluate this complex issue and should not have its power usurped by the court.[23]

Patient Self-Determination Act of 1990

The *Patient Self-Determination Act of 1990* (PSDA)[24] was enacted to ensure that patients are informed of their rights to execute advance directives and accept or refuse medical care. On December 1, 1991, the PSDA[25] took effect in hospitals, skilled nursing facilities, home health agencies, hospice organizations, and health maintenance organizations serving Medicare and Medicaid patients. As a result of implementation of the PSDA,[26] healthcare organizations participating in the Medicare and Medicaid reimbursement programs must address patient rights regarding life-sustaining decisions and other advance directives. Healthcare organizations have a responsibility to explain to patients, staff, and families that patients have a legal right to direct their own medical and nursing care as it corresponds to existing state law, including right-to-die directives. A person's right to refuse medical treatment is not lost when his or her mental or physical status changes. When a person is no longer competent to exercise his or her right of self-determination, the right still exists, but the decision must be delegated to a surrogate decision maker. Those organizations that do not comply with a patient's medical directives or those of a legally authorized decision maker are exposing themselves to the risk of a lawsuit.

Each state is required under PSDA to provide a description of the law in the state regarding advance directives to providers, whether such directives are based on state statutes or judicial decisions. Providers must ensure that written policies and procedures with respect to all adult individuals regarding advance directives are established as follows:

    a. to provide written information to each such individual concerning

        i. an individual's rights under State law (whether statutory or as recognized by the courts of the State) to make decisions concerning such medical care, including the right to accept or refuse medical or surgical treatment and the right to formulate advance directives . . . and

        ii. written policies of the provider organization respecting the implementation of such rights;

    b. to document in the individual's medical record whether or not the individual has executed an advance directive;

    c. not to condition the provision of care or otherwise discriminate against an individual based on whether or not the individual has executed an advance directive;

    d. to ensure compliance with requirements of State law (whether statutory or recognized by the courts of the State) respecting advance directives at the facilities of the provider or organization; and

    e. to provide (individually or with others) for education for staff and the community on issues concerning advance directives.[27]

Although the PSDA is being cheered as a major advancement in clarifying and nationally regulating this often-obscure area of law and medicine, there are continuing problems and new issues that must be addressed. Providers of care who do not comply with the PSDA are not entitled to reimbursement under the Medicare program if they fail to meet PSDA requirements.

▶ DEFINING DEATH

When is a patient considered to be legally dead, and what type of treatment can be withheld or withdrawn? Most cases dealing with euthanasia speak of the necessity for a physician to diagnose a patient as being either in a persistent vegetative state or terminally ill.

Traditionally, the definition of death adopted by the courts has been the *Black's Law Dictionary* definition: "cessation of respiration, heartbeat, and certain indications of central nervous system activity, such as respiration and pulsation."[28] Currently, however, modern science has the capacity to sustain vegetative functions of those in irreversible comas. Medical equipment can sustain heartbeat and respiration even in the face of brain death. With thousands of patients existing in the twilight state of life at this time, every appellate court that has ruled on the question has recognized that the irreversible cessation of brain function constitutes death.

Ethicists who advocate the prohibition on taking action to shorten life agree that, "where death is imminent and inevitable, it is permissible to forgo treatments that would only provide a precarious and painful prolongation of life, as long as the normal care due to the sick person in similar cases is not interrupted."[29]

Brain Death Criteria

The Harvard Ad Hoc Committee on Brain Death published a report in 1968 describing the characteristics of a permanently nonfunctioning brain, a condition it referred to as "irreversible coma," now known as brain death:

1. Patient shows total unawareness to external stimuli and unresponsiveness to painful stimuli.
2. No movements or breathing: All spontaneous muscular movement, spontaneous respiration, and response to stimuli are absent.
3. No reflexes: Fixed, dilated pupils; no eye movement even when hit or turned, or when ice water is placed in the ear; no response to noxious stimuli; no tendon reflexes.

In addition to these criteria, a flat electroencephalogram was recommended.[30]

Relying on the 1968 Harvard Criteria set forth by the Ad Hoc Committee of the Harvard Medical School to Examine the Definition of Brain Death, the American Medical Association (AMA) in 1974 accepted that death occurs when there is "irreversible cessation of all brain functions including the brain stem."[31] Most states recognize brain death by statute or judicial decision. New York, for example, in *People v. Eulo*,[32] in rejecting the traditional cardiopulmonary definition of death, announced that the determination of brain death can be made according to acceptable medical standards. The court also repeated its holding in *In re Storar*[33] that clear and convincing evidence of a person's desire to decline extraordinary medical care may be honored and that a third person may not exercise this judgment on behalf of a person who has not or cannot express the desire to decline treatment. Following the *Bludworth* logic, the court noted that healthcare professionals acting within these cases should not face liability.

The clear and convincing evidence standard was defined more succinctly by the New York Court of Appeals in *In re Westchester County Medical Center ex rel. O'Connor*.[34] There, the court determined that artificial nutrition could be withheld from O'Connor, a stroke victim who was unable to converse or feed herself. The court held that "nothing less than unequivocal proof of a patient's wishes will suffice when the decision to terminate life support is at issue."[35] Factors outlined by the court in determining the existence of clear and convincing evidence of a patient's intention to reject the prolongation of life by artificial means were the following:

- The persistence of statements regarding an individual's beliefs
- The desirability of the commitment to those beliefs
- The seriousness with which such statements were made
- The inferences that may be drawn from the surrounding circumstances

▶ FUTILITY OF TREATMENT

Futility of treatment, as it relates to medical care, occurs when a physician recognizes that the effect of continuing treatment will be of no benefit to the patient. Morally, a physician has a duty to inform the patient when there is little likelihood of success. The determination as to futility of treatment is based on the physician's assessment and medical judgment.

After a diagnosis has been made that a person is terminally ill with no hope of recovery and is in a chronic vegetative state with no possibility of attaining cognitive function, a state generally has no compelling interest in maintaining life. The decision to forgo or terminate life support measures is, at this point, simply a decision that the dying process will not be artificially extended. Although the state has an interest in the prolongation of life, it has no interest in the prolongation of dying, and although there is a moral and ethical decision to be made to end the process, that decision can be made only by the surrogate. The decision of whether to end the dying process is a personal decision for family members or those who bear a legal responsibility for the patient.

A determination as to the futility of medical care is a decision that must be made by a physician. Even if death is not imminent, but a patient's coma is irreversible beyond doubt and there are adequate safeguards to confirm the accuracy of the diagnosis with the concurrence of those responsible for the patient's care, it is not unethical to discontinue all means of life-prolonging medical treatment.

▶ DO-NOT-RESUSCITATE ORDERS

Cardiopulmonary resuscitation (CPR) is an emergency procedure performed on individuals who experience a cardiac arrest. It involves chest compressions and exhaling into the patient's mouth in order to restore circulation and preserve brain function. In 1960, the American Heart Association began a program that was initially designed to educate physicians on closed-chest cardiac resuscitation. CPR has generated a variety of ethical dilemmas that include the use of limited resources on those who have been determined to be in a comatose, vegetative state with no hope of recovery.

Do-not-resuscitate (DNR) orders, or "no-code" orders, are those prescribed by a physician indicating that, in the event of a cardiac or respiratory arrest, no resuscitative measures should be used to revive the patient. A DNR order is an extremely difficult decision to make for both the patient and family. It is generally made when one's quality of life has been so diminished that "heroic" rescue methods are no longer in the patient's best interest. The attending physician or his or her designee may initiate a DNR order at the request of or with the agreement of the patient or the legally appointed healthcare decision maker. A DNR order may be written if the patient has an executable advance directive with instructions regarding DNR status and/or if the transfer information from an extended-care facility indicates the patient should have a DNR order. If a patient lacks the ability to make a decision regarding a DNR order, the patient's legally appointed decision maker can make such decisions provided it can be demonstrated that the decision maker is following the patient's wishes. Advance directives, such as living wills, are helpful in determining a patient's wishes.

DNR orders must be in writing and signed and dated by the physician (**FIGURE 17-1**). Appropriate consents must be obtained either from the patient or his or her healthcare agent. Many states have acknowledged the validity of DNR orders in cases involving terminally ill patients in which the patients' families make no objections to such orders.

FIGURE 17-1 Do-not-resuscitate (DNR) orders.

DNR orders must comply with statutory requirements, be of short duration, and be reviewed periodically to determine whether the patient's condition or other circumstances (e.g., change of mind by the patient or family) surrounding the no-code orders have changed. Presently, it is generally accepted that if a patient is competent, the DNR order is considered to be the same as other medical decisions in which a patient may choose to reject life-sustaining treatment. In the case of an incompetent, absent any advance written directives, the best interests of the patient would be considered.

Competent Patients and No-Code Orders

Should relatives of a patient agree to a no-code order when the patient is competent to make his or her own decision? In *Payne v. Marion General Hospital*,[36] the Indiana Court of Appeals overturned a lower court decision in favor of the physician. The physician had issued a no-code status on Payne despite evidence given by a nurse that, up to a few minutes before his death, Payne could communicate. The physician had determined that Payne was incompetent, thereby rendering him unable to give informed consent to treatment. Because Payne left no written directives, the physician relied on one of Payne's relatives, who asked for the DNR order. The court found that there was evidence that Payne was not incompetent and should have been consulted before a DNR order was given. Furthermore, the court reviewed testimony that, 1 year earlier, Payne had suffered and recovered from the same type of symptoms, leading to the conclusion that there was a possibility that he could have survived if resuscitation had continued. There was no DNR policy in place at the hospital to assist the physician in making his decision. To avoid this type of problem, healthcare providers should adopt an appropriate process with respect to issuing no-code orders.

▶ WITHHOLDING AND WITHDRAWAL OF TREATMENT

Withholding of treatment is a decision not to initiate treatment or medical intervention for the patient. This is a decision often made when death is imminent and there is no hope of recovery. *Withdrawal of treatment* is a decision to discontinue treatment or medical interventions for the patient when death is imminent and cannot be prevented by available treatment. Withholding or withdrawing treatment should be considered in the following circumstances:

- The patient is in a terminal condition and there is a reasonable expectation of imminent death of the patient.
- The patient is in a noncognitive state with no reasonable possibility of regaining cognitive function.
- Restoration of cardiac function will last for a brief period.

Theologians and ethicists have long recognized a distinction between ordinary and extraordinary medical care. The theological distinction is based on the belief that life is a gift from God that should not be destroyed deliberately by humans. Therefore, extraordinary therapies that extend life by imposing grave burdens on the patient and family are not required.

Although the courts have accepted decisions to withhold or withdraw extraordinary care, especially the respirator, from those who are comatose or in a persistent vegetative state with no possibility of emerging, they have been unwilling until recent years to discontinue feeding, which they have considered to be ordinary care. For example, the Illinois Supreme Court, in *In re Estate of Longeway*,[37] found that the authorized guardian of a terminally ill patient in an irreversible coma or persistent vegetative state has a common law right to refuse artificial nutrition and hydration. The court found that there must be clear and convincing evidence that the refusal is consistent with the patient's interest. The court also required the concurrence of the patient's attending physician and two other physicians. Court intervention is also necessary to guard against the possibility that greed may taint the judgment of the surrogate decision maker. Although there may be a duty to provide life-sustaining equipment in the immediate aftermath of cardiopulmonary arrest, there is no duty to continue its use when it has become futile and ineffective to do so in the opinion of qualified medical personnel.

The New Jersey Supreme Court in 1985 heard the case of *In re Claire C. Conroy*.[38] The case involved an

84-year-old nursing home patient whose nephew petitioned the court for authority to remove the nasogastric tube that was feeding her. The court overturned the appellate division decision and held that life-sustaining treatment, including nasogastric feeding, could be withheld or withdrawn from incompetent nursing home patients who will, according to physicians, die within 1 year, in three specific circumstances. These are as follows:

1. When it is clear that the particular patient would have refused the treatment under the circumstances involved (the subjective test)
2. When there is some indication of the patient's wishes (but he or she has not "unequivocally expressed" his or her desires before becoming incompetent) and the treatment "would only prolong suffering" (the limited objective test)
3. When there is no evidence at all of the patient's wishes, but the treatment "clearly and markedly outweighs the benefits the patient derives from life" (the pure objective test based on pain)[39]

A procedure involving notification of the state Office of the Ombudsman is required before withdrawing or withholding treatment under any of the three tests. The ombudsman must make a separate recommendation.

The court also found tubal feeding to be a medical treatment, and as such, it is as intrusive as other life-sustaining measures. If physicians follow the *Quinlan/Conroy* standards and decide to end medical treatment of a patient, the duty to continue treatment ceases. Thus, the termination of treatment becomes a lawful act.

Although *Conroy* presents case-specific guidelines, there is concern that the opinion will have far-reaching repercussions. There is fear that decisions to discontinue treatment will not be based on the "balancing-of-interests" test, but based on the "quality-of-life." Those quality-of-life judgments would be most dangerous for nursing home patients in which age would be a factor in the decision-making process. "Advocates of 'the right to life' fear that the 'right to die' for the elderly and handicapped will become a 'duty to die.'"[40] In both the *Saikewicz* and *Spring* cases, age was a determining factor weighing against life-sustaining treatment. Furthermore, in *In re Hier*,[41] the court found that Mrs. Hier's age of 92 years made the "proposed gastrostomy substantially more onerous or burdensome . . . than it would be for a younger, healthier person." Moreover, a New York Superior Court held that the burdens of an emergency amputation for an elderly patient outweighed the benefit of continued life.[42] Finding that prolonging her life would be cruel, the court stated that life had no meaning for her. Although some courts have recognized the difference, other courts must still address the difference between *Quinlan*-type patients and older, confined, and conscious patients who can interact but whose mental or physical functioning is impaired.

In a New Jersey case, however, the ombudsman denied a request to remove feeding tubes from a comatose nursing home patient.[43] In applying the *Conroy* tests, the ombudsman decided that Hilda Peterson might live more than 1 year, the period that *Conroy* used as a criterion for determining whether life support can be removed.

To complicate this issue further, on March 17, 1986, the AMA changed its code of ethics on comas.[44] Now, physicians may ethically withhold food, water, and medical treatment from patients in irreversible comas or persistent vegetative states with no hope of recovery—even if death is not imminent.[45] Although physicians can consider the wishes of the patient and family or the legal representatives, they cannot cause death intentionally. The wording is permissive, and thus, those physicians who feel uncomfortable withdrawing food and water may refrain from doing so. The AMA's decision does not comfort those who fear abuse or mistake in euthanasia decisions, nor does it have any legal value as such. There are physicians, nurses, and families who are unscrupulous and have their own, and not the patient's, interests in mind. Even with the *Conroy* decision and the AMA's Code of Ethics change, the feeding tube issue is not settled.

On April 23, 1986, the New Jersey Superior Court ruled that the husband of severely brain-damaged Nancy Jobes could order the removal of her life-sustaining feeding tube, which would ultimately cause the 31-year-old comatose patient, who had been in a vegetative state in a hospice for 6 years, to starve to death.[46] Dr. Fred Plum created and defined the term *persistent vegetative state* as one in which:

> [t]he body functions entirely in terms of its internal controls. It maintains temperature. It maintains digestive activity. It maintains heart beat and pulmonary ventilation. It maintains reflex activity of muscles and nerves for low-level conditioned responses. But there is no behavioral evidence of either self-awareness or awareness of the surroundings in a learned manner.[47]

Medical experts testified that the patient could, under optimal conditions, live another 30 years.

Relieving the nursing home officials from removing the feeding tube, the court ruled that the patient could be taken home to die (with the removal to be supervised by a physician and medical care to be provided to the patient at home).

The nursing home had petitioned the court for the appointment of a "life advocate" to fight for continuation of medical treatment for Jobes, which, it argued, would save her life. The court disallowed the appointment of a life advocate, holding that case law does not support requiring the continuation of life support systems in all circumstances. Such a requirement, according to the court, would contradict the patient's right of privacy.

The court's decision applied the principles enunciated in *Quinlan* and *Conroy* and the ruling by the AMA's Council on Judicial Affairs that the provision of food and water is, under certain circumstances, a medical treatment like any other and may be discontinued when the physician and family of the patient feel it is no longer benefiting the patient.

A mentally competent cerebral palsy patient, in *Bouvia v. Superior Court*, won her struggle to have feeding tubes removed even though she was not terminally ill.[48] The California Court of Appeals announced on April 16, 1986, that she could go home to die. The court found that Bouvia's decision to let nature take its course did not amount to a choice to commit suicide with people aiding and abetting it. The court stated that it is not "illegal or immoral to prefer a natural, albeit sooner, death than a drugged life attached to a mechanical device."[49] The court's finding that it was a moral and philosophic question, not a legal or medical one, leaves one wondering whether the courts are opening the door to permitting legal starvation to be used by those who are not terminally ill but who do wish to commit suicide.

Life-Sustaining Measures Became Futile

Although there may be a duty to provide life-sustaining equipment in the immediate aftermath of cardiopulmonary arrest, there is no duty to continue its use after it has become futile and ineffective to do so in the opinion of qualified medical personnel. Two physicians in *Barber v. Superior Court*[50] were charged with the crimes of murder and conspiracy to commit murder based on their acceding to requests of the patient's family to discontinue life support equipment and intravenous tubes. The patient had suffered a cardiopulmonary arrest in the recovery room after surgery. A team of physicians and nurses revived the patient and placed him on life support equipment. The patient had suffered severe brain damage, placing him in a comatose and vegetative state from which, according to tests and examinations by other specialists, he was unlikely to recover. On the written request of the family, the patient was taken off life support equipment. The family, his wife and eight children, made the decision together after consultation with the physicians. Evidence had been presented that the patient, before his incapacitation, had expressed to his wife that he would not want to be kept alive by a machine. There was no evidence indicating that the family was motivated in their decision by anything other than love and concern for the dignity of their loved one. The patient continued to breathe on his own. Because the patient showed no signs of improvement, the physicians again discussed the patient's poor prognosis with the family. The intravenous lines were removed, and the patient died sometime thereafter.

A complaint was then filed against the two physicians. The magistrate who heard the evidence determined that the physicians did not kill the deceased because their conduct was not the proximate cause of the patient's death. On motion of the prosecution, the superior court determined as a matter of law that the evidence required the magistrate to hold the physicians to answer and ordered the complaint reinstated. The physicians then filed a writ of prohibition with the court of appeals. The court of appeals held that the physicians' omission to continue treatment, although intentional and with knowledge that the patient would die, was not an unlawful failure to perform a legal duty. The evidence amply supported the magistrate's decision. The superior court erred in determining that, as a matter of law, the evidence required the magistrate to hold the physicians to answer. The preemptory writ of prohibition to restrain the Superior Court of Los Angeles from taking any further action in this matter—other than to vacate its order reinstating the complaint and to enter a new and different order denying the people's motion—was granted.

▶ EUTHANASIA

There is nothing more sacred than life and there is nothing more natural in life to wish to cling on to it for those you love! And nothing more cruel than to play God by artificially holding onto that which God wants to bring home.

—Author Unknown

When patients and their families perceive a deterioration of the quality of life and no end to unbearable pain, conflict often arises between healthcare professionals, who are trained to save lives, and patients and their families, who wish to end the suffering. This conflict centers on the concept of euthanasia and its place in the modern world. There seems to be an absence of controversy only when a patient who is kept alive by modern technology is still able to appreciate and maintain control over his or her life.

Even the connotation of the word *euthanasia* has changed with time depending on who is attempting to define it. Euthanasia originated from the Greek word *euthanatos*, meaning "good death" or "easy death," and was accepted in situations in which people had what were considered to be incurable diseases. Euthanasia is defined broadly as "the mercy killing of the hopelessly ill, injured, or incapacitated."[51]

Any discussion of euthanasia obliges a person to confront humanity's greatest fear—death. The courts and legislatures have faced it and have made advances in setting forth some guidelines to assist decision makers in this arena; however, much more must be accomplished. Society must be protected from the risks associated with permitting the removal of life support systems. Society cannot allow the complex issues associated with this topic to be simplified to the point where it is accepted that life can be terminated based on subjective quality-of-life considerations. The legal system must ensure that the constitutional rights of the patient are maintained, while protecting society's interests in preserving life, preventing suicide, and maintaining the integrity of the medical profession. For example, can competent adult patients who ask that no extraordinary lifesaving measures be taken recover damages for finding themselves alive after unwanted resuscitative measures? During a medical emergency, it seems unrealistic to ask a caregiver to first look in a patient's medical record for an advance directive before tending to the immediate needs of the patient. In the final analysis, the boundaries of patient rights remain uncertain.

From its inception, euthanasia has evolved into an issue with competing legal, medical, and moral implications that continues to generate debate, confusion, and conflict. Currently, there is a strong movement advocating death with dignity, which excludes machines, monitors, and tubes. **FIGURE 17-2** and **FIGURE 17-3** illustrate and summarize the numerous ramifications of euthanasia discussed in this chapter.

In the Confucian and Buddhist religions, suicide is an acceptable answer to unendurable pain and incurable disease. The Celts went a step farther, believing that those who chose to die of disease or senility, rather than committing suicide, would be condemned to Hell. Such acceptance began to change during the 1800s when Western physicians refused to lessen suffering by shortening a dying patient's life. Napoleon's physician, for example, rejected Napoleon's plea to kill plague-stricken soldiers, insisting that his obligation was to cure, rather than kill, people.

In the late 1870s, writings on euthanasia began to appear, mainly in England and the United States. Although such works were written, for the most part, by lay authors, the public and the medical community began to consider the issues raised by euthanasia. Then defined as the act or practice of painlessly putting to death persons suffering from incurable conditions or diseases, it was considered to be a merciful release from incurable suffering. By the beginning of the 20th century, however, there were still no clear answers or guidelines regarding the use of euthanasia. Unlike in prior centuries when society as a whole supported or rejected euthanasia, different segments of today's society apply distinct connotations to the word, generating further confusion. Some believe euthanasia is meant to allow a painless death when one suffers from an incurable disease, yet is not dying. Others, who remain in the majority, perceive euthanasia as an instrument to aid only dying people in ending their lives with as little suffering as possible.

It has been estimated that of the 2 million Americans who die each year, 80% die in hospitals or nursing homes, and 70% of those die after a decision to forgo life-sustaining treatment has been made. Although such decisions are personal in nature and based on individual moral values, they must comply with the laws applicable to the prolonging of the dying process. Courts have outlined the ways in which the government is allowed to participate in the decision-making process. Yet the misconceptions and lack of clear direction regarding the policies and procedures have resulted in wide disparity among jurisdictions, both in legislation and in judicial decisions. As a result, the AMA, the American Bar Association, legislators, and judges are actively attempting to formulate and legislate clear guidelines in this sensitive, profound, and not yet fully understood area. To ensure compliance with the law, while serving the needs of their patients, it is incumbent on healthcare providers to keep themselves informed about the legislation enacted in this ever-changing field.

To address the topic of euthanasia properly, it is necessary to understand the precise meaning of its recognized forms. Rhetorical phrases such as right to die, right to life, and death with dignity have obfuscated, rather than clarified, the understanding of euthanasia. The dividing of euthanasia into two categories, active or passive, is for many the most controversial aspect of this topic.

Euthanasia

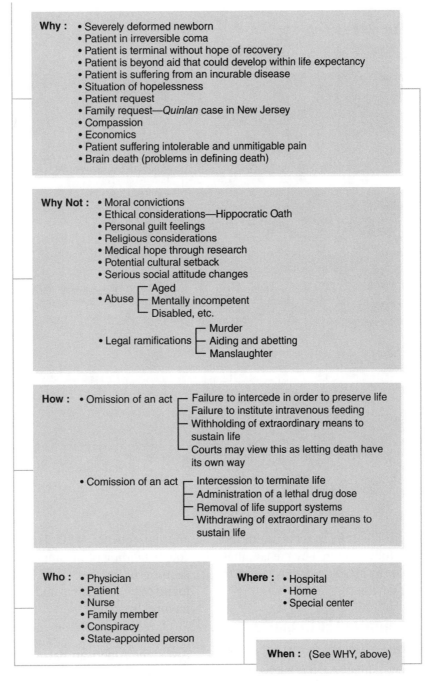

Why :
- Severely deformed newborn
- Patient in irreversible coma
- Patient is terminal without hope of recovery
- Patient is beyond aid that could develop within life expectancy
- Patient is suffering from an incurable disease
- Situation of hopelessness
- Patient request
- Family request—*Quinlan* case in New Jersey
- Compassion
- Economics
- Patient suffering intolerable and unmitigable pain
- Brain death (problems in defining death)

Why Not :
- Moral convictions
- Ethical considerations—Hippocratic Oath
- Personal guilt feelings
- Religious considerations
- Medical hope through research
- Potential cultural setback
- Serious social attitude changes
- Abuse
  - Aged
  - Mentally incompetent
  - Disabled, etc.
- Legal ramifications
  - Murder
  - Aiding and abetting
  - Manslaughter

How :
- Omission of an act
  - Failure to intercede in order to preserve life
  - Failure to institute intravenous feeding
  - Withholding of extraordinary means to sustain life
  - Courts may view this as letting death have its own way
- Comission of an act
  - Intercession to terminate life
  - Administration of a lethal drug dose
  - Removal of life support systems
  - Withdrawing of extraordinary means to sustain life

Who :
- Physician
- Patient
- Nurse
- Family member
- Conspiracy
- State-appointed person

Where :
- Hospital
- Home
- Special center

When : (See WHY, above)

FIGURE 17-2 Ramifications of euthanasia.

Active and Passive Euthanasia

Active euthanasia is commonly understood to be the intentional commission of an act, such as providing a patient a lethal dose of a medication that results in death. The act, if committed by the patient, is thought of as suicide. Moreover, because in most states the patient cannot take his or her own life, any person who assists in the causing of the death could be subject to criminal sanction for aiding and abetting suicide.

Passive euthanasia occurs when lifesaving treatment (such as a respirator) is withdrawn or withheld, allowing a patient diagnosed as terminal to die a natural death. Passive euthanasia is generally accepted pursuant to legislative acts and judicial decisions.[52] These decisions, however, generally are based on the facts of a particular case. Regardless of the definitional differences, though, in both active and passive euthanasia, the end result is the same.

The distinctions are important when considering the duty and the liability of a physician who must decide whether to continue or initiate treatment of a comatose or terminally ill patient. Physicians are

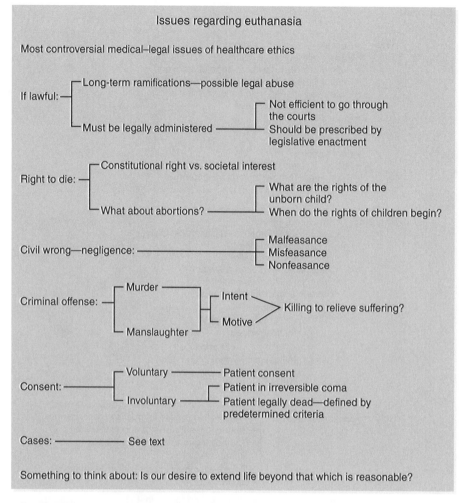

FIGURE 17-3 Issues of euthanasia.

obligated to use reasonable care to preserve health and to save lives, so unless fully protected by the law, they will be reluctant to abide by patient or family wishes to terminate life support devices.

Voluntary and Involuntary Euthanasia

Both active and passive euthanasia may be either voluntary or involuntary. *Voluntary euthanasia* occurs when the suffering, incurable patient makes the decision to die. To be considered voluntary, the request or consent must be made by a legally competent adult and be based on material information concerning the possible ramifications and alternatives available. The term *legally competent* was addressed in a case concerning the right to refuse treatment, *Lane v. Candura*.[53] The case involved a patient who twice refused to permit surgeons to amputate her leg to prevent gangrene from spreading. The patient's daughter sought to be appointed as a legal guardian to enable her to consent to her mother's surgery. The appellate court, finding no evidence indicating that Mrs. Lane was incapable of appreciating the nature

and consequence of her decision, overturned the trial court's holding of incompetence. Even though Lane's decision ultimately would lead to her death, she was found to be competent and thus was allowed to reject medical treatment.

Involuntary euthanasia occurs when a person other than the incurable person makes the decision to terminate the life of the incurable person (i.e., in cases of an incompetent or nonconsenting competent person).

The patient's lack of consent could be a result of mental impairment or a comatose state. Important value questions face courts grappling with making decisions regarding involuntary euthanasia, including the following:

- Who should decide to withhold or withdraw treatment?
- On what factors should the decision be based?
- Are there viable standards to guide the courts?
- Should criminal sanctions be imposed on a person assisting in ending a life?
- When does death occur?

▶ PHYSICIAN-ASSISTED SUICIDE

Derek Humphry's popular book, *Final Exit: The Practicalities of Self-Deliverance and Assisted Suicide for the Dying*, hit the headlines and the bestseller lists in 1992 with its startling subject matter. There were calls for it to be banned, but this is not possible under the U.S. Constitution. Humphry founded the Hemlock Society, which advocated the right to physician-assisted dying for the terminally ill, mentally competent patient. The mission of the society was to provide information to dying patients and support legislation for physician-assisted suicide. Following publication of his book, Humphry left the society. The Hemlock Society later merged with another group and is known today as Compassion and Choices; it is the leading nonprofit organization committed to helping everyone have the best death possible.[54]

The issue of physician-assisted suicide presents profound questions of medicine and medical ethics, theology and sociology, and numerous other far-reaching public policy issues (**FIGURE 17-4**). These are precisely the kinds of issues in which public input is vital, and courts are simply not equipped to conduct the type of comprehensive, broad-based hearings at which witnesses and experts on all sides of the question would testify about the broader policy ramifications of creating and regulating a right to assisted suicide.

The legislative and executive branches in our system of government are uniquely well equipped to pursue these issues. Courts have before them only the legal arguments of lawyers, and although questions of law are certainly part of the equation, the core issues presented are fundamentally grounded in questions of policy and how we view ourselves as a society.[55] It is well established that competent, terminally ill patients may

🅽🅴🆆🆂 *DOCTOR SAYS INSURERS PUSH SUICIDE OVER MEDICAL CARE*

Brian Callister, associate professor of internal medicine at the University of Nevada, said he tried to transfer two patients to California and Oregon for procedures not performed at his hospital. Representatives from two different insurance companies denied those transfer requests by phone, he said.

"And in both cases, the insurance medical director said to me, "Brian, we're going to cover that procedure or the transfer, but would you consider assisted suicide?"
—Bradford Richardson, *The Washington Times*,
June 1, 2017

refuse life-sustaining treatment; physician-assisted suicide, however, continues to raise much debate.

The competing concerns of privacy, morality, patient autonomy, legislation, and states' interests swirl around those involved in the decision-making process. States have been confronted with the question of whether it is ever right for a physician to provide a patient with aid in dying. On July 26, 1991, a Monroe County, New York, grand jury answered "yes" when it failed to indict Dr. Timothy Quill for giving a leukemia patient a lethal dose of sedatives to enable her to take her own life.[56] Dr. Quill wrote an article in *The New England Journal of Medicine* focusing on the suffering of terminally ill patients. He discussed how physicians could relieve an individual's suffering.

In a Florida case, the court ruled that a man dying of acquired immunodeficiency syndrome (AIDS) had

FIGURE 17-4 Physician-assisted suicide.

a right to physician-assisted suicide under the privacy issues of the state's constitution. The court emphasized that the patient had to administer the lethal dose of medication, which was prescribed by his physician. Prosecutors were enjoined from bringing criminal charges against the physician. "The state has a clear interest in preserving life, but not at the unbridled expense of individual autonomy in matters concerning a person's medical treatment decisions," wrote Circuit Judge S. Joseph Davis, Jr.[57]

Michigan and Assisted Suicide

Michigan's Dr. Jack Kevorkian became a controversial figure when he announced in October 1989 that he had developed a device that would end one's life quickly, painlessly, and humanely. The news of his invention was disconcerting because of fears that individuals would abuse the practice of euthanasia, which Kevorkian referred to as a medicide, despite any safeguards that are in place.

Kevorkian assisted Janice Adkins, a 54-year-old Alzheimer's disease patient, in committing suicide on June 4, 1990. In December 1990, he was charged with first-degree murder, but the charge was later dismissed because Michigan had no law against assisted suicide. He was ordered, however, not to help anyone else commit suicide or to give advice about it. On February 6, 1991, he violated the court order by giving advice about the preparation of a drug to a terminally ill cancer patient.[58] Additional murder charges were lodged against Kevorkian in October 1991, when he instructed two Michigan women in the use of his "suicide machine." In dismissing the charges against him on July 21, 1992, Oakland County Circuit Court Judge David Breck stated that some people with intractable pain cannot benefit from treatment. While emphasizing that Michigan has no law against assisting suicide, the judge also expressed his belief that physician-assisted suicide remains an alternative for patients experiencing "unmanageable pain."[59]

The Michigan House, however, approved legislation placing a temporary ban on assisted suicide on November 24, 1992. The Senate approved the temporary ban after Kevorkian assisted a sixth terminally ill patient to end her life. On December 15, 1992, Michigan Governor John Engler signed the law just hours after two more women committed suicide with Kevorkian's aid. The new law, which became effective on April 1, 1993, made assisting suicide a felony punishable by up to 4 years in prison and a $2,000 fine. Under the new law, assisted suicide was banned for 15 months. During this period, a special commission studied assisted suicide and submitted its recommendations to the Michigan legislature for review and action. The new law apparently raised constitutional questions and was challenged by the Civil Liberties Union of Michigan because of the claim that it

fails to recognize that the terminally ill have the right to end their lives painlessly and with dignity.

The Supreme Court of Michigan ruled on December 13, 1994, that assisted suicide is illegal in the state of Michigan. The ruling overturned several lower court decisions. The court determined that there is no constitutional right to aid in carrying out a suicide in Michigan. Dr. Kevorkian, a physician, assisted terminally ill patients in suicide outside the boundaries of the law.

Kevorkian faced prosecution for murdering two people and for assisting in the suicides of three others. As a result, he appealed to a Michigan Supreme Court ruling that found there is no right to assisted suicide.[60] The U.S. Supreme Court rejected Kevorkian's argument that assisted suicide is a constitutional right. The high court's decision allowed the state of Michigan to move forward and prosecute Kevorkian on the pending charges. At the time of the high court's ruling, Kevorkian had attended his 22nd suicide, involving a retired clergyman, less than a month after he was left facing murder charges in Michigan.[61] In 1998, Kevorkian administered a lethal injection to Thomas Youk, a 52-year-old man with Lou Gehrig's disease, on national television. By March 1998, Kevorkian had aided in or witnessed 100 suicides. In the same year Michigan voters defeated a ballot measure that would legalize physician-assisted suicide. In 1999, he was convicted of second-degree murder and was released on June 1, 2007, after serving 8 years of the 10- to 25-year sentence for physician-assisted suicide.

Oregon's Death with Dignity Act

Ironically, while Kevorkian was serving time in a Michigan prison for physician-assisted suicide, Oregon was the first state to legalize assisted suicide by passing the *Death with Dignity Act* on October 27, 1997, allowing terminally ill Oregon residents to obtain prescriptions from their physicians for self-administered, lethal doses of medications. The act legalizes physician-assisted suicide but specifically prohibits euthanasia, where a physician or other person directly administers a medication to end another's life. Physician-assisted suicide, through referendum, became a legal medical option within narrowly prescribed circumstances for terminally ill Oregon residents. In 1998, Oregon voters reaffirmed their support for the Death with Dignity Act by a 60% majority. The Death with Dignity Act provides that the attending physician shall:

1. Make the initial determination of whether a patient has a terminal disease, is capable, and has made the request voluntarily.
2. Inform the patient of:

    a. His or her medical diagnosis;
    b. His or her prognosis;

c. The potential risks associated with taking the medication to be prescribed;

d. The probable result of taking the medication to be prescribed; and

e. The feasible alternatives, including, but not limited to, comfort care, hospice care, and pain control.

3. Refer the patient to a consulting physician for medical confirmation of the diagnosis,

and for a determination that the patient is capable and acting voluntarily.[62]

The request for medication is illustrated in **EXHIBIT 17-1**.

The Oregon Death with Dignity Act[63] allows physicians to prescribe but not administer lethal drugs to the requester, who must be terminally ill with fewer than 6 months to live. The patient must convince doctors that the decision is voluntary, sincere, and not based

---

Request for Medication to End My Life in a Humane and Dignified Manner

I, _____, am an adult of sound mind.

I am suffering from _____, which my attending physician has determined is a terminal disease and which has been medically confirmed by a consulting physician.

I have been fully informed of my diagnosis, prognosis, the nature of medication to be prescribed and potential associated risks, the expected result, and the feasible alternatives, including comfort care, hospice care, and pain control.

I request that my attending physician prescribe medication that will end my life in a humane and dignified manner.

Initial One:

_____ I have informed my family of my decision and taken their opinions into consideration.

_____ I have decided not to inform my family of my decision.

_____ I have no family to inform of my decision.

I understand that I have the right to rescind this request at any time.

I understand the full import of this request and I expect to die when I take the medication to be prescribed. I make this request voluntarily and without reservation, and I accept full moral responsibility for my actions.

Signed: _____ Dated: _____

Declaration of Witnesses

We declare that the person signing this request:

a. Is personally known to us or has provided proof of identity;

b. Signed the request in our presence;

c. Appears to be of sound mind and not under duress, fraud or undue influence;

d. Is not a patient for whom either of us is the attending physician.

EXHIBIT 17-1 Oregon request form to end life.

on being depressed. The waiting period is 15 days. The medication only can be given orally. Two physicians must examine the patient to confirm the diagnosis and prognosis. The patient must have made a witnessed request both orally and in writing. All prescriptions must be reported to the state health department.

Prohibition of Assisted Suicide Ruled Constitutional

The U.S. Supreme Court, in June 1997, made two unanimous and separate decisions, ruling that the laws in Washington and New York prohibiting assisted suicide are constitutional. In the Washington case, *Washington v. Glucksberg*,[64] the Supreme Court applied the same "rationally related to the state's interest in preserving life" test (which includes preventing suicide and studying, identifying, and treating its causes; protecting vulnerable groups; and preventing the state from allowing euthanasia). The Court held that assisted suicide is not a liberty protected by the Constitution's due process clause.

The U.S. Supreme Court, in *Quill v. Vacco*,[65] found that neither the assisted-suicide ban nor the law permitting patients to refuse medical treatment treats anyone differently from anyone else or draws any distinctions between persons. There is a distinction, however, between letting a patient die and making one die. Most legislatures have allowed the former, but have prohibited the latter. The Supreme Court disagreed with the respondents' claim that the distinction is arbitrary and irrational. In its decision, the Supreme Court determined that New York had valid reasons for distinguishing between refusing treatments and assisting suicide. Those reasons included prohibiting intentional killing and preserving life; preventing suicide; maintaining the physician's role as his or her patient's healer; and protecting vulnerable people from indifference, prejudice, and psychological and financial pressure to end their lives. All of those reasons, the Court decided, constitute valid and important public interests fulfilling the constitutional requirement that a legislative classification bear a rational relation to a legitimate end.

Assisted Suicide Law Ruled Constitutional

U.S. Attorney General John Ashcroft, in 2001, challenged Oregon's Death with Dignity Act by claiming that physician-assisted suicide was a violation of the federal Controlled Substances Act because it served no "legitimate medical purpose." In *State of Oregon v. Ashcroft*, CV 01-1647 (D. Oregon), the court allowed Oregon's law to remain in effect. In 2002, the U.S. District Court upheld Oregon's Death with Dignity Act and Attorney General John Ashcroft filed an appeal, asking the Ninth U.S. Circuit Court of Appeals to lift the district court's ruling. On May 26, 2004, a three-judge panel of the Ninth U.S. Circuit Court of Appeals voted two to one to uphold the Oregon lawsuit initiated in 2002. This blocked the attempt by the U.S. Justice Department, under Attorney General Ashcroft, to use the federal Controlled Substances Act to prevent doctors in the state from prescribing drugs to assist the suicide of their patients. The Ashcroft directive interfered with Oregon's authority to regulate medical care within its borders and therefore altered the usual constitutional balance between state and the federal governments.[66]

The U.S. Supreme Court on January 17, 2006, in *Gonzales v. Oregon*,[67] ruled that the states could allow physicians to assist in the suicide of their terminally ill patients. In a six-to-three vote, the court upheld Oregon's physician-assisted suicide law. Former Attorney General John Ashcroft was found to have overstepped his authority in seeking to punish doctors who prescribed drugs to help terminally ill patients end their lives. The Supreme Court determined that the Oregon law supersedes federal authority to regulate physicians and that the Bush administration improperly attempted to use the Controlled Substances Act to prosecute Oregon physicians who assist in patient suicides. The Supreme Court blocked the Bush administration's attempt to punish doctors who help terminally ill patients die, protecting Oregon's one-of-a-kind assisted suicide law.[68]

Legalization of Assisted Suicide

At the time of this writing, California, Colorado, District of Columbia, Montana, Oregon, Vermont, and Washington have legalized physician-assisted suicide. Vermont became the third state to legalize physician-assisted suicide, when Governor Peter Shumlin signed into law a bill allowing physicians to legally prescribe lethal doses of medication for terminally ill patients.

The Montana Supreme Court ruled that state law protects physicians from prosecution for assisting terminally ill patients in committing suicide. The court, however, did not address whether assisted suicide was guaranteed under the state's constitution.[69] Montana "HB 505 which would have explicitly prohibited doctor-prescribed suicide was introduced by Rep. Krayton Kerns. The bill passed in the House and was sent to the Senate, where it failed on April 15, 2013 in a 27–23 vote."[70]

California's physician-assisted dying law, ABX2-15n(AB-15), the End of Life Option Act, took effect on June 9, 2016. The physician-assisted suicide debate and rulings from the various states continue, as noted in the Massachusetts ballot question 2, Death with Dignity initiative, where legalized physician-assisted suicide was defeated by a narrow margin.[71]

▶ ADVANCE DIRECTIVES

(NEWS) *EVEN DOCTORS FIND IT HARD TO THINK ABOUT MORTALITY*

[L]iving wills or designated proxies cannot exist in isolation. Instead, these questions must begin with a lot of self-reflection and difficult conversations with our loved ones. But none of that can happen until we come to terms with the unsettling reality of our own mortality.
— Daniel Marchalik, *The Washington Post*, August 16, 2016

Advance directives for health care are instructions given by individuals specifying what actions should be taken for their health in the event that they are no longer able to make healthcare decisions as a result of illness or incapacity. Patients have a right to make decisions about their health care with their physician. They may agree to a proposed treatment, choose among offered treatments, or say no to a treatment. Patients have this right even if they become incapacitated and are unable to make decisions regarding their health care.

Because of the advances in modern medical technology, each person should give serious consideration as to their healthcare wishes, decide what they would want done should they become incapacitated, execute advance directives, and make their wishes known so that family and healthcare providers can respect their decision.

Advance directives include, for example, a living will and/or *durable power of attorney*. They both provide that a person may state in advance the kinds of medical care that he or she considers acceptable or not acceptable. The patient can appoint an *agent*, or a *surrogate decision maker*, to make those decisions on his or her behalf. A patient should be asked at the time of admission whether he or she has an advance directive. If a patient does not have an advance directive, the organization should provide the patient with information about an advance directive and the opportunity to execute one. A patient should clearly understand that an advance directive is a guideline for caregivers describing his or her wishes for medical care—what he or she would and would not want—in the event of incapacitation and inability to make one's own decisions. This interaction should be documented in the patient's medical record. If the patient has an advance directive, a copy should be requested for insertion into the patient's record. If the patient does not have a copy of the advance directive at the time of surgery, the substance thereof should be documented and flagged in the patient's medical record. Documentation should

include the location of the advance directive, the name and telephone number of the designated healthcare agent, and any information that might be helpful in the immediate care situation (e.g., patient's desire for food and hydration). The purpose of such documentation should not be considered to be a need to recreate a new directive, but should be considered a need to adhere to a patient's wishes in the event some untoward event occurs while waiting for a copy of the directive.

The patient can execute a new directive at any time if desired. Patient and family education should be provided regarding the existence of the directive and its contents. The patient should be periodically queried about whether he or she wishes to make any changes with regard to an advance directive.

Obligation to Make Preferences Known

Patients have an obligation to make medical preferences known to the treating physician. Any glimmer of uncertainty regarding a patient's desires in an emergency situation should be resolved in favor of preserving life.

The patient in *Matter of Hughes*[72] signed a standard hospital form entitled "Refusal to Permit Blood Transfusion." There was no indication on the form that the consequences of her refusal had been explained to her in the context of the elective surgical procedure she was about to undergo. The form should have contained an unequivocal statement that under any and all circumstances, blood is not to be used and an acknowledgment that the consequences of the refusal were fully explained. The form should have fully released the physician, all medical personnel, and the hospital from liability should complications arise from the failure to administer blood, thereby resolving any doubt as to the physician's responsibility to his patient. If Hughes would have refused to sign such a form, her physician could then decide whether to continue with Hughes's treatment or aid her in finding a physician who would carry out her wishes.

The court emphasized that this case arose in the context of elective surgery. This was not an emergency situation in which the physician and patient did not have time to fully discuss the potential risks, benefits, and alternatives of the planned surgery and the conflict arising over the patient's religious beliefs. Patients have an obligation to make medical preferences known to the treating physician, including the course to follow if life-threatening complications should arise. This protects the patient's right to freedom of religion and self-determination. In addition, it is helpful to the hospital when faced with the dilemma of trying to preserve life whenever possible versu⁄ honoring the patient's wishes to forgo life-sustaini⁄ treatment.

Living Will

A *living will* is the instrument or legal document that describes those treatments an individual wishes or does not wish to receive should he or she become incapacitated and unable to communicate treatment decisions (see **FIGURE 17-5**). The first living will legislation was enacted in California in 1976, permitting a person to sign a declaration stating that if there is no hope of recovery, no heroic measures need to be taken to prolong life. This provision is now available in every state. In 2010, legislation was introduced in California that would make it the first state in the country to build a Living Donor Registry. "Senate Bill 1395 by Sen. Elaine Alquist, D-Santa Clara, would make it easier for people to decide whether they want to donate their organs when they die, by requiring them to check a box when they get their driver's license."[73]

Typically, a living will allows a person, when competent, to inform caregivers in writing of his or her wishes with regard to withholding and withdrawing life support treatment, including nutrition and hydration. The living will is helpful to healthcare professionals because it provides guidance about a patient's wishes for treatment, provides legally valid instructions about treatment, and protects the patient's rights and the provider who honors them.

The Supreme Court determined that Kentucky's Living Will Directive Act was constitutional in *T. Bruce Simpson, Jr. v. Commonwealth of Kentucky and Cabinet for Human Resources*.[74] The act allows a judicially appointed guardian or other designated surrogate to remove life support. After suffering cardiac arrest, it was agreed the patient, Woods, would never regain consciousness. After a recommendation of the hospital's ethics committee, Woods' guardian asked for the removal of Woods' life support. If there is no legal guardian but the physicians, family, and ethics committee all agree with the surrogate's decision—in this case, the state's—there is no need for judicial approval.

FIGURE 17-5 Living will.

© Jim Barber/ShutterStock, Inc.

The Supreme Court did determine that when there is disagreement in a particular case, withdrawal of life support would be prohibited absent clear and convincing evidence that the patient is permanently unconscious or in a persistent vegetative state and that withdrawal of life support was in the patient's best interest. In support of its holding, the Supreme Court cited the ethical standards of the National Center for State Courts, the Council on Ethical and Judicial Affairs of the AMA, an Address to an International Congress of Anesthesiologists by Pope Pius XII, and the Declaration on Euthanasia by Pope John Paul II:

> In determining the patient's best interests, courts may consider, but are not limited to considering: (1) the patient's present level of physical, sensory, emotional, and cognitive functioning and possibility of improvement thereof; (2) any relevant statements or expressions made by the patient, when competent, as to his or her own wishes with a rebuttable presumption attaching to a valid living will or a designation of a health care surrogate; (3) to the extent known, the patient's own philosophical, religious, and moral views, life goals, values about the purpose of life and the way it should be lived, and attitudes toward sickness, medical procedures, suffering, and death; (4) the degree of physical pain caused by the patient's condition, treatment, and termination of treatment; (5) the degree of humiliation, dependence, and loss of dignity probably resulting from the condition or treatment; (6) the life expectancy and prognosis for recovery with and without the treatment; (7) the various treatment options and their risks, benefits, and side effects; whether any particular treatment would be proportionate or disproportionate in terms of the benefits gained; and (8) the impact on the patient's family (the assumption being that the patient would be concerned about the well-being and happiness of his or her own family members).

The living will should be signed and dated by two witnesses who are not blood relatives or beneficiaries of the patient's property. A living will should be discussed with the patient's physician, and a signed copy should be placed in the patient's medical record. A copy also should be provided to the individual designated to make decisions in the event the patient is unable to do so. A person who executes a living will when healthy and mentally competent cannot predict how he or she will feel at the time of a terminal illness; therefore, it should be updated regularly so that it accurately reflects a patient's wishes. The written instructions become effective when a patient is either in a terminal condition, permanently unconscious, or suffering irreversible brain damage. An example of a *living will* is illustrated in **EXHIBIT 17-2**.

Dying Without a Living Will

In *San Juan-Torregosa v. Garcia*,[75] the evidence at trial established that Garcia suffered a cardiac arrest. Although she was later resuscitated, she suffered oxygen deprivation to her brain for more than 10 minutes and

---

My Living Will

To my Family, Doctors, and All Those Concerned with my Care:

I, _____, being of sound mind, make this statement as a directive to be followed if for any reason I become incapacitated and unable to participate in decisions regarding my medical care.

If I should be in an incurable or irreversible mental or physical condition with no reasonable expectation of recovery, I direct my attending physician to withhold or withdraw treatment that merely prolongs my dying. I direct that my treatment in this instance be limited to comfort care and the control of and relief from pain.

Care I Want:

_____
_____
_____
_____

To live as long as possible regardless of the quality of life that I may experience:

☐ I direct that all appropriate medical/surgical measures be provided to sustain my life regardless of my mental or physical condition.

☐ Upon my death, I want to donate any parts of my body that may be of benefit to others.

Care I Do Not Want:

_____
_____
_____
_____

☐ I am permanently unconscious with and permanently connected to a ventilator.
☐ I am permanently unconscious with a feeding tube and/or intravenous hydration.
☐ I am on a ventilator when there is little or no chance of recovery.
☐ I am conscious but unable to communicate, being fed with a feeding tube and/or hydrated.
☐ I am in the end stage of a fatal irreversible mental or physical illness, disease, or condition.
☐ I do not want: _____ Mechanical ventilation _____
    CPR _____ Dialysis _____ Feeding tubes _____
☐ Other exceptions and/or comments:

_____
_____
_____
_____

Additional Comments or Exceptions:

This living will describes my express wishes and legal right to accept or refuse treatment. As I am of sound mind, I expect my family, physician(s), and all those concerned with my care to regard themselves as legally and morally bound to act in accord with my wishes.

Signed _____ Date _____

Witness (cannot be designated healthcare agent). I declare that the person who signed the document or asked another to sign this document on his/her behalf did so in my presence and that he/she appears to be of sound mind and free of duress or undue influence.

Signed _____ Date _____

Signed _____ Date _____

Note: A copy of the executed living will should be provided to the patient's physician and healthcare agent.

EXHIBIT 17-2 My living will.

was in a chronic vegetative state. There was no evidence that she would be able to recover "cortical functions." Garcia's treating physician, Dr. Parrish, testified that Garcia was functioning on a low brain level, whereby the brain stem kept her blood circulating, maintained blood pressure, and maintained respiration and that she was in a persistent vegetative state with a zero chance of recovering any cortex activity. Dr. Parrish further stated that he discussed the discontinuation of artificial nutrition and hydration with the family and that they had ultimately decided to continue the fluids but stop the nutrition, which he felt was reasonable.

When asked why Garcia had been given life support in the first place, Dr. Parrish explained that although Garcia's injury initially seemed very severe, he could not say from the beginning whether she would recover and wanted to give her every chance to improve if she could. The trial court ruled that because Garcia, who was in a chronic vegetative state, had not executed a living will, the court had no authority to authorize discontinuance of artificial nutrition. On appeal, the appellants asserted that the trial court erred in refusing to allow Garcia's family to terminate the artificial nutrition and hydration, thereby failing to honor her wishes and denying her constitutional right to bodily integrity.

The Court of Appeals of Tennessee at Knoxville concurred with the Trial Court's fact finding that the evidence was clear and convincing that Ms. Garcia would not want to be kept alive by artificial means and that her wishes, expressed while she was competent, would be to have these services discontinued. The appeals court ruled that the courts have a duty to protect, and when necessary, enable individuals to exercise their constitutional rights. Since Ms. Garcia had no written preference, her husband would be the first choice to act as her conservator and make medical decisions for her. The judgment of the trial court was remanded for proceedings in accordance with this opinion.[76]

Living Will Declaration Upheld

The plaintiff-sister (Oris Pettis) was not entitled to enjoin her brother and sister from implementing the living will in which their mother, Doris Smith, directed the withdrawal of life-sustaining medical procedures in the event she should have a terminal and irreversible condition. Smith, at the age of 89, suffered a debilitating stroke in March 2004. Although she survived, she no longer had any significant brain function. Dr. Maran examined Ms. Smith and assessed her condition as being in a vegetative state with no chance of improvement. After consideration of their mother's condition, Steve Smith and Dianne Braddock indicated that the hospital should stop providing nutrition to their mother through the gastric feeding tube that had been inserted. Mr. Smith

and Mrs. Braddock informed Dr. El-Malah, her treating physician, that their mother had executed a living will in March 2001. Drs. Maran and El-Malah signed the form, attesting that the resident would die whether or not life-sustaining procedures were used and that the application of such procedures would serve only to artificially prolong the dying process. The patient's declarations specifically prohibited her daughters from making decisions about life-sustaining procedures pursuant to La. R.S. 40:1299.58.1, et seq. The second section, captioned "Declaration of living will for terminal illness pursuant to La. R.S. 40:1299.58.1," declares:

> I willfully and voluntarily make known my desire that my dying shall not be artificially prolonged under the circumstances set forth below and do hereby declare:
>
> If at any time I should be diagnosed as having incurable injury, disease, or illness certified to be a terminal and irreversible condition by two physicians who have personally examined me, one of whom shall be my attending physician, and the physicians have determined that my death will occur whether or not life-sustaining procedures are utilized and where the application of life-sustaining procedures would serve only to prolong artificially the dying process; I direct that such procedures be withheld or withdrawn and that I be permitted to die naturally with only the administration of medication or the performance of any medical procedure deemed necessary to provide me with comfort care.
>
> In the absence of my ability to give directions regarding the use of such life-sustaining procedures, it is my intention that this declaration shall be honored by my family and physician(s) as the final expression of my legal right to refuse medical or surgical treatment and accept the consequences of such refusal. I understand the full import of this declaration and appointment of my attorney-in-fact and I am emotionally and mentally competent to make this declaration.[77]

Healthcare Proxy

A *healthcare proxy* is a legal document that allows a person to appoint a healthcare agent to make treatment decisions in the event he or she becomes incapacitated and is unable to make decisions for him or herself. The agent must be made aware of the patient's wishes regarding nutrition and hydration in order to be allowed to make a decision concerning withholding or withdrawing them. In contrast to a living will, a healthcare proxy does not require a person to know about and consider in advance all situations and decisions that could arise. Rather, the appointed agent would know about and interpret the expressed wishes of the patient and then make decisions about the medical care and treatment to be administered or refused.

Most states allow the document to be effective until revoked by the individual. To revoke, the patient must sign and date a new writing, personally destroy the first document, direct another to destroy the first document in his or her presence, or orally state to the physician one's intent to revoke the healthcare proxy document. The effect of the directive varies among jurisdictions. However, there is unanimity in the promulgation of regulations that specifically authorize healthcare personnel to honor the directives without fear of incurring liability.

The highest court of New York in *In re Eichner*[78] complied with the request of a guardian to withdraw life support systems from an 83-year-old brain-damaged priest. The court reached its result by finding the patient's previously expressed wishes to be determinative. Prior to exercising an incompetent patient's right to forgo medical treatment, the surrogate decision maker must satisfy the following conditions:

1. The surrogate must be satisfied that the patient executed a document (e.g., durable power of attorney for health care and healthcare proxy) knowingly, willingly, and without undue influence, and that the evidence of the patient's oral declaration is reliable.
2. The patient must not have reasonable probability of recovering competency so that the patient could exercise the right.
3. The surrogate must take care to ensure that any limitations or conditions expressed either orally or in written declarations have been considered carefully and satisfied.

Before declaring an individual incapacitated to make end-of-life decisions, the attending physician must find, with a reasonable degree of medical certainty, that the patient lacks capacity. A notation should be placed in the patient's medical record describing the cause, nature, extent, and probable duration of incapacity. Before withholding or withdrawing life-sustaining treatment, a second physician must confirm the incapacity determination and make an appropriate entry on the medical record before honoring any new decisions by a healthcare agent.

Durable Power of Attorney

A *durable power of attorney* is a legal device that permits one individual, known as the principal, to give to another person, called the *attorney-in-fact*, the authority to act on his or her behalf. The attorney-in-fact is authorized to handle banking and real estate affairs, incur expenses, pay bills, and handle a wide variety of legal affairs for a specified period. The power of attorney may continue indefinitely during the lifetime of the principal so long as that person is competent and capable of granting power of attorney. If the principal becomes comatose or mentally incompetent, the power of attorney automatically expires, just as it would if the principal dies. California passed the first durable power of attorney statute in 1983, permitting an advance directive to be made describing the kind of health care that one would desire when facing death by designating an agent to act on the patient's behalf.

Because a power of attorney is limited by the competency of the principal, some states have authorized a special legal device for the principal to express intent concerning the durability of the power of attorney to allow it to survive disability or incompetency. The durable power of attorney is more general in scope, and the patient does not have to be in imminent danger of death, as is necessary in a living will situation. Although it need not delineate desired medical treatment specifically, it must indicate the identity of the principal's attorney-in-fact and that the principal has communicated his or her healthcare wishes to the attorney-in-fact. Although the laws vary from state to state, all 50 states and the District of Columbia have durable power of attorney statutes. This legal device is an important alternative to guardianship, conservatorship, or trusteeship. Because a durable power of attorney places a considerable amount of power in the hands of the attorney-in-fact, an attorney in the state where the client resides should draw up the power of attorney. In the healthcare setting, a durable power of attorney for health care is a legal instrument that designates and grants authority to an agent. An example of a *durable power of attorney* is illustrated in **EXHIBIT 17-3**.

Surrogate Decision Making

A *surrogate decision maker* is an agent who acts on behalf of a patient who lacks the capacity to participate in a particular decision. A healthcare agent's rights are no greater than those of a competent patient; however, the agent's rights are limited to any specific instructions included in the proxy document. An agent's decisions take priority over any other person except the patient. The agent has the right to consent or refuse to consent to any service or treatment, routine or otherwise; to refuse life-sustaining treatment; and to access all of the patient's medical information to make informed decisions. The agent must make decisions based on the patient's moral and religious beliefs. If a patient's wishes are not known, decisions must be based on a good faith judgment of what the patient would have wanted.

Durable Power of Attorney for Health Care

I, _____, appoint:

1. Name _____ Phone _____ Address _____ as my attorney-in-fact or agent to make my health and personal care decisions for me if I become unable to make my own decisions. If the person I have named above is unable to act as my agent, I hereby designate the following person to serve as my agent:

2. Name _____ Phone _____ Address _____

This *durable power of attorney* shall become effective upon my incapacity to make health or personal care decisions. (Please initial the statement/s below that best expresses your wishes.)

_____ I authorize my admission to or discharge from any medical, nursing, residential, or similar facility and to enter into agreements for my care.

_____ I authorize my agent to refuse or withdraw consent to any and all types of treatment, including, but not limited to, nutrition and hydration administered by artificial or invasive means.

I have discussed with my agent my wishes for health care. If my agent is not able to determine what I would want, I trust my agent to make his/her decision based on what he/she believes would be my wishes. This durable power of attorney is meant to replace all others.

Signed _____ Date _____

Witness (Cannot be the principal's designated healthcare agent). I declare that the person who signed this document or asked another to sign this document on his/her behalf did so in my presence and that he/she appears to be of sound mind and free of duress or undue influence.

Signed _____ Date _____

Signed _____ Date _____

Primary Agent

I, _____, have read the above durable power of attorney and am the person identified as the agent for _____. My signature below indicates that I acknowledge and accept responsibility to act as the agent and will exercise the powers herein granted in the best interest of the principal.

Signed _____ Date _____

Substitute Agent

I, _____, have read the above durable power of attorney and am the person identified as the agent for _____. My signature below indicates that I acknowledge and accept responsibility to act as the agent and will exercise the powers herein granted in the best interest of the principal.

Signature _____ Date _____

State of _____

County of _____

On this date, the _____ day of, 20 _____, before me, the undersigned officer, personally appeared, _____ known to me (satisfactorily proven) to be the person whose name is subscribed to the foregoing instrument, and acknowledged that he/she executed it for the purposes therein contained.

Witness my hand and official seal the day and year aforesaid _____

Notary Public

Note: A copy of the executed durable power of attorney should be provided to the patient's physician and healthcare agent.

EXHIBIT 17-3 Durable power of attorney for health care.

Substituted judgment is a form of surrogate decision making where the surrogate attempts to establish what decision the patient would have made if that patient were competent. This conclusion can be based on the patient's preference expressed in previous statements or the surrogate's knowledge of the patient's beliefs (e.g., religious) and values.[79]

In 1976, the New Jersey Supreme Court, in the matter of Karen Ann Quinlan,[80] rendered a unanimous decision providing for the appointment of Joseph Quinlan as personal guardian of his daughter.

Guardianship

Guardianship is a legal mechanism by which the court declares a person incompetent and appoints a guardian. The court transfers the responsibility for managing financial affairs, living arrangements, and medical care decisions to the guardian.

The right to refuse medical treatment on behalf of an incompetent person is not limited to legally appointed guardians, but may be exercised by healthcare proxies or surrogates such as close family members or friends. When a patient has not expressed instructions concerning his or her future health care in the event of later incapacity, but has merely delegated full responsibility to a proxy, designation of a proxy must have been made in writing.

When a person has been declared incompetent as a result of being in a persistent vegetative state and has left no advance directive, life-sustaining decisions become more complex. Since 1990, Terri Schiavo from Clearwater, Florida, had been in a persistent vegetative state after a heart attack cut off the supply of oxygen to her brain. Her husband Michael became her legal guardian and fought to have her feeding tube removed, which was against her parents' wishes. Michael argued that Terri had articulated her desire not to be kept alive by artificial means.

In an unprecedented move, on October 21, 2003, Governor Jeb Bush signed an order based on a hastily passed law called Terri's Law, mandating the reinsertion of Ms. Schiavo's feeding tube, which had been removed 6 days earlier. Mr. Schiavo filed an appeal based on a violation of his wife's right to privacy under the Florida Constitution, asserting that the law intruded on the separation of powers. This case is the first time a governor and legislative branch of government have usurped not only the authority of the judiciary, but also the rights of legal guardians to make decisions.

The law was narrowly tailored to fit Terri Schiavo's circumstances: a patient has not left a living will, is in a persistent vegetative state, has had feeding tubes removed, and a family member challenges the removal.

Florida law Chapter 2003-418 was passed by the Florida legislature. It directly affected the patient, Terri Schiavo, who had been in a persistent vegetative state since 1990. The act provided that the governor shall have authority to issue a one-time stay to prevent the withholding of nutrition and hydration from the patient. The act was determined to be unconstitutional as applied in the *Schiavo* case. The Supreme Court of Florida in *Schiavo* concluded:

> The continuing vitality of our system of separation of powers precludes the other two branches from nullifying the judicial branch's final orders. If the Legislature with the assent of the Governor can do what was attempted here, the judicial branch would be subordinated to the final directive of the other branches. Also subordinated would be the rights of individuals, including the well established right to self-determination. See *Browning*, 568 So.2d at 11–13. No court judgment could ever be considered truly final and no constitutional right truly secure, because the precedent of this case would hold to the contrary. Vested rights could be stripped away based on popular clamor. The essential core of what the Founding Fathers sought to change from their experience with English rule would be lost, especially their belief that our courts exist precisely to preserve the rights of individuals, even when doing so is contrary to popular will.[81]

The U.S. Supreme Court, on January 24, 2005, denied an appeal by Florida Governor Jeb Bush to overturn a decision by the Florida Supreme Court, which ruled Terri's Law unconstitutional.

▶ AUTOPSY

Autopsies, or postmortem examinations, are conducted to ascertain the cause of a person's death, which, in turn, may resolve several legal issues. An autopsy may reveal whether death was the result of criminal activity, whether the cause of death was one for which payment must be made in accordance with an insurance contract, whether the death is compensable under workers' compensation and occupational disease acts, or whether death was the result of a specific act or a culmination of several acts. Aside from providing answers to these specific questions, the information gained from autopsies adds to medical knowledge. As such, medical schools have an interest in autopsies for educational purposes.

In those instances when the death of a patient is the result of criminal activity or unusual or suspicious circumstances, the patient's death must be reported to the medical examiner. Deaths resulting from natural causes within 24 hours of admission to a hospital do not need

SPOUSE'S GUARDIANSHIP RIGHTS QUESTIONED

Citation: *In re Martin*, 517 N.W.2d 749 (Mich. Ct. App. 1994)

Facts

Martin sustained debilitating injuries as the result of an automobile accident. His injuries left him totally paralyzed on the left side. He could communicate to a very minimal degree through head nods.

The trial court determined that Martin did not have nor would he ever have the ability to have the requisite capacity to make decisions regarding the withdrawal of life support equipment. Evidence demonstrated that Martin's preference would have been to decline life support equipment given his medical condition and prognosis. The trial court's decision was based on the following four-part test for determining whether a person has the requisite capacity to make a decision: the person (1) has sufficient mind to reasonably understand the condition, (2) is capable of understanding the nature and effect of the treatment choices, (3) is aware of the consequences associated with those choices, and (4) is able to make an informed choice that is voluntary and not coerced. The trial court determined that the spouse was a suitable guardian for Martin.

Mrs. Martin petitioned to withdraw her husband's life support. Martin's mother and sister counter-petitioned to have Mrs. Martin removed as the patient's guardian.

Issue

Was there sufficient evidence to support a finding that: (1) the patient lacked capacity to make decisions regarding the removal of life-sustaining treatment; (2) the patient would have had a medical preference to decline life-sustaining treatment under the circumstances; and (3) Mrs. Martin would be a suitable individual to represent her husband as to the withdrawal of life-sustaining medical treatment?

Holding

The Michigan Court of Appeals held there was sufficient evidence to support a finding that: (1) the patient lacked capacity to make decisions regarding the withholding or withdrawal of life-sustaining treatment; (2) the patient would have declined treatment under the circumstances such as those that occurred; and (3) there was sufficient evidence to show that the patient's spouse was a suitable guardian.

Reason

The burden of proof for determining whether Martin had the requisite capacity to make a decision regarding the withholding or withdrawing of life-supporting medical treatment was clear and convincing. It was the general consensus of all of the experts that Martin's condition and cognitive level of functioning would not improve in the future.

Testimony from two of Martin's friends described statements made by him that he would never want to be maintained in a coma or in a vegetative state. In addition, Mrs. Martin described numerous statements made to her by Martin prior to the accident that he would not want to be maintained alive given the circumstances described here. The trial court found that Mrs. Martin was credible. The court of appeals found no reason to dispute the trial court's finding as to Mrs. Martin's credibility.

Contrary to allegations made by the patient's mother and sister, the evidence was clear that Mrs. Martin's testimony was credible. There was no evidence that Mrs. Martin had anything but her husband's best interest at heart. There were allegations, but no evidence, of financial considerations or pressure from another individual that would indicate that Mrs. Martin's testimony was influenced by other individuals.

---

to be reported as long as the patient was in the hospital at the time of death and as long as an appropriate physician signs the death certificate and records the cause of death.

Deaths that occur during a surgical procedure are generally reportable events to the medical examiner. If an autopsy for medical evaluation is desired by the hospital, consent must be obtained from the next of kin. An unauthorized autopsy may disturb persons whose religious beliefs prohibit such a procedure as well as those persons who have a general aversion to the procedure. When autopsies are performed without statutory authorization and without the consent of the

decedent, the surviving spouse, or an appropriate relative, liability may be imposed.

Damages awarded in cases of liability through interference with the rights of a surviving spouse or near-relative with regard to the body of a decedent are based on the emotional and mental suffering that results from such interference. For damages to be awarded, the conduct of the alleged wrongdoer must be sufficiently disturbing to a person of ordinary sensibilities as to cause emotional harm. Cases involving the wrongful handling of dead bodies may be classified into four groups: (1) mutilation of a body, (2) unauthorized autopsy, (3) wrongful detention, and (4) unauthorized use or publication of photographs taken after death.

To limit lawsuits regarding the disposition of dead bodies, appropriate handling and release procedures should be established. Legal counsel should review such procedures. Interfering with rights to a body can result in liability. For example, in the case of *Lott v. State*,[82] two bodies were improperly tagged. The body of a person of the Roman Catholic faith was prepared for Orthodox Jewish burial, and the person of the Orthodox Jewish faith was prepared for Roman Catholic burial. This negligent conduct interfered with burial plans and caused mental anguish, for which liability was imposed.

Autopsy Consent Statutes

Recognizing both the need for information that can be secured only through the performance of a substantial volume of autopsies and the valid interests of relatives and friends of the decedent, most states have enacted statutes dealing with autopsy consent. Such legislation seems intended to have a twofold effect: first, to protect the rights of the decedent's relatives, and second, to guide those performing autopsies in establishing procedures for consent to autopsy. Most autopsy consent statutes establish an order for obtaining consent to autopsy based on the degree of family relationship.

Authorization by Decedent

Most autopsy consent statutes provide that persons may authorize an autopsy prior to death. Ordinarily, such consent must be in writing. There may be legal as well as practical problems in obtaining authorization for an autopsy from a patient before death if the state does not statutorily provide for such authorization.

In states where there is neither an autopsy consent statute nor a statute permitting donation that may be construed to include autopsy, it is unwise to rely exclusively on the authorization of a decedent to perform an autopsy. This is especially true when relatives of the deceased who assume custody of the body for burial object to an autopsy.

Although the courts have upheld the wishes of the deceased with respect to the place of internment or the manner of disposition of the remains (i.e., by burial or cremation), it is possible that the courts will not afford the same weight to the decedent's wishes concerning an autopsy. In such instances, compelling reasons presented by certain next of kin of the decedent, especially the surviving spouse, may prevail over the wishes of the decedent.

Authorization by Someone Other Than Decedent

Generally, the primary right to custody of a deceased person belongs to the surviving spouse. When there is no spouse, the right passes (in the absence of statutes furnishing a preference order of responsibility for burial and consent for autopsy) to the adult children of the deceased, parents, adult siblings, grandparents, uncles and aunts, and finally cousins. A court may find that a surviving spouse's unwillingness to assume responsibility for burial is sufficient to permit the right to custody of the body to devolve on a relative who is willing to assume such responsibility.

In *Callsen v. Cheltenham York Nursing Home*,[83] the relatives of the decedent, Mrs. Callsen, sued the defendants regarding the transfer of her body to a teaching hospital for dissection purposes. The defendants claimed immunity from liability under good faith provisions of the Uniform Anatomical Gift Act. An amended complaint named 22 separate defendants. The complaint recited that Callsen was the mother of the plaintiffs and that, prior to her death she resided at the Cheltenham York Nursing Home. The nursing home maintained records of family and friends who visited her. On May 27, 1990, the nursing home transferred Callsen (who died on or about June 9, 1990) to the Einstein Medical Center. The medical center was notified that there was no family information for Callsen. In an amended complaint that, following Callsen's death, no efforts were made by the medical center to locate and notify family members regarding the transfer of the decedent's remains. The family did not discover her whereabouts until approximately 10 days after her death, and by that time, the body had been partially dissected. The plaintiffs also claim that the defendants were negligent in failing to follow the statutory procedures for disposition of a deceased person's remains and that their conduct was grossly negligent and outrageous.

The common pleas court sustained the medical center's preliminary objections and dismissed the complaint. An appeal was taken as to whether or not there were triable issues of fact with regard to the medical center making appropriate efforts to locate the patient's family.

The commonwealth court held that there were triable issues of fact whether appropriate efforts to locate the patient's family had been made. Although the nursing facility had access to the names of family members, the nursing facility agreement did not record their names. One of the facility's nurses reported to Einstein Medical Center that there was no family information for the decedent. The complaint does not disclose what efforts, if any, were made to locate the relatives or to notify any of them as to the proposed disposition of the decedent's remains. The court held that the ultimate decision as to the presence or absence of the exercise of good faith by any of the three parties must await the filing of further pleadings, the completion of any necessary discovery, and possible motions for summary judgment.

Scope and Extent of Consent

Legal issues may arise as a result of an autopsy even if consent has been obtained from the person authorized by law to grant such consent. If autopsy procedures go beyond the limits imposed by the consent or if the consent to an autopsy is obtained by fraud or without the formal requisites, liability may be incurred. It is a fundamental principle that a person who has the right to refuse permission for the performance of an act also has the right to place limitations or conditions on consent.

It is especially important that the hospital and its personnel adhere to any limitations or conditions placed on the permission to autopsy; if such limitations are exceeded, the physician or the hospital has no defense on the ground of emergency or medical necessity.

Although consent to autopsy also may encompass authorization for removal of body parts for examination, a separate question may arise concerning disposal of tissues and organs on completion of the examination: May the hospital and its personnel dispose of such material in a routine manner or use it for the hospital's own purposes, or must the hospital return the tissue and body organs before burial? In *Hendriksen v. Roosevelt Hospital*,[84] permission had been granted for a complete autopsy, including an examination of the central nervous system by a scalp incision. Yet the court held that liability might be imposed on the hospital if the jury found that the hospital retained parts of the body. Pursuant to a New York statute requiring the authorization of the next of kin, consent was given for dissection; however, the court held that this statute should be construed narrowly and that special consent would have to be obtained to retain the internal organs of the decedent.

Consent given with the understanding that organs and tissue could be removed and retained for examination would seem to authorize the hospital to dispose of such materials in a suitable manner or to use them after the autopsy. However, the *Hendriksen* decision raises doubts on this matter. When the party giving consent expressly stipulates that parts severed from the body are to be returned to the body for burial, conduct deviating from this provision may result in liability. Also, it would appear that consent to autopsy does not include authorization to mutilate or disfigure the body. Therefore, when autopsy involves the removal of exterior body parts and the physical appearance of the body cannot be restored without return of such parts,

the hospital may be subject to liability for **exceeding** the scope of the authorization if the removed **parts are** not returned. In general, hospitals should **periodically** review protocols for obtaining consent, **limitations** placed on an autopsy, and the disposition of body parts.

Fraudulently Obtained Consent

It is a long-accepted principle that consent obtained through fraud or material misrepresentation is not binding and that the person whose consent is so obtained stands in the same position as if no consent had been given. This principle can apply to autopsies when facts are misrepresented to the person who has the right to consent to induce his or her consent. If a physician or a hospital employee states, as fact, something known to be untrue to gain consent, the autopsy would be unauthorized, and liability might follow.

Unclaimed Dead Bodies

Persons entitled to possession of a dead body must arrange for release of the body for transfer to an undertaker for final disposal. The body of a deceased person imposes a duty on a healthcare facility to make reasonable efforts to give notice to persons entitled to claim the body. When there are no known relatives or friends of the family who can be contacted by the facility to claim the body, the facility has a responsibility to dispose of the body in accordance with law.

Most states have statutes providing for the disposal of unclaimed bodies by delivery to institutions for

📰 ORGANS FOR SALE

All over the world, the organs of human beings are being trafficked, sometimes with, and sometimes without, the consent of those to whom they belong. People are directly, or indirectly, being forced to sell their own organs for a low price, often to middlemen, who make thousands of Euros from poor vulnerable persons.

• • •

The organs commonly transplanted include kidney, liver, heart, lung and pancreas. The organ most frequently given by a living donor is kidney as humans have two kidneys and you can live easily with only one. But also parts of other organs including liver, lung and pancreas can be transplanted from living donors. And a variety of tissues and cells are routinely implanted for a wide range of procedures.

—*United Nations Regional Information Centre for Western Europe*, April 19, 2017.[85]

educational and scientific purposes. The public official in charge of the body has a duty to notify the government agency of the presence of the body, which then arranges for the transfer of the body in accordance with the statute. If no such agency exists under the statute, the healthcare facility or a public official may be authorized to allow a medical school or other institution or person, designated by the statute as an eligible recipient of unclaimed dead bodies, to remove the body for scientific use. For public health reasons, the statutes usually do not permit distribution of the bodies of persons who have died from contagious diseases.

Although most statutes explicitly require notification of relatives and set time limits for holding the body to allow relatives an opportunity to claim it, strict compliance with the statutory provisions is often impossible because of the very nature of the problems that arise in the handling of dead bodies and in the required procedures themselves. An example of such a provision is the requirement that relatives be notified immediately on death and that the body be held for 24 hours subject to claim by a relative or friend. The procedure of locating and notifying relatives may consume the greater part of the 24-hour period after death. If relatives who are willing to claim the body are located, the body should be held for a reasonable time to allow them to arrange custody for burial.

▶ ORGAN DONATIONS AND TRANSPLANTATION

There are approximately 119,000 men, women, and children on the national transplant waiting list. In 2015 there were 30,970 transplants performed while at the same time 22 people die each day waiting for a transplant. Although 95% of adults believe in organ transplantations only 48% have actually registered as donors. To help resolve the shortage of donors, every eligible person is encouraged to register in their state as a donor.[86]

Federal regulations require that hospitals have, and implement, written protocols regarding the organization's organ procurement responsibilities. The regulations impose specific notification duties, as well as other requirements concerning informing families of potential donors. They encourage discretion and sensitivity in dealing with the families and in educating hospital staff on a variety of issues involved with donation matters in order to facilitate timely donation and transplantation. The Joint Commission standards require that hospitals comply with the rules of the "Organ Procurement and Transplantation Network" (https://optn.transplant.hrsa.gov).[87]

The first kidney transplant[88] was conducted in 1954. The transplantation of human organs has generated numerous ethical issues (e.g., the harvesting and selling of organs, who should have first access to freely donated human organs, how death is defined).

Organ transplantation is done to treat patients with end-stage organ disease who face organ failure. Developments in medical science have enabled physicians to take tissue from persons immediately after death and use it to replace or rehabilitate diseased or damaged organs or other parts of living persons. Interest in organ transplantation began approximately 25 years ago when attempts were made to transplant kidneys between twins.[89] Success rates have improved because of better patient selection, improved clinical and operative management and skills, and immunosuppressant drugs that aid in decreasing the incidence of tissue rejection (e.g., cyclosporine, which acts to suppress the production of antibodies that attack transplanted tissue); nevertheless, this progress has created the problem of obtaining a sufficient supply of replacement body parts. There is a corresponding cry for more organs as the success rate in organ transplantation increases. Because of the fear of people buying and selling organs, the National Organ Procurement Act was enacted in 1984, making it illegal to buy or sell organs. Throughout the country, there are tissue banks and other facilities that store and preserve organs and tissue that can be used for transplantation and other therapeutic services.

The ever-increasing success of organ transplantations and the demand for organ tissue require the close scrutiny of each case, ensuring that established procedures have been followed in the care and disposal of all body parts. Section 1138, Title XI, of the Omnibus Budget Reconciliation Act of 1986 requires hospitals to establish organ procurement protocols or face a loss of Medicare and Medicaid funding. Physicians, nurses, and other paramedical personnel assigned with this responsibility often are confronted with several legal issues. Liability can be limited by complying with applicable regulations. Organs and tissues to be stored and preserved for future use must be removed almost immediately after death; therefore, it is imperative that an agreement or arrangement for obtaining organs and tissue from a body be completed either before death or soon after death, to enable physicians to remove and store the tissue promptly.

Who Lives? Who Dies? Who Decides?

Who lives? Who dies? Who decides? These are but a few of the ethical questions that arise when deciding to whom an organ shall be given. The answers are not easy. The decision makers, even with guidelines to follow, often become the judge and jury and find that answers to questions such as who lives and dies are not always easy decisions to make. If there were unlimited sources of organs, there would be no supply and demand issues. Because there is not an unlimited supply, numerous ethical principles come into play. In the case of a 70-year-old patient with multiple life-threatening health problems, the patient may not be considered a suitable candidate for transplantation, whereas a 15-year-old patient with few health issues would be considered a more appropriate candidate.

Determination of Death

The time of a patient's death must be determined by a physician in attendance at the donor's death, or a physician certifying death, who shall not be a member of the team of physicians engaged in the transplantation procedure.

Consideration of legal duties regarding the use, handling, and disposition of dead bodies cannot be divorced from the legal questions involved in determining when death occurs. In many contexts, such as deciding rights to the property of the deceased person, the determination of death does not involve the hospital or its personnel. However, when permission has been granted for use of a patient's body or organs for the benefit of another or science in general, determination of the point of death becomes critical. New technology, specifically medical advancement in artificially sustaining life and transplanting vital organs, raises both legal and moral questions regarding the viability of the traditional methods of determining death.

Uniform Anatomical Gift Act

The American Bar Association has endorsed a Uniform Anatomical Gift Act drafted by the Commission on Uniform State Laws. This statute has been enacted by all 50 states and has many detailed provisions that apply to the wide variety of issues raised in connection with the making, acceptance, and use of anatomic gifts. The act allows a person to make a decision to donate organs at the time of death and allows potential donors to carry an anatomic donor card. State statutes regarding donation usually permit the donor to execute the gift during his or her lifetime.

The right to privacy of the donor and his or her family must be respected. Information should not be disseminated regarding transplant procedures that publish the names of the donor or donee without adequate consent.

Virtually all of the states have based their enactments on the Uniform Anatomical Gift Act, but it should be recognized that in some states, there are deviations from this act or additional laws dealing with donation.

Individuals who are of sound mind and 18 years of age or older are permitted to dispose of their own bodies or body parts by will or other written instrument for medical or dental education, research, advancement of medical or dental science, therapy, or transplantation.

Among those eligible to receive such donations are any licensed, accredited, or approved hospitals; accredited medical or dental schools; surgeons or physicians; tissue banks; or specified individuals who need the donation for therapy or transplantation. The statute provides that when only a part of the body is donated, custody of the remaining parts of the body shall be transferred to the next of kin promptly after removal of the donated part.

A donation by will becomes effective immediately on the death of the testator, without probate, and the gift is valid and effective to the extent that it has been acted on in good faith. This is true even if the will is not probated or is declared invalid for testimonial purposes.

Failure to Obtain Consent

There is a shortage of cadavers needed for medical education and transplantation. Some people may wish to make arrangements for the use of their bodies after death for such purposes. A surviving spouse may, however, object to such disposition. In such cases, the interest of the surviving spouse or other family member could supersede that of the deceased.

Although failure to obtain consent for removal of body tissue can give rise to a lawsuit, not all such claims are successful. In *Nicoletta v. Rochester Eye & Human Parts Bank*,[90] emotional injuries resulted from the removal of the eyes of Nicoletta's son for donation after a fatal motorcycle accident. The hospital was immune from liability under the provisions of the Uniform Anatomical Gift Act because the hospital had neither actual nor constructive knowledge that the woman who had authorized the donation was not the decedent's wife. The hospital was entitled to the immunity afforded by the "good faith" provisions of Section 4306(3) of the act in which its agents had made reasonable inquiry as to the status of the purported wife, who had resided with the decedent for 10 years and was the mother of their two children. The hospital had no reason to believe that any irregularity existed. The father, who was present at the time his son was brought to the emergency department, failed to object to any organ donation and failed to challenge the authority of the purported wife to sign the emergency department authorization.

There are several methods by which a donation may be revoked. If the document has been delivered to a named donee, it may be revoked by:

- A written revocation signed by the donor and delivered to the donee
- An oral revocation witnessed by two persons and communicated to the donee
- A statement to the attending physician during a terminal illness that has been communicated to the donee

- A written statement that has been signed and is on the donor's person or in the donor's immediate effects

If the written instrument of donation has not been delivered to the donee, it may be revoked by destruction, cancellation, or mutilation of the instrument. If the donation is made by a will, it may be revoked in the manner provided for revocation or amendment of wills. Any person acting in good faith reliance on the terms of an instrument of donation will not be subject to civil or criminal liability unless there is actual notice of the revocation of the donation.

▶ RESEARCH, EXPERIMENTATION, AND CLINICAL TRIALS

Research studies are designed to answer specific questions, sometimes about a drug or device's safety and effectiveness. Participating in a research study is different from being a patient. As a patient, one's personal physician has a great deal of freedom in making healthcare decisions. As a research subject, the protocol director and the research staff follow the rules of the research study (protocol) as closely as possible, without compromising the patient's health.[91]

Ethical principles relevant to the ethics of research involving human subjects include respect for person, beneficence, and justice. These principles cannot always be applied to resolve ethical problems beyond dispute. The objective in applying ethical principles is to provide an analytical framework that will guide the resolution of ethical problems arising from research involving human subjects.

(NEWS) *CODDLING HUMAN GUINEA PIGS*

Endless Red Tape . . . Is Having a Stifling Effect on Clinical Research

Let's agree that people who are altruistic enough to volunteer for experiments should know what they're in for if the study is testing a drug that has harmed lab animals, for instance, or if it involved a psychological manipulation that might have emotional scars. . . .

Doing studies on people "is so full of red tape that even experienced researchers are increasingly reluctant to tackle it," a scientist from the University of California, told me. "It is so much simpler to deal with a mouse." But haven't we cured enough of them?

—Sharon Begley, *Newsweek*, August 25, 2008

The Cures Act

The *Cures Act*, formally known as H.R. 34 or the 21st Century Cures Act, passed in the U.S. House of Representatives and Senate in the 114th Congress and was signed into law by President Barack Obama on December 13, 2016. It included important changes affecting the Food and Drug Administration and the National Institutes of Health.[92] The *Cures Act* established and appropriated funds "(1) for biomedical research, including high-risk, high-reward research and research conducted by early stage investigators; (2) to develop and implement a strategic plan for biomedical research; and (3) to carry out specified provisions of this Act." The following describes some of the relevant provisions of the *Cures Act*.[93]

TITLE I—DISCOVERY
(Sec. 1002) The NIH must establish an Innovation Prizes Program to fund areas of biomedical science that could realize significant advancements or improve health outcomes.
(Sec. 1023) The NIH must reduce the administrative burdens of researchers funded by the NIH.
(Sec. 1027) The support the National Center for Advancing Translational Sciences may provide to clinical trials is extended through a later clinical trial phase.
(Sec. 1028) Each national research institute must conduct or support high-risk, high-reward research.[94]

Title II of the Act requires the FDA to establish processes under which patient experience data may be considered in the risk–benefit assessment of a new drug.

(Sec. 2441) The FDA must define "precision" drugs and the evidence needed to support their use in a subset of patients. To expedite clinical development of precision drugs for the treatment of serious or rare conditions, the FDA may rely upon data previously submitted for a different approved drug or indication.
Subtitle E—Expediting Patient Access
(Sec. 2082) Manufacturers and distributors of investigational drugs for serious conditions must publish their policies on expanded access (also known as "compassionate use").
(Sec. 2201) The FDA must establish a program for priority review of breakthrough medical devices."[95]

Ethical considerations that must be addressed when conducting research on human subjects include personal autonomy; self-determination; the moral issues involved in using persons as subjects of research, the Hippocratic maxim of "do no harm" and the Hippocratic Oath's requirement that physicians benefit their patients "according to their best judgment"; and various meanings of the term "justice," such as whether burdens are to be distributed to each person equally, to each according to his or her needs, to each according to his or her societal contribution, or to each according to merit.

The Holocaust that occurred from 1932–1945 was one of the most violent events in human history. Over 6 million Jews perished, as well as millions of others, including Slavs, homosexuals, and Gypsies. In 1946, a military tribunal for war crimes began criminal proceedings against 23 German physicians and administrators for war crimes. As a direct result of these proceedings, the Nuremberg Code was established, which made it clear that the voluntary and informed consent of human subjects is essential to research and that benefits of research must outweigh risks to the human subjects involved.[96] The code requires that human subjects be fully informed as to the nature and societal benefits of the research being undertaken and provides guidelines for the development of federal regulations for medical research and the protection of human subjects.

By 1946, following the Nuremberg trials, the *International Code of Medical Ethics* was adopted in the wake of the numerous experiments conducted by the Nazis on prisoners in concentration camps. Prisoners were exposed to cholera, diphtheria, malaria, mustard gas, yellow fever, typhus, and other horrendous experiments, ultimately claiming thousands of lives. This exploitation of unwilling prisoners as research subjects in Nazi concentration camps was condemned as a particularly flagrant injustice.

Medical progress and improved patient care are dependent on advances in medicine made through research. The basic principle of research is honesty, which must be ensured through institutional protocols. Fraud in research is not uncommon, and it must be condemned and punished. Honesty and integrity must govern all stages of research.

In 1964, the World Medical Association developed the Declaration of Helsinki, which contains ethical principles that provide guidance to physicians and other participants in medical research involving human subjects. The declaration includes medical research that involves readily identifiable human material or identifiable data. The declaration contains strict guidelines for protecting the life, health, and privacy of the human subject.

Federal regulations control federal grants that apply to experiments involving new drugs, new medical devices, or new medical procedures. Generally, a combination of federal and state guidelines

and regulations ensures proper supervision and control over experimentation that involves human subjects. For example, federal regulations require hospital-based researchers to obtain the approval of an institutional review board (IRB). This board functions to review proposed research studies and conduct follow-up reviews on a regular basis.

Federal regulations control federal grants that apply to experiments involving new drugs, new medical devices, stem cell research and human cloning, or new medical procedures. Generally, a combination of federal and state guidelines and regulations ensures proper supervision and control over experimentation that involves human subjects. For example, federal regulations require hospital-based researchers to obtain the approval of an IRB prior to conducting clinical trials. This board functions to review proposed research studies and conduct follow-up reviews on a regular basis.

Research and ethical guidelines are helpful when followed. Even so, public disclosure of questionable research practices has raised many alarms over the years as noted in the following "Failed Research" *reality check*.

✓ FAILED RESEARCH?

Was it the failures of research we saw or was it cruelty inflicted on the helpless? As students in healthcare administration in 1967–68, something was not quite right as we toured several psychiatric facilities somewhat close to the university. At one facility we were taken to an underground, dark, dingy corridor where we observed iron-barred cells with patients who appeared to lack the attributes that reflect a human being. There seemed to be no dignity related to their care. They were caged in like animals without clothes. As we walked down the corridor we were told not to get too close to the caged cells. An eerie feeling came over us as we looked into each barred cage. There appeared to be distinct species of humans totally different from what we would expect to see above ground. What cruelties were inflicted on these people? It was unsettling to see and unnerving to describe. We just thought to ourselves, how ghastly, there are people like this in the world. We asked ourselves many questions.

- Were they born this way and if they were, why were they hidden away in a dungeon?
- Were these the results of failed experiments?
- Do such facilities exist today?
- Was this really the state of affairs across the nation for patients with mental illness?
- What are the legal implications and ethical responsibilities of government to regulate medical research?

Institutional Review Board

Each organization conducting medical research should have a mechanism in place for approving and overseeing the use of investigational protocols. This is accomplished through the establishment of an IRB, which should include community representation. The IRB is responsible for reviewing, monitoring, and approving clinical protocols for investigations of drugs and medical devices involving human subjects and ensuring that the rights of each individual are protected and that all research is conducted within appropriate state and federal guidelines (e.g., Food and Drug Administration guidelines).

> Under FDA regulations, an IRB is an appropriately constituted group that has been formally designated to review and monitor biomedical research involving human subjects. In accordance with FDA regulations, an IRB has the authority to approve, require modifications in (to secure approval), or disapprove research. This group review serves an important role in the protection of the rights and welfare of human research subjects.
>
> The purpose of IRB review is to assure, both in advance and by periodic review, that appropriate steps are taken to protect the rights and welfare of humans participating as subjects in the research. To accomplish this purpose, IRBs use a group process to review research protocols and related materials (e.g., informed consent documents and investigator brochures) to ensure protection of the rights and welfare of human subjects of research.[97]

Informed Consent

Physicians have a clear duty to warn patients as to the risks and benefits of an experimental procedure, as well as the alternatives to a proposed experimental procedure. Written consent should be obtained from each patient who participates in a clinical trial. Consent should include the risks, benefits, and alternatives to the proposed treatment protocol. The consent form must not contain any coercive or exculpatory language through which the patient is forced to waive his or her legal rights, including the release of the investigator, sponsor, or organization from liability for negligent conduct.

Federal and state regulations impose several other requirements on experiments involving human subjects. Organizations conducting clinical trials on human subjects, at the very least, must do the following:

- Fully disclose to the patient the inherent risks, benefits, and treatment alternatives to the proposed research protocol(s).
- Determine the competency of the patient to consent.
- Obtain written consent from the patient.
- Educate the staff as to the potential side effects, implementation of, and ongoing monitoring of protocols.
- Require financial disclosure issues associated with the protocols.
- Promote awareness of ethical issues.
- Promote education in regard to ethical decision making.
- Increase nurse participation in ethical decision making.
- Have ongoing monitoring of approved protocols.

Research Subject's Bill of Rights

The following is a bill of rights developed by the Veterans Administration system for patients involved in research studies.

> As a human subject, you have the following rights. These rights include, but are not limited to, the subject's right to be:

- informed of the nature and purpose of the experiment;
- provided with an explanation of the procedures to be followed in the medical experiment and any drug or device to be used;
- provided with a description of any attendant discomforts and risks reasonably to be expected;
- provided with an explanation of any benefits to the subject reasonably to be expected, if applicable;
- provided with a disclosure of any appropriate alternatives, drugs, or devices that might be advantageous to the subject, their relative risks, and benefits;
- informed of the avenues of medical treatment, if any, available to the subject after the experiment if complications should rise;
- provided with an opportunity to ask questions concerning the experiment or the procedures involved;
- instructed that consent to participate in the medical experiment may be withdrawn at any time and the subject may discontinue participation without prejudice;
- provided with a copy of the signed and dated consent form; and

- provided with the opportunity to decide to consent or not to consent to a medical experiment without the intervention of any element of force, fraud, deceit, duress, coercion, or undue influence on the subject's decision.[98]

Failure to Obtain Informed Consent

The necessity of informed consent cannot be overemphasized. In *Friter v. Iolab Corp.*,[99] the hospital contracted with the FDA to participate in a clinical study involving the implantation of experimental intraocular lenses. They were so experimental that they had not yet obtained FDA approval; hence, the FDA promulgated regulations requiring the hospital to obtain informed consent, using a very detailed, five-page consent form, setting forth with particularity the possibility of the existence of unknown risks because the lenses were still being tested. The court held in this case that the failure to obtain informed consent is actionable.

Federal regulations require that the nature of experimental drugs and possible adverse consequences must be explained to the patient. Failure to obtain consent for the administration of experimental drugs can give rise to a lawsuit. The district court, in *Blanton v. United States*,[100] held that when a new drug of unknown effectiveness was administered to a patient at a Navy medical center, despite the availability of other drugs of known effectiveness, the hospital violated the accepted medical standards and its duty of due care, so that in the absence of the patient's consent to the experiment, the United States was liable for the resulting injury.

Duty to Warn

Even if patient consent is obtained, the consent must adequately inform the patient of a treatment's potential side effects. Approximately 5,000 patients at the Michael Reese Hospital and Medical Center, located in Chicago, were treated with X-ray therapy for benign conditions of the head and neck from 1930 to 1960. Among them was Joel Blaz, who received this treatment for infected tonsils and adenoids.

In 1974, Michael Reese set up a thyroid follow-up project to conduct research among those who had been subjected to the X-ray therapy. In 1975, Blaz was notified by mail that he was at increased risk of developing thyroid tumors because of the treatment. In 1976, someone associated with the program gave him similar information by phone and invited him to return to Michael Reese for evaluation and treatment at his own expense, which he declined to do.

Dr. Schneider was put in charge of the program in 1977. In 1979, Dr. Schneider and Michael Reese submitted a research proposal to the National Institutes of Health stating that a study based on the program showed evidence of a connection between X-ray treatments of the sort administered to Blaz and various sorts of tumors, including thyroid and neural. In 1981, Blaz received but did not complete or return a questionnaire attached to a letter from Dr. Schneider in connection with the program. The purpose of the questionnaire was to investigate the long-term health implications of childhood radiation treatments and to determine the possible associated risks. It did not say anything about strong evidence of a connection between the treatments and any tumors. In 1996, after developing neural tumors, Blaz sued Michael Reese's successor, Galen Hospital, and Dr. Schneider, alleging that they failed to notify and warn him of their findings that he might be at greater risk of neural tumors in a way that might have permitted their earlier detection and removal or other treatment.

The court here found that the harm alleged—neural and other tumors—would here be reasonably foreseeable as a likely consequence of a failure to warn and was, in fact, foreseen by Dr. Schneider. A reasonable physician could foresee that if someone were warned of "strong evidence" of a connection between treatments to which he had been subjected and tumors, he would probably seek diagnosis or treatment to perhaps avoid these tumors; and if he were not warned, he probably would not seek diagnosis or treatment, increasing the likelihood that he would suffer from such tumors.[101]

Patents Delay Research

The legal system—caught up in the rights of patent holders—has resulted in delayed cures. What happens to the rights of those who would have benefited from the cures?

Nursing Facilities

The review process of the Centers for Medicare and Medicaid Services includes a review of the rights of any nursing facility residents participating in experimental research. Surveyors will review the records of residents identified as participating in a clinical research study. They will determine whether informed consent forms have been executed properly. The form will be reviewed to determine whether all known risks have been identified. Appropriate questions may be directed to both the staff and residents or the residents' guardians.

Possible questions to ask staff include:

- Is the facility participating in any experimental research?
- If yes, which residents are involved? (Interview a sample of these residents.)

Residents or guardians may be asked questions such as the following:

- Are you participating in the study?
- Was this explained to you well enough so that you understand what the study is about and any risks that might be involved?[102]

Patients participating in research studies should fully understand the implications of their participation. Healthcare organizations involved in research studies should have appropriate protocols in place that protect the rights of patients. Consent forms should describe both the risks and benefits involved in the research activity.

Patient Understood the Risks

Most people understand the risks associated with clinical trials, yet they are willing to take those risks so that those with similar illnesses may benefit from their sacrifice. This takes *courage*, the foundation of all other virtues. As reported in the following excerpt from *The Wall Street Journal*, one couple took the risk so others may live.

> Three years later, we have just learned of the disease's progression, but we continue to look forward, remain optimistic, and support those who dedicate their lives for the betterment of those afflicted with these cursed cancers. The reality is that someday, probably sooner than later, my husband will lose the battle with this tenacious enemy, but we are still thankful for the compassionate and learned members of all those who participate in research.[103]

▶ HUMAN GENETICS

Human genetics describes the study of inheritance as it occurs in human beings. It includes such areas as stem cell research, clinical genetics (e.g., genetic disease markers), and molecular genetics. In 1975, scientists conducted the first successful cloning of a frog; in 1996, cloning was revolutionized when Ian Wilmut and his colleagues at the Roslin Institute in Edinburgh, Scotland, successfully cloned a sheep named Dolly, the first cloned mammal. By 2003, the human genome system had been fully sequenced, allowing molecular genetics and medical research to accelerate at an unprecedented rate. The ethical implications of human genome research are as immense as the undertaking of the totality of the research that was conducted to map the human genome system.

Few New Cures But Hope Looms

The New York Times in 2010 reported "Ten years after President Bill Clinton announced that the first draft of the human genome was complete, medicine has yet to see any large part of the promised benefits."[104] Since that time "Genomics has become a fast-moving field, with findings pouring out of labs all over the world. Each month, the National Human Genome Research Institute will highlight what it considers the coolest genomic advances, broadly defined, of the previous month."[105] The National Human Genome Research Institute's "Genome Advance by Month" can be found at its website (www.genome.gov/27543594/). In February 2016, the following news was reported, "a leap forward in understanding the heritability and progression of schizophrenia in a study by researchers at Harvard Medical School and the Broad Institute."[106] One of the most exciting projects was reported in February 2017 as follows:

> February 2, 2017: NIH to expand critical catalog for genomics research
> Bethesda, Md., Wed., February 1, 2017—The National Institutes of Health (NIH) plans to expand its Encyclopedia of DNA Elements (ENCODE) Project, a fundamental genomics resource used by many scientists to study human health and disease. Funded NHGRI, a part of the NIH, the ENCODE Project strives to catalog all genes and regulatory elements—the parts of the genome that control whether genes are active or not—in humans and select model organisms. Four years of additional support will build on a long-standing commitment to developing freely available genomics resources for use by the scientific community.[107]

Inevitably, ethical issues will continue to arise. The ethics of modern science is a challenging and evolving area, but it is nothing new. In ancient China, for instance, physician Sun Simiao (580–682 AD) had a difficult medical ethical dilemma. In his book *Qianjinfang* (*Prescriptions Worth a Thousand Pieces of Gold*), he is credited with formulating the first ethical basis for the practice of medicine in China. The ethical conundrum he faced was the clash between Confucian and

Buddhist ethics. The relatively new religion of Buddhism had taboos against using any animal-derived product for the treatment of disease, as this violated the principle of respect for all life. The more ancient Confucian idea of compassion and kindness could be interpreted to overrule this, however. Sun Simiao dealt with this conflict by prohibiting a "standard physician" from using any medication derived from an animal source. He then included many prescriptions in his book that did have animal-sourced remedies. In other words, he seems to have artfully navigated an ethical gray zone between the two philosophies, but with a less than clear distinction between right and wrong. In modern times, we are still faced with continuing and evolving issues of ethics in the practice of medicine.[108]

Genetic Markers

Genetic markers are genes or DNA sequences with a known location on a chromosome that can be used to identify specific cells and diseases, as well as individuals and species. They are often used to study the relationship between an inherited disease and its genetic cause in order to determine an individual's predisposition/proclivity to a specific disease. Genetic markers show observable information in DNA sequence variation, which may arise as a result of mutation of a specific gene. There are companies that can evaluate a person's DNA for these markers and provide a person with a report of his or her potential health risks. Health insurers, life insurers, employers, and others could potentially use this information to determine one's insurance premiums and even one's job future and so forth; the potential use (and misuse) of this information means that ethical issues will arise. For instance, suppose a woman has a family history of breast cancer and has a genetic marker for it, but she is young (e.g., 30 years old) and free of any evidence of cancer. If a physician recommends prophylactic mastectomies or if the patient wants prophylactic mastectomies, should this be covered by insurance?

Genetic Information Nondiscrimination Act of 2008

President Bush signed into law the *Genetic Information Nondiscrimination Act* (GINA) on May 21, 2008, resulting largely from the efforts of Senator Ted Kennedy. The law prohibits discrimination on the basis of genetic information with respect to the availability of health insurance and employment. GINA prohibits group health plans and insurers from denying coverage to a healthy individual or charging that person higher premiums based solely on a genetic predisposition to developing a specific disease (e.g., cancer or heart disease) at some future time. GINA also prohibits employers from using an individual's genetic information when making hiring, firing, job placement, or promotion decisions.

The relatively recent mapping of the human genome and the likelihood of increasing clinical application of advances in genetic disease markers make this an issue of potential increasing importance in the practice of medicine. Most states have legislation that addresses this issue. Unfortunately, however, there is still no federal legislation that protects people from discrimination in the availability of life insurance, disability insurance coverage, or long-term care insurance. Because of this loophole, patients and their doctors need to consider the potential downside of ordering prognostic genetic tests.

▶ STEM CELL RESEARCH

Stem cell research involves the use of embryonic stem cells to create organs and various body tissues. The use of fetal stem cells versus adult stem cells for research and therapy continues to be a highly controversial issue, generally involving religious beliefs and fears about how far scientists might go in their attempt to create, for example, another human being. After all, a sheep named Dolly was already cloned and born in 1996, and who knows what goes on behind the doors of research, which are closed to the outside world.

The search for cures for cancer, autoimmune disorders, heart disease, and so on is often slowed by political, religious, and personal beliefs and conflicts. The moral issues surrounding embryonic stem cell research, for example, slowed the wheels of progress for many years.

Opponents of stem cell research argue that this practice is a slippery slope to reproductive cloning and fundamentally devalues the worth of a human being. Contrarily, some medical researchers in the field argue that it is necessary to pursue embryonic stem cell research because the resultant technologies could have significant medical potential and that excess embryos created for in vitro fertilization could be donated with consent and used for research. This, in turn, conflicts with opponents in the pro-life movement, who advocate for the protection of human embryos. The ensuing debate has prompted authorities around the world to seek regulatory frameworks and highlighted the fact that embryonic stem cell research represents a social and ethical challenge that includes concerns about the natural order of the ecosystem and, ultimately, the survival of the human race.

OBAMA REVERSING STEM CELL LIMITS IMPOSED BY BUSH

"By removing politics from science," said Peter T. Wilderotter, the organization's [Christopher and Dana Reeve Foundation] president and chief executive, "President Obama has freed researchers to explore these remarkable stem cells, learn from them and possibly develop effective therapies using them."

—David Stout, *The New York Times*, March 6, 2009

▶ CHAPTER REVIEW

1. The *right of self-determination* provides that every human being of adult years and sound mind has the right to determine what shall be done with his or her own body.

2. When there is uncertainty regarding a patient's wishes in an emergency situation, the dilemma should be resolved in a way that favors the preservation of life.

3. According to the *Patient Self-Determination Act of 1990*, healthcare organizations have a responsibility to explain to patients, staff, and families that patients have legal rights to direct their medical and nursing care as it corresponds to existing state law.

4. The Harvard Ad Hoc Committee on Brain Death published a report in 1968 describing the characteristics of a permanently nonfunctioning brain.

5. *Futility of treatment* occurs when a physician recognizes that the effect of continuing treatment will be of no benefit to the patient.

   - Morally, there is a duty to inform the patient when there is little likelihood of success.
   - The determination as to futility of treatment is based on the physician's assessment and medical judgment.

6. *Cardiopulmonary resuscitation* (CPR) is an emergency procedure performed on individuals who experience a cardiac arrest.

7. *Do-not-resuscitate* (DNR) *orders* are those prescribed by a physician indicating that, in the event of a cardiac or respiratory arrest, no resuscitative measures should be used to revive the patient.

8. Withholding and withdrawal of treatment:

   - *Withholding of treatment* is a decision not to initiate treatment or medical intervention for the patient.
   - *Withdrawal of treatment* is a decision to discontinue treatment or medical interventions for the patient.

9. *Euthanasia* is the mercy killing of the hopelessly ill, injured, or incapacitated. Euthanasia is complex, and the legal system must maintain a balance between ensuring that the patient's constitutional rights are protected while protecting public interests in preserving life, preventing suicide, and maintaining the integrity of the medical profession.

   - *Active euthanasia* is the intentional commission of an act that will result in death.
   - *Passive euthanasia* involves the withdrawal or withholding of lifesaving treatment.
   - *Voluntary euthanasia* occurs when a suffering, incurable patient makes the decision to die.
   - *Involuntary euthanasia* occurs when a person other than the incurable person makes the decision to terminate the life of an incurable person.

10. Physician-assisted suicide:

    - The right to allow a physician to assist patients in dying who are terminally ill and mentally competent to determine how they wish to spend the remaining days of their lives.
    - The *Oregon Death with Dignity Act* was the first statute allowing terminally ill Oregon residents to obtain prescriptions from their physicians for self-administered, lethal medications.
    - Washington and Vermont now have similar statutes.

11. *Advance directives for health care* are instructions, preferably executed in writing, by individuals specifying what actions should be taken for their care in the event that they become unable to make healthcare decisions.

    - A *living will* is the instrument or legal document that describes those treatments an individual wishes or does not wish to receive should he or she become incapacitated and unable to communicate treatment decisions.
    - A *living will* provides specific instructions as to a patient's wishes, such as a desire not to be maintained on a respirator.
    - A *healthcare proxy* is a legal document that allows a person to appoint a healthcare agent to make treatment decisions in the event he or she becomes incapacitated and is unable to make decisions for him or herself.

- A *durable power of attorney* is a legal device that permits one individual, known as the principal, to give to another person, called the *attorney-in-fact*, the authority to act on his or her behalf.

- A *surrogate decision maker* is an agent who acts on behalf of a patient who lacks the capacity to participate in a particular decision.

- *Guardianship* is a legal mechanism by which the court declares a person incompetent and appoints a guardian.

12. *Autopsies* are postmortem examinations conducted to ascertain the cause of death. Most states have enacted autopsy consent statutes that establish an order to obtain consent to autopsy based on the degree of family relationship.

13. Organ donations and transplantations are guided by federal regulations and accreditation standards of accrediting bodies such as *The Joint Commission*. Hospitals are required to implement written protocols regarding the organization's responsibilities.

    - The *Uniform Anatomical Gift Act* allows a person to make a decision to donate organs at the time of death.

14. Research, experimentation, and clinical trials are, in most states, subject to a combination of federal and state guidelines and regulations to ensure the proper supervision and control over research and experimentation involving human subjects. An *institutional review board* is responsible for reviewing, monitoring, and approving clinical investigations of drugs and medical devices that involve human subjects. Written consent must be obtained from patients participating in clinical investigations.

15. *Human genetics* describes the study of inheritance as it occurs in human beings. It includes such areas as stem cell research, clinical genetics (e.g., genetic disease markers), and molecular genetics.

    - *Genetic markers* are genes or DNA sequences with a known location on a chromosome that can be used to identify specific cells and diseases, as well as individuals and species.

    - The *Genetic Information Nondiscrimination Act of 2008* prohibits discrimination based on genetic information with respect to the availability of health insurance and employment.

    - *Stem cell research* involves the use of embryonic stem cells to create organs and various body tissues.

▶ REVIEW QUESTIONS

1. Describe how patient autonomy in making healthcare decisions has been impacted by case law and legislative enactments.
2. Discuss the following concepts: euthanasia, advance directives, futility of treatment, withholding and withdrawal of treatment, and do-not-resuscitate orders.
3. Explain end-of-life issues as they relate to autopsy, organ donations, research experimentation, and clinical trials.
4. Describe how human genetics and stem cell research can have an impact on end-of-life issues.
5. Discuss the importance of genetic markers.
6. Explain why the Genetic Information Nondiscrimination Act was enacted.

▶ NOTES

1. *Union Pac. Ry. Co. v. Botsford*, 141 U.S. 250, 251 (1891).
2. Desmond Tutu, "When My Time Comes, I Want the Option of Assisted Death," *The Washington Post*, October 6, 2016. https://www.washington post.com/opinions/global-opinions/archbishop -desmond-tutu-when-my-time-comes-i-want -the-option-of-an-assisted-death/2016/10/06 /97c804f2-8a81-11e6-b24f-a7f89eb68887_story .html?utm_term=.3515aa6e8fbc.
3. 105 N.E. 92, 93 (N.Y. 1914).
4. *Id.*
5. 438 N.Y.S.2d 266, 272 (N.Y. 1981).
6. 410 U.S. 113 (1973).
7. *Quinlan*, 355 A.2d at 663 (N.J. 1976).
8. 370 N.E.2d 417 (Mass. 1977).
9. *Id.* at 434.
10. Gregory Gelfand, "Euthanasia and the Terminally Ill Patient," *Nebraska Law Review* 63 (1984): 741, 747. http://digitalcommons.unl.edu/nlr/vol63 /iss4/7.
11. 380 N.E.2d 134 (Mass. 1978).
12. 405 N.E.2d 115 (Mass. 1980).
13. 452 So. 2d 925 (Fla. 1984).
14. 362 So. 2d 160 (Fla. Dist. Ct. App. 1978).
15. *Severns v. Wilmington Med. Ctr.*, 425 A.2d 156 (Del. Ch. 1980) (incompetent's right to refuse medical treatment may be expressed through a guardian when the patient is in a chronic vegetative state); *Leach v. Akron Gen. Med. Ctr.*, 426 N.E.2d 809 (Ohio Com. Pl. 1980) (right to privacy includes right of terminally ill patient in

a vegetative state to determine his or her own course of treatment).

16. *Satz v. Perlmutter*, 379 So. 2d 359 (Fla. 1980) (constitutional right to privacy supports decision of competent adult suffering from a terminal illness to refuse extraordinary treatment); *Superintendent of Belchertown State Sch. v. Saikewicz*, 370 N.E.2d 417 (Mass. 1977) (right to refuse medical treatment for terminal illness extends to incompetent patients).

17. *Cruzan v. Harman*, 760 S.W.2d 408 (Mo. 1988).

18. *Id.* at 425.

19. *Cruzan v. Director of the Mo. Dep't of Health*, 497 U.S. 261 (1990).

20. Pa. S.646, Amendment A3506, Printer's No. 689, Oct. 1, 1990.

21. 20 PA. Cons. Stat. Ann. § 5602(a)(9) (1988).

22. "Hospital Wants to Let Wife Die," *Newsday*, January 11, 1991: 13.

23. *Farnam v. Crista Ministries*, 807 P.2d 830, 849 (Wash. 1991).

24. 42 U.S.C. 1395cc(a)(1).

25. Public Law 101–508, November 5, 1990, sections 4206 and 4751 of the Omnibus Budget Reconciliation Act.

26. 42 U.S.C. 1395 (1992).

27. 42 U.S.C. 1395cc (1992).

28. *Schmitt v. Pierce*, 344 S.W.2d 120 (Mo. 1961).

29. John Connery, "Prolonging Life: The Duty and Its Limits," *Linacre Quarterly* 47.2 (May 1980).

30. Ascension Health, "Issues and Concepts," http://www.ascensionhealth.org/ethics/public/issues/harvard.asp.

31. American Medical Association, *Statement of Medical Opinion Re: "Brain Death,"* AMA House of Delegates Res. (June 1974).

32. 482 N.Y.S.2d 436 (1984).

33. 438 N.Y.S.2d 266 (1981).

34. 534 N.E.2d 886 (N.Y. 1988).

35. *Id.* at 891.

36. 549 N.E.2d 1043 (Ind. Ct. App. 1990).

37. 549 N.E.2d 292 (Ill. 1989).

38. 486 A.2d 1209 (N.J. Sup. Ct. 1985).

39. *Id.*

40. United States Congress, Office of Technology Assessment, *Life-Sustaining Technologies and the Elderly*, OTA-BA-306 (Washington, DC: US Government Printing Office, 1987), 48.

41. 464 N.E.2d 959 (Mass. 1984).

42. *In re Beth Israel Med. Ctr.*, 519 N.Y.S.2d 511, 517 (N.Y. Sup. Ct. 1987).

43. Ronald Sullivan, "Ombudsman Bars Food Tube Removal," *The New York Times*, March 7, 1986: 82.

44. *John F. Kennedy Mem'l Hosp. v. Bludworth*, 452 So. 2d 921, 925 (Fla. 1984) (citing *In re Welfare of Colyer*, 660 P.2d 738 [Wash. 1983], in which the court found prior court approval to be "unresponsive and cumbersome").

45. "AMA Changes Code of Ethics on Comas," *Newsday*, March 17, 1986: 2.

46. *In re Jobes*, 529 A.2d 434 (N.J. 1987).

47. *Id.* at 438.

48. *Bouvia v. Superior Court (Glenchur)*, 225 Cal. Rptr. 297 (Cal. Ct. App. 1986).

49. *Id.* at 306.

50. 147 Cal. App. 3d 1006 (Cal. Ct. App. 1983).

51. James Podgers, "Matters of Life and Death," *ABA Journal* 78 (1992): 60.

52. *In re Estate of Brooks*, 205 N.E.2d 435 (Ill. 1965); *Superintendent of Belchertown State Sch. v. Saikewicz*, 370 N.E.2d 417 (Mass. 1977); *In re Quinlan*, 355 A.2d 647 (N.J. 1976).

53. 376 N.E.2d 1232 (Mass. App. Ct. 1979).

54. Compassion and Choices, "About C&C Oregon: What We Do." https://www.compassionandchoices.org/who-we-are/about/.

55. *Kevorkian v. Thompson*, 947 F. Supp. 1152 (1997).

56. Lawrence K. Altman, "Doctor Says He Gave Patient Drug to Help Her Commit Suicide," *The New York Times*, March 6, 1991.

57. *McIver v. Krischer*, No. CL-96-1504-AF (Jan. 31, 1997) (stay issued February 11, 1997).

58. "Dr. Death at Work," *Newsday*, February 7, 1991: 12.

59. "Kevorkian Charges Dropped," *Newsday*, July 22, 1992: 4.

60. *Hobbins v. Attorney Gen. of Mich.*, No. 94-1473 (Mich. 1994); *Kevorkian v. Michigan*, No. 94-1490 (Mich. 1994).

61. "22nd Death for 'Dr. Death,'" *USA Today*, May 9, 1995: 2A.

62. Or. Rev. Stat. Sects. 127.800–897.

63. *Id.*

64. 117 S. Ct. 2258 (1997).

65. *Id.*

66. *State of Oregon v. Ashcroft*, No. 02-35587 (C.A. 9, Ore. 2004).

67. 126 S. Ct. 904 (2006).

68. Death with Dignity National Center, "Legal and Political Timeline in Oregon," http://www.deathwithdignity.org/historyfacts/oregontimeline.asp.

69. *Baxter v. State*, 354 Mont. 234, 224 P.3d 1211 (2009).

70. Patients' Rights Council, "Montana," http://www.patientsrightscouncil.org/site/montana/.

71. *Associated Press*, Boston.com, November 7, 2012.

72. 611 A.2d 1148 (N.J. Super. Ct. 1992).

73. Erin Allday, "Living Donor Registry Would Be First in Nation," *SF Gate*, http://www.sfgate.com/health/article/Living-Donor-Registry-would-be-1st in-nation-3266707.php.

74. 142 S.W3d 24 (Ky. 2004).

75. No. E2001-02906-COA-R3-CV (2002).

76. *Id.* at 7.

77. *Pettis v. Smith*, 880 So.2d 145 (La. Ct. App. 2004).

78. 420 N.E.2d 64 (N.Y. 1981).

79. Ascension Health, "Issues and Concepts," http://www.ascensionhealth.org/ethics/public/issues/substituted.asp.

80. *In re Quinlan*, 355 A.2d 647 (N.J. 1976).

81. *Bush v. Schiavo*, No. SC04-925 (Fla. App. 2004).

82. 225 N.Y.S.2d 434 (N.Y. Ct. Cl. 1962).

83. 624 A.2d 663 (Pa. Comm. Ct. 1993).

84. 297 F. Supp. 1142 (S.D.N.Y. 1969).

85. United Nations Regional Information Centre for Western Europe, "Organs for Sale," April 19, 2017. http://www.unric.org/en/human-trafficking/27447-organs-for-sale.

86. U.S. Department of Health and Human Services, "Organ Donation Statistics," https://www.organdonor.gov/statistics-stories/statistics.html.

87. Transplant Safety, TS.02.01.01, Comprehensive Accreditation Manual for Hospitals, 2017.

88. PBS, "First Successful Kidney Transplant Performed," http://www.pbs.org/wgbh/aso/databank/entries/dm54ki.html.

89. *Associated Press*, "Errors Possible in Maryland HIV Tests," http://msnbc.msn.com/id/4505640.

90. 519 N.Y.S.2d 928 (N.Y. Sup. Ct. 1987).

91. Stanford University, "Human Subjects Research and IRB," http://researchcompliance.stanford.edu/hs/index.html.

92. Kathy L. Hudson and Francis S. Collins, "The 21st Century Cures Act—A View from the NIH," *The New England Journal of Medicine*, January 12, 2017. http://www.nejm.org/doi/full/10.1056/NEJMp1615745?query=TOC.

93. H.R.6 21st Century Cures Act, https://www.congress.gov/bill/114th-congress/house-bill/6.

94. *Id.*

95. *Id.*

96. U.S. Department of Health and Human Services, Office for Human Research Protections, "Ethical Codes & Research Standards: Nuremberg Code," http://www.hhs.gov/ohrp/archive/nurcode.html.

97. U.S. Food and Drug Administration, "Institutional Review Boards: Frequently Asked Questions - Information Sheet," https://www.fda.gov/RegulatoryInformation/Guidances/ucm126420.htm.

98. *Id.*

99. 607 A.2d 1111 (1992).

100. 428 F. Supp. 360 (D.D.C. 1977).

101. *Blaz v. Michael Reese Hosp. Found.*, 74 F. Supp. 2d 803 (D.C. Ill. 1999).

102. 2 C.F.R. § 488.115 (1989).

103. Bill and Mary Ellen Stokes, "Relentless Assault on a Research Hospital," *The Wall Street Journal*, March 15, 2004: A17.

104. Nicholas Wade, "A Decade Later, Genetic Map Yields Few New Cures," *The New York Times*, June 12, 2010. http://www.nytimes.com/2010/06/13/health/research/13genome.html?pagewanted=all

105. National Human Genome Research Institute, "Genome Advance of the Month," https://www.genome.gov/27543594/.

106. *Id.*

107. National Human Genome Research Institute, "Current News Releases: NIH to expand critical catalog for genomics research," February 2, 2017. https://www.genome.gov/10000475/current-news-releases/.

108. S. Yuanyi and G. Chun, *History of Medicine* (Wuhan, China: People's Health Publishing House, 1988).

© Bacho/Shutterstock

CHAPTER 18

Legal Reporting Requirements

🔨 IT'S YOUR GAVEL...

ALLEGED ABUSE: IMMUNITY PROVIDED

Two children were placed in the temporary custody of a foster family. One child was referred to a licensed psychologist for evaluation. After two interviews, the psychologist formed a professional opinion that the child had been sexually molested. Based in part on statements made by the child, the psychologist further believed that the perpetrator of the suspected molestation was the father. At a hearing before a juvenile court, the court determined that the evidence did not support a finding that the father had abused his child. Custody was returned to the parents. The child's parents subsequently initiated an action for medical malpractice against the psychologist. The psychologist claimed immunity from liability as provided by a state child abuse reporting statute. The parents argued that the immunity provisions of the statute do not apply to the psychologist because she was not a "mandatory reporter" under that statute.[1]

WHAT IS YOUR VERDICT?

Love and knowledge led upwards to the heavens, but always pity brought me back to earth; cries of pain reverberated in my heart of children in famine, of victims tortured, and of old people left helpless. I long to alleviate the evil, but I cannot, and I too suffer. This has been my life; I found it worth living.

—Bertrand Russell (Adapted)

▶ LEARNING OBJECTIVES

The reader, upon completion of this chapter, will be able to:

- Describe various forms of child abuse, how to recognize it, and reporting requirements.
- Describe various forms of elder abuse, how to recognize it, and reporting requirements.
- Explain why it is important to report communicable diseases, adverse drug reactions, and infectious diseases.
- Discuss the importance of reporting births and deaths.
- Explain how and why physician incompetence is reported.
- Understand the importance of incident reporting, sentinel events, and the purpose of root cause analyses.

This chapter provides an overview of a variety of legal reporting requirements mandated by both federal and state regulatory agencies. Through such reporting, appropriate measures are taken to safeguard the health of the nation's population. Most states have legislative reporting requirements for child abuse, elder abuse, and diseases that pose a threat to public health and safety (e.g., anthrax, smallpox). Although most statutory reporting requirements do not contain an express immunity from liability for disclosure without the permission of the person affected, as a general rule, a person making a report in good faith and under statutory command is protected.

▶ ABUSE

The physically abused or neglected person presents a medical, social, and legal problem. What constitutes abuse is sometimes difficult to determine because it is often impossible to ascertain whether the injury was intentional or accidental. Abuse in the healthcare setting often occurs to those who are most vulnerable and dependent on others for care (e.g., patients diagnosed with dementia and Alzheimer's disease, those who are physically weak). Abuse is not limited to an institutional setting; it may occur in an individual's home as well as in a healthcare organization. Abuse can take many forms, such as physical, psychological, medical, and financial. It is not always easy to identify because injuries often can be attributed to other causes. This chapter reviews both child and elder abuse.

▶ CHILD ABUSE

Child abuse is the intentional serious mental, emotional, sexual, and/or physical injury inflicted by a family member or other person responsible for a child's care. Some states extend the definition to include a child suffering from starvation. Other states include moral neglect in the definition of abuse, along with immoral associations; endangering a child's morals; and the location of a child in a disreputable place or in association with vagrant, vicious, or immoral persons.

The federal Child Abuse Prevention and Treatment Act (CAPTA) provides minimum standards that states must incorporate in their statutory definitions of child abuse and neglect. The CAPTA definition of "child abuse and neglect," at a minimum, refers to: "Any recent act or failure to act on the part of a parent or caregiver, which results in death, serious physical or emotional harm, sexual abuse, or exploitation, or an act or failure to act which presents an imminent risk of serious harm."[2]

A wealth of information on child abuse and state statutes can be found at the Administration for Children and Families website: www.childwelfare.gov. This site is a child welfare information gateway that provides access to information and resources to help protect children and strengthen families. Topics include child welfare, preventing and responding to child abuse and neglect, supporting and preserving families, foster care, and adoption.

Who Should Report?

Presently, all states have enacted laws to protect abused children. Most states protect the persons required to report cases of child abuse. In a few states, certain identified individuals who are not required to report instances of child abuse, but who do so, are protected. Child abuse laws may provide penalties for failure to report. Persons in the healthcare setting who are required to report, or cause a report to be made, when they have reasonable cause to suspect that a child has been abused include administrators, physicians, interns, registered nurses, chiropractors, social service workers, psychologists, dentists, osteopaths, optometrists, podiatrists, mental health professionals, and volunteers in residential facilities.

How to Detect Abuse?

An individual who reports child abuse should be aware of the physical and behavioral indicators of abuse and maltreatment that appear to be part of a pattern (e.g., bruises, burns, broken bones). In reviewing the indicators of abuse and maltreatment, the reporter does not have to be absolutely certain that abuse or maltreatment exists before reporting. Rather, abuse and maltreatment should be reported whenever they are suspected, based on the existence of the signs of abuse and maltreatment and in light of the reporter's training and experience. Behavioral indicators include, but are not limited to, substantially diminished psychological or intellectual functioning, failure to thrive, no control of aggression, self-destructive impulses, decreased ability to think and reason, acting out and misbehavior, or habitual truancy. Such impairment must be clearly attributable to the unwillingness or inability of the person responsible for the child's care to exercise a minimum degree of care toward the child.

Good Faith Reporting

Reports of suspected child abuse must be made with a *good faith* belief that the facts reported are true. The definition of good faith as used in a child abuse statute may vary from state to state. However, when a healthcare practitioner's medical evaluation indicates reasonable cause to believe a child's injuries were not accidental and when the healthcare practitioner is not acting from his or her desire to harass, injure, or embarrass the child's parents, making the report will not result in liability. Statutes generally require that when a person covered by a statute is attending a child and suspects child abuse, that person must report such concerns. Typical statutes provide that an oral report be made immediately, followed by a written report. Most states require the report to contain the following information:

- The child's name and address
- The person(s) responsible for the child's care
- The child's age
- The nature and extent of the child's injuries (including any evidence of previous injuries)
- Any other information that might be helpful in establishing the cause of the injuries, such as photographs of the injured child, and the identity of the alleged abuser

Psychologist Immune to Liability

A minor child and his mother brought an action for damages against physicians for failing to diagnose disease and filing erroneous child abuse reports in *Awkerman v. TriCounty Orthopedic Group.*[3] The Wayne County Circuit Court granted the physicians' motions for partial summary judgment, and the plaintiffs appealed. The Michigan Court of Appeals held that the child abuse reporting statute provides immunity to persons who file child abuse reports in good faith even if the reports were filed because of negligent diagnosis of the cause of the child's frequent bone fractures, which eventually was diagnosed as osteogenesis imperfecta. The court of appeals also held that damages for shame and humiliation were not recoverable pursuant to Michigan statute. Immunity from liability did not extend to damages for malpractice that may have resulted from the failure to diagnose the child's disease as long as all the elements of negligence are present.

In another case, the psychologist in *E.S. by D.S. v. Seitz*[4] was immune from liability in a suit charging her with negligence in formulating and reporting her professional opinion to a social worker that a father had sexually abused his 3-year-old daughter. The psychologist made the report in compliance with the Wisconsin statute, after having examined the child in the course of her professional duties as a mental health professional. The patient in *Marks v. Tenbrunsel*[5] had been assured that anything he disclosed during his treatment sessions would remain confidential. During the treatment sessions, the patient disclosed that he had fondled two children under the age of 12. As a result of that disclosure, two psychologists made a good faith report to Child Protective Services. The report caused the patient to be prosecuted for his admitted sexual misconduct. Because the patient admitted to the abuse of two children, the psychologists had reasonable cause to believe that the children currently were being abused. The psychologists were found immune from both civil and criminal liability as a result of their good faith report.

Failure to Report Child Abuse

The criminal and civil risks for healthcare professionals lie not in good faith reporting of suspected incidents of child abuse, but rather in failing to report such incidents. Most states have legislated a variety of civil and criminal penalties for failure to report suspected child abuse incidents. Penalties are "in the form of either fines or jail time or both, on mandatory reporters who fail to report cases of suspected child abuse and neglect as required by the reporting laws. State laws also may impose penalties on any person who knowingly makes a false report of abuse or neglect."[6]

Psychologist's Failure to Report Past Abuse

The Minnesota Board of Psychology was found to have acted properly when it placed the license of a psychologist on conditional status.[7] The psychologist argued that he was not required to report past abuse that was not ongoing, that a report made 5 weeks after the incident was not untimely, and that the reporting laws were unconstitutional because they violated the privacy rights of clients and the privilege against self-incrimination. The psychologist had failed to report incidents of sexual child abuse. The court held that there was no merit to the psychologist's contentions that the child abuse reporting laws were unclear and that they did not apply to one patient, who was a grandfather responsible for the child's care at the time of the incident in question.

Nurse's Failure to Document and Report

In *State v. Brown*,[8] rescue personnel were summoned to the scene of an emergency and found a 2-year-old foster child unconscious; not breathing; and "posturing," an abnormal rigidity of the body and a sign of brain damage. While performing emergency medical treatment, rescue personnel discovered a series of small, round, dime-to-quarter size bruises running parallel along the child's spine. They also noticed a red bruise under his eye. This information was relayed to the flight crew who airlifted the child to the hospital. The flight crew then reported the information to a nurse employed at the hospital. The child recovered after treatment and was released from the hospital on August 14, 2002. Four days later, on August 18, the child was returned to the hospital where he died of abusive head trauma. The nurse did not document the bruises or call the state's child abuse hotline because the boy's foster mother said the bruises were the result of the boy leaning back in a booster seat. In February 2003, the prosecutor alleged that the nurse had reasonable cause to suspect that the child had been abused or neglected. She was charged with failure to report child abuse to the division of family services under Section 210.115.1, Revised Statutes of Missouri, and to a physician under Section 210.120, Revised Statutes of Missouri. The nurse sought to dismiss the charges, alleging the statutes were unconstitutionally vague. In September 2003, the court held that the sections were unconstitutionally vague and dismissed the case. The state appealed. The appellate court determined that the statutes were not vague. The test for determining whether a law is void for vagueness is whether its language conveys to a person of ordinary intelligence a sufficiently definite warning as to the proscribed conduct when measured by common understanding and practices. The statute criminalizing a health professional's failure to report child abuse upon "reasonable cause to suspect" abuse was not unconstitutionally vague. The phrase "reasonable cause to suspect" has been in use for more than a century and is understandable by ordinary persons.

Physician Entitled to Immunity

A physician who was not the initial reporter of suspected child abuse, but who performed a medical examination of a child at the request of the Department of Children and Families to determine whether reasonable cause existed to suspect child abuse, was entitled to the immunity from liability provided by statutory law. It was clear that the physician, a mandated reporter under the law, examined the child in the ordinary course of his employment in the emergency department. He complied with applicable statutes when he relayed his findings that there was a reasonable suspicion of child abuse to the department. Inasmuch as the plaintiffs did not allege that the physician acted in bad faith during the examination and reporting process, his actions constituted a report of suspected child abuse protected by statutory law. The trial court, therefore, properly granted the medical defendants' motion for summary judgment.[9]

✔ *CHILD ABUSE CAN BE ELUSIVE*

Child abuse is not always obvious to the caregiver and can unfortunately go undetected to the detriment of the child. I learned this early on in my training. I was a first-year resident at General Medical Center and was on tour in the hospital's pediatric unit with Peggy, the unit charge nurse. As we walked down the corridor I noticed a young child in room 106 in a full leg cast, which had been placed in traction. I asked Peggy what had happened to the patient? Peggy said, "Oh that's Gracie. Poor thing. She broke her femur tripping over a toy in her home." I thought to myself that was a major injury for tripping over a toy. I questioned Peggy further and she told me that she knew where I was leading by my questions and said, "Oh you can be assured that Gracie had not been abused. She has the sweetest mother and father. Although they are divorced one of her parents is here every day. I even questioned the mother and she assures me it was an accident." I had an uneasy feeling about the mother's story and decided to visit the radiology department to review Gracie's X-rays with the radiologist on duty. I walked into the imaging reading room where I found three radiologists reviewing various imaging studies. I introduced myself as a first-year resident to Dr. Patrick Williams, the medical director of radiology. I asked Dr. Williams, "Do you have time to review Gracie's X-rays with me?" The radiologist replied, "No problem. What is Gracie's last name?" I told him and he pulled up Gracie's X-rays electronically on a computer screen. As soon as the he pulled up the X-rays he said, "Oh yes, Gracie has a compound fracture of the femur." He was very patient as he thoroughly reviewed with me Gracie's case. He pointed out the compound fracture of the femur with the computer cursor. I asked him, "Do you think the injury could have occurred from Gracie tripping over a toy at home on a plush carpet?" He replied, "That would be highly unlikely." He called over one of his partners and said, "Does this patient's injury look like she tripped over a toy?" Looking at me he said, "Is this what you were told?" I said, "Well, yes, I was." He looked at me and said, "I have been reading imaging studies for over 20 years. It is highly unlikely that Gracie's compound fracture of her left femur is the result of her tripping over a toy." The third radiologist in the room commented, "Definitely not caused by a slip on a toy." Following my review with the radiologists, I called Peggy and asked if she had time to review Gracie's medical record with me after lunch. Peggy replied, "Sure thing, I will see you after lunch." After lunch I went to the pediatric unit. Upon arriving on the unit Peggy and Caroline, a hospital social service worker, greeted me. Caroline said, "I contacted child welfare in the county in which Gracie resides. They informed me that Gracie was an active child abuse case, which they have been following for the past 6 months. They thanked me for the information and will be in the hospital late this afternoon to follow up."

The lesson here for every caregiver is to be continuously observant regarding the signs and symptoms of abuse. Caregiver in-service education programs should include the procedures for reporting suspected abuse according to applicable laws and an organization's policies and procedures.

▶ SENIOR ABUSE

People at their weakest are often treated the worst.

—NS

Elder abuse generally refers to mistreatment of an older person by someone who has a special relationship with the adult such as a spouse, sibling, child, relative, friend, or caregiver. It can involve physical abuse (that results in bodily injury, pain, or impairment and includes assault, battery, and inappropriate restraint), sexual abuse (nonconsensual sexual contact of any kind with an older person), domestic violence (an escalating pattern of violence by an intimate partner where the violence is used to exercise power and control), emotional or psychological abuse (the willful infliction of mental or emotional anguish by threat, humiliation, or other verbal or nonverbal conduct), or financial abuse or exploitation (the illegal or improper use of an older person's funds, property, or resources),[10] *neglect* by failing to provide the care necessary to avoid physical harm (e.g., the failure of staff to turn a patient periodically to prevent pressure sores), mental anguish, or abandonment. Abusers themselves may suffer from alcohol or drug abuse. Sometimes the abusers were abused themselves as children. The abuser may be emotionally unstable. In other situations, a caregiver may be overwhelmed and unable to cope with a stressful situation and not know where to turn for help.

The abuse of senior individuals is not a localized or isolated problem. Unfortunately, it permeates our society. *Behind Closed Doors*, a landmark book on family violence, stated that the first national study of violence in American homes estimated that one in two homes was the scene of family violence at least once a year.[11]

> We have always known that America is a violent society. . . . What is new and surprising is that the American family and the American home are perhaps as much or more violent than any other single institution or setting (with the exception of the military, and only then in the time of war). Americans run the greatest risk of assault, physical injury and even murder in their own homes by members of their own families.[12]

It is difficult to determine the extent of senior abuse because the abused are reluctant to admit that their children or loved ones have assaulted them. Unfortunately, the abuse of senior persons remains hidden from the public, and the findings of the 1990 report are as current today as when they were first published. The Senate Select Committee on Aging reported:

- Senior abuse is less likely to be reported than child abuse.
- Physical violence, including negligence, and financial abuse appear to be the most common

forms of abuse, followed by abrogation of basic constitutional rights and psychological abuse.

- Most instances of senior abuse are repeated events rather than one-time occurrences.
- Victims are often 75 years of age or older, and women are more likely to be abused than men.
- Senior people are often ashamed to admit that their children or loved ones abuse them, or they may fear reprisals if they complain.
- Many middle-aged family members, finally ready to enjoy time for themselves, are resentful of a frail and dependent senior parent.
- The majority of the abusers are relatives.[13]

A *USA Today* review of 2 years of inspection records (between 2000 and 2002) for more than 5,300 assisted-living facilities found that what should be havens for senior persons may, in reality, be exposing them to deadly risks. The study indicates that medication errors and poor staff training resulted in many of the injuries identified.[14]

Most states have enacted statutes mandating the reporting of senior abuse. Seniors often fail to report incidents of abuse because they fear retaliation and not being believed. Threats of placement in a nursing home or shame that a family member is involved often prevent the person from seeking help.

National Center on Elder Abuse

The National Center on Elder Abuse (NCEA), directed by the U.S. Administration on Aging, is committed to helping national, state, and local partners in the field to be fully prepared to ensure that older Americans will live with dignity; integrity; independence; and without abuse, neglect, and exploitation. The NCEA is a resource for policymakers, social service and healthcare practitioners, the justice system, researchers, advocates, and families.[15]

Abusers of older adults are both women and men. Family members are more often the abusers than any other group. For several years, data showed that adult children were the most common abusers of family members; recent information indicates spouses are the most common perpetrators when state data concerning elders and vulnerable adults is combined.[16]

Proving charges is often difficult. Signs of abuse or neglect include unexplained or unexpected death; development of pressure sores; heavy medication and sedation used in place of adequate nursing staff; occurrence of broken bones; sudden and unexpected emotional outbursts, agitation, or withdrawal; bruises, welts, discoloration, and burns; absence of hair and/or presence of hemorrhaging below the scalp; dehydration and/or malnourishment without an illness-related

cause; hesitation to talk openly; implausible stories; unusual or inappropriate activity in bank accounts; signatures on checks and other written materials that do not resemble the patient's signature; power of attorney given, or recent changes or creation of a will, when the person is incapable of making such decisions; missing personal belongings such as silverware or jewelry; an untreated medical condition; and the person not being permitted to speak for himself or herself or see others or is discouraged from speaking for himself or herself or seeing others without the presence of the caregiver (suspected abuser).

Policies and Procedures

Policies and procedures that include prohibition of mistreatment, description of reporting procedures regarding alleged abuse, maintenance of evidence of alleged abuse, investigation of alleged abuse, and prevention of further potential abuse while an investigation is in progress should be developed.

Documentation and Reporting Abuse

The warning signs of abuse include frequent arguments or tension, sudden changes in the elder's financial condition, changes in the elder's personality or behavior (self-neglect), visible injuries such as broken bones, cuts, scars, and bed sores. Neglect can be suspected when observing weight loss, signs of dehydration, and personal grooming. Caregivers should be educated about the signs of abuse. Symptoms and conditions of suspected abuse should be defined clearly and objectively.

- Witnesses: Reporters of abuse must describe statements made by others as accurately as possible and what actions were taken, by what, whom, how, when, and where. Information should be included about how witnesses may be contacted.
- Photographs: It may be necessary to photograph wounds or injuries. A hospital emergency department or the police department can be asked to take photographs in emergency situations.

Caregivers must observe and listen to elders and intervene as required by reporting suspected abuse per state requirements and organizational policies and procedures for reporting abuse.

▶ COMMUNICABLE DISEASES

Most states have enacted laws that require the reporting of actual or suspected cases of communicable diseases. The need for statutes requiring the reporting of communicable diseases is clear: If a state is to protect its citizens' health through its power to quarantine, it must ensure the prompt reporting of infection or disease. The mandatory reporting of communicable diseases by clinicians is vital to protection of society as noted in the following excerpt from a 1990 Centers for Disease Control and Prevention (CDC; http://www.cdc.gov) report:

> Reporting of cases of infectious diseases and related conditions has been and remains a vital step in controlling and preventing the spread of communicable disease. These reports are useful in many ways, including assurance of provision of appropriate medical therapy (e.g., for tuberculosis), detection of common-source outbreaks (e.g., in foodborne outbreaks), and planning and evaluating prevention and control programs (e.g., for vaccine-preventable diseases). The epidemic of the acquired immunodeficiency syndrome, the recent increase in tuberculosis in young adults, the reemergence of malaria as a health threat to travelers, and the potential spread of dengue fever to the continental United States have all contributed to the renewed interest in the surveillance of infectious diseases.[17]

▶ AIDS

Acquired immunodeficiency syndrome (AIDS) is a reportable communicable disease in every state. Physicians and hospitals must report cases of AIDS, along with the patient's name, to government public health authorities. Cases reported to local health authorities also are reported to the CDC, with the patients' names encoded by a system known as Soundex. CDC records come under the general confidentiality protections of the Federal Privacy Act of 1974. However, the statute permits disclosures to other federal agencies under certain circumstances. The Occupational Safety and Health Administration (OSHA) require that healthcare organizations implement strict procedures, developed by the CDC, to protect employees against the human immunodeficiency virus (HIV).

State HIV Required Reporting

Medical providers and laboratories are expected to counsel an HIV-positive patient to notify his or her sexual or needle-sharing partners or to seek help in doing so from public health officials. If a patient refuses to do so, a physician may, without the patient's consent, notify public health officials of a patient's sexual partner

known to be at risk of HIV infection. Some states have developed informational brochures and consent, release, and partner notification forms. In Virginia, HIV surveillance activities are authorized under the Virginia Department of Health Regulations Section 32.1-39 and Section 32.1-40 of the Code of Virginia.

> Medical providers and laboratories are required by law to report all HIV and AIDS cases. In May of 2007, Virginia's health reporting regulations were revised to require laboratories to report all HIV CD4 counts and viral load test results. The Virginia Department of Health [VDH] relies on medical providers and laboratories to identify and report conditions of public health importance, including HIV infection, and encourages providers to consider the impact that patients' health may have on the larger community. Providers and VDH partner to control the spread of disease in Virginia.[18]

Mandatory Testing

The U.S. District Court found that routine testing of firefighters and paramedics for HIV does not violate an individual's Fourth Amendment or constitutional privacy rights.[19] Because the tested employees are a high-risk group for contracting and transmitting HIV to the public, the city has a compelling interest and legal duty to protect the public from contracting the virus.

Firefighters and paramedics are in a higher risk category than hospital personnel because they work in an uncontrolled setting. *Skinner v. Railway Executives Association* confirmed "society's judgment that blood tests do not constitute an unduly extensive imposition on an individual's privacy and bodily integrity."[20] However, "mandatory testing by a governmental agency for the sole purpose of obtaining a baseline to determine whether an employee contracted AIDS on the job, and thereby to determine the validity of any future workers' compensation claim, is not valid. Mandatory AIDS testing of employees can be valid only if the group of employees involved is at risk of contracting or transmitting AIDS to the public."[21]

▶ BIRTHS AND DEATHS

All births and deaths are reportable by statute. Births occurring outside of a healthcare facility should be reported by the legally qualified physician in attendance at a delivery or, in the event of the absence of a physician, by the registered nurse or other attendant. The physician who pronounces death must sign the death certificate.

Statutes requiring the reporting of births and deaths are necessary to maintain accurate census records.

Suspicious Deaths

Greater than a state's interest in the recording of all births and deaths is the state's desire to review suspicious deaths that may be the result of some form of criminal activity. Unnatural deaths must be referred to the medical examiner for review. Such cases include violent deaths, deaths caused by unlawful acts or criminal neglect, and deaths that may be considered suspicious or unusual. The medical examiner may conduct an investigation as to the cause of death through an autopsy and report the findings to the police department or prosecutor assigned to the case. The purpose of a medical examiner's investigation is to determine the actual cause of death and thereby provide assistance for any further criminal investigation that may be considered necessary. If a medical examiner determines a death is due to an intentional act, he or she can be called as a witness to testify with regard to the findings if a trial ensues.

▶ ADVERSE DRUG REACTIONS

Adverse drug reactions (ADRs) are unwanted or harmful reactions that occur as a result of the administration of a drug or combination of drugs. Pharmacies must maintain and report adverse drug reactions to the Food and Drug Administration (FDA). MedWatch is the FDA's "program for reporting serious reactions, product quality problems, therapeutic inequivalence/failure, and product use errors with human medical products, including drugs, biologic products, medical devices, dietary supplements, infant formula, and cosmetics."[22] Timely reporting helps the FDA to provide prompt notification to pharmacies, physicians, and patients of harmful drug reactions.

Consumers can report ADRs via an online form; printing a form located on the FDA website (https://www.accessdata.fda.gov) and faxing or mailing it to the U.S. Food and Drug Administration, 10903 New Hampshire Avenue, Silver Spring, MD 20993; or by calling the FDA (800-332-1088 or 888-463-6332).

▶ PHYSICIAN COMPETENCY

Congress enacted the *Health Care Quality Improvement Act* (HCQIA)[23] of 1986 to improve the quality of medical care by encouraging physicians to participate in peer review and by restricting the ability of incompetent physicians to move from state to state without disclosure or discovery of their previous substandard

NEWS *AFTER HE FELL OFF A LADDER, ONE MEDICAL ERROR LED TO ANOTHER*

. . . I left the medical system damaged and broke. I believe that if I had access to some solid, physician-specific outcome data and better information on the risks and benefits of the medical devices my doctors were proposing, even I could have made health care decisions that wouldn't have resulted in my having to type this essay with one hand.

—Kerry O'Connell, *The Washington Post*, August 25, 2012

performance or unprofessional conduct. The HCQIA was enacted in part to provide those persons giving information to professional review bodies and those assisting in review activities with limited immunity from damages that may arise as a result of adverse decisions that affect a physician's medical staff privileges.

Prior to enacting the HCQIA, Congress found that "[t]he increasing occurrence of medical malpractice and the need to improve the quality of medical care . . . [had] become nationwide problems," especially in light of "the ability of incompetent physicians to move from State to State without disclosure or discovery of the physician's previous damaging or incompetent performance."[24] HCQIA was enacted to facilitate the frank exchange of information among professionals who conduct peer review inquiries without the fear of reprisals in civil lawsuits. The statute attempts to balance the chilling effect of litigation on peer review with concerns for protecting physicians who are improperly subjected to disciplinary action.

National Practitioner Data Bank

The National Practitioner Data Bank (NPDB) was created by Congress as a national repository of information with the primary purpose of facilitating a comprehensive review of physicians' and other healthcare practitioners' professional credentials. The NPDB operates under the authority of the Secretary of the Department of Health and Human Services (DHHS). The NPDB was established by law to protect the public and patient safety by restricting the ability of unethical or incompetent practitioners to move from state to state without disclosure or discovery of previously damaging or incompetent performance. The NPDB provides hospitals with a snapshot of a professional's history before credentialing. The repository of information streamlines a patchwork of state laws governing the reporting of adverse actions against professionals seeking privileges.

Hospitals are required to report to the NPDB professional review actions related to a professional's competence or conduct that adversely affect clinical privileges for more than 30 days and a physician's voluntary surrender or restriction of clinical privileges.

The NPDB presents a number of challenges to healthcare organizations. Healthcare professionals, for example, need to be educated regarding the purpose of the data bank so it will not erode trust and staff participation in risk management activities. The purpose of the data bank is not punishment; rather, it is prevention and deterrence.

Reporting Requirements

The regulations establish reporting requirements applicable to hospitals; healthcare entities; boards of medical examiners; professional societies of physicians, dentists, or other healthcare practitioners that take adverse licensure or professional review actions (e.g., reduction, restriction, suspension, revocation, or denial of clinical privileges or membership in a healthcare entity of 30 days or longer); and individuals and entities (including insurance companies) making payments as a result of medical malpractice actions or claims. A *medical malpractice action* (or claim) has been defined as a written complaint or claim demanding payment based on a healthcare practitioner's provision of or failure to provide healthcare services, including the filing of a cause of action based on tort law, brought in any state or federal court or other adjudicative body.

Required Queries

Healthcare organizations must query the data bank every 2 years on the renewal of staff privileges. The data bank serves as a flagging system whose principal purpose is to facilitate a more comprehensive review of professional credentials. As a nationwide flagging system, it provides another resource to assist state licensing boards, hospitals, and other healthcare entities in conducting extensive independent reviews of the qualifications of healthcare practitioners they seek to license or hire or to whom they wish to grant clinical privileges.

Required Reporting

For those healthcare providers who question whether they are covered under this law, the DHHS defines the term *entity* broadly, rather than attempting to focus on the myriad healthcare organizations, practice arrangements, and professional societies, to ensure that the

regulations include all entities within the scope of the statute. A healthcare entity is any entity that provides healthcare services and engages in professional review activity through a formal peer-review process for the purpose of furthering quality health care or a committee of that entity. Healthcare practitioners include all healthcare practitioners authorized by a state to provide healthcare services by whatever formal mechanism the state uses (e.g., certification, registration, licensure).

Data Bank Queries

Data bank queries can be made by state licensing boards, hospitals, other healthcare entities, and professional societies that have entered or may be entering employment or affiliation relationships with a physician, dentist, or other healthcare practitioner who has applied for clinical privileges or appointment to a medical staff. A plaintiff's attorney is permitted to obtain information from the data bank when a malpractice action has been filed and the practitioner on whom information has been sought is named in a suit.

Query Fees

Under data bank rules, there is a nominal fee for data bank queries each time a physician and dentist apply for medical staff privileges at their facilities.[25]

Penalties for Failing to Report

Hospitals or other healthcare entities that fail to report adverse professional review actions limiting the clinical privileges of physicians or dentists lasting more than 30 days can lose immunity protection provided by Title IV of the HCQIA for a 3-year period.

Confidentiality of Data Bank Information

Information reported to the data bank is considered strictly confidential and cannot be disclosed except as specified in the NPDB regulations. Individuals and entities that knowingly and willfully report to or query the data bank under false pretenses or fraudulently access the data bank directly are subject to civil penalties. The data bank follows the following guidelines on disclosure:

§ 60.13 Confidentiality of National Practitioner Data Bank information.

(a) Limitations on disclosure. Information reported to the Data Bank is considered confidential and shall not be disclosed outside the Department of Health and Human Services, except as specified in §60.10, §60.11 and §60.14. Persons and entities which receive information from the Data Bank either directly or from another party must use it solely with respect to the purpose for which it was provided. Nothing in this paragraph shall prevent the disclosure of information by a party which is authorized under applicable State law to make such disclosure.

(b) Penalty for violations. Any person who violates paragraph (a) shall be subject to a civil money penalty of up to $10,000 for each violation. This penalty will be imposed pursuant to procedures at 42 CFR part 1003.[26]

The Privacy Act of 1974 protects the contents of federal systems of records, such as those contained in the NPDB, from disclosure, unless the disclosure is for a routine use of the system of records as published annually in the *Federal Register*. The published routine uses of NPDB information do not allow for disclosure of information to the general public.

▶ INCIDENT REPORTING

Incident reports contain statements made by employees and physicians regarding a deviation from acceptable patient care. Some state health codes provide that hospitals and nursing facilities must investigate incidents regarding patient care and require that certain incidents must be reported in a manner prescribed by regulation. Reportable incidents often include such things as those incidents that have resulted in a patient's serious injury or death, an event such as fire or loss of emergency power, certain infection outbreaks, and strikes by employees. Incident reports should not be placed in the medical record. They should be directed to counsel for legal advice. This will help prevent discovery on the basis of client–attorney privilege.

There is conflicting case law in that some courts will not permit incident reports to be discovered, whereas others will allow discovery. A Florida appeals court ruled that incident reports prepared in anticipation of litigation are not discoverable, even though the information contained in the report was not available by any other means.[27] In *Berg v. Des Moines General Hospital Co.*,[28] the Iowa Supreme Court ruled that, because of the time lapse between the actual incident and the inability of the nurses to recall the incident, discovery of the written incident report was allowed.

Incident/Occurrence Reports Discoverable

Occurrence reports in *Columbia/HCA Healthcare Corp. v. Eighth Judicial District Court*[29] were found

to have been prepared in the ordinary course of the hospital's business and were therefore not protected by the "work product doctrine." The hospital's petition implicitly admitted that it required its personnel to fill out preprinted forms in the event of an unexpected occurrence.

Occurrence reports consisted of a four-page form, which are completed by hospital employees who have information regarding unusual events that occurred in the hospital. The hospital admitted that the purpose, at least in part, for creating occurrence reports was to improve the quality of care given at the hospital. The documents were not privileged merely because an attorney was involved in the investigative process. The investigation occurred in the ordinary course of business. The Nevada legislature never intended to exempt occurrence reports from discovery under Nevada Revised Statute § 49.265.

Occurrence reports, which the hospital admitted are nothing more than factual narratives, contain the very type of information that will most likely be uncovered through traditional discovery procedures. In those instances where the information can be obtained only through the occurrence report, prospective plaintiffs should not be denied access. Allowing Nevada Revised Statute § 49.265 to become an impenetrable bulwark of damaging factual information defeats the very purposes of Nevada's evidence code for which Nevada Revised Statute § 49.265 is a part: "The purposes of this [evidence code are] to secure fairness in administration . . . to the end that truth may be ascertained and proceedings justly determined."[30] The court concluded that the occurrence reports are neither work product nor protected by the peer-review privilege embodied in Nevada Revised Statute § 49.265.

State Reportable Incidents

State reportable events include the reporting of communicable diseases, infections, and an unusual or an unexpected cluster of patients with symptoms/diseases or exposures suggestive of a health emergency or terrorism event. Many states have enacted legislation requiring hospitals to report incidents that result in patient injury. The Pennsylvania Medical Care Availability and Reduction of Error Act (MCARE Act) reporting requirements, for example, are intended to help reduce and eliminate medical errors by identifying problems and implementing solutions to improve patient safety. The MCARE Act requires healthcare facilities to report serious events and incidents to a newly established patient safety authority. The act defines a *serious event* as an event, occurrence, or situation involving the clinical care of a patient in a medical facility that results in death or compromises patient safety and results in an unanticipated injury, requiring the delivery of additional healthcare services to the patient. Physicians are also required to report complaints, disciplinary actions, and criminal offenses to the professional licensure board. Physicians are required to report the following events:[31]

- Medical professional liability actions filed against the physician
- Disciplinary actions by a healthcare licensing authority of another state
- Convictions for offenses above summary offenses
- Arrests for a felony (criminal homicide, aggravated assault, sexual offenses) or an offense under the Controlled Substance, Drug, Devise [sic] and Cosmetic Act

Managers must be aware of specific state reporting requirements. Hospital procedures for reporting patient care incidents must comply with state regulations. As with The Joint Commission requirements, the Pennsylvania law prohibits retaliatory action against the healthcare worker for reporting patient care incidents and provides for written notification to patients.

Individuals designated to report incidents must do so if required by a state's statute. The director of nursing at a nursing facility in *Choe v. Axelrod*[32] was fined $150 for failure to report an instance of patient neglect. An anonymous telephone call had been placed with the Department of Health regarding two incidents of alleged patient neglect. In one incident, a patient had been left unattended in a shower by an orderly and the patient sprayed himself with hot water, which resulted in second-degree burns on his forehead. On a second occasion, a similar incident occurred, but no one was injured.

On investigation by the Department of Health, a determination was made that both incidents constituted patient neglect and that failure to report these incidents was a violation of New York public health law. After a hearing by an administrative law judge, the charge in the first incident was sustained, and the charge in the second incident was dismissed. The nursing director petitioned to annul the administrative determination. She contended that the Department of Health failed to establish a prima facie case of patient neglect, that the incident was an unavoidable accident, and that the Department of Health's proof was based on hearsay evidence. The court held that evidence supported a finding that the director of nurses failed to report an incident of patient neglect as required by statute. On the question of hearsay evidence:

It is . . . well established that an agency can prove its case through hearsay evidence . . . In the final analysis, the evidence showed that the patient was left unattended, albeit momentarily, O'Brien (the orderly) was disciplined for that act, and petitioner did not report the incident. The finding is thus supported by the kind of evidence on which reasonable persons are accustomed to rely in serious affairs.[33]

Although it may not always be clear as to when an incident report should be filed, appropriate procedures should be in place addressing how questionable events should be handled.

▶ SENTINEL EVENTS

The Joint Commission encourages healthcare organizations to self-report sentinel events. The Joint Commission defines a *sentinel event* as "a patient safety event (not primarily related to the natural course of the patient's illness or underlying condition) that reaches a patient and results in death, permanent harm, or severe temporary harm."[34] Sentinel events subject to review by The Joint Commission include: patient suicide, the unanticipated death of a full-term infant, discharge of an infant to the wrong family, abduction of a patient, patient elopement, hemolytic reaction to a transfusion, rape, assault, invasive procedure on the wrong patient, retention of a foreign object in the patient's body, and radiation overdose.[35] Although The Joint Commission encourages the reporting of sentinel events, it does not require such reporting. It does, however, expect organizations to conduct a root cause analysis when sentinel events do occur.

Root Cause Analysis

A root cause analysis (RCA) is a chronologic review of an event to identify what, how, why, when, and where an unwanted event occurred in order to prevent reoccurrence of the event. The Joint Commission describes an RCA as focusing "on systems and processes . . . for identifying the factors that underlie a sentinel event."[36]

The National Patient Safety Foundation has a wealth of information on root cause analysis on its website, including slides for conducting a root cause analysis, webcast archives, and patient safety awareness week.[37] The vision of the National Patient Safety Foundation is "to create a world where patients and those who care for them are free from harm. A central voice for patient safety since 1997, NPSF partners with patients and families, the health care community, and key stakeholders to advance patient safety and health care workforce safety and disseminate strategies to prevent harm."[38]

An RCA is a process for identifying the basic or causal factor(s) underlying variation in performance, including the occurrence or possible occurrence of a sentinel event. The basic purpose of an RCA is to improve organizational performance outcomes. Organizations often are concerned with the possibility that RCAs could be subject to discovery by a plaintiff's attorney and could then be used against them in civil trials. To address this concern and minimize the risks of additional liability exposure, The Joint Commission continues to work on ways to prevent the disclosure of the substance of RCAs.

The RCA process involves investigating an unfortunate occurrence to determine the main cause of the event; conducting a thorough and credible analysis; investigating both general and special causes instigating the event; researching and reviewing the literature; searching for best practices on the Internet; contacting and consulting with other organizations that have implemented best practices to limit the likelihood of such events from occurring in the future; identifying changes that can be made to reduce or eliminate the likelihood of similar occurrences in the future; identifying who will be responsible for implementing changes; pilot testing the new design/best practice prior to full implementation; determining a time line for implementing changes; determining how changes will be communicated to those who will be working under the new design; educating staff, who will be responsible for operating under the newly designed practice; and determining how implementation of new processes will be monitored and evaluated.

🔍 THE COURT'S DECISION

The Georgia Court of Appeals held that the statute's grant of immunity from liability extended to the psychologist. The evidence did not establish bad faith on the part of the psychologist so as to deprive her of such immunity. The statute provides that any person participating in the making of a report, or participating in any judicial proceeding or any other proceeding resulting in a report of suspected child abuse, is immune from any civil or criminal liability that might otherwise be incurred or imposed, provided such participation pursuant to the statute is made in good faith. The grant of qualified immunity covers every person who, in good faith, participates over time in the making of a report to a child welfare agency. There was no competent evidence that the psychologist acted in bad faith.

▶ LOOK CLOSER, SEE ME

Donna Fannin read the poem "Look Closer, See ME" to every nursing assistant class she ever taught. This powerful poem was found among the meager belongings of an 89-year-old nursing home patient in Scotland following her death. It has been widely published since her passing. It is a reminder to us all that our bodies and relationships continue to change, and someday many of us will experience what she had felt.[39]

✒ Look Closer, See ME

What do you see, Nurses?/What do you see?/What are you thinking?/When you're looking at me?

A crabbit old woman,/Not very wise,/Uncertain of habit/With faraway eyes?

Who dribbles her food/And makes no reply/When you say in a loud voice,/"I do wish you'd try!"

Who seems not to notice/The things that you do,/And forever is losing/A stocking or shoe?

Who, resisting or not,/Lets you do as you will,/With bathing and feeding,/The long day to fill.

Is that what you're thinking?/Is that what you see?/Then open your eyes, Nurse,/You're not looking at ME.

I'll tell you who I am/As I sit here so still/As I do at your bidding/As I eat at your will.

I'm a small child of ten,/With a Mother and Father,/Brothers and sisters/Who love one another.

A young girl of sixteen,/With wings on her feet,/Dreaming that soon,/A lover she'll meet.

A bride soon at twenty,/My heart gives a leap./Remembering the vows/We have promised to keep.

At twenty-five now,/I have young of my own,/Who need me to guide them,/And a secure happy home.

A woman of thirty/My young they grow fast,/Bound to each other/With ties that should last.

At forty, my young sons/Have grown and have gone,/But my man's beside me/To see I don't mourn.

At fifty, once more/Babies play round my knee,/Again we know children,/My husband and me.

Dark days are upon me,/My husband is dead./I look to the future/And shudder with dread.

For my young are all rearing/Young of their own,/And I think of the years/And the love I have known.

I'm an old woman now,/And nature is cruel,/'Tis her jest to make old age/Look like a fool.

The body, it crumbles,/Grace and vigor depart/There is now a stone,/Where I once had a heart.

But inside this old carcass,/A young girl still dwells,/And now and again,/My battered heart swells.

I remember the joys,/I remember the pain,/And I'm living and loving/All over again.

I think of the years,/All too few, gone too fast,/And accept the stark fact/That nothing can last.

So, open your eyes, people,/Open and see,/Not a crabbit old woman,/Look closer, See ME.

—Anonymous

▶ CHAPTER REVIEW

1. An *abused child* is defined as one who has suffered intentional and serious mental, emotional, sexual, and/or physical injury inflicted by a parent or other person charged with the child's care.

2. Child abuse laws differ from state to state, but, in most states, persons required to report cases of child abuse are protected.

   - The person reporting abuse does not have to be absolutely certain that abuse has taken place before he or she reports.
   - Reports must be made with a good faith belief that the facts reported are true.

3. Senior abuse is less likely to be reported than child abuse, and proving senior abuse charges is often difficult. Types of senior abuse include abandonment, emotional or psychological abuse, physical abuse, neglect, financial exploitation, sexual abuse, and self-neglect.

4. The prompt reporting of communicable diseases is necessary in order for states to protect citizens' health by invoking the power to quarantine.

5. All births and deaths are reportable by statute. Unnatural deaths are to be referred to the medical examiner to determine the actual cause of death and provide related assistance for further criminal investigation, when necessary.

6. Timely reporting of drug interactions is necessary to help prevent harmful occurrences by those dispensing, prescribing, and taking the medication reported.

7. The *National Practitioner Data Bank* is used to collect and release information on the professional competence and conduct of physicians, dentists, and other healthcare practitioners.

8. Information in the data bank is considered strictly confidential. Data bank queries can be made by state licensing boards, hospitals, other healthcare organizations, and professional societies that have entered or may be entering into employment or affiliation relationships with a physician, dentist, or other healthcare practitioner who has applied for clinical privileges or appointment to a medical staff.

9. Incident reports include statements from employees and physicians regarding significant or noteworthy deviation from acceptable patient care. Some states require the reporting of specific incidents.

10. A *sentinel event* is an unexpected occurrence involving death or serious physical or psychological injury, or the risk thereof. The Joint Commission encourages self-reporting of sentinel events.

▶ REVIEW QUESTIONS

1. Describe various forms of child abuse, how to recognize it, and reporting requirements.
2. Describe various forms of elder abuse, how to recognize it, and reporting requirements.
3. Discuss the importance of reporting births and deaths.
4. Explain why it is important to report communicable diseases, adverse drug reactions, and infectious diseases.
5. Explain how and why physician incompetence is reported.
6. Explain the importance of incident reporting, sentinel events, and the purpose of root cause analyses.

▶ NOTES

1. *Michaels v. Gordon*, 439 S.E.2d 722 (Ga. Ct. App. 1993).
2. 42 U.S.C.A. § 5106g (2) (2003).
3. 373 N.W.2d 204 (Mich. Ct. App. 1985).

4. 413 N.W.2d 670 (Wis. Ct. App. 1987).

5. No. 1031515 (Ala. 2005).

6. Child Welfare Information Gateway, "Penalties for Failure to Report and False Reporting of Child Abuse and Neglect," https://www.childwelfare.gov/topics/systemwide/laws-policies/statutes/report/.

7. 415 N.W.2d 436 (Minn. Ct. App. 1987).

8. 140 S.W.3d 51 (Mo. banc).

9. *Manifold v. Ragaglia*, No. SC 17150 (Conn. 2004).

10. National Committee for the Prevention of Elder Abuse, "What Is Elder Abuse?" http://www.preventelderabuse.org/elderabuse/.

11. Richard J. Gelles, Murray A. Strauss, and Suzanne K. Steinmetz, *Behind Closed Doors: Violence in the American Family* (Garden City, NY: Anchor Press/Doubleday, 1980).

12. *Id.*

13. Senate Subcommittee on Health and Long-Term Care, *supra* note 53.

14. Kevin McCoy and Barbara Hansen, "Havens for Elderly May Expose Them to Deadly Risks," *USA Today*, May 25, 2004: 1.

15. National Center on Elder Abuse, "About NCEA," http://www.ncea.aoa.gov/ncearoot/Main_Site/index.aspx.

16. National Center on Elder Abuse, "Frequently Asked Questions," http://www.ncea.aoa.gov/NCEAroot/Main_Site/FAQ/Questions.aspx.

17. Centers for Disease Control and Prevention, "Mandatory Reporting of Infectious Diseases by Clinicians," *Morbidity and Mortality Weekly Report* 39 (June 22, 1990): 1–11, 16–17, http://www.cdc.gov/mmwr/preview/mmwrhtml/00001665.htm.

18. Virginia Department of Health, "HIV Reporting," http://www.vdh.virginia.gov/epidemiology/DiseasePrevention/Programs/HIV-AIDS/SurveillanceProgram/Reporting.htm.

19. *Anonymous Fireman v. Willoughby*, No. C88-1182 (D.C. N. Ohio Dec. 31, 1991) (unpublished).

20. 489 U.S. 602, 625 (1989).

21. *Anonymous Fireman*, No. C88-1182.

22. U.S. Food and Drug Administration, "How Consumers Can Report an Adverse Event or Serious Problem to the FDA," February 11, 2014, http://www.fda.gov/Safety/MedWatch/HowToReport/ucm053074.htm.

23. PUB. L. No. 99-660, tit. IV (1986).

24. 42 U.S.C. § 11101[0].

25. There is a guidebook that is meant to serve as a resource for the users of the NPDB. It is one of a number of efforts to inform the U.S. healthcare community about the data bank and what is required to comply with the requirements established by the HCQIA. The NPDB Help Line (1-800-767-6732) is a toll-free telephone service that provides healthcare entities and healthcare practitioners with information about the data bank.

26. 45 C.F.R. § 60.13.

27. 551 So. 2d 532 (Fla. Dist. Ct. App. 1990).

28. 456 N.W.2d 173 (Iowa 1990).

29. 936 P.2d 844 (Nev. 1997).

30. Nev. Rev. Stat. § 47.030.

31. Anna Bamonte Torrance, "Patient Safety Reporting Requirements," *Physician's News*, http://www.physiciansnews.com/law/902torrance.html.

32. 534 N.Y.S.2d 739 (N.Y. App. Div. 1988).

33. *Id.* at 741.

34. The Joint Commission, *2017 Hospital Accreditation Standards* (Oakbrook Terrace, IL: The Joint Commission, 2017), SE–1.

35. *Id.*

36. *Id.* at SE–6.

37. Institute for Healthcare Improvement, "How to Do a Root Cause Analysis of Diagnostic Error," [Slides], http://www.npsf.org/search/all.asp?bst=root+cause+analysis.

38. Institute for Healthcare Improvement, "About IHI/NPSF," http://www.npsf.org/?page=aboutus.

39. http://nursing.uc.edu/advantage/aging_with_dignity/Look_Closer_See_Me/look_closer_see_mepoem.html

© Orhan Cam/Shutterstock

CHAPTER 19

Labor Relations

UNFAIR LABOR PRACTICES

Ms. Welton attended a union organization meeting on July 5. At a hearing before an administrative law judge, she testified that the day after the meeting, her supervisor asked whether she or anyone from the dietary department attended the meeting. Welton's supervisor denied having any conversation with Welton about the union meeting. The National Labor Relations Board (NLRB) found that the questioning of Welton constituted unlawful interrogation.

Mr. Hopkins worked as a janitor for the nursing facility. He also attended the meeting on July 5. He testified that his supervisor approached him at work and questioned him as to whether any of the nurses or aides harassed him about the union. The board credited Hopkins's and Welton's version of the events, noting that they had nothing to gain by fabricating their testimony.

On July 18, the facility circulated a memorandum to all employees that stated: "This is to advise that the NLRB has tentatively set a hearing on Wednesday, July 25th, to decide who can vote in a union election. Our position is that supervisors, RNs, and LPNs cannot vote. We will keep you advised."

On July 19, the facility held a mandatory meeting for all nurses and supervisors. The facility's administrator, Mr. Wimer; the facility's attorney, Mr. Yocum; and the chief executive officer, Mr. Colby, told the nurses that, in the facility's

(continues)

opinion, nurses could not vote in the upcoming election but must remain loyal to the facility. When asked by Sands, a union supporter, what he meant by loyalty, Yocum replied that all nurses were prohibited from engaging in union activities. When asked by Sands why the facility opposed the union, Yocum responded, "Well, for one thing, they cost too . . . much money. . . . Do you think those dues come out of thin air?"

The board concluded that the facility, through Yocum, violated the National Labor Relations Act by telling nurses present at the meeting that they could not vote in the upcoming union election or participate in union activities and that such activities could subject them to dismissal.[1]

WHAT IS YOUR VERDICT?

▶ LEARNING OBJECTIVES

The reader, upon completion of this chapter, will be able to:

- Describe the various federal labor acts.
- Discuss the rights and responsibilities of unions and management.
- Describe the purpose of an affirmative action plan.
- Describe a patient's rights during labor disputes.
- Discuss the types of discrimination that occur in the workplace.
- Describe what sexual harassment is and what forms it can take.

Federal or state regulation generally pervades all areas of employer–employee relationships. Healthcare organizations are not exempt from the impact of these laws and therefore are required to take into account such matters as employment practices (wages, hours, and working conditions), union activity, workers' compensation laws, occupational safety and health laws, and employment discrimination law.

The most significant piece of federal legislation dealing with labor relations is the National Labor Relations Act. Although federal laws generally take precedence over state laws when there is a conflict between the state and the federal laws, state laws are applicable and must be considered, especially when state regulations are more rigid than federal legislation. This chapter provides an overview of a variety of laws affecting the healthcare industry.

▶ U.S. DEPARTMENT OF LABOR

The *U.S. Department of Labor* is a department within the executive branch of government. The Secretary of Labor advises the president on labor policies and issues. The functions of the department of labor are to foster, promote, and develop the welfare of wage earners; to improve working conditions; and to advance opportunities for profitable employment. In carrying out this mission, the department administers a variety of federal labor laws guaranteeing workers' rights to safe and healthy working conditions, a minimum hourly wage and overtime pay, freedom from discriminatory practices, unemployment insurance, and workers' compensation. As the department seeks to assist all Americans who need and want to work, special efforts are made to meet the unique job market problems of older workers, youths, minority group members, women, the handicapped, and other groups. Within the Department of Labor are various agencies responsible for carrying out the purpose of the department (e.g., Occupational Safety and Health Administration [OSHA]).

▶ UNIONS AND HEALTHCARE ORGANIZATIONS

Union organizational activity in the healthcare industry was minimal until the late 1950s. Many labor organizations have attempted to become the recognized collective bargaining representatives for employees in healthcare settings. Craft unions devote their primary organizing efforts to skilled employees, such as carpenters and electricians, and industrial unions and unions of governmental employees seek to represent large groups of unskilled or semiskilled employees. Professional and occupational associations, such as state nurses' associations, historically known for their social and academic efforts, have involved themselves in collective bargaining for their professions. To the extent that professional organizations seek goals directly concerned with wages, hours, and other employment conditions and engage in bargaining on behalf of employees, they perform the functions of labor unions.

Limitations on Bargaining Units

A major area of concern for healthcare institutions is the number of bargaining units allowed in any one institution. Rules and regulations issued on April 21, 1989, by the NLRB allow up to eight collective bargaining units in healthcare organizations, as opposed to the three normally allowed before the regulations. The American Hospital Association brought an action to enjoin the NLRB from enforcing the newly promulgated regulation recognizing up to eight bargaining units in *American Hospital Association v. NLRB*.[2] A federal district court enjoined enforcement of the rule. The NLRB and intervening unions appealed. The U.S. Court of Appeals for the Seventh Circuit held that the rule was not arbitrary and was within the authority of the NLRB. No rule is necessary to confer the rights already conferred by statute entitling guards and professional employees to form separate bargaining units.

In making unit determinations, the NLRB is required to strike a balance among the competing interests of unions, employees (whose interests are not always compatible with those of unions), employers, and the broader public. The statute can be read to suggest that the tilt should be in favor of unions and toward relatively many, rather than relatively few, units.

This balancing act is not spelled out in the statute, thus requiring an NLRB decision. The decision is particularly difficult and delicate in the healthcare industry because the workforce of a hospital, nursing home, or rehabilitation center tends to be small and heterogeneous.

On appeal, the U.S. Supreme Court, on April 23, 1991, by unanimous decision, upheld the NLRB rule allowing hospital workers to form up to eight separate bargaining units, including those for physicians, registered nurses, other professionals, technical employees, clerical employees, skilled maintenance employees, other nonprofessional employees, and security guards.[3]

▶ NATIONAL LABOR RELATIONS ACT

Congress enacted the *National Labor Relations Act* (NLRA)[4] in July 1935 to govern the labor–management relations of business firms engaged in interstate commerce. The Act is generally known as the Wagner Act, after Senator Robert R. Wagner of New York. The Act defines certain conduct of employers and employees as unfair labor practices and provides for hearings on complaints that such practices have occurred. The Taft–Hartley amendments of 1947 and the Landrum–Griffin amendments of 1959, modified the NLRA.

National Labor Relations Board

The *National Labor Relations Board* (NLRB), which is entrusted with enforcing and administering the NLRA, has jurisdiction over matters involving proprietary and not-for-profit healthcare organizations. The NLRB is an agency, independent of the Department of Labor, that is responsible for preventing and remedying unfair labor practices by employers and labor organizations or their agents. The NLRB conducts secret ballot elections among employees in appropriate collective bargaining units to determine whether they desire to be represented by a labor organization and among employees under union-shop agreements to determine whether they wish to revoke their union's authority. The general counsel of the NLRB has final authority to investigate charges of unfair labor practices, issue complaints, and prosecute such complaints before the NLRB. There are regional directors, under the direction of the general counsel, who are responsible for processing representation, unfair labor practice, and jurisdictional dispute cases.

The NLRB's basic method of operation is to investigate claims or complaints of unfair practices submitted by the employer, employees, or both. The board reviews the claim to determine whether there have been unfair labor practices and recommends a remedy. Most questions submitted to the board involve claims by employees that their rights of self-organization or of choosing their collective bargaining representative have been interfered with by the employer. Employers also may submit complaints to the NLRB (e.g., when two unions are seeking recognition and one of them intimidates employees by making allegations that a sweetheart relationship exists between the employer and the competing union in an effort to disrupt the certification process).

An exemption for governmental institutions was included in the 1935 enactment of the NLRA, and charitable healthcare institutions were exempted in 1947 by the Taft–Hartley Act amendments to the NLRA. However, a July 1974 amendment to the NLRA extended coverage to employees of nonprofit healthcare organizations, who previously had been exempted from its provisions. In the words of the amendment, a healthcare facility is "any hospital, convalescent hospital, health maintenance organization, health clinic, nursing home, extended care facility, or other institution devoted to the care of the sick, infirm or aged."[5]

The amendment also enacted unique, special provisions for employees of healthcare organizations who oppose unionization on legitimate religious grounds. These provisions allow a member of such an organization to make periodic contributions to one of three nonreligious charitable funds selected jointly by the labor organization and the employing institution rather than paying periodic union dues and initiation fees. If the collective bargaining agreement does not specify an acceptable fund, the employee may select a tax-exempt charity.

Elections

The NLRA sets out the procedures by which employees may select a union as their collective bargaining representative to negotiate with healthcare organizations over employment and contract matters. A healthcare organization may choose to recognize and deal with the union without resorting to the formal NLRA procedure. If the formal process is adhered to, employees vote on union representation in an election held under NLRB supervision.

The NLRA provides that the representative, having been selected by a majority of employees in a bargaining unit, is the exclusive bargaining agent for all employees in the unit. The scope of the bargaining unit is often the subject of dispute, for its boundaries may determine the outcome of the election, the employee representative's bargaining power, and the level of labor stability.

When the parties cannot agree on the appropriate unit for bargaining, the NLRB has broad discretion to decide the issue; however, the NLRB's discretion is limited to determining appropriate units for only those employees who are classified as professional, supervisory, clerical, technical, or service and maintenance employees when they are included in units outside their particular category. This is the case unless there has been a self-determination election in which the members of a certain group vote, as a class, to be included within the larger bargaining unit. For example, nurses and other professional employees can be excluded from a bargaining unit composed of service and maintenance employees unless the professionals are first given the opportunity to choose separate representation and reject it. Supervisory nurses also have been held entitled to a bargaining unit separate from the unit composed of general-duty nurses.

Although the NLRA does not require employee representatives to be selected by any particular procedure, the Act provides for the NLRB to conduct representation elections by secret ballot. The NLRB may conduct such an election when an employee, a group of employees, an individual, a labor union acting on the employees' behalf, or an employer has filed a petition for certification. When the petition is filed, the NLRB must investigate and direct an election if it has

reasonable cause to believe a question of representation exists. Any party to an election who believes that certain conduct created an atmosphere that interfered with free choice may file objections with the NLRB.

Unfair Labor Practices

The NLRA prohibits healthcare organizations from engaging in certain conduct classified as employer unfair labor practices. For example, discriminating against an employee for holding union membership is not permitted. The NLRA stipulates that the employer must bargain in good faith with representatives of the employees; failure to do so constitutes an unfair labor practice. The NLRB may order the employer to fulfill the duty to bargain.

If the employer dominates or controls the employees' union or interferes with and supports one of two competing unions, the employer is committing an unfair labor practice. Such employer support of a competing union is illustrated clearly in a situation in which two unions are competing for members in the same facility, as well as for recognition as the employees' bargaining organization. If the organization permits one of the unions to use its facilities for its organizational activities but denies the use of the facilities to the other union, an unfair labor practice is committed. Financial assistance to one of the competing unions also constitutes an unfair labor practice.

The NLRA places duties on labor organizations and prohibits certain employee activities that are considered unfair labor practices. Coercion of employees by the union constitutes an unfair labor practice; such activities as mass picketing, assaulting nonstrikers, and following groups of nonstrikers away from the immediate area of the facility plainly constitute coercion and can be ordered stopped by the NLRB. Breach of a collective bargaining contract by the labor union is another example of an unfair labor practice.

State Employees Excluded from Paying Union Dues

The U.S. Supreme Court, in a five-to-four decision in *Harris v. Quinn*,[6] on June 28, 2014, struck down an Illinois "fair share" statute that compelled home healthcare workers to pay union dues even if they were not members of the union. The Court ruled that home care workers in Illinois paid by the state are not similar enough to government employees to be compelled to pay union dues. Government employees who provide in-home care for family members and others with disabilities were not considered full-fledged public employees. The decision left undisturbed its 1977

Michigan ruling in *Abood v. Detroit Bd. of Educ.*[7] that allowed unions to collect compulsory dues used for nonpolitical activities under collective bargaining agreements. Michigan statute allows for an *agency shop* arrangement, whereby employees represented by a union, even though not union members, must pay to the union, as a condition of employment, a service charge equal in amount to union dues.

▶ NORRIS–LAGUARDIA ACT

Congress enacted the *Norris–LaGuardia Act*[8] to limit the power of federal courts to issue injunctions in cases involving or growing out of labor disputes. The Act's strict standards must be met before such injunctions can be issued. Essentially, a federal court may not apply restraints in a labor dispute until after the case is heard in open court and the finding is that unlawful acts will be committed unless restrained and that substantial and irreparable injury to the complainant's property will follow.[9]

The Norris–LaGuardia Act is aimed at reducing the number of injunctions granted to restrain strikes and picketing. An additional piece of legislation designating procedures limiting strikes in healthcare institutions is the 1974 amendment to the NLRA. This amendment sets out special procedures for handling labor disputes that develop from collective bargaining at the termination of an existing agreement or during negotiations for an initial contract between a healthcare institution and its employees. The procedures were designed to ensure that the needs of patients would be met during any work stoppage (strike) or labor dispute in such an institution.

The amendment provides for creating a board of inquiry if a dispute threatens to interrupt health care in a particular community. The board is appointed by the director of the Federal Mediation and Conciliation Service (FMCS) within 30 days after notification of either party's intention to terminate a labor contract. The board then has 15 days in which to investigate and report its findings and recommendations in writing. After the report is filed with the FMCS, both parties are expected to maintain the status quo for an additional 15 days. The board's findings provide a framework for arbitrators' decisions, while recognizing both the community's need for continuous health services and the good faith intentions of labor organizations to avoid a work stoppage whenever possible and to accept arbitration when negotiations reach an impasse.

The amendment also mandates certain notice requirements by labor groups in healthcare institutions:

(1) the institution must be given 90 days' notice before a collective bargaining agreement expires, and (2) the FMCS is entitled to 60 days' notice. Previously, only 60 days' notice to the employer and 30 days' notice to the FMCS were required. However, if the bargaining agreement is the initial contract between the parties, only 30 days' notice needs to be given to the FMCS.

More significantly, 10 days' notice is required in advance of any strike, picketing, or other concerted refusal to work, regardless of the source of the dispute. This allows the NLRB to determine the legality of a strike before it occurs and also gives healthcare institutions ample time to ensure the continuity of patient care. At the same time, any attempt to use this period to undermine the bargaining relationship is implicitly forbidden. The 10-day notice may be concurrent with the final 10 days of the expiration notice. Any employee violation of these provisions amounts to an unfair labor practice and automatically may result in the discharge of the employee. Also, injunctive relief may be available from the courts if circumstances warrant. In summary, the amendment's provisions are designed to ensure that every possible approach to a peaceful settlement is explored fully before a strike is called.

▶ LABOR–MANAGEMENT REPORTING AND DISCLOSURE ACT

The *Labor–Management Reporting and Disclosure Act of 1959*[10] was enacted to place controls on labor unions and the relationships between unions and their members. Also, it requires that employers report payments and loans made to officials or other representatives of labor organizations or any promises to make such payments or loans. Expenditures made to influence or restrict the way employees exercise their rights to organize and bargain collectively are illegal unless the employer discloses them. Agreements with labor consultants, under which such persons undertake to interfere with certain employee rights, also must be disclosed.

Reports required under the Act must be filed with the Secretary of Labor and are then made public. Both charitable and proprietary healthcare organizations that make such payments or enter into such agreements must file reports. Penalties for failing to make the required reports or for making false reports include fines up to $10,000 and imprisonment for 1 year.

FAIR LABOR STANDARDS ACT

The *Fair Labor Standards Act* (FLSA)[11] of 1938 established a national minimum wage, guaranteed time and one half for overtime, established maximum hours of employment, and prohibited most employment for minors. The Wage and Hour Division of the U.S. Department of Labor, which conducts audits and workplace inspections, administers the FLSA. The FLSA provides for direct federal actions by employees and offers substantial financial incentives for private litigants and their counsel.

Employees of all governmental, charitable, and proprietary healthcare organizations are covered by the FLSA. Employers must conform to the minimum wage and overtime pay provisions. However, bona fide executive, administrative, and professional employees are exempted from the wage and hour provisions.

The law permits employers to enter into agreements with employees, establishing a work period of 14 consecutive days as an alternative to the usual 7-day week. If the alternative period is chosen, the employer must pay the overtime rate only for hours worked in excess of 80 hours during the 14-day period. The alternative 14-day work period does not relieve a facility from paying overtime for hours worked in excess of 8 hours in any 1 day, even if no more than 80 hours are worked during the period.

Hospital's Unfair Labor Practice

The NLRB, in *St. John's Mercy Health Systems v. National Labor Relations Board*,[12] was found to have properly upheld a union's unfair labor practice charge against a hospital that had refused to discharge registered nurses who had not paid union dues, as required by the applicable collective bargaining agreement. There was no Missouri public policy that prevented enforcement of union security provision of the collective bargaining agreement, notwithstanding statistical evidence of a regional or national nursing shortage that would make it difficult to replace nurses. In addition, the hospital was not exempt from the NLRA union security provisions.

CIVIL RIGHTS ACT

Title VII of the Civil Rights Act of 1964, as amended by the Equal Employment Opportunity Act of 1972,[13] prohibits private employers and state and local governments from discrimination in employment in any business based on race, color, religion, sex, or national origin. The Act prohibits harassment based on one's affiliation (e.g., religion), physical and cultural traits and clothing (e.g., skin color, headscarf), perception (e.g., as a result of national origin: he is from Pakistan and must, therefore, be a terrorist), and association (e.g., discrimination based on association with an individual or organization). The federal antidiscrimination law provides that it is unlawful for most public and private employers to discriminate against, fail or refuse to hire, or to discharge any individual, with respect to his or her compensation, terms, conditions, or privileges of employment because of such individual's race, color, religion, sex (including pregnancy), or national origin.

Title VII also prohibits retaliation against employees who oppose such unlawful discrimination. The Equal Employment Opportunity Commission (EEOC) enforces Title VII. The EEOC investigates, mediates, and sometimes files lawsuits on behalf of employees. Title VII also provides that an individual can bring a private lawsuit.

An exception to prohibited employment practices may be permitted when, for example, religion, sex, or national origin is a bona fide occupational qualification necessary to the operation of a particular business or enterprise.

This Act does not apply to a religious corporation (e.g., hospital), association, educational institution, or society with respect to the employment of individuals of a particular religion to perform work connected with the carrying on by such corporation, association, educational institution, or society of its activities.

Many states have enacted protective laws with respect to the employment of women. The EEOC guidelines on sex discrimination make it clear that state laws limiting the employment of women in certain occupations are superseded by Title VII and are no defense against a charge of sex discrimination.

OCCUPATIONAL SAFETY AND HEALTH ACT

Congress enacted the *Occupational Safety and Health Act of 1970* (OSH Act)[14] to establish an administrative mechanism for the development and enforcement of standards for occupational health and safety. The legislation was enacted based on congressional findings that personal injuries and illnesses arising out of work situations impose a substantial burden on and are substantial hindrances to interstate commerce in terms of lost production, wage loss, medical expenses, and disability compensation payments. Congress declared that its purpose and policy were to ensure, so far as possible, every working man and woman in the nation safe and healthful working conditions and to preserve human resources by implementing the following:

1. by encouraging employers and employees in their efforts to reduce the number of occupational safety and health hazards at their places of employment, and to stimulate employers and employees to institute new and to perfect existing programs for providing safe and healthful working conditions;

2. by providing that employers and employees have separate but dependent responsibilities and rights with respect to achieving safe and healthful working conditions;

3. by authorizing the Secretary of Labor to set mandatory occupational safety and health standards applicable to businesses affecting interstate commerce, and by creating an Occupational Safety and Health Review Commission for carrying out adjudicatory functions under the Act;

4. by building upon advances already made through employer and employee initiatives for providing safe and healthful working conditions;

5. by providing for research in the field of occupational safety and health, including the psychological factors involved, and by developing innovative methods, techniques, and approaches for dealing with occupational safety and health problems;

6. by exploring ways to discover latent diseases, establishing causal connections between diseases and work in environmental conditions, and conducting other research relating to health problems, in recognition of the fact that occupational health standards present problems often different from those involved in occupational safety;

7. by providing medical criteria which will assure insofar as practicable that no employee will suffer diminished health, functional capacity, or life expectancy as a result of his work experience;

8. by providing for training programs to increase the number and competence of personnel engaged in the field of occupational safety and health; affecting the OSH Act since its passage in 1970 through January 1, 2004;

9. by providing for the development and promulgation of occupational safety and health standards;

10. by providing an effective enforcement program which shall include a prohibition against giving advance notice of any inspection and sanctions for any individual violating this prohibition;

11. by encouraging the States to assume the fullest responsibility for the administration and enforcement of their occupational safety and health laws by providing grants to the States to assist in identifying their needs and responsibilities in the area of occupational safety and health, to develop plans in accordance with the provisions of this Act, to improve the administration and enforcement of State occupational safety and health laws, and to conduct experimental and demonstration projects in connection therewith;

12. by providing for appropriate reporting procedures with respect to occupational safety and health which procedures will help achieve the objectives of this Act and accurately describe the nature of the occupational safety and health problem; and

13. by encouraging joint labor–management efforts to reduce injuries and disease arising out of employment.[15]

The employer must comply with the occupational and health standards under the Act, and employees must follow the rules, regulations, and orders issued under the Act that are applicable to their actions and conduct on the job. The duties of employers and employees under the Act are as follows:

a. Each employer—
   1. shall furnish to each of his employees employment and a place of employment which is free from recognized hazards that are causing or are likely to cause death or serious physical harm to his employees;
   2. shall comply with occupational safety and health standards promulgated under this Act.

b. Each employee shall comply with occupational safety and health standards and all rules, regulations, and orders pursuant to this Act which are applicable to his own actions and conduct.[16]

Promulgation and Enforcement of OSHA Standards

OSHA develops and promulgates occupational safety and health standards for the workplace. It develops and issues regulations, conducts investigations and inspections to determine the status of compliance, and issues citations and proposes penalties for noncompliance. Inspections are conducted without advance notice.

Employers are responsible for becoming familiar with standards applicable to their businesses and for ensuring that employees have and use personal protective equipment when required for safety. Employees must comply with all rules and regulations that are applicable to their work environment. Where OSHA has not promulgated specific standards, the employer is responsible for following the Act's general duty clause. The general duty clause states that each employer must furnish a place of employment that is free from recognized hazards that are causing or likely to cause death or serious physical harm.

Recordkeeping

Employers with 11 or more employees are required to maintain records of occupational injuries and illnesses. The purpose of maintaining records is to permit the Bureau of Labor Statistics to help define high-hazard industries and to inform employees of the status of their employer's record.

Education

Employers are responsible for keeping employees informed about OSHA and about the various safety and health matters with which they are involved. OSHA requires that employers post informational materials at prominent locations in the workplace (e.g., a job safety and health protection workplace poster informing employees of their rights and responsibilities under the OSHA).

The ever-increasing likelihood that healthcare workers will come into contact with persons carrying infectious diseases demands compliance with approved safety procedures. This is especially important for workers who come into contact with the blood and body fluids of, for example, HIV-infected persons. The CDC expanded its infection control guidelines and has urged hospitals to adopt standard precautions to protect their workers from exposure to patients' blood and other body fluids.

The CDC recommends Standard Precautions for the care of all patients, regardless of their diagnosis or presumed infection status.

- Standard Precautions apply to 1) blood; 2) all body fluids, secretions, and excretions, *except sweat*, regardless of whether or not they contain visible blood; 3) non-intact skin; and 4) mucous membranes. Standard precautions are designed to reduce the risk of transmission of microorganisms from both recognized and unrecognized sources of infection in hospitals.
  - Standard precautions includes the use of: hand washing, appropriate personal protective equipment such as gloves, gowns, masks, whenever touching or exposure to patients' body fluids is anticipated.
- **Transmission-Based Precautions** (i.e., Airborne Precautions, Droplet Precautions, and Contact Precautions), are recommended to provide additional precautions beyond Standard Precautions to interrupt transmission of pathogens in hospitals.
  - Transmission-based precautions can be used for patients with known infections or suspected to be infected or colonized with epidemiologically-important pathogens that can be transmitted by airborne or droplet transmission or by contact with dry skin or contaminated surfaces. These precautions should be used in addition to standard precautions.
    - **Airborne Precautions** used for infections spread in small particles in the air such as chicken pox.
    - **Droplet Precautions** used for infections spread in large droplets by coughing, talking, or sneezing such as influenza.
    - **Contact Precautions** used for infections spread by skin-to-skin contact or contact with other surfaces such as herpes simplex virus.
  - Airborne Precautions, Droplet Precautions, and Contact Precautions may be combined for diseases that have multiple routes of transmission. When used either singularly or in combination, they are to be used in addition to Standard Precautions. (https://www.osha.gov/SLTC/etools/hospital/hazards/univprec/univ.html)

Although transmission of an infectious disease from an infected caregiver to his or her patient during invasive surgery may be unlikely, it is possible and therefore foreseeable. Because of the potentially deadly consequence of such transmission, infected caregivers must not engage in activity that creates a risk of transmission.

The process of staff education in preparing to care for patients with AIDS is extremely important and must include a training program on prevention and transmission in the work setting. Educational requirements specified by OSHA for healthcare employees include epidemiology, modes of transmission, preventive practices, and universal precautions.

Infectious Body Fluids

OSHA issued standards on December 2, 1991, that are to be followed by employers to protect employees from blood-borne infections. Universal precautions are mandatory, and employees who are likely to be exposed to body fluids must be provided with protective clothing (e.g., masks, gowns, gloves). In addition, postexposure testing must be available to employees who have been exposed to body fluids.

Employee Complaints

Employees should inform their supervisors if they suspect or detect a dangerous situation in the workplace, and employers are expected to address reported hazards in the workplace. Employees or their representatives have the right to file complaints with an OSHA office and request a survey when they believe that conditions in the workplace are unsafe or unhealthy. If a violation of the Act is found at the time of a survey, the employer may receive a citation stating a time frame within which the violation must be corrected.

State Regulation

The states have statutes charging employers with the duty to furnish employees with a safe working environment. The city and county in which a healthcare facility is located also may prescribe rules regarding the health and safety of employees. Many communities have enacted sanitary and health codes that require certain standards.

Legal Liability

From a liability point of view, an employer can be held legally liable for damages suffered by employees through exposure to dangerous conditions that are in violation of OSHA standards. Proof of an employee's exposure to noncompliant conditions is generally necessary to find an employer liable.

▶ REHABILITATION ACT

The essential purpose of the *Rehabilitation Act of 1973*[17] is to provide protection to handicapped people from discrimination. The law basically is administered by the Department of Health and Human Services (DHHS), which derives its jurisdiction from the fact that healthcare organizations participate in such federal programs as Medicare, Medicaid, and the Hill–Burton Act. Therefore, the law is applied to both public and private organizations, because both participate in these programs.

Section 503 of the Act applies to government contractors whose contracts exceed $2,500 in value. Section 504, which applies to employers who are recipients of federal financial assistance, states, "[n]o . . . qualified handicapped individual in the United States . . . shall solely by reason of his handicap, be excluded from participation in, be denied the benefits of, or be subjected to discrimination under any program as actively receiving federal financial assistance." Section 504 applies to virtually every area of personnel administration, including recruitment, advertising, processing of applications, promotions, rates of pay, fringe benefits, and job assignments.

Since July 1977, all institutions receiving federal financial assistance from the DHHS have been required to file assurances of compliance forms. Each employer must designate an individual to coordinate compliance efforts. A grievance procedure should be in place to address employee complaints alleging violation of the regulation. All employment decisions must be made without regard to physical or mental handicaps that are not inherently disqualifying (e.g., an employer is not obligated to employ a person with a highly contagious disease that can be easily transmitted to others).

Employers receiving federal funds are required to perform a self-evaluation regarding their compliance with Section 504 of the Rehabilitation Act of 1973. If discriminatory practices are identified through the self-evaluation process, remedial steps are to be taken to eliminate the effects of any discrimination. Records of the evaluation are to be maintained on file for at least 3 years after the review for public inspection.[18]

Jobs should not be purposely designed to eliminate the hiring of disabled persons. Employers, however, are not required to change the essential elements of a job in order to create a position for a disabled person. The Iowa Supreme Court, in *Schlitzer v. University of Iowa Hosp. and Clinics*,[19] decided that an employer is not required to create a vacancy or a job for a disabled person. The court found that a nurse's 20-pound lifting restriction, as a result of a car accident, limited her ability to lift, thus making the demands of her job incompatible with her physical disability. The law does not require that an employer change the essential elements of a job in order to meet a claimant's disability.

In this case, the job required that the nurse be able to work with severely disabled persons. The 20-pound limitation, in this case, was an impossible hurdle to overcome.

► FAMILY AND MEDICAL LEAVE ACT

The *Family and Medical Leave Act of 1993* (FMLA) was enacted to grant temporary medical leave to employees under certain circumstances. The Act provides that covered employers must grant an eligible employee up to a total of 12 workweeks of unpaid leave during any 12-month period for one or more of the following reasons: the birth and care of an employee's child, placement of an adopted or foster child with the employee, the care of an immediate family member (spouse, child, or parent) with a serious health condition, or inability to work because of a serious health condition. It is illegal to terminate health insurance coverage for an employee on FMLA leave. Following an FMLA leave, the employee's job—or an equivalent job with equivalent pay, benefits, and other terms and conditions of employment—must be restored.

While an employee is on FMLA-approved leave, benefits cannot be denied as well as the rights the employee is entitled to, including the right to not have to perform work-related tasks while on leave. In *Vess v. Scott Medical Corporation*,[20] Julie Vess was on FMLA leave from her position as the director of respiratory therapy at Regency Hospital in Toledo, Ohio. While on leave from knee surgery needed to treat an injury that occurred in the Regency parking lot, Vess claimed that she was ordered to do so much work that her FMLA leave was interfered with. The court ruled that Vess's statements outlining the tasks she was asked to do while she was on leave were sufficient to demonstrate that she may have been denied FMLA benefits. In the ruling, the court stated that employers ask workers who are out on FMLA to perform the following tasks:

- Pass along institutional knowledge to new staff.
- Provide computer passwords.
- Seek closure on completed assignments.
- Identify other employees to fill voids.[21]

► STATE LABOR LAWS

The federal labor enactments serve as a pattern for many state labor laws that comprise the second labor regulation system affecting healthcare organizations. State labor acts vary from state to state; therefore, it is important that each institution familiarize itself not only with federal regulations but also with state regulations affecting labor relations within the institution.

Because the NLRA excludes from coverage healthcare organizations operated by the state or its political subdivisions, regulation of labor–management relations in these organizations is left to state law. Unless the constitution in such a state guarantees the right of employees to organize and imposes the duty of collective bargaining on the employer, healthcare organizations do not have to bargain collectively with their employees. However, in states that do have labor relations acts, the obligation of an organization to bargain collectively with its employees is determined by the applicable statute.

State laws vary considerably in their coverage, and often employees of state and local governmental organizations are covered by separate public employee legislation. Some of these statutes cover both state and local employees, whereas others cover only state or only local employees.

Some of the states that have labor relations acts granting employees the right to organize, join unions, and bargain collectively have specifically prohibited strikes and lockouts and have provided for compulsory arbitration whenever a collective bargaining contract cannot otherwise be executed amicably. Anti-injunction statutes would not forbid injunctions to restrain violations of these statutory provisions.

The doctrine of federal preemption, as applied to labor relations, displaces the states' jurisdiction to regulate an activity that is arguably an unfair labor practice within the meaning of the NLRA. Nonetheless, the U.S. Supreme Court has ruled that states can still regulate labor relations activity that also falls within the jurisdiction of the NLRB when deeply rooted local feelings and responsibility are affected.

Union Security Contracts and Right-to-Work Laws

Labor organizations frequently seek to enter union security contracts with employers. Such contracts are of two types: (1) the closed-shop contract, which provides that only members of a particular union may be hired, and (2) the union-shop contract, which makes continued employment dependent on membership in the union, although the employee does not need to have been a union member when applying for the job.

Various states have made such contracts unlawful. Statutes forbidding such agreements generally are called *right-to-work laws* on the theory that they protect everyone's right to work even if a person refuses to join a union. Several state statutes or court decisions purport to restrict union security contracts or specify procedures to be completed before such agreements may be made.

Wage and Hour Laws

When state minimum wage standards are higher than federal standards, the state's standards are applicable.

Child Labor Laws

Many states prohibit the employment of minors younger than a specified age and restrict the employment of other minors. Child labor legislation commonly requires that working papers be secured before a child may be hired, forbids the employment of minors at night, and prohibits minors from operating certain types of dangerous machinery.

This kind of legislation rarely exempts charitable institutions, although some exceptions may be made with respect to the hours when student nurses may work.

▶ WORKERS' COMPENSATION

Workers' compensation is a program by which an employee can receive certain wage benefits because of work-related injuries. An employee who is injured while performing job-related duties is generally eligible for workers' compensation. Workers' compensation programs are administered by the states.

State legislatures have recognized that it is difficult and expensive for employees to recover from their employers and, therefore, have enacted workers' compensation laws. Employers are required to provide workers' compensation as a benefit. Workers' compensation laws give the employee a legal way to receive compensation for injuries incurred while on the job. The acts do not require the employee to prove that the injury was the result of the employer's negligence. Workers' compensation laws are based on the employer–employee relationship and not on the theory of negligence.

The scope of workers' compensation varies widely. Some states limit an employee's compensation to the amount recoverable by the workers' compensation law, and further lawsuits against the employer are barred. Other states permit employees to choose whether to accept the compensation provided by law or to institute a lawsuit against the employer. Some acts go further and provide a system of insurance that may be under the supervision of state or private insurers.

Physical Injury

The courts have been somewhat liberal in allowing workers' compensation benefits to be paid to employees injured while on duty, even when challenged by the employer under seemingly justifiable circumstances. The employee in *Fondulac Nursing Home v. Industrial Commission*[22] was entitled to workers' compensation despite orders that she was not to lift patients because of a back injury. When a patient was being transferred from her wheelchair to her bed and began to fall, the nurse attempted to prevent the fall, injuring herself. The nurse acted within her scope of employment by attempting to prevent the fall to her own detriment and in her employer's best interests by protecting the patient from injury.

Job Stress

Workers' compensation has been awarded for depression related to job stress. In *Elwood v. SAIF*,[23] a registered nurse filed a workers' compensation claim for an occupational disease based on depression. The referee and the workers' compensation board affirmed the insurer's denial of the claim, and the claimant sought judicial review. The questions that needed to be answered to determine job stress were as follows:

- What were the "real" events and conditions of the plaintiff's employment?
- Were those real events and conditions capable of producing stress when viewed objectively, even though an average worker might not have responded adversely to them?
- Did the plaintiff suffer a mental disorder?
- Were the real stressful events and conditions the major contributing cause of the plaintiff's mental disorder?

The record established that many events and conditions of her employment, including her termination, were real and capable of producing stress when viewed objectively. The claimant's treating physician advised her that she was suffering from anxiety, depression, and stress and advised her to seek a psychiatric evaluation. The court held that the claimant established that her condition was compensable.

Influenza Vaccination

A hospital employee's reaction to an influenza vaccination given by an emergency department employee while he or she is on duty most likely will be a compensable injury under workers' compensation. A housekeeping employee in *Monette v. Manatee Memorial*

Hospital[24] suffered a serious reaction to the influenza vaccination administered to her while on duty and was entitled to workers' compensation.

Exposure to Hazardous Materials

Workers' compensation benefits, in *Caldwell v. District of Columbia Dep't of Employment Svcs.*,[25] were improperly denied to an employee of a university hospital who had sought benefits for medical problems and expenses resulting from her contact with certain chemical agents. There was no substantial evidence to support a finding that the employee's initial symptoms were not attributable to the laboratory environment. Doctors agreed that chemical solvents in the laboratory, when combined with defective ventilation at the laboratory, could cause or significantly contribute to various conditions of which the employee complained. The medical reports revealed no substantial evidence that the effects of conditions at the hospital had been entirely resolved.

▶ LABOR RIGHTS

Rights and responsibilities run concurrently. Employee rights include the following:

- The right to organize and bargain collectively
- The right to solicit and distribute union information during nonworking hours (i.e., mealtimes and coffee breaks)
- The right to picket (Picketing is the act of patrolling, by one or more persons, a place related to a labor dispute. It varies in purpose and form. It may be conducted by employees or nonemployees, and, like strikes, some picketing may be legislatively or judicially disapproved and subject to regulation.)
- The right to strike (A strike may be defined as the collective quitting of work by employees as a means of inducing the employer to assent to employee demands. Employees possess the right to strike, although this right is not absolute and is subject to limited exercise. The 1974 amendments to the NLRA have added requirements with respect to strikes and picketing in an attempt to reduce the interruption of healthcare services. The NLRB is urged to give top priority to settling labor–management disputes resulting in the loss of healthcare personnel or medical services.)

Employees granted these rights have the concomitant responsibility to perform their work duties properly. A nursing home housekeeper, for example, was terminated properly after repeated oral and written reprimands concerning her improper cleaning of rooms in *Ford v. Patin*.[26] Her substandard performance, despite repeated warnings, evidenced willful and wanton disregard of her employer's interest and constituted misconduct within purview of Section 23:1601(2) of the Louisiana Revised Statutes Annotated.

▶ MANAGEMENT RIGHTS

As with labor, management also has certain rights and responsibilities. Specific management rights are reviewed here.

Receive Strike Notice

Management has a right to a 10-day advance notice of a bargaining unit's intent to strike.

Hire Replacement Workers

Although management may not discharge employees in retaliation for union activity, concomitant with the employees' right to strike is management's right to hire replacement workers in the event of a strike. The nursing home in *Charlesgate Nursing Center v. State of Rhode Island*[27] brought an action against the state, seeking a determination that a state statute prohibiting strike-affected employers from using the services of a third party to recruit replacement workers during a strike was unconstitutional. Employees of the nursing home went on strike on June 2, 1988, and Charlesgate hired temporary replacement workers to provide continued services for its patients. The temporary employees were hired through employment agencies. The actions of Charlesgate and the agencies violated Sections 28-10-10 and 28-10-12 of the General Laws of Rhode Island (1956) (1986 Reenactment), which read:

> 28-10-10. Recruitment prohibited—It shall be unlawful for any person, partnership, agency, firm or corporation, or officer or agent thereof, to knowingly recruit, procure, supply or refer any person who offers him or herself for employment in the place of an employee involved in a labor strike or lockout in which such person, partnership, agency, firm, or corporation is not directly interested.
>
> 28-10-12. Agency for procurement—It shall be unlawful for any person, partnership, firm or corporation, or officer or agent thereof, involved in a labor strike or lockout to contract or arrange with any other person,

partnership, agency, firm or corporation to recruit, procure, supply, or refer persons who offer themselves for employment in the place of employees involved in a labor strike or lockout for employment in place of employees involved in such labor strike or lockout.

Citing these statutes, the labor unions involved in the strike notified nursing pools throughout the state that it was unlawful to provide Charlesgate with replacement workers. At the same time, the unions urged the city of Providence and the Rhode Island attorney general to prosecute Charlesgate, at which time Charlesgate filed its suit claiming that the Rhode Island statutes were unconstitutional.

Although the strike was settled, the federal district court held that the statute was unconstitutional because it prohibited activity that Congress had intended to leave open to strike-affected employers as a peaceful weapon of economic self-help.

Restrict Union Activity to Prescribed Areas

Management has the right to reasonably restrict union organizers to certain locations in the healthcare facility and to certain time periods to avoid interference with facility operations.

Prohibit Union Activity During Working Hours

Management has the right to prohibit union activities during employee working hours.

Prohibit Supervisors from Participating in Union Activity

Management has the right to prohibit supervisors from engaging in union organizational activity. A nursing supervisor brought a lawsuit for wrongful discharge against a nursing facility and its director of nursing. She had been dismissed for her activities in attempting to form an organization to represent the nurses. The circuit court granted summary judgment for the defendants, and the appeals court affirmed. On review, the Wisconsin Supreme Court held, in *Arena v. Lincoln Lutheran of Racine*,[28] that after the NLRB had determined that the nurse in this case was a supervisor rather than an employee within the meaning of the NLRA, federal labor law preempted the state court from determining whether the nurse's discharge for engaging in concerted activities was wrongful under Wisconsin law. Employees who are supervisors as defined in the NLRA are treated differently than

professional employees. The definition of the term supervisor found in Section 2(11) provides:

> The term "supervisor" means any individual having authority, in the interest of the employer, to hire, transfer, suspend, lay off, recall, promote, discharge, assign, reward, or discipline other employees, or responsibly to direct them, or to adjust their grievances, or effectively to recommend such action, if in connection with the foregoing the exercise of such authority is not merely a routine or clerical nature, but requires the use of independent judgment.

The petitioner alleged in her complaint that she had become concerned with certain policies that included nurses being treated in an arbitrary manner. The petitioner held a meeting outside of Racine with the nurses to discuss their concerns and the possibility of forming an association to represent the collective interests of the nurses. The NLRA did not protect the nursing supervisor because she was a supervisor rather than an employee. Congress excluded supervisors from protection afforded rank-and-file employees engaged in concerted activity for their mutual benefit to assure management of the undivided loyalty of its supervisory personnel by making sure that no employer would have to retain as its agent one who is obligated to a union.

Seven registered nurses (RNs) at a small, 72-bed nursing home were found not to function as supervisors and were, therefore, eligible for a separate bargaining unit in *NLRB v. Res-Care, Inc.*[29] Although the nurses had the authority to assign nurses' aides, their exercise of this authority was merely routine and did not require independent judgment. The nurses were not shown to have any authority to hire, discipline, and/or fire any of the nursing aides. Such authority, if present, would have indicated some sort of supervisory status. Allowing seven nurses to form their own collective bargaining unit rather than merging them into a unit consisting of nurses' aides and other workers was not found to be improper and was not an undue proliferation of bargaining units at the facility.

Certification of 17 RNs as an employee bargaining unit in *NLRB v. American Medical Services*[30] was shown to be improper. The nursing home contended that a very low ratio of supervisors to employees would occur if the NLRB's decision was upheld. Substantial evidence had been presented to the court showing that the nurses exercised substantial supervisory powers, including the authority to issue work assignments and discipline employees.

The Taft–Hartley Act, as applied in this case, illustrates the importance of balancing the rights of both employees and employers.

> Taft–Hartley applied some brakes, so that the balance of power between companies and unions would not shift wholly to the union side. The exclusion of supervisors is one of the brakes. If supervisors were free to join or form unions and enjoy the broad protection of the Act for concerted activity, see Sec. 7, 29 U.S.C. Sec. 157, the impact of a strike would be greatly amplified because the company would not be able to use its supervisory personnel to replace strikers. More important, the company with or without a strike could lose control of its work force to the unions, since the very people in the company who controlled hiring, discipline, assignments, and other dimensions of the employment relationship might be subject to control by the same union as the employees they were supposed to be controlling on the employer's behalf.[31]

▶ AFFIRMATIVE ACTION PLAN

Healthcare organizations are required to comply with all applicable DHHS regulations "including but not limited to those pertaining to nondiscrimination on the basis of race, color, or national origin (45 C.F.R. part 80), nondiscrimination on the basis of handicap (45 C.F.R. part 84), nondiscrimination on the basis of age (45 C.F.R. part 91), protection of human subjects of research (45 C.F.R. part 46), and fraud and abuse (42 C.F.R. part 455). Although these regulations are not in themselves considered requirements under this part, their violation may result in the termination or suspension of or the refusal to grant or continue payment with federal funds."[32] To comply with the spirit of these regulations and Executive Order 11246, healthcare organizations should have an equal employment opportunity or affirmative action plan in place.

An affirmative action program includes such things as the collection and analysis of data on the race and sex of all applicants for employment, as well as a statement in the personnel policy/procedure manuals and employee handbooks that would read, for example, "Health Care Facility, Inc., is an equal opportunity/affirmative action employer and does not discriminate on the basis of race, color, religion, sex, national origin, age, handicap, or veteran status."

▶ PATIENT RIGHTS DURING LABOR DISPUTES

Patient rights take precedence over employee and management rights when a patient's right to privacy and health are in jeopardy as a result of labor disputes. Patients have a right to receive continuing quality care and not be used as a sounding board for disgruntled employees.

▶ INJUNCTIONS

An injunction is an order by a court directing that a certain act be performed or not performed. Persons who fail to comply with court orders are said to be in contempt of court. The earliest use of injunctions in labor relations was by employers to stop strikes or picketing by employees. Today, the general rule limits the availability of injunctive relief to halt work stoppages. The federal government and many states have enacted anti-injunction acts. These acts restrict the power of the courts to limit injunctions in labor disputes by setting strictly defined standards that must be met before injunctions can be granted to restrain activities such as strikes and picketing.

▶ ADMINISTERING COLLECTIVE BARGAINING AGREEMENT

When a collective bargaining agreement has been negotiated in good faith, it should be administered with care and good faith as well. The first-line supervisors are responsible for administering the agreement at the grassroots level. They should familiarize themselves with the provisions of the agreement. Educational programs should be provided by the organization, with special emphasis on the use of corrective discipline, as provided under the contract, and on how to respond to grievances. The organization's management, through its human relations department, maintains the ultimate responsibility in the facility for the fair and effective administration of its union contract(s).

Maintaining propitious records of all grievances, grievance meetings, and grievance resolutions is the responsibility of supervisors and management. Regardless of whether a grievance is meritorious and settled by management or whether it is spurious and therefore denied, clear and complete records should be maintained. The ability to document resolutions of particular problems, as well as management's approach to grievances, are especially important if arbitration is required to settle a grievance.

Arbitration procedures are set in motion when the union files a demand for arbitration either with the employer or with the arbitration agency named in the contract. The arbitration hearing is a relatively informal proceeding at which labor and management frequently choose to be represented by counsel. The arbitrator's decision is binding on both parties.

Showing any of the following can upset the arbitrator's decision:

- The arbitrator has clearly exceeded his or her authority under the collective bargaining agreement.
- The decision is the product of fraud or duress.
- The arbitrator has been guilty of impropriety.
- The award violates the law or requires a violation of the law.

▶ DISCRIMINATION IN THE WORKPLACE

Discrimination in the workplace comes in many forms and occurs in numerous ways, and each has its own little twist of facts: You are either too old or too young for the job; you are either overqualified or under qualified. There are laws prohibiting discrimination against any individual because of his or her race, color, religion, sex, or national origin, or to classify or refer for employment any individual on the basis of his or her race, color, religion, sex, or national origin. Unfortunately, prohibition and practice do not always match up. A variety of cases are presented in this section that describe but a few of the various forms of discrimination prohibited by law.

Age Discrimination

The *Age Discrimination in Employment Act of 1967* (ADEA)[33] prohibits age-based employment discrimination against persons 40 years of age or older. The purpose of this law is to promote employment of older persons based on their ability without regard to their age. The law prohibits arbitrary age discrimination concerning hiring, discharge, or pay, and terms, conditions, or privileges of employment. The ADEA covers private employers with 20 or more employees, state and local governments, employment agencies, and most labor unions. The Age Discrimination and Claims Assistance Amendment of 1990 extends the suit filing period for ADEA charges meeting certain criteria. There are strict time frames in which charges of age discrimination must be filed.

According to the U.S. Supreme Court in *Texas Department of Community Affairs v. Burdine*,[34] a prima facie case of age discrimination requires that evidence sufficient to support a finding for the complainant must establish all of the following:

- The complainant is in a protected age group.
- The complainant is qualified for his or her job.
- The complainant was discharged.
- The discharge occurred in circumstances that give rise to the inference of age discrimination.

Disability

The *Americans with Disabilities Act of 1990* (ADA) was enacted by Congress to prohibit employers from discriminating against job applicants and employees based on disability.[35] It applies to employers with 15 or more employees working for 20 or more weeks during a calendar year. The ADA protects employees who are qualified individuals with disabilities capable of performing the essential functions of the job in question, with or without reasonable accommodation, from discrimination by the employer.

The number of disabled Americans is increasing as the population grows older. Society tends to isolate and segregate individuals with disabilities. Despite some improvements, discrimination against individuals with disabilities continues to be a serious and pervasive social problem. Discrimination continues in such crucial areas as employment, housing, public accommodations, education, transportation, and health services. Unlike individuals who have experienced discrimination based on race, color, sex, national origin, religion, or age, those who are disabled have had no legal recourse to redress such discrimination. Individuals with disabilities continually encounter different forms of discrimination, including outright intentional exclusion; the discriminatory effects of architectural, transportation, and communication barriers; the failure to make modifications to existing organizations and practices; exclusionary qualification standards and criteria; segregation; and relegation to lesser services, programs, activities, benefits, jobs, or other opportunities.

Census data, national polls, and other studies have documented that people with disabilities, as a group, occupy an inferior status in society. The nation's proper goals regarding individuals with disabilities are to ensure equality of opportunity, full participation, independent living, and economic self-sufficiency for such individuals.

The ADA prohibits job discrimination in hiring, promotion, or other provisions of employment against qualified individuals with disabilities by private employers, state and local governments, employment agencies, and labor unions. On July 26, 1991, the EEOC issued final regulations implementing Title 1 of the ADA. The purpose of the ADA is as follows:[36]

- Provide a clear and comprehensive national mandate for the elimination of discrimination against individuals with disabilities.
- Provide clear, strong, consistent, enforceable standards addressing discrimination against individuals with disabilities.
- Ensure that the federal government plays a central role in enforcing the standards established in the Act on behalf of individuals with disabilities.
- Invoke the sweep of congressional authority, including the power to enforce the Fourteenth Amendment and to regulate commerce to address the main areas of discrimination faced day to day by people with disabilities.

The general rule of discrimination under Title I of the Act provides that "no covered entity shall discriminate against a qualified individual with a disability because of the disability of such individual in regard to job application procedures, the hiring, advancement, or discharge of employees, employee compensation, job training, and other terms, conditions, and privileges of employment."[37]

A defense to a charge of discrimination under the Act would require showing that the screening out of a specific disability was job-related and consistent with business necessity and that performance cannot be accomplished by reasonable accommodation.

Disability Requires Reasonable Accommodation

The appellee Alley, in *Alley v. Charleston Area Med. Ctr., Inc.*,[38] worked for Charleston Area Medical Center (CAMC) for over 17 years and suffered from epilepsy and asthma, with the asthma becoming increasingly aggravated by on-the-job exposure to certain chemicals. Alley requested a 12-week family medical leave of absence, which the hospital approved, with the agreement that the leave could be taken intermittently as needed. Alley began seeing Dr. Douglas with CAMC Physician Health Group for treatment of her asthma and epilepsy.

Alley's physician wrote a letter explaining her physical conditions and requested that Alley be allowed to work in an outpatient setting and not be exposed to people with multiple infections. Although Alley presented her request for accommodation to various CAMC supervisory personnel and to

employee health services at the hospital, she was told that no accommodation would be made. The employee health services physician, Dr. Ranadive, met with Alley for 5 minutes. He did not perform any tests. Ranadive called the physician who had written the request and summarily concluded that there was no medical reason why Alley could not continue her employment and that CAMC would not accommodate her.

Alley was eventually terminated, and she filed suit against CAMC in the circuit court alleging that she had been subjected to retaliatory discharge based on physical and mental impairment. Alley claimed that CAMC refused to make reasonable accommodations for her known impairments, that this was a violation of the West Virginia Human Rights Act, and that CAMC, with knowledge of Alley's asthma, exposed her to substances that exacerbated her condition.

The jury returned a verdict in favor of Alley, awarding $325,000 in damages. On appeal, the court determined that the evidence was sufficient for a jury to find that Alley was a qualified person with a disability, that CAMC was aware of her disability, and that a reasonable accommodation could have been made. The jury award was fair, considering all of the evidence and the instructions it received. The trial court did not abuse its discretion in refusing to grant a new trial.

National Origin

The *Immigration Reform and Control Act of 1986, 1990, and 1996* (IRCA) prohibits most employers from discriminating against employees or applicants because of national origin or U.S. citizenship status with respect to hiring, referral, or discharge. The Act establishes penalties for employers who knowingly hire undocumented immigrants.

Determining the legality of the employee's status is the employer's responsibility. Consider the following example:

A 1999 settlement with *Woodbine Healthcare Center* resolving allegations that the defendant recruited Filipino nurses with promises of hiring them as registered nurses in the United States, but instead placed them in nurse assistant positions at substantially lower pay, or in registered nurse assignments at reduced pay. EEOC also claimed that the employer harassed the victims with threats of deportation when they complained. EEOC obtained relief of $2.1 million for sixty-five class members.[39]

NEWS NEW LAWS BAN THE SALARY QUESTION

It's that job interview question you'd love to dodge: What's your current or most recent salary?

A low figure could limit your starting pay. A high number might make you seem expensive.

Now some states are banning the question as part of efforts to ensure pay equity for women . . .

—Paul Davidson, *USA Today*, May 1, 2017

Pay Discrimination

In an effort to assist in the prevention of wage and salary discrimination, New York City has banned employers from asking employees about their salary history. This follows a similar law in Massachusetts titled Act 2016 Chapter 177 Section 105, which reads in part as follows:

(b) No employer shall discriminate in any way on the basis of gender in the payment of wages, or pay any person in its employ a salary or wage rate less than the rates paid to its employees of a different gender for comparable work; provided, however, that variations in wages shall not be prohibited if based upon: (i) a system that rewards seniority with the employer; provided, however, that time spent on leave due to a pregnancy-related condition and protected parental, family and medical leave, shall not reduce seniority; (ii) a merit system; (iii) a system which measures earnings by quantity or quality of production, sales, or revenue; (iv) the geographic location in which a job is performed; (v) education, training or experience to the extent such factors are reasonably related to the particular job in question; or (vi) travel, if the travel is a regular and necessary condition of the particular job.

• • •

(c) It shall be an unlawful practice for an employer to: . . .

(2) seek the wage and salary history of a prospective employee from the prospective employee or a current or former employer or too require that a prospective employee's prior wage or salary history meet certain criteria; provided, however, that: (i) if a prospective employee has voluntary disclosed such information, a prospective employer may confirm prior wages or salary or permit a prospective employee to confirm prior wages or salary; and (ii) a prospective employer may seek or confirm a prospective employee's wage or salary history after an offer of employment has been negotiated and made to the prospective employee . . .[40]

Philadelphia and Puerto Rico have also banned employers from asking wage and salary information on applications and during employment interviews. Other jurisdictions are considering similar bans.

The *Equal Pay Act of 1963* and Title VII of the Civil Rights Act of 1964 were violated when a female nurse's aide was paid less than male orderlies for similar work in *Odomes v. Nucare, Inc.*[41] The nursing facility argued that the orderlies performed heavy lifting chores and provided a form of security for the mostly all-female shift. Testimony of the orderlies for Odomes indicated that the orderlies did little or nothing more than the nurse's aides. The security aspects of an orderly's job were at best his presence on the shift and his periodic checking of the facility's premises. The facility argued that the orderlies were involved in a training program that justified higher pay. The court considered this an "illusory post event justification for unequal pay for equal work."[42]

The Supreme Court stated, in *Corning Glass Works v. Brennan*,[43] that Congress's purpose in enacting the Equal Pay Act was to remedy what was perceived to be a serious and endemic problem of employment discrimination in private industry. The wage structure of many segments of American industry has been based on an ancient outmoded belief that a man, because of his role in society, should be paid more than a woman even though his ideas are the same.

Filing of a claim for pay discrimination can be a difficult decision to make as noted in the following *reality check*.

Pregnancy Discrimination

The *Pregnancy Discrimination Act* is an amendment to Title VII of the Civil Rights Act of 1964. Discrimination based on pregnancy, childbirth, or a related medical condition constitutes unlawful sex discrimination under Title VII. Women affected by pregnancy or related conditions must be treated in the same manner as other applicants or employees with similar abilities or limitations by, for example, providing modified tasks, alternative assignments, disability leave, or leave without pay. The X-ray technician in *Hayes v. Shelby Memorial Hospital*[44] brought an employment

✅ *EQUAL PAY FOR EQUAL WORK*

The annual Health Systems Consulting, Inc. conference was held at the New York City Hilton. During the closing session on Friday, the company's leadership sat onstage summarizing the week's training and conducting a question-and-answer period. Prior to the session, Frank, an administrator consultant, questioning his manager inquired, "Jerome, I have heard that the nurses wages have recently been increased substantially higher than that of administrators." Jerome replied, "You asked a direct question, so I will give you a direct answer, even though per company policy we have been advised not to share that sort of information. So, yes, the answer is yes. It was implemented several weeks ago. The consulting process is more and more clinical and therefore nurses are getting a higher starting salary then lay administrators." Frank answered, "We still all do the same work. As you know, the skill levels vary between the clinical expertise of a psychiatric nurse and that of an obstetrics nurse. Yet we all follow the same consulting guidelines. As we have discussed before, when I am assigned to work with a psychiatrist or psychiatric nurse they often shy away from consulting in the operating suite or obstetrics unit. I have never rejected or felt uncomfortable consulting in any clinical or nonclinical clinical service. Furthermore, we are asked to consult as to company guidelines and not make clinical judgments." Jerome replied, somewhat frustrated, "I know that, but that's the way it is."

Frank discussed what he considered a discriminatory practice with Shelia, a representative from Wage and Hour Division of the Department of Labor (1-866-487-9243). Shelia researched Frank's complaint and discussed with Frank his options over a several month period. On several occasions Shelia reminded Frank, "Although you most certainly have what appears to be a legitimate complaint, there is always a price to pay when reporting your employer for wage discrimination practices." Frank said, "I understand what you are saying" and did not pursue his complaint.

Even though Frank presented a legitimate complaint if pursued, the outcome could have resulted in an unhealthy atmosphere and working relationship with Jerome. Frank decided not to proceed with his complaint because he was nearing retirement. Ethical and questions of right and wrong, as noted in this *reality check*, will forever loom in the employee–employer relationship.

---

discrimination action against the hospital. The technician had been fired by the hospital when it learned that she was pregnant. The federal district court found that the hospital had violated the Pregnancy Discrimination Act. In affirming the lower court's decision, the appellate court held that the hospital failed to consider less discriminatory alternatives to firing the technician.

Race Discrimination

Discharge of an employee based on racial bias is actionable under state and federal laws. Title VII of the Civil Rights Act of 1964 "requires the elimination of artificial, arbitrary, and unnecessary barriers to employment that operate invidiously to discriminate on the basis of race."[45] An at-will employee's claim of racially motivated retaliatory discharge for filing a discrimination complaint can be actionable in tort as a violation of public policy.

The Civil Service Commission was found to have acted improperly in suspending a black licensed practical nurse as a result of a physical altercation with a white coworker in *Theodore v. Department of Health & Human Services*.[46] A crib being pushed by the black nurse had accidentally struck the white nurse. Evidence at trial supported the black nurse's contentions

that she apologized for the accident. The white nurse struck the first blow and spoke inflammatory slurs. The black nurse's reaction had been defensive. The facts revealed no grounds for suspension or disciplinary action against the black nurse.

The Bethany Methodist Corporation's medical and skilled nursing care facility terminated a black certified nursing assistant because of its determination that she abused a patient on four separate occasions in *Billups v. Methodist Hospital of Chicago*.[47] The appellate court upheld a lower court order entering a summary judgment in favor of the defendant. The plaintiff did not offer traditional forms of indirect evidence to prove racial discrimination, such as statistics or evidence of comparable situations. There was no evidence in the record suggesting that Bethany terminated black employees more frequently for physically abusing a patient, while retaining nonblack employees.

In *Buckley Nursing Home v. Massachusetts Commission Against Discrimination*,[48] Young, a black applicant for a nurse's aide position, filed a complaint alleging racial discrimination. Young responded to a newspaper advertisement for a nurse's aide position, filing her application on March 1, 1974, and was interviewed by the acting supervisor of nursing. The applicant called to inquire about the position on several occasions and eventually was told that the position had been filled. The advertisement ran again in the newspaper, and the applicant again called in response to the advertisement. Young was told that her application was on file and that she would be called as needed. The facility hired four full-time and one part-time nurse's aide for evening shifts between March 1, 1974, and July 1, 1974.

On the upper right hand corner of Young's application, there is a handwritten notation reading "no openings," even though during the relevant time periods there were openings and other persons were hired for the evening shift. That notation does not appear on any other application, and none of Buckley's witnesses could identify who wrote it or when it appeared.

Despite testimony to the contrary, the commission found that Buckley had entered discussion about Young's race and had decided not to hire her on that basis. The commission thus concluded that Buckley's reason for not hiring Young (that she was not the best-qualified applicant for the job) was a pretext and that she would have been hired but for her race.

The commission awarded Young $6,986 plus interest for lost wages and $2,000 for emotional distress. Besides the monetary award to Young, the nursing facility had been instructed by the commission to develop a minority recruitment program. On appeal by the facility, the trial court upheld the commission's decision. On further appeal, the appeals court held that the evidence was sufficient to support a reasonable inference that the nursing facility's rejection of the applicant occurred after consideration of her race.

Religious Discrimination

Discrimination based on religion is valuing a person or group lower because of their religion or treating someone differently because of what they do or do not believe. Although many religious and secular authorities tend to stress that religion is something personal, the highly social nature of most religions makes conflicts between religious groups, and thus discrimination, still very probable. Reasonable accommodations should be made for an employee's religious beliefs.

Sex Discrimination

In *Jones v. Hinds General Hospital*,[49] a prima facie case of sex discrimination was established by evidence showing that a hospital terminated female nursing assistants while retaining male orderlies who performed the same functions. The court, however, held that Title VII of the Civil Rights Act was not violated by the hospital's use of gender as a basis for terminating employees. Gender was a bona fide occupational qualification for orderlies because a substantial number of male patients objected to the performance of catheterizations and surgical preparation by female assistants.

Sexual Harassment

Section 703 of Title VII and the EEOC define sexual harassment in employment as unwelcome sexual advances, requests for sexual favors, and other verbal or physical conduct of a sexual nature when this conduct explicitly or implicitly affects an individual's employment; unreasonably interferes with an individual's work performance; or creates an intimidating, hostile, or offensive work environment.

Sexual conduct becomes unlawful only when it is unwelcome by the victim. The victim must not have solicited or invited the actions and must have considered the conduct undesirable or offensive. To determine if the victim may have solicited or encouraged the claimed sexual harassment, a court may assess the victim's sexual aggressiveness or consistent use of sexually oriented language in the work environment. Of course, indications of an employee's sexually aggressive nature will not necessarily negate a claim of sexual harassment, just as voluntary participation in sexual conduct by the victim will not necessarily negate the claim. An employee may participate in sexual conduct for fear of repercussions; thus, each claim must be examined individually to determine whether the particular conduct complained of was unwelcome. Unwelcome sexual conduct becomes harassment when it creates a working environment that is unreasonably intimidating or offensive. A reasonable person must find the work environment offensive, and the complaining employee must have perceived the conduct as offensive.

When sexual conduct is determined to be unwelcome, the court must evaluate its level of interference with the employee's job and whether the harassment created a hostile work environment. The court will consider the type of harassment (verbal, physical, or both), as well as the frequency of the harassment. A hostile work environment usually requires a pattern of conduct that has a repetitive effect. An isolated incident of physical advance is more likely to constitute a hostile environment (such as unwanted touching of the intimate body parts) than would a single case of verbal advance. In the same respect, sexual flirtation or vulgar language often will not constitute a hostile work environment as readily as would pervasive and continuous proliferation of pornography and demeaning comments.

An employer may be held liable for harassment inflicted by a supervisor that results in a tangible employment action or a significant change in the victim's employment status. Such tangible employment action may fall under categories such as hiring, firing, promotion, demotion, undesirable reassignment, decision causing a significant change in benefits, compensation decisions, and work assignment. The victim of sexual harassment and the harasser may be a man or woman. The harasser can be the victim's supervisor, an agent of the employer, a supervisor in another area, a coworker, or a nonemployee. The victim does not have to be the person harassed but could be anyone affected by the offensive conduct. Unlawful sexual harassment may occur without economic injury.

An employee who claims harassment based on a hostile work environment must demonstrate that the conduct complained of was sufficiently severe and/or pervasive to alter the conditions of employment and create a work environment that would qualify as hostile or abusive to employees because of their sex. An employer, however, will not always be held liable for sexual harassment that occurs in the workplace if the employer can prove: (1) it had in place an antiharassment policy with an effective complaint procedure; (2) it promptly took action to prevent and correct any harassment; and (3) the employee unreasonably failed to avoid further harm by complaining to management. If a nonsupervisor commits the harassment, the lower courts have held that the employer will only be liable if it knew or should have known about the conduct and failed to take appropriate corrective action.

THE COURT'S DECISION

The U.S. Court of Appeals for the Seventh Circuit found that the employer's interrogation of nursing facility employees about a union meeting constituted an unfair labor practice. On the record as a whole, substantial evidence supported the board's conclusions that the questioning of Welton and Hopkins amounted to unlawful interrogation. The record revealed "that the Home was actively hostile toward the union organization efforts of its employees, and substantial evidence supports the challenged findings of violations of Sec. 158(a) (1), (3), and (4). Accordingly, the Board's applications for enforcement are granted in their entirety."[50]

▶ CHAPTER REVIEW

1. The *U.S. Department of Labor* is a department within the executive branch of government.
2. Functions of the department of labor include: fostering, promoting, and developing the welfare of wage earners; improving working conditions; and advancing opportunities for profitable employment.
3. The *National Labor Relations Act* (NLRA) governs the labor–management relations of business firms engaged in interstate commerce.
4. The *National Labor Relations Board* (NLRB) is responsible for administering and enforcing the NLRA. It also provides procedures through which employees can choose a union as a collective bargaining representative.
5. The *Norris–LaGuardia Act* was enacted by Congress to limit the power of the federal courts to issue injunctions in cases that involve or have grown out of labor disputes.
6. In 1974, an amendment designating procedures that limit strikes in healthcare organizations was added to the NLRA. The amendment: requires a 10-day strike notice; allows the NLRB to determine the legality of the strike; and allows time for the organization time to establish provisions that protect the health of patients.
7. *Title VII of the Civil Rights Act of 1964*, as amended by the *Equal Employment Opportunity Act of 1972*, prohibits discrimination in employment based on race, color, religion, sex, or national origin.
8. The *Fair Labor Standards Act* (FLSA) established minimum wages and maximum hours of employment.
9. The *Equal Pay Act*, essentially an amendment to the FLSA, prohibits sex discrimination in the payment of wages.
10. The *Age Discrimination in Employment Act of 1967* addresses age discrimination.
11. The *Occupational Safety and Health Act of 1970* was enacted by Congress to ensure safe and healthful working conditions and to preserve human resources. Employers are required to provide a place of employment that is without recognized hazards that cause or are likely to cause death or serious physical harm.
12. The *Rehabilitation Act of 1973* provides protection from discrimination to handicapped employees and is applied to both public and private organizations.

13. The *Americans with Disabilities Act of 1990* is legislation that further protects the rights of the disabled. The Act prohibits job discrimination in hiring, promotion, and other requirements of employment against qualified individuals with disabilities.

14. There are two kinds of union security contracts:

    ■ *Closed-shop contracts* provide that only members of a particular union may be hired.

    ■ *Union-shop contracts* hold that continued employment is dependent on membership in the union.

15. *Workers' compensation* is a reimbursement program for employees with work-related injuries. These programs are administered on a state-by-state basis.

16. Labor rights include the right to organize and bargain collectively, solicit and distribute union information, picket, and strike.

17. Management rights include the right to receive a strike notice, hire replacement workers, restrict union activity to prescribed areas, prohibit union activity during working hours, and prohibit unionization of supervisors.

18. Affirmative action programs include: collection and analysis of data on the race and sex of all applicants for employment; and a nondiscrimination statement in personnel policy and procedure manuals and employee handbooks.

19. An *injunction* is an order by a court that instructs that a certain act be performed or not performed.

20. *Arbitration* procedures begin when a union files a demand for arbitration either with the employer or with the arbitration agency named in the contract. The arbitrator's decision is binding on both parties.

21. Discrimination in the workplace is often based on age, disability, national origin, pay, pregnancy, race, religion, and sexual harassment.

▶ REVIEW QUESTIONS

1. Describe the various federal labor acts.
2. Discuss the rights and responsibilities of unions and management.
3. Describe the purpose of an affirmative action plan.
4. Describe a patient's rights during labor disputes.

5. Discuss the types of discrimination that occur in the workplace.
6. Describe what sexual harassment is and what forms it can take.

▶ NOTES

1. *NLRB v. Shelby Mem'l Hosp. Ass'n*, 1 F.3d 550 (7th Cir. 1993).
2. 899 F.2d 651 (7th Cir. 1990).
3. "Supreme Court Upholds NLRB Bargaining-Unit Rule," *AHA News*, April 29, 1991: 1.
4. 29 U.S.C. § 151.
5. NLRA § 2 (14) (1974).
6. 34 S.Ct. 2618 (2014).
7. 431 U.S. 209 (1977).
8. Norris–LaGuardia Act 29 U.S.C. ch. 6 (1932).
9. *United States v. Hutcheson*, 312 U.S. 219 (1941).
10. Labor-Management Reporting and Disclosure Act of 1959, Pub. L. No. 86-257 (29 U.S.C. ch. 11).
11. Fair Labor Standards Act of 1938, 29 U.S.C. ch. 8.
12. 436 F.3d 843 (C.A. 8, Mo. 2006).
13. Equal Employment Opportunity Act of 1972, 42 U.S.C. § 2000e et seq.
14. Occupational Safety and Health Act of 1970, 29 U.S.C. § 651.
15. Pub. L. No. 91-596, § 2, 84 Stat. 1590 (Dec. 29, 1970); see also 29 U.S.C.A. § 651 (1990).
16. *Id.* at § 5, 84 Stat. 1593; *Id.* at § 654.
17. Rehabilitation Act of 1973, 29 U.S.C. ch. 14.
18. 45 C.F.R. § 4.6[c].
19. 641 N.W.2d 525 (Iowa 2002).
20. No. 3:11 CV 2549, 2013 WL 1100068, United States District Court, ND Ohio, Western Division 2013.
21. *Id.*
22. 460 N.E.2d 751 (Ill. 1984).
23. 676 P.2d 922 (Or. Ct. App. 1984).
24. 579 So. 2d 195 (Fla. Dist. Ct. App. 1991).
25. 916 A.2d 896 (D.C. App. 2007).
26. 534 So. 2d 1003 (La. Ct. App. 1988).
27. 723 F. Supp. 859 (D.R.I. 1989).
28. 437 N.W.2d 538 (Wis. 1989).
29. 705 F.2d 1461 (7th Cir. 1983).
30. *NLRB v. American Medical Services, Inc.*, 705 F.2d 1472, 1474–75 (7th Cir. 1983).
31. *NLRB v. Res-Care, Inc.*, 705 F.2d 1461, 1465 (7th Cir. 1983).
32. 42 C.F.R. § 483.75 (1989).
33. Age Discrimination in Employment Act of 1967, 29 U.S.C. ch. 14, as amended.
34. 450 U.S. 248, 253 (1981).

35. Americans with Disabilities Act of 1990, Pub. L. No. 101–336, 104 Stat. 327 (July 26, 1990).

36. *Id.* at 329.

37. *Id.* at 331–332.

38. No. 31591 (W.Va. 2004).

39. Equal Employment Opportunity Commission, "Furthering the Protections Against Workplace Discrimination and Harassment," http://www .eeoc.gov/eeoc/history/35th/1990s/furthering .html.

40. The General Court of the Commonwealth of Massachusetts, "Chapter 177: An Act to Establish Pay Equity," https://malegislature.gov /Laws/SessionLaws/Acts/2016/Chapter177.

41. 653 F.2d 246 (6th Cir. 1981).

42. *Id.* at 247.

43. 417 U.S. 188, 195 (1974).

44. 726 F.2d 1543 (11th Cir. 1984).

45. *Griggs v. Duke Power Co.*, 401 U.S. 424 (1971).

46. 515 So. 2d 454 (La. Ct. App. 1987).

47. 922 F.2d 1300 (7th Cir. 1991).

48. 478 N.E.2d 1292 (Mass. App. Ct. 1985).

49. 666 F. Supp. 933 (D. Miss. 1987).

50. *See NLRB v. Shelby Mem'l Hosp. Ass'n.*

© Raif Kleemann/Shutterstock

CHAPTER 20

Employment at Will, Rights, and Responsibilities

▶ LEARNING OBJECTIVES

The reader, upon completion of this chapter, will be able to:

■ Discuss the employment-at-will doctrine.
■ Explain public policies that protect employees from unlawful discharge.
■ Describe what is meant by retaliatory and constructive discharge and how to defend a claim for unfair discharge.

■ Describe under what circumstances employers often discharge an employee.
■ Describe effective hiring practices and the importance of clear communications.
■ Describe and understand the rights of employees.
■ Describe and understand the responsibilities of employees.

This chapter provides an overview of the employment process in the healthcare setting. Fairly balancing the rights and responsibilities of the employee and the needs of the organization is particularly challenging in the healthcare setting. Because the employment-at-will doctrine remains viable in all but one state, it is reviewed here in terms of its definition, exceptions, and the rights and responsibilities of both the employers and employees.

▸ EMPLOYMENT AT WILL

An at will prerogative without limits could be suffered only in an anarchy, and there not for long; it certainly cannot be suffered in a society such as ours without weakening the bond of counter balancing rights and obligations that holds such societies together.

—Sides v. Duke Hospital[1]

The common law *employment-at-will* doctrine provides that employment without a contract or end date of the employment is at the will of either the employer or the employee, where the employer or employee may terminate employment for any or no reason. For the healthcare worker, an unexpected termination may mean a significant setback in career progression, financial hardship, and loss of self-esteem. For the organization and its community, a termination can foster ill will and lead to possible disruption and realignment of services. A growing consensus is that high turnover rates are unhealthy and provide a disservice to an industry plagued with financial and staffing hardships. The high cost of human errors and greed that lead to so many patient injuries and deaths often result in negative news coverage, thus exacerbating the poor image many have of the healthcare industry.

Employment at will does not abrogate employee rights. Employees have faced discrimination involving age, race, creed, color, gender, wages, benefits, wrongful termination, as well as a host of other common labor issues. A variety of federal and state laws protect employee rights to be treated fairly in the workplace. Termination of an employee in violation of public policy or a legal contract that specifies the terms and duration of employment is actionable for damages in a court of law. Historically, termination of employees for any reason was widely accepted.

> In recent years, the rule that employment for an indefinite term is terminable by the employer whenever and for whatever cause he chooses without incurring liability has been the subject of considerable scholarly debate and judicial and legislative modification. Consequently, there has been a

growing trend toward a restricted application of the at-will employment rule whereby the right of an employer to discharge an at-will employee without cause is limited by either public policy considerations or an implied covenant of good faith and fair dealing.[2]

In *Sides v. Duke Hospital*, the North Carolina Court of Appeals found it to be:

> An obvious and indisputable fact that in a civilized state where reciprocal legal rights and duties abound, the words "at will" can never mean "without limit or qualification," as so much of the discussion and the briefs of the defendants imply; for in such a state the rights of each person are necessarily and inherently limited by the rights of others and the interests of the public.

> • • •

> If we are to have law, those who so act against the public interest must be held accountable for the harm inflicted thereby; to accord them civil immunity would incongruously reward their lawlessness at the unjust expense of their innocent victims.[3]

The concept of the employment-at-will doctrine is embroiled in a combination of legislative enactments and judicial decisions. Some states have a tendency to be more employer-oriented, such as New York, whereas others, such as California, emerge as being much more forward thinking and in harmony with the constitutional rights of the employee. "The late twentieth century saw many states abandoning the 'at-will' doctrine and an increase in protection of employee rights at work under a variety of theories including tort, contract, and property theories."[4] Although employment relationships are presumed to be at will in all states (except Montana) the courts have, over the years, carved out exceptions to the at-will presumption.

> The employment-at-will common law doctrine is not truly applicable in today's society and many courts have recognized this fact. In the last century, the common law developed in a laissez-faire climate that encouraged industrial growth and improved the right of an employer to control his own business, including the right to fire without cause an employee at will. . . . The twentieth century

has witnessed significant changes in socio-economic values that have led to reassessment of the common law rule. Businesses have evolved from small and medium-size firms to gigantic corporations in which ownership is separate from management. Formerly there was a clear delineation between employers, who frequently were owners of their own businesses, and employees. The employer in the old sense has been replaced by a superior in the corporate hierarchy who is himself an employee.[5]

As discussed here, exceptions to the employment-at-will doctrine involve contractual relationships, public policy issues, defamation, retaliatory discharge, and fairness.

▶ PUBLIC POLICY ISSUES AND TERMINATION

The public policy exception to the employment-at-will doctrine provides that employees may not be terminated for reasons that are contrary to a public interest. Public policy originates with legislative enactments that prohibit, for example, the discharge of employees on the basis of disability, age, race, color, religion, sex, national origin, pregnancy, union membership, and/or filing of safety violation complaints with various agencies (e.g., the Occupational Safety and Health Administration). Any attempt to limit, segregate, or classify employees in any way that would tend to deprive any individual of employment opportunities on these bases is contrary to public policy.

Brandi Cochran, who had been a presenter on "The Price Is Right," said she was fearful of losing her job if she got pregnant. She was right: she lost her job. She sued the game show, claiming wrongful termination based on her pregnancy. The jury awarded her more than $7.7 million in punitive damages. Discrimination based on her pregnancy was both illegal and unfair.

> If a woman is temporarily unable to perform her job due to a medical condition related to pregnancy or childbirth, the employer or other covered entity must treat her in the same way as it treats any other temporarily disabled employee. For example, the employer may have to provide light duty, alternative assignments, disability leave, or unpaid leave to pregnant employees if it does so for other temporarily disabled employees.[6]

Public policy also can arise as a result of judicial decisions that address those issues not covered by statutes, rules, and regulations. "[I]t can be said that public policy concerns what is right and just and what affects the citizens of the state collectively. It is to be found in the state's constitution and statutes and, when they are silent, in its judicial decisions."[7]

Public policy favors the exposure of crime, and the cooperation of citizens possessing knowledge thereof is essential to effective implementation of that policy. Those persons acting in good faith, who have probable cause to believe crimes have been committed, should not be deterred from reporting them for fear of unfounded suits by those accused.[8]

In those instances in which state and federal laws are silent, not all courts concur with the use of judicial decisions as a means for determining public policy. A California court determined that a public policy exception to the employment-at-will doctrine must be based on constitutional or statutory provisions rather than judicial policy making.[9]

Whistleblowing

A *whistleblower* is a person who reports corruption and criminal and unethical business practices in the workplace to appropriate government authorities. This often occurs when one believes that the public interest overrides the interest of the organization and can involve illegal or fraudulent activities. A whistleblower provides information he or she reasonably believes evidences violation of any law, rule, or regulation; gross mismanagement; a gross waste of funds; an abuse of authority; a substantial and specific danger to public health; and/or a substantial and specific danger to public safety.[10]

The False Claims Act of 1863 was enacted to prevent scams against the federal government in response to frauds that were costing the U.S. Treasury millions of dollars. Under the 1986 amendments to the False Claims Act, financial rewards to whistleblowers were expanded.[11] The purpose of the False Claims Act is to discourage fraud against the federal government in areas such as billing for services not rendered; unnecessary procedures, such as knowingly placing cardiac stents into patients; and home care visits that never occurred.

According to the public policy exception, an employer may not rely on the at-will doctrine as a basis for escaping liability for discharging an employee because of refusing to perform an illegal act. Moreover, statutes in several jurisdictions protect an employee from an employer's retaliation for engaging in certain types of protected activities, such as whistleblowing.[12]

Given the concern of the public about ethical behavior in government, the strong policy statement of the legislature in enacting the whistle-blower statute and the explicit inclusion of the state within its reach, the Whistleblower Act operates as an implied waiver of the statutory immunity provision of Minn. Stat. A4 3.736. A decision to shield potential government wrongdoing, as urged by the state, would exacerbate public cynicism about the ethics of public officials, and this we do not choose to do.[13]

Dr. Steven Bander was awarded a "2010 Director's Community Leadership Award" for his part as a whistleblower in reporting Medicare and Medicaid fraud.

Dr. Steven Bander knew he would lose his career and would have to pay upfront lawyer fees and costs when he became a whistle blower in April 2001. What he didn't know was whether his case would prevail or how it would affect his family. But as the chief medical officer for Gambro Healthcare U.S., the world's third-largest supplier of kidney dialysis services, he knew he had to do what was right.

In an agreement three-and-a-half years later, Gambro paid $350 million in civil and criminal penalties to settle claims it defrauded Medicare and Medicaid out of hundreds of millions of dollars. This agreement, made in December 2004, remains the largest fraud settlement in Missouri history and, at the time, was the sixth largest in the country.

Under the federal whistle-blower law, Dr. Bander received a $56 million share of the settlement. To this day, Dr. Bander lives in the same house. He has donated more than 20 percent of his money, after legal fees, to establish a charitable foundation that focuses on business ethics in health care.[14]

Cases such as this serve as a reminder to healthcare practitioners and organizations that reporting of criminal activity within one's medical practice or healthcare organization can result in monetary rewards for the whistleblower, thus encouraging the reporting of illegal activity.

Whistleblower lawsuits must be brought forward on a timely basis. For example, the lawsuit was found to be untimely in *HCA Health Services of Florida, Inc. v. Hillman*.[15] The nurses working in an intensive care unit had been complaining to their supervisors about deficient patient care. Because of subsequent disciplinary action taken by their supervisors, the plaintiffs retained counsel to file a whistleblower action pursuant to section 448.103, which authorizes an aggrieved employee who has been the object of retaliation to institute a civil action in a court within 2 years of discovering the alleged retaliatory personnel action or within 4 years after the personnel action was taken, whichever comes first. The Florida District Court of Appeals determined that the trial court erred by allowing the nurses to pursue their claim after the statute of limitations period expired. The final judgment awarding the nurses damages and attorney fees was reversed.

Rest and Lunch Breaks

Pursuant to public policy, reversal was required with respect to granting of a directed verdict against a dental assistant who brought an action against her former employer in *Bonidy v. Vail Valley Ctr. for Aesthetic Dentistry, P.C.*[16] for wrongful discharge in violation of public policy. She alleged that the employer had terminated her for asserting her legal right to receive rest and lunch breaks. The Department of Labor and Employment's wage order, providing that employees were entitled to meal period and pay rest breaks for work shifts of a specified length, was clearly expressed public policy, and the dental assistant had presented evidence that she was employed in a position that implicated public safety if she were not permitted to have rest and lunch breaks.

Report Patient Abuse

An employer may not discharge an employee for fulfilling societal obligations or in those instances in which the employer acts with a socially undesirable motive.[17] A tort claim for wrongful discharge was stated in *McQuary v. Air Convalescent Home*[18] by allegations that the plaintiff was wrongfully discharged from her position at the nursing facility in retaliation for threatening to report to state authorities instances of alleged patient mistreatment. Such mistreatment purportedly involved violation of a patient's rights under the Nursing Home Patient's Bill of Rights. To prevail, the discharged employee was not required to prove that patient abuse actually had occurred but only that she acted in good faith.

This conclusion is consistent with established Oregon law. Statutes which protect employees against retaliation do not require that the alleged violation which the employee claims be ultimately proved. See, e.g., ORS 652.355 (protects an employee who merely consults an attorney or agency about a wage claim); ORS 654.062(5) (protects any employee who makes a complaint under the Oregon Safe Employment Act); ORS 659.030(1)(f) (prohibits discrimination against an employee who filed a civil rights complaint); ORS 633.120(3) (prohibits discrimination against an employee for filing an unfair labor practices complaint). We have, in fact, upheld awards for retaliation despite holding that the original complaint did not show discrimination. . . .

Similar considerations of public policy lead to our conclusion that an employee who reports a violation of a nursing home patient's statutory rights in good faith should be protected from discharge for that action.[19]

This case, which had been dismissed in the lower court, was reversed and remanded for trial.

▶ TERMINATION

A decision to terminate an employee should be reviewed carefully by a member of management familiar with the issues of wrongful discharge. Oral counseling, written counseling, written counseling with suspension, and written counseling with termination are the textbook responses to disciplinary action and discharge. Whatever form of discipline is used, it should be designed to produce a more effective and productive employee.

The employer's right to terminate an employee is not absolute. It is limited by fundamental principles of public policy and by express or implied terms of agreement between the employer and the employee.

Formulating a standard for substantive fairness in employee dismissal law requires accommodating a number of different interests already afforded legal recognition. The legal interest of employees to be protected against certain types of unfair and injurious action . . . are at the core of any employee dismissal proposal. Arrayed against these interests are employer and societal interests in effective management of organizations, which require that employees not be shielded from the consequences of their poor performance or misconduct, and that supervisors not be deterred from exercising their managerial responsibilities by the inconvenience of litigating employees' claims.[20]

Prior to termination of an employee, the employer should determine whether the termination was: a violation of public policy; a violation of the organization's policies and procedures (e.g., employee handbook); retaliatory in nature; arbitrary and capricious; discriminatory on the basis of age, disability, race, creed, color, religion, sex, national origin, or marital status; a violation of any contract, oral or written; consistent with the reasons for discharge; discriminatory against an employee for filing a lawsuit; fixed before any appeal actions could be taken; and/or an interference with an employee's rights as secured by the laws or Constitution of the United States (e.g., right to freedom of speech).

Provision for Termination in Employment Contracts

A termination-for-cause-only clause in an employment contract was determined to be binding in *Eales v. Tanana*.[21] In this case, James Eales, who had been a physician assistant at the Tanana Valley Medical-Surgical Group (Tanana Clinic) was fired from his job. The defendant Eales decided to sue the Tanana Clinic for wrongful discharge. Tanana Clinic filed a motion for summary judgment and the trial court granted the motion. On Appeal, the Supreme Court of Alaska reversed the trial court's decision, holding that an employee hired up to retirement age could be terminated *only for cause*.

While there are many cases supporting the rule that contracts for permanent employment are necessarily terminable at will by the employer unless supported by independent consideration . . . there is a substantial body of authority which recognizes, correctly in our view, the unsound foundation of that rule.[22]

Financial Necessity to Reduce Staff

Termination of employees for financial or other legitimate business reasons does not constitute a breach of employment contract. No breach of employment contract occurred in *Wilde v. Houlton Regional Hospital*[23] when, because of financial difficulties, a hospital terminated the employment of two nurses, a ward clerk, and a dietary supervisor. Even if the employees were correct in contending that their indefinite contracts of employment had been modified by virtue of a dismissal for cause provision in the employee's handbook and by management's oral assurances that they were permanent, full-time employees whose jobs were secure so long as they performed satisfactorily, the employees' discharge for financial or other legitimate business reasons did not offend the employment contracts as thus modified. A private employer had an essential business prerogative to adjust its workforce as market forces and business necessity required, and the layoffs in question violated no compelling public policy.

> [T]he appellants have failed to set forth specific facts showing that they were discharged for any reasons other than financial difficulties and overstaffing. The record does not suggest, for example, that financial difficulties were a pretext for discharges that were actually motivated by Houlton Regional's bad faith or retaliatory purpose.[24]

Hostile Attitude

Dismissal was ordered properly for claims of wrongful termination and defamation in *Eli v. Griggs County Hospital & Nursing Home*,[25] in which a nurse's aide was terminated based on an incident in the hospital dining room. In the presence of patients and visitors, she cursed her supervisor and complained that personnel were working short staffed. Given the nature of her employment and the high standard of care that persons reasonably expected from a nursing care facility, such behavior justified her termination on a charge of reported breach of patient-specific and facility-specific information. No defamation resulted from the entry of such charges in the aide's personnel file because the record established that the charges were true.

The chief X-ray technician in *Paros v. Hoemako Hospital*[26] was dismissed because of a chronic argumentative and hostile attitude inconsistent with the performance of supervisory duties. The trial court entered a summary judgment in favor of the hospital and the administrator. On appeal, the appeals court held that the discharge was properly based on good cause and precluded recovery for breach of contract and wrongful discharge.

✅ *HOSPITAL SURVEY: I COULD SHOOT HIM!*

It was early on in the survey process and I was in training. I was being monitored and evaluated by my assigned mentor. I remember it well. We were in Florida where I was conducting my last mentored survey. I was reviewing a sampling of employee personnel records to determine, amongst other things, if there was ongoing age-specific education and training documented in employee records that would indicate that employees had the appropriate training, skills and competencies to work with various age groups. I noted in one record that a contract agency nurse was assigned to work with various age groups. Documentation of age-specific education and training could not be found in the record. I looked at my mentor and said, "The rest of the records look OK. The hospital's staffing and credentialing processes are well organized and thorough. I don't think one record warrants a major citation." Looking around the room to be sure no one was watching, he turned and looked at me, "If I were you, I would score the missing documentation." Of course I did, he was my mentor and I was in training.

I later explained to the survey coordinator what I had found. She was very unhappy with my decision to score the missing documentation. She looked at me and said with frustration, "I will talk to your mentor about this." She walked over to complain to my mentor. He replied to her complaint, "It's up to him; I am just observing his work."

Looking at me, the coordinator said, "This is just 1 record out of 600 and I can get you the documentation faxed today from the contracting agency." After she walked away my mentor looked at me and said, "I would score this, if I were you, but it's your decision." The decision was not so difficult. The lack of documentation on hand at the time was cited.

Later that afternoon, at the exit conference, each of the surveyors presented their findings to the hospital's leadership. After I presented my findings, the CEO of the hospital, looking around the table at his staff sitting at the table asked, "Is there anything you would like to say to the surveyors." My mentor was sitting between the coordinator and myself. She looked at me leaning forward against the table to look past my mentor and said, "I could shoot him." From what I could gather as the years passed, survey coordinators felt responsible for any citations received. Each hospital wanted a score of 100. Following the exit interview, the surveyor coordinator hugged my mentor goodbye. Looking angry, she walked away. The CEO was speechless and the room became eerily quiet.

Improper Billing Practices

The hospital in *Jagust v. Brookhaven Memorial Association*[27] was found to have properly dismissed a staff physician from his administrative position as director of the hospital's family practice residency program without a hearing. The hospital learned that the physician had engaged in improper billing practices by submitting bills for services that he never rendered. The physician was an employee at will as far as his administrative position was concerned. Neither the hospital's administrative procedure manual nor the employee handbook stated that the employee was subject to discharge for cause. Procedural protection was provided in the medical staff bylaws; however, the bylaws pertained to medical staff privileges and not administrative positions.

> Further, the bylaws at issue provide a hearing and review procedure to any member of the medical staff receiving notice of a hospital decision which "adversely affects" his (1) appointment or reappointment to the medical staff, (2) status as a member of the medical staff, or (3) exercise of clinical privileges. We conclude that the plaintiff would be entitled to a hearing under this provision of the bylaws only upon any decision affecting his membership on the Hospital medical staff.[28]

Poor Work Performance

In *Matter of Yerry v. Ulster County*,[29] a nurse's aide had been terminated from a county infirmary for misconduct. Among other things, she failed to report, in a timely manner, bumping and injuring a resident's leg, failed to feed a resident properly as ordered by the resident's physician, and, on another occasion, fed a resident food that burned the resident's mouth. The court held that eyewitness testimony and believable hearsay evidence were sufficient to sustain the findings of the hearings officer who recommended her termination. The court found that the penalty imposed was not disproportionate to the offenses. She showed insensitivity and a lack of ability that made her unsuitable for the work and thus constituted a danger to the well-being of the infirmary's elderly residents.[30]

The plaintiff in *Silinzy v. Visiting Nurse Association*[31] brought an action claiming racial discrimination and retaliatory discharge. The court granted a motion for summary judgment by the defendant-employer. The district court held that the plaintiff failed to establish a prima facie case of racial discrimination and retaliatory discharge. The plaintiff's poor job performance was the reason for her discharge.

The defendant was found to have produced ample evidence that the plaintiff was not performing her job adequately. Numerous complaints regarding her negative attitude and poor job performance, from a variety of sources, were documented.

> Although plaintiff may have felt that "the nurses are out to get me," she provides no evidence to support this contention. The evidence instead shows that patients, patients' families, and medical personnel unaffiliated with VNA filed most of the complaints about plaintiff with VNA. She was counseled and warned to change her ways on at least two occasions, but for reasons unknown, she did not. Plaintiff has failed to provide the Court with any evidence to show the plaintiff's discharge was racially motivated. Instead, the proffered evidence supports defendant's contention that plaintiff was not treated any differently than any other employee and that plaintiff's poor job performance was the reason for her discharge.[32]

Alcoholism

Discharge of an employee because of alcoholism is not necessarily a discriminatory practice, as evidenced by the hospital's discharge of a staff physician in *Soentgen v. Quain & Ramstad Clinic*.[33] A board-certified neonatologist at the Fargo Clinic reviewed and evaluated records for some of Soentgen's patients. In the neonatologist's opinion, Soentgen needed additional education in intubation, ventilation, and nutrition management. Although the CEO had received reports from the nursing staff that the physician had reported for work with alcohol on her breath and slurred speech, it was not the sole reason for a suggested leave of absence by the CEO and the administrator of Q & R. Both mutually decided to offer Soentgen a voluntary leave of absence for 4 to 6 weeks and to request that she obtain continuing medical education during that time. Soentgen stated she believed that alcohol was the determining factor leading to a suggested voluntary leave of absence. Soentgen had been discharged on bona fide occupational qualifications reasonably necessary for a physician in Soentgen's position.[34]

Insubordinate Behavior

Substantial evidence in *Daniul v. Commissioner of Labor*[35] supported a finding that the claimant's employment as a certified nurse's aide in a residential healthcare facility was terminated as a result of misconduct where the record indicated that the nurse's aide had been terminated after she refused to attend a meeting to discuss her job performance. She did this despite the request of her supervisor, who had warned her that she would be discharged if she did not attend the meeting. Although the nurse's aide asserted that her refusal was because she was upset and feared she might say something prompting her termination, her insubordinate conduct in failing to comply with her employer's reasonable request constituted disqualifying misconduct.

> Here, the employer's request was reasonable and claimant's fear of discharge did not constitute a good reason for her failure to attend the meeting. She was fully aware that she was placing her job in jeopardy by refusing to do so. Under these circumstances, substantial evidence supports the Board's decision.[36]

▶ UNEMPLOYMENT COMPENSATION

Unemployment compensation is a government sponsored program that provides unemployment insurance to qualified former employees. The federal government and states manage the program together. The program is funded with taxes collected from employers. The various states have different rules and regulations regarding administering their unemployment insurance programs. Former employees are eligible for unemployment compensation when they are terminated due to no fault of their own (e.g., organization downsizing). However, voluntary separation or misconduct can lead to denial of unemployment insurance benefits.

Unemployment insurance was granted in *Mankato Lutheran Home v. Miller*.[37] In this case a nursing assistant was found not to be disqualified from receiving unemployment benefits because of a single episode of profanity directed toward her supervisor. The nurse claimed she was ill, frustrated, and, in part, provoked by actions of her supervisor. The nursing assistant had no prior record of misconduct during her 5 years of employment. The nurse claimed that her illness and frustration at having to work after she repeatedly indicated she was not feeling well and that over the course of several hours of work she exploded emotionally. She had asked her supervisor, Ms. Darkow, if she could go home but was refused because of the probability of being unable to replace her in the middle of a shift.

At about 5:30 AM Darkow entered a patient's room where Miller was helping a resident get dressed. When she asked how Miller was feeling, Miller became upset and said, "What the … do you care, you don't think I'm sick anyway. I could drop over dead and still have to do these … people." Darkow retorted that Miller should not have come to work if she was so sick, and Miller yelled back, "I never had this … pain until I came to this … hole."[38]

The episode in this case did not represent a disregard for the employer's interests or of the nursing assistant's duties and responsibilities. The Court of Appeals of Minnesota determined that:

> The record supports the Commissioner's finding that Miller should not be disqualified from unemployment compensation benefits. Her conduct was an isolated outburst, provoked in part by her supervisor. It does not demonstrate an intentional disregard of the employer's interests or of her duties and obligations.[39]

Threatening Coworkers

In *Perkins v. Commissioner of Labor*,[40] in which a nursing assistant's employment was terminated as a result of misconduct, denial was deemed proper where the assistant admitted he had become involved in an argument with a registered nurse over the use of a copy machine. Although the nursing assistant maintained that the nurse threatened him by stating that she was going to get him, the nurse indicated that the nursing assistant threatened her by telling her to watch her back and car. The Unemployment Insurance Appeal Board (UIAB) "disqualified claimant from receiving unemployment insurance benefits on the ground that his employment was terminated due to misconduct."[41] The claimant appealed the UIAB's decision to the Appellate Division of the Supreme Court of New York. The appeals court determined that the conflicting account of the incident presented an issue of credibility for the UIAB to resolve, and threatening conduct toward a coworker was misconduct disqualifying one from receiving unemployment insurance benefits.

Theft

In *Forbis v. Wesleyan Nursing*,[42] unemployment compensation was denied because of an employee's theft of a patient's clock. The theft constituted willful and wanton disregard for the nursing home's interests.

The Employment Security Commission, on its investigation, made the following findings of fact: The claimant was discharged for theft of patient property; the patient accused the claimant of taking the patient's clock; and, upon being confronted with the patient's accusation, the claimant produced the missing clock from her pocket and admitted taking it.[43]

Poor Work Performance

Poor work attendance was found to be grounds for denial of unemployment benefits, in *Love v. Heritage House Convalescent Ctr.*,[44] even though the employee's most recent absence had been excused. The employee's record indicated that the center had shown exceptional tolerance in allowing the employee to continue employment for as long as it did.

> It is the responsibility of the employee to arrive at work on time. General road conditions do not constitute good cause for chronic tardiness. Since the claimant was tardy on thirteen different occasions because of general road conditions, the referee concludes that the claimant did not have good cause for such tardiness. As a result, the referee concludes that the claimant was discharged for just cause. . . .[45]

The appellant challenged the Board's decision. The Court of Appeals of Indiana, after reviewing the facts of the case determined:

> . . . we cannot say that reasonable minds would be compelled to reach a conclusion other than that reached by the Board. Moreover, we are reminded that the Employment Security Act was intended to protect only those who are discharged "through no fault of their own." We do not deem claimant to fall within that class of persons which the Act was designed to benefit. The Board's determination that appellant was discharged for just cause is therefore affirmed.[46]

Voluntary Termination

Voluntary termination because of a change in working conditions will not necessarily make an employee eligible for unemployment benefits. In *Montclair Nursing Home v. Wills*,[47] a licensed practical nurse was found to be ineligible for unemployment benefits when she resigned after reassignment to a night shift. Voluntary termination because of a change in working hours

was not considered sufficient cause to grant unemployment benefits, absent an "improper" purpose or motive in the change in the employee's work hours.

Violation of Smoking Policy

Unemployment compensation was properly denied a nursing assistant for breach of a no-smoking rule in *Selan v. Commonwealth Unemployment Compensation Board of Review*.[48] The nursing facility's personnel handbook clearly provided that smoking was allowed only in specified areas. The handbook provided that employees must refrain from smoking in offices, resident areas, elevators, corridors, or any area where it might be hazardous.

The nursing home assistant admitted that she was smoking but argued that she did not break the facility's smoking rules. The court disagreed. Evidence was sufficient to show that the employee knowingly violated Methodist Home's rule by smoking in a patient's bathroom. Deliberate violation of a reasonable employer rule, without due cause, constitutes willful misconduct warranting disqualification for unemployment compensation.

▶ WRONGFUL DISCHARGE

Wrongful discharge claims are difficult, time-consuming, and expensive lawsuits to defend. Employers who experience favorable court decisions in wrongful discharge claims often have unfavorable repercussions because of bad press and the negative effects a discharge can have on employee morale. An employee who is wrongfully discharged can maintain a cause of action in contract or tort, or both. In a tort action for wrongful discharge, the court can award punitive damages. This remedy is not available when there is a breach of a contract by the employer.

A California Supreme Court decision prohibits plaintiffs from seeking punitive and emotional distress damages from former employers in wrongful dismissal cases applied retroactively to thousands of cases pending in that state's courts. In *Newman v. Emerson Radio Corp.*,[49] the court, by a four-to-three vote, decided that its previous decision in *Foley v. Interactive Data Corp.*[50] applies to all wrongful dismissal cases pending as of January 30. The California Supreme Court held in *Foley* that a wrongful discharge claim asserting a breach of an implied covenant of good faith and fair dealing may give rise to contract, but not tort, damages. As a result of this ruling, punitive damages will not ordinarily be available to wrongfully discharged plaintiffs.

The Montana Supreme Court held that a Montana statute that limits the damages recoverable in

JUSTICES SAY LAW BARS RETALIATION OVER BIAS CLAIMS

(NEWS) **JUSTICES SAY LAW BARS RETALIATION OVER BIAS CLAIMS**

Retaliation complaints are a growing subset of workplace discrimination cases, because it is often easier for employees to demonstrate that they were retaliated against than that they were victims of discrimination in the first place. Retaliation complaints filed annually with the Equal Employment Opportunity Commission doubled in the last 15 years to 22,000 from 11,000.

—Linda Greenhouse, *The New York Times*, May 28, 2008[52]

wrongful discharge suits to 4 years of wages and benefits does not violate the state constitution.[51] According to the court, the state constitution's guarantee of full legal redress afforded the plaintiff, a former nursing home administrator, only a right to judicial access to obtain remedies, not a fundamental right to full redress. The statute abolishes common law causes of action for discharge and creates a statutory action in which punitive damages are available only on clear and convincing evidence that the employer acted with actual malice or committed actual fraud.

Retaliatory Discharge

Retaliatory discharge is a term used when an employer terminates an employee generally for reasons other than work-performance related causes, such as reporting an employer for illegal conduct, filing a discrimination charge, or opposing unlawful activity. The Supreme Court ruled in 2008 that

> [E]mployees are protected from retaliation when they complain about discrimination in the workplace, adopting a broad interpretation of workers' rights under two federal civil rights laws.[53]
>
> Congress has provided explicit protection against retaliation in two major federal statutes. One is Title VII of the Civil Rights Act of 1964, which prohibits employment discrimination on the basis of race and sex. The other is the provision of the Age Discrimination in Employment Act that applies in the private sector.[54]

Abuse of power through threats, abuse, intimidation, and retaliatory discharge are cause for legal action. Employees who become the targets of a vindictive supervisor often have difficulty proving a bad-faith motive. In an effort to reduce the probability of wrongful discharge, some states, such as Connecticut,[55] Maine,[56] Michigan,[57] and Montana,[58] have enacted legislation that protects employees from terminations found to be arbitrary and capricious. The Montana Supreme Court upheld state legislation that protects workers against arbitrary discharge, while at the same time limiting the damages they can win.

Employees have brought claims alleging abusive discharge in violation of public policy. This type of action is usually found to be an actionable tort, and thus in certain circumstances, punitive damages have been awarded. The burden of proof for establishing some hidden motive for discharge from employment rests on the discharged employee(s).

> The National Labor Relations Act and other labor legislation illustrate the governmental policy of preventing employers from using the right of discharge as a means of oppression. . . . Consistent with this policy, many states have recognized the need to protect employees who are not parties to a collective bargaining agreement or other contract from abusive practices by the employer. . . . Those states have recognized a common law cause of action for employees-at-will who were discharged for reasons that were in some way "wrongful." The courts in those jurisdictions have taken various approaches: some recognizing the action in tort, some in contract.[59]

The court in *Khanna v. Microdata Corp.*[60] held that substantial evidence supported a finding that the employer fired the employee in bad-faith retaliation for bringing a lawsuit against the employer, thus violating an implied covenant of good faith and fair dealing.

> Under the traditional common-law rule, codified in section 2922 of the [California] Labor Code, an employment contract of indefinite duration is in general terminable at the will of either party. During the past several decades, however, judicial authorities in California and throughout the United States have established the rule that, under both common law and the statute, an employer does not enjoy an absolute or totally unfettered right to discharge even an at-will employee.[61]

In *Shores v. Senior Manor Nursing Center*,[62] a formerly employed nurse's assistant brought an action against the nursing facility for retaliatory discharge for reporting to the nursing home administrator that the charge nurse was performing her nursing functions improperly. The circuit court dismissed the complaint for failure of the plaintiff to state a cause of action. On appeal, the appellate court held that the allegation of the former employee that she was discharged in retaliation for reporting that the charge nurse was performing her nursing functions improperly, allegedly violating the Nursing Home Care Reform Act, therefore stating a cause of action for retaliatory discharge. The circuit court was reversed, and the case was remanded for further proceedings.

In another case, dismissal of an employee shortly after a request for a grievance hearing regarding a salary discrepancy with another employee can raise an issue of liability for retaliatory discharge. The physician in *Jones v. Westside-Urban Health Center*[63] was found to have established a prima facie case of retaliatory discharge in which the record indicated that he had been fired from the hospital 5 days after his request for a grievance hearing on an alleged salary discrepancy. "As staff physicians, both Jones and Larned had the same job description and each was required to have the same minimum qualifications."[64]

The defendants in this case argued that Jones was fired because of his excessive absences from work. Jones argued that his attendance record was better than Larned's. He claimed that his time sheets were altered, making it appear that he missed more work than he actually did. Westside's bookkeeper, Alyce Martin, stated that "Jones' time sheets do appear to have been altered in some way. These material factual discrepancies make summary judgment improper."[65]

The United States District Court of Georgia determined that the plaintiff established a prima facie case under the Equal Pay Act. The plaintiff made less money than Larned, a female physician, and he showed that both he and Larned are staff physicians.

> As Westside's job description bulletin makes clear, the skills and qualifications necessary for each of them to obtain the position of staff physician are identical. Both doctors had to have completed an internship and obtained a medical degree and a license to practice medicine in the State of Georgia. Both were responsible for patient treatment and hospital visitations. They even treated the same patients occasionally. Thus, plaintiff has met his burden of proving that Westside paid different wages to him and Larned for equal work on substantially equal jobs."[66]

Because factual disputes surrounded the plaintiff's claims under the Equal Pay Act, the defendants' motion for summary judgment and plaintiff's cross-motion for summary judgment were denied. "The Court finds that plaintiff's claims have an adequate factual base and are well grounded in existing law. Furthermore, the Court finds that plaintiff asserted his claims for a proper purpose. Therefore, defendants' motion for sanctions pursuant to Rule 11 is DENIED."[67]

Constructive Discharge

The term *constructive discharge* describes a work environment where an employee is pushed to quit a job because the employer has made working conditions intolerable—for example, an employee is discriminated against based on race, creed, color, or disability; is sexually harassed; and/or has a negative change in job responsibilities, pay, and benefits for reasons not associated with the employee's performance. Employers who make workers' jobs so unbearable that they would rather resign than agonize over continuing abuse cannot be tolerated in a free society.

> A constructive discharge occurs when an employer deliberately makes or allows an employee's working conditions to become so intolerable that the employee has no other choice but to quit. For example, *Irving v. Dubuque Packing Co.*, 689 F.2d 170 (10th Cir. 1982). A party seeking to recover on a claim of constructive discharge must show that a reasonable person in that party's position would not have returned to work. The focus is not how the plaintiff felt but whether a reasonable person in that position would not have returned to work.[68]

Although employers can disapprove of an employee's job performance and deny benefits for reasons that are business-related, improper disciplinary actions can lead to a complaint for constructive discharge. An employee may be successful in a constructive discharge lawsuit even though the employee does not sever employment, for example, if an employer intentionally allowed such an intolerable workplace situation to exist that the employee ends up on permanent unpaid medical leave.

In a constructive discharge action, an employee must prove that (1) working conditions were constructively made intolerable and were directly aimed at the employee by the employer, (2) there was a continuous pattern of employer misconduct, and (3) conditions were so egregious and intolerable that any reasonable person would or did resign.

🔍 *RETALIATORY DISCHARGE AND EMOTIONAL DISTRESS*

Citation: *Dalby v. Sisters of Providence*, 865 P.2d 391 (Or. Ct. App. 1993)

Facts

Dalby, a pharmacy technician, alleged that she was discharged for reporting to her supervisor on several occasions that there were inaccuracies in the drug inventory and that recordkeeping regarding these inaccuracies was in violation of Oregon administrative rules. Dalby alleged that rather than comply with the regulations, her supervisor retaliated against her because of her insistence that her employer comply with the rules.

Retaliatory actions against Dalby included accusations of stealing cocaine from the hospital's drug inventory. Dalby learned that the sheriff's department had been asked to arrest her for stealing the cocaine. The sheriff's department refused to make the arrest. Dalby also alleged that her supervisor refused to talk to her except for job-related purposes and that hospital attendance policies were rigidly applied against her. As a result of the defendant's actions, Dalby resigned her position.

Dalby's former employer argued that the allegations did not demonstrate constructive discharge by deliberately creating difficult working conditions with the intention of forcing the employee to leave employment and that the employee left employment because of the working conditions.

The circuit court dismissed Dalby's claim, and she appealed.

Issue

Did the plaintiff state a cause of action for wrongful discharge and emotional distress?

Holding

The Oregon Court of Appeals, assuming the plaintiff's allegation to be true, reversed and remanded the case for trial, holding that the pharmacy technician stated a cause of action for wrongful discharge and intentional infliction of emotional distress.

Reason

Dalby made a good-faith report as to the hospital's noncompliance with the drug inventory and recordkeeping requirements required under Oregon regulations. Her report fulfilled an important societal obligation. An employer may not discharge an employee for making such reports. The conduct of the employer, including false accusations that she had taken cocaine, gave rise to an action for the infliction of emotional distress.

Damages for constructive discharge can be awarded for wages the employee would have been paid, wages while the employee searches for a comparable job, legal fees, compensatory damages for pain and suffering or mental distress, and punitive damages.

Sexual Harassment Based on Constructive Discharge

Rivera, the plaintiff in *Rivera Maldonado v. Hospital Alejandro Otero Lopez*, filed a lawsuit for constructive discharge alleging her supervisor subjected her to sexual harassment. According to Rivera, the defendant offered her unsolicited gifts, made unsolicited comments about her physical appearance, stalked her, touched her, intimidated her, and requested sexual favors. The plaintiff also alleged to the extent she rejected the defendant's advances that he threatened her with unjust disciplinary actions, including suspension without pay. Rivera claims that she began to suffer both physically and emotionally as a result of the defendant's sexual harassment. Puerto Rico's Law 80

(P.R. LAWS ANN., tit. 29 § 185e) defines constructive discharge as "The resignation of the employee caused by the actions of the employer directed to induce or compel him to resign, such as imposing or trying to impose on him more onerous working conditions, reducing his salary, lowering his category or submitting him to derogatory criticisms or humiliations by deed or word."

The basic elements for a constructive discharge claim [under Law No. 80] are: (1) considerably serious actions by the employer that create an intimidating, hostile, and offensive work environment; and (2) for the employee to have no other available alternative but to resign.[69]

The United States District Court, D. Puerto Rico found that issues of fact remained as to whether or not Rivera was informed that the defendant had been terminated following the investigation of her complaint. Accordingly, the court was unable to make the necessary inferences to determine whether or not, judging from Rivera's state of mind, she was unable to return to work because her working conditions were going to continue to be so intolerable that the only reasonable alternative for her was to not return to work. The defendant's motion for summary judgment on the Law No. 80 claim was, therefore, denied.[70]

▶ DEFENDING A CLAIM FOR UNFAIR DISCHARGE

An employee who believes that he or she has been unfairly discharged will most likely seek access to the following information in defense of his or her claim:

- Employment contracts
- Employee handbooks
- Human resources policies and procedures
- Minutes of pertinent meetings
- Written reports, typed or handwritten
- Personnel file
- Tapes (e.g., audio, video)
- Letters, cards, and handwritten notes written on the employee's behalf from the public
- Oral testimony from fellow employees and supervisors

Employers must document carefully and fairly any disciplinary proceedings that might be subject to discovery by a disgruntled employee; failure to do so could place the organization or supervisor at a disadvantage should a complaint reach the courts.

Employment Disclaimers

An *employment disclaimer* is the denial of a right that is imputed to a person or that is alleged to belong to him or her. Although a disclaimer is often a successful defense for employers in wrongful discharge cases, it should not be considered a license to discharge at will and at the whim of the supervisor in an arbitrary and capricious manner.

Employers can help prevent successful lawsuits for wrongful discharge that are based on the premise that an employee handbook or departmental policy and procedure manual is an implied contract by incorporating disclaimers in published manuals, such as that described in *Battaglia v. Sisters of Charity Hospital*,[71] in which a personnel manual could not be interpreted to limit the hospital's power to terminate an at-will employee. Language in the manual indicated that the personnel manual was not a contract; that it could be modified, amended, or supplemented; and that the hospital retained the right to make all necessary management decisions for the delivery of patient care services and the selection, direction, compensation, and retention of employees.

Handbooks that do not contain disclaimers can alter an employee's at-will status. An appeals court in *Trusty v. Big Sandy Health Care Center*[72] noted that the handbook did not contain any disclaimer or any other language that indicated that employment was at will. The court held that there was sufficient evidence to establish that the handbook had altered the employee's at-will status and determined that the employee could bring a wrongful discharge suit.

Disclaimers must be clear to the employee. The court in *Harvet v. Unity Medical Center*[73] held, in a wrongful discharge suit, that the hospital's employee handbook was sufficiently definite to form an employment contract.

> Unity's handbook contained detailed provisions on conduct and procedures for discipline. As the trial court observed, "there can be no question that [respondent's] handbook provisions are sufficiently definite to form a contract." The handbook represents much more than Unity's general statement of policy. Moreover, the terms of the handbook were sufficiently definite to allow a fact finder to determine whether there had been a breach. . . .
>
> Respondent contends the handbook contained the following reservations on the part of the employer indicating it was not being offered as a contract: "Exceptions to any personnel policy or procedure may be permitted on a documented form showing of good and sufficient cause." . . .
>
> In the present case the trial court correctly found, "the clause does not clearly tell employees that the handbook is not part of an employment contract."[74]

The employer's disclaimers were considered clear in *Simonson v. Meader Distribution Co.*,[75] in which an employee filed a breach of contract suit alleging a dismissal was outside the company's adopted disciplinary guidelines. The court held that the company could and did reserve the discretion to discipline employees outside of adopted guidelines. The policy manual contained the following three specific reservations of management discretion:[76]

1. Management reserves the right to make any changes at any time by adding to, deleting, or changing any existing policy.
2. The rules set out below are as complete as we can reasonably make them. However, they are not necessarily all-inclusive, because circumstances that we have not anticipated may arise. Some currently unanticipated

circumstances may warrant the application of discipline, including discharge.

3. Management may vary from the above policies if, in its opinion, the circumstances require.

Healthcare organizations can be successful when confronted with wrongful discharge suits based on breach of contract by placing similar language in their personnel manuals.

▶ FAIRNESS: THE ULTIMATE TEST

"Is it fair?" is the ultimate question that a supervisor must ask when considering discipline or termination. In general, bad-faith and inexplicable terminations are subject to the scrutiny of the courts. Some courts and legislative enactments have overturned the view that employers have total discretion to terminate workers who are not otherwise protected by collective bargaining agreements or civil service regulations. Montana legislation grants every employee the right to sue the employer for wrongful discharge. The mere fact that an employment contract is terminable at will does not give the employer an absolute right to terminate it in all cases.[77]

The court in *Cleary v. American Airlines*[78] held that the longevity of the employee's services, together with the express policy of the employer, operated as a form of estoppel, precluding any discharge of the employee by the employer without good cause, and thus, the employee stated a cause of action for wrongful discharge.

> In the case at bench, we hold that the longevity of the employee's service, together with the expressed policy of the employer, operate as a form of estoppel, precluding any discharge of such an employee by the employer without good cause. We recognize, of course, that plaintiff has the burden of proving that he was terminated unjustly, and that the employer, American Airlines, will have its opportunity to demonstrate that it did in fact exercise good faith and fair dealing with respect to plaintiff. Should plaintiff sustain his burden of proof, he will have established a cause of action for wrongful discharge that sounds in both contract and in tort. He will then be entitled to an award of compensatory damages, and, in addition, punitive damages if his proof complies with the requirements for the latter type of damages.[79]

There is an implied covenant of good faith and fair dealing in every contract—that neither party will do anything that will injure the right of the other to receive benefits from the agreement. An employee in *Pugh v. See's Candies*[80] was found to have shown a prima facie case of wrongful termination in violation of an implied promise that the employer would not act arbitrarily in dealing with the employee. The employer's right to terminate an employee is not absolute. It is limited by fundamental principles of public policy and by expressed or implied terms of agreement between the employer and the employee.

Procedural issues are as important as issues of discrimination. In *Renny v. Port Huron Hospital*,[81] the Michigan Supreme Court found, as did the jury, that the employee's discharge hearing was not final and binding because it did not comport with elementary fairness. The court found that there was sufficient evidence for the jury to find that the employee had not been discharged for just cause. The existence of a just-cause contract is a question of fact for the jury when the employer establishes written policies and procedures and does not expressly retain the right to terminate an employee at will. That the hospital followed the grievance procedure with the plaintiff is evidence that a just-cause contract existed on which the plaintiff relied.

The employee handbook provided for a grievance board as a fair way to resolve work-related complaints and problems. This was not a mandatory procedure to which the hospital's employees had to submit. The employee was not bound by the grievance board's determination that her discharge was proper because evidence supported a finding that she was not given adequate notice of who the witnesses against her would be. She was not permitted to be present when the witnesses testified, and she was not given the right to present certain evidence.

There was sufficient evidence for the jury to conclude that the plaintiff had suffered damages. Evidence presented indicated that her subsequent professional employment did not equal her earnings before discharge and that she experienced increased expenses because of the loss of her health insurance as well as other financial losses that she suffered as a result of her discharge.

Employee References

Employee references, fairly drafted, can protect both the employer and employee, as noted in *Passmore v. Multi-Management Services, Inc.*[82] In this case, Mark Passmore believed that a bruise on his mother was the result of an assault by Parke County's maintenance supervisor, Richardson. Passmore sued Parke County and Richardson's former employer, Lee Alan Bryant Nursing Care Facilities, Inc., asserting that Lee Alan wrongly gave Richardson a favorable recommendation and thus should be liable for the injury. Richardson was a maintenance worker at Lee Alan. Bratcher, Richardson's supervisor at the time, received several reports from residents alleging misconduct between Richardson and some female residents. These were not formal complaints, but Bratcher looked into the matter and was unable to verify them. Lee Alan administrator Hein completed a reference form indicating Richardson would be eligible for rehire. The plaintiff asserted that the former employer wrongly gave a favorable recommendation and thus should be liable for the injury.

The Parke Circuit Court granted summary judgment in favor of Lee Alan. The Court of Appeals affirmed summary judgment for Parke County, holding there was no basis for liability. The nursing home hired a new worker in part on the basis of a favorable recommendation from his former employer. Passmore appealed asking the Supreme Court of Indiana to hold that a regulated nursing facility owes a duty to third persons not to misrepresent material facts that describe qualifications and character of a former employee.

The Supreme Court of Indiana found that such was not the case here. Conscious misrepresentation could have led to a different outcome in this case. The facts before the trial court on summary judgment did not reflect that Lee Alan had any substantial information indicating that Richardson committed sexual misconduct with residents at Lee Alan when Hein completed the reference form. Bratcher had been unable to substantiate what she had heard about Richardson. This may have constituted negligence, but could not be considered purposeful misrepresentation.

Declaring employers liable for negligence in providing employment references has resulted in reluctance by employers to provide information other than name, position held, and dates of employment.

A legal policy that discourages providing performance assessments to subsequent employers will not make for safer healthcare facilities.

▶ EFFECTIVE HIRING PRACTICES

The best way for the human resources manager to prevent negligent hiring litigation for the employer is to become familiar with the risks and avoid hiring workers who are likely to become problematic employees. The organization should:

- Communicate clearly to prospective employees that their employment is at will and can be terminated at any time by either the employer or the employee. During the course of employment, handbooks and personnel manuals must provide fair and unambiguous standards for employee discipline and termination.
- Develop clear policies and procedures on hiring, disciplining, and terminating employees.
- Include appropriate language in the organization's policies and procedures, reserving the right to add, delete, and/or revise the same.
- Develop an application that realistically determines an applicant's qualifications before hiring.
- Take appropriate precautions to prevent the hiring of those who might be a hazard to others.
- Review each applicant's background and past work behavior.
- Become familiar with any state laws that might be applicable when hiring an individual with a past criminal record.
- Develop an effective system for screening applicants (the interviews should be conducted first by an appropriately trained member of the human resources department and then by the supervisor of the service to which the applicant is applying).
- Solicit references with the applicant's permission by using a release form, and follow up with a telephone call for further information.
- Provide an employee handbook and present a job description to each new employee (signed

📰 JOB APPLICANTS NOT ALWAYS SCREENED

Despite the danger of hiring an employee who might jeopardize assisted living residents, some facilities neglect background screening of new workers.

More than 1 in 10 facilities inspected by state regulators in seven states during a two-year period within 2000–2002 picked up at least one citation for neglecting background checks on prospective caregivers . . .

—Kevin McCoy, *USA Today*, May 26, 2004

documentation should be maintained in the employee's personnel folder indicating that the employee received, read, and understood the employee handbook and job description).

- Develop constructive performance evaluations that reinforce good behavior and provide instruction in those areas needing improvement (the performance evaluation should include a written statement regarding the employee's performance).
- Develop a progressive disciplinary action policy.
- Provide in-service education programs for supervisors on such subjects as interviewing techniques, evaluations, and discipline. (Various colleges, universities, and consultants provide in-service education programs for employers.)
- Be mindful of the importance of developing appropriate employment contract language.

▶ EMPLOYEE RIGHTS

Man never fastened one end of a chain around the neck of his brother that God did not fasten the other end round the neck of the oppressor.

—Lamartine (1790–1869)

This section presents an overview of the rights of employees in the healthcare setting, many of which are expressed in both federal and state laws. Healthcare organizations are not exempt from the impact of these laws and are required to take into account employment practices, such as wages, hours, working conditions, union activity, workers' compensation laws, occupational safety and health laws, and employment discrimination laws.

© Andrey Burmakin/Shutterstock

Equal Pay for Equal Work

The *Equal Pay Act (EPA) of 1963* prohibits gender discrimination in the payment of wages for women and men performing substantially equal work in the same establishment and requires that employees who perform equal work receive equal pay. There are situations in which wages may be unequal as long as they are based on factors other than gender, such as in the case of a formalized seniority system or a system that objectively measures earnings by the quantity or quality of production.

Refuse to Participate in Care

Caregivers have a right to refuse to participate in certain aspects of patient care and treatment. This can occur when there is conflict with one's cultural, ethical, and/or religious beliefs, such as the administration of blood or blood products, participation in elective abortions, and end-of-life issues such as disconnecting a respirator. Questionable requests not to participate in certain aspects of a patient's care should be referred to an organization's ethics committee for review and consultative advice.

Some pharmacists' religious beliefs prohibit abortion or the use of birth control. They believe that dispensing such medications to others is an infringement on their freedom of religion. There are others who believe that pharmacists have an obligation to fill all prescriptions, and that refusing to fill them violates the patients' freedom of conscience. The First Amendment protects individual free exercise of religion. The question here is "Does requiring pharmacists to fill prescriptions conflict with religious beliefs and violate their rights under the First Amendment?" Some say yes, because people whose religious beliefs prohibit birth control or abortion cannot freely exercise their religion if they are forced to dispense these medications. Others say no, because the patients' need to obtain their medication outweighs the pharmacists' rights.[83]

> Some states have subsequently proposed legislation and passed laws designed to allow doctors and other direct providers of health care to refuse to perform or assist in an abortion, and hospitals to refuse to allow abortion on their premises. Now, the issue is expanding as pharmacists are refusing to fill emergency contraception and contraception prescriptions.[84]

As each state often has different rulings on this issue, the reader should review applicable state statutes.

Balancing Employee and Patient Rights

In the attempt to honor staff rights, a patient's health must not be compromised. The New York Supreme Court, Appellate Division in *Larson v. Albany Medical Center* held that although a nurse has the right to refuse to participate in an elective termination of pregnancy on grounds of freedom from religious discrimination in employment, the case at issue did not involve an elective procedure. The mother was in need of emergency care and the nurses were asked by their nursing supervisor to assist in an "emergency" evacuation of a dead fetus. The nurses launched an argument about elective abortions, and the court ruled their action as insubordinate behavior.[85]

In a Missouri case, *Doe v. Poelker*,[86] the city was ordered to obtain the services of physicians and personnel who had no moral objections to participating in abortions. The city also was required to pay the plaintiff's attorneys' fees because of the wanton disregard of the indigent woman's rights and the continuation of a policy to disregard and/or circumvent the U.S. Supreme Court's rulings on abortion.

Question Patient Care

A caregiver has the right to question the care being rendered to a patient by another caregiver if there is reason to believe that the care is likely to be detrimental to the well-being of the patient. If, for example, a caregiver believes that a particular order appears to be questionable, the caregiver has the responsibility to seek verification from the prescribing physician. If the prescribing physician believes the order to be correct and the caregiver still questions the order, the concern must be relayed to the employee's supervisor for verification and further follow-up if necessary.

Suggest Changing Physician

There are circumstances in which a caregiver has a right to suggest that a patient or patient's family change their physician. In one case, a patient began losing weight and having hallucinations. A nurse documented the patient's difficulties and attempted on several occasions to call the patient's physician. The physician failed to return the nurse's calls. Because of the patient's deteriorating condition, the family contacted the nurse. After the nurse advised the patient's family about her concerns, a member of the patient's family asked her what they should do. The nurse advised that she would reconsider their "choice of physicians." The nurse was terminated because she had advised the patient's family to consider changing physicians.

The nurse brought a lawsuit for wrongful discharge in violation of public policy. The language in the Nursing Practice Act of North Carolina and regulations of the Board of Nursing describe the practice of nursing as assessing a patient's health, which entails a responsibility to communicate, counsel, and provide accurate guidance to clients and their families. The nurse's comments that resulted in her termination were made in fulfillment of these responsibilities.

The North Carolina Court of Appeals held that the nurse stated a claim for wrongful discharge in violation of public policy. The nurse's termination for fulfilling her responsibilities as a practicing nurse violated state public policy and was a factual question for jury determination. Although there may be a right to terminate at-will employment for no reason or for an

🔍 *PAVING HER WAY TO HEAVEN*

Citation: *Kirk v. Mercy Hosp. Tri-County*, 851 S.W.2d 617 (Mo. Ct. App. 1993)

Facts

A short time after a patient had been admitted to Mercy Hospital, Kirk, the charge nurse, determined the patient was suffering from toxic shock syndrome. Knowing that death would result if left untreated, Kirk assumed the physician would order antibiotics. After a period of time passed without having received such orders, Kirk discussed the patient's condition with the nursing director. The director asked Kirk to document, report the facts, and "stay out of it."

Kirk discussed the patient's condition and lack of orders with the chief of staff. Although the chief of staff took appropriate steps to treat the patient, the patient later died. A member of the patient's family informed the nursing director that Kirk offered to obtain a copy of the medical records. The director was later told that Kirk was heard to say that the physician was "paving the patient's way to heaven." Kirk was later terminated. After her termination, Kirk received a letter from the hospital that directed her to refrain from making any further false statements about the hospital and its staff. Kirk then filed a lawsuit.

(continues)

🔍 *PAVING HER WAY TO HEAVEN*   *(Continued)*

The trial court entered a summary judgment for the defendant-hospital, stating that there were no triable issues of fact and there was no public policy exception to Kirk's at-will termination. The court could not find any law or regulation prohibiting the hospital from discharging Kirk, who later appealed the court's decision.

Issue
Was there a public policy exception to the Missouri employment-at-will doctrine?

Holding
The Missouri Court of Appeals reversed the granting of summary judgment and remanded the case for trial, holding that the Nursing Practice Act (NPA) provided a clear mandate of public policy that nurses had a duty to provide the best possible care to patients.

Reason
Public policy clearly mandates nurses have an obligation to serve the best interests of patients. Therefore, if Kirk refused to follow her supervisor's orders to stay out of a case where the patient was dying from a lack of proper medical treatment, there would be no grounds for her discharge under the public policy exception to the employment-at-will doctrine. Pursuant to the NPA, the plaintiff risked discipline if she ignored improper treatment of the patient. Kirk's persistence in attempting to get the proper treatment for the patient was her absolute duty. The hospital could not lawfully require that Kirk stay out of a case that would have obvious injurious consequences to the patient. Public policy, as defined in case law, holds that no one can lawfully do that which tends to be injurious to the public or against the public good.

arbitrary or irrational reason, there can be no right to terminate such employment for an unlawful reason or purpose that contravenes public policy.[87]

Freedom from Sexual Harassment

Employees and staff have a right to be free from sexual harassment. Sexual harassment can be verbal or physical, and it includes a request for a sexual favor, sexual advances made as a condition of employment and unreasonably interfering with an employee's work performance, and creating an intimidating or offensive working environment. In 1980, the Equal Employment. Opportunity Commission (EEOC) issued landmark sexual harassment guidelines that prohibit unwelcome sexual advances or requests that are made as a condition of employment. The guidelines also prohibit conduct that creates a hostile work environment. The U.S. Supreme Court held that a hostile work environment refers not only to conduct that is psychologically injurious, but also to conduct that is perceived as abusive.

Treated with Dignity and Respect

One's dignity may be assaulted, vandalized, and cruelly mocked, but it cannot be taken away unless it is surrendered.

—Author Unknown

Each employee has the right to be treated with dignity, respect, and in a fair and consistent manner by his or her employer. Employers have a responsibility to address in a timely manner employee complaints and concerns regarding their rights. Furthermore, employers should respond promptly to employee questions, especially when they are working away from the corporate site, as noted in the following *reality check.*

✔ *CALL FOR HELP—NO RESPONSE*

Three consultants were assigned by their employer, International Consulting (IC), to review the quality of care being delivered at Newtown Medical Center in Boston. Newtown was larger and more complex than the consultants were expecting. In addition, it was located in a different state than IC's headquarters. On the first day of the consulting assignment, the IC's consulting team leader called the IC corporate office to discuss the need for additional help, as required by corporate policy. The manager responsible for addressing field requests did not respond. Despite the lack of a follow-up call from the corporate manager, the team covered the assigned task. Newtown's leadership expressed their appreciation to the consultants by writing to IC's CEO, expressing their appreciation for how well the consultants conducted their work.

🅝 *THE PRICE WHISTLE-BLOWERS PAY FOR SECRETS*

"It's a life-changing experience," said John R. Phillips, founder of the law firm Phillips & Cohen and the man credited with devising the amendments that strengthened the government antifraud law, the False Claims Act, in 1986. "If you look at the field of whistle-blowers, you see a high degree of bankruptcies. You may find yourself unemployable. Home foreclosures, divorce, suicide, and depression all go with this territory."

—Paul Sullivan, *The New York Times*, September 21, 2012

Whistleblowing

Employees have both a right and responsibility to report unethical conduct. Whistleblowing has been defined as an act of someone "who, believing that the public interest overrides the interest of the organization he serves, publicly blows the whistle if the organization is involved in corrupt, illegal, fraudulent, or harmful activity."[88]

> Given the concern of the public about ethical behavior in government, the strong policy statement of the legislature in enacting the whistle-blower statute and the explicit inclusion of the state within its reach, the Whistleblower Act operates as an implied waiver of the statutory immunity provision of Minn. Stat. A4 3.736. A decision to shield potential government wrongdoing, as urged by the state, would exacerbate public cynicism about the ethics of public officials, and this we do not choose to do.[89]

Healthcare organizations often describe their whistleblower policy in their compliance manuals. Compliance officers are responsible for providing information to employees regarding the organization's compliance program. The policies provide reporting procedures that ensure anonymity for employees through, for example, the use of phone hotlines answered by third parties not affiliated with the organization. Organizations must not retaliate against an employee for disclosing activities that he or she reasonably believes are in violation of public policy, such as fraudulent billing practices. The Occupational Safety and Health Act's (OSH Act's) whistleblower protection program, for example

> . . . enforces the whistleblower provisions of more than twenty whistleblower statutes protecting employees who report violations of various workplace safety, airline, commercial motor carrier, consumer product, environmental, financial reform, food safety, health insurance reform, motor vehicle

safety, nuclear, pipeline, public transportation agency, railroad, maritime, and securities laws. Rights afforded by these whistleblower acts include, but are not limited to, worker participation in safety and health activities, reporting a work-related injury, illness or fatality, or reporting a violation of the statutes.[90]

Freedom from Intimidation

Employees have a right to be free from intimidation by disgruntled physicians, patients, visitors, and fellow employees and managers in the workplace. Employees have a right to be protected from the mistreatment by others regardless of their position in the healthcare setting. As noted in the following news clipping, physicians can be intimidating to both employees and patients.

Patients also present a challenge to employees. They are at times disrespectful or angry, often because they are in a place they do not wish to be. Hospitals are high-stress, demanding environments in which

🅝 *HOSPITALS CRACK DOWN ON TIRADES BY ANGRY DOCTORS*

At a critical point in a complex abdominal operation, a surgeon was handed a device that didn't work because it had been loaded incorrectly . . . the surgeon slammed it down, accidentally breaking the technician's finger . . .

The 2011 incident illuminates a long-festering problem that many hospitals have been reluctant to address: disruptive and often angry behavior by doctors. Experts estimate that 3 to 5 percent of physicians engage in such behavior, berating nurses who call them in the middle of the night about a patient . . . demeaning co-workers they consider incompetent or cutting off patients who ask a lot of questions.

—Sandra G. Boodman,
The Huffington Post, March 5, 2013

✅ *YOUR MAIL WAS OPENED*

The XYZ Corporation decided to open all mail sent to employees who work at various consulting sites in various states. The following memorandum was sent to field consultants describing this new corporate policy:

> *Important Notice to ALL Employees*
>
> *All mail with a hospital return address directed to field consultants will be opened by corporate office staff to determine if its contents appears to be related to company business. All other mail will be labeled "return to sender." Consultants who have their professional magazines addressed to the corporate office address will be discarded. This action is necessary from a cost-savings standpoint. XYZ does not have sufficient staff to forward personal mail and magazines that it receives each month addressed to field representatives. This policy is necessary because vital company business matters end up being sent to the field consultants and can delay responses to clients.*

Although it is legal for an organization to open all mail prior to sorting and delivering it, employees should be made aware of company policy. Managers should not open an employee's mail indiscriminately; such invasion of privacy will undermine employee morale and could result in legal action. An employee's right to privacy must be honored and safeguards implemented to protect personal information from being indiscriminately disseminated.

to work. Patient handbooks and employee training are helpful tools in dealing with both the anxious and angry patient. Patients, as well as employees, have rights and responsibilities. The responsibilities of both patients and visitors should be described in the patient handbook.

Privacy and Confidentiality

Employees have a right to privacy and confidentiality in regard to information about their health status. However, modern technology makes it possible for employers to monitor their employees' activities through their computer site visits, electronic communications, voicemail, and video monitoring. Such monitoring is generally unregulated, and unless an organization's policy specifically states otherwise, the employer may listen to, watch, and read an employee's workplace communications. Employee rights often ride a fine line as related to privacy. As the following *reality check* illustrates, it is sometimes difficult to know where to make a distinction between corporate rights and employee rights.

Safe Environment

Employees have a right to work in a safe environment that includes: security inside and outside the hospital (e.g., sitting areas, parking lots); providing appropriate equipment (e.g., ventilation systems as required throughout the hospital, patient gowns, gloves, goggles); and signage posted as required in hazardous areas (e.g., isolation rooms for protection of both the employee and patient, hazardous medical gas storage areas).

▶ EMPLOYEE RESPONSIBILITIES

> *I believe that every right implies a responsibility; every opportunity, an obligation; every profession, a duty.*
>
> —John D. Rockefeller, Jr.

Employees have duties and responsibilities as defined in their job descriptions and the organization's policies and procedures. Rights and responsibilities run parallel to one another. With every right, there is a corresponding duty; for example, although there is a right to expect respect from others, there is a corresponding duty and responsibility to respect the rights of others. The following sections describe a variety of the many responsibilities required of healthcare employees.

Compassion

> *How far you go in life depends on you being tender with the young, compassionate with the aged, sympathetic with the striving and tolerant of the weak and strong. Because someday in your life you will have been all of these.*
>
> —George Washington Carver

The ability to show strength of character through compassion is truly an important employee responsibility. Compassionate caregivers make the difference in the life of both patients and coworkers. It is the compassionate caregiver who guides the patient as he or she struggles through illness, pain, and suffering. It is the compassionate caregiver who provides hope when there seems to be no hope.

✓ COMPASSION AND SENSITIVITY LACKING

Mark was waiting to be seen by his physician in a multispecialty physician office practice. As Mark was waiting to see his physician, he observed a woman, most likely in her late 70s, limping into the office. She had a large leg brace that ran from her thigh to the calf of her leg. She struggled to push her husband in a wheelchair into the office. She carefully parked the wheelchair and approached the check-in counter. She apologized for being late for her appointment because she was delayed leaving another physician's office. The patient was told, "You are late for your appointment. The office has a 15-minute late arrival rule. You will have to reschedule your appointment." She apologized for being late but said that she did call the physician's office to notify them that she would be late. She was then told, "You can wait, and I will try to squeeze you into the schedule, but I don't know how long you will have to wait." The lady said, "I don't want to bother anyone. I will reschedule my appointment." She was directed around the corner to another desk to reschedule her appointment. Mark got up out of his chair, walked over to the scheduler, and said, "I don't believe this. Her husband is sitting in a wheelchair, and she is having difficulty walking. She can have my appointment, and I can reschedule." The lady suddenly turned to Mark and gave him a big hug. The scheduler asked, "Who is your physician?" Mark told her, and she said, "I am sorry, but this lady has a different physician." The lady, now a bit teary eyed, continued to reschedule her appointment.

Mark saw what he perceived to be a wrong and tried to make a right. Employees at the reception desk, who are often the patient's first exposure to the healthcare system, can leave a good or bad impression on patients. Compassion requires all employees, regardless of the setting to be sensitive to patient needs.

Honor Patient Wishes

Caregivers have a responsibility to honor a patient's right to participate in decisions regarding his or her care, including the right to formulate advance directives and have those directives honored.

Maintain Confidentiality

The duty to maintain confidentiality encompasses both verbal and written communications. This requirement also applies to consultants, contracted individuals, students, and volunteers. Information about a patient, regardless of the method in which it is acquired, is confidential and should not be disclosed without the patient's permission. Those who come into possession of the most intimate personal information about patients have both a legal and an ethical duty not to reveal confidential communications.

Patient Confidentiality

The legal duty arises because the law recognizes a right to privacy. To protect this right, there is a corresponding duty to comply with the law. The ethical duty is broader and applies at all times.

Healthcare professionals who have access to medical records have a legal, ethical, and moral obligation to protect the confidentiality of the information in the records. The communications between a physician and his or her patient and the information generated during the course of the patient's illness are generally accorded the protection of confidentiality.

Healthcare professionals have a clear legal and moral obligation to maintain this confidentiality. As noted previously, medical records, with proper authorization, may be used for the purposes of research, statistical evaluation, and education. The information obtained from medical records must be dealt with in a confidential manner; otherwise, an organization could incur liability.

Employee Confidentiality

The duty of employees to maintain confidentiality is applicable to other employees as well as patients. Those in positions of trust can only maintain their individual integrity by being trustworthy. If there is illegal activity or unethical conduct being perpetrated by another employee, that employee has given up his or her right to privacy, regardless of his or her rank in the organization.

Adhere to Safe Practices

Caregivers have a responsibility to adhere to safe practices in order to minimize patient injuries. This responsibility requires employees to adhere to national patient safety goals (e.g., hand washing, patient identification, verification of operative site), the purpose of which is to protect the health and welfare of the patient.

Comply with Sterile Technique Protocols

The Centers for Disease Control and Prevention has estimated that "nosocomial [hospital-acquired] bloodstream infections are a leading cause of death in the United States. If we assume a nosocomial infection rate of 5%, of which 10% are bloodstream infections, and an attributable mortality rate of 15%, bloodstream infections would represent the eighth leading cause of death in the United States."[91] It is believed that such infections have resulted in as many as 100,000 deaths and billions of dollars in additional healthcare costs. These numbers do not reflect nonhospital-acquired infections that have occurred in physicians' offices.

The seriousness of these numbers encourages all caregivers to comply with sterile practice techniques through recommended hand washing and maintaining a sterile environment for patients.

Exercise Appropriate Judgment

Caregivers have a responsibility to exercise discretion and good judgment. This is especially true of physicians who are bound to exercise their judgment without interference from others. The Hippocratic Oath requires that the physician use his power to help the sick to the best of his or her ability and judgment. Such discretion, however, has limits and must consider the autonomous rights of patients.

Adhere to Professional Standards

Caregivers have a responsibility to be professional in the performance of their work. The operation of a hospital requires the coordination of numerous employees and departments, each with different responsibilities that depend on each other. Thus, staff cooperation and communication are essential for ensuring professionalism in the provision of high-quality patient care.

Report Unethical Behavior

Caregivers have both a right and responsibility to report impaired, incompetent, and unethical colleagues in accordance with the legal requirements of each state. Unethical behavior includes conduct that threatens patient care, violation of state licensing provisions, and other applicable laws, rules, and regulations as reviewed previously.

Protect Patients from Harm

Caregivers have an ethical and legal responsibility to protect patients from harm. Such responsibilities are not duties invented by courts of equity, but rather

are the tenets of ethical responsibility described in the codes of ethics of various health professionals. The rules of ethics applicable to nurses, for example, specifically recognize a nurse's obligation to safeguard not only a patient's health, but his or her safety as well.

Report Patient Abuse

Caregivers have both a right and responsibility to report patient abuse. An employer may not discharge an employee for fulfilling societal obligations or one who acts with a socially desirable motive. Statutes protect employees against retaliation for reporting patient abuse.

Maintain Respect in All Professional Relationships

 Without the feelings of respect, what is there to distinguish men from beasts?

—*Confucius*

Employees are responsible for maintaining appropriate professional relationships with patients, families, coworkers, and others with whom they may come into contact in the organization, such as hospital consultants, as noted in the following *reality check*.

Play the Role of Patient Advocate

All caregivers should consider themselves as patient advocates for the patients for whom they are assigned to care, as noted in the *reality check*.

Teamwork and Professional Relationships

Teamwork is the ability to work together toward a common vision. The ability to direct individual accomplishments toward organizational objectives. It is the fuel that allows common people to attain uncommon results.

—*Author Unknown*

Employees are responsible for maintaining appropriate professional relationships with patients, families, coworkers, and others with whom they may come into contact in the organization, such as hospital survey teams, as noted in the following *reality check*.

✔ *RESPECT AND INTEGRITY HAS LIMITS*

Bill, a quality improvement consultant hired by a hospital board, was praised during the presentation for his quality improvement report. He was treated with kindness and given assurances as to how well he helped the staff and how employees appreciated his suggestions for improvement. Prior to exiting the conference room, Bill asked whether there were any questions about his report. No questions, just smiles, accolades, and good-byes. Jeff, who was still in the room and was not scheduled to finish his assignment for another 2 weeks, thought to himself: Wow, it is good to see good people take suggestions and be so willing to make the suggested changes.

However, it turns out Bill wasn't considered as wonderful as he appeared to have been. The group was disgruntled by his report. Now that Bill was gone, he was criticized and berated. Jeff asked, "Why didn't you ask questions while Bill was here?"

Carol, the finance director, replied, "I spent 2 weeks with Bill. He just made up his mind. There was just no changing his mind." Jeff asked, "Are you saying that you disagree with Bill's report?" Carol replied, "Yes, I do disagree with it." Jeff continued, "But you did not state that while he was here. You told him you liked his suggestions and that you were already in the process of implementing them." Carol replied, "That's true, but since we made the suggested changes while he was here, he did not have to include them in his report. Now I look bad in that report." Jeff replied, "It speaks well of your organization that you have done so; however, it is the board that asked for the audit. We must report what we found." Carol, disgruntled, said, "Well Jeff, you are doing a super job, and the feedback from staff has been nothing but praise, but as to Bill, ugh."

Carol's remarks after Bill left the conference room were disrespectful and disingenuous, and they illustrate how an employee can be more concerned with his or her own interests rather than those of the patients. Bill's responsibility was to the board members who hired him and to other members of the consulting team charged with evaluating the hospital's operations in order to identify how the hospital could improve its services and the quality of patient care.

✔ *MOM NEEDED AN ADVOCATE*

My mom received the dreaded diagnosis of colon cancer. She underwent surgery that entailed a partial resection of her colon. When visiting her the second day post surgery I noticed there were solid foods on her food tray.

Looking at her dinner plate I thought to myself: What are they serving my mom? She looked up at me and said, "Are you hungry?" I said, "No mom, I am not hungry." Looking oh-so-sad, she continued, "Can you believe they want me to eat a pork chop? I can barely drink a glass of water. Why would they serve me a pork chop? My doctor told me I would be on a liquid diet for several days."

I went to the nursing station and asked the nurse about mom's diet orders.

She looked in the medical record and said, "The surgeon ordered a regular diet. It is documented on the patient care order sheet. The doctor documented in his notes 'regular diet.' I cannot change his orders." I replied, "Then he wrote the wrong diet order." The nurse continued, "I can't change his order. I will call the doctor and clarify his diet orders."

About 20 minutes later I went back to the nurses' station, and the nurse said that the doctor had not yet returned her call. As the nurse looked up at me from her desk at the nursing station, I said, "Could you call the dietitian and check? The doctor wrote the wrong note. Please call him again as well. Even if he had written his diet order correctly, she cannot eat solid foods at this time. Some nutrition is better than no nutrition." The nurse persisted, "I can only do what the doctor has ordered." I replied, "Please call him and tell him I am here now and he needs to correct his mistake." Frustrated, I said, "If I was to survey your hospital and observed this unresolved, I would fail your hospital." The nurse looked at me and said, "What do you do for a living?" I replied, "I inspect hospitals for accreditation purposes." Problem resolved.

It's a sad message—knowing compassion should trump all words—regardless of a person's position in life. When a doctor mistakenly writes a wrong order and the caregiver becomes aware of that mistake, he or she is obligated by law and ethics to intervene to prevent a continuing harm to the patient. In general, all caregivers must advocate for the patients to whom they are assigned to provide care and address the needs of patients in a timely fashion. This is their right.

—Mike

✓ *MULTIDISCIPLINARY APPROACH TO PATIENT CARE*

Bill visited a pain center where Dr. Jones, the medical director, had recently included a physical therapist on his pain management team. After several visits to the pain management program, Bill complimented the staff as to their multidisciplinary approach to his care. Dr. Jones discussed with Bill how patient outcomes had improved over time, as treatment plans became more multidisciplinary. He went on to explain how patients are encouraged to ask questions of the caregiver, such as the following:

- Have you reviewed my medical records?
- Have you discussed my treatment plan with my physician?
- What were my physician's specific orders?
- May I see them?
- What precautions have you been asked to follow with me?
- Have you seen my imaging studies?
- Has anyone discussed them with you?

Bill, before leaving, said to Dr. Jones, "I truly am getting individualized care and treatment in your pain center in a style worthy of the words, 'quality care is alive and well here.'"

The multidisciplinary approach to patient care improves patient outcomes through improved planning and cooperation between caregivers. Patients undergoing treatment quickly recognize when caregiver decisions are based on a cooperative effort between caregivers who are committed to improving patient care. In the words of Andrew Carnegie, "It marks a big step in a man's development when he comes to realize that other men can be called in to help him do a better job than he can do alone." And so it is in the care of patients, the success of quality patient care is dependent on teamwork.

▶ THE CAREGIVER'S PLEDGE

- I will be compassionate.
- I will not neglect my duties and responsibilities.
- I will read instructions and follow protocols.
- I will seek verification of questionable orders.
- I will report concerns for patient safety (e.g., staffing concerns).
- I will not assume responsibilities beyond my capabilities.
- I will call for help when a patient's medical needs suddenly change.
- I will continuously improve my skills and participate in continuing education opportunities.

▶ CHAPTER REVIEW

1. *Employment at will* is a doctrine by which employment can be terminated at any time by either the employee or employer. Exceptions to this doctrine include employment contracts and issues involving public policy.

2. *Public policy* prohibits the termination of an employee based on factors such as disability, age, race, color, religion, sex, national origin, pregnancy, filing safety violation complaints with various agencies, membership in a union, whistleblowing, rest and lunch breaks, and reporting patient abuse.

3. Termination for cause can be due to provisions for termination in employment contracts, financial necessity, hostile attitude, improper billing practices, poor work performance, alcoholism, and insubordinate behavior.

4. Unemployment compensation can be denied, for example, in cases of profanity, threatening coworkers, theft, poor work attendance, voluntary termination, and violation of no-smoking policies.

5. Wrongful discharge can be *retaliatory* or *constructive discharge*.

6. An employee who believes that he or she has been unfairly discharged should seek access to his or her employment contract (if applicable), employee handbook, human resources policies and procedures, minutes of pertinent meetings, written reports (typed or handwritten), as well as any employment files maintained by the organization.

7. The fact that an employment contract is terminable at will does not, in all cases, allow an employer the absolute right to terminate the contract.

8. Employers can reduce exposure to liability for wrongful discharge by establishing and maintaining effective hiring practices.

9. Fairly balancing the rights and responsibilities of the employee and the needs of the organization is an extremely complex objective.

   ■ Rights and responsibilities run parallel to one another.

   ■ There is a corresponding duty to accept one's responsibilities and at the same time respect the rights of others.

10. Employee rights include: equal pay for equal work; refuse to participate in care for religious reasons, question patient care; freedom from sexual harassment; treatment with dignity and respect; report the employer for violation of the law; freedom from intimidation; privacy and confidentiality; and, work in a safe environment.

11. Staff responsibilities include: compassion; honor patient wishes; maintain confidentiality for both patients and employees; adhere to safe practices (e.g., comply with sterile technique protocols); exercise appropriate judgment; adhere to professional standards; report unethical behavior; protect patients from harm; report patient abuse; and, maintain professional relationships.

▶ REVIEW QUESTIONS

1. Discuss the employment-at-will doctrine.
2. Explain public policies that protect employees from unlawful discharge.
3. Discuss under what conditions unemployment compensation can be denied to a claimant.
4. Describe what is meant by retaliatory and constructive discharge and how to defend a claim for unfair discharge.
5. Describe under what circumstances employers often discharge an employee.
6. Describe effective hiring practices and the importance of clear communications.
7. Discuss why employment disclaimers are important to the employer.
8. Describe the rights and responsibilities of employees.
9. Discuss in what ways the rights and responsibilities of patients and employees are similar.

▶ NOTES

1. 328 S.E.2d 818 (N.C. Ct. App. 1985).
2. 44 A.L.R. 4th 1136 (1986).
3. *Sides v. Duke Hosp.*, 328 S.E.2d 818 (N.C. Ct. App. 1985).
4. Cornell Law School, "Employment-at-will Doctrine," https://www.law.cornell.edu/wex/employment-at-will_doctrine.
5. *Pierce v. Ortho Pharm. Corp.*, 417 A.2d 505, 509 (N.J. 1980).
6. U.S. Equal Employment Opportunity Commission, "Pregnancy Discrimination," http://www.eeoc.gov/laws/types/pregnancy.cfm.
7. *Palmateer v. International Harvester Co.*, 421 N.E.2d 876, 878 (Ill. 1981).
8. *Joiner v. Benton Community Bank*, 411 N.E.2d 229, 231 (Ill. 1980).
9. *Gantt v. Sentry Ins.*, 824 P.2d 680, 687–688 (Cal. 1992).
10. https://en.wikipedia.org/wiki/Whistleblower.
11. 31 U.S.C.A. § 3729.
12. Annotation, 99 A.L.R. Fed. 775.
13. *Gambee v. State Bd. of Med. Exam'rs*, 923 P.2d 679 (1996).
14. Federal Bureau of Investigation, "Honoring Community Leaders," http://www.fbi.gov/about-us/partnerships_and_outreach/community_outreach/dcla/2010/stlouis.
15. *HCA Health Services of Florida, Inc. v. Hillman*, No. 2D03-1534 (Fla. Dist. Ct. App. 2004).
16. No. 06CA1849 (Colo. App. 2008).
17. *Delaney v. Taco Time Int'l*, 681 P.2d 114 (Or. 1984). This case involved an employer found liable by the Oregon Supreme Court for the wrongful discharge of an at-will employee who was discharged for fulfilling a societal obligation because he refused to sign a false and arguably tortious statement that cast aspersions on the work habits and moral behavior of a former employee.
18. 684 P.2d 21 (Or. Ct. App. 1984).
19. *Id.* at 24.
20. H. H. Perritt, *Employee Dismissal Law and Practice* (New York, NY: John Wiley & Sons, 1984), 354.
21. 663 P.2d 958 (Alaska 1983).
22. *Id.* at 659.
23. 537 A.2d 1137 (Me. 1987).
24. *Id.* at 1138.
25. 385 N.W.2d 99 (N.D. 1986).
26. 681 P.2d 918 (Ariz. Ct. App. 1984).
27. 541 N.Y.S.2d 41, 150 A.D.2d 432 (1989).
28. *Id.* at 433.
29. 512 N.Y.S.2d 592, 128 A.D.2d 941 (1987).
30. *Id.* at 593.
31. 777 F. Supp. 1484 (E.D. Mo. 1991).
32. *Id.* at 1488.
33. 467 N.W.2d 73 (N.D. 1991).
34. *Id.* at 76.
35. 807 N.Y.S.2d 477 (N.Y. App. Div. 2006).

36. *Id.*

37. 358 N.W.2d 96 (Minn. Ct. App. 1984).

38. *Id.* at 98.

39. *Id.*

40. 16 A.D.3d 756, 790 N.Y.S.2d 313 (N.Y. 2005).

41. *Id.*

42. 325 S.E.2d 651 (N.C. Ct. App. 1985).

43. *Id.* at 652.

44. 463 N.E.2d 478 (Ind. Ct. App. 1983).

45. *Id.* at 481.

46. *Id.* at 483.

47. 371 N.W.2d 121 (Neb. 1985).

48. 415 A.2d 139 (Pa. Commw. Ct. 1980).

49. 772 P.2d 1059 (Cal. 1989).

50. 765 P.2d 373 (Cal. 1988).

51. *Meech v. Hillhaven W., Inc.*, 776 P.2d 488 (Mont. 1989).

52. Linda Greenhouse, "Justices Say Law Bars Retaliation Over Bias Claims," *The New York Times*, May 28, 2008. http://www.nytimes.com/2008/05/28/washington/28scotus.html.

53. *Id.*

54. *Id.*

55. Conn. Gen. Stat. Ann. § 31-51m(a) (West 1987).

56. Me. Rev. Stat. Ann. 26, §§ 831–840 (West 1987).

57. Mich. Comp. Laws Ann. §§ 15.361-369 (West 1981).

58. Mont. Code Ann. § 39-2-901 (1987).

59. *Pierce v. Ortho Pharm. Corp.*, 417 A.2d 505, 509 (N.J. 1980).

60. 215 Cal. Rptr. 860 (Cal. Ct. App. 1985).

61. *Id.* at 865.

62. 518 N.E.2d 471 (Ill. App. Ct. 1988).

63. 760 F. Supp. 1575 (D.C. Ga. 1991).

64. *Id.* at 1577.

65. *Id.* at 1578.

66. *Id.* at 1579.

67. *Id.* at 1582.

68. *Soentgen v. Quain & Ramstad Clinic*, 467 N.W.2d 73 (N.D. 1991).

69. *Rivera Maldonado v. Hospital Alejandro Otero Lopez*, 614 F. Supp. 2d 181 (Dist. Court, D. Puerto, 2009).

70. *Id.*

71. 508 N.Y.S.2d 802 (N.Y. App. Div. 1986).

72. No. 89-CA-2272-MR (Ky. Ct. App. Mar. 22, 1991).

73. 428 N.W.2d 574 (Minn. Ct. App. 1988).

74. *Id.* at 577.

75. 413 N.W.2d 146 (Minn. Ct. App. 1987).

76. *Id.* at 147.

77. *HCA Health Services of Florida, Inc. v. Hillman*, No. 2D03-1534 (Fla. Dist. Ct. App. 2004).

78. 168 Cal. Rptr. 722, 111 Cal.App.3d 433 (1980).

79. *Id.* at 457.

80. 171 Cal. Rptr. 917 (Cal. Ct. App. 1981).

81. 398 N.W.2d 327 (Mich. 1986).

82. 810 N.E.2d 1022 (2004).

83. http://www.ncsl.org/research/health/pharmacist-conscience-clauses-laws-and-information.aspx (accessed December 10, 2014).

84. *Id.*

85. 676 N.Y.S. 2d 293 (N.Y. App., 1998).

86. 515 F.2d 541 (8th Cir. 1975).

87. *Deerman v. Beverly Cal. Corp.*, 518 S.E.2d 804 (N.C. App. 1999).

88. Ralph Nader, Peter J. Petkas, and Kate Blackwell (editors), *Whistle Blowing: The Report of the Conference on Professional Responsibility* (New York: Grossman, 1972).

89. *Gambee v. State Bd. of Med. Exam'rs*, 923 P.2d 679 (1996).

90. Occupational Safety and Health Administration, "The Whistleblower Protection Programs," http://www.whistleblowers.gov.

91. Richard P. Wenzel and Michael B. Edmond, "The Impact of Hospital-Acquired Bloodstream Infections," *Emerging Infectious Diseases*, April 2001. http://wwwnc.cdc.gov/eid/article/7/2/70-0174_article.htm.

CHAPTER 21

Professional Liability Insurance

🔍 IT'S YOUR GAVEL . . .

CRIMINAL ACTS AND INSURANCE COVERAGE

A physician was convicted for the sexual assault of a minor. He was then sued in federal court for civil damages. An insurer had issued medical malpractice policies to the physician. Under the policies, the insurer agreed to pay on behalf of the insured all sums that the insured became legally obligated to pay as damages because of bodily injury or personal injury resulting from rendering or failing to render, during the policy period, professional services by the insured. The policies contained an express exclusion barring liability of the insurer for any acts of the insured arising out of the performance of a criminal act.

Does sexual assault constitute rendering professional services within the coverage provisions of the physician's insurance policy? Should a malpractice insurer be required to indemnify a physician for liability resulting from the sexual assault of a minor?[1]

WHAT IS YOUR VERDICT?

I never was ruined but twice—once when I gained a lawsuit, and once when I lost one.

—Francois Marie de Voltaire (1694–1778)

▶ LEARNING OBJECTIVES

The reader, upon completion of this chapter, will be able to:

- Describe the purpose of a malpractice insurance policy, including risk categories, and the importance to professionals of carrying professional liability insurance.
- Explain the elements and conditions of an insurance policy.
- Describe the investigation and settlement of claims.

This chapter introduces the reader to some of the basic concepts related to professional liability insurance. The purpose of liability insurance is to spread the risk of economic loss among members of a group who share common risks (for example, an obstetrician would share risk with other obstetricians). As risks increase, premiums increase to cover the associated risks. The premiums are placed in a shared risk fund from which monies are drawn to cover the costs of lawsuits. Because of skyrocketing malpractice premiums, some physicians limit their practice to less costly procedures, restrict their practices by not accepting new patients, decide to close their practice, or accept a position as an employee in a hospital setting.

Medical malpractice insurance is subject to the cyclical nature of the insurance market. Problems intrinsic in malpractice insurance include the uncertainty of the U.S. legal system, inflation, damages awarded, emerging technology, and high-risk procedures.

▶ INSURANCE POLICIES

Insurance is a contract that creates legal obligations on the part of both the insured and the insurer. It is a contract in which the insurer agrees to assume certain risks of the insured for consideration or payment of a premium. Under the terms of the contract, also known as the *insurance policy*, the insurer promises to pay a specific amount of money if a specified event takes place. An insurance policy contains three necessary elements: (1) identification of the risk covered, (2) the specific amount payable, and (3) the specified occurrence.

Insurance companies are required by the laws of the different states to issue only policies that contain certain mandated provisions and to maintain certain financial reserves to guarantee to policyholders that their expectations will be met when coverage is needed. The basic underlying concept of insurance is the spreading of risk. By writing coverage for a large enough pool of individuals, the company has determined actuarially that a certain number of claims will arise within that pool, and if the premium structure has been established correctly and the prediction of claims made accurately, the company ought to be able to meet those claims and return a profit to its shareholders.

Insurance policies include occurrence policies, which cover all incidents that arise during a policy year, regardless of when they are reported to the insurer; and claims-made policies, which cover only those claims made or reported during the policy year. Tail coverage policies provide for an uninterrupted extension of an insurance policy period. Umbrella policies cover awards over the amount provided in the basic policy coverage. The dollar amount of coverage is specified in the policy.

Risk Categories

A *risk* is the possibility that a financial loss will occur. The main function of insurance is to provide security against this loss. Insurance does not prevent or hinder the occurrence of the loss, but it does compensate for the damages.

An insured individual may be exposed to three categories of risk:

1. *Property loss or damage*: the possibility that an insured's property may be damaged or destroyed by fire, flood, tornado, hurricane, or other catastrophe.
2. *Personal injury*: the possibility that the insured may be injured in an accident or may become ill; the possibility of death is a personal risk covered in the typical life insurance plan.
3. *Legal liability risk*: the possibility that the insured may become legally liable to pay money damages to another and includes accident and professional liability insurance. The insured is protected from the risk of liability imposed by lawsuits or claims that come within the coverage of the insurance policy.

Telemedicine

Telemedicine can involve misdiagnosis and thus result in a lawsuit. Failure by a radiologist, for example, who incorrectly interprets a patient's radiology images on an offsite remote electronic device, can lead to a patient's injury and thus a lawsuit could ensue. Although insurance companies often provide coverage for telemedicine-related lawsuits, some insurance plans only cover telemedicine-related lawsuits within the state in which the provider is licensed. Therefore, healthcare providers should confirm with their insurance companies that their policies adequately cover patient injuries related to telemedicine services within the states they practice. Written verification of such coverage from the insurer is preferable. If a healthcare professional practices in multiple states, the insurance policy should include a provision for those states, and in some cases the countries, within which one practices.

▶ INSURANCE POLICY PROVISIONS

Healthcare organizations, nurses, physicians, and other healthcare practitioners who are covered by insurance should become familiar with the rights and duties inherent in the policy. The insurance policy includes coverage agreements, exclusions, defense and settlement provisions, limits on liability, and conditions. The insured should be able to identify the risks covered, description of the coverage, as well as conditions of the contract.

Although policies of different insurance companies vary, the standard policy typically provides that the insurance company will pay the economic damages on behalf of the insured. The insurer, under the terms of an insurance policy, is obligated to reimburse the insured up to the policy limits, including legal fees for damages that arise from the professional's negligent acts.

Policy Period

The period of the policy is stated in the insurance contract. Under an *occurrence policy*, the contract provides protection only for claims that occur during the time frame within which the policy is stated to be in effect. Any incident that occurs before or after the policy period would not be covered under the insuring agreement. Occurrence policies provide coverage for all claims that may arise out of a policy period. The actual reporting time has no bearing on the validity of the claim, so long as it is filed before the applicable statute of limitations tolls. Although the reporting time has no bearing on the validity of the claim from the standpoint of coverage under the policy,

the conditions of the policy will require notice within a specified time. Failure to provide such notice could void the insurer's obligation under the policy if it can be demonstrated that the carrier's position was compromised as a result of filing an untimely claim or report.

A *claims-made policy* provides coverage for only those claims instituted during the policy period. Notice of a claim is required during the policy period. Failure to give notice of a claim to the insurer in a claims-made policy until after the policy expires can result in denial by the insurance company to cover the claim.

Defense and Settlement

In the defense and settlement portion of the insurance policy, the insured and the insurance company agree that the company will defend any lawsuit against the insured arising from performance or nonperformance of professional services. The insurance company is delegated the power to effect a settlement of any claims as it deems necessary. In a professional liability policy, the duty of the insurer under this clause is limited to the defense of lawsuits against the insured that are a consequence of the insured's negligent act(s) that result in patient injury.

The insurance company fulfills its obligation to provide legal defense by engaging the services of an attorney on behalf of the insured. The obligation of the attorney is to the insured directly, because the insured is the attorney's client. There is, to some extent, a divided loyalty because the attorney looks to the insurance company to obtain business. Nevertheless, the attorney–client relationship exists between the attorney and the insured. The insured thus has the right to expect the attorney to fulfill attorney–client responsibilities.

Coverage: Amount Payable

The amount to be paid by an insurer is determined by the amount of damages incurred by the injured party. The insurance company and the injured party may negotiate a settlement prior to or during trial. Some states have provisions mandating that consent of the court must be obtained prior to the settlement of a negligence claim on behalf of a minor.

In any event, the insurance company will pay the injured party no more than the maximum limit stated in the insurance policy. The insured professional must personally pay any damages that exceed the policy limits. For example, under a policy with a maximum coverage of $1 million for each claim and $3 million for aggregate claims (the total amount payable to all injured parties), the insured must pay any amount over $1 million on each individual claim and any amount over $3 million in a policy period.

Punitive Damages

A claim for punitive damages awarded in a malpractice suit was submitted to an insurance carrier for payment but was subsequently denied by the carrier.[2] The insurance carrier cited Florida public policy, which prohibits coverage of punitive damage awards.

> In this case, the injuries suffered by Charlotte Cohen gave rise to a compensatory damage award of $25,000. Looking beyond the injury to the nature of plaintiff's conduct, the jury in the Florida state court action determined that that conduct warranted imposition of punitive damages in the amount of $750,000, none of which fits the definition of a "malpractice loss" for which plaintiff may claim reimbursement.
>
> Furthermore, the result which plaintiff seeks would contravene federal public policy considerations which counsel against allowing reimbursement of punitive damage assessments. The purpose of assessing punitive damages is "to punish the tortfeasor . . . and to deter him and others from similar extreme conduct." *City of Newport v. Fact Concerts, Inc.*, 453 U.S. 247, 266–67, 101 S. Ct. 2748, 2759–60, 69 L. Ed. 2d 616 (1981). That purpose would be ill served by reimbursement, which would shift the responsibility for paying the damages from Greenbrook to the Medicare trust fund, and ultimately to this nation's taxpayers who would bear the burden of plaintiff's wrong-doing.
>
> Plaintiff can identify no case in which a punitive damage award has been held to be a reimbursable malpractice loss.[3]

▶ CONDITIONS OF INSURANCE POLICIES

Each insurance policy contains a number of important conditions. Failure to comply with these conditions may cause forfeiture of the policy and nonpayment of claims against it. Generally, insurance policies contain the following conditions:

1. *Notice of occurrence*: When the insured becomes aware that an injury has occurred as a result of acts covered under the contract, the insured must notify the insurance company promptly. The form of notice may be either oral or written, as specified in the policy.

2. *Notice of claim*: Whenever the insured receives notice that a claim or suit is being instituted, prompt notice must be sent by the insured to the insurance company. This provides the insurance company with an opportunity to investigate the facts of a case. The policy will specify what papers are to be forwarded to the company. The mere failure to advise in a timely manner may be in and of itself a breach of the insurance contract, entitling the insurer to decline coverage. It may not matter that the insurer has in no way been prejudiced by the late notification—the mere fact that the insured failed to carry out obligations under the policy may be sufficient to permit the insurer to avoid its obligations. When the insurer has refused to honor a claim because of late notice and the insured wishes to challenge such refusal, an action can be brought, asking a court to determine the reasonableness of the insurer's position.

3. *Assistance of the insured*: The insured must cooperate with the insurance company and render any assistance necessary to reach a settlement.

4. *Other insurance*: If the insured has pertinent insurance policies with other insurance companies, the insured must notify the insurance company so that each company may pay the appropriate amount of the claim.

5. *Assignment*: The protections contracted for by the insured may not be transferred unless the insurance company grants permission. Because the insurance company was aware of the risks the insured would encounter before the policy was issued, the company will endeavor to avoid protecting persons other than the policyholder.

6. *Subrogation*: This is the right of a person who pays another's debt to be substituted for all rights in relation to the debt. When an insurance company makes a payment for the insured under the terms of the policy, the company becomes the beneficiary of all the rights of recovery the insured has against any other persons who also may have been negligent. For example, if several nurses were found liable for negligence arising from the same occurrence and the

insurance company for one nurse pays the entire claim, the company will be entitled to the rights of that nurse and may collect a proportionate share of the claim from the other nurses.

7. *Changes*: The insured cannot make changes in the policy without the written consent of the insurance company. Thus, an agent of the insurance company ordinarily cannot modify or remove any condition of the liability contract. Only the insurance company, by written authorization, may permit a condition to be altered or removed.

8. *Cancellation*: A cancellation clause spells out the conditions and procedures necessary for the insured or the insurer to cancel the liability policy. Written notice usually is required. The insured person's failure to comply with any terms of the policy can result in cancellation and possible nonpayment of a claim by the insurance company. As a legal contract, failure to meet the terms and conditions of an insurance policy can result in a breach of contract and voidance of coverage.

▶ LIABILITY OF THE PROFESSIONAL

An individual who provides professional services to another person may be legally responsible for any harm the person suffers as a result of negligence. Many professionals protect themselves from their exposure to a legal loss by acquiring a professional liability insurance policy.

All Professionals Need Insurance

All healthcare professionals should carry malpractice insurance. Even though a hospital, for example, as an employer can be held liable for the acts of its employees under the doctrine of *respondeat superior*, the employee can be financially liable to the employer for his or her own negligent acts. From a cost–benefit standpoint, the answer to the question, "Do I really need insurance?" is yes. Insurance premiums for allied health professionals are relatively reasonable.

No matter how educated, confident, and careful the nurse is, unintentional mistakes can and will happen. Accidents will occur. And, unfortunately, willful neglect can be an issue. Injury and death very often are the results of mistakes, accidents, and neglect. Families want to know what happened. Even in the best

scenario, the nurse feels embarrassed and ultimately fears what the damage could do to a perfect professional reputation. Nurses must have the option of protecting their professional reputations and personal assets. Having individual liability insurance is a smart solution.[4]

Malpractice insurance coverage is especially important if a caregiver is working:

- As a volunteer at a clinic or health fair not sponsored by his or her employer
- As an independent contractor providing a service in a patient's home
- For an independent agency or registry
- For an organization that is covered by an insurance policy that has an exclusionary provision by which the insurance company disclaims liability for malpractice actions brought against the insured organization

If a private agency has inadequate insurance coverage, there is always a possibility that recovery will be sought against a nurse's estate.

There are disadvantages to nurses obtaining malpractice insurance. First, acquisition of malpractice coverage by nurses could encourage naming nurses as defendants in malpractice suits. Second, an increase in complaints against nurses could cause an increase in insurance premiums, eventually placing the cost of malpractice insurance outside their financial means. The cost of insurance for nurses, however, has been reasonably low and affordable. The peace of mind is well worth the cost.

The cost of a policy is economical and reasonable. For example, the annual premium could cover the first hour billed by an attorney. For coverage amounts of $1 million/$6 million, premiums are approximately $100 per year in most states for a registered nurse (RN) or licensed practical/vocational nurse (LPN/LVN).[5]

Advanced Practice Nurse Practitioner

Nurse practitioners are experiencing, on average, a 2.3% increase on indemnity and expense payments. This is due in part to the expanding roles of nurse practitioners as they take on various responsibilities that have historically been performed by physicians. As with physicians, claims often involve the failure to properly assess and diagnose patients.[6]

Registered Nurse

The scope of practice for nurses, particularly advanced nurse practitioners, continues to expand. State laws describe the procedures and services nurses are permitted to provide to patients. They are based on education, experience, competencies, and licensing laws. As the scope of practice of nurses expands, the risk of lawsuits and insurance payouts increases, as noted in the following cases.

A nurse's insurance policy was primary with respect to the first $100,000 of a settlement that resulted from a malpractice action against the nurse in *American Nurses Association v. Passaic General Hospital*.[7] The National Fire Insurance Company had issued an insurance policy covering the contractual obligation of the American Nurses Association to its members. The New Jersey Supreme Court held that the judgment against the nurse in excess of $100,000 was properly apportioned equally between the hospital's liability insurer and the association's liability insurer.

The court in *Jones v. Medox, Inc.*[8] held that only the nurse's insurance carrier, Globe Insurance, was liable for injuries sustained by the plaintiff while at Doctors Hospital; these injuries resulted from an injection administered by the nurse. Medox, Inc., a corporation providing temporary medical personnel to Doctors Hospital, employed Ms. Jones. After settlement of the claim against the nurse, the hospital, and the nurse's employer, the nurse and her insurer brought an action against Doctors Hospital, Medox, Inc. and their insurers. The trial court granted summary judgment in favor of the hospital and its insurer, and they dismissed the claim against Medox, Inc. and its insurer.

Private Duty Nurse

Private duty nurses are not considered employees; they are engaged by the patient (or the patient's family) to provide services to that patient. As independent contractors, they set their own fees and are reimbursed for services provided to the client-patient. As such, private duty nurses should obtain their own malpractice insurance coverage. Even though a patient employs a special duty nurse, a hospital, for example, can be held jointly and severally liable for damages resulting from a nurse's negligence during that time the patient is in the hospital.

A hospital has the right to seek recovery not only from the nurse but would include the nurse's agency if the nurse works as an agency nurse. Whether home care, hospital, nursing home, or other healthcare entity, all such entities and patients should ensure that private duty nurses and agency nurses have a stipulation in their contract that all providers of care have malpractice insurance coverage that sets minimally acceptable limits in the event of a malpractice award.

Students

The potential for liability is not limited to licensed professionals. Students engaged in learning a profession who engage in activities involving the care and treatment of others face potential liability for their acts. For this reason, these individuals often obtain personal insurance coverage or assure themselves of such coverage through the organization in which they are employed or the educational institution in which they are enrolled.

▶ INTENTIONAL TORTS: COVERAGE DENIED

An insurer has no duty to defend or provide coverage for intentional torts. Contracts insuring against loss from intentional wrongs are generally void as being against public policy, as noted in the following cases.

No Duty to Cover Intentional Torts

An action was brought by a comprehensive liability insurer for declaratory judgment as to its duty to defend the insured in civil actions alleging slander, interference with business relations, and violations of the federal antitrust laws in *St. Paul Insurance Co. v. Talladega Nursing Home*.[9] The federal district court ruled for the insurer, and the nursing facility appealed. The Fifth Circuit held that the insurer has no duty to defend or provide coverage for alleged intentional torts. Under Alabama law, all contracts insuring against loss from intentional wrongs are void as being against public policy.

Therapist's Sexual Affair with Patient

A therapist's sexual affair with a patient was not covered by the provider's liability insurance in *Scottsdale Ins. Co. v. Flowers*.[10] The district court was found not to have abused its discretion in exercising jurisdiction over a patient's emotional distress action arising out of the therapist's sexual affair with the patient. The court properly ruled that the therapist, an employee of the insured mental health services provider, was not covered by the provider's liability insurance policy for tort damages arising from the sexual affair. The conduct in question was outside the scope of the therapist's employment and thus outside tort liability coverage of the liability insurance policy of the therapist's employer, which included only employees' acts "within the scope of their employment."

Sexual Assault

Sexual assault does not constitute rendering professional services within the coverage provisions of insurance policies. As a result, malpractice insurers are not required to indemnify the insured for liability resulting from the sexual assault. The Medical Protective Company, in *R. W. v. Schrein*,[11] a physician's professional liability insurer, sought a judgment determining that it had no duty to defend or indemnify the physician with respect to five former patients who claimed that they were sexually abused during examination and treatment. The Supreme Court of Nebraska held that there is no clearly articulated public policy that would permit or require the court to disregard the fact that the physician's acts did not fall within the coverage provided. The physician's liability to the appellants was not based on the provision or failure to provide professional services.

There was no duty by the malpractice insurer in *Sanzi v. Shetty*[12] to defend the pediatric neurologist who allegedly sexually abused a patient for a period of 8 years, beginning when she was just 14 years old. It was asserted that such abuse led to the patient's suicide approximately 12 years after the neurologist ended his relationship with the patient. It was alleged that the neurologist had deceived the patient's parents into believing that it would be beneficial to the patient to spend Saturdays working in his office, where he allegedly sexually abused the patient during regular medical visits and on the purported Saturday workdays. A hearing justice found that the malpractice insurer had no duty to defend or indemnify the neurologist. The state supreme court held that because the claim against the doctor did not allege injury arising from the rendering or failure to render professional services, it was not covered by the policy. The only connection between the doctor's acts and his profession was that the sexual abuse of the deceased occurred at his office while she worked there. Because the alleged sexual abuse carried with it an inferred intent to harm, there was no accidental nature to the resulting injuries. Consequently, the insurer was relieved from its duty to defend or indemnify the insured physician.

▶ MEDICAL LIABILITY INSURANCE

The fundamental tenets of insurance law and their application to the typical liability insurance policy are pertinent to the provisions of medical professional liability insurance as applied to individuals and institutions. Professional liability policies vary in the broadness, the exclusions from coverage, and the interpretations a company places on the language of the contract.

There are three medical professional liability classes:

1. Individuals, including (but not limited to) physicians, surgeons, dentists, nurses, osteopaths, chiropractors, opticians, physiotherapists, optometrists, and different types of medical technicians. (This category may include medical laboratories and blood banks.)
2. Healthcare institutions, such as hospitals, extended-care facilities, homes for the aged, institutions for the mentally ill, and other healthcare facilities where bed and board are provided for patients or residents.
3. Outpatient facilities and clinics where there are no regular bed or board facilities. (These institutions may be related to industrial or commercial enterprises; however, they are to be distinguished from facilities operated by dentists or physicians, which usually are covered under individual professional liability contracts.)

The insuring clause usually will provide for payment on behalf of the insured if an injury arises from either of the following:

■ Malpractice, error, or mistake in rendering or failing to render professional services in the practice of the insured's profession during the policy period
■ Acts or omissions on the part of the insured during the policy period as a member of a formal accreditation or similar professional board or committee of a healthcare facility or a professional society

Although injury is not limited to bodily injury or property damage, it must result from malpractice, error, mistake, or failure to perform acts that should have been performed.

The most common risks covered by medical professional liability insurance are as follows:

■ Negligence
■ Assault and battery as a result of failing to obtain consent to a medical or surgical procedure
■ Libel and slander
■ Invasion of privacy for betrayal of professional confidences

Coverage may vary from company to company, but standards of policy coverage generally are followed. Rates will differ according to the risks that might be incurred for individuals by profession, specialty, and type of healthcare facility (e.g., nursing facility or hospital).

▶ SELF-INSURANCE

Exorbitant malpractice insurance premiums often have produced situations in which the premium cost of insurance has approached and, on occasion, reached the face amount of the policy. Because of the extremely high cost of maintaining such insurance, some institutions have sought alternatives to this conventional means of protecting against medical malpractice. One alternative is self-insurance. When a healthcare facility self-insures its malpractice risks, it no longer purchases a policy of malpractice insurance but instead periodically sets aside a predetermined amount of its own funds as a reserve against malpractice losses and expenses that might occur. An institution that self-insures generally retains the services of a self-insurance consulting firm and of an actuary to determine the proper level of funding that the institution should maintain.

A self-insurance program need not involve the elimination of insurance coverage in its entirety. A healthcare organization may find it prudent to purchase excess coverage whereby the organization self-insures the first agreed-on dollar amount of risk and the insurance carrier insures the balance. For example, in a typical program, the organization may self-insure the first $1 million of professional liability risk per year. Because most claims will be disposed of within such limitation, the cost of excess insurance may be quite reasonable.

Before a corporation makes a decision to self-insure, not only must it determine the economic aspects of such a decision and the necessary funding levels to maintain an adequate reserve for future claims, it also must determine whether there are any legal impediments to such a program. A corporation that has obtained funding from governmental sources or that has issued bonds or other obligations containing certain covenants may find itself unable to self-insure because of these prior commitments. Healthcare organizations should consult legal counsel to review appropriate and applicable documentation before making the self-insurance decision.

▶ TRUSTEE COVERAGE

Board members/trustees/officers of both profit and not-for-profit organizations are at risk for exposure to a variety of lawsuits, ranging from allegations of wrongful acts to financial mismanagement, errors in judgment, and negligence. Claims against directors and officers can be costly and disruptive to any organization. Board members, if found guilty of wrongdoing, can be personally liable, placing their personal assets at risk. For this reason, they should be provided liability insurance in the event a lawsuit arises out of their fiduciary duties and responsibilities to the organization. Such coverage is generally provided for by the organization and is helpful in attracting qualified board members. Before an insurer writing a trustee policy (generally known as directors' and officers' liability insurance) will respond to defend or pay a claim on behalf of a trustee, it must be shown that the trustee acted in good faith and within the scope of his or her responsibilities. Ordinarily, coverage would not be afforded when a trustee is accused of acting improperly in his or her relationship with the corporation. In addition, insurance coverage for officers' and directors' liability generally excludes, as a covered event, the failure to obtain other necessary insurance for the institution (e.g., fire insurance).

Insurance coverage for officers and directors of a corporation should include indemnification, to the extent possible by law, for all liabilities and expenses, including the following:

- Counsel fees and expenses that are reasonably incurred as the result of any legal proceeding stemming from lawsuits that might arise in connection with an officer or director's position within the corporation
- Funds paid in satisfaction of judgments
- Fines and penalties
- Coverage that extends to actions taken while in office or thereafter, by reason of being or having been a director or officer of the corporation, excepting when the officer or director has not acted in good faith or when there is reasonable belief that an officer's or director's action was not in the best interest of the corporation

▶ MANDATED MEDICAL STAFF INSURANCE COVERAGE

Physicians are often required by healthcare organizations to carry their own malpractice insurance. Physicians who fail to maintain such coverage can be suspended from a hospital's medical staff.

Right to Suspend Physician

A federal district court in *Pollack v. Methodist Hospital*[13] ruled that a hospital has the legal right to suspend a staff physician for failing to comply with its requirement that physicians carry medical malpractice insurance coverage. The decision resulted from a suit brought against a hospital by a physician whose staff privileges were suspended because he failed to comply with a newly adopted hospital requirement that all staff physicians provide proof of malpractice coverage of at least $1 million. The court rejected the physician's charges that the requirement violated his civil rights and antitrust laws.

As held in *Wilkinson v. Madera Community Hospital*,[14] a healthcare organization can require its medical staff to show evidence of professional liability insurance. The physician in this case was refused reappointment because he failed to maintain malpractice insurance with a recognized insurance company as required by the hospital.

▶ INVESTIGATION AND SETTLEMENT OF CLAIMS

An injured party may request settlement of a claim prior to instituting legal action. As a first step toward settlement of a claim, the insurance carrier may have an investigator interview a claimant regarding the details of the alleged occurrence that led to the injury. After an investigation, the insurance company may agree to a settlement if liability is questionable and the risks of proceeding to trial are too great. Should settlement negotiations fail, an attorney may be employed by the injured party to negotiate a settlement. If the

🔍 *THE COURT'S DECISION*

Sexual assault did not constitute rendering professional services within coverage provisions of the physician's insurance policy. The New Mexico Supreme Court held that the malpractice insurer was not required to indemnify a physician for liability resulting from the sexual assault of a minor. The physician's conviction was admitted into evidence not to prove negligence but to prove that the physician's misconduct constituted criminal acts within exclusions of liability policies.[15] The New Mexico Supreme Court added: "Furthermore, our evaluation of insurance coverage centers on LaMure's insurance policies and the federal complaint, which, supported by evidence of LaMure's indictment and conviction, provides sufficient evidence regarding LaMure's alleged misconduct to resolve the coverage issue."[16]

attorney fails to obtain a settlement, either the claim can be dropped or legal action commenced.

When a claim is settled, a general release, signed by the plaintiff, surrenders the right of action against the defendant. If the claimant is married, a general release also should be obtained from the spouse, because there may be a cause of action as a result of loss of the injured spouse's services (e.g., companionship). A parent's release surrenders only a parental claim. Approval of a court may be necessary to release a child's claim. A minor, upon reaching majority, may repudiate a release in some instances. A general release can be voided if the releasee:

- Is intoxicated, under the influence of drugs, in shock, or in extreme pain that prevents sufficient understanding of a general release and therefore prevents or voids its execution
- Does not understand the language of the release
- Has not had the opportunity to obtain appropriate legal consultation
- Has been the victim of mental or physical duress
- Has executed the release as a result of misrepresentation or fraud
- Is mentally incompetent and cannot give a valid release. (In this instance, a court-appointed guardian is required to execute a release on behalf of a mental incompetent, and a court must pass on the terms of any settlement.)

▶ CHAPTER REVIEW

1. Medical malpractice insurance is affected by the cyclical nature of the insurance market.
2. *Insurance* is a contract in which the company providing the insurance agrees to assume some of the risks of the insured party for consideration or the payment of a premium. The three primary components of an insurance policy are identification of the covered risks, specification of the amounts payable, and specification of the occurrence.
3. By creating a large pool of individuals, an insurance company can balance its risk—the possibility that loss will occur—enough that it should be able to both cover claims and return a profit to shareholders.
4. The three primary categories of risks are property loss, personal liability, and legal liability.
5. *Occurrence policies* cover all accidents during a policy year, regardless of when they are reported, whereas *claims-made policies* cover claims made or reported during the policy year, no matter when they occurred.

6. Standard liability policies include: (1) insurance agreement, (2) defense and settlement, (3) policy period, and (4) amount payable by the insurance company.

7. Policy conditions: if the insured does not comply with the conditions of the policy, forfeiture of the policy and nonpayment of claims against it could result.

8. Professional liability insurance covers negligence and assault and battery that result from failing to obtain consent to a medical or surgical procedure.

9. Conditions of an insurance policy include notice of occurrence, notice of claim, assistance of the insured, other insurance, assignment, subrogation, changes, and cancellation.

10. Healthcare professionals are encouraged to obtain malpractice insurance because they can be held liable for their own negligence. The drawbacks include the encouragement of being named in malpractice suits.

11. Professional liability does not cover intentional torts and sexual assault.

12. *Self-insurance* is a practice in which a healthcare organization periodically sets aside a certain amount of money to cover malpractice losses and expenses.

13. An injured party may request settlement of a claim prior to instituting legal action.

14. When a claim is settled, the plaintiff signs a *general release*, which states that the plaintiff surrenders the right of action against the defendant.

▶ REVIEW QUESTIONS

1. What is the purpose of an insurance policy?
2. Describe the conditions of an insurance policy.
3. What are the primary components of an insurance policy?
4. What are the primary categories of a risk?
5. What are the distinct parts of an insurance policy?
6. Under what circumstances should a healthcare professional self-insure?
7. Should a board member have personal liability insurance coverage?
8. Describe what acts a professional liability policy covers, as well as the risks it does not cover.

▶ NOTES

1. *New Mexico Physicians Mut. Liab. Co. v. LaMure*, 860 P.2d 734 (N.M. 1993).
2. *American Nursing Ctr. Greenbrook v. Heckler*, 592 F. Supp. 1311, 1312 (D.D.C. 1984).
3. *Id.*
4. AllNurses.com, "Should I Carry Nursing Malpractice (Liability) Insurance?" Updated June 29, 2017. http://allnurses.com/general-nursing-discussion/should-i-carry-391596.html.
5. *Id.*
6. "Nurse Practitioner Liability Claims Costs Rising 2.3% a Year: CAN Health Pro," *Claims Journal*, March 26, 2010. http://www.claimsjournal.com/news/national/2010/03/26/108490.htm.
7. 484 A.2d 670 (N.J. 1984).
8. 430 A.2d 488 (D.C. 1981).
9. 606 F.2d 631 (5th Cir. 1979).
10. *Scottsdale Ins. Co. v. Flowers*, Nos. 06-6385, 06-6412, U.S. Court of App. (6th Ct. App., 2008).
11. 263 Neb. 708, 642 N.W.2d 505 (2002).
12. 864 A.2d 614 (R.I. 2005).
13. 392 F. Supp. 393 (E.D. La. 1975).
14. 192 Cal. Rptr. 593 (Cal. Ct. App. 1983).
15. *New Mexico Physicians Mut. Liab. Co. v. LaMure*, *supra* at 742.
16. *Id.*

© Isak55/Shutterstock

CHAPTER 22

Managed Care and National Health Insurance

🔍 IT'S YOUR GAVEL...

FAILURE TO DISCLOSE FINANCIAL INCENTIVES

The patient in *Shea v. Esensten* died after suffering a heart attack. Although the patient had recently visited his primary care physician and presented symptoms of cardiac problems, including a family history of cardiac trouble, the physician did not refer the patient to a cardiologist. The patient's widow sued the health maintenance organization for failing to disclose the financial incentive system it provided to its physicians to minimize referrals to specialists.[1]

WHAT IS YOUR VERDICT?

▶ LEARNING OBJECTIVES

The reader, upon completion of this chapter, will be able to:

- Describe the common models of managed care organizations.
- Describe the purpose and process of *utilization review*.
- Discuss the purpose and various titles of the Patient Protection and Affordable Care Act (ACA) of 2010.
- Describe various court rulings involving the ACA.

Health care has come a long way from the days of the doctor who made house calls and tended to entire families, often being present for both the births and deaths of many of his patients. Today, mergers, cost controls, regulations, and the inability of many to access health care because of the high cost of insurance premiums, plague the healthcare system. This chapter discusses the role of managed care organizations in the U.S. healthcare system and the current state of national health insurance.

▶ MANAGED CARE

Managed care organizations (MCOs) represent a major shift away from the domination of the fee-for-service system toward networks of providers supplying a full range of services. Managed care is the process of structuring or restructuring the healthcare system in terms of financing, purchasing, delivering, measuring, and documenting a broad range of healthcare services and products. Managed care is nothing new to the U.S. healthcare delivery system; it has been around in some form for decades, and it has not been replaced by the Affordable Care Act.

> The term managed care or managed health-care is used in the United States to describe a group of activities ostensibly intended to reduce the cost of providing health care while improving the quality of that care ("managed care techniques"). It has become the essentially exclusive system of delivering and receiving American health care since its implementation in the early 1980s, and has been largely unaffected by the Affordable Care Act.[2]

The relationships that are being restructured are those among employers, physicians, a wide variety of healthcare organizations, payers, and consumers. The two major constraints of MCOs are (1) limitations on the choice of providers by the consumer, and (2) requirements for prior authorization in order to obtain services. As reviewed in this chapter, managed care comes in a variety of packages.

▶ MODELS OF MANAGED CARE ORGANIZATIONS

There are a wide variety of managed care models that integrate financing and management with the delivery of healthcare services to an enrolled population. The following sections describe some of the common models.

Health Maintenance Organizations

Health maintenance organizations (HMOs) are organized healthcare systems that are responsible for both the financing and the delivery of a broad range of comprehensive health services to an enrolled population. HMOs act both as insurer and provider of healthcare services. They charge employers a fixed premium for each subscriber. An *independent practice association* (IPA)–model HMO provides medical care to its subscribers through contracts it establishes with independent physicians. In a staff-model HMO, the physicians are normally full-time employees of the HMO. Individuals who subscribe to an HMO are often limited to the panel of physicians who have contracted with the HMO to provide services to its subscribers.

Preferred Provider Organizations

Preferred provider organizations (PPOs) are entities through which employer health benefit plans and health insurance carriers contract to purchase healthcare services for covered beneficiaries from a selected group of participating providers. Most states have specific PPO laws that directly regulate such entities. Common characteristics of PPOs include the following:

- Select provider panel
- Negotiated payment rates
- Rapid payment terms
- Utilization management (programs to control the utilization and cost)
- Consumer choice (allows covered beneficiaries to use non-PPO providers for an additional out-of-pocket charge [point-of-service option])

In PPOs, a payer, such as an insurance company, provides incentives to its enrollees to obtain medical care from a panel of providers with whom the payer has contracted a discounted rate.

Exclusive Provider Organizations

Exclusive provider organizations (EPOs) limit their beneficiaries to participating providers for any health-care services.

EPOs use a gatekeeper approach to authorize non–primary care services. The main difference between an HMO and an EPO is that the former is regulated under HMO laws and regulations, whereas the latter is regulated under insurance laws and regulations. Characteristics of EPOs include the following:

- Primary care physicians are reimbursed through capitation payments or other performance-based reimbursement methods.
- Primary care physicians act as gatekeepers.

Point-of-Service Plans

Point-of-service (POS) plans use primary care physicians as gatekeepers to coordinate and control medical care. Subscribers covered under POS plans may decide whether to use HMO benefits or indemnity-style benefits for each instance of care. In other words, the member is allowed to make a coverage choice at the POS, though a patient who chooses a provider outside the plan is responsible for higher copayments.

Experience-Rated HMOs

Under *experience-rated HMO* benefit options, an HMO receives monthly premium payments much as it would under traditional premium-based plans. Typically, to arrive at a final premium rate, there is a settlement process in which the employer is credited with some portion, or all, of the actual utilization and cost of its group. Refunds or additional payments are then calculated and provided to the appropriate party.

Specialty HMOs

Specialty HMOs provide limited components of health-care coverage. Dental HMOs, for example, have become more common as an option to indemnity dental insurance coverage.

Independent Practice Association

An IPA is a legal entity comprising physicians organized for the purpose of negotiating contracts to provide physician services. For example, an IPA might contract with an HMO or a physician–hospital organization. The associated physicians maintain their own practices and do not share services, such as claims, billing, scheduling, accounting, and so forth.

Group Practice

A *physician group* that has only one or a small number of service delivery locations is a group practice. It is completely integrated economically, sharing costs and revenues. Group practices often are either specialty or primary care dominated.

Group Practice Without Walls

A *group practice without walls* is a physician organization formed for the purpose of sharing some administrative and management costs while physicians continue to practice at their own locations, rather than at a centralized location.

Physician–Hospital Organizations

A *physician–hospital organization* (PHO) is a legal entity consisting of a joint venture of physicians and a hospital. It is formed to facilitate managed care contracting, to improve cost management and services, and to create new healthcare resources in the community.

Medical Foundations

In a *medical foundation*, the foundation employs or contracts with physicians to provide care to the foundation's patients.

Management Service Organizations

A *management service organization* (MSO) is an entity that provides administrative and management services, such as practice management, marketing, managed care contracting, accounting, billing, and personnel management, to physicians. The MSO can be hospital affiliated, a hospital–physician joint venture, physician owned, or investor owned.

Vertically Integrated Delivery System

A *vertically integrated delivery system* is any organization (e.g., rehabilitation facility, physician practice) that merges in order to provide a broader range of services to their patients. A vertically integrated delivery system achieves this goal by providing services ranging from primary outpatient care to tertiary inpatient care. An ever-increasing number of vertically integrated delivery systems include such services as preventive medicine programs, community education, home health care, long-term care, rehabilitation, and mental health care.

Horizontal Consolidations

A *horizontal consolidation* involves a merger of similar or identical businesses in the same consumer marketplace. A horizontal merger occurs when two or more healthcare entities combine, offering similar or compatible healthcare services. For example, a new healthcare entity is created when a hospital medical center merges with one or more smaller community hospitals in the same or surrounding communities. This, in turn, allows the new entity to expand into new consumer markets. Each merger of this sort gives rise to legal questions as to whether a proposed merger is permissible. Recognizing a congressional intent to preserve competition by preventing undue market concentration, the courts have focused primarily on the possibility that consolidation will substantially lessen competition.

▶ FEDERALLY QUALIFIED HMO

Many HMOs are federally qualified. Federal qualification, which is entirely voluntary, requires HMOs to meet federal standards for legal and organizational status, financial viability, marketing, and health service delivery systems, as delineated in the federal HMO Act and its implementing regulations. The disadvantage of federal qualification—beyond the fees involved—is that a federally qualified HMO has less flexibility in its benefits package and in developing premium rates.

The standards for federal qualification were introduced in 1973, when Congress enacted Title XIII of the Public Health Service Act, commonly known as the HMO Act.[3] This law was intended to foster the growth of HMOs, which were considered to be a cost-effective method of healthcare delivery.

The law was amended in 1976 to ease some of the restrictions on open enrollment, community rating, and medical staffing. It was amended again in 1978 for financial disclosure and in 1981 for solvency protection. In 1986, certain HMO grant and loan programs were abolished.[4]

The most dramatic amendments, however, occurred in 1988. They permitted federally qualified HMOs to provide up to 10% of their physician services through non-HMO-affiliated physicians and authorized reasonable deductibles for those services. They also repealed the dual choice requirement, effective in 1995; broadened the definition of restrictive state laws; required disclosure of rate-making methods and data; addressed nondiscrimination in the financing of employee plans; deleted the requirement that one-third of the policymaking body be composed of HMO members; and repealed the requirement that the policymaking body include equitable representation from underserved communities.

Federally qualified HMOs must provide or arrange for basic health services for their members as needed and without limitation as to time, cost, frequency, extent, or kind of services actually provided. Basic health services include the following:

- Physician services, including consultant and referral services by a physician
- Inpatient and outpatient services, including short-term rehabilitation services and physical therapy
- Medically necessary emergency health services
- Twenty outpatient visits per member per year for short-term, evaluative, or crisis intervention mental health services
- Medical treatment and referral services
- Diagnostic laboratory and diagnostic and therapeutic radiology services
- Home health services
- Preventive health services, including immunizations and well-child care from birth

▶ STATE HMO LAWS

Most states have enacted comprehensive HMO laws that are often based on the National Association of Insurance Commissioners' Model HMO Act. State laws generally specify what type of entities can apply for a certificate of authority to operate an HMO. Typically, the state insurance department is the primary regulatory body.

Generally, state HMO laws require that an application for a certificate of authority be accompanied by a description of the proposed marketing plan that the regulator must approve. HMO laws generally specify that a schedule of charges and amendments must be filed and approved by the commissioner.

The majority of state HMO laws require that the provision of basic health services includes emergency care, inpatient care, physician care, and outpatient care. State HMO laws contain several provisions designed to protect enrollees in the event that the HMO becomes insolvent. These include deposit, capital, reserve, and net worth requirements. State laws pertaining to HMOs generally require the following:

- The HMO cannot cancel or refuse to renew an enrollee solely because of the individual's health.
- If an individual terminates employment or membership in a group, that person must be permitted to convert to a direct payment basis.
- Grievance procedures must be in place.
- State HMO laws usually condition issuance of a certificate of authority on the submission and approval of a quality assurance program.

▶ CASE MANAGEMENT FIRMS

Case management firms assist employers and insurers in managing catastrophic cases. They identify cases that will become catastrophic, negotiate services and reimbursement with providers who can treat the patient's condition, develop a treatment protocol for the patient, and monitor the treatment. Failure to manage a case appropriately can give rise to a lawsuit and result in damages paid to the plaintiff as noted in a jury award amounting to $7.4 million in a wrongful death lawsuit against Humana HMO.[5] An outline of the case is as follows:

> The Smeliks alleged that the care delivered by Humana and its physicians to Joan Smelik was substandard. Testimony showed that Mrs. Smelik had been under case management when Humana had outsourced that service to another health care provider. But when that contract ended and Humana began handling case management on its own, Mrs. Smelik's case reportedly was not given the necessary extra oversight.[6]

▶ THIRD-PARTY ADMINISTRATORS

A *third-party administrator* (TPA) is a firm that provides services for employers and associations that have group insurance policies. The TPA acts as a liaison between the employer and the insurer. The TPA performs administrative activities, such as claims processing, certifying eligibility, and a preparation of report required by the staff.

▶ UTILIZATION REVIEW

Utilization review (UR) is a process whereby a third-party payer evaluates the medical necessity of a course of treatment. MCOs use a UR process to compare a patient's request for care with what treatment doctors commonly practice in similar medical circumstances. Medical care is considered necessary when it is needed to prevent, diagnose, and treat a patient's medical condition. Generally, UR is performed prospectively, concurrently, or retrospectively.

- *Prospective review*: The payer determines whether to pay for treatment before treatment is initiated. If review of a case reveals that a particular treatment is not medically appropriate or necessary, the payer then makes known to the provider its decision not to reimburse for the recommended medical care.
- *Concurrent review*: This review is performed during the course of treatment. Concurrent review entails monitoring whether medical care continues to be appropriate and necessary. If it is not, the payer will discontinue payment for additional care.
- *Retrospective review*: This type of review is performed after treatment has been completed. If the review indicates that medical care was not necessary, the insurer can deny the claim.

Most insurance companies and MCOs rely on prospective and concurrent UR to determine whether care is necessary and what level of care is appropriate for each patient reviewed. UR has become an accepted and essential part of cost containment.

Case management is an increasingly important aspect of utilization management. It involves identifying, at an early stage, those patients who can be treated more cost effectively in an alternative setting or at a lower level of care without negatively affecting the quality of care. Case management is often necessary in catastrophic or high-cost cases.

Utilization Management Firms

Utilization management firms perform utilization management activities for managed care entities, insurers, or employers. Mental health and dental care are two common types of such firms. In recent years, the regulation of utilization by private review agents or utilization review organizations (UROs) has noticeably increased.

Just as healthcare entities have a corporate duty to select and monitor physicians carefully, they also have a duty to carefully select the URO with which they contract. That duty entails investigating the URO before contracting with it to ensure that its procedures are adequate and its personnel are qualified to perform UR activities.

Negligent UR Decisions

MCOs that perform UR may be found liable for undesirable patient outcomes because of defects or failures in the UR process or because of a negligent UR decision. The first reported case involving liability for UR was *Wickline v. State of California*.[7] In that case, the court stated that a third-party payer of healthcare services could be held legally accountable when medically inappropriate decisions result from defects in the design or implementation of cost-containment mechanisms. Liability in the UR process can arise from several sources, including failure to gather information adequately before making a decision regarding medical necessity, failure to initiate a meaningful dialogue between UR personnel and the treating physician, failure to inform members of their right to appeal an adverse UR decision, and failure to issue a timely UR decision.

► LIABILITY FOR NONPARTICIPATING HOSPITALS

MCOs may be liable for the medical malpractice of nonemployee, participating physicians under an ostensible or apparent agency theory if (1) the patient reasonably views the entity (e.g., hospital) rather than the individual physician as the source of care, and (2) the entity engages in conduct that leads the patient reasonably to believe that the source of care is the entity or that the physician is an employee of the entity.

The doctrine of corporate negligence clearly applies to staff-model HMOs in which the HMO employs the physicians and provides the facility within which they offer care. If an HMO employs physicians, such as in a staff-model HMO, the HMO can be held liable for the negligence of its employees under the doctrine of respondeat superior.

► EMPLOYEE RETIREMENT INCOME SECURITY ACT

Congress enacted the *Employee Retirement Income Security Act of 1974* (ERISA) to ensure that employee welfare and benefit plans conform to a uniform body of benefits law. ERISA sets minimum standards for most voluntarily established pension and health plans in private industry to provide protection for individuals in these plans. ERISA requires plans to provide participants with plan information, including important information about plan features and funding; provides fiduciary responsibilities for those who manage and control plan assets; requires plans to establish a grievance and appeals process for participants to get benefits from their plans; and gives participants the right to sue for benefits and breaches of fiduciary duty.

The law does not, however, regulate the contents of the welfare benefit plans. For example, it does not mandate that specific benefits be provided to beneficiaries. To qualify as an employee benefit plan, the plan must be maintained by an employer or employee

organization for the benefit of its employees. ERISA requires that every plan (1) describe procedures for the allocation of responsibilities for its operation and administration, and (2) specify the basis on which payments are made to and from the plan.

The Consolidated Omnibus Budget Reconciliation Act (COBRA) included an amendment that expanded benefits, providing some workers and their families with the right to continue their health coverage for a limited time under certain circumstances, such as the loss of a job. Another amendment to ERISA is contained in the Health Insurance Portability and Accountability Act (HIPAA), which provides protection for employees and their families who have preexisting medical conditions or who might otherwise suffer discrimination in health coverage based on factors that relate to an individual's health. In general, ERISA does not cover group health plans established or maintained by governmental entities or churches for their employees or plans that are maintained solely to comply with applicable workers' compensation, unemployment, or disability laws.

Although ERISA generally preempts state law affecting employee benefit plans, the following case illustrates that this is not universally true. Ms. Moran, in *Rush Prudential HMO, Inc. v. Moran*,[8] sought treatment from Dr. LaMarre, her primary care physician under her HMO plan (Rush Prudential HMO, Inc.), because of numbness, pain, and decreased mobility in her right shoulder.

During a series of physiotherapy treatments under LaMarre, Moran obtained the name of an out-of-network physician, Dr. Terzis, and submitted a request to Rush for a referral to consult with this physician. Her request was denied. Moran had the consult anyway and was diagnosed with plexopathy and thoracic outlet syndrome. Terzis recommended a more involved and expensive surgery. Two plan physicians recommended a less complicated surgery. LaMarre formally asked Rush to approve Terzis's recommended surgery. Rush denied approval of the surgery. Moran made a written demand to Rush seeking its compliance with the Illinois Health Maintenance Organization Act, Section 4-10, which requires HMOs to provide an independent physician review when a patient's primary care physician disagrees with an HMO about the medical necessity of a proposed treatment. Moran eventually decided to undergo the surgery with Terzis at her own expense. She later submitted the bill to Rush and sought a court order requiring Rush to comply with Section 4-10. Rush moved the case to a federal court citing the statute's conflict with ERISA. The district court agreed with Rush that ERISA preempted Moran's claims and granted summary judgment to Rush. The case eventually reached the

U.S. Supreme Court, which upheld Section 4-10 of the Illinois Health Maintenance Organization Act, which provides a mechanism whereby insured patients are permitted to have an independent physician review enforced when there is disagreement between the HMO and the patient's primary care physician.

▶ REDUCING EXPOSURE TO LIABILITY

Employers, managed care entities, and providers can reduce liability exposure by complying with all formalities, considering contracting through the plan itself, and clearly defining discretionary responsibilities. Employers should seek and employ competent advisers. A managed contract should be developed between the employer and the selected fiduciary that ensures the following:

- The fiduciary is responsible for monitoring its discretionary authority.
- The fiduciary is committed to supplying the employer with data on the various aspects of its performance.
- Proper indemnities are negotiated on behalf of the employer and its employees.
- Hold-harmless clauses are provided for employees for payment for services rendered.
- Financial disclosures are made as appropriate.
- Sufficient reinsurance, fiduciary insurance, and liability insurance are maintained, and proof is supplied to the employer.
- Confidentiality agreements are established and observed.
- Quality assurance programs are maintained.
- Claims and appeal procedures are available, and assurances are given as to the program's operation and improvement.
- A description of the fiduciary's utilization control mechanism, methods for preadmission review of elective procedures, continuous stay review procedures, systems for retrospective review of ancillary services provided, retrospective review of surgical procedures, quality assurance programs, mechanisms for denial of coverage or charges, and methods used for dispute resolution is provided.

▶ HEALTH CARE QUALITY IMPROVEMENT ACT OF 1986

The *Health Care Quality Improvement Act of 1986* (HCQIA) was enacted in part as a response to numerous antitrust suits against participants in peer-review and credentialing activities. Congress passed the act to encourage continued participation in these activities. The purpose of the HCQIA is to provide those persons giving information to professional review bodies and those assisting in review activities limited immunity from damages that may arise as a result of adverse decisions that affect a physician's medical staff privileges. The immunity does not extend to civil rights litigation or suits filed by the United States or an attorney general of a state.

Open Enrollment

Federal HMO regulations require federally qualified HMOs to hold an open enrollment period of not less than 30 days per year, during which the HMO must accept individual applicants for coverage regardless of their health status. Not all state HMO laws require open enrollment periods.

Emergency Care

HMOs can refuse benefit coverage to patients if they determine retrospectively that a patient's condition did not require emergency department care. Of course, hindsight is 20/20. Determining whether one's chest pains are because of diet or a coronary condition requires expensive testing. To refuse a patient care before determining the etiology of a patient's condition could be financially disastrous to an organization. In addition, federal law prohibits hospital emergency departments from turning away patients seeking emergency care. Unfortunately, retrospective denial places the burden on the provider to seek reimbursement from the patient if the insurer denies the charges.

▶ ETHICS IN PATIENT REFERRAL ACT (1989)

In 1989, the *Ethics in Patient Referral Act* (frequently referred to as the Stark bill for its author, Rep. Fortney [Pete] Stark [D-Cal.]) was enacted as part of the Omnibus Budget Reconciliation Act of 1989. Effective January 1, 1992, the act prohibits physicians who have ownership interest or compensation arrangements with a clinical laboratory from referring Medicare patients to that laboratory. The law also requires all Medicare providers to report the names and provider numbers of all physicians or their immediate relatives with ownership interests in the provider entity prior to October 1, 1991. Failure to comply with the disclosure requirements exposes providers to a civil monetary penalty of up to $10,000 per day.

▶ MANAGED CARE AND LEGAL ACTIONS

The following cases describe just a few of the many legal actions involving managed care.

Financial Incentives Disclosed

In 1996, Dr. Linda Peeno, featured in Michael Moore's 2007 film, *Sicko*, testified before Congress regarding her prior work as a medical reviewer for Humana. Her testimony included the following remarks, after which she embarked on a journey to become one of the best-known whistleblowers regarding HMOs and the healthcare industry.

> I am here primarily today to make a public confession. In the spring of 1987, as a physician, I denied a man a necessary operation that would have saved his life and thus caused his death. No person and no group has held me accountable for this, because in fact, what I did was I saved a company a half a million dollars for this.

Dr. Peeno, now a physician in Louisville, Kentucky, remains unsanctioned by her peers and unpunished by the justice system for the act described above and others she admitted to committing because the medical profession remains self-regulating and the medical licensing boards are comprised mostly of physicians. Moreover, courts are generally reluctant to get involved with the internal affairs of a professional society unless the sanctions they impose violate public policy.

The medical community has turned its attention to the authority of state medical boards to police improper physician expert testimony in medical malpractice actions. The discussion has been broadened to consider whether or not the presentation of testimony constitutes the carrying out of the practice of medicine. Depending on the state, some cases have held that the "carrying out" requirement means that the medical judgment must affect or have the possibility of affecting the patient. For example, in *Murphy v. Board of Medical Examiners*,[9] an Arizona court held that a physician performing prospective UR was practicing medicine because his decisions "could affect" a patient's health. Dr. Peeno was engaging in prospective UR. However, several federal courts have held that neither prospective nor retrospective review constitutes the practice of medicine.[10]

The public has the right to expect expert physicians to be accurate and truthful when giving testimony.

If the profession cannot police itself, then the states will be forced to intervene in order to protect the public from other unrepentant Dr. Peenos.

Insurer and Tortfeasor

The plaintiff in *Karsten v. Kaiser Foundation Health Plan*[11] brought a legal action against her HMO for malpractice. The plaintiff alleged that Kaiser's negligent care caused her to deliver a premature stillborn fetus. Although Kaiser denied any wrongdoing, the jury awarded the plaintiff $210,000 in damages. At trial, the plaintiff introduced hospital bills incurred as a result of the incident in question. Kaiser had paid these bills prior to trial. Although Kaiser agreed that, based on its contract with the plaintiff, it was required to pay these bills regardless of fault, Kaiser objected to the medical bills as part of the plaintiff's compensatory damages because they had already been paid by Kaiser.

The issue under Virginia law was: Does the collateral source rule allow the plaintiff to recover compensatory damages for medical bills previously satisfied by her HMO?

The U.S. District Court held that, under Virginia law, the collateral source rule allows a member to receive from the HMO compensatory damages for medical bills that the HMO previously paid under the HMO contract, when the HMO was also liable to the plaintiff as a tortfeasor. The court focused on the nature of each payment Kaiser was being asked to make. The first payment made by Kaiser was for the plaintiff's medical bills. The defendant made this payment in its capacity as the plaintiff's insurer. The defendant was then being asked to pay these same medical expenses as compensatory damages. Even though the defendant was being asked to pay the same damages twice, it is patent that the nature of the two payments is different.

Benefit Denials

The California Supreme Court has ruled that insurers must inform beneficiaries of their right to contest a benefit denial. The court in *Davis v. Blue Cross of N. California*[12] held that the insurer breached its duty of good faith and fair dealing by failing to adequately apprise an insured of his rights under the policy's arbitration clause.

The insured in *Katskee v. Blue Cross/Blue Shield*[13] brought action against the health insurer for breach of contract. In January 1990, on recommendation of her gynecologist, Dr. Roffman, the appellant consulted with Dr. Lynch regarding her family's history of breast and ovarian cancer and particularly her health in relation to such a history. After examining the appellant and investigating her family's medical history, Lynch diagnosed her as suffering from a genetic condition known as breast-ovarian carcinoma syndrome. Lynch then recommended that the appellant have a total abdominal hysterectomy and bilateral salpingo-oophorectomy. Roffman concurred with Lynch's diagnosis and agreed that the recommended surgery was the most medically appropriate treatment available.

Initially, Blue Cross/Blue Shield sent a letter to the appellant and indicated that it might pay for the surgery. Two weeks before surgery, Dr. Mason, the chief medical officer for Blue Cross/Blue Shield, wrote to the appellant and stated that Blue Cross/Blue Shield would not cover the cost of the surgery. Nonetheless, the appellant had the surgery. She filed an action for breach of contract, seeking to recover $6,022.57 in costs associated with the surgery. Blue Cross/Blue Shield filed a motion for summary judgment. The district court granted the motion. It found that there was no genuine issue of material fact and that the policy did not cover the appellant's surgery.

The appellant filed a notice of appeal to the Nebraska Court of Appeals, contending that the district court erred in finding that no genuine issue of material fact existed and in granting summary judgment in favor of the appellee. Blue Cross/Blue Shield denied coverage because it concluded that the appellant's condition did not constitute an illness and, thus, the treatment she received was not medically necessary.

On further appeal, the Nebraska Supreme Court held that the insured's breast-ovarian carcinoma syndrome was an illness within the meaning of the health insurance policy, notwithstanding the insurer's contention that the syndrome was merely predisposition to cancer. The court found that whether a policy is ambiguous is a matter of law for the court to determine. A general principle of construction, which the courts apply to ambiguous insurance policies, holds that an ambiguous policy will be construed in favor of the insured. The language used in the policy at issue in the present case was not reasonably susceptible to differing interpretations and thus not ambiguous. The issue, then, becomes whether the appellant's condition—breast-ovarian carcinoma syndrome—constituted an illness. For women at an inordinately high risk for ovarian cancer, such as the appellant, the standard of care may require radical surgery that involves the removal of the uterus, ovaries, and fallopian tubes. Blue Cross/Blue Shield did not provide any evidence disputing the premise that the origin of this condition is in the genetic makeup of the individual and that, in its natural development, it is likely

to produce devastating results. The medical evidence regarding the nature of breast-ovarian carcinoma syndrome persuaded the court that the appellant suffered from a bodily disorder or disease and, thus, suffered from an illness as defined by the insurance policy. Blue Cross/Blue Shield was, therefore, not entitled to judgment as a matter of law.

False and Misleading Statements

The plaintiff in *Drolet v. Healthsource, Inc.*[14] was a beneficiary of a healthcare plan administered by her employer, the Mitre Corporation. The plaintiff brought a class-action complaint alleging that Healthsource New Hampshire, Inc., and its parent corporation, Healthsource, Inc., are liable under ERISA for several materially false and misleading statements that Healthsource New Hampshire allegedly made to the plan's beneficiaries.

The benefits provided by the plan require a member to choose a primary care physician to be responsible for providing the member with routine medical care and coordinating the member's specialty care referrals. In defining the term *primary care physician*, the agreement emphasized that the physician has a contractual relationship with Healthsource, which does not interfere with the exercise of the physician's independent medical judgment. The plaintiff contended that the physician–patient relationship is compromised by various undisclosed financial incentives that are provided to the plan's physicians to reduce expenditures on specialty care services. Among these incentives, the plaintiff alleged, are referral funds that permit a physician to earn up to 33% in additional income by minimizing the use of specialty services such as diagnostic tests, referrals, and hospitalizations. The plaintiff argued that the company breached the fiduciary duty it allegedly owed to the Mitre plan's participants and beneficiaries under ERISA.

The duty to disclose material information is the core of a fiduciary's responsibility. Therefore, if Healthsource New Hampshire made material misrepresentations in the group subscriber agreement and other plan documents, it can be enjoined under ERISA to prevent further breaches of its fiduciary duty. Regulations do not authorize Healthsource New Hampshire, as a fiduciary, from making misrepresentations to beneficiaries.

▶ PRICE FIXING

Price fixing is considered a per se violation of the antitrust laws. Price fixing occurs when two or more competitors come together to decide on a price that will be charged for services or goods. The per se rule applies to restraints in trade that are so inimical to competition and so unjustified that they are presumed to be unreasonable and, therefore, are illegal. Examples of per se violations include price fixing, horizontal market allocation, tying, and group boycotts.

The provider-controlled MCO is at significant antitrust risk when setting provider reimbursement and bargaining with payers. There is a danger that provider-controlled organizations will be viewed as a horizontal conspiracy between competitors that acts as a mechanism for price fixing.

Even without organizational control, providers may have practical control of the plan.

One of the leading cases involving price fixing is *Maricopa County Medical Society v. Arizona University*,[15] a U.S. Supreme Court case that involved the exercise of provider control over the level of physician reimbursement. Because the physicians had no financial stake in the success of the plan, the Supreme Court found that the maximum fee schedule set by the physicians constituted illegal price fixing.

In *Maine v. Alliance Healthcare, Inc.*,[16] an entity composed of four hospitals and their affiliated physician groups was formed to contract with managed care plans. The state attorney general charged that the entity was engaged in price fixing because it allegedly forced HMOs to pay physicians on a fee-for-service basis instead of a capitation basis. In the resulting consent decree, the entity agreed to cease collectively negotiating prices for its members. In *Hassan v. Independent Practice Assoc.*,[17] the court found that a capitated IPA arrangement was appropriate in the following circumstances:

- Physicians shared the risk of loss through acceptance of capitation payments.
- The plan did not dictate what participating physicians could charge to nonplan patients, including those belonging to competing health carriers.
- The plan constituted a new product, namely, guaranteed comprehensive physician services, for a prepaid premium different from fee-for-services.

In this context, the court held that the maximum reimbursement rates established by the IPA were lawful as a necessary part of the joint venture's integration of resources.

▶ MARKET POWER

Whenever an MCO possesses significant market power or deals with a group that has significant market power, antitrust implications should be considered.

To determine market power, it is necessary first to identify the market in which the entity exercises power. For antitrust purposes, the relevant market has two components: (1) a product component and (2) a geographic component.

Product Market

The relevant product market involves the product or service at issue and all substantially acceptable substitutes for it. The relevant product market for MCOs is the market for healthcare financing. Broadly defined, this market includes traditional insurers, HMOs, PPOs, IPAs, and so on, along with their subscriber members.

Market power results from the ability to cut back the market's total supply and then raise prices because of consumer demand for the product. Generally, the market in healthcare financing is competitive because the customers can switch companies readily, new suppliers can enter the market quickly, and existing suppliers can expand their sales rapidly.

Geographic Market

The relevant geographic market is the market area in which the seller operates and to which the purchaser can practically turn for supplies. The primary factors that courts have examined to determine the geographic scope of the market for hospital services are as follows:

- Patient flow statistics
- Location of physicians who admit patients
- Determinations of health planners
- Public perception

Provider Exclusion

Providers who are excluded from managed care systems may bring group boycott charges alleging that the exclusion constitutes an illegal restraint of trade. Traditionally, group boycotts have been considered inherently anticompetitive and, therefore, characterized as per se violations of the Sherman Antitrust Act.[18] In *Northwest Wholesale Stationers, Inc. v. Pacific Stationery and Printing Co.*,[19] the U.S. Supreme Court identified three characteristics as indicative of per se illegal boycotts:

1. The boycott cuts off access to a supply, facility, or market necessary to enable the victim firm to compete.
2. The defendant possesses a dominant market position.

3. The practices are not justified by plausible arguments as enhancing overall efficiency or competition.

Essentially, competitors who agree with each other not to deal with a supplier or distributor if it continues to serve a competitor whom they both seek to injure are in violation of the Sherman Antitrust Act.

Antitrust and Market Share

Competition between HMOs can bring about market share actions in antitrust. For example, in *U.S. Healthcare, Inc. v. Healthsource, Inc.*,[20] several HMOs—U.S. Healthcare, Inc.; U.S. Healthcare of Massachusetts, Inc.; and U.S. Healthcare of New Hampshire, Inc. (collectively U.S. Healthcare)—brought an action against Healthsource, Inc. (also an HMO), alleging that an exclusive dealing clause in Healthsource's service agreements with physicians violated antitrust laws. Both sides are engaged in providing medical services through HMOs in New Hampshire.

Healthsource, founded in 1985 and an IPA-model HMO, was the first HMO established in New Hampshire. Aware that other HMOs were considering marketing in New Hampshire, Healthsource, in order to maintain its market share, offered its panel of physicians greater compensation if they agreed to an exclusive contract. Healthsource's new agreement provided the following optional paragraph:

> 11.01 Exclusive Services of Physicians. Physician agrees during the term of this agreement not to serve as a participating physician for any other HMO plan; this shall not, however, prevent Physician from providing professional courtesy coverage arrangements for brief periods of time or emergency services to members of other HMO plans.[21]

U.S. Healthcare entered the New Hampshire market by applying for and obtaining a license on February 21, 1991, to market its HMO in New Hampshire. U.S. Healthcare claimed a per se violation of the Sherman Antitrust Act, in that the exclusivity clause consisted of a group boycott.

The U.S. Court of Appeals held that the exclusive dealing clause in Healthsource's service agreements with physicians did not give rise to a per se violation of the Sherman Antitrust Act. The court found that there was no evidence of a horizontal agreement among Healthsource's physicians. The exclusivity agreement challenged by U.S. Healthcare was vertical in form. It is "clear that a purely vertical arrangement, by which (for example) a supplier or dealer makes an arrangement, exclusively to supply or serve a manufacturer, is not a group boycott. Were the law otherwise, every distributor or retailer who agreed with a manufacturer to handle only one brand of television or bicycle would be engaged in a group boycott of other manufacturers."[22]

The competitors of Healthsource, Inc., failed to establish violation of the Sherman Antitrust Act under the rule of reason. U.S. Healthcare asserted that the exclusivity clause completely foreclosed U.S. Healthcare and any other non-staff HMO from operation in New Hampshire. Although the number of physicians tied to Healthsource represented 25% of the total number of primary care physicians practicing in the state of New Hampshire, a significant number of physicians were not tied to an exclusive arrangement with Healthsource. In addition, physicians who signed into the exclusivity contract were not tied in permanently. U.S. Healthcare could have competed for Healthsource physicians by offering greater financial incentives to switch over. Furthermore, there is a constant stream of new physicians entering the marketplace, who are a source for recruitment for any competitor. Absent the showing of a properly defined market in which Healthsource could approach monopoly size, there was no reason to consider the geographic dimension of the market.

▶ NATIONAL HEALTH INSURANCE

The declining trust in the nation's ability to deliver quality health care is evidenced by a system caught up in the morass of managed care companies, which have in some instances inappropriately devised ways to deny healthcare benefits to their constituency. This, coupled with the increased cost of insurance premiums and of health care itself, leads to a lack of or inadequate insurance coverage for many. The vast number of un- and underinsured Americans has led to demands for changes in the way the healthcare system functions in the United States.

Congress, after months of contentious debate, by a slim margin enacted the Patient Protection and Affordable Care Act (ACA), often referred to as Obamacare. Its dual purposes were to increase by approximately 30 million people the number of Americans covered by health insurance and to lower the costs associated with health insurance. The purpose of the ACA was to transform U.S. health insurance and make it more affordable through shared responsibility and to eliminate discriminatory acts such as exclusion because of preexisting conditions, health status, and gender.

Upon being signed into law, of the 10 titles that the Act contains in its 900 pages, several reforms were put into place immediately. The following are those reforms:

- Eliminate lifetime and unreasonable annual limits on benefits.
- Prohibit rescissions of health insurance policies.
- Provide assistance for those who are uninsured because of preexisting conditions.
- Require coverage of preventive services and immunizations.
- Extend dependent coverage up to age 26 years.
- Develop uniform coverage documents so consumers can make equal comparisons when shopping for health insurance.
- Cap insurance companies' nonmedical, administrative expenditures.
- Ensure consumers have access to an effective appeals process, and provide a place to turn for help in navigating the appeals process and assessing their coverage.
- Create a temporary reinsurance program to support coverage for early retirees.
- Establish an Internet portal to assist Americans in identifying coverage options.
- Facilitate administrative simplification to lower health system costs.

The ACA's provisions were implemented on a rolling basis, with some changes becoming effective immediately and others taking effect in subsequent years.

Since implementation of the ACA began, political controversy has continued to raise doubts regarding what direction and form of coverage will be available to the general public. The future of national health insurance in its present form will continue to evolve. A variety of cases that have occurred as a result of the ACA are reviewed next.

Act Titles

Most of the ACA's provisions contained in the titles did not go into effect until 2014, because those provisions would take some time to implement.

Title I. Quality Affordable Health Care for All Americans

This Act puts individuals, families and small business owners in control of their health care. It reduces premium costs for millions of working families and small businesses by providing hundreds of billions of dollars in tax relief—the largest middle class tax cut for health care in history. It also reduces what

families will have to pay for health care by capping out-of-pocket expenses and requiring preventive care to be fully covered without any out-of-pocket expense. For Americans with insurance coverage who like what they have, they can keep it. Nothing in this act or anywhere in the bill forces anyone to change the insurance they have, period.

Americans without insurance coverage will be able to choose the insurance coverage that works best for them in a new open, competitive insurance market—the same insurance market that every member of Congress will be required to use for their insurance. The insurance exchange will pool buying power and give Americans new affordable choices of private insurance plans that have to compete for their business based on cost and quality. Small business owners will not only be able to choose insurance coverage through this exchange, but will receive a new tax credit to help offset the cost of covering their employees.

It keeps insurance companies honest by setting clear rules that rein in the worst insurance industry abuses. And it bans insurance companies from denying insurance coverage because of a person's preexisting medical conditions while giving consumers new power to appeal insurance company decisions that deny doctor-ordered treatments covered by insurance.

The Secretary has the authority to implement many of these new provisions to help families and small business owners have the information they need to make the choices that work best for them.

Title II. The Role of Public Programs

The Act extends Medicaid while treating all States equally. It preserves CHIP, the successful children's insurance plan, and simplifies enrollment for individuals and families.

It enhances community-based care for Americans with disabilities and provides States with opportunities to expand home care services to people with long-term care needs.

The Act gives flexibility to States to adopt innovative strategies to improve care and the coordination of services for Medicare and Medicaid beneficiaries. And it saves taxpayer money by reducing prescription drug costs and payments to subsidize care for uninsured

Americans, as more Americans gain insurance under reform.

The Secretary has the authority to work with states and other partners to strengthen key public programs.

Title III. Improving the Quality and Efficiency of Health Care

The Act will protect and preserve Medicare as a commitment to America's seniors. It will save thousands of dollars in drug costs for Medicare beneficiaries by closing the coverage gap called the "donut hole." Doctors, nurses and hospitals will be incentivized to improve care and reduce unnecessary errors that harm patients. And beneficiaries in rural America will benefit as the Act enhances access to healthcare services in underserved areas.

The Act takes important steps to make sure that we can keep the commitment of Medicare for the next generation of seniors by ending massive overpayments to insurance companies that cost American taxpayers tens of billions of dollars per year. As the numbers of Americans without insurance falls, the Act saves taxpayer dollars by keeping people healthier before they join the program and reducing Medicare's need to pay hospitals to care for the uninsured. And to make sure that the quality of care for seniors drives all of our decisions, a group of doctors and healthcare experts, not Members of Congress, will be tasked with coming up with their best ideas to improve quality and reduce costs for Medicare beneficiaries.

The Secretary has the authority to take steps to strengthen the Medicare program and implement reforms to improve the quality and efficiency of health care.

Title IV. Prevention of Chronic Disease and Improving Public Health

The Act will promote prevention, wellness, and the public health and provides an unprecedented funding commitment to these areas. It directs the creation of a national prevention and health promotion strategy that incorporates the most effective and achievable methods to improve the health status of Americans and reduce the incidence of preventable illness and disability in the United States.

The Act empowers families by giving them tools to find the best science-based nutrition information, and it makes prevention and screenings a priority by waiving copayments for America's seniors on Medicare.

The Secretary has the authority to coordinate with other Departments, develop and implement a prevention and health promotion strategy, and work to ensure more Americans have access to critical preventive health services.

Title V. Health Care Workforce

The Act funds scholarships and loan repayment programs to increase the number of primary care physicians, nurses, physician assistants, mental health providers, and dentists in the areas of the country that need them most. With a comprehensive approach focusing on retention and enhanced educational opportunities, the Act combats the critical nursing shortage. And through new incentives and recruitment, the Act increases the supply of public health professionals so that the United States is prepared for health emergencies.

The Act provides state and local governments flexibility and resources to develop health workforce recruitment strategies. And it helps to expand critical and timely access to care by funding the expansion, construction, and operation of community health centers throughout the United States.

The Secretary has the authority to take action to strengthen many existing programs that help support the primary care workforce.

Title VI. Transparency and Program Integrity

The Act helps patients take more control of their health care decisions by providing more information to help them make decisions that work for them. And it strengthens the doctor–patient relationship by providing doctors access to cutting edge medical research to help them and their patients make the decisions that work best for them.

It brings greater transparency to nursing homes to help families find the right place for their loved ones and enhances training for nursing home staff so that the quality of care continuously improves. The Act promotes nursing home safety by encouraging self corrections of errors, requiring background checks for employees who provide direct care and by encouraging innovative programs that prevent and eliminate elder abuse.

The Act reins in waste, fraud, and abuse by imposing tough new disclosure requirements to identify high-risk providers, who have defrauded the American taxpayer. It gives states new authority to prevent providers who have been penalized in one state from setting up in another. And it gives states flexibility to propose and test tort reforms that address several criteria, including reducing health care errors, enhancing patient safety, encouraging efficient resolution of disputes, and improving access to liability insurance.

The Secretary has new and improved authority to promote transparency and ensure that every dollar in the Act and in existing programs is spent wisely and well.

Title VII. Improving Access to Innovative Medical Therapies

The Act promotes innovation and saves consumers money. It extends drug discounts to hospitals and communities that serve low-income patients. And it creates a pathway for the creation of generic versions of biological drugs so that doctors and patients have access to effective and lower cost alternatives.

The Secretary of Health and Human Services has the authority to implement these provisions to help make medications more affordable.

Title VIII. CLASS Act

The Act provides Americans with a new option to finance long-term services and care in the event of a disability.

It is a self-funded and voluntary long-term care insurance choice. Workers will pay in premiums in order to receive a daily cash benefit if they develop a disability. Patient need will be based on difficulty in performing basic activities such as bathing or dressing. The benefit is flexible: it could be used for a range of community support services, from respite care to home care.

No taxpayer funds will be used to pay benefits under this provision. The program will actually reduce Medicaid spending, as people are able to continue working and living in their homes and not enter nursing homes. Safeguards will be put in place to ensure its premiums are enough to cover its costs.

The Secretary has the authority to establish the CLASS Program.

Title IX. Revenue Provisions

The Act makes health care more affordable for families and small business owners by providing the largest middle class tax cuts for health care in American history. Tens of millions of families will benefit from new tax credits which will help them reduce their premium costs and purchase insurance. Families making less than $250,000 will see their taxes cut by hundreds of billions of dollars.

When enacted, health reform is completely paid for and will reduce the deficit by more than one hundred billion dollars in the next ten years.

This title will be implemented by the U.S. Department of the Treasury.

Title X. Strengthening Quality

The Act reauthorizes the Indian Health Care Improvement Act (ICHIA) which provides health care services to American Indians and Alaska Natives. It will modernize the Indian health care system and improve health care for 1.9 million American Indians and Alaska Natives.

The Secretary, in consultation with the Indian Health Service, has the authority to implement the Indian Health Care Improvement Act.

—Reproduced from www.healthcare.gov/law/full/index.html

Court Challenges and Rulings

Soon after the president signed the ACA into law, the legal battles began. The initial challenges were at first viewed as essentially harmless; however, as more states joined the dispute, a central theme emerged: the worry that if Congress had the power to require its citizens to follow this law and its mandates (specifically, the requirement to purchase health insurance), then it could basically require Americans to buy food, for example, deemed healthy for them.

Finally, the Supreme Court accepted a suit brought by Florida and 25 other states in addition to a challenge by the National Federation of Independent Business. On June 28, 2012, in a five-to-four ruling, the Court upheld the major portions of the ACA. The decision agreed that the requirement for nearly all Americans to buy health insurance is permissible under Congress's taxing authority. The decision created state-run *insurance exchanges* where Americans would be able to buy private insurance at a more affordable price.

The ACA requires insurance companies to provide improved access to preventive services, and it provides refundable tax credits for those with incomes between 100% and 400% of the federal poverty level (FPL).

The high court did excise one major portion of the law, which required states to expand their Medicaid coverage, in a joint federal–state effort, to families with incomes up to 133% of the FPL and who are not entitled to Medicare. The Court held that the law's requirement that states rapidly extend coverage or lose existing federal payments was unduly coercive. Most state governors have reservations about expansions, in spite of the federal government's promise of covering 100% of the cost of new eligible beneficiaries between 2014 and 2017. Their major concerns center around questions such as whether or nor a state may opt out and then opt back in at a later date and whether a state can partially participate by raising the income cutoff to a level lower than the law's 133%.

If many states opt out, the cost of the health law would decrease, as would the number of new beneficiaries. This would defeat two of the goals of the ACA: expanding access to insurance coverage and controlling the rising cost of health care.

In response to the Supreme Court decision, the House voted on July 11, 2012 (for the 33rd time) to repeal the law in its entirety. This was viewed at the time as a purely symbolic gesture.

As of this writing, the U.S. Court of Appeals for the District of Columbia, on appeal from the United States District Court, ruled that the insurance subsidies are illegal in three dozen states. Several hours after that ruling, the U.S. Court of Appeals for the Fourth District in Richmond in *King v. Burwell*[23] handed down a contradictory ruling by holding that it is not specified as to whether the subsidies should be available in states that declined to set up marketplaces. Meanwhile, President Obama asked the full D.C. District Court to review the *Halbig v. Burwell*[24] case.

Affordable Care Act Controversy

Controversy continues to swirl around the ACA by politicians, insurers, and policyholders. The success of the ACA is based on the premise that when more people sign up for health insurance, the lower costs associated with healthy policyholders will help defray the costs associated with those who have more costly medical conditions. However, an increasing number of insurance companies have decided not to provide coverage in certain markets because of the excessive losses they are experiencing due to enrollment numbers that are lower than projected. Insurers claim that premiums cannot keep up

with costs associated with the claims made. Those who have failed to obtain policies have argued that the costs are too high even for those who qualify for subsidized premiums.

Both political parties continue to look for ways to address the problems that are emerging as health insurance premiums continue to rise. The high costs associated with the ACA have led to a dwindling number of insurers willing to serve geographical locations associated with high-risk patients who access health care more frequently, often due to age, thus driving up the costs to insurers. Fewer insurance companies are willing to take on the risks associated with the ACA. Aetna Inc., for example, is expected to pull out of Delaware's health insurance marketplace in 2018.

▶ VETERANS CARE

I hate all the bungling as I do sin, but particularly bungling in politics, which leads to the misery and ruin of many thousands and millions of people.

—Johann Wolfgang von Goethe

The Veterans Health Administration (VA) provides healthcare benefits for over 8.76 million veterans at more than 1,700 sites. Detailed information about the benefits program can be found at www.va.gov/health/. Although there are a lot of happy endings in the care provided, there remain a variety of problems in the system including ethical issues, inadequate staffing, long waits for care, falsified records, and in some cases, denial of benefits, as noted in the following *reality check*.

Improvement of the quality of health care for veterans has been making progress. President Obama signed a healthcare bill to provide easier access to health benefits in response to systemic problems in the delay, as well as the care and treatment of veterans. The bill allows for hiring additional health professionals to help meet the demand for more timely care. The bill will also make it less complicated to discipline VA executives who are negligent or inadequately performing their duties and responsibilities. The legislation is in response to reports of veterans dying while waiting for appointments. President Trump, as did President Obama, continues to make progress by improving access to quality care for veterans by signing a bill that extended the stopgap services for veterans to go outside the VA medical system for care. There is still much more to be done as progress continues. The reader is encouraged to follow the progress by connecting with the veterans administration's official website at https://www.va.gov.

☑ *VETERAN DENIED DENTAL CARE*

Marc arrived early to survey the Veterans Hospital in a major city. Prior to entering the hospital, Marc noticed several vets sitting near the entrance to the hospital. As was the norm with Marc, he always arrived early so he could chat with the vets about their healthcare benefits before beginning his day's work. Most seemed satisfied. Joe, one of the veterans, opening his mouth wide to show Marc, said, "Look at my teeth. [He had but a few decayed teeth in his mouth.] They won't fix them because they are not considered a war-related injury." He turned his head sideways, and Marc noticed that an ear was missing. Joe, with a big grin observing Marc's eyes looking at his head, continued, "Now this ear, well as you can see, it's gone." The vets watching and listening to Joe's war story all had smiles on their faces. Joe continued, "Marc, you look worried about my missing ear? I lost it somewhere during the Viet Nam War. I woke up in a hospital tent and it was gone. No one told me until I asked for a mirror to shave." Joe and his fellow vets all cracked up laughing. Joe continued, "I was, however, able to get a prosthesis. It needs some work, so I didn't wear it. I guess they will provide me with a new one. You see, I am able to get care for it because it is a war-related injury, but I really could use some teeth."

When Marc began his survey, he queried hospital staff about Joe's teeth. A hospital manager replied, "It's hospital policy. The present condition of Joe's teeth is not due to a war-related injury, so there is nothing we can do for him." The manager did, however, suggest Joe could go to the University Hospital Dental School, which was only a few blocks away, and get a set of false teeth that should be relatively inexpensive.

Marc asked to see the hospital's dental area. Following a tour of the dental suite, Marc commented, "This is the most modern dental facility I have ever seen." The staff was happy that Marc was pleased with the facility. After observing ample staff, workspace, modern equipment, top-of-the-line dental chairs, and unoccupied rooms, he asked, "Are you open for business? Where are the patients?" The staff in unison responded, "Oh yes, we are open but we don't have any patients at the moment. We should have a few later." The staff proceeded to discuss with enthusiasm the wide variety of dental procedures they could provide, including complicated extractions, implants, and dentures.

Later, Bill, one of the dentists, asked to speak privately with Marc. The dentist proceeded to explain his disgust with a policy that forbids him from providing care for Joe, saying, "We have all this new equipment and we ourselves are sitting here idle."

🔍 *THE COURT'S DECISION*

The U.S. Court of Appeals for the Eighth Circuit agreed that knowledge of financial incentives that affect a physician's decisions to refer patients to specialists is material information requiring disclosure, and it reversed a lower court's dismissal of the claim.

In sum, we believe Mrs. Shea has stated a claim against Medics for breaching the fiduciary obligation to disclose all the material facts affecting her husband's health care interests. When an HMO's financial incentives discourage a treating doctor from providing essential health care referrals for conditions covered under the benefit plan structure, the incentives must be disclosed and the failure to do so is a breach of ERISA's fiduciary duties.[25]

▶ CHAPTER REVIEW

1. *Managed care* is the process of structuring or restructuring the healthcare system in terms of financing, purchasing, delivering, measuring, and documenting a broad range of healthcare services and products.
2. *Health maintenance organizations* (HMOs) are the most highly regulated form of managed care organizations (MCOs) and are health systems that are responsible for the financing and delivery of a wide range of comprehensive services to their enrolled populations.
3. *Independent practice association* (IPA) models provide care to subscribers through contracts with independent physicians.
4. Staff models normally contract with physicians as full-time employees.
5. Entities through which employer health benefit plans and health insurance carriers contract to purchase services for covered beneficiaries from a selected group of providers are called *preferred provider organizations* (PPOs). *Exclusive provider organizations* (EPOs) limit beneficiaries to participating providers.
6. IPAs are legal entities of physicians who have organized to negotiate contracts to provide their services. Group practices are physician groups that have only one or a small number of service delivery locations; whereas, in a group practice without walls, physicians organize to share administrative and management costs but practice at their own locations.

7. *Management service organizations* (MSOs) provide services such as practice management, marketing, managed care contracting, billing, and personnel management for physicians.

8. A *vertically integrated delivery system* is any organization (e.g., rehabilitation facility, physician practice) that merges to provide a broader range of services to patients.

9. A *horizontal consolidation* involves a merger of similar or identical businesses in the same consumer marketplace. A new healthcare entity, for example, is created when a hospital medical center merges with one or more smaller community hospitals in the same or surrounding communities.

10. Federal qualification of HMOs is voluntary, and those that are federally qualified must provide or arrange for basic services for members as needed and without limitations on time, cost, frequency, extent, or nature of services provided.

11. Most state HMO laws require that an application for a certificate of authority be accompanied by a description of proposed marketing plans. A regulator must approve this plan.

12. *Utilization review* (UR) is a process through which a third-party payer assesses the medical necessity of a course of treatment. Prospective review is the determination of whether to pay for a treatment before the treatment is administered, concurrent review takes place during the treatment, and retrospective review takes place after the treatment.

13. Congress passed the *Health Care Quality Improvement Act* (HCQIA) of 1986 to encourage continued participation in peer-review and credentialing activities. The Act grants immunity to persons who supply to professional review bodies information that may result in adverse decisions against a physician.

14. A *fiduciary* is obligated to deal fairly and honestly with plan members. The duty not to mislead is derived both from the common law of trusts and the statutory language in the *Employee Retirement Income Security Act of 1974.*

15. *Price fixing* is when two or more competitors collude to decide on the price that will be charged for services or goods. For MCOs, there is a danger that provider-controlled organizations will be seen as a horizontal conspiracy between competitors that acts as a mechanism for price fixing.

16. The Affordable Care Act (ACA) is designed to increase the number of Americans covered by health insurance, while decreasing the cost of the insurance. Controversy, however, continues to swirl around the ACA by politicians, insurers, and policyholders.

▶ REVIEW QUESTIONS

1. Describe the common models of managed care organizations.
2. Describe the difference between a vertically integrated delivery system and a *horizontal consolidation* healthcare delivery system.
3. Describe the purpose and process of *utilization review.*
4. Describe the various titles of the ACA.
5. Describe the various court rulings in the ACA.
6. Describe the purpose of price fixing as discussed in this chapter.

▶ NOTES

1. 107 F.3d 625 (8th Cir. 1997).
2. "Managed care," https://en.wikipedia.org/wiki/Managed_care.
3. 42 U.S.C. § 300 (1995).
4. See 42 U.S.C. § 300e (1995) (Historical and Statutory Notes).
5. Physicians for a National Health Plan, "Jury Awards $7.4 Million in Wrongful Death Lawsuit Against Humana HMO," July 21, 2005. http://www.pnhp.org/news/2005/july/jury-awards-74-million-in-wrongful-death-lawsuit-against-humana-hmo.
6. "Texas Jury Finds Humana HMO Liable in Wrongful Death Lawsuit," *Insurance Journal*, July 21, 2005. http://www.insurancejournal.com/news/southcentral/2005/07/21/57517.htm.
7. 239 Cal. Rptr. 810 (Cal. Ct. App. 1986).
8. 536 U.S. 355 (2002).
9. 949 P.2d 530, 535 (Ariz. Ct. App. 1997).
10. *Adnan Varol, M.D., P.C. v. Blue Cross Blue Shield of Mich.*, 708 F. Supp. 826 (E.D. Mich. 1989); *Corcoran v. United Health Care*, 956 F.2d 1321 (5th Cir. 1992).
11. 808 F. Supp. 1253 (E.D. Va. 1992).
12. 600 P.2d 1060 (Cal. 1979).
13. 515 N.W.2d 645 (Neb. 1994).
14. 968 F. Supp. 757 (D.C. N.H. 1997).
15. 457 U.S. 332 (1982).
16. 1991-1 Trade Cas. (CCH) || 69,339.

17. 698 F. Supp. 679 (D. Mich. 1988).

18. *Eastern States Retail Lumber Dealers Ass'n v. United States*, 234 U.S. 600 (1914).

19. 472 U.S. 284 (1985).

20. 986 F.2d 589 (1st Cir. 1993).

21. *Id.* at 592.

22. *Id.* at 594.

23. *Jacqueline Halbig v. Sylvia Mathews Burwell*, No. 14-5018 (D.C. Cir. 2014).

24. *King v. Burwell*, No. 14–1158 (U.S. 4th Circuit 2014).

25. *Supra*, 107 F.3d 625 (8th Cir. 1997).

Author's Afterword: Journey to Excellence—Dare to Dream

Excellence can be attained if you . . .
Care more than others think is wise.
Risk more than others think is safe.
Dream more than others think is practical.
Expect more than others think is possible.

—Author Unknown

This book is not the end, but a beginning of a long and rewarding journey to excellence. Progress occurs when those of vision see and act on the limitless possibilities for improving patient care. The *Journey to Excellence* begins with a vision by each organization's leadership to continuously improve the way care is provided in multiple settings. To be successful, leadership must be committed to charting new waters and improving patient care. The journey to excellence is not an easy path to follow. But then it is a journey worthwhile, filled with tears, sweat and ultimately success.

There is nothing more difficult to take in hand, more perilous to conduct, or more uncertain in its success, than to take the lead in the introduction of a new order of things. Because the innovator has for enemies all those who have done well under the old conditions, and lukewarm defenders in those who may do well under the new. This coolness arises partly from fear of the opponents, who have the laws on their side, and partly from the incredulity of men, who do not readily believe in new things until they have had a long experience of them.

—Niccolo Machiavelli (*The Prince*, 1513)

© My Life Graphic/Shutterstock

The ideas and the dreams presented below are but a few of the many to challenge healthcare professionals and organizations as they begin their *Journey to Excellence*. They are offered as a starting point for a new beginning. Although there are many past practices that have long been implemented successfully, they are not an ending—they are of historical value and a measure of the journey to a new beginning. To be successful, leadership must be committed to charting new waters towards the ultimate goal of improving patient care.

▶ THE HEALTHCARE WAR ROOM

No one can predict to what heights you can soar. Even you will not know until you spread your wings.

Author Unknown

The *healthcare war room* is a designated place, a room that inspires the imagination, where healthcare professionals meet to brainstorm ways to improve the quality of patient care. The war room must be conducive to brainstorming with sleeves rolled up, all in a comfortable, inviting setting, with pleasant decor free of cell phones and pagers. It is in such an environment that inspires creativity. The war room is a working, living, breathing think tank dedicated to brainstorming, storyboarding, strategizing, and coordinating a course of action. It is a room where ideas are created, prioritized, and assigned to a team player who has leadership skills, abilities, knowledge, vision, and passion to bring an idea to life, to make it happen. It is a room for turning what seems impossible into

reality. It is not just about "doing the right thing." It is about "doing the right thing" and doing it well. It is a room where caregivers are provided the opportunity to dream what they dare, and are empowered in providing the resources to bring the dream to life. The doors of the war room are always open and the search never ending. Competent leadership in the war room demands each individual dream in the stars, not in the clouds.

The main resources of the war room are the people, for they create the ideas and design the plans for implementation. The process requires a lot of hard work from a lot of people. The war room should include a "medical librarian," one who has been trained to assist others in navigating through the maze of information resources. The healthcare war room is a room of possibility thinking, not impossibility thinking. It is a room for freethinking people to generate creative new ideas.

The bigger dream is the establishment of an international Healthcare War Room that expands into a larger worldwide community of experts from every corner of the world. On an international level, the information shared at such meetings should be posted on the Internet, available to all to have input and the freedom to express their opinions and make constructive contributions. In time, more and more experts will contribute to the war room files on the Internet. The Internet allows for the continuous updating of information in the war room.

The road to success will uncover many obstacles to slow the wheels of progress. The war room, however, helps individuals to focus on ways to plow through or navigate around these challenges as they strive for excellence.

The Journey to Excellence requires leadership by an executive who is confident in any setting. A successful leader *Dares to Dream*, create, and champion new ideas and has the determination to fulfill an organization's mission and vision. The leader must be committed to the appointment of those who believe in the limitless potential to carry a project forward as a team. The visionaries and the innovators need to be identified and their energies given focus and direction.

AMBASSADORS WORLDWIDE

The structure of world peace cannot be the work of one man, or one party, or one nation. . . . It must be a peace, which rests on the cooperative effort of the whole world.

—Eleanor Roosevelt

Eleanor Roosevelt's words apply to the world of health care. The need for current healthcare information requires a collaborative effort of healthcare professionals from around the world. A first-class healthcare system cannot be the work of one person or one nation. It must be a system that depends on the cooperative effort of the world community.

Leaders of healthcare organizations should consider sponsoring an *Ambassadors Worldwide* program that encourages staff to contact other caregivers in their discipline from around the world. A dialogue can begin by contacting healthcare professionals in the same discipline as the staff member, introducing oneself, and discussing common problems associated with treating patients in that discipline. From there, a professional relationship may ensue where each professional is able to learn about best practices in each other's country and how to best apply that knowledge in their home countries. Such sharing of information will create worldwide ambassadors for health care, leading to a melding of resources and knowledge for the most effective care of patients.

Hospitals that implement such a program should then share the program's findings with their local community by publishing a hospital newsletter highlighting the most interesting and informative results, including the unique experiences that their staff members have had with other caregivers from around the world.

TELEMEDICINE

Telemedicine is the delivery of healthcare services by means of telecommunications. The use of telemedicine brings modern health care to remote areas of the world. Telecommunications includes *medical consultations* by specialists at a site remote from where a patient is being examined and or treated by a health care practitioner. *Teleradiology* involves the interpretation of imaging procedures and consultation at a site remote from the patient where the diagnostic procedure was performed. *Telepathology* involves the interpretation of slides at a location far from where the slides are prepared. Not only are the slides interpreted by the pathologist but consultation is a *value-added* tool to assist the remote caregiver in making patient care decisions. *Electroencephalograms* and *electrocardiograms* can also be transmitted almost anywhere in the world.

The possibilities of telemedicine are endless. The benefits include improving access to high-tech care in remote areas of the nation and the world while at the same time reducing the transportation hardships for patients. Patients can remain in their community and still have access to the marvels of modern medicine. Global telemedicine can provide:

- Worldwide medical consultations conducted by specialty.
- Continual access to updated physiologic data about patients in remote areas.
- Electronic medical records.
- Remote examination of patients at the primary site.
- Remote review of imaging studies, for example, at a secondary site.
- Interpretation of pathology slides at a location far from where the slides are prepared (telepathology).
- Transmission of electroencephalograms and electrocardiograms.
- Consultations between primary care physicians and medical specialists.

PROFESSIONAL EXCHANGE PROGRAM

This concept involves an exchange program whereby international host families sponsor a healthcare professional in their home for a selected period of time (e.g., 2 or more weeks). The professional would work in a foreign university hospital setting to learn the practices used in that healthcare setting, while also

📰 DOCTORS BRING EXTRA EYES AND EARS INTO EXAM ROOM

As the doctor examines Andrew, a new kind of medical scribe is watching the examination, transcribing everything he sees. The scribe, named Andrew, is thousands of miles away in India, and he is viewing the office visit live through the pint-size, Wi-Fi–connected camera attached to the doctor's glasses.

Paul Schwartzman, *The Washington Post*,
September 28, 2016

sharing with the host hospital best practices from his or her hospital. These programs would provide an environment in which caregivers can learn on site each other's best practices.

▶ PARTNERS IN EDUCATION

Partners in healthcare education programs, created by hospital–school partnerships, support and enrich student learning by introducing students to opportunities in the healthcare professions. Partners in education can take the form of a school lunch program whereby healthcare professionals (e.g., nurses, pharmacists, physical therapists, physicians) from a local community hospital are matched with students from a local middle school or high school who have an interest in a particular health career. Hospital employee volunteers are matched with one or more students for a semester and have lunch with them during a set day and time

each week. Students may even choose to learn about a different discipline the following semester. The earlier this process begins, the greater the opportunity a student has to discover a successful career path. The *Dunbar High School Health Partnership*, for example, is a partnership between Johns Hopkins and Dunbar High School in Baltimore, Maryland "that encourages students to reach their fullest potential by preparing them for entrance into post-secondary education institutions and/or careers in health care. Students have access to resources that help them increase test scores, broaden their awareness of biotechnology and health professions, and expose them to overall academic enrichment and personal development."[1] Information on a wide variety of middle school, high school, and undergraduate college programs can be found by searching *schools partner early for health careers*.

▶ BEST PRACTICES

The journey to excellence involves searching for best practices worldwide. It is a journey to the far corners of the earth in search of answers to difficult healthcare issues. It is the "worldwide search" to improve the quality of life on a global basis. It involves providing information to those individuals unwilling to accept an end without a fight. It recognizes that the answers to complex disease processes may lead the reader to exotic lands in search of a remedy. Although many issues may seem overwhelming, the answer to many healthcare issues may be just a click away.

The sharing of best practices among hospitals should be conducted on a not-for-profit basis. All too

✅ TIME TO SHARE

Joe was a healthcare consultant who collected thousands of documents of helpful information that he shared with healthcare organizations. His thinking was this: Why should hospitals have to reinvent the wheel? If organizations are willing to share with others, he became a conduit for that sharing for the benefit of other hospitals and ultimately for their patients. His hopes were that larger trade organizations would eventually collect the information and freely share with their constituents. Joe provided copies of his CD to fellow consultants and encouraged them to share the information with others. On the second day of his work, one work assignment he noticed that one of the consultants to whom he had given a copy of the CD the day before had various newspaper clippings about hospitals spread out on the organization's conference room table. Joe thought they looked interesting and asked, "Could I have a copy of your clippings?" The consultant said, "No, these are proprietary information." Joe was thinking to himself, "wow, I just gave you ten thousand pages of documents that I have collected over the years and you are unwilling to share four or five newspaper clippings."

The road to success in treating patients requires sharing of information so that each new generation can improve from the generations that preceded them.

often, hospitals spend hundreds of thousands of dollars to implement a hybrid of an idea that is already in the marketplace free of charge. The sharing of information such as job descriptions, performance evaluations, employee handbooks, age-specific educational materials, and infection control PowerPoint presentations should be shared freely among healthcare organizations and tweaked as necessary for the individual organization.

▶ INFORMATION TECHNOLOGY

Healthcare organizations need to improve their information technology systems in order to reduce the tremendous amount of paperwork required of caregivers, allowing more time for direct patient care. In addition, physicians should be able to access best practices. Electronic patient information–based technology coupled with computer-assisted diagnosis and treatment options will improve the decision-making process and ultimately patient care outcomes.

The medical record has become a cumbersome compilation of illegible notes from many healthcare disciplines. It has become an unfriendly and far-from-effective communications tool in the care and treatment of patients. Its purpose has shifted from being a useful communications tool between caregivers to becoming a tool for satisfying regulatory bodies. The proverbial wheel is broken, so reinventing the "medical record" wheel is a must, requiring serious attention by the healthcare industry and regulatory bodies in order to provide patients with increased quality of bedside care and time with each patient.

Nurses claim they often spend up to 2 hours or more of an 8-hour shift documenting in-patient records. Getting the nurses and other professionals back to the patient's bedside and away from the computer keyboard or pen requires ongoing reengineering of information systems.

▶ ARTIFICIAL INTELLIGENCE

Artificial intelligence (AI)-based medical decision support systems, utilizing electronic tools and super computers for entering a patient's health information into a computer program to assist in suggesting clinical tests for diagnosing a patient's illness and suggesting alternate treatment plans, including the potential for success of each alternative plan with statistical evidence.

Meet Watson the supercomputer developed by IBM. Actually, more of an artificial intelligence system…. Watson's ability to analyze huge volumes of data and reduce it down to critical decision points would obviously make it perfect for a clinical decision support system. Doctors or assistants could simply input symptoms and related factors, then Watson could make suggestions based on thousands upon thousands pieces of data it has stored from medical books, EMR data, clinical studies, journal articles, doctors notes and patient information.[2]

The use of AI involves the following:

- Ensuring that the data collected are easily accessible and user friendly to healthcare practitioners, organizations, and consumers of health care, and are used to synergize activities between clinical care, education and training, and research.
- Evaluating computer decision models and continue to improve the value of AI tools.
- Reassuring practitioners that AI is designed to be an aide to enhance their knowledge base and skills and, like any other clinical test, to be used as a tool in the decision-making process to diagnose and treat the patient.
- Encouraging research to better integrate conventional and traditional medicine in such a way that they complement each other.
- Establishing medical field teams (e.g., journalists, physicians, and other healthcare practitioners, as appropriate) who go into the field to investigate what appears to be promising *new medical treatments*.
- Providing distant learning through worldwide educational conference programming using the conferencing capabilities of major hotel chains, such as Marriott, which have worldwide conferencing center capabilities.

▶ STREAMLINE DATA COLLECTION AND EVALUATION

It's better to have no data than to have data that leads to the wrong conclusions.

—Author Unknown

The collection of data must be meaningful and lead to improved patient outcomes. With limited financial resources, data gathering should have a recognizable clinical payoff for the patient. Hospitals should set their goals by reducing paperwork thus giving caregivers more time with patients and less with paperwork.

▶ MEDICAL INFORMATION REPOSITORY

The loftier your goals, the higher the risk, the greater your glory.

—Author Unknown

There is a need to develop a comprehensive *medical information repository* (MIR) database for use in computer-assisted diagnosis and treatment. Such a repository should integrate both conventional and traditional medicines.

Conventional medicine is often referred to as evidence-based medicine, meaning that the value of medicine has statistical reliability as to its safety, effectiveness, and efficacy. It is practiced by physicians holding an M.D. (medical doctor) or D.O. (doctor of osteopathy) degree and by their allied health professionals, such as physical therapists, psychologists, nurse practitioners, and physician assistants.

Traditional medicine, as defined by the World Health Organization, "is the sum total of the knowledge, skills, and practices based on the theories, beliefs, and experiences indigenous to different cultures, whether explicable or not, used in the maintenance of health as well as in the prevention, diagnosis, improvement or treatment of physical and mental illness."[3] Traditional medicines include herbal medicine and acupuncture. The safe use of some traditional medicines remains in doubt as a result of the fact that science has yet to substantiate their value, effectiveness, and efficacy. As an example, in herbal medicine, there are a variety of herbal medications that have yet to show value and, in some cases, have contributed to the injury or death of the user. Moreover, there have been reports of drug–herbal interactions; complicating the problem is the fact that herb and vitamin-based over-the-counter "medicines" are not Food and Drug Administration regulated.

The *medical information repository* should be carefully analyzed and verified for reliability. Dissemination of the most current and exhaustive medical information must be continuously updated on a 24-hour, 365-day-per-year basis. The information gathered should be designed to assist and provide clinicians with the most effective curative and rehabilitative regimens to enhance the quality of patient care. Web-based health information should be available and *assessable by the public.*

▶ FOCUS ON PREVENTATIVE MEDICINE

Hospitals and physicians are often so busy treating symptoms, diseases, conditions, and injuries that preventative care is often not addressed. By committing more time and resources to preventative medicine, the risks of early onset of disease can be reduced.

▶ THE FIVE SENSES

Some things are not always easy to imagine until you have seen the vision. The closest to the vision of what a patient should experience in the hospital setting lies in the theatre play version of *Dirty Dancing*.

It has been difficult to explain over the years how I envision the patient's room. Watching the theatre production demonstrates that all things are possible. Adapting what is seen in the theatre play takes the imagination to new heights. A better life experience for all whether it is a temporary nursing home or hospital stay or what you would like your end-of-life experience to be like.

> "It's long been a dream of mine to mount a North American tour of Dirty Dancing," said Ken Gentry, CEO of NETworks Presentations LLC, in a statement. "The proven global appeal for this story is undeniable and I know audiences, both fans of theatre and fans of the film, will be captivated with the way this production re-imagines the movie through an incredible fusion of storytelling, classic songs and electrifying choreography."[4]

Bedside care involves more than recordkeeping. Imagine for a moment Patient A's and Patient B's experiences through the five senses as described here.

Patient A

> See: Your favorite scenes from Africa on a screen that encompasses the room giving the feeling that you are there; you have a private room, a private world.

> Hear: Your favorite music by Enya playing in the background; the corridors are quiet.

Smell: You have fresh flowers, and the bathroom is clean with no harsh chemical odors.

Taste: You have your favorite foods.

Touch: Your pain is controlled, the room is the right temperature, and you have had caring caregivers and family . . .

Patient B

See: The walls are cracked, the paint is peeling, and mold is growing in the vents.

Hear: The corridor is noisy. You have no visitors, but your roommate has eight of them.

Smell: A sewage plant is nearby, and the wind from its direction is blowing in your open screened window.

Taste: You are on a liquid diet; your water is warm and has a weird taste.

Touch: Your pain is unrelenting, and the room is hot.

Patient A and Patient B are two different patients with two very different experiences. Clearly, the health profession must do more to better address the five senses. Each sense has many components. For example, the sense of touch includes physical, psychological, social, and spiritual elements, each of which needs to be addressed. The physical aspect includes the effective control of a patient's pain. The social aspect involves family, caregivers, visitors, friends, and spiritual guidance. All healthcare entities may have the resources to create such an environment and so may not be able to address every need they would like to fulfill for their patients and residents, but they can better address their sensory needs.

▶ DREAM BOARDS

From the war room have come many dreams, the visions, the plans, and, most importantly, the assignment of a leader to take ownership and carry the agreed-upon projects forward. This part of the journey represents the fruits of the warriors who worked diligently in the war room to create the dream. To help make a dream become reality, it is important for others to understand the dream and take ownership of it. This can be accomplished effectively by graphically displaying the vision on an oversized "Dream Board" easily visible to all who pass by. The dream board should be displayed in high-traffic areas (e.g.,

emergency department waiting area, intensive care unit, oncology unit, rehabilitation unit, or wellness center).

Dreams realized should be displayed in what might be termed the "Hall of Dreams."

▶ ADOPT A HOSPITAL

Why not *adopt a hospital*? Highways and rivers are adopted. Creating change on a grand scale requires financial backing by mission-driven individuals and corporations willing to adopt hospitals and provide funding for their capital needs for new or expanded programs and services. With fewer than 6,000 hospitals and numerous for-profit corporations in the United States, the healthcare system would be able to continuously grow and provide quality services with an Adopt a Hospital sponsorship from the nation's wealthiest people and corporations such as Apple, Johnson and Johnson, Google, IBM, Intel, Facebook, and Microsoft. In such a program, hospitals would be matched with corporations based on size and needs.

Fundraising is everybody's job, and everybody has a role to play. Seniors can knit, crochet, and have their items sold in a gift or thrift shop. Young people can organize a car wash. Volunteers can have bake sales, sell raffle tickets, or sponsor dinner dances. The possibilities are endless.

▶ FUNDING YOUR DREAMS

The way to predict the future is to create it. Vision is the gift to see or do what others only dream.

—Author Unknown

To help make a dream become reality, it is important for others to see and understand the dream. This can be accomplished effectively by visually displaying the vision on an electronic dream board and making it easily visible to all. The dream board could be placed, for example, in high-traffic areas such as the hospital lobby or in the emergency department, intensive care, oncology, and rehabilitation waiting areas. It is important to remember that there can be multiple dreams displayed in various locations within the organization. Dreams accomplished should be displayed in a hospital corridor, for example, in what might be termed the "Hall of Dreams," celebrating the successes of those who worked hard to achieve them.

▶ BALDRIGE PERFORMANCE EXCELLENCE PROGRAM

The Pathway to Excellence and the accomplishments of an organization's successes are often recognized on a national basis through the *Malcolm Baldrige National Quality Award* (MBNQA). Malcolm Baldrige was Secretary of Commerce from 1981 to July 1987. He was a proponent of quality management. In recognition of his contributions, Congress named the award, which is the highest level of national recognition for performance excellence that a U.S. organization can receive. Congress established the Baldrige Program in 1987 to recognize U.S. companies for their achievements in quality and business performance and to raise awareness about the importance of quality and performance excellence in gaining a competitive edge. Education and healthcare organizations are eligible to qualify for the highly competitive award by meeting stringent Health Care *Criteria for Performance Excellence.*[6] To receive the BNQA, an organization must have a role-model organizational management system that ensures continuous improvement in the delivery of products and/or services, demonstrates efficient and effective operations, and provides a way of engaging and responding to customers and other stakeholders.[7]

The journey to excellence involves searching for best practices worldwide. It is a journey to the far corners of the earth in search of answers to difficult health care issues. It is the "worldwide search" to improve the quality of life on a global basis. It involves providing information to those individuals unwilling to accept an end "without a fight." It recognizes that the answers to difficult disease processes may lead the reader to exotic lands in search of a remedy. Although many issue(s) may seem overwhelming, the answer to many health care issues may be a click away.

▶ BEGIN THE JOURNEY

The beginnings of conducting a "Worldwide Search" of healthcare information (e.g., treatment of rare diseases described as orphan diseases [e.g., systemic sclerosis], pain management) begins with the collection, validation, and sharing of health information worldwide, utilizing the Internet as an effective source for building a database. Proven experts and specialists will contribute to the edification of this database. The World Wide Web (WWW) is the universe of network-accessible information, an embodiment of human knowledge. Therefore, it is appropriate that a major component of success begins with an ongoing and continuous search of the Internet.

This is the beginning of a new adventure. The search begins with a journey through the National Library of Medicine's Web site at http://www.nlm.nih.gov/. The library, located on the grounds of the National Institutes of Health in Bethesda, Maryland, is the world's largest medical library, where more than 6 million items, including books, journals, photographs, and images can be found in its collections.

The following template is helpful to better understand and begin the journey to excellence on a local or international basis.

The pathway to excellence involves searching for the best practices worldwide. It is a journey to the far corners of the Earth in search of answers to difficult health care issues. It is the "worldwide search" to improve the quality of life on a global basis. It involves providing information to those individuals unwilling to accept an end "without a fight." It recognizes that the answers to difficult disease processes may lead the reader to exotic lands in search of a remedy. Although many issue(s) may seem overwhelming, the answer to many health care issues may be just a click away.

🔍 FOUR U.S. ORGANIZATIONS RECEIVE NATION'S HIGHEST HONOR FOR PERFORMANCE EXCELLENCE

- For seven consecutive years, **Kindred Nursing and Rehabilitation Center—Mountain Valley** has achieved a five-star quality rating—the highest possible—from the Centers for Medicare and Medicaid, a ranking designed to help potential residents, families and caregivers compare nursing homes. Less than one percent of 15,600 skilled nursing facilities nationwide received the five-star rating over that period of time.
- **Memorial Hermann Sugar Land Hospital** ranks among the top 10 percent nationally for a number of performance metrics, including emergency center arrival-to-discharge time, compliance with regulations to reduce medication errors, bed turnaround times, radiology and laboratory result turnaround times, and the use of computerized physician order entry.[5]

Mission
Improve the quality of healthcare on a worldwide scale.

Vision
To find, verify, disseminate, and make available the most current medical information to health care practitioners and provide the tools to assist physicians in computer programming techniques for selecting care and treatment options for their patients. To provide opportunities for improving the practice of medicine:

1. Develop the structure, incentives, and support for hospitals to include proven (widely accepted) traditional medicines from around the world in treatment programs.
2. Train health care professionals in the various treatment modalities from around the world.
3. Promote health care standards and encourage the safe production and manufacturing of herbal medicines.
4. Provide continuing educational support for practitioners of traditional medicine.
5. Encourage research and the use of traditional medicine, along with modern medicine, in curing diseases.

Objectives
The objective here is to describe a plan for:

1. Developing a worldwide health care information data base that includes
   a. 24-hours-a-day, 365-days-a-year research in a Healthcare War Room
   b. Inclusion of health care information technology experts in the data collection process
      i. Professional researchers responsible for conducting an ongoing search for information about the latest in health care treatments (e.g., system by system, disease by disease)
      ii. Knowledge of health care terminology and disease processes
      iii. Knowledge of and ability to collect worldwide data
      iv. Ability to verbally communicate with practitioners from around the world
      v. Assignment to research countries within which the researcher has working skills in the language of the nation assigned
   c. Establishment of a data analysis team to
      i. Assess the validity of data collected
      ii. Identify both low and high-risk treatment options
      iii. Identify combinations of treatment options
      iv. Accept that as there are cocktails of medications for patients (e.g., HIV); there are cocktails that include not only medications but the use of a variety of treatment modalities, such as those described below in the treatment of MS patients
   d. Establishment of field teams (e.g., journalists, physicians, and other health care practitioners, as appropriate) who go into the field to investigate what appears to be promising "new medical finds"
   e. Development of a data base that includes both contemporary and traditional medicines
   f. Guarantee that the data collected are easily accessible and user friendly to health care practitioners, organizations, and consumers of health care
   g. Provision of computer-assisted diagnosis, treatment options, and comprehensive care planning
      i. For example, Harvard and University of Pittsburg Software for computer assisted diagnosis
   h. Provision of distant learning through worldwide educational conference programming
      i. Utilization of the conferencing capabilities of Marriott hotels or other major hotel chains with worldwide conferencing center capabilities
      ii. Selection of world-renowned speakers to discuss major success stories
      iii. Teleconferencing capabilities
      iv. Provision of teleconferencing breakout sessions for special topics and interests
   i. Collection of end-user feedback
   j. Continuous utilization of end-user feedback to improve data collection, dissemination, treatment successes, etc.
2. Encouraging the establishment of hospital war rooms
3. Encouraging the sharing of best practices among hospitals
4. Implementing Projects Teams
   a. Planning, Design, and Operations Team
   b. Data Collection Team
      i. Utilize existing data bases, libraries, etc.
      ii. Utilize the World Wide Web (WWW) as a tool for data collection. The WWW is the universe of network-accessible information, an embodiment of human knowledge. Therefore, it is appropriate that a major

component of this project begins with an ongoing Internet search for current health information from around the world

   c. Fund-raising Team
   d. Pain Centers for Excellence Design Teams
      i. Program design
      ii. Costs and design characteristics
      iii. Recruiting
   a. Quality monitoring team

Strategy

1. Implement the Plan
2. Execute the Plan
   a. Conduct an enduring, continuing "worldwide search" for healthcare information (e.g., clinical trials, pain management)
   b. Solicit the assistance of librarians worldwide to participate in
      i. Developing the plan for the sharing of medical information freely to all persons
3. Obtain financing for constructing a command and data base collection center, as depicted in the image above

Worldwide Health Conferences and Tele-Education

Tele-education here refers to a conference center site for linking lectures and formal education programs to multiple secondary conference sites worldwide. "As telecommunication technology has advanced and costs have declined over the past decade, there has been a steady growth in telemedicine."[8] Establish a relationship with Marriott or comparable hotel chain to establish worldwide conferencing for various healthcare specialties. This would involve world-renowned speakers, which would in turn encourage the replication of superior practices.

> May your journey to excellence be rewarding as you dare to champion new ideas,
> and most of all,
> May your successes bring healing to all.
> —George

Begin the journey template

► NOTES

1. https://www.hopkinsmedicine.org/human_resources/education_programs/youth/dunbar_health_partnership.html.

2. http://www.bcsolutionsrfn.com/calling-dr-watson/.

3. World Health Organization, Traditional Medicine: Definitions, http://www.who.int/medicines/areas/traditional/definitions/en/index.html.

4. http://www.playbill.com/news/article/dirty-dancing-the-classic-story-on-stage-will-launch-new-north-american-tou-217451.

5. https://www.nist.gov/news-events/news/2016/11/four-us-organizations-receive-nations-highest-honor-performance-excellence.

6. http://www.nist.gov/baldrige/publications/hc_criteria.cfm.

7. http://www.nist.gov/baldrige/about/baldrige_faqs.cfm.

8. http://www.ncbi.nlm.nih.gov/pmc/articles/PMC1121135/.

Glossary

Abandonment Unilateral severance by the physician of the professional relationship between himself or herself and the patient, without reasonable notice at a time when the patient still needs continuing care.

Abortion Premature termination of pregnancy at a time when the fetus is incapable of sustaining life independent of the mother.

Acquired Immune Deficiency Syndrome Generally accepted as a collection of specific, life-threatening opportunistic infections and manifestations that are the result of an underlying immune deficiency. It is caused by the human immunodeficiency virus (HIV), a highly contagious blood-borne virus. HIV destroys the body's immune system and thus its capacity to ward off infections that ordinarily would be fought off by a properly functioning immune system.

Ad litem A Latin term meaning "for the suit." A guardian ad litem is a person appointed by a court to defend a legal action on the part of a child or incapacitated person. A guardian ad litem is specifically appointed for the purposes of a suit.

Admissibility (of evidence) Refers to the issue of whether a court, applying the rules of evidence, is bound to receive or permit introduction of a particular piece of evidence.

Advance directives Written instructions expressing one's healthcare wishes in the event that he or she becomes incapacitated and is unable to make such decisions.

Adverse drug reaction An unusual or unexpected response to a normal dose of a medication; an injury caused by the use of a drug in the usual, acceptable fashion.

Affidavit A voluntary statement of facts, or a voluntary declaration in writing of facts, that a person swears to be true before an official authorized to administer an oath.

Agent An individual who has been designated by a legal document to make decisions on behalf of another individual; a substitute decision maker.

Americans with Disabilities Act (ADA) Federal act that bars employers from discriminating against disabled persons in hiring, promotion, or other provisions of employment.

Appellant Party who appeals the decision of a lower court to a court of higher jurisdiction.

Appellee Party against whom an appeal to a higher court is taken.

Artificial nutrition and hydration Providing food and liquids when a patient is unable to eat or drink, such as intravenous feedings.

Assault Intentional act that is designed to make the victim fearful and produces reasonable apprehension of harm.

Attestation Act of witnessing a document in writing.

Autonomy Right of an individual to make his or her own independent decisions.

Battery Intentional touching of one person by another without the consent of the person being touched.

Beneficence Describes the principle of doing good, demonstrating kindness, and helping others.

Best evidence rule Legal doctrine requiring that primary evidence of a fact (such as an original document) be introduced or that an acceptable explanation be given before a copy can be introduced or testimony given concerning the fact.

Borrowed servant doctrine Refers to a situation in which an employee is temporarily placed under the control of someone other than his or her primary employer. It may involve a situation in which an employee is carrying out the specific instructions of a physician. The traditional example is that of a nurse employed by a hospital who is "borrowed" and under the control of the attending surgeon during a procedure in the operating room. The temporary employer of the borrowed servant can be held responsible for the negligent acts of the borrowed servant under the doctrine of respondeat superior. This rule is not easily applied, especially if the acts of the employee are for the furtherance of the objectives of the employer. The courts apply a narrow application if the employee is fulfilling the requirement of his or her position.

Captain of the ship doctrine A doctrine making the physician responsible for the negligent acts of other professionals because he or she had the right to control and oversee the totality of care provided to the patient.

Cardiopulmonary resuscitation A lifesaving method used by caregivers to restore heartbeat and breathing.

Case citation Describes where a court's opinion in a particular case can be located. It identifies the parties in the case, the text in which the case can be found, the court writing the opinion, and the year in which the case was decided. For example, the citation *Bouvia v. Superior Court (Glenchur)*, 225 Cal. Rptr. 297 (Ct. App. 1986), is described as follows:

- *Bouvia v. Superior Court (Glenchur)* identifies the basic parties involved in the lawsuit.
- 225 Cal. Rptr. 297 identifies the case as being reported in volume 225 of the California Reporter at page 297.
- Ct. App. 1986 identifies the case as being decided in the California Court of Appeals in 1986.

601

Case law Aggregate of reported cases on a particular legal subject as formed by the decisions of those cases.

Certiorari Writ that commands a lower court to certify proceedings for review by a higher court. This is the common method of obtaining review by the U.S. Supreme Court.

Charitable immunity Legal doctrine that developed out of the English court system that held charitable institutions blameless for their negligent acts.

Civil law Body of law that describes the private rights and responsibilities of individuals. The part of law that does not deal with crimes; it involves actions filed by one individual against another (e.g., actions in tort and contract).

Clinical privileges On qualification, the diagnostic and therapeutic procedures that an institution allows a physician to perform on a specified patient population. Qualification includes a review of a physician's credentials, such as medical school diploma, state licensure, and residency training.

Closed-shop contract Labor–management agreement that provides that only members of a particular union may be hired.

Common law Body of principles that has evolved and continues to evolve and expand from court decisions. Many of the legal principles and rules applied by courts in the United States had their origins in English common law.

Comorbidities Two or more coexisting medical conditions or disease processes that are additional to an initial diagnosis.

Complaint The first pleading in an alleged negligence action, filed in a court by the plaintiff's attorney. It is the first statement of a case by the plaintiff against the defendant and states a cause of action, notifying the defendant as to the basis for the suit.

Congressional Record Document in which the proceedings of Congress are published. It is the first record of debate officially reported, printed, and published directly by the federal government. Publication began in March 4, 1873.

Consent *See* Informed consent.

Consequentialism A moral theory that determines good or bad, right or wrong, based on good outcomes or consequences.

Contextualism An ethical doctrine that considers the rightness or wrongness of an action, such as lying, to be based on the particular circumstances of a given situation. The implication is that lying is acceptable in one situation but not in another, even though the situations may be similar. In other words, it depends on the context within which something occurs.

Criminal negligence Reckless disregard for the safety of others. It is the willful indifference to an injury that could follow an act.

Decision capacity Having the mental capacity to make one's own decisions. Mental capacity refers to the ability to understand the risks, benefits, alternatives, and consequences of one's actions. Inferred in this interpretation is knowing the decision maker can reasonably distinguish right from wrong and good from bad.

Defamation Injury of a person's reputation or character caused by the false statements of another made to a third person. It includes both libel and slander.

Defendant In a criminal case, the person accused of committing a crime. In a civil suit, the party against whom the suit is brought, demanding that he or she pay the other party legal relief.

Demurrer Formal objection by one of the parties to a lawsuit that the evidence presented by the other party is insufficient to sustain an issue or case.

Deontological ethics An ethical approach that focuses on duty, rather than on the consequences, when determining the right conduct to be followed.

Deposition A method of pretrial discovery that consists of statements of fact taken by a witness under oath in a question-and-answer format, as it would be in a court of law, with opportunity given to the adversary to be present for cross-examination. Such statements may be admitted into evidence if it is impossible for a witness to attend a trial in person.

Determinism The view that nothing happens without a cause.

Directed verdict When a trial judge decides that the evidence and/or law is clearly in favor of one party, the judge may direct the jury to return a verdict for the appropriate party. The conclusion of the judge must be so clear and obvious that reasonable minds could not arrive at a different conclusion.

Discharge summary The part of a medical record that summarizes a patient's initial complaints, course of treatment, final diagnosis, and instructions for follow-up care.

Discovery An ascertion of that which was previously unknown through a pretrial investigation; it includes testimony and documents that may be under the exclusive control of the other party.

Do not resuscitate (DNR) Directive of a physician to withhold cardiopulmonary resuscitation in the event that a patient experiences cardiac arrest.

Durable power of attorney Legal instrument enabling an individual to act on another's behalf. In the healthcare setting, it grants the authority to make medical decisions for another.

Ethical conduct Conducting oneself in a manner consistent with acceptable principles of right and wrong. Such conduct may relate to one's community, country, profession, and so on.

Ethical dilemma A situation that forces a person to make a decision that involves breaking some ethical norm or contradicting some ethical value. It involves making a decision between two or more possible actions where any one of the actions can be justified as being the right decision, but, whatever action is taken, there always remains some doubt as to whether the correct course of action was chosen. The effect of an action may put others at risk, harm others, or violate the rights of others.

Ethicist One who specializes in ethics.

Ethics A set of principles of right and wrong conduct; a theory or system of moral values, of what is right and what is wrong; a system of values that guides behavior in relationships among people in accordance with certain social roles.

Ethics committee A committee created to deal with ethical problems and dilemmas in the delivery of patient care.

Euthanasia A Greek word meaning "good death." It is an act conducted for the purpose of causing the merciful death of a person who is suffering from an incurable condition, such as providing a patient with medications to hasten his or her death.

Evidence Proof of a fact, which is legally presented in a manner prescribed by law, at trial.

Expert witness Person who has special training, experience, skill, and knowledge in a relevant area and who is allowed to offer an opinion as testimony in court.

Feres doctrine A legal doctrine that bars legal claims by members of the military and their families from successfully suing the federal government.

Futility Having no useful result. As it relates to medical care or treatment, it occurs when the physician recognizes that the effect of treatment will be of no benefit to the patient. Morally, the physician has a duty to inform the patient when there is little likelihood of success.

Good Samaritan laws Laws designed to protect those who stop to render aid in an emergency. These laws generally provide immunity for specified persons from a civil suit arising out of care rendered at the scene of an emergency, provided that the one rendering assistance has not done so in a grossly negligent manner.

Grand jury Jury called to determine whether there is sufficient evidence that a crime has been committed to justify bringing a case to trial.

Grievance The process undertaken to resolve a labor–management dispute when there is an allegation by a union member that management has failed in some way to meet the terms of a labor agreement.

Guardian Person appointed by a court to protect the interests of and make decisions for a person who is incapable of making his or her own decisions.

Health According to the World Health Organization, "[a] state of complete physical, mental, and social well-being and not merely the absence of disease or infirmity."

Healthcare proxy Document that delegates the authority to make one's own healthcare decisions to another, known as the healthcare agent, when a person has become incapacitated or is unable to make his or her own decisions.

Hearsay rule Rule of evidence restricting the admissibility of evidence that is not the personal knowledge of the witness.

Holographic will A will handwritten by the testator.

Home health agency An agency that provides home health services. Home health care involves an array of services provided to patients in their homes or foster homes because of acute illness, exacerbation of chronic illness, and disability. Such services are therapeutic and/or preventive.

Home health care Home health care is an alternative for those who fear leaving the secure environment of their home. Such care is available through home health agencies. These agencies provide a variety of services for the elderly living at home. Such services include part-time or intermittent nursing care; physical, occupational, and speech therapy; medical social services, home health aide services, and nutritional guidance; medical supplies other than drugs and biologicals prescribed by a physician; and the use of medical appliances.

Hospice care Care provided for terminally ill persons, in a setting more economical than that of a hospital or nursing facility. Hospice care is often sought after a decision has been made to discontinue aggressive efforts to prolong life. A hospice program includes such characteristics as support services by trained individuals, family involvement, and control of pain and discomfort.

Hydration Intravenous addition of fluids to the circulatory system.

Immoral Behavior that is in opposition to accepted societal, religious, cultural, and/or professional standards.

Incapacity An individual's lack of ability to make decisions for himself or herself.

Incompetent Individual determined by a court to be incapable of making rational decisions on his or her own behalf.

Independent contractor One who agrees to undertake work without being under the direct control or direction of an employer.

Indictment Formal written accusation presented by a grand jury charging a person therein named with criminal conduct.

Informed consent Legal concept that provides that a patient has the right to know the potential risks, benefits, and alternatives of a proposed procedure prior to undergoing a particular course of treatment. Informed consent implies that a patient understands a particular procedure or treatment, including the risks, benefits, and alternatives; is capable of making a decision; and gives consent voluntarily.

Injunction Court order either requiring a person to perform a certain act or prohibiting the person from performing a particular act.

In loco parentis Legal doctrine that permits the courts to assign a person to stand in the place of parents and possess their legal rights, duties, and responsibilities toward a child.

Interrogatories List of questions sent from one party in a lawsuit to the other party to be answered under oath.

Joint Commission A not-for-profit, independent organization dedicated to improving the quality of health care in organized healthcare settings. Its major functions include developing organizational standards, awarding accreditation decisions, and providing education and consultation to healthcare organizations.

Judicial notice An act by which a court, in conducting a trial or forming a decision, will, of its own motion and without evidence, recognize the existence and truth of certain facts bearing on the controversy at bar (e.g., serious falls require X-rays).

Jurisdiction Right of a court to administer justice by hearing and deciding controversies.

Jurisprudence Philosophy or science of law on which a particular legal system is built.

Justice The obligation to be fair in the distribution of benefits and risks.

Kennedy Institute of Ethics The world's oldest and most comprehensive bioethics center. The Institute was established at Georgetown University in 1971 by a grant from the Joseph P. Kennedy, Jr. Foundation.

Larceny Taking another person's property without consent with the intent to permanently deprive the owner of its use and ownership.

Legal wrong Invasion of a protected right.

Liability As it relates to damages, an obligation one has incurred or might incur through a negligent act.

Libel False or malicious writing that is intended to defame or dishonor another person and is published so that someone other than the one defamed will observe it.

Life support Medical intervention(s) designed to prolong life (e.g., respirator, kidney dialysis machine, tube feedings).

Living will A document in which an individual expresses, in advance, his or her wishes regarding the application of life-sustaining treatment in the event that he or she is incapable of doing so at some future time. It describes in advance the kind of care one wants to receive or does not wish to receive in the event that he or she is unable to make decisions for himself or herself. It takes effect when a person is in a terminal condition or permanent state of unconsciousness.

Malfeasance Execution of an unlawful or improper act.

Malpractice Professional misconduct, improper discharge of professional duties, or failure to meet the standard of care of a professional that results in harm to another; the negligence or carelessness of a professional person such as a nurse, pharmacist, physician, or accountant.

Mandamus Action brought in a court of competent jurisdiction to compel a lower court or administrative agency to perform—or not to perform—a specific act.

Medicaid Medical assistance provided in Title XIX of the Social Security Act. Medicaid is a state-administered program for the medically indigent.

Medicare Medical assistance provided in Title XVIII of the Social Security Act. It is a health insurance program administered by the Social Security Administration for persons aged 65 years and older and for disabled persons who are eligible for benefits. Part A benefits provide coverage for inpatient hospital care, skilled nursing facility care, home health care, and hospice care. Part B benefits provide coverage for physician services, outpatient hospital services, diagnostic tests, various therapies, durable medical equipment, medical supplies, and prosthetic devices.

Meta-ethics The branch of ethics that seeks to understand the nature of ethical properties, statements, attitudes, and judgments. (en.wikipedia.org/wiki/Meta-ethics)

Misdemeanor Unlawful act of a less serious nature than a felony, usually punishable by a jail sentence for a term of less than 1 year and/or a fine.

Misfeasance Improper performance of an act.

Monotheism The worship of one God, who is immortal, omniscient, omnipotent, and omnipresent.

Nasogastric tube, insertion of Involves placing a tube through a patient's nose, down the back of the throat into the esophagus, and then into the stomach. Its purpose is to suction out the contents of the stomach or to deliver food or medicine.

Negligence Omission or commission of an act that a reasonably prudent person would or would not do under given circumstances. It is a form of heedlessness or carelessness that constitutes a departure from the standard of care generally imposed on members of society.

Non compos mentis "Not of sound mind"; suffering from some form of mental defect.

Nonfeasance Failure to act, when there is a duty to act, as a reasonably prudent person would in similar circumstances.

Normative ethics The study of what is right and wrong.

Norms Accepted rules and ways of doing things.

Nuncupative will An oral statement intended as a last will made in anticipation of death.

Obamacare The informal name ascribed to the Patient Protection and Affordable Care Act (PPACA).

Objectivism The belief that morality is based on some universal, external, and unchangeable fact. For example, murder is always wrong.

Ombudsman Person who is designated to speak and act on behalf of a patient/resident, especially in regard to his or her daily needs.

Opined To give or express as an opinion.

Paternalism A doctrine that literally means "rule by the father." In health care, it is the concept of physicians making decisions for their patients, whereas the more acceptable approach is autonomy, whereby the physician informs the patient as to the risks, benefits, and alternatives to care and treatment, and then the patient makes the final choice as to what is best.

Patient Protection and Affordable Care Act A federal act passed by Congress, signed into law by President Obama in March 2010, upheld as constitutional by the Supreme Court in 2012, designed to provide better health security by enacting comprehensive health insurance reforms that hold insurance companies accountable, lower health care costs, guarantee more choice, and enhance the quality of care for all Americans.

Perjury Willful act of giving false testimony under oath.

Plaintiff Party who brings a civil suit seeking damages or other legal relief.

Privileged communication Statement made to an attorney, physician, spouse, or anyone else in a position of trust. Because of the confidential nature of such information, the law protects it from being revealed even in court. The term is applied in two distinct situations. First, the communications between certain persons, such as physician and patient, cannot be divulged without the consent of the patient. Second, in some situations, the law provides an exemption from liability for disclosing information for which there is a higher duty to speak, such as statutory reporting requirements.

Probate A judicial proceeding that determines the existence and validity of a will.

Probate court A court with jurisdiction over wills. Its powers range from deciding the validity of a will to distributing property.

Process A series of related actions to achieve a defined outcome.

Prognosis Informed judgment regarding the likely course and probable outcome of a disease.

Proximate cause In immediate relation with something else. In negligence cases, the careless act must be the proximate cause of injury.

Rational Having the capacity to think logically.

Real evidence Evidence furnished by tangible things (e.g., medical records and equipment).

Rebuttal Giving of evidence to contradict the effect of evidence introduced by the opposing party.

Relativism The belief that morality is relative to each individual culture. What is right in one culture may be wrong in another culture. In ethics, it is a theory that conceptions of truth and moral values are not absolute but are relative to the persons or groups holding them.

Relativist A person who is a proponent of relativism.

Release Statement signed by one person relinquishing a right or claim against another.

Remand Referral of a case by an appeals court back to the original court, out of which it came for the purpose of having some action taken there.

Res gestae "The things done"; all the surrounding events that become part of an incident. If statements are made as part of the incident, they are admissible in court as res gestae despite the hearsay rule.

Res ipsa loquitur "The thing speaks for itself"; a doctrine of law applicable to cases in which the defendant had exclusive control over the thing that caused the harm and where the harm ordinarily could not have occurred without negligent conduct.

Res judicata "The thing is decided"; that which has been acted on or decided by the courts.

Respirator A machine used to assist in keeping a patient breathing.

Respondeat superior "Let the master answer"; an aphorism meaning that the employer is responsible for the legal consequences of the acts of the servant or employee who is acting within the scope of his or her employment.

Restraint Can be either physical or chemical (medication). Physical involves a device (e.g., safety belt, safety bar, geriatric chair, bed rail) that restricts or limits voluntary movement that cannot be removed by the patient.

Scope of practice In the hospital setting, describes the procedures that a healthcare provider can perform based on educational and other applicable training requirements that may be established by the hospital and licensing bodies. Healthcare professionals who perform procedures they are not privileged to perform can be held responsible for any financial harm suffered by the patient, and this action can result in the loss of licensure to practice in one's profession.

Slander False oral statement made in the presence of a third person that injures the character or reputation of another.

Standard of care Description of the conduct that is expected of an individual in a given situation. It is a measure against which a defendant's conduct is compared.

Stare decisis "Let the decision stand"; the legal doctrine that prescribes adherence to those precedents set forth in cases that have been decided.

Statute of limitations Legal limit on the time allowed for filing suit in civil matters, usually measured from the time of the wrong or from the time when a reasonable person would have discovered the wrong.

Statutory law Law that is prescribed by legislative enactments.

Stipulation Agreement, usually in writing, by attorneys on opposite sides of an issue as to any matter pertaining to the proceedings. Such agreement is not binding unless agreed on by the parties involved in the issue.

Subjectivism A doctrine that says moral judgments are based on personal preferences.

Subpoena ad testificandum Court order requiring one to appear in court to give testimony.

Subpoena duces tecum Court order that commands a person to come to court and to produce whatever documents are named in the order.

Subrogation Substitution of one person for another in reference to a lawful claim or right.

Substituted judgment In the healthcare setting, a surrogate decision maker's decisions are accepted as a substitute for the patient in the event the patient becomes incapacitated and unable to make decisions. Decisions are made on the basis of the patient's known healthcare preferences. Such preferences are generally described in the document appointing the surrogate and/or other documents such as a "living will" or "durable power of attorney for health care."

Summary judgment Generally, an immediate decision by a judge, without jury deliberation.

Summons Court order directed to the sheriff or other appropriate official to notify the defendant in a civil suit that a suit has been filed and when and where to appear.

Supra (above) In legal terms, supra refers to *a citation previously mentioned*, such as in a case, legal document, or chapter in a book.

Surrogate decision maker Individual who has been designated to make decisions on behalf of an individual determined incapable of making his or her own decisions.

Teleological ethics A theory of morality that derives duty or obligation from what is good or desirable as an end to be achieved.

Terminal condition A medical condition that is incurable and because of which death will occur.

Testimony Oral statement of a witness given under oath at trial.

Tort A civil wrong committed by one individual against another that may be classified as either intentional or unintentional. When it is classified as a criminal wrong (e.g., assault, battery, false imprisonment), the wrongdoer can be held liable in a criminal and/or civil action.

Tortfeasor Person who commits a tort.

Trial court Court where evidence is first presented to a judge and/or jury for decision.

Unethical behavior Character that describes behavior contrary to admirable traits or a code of conduct that has been endorsed by one's society, community, or profession.

Union-shop contract Labor–management agreement making continued employment contingent on joining the union.

Utilitarianism A moral theory that treats pleasure and happiness as the only absolute moral good. Acts that bring about happiness and pleasure are good, and acts that bring about pain and suffering are morally bad.

Value Worth or usefulness. Intrinsic is something that has merit in and of itself (e.g., happiness). Instrumental is something that helps to give worth to something else (e.g., currency is valuable for what it can buy).

Value judgment A judgment that assigns worth to an action.

Venue Geographic district in which an action is or may be brought.

Verdict Formal declaration of a jury's "findings of fact," signed by the jury foreperson and presented to the court.

Virtue A moral trait that refers to excellence and righteousness.

Waiver Intentional giving up of a right, such as allowing another person to testify to information that ordinarily would be protected as a privileged communication.

Will Legal declaration of the intentions that a person wishes to have carried out after death concerning property, children, or estate. It designates a person or persons to serve as the executor(s), who are responsible for carrying out the instructions it contains.

Witness Person who is called to give testimony in a court of law.

Writ Written order that is issued to a person or persons requiring the performance of some specified act or giving authority to have it done.

Wrongful birth Applies to a cause of action of the parents of a child who claim that the negligent advice or treatment by the defendant(s) deprived them of the choice of terminating the pregnancy.

Wrongful life Refers to a cause of action brought by the plaintiff(s) on behalf of a defective child who claims that but for the defendant(s) negligence (e.g., a laboratory's negligent genetic testing procedures or a physician's negligent advice or treatment), the child would not have been born.

Index